# Direct Roots

## A guide to folk, roots and related music and arts in the British Isles

Foreword by Martin Carthy MBE

Mrs Casey Music

Musicians Union

Ledgard Jepson creative design

The Association of Festival Organisers

## Acknowledgements

| | |
|---|---|
| Editor | **Alan Bearman** |
| Assistant Editors | **Laurel Swift** and **Gill Brice** |
| Database Design | **Harvey French** |
| Design and Layout | **Bryan Ledgard** |
| Typesetting Assistant | **Gordon Thompson** |
| Internet Research | **Kevin Sheils** |
| Advertising | **Ross McKinlay** and **Ali Rawlings** |
| Copy Editor & Research Assistant | **Pauline Bailey** |
| Copy Editor | **Lioux Heap** |
| Project Management | **Steve Heap** for **Mrs. Casey Music** |

Thanks to all those who have contributed data, articles, information, advice and enthusiasm. Your invaluable assistance is much appreciated. May your projects prosper !

**Victor Ryan** and **Association of Irish Festival Events (AOIFE)**, **Association of Festival Organisers (AFO)**, **fRoots**, **Elspeth Cowie** and **Traditional Music and Song Association of Scotland (TMSA)**, **Jim Hancock** and **Guestbook**, **Mick Tems** and **Celfyddydau Mari Arts**, **Becky Morris** and **Smallworld Music**, **John Leonard** and **Smooth Operations**, **John Turner** and **The Music Room**, **Richard Porter** and **Proper Distribution**, **Jacey Bedford**, **Fee Lock** and **The Morris Federation**, **John Frearson** and **The Morris Ring**, **Open Morris**, **Songlines**, **Trevor Gilson** and **ScoFF**, **Sam Satyanadhan** and **Folk on Tap**, **Folk Arts Network**, **Martin Carthy**, **Derek Schofield**, **Andrew Cronshaw**, **Ian Anderson**, **John Howson**, **John Kirkpatrick**, **Mike Bettison**, **Patrick Ryan**, **Chris Wade**, **Penny Allen**, **Jackie Allen**, **Ross Allen**, **Ayla Bedri** of **On Bouge**, **Graham Breakwell**, **Alan O'Leary**, **Gordon Potts**, **Mark Allan**, **Sue Swift**, **Colin Irwin**, **Chris Jaeger** and **Speaking Volumes**, **Ray and Bev Langton**, **Paul Saunders**, **Ross McKinlay**, **Linda Fisher** of **The Blues Line**, **Rick Townend**, **Chris Turner** and **Set and Turn Single**, **Keith Johnson**, **Tim Phillips**, **John Ward**, **Eddie Walker**, **John Crosby**, **Martin Nail**, **Peter Chegwyn**, **Mike O'Connor**, **Pete and Sue Coe**, **Alison Smith**, **Philip Freeman**, **Scottish Folk Arts Group**, **Ken and Sue Bradburn**, **Michael Catovsky**, **Alistair Anderson**, **Folkworks**, **Folktalk**, **Ian Smith (Prego)**, **Folk Roundabout**, **Gail Duff** and **TRADS**, **Mark Ringwood** of **Marko Polo**, **Sheila Mainwaring** and **Shreds and Patches**, **John Halliwell** and **Mardles**, **Katie Howson** and **East Anglian Traditional Music Trust**, **John New** and **efn**, **Gerry Milne** and **Folk London**, **Alan Bell**, **Folkus**, **North West Folk Federation**, **Richard Ashe**, **Sain**, **Fflach Tradd**, **Danny Kilbride**, **Gerard Kilbride**, **Frank Warren** of **Matters Musical**, **Sarah Coxson**, **Kerry Fletcher**, **Frances Watt**, **John Barrow** of **Stoneyport Agency**, **Greentrax** and **Dave Smith (NEM Productions)**.





ISBN 0-9540723-0-8

First published June 2001 by Mrs. Casey Music and supported by The Musicians' Union, Ledgard Jepson Ltd. and The Association of Festival Organisers

Published by **Mrs Casey Music**
PO Box 296, Aylesbury, Bucks, HP19 9TL
**Phone** +44 (0)1296 394411
**Fax** +44 (0)1296 392300
**Email** pub@direct-roots.com
**Web** www.direct-roots.com

The Publications Officer of Mrs Casey Music would be happy to hear from other potential authors, or individuals, who wish to submit information relevant to this directory. You may contact the Officer via Mrs Casey Music at the address above. The views expressed in this publication are those of the authors and do not necessarily represent those of Mrs Casey Music.

All entries supplied by authors, groups, organisations and individuals were deemed correct at date of publication. The publishers take no responsibility for any errors, omissions or inaccuracies.

Designed and typeset by **Ledgard Jepson Limited**
Mortimer Heights, Cubley, Penistone, S36 9UY
**Phone** +44 (0)1226 766608
**Fax** +44 (0)1226 766619
**Email** studio@ledgardjepson.com
**Web** www.ledgardjepson.com

Printed and bound in England

welcome
from the editor

## Welcome to Direct Roots

Publication of this guide feels like both an end and a beginning. The concept of such a directory/ guide is one I've pondered for many years now, so getting to this point is a pleasure and a relief. However, it is also just the start. The ultimate directory/guide is still a year or two away with countless developments, refinements and ideas yet to be explored.

It has never been a realisable goal to provide listings of every artist, club, service and festival for every genre of music within the folk and roots world. Instead, we have set about providing signposts to such information. So we may not have every UK Blues singer, storyteller or salsa class but we do tell you where to look. Similarly with information for promoters and festival organisers; we haven't attempted to list every marquee company, caterer or PA company but we point you in the right direction.

The vast majority of the information included in the main listings has been verified through thousands of forms, emails and phone calls. However, the nature of the "folk scene" means that if we just relied on such information being sent in we would be missing a lot of key people. So, we've gone to the grass roots and asked magazine editors, web masters, development agencies, agents and promoters for their recommendations and listings. The best sources for accurate up to date information are always the smaller local and specialist organisations. These are the real grass roots of the business. We have highlighted the work of many of these and hope that you discover new web sites, magazines, or organisations that can heighten your enjoyment of the music we all enthuse about.

It always seemed vital to provide some information that would help the reader select the appropriate entry for their particular purpose. So in most cases we have added a line or two of information to clarify the nature of the artist, service, festival etc. These are usually edited versions of the copy we received, but in some cases we have added our own descriptions. We've tried to cut out the hype but leave in enough to help you judge the Martin Carthys from the wannabe Martin Carthys. We hope it helps.

When we decided to invite a number of key players in the folk and roots sector of the music business to write articles we gave ourselves some impossible choices. Dozens of possibilities came to mind and only a few could be included. Each contributor has their own viewpoint and there will be plenty of alternative opinions: in this lies the core of Volume 2. We have included Resource sections on specific musics and art forms in order to provide a number of signposts to help in further exploration.

This is, as I said some four hundred words ago, just a start. Our ever-developing sector of the music business needs an appropriate resource bank. I'd like to think that this first volume goes some way to achieving this.

Thanks to the dozens of contributors. I hope I have credited you all appropriately. Special thanks are due to Laurel Swift, Gill Brice, Harvey French and Kevin Sheils.

Thanks also to Martin Frost for early encouragement and to Mrs Casey Music, The Musicians' Union and Bryan Ledgard of Ledgard Jepson for helping to turn a worthy intention into something close to reality.

**Alan Bearman**
*Editor*

# foreword

**Martin Carthy MBE**

**Direct Roots** has been a long time coming. The original Folk Directory was badly needed at the time of its inception, but enormously valuable as it is, there grows the feeling of 'Things Moving On' and, in consequence, its possible marginalisation by the growth of interest in other folk musics native born to this country as well as folk musics from "outside". It may seem to be stating the obvious but old fashioned, country (with a small "c") music is not our only native born music. Truly we are not alone.

It was the tremendous acceleration in the growth of folk clubs in the early 1960s which prompted people in the EFDSS to put together a directory of clubs and club organisers in England, Scotland and Wales to include as comprehensive a directory of performers as was possible. We are talking about a scene that in the 1960s boasted between 400 and 500 clubs in London alone. For years, and especially during the 1970s when the number of clubs reached its peak, this directory proved itself to be a quite invaluable source of information for people needing - for whatever reason - to know about the folk scene of the time. The 1970s also saw this folk scene collapse almost catastrophically in upon itself as clubs which had held on well past their sell-by date disappeared, along with many performers who were frankly not good enough, but were able to make a decent living in the far-too-tolerant atmosphere which prevailed. The cold reality which laid its hand upon us was certainly given extra weight by that revolution visited on the rock 'n' roll scene by the Sex Pistols and others which, having seemed initially to have passed us by, actually caught us in a quite vicious undertow.

It took a long time for any kind of a recovery to take hold and when it did it was a very different folk scene that began to take shape. Much smaller and leaner, no longer simply confined to the back rooms of pubs but, for better or worse, spreading out and making its presence felt in Arts Centres, even in straight rock 'n' roll venues and once more in some of the concert venues in which it had thrived for a brief period twenty years earlier. But the fundamental change was that no longer did the folk clubs feed the folk festivals, but instead the reverse had become true and the festival held sway. Perhaps that in itself was one reason young people, who generally speaking had seemed to feel a certain discomfort in clubs, found and embraced the music. This fresh generation certainly took its time making its appearance and indeed, there were those of us who had been wondering whether what we had was simply something which had hung on from the perceived glory days of the 1960s and which was about to die a natural death. It was because we were hoping that it could be otherwise, that we pounced on anyone who looked as though they might be showing an interest in traditional music - but at the same time (and very stupidly) doors were shut firmly in the faces of new writers who could and would have galvanised us one more time. New writing always was and will remain a crucial factor in the regeneration of traditional music and in the choices that are made on its behalf.

It is not my place to say why younger people take an interest, except that a memory of my own discovery as a seventeen year-old of something which was as foreign/exotic to me as the Indian music which I was also discovering at the time, is one of unearthing something quite unique and, crucially, of doing it for myself. As younger performers at last stuck their heads above the parapet in the late 1980s and early 1990s, they found themselves occupying a massively altered stage and facing an audience which demanded more than just music and song. The range of performers to be found at festivals by then better reflected both the astonishing variety of recorded music available to people and more properly reflected the society in which we now find ourselves. It is true to say that previously the fare had been almost entirely English speaking. While developments there - including storytelling, a belated connection with the Welsh Language folk scene and a desire to connect with some of the past struggles of those ordinary people to whose legacy we are all tied using theatre - have broadened its base in an exciting way, there is nothing quite like the understanding to be gained from viewing your music in a wider international context, and the wonderfully skilled performers from all over Europe (which alone is representative of an enormous variety of music), from West and Southern Africa, and the wildly different Asian and South and Central American musics offer just that. It is true that in the end all of these musics speak with one voice and have one thing in common. All of them are made up from nothing by people who have had nothing, and that in itself represents humanity triumphant.

It is quite clear not simply that a new directory is needed, but that such a directory will need to widen its horizons and reflect all these developments if it is to be of any use to anyone who has an interest in folk or traditional music. In no way does **Direct Roots** pretend that this is going to be THE definitive tome. Indeed it is just the beginning of a major and ongoing project which will seek to draw together as many strands of - geographically speaking - the British Isles Body Musical as it possibly can, however long it takes.

introductions

- **Ian Smith**, Musicians' Union
- **Andy Knight**, Musicians' Union

## Ian Smith

### Organiser, Musicians' Union Folk Roots and Traditional Music Section

The Folk, Roots and Traditional Music Section of The Musicians' Union was established in 1998 following pressure from Union members for more specialist recognition for this growing section of the industry within Europe's largest representative organisation for musicians. The Section has grown in membership and influence, quickly becoming a credible focal point for this sector. Folk, Roots, Traditional and associated musics can no longer be seen as a "minority" interest but as a vitally essential part of the music industry. The Musicians' Union, through its FRTM Section, is now seen to properly represent the sector, both by its members and by the service industry with whom we have established such close working relationships over the past three years. This is clearly evidenced by our support for many festivals and organisations including Sidmouth International Festival and Cambridge Folk Festival who both provide dedicated facilities for us. We are associate members of the AFO (Association of Festival Organisers) and are now working ever more closely with PRS, where three members of the FRTM Section Committee, including the Chairperson Steafan Hannigan, serve on the PRS Specialist Music Group.

In 1999, we published our first FRTM Directory, which was well received by the industry. We are therefore delighted to collaborate with Mrs Casey Music in publishing **Direct Roots**, which we hope will become the "White Book" of the folk and associated sectors and become an invaluable and essential reference book, not only for all those practitioners at every level working within it, but also for the service industry that supports it.

## Andy Knight

### Assistant General Secretary (Administration), Musicians' Union

When the Amalgamated Musicians' Union was born in May 1893, little did Joe Williams realise that the organisation he had founded and of which he had become the first General Secretary, would evolve today into the largest and most influential body representing musicians in Europe. In June 1921, the AMU became the Musicians' Union and has continued to serve the professional needs of musicians throughout the UK for more than 100 years, occupying a unique and vitally important role, in both representing its members and earning the respect of the music industry world-wide.

The Union, through its Executive Committee, branch, district and section structures, continues to evolve to ensure that we meet the needs of all our members in an ever changing world, where technological advances, in particular, require that we adapt and change to meet those needs wherever our members work and within whatever genre of music they perform.

The Folk, Roots and Traditional Music Section is the Union's most recent section and demonstrates the Union's commitment to its members, who requested this specialist representative section be founded at our own Biennial Delegate Conference in 1997. The FRTM Section has quickly gained enormous credibility through the strength of its committee and the hard work of its organiser, Ian Smith It is now seen as one of the most influential bodies within the folk world and its work complements the Union's policy of keeping music live.

**Direct Roots** is further evidence of the Section's credibility and influence and the Musicians' Union is delighted to be associated with Mrs Casey Music in publishing the first directory of its type specifically dedicated to all the needs of this specialist genre. It follows on from our first FRTM Directory in 1999 and will be a necessary and essential reference book, not only for this growth sector, but for the entire UK music industry.

# contents

## foreword



## introductions



## finding the right root!

## artists



## agents



## spotlight



## morris and percussive dance



## folk arts



## festivals



## services



## rooting in the regions

contents

# Finding the right root!

**Contents page opposite**
This lists the subjects covered in each section.

***All listings on a white background have been verified by Direct Roots staff.***

***Information on tinted background has been provided by key figures in the appropriate music or area, it is usually additional to the central listings.***

The **Regional**, **Spotlight** and **National Focus** sections bring together a wide range of resources.

Generally you should start looking in the section for the specific region, country or type of music that you want to explore before consulting listings such as Media or Organisations. e.g. if you want to know about a folk magazine or website for Cornwall start in the South West section rather than in Magazines.

**Notes in the margins and at the end of entries**
These will guide you from one section to another for more detail.

There is a large number of non UK/ Ireland resident artists featured in the main listings. These are generally artists who tour here regularly and are available through named agents.
**Ceilidh and Social Dance Bands** are included in the main listings. There is a list of local bands in each Regional section where sources for more extensive local lists are usually provided.

**Social Dance Clubs**
Some have asked to be included and are found in the Venues and Regular Events section. More comprehensive listings of Dance Clubs will be found in Chris Turner's Set and Turn Single magazine and at The English Folk Dance and Song Society's Root Source web site. www.rootsource.co.uk

**The English Regions**
These are based on Regional Arts Board representation with some variation (see page 307). The RAB definitions are used here as a generally helpful way of splitting up England for a more detailed look at local resources. Also check sections for neighbouring regions for the band, caller or venue you are looking for. Contributors and magazine listings often mention venues and services based in adjacent regions.

**Alphabetical Order**
Listings are arranged alphabetically by the first letter of the first name or band name. E.g. John Tams will appear under J not T. Bands having 'The' in their title are also sorted by the first letter of the first name E.g. The Gloworms will appear under G.
**Regional Arts Boards and Arts Council**
Where known the Regional Arts Board (RAB) or Arts Council (AC) is given in the listings as an aid to locating an appropriate artist or service. This does not mean that they restrict themselves to the named Region but may be useful in some cases - e.g finding a local band or P.A. Company.

**M.U. Membership**
Where known, membership of Musicians' Union is indicated. See pages 423-424 for the membership list of Musicians' Union Folk Roots and Traditional Music Section.

**Annotations**
Above all, we have sought quality information rather than quantity. We hope the annotations are helpful and contribute to recognition of the reputations of many well established artists without detracting from others. The listings sections are open to all comers. Sections on particular genres give recommendations but these are generally the opinion of the writer and should not be considered exhaustive.

**Alan Bearman**
*Editor*

artists

# artists

# artists

*Artists in the main A-Z listing are mostly available for concert and club bookings.*

# BOB FOX

"Bob Fox, possibly the most complete artist in English folk, his quietly impressive 'Dreams Never Leave You' is my album of 2000." **COLIN RANDALL**, Daily Telegraph

"Deservedly popular on the folk circuit, Bob Fox's first solo album mixes traditional themes with more contemporary material... a must-have for folk enthusiasts." **ANDY FARQUARSON**, Independent on Sunday

## Dreams never leave you

"...an album which absolutely demands to be heard... a total delight from first note to last." **DOUG PORTER**, Folk On Line

"Anyone who appreciates great singing and excellent accompaniment should buy this CD... better still, go see Bob live." **PHIL CROSS**, Folkmag.co.uk

For bookings and gig details phone/fax **0191 388 6505**.
Further details fom www.bobfoxmusic.com

Woodworm Records WRCD035
PO Box 37, Banbury, Oxon OX16 8YN
Fax 01869 337142

a major multi-media show based on the album

# ON THE SHOULDERS OF THE GREAT BEAR

ANDREW CRONSHAW    Cloud Valley CV2007    dist. by PROPER

## TOUR - MARCH 2002

featuring

**Andrew Cronshaw, Jenny Wilhelms**
**Heikki Laitinen, Bernard O'Neill**
**Hannu Saha, Ian Blake, Reijo Kela**

London (Ocean), Kendal (Brewery), Newcastle (Live Theatre), Bracknell (Wilde Theatre), Nottingham, Southampton (Gantry)

*Details in the press and from:*
CMN: www.cmntours.org.uk, Folkworks: www.folkworks.co.uk
Cloud Valley Music: (020)-8521-4649 cloudval@aol.com
http://members.aol.com/cloudval

Supported by the Arts Council of England and the Finnish Cultural Fund

## 422
**Contact** Ian Stephenson
**Mail address** Marsh Lane House, Hirst Courtney, SELBY, N Yorks, YO8 8QT
**Email** iancollege@yahoo.com
**Web** www.the-422.co.uk
**Alt contact** Sam Pirt
**Alt address** 97 Hook Road, GOOLE, E Yorks
**Phone** 01405 769010
**Email** sampirt@folkmusic.freeserve.co.uk
*5 piece band. Winners of BBC Radio 2 Young Folk Award 1999*
***Musicians' Union member***

## AAAAG
**Contact** Sam Pirt
**Mail address** 97 Hook Road, GOOLE, E Yorks, DN14 5JR
**Phone** 01405 769010
**Email** sampirt@folkmusic.freeserve.co.uk
**Web** www.sampirt.co.uk
*Sam Pirt and David Wood. Young accordion and guitar traditional music duo.*
**RAB** Yorkshire Arts

## Aardvark Ceilidh Band
**Contact** Pete Grassby
**Mail address** 22 Derwent Road, COVENTRY, W Midlands, CV6 2HB
**Phone** 024 7633 6740
07768 683015
**Web** www.laity.freeserve.co.uk/aardvarks.htm
*Folk rock ceilidh band with/ without caller.*
**RAB** West Midlands Arts

## Abana
**Contact** Matters Musical
**Web** www.mattersmusical.com
*Dance music from Sierra Leone on African guitar, bass, percussion, keyboard, drums and vocals. Onstage dancers available*

## Abdelkader Saadoun
**Contact** Matters Musical
**Web** www.mattersmusical.com
*Algerian Rai singer with Arabic Rai band. Based on percussive rhythms, featuring French and Arabic rapping*

## Abdul Teejay's Rokoto
**Contact** Adastra
**Web** www.adastra-music.com
*Sierrra Leone roots band. Abdul is also avaliable solo or with a trio for acoustic sets and workshops*

## Acaysha
**Contact** Adastra
**Web** www.adastra-music.com
*All female band playing mix of bluegrass, old-time and new roots*

## Aces High
**Contact** ABDC Entertainments
**Web** members.tripod.co.uk/abdc/aceshigh.html
*Country & Bluegrass band for barn, square and line dancing*
**RAB** Southern Arts

## Achanak
**Contact** Access All Areas
*UK/ Punjab Bhangra group with voice, tabla,dholak and dancers*

## Adam McNaughton
**Phone** 0141 5522665
*Glasgow singer/ songwriter.*
**AC** Scotland

## The Adamant Band
**Contact** Artists Connect
**Web** www.artistsconnect.com
*Traditional New Orleans Marching Band*

## Adderstone
**Contact** Elizabeth Jones Entertainments
**Web** www.bromyard.co.uk/ejones
*4 piece Northumbrian band featuring harp and Northumbrian small pipes*
**Agent** Bogle Music, Elizabeth Jones Entertainments

## Adel Salameh
**Contact** Matters Musical
**Web** www.mattersmusical.com
*Arabic classical virtuoso oud player. Available solo or with accompaniment*
**RAB** London Arts

## Adrian Spendlow
**Contact** Bright Light Arts
*Performance poet & MC. Music collaborator with wide range of line ups.*
**RAB** Yorkshire Arts

## Adrian Y Gof
**Mail address** "Ys" 10 Cwrt Ty Mawr, Y Fan, CAERFFILI, Morgannwg Ganol, CF83 3EQ, Wales
**Email** BrasigProd@aol.com
**Alt contact** Ben Newman - Agent Litiez, 29690, LA FEUILEE, Breizh, France
**Phone** 00 33 2 9899 6618
*Traditional and contemporary French and Breton music and song accompanied on guitar and bodhran.*
***Musicians' Union member***
**AC** Wales

## Afro Celt Sound System
**Contact** Primary Talent
*High profile band fusing African dance rhythms with synthesisers and Celtic musicians*

## Afroshock
**Contact** Matters Musical
**Web** www.mattersmusical.com
*Vocal duo, singing in ancient African languages over syncopated Afro-Cuban beats*

## Ahanan
**Contact** Chris James
**Mail address** Lanherch, Bridge, REDRUTH, Cornwall, TR16 4QE
**Phone** 01209 843299
07788 136089
**Email** cadwur@zoom.co.uk
*Acoustic trio. Guitar, drum & fiddle. Traditional Cornish & Celtic plus other music & songs.*
**RAB** South West Arts

## Aidan O'Rourke
**Mail address** 2/3 13 Church Street, Partick, GLASGOW, G11 5JP
**Phone** 0141 581 6147
0777 9293527
**Email** aidanorourke@aol.com
*Scottish fiddle player and composer.*
***Musicians' Union member***
**AC** Scotland

## Aileen Carr
**Contact** Greentrax
**Mail address** Cockenzie Business Centre, Edinburgh Road, COCKENZIE, East Lothian, EH32 0XL, Scotland
**Phone** 01875 814155
01875 815888
**Fax** 01875 813545
**Email** greentrax@aol.com
**Web** www.greentrax.com
*Scottish singer.*
**AC** Scotland

## Akmed's Camel
**Contact** Mark Addison
**Mail address** 'Squirrel's Haunt', Main Road, Sibsey, BOSTON, Lincs, PE22 0TN
**Phone/Fax** 01205 750753
**Phone** 07780 831385
**Email** mark@addisonfolk.freeserve.co.uk
*Concert and ceilidh band, own caller and PA.*
***Musicians' Union member***
**RAB** East Midlands Arts



*Artists in the main A-Z listing are mostly available for concert and club bookings.*

*See page 11 for details of other artist listings (Dance Display, Solo Musicians, Composers, Arrangers, Session Musicians, Band Deps. Lecturers, MCs Tutors, Street Theatre Children's Entertainers, Theatre Companies).*

*Agents section appears on pages 119-131.*

# artists
## a

Artists in the main A-Z listing are mostly available for concert and club bookings.

See page 11 for details of other artist listings (Dance Display, Solo Musicians, Composers, Arrangers, Session Musicians, Band Deps. Lecturers, MCs, Tutors, Street Theatre, Children's Entertainers, Theatre Companies).

Agents section appears on pages 119-131.

### Alain Genty Band
**Contact** Adastra
**Web** www.adastra-music.com
*Acclaimed French bass player and his band, fusing Breton and Gaelic tunes*

### Alan Bell Band
**Contact** Alan Bell
**Mail address** 55 The Strand, Rossall, FLEETWOOD, Lancs, FY7 8NP
**Phone** 01253 872317
**Fax** 01253 878382
**Email** alanbell@fylde-folk-fest.demon.co.uk
**Web** www.fylde-folk-fest.com
*Respected North-West English singer/songwriter with band.*
**RAB** North West Arts

### Alan Burke
**Contact** The Event Shop
*Singer/ songwriter, former Afterhours frontman*
**Agent** Event Shop, OTB Productions
***Musicians' Union member***

### Alan Burton and Steve Hunt
**Contact** Alan Burton
**Mail address** Flat 4, 4 Great Bedford Street, BATH, BA1 2TZ
**Phone** 01225 314815
**Alt contact** Steve Hunt
**Alt address** 25 Haywards Mead, Eton Wick, WINDSOR, Berks, SL4 6JN
**Phone** 01753 863378
**Email** bodhran41@hotmail.com
*Traditional and new tunes and songs; uillean pipes, whistles, guitar and bodhran.*
***Musicians' Union member***
**RAB** South East Arts

### Alan Kelly
**Contact** Smallworld Music
*Celebrated accordionist also with band*
**AC** Ireland

### Alan O'Leary
**Mail address** 68 Belleville Road, LONDON, SW11 6PP
**Phone/Fax** 020 7585 0357
**Email** olearyam@ukonline.co.uk
*Irish traditional music on flute & tin whistle.*
**RAB** London Arts

### Alan Simpson
**Mail address** 12 Talbot Avenue, WATFORD, Herts, WD19 4AX
**Phone** 01923 221555
01923 229387
**Email** alsim@btinternet.com
*Caller for barn dances, ceilidhs, etc.*
**RAB** South East Arts

### Alan Stivell Band
**Contact** Adastra
**Web** www.adastra-music.com
*Renowned Breton multi-instrumentalist and his band*

### Alan Woolley
**Contact** Elizabeth Jones Entertainments
**Web** www.bromyard.co.uk/ejones
*Ex Rattlers singer/ songwriter*

### Albert Nyathi and Imbongi
**Contact** Equator Company Ltd (The)
**Web** www.equatorcompany.com
*Poet Albert Nyathi fronts 12 piece contemporary Zimbabwean group including 4 female vocalists and brass section*

### The Albion Band
**Contact** Speaking Volumes
**Web** www.speakingvolumes.co.uk
*Long established electric/ acoustic 5 piece, led by Ashley Hutchings, prime mover in English folk rock.*
***Musicians' Union member***
**RAB** North West Arts

### Alexander D Great and The Great Band
**Contact** Matters Musical
**Web** www.mattersmusical.com
*Solo singer, poet, social commentator in Trinidadain tradition of Kaiso (precursor of Calypso) with up to 10 piece band including brass and steel pans*

### Alex Debnam
**Mail address** 71 Millias Road, Itchen, SOUTHAMPTON, SO14 2FX
**Phone** 023 8044 0835
0771 235 7443
**Fax** 023 8034 6326
**Email** pauldrums@aol.com
**Web** www.pauldrums.com
*Musician; drums and bodhran.*
***Musicians' Union member***
**RAB** Southern Arts

### Alf Alfalfa and The Wild Oats
**Contact** Jason Hill
**Mail address** 54 Price Street, Burslem, STOKE ON TRENT, Staffs, ST6 4EN
**Phone** 01782 813401
07778 913528
**Email** jason@burslem.demon.co.uk
**Web** www.wildoats.fsnet.co.uk
**Alt contact** Trevor Carter
**Alt address** 82 Uttoxeter Road, Blythe Bridge, STOKE ON TRENT, Staffs, ST11 9JG
**Phone** 01782 398657
**Email** carter@edgemusic.fsnet.co.uk
*5 piece ceilidh band and caller. Melodeon, fiddle, recorders, percussion, etc.*
***Musicians' Union member***
**RAB** West Midlands Arts

### Alicia Davies
**Mail address** 282 Loughborough Park, Brixton, LONDON, SW9 8TD
**Phone** 020 7738 3817
07718 178682
*Percussion including djembe, balafon, bougarabom etc. Session work, performance, workshops and tuition.*
***Musicians' Union member***
**RAB** London Arts

### Alistair Anderson
**Mail address** Mount Hooley, Whittingham, ALNWICK, Northumberland, NE66 4RN
**Phone** 01665 574631
07720 451496
**Fax** 01665 574354
*Illustrious concertina and Northumbrian pipes player. Solo and workshop leader. Dance caller and band leader.*
***Musicians' Union member***
**RAB** Northern Arts

### Alistair Hulett
**Mail address** 0/29 Albert Ave, GLASGOW, G42 8RB, Scotland
**Phone** 0141 4339446
**Email** a.hulett@talk21.com
**Web** www.folkicons.co.uk/alistair.htm
**Alt contact** Emerging Music
**Alt address** Burncrook Cottage, Faugh, Heads Nook, CARLISLE, CA4 9BS
**Phone** 01228 670580
**Email** ken@emerging.demon.co.uk
*Singer and guitarist performing traditional UK and political songs. Also with Dave Swarbrick.*
***Musicians' Union member***
**AC** Scotland

## Alistair Kildare
**Mail address** PO Box 560, ADDLESTONE, Surrey, KT15 1RF
**Phone** 01932 842518
*Solo singer & songwriter, guitarist and bodhran player.*
***Musicians' Union member***
**RAB** South East Arts

## Alistair McCulloch
**Contact** The Lighthouse Music Agency
**Web** www.lighthouse-music.co.uk
*Scottish fiddler player, duo with Ross Kennedy.*

## Alistair McDonald
**Mail address** c/o Corban Records, PO Box 2, GLASGOW, G44 3LB
**Phone** 0141 6375277
**Email** alcorban@hotmail.com
*Traditional/ contemporary singer & songwriter and guitar/ banjo player.*
**AC** Scotland

## Alistair Russell
**Phone/Fax** 0113 226 9209
**Email** soundout@clara.net
**Web** http://home.clara.net/soundout/
*Solo singer, guitar/ cittern accompaniment. Scottish/ Irish traditional and own songs. Ex Battlefield Band.*
***Musicians' Union member***
**RAB** Yorkshire Arts

## Alistair Russell and Chris Parkinson
**Contact** Alistair Russell
**Phone/Fax** 0113 226 9209
**Email** soundout@clara.net
**Web** http://home.clara.net/soundout/
*Duo; vocals, guitar, cittern, accordion, melodeon, harmonica. etc. Mainly Irish plus own songs.*

## Alkasalsa
**Contact** mARKO pOLO
**Web** www.markopolo.co.uk
*Devon based 10 piece Salsa band*
**RAB** South West

## All Blacked Up
**Contact** Phil Speight
**Mail address** Datfords Wharf, Mill Street, Wordsley, STOURBRIDGE, W Mids, DY8 5SX
**Phone** 01384 435554
07378 055540
**Email** p.speight@virgin.net
**Alt contact** Coughing Dog Music
**Alt address** 58 Kings Street, BROSELEY, Shrops, TF12 5NA
**Phone** 01952 882909
07973 866198
**Email** alistair@agpstudio.demon.co.uk
*English ceilidh band, mix of acoustic & electric instruments plus traditional and new music.*
**RAB** West Midlands Arts

## All Hands Around
**Contact** Alison Macfarlane
**Mail address** 40 Warwick Road, ST ALBANS, Herts, AL1 4DL
**Phone/Fax** 01727 852111
**Email** alison.macfarlane@perinat.ox.ac.uk
*5 piece band playing English & Irish music for ceilidhs & barn dances.*
**RAB** East England Arts

## Allan Johnston
**Mail address** 23 Dudley Terrace, EDINBURGH, EH6 4QQ
**Phone** 0131 5533271
**Email** a.johnston3@ntlworld.com
**Web** www.musicscotland.com/alljohn
*Singer, guitarist and songwriter. Scottish & Irish traditional and new songs. Solo or duo with fiddle player.*
***Musicians' Union member***
**AC** Scotland

## Allan Taylor
**Contact** Stoneyport Agency
**Web** www.allantaylor.com
*Respected singer/songwriter*
**RAB** Yorkshire Arts

## Allie Fox
**Contact** Elizabeth Jones Entertainments
**Web** www.vixenrecords.com
*Singer/ songwriter*
**Agents** Access All Areas, Elizabeth Jones Entertainments

## Altan
**Contact** Tom Sherlock
**Mail address** 71 Carysfort Avenue, BLACKROCK, Co Dublin, Ireland
**Phone** +353 1 2781090
**Fax** +353 1278 1093
**Email** sherlock@altan.ie
*Leading Irish traditional group*
**Agent** Asgard Promotions

## Altar Native
**Contact** David Camlin
**Mail address** Ghyll Cottage, Lamplugh Green, WORKINGTON, Cumbria, CA14 4TY
**Phone** 01946 861080
0771 2322826
**Email** Mark@alternative.freeserve.co.uk
**Alt contact** Mark Newport
**Alt address** 8 The Brow, Bullgill, MARYPORT, Cumbria, CA15 6TW
**Phone** 01900 813720
0771 4071914
**Email** Altar.Native@btinternet.com
*Electronic folk duo. Fiddle/guitar with natural sound samples/ looped ambient resonance. Full band with DJ and bass available*
**Agent** Elizabeth Jones Entertainments
***Musicians' Union member***
**RAB** Northern Arts

## Aly Bain and Phil Cunningham
**Contact** Adastra
**Web** www.adastra-music.com
*Celebrated duo: Shetland fiddler and Scottish accordionist*
**AC** Scotland

## Alyth McCormack
**Phone** 0777 1787377
**Email** bratach2@aol.com
**Web** www.alyth.com
*Singer of mainly Gaelic song, with piano, guitar & fiddle accompanists. Sings with Shine & Sunhoney. Available for workshops/ vocal coaching.*
***Musicians' Union member***
**AC** Scotland

## Amanda Hall
**Mail address** The Shadowhouse, 71 Cromwell Road, CAMBRIDGE, CB1 3EB
**Phone** 01223 515137
*Singer/ guitarist; American blues, jazz ballad & country styles. Solo, duo or band.*
***Musicians' Union member***
**RAB** East England Arts

## Amanda Lowe
**Mail address** Molescroft Grange Farmhouse, Grange Way, BEVERLEY, East Yorks
**Phone** 01482 865604
**Email** grinnigogs@pop3.poptel.org.uk
*Solo hammer dulcimer player and vocalist.*
**RAB** Yorkshire Arts

## Amaru III
**Contact** Matters Musical
**Web** www.mattersmusical.com
*South American pan pipe and flute band with rhythm section. Costumed.*



*Artists in the main A-Z listing are mostly available for concert and club bookings.*

*See page 11 for details of other artist listings (Dance Display, Solo Musicians, Composers, Arrangers, Session Musicians, Band Deps. Lecturers, MCs, Tutors, Street Theatre, Children's Entertainers, Theatre Companies).*

*Agents section appears on pages 119-131.*

# artists

*Artists in the main A-Z listing are mostly available for concert and club bookings.*

*See page 11 for details of other artist listings (Dance Display, Solo Musicians, Composers, Arrangers, Session Musicians, Band Deps. Lecturers, MCs, Tutors, Street Theatre, Children's Entertainers, Theatre Companies).*

*Agents section appears on pages 119-131.*

"a one man folk industry"

## Pete Coe

songs & tunes, with bouzouki, banjo, melodeon, dulcimer & feet, sometimes all at once

dance caller & musician, workshops, schools projects

recording and touring professionally for 30 years

"one of our most versatile and impressive performers"
*Sidmouth International Festival*

**website**
www.backshift.demon.co.uk/petehome.htm

103 Oldham Road, Ripponden, Sowerby Bridge, West Yorks, HX6 4EB
Tel & Fax 01 422 822 569
*e-mail :* petecoe@backshift.demon.co.uk

## RICK PAYNE

*acoustic blues/slide guitar...held this sell-out audience spellbound from start to finish...*
SPALDING BLUES CLUB

*Impressive slide guitar playing...bears comparison with early Ry Cooder*
COLIN RANDALL

## PETER WYTON

*poetry performed with panache*
*...a star of the performance poetry world...ready with irony, riddled with wordplay, acute with enquiry.*
CHAIRMAN LEDBURY POETRY FESTIVAL

**SEPARATELY THESE GUYS ARE IMPRESSIVE TOGETHER THEY ARE**

## RHYME & BLUES

*This splendid combination of blues and poetry really worked...the audience was calling out for more.*
DEVIZES CARNIVAL

*...a match winning combination...*
ARTISTIC DIRECTOR RIBCHESTER FESTIVAL

The Blues Line 01452 532081
linda@bluesline.freeserve.co.uk or www.bluesline.freeserve.co.uk

## BLUE C

'. . . tastefully subtle yet powerful . . . a unique blues sound that has, at its heart, a thorough soaking in Anglo-Irish folk traditions'
***– Blues Revue (USA) April 2001***

**BLUE C are Raphael Callaghan (vocal, slide guitar, harmonica) & Christine Purnell (bass, vocal)**

New album Swimming Against The Tide (BCR 51). Order direct or through Red Lick mail order

***BLUE C, available for clubs, concerts, festivals worldwide. Contact:***

**Raphael Callaghan, PO Box 48, Old Hall Street, Liverpool L69 3EB, England.**
**Tel: 0151 709 5484**
**email: raphaelcuk@yahoo.co.uk**

## DALTA

**A New Generation of Celtic Music**

"An exceptional group writing original material sympathetic to its traditional inspiration whilst being thoroughly modern in outlook" - Folk Roots

For bookings and all other enquiries contact Gareth Banks
Tel: 07740 224 329 Email: gareth@dalta.com

www.dalta.com

**AROUND THE WORLD IN 80 MINUTES WITH**

## EAST OF EALING

**GOODTIME GLOBAL GROOVES**

**BRING YA DANCIN' BOOTS!**

**A DASH OF CAJUN TO CELTIC**
**REGGAE TO RUSSIAN**
**DUB TO DERVISH**
**SOUTH AFRICAN TO SAMBA**
**GREEK TO GROOVE**
**CALL 0208 891 0623**
**www.eastofealing.fsnet.co.uk**

### Amaryllis
**Contact** Tracey Middleton
**Mail address** 16 Norgrave Road, SOLIHULL, W Midlands, B92 9JH
**Phone** 0121 7436637
**Email** amaryllis@amaryllis.force9.net
**Web** www.amaryllis.force9.net
*Accordion duo for folk/ barn dances, Playford balls, ballroom, etc. Trio with guitarist available.*
***Musicians' Union member***
**RAB** West Midlands Arts

### Amazing Blondel
**Contact** Elizabeth Jones Entertainments
**Web** www.bromyard.co.uk/ejones
*3 piece acoustic close harmony song group*

### The Amazing Mr Smith
**Contact** Derek Smith
**Mail address** Church Farm House, Loders, BRIDPORT, Dorset, DT6 3SA
**Phone/Fax** 01308 425649
**Email** amazingmrsmith@lineone.net
**Web** www.the-amazing-mr-smith.co.uk
*Eccentric, comic musician playing a variety of homemade instruments and guitar.*
***Musicians' Union member***
**RAB** South West Arts

### The Ambling Band
**Contact** Artists Connect
**Web** www.artistsconnect.com
*Afro-Latin 20 piece brass band*

### Amos Garrett
**Contact** Stoneyport Agency
**Mail address** 44 Queens Drive, GLASGOW, G42 8DD, Scotland
**Phone** 0141 4240280
0771 201 4248
**Fax** 0141 401 9741
**Email** jimcondie@aol.com
**Web** www.melmusic.com/amos_garrett
*American Blues guitarist*

### Ana Leon Flamenco Group
**Contact** Matters Musical
**Web** www.mattersmusical.com
*Group of 2 - 8 Flamenco guitarists*

### Anam
**Contact** Brian O hEadhra
**Phone** 07802 433294
**Email** office@anam.co.uk
**Web** www.anam.co.uk
*Traditional & contemporary Celtic music group. Music from Scotland, Ireland, Cornwall, etc*
**Agent** CTM UK/Celtic Traditional Music
***Musicians' Union member***
**AC** Scotland

### Ancillary Folk Dance Band
**Contact** Ann Steward
**Mail address** 104 High Street, Sutton, ELY, Cambs, CB6 2NW
**Phone** 01353 778655
*2-3 piece social dance band. Can run mixed ability workshops.*
**RAB** East England Arts

### Andalus
**Contact** Matters Musical
**Web** www.mattersmusical.com
*3 Spanish guitarists/vocalists plus bass and drums. Latin rumba and flamenco styles*

### Andrew Cronshaw
**Contact** Cloud Valley Music
**Mail address** 51 Hainault Court, Forest Rise, LONDON, E17 3NW
**Fax** 020 8521 4649
**Email** cloudval@aol.com
**Web** http://members.aol.com/cloudval
*Journalist, multi-instrumentalist: zithers, wind instruments, etc. Producer and sound engineer.*
***Musicians' Union member***
**RAB** London Arts

### Andy Caven
**Mail address** 20 Meyrick Crescent, COLCHESTER, Essex, CO2 7QY
**Phone** 01206 549582
**Email** andy@andycaven.freeserve.co.uk
**Web** www.andycaven.co.uk
*Singer & guitarist; rock n roll, blues, folk, love songs plus own songs.*
**RAB** East England Arts

### Andy Guttridge
**Contact** Elizabeth Jones Entertainments
**Web** www.bromyard.co.uk/ejones
*Singer/songwriter*

### Andy Guttridge and Martin Green
**Contact** Karisma Music Management
**Web** www.karisma.net
*Available as a duo or with Roger Inniss (bass) and Tom Leary (fiddle)*

### Andy Irvine
**Contact** The Bechhofer Agency
*Renowned Irish singer/ musician, also with Patrick Street.*

### Andy Lambert
**Mail address** 50 Riversdale Road, LONDON, N5 2JT
**Phone** 07767 607717
**Phone/Fax** 020 7226 5477
**Email** andrew@lamcon.demon.co.uk
*Plays strummed strings and sings. Irish, Scots, Bluegrass.*
***Musicians' Union member***
**RAB** London Arts

### Andy M Stewart and Gerry O'Beirne
**Contact** Stoneyport Agency
**Web** www.stoneyport.demon.co.uk

### Andy Perkins
**Mail address** 21 Stone Street, FAVERSHAM, Kent, ME13 8PU
**Phone** 01795 533864
01795 590374
**Email** andybanjo@aol.com
*Tenor banjo player, teacher and barn dance band leader.*
***Musicians' Union member***
**RAB** South East Arts

### Andy Smythe
**Contact** Elizabeth Jones Entertainments
**Web** www.bromyard.co.uk/ejones
*Singer/ songwriter. Also available as a duo with Chris Payne*

### Andy Stafford
**Mail address** 22 Flamborough Close, Lower Earley, READING, Berks, RG6 3XB
**Phone** 0118 935 3382
07715 478822
**Email** Andy@mnemonic.uk.com
*Dance caller*
**RAB** Southern Arts

### Andy Thorburn
**Phone** 01349 830132
**Email** andythorburn@madasafish
**Web** www.musicscotland.com/andy
*Scottish pianist, composer, musical director and teacher.*
**AC** Scotland

### Andy Turner
**Mail address** 37 Orwell Drive, DIDCOT, Oxon, OX11 7RX
**Phone** 01235 811757
**Email** andyturner@britishlibrary.net
**Web** http://homepages.tesco.net/~andy.auds
*Solo performer mainly of Southern English songs and tunes. Vocals with anglo-concertina.*
**RAB** Southern Arts

### Angela Brown and The Mighty 45s
**Contact** GTA Music Agency
*Major Blues act*

### Angelique Kidjo
**Contact** Primary Talent
*Popular Afro-pop singer*

### Angelou
**Contact** Moneypenny
*Contemporary folk band, performing songs written by Holly Terski*

## artists
## a

*Artists in the main A-Z listing are mostly available for concert and club bookings*

*See page 11 for details of other artist listings (Dance Display, Solo Musicians, Composers, Arrangers, Session Musicians, Band Deps, Lecturers, MCs, Tutors, Street Theatre, Children's Entertainers, Theatre Companies).*

*Agents section appears on pages 119-131.*

*Artists in the main A-Z listing are mostly available for concert and club bookings.*

*See page 11 for details of other artist listings (Dance Display, Solo Musicians, Composers, Arrangers, Session Musicians, Band Deps. Lecturers, MCs, Tutors, Street Theatre, Children's Entertainers, Theatre Companies).*

*Agents section appears on pages 119-131.*

## Angels Of The North
**Contact** Noel Jackson
**Mail address** 3 East Law, EBCHESTER, Co Durham, DH8 0QH
**Phone** 01207 560684
**Email** info@angelsofthenorth.org
**Web** www.angelsofthenorth.org
*6 piece ceilidh and concert band specialising in ancient and modern Northumbrian material. Own caller.*
**RAB** Northern Arts

## Ani Difranco
**Contact** Primary Talent
*Major league singer songwriter from Buffalo, New York*

## Anna Ryder
**Contact** Rowdy Music
**Mail address** PO Box 1596, WARWICK CV34 6ZR
**Phone** 01926 400927
**Email** rowdy.music@virgin.net
**Web** www.rowdymusic.net
**Alt contact** Richard Hamilton
**Phone** 01295 268313
*Singer-songwriter, multi-instrumentalist.*
***Musicians' Union member***
**RAB** West Midlands Arts

## Anne Duggan
**Contact** Elizabeth Jones Entertainments
**Web** www.bromyard.co.uk/ejones
*Singer/songwriter available with band*

## Anne Lister
**Mail address** 34 Nightingale House, Thomas More Street, LONDON, E1 9UA
**Phone** 020 7481 3619
**Email** anne.lister@virgin.net
**Web** http://freespace.virgin.net/anne.lister
*Singer-songwriter, storyteller, workshop leader.*
**RAB** London Arts

## Anne Lorne Gillies
**Contact** Kevin Bree
**Email** kevinbree@bigfoot.com
**Email** annelornegillies@bigfoot.com
*Gaelic singer/ songwriter/ pianist. Teacher and writer of Gaelic and English books/ stories.*
**AC** Scotland

## Anne Martin
**Contact** Whitewave Music
**Web** www.whiteact.demon.co.uk
*Traditional Gaelic song from the Isle of Skye and West Coast of Scotland. Available solo, with Ingrid Henderson or with full band.*
***Musicians' Union member***
**AC** Scotland

## Annies Blues
**Contact** Geoff Palfreman
**Mail address** Teversall, Thornton Road, Goxhill, BARROW ON HUMBER, North Lincs, DN19 7LW
**Phone** 01469 531344
**Web** pages.eidosnet.co.uk/zippynbungle
*Acoustic style blues.*
**RAB** Yorkshire Arts

## Apicella
**Contact** Roger Courtney
**Phone** 023 9267 2087
**Email** rogcourtney@aol.com
*4 piece folk, blues, boogie & swing band.*

## April Verch Band
**Contact** Emerging Music
**Web** www.emerging.demon.co.uk
*Canadian fiddler and step-dancer with band*

## Apu
**Contact** Matters Musical
**Web** www.mattersmusical.com
*Andean pan pipe and flute group with percussion. Traditional and contemporary tunes*

## Ar Log
**Contact** Gwyndaf Roberts
**Mail address** 25 Briarmeadow Drive, Thornhill, CARDIFF, CF4 9FB, Wales
**Phone/Fax** 029 2075 6931
**Phone** 07836 318960
**Email** gwyndafroberts@tinyworld.co.uk
*Folk group playing traditional Welsh music arranged for the 21st century. Triple harp, fiddles, flute, guitars and percussion.*
***Musicians' Union member***
**AC** Wales

## Aranmore
**Contact** Elizabeth Jones Entertainments
**Web** www.bromyard.co.uk/ejones
*Fiddle, keyboards & vocals*
**RAB** West Midlands Arts

## The Armpit Jug Band
**Contact** Karisma Music Management
**Web** www.karisma.net

## Arnie Cottrell and Tim Payne
**Contact** Arnie Cottrell
**Mail address** 20 Roseland Gardens, Highfield, SOUTHAMPTON, Hants
**Phone** 023 8031 5048
**Alt contact** Mutiny Music
**Alt address** 51 Brunel Drive, Preston, WEYMOUTH, Dorset, DT3 6NY
**Phone** 01305 832447
**Email** tim@talkingheads.freeserve.co.uk
*Acoustic duo playing range of country blues, cajun, appalachian and bluegrass.*
**RAB** Southern Arts

## Arthur Knevett
**Mail address** 130 Clee Road, GRIMSBY, Lincs, DN32 8NP
**Phone** 01472 699432
**Email** Carol.arthur@btinternet.com
*Unaccompanied traditional singer, mostly English ballads and songs.*
**RAB** East England Arts

## Artisan
**Contact** Jacey Bedford Tour Management
**Web** www.artifact.demon.co.uk
*Yorkshire vocal harmony trio. Songs and humour.*
**RAB** Yorkshire Arts

## Arve Haland's Cajun Gumbo
**Contact** Access All Areas
*Norwegian Cajun group*

## Asha
**Contact** Shindy Arts
**Web** www.shindy.org.uk
*3 piece ceilidh and concert band playing folk tunes with blues, soul, jazz & latin influences*
**RAB** Southern Arts

## Atlantic Bridge
**Contact** Terry Arsenault/Penny Phenix
**Mail address** 10 Penrith Road, BASINGSTOKE, Hants, RG21 8XW
**Phone** 01256 329702
0778 873 3593
**Fax** 01256 475381
**Email** penny.phenix@lineone.net
*4 piece Celtic music band. Fiddle, uilleann pipes, vocals, etc. Caller available for ceilidhs.*
***Musicians' Union member***
**RAB** Southern Arts

## Babysnakes
**Contact** Sonia Oakes-Stuart
**Mail address** 79a Adelaide Avenue, Ladywell, LONDON, SE4 1JY
**Phone** 020 8690 5817
07946 467626
**Fax** 020 8690 1022
**Email** jimsos@ukonline.co.uk
**Alt contact** Catherine Wood
**Alt address** 129 Mitcham Road, East Ham, LONDON
**Phone** 020 84712185
07940 719297
*4 piece all female acoustic instrumental band. Music from around the world on cello, mandolin, guitar, accordion and fiddle.*
***Musicians' Union member***
**RAB** London Arts

## Bachue
**Contact** Corrina Hewat
**Mail address** 11A Ettrick Road, SELKIRK, TD7 5AJ, Scotland
**Phone/Fax** 01750 22023
**Phone** 07711 512692
**Email** bachue@bachue.co.uk
**Web** www.bachue.co.uk
*Duo playing traditional and contemporary mix on harp, piano and vocals.*
***Musicians' Union member***
**AC** Scotland

## Back Of The Moon
**Contact** Back of The Moon Music
**Mail address** White Heather Cottage, Gartocharn, ALEXANDRIA, G83 8ND, Scotland
**Phone** 07929 237436
0141 564 5679
**Email** botmusic@hotmail.com
**Web** http://backofthemoon.tripod.com/backofthemoon
*4 piece Scottish folk group, pipes, fiddle, guitar, piano plus vocals. Featutures Gillian Frame, Young Scottish Traditional Musician of the Year 2001.*
**AC** Scotland

## Bag O'Cats
**Contact** Stoneyport Agency
**Web** www.bagocats.org.uk
*Scottish 5 piece instrumental Folk-Jazz-improvisational band with influences from the Cairngorms to the Himalayas*
**AC** Scotland

## The Baggettes
**Contact** Paul Saunders
**Mail address** 6 Swan Meadow, MUCH WENLOCK, Shropshire, TF13 6JQ
**Phone/Fax** 01952 728283
**Email** ps@workingjo.co.uk
**Web** www.workingjoe.co.uk
*14-18th century costumed street band. Authentic sounds & sights. Medieval ceilidhs with caller.*
***Musicians' Union member***
**RAB** West Midlands Arts

## Baggyrinkle
**Contact** Dave Robinson
**Mail address** 267 Llangyfelach Road, Brynhyfryd, SWANSEA, SA5 9LB, Wales
**Phone** 01792 464871
**Fax** 01792 415725
**Email** david.robinson2@ntlworld.com
**Web** www.baggyrinkle.freeservers.com
*Sea songs & shanties, drinking songs etc. Traditional and new. 3 part harmony with some concertina.*
**AC** Wales

## Baghdaddies
**Contact** CTM UK/Celtic Traditional Music
**Web** www.ctmuk.com
*Eastern Europe, Middle East and world roots dance band*
**Agent** Access All Areas, CTM UK/ Celtic Traditional Music

## Baka Beyond
**Contact** OTB Productions
**Web** www.otbproductions.co.uk
*Global dance music fusing musicians from Europe and the West Coast of Africa*

## Balalaika Orchestra
**Contact** Matters Musical
**Web** www.mattersmusical.com
*Balalaika Orchestra, variety of sizes available*

## Balfa Toujours
**Contact** Access All Areas
*Louisiana traditional Cajun band*

## Baluji Shrivastav
**Contact** Matters Musical
**Web** www.mattersmusical.com
*Hindustani classical singer and sitar player. Available solo or with his jazz-Indian band, Jazz Orient*
**RAB** London Arts

## Band B Band
**Contact** Keith Leech
**Mail address** 205 Priory Road, HASTINGS, Sussex, TN34 3JB
**Phone/Fax** 01424 716576
**Email** chiefbogie@hotmail.com
*Band for ceilidhs/ barn dances. East Sussex & surrounding area. Ex members of Banjax, etc.*
**RAB** South East Arts

## Band of Rack and Ruin
**Contact** Elizabeth Jones Entertainments
**Web** www.bromyard.co.uk/ejones
*4 piece folk/ rock band*

## Band Of Two
**Contact** Pete Fyfe
**Mail address** 26 Cumberland Court, Cross Road, CROYDON, Surrey, CR0 6TE
**Phone** 020 8680 4302
**Email** petefyfe@aol.com
*Goodtime celtic folk duo and folk dance band*
**Agent** Elizabeth Jones Entertainments
***Musicians' Union member***
**RAB** South East Arts

## Banish Misfortune
**Contact** ABDC Entertainments
**Web** www.abdc.co.uk
*3-6 piece barn dance band with caller. Wide mix of traditional and modern dances*
**RAB** Southern Arts

## Banoffi
**Contact** Dave Moss
**Mail address** The Toft, Bank House Farm, Glaisdale, WHITBY, North Yorks, YO21 2QA
**Phone** 01947 897313
**Email** david@banoffi.com
**Web** www.banoffi.com
**Alt contact** Ian Hulme
**Alt address** Airy Hill Manor, Waterstead Lane, WHITBY, North Yorks
**Phone** 01947 821087
**Email** ian@banoffi.com
*3 piece Anglo-European-Celtic acoustic band. Fiddle, bouzouki, bodhran, song, etc*
**Agent** Porthole Promotions
**RAB** Yorkshire Arts

## Banter
**Contact** Kirsty Cotter
**Mail address** 23 Moorfield Rd, WOODBRIDGE, Suffolk, IP12 4JN
**Phone** 01394 388221
07796 184981
**Email** kirsty.cotter@btinternet.co.uk
*3 piece all female band playing traditional & contemporary Scottish music on clarsach, fiddle, cello, viola & voice.*
**AC** Scotland



*Artists in the main A-Z listing are mostly available for concert and club bookings.*

*See page 11 for details of other artist listings (Dance Display, Solo Musicians, Composers, Arrangers, Session Musicians, Band Deps. Lecturers, MCs, Tutors, Street Theatre, Children's Entertainers, Theatre Companies).*

*Agents section appears on pages 119-131.*

# artists
## b

*Artists in the main A-Z listing are mostly available for concert and club bookings.*

*See page 11 for details of other artist listings (Dance Display, Solo Musicians, Composers, Arrangers, Session Musicians, Band Deps. Lecturers, MCs, Tutors, Street Theatre, Children's Entertainers, Theatre Companies).*

*Agents section appears on pages 119-131.*

### Barachois
**Contact** Adastra
**Web** www.adastra-music.com
*Canadian band playing music from the Acadian (French) tradition, with an element of physical comedy*

### Barnstorm
**Contact** Matters Musical
**Web** www.mattersmusical.com
*American-style dances. Led by Dave Evans calling in patter style.*

### The Barra MacNeils
**Contact** mARKO pOLO
**Web** www.markopolo.co.uk
*Cape Breton band, playing a range of instruments, singing in Gaelic and English*

### Barry Charles
**Mail address** The Barn, Moorstead House, Widdicombe Lane, COMPTON, Devon, TQ3 1TD
**Phone** 01803 875437
07957 975981
**Email** barrycharles@btinternet.com
*UK based Australian vocalist, songwriter, guitarist. Plus scatting, Tibetan chant/ split harmonics. Rhythmic/ percussive guitar.*
**RAB** South West Arts

### Barry Goodman
**Mail address** 54 Ickleford Road, HITCHIN, Herts, SG5 1TR
**Phone** 01462 456811
**Email** barry.goodman1@ntlworld.com
**Web** www.good-man.freeserve.co.uk
*Caller for English ceilidhs, barn dances, weddings etc.*
**RAB** East England Arts

### Baton Rouge
**Contact** Access All Areas
*Welsh band mixing Cajun, Hillbilly, Irish, Delta Blues, etc*
**Agent** Access All Areas, Artists Connect

### The Battlefield Band
**Contact** Robin Morton - Manager
**Mail address** Temple Records, Shillinghill, TEMPLE, Midlothian, EH23 4SH, Scotland
**Phone** 01875 830328
**Fax** 01875 830392
**Web** www.battlefieldband.co.uk
*One of Scotlands leading traditional music bands, under the banner "forward with Scotland's past".*
***Musicians' Union member***
**AC** Scotland

### Bayou Seco
**Contact** Access All Areas
*USA Cajun/ "old music" trio*

### The Bearcats
**Contact** Swamp Music
**Web** www.swampmusic.co.uk
*4/5 piece traditional cajun band featuring members of R Cajun, the Flatville Aces and Bearcat Trio.*
**Agent** Matters Musical, Swamp Music

### Becky Taylor
**Contact** Becky Speller
**Mail address** 10 Langton Street, Sowerby Bridge, HALIFAX, West Yorks, HX6 2HD
**Phone** 01422 839262
07980 600476
**Email** rebecca.taylor@eu.interfaceinc.com
*Performer and teacher of Uilleann pipes, Northumbrian smallpipes, fiddle & whistles. Composer & arranger*
**Agent** Artists Connect
**RAB** Yorkshire Arts

### Bedlam
**Contact** James McKinlay
**Mail address** 2 Towngate, Botany Lane, Lepton, HUDDERSFIELD, Yorks, HD8 0NR
**Phone/Fax** 01484 604704
**Email** bedlam@selwynmusic.co.uk
**Phone** 07961 157128
*Popular young 4 piece ceilidh and concert band. Fiddle, box, recorder, guitar, drums & didgeridoo.*
**RAB** Yorkshire Arts

### Beehive Band
**Contact** Roger Edwards
**Mail address** 199 Town Lane, Whittle-le-Woods, CHORLEY, Lancs, PR6 8AG
**Phone** 01257 276022
*5 piece ceilidh/barndance band. English music on melodeon, concertina, viola, mandola, cello.*
**RAB** North West Arts

### Beggar's Row Folk Band
**Contact** Harry Morris
**Mail address** Carrymor Cottage, East Greenlees Road, Cambuslang, GLASGOW, G72 8TU, Scotland
**Phone** 0141 6460086
**Fax** 01505 815729
**Email** beggarsrow@supanet.com
**Web** www.beggarsrow.supanet.com
**Phone** 0141 5503388
*6 piece band, Scottish/ Irish traditional song and music.*
**AC** Scotland

### Beginish
**Contact** Artistic Upstarts
**Web** www.taramusic.com/begin.htm
*Respected Irish 5 piece band*
**Agent** Artistic Upstarts, Stoneyport Agency

### Bella MacNab's Dance Band
**Contact** David Francis
**Mail address** 214 Portobello High Street, EDINBURGH, EH15 2AO
**Phone/Fax** 0131 6698824
**Email** dfrancis@musicscotland.com
**Web** www.ceilidhdance.com
*5 piece fiddle-led ceilidh band. Caller for Scottish dancing. Includes members of The Cast, Salsa Celtica, Anam, etc.*
***Musicians' Union member***
**AC** Scotland

### Belshazzar's Feast
**Contact** Paul Sartin
**Mail address** May Cottage, WHERWELL, Hants, SP11 7JS
**Phone** 01264 860791
07711 485798
**Web** www.2pauls.com
*Concerts/dance duo. Paul Sartin (oboe, violin, vocals), Paul Hutchinson (accordion).*
**RAB** Southern Arts

### Benji Kirkpatrick
**Contact** Elizabeth Jones Entertainments
**Web** www.benjikirkpatrick.co.uk
*Noted young singer and guitarist/ bouzouki player. Also in Magpie Lane and Dr. Faustus.*
**Agent** The Amber Agency, Elizabeth Jones Entertainments
**RAB** West Midlands Arts

### Beppe Gambetta
**Contact** mARKO pOLO
**Web** www.markopolo.co.uk
*US flat picking guitarist. Also with Dan Crary.*

### Bernard Hoskin
**Mail address** 43 Broadmeadow, SAWSTON, Cambs, CB2 4EB
**Phone** 01223 834731
**Fax** 01223 565532
**Email** bernard@bhoskin.com
**Web** www.bernardhoskin.com
*Singer, songwriter, guitarist. Acoustic roots.*
**RAB** East England Arts

### Bernard Wrigley
**Mail address** 'Brewin', 1a Ansdell Road, Horwich, BOLTON, Lancs, BL6 7HJ
**Phone** 01204 697716
**Email** loofyman@aol.com
**Web** www.bernardwrigley.com
*Storyteller, singer and instrument-alist. Solo or sea song, fiddle and concertina duo with Wilf Darlington.*
**RAB** North West Arts

## Bert Jansch
**Contact** Stoneyport Agency
**Web** www.stoneyport.demon.co.uk
*Highly influential guitarist, and singer/songwriter*

## Beverley Martyn
**Contact** Elizabeth Jones Entertainments
**Web** www.bromyard.co.uk/ejones
*Singer/ songwriter*

## Beware Of The Dog
**Contact** mARKO pOLO
**Web** www.markopolo.co.uk
*Twin fiddle-led band with Pat Kilbride and Brian Mullan on cello*

## Beyond The Pale
**Contact** Matters Musical
**Web** www.mattersmusical.com
*4 piece Irish - bluegrass band, 2 female vocalists*

## Bhodan Chomenko
**Contact** Matters Musical
**Web** www.mattersmusical.com
*Ukranian accordionist/ vocalist. Hungarian, French, Macedonian, etc*

## Bibs Ekkel's Tziganka
**Contact** Matters Musical
**Web** www.mattersmusical.com
*11 piece Russian folk music and dance group*

## Big Bad Contra
**Contact** Fiona Maurice-Smith
**Mail address** 47 Mill Lane, KEGWORTH, Derbys, DE74 2FX
**Phone** 01509 673867
07946 703302
**Email** fiona@maurice-smith99.freeserve.co.uk
**Web** www.bandsandmusicians.co.uk
**Alt contact** Flos Headford
**Alt address** 38 Upton Street, Tredworth, GLOUCESTER, GL1 4LA
**Phone** 01592 240989
01452 310372
**Email** flos@madasafish.com
*Contra dance music with attitude! Ian Wilson, Alan Harris, Fiona Maurice-Smith, Flos Headford.*
**RAB** South West Arts

## Big Bashooey
**Contact** Corrina Hewat
**Mail address** 11A Ettrick Road, SELKIRK, TD7 5AJ, Scotland
**Phone/Fax** 01750 22023
**Phone** 07711 512692
**Email** bachue@bachue.co.uk
**Web** www.bachue.co.uk
*Eight piece band, influences from traditional Scottish to contemporary music, with Scots & Gaelic vocals.*
**AC** Scotland

## Big Bill Morganfield
**Contact** mARKO pOLO
**Web** www.markopolo.co.uk
*Muddy Waters' son and band. Winner of WC Handy Award 2000 for Best New Artist*

## The Big Hum
**Contact** UK Touring
**Web** www.uktouring.org.uk
*Trio performing a capella song, dance and rural debate*

## The Big Nite Out
**Contact** mARKO pOLO
**Web** www.markopolo.co.uk
*Pat Kilbride and Miriam Kavana's Irish session band*

## Big Sky
**Contact** Active
*Scottish band with Charlie McKerron and John Saich of Capercaillie, Laura McKerron and others. Essence of tradition with a modern sound*
**AC** Scotland

## Bill Barclay
**Mail address** 39 Shandon Crescent, EDINBURGH EH11 1QF Scotland
**Phone** 0131 3394279
**Email** bb003@almac.co.uk
*Singing comic and compere of folk festivals*
**Agent** Stoneyport Agency
**AC** Scotland

## Bill Caddick
**Mail address** Flat 8, Maws Craft Centre, Jackfield, TELFORD, Shrops, TF8 7LS
**Phone** 01952 883009
**Fax** 01952 833923
**Email** caddick.family@virgin.net
**Web** www.billcaddick.co.uk
*Singer/ songwriter. Mainly own songs accompanied on 6, 12 string and steel guitars. Former member of Albion Band, Home Service, etc. Clubs, festivals, TV, radio, film.*
**Agent** Working Joe Music
**RAB** West Midlands Arts

## Bill Jones
**Contact** Felicity Jones
**Mail address** Brick Wall Music, PO Box 391, SUNDERLAND, SR6 8YN
**Phone** 01889 271858
**Email** bookings@brickwallmusic.com
**Web** www.brickwallmusic.com
*Fast rising young singer and musician. Recipient of Horizons Award at BBC Folk Awards 2001.*
**RAB** Northern Arts

## Bill Taylor
**Mail address** Orchard House, Castle Leod, STRATHPEFFER, Ross-shire, IV14 9AA
**Phone** 01997 421143
**Email** bill@clarsach.net
**Web** www.clarsach.net/bill_taylor.htm
*Harp player of ancient music of Ireland, Scotland, Wales. Solo or with male singer and recorder player.*
***Musicians' Union member***
**AC** Scotland

## Bill Whaley and Dave Fletcher
**Contact** Dave Fletcher
**Mail address** Amulree Holme Road, Kirton Holme, BOSTON, Lincs PE20 1TE
**Phone** 01205 290562
*Vocal duo accompanied by concertinas and other reeds. Mainly traditional chorus songs.*
***Musicians' Union member***
**RAB** East Midlands Arts

## Billy Ross
**Contact** Greentrax
**Mail address** Cockenzie Business Centre, Edinburgh Road, COCKENZIE, East Lothian, EH32 0XL, Scotland
**Phone** 01875 814155
01875 815888
**Fax** 01875 813545
**Email** greentrax@aol.com
**Web** www.greentrax.com
**Alt contact** Brenda McCulloch
*Scottish/ Gaelic traditional singer, former member of Ossian.*
**AC** Scotland

## The Bisserov Sisters
**Contact** mARKO pOLO
**Web** www.markopolo.co.uk
*Female Bulgarian vocal trio*

## The Black Cat Theory
**Contact** Josh Clark
**Mail address** 6 Rockcliffe Road, Bathwick, BATH, BA2 6QN
**Phone** 07866 749862
**Email** josh@theblackcattheory.co.uk
**Web** www.theblackcattheory.co.uk
*4 piece jazz roots band; banjo, piano, double bass and drums. Winners of the BBC Young Folk Award, 2000.*
***Musicians' Union member***
**RAB** South West Arts



*Artists in the main A-Z listing are mostly available for concert and club bookings.*

*See page 11 for details of other artist listings (Dance Display, Solo Musicians, Composers, Arrangers, Session Musicians, Band Deps. Lecturers, MCs, Tutors, Street Theatre, Children's Entertainers, Theatre Companies).*

*Agents section appears on pages 119-131.*

*Artists in the main A-Z listing are mostly available for concert and club bookings.*

*See page 11 for details of other artist listings (Dance Display, Solo Musicians, Composers, Arrangers, Session Musicians, Band Deps. Lecturers, MCs, Tutors, Street Theatre, Children's Entertainers, Theatre Companies).*

*Agents section appears on pages 119-131.*

## Black Sheep Ceilidh Band
**Contact** Richard Watkinson
**Mail address** 126 Onslow Road, SHEFFIELD, S11 7AG
**Phone** 0114 266 8280
**Email** blacksheep@argonet.co.uk
**Email** rwatki@argonet.co.uk
*4 piece barn dance/ceilidh band. English, Irish, Scottish and American music. South Yorks area. With caller.*
**RAB** Yorkshire Arts

## Blackthorn
**Phone** 01273 455202
**Email** pete@mcmail.demon.co.uk
**Web** www.hobgoblin.com/blackthorn
*Music from around the British Isles, especially Ireland*

## Black Umfolosi
**Contact** Adastra
**Web** www.adastra-music.com
*Traditional Zimbabwean song and dance group. Workshops and community residencies available*

## Blazin' Fiddles
**Contact** Bruce MacGregor
**Mail address** Holm Burn, Essich Road, INVERNESS, IV2 6AH, Scotland
**Phone** 01463 238070
**Email** bruce.mac@virgin.net
**Web** www.blazin-fiddles.co.uk
*6 of Scotlands finest fiddle players from the Highlands and Islands, with guitar and piano. Solo to ensemble playing. Workshop leaders*
**Agent** Adastra
**AC** Scotland

## Bleizi Ruz
**Contact** Adastra
**Web** www.adastra-music.com
*One of Brittany's best known bands.*

## Blowzabella
**Contact** Nigel Eaton
**Mail address** 15 Becondale Road, Upper Norwood, LONDON, SE19 1QS
**Phone** 020 8653 9059
*Influential band playing European dance music. Hurdy gurdy, pipes, fiddle, accordeon, etc*
**RAB** London Arts

## Blue C
**Contact** Raphael Callaghan
**Mail address** PO Box 48, Old Hall Street, LIVERPOOL, L69 3EB
**Phone** 0151 709 5484
**Email** raphaelcuk@yahoo.co.uk
*Blues, gospel & roots duo. Raphael Callaghan (vocal, slide guitar & harmonica) & Christine Purnell (bass guitar, vocal).*
***Musicians' Union member***
**RAB** North West Arts

## Blue Hyenas
**Contact** Stoneyport Agency
**Web** www.stoneyport.demon.co.uk
*4/5 piece Edinburgh R 'n B band, with brass if required*

## Blue Yonder
**Contact** Ken Morris
**Mail address** 4 Bannerman Road, NOTTINGHAM, NG6 9HZ
**Phone** 0115 9169681
**Email** B123yonder@aol.com
**Phone** 01773 762723
*Contemporary folk/ roots trio, vocal and instrumental.*
**RAB** East Midlands Arts

## Bluehorses
**Contact** Nic Waulker
**Mail address** PO Box 51, PONTYPRIDD, CF37 2YQ, Wales
**Phone/Fax** 01443 686963
**Email** nic@nativespirit.demon.co.uk
**Web** www.bluehorses.co.uk
*Twin fiddle driven rock-folk band from Wales*
**Agent** Adastra
**AC** Wales

## The Blues Band
**Contact** GTA Music Agency
**Alt contact** Toni Weekes
*Renowned line-up of Paul Jones, Dave Kelly, Tom McGuinness, Gary Fletcher, Rob Townsend*

## Boat Band
**Contact** Kate Barfield
**Mail address** 19 Croft Crescent, Penkhull, STOKE ON TRENT, ST4 5EP
**Phone** 01782 871691
**Email** boatband@cwctv.net
**Web** www.rootsworld.com/harbour town/boatband.html
*4 piece band, mainly traditional dance music & song. Cajun, English, Caribbean. Stage, street & dances. Workshops on song, NW tunes, fiddle, melodeon*
**Agent** Matters Musical, Swamp Music
***Musicians' Union member***
**RAB** North West Arts

## Bob and Gill Berry
**Contact** Robert Berry
**Mail address** 19 Whistley Road, Potterne, DEVIZES, Wilts, SN10 5QY
**Phone** 01380 726597
07714 550990
**Email** bobandgill@aol.com
**Web** http://hometown.aol.com/potfolk/myhomepage/business.html
*Duo singing traditional and contemporary folk songs in harmony.*
**RAB** Southern Arts

## Bob Adams
**Contact** Shindy Arts
**Web** www.shindy.org.uk
*Caller for barn dances and ceilidhs*
**RAB** Southern Arts

## Bob Brozman
**Contact** NEM Productions (UK)
**Web** www.nemproductions.com
*American musician, author and ethnomusicologist*

## Bob Everhart
**Contact** Access All Areas
*USA Old Timey and Bluegrass musician*

## Bob Fox
**Mail address** 33 Chillingham Drive, CHESTER-LE-STREET, Co Durham, DH2 3TJ
**Phone/Fax** 0191 388 6505
**Phone** 07885 213691
**Email** bob@bobfoxmusic.com
**Web** www.bobfoxmusic.com
*Solo North East singer & guitarist. Folksongs from NE & beyond, traditional and modern*
**Agent** Iconic Music & Media, The Other Agency
**RAB** Northern Arts

## Bob Hall
**Contact** Prospect Music
**Mail address** 5 Prospect Place, Totley Rise, SHEFFIELD, S17 4HZ
**Phone/Fax** 0114 2363309
**Email** prospect@boogie.demon.co.uk
**Web** www.boogie.demon.co.uk
**Alt contact** Lesley Carr
**Alt address** Able Records, Red House Cottage, Botley Road, SHEFFIELD, Hants, SO32 2HN
**Phone/Fax** 01329 833359
**Email** gone@globalnet.co.uk
*Boogie Woogie pianist & vocalist, original material. Duo with Hilary Blythe, trio with Stewart Carr*
**Agent** GTA Music Agency
***Musicians' Union member***
**RAB** Yorkshire Arts

## Bobby Eaglesham
**Contact** The Bechhofer Agency
*Scottish*
**AC** Scotland

## Bobby Valentino
**Contact** Matters Musical
**Web** www.mattersmusical.com
*Renowned fiddle player and crooner. Swing, jazz and country*

## Bohinta
**Contact** CTM UK
**Web** www.ctmuk.com
*Irish traditional & contemporary music and song*

## Boka Halat
**Contact** Hemlock Music
**Web** www.hemlockmusic.demon.co.uk
*6 piece dance band fusing English tunes with rhythms from the Gambia, India, etc. Workshops on multicultural dance, percussion, improvisation, etc*
**Agent** Hemlock Music
**RAB** Southern Arts

## The Bollywood Brass Band
**Contact** Emergency Exit Arts
**Web** www.eea.org.uk
*Bollywood meets Brass meets Bhangra. Stage or costumed procession*
***Musicians' Union member***
**RAB** London Arts

## Bon Accord Ceilidh Band
**Contact** ABDC Entertainments
**Web** www.abdc.co.uk
*3-6 piece Scottish ceilidh and country dance band*
**RAB** Southern Arts

## Bon Temps Playboys
**Contact** Clare Gilliam
**Mail address** 70a Mansfield Road, LONDON, NW3 2HU
**Phone/Fax** 020 7267 1374
**Email** bontemps@playboys1.freeserve.co.uk
**Web** http://members.aol.com/bontempsplayboys
*7-piece Herts/London based band playing Cajun, Zydeco, Swamp Pop*
**Agent** Swamp Music
***Musicians' Union member***
**RAB** London Arts

## Boneshaker
**Contact** UK Touring
**Web** www.uktouring.org.uk
*Stiltdancing percussionists, mix of carnival, house and experimental sound. Trombone, melodeon, percussion, kit, bass and dj. Son of Salt*

## Boo Hewerdine
**Contact** Emerging Music
**Web** www.emerging.demon.co.uk
*Singer songwriter covered by kd lang, Paul Young and Eleanor Shanley*

## Boogalusa
**Contact** Mesmerist Productions
**Web** www.mesmerist.com
*Scotland based Cajun band*
***Musicians' Union member***
**AC** Scotland

## The Border Directors
**Contact** Derek Poxton
**Mail address** 17 Northbourne Avenue, MORPETH, Northumberland, NE61 1JG
**Phone** 01670 519037
**Email** DPO1234@aol.com
**Web** www.dragonflymusic.co.uk
**Alt contact** Matt Seattle
**Alt address** PO Box 13772, PEEBLES, EH45 8YE, Scotland
**Phone/Fax** 01721 724707
**Email** matt@dragonflymusic.co.uk
*Northumberland and Scottish Borders music for ceilidhs, concerts, etc. With caller.*
**RAB** Northern Arts

## Boreen
**Contact** Helen Akitt
**Mail address** 105 Green Hill, HIGH WYCOMBE, Bucks, HP13 5QB
**Phone** 01494 513105
07768 618962
**Email** helenakitt@compuserve.com
**Alt contact** Paul Draper
**Phone** 020 8548 1941
*Duo to 4 piece ceilidh/ barn dance/ pub band*
**Agent** ABDC Entertainments
**RAB** Southern Arts

## Boys From The Hill
**Contact** Chris Pitson 115 Powys Avenue, Townhill, SWANSEA, West Glamorgan, SA1 6PJ, Wales
**Phone** 01792 421881
**Email** bfth2001@ntlworld.com
**Web** homepage/ntlworld.com/bfth2001
*Urban Welsh acoustic trio.*
**AC** Wales

## Boys Of The Lough
**Contact** Dave Richardson
**Mail address** 31 Fountainhall Road, EDINBURGH, EH9 2LN, Scotland
**Phone/Fax** 0131 662 0956
*Long established and influential traditional celtic music band.*
**AC** Scotland

## Bracken Rigg Band
**Contact** Geoff Wright
**Mail address** 10 Woodside Road, Scawthorpe, DONCASTER, Yorks, DN5 9LE
**Phone** 01302 784561
**Email** brackenriggband@hotmail.com
**Web** www.brackenrigg.homepage.com
*Scottish/ Irish ceilidh/ barn dance band. Accordion & fiddle.*
***Musicians' Union member***
**RAB** Yorkshire Arts

## Bram Taylor
**Mail address** 64 Arlington Drive, LEIGH, Lancs, WN7 3QP
**Phone** 01942 602864
0777 1690617
**Email** bram.taylor@freeuk.com
**Web** www.bramtaylor.freeuk.com
*Sings traditional & contemporary material, also plays guitar & concertina*
**Agent** Oscar Music Agency
***Musicians' Union member***
**RAB** North West Arts

## Branco Stoysin
**Mail address** 59A East Dulwich Grove, LONDON, SE22 8PR
**Phone/Fax** 020 8693 2398
*Guitarist, composer, tutor. Duo or trio with bass & percussion. Eastern European influences. See Sun Recordings.*
***Musicians' Union member***
**RAB** London Arts

## Brass Monkey
**Contact** Mrs Casey Music
**Web** www.mrscasey.co.uk/brass
*5 piece 'Quintessentially English' folk group with Martin Carthy, John Kirkpatrick, Howard Evans, Richard Cheetham & Martin Brinsford*
**Agent** Mrs Casey Music
**RAB** Southern Arts

## The Brasshoppers
**Contact** Toby Rathbone
**Mail address** 65 Radnor Street, SWINDON, SN1 3PS
**Phone/Fax** 01793 421856
**Email** toby@brasshoppers.com
**Web** www.brasshoppers.com
*8 piece brass band drawing on Latin/ African influences.*
**RAB** Southern Arts

## Brendan Croker
**Contact** Adastra
**Web** www.adastra-music.com
*Renowned blues musician.*

## Brendan McGlinchey
**Mail address** 50 Highfield Lane, Oving, CHICHESTER, W Sussex, PO20 6DL
**Phone** 01243 778845
**Email** McGlinchey100@hotmail.com
*Solo fiddle artist, workshop and masterclass leader.*
**RAB** South East Arts

## Brian McNeill
**Email** brian@b-mcneill.demon.co.uk
**Web** www.brianmcneill.co.uk
*Multi-instrumentalist, singer and songwriter. Solo performer and producer. Founderr member of Battlefield Band, also with Dick Gaughan.*
**AC** Scotland

*Artists in the main A-Z listing are mostly available for concert and club bookings.*

*See page 11 for details of other artist listings (Dance Display, Solo Musicians, Composers, Arrangers, Session Musicians, Band Deps, Lecturers, MCs, Tutors, Street Theatre, Children's Entertainers, Theatre Companies).*

*Agents section appears on pages 119-131.*

artists
b

*Artists in the main A-Z listing are mostly available for concert and club bookings.*

*See page 11 for details of other artist listings (Dance Display, Solo Musicians, Composers, Arrangers, Session Musicians, Band Deps. Lecturers, MCs, Tutors, Street Theatre, Children's Entertainers, Theatre Companies).*

*Agents section appears on pages 119-131.*

## Brian O hEadhra
**Contact** Brian O hEadhra
**Phone** 07802 433294
**Email** brian@anam.co.uk
**Web** www.brianoheadhra.com
*Singer, songwriter and teacher. Manager and musician with celtic group Anam. Gaelic and English.*
***Musicians' Union member***
**AC** Scotland

## Brian Peters
**Mail address** 72 Sheffield Road, GLOSSOP, Derbys, SK13 8QP
**Phone** 01457 862 560
**Email** brian.peters@cwcom.net
*Solo performer of traditional songs, ballads, English tunes. Melodeon, anglo-concertina and guitar. Teacher and workshop leader.*
***Musicians' Union member***
**RAB** North West Arts

## Brian Peters and Gordon Tyrrall
**Contact** Brian Peters
**Mail address** 72 Sheffield Road, GLOSSOP, Derbys, SK13 8QP
**Phone** 01457 862560
**Email** brian.peters@cwcom.net
**Alt contact** Gordon Tyrrall
**Alt address** 12 Nettletow Court, Whitkirk, LEEDS, LS15 9AW
**Email** gordon@tyll.telinco.co.uk
*Duo performing traditional songs and tunes. Originals and covers. Voices, guitar, melodeon, flute, etc.*
**RAB** North West Arts

## Brian Stafford
**Mail address** 21 Bright Street, SKIPTON, N Yorks, BD23 1QQ
**Phone** 01756 798285
07968 726191
**Email** brian.stafford@ukonline.co.uk
**Web** web.ukonline.co.uk/brian.stafford
*Solo uillean piper, mainly traditional Irish and Scottish music.*
***Musicians' Union member***
**RAB** Yorkshire Arts

## The Broadside Ceilidh Band
**Contact** John Conolly
**Mail address** 18 Scrivelsby Court, CLEETHORPES, NE Lincs, DN35 OHJ
**Phone** 01472 695836
*Ceilidh band for barn dances, weddings, etc*

## Broderick
**Contact** Mutiny Music
**Web** www.broderickonline.co.uk
*Traditional and new Irish and Breton music. Luke Daniels (accordion), Colm Murply (fiddle), Clare Garrand (fiddle & viola) and Don Oteors (guitar). Vocalist available*
**Agents** Mutiny Music, The Other Agency
***Musicians' Union member***
**RAB** Southern Arts

## Brolum
**Contact** Martin O'Neill
**Mail address** 189 Carfin Street, New Stevenson, MOTHERWELL, ML1 4EU
**Phone** 07092 114070
0781 8405793
**Fax** 07092 1140703
**Email** info@brolum.co.uk
**Web** www.brolum.co.uk
*7 piece Scottish band.Elements of traditional & contemporary celtic music.*
***Musicians' Union member***
**AC** Scotland

## Bruce MacGregor and Friends
**Contact** Bruce MacGregor
**Mail address** Holmburn, Essich Road, INVERNESS, IV2 6AH, Scotland
**Phone** 01463 238070
**Email** bruce.mac@virgin.net
*Tuition & performance from founding member of Blazin Fiddles.*
**AC** Scotland

## Bucharest String Duo
**Contact** Matters Musical
**Web** www.mattersmusical.com
*Romanian gypsy duo, classical, jazz, folk and roots*

## The Bucket Band
**Contact** Artists Connect
**Web** www.artistsconnect.com
*Street band using improvised instruments: buckets and homemade bass, plus strings and guitar. UK traditional tunes with American roots*

## Buddy Mondlock
**Contact** themusictree. (uk) ltd
**Web** www.songs.com/buddy
*American singer songwriter, occasional UK tours*

## Budowitz
**Contact** Elizabeth Jones Entertainments
**Web** www.bromyard.co.uk/ejones
*5 piece Klezmer band from Austria/Hungary/Germany*

## The Bumblebees
**Contact** Smallworld Music
**Web** www.anu.ie/bumblebees
*All women 4 piece Irish traditional music band*
**AC** Ireland

## Burach
**Contact** Stoneyport Agency
**Web** www.accordions.com/sandy
*Full-time touring 6 piece Scottish celtic rock band featuring Sandy Brechin, mostly new material*
***Musicians' Union member***
**AC** Scotland

## The Burning Bush
**Contact** Lucie Skeaping
**Mail address** 19 Patshull Road, LONDON, NW5 2JX
**Phone** 020 7485 3957
07931 373133
**Fax** 020 7267 2957
**Email** lucieskeaping@hotmail.com
**Web** www.theburningbush.co.uk
*UK band playing traditional music of the old Jewish world. Female lead singer plus 5 instrumentalists. Oud, clarinet, accordion, etc. Concerts, workshops & talks*
**Agent** Adastra
**RAB** London Arts

## The Bushburys
**Contact** c/o The Eye of Horus
**Mail address** 1786 Pershore Road, Cotteridge, BIRMINGHAM, B30 3BG
**Phone** 0121 4513081
**Fax** 0709 2223081
**Email** info@bushburys.com
**Web** www.bushburys.com
*UK Roots band; acoustic rock, folk and blues plus own songs.*
***Musicians' Union member***
**RAB** West Midlands Arts

## Bushes and Briars
**Contact** Paul Kiff
**Mail address** 14 North Road, Tollesbury, Essex, CM9 8RQ
**Phone** 01621 868219
07710 647706
*Folk-rock barn dance and ceilidh band.*
**RAB** East England Arts

## Buz Collins
**Contact** c/o 153 Jordanhill Drive, GLASGOW, G13 1UQ
**Phone** 07889 060810
**Email** buz@buzmusic.co.uk
**Web** www.buzmusic.co.uk
*Songwriter, singer, player of stringed & keyed instruments. Traditional/contemporary mix. Not resident in Scotland, address is mail only.*
***Musicians' Union member***

## Café Aman
**Contact** Matters Musical
**Web** www.mattersmusical.com
*Large ensemble combining Greek rembetica with roots and jazz*

## Caim
**Contact** Clunie Creative Enterprises
**Web** www.come.to/clunie
*Vocal harmony duo, occasional session musicians. Irish & Scottish folk song.*
**AC** Scotland

## Cajun Aces
**Contact** Mannings Musicals
**Mail address** 75 Westgate, BRADFORD, W Yorks, BD1 2RD
**Phone/Fax** 01274 723539
*Long established British Cajun band*
**Agent** Access All Areas
**RAB** Yorkshire Arts

## Cajun Company
**Contact** Access All Areas
*Netherlands twin-fiddle led Cajun band*

## Cajun Hurricane
**Contact** Access All Areas
*Swedish Cajun group*

## Cajun Pioneers (The)
**Contact** Access All Areas
*German Cajun band*

## Cajuns Denbo
**Contact** Access All Areas
*Welsh Cajun big band*
**AC** Wales

## Cal
**Contact** Michael Callaghan
**Mail address** 14 Bank Street, GRANGEMOUTH, Stirlingshire, FK3 8EY, Scotland
**Phone/Fax** 01324 474967
**Email** cal.music@ic24.net
**Web** www.calmusic.co.uk
*Singer/ guitarist. Traditional and contemporary.*
***Musicians' Union member***
**AC** Scotland

## Caleb Jarvis
**Mail address** Flat 3, 79 Abbotsham Road, BIDEFORD, Devon, EX39 3AQ
**Phone** 01237 473804
**Email** jarviscribe@talk21.com
*Vocalist, guitarist, songwriter*
***Musicians' Union member***
**RAB** South West Arts

## Calennig
**Contact** Mick Tems & Pat Smith
**Mail address** 1 Ty Clwyta Cottages, Cross Inn, LLANTRISANT, Rhondda Cynon Taf, CF72 8AZ, Wales
**Phone/Fax** 01443 226892
**Phone** 07773 075962
**Email** calennig@folkwales.org.uk
**Web** www.folkwales.org.uk
*Songs, dances & tunes from South Wales. Concerts, tympaths and ceilidhs, etc.*
**AC** Wales

## Calico
**Contact** Black Hat Music Management
**Web** www.blackhatmusic.com
*Contemporary and traditional Irish music band fusing original songs & tunes with Irish & Breton traditional music*
**AC** Ireland

## Calum Mor (pipe major)
**Contact** Artists Connect
**Web** www.artistsconnect.com
*Uniformed Highland piper.*

## Calypso Rose, Mighty Shadow and Reasons Orchestra
**Contact** mARKO pOLO
**Web** www.markopolo.co.uk
*Caribbean singers Rose and Shadow backed by the soca-style Reasons Orchestra*

## Cambridge and Napier
**Contact** Findlay Napier
**Mail address** 0/2 239 Craigpark Drive, Dennistoun, GLASGOW, G31 2TG
**Phone** 07989 332407
0141 5645679
**Email** findlaynapier@ntlworld.com
**Web** http://findlaynapier.tripod.com/findlaynapier
*Blues duo. Singer, songwriter and guitarist with harmonica player.*
**AC** Scotland

## Capercaillie
**Contact** Primary Talent
*Celebrated Scottish Celtic Roots band.*
***Musicians' Union member***

## Captain Swing
**Contact** Mike Griffiths
**Phone** 01527 402644
0794 1288474
**Email** mike.griffiths@virgin.net
**Web** www.freespace.virgin.net/mike.griffiths/cswing.htm
*4 piece English country dance band, own caller.Melodeon, sax, guitar, bass etc.*
**RAB** West Midlands Arts

## Captain Thunderbolt
**Contact** David Milner
**Mail address** 14a Rectory Close, BROADMAYNE, Dorset, DT2 8EQ
**Phone** 01305 852773
**Email** dmilner@thomas-hardye.dorset.sch.uk
**Alt contact** Teresa Rideout
**Alt address** 27 Fordington High Street, DORCHESTER, Dorset
*Ceilidh/ barndance band with caller. Melodeon led, bass & drums available.*
**RAB** South West Arts

## Cara Dillon
**Contact** The Concert Clinic
**Web** www.concertclinic.com
*Acclaimed young Irish singer. Available as a duo with Sam Lakeman or with a 4 piece band.*

## Caribbean Carnival Extravaganza
**Contact** mARKO pOLO
**Web** www.markopolo.co.uk
*Caribbean street carnival tradition, with spectacular costumes*

## Carlos Sisters
**Contact** Adastra
**Web** www.adastra-music.com
*Young bluegrass duo*

## Carmen Higgins
**Contact** Mesmerist Productions
**Web** www.mesmerist.com
*Solo traditional fiddle player from the North of Scotland*
**AC** Scotland

## Carmina
**Contact** CTM UK
**Web** www.ctmuk.com
*Folk/ jazz/ Irish band.Contemporary and traditional*
**Agents** CTM UK, Spadger Productions

## The Carol Harrison Band
**Contact** Laurie Harrison
**Mail address** 2A Kirkmoor Road, CLITHEROE, Lancs, BB7 2DU
**Phone** 01200 424787
01200 426185
**Alt contact** Seamus Heffernan
**Alt address** "The Garth", Commons Lane, Balderstone, BLACKBURN, Lancs, BB2 7LL
**Phone** 01254 812131
**Email** s.hefferernan@btinternet.com
*4 piece jazz-folk band. Guitar, bass, twin fiddles, 3 voices.*
***Musicians' Union member***
**RAB** North West Arts



*Artists in the main A-Z listing are mostly available for concert and club bookings.*

*See page 11 for details of other artist listings (Dance Display, Solo Musicians, Composers, Arrangers, Session Musicians, Band Deps. Lecturers, MCs, Tutors, Street Theatre, Children's Entertainers, Theatre Companies).*

*Agents section appears on pages 119-131.*

## artists
## C

*Artists in the main A-Z listing are mostly available for concert and club bookings.*

*See page 11 for details of other artist listings (Dance Display, Solo Musicians, Composers, Arrangers, Session Musicians, Band Deps. Lecturers, MCs, Tutors, Street Theatre, Children's Entertainers, Theatre Companies).*

*Agents section appears on pages 119-131.*

### Carolyn Francis
**Mail address** 16 Hinde Street, LANCASTER, LA1 1DX
**Phone/Fax** 01524 35391
**Email** carolyn@striding-edge.demon.co.uk
*Performer; fiddle, vocals, trombone, percussion; one-woman-band street act. Workshop leader; community & schools workshops, fiddle teacher.*
***Musicians' Union member***
**RAB** Northern Arts

### Carolyn Robson
**Mail address** 70 Burnt Hill Road, Lower Bourne, FARNHAM, Surrey, GU10 3LN
**Phone/Fax** 01252 722938
**Email** carolyn.robson@virgin.net
**Web** www.carolynrobson.com
*Solo singer of mostly traditional songs from NE England & Scotland. Workshops, clubs & festivals.*
**RAB** South East Arts

### Carousel Ceilidh
**Contact** Guy & Aileen Hindley
**Phone** 01253 737832
*Barn dance & ceilidh band. Accordions and percussion with caller.*
***Musicians' Union member***
**RAB** North West Arts

### Carreg Lafar
**Contact** Antwn Owen Hicks
**Mail address** 10 Stryd Eyre, Sblot, CAERDYDD/CARDIFF, CF24 2JR
**Phone** 029 2025 7589
**Email** info@carreglafar.co.uk
**Web** www.carreglafar.co.uk
*Traditional music of Wales. 5 piece band – vocals, fiddle, flute, Welsh pipes and guitar*
**Agent** Nancy Carlin Associates
**AC** Wales

### Carrig
**Contact** Matters Musical
**Web** www.irishmusic.fsbusiness.co.uk
*Irish band covering traditional and contemporary tunes and songs*
**RAB** London Arts

### Casa Latina Allstars
**Contact** Matters Musical
**Web** www.mattersmusical.com
*10 piece brass and percussion band playing Latin, etc*

### The Casablanca Steps
**Contact** Matters Musical
**Web** www.mattersmusical.com
*Quartet performing music from the 1920s -1940s with tongue-in-cheek visual humour*

### Cass Meurig
**Mail address** Min Y Nant, Allt Goch, CWM-Y-GLO, Caernarfon, LL55 4DW
**Phone** 01286 871042
**Email** cassmeurig@aol.com
*Fiddler and Welsh Crwth player, mainly traditional Welsh music. Member of Fernhill & Pigyn Clust. Workshops in Welsh fiddle/Crwth, led in English or Welsh.*
***Musicians' Union member***
**AC** Wales

### The Cast
**Contact** Stoneyport Agency
**Phone/Fax** 0131 5571050
**Email** dfrancis@musicscotland.com
*Scottish duo; Mairi Campbell and Dave Francis on fiddle, viola, guitar and vocals*
***Musicians' Union member***
**AC** Scotland

### Cat In The Mangle
**Contact** Hilary Blagbrough
**Mail address** 127 Mill Road, Buckden, HUNTINGDON, Cambs, PE19 5SN
**Phone** 01480 810756
**Alt contact** Pat Simpson
**Alt address** Orchard House, 64 High Street, Toseland, ST. NEOTS, Cambs
**Phone** 01480 880351
*Female song and music duo, various UK traditions.*
**RAB** East England Arts

### Cat.Fish.Dog
**Contact** Chris Broderick
**Mail address** Gleaners, Buckland Road, Cliffe, ROCHESTER, Kent, ME3 7RR
**Phone/Fax** 01634 221872
**Email** chris.broderick@tinyworld.co.uk
**Web** www.catfishdog.com
**Alt contact** John Gibson
**Phone** 01634 400521
*3 piece "UK urban acoustic, skiffle, punk, folk, country, pyscho-ballad, blues-a-billy".*
**RAB** South East Arts

### Catch 22
**Contact** Dave Rawlinson
**Mail address** 1 Bowter Gardens, SALISBURY, SP1 2RL
*6 piece Irish folk band.*
**RAB** Southern Arts

### Cathal Hayden and Eamon McElholm
**Contact** Smallworld Music
*Former 4 men & a Dog fiddle/ banjo player with Stockton's Wing vocalist/ guitarist*

### Cathryn Craig and Brian Willoughby
**Contact** Brian Willoughby
**Phone/Fax** 020 8891 5929
**Phone** 07967 562213
**Email** cabritour@aol.com
**Web** www.brianwilloughby.com
*American-English singer songwriter and guitar roots duo*
**Agent** GTA Music Agency
***Musicians' Union member***
**RAB** London Arts

### Catriona MacDonald
**Contact** Peerie Angel Productions
**Web** www.peerieangel.demon.co.uk
*Scottish fiddle artist and teacher playing in the Shetland tradition. Member of Blazin Fiddles*
***Musicians' Union member***
**AC** Scotland

### The Cat's Whiskers
**Contact** David Pattenden
**Mail address** 10 Wordsley Close, REDDITCH, Worcs, B98 8RT
**Phone** 01527 65483
**Email** dpattend@cksys.com
**Alt contact** Mike Smith
**Phone** 01295 255468
*3 piece folk dance band. Traditional music from England, America and Scotland.*
**RAB** West Midlands Arts

### Causeway
**Contact** Marc Duff
**Mail address** Flat 2/2, 62A Albert Road, Crosshill, GLASGOW, G42 8DW
**Phone** 0141 423 6996
**Email** duffhouse@supanet.com
**Alt contact** Fraser Fifield
**Alt address** 10 Linlithgow Terrace, Ormiston, TRANENT, E Lothian, EH35 5LJ
**Phone** 01875 612196
**Email** fraserfifield@onetel.net.uk
*4 piece instrumental band. New and traditional music from Scotland and Europe. Low whistle, sop sax, guitars and percussion.*
***Musicians' Union member***
**AC** Scotland

### Ceili House
**Contact** Chris Maguire
**Phone** 01977 614409
**Web** www.stirrings.co.uk/folkzone/bands/ceilihouse
*Traditional Irish music & song. Flute, pipes, fiddle, guitar, concertina*
**Agent** Carrick Music Agency
**RAB** Yorkshire Arts

## Celfyddydau Mari Arts
**Contact** Mick Tems
**Mail address** 1 Ty Clwyta Cottages, Cross Inn, LLANTRISANT, Rhondda Cynon Taf, CF72 8AZ, Wales
**Phone/Fax** 01443 226892
**Phone** 07773 075962
**Email** mariarts@folkwales.org.uk
**Web** www.folkwales.org.uk
*Creation & performance of new work based on traditional themes.*
**AC** Wales

## Celtarabia
**Contact** Quentin Budworth
**Mail address** Molescroft Grange Farmhouse, BEVERLEY, Yorks, HU17 9RS
**Phone** 01482 865604
**Email** grinnigogs@pop3.poptel.org.uk
**Web** www.celtarabia.co.uk
*Global dance band featuring hurdy-gurdy, pipes, dulcimer and voice*
**Agent** Artists Connect, Matters Musical
**RAB** Yorkshire Arts

## Celtic Fiddle Festival
**Contact** Adastra
**Web** www.adastra-music.com
*Irish/ Scottish/French fiddle trio - Kevin Burke, Johnny Cunningham, Christian LeMaitre plus guitarist Soig Siberil*

## Ceolbeg
**Contact** Stoneyport Agency
**Phone/Fax** 0131 5571050
**Email** dfrancis@musicscotland.com
**Web** www.ceolbeg.com
*Scottish Celtic roots band*
**AC** Scotland

## The Chain Gang
**Contact** Richard Heath
**Mail address** Flat 1, 65 Mayfield Road, Moseley, BIRMINGHAM, B13 9HT
**Phone** 0121 6842485
**Fax** 0709 2223081
**Email** buzby@cableinet.co.uk
**Web** www.buzby.pwp.blueyonder.co.uk
Band, contemporary songs, Bluegrass style. Double bass, 5 string banjo, mandolin, guitar & fiddle.
***Musicians' Union member***
**RAB** West Midlands Arts

## Chalktown
**Contact** Paul Scourfield
**Mail address** 9 Victoria Road, HITCHIN, Herts, SG5 2LS
**Phone** 01462 458031
**Email** pscourfield@mad-river.co.uk
**Web** www.pgsystems.demon.co.uk/workingparty/chalktown.htm
*Folk, rock and jazz influenced dance band for ceilidhs, weddings, concerts, etc.*
**RAB** East England Arts

## Charles Bolton
**Mail address** 20 The Woodlands, Broom, BIGGLESWADE, Beds, SG18 9NH
**Phone** 01767 312315
**Email** cboltbroom@aol.com
**Web** www.charles-bolton.co.uk
*Caller, teacher and composer of Playford and Playford-style dances.*
**RAB** East Midlands Arts

## Charles Spicer
**Mail address** 3 The Square, Spencers Wood, READING, Berks, RG7 1BS
**Phone** 0118 988 4337
*Player of period and modern oboe and cor anglais, bagpipes, shawm. Musical arranger. Member of Mellstock band, Oxford Waits, Boka Halat. Workshop leader.*
***Musicians' Union member***
**RAB** Southern Arts

## The Chase
**Contact** Kerry Fletcher
**Mail address** 80 Ryarsh Road, BIRLING, Kent, ME19 5JR
**Phone/Fax** 01732 849163
**Phone** 07703 639720
**Email** TheChase@bigfoot.com
**Web** www.bigfoot.com/~thechase
*New music and dance performance based on European traditions. 5-7 performers, element of audience participation. Range of music and dance workshops.*
***Musicians' Union member***

## Cheap Jack
**Contact** Hemlock Music
**Web** www.hemlockmusic.demon.co.uk
*4 piece ceilidh band, hurdy gurdy, fiddles and melodeon, etc*
**RAB** London Arts

## Cheb Nacim
**Contact** Matters Musica
**Web** www.mattersmusical.com
*Algerian Rai singer, superimposing modern rai on a traditional musical base. Available with 5-piece band*

## Chipolata 5
**Contact** Tristan Glover, Hoodlum Productions
**Mail address** PO Box 160, CHELTENHAM, Glos, GL5 2ZQ
**Phone** 01242 577745
**Fax** 01242 577702
**Email** chipolatas@hotmail.com
**Web** www.chipolatas.com
*High energy dance music*
**Agents** Hoodlum Productions, Fool's Paradise
**RAB** South West Arts

## Chouchenn
**Contact** Ben Farmer
**Mail address** 27 Regent Street, LANCASTER, LA1 1SQ
**Phone** 01524 847135
**Email** info@chouchenn.net
**Web** www.chouchenn.net
**Alt contact** Maurice Pennance
**Alt address** 7 Mill Street, LANCASTER, LA1 3PL
**Phone** 01524 847013
*Band blending traditional and new tunes with roots of Central France, Brittany and Sweden. Workshops in French/ Swedish dance & range of instruments.*
**RAB** North West Arts

## Chris Bartram
**Mail address** Granway House, 3 Coldharbour, Uffculme, CULLOMPTON, Devon, EX15 3EE
**Phone/Fax** 01884 841499
**Phone** 07968 193555
**Email** chris@chris-bartram.co.uk
**Web** www.chris-bartram.co.uk
*Southern English traditional fiddle player & singer. Workshop leader. Extensive research on English fiddle music.*
***Musicians' Union member***
**RAB** South West Arts

## Chris Bartram and Keith Holloway
**Contact** Chris Bartram
**Mail address** Granway House, 3 Coldharbour, Uffculme, CULLOMPTON, Devon, EX15 3EE
**Phone/Fax** 01884 841499
**Email** chris@chris-bartram.co.uk
**Web** www.bartram-holloway.co.uk
**Alt contact** Keith Holloway
**Phone** 01264 735252
*Traditional songs & music from the Vale of the White Horse.*
***Musicians' Union member***
**RAB** South West Arts

## Chris Butler
**Email** efcbutler@hotmail.com
**Web** www.morton45.fsnet.co.uk
*Solo singer/ songwriter/ guitarist. Political/ social comment.*
**RAB** East Midlands Arts

## Chris Coe
**Mail address** 21 Halifax Road, Ripponden, SOWERBY BRIDGE, West Yorks, HX6 4AH
**Phone** 01422 822413
07870 337603
**Email** chris.coe@tesco.net
*Respected singer of traditional songs accompanied by dulcimers and concertina. Step dancer. Workshop leader for voice, traditional song and dance.*
**RAB** Yorkshire Arts



*Artists in the main A-Z listing are mostly available for concert and club bookings.*

*See page 11 for details of other artist listings (Dance Display, Solo Musicians, Composers, Arrangers, Session Musicians, Band Deps. Lecturers, MCs, Tutors, Street Theatre, Children's Entertainers, Theatre Companies).*

*Agents section appears on pages 119-131.*

Artists in the main A-Z listing are mostly available for concert and club bookings.

See page 11 for details of other artist listings (Dance Display, Solo Musicians, Composers, Arrangers, Session Musicians, Band Deps. Lecturers, MCs, Tutors, Street Theatre, Children's Entertainers, Theatre Companies).

Agents section appears on pages 119-131.

## Chris Conway
**Contact** Elizabeth Jones Entertainments
**Web** www.bromyard.co.uk/ejones
*American born singer, songwriter and multi-instrumentalist.*

## Chris Foster
**Mail address** 11 Osborne Street, BURTON-UPON-TRENT, DE15 0JL
**Phone/Fax** 01283 561473
**Email** 106056.642@compuserve.com
**Web** www.folkmusic.net/chrisfoster
*Highly regarded singer/ guitarist. Mainly traditional English songs, with some issue-based contemporary material*
**RAB** West Midlands Arts

## Chris Haigh
**Mail address** 232 Sebert Road, Forest Gate, LONDON, E7 0NP
**Phone** 020 8534 3887
**Email** Chris@fiddlingaround.co.uk
**Web** www.fiddlingaround.co.uk
*Fiddle player (all styles). Band leader for East European music trio Tziganarama. Tutor and workshop leader.*
***Musicians' Union member***
**RAB** London Arts

## Chris Hawes
**Mail address** 3 Roe's Close, Sawston, CAMBRIDGE, CB2 4TH
**Phone** 01223 834678
*Concertina (duet) and keyboard player. Workshop leader.*
**RAB** East England Arts

## Chris Manners
**Mail address** 51 Cowpasture Road, ILKLEY, West Yorks, LS 29 8SY
**Phone** 01943 601807
07951 399272
**Email** spanners@cmanners.fsnet.co.uk
*Performing songwriter with traditional roots.*
**RAB** Yorkshire Arts

## Chris Parkinson
**Mail address** 6 Blackburn's Yard, WHITBY, N Yorks, YO22 4DS
**Email** chris@parkymusic.fsnet.co.uk
*Prolific performer, keyboards, piano accordion, melodeon, harmonica. Member of New House Band. Session work with Ralph McTell, Martin Simpson, Kieran Halpin, Mike Harding, Norma Waterson and Martin Carthy, Steve Phillips and others.*
***Musicians' Union member***
**RAB** Yorkshire Arts

## Chris Pitt
**Mail address** 66a Granville Road, Walthamstow, LONDON E17 9BT
**Phone** 020 8509 2138
07947 522172
**Email** pittchristopher@hotmail.com
*Ceilidh dance caller, festival MC and singer.*
**RAB** London Arts

## Chris Rogers
**Mail address** 4 McLaren Grove, Kittochglen, EAST KILBRIDE, G74 4SR
**Phone** 01355 234736
**Email** library@ngcb.u-net.com
**Web** www.ngcb.u-net.com/kagan.htm
*Singer-songwriter and member of Kagan.*
***Musicians' Union member***
**AC** Scotland

## Chris Smither
**Contact** Young/Hunter Management (USA)
**Phone** +1 781 643 2773
**Email** carol@younghunter.com
**Web** www.smither.com
*One of American roots music's most passionate, soulful songsmiths and interpreters.*

## Chris Sugden
**Mail address** 10 Perseverence Road, Queensbury, BRADFORD, W Yorks, BD13 1LY
**Phone** 01274 831745
*Performances, talks and workshops built around unaccompanied songs in English.*
***Musicians' Union member***
**RAB** Yorkshire Arts

## Chris Taylor
**Mail address** 35 Stoney Road, DUNKIRK, Kent, ME13 9TN
**Phone** 01227 750392
*Multi-instrumentalist. Celtic, Cajun, Blues, etc. Harmonica, banjo, guitar, etc. Band available for ceilidhs.*
***Musicians' Union member***
**RAB** South East Arts

## Chris Thomas King
**Contact** mARKO pOLO
**Web** www.markopolo.co.uk
*Solo guitarist*

## Chris Turner
**Mail address** 9 Glendale Avenue, LONDON, N22 5HL
**Phone** 020 8889 0634
*Dance caller & teacher. Melodeon/ concertina player and singer/ guitarist. Folk animateur.*
***Musicians' Union member***
**RAB** London Arts

## Chris Wood
**Mail address** 40 Whitstable Road, FAVERSHAM, Kent, ME13 8DL
**Phone** 01795 537906
**Email** cw@rurecords.com
**Web** www.rufrecords.com
*Musician, composer, arranger, producer & teacher. Violinist & singer. See entries for RUF Records; English Acoustic Collective; Wood, Wilson, Carthy; Two Duos Quartet.*
**RAB** South East Arts

## Chris Wood and Andy Cutting
**Contact** Chris Wood
**Mail address** 40 Whitstable Road, FAVERSHAM, Kent, ME13 8DL
**Phone** 01795 537906
**Email** cw@rurecords.com
**Web** www.rufrecords.com
*Highly influential violin/ vocal and diatonic accordion duo.*
**RAB** South East Arts

## Chris Wood Trio
**Contact** Chris Wood
**Mail address** 40 Whitstable Road, FAVERSHAM, Kent, ME13 8DL
**Phone** 01795 537906
**Email** cw@rurecords.com
**Web** www.rufrecords.com
*Original ensemble playing new work. Nick Cooper (cello), Anne Wood (violin) and Chris Wood (violin & voice).*
**RAB** South East Arts

## Christian Laverick
**Contact** Elizabeth Jones Entertainments
**Web** www.bromyard.co.uk/ejones
*Singer/ songwriter*

## Christine Collister
**Contact** Asgard Promotions
*Celebrated singer of mostly contemporary songs.*

## Christine Kydd
**Contact** Stockbridge Music
**Mail address** 3 Leslie Place, EDINBURGH, EH4 1NG, Scotland
**Phone/Fax** 0131 332 7067
**Email** johnbrown@stockbridgemusic.demon.co.uk
**Web** www.musicscotland.com/kydd
*Scottish singer, respected interpreter of the Scots song tradition. Teacher of Scots song and voicework.*
**Agent** Stoneyport Agency
***Musicians' Union member***
**AC** Scotland

## Christine Michael (The Singing Poet)
**Mail address** 54 Kingswood Road, West Bridgford, NOTTINGHAM, NG2 7HS
**Phone** 0115 9819397
07973 296444
**Email** christinemichael@yahoo.com
**Web** homepages.ntlworld.com/christine.michael
**Alt address** PO Box 30, South PDO, NOTTINGHAM, NG2 7JP
**Email** expansionspress@yahoo.co.uk
*Singer & 12 string guitarist, traditional & contemporary. Storyteller (adults and children), poetry readings.*
**RAB** East Midlands Arts

## Christine Primrose
**Mail address** Sabhal Mor, Ostaig, TEANGUE, Isle of Skye, IV44 8RQ, Scotland
**Phone** 01471 888000
**Email** sm00cp@groupwise.uhi.ac.uk
**Alt contact** Robin Morton
**Alt address** Shillinghill, TEMPLE, Midlothian, EH23 4SH, Scotland
**Phone** 01875 830392
*Gaelic traditional singer from the Isle of Lewis. Duo with Alison Kinnaird.*
**AC** Scotland

## Citizen Camembert
**Contact** Hemlock Music
**Web** www.citizencamembert.com
*Traditional and comtemporary French dance music for bals, concerts, ceilidhs, etc*
**RAB** South East Arts

## The City Waites
**Contact** Lucie Skeaping
**Mail address** 19 Patshull Road, LONDON, NW5 2JX
**Phone** 020 7485 3957
**Fax** 020 7267 2957
**Email** lucieskeaping@hotmail.com
**Web** www.citywaites.com
*Early and traditional English music. Period instruments and voices.*
**RAB** London Arts

## Claret
**Contact** Sandra & Tim Robinson
**Mail address** Tudor Rose Cottage, 55 Coleshill Street, SUTTON COLDFIELD, W Mids, B72 1SH
**Phone** 0121 3544234
**Email** michael@mrcropp.freeserve.co.uk
*3 piece multi-instrumental folk based band. Barn dances and ceilidhs catered for.*
**RAB** West Midlands Arts

## Clarty Sough
**Contact** Jim Hancock
**Phone** 01724 844241
**Email** jim@guestlist.freeserve.co.uk
*Derbyshire unaccompanied traditional song duo.*
**RAB** East Midlands Arts

## Claudio Allodi Italian Orchestra
**Contact** Matters Musical
**Web** www.mattersmusical.com
*Solo accordion to 5 piece or larger. Music and European songs*

## Cliff Stapleton
**Contact** 31 Meynell Road, Hackney, LONDON, E9 7AP
**Phone** 020 8986 0531
**Email** j.stapleton@talk21.com
*Composer and hurdy-gurdy player, performer and teacher. Commissions to write music for dance, theme, song, ambience, etc.*
***Musicians' Union member***
**RAB** London Arts

## Clive Carroll
**Contact** NEM Productions (UK)
**Web** www.nemproductions.com
*Young virtuoso guitarist. Solo or with various groups*
**RAB** London Arts

## Clive Gregson
**Contact** Emerging Music
**Web** www.emerging.demon.co.uk
*Respected guitarist, singer and songwriter*

## Clive Gregson and Boo Hewerdine
**Contact** Emerging Music
**Web** www.emerging.demon.co.uk
*Renowned songwriters and performers.*

## Cluanas
**Contact** Mesmerist Productions
**Web** www.mesmerist.com
*Scottish concert band from the West Coast*
**Agent** Mesmerist Productions
**AC** Scotland

## cMc
**Contact** Stoneyport Agency
**Web** www.deafshepherd.com
*Scottish fiddle duo: Maireanne Campbell and Claire McLaughlin. Workshop leaders*
**AC** Scotland

## The Coal Porters
**Contact** Matters Musical
**Web** www.mattersmusical.com
*Contemporary country flavoured rock with witty lyrics*
**RAB** London Arts

## Coblers Monday
**Contact** Mick Haywood
**Mail address** 3 Woodwarks Yard, Church Street, WHITBY, N Yorks, YO22 4DG
**Phone** 01947 601963
**Email** mick.angi@btinternet.com
*Group singing sea and humorous songs, socio-political anthems.*
**RAB** Yorkshire Arts

## The Cock and Bull Band
**Contact** Hemlock Music
**Web** www.hemlockmusic.demon.co.uk
*Long established and popular dance band. Anglo-French music for ceilidhs and concerts. Bagpipes, mandola/ dulcimer, saxophone & bass guitar*
**RAB** Southern Arts

## Coco Xpress
**Contact** Matters Musical
**Web** www.salasadirect.co.uk
*3-5 piece Latin dance band*

## Cofa
**Contact** Karisma Music Management
**Web** www.karisma.net

## Coinneach
**Contact** Beyond
*Scottish celtic pop band*

## Colin Andrews
**Mail address** Bonny Green, Morton Bishop, CREDITON, Devon, EX17 6PG
**Phone/Fax** 01363 877216
**Email** colin@bonnygreeen.co.uk
**Web** www.bonnygreen.co.uk
*Caller, musician (melodeon, guitar, whistle), singer and morris dance teacher. Duo with Sonja Andrews; accompanied & unaccompanied songs.*
**RAB** South West Arts

## Colin Pitts
**Mail address** 37 Coxlea Close, EVESHAM, Worcs, WR11 4JS
**Phone** 01386 41760
*Solo singer, own, traditional & contemporary material.*
**RAB** West Midlands Arts



*Artists in the main A-Z listing are mostly available for concert and club bookings.*

*See page 11 for details of other artist listings (Dance Display, Solo Musicians, Composers, Arrangers, Session Musicians Band Deps. Lecturers, MCs, Tutors, Street Theatre, Children's Entertainers, Theatre Companies).*

*Agents section appears on pages 119-131.*

artists

C

Artists in the main A-Z listing are mostly available for concert and club bookings.

See page 11 for details of other artist listings (Dance Display, Solo Musicians, Composers, Arrangers, Session Musicians, Band Deps. Lecturers, MCs, Tutors Street Theatre, Children's Entertainers, Theatre Companies).

Agents section appears on pages 119-131.

## Colin Reid
**Contact** Artistic Upstarts
**Web** http://members.xoom.com/colin_reid
*Virtuoso solo guitarist*
**Agent** Artistic Upstarts, themusictree.(uk) ltd

## Colin Thompson
**Mail address** 80 Dorchester Road, MAIDEN NEWTON, Dorset, DT2 0BG
**Phone** 01300 320558
*Fiddle player, all UK traditional styles, American & Swedish.*
**RAB** South West Arts

## Collen Gregory
**Contact** The Other Agency
*Singer, guitarist, songwriter. Also traditional songs and tunes*
***Musicians' Union member***

## Colm Daly
**Mail address** 184 Liverpool Road, READING, Berks, RG1 3PH
**Phone** 0118 967 7408
**Email** oldtimejoanna@riff.com
**Web** www.riff.com
*Fiddle and piano player working with local Reading bands & dance groups. Old time & American music.*
**RAB** Southern Arts

## Colvin Quarmby
**Contact** Nick Quarmby
**Mail address** 88 Orchard Park, Twigworth, GLOUCESTER, GL2 9QR
**Phone** 07780 982168
**Phone/Fax** 01594 510260
**Email** gerry@colvin.freeserve.co.uk
**Web** www.colvinquarmby.com
*Three piece band playing original songs in the acoustic roots style.*
***Musicians' Union member***
**RAB** South West Arts

## The Committee Band
**Contact** Jeff Dent
**Mail address** Working Party Music, 6 Riverside Walk, ISLEWORTH, Middlesex, TW7 6HW
**Phone** 020 8560 5049
020 8737 7307
**Email** jeffdent@yahoo.co.uk
**Web** www.workingparty.com
*Large and popular ceilidh band with caller. English & European influences.*
***Musicians' Union member***
**RAB** London Arts

## Confluence
**Contact** Laurel Swift
**Mail address** 62 Eade Road, LONDON, N4 1DH
**Phone** 07855 389360
**Email** laurel@beam.freeserve.co.uk
**Alt contact** John Dipper
**Alt address** West End House, High Street , Heytesbury, WARMINSTER, Wilts, BA12 0BA
**Phone** 07811 839997
*Fiddle duo playing English and other traditional music with baroque to atonal influences, plus clog, concertina and viola.*
**RAB** London Arts

## Connie Lush and Blues Shouter
**Contact** Access All Areas
*UK blues vocalist with her band*

## Contradition
**Contact** Dave Brown
**Mail address** 3 Fanshaw Way, Lower Marsh Road, WARMINSTER, Wilts, BA12 9QX
**Phone** 01985 847417
**Fax** 01985 219548
**Email** dave@dlbmusic.freeserve.co.uk
**Web** www.dlbmusic.freeserve.co.uk
*Folk dance band. Playford to contras.*
**RAB** Southern Arts

## Coope Boyes and Simpson
**Contact** Georgina Boyes
**Mail address** 78 Moorgate Road, ROTHERHAM, S Yorks, S60 2AY
**Phone/Fax** 01709 375063
**Email** georgina@nomasters.co.uk
**Web** www.coopeboyesandsimpson.co.uk
*Illustrious three part acapella singers and songwriters touring in Britain, Europe and North America. Workshops in songwriting, harmony singing and arranging.*
***Musicians' Union member***
**RAB** Yorkshire Arts

## Cordas et Cannas
**Contact** mARKO pOLO
**Web** www.markopolo.co.uk
*World roots band*

## Cornfield Perambulation
**Contact** Derek Morris
**Mail address** The Old School House, CHEBSEY, Staffs, ST21 6JU
**Phone** 01785 760660
**Email** cornper@aol.com
*Barn dance band for weddings, ceilidhs, etc. Tunes from UK, America & beyond.*
**RAB** West Midlands Arts

## Corrina Hewat
**Mail address** 11A Ettrick Road, SELKIRK, TD7 5AJ, Scotland
**Phone/Fax** 01750 22023
**Phone** 07711 512692
**Email** bachue@bachue.co.uk
**Web** www.corrinahewat.com
*Traditional Scottish harp player and singer (Scots and Gaelic). Teacher of harp & voice.*
***Musicians' Union member***
**AC** Scotland

## Cosmic Sausages
**Contact** Artists Connect
**Web** www.artistsconnect.com
*Streetfolk band, pop classics, theatre, circus, slapstick and crowd participation*

## Cottage Industry
**Contact** Peter Aston Orchard End, Gaunts Common, WIMBOURNE, Dorset, BH21 4JR
**Phone** 01258 840844
01929 557221
**Email** cottageindustry@hotmail.com
*4 piece ceilidh/ barn dance band with caller. Recording studio.*
***Musicians' Union member***
**RAB** South West Arts

## The Coyotes
**Contact** Matters Musical
**Web** www.mattersmusical.com
*Country blues. Winners of Best British Country Album 1997*

## Cragg Vale Gamelan
**Contact** Jan Scott
**Mail address** 3 Regent Place, HEBDEN BRIDGE, W Yorks, HX7 7DF
**Phone** 01422 843315
07808 854664
**Email** jan.scott@u.genie.co.uk
**Web** www.craggvalegamelan.co.uk
*Wide reportoire of Indonesian inspired music, plus world influences. New street theatre & shadow play. Educational workshops.*
**RAB** Yorkshire Arts

## Craobh Rua
**Contact** CTM UK
**Web** www.ctmuk.com
*Traditional Irish music and song band*

## Crasdant
**Contact** Stephen Rees
**Mail address** 8 Bron Arfon, LLANLLECHID, Gwynedd, LL57 3LW
**Phone/Fax** 01248 600427
**Phone** 07880 602897
**Email** crasdant@btinternet.com
*Traditional Welsh music & clogging from Robin Huw Bowen, Stephen Rees, Andy McLauchlin & Huw Williams. Workshop leaders*
***Musicians' Union member***
**AC** Wales

## Crediton World Music Choir
**Contact** Alise Ojay
**Mail address** Kerlistz, The Green, Morchard Bishop, CREDITON, Devon
**Phone** 01392 216633
**Email** patten@kerlistz.freeserve.co.uk
**Phone** 01363 877503
*Friendly community choir, meets weekly. Repertoire of traditional music from all continents. Performs concerts locally.*
**RAB** South West Arts

## Crocodile Style
**Contact** Emergency Exit Arts
**Web** www.eea.org.uk
*7 piece street band playing music from all over the world. Costumes and dance*
***Musicians' Union member***
**RAB** London Arts

## Croft No. Five
**Contact** Martin Coull Music Management
**Mail address** Studio 7, 6 New Street, EDINBURGH, EH8 8BH, Scotland
**Phone/Fax** 0131 557 5330
**Phone** 07803 137509
**Email** marticoull@aol.com
*Scottish band combining traditional and new tunes with dance and funk grooves*
**Agent** Stoneyport Agency
**AC** Scotland

## Cross O' Th Hands
**Contact** John Adams
**Mail address** 13 Chevin Rroad, BELPER, Derbys, DE56 2UW
**Phone** 01773 829602
07941 534968
**Email** jadams@cothrecords.co.uk
**Web** www.cothrecords.co.uk
**Alt contact** Sarah Matthews
**Alt address** 10 Hamblin Crescent, SINFIN, Derbys, DE24 9PL
**Phone** 07941 366319
01332 273383
**Email** sarah@folkspace.idps.co.uk
*4 piece acoustic band playing English and European,traditional and new,tunes and songs*
**Agent** Access All Areas
***Musicians' Union member***
**RAB** East Midlands Arts

## The Cuckoo Ale Band
**Contact** Bev Langton
**Mail address** Lacon Hall, Lacon, WEM, Shrops, SY4 5RP
**Phone** 01939 233977
**Email** bev.langton@talk21.com
**Alt contact** Ray Langton
**Email** ray.langton@talk21.com
*3 piece ceilidh band with own caller. Melodeon, percussion and guitar. Please call evenings/ weekends.*
**RAB** West Midlands Arts

## Cuckoo's Nest
**Contact** Pam Bishop
**Mail address** 35 Waterloo Road, Kings Heath, BIRMINGHAM, B14 7SD
**Phone** 0121 244 3513
**Email** pam@cabaret.free-online.co.uk
*Traditional dance music band with fiddle, concertina, whistle, melodeon, guitar. Dances and concerts.*
***Musicians' Union member***
**RAB** West Midlands Arts

## Cyril Jones
**Mail address** 3 Uplands Way, Grange Park, LONDON, N21 1DH
**Email** cydorjones@aol.com
*MC & barn dance caller. Qualified EFDSS tutor for English country dance workshops.*
**RAB** London Arts

## Cyril Tawney
**Contact** Rosemary Tawney
**Mail address** 10 Sivell Place, Heavitree, EXETER, Devon, EX2 5ET
**Phone** 01392 426055
*Eminent solo singer, with guitar or unaccompanied. Traditional West Country and maritime songs plus own songs e.g. "Grey Funnel Line", "Sally Free and Easy" etc.*
**RAB** South West Arts

## Da Capo
**Contact** Cathy Turner
**Mail address** 4 De Aston Field, Willingham Road, MARKET RASEN, Lincs, LN8 3DX
**Phone** 01673 843571 - eve & weekend
**Email** cathy.turner@lineone.net
**Alt address** Mill Corner, High Street, FALDINGWORTH, Lincs, LN8 3SE
**Phone** 01673 885571
*12 piece group singing traditional and new songs with string and wind accompaniment.*
**RAB** East Midlands Arts

## The Dagmars
**Contact** Matters Musical
**Web** www.mattersmusical.com
*Lamé-clad 3 piece Scottish Glam-a-billy band. Covers with a twist*

## Dai Thomas
**Contact** D J Thomas
**Mail address** 42 Lancaster Road, SALFORD, Lancs, M6 8AW
**Phone** 0161 707 4063
07773 492975
**Email** d.thomas@which.net
*Solo blues & old timey singer & guitarist. Plus 12 string banjo, mandolin and autoharp.*
***Musicians' Union member***
**RAB** North West Arts

## Daisy-Belle
**Contact** Access All Areas
*5 piece Cajun and Zydeco band from France*

## Dalcassian
**Contact** Matters Musical
**Web** www.mattersmusical.com
*3 or 4 piece Scottish ceilidh band. Caller available*

## Dalta
**Contact** Gareth Banks
**Mail address** 18 Birchfield Way, Lydiate, LIVERPOOL, L31 4DS
**Phone** 0151 5319525
**Email** gareth@dalta.com
*Contemporary Celtic band, songs and instrumentals. Workshops available.*
***Musicians' Union member***
**RAB** Yorkshire Arts

## Damian Clarke
**Contact** Damian Clarke
**Mail address** 25 Kings Road, DORCHESTER, Dorset, DT1 1NH
**Phone/Fax** 01305 267510
**Email** damian@voxpop.demon.co.uk
**Web** www.voxpop.demon.co.uk
*Solo singer, traditional/self-penned political. Rural touring and schools.*
**RAB** South West Arts

## Damien Barber
**Mail address** The Flat, 11 Bridgehouse Lane, HAWORTH, W Yorks, BD23 8QE
**Phone** 01535 646605
**Email** damienbarber@hotmail.com
**Web** www.damienbarber.com
*Singer of traditional songs accompanied on concertina, guitar and button accordion. Solo or with band.*
**RAB** Yorkshire Arts

## Damn Heart
**Contact** Bright Light Arts
*Poet and singer/ guitarist duo; spontaneous words and music*



*Artists in the main A-Z listing are mostly available for concert and club bookings.*

*See page 11 for details of other artist listings (Dance Display, Solo Musicians, Composers, Arrangers, Session Musicians, Band Deps. Lecturers, MCs, Tutors, Street Theatre, Children's Entertainers, Theatre Companies).*

*Agents section appears on pages 119-131.*

## artists
## d

*Artists in the main A-Z listing are mostly available for concert and club bookings.*

*See page 11 for details of other artist listings (Dance Display, Solo Musicians, Composers, Arrangers, Session Musicians, Band Deps. Lecturers, MCs, Tutors, Street Theatre, Children's Entertainers, Theatre Companies).*

*Agents section appears on pages 119-131.*

### Damon and Naomi
**Contact** Moneypenny
*US alternative rock veterans, quiet & melancholy*

### Dan Evans
**Mail address** 61 Sillswood, OLNEY, Bucks, MK46 5PN
**Phone/Fax** 01234 241976
**Email** dansing.music@virgin.net
**Web** www.musiclink.co.uk/dansing
*Mountain dulcimer player and guitarist, mixed folk repertoire. Performs solo and with violinist Sylvia Seaton.*
***Musicians' Union member***
**RAB** East England Arts

### Dan Quinn
**Mail address** 87 St Andrews Road, Portslade, BRIGHTON, Sussex, BN41 1DD
**Phone** 01273 881316
**Email** quinn@unisonfree.net
*Solo singer of traditional and humorous songs accompanied on melodeon.*
***Musicians' Union member***
**RAB** South East Arts

### Dana Robinson
**Contact** The Other Agency
*American singer, old-time fiddle, guitar, banjo. Workshops in old-time fiddle, flat-picking guitar styles*

### Dangerous Curves
**Contact** Viva Smith
**Mail address** Church Farm House, Looers, BRIDPORT, Dorset, DT6 3SA
**Phone** 01308 425649
**Email** dancurves@lineone.net
**Email** paulm.downes@virgin.net
*Vocal trio traditional songs with jazz and countrry influences.*
**RAB** South West Arts

### Danu
**Contact** themusictree. (uk) ltd
**Web** www.danu.net
*Irish 7 piece all male traditional music band. 'Best Group' winners, BBC Folk Awards 2001 recipients.*

### Dave and Dave
**Contact** Dave Trenow
**Mail address** 82 Shrub End Road, COLCHESTER, Essex, CO3 4RX
**Phone** 01206 544447
**Email** trenow@talk21
*Unaccompanied traditonal English songs*
**RAB** East England Arts

### Dave and Ruth Cooper
**Mail address** 94 Pasture Road, Stapleford, NOTTINGHAM, NG9 8GL
**Phone** 0115 9399730
**Email** rcooper@stapleford-centre.org
*A capella harmony duo. English, American traditional & Gospel songs.*
**RAB** East Midlands Arts

### Dave (Floodgates) Robertson and Circle
**Mail address** c/o Chris Vernal, 1 Owens Place, Bridge Street, KINGTON, HR5 3DH
**Phone** 07967 005410 - Dave
01544 231734
**Web** www.dave.robertson.com
**Alt address** Tibet Foundation, 1 St James Market, LONDON, SW1Y 4SB
**Phone** 020 7930 6001
**Fax** 020 7930 6002
*Singer/songwriter/guitarist. Also available with other musicians.*
**RAB** London Arts

### Dave and Mike
**Contact** Mike Longhurst
**Mail address** Briat Croft, The Square, HARROW BARROW, Cornwall, PL17 8BA
**Phone** 01579 351201
**Email** mrlonghurst@talk21.com
*Songs, stories, workshops on "the great days of sailing" for schools (suits key stages)/ festivals.*
**RAB** South West Arts

### Dave Burland
**Mail address** 14 Longman Road, BARNSLEY, S Yorks, S70 2LD
**Phone/Fax** 01226 298985
**Email** s.burland14@aol.com
**Web** www.daveburland.co.uk
*Respected and influential solo singer of traditional and contemporary material, mostly with guitar accompaniment. "One of the leading folk voices of the 60s and 70s revival".*
**RAB** Yorkshire Arts

### Dave East
**Mail address** 21 Fernthorpe Road, Streatham, LONDON, SW16 6DP
**Phone** 020 8677 9989
*Multi instrumentalist; concertina, guitar, banjo, voice, etc. UK & American styles.*
**RAB** London Arts

### Dave Evans
**Mail address** 75 Oakleigh Park South, Whetstone, LONDON, N20 9JL
**Phone** 020 8446 4137
*Patter style caller for western barn dances & line dance instructor.*
**RAB** London Arts

### Dave Gardner and Anne Topping
**Contact** Dave Gardner
**Mail address** 805 Garstang Road, Barton, PRESTON, Lancs, PR3 5AA
**Phone** 01772 866058
**Email** davegardner@songwriter01.freeserve.co.uk
**Web** www.ammoniterecords.demon.co.uk/davegardner/
*New songs with guitar, piano & violin. Rock/ folk/ country/ classical style.*
**RAB** North West Arts

### Dave Gibb
**Contact** Isobel Gibb
**Mail address** 9 The Glade, LARKHALL, ML9 2JA, Scotland
**Phone** 01698 883294
**Email** davewg@hotmail.com
**Web** fp.davegibb.f9.co.uk
*Singer, guitarist and songwriter. Traditional and new.*
***Musicians' Union member***
**AC** Scotland

### Dave Hunt
**Mail address** 74A King Street, Dawley, TELFORD, Shropshire, TF4 2AQ
**Phone** 01952 505073
**Email** davehunt@aol.com
*Established caller for ceilidhs/ barn dances. Workshops for adults & schools. Available full time.*
***Musicians' Union member***
**RAB** West Midlands Arts

### Dave Illingworth
**Mail address** 87 Palmerston Road, Wimbledon, LONDON, SW19 1PB
**Phone** 020 8540 2919
*Singer/ guitarist: folk, jazz, blues*
**RAB** London Arts

### Dave James
**Phone** 07877 698182
**Alt contact** Mad Moggy's Agency
**Phone** 01384 897386
*Singer, songwriter, instrumentalist. Humorous, traditional, new songs and monologues.*

### Dave Kelly
**Contact** GTA Music Agency
*Solo acoustic blues*

### Dave Peabody
**Contact** The Blues Line
**Web** www.bluesline.freeserve.co.uk
*Respected Blues artist*

## Dave Robinson
**Mail address** 267 Llangyfelach Road, Brynhyfryd, SWANSEA, SA5 9LB, Wales
**Phone** 01792 464871
**Fax** 01792 415725
**Email** david.robinson2@ntlworld.com
*Sea-songs/shanties*
**AC** Wales

## Dave Swarbrick and Alistair Hulett
**Contact** Emerging Music
**Web** www.emerging.demon.co.uk
*Revered fiddle player with Scottish singer songwriter.*

## Dave Swarbrick and Kevin Dempsey
**Agent** Karisma Music Management

## Dave Townsend
**Mail address** 22 Swinbourne Road, Littlemore, OXFORD, OX4 4PQ
**Phone** 01865 714778
07798 520552
**Fax** 01865 749428
**Email** mellstock@aol.com
**Alt address** Huntingdon Hall, Crowngate, WORCESTER, WR1 3LD
**Phone** 01905 611323
*English traditional songs and music with concertina, fiddle and accordion. Workshop leader and dance caller.*
***Musicians' Union member***
**RAB** Southern Arts

## Dave Webber and Anni Fentiman
**Contact** Dave Webber
**Mail address** 64 Oxhey Avenue, Oxhey, WATFORD, Herts, WD1 4HA
**Phone** 01923 228468
07976 521788
**Fax** 01923 441869
**Email** daveandanni@oldandnew tradition.com
**Web** http://freespace.virgin.net/ daveandanni.music
*Traditional & traditional idiom songs in harmony.*
**RAB** East England Arts

## Dave Wright
**Contact** Blue Balloon Records
**Mail address** PO Box 743, BRISTOL, Avon, BS99 5GU
**Phone** 0117 942 3715 before 8.30pm
07929 864573
**Email** 113040.3101@compuserve. com
**Web** www.blueballoonrecords.com
*Blues/ country singer- songwriter.*
***Musicians' Union member***
**RAB** South West Arts

## Davey Graham
**Contact** Kay Thomson
**Mail address** 31 Severus Street, Acomb, YORK, YO24 4NL
**Phone** 01904 782410
**Email** kaythomson@yahoo.co.uk
**Web** www.geocities.com/daveygraham
*Virtuoso guitar player, writer of "Angi". Fanzine "Midnight Man" & mail order service for CDs etc.*
***Musicians' Union member***
**RAB** Yorkshire Arts

## David Camlin
**Mail address** Ghyll Cottage, Lamplugh Green, WORKINGTON, Cumbria, CA14 4TY
**Phone** 01946 861080
0771 232 2826
**Email** David.Camlin@btinternet.com
*Singer-songwriter delivering mellow, personal songs of warmth & depth.*
***Musicians' Union member***
**RAB** Northern Arts

## David Milner
**Mail address** 14a Rectory Close, BROADMAYNE, Dorset, DT2 8EQ
**Phone** 01305 852773
**Email** dmilner@thomas-hardye.dorset. sch.uk
*Caller of English style barndances/ ceilidhs. Leader of Breton dance workshops.*
**RAB** South West Arts

## De Dannan
**Contact** Stoneyport Agency
**Phone/Fax** 0131 5571050
**Email** dfrancis@musicscotland.com
**Web** home.att.net/~frankiegavin/ index.html
*Legendary Irish band, led by fiddle player, Frankie Gavin*

## Deaf Shepherd
**Contact** Martin Coull Music Management
**Mail address** Studio 7, 6 New Street, EDINBURGH, EH8 8BH, Scotland
**Phone/Fax** 0131 557 5330
**Phone** 07803 137509
**Email** marticoull@aol.com
**Web** www.deafshepherd.demon.co.uk
*Scottish upbeat traditional music band. Twin fiddles, pipes, guitar, etc*
**Agent** Stoneyport Agency

## Dean Johnson
**Contact** Elizabeth Jones Entertainments
**Web** www.bromyard.co.uk/ejones
*Singer songwriter*

## Dean Owens
**Contact** Active
*Scottish songwriter and The Felsons frontman with his own band*
**AC** Scotland

## Dearman, Gammon and Harrison
**Contact** Vic Gammon
**Mail address** 12 Beechfield Road, HUDDERSFIELD, HD2 2XQ
**Phone** 01484 424465
0113 2334566
**Email** gammon@dial.pipex.com
**Alt contacts** Annie Dearman/ Steve Harrison
**Phone** 01484 844055
**Email** gamut@dial.pipex.com
*English traditional songs, accompanied on banjo, melodeon, concertina, mouth organ. Associated with Ryburn 3 Step.*
***Musicians' Union member***
**RAB** Yorkshire Arts

## Debby McClatchy
**Contact** Neil White - UK Agent
**Mail address** 28 Bovingdon Heights, MARLOW, Bucks, SL7 2JS
**Phone/Fax** 01628 473292
**Email** Appalcore@neilart.force9.co.uk
*US Old time banjo player and singer, fiddler and step dancer. Banjo and song workshops.*
**RAB** South East Arts

## Deborah Kermode
**Mail address** 60 Soutergate, Ulverston, Cumbria, LA12 7ES
**Phone** 01229 582704
**Email** Kmode@onetel.net.uk
*Ceilidh dance caller specialising in Cumbrian Lakes dances.*
**RAB** Northern

## The Deep Ellum Playboys
**Contact** Jason Hill
**Mail address** 54 Prince Street, Burslem, STOKE ON TRENT, Staffs, ST6 4EN
**Phone** 01782 813401
07778 913528
**Email** jason@burslem.demon.co.uk
**Alt contact** Trevor Carter
**Phone** 01782 398657
**Email** carter@edgemusic.fsnet.co.uk
*6 piece western swing band. Jazz-influenced rural dance music from pre-war Texas.Banjo, fiddle, steel guitar, sax, etc.*
***Musicians' Union member***
**RAB** West Midlands Arts

## Delyth Jenkins
**Contact** Elizabeth Jones Entertainments
**Web** www.bromyard.co.uk/ejones
*Welsh harpist*
**AC** Wales



*Artists in the main A-Z listing are mostly available for concert and club bookings.*

*See page 11 for details of other artist listings (Dance Display, Solo Musicians, Composers, Arrangers, Session Musicians, Band Deps. Lecturers, MCs, Tutors, Street Theatre, Children's Entertainers, Theatre Companies).*

*Agents section appears on pages 119-131.*

*Artists in the main A-Z listing are mostly available for concert and club bookings.*

*See page 11 for details of other artist listings (Dance Display, Solo Musicians, Composers, Arrangers, Session Musicians, Band Deps. Lecturers, MCs, Tutors, Street Theatre, Children's Entertainers, Theatre Companies).*

*Agents section appears on pages 119-131.*

## Derek Brimstone
**Mail address** 48 Lyne Way, HEMEL HEMPSTEAD, Herts, HP1 3PN
**Phone** 01442 264924
**Email** brimo1@mcmail.com
**Web** www.derekbrimstone.mcmail.com
*Singer, guitarist, banjo player, raconteur and comedian*
**Agent** Karisma Music Management
**RAB** East England Arts

## Derek Gifford
**Mail address** 22 Stoney Brow, Roby Mill, UP HOLLAND, Lancs, WN8 0QE
**Phone** 01695 625097
**Email** derek.gifford@talk21.com
*Singer, traditional style songs. Unaccompanied/ with guitar & bowed psaltery. Talks and workhops.*
***Musicians' Union member***
**RAB** North West Arts

## Derek Gregory
**Mail address** 52 Oakhampton Road, Mill Hill, LONDON, NW7 1NH
**Phone/Fax** 020 8349 2893
**Email** dgregor@tesco.net
*Barn dance & ceilidh caller. Band available: The Friday Folk Band.*
**RAB** London Arts

## Derrin Nauendorf and David Downing
**Mail address** 134 Richmond Road, IPSWICH, Suffolk, IP1 4AP
**Phone** 07765 116294
01473 431165
**Email** thekegster@hotmail.com
**Alt contact** David Downing
**Alt address** PO Box 129, North Carlton, VICTORIA, 3054, Australia
**Phone** 0061 41738 4152
*Professional international rott/ blues duo. Annual UK visits.*
***Musicians' Union member***
**RAB** East England Arts

## Dervish
**Contact** Adastra
**Web** www.adastra-music.com
*Celebrated 7-piece Irish traditional music group*

## Desperate Men
**Contact** John Richards
**Mail address** Crescent Lodge, Newbridge Crescent, Tettenhall, Wolverhampton, WV6 0LN
**Phone** 01902 746577
**Email** desperate@workingjoe.co.uk
**Alt contact** Dave Jones
**Phone** 01902 711236
*Six piece roots/rock/r&b band, performing mainly original material from John Richards.*
**RAB** West Midlands Arts

## Devana
**Contact** Mutiny Music
*Irish music band*
**AC** Ireland

## Dezi Donnelly
**Contact** Smallworld Music
*Acclaimed solo Irish traditional fiddle player (Manchester based)*
**RAB** North West Arts

## Dick Gaughan
**Contact** Stoneyport Agency
**Web** www.dickalba.demon.co.uk/main.htm
*Celebrated Scottish singer/ song-writer and guitarist. Traditional/ contemporary/political material.*
**AC** Scotland

## Dick Gaughan and Brian McNeill
**Contact** Stoneyport Agency
**Web** www.brianmcneill.co.uk
*Pairing of Scottish political singer/ songwriter/ guitarist and fiddler/ singer / multi-instumentalist*
**AC** Scotland

## Dick Glasgow
**Mail address** 18 Main Street, Ballintoy, Co. Antrim BT54 6LX
**Phone/Fax** 028 2076 3116
**Email** afm06@dial.pipex.com
**Web** causewaymusic.co.uk
*Irish and Scottish music on fiddle, tenor banjo and anglo concertina. Also bands, classes, concerts, ceilis etc.*
**AC** Northern Ireland

## Diego Brown and The Good Fairy
**Contact** Adam Bradbury
**Mail address** PO Box 33601, LONDON, N16 7ZF
**Phone** 07949 226421
**Email** good.fairy@virginnet.co.uk
**Web** www.diegobrown.com
**Alt contact** Andy Lambert
**Alt address** 50 Riversdale Road, LONDON, N5 2JT
**Phone/Fax** 020 7226 5477
**Phone** 07767 607717
*Songs, offbeat humour and audience participation*
**Agent** Matters Musical
***Musicians' Union member***
**RAB** London Arts

## Dirk Powell
**Contact** Access All Areas
*USA Appalachian & Old Timey accordion player. Member of Balfa Toujours*

## Don Mescall
**Contact** themusictree. (uk) ltd
*London based Irish singer songwriter*
**RAB** London Arts

## Donal Lunny
**Contact** Asgard Promotions
*Founder member of Planxty, Bothy Band & Moving Hearts. Composer, record producer and leading figure in Irish traditional music*

## Donal Maguire
**Mail address** 5 Tor View, Haslingden, ROSSENDALE, Lancs, BB4 6PN
**Phone** 01706 214994
**Email** rossrecs@talk21.com
**Web** www.donalmaguire.co.uk
*Solo singer, mainly traditional Irish & contemporary. Guitar, mandolin, tenor banjo player. Seminars/ workshops in singing styles.*
**RAB** North West Arts

## Donnie Munro
**Contact** Active
*Ex Runrig frontman with his own band*
**AC** Scotland

## Dordan
**Contact** Martina Goggin
**Mail address** Bothuna, AN SPIDDEAL, Co Galway, Ireland
**Phone/Fax** +353 91 553255
**Phone** 00353 86 8814101
**Email** dordan@eircom.net
*Irish all-female traditional music quartet.*
**RAB** Ireland

## The Doonan Family Band
**Contact** Mick Doonan
**Mail address** 51 Jacob's Well Lane, Wakefield WF1 3PB
**Phone** 01924 366126
**Email** mick@mdoonan.freeserve.co.uk
*3 generations of Irish traditional performers including All-Ireland and World Piccolo Champion John Doonan. Also includes two Irish dancers.*

## Doreen Lighter
**Mail address** 21 Fernthorpe Road, Streatham, LONDON, SW16 6DP
**Phone** 020 8677 9989
*Unaccompanied singer of American & French traditional songs. Solo and duo with Dave East.*
**RAB** London Arts

## Dorothy Dearnley

**Mail address** Eleven North Drive, Heswall, WIRRAL, Merseyside, CH60 0BB
**Phone** 0151 342 4490
*Singer/ storyteller of Lancashire and Cheshire material.*
***Musicians' Union member***
**RAB** North West Arts

## Doug Hudson

**Mail address** 182 Windmill Road, GILLINGHAM, Kent, ME7 5PE
**Phone/Fax** 01634 574837
**Phone** 07941 238377
**Email** doug.hudson@lineone.net
**Web** www.doughudson.com
*Singer & stand-up comedian.*
**RAB** South East Arts

## Doughboy Zydecajun

**Contact** Mr Robin Hillman
**Mail address** 4 Saxon Rise, EARLS BARTON, Northants, NN6 0NY
**Phone** 01604 810896
**Email** hillmanimps@talk21.com
**Alt contact** Mr Janis Zakis
**Alt address** 7 Broadlands, RAUNDS, Northants, NN9 6QL
**Phone** 01933 623172
01933 277717
**Fax** 01933 270277
*Cajun & Zydeco dance band with fiddle, accordion, guitar and percussion*
**Agent** Access All Areas
**RAB** East Midlands Arts

## Dougie MacLean

**Contact** NEM Productions (UK)
**Web** www.dunkeld.co.uk
*Scottish singer and songwriter of international repute*
**AC** Scotland

## Douglas Keir and The Bluebell Scottish Dance Band

**Contact** Douglas Keir
**Mail address** 7 Pitfirrane Park, CROSSFORD, Fife, KY12 8NU Scotland
**Phone** 01383 725359
*Traditional dance band with accordions, fiddle, drums, double bass.*
***Musicians' Union member***
**AC** Scotland

## DPN Plus One

**Contact** Dave Illingworth
**Mail address** 87 Palmerston Road, Wimbledon, LONDON, SW19 1PB
**Phone** 020 8540 2919
**Email** normfairey@aol.com
**Alt contact** Norman Fairey
**Fax** 020 8647 7018
*Quartet playing swing, ballads, blues, skiffle, etc. on clarinet, harmonica, guitars, etc.*
**RAB** London Arts

## Dr Faustus

**Contact** Robert Harbron
**Mail address** 94 Roxeth Green Avenue, HARROW, Middx, HA2 8AQ
**Phone** 020 8357 3261
07973 717786
**Fax** 020 8537 8335
**Email** rob.harbron@virgin.net
**Web** www.drfaustus.co.uk
**Alt contact** Paul Sartin
**Alt address** May Cottage, WHERWELL, Hants, SP11 7JS
**Phone** 01264 860791
07711 485798
**Email** psartin@attglobal.net
*4 piece traditional English band. Melodeon, concertina, fiddle, guitar, voice, etc. Concerts or dances, own PA and caller.*
**RAB** Southern Arts

## Dr Q's Strange Karaoke

**Contact** Quentin Budworth
**Mail address** Molescroft Grange Farmhouse, BEVERLEY, Yorks, HU17 9RS
**Phone** 01482 865604
**Email** grinnigogs@pop3.poptel.org.uk
*Live PA with programmed beats, hurdy-gurdy, bagpipes, shawm and low whistle!*
**RAB** Yorkshire Arts

## Dragon's Breath

**Contact** Mark Takel
**Mail address** 56 Heathfield Road, Gabalfa, CARDIFF, CF4 3JY, Wales
**Phone** 029 2061 5403
**Alt contact** Barry Scouse
**Alt address** 'Newlands', Rhadyr Llanbadoc, USK, Monmouthshire, Wales
**Phone** 01291 672612
*Ceilidh or barn dance band, emphasis on Celtic repertoire.*
**AC** Wales

## Dragonsfire

**Contact** Matters Musical
**Web** www.mattersmusica .com
*Early music vocal and instrumental quartet. Themed and costumed shows covering Victorian, Folk, Christmas etc*

## Drop The Box

**Contact** CTM UK
**Web** www.ctmuk.com
*Shetland 5-piece Celtic folk/jazz/ pop band*
**Agent** CTM UK, Organic Arts
***Musicians' Union member***
**AC** Scotland

## Dropping Clangers

**Contact** Robert Mulford
Ashwood Cottage, 23 Bramley Road, Southgate, LONDON, N14 4HD
**Phone** 020 8373 1282
07768 960896
**Email** robert@dropping-clangers.co.uk
**Web** www.dropping-clangers.co.uk
*Barn dance band with caller.*
***Musicians' Union member***
**RAB** London Arts

## DRQ DJ & Compere

**Contact** Quentin Budworth
Molescroft Grange Farmhouse, BEVERLEY, Yorks, HU17 9RS
**Phone** 01482 865604
**Email** grinnigogs@pop3.poptel.org.uk
*World music DJ and compere*

## Duck Baker

**Contact** The Bechhofer Agency
*American guitarist: Blues, Ragtime, Celtic and original compositions*

## Dulaman

**Contact** Clunie Creative Enterprises
**Web** www.come.to/clunie
*Irish/Gaelic song band with guitar and light percussion*

## Dunav Balkan Group

**Contact** Caroline Thomas
**Mail address** 77 Forest Road, Walthamstow, LONDON, E17 6HF
**Phone/Fax** 020 8527 4896
**Email** dunav@classical-artists.com
**Web** www.classical-artists.com/ dunav-balkan
*Vocal and instrumental group playing music from SE Europe. Also workshops in Balkan dance.*
**RAB** London Arts

## Duncan McCrone

**Mail address** East End Cottage, GARTMORE, Stirlingshire, FK8 3RW, Scotland
**Phone** 01877 382259
**Email** duncan@ranzamusic.com
*Singer/songwriter, formerly with the Clydesiders.*
***Musicians' Union member***
**AC** Scotland

## Durga Rising

**Contact** Matters Musical
**Web** www.mattersmusical.com
*Vocal/ piano/ percussion trio fusing ragas, blues, rhythm, bhangra, jazz. Features Barb Jungr, Russell Churney and Kuljit Bhamra*



*Artists in the main A-Z listing are mostly available for concert and club bookings.*

*See page 11 for details of other artist listings (Dance Display, Solo Musicians, Composers, Arrangers, Session Musicians, Band Deps. Lecturers, MCs, Tutors, Street Theatre, Children's Entertainers, Theatre Companies).*

*Agents section appears on pages 119-131.*

*Artists in the main A-Z listing are mostly available for concert and club bookings.*

*See page 11 for details of other artist listings (Dance Display, Solo Musicians, Composers, Arrangers, Session Musicians, Band Deps. Lecturers, MCs, Tutors, Street Theatre, Children's Entertainers, Theatre Companies).*

*Agents section appears on pages 119-131.*

## The Dylan Project
**Contact** Rob Braviner
**Mail address** PO Box 37, BANBURY, Oxon, OX16 8YN
**Phone** 01869 338853
**Fax** 01869 337142
**Web** www.fairportconvention.com
*Steve Gibbons, PJ Wright, Dave Pegg and Simon Nicol playing Bob Dylan songs.*
***Musicians' Union member***
**RAB** South East Arts

## e2K
**Contact** Jon Moore
**Mail address** 49 Kirkes Road, LANCASTER, LA1 3DW
**Phone** 01524 843413
0794 1151844
**Email** moorejon@compuserve.com
**Web** www.e2kmusic.co.uk
*8 piece multicultural roots act based in UK folk and West African music.*
**Agent** Adastra
***Musicians' Union member***
**RAB** North West Arts

## The East Kent Hoppers
**Contact** Keith Kendrick
**Mail address** 88 Highfield Road, ASHBOURNE, Derbys, DE6 1DX
**Phone/Fax** 01335 345675
**Phone** 07885 345367
**Email** eyup@freeuk.com
**Web** www.freeuk.com
*Trio playing music for English Country dance on concertina, piano & tenor banjo.*
**RAB** East Midlands Arts

## East Of Ealing
**Contact** Helene Hambrook
**Mail address** Sober Promotions, 64 Talbot Road, OLD ISLEWORTH, Middx, TW7 7HF
**Phone/Fax** 020 8891 0623
07870 326133
**Email** mail@eastofealing.fsnet.co.uk
**Web** www.eastofealing.fsnet.co.uk
*Fiddle-led global dance band*
**Agent** Adastra
***Musicians' Union member***
**RAB** London Arts

## Ebony Steel Band
**Contact** Matters Musical
**Web** www.mattersmusical.com
*UK Steel band*

## Ed Miller
**Contact** The Bechhofer Agency

## Ed Wolstenholme
**Contact** Ed Wolstenholme
**Mail address** 34 Dale Street, Longwood, HUDDERSFIELD, W Yorks, HD3 4TG
**Phone** 01484 649544
07778 676370
**Email** ed@webshopmedia.com
*Various styles on electric violin, mandolin*
***Musicians' Union member***
**RAB** Yorkshire Arts

## Eddie Walker
**Mail address** 33 The Grove, Brookfield, MIDDLESBROUGH, Teesside, TS5 8DT
**Phone** 01642 593780
**Email** eddiewalker@raggedrecords.freeserve.co.uk
**Web** ww.folkmusic.net/eddiewalker
*Singer, guitarist, songwriter. Old blues, rags, folk and instrumentals.*
***Musicians' Union member***
**RAB** Northern Arts

## The Eel Grinders
**Contact** David Faulkner
**Mail address** 7 Bowring Mead, MORETONHAMPSTEAD, Devon, TQ13 8NP
**Phone** 01647 440020
**Email**
eelgrinders@netscapeonline.co.uk
**Alt contact** Steve Turner
**Alt address** 8 Nattadon Road, CHAGFORD, Devon, TQ13 8BC
**Phone** 01647 433646
*4 piece ceilidh, dance and concert band playing English and European tunes with classical and jazz elements. Fiddle, pipes, percussion.*
**RAB** South West Arts

## Eh, La-Bas! with Moise and Alida Viator
**Contact** Access All Areas
*8 piece US New Orleans Creole jazz group, fronted by young Creole-Cajun fiddle & guitar duo*

## Eileen McGann
**Contact** Jacey Bedford Tour Management
**Web** www.borealisrecords.com
*Canadian songwriter and traditional/ contemporary singer. Tours with guitarist/ vocalist*
**Agent** Jacey Bedford Tour Management

## El Adivino
**Contact** Matters Musical
**Web** www.mattersmusical.com
*Solo guitarists/ vocalists up to big band, dancers available*

## Elaine Barker
**Mail address** Holly Cottage, Lower Road, PELDON, Essex, CO5 7PR
**Phone** 01206 735606
*Barn dance caller. Singer and guitarist. Guitar teacher and guitar tutor books. Promoter of folk events and parties.*
**RAB** East England Arts

## Elaine Samuels and Kindred Spirit
**Contact** Elaine Samuels
**Mail address** 9 Church Stretton Road, HOUNSLOW, Middlesex, TW3 2QP
**Phone/Fax** 020 8898 6040
**Email** elaine_samuels@email.com
**Web** members.nbci.com/elaine_samuels
*Solo singer and guitar/ banjo player. Also with band; violin, bass and drums. Please book via agent*
**Agent** Elizabeth Jones Entertainments
***Musicians' Union member***
**RAB** London Arts

## Elderberries
**Contact** Cath McGrother
**Mail address** 209 Leicester Road, MARKFIELD, Leics, LE67 9RF
**Phone** 01530 4244667
**Email** cath@McGrother.freeserve.co.uk
**Web** www.elderberries.co.uk
**Alt contact** Dave Yeomans
**Alt address** 98 Woodside, ASHBY DE LA ZOUCH, Leics, LE65 2NU
**Phone** 01530 414719
Contemporary folk songwriting duo.
***Musicians' Union member***
**RAB** East Midlands Arts

## The Electric Bluebirds
**Contact** Matters Musical
**Web** www.mattersmusical.com
*English band incorporating Cajun and other American roots into mainstream Rock*

## Elephant Talk
**Contact** Artists Connect
**Web** www.infrasound.co.uk
*African & Asian beats fused with Celtic saxophone and flute plus didgeridoo and Spanish guitar*
**Agent** Artists Connect, Matters Musical
**RAB** Yorkshire Arts

## Elephant Talk featuring special guest Eddi Reader
**Contact** Matters Musical
**Web** www.mattersmusical.com
*Afro-Asian roots band with acclaimed singer/songwriter. Available for selected shows*

### Eliot Mackrell
**Contact** Matters Musical
**Web** www.mattersmusical.com
*Didgeridoo player. Also performs folk-based violin music*

### Eliza Carthy
**Contact** Moneypenny
*Groundbreaking English singer and fiddle player*
***Musicians' Union member***

### Eliza Carthy Band
**Contact** The Concert Clinic
**Web** www.concertclinic.com
***Musicians' Union member***

### Elspeth Cowie
**Mail address** 3 Rockville Terrace, BONNYRIGG, Midlothian, EH19 2AG, Scotland
**Phone/Fax** 0131 6637647
**Email** elspeth@scotfolk.com
**Web** www.scotfolk.com/cowie
*Singer of unaccompanied Scots traditional songs. Solo/ duo with guitarist Ronnie Lang. Teacher of Scots song & bodhran.*
***Musicians' Union member***
**AC** Scotland

### Emily Druce
**Mail address** 32 Berry Croft, Honley, HUDDERSFIELD, Yorks, HD7 2BP
**Phone** 01484 667738
*Country blues singer/ guitarist.*
**RAB** Yorkshire Arts

### Emily Slade
**Mail address** PO Box 61, HITCHIN, Herts, SG5 3GL
**Phone** 07941 013943
**Email** rusticthorn@emilyslade.co.uk
**Web** www.emilyslade.co.uk
*Singer & guitarist. Traditional, contemporary and own songs.*
**RAB** East England Arts

### Emmylou Harris
**Contact** Asgard Promotions
*Major league Country singer and songwriter*

### The English Country Dance Band
**Contact** Rod Stradling
**Mail address** 1 Castle Street, STROUD, Glos, GL5 2HP
**Phone** 01453 759475
**Email** rod@mustrad.org.uk
**Web** www.mustrad.org.uk/english.htm
**Alt contact** Paul Burgess
**Alt address** 23 Haywards Road, Charlton Kings, CHELTENHAM, GL52 6RQ
**Phone** 01242 518676
**Email** paul_burgess@bigfoot.com
*5 piece band specialising in traditional style English music for dancing, as played in the villages during late 19th/early 20th Centuries. Caller and full PA. Concerts; songs & tunes.*
**RAB** South West Arts

### enQ
**Contact** c/o AMS
**Mail address** PO Box 649, DUNSTABLE, Beds, LU5 4XD
**Phone** 01582 475655
**Fax** 01582 475739
**Email** enq@route66.cix.co.uk
**Web** www.enq.org.uk
*Celtic funk/ folk/ rock/ jazz fusion. Mix of new songs and tradition-influenced instrumentals.*
***Musicians' Union member***
**RAB** East England Arts

### Equation
**Contact** NEM Productions (UK)
**Web** www.nemproductions.com
*6 piece pop-folk band*

### Eric Bibb
**Contact** Alan Robinson Management
**Web** www.ericbibb.com
*Highly respected American blues guitarist/ vocalist*
**Agents** Alan Robinson Management, Asgard Promotions

### Eric Bogle
**Contact** Stoneyport Agency
**Web** www.windbourne.com/ebogle/
*Writer of frequently covered songs, & singer with guitar accompaniment. Originally from Scottish Borders, long-term Australian resident. Occasional tours.*

### Eric Roche
**Mail address** 35 Chauntry Road, HAVERHILL, Suffolk, CB9 8BE
**Phone** 07976 293299
01440 709212
**Email** info@innerearmusic.com
**Web** www.innnerearmusic.com
**Alt address** c/o Academy of Contemporary Music, 4 Bridge Street, GUILDFORD, Surrey, GU1 4SB
**Phone** 01483 456788
*Solo guitar. Fingerstyle instrumental/ vocal accompaniment.*
***Musicians' Union member***
**RAB** South East Arts

### Errol Linton's Blues Vibe
**Contact** Matters Musical
**Web** www.mattersmusical.com
*Blues harmonica player and hollerer plus band, 1950s Chicago style*

### Esyllt Harker
**Mail address** 7/1 Stryd Y Ffynon, Gerlan, BETHESDA, Gwynedd, LL57 3TN
**Phone** 01248 602033
*Teller of Welsh and other stories, singer & actor. Workshops in voice & movement, led in English or Welsh.*
**AC** Wales

### Extra
**Contact** Hemlock Music
**Web** www.hemlockmusic.demon.co.uk
*Folk arts teaching group. Workshops include Morris (most styles), percussive dance, ceilidh dance, mummers plays, music & song*

### The Fairfield Four
**Contact** Adastra
**Web** www.adastra-music.com
*Legendary USA group, rooted in Gospel music and mixing it with modern American music styles*

### Fairport Convention
**Contact** Rob Braviner
**Mail address** Woodworm Records, PO Box 37, BANBURY, Oxon, OX16 8YN
**Phone** 01295 780400
**Fax** 01869 337142
**Web** www.fairportconvention.com
*Long established pre-eminent folk rock band; Simon Nicol, Dave Pegg, Ric Sanders, Chris Leslie and Gerry Conway*
**Agent** Stoneyport Agency, Woodworm
***Musicians' Union member***
**RAB** Southern Arts

*Artists in the main A-Z listing are mostly available for concert and club bookings.*

*See page 11 for details of other artist listings (Dance Display, Solo Musicians, Composers, Arrangers, Session Musicians, Band Deps. Lecturers, MCs, Tutors, Street Theatre, Children's Entertainers, Theatre Companies).*

*Agents section appears on pages 119-131.*

artists

f

*Artists in the main A-Z listing are mostly available for concert and club bookings.*

*See page 11 for details of other artist listings (Dance Display, Solo Musicians, Composers, Arrangers, Session Musicians, Band Deps. Lecturers, MCs, Tutors, Street Theatre, Children's Entertainers, Theatre Companies).*

*Agents section appears on pages 119-131.*

## The Famous Potatoes

**Contact** Paul McDowell
**Mail address** 13 Marine Avenue, LEIGH ON SEA, Essex, SS9 2JD
**Phone** 01702 474255
07790 061381
**Fax** 0703 115 0626
**Email** paul.mcdowell@easynet.co.uk
**Web** www.famouspotatoes.co.uk
*Eight piece barn dance band with caller.*
**RAB** East England Arts

## Fantazia

**Contact** Matters Musical
**Web** www.mattersmusical.com
*Afro-Oriental jazz fusion. Oud and derbouka, saxophones, drums and bass. Plus dancer*
**RAB** London Arts

## Fay Hield

**Mail address** 63 Nelson Street, Cross Roads, KEIGHLEY, Yorkshire, BD22 9EA
**Phone** 01535 643249
**Email** fayhield@hotmail.com
*Unaccompanied singer of mainly traditional songs. Solo or with Maggie Boyle.*
**RAB** Yorkshire Arts

## Faye Rochelle

**Contact** The Other Agency
*Singer/ songwriter. With guitar or backing band*

## Fee Lock

**Mail address** 28 Fairstone Close, HASTINGS, E Sussex, TN35 5EZ
**Phone** 01424 436052
**Email** feelock@hotmail.com
**Web** www.feecallsceilidhs.co.uk
*Caller for ceilidhs and barn dances in the English ceilidh style.*
**RAB** South East Arts

## Fernhill

**Contact** Beautiful Jo Records
**Phone** 01865 249194
**Fax** 01865 792765
**Email** tim@bejo.com
**Web** www.bejo.co.uk
**Alt contact** Julie Murphy
**Phone** 01559 384962
*4-7 piece Internationally recognised Welsh traditional band setting folk poetry over traditional Welsh dance rhythms.*
***Musicians' Union member***
**AC** Wales

## Ffynnon

**Contact** Lynne Denman
**Mail address** Y Winllan, Brechfa, SIR GAR, SA32 7QZ, Wales
**Phone/Fax** 01267 202333
**Phone** 01267 202474
**Email** huw.denman@newscientist.net
**Alt contact** Stacey Blythe
**Alt address** 15 Roath Court Road, Roath, CARDIFF, CF24 3SD, Wales
**Fax** 029 2048 1949
*3 piece band, voice, piano, bass. Welsh, English, Breton & French, mostly traditional.*
**AC** Wales

## Fiddlers' Bid

**Contact** Stoneyport Agency
**Phone/Fax** 0131 5571050
**Email** dfrancis@musicscotland.com
**Web** www.fiddlersbid.com
*Young Shetland 7 piece band, led by 4 fiddlers including Chris Stout, plus Catriona McKay on clarsach*

## Fiddler's Elbow

**Contact** Robin Dunn
**Mail address** 1020 Sheilds Road, NEWCASTLE UPON TYNE, NE6 4SQ
**Phone** 0191 295 5851
*Ceilidh band with caller. Suitable for all levels of dancers.*
***Musicians' Union member***
**RAB** Northern Arts

## Fiddlin' Around

**Mail address** Matters Musical
**Web** www.mattersmusical.com
*Twin fiddle led acoustic ceilidh band, traditional dance styles from UK and America*
**RAB** London Arts

## Finality Jack

**Mail address** Matters Musical
**Web** www.mattersmusical.com
*English and French tunes on violins, bouzouki, kantele etc*

## Findlay Napier

**Mail address** 0/2 239 Craigpark Drive, Dennistoun, GLASGOW, G31 2TG
**Phone** 07989 332407
0141 5645679
**Email** findlaynapier@ntlworld.com
**Web** http://findlaynapier.tripod.com/findlaynapier
*Scottish traditional singer, songwriter and guitarist.*
**AC** Scotland

## The Finlay MacDonald Band

**Contact** Finlay MacDonald
**Mail address** 11 Crofthead Cottages, NEILSTON, E Renfrewshire, G78 3NB
**Phone** 0141 8811739
07957 586266
**Email** finlaypipes@yahoo.com
**Web** www.tartantapes.com
**Alt contact** Martin Coull Music Management
**Phone** 0131 5575330
**Email** MartiCoull@aol.com
*Scottish traditional music band with a contemporary edge, featuring pipes and fiddle*
**Agent** Stoneyport Agency
***Musicians' Union member***
**AC** Scotland

## Fintan Vallely

**Mail address** 15 Castlewood Terrace, Rathmines, DUBLIN 6, Ireland
**Fax** +353 1 497 2979
**Phone** +353 86 603 9461
**Email** f@fidil.com
**Web** www.fidil.com
*Irish flute player and teacher. Writer and lecturer on flute and Irish traditional music. Concert bookings via agency*
**Agent** The Bechhofer Agency
**RAB** Ireland

## Fiona Branson

**Phone** 020 7732 1503
*Singer-songwriter, contemporary folk.*
***Musicians' Union member***
**RAB** London Arts

## Fiona Davidson

**Mail address** Duncauld, Cauldhame, KIPPEN, Stirlingshire, FK8 3HL, Scotland
**Phone/Fax** 01786 870626
**Phone** 07720 894332
**Email** fionadavidson@x-stream.co.uk
**Web** www.the-bard.co.uk
*One woman show of Celtic harp, song (Scottish, Gaelic, Irish) and legend.*
***Musicians' Union member***
**AC** Scotland

## Fiona MacKenzie

**Phone** 07802 433294
**Email** fiona@anam.co.uk
**Web** www.fionamackenzie.com
*Singer/ songwriter with the celtic group Anam. Solo singer in Gaelic and English. Gaelic song tutor.*
**AC** Scotland

## Firedaze

**Contact** Steff or String
**Mail address** DeAD Music, PO Box 213, LEAMINGTON SPA, Warks, CV31 1ZP
**Phone/Fax** 01926 421830
**Phone** 07989 775730
**Email** deadafterdark@dial.pipex.com
**Web** www.deadafterdark.dial.pipex.com/fire.html
*Roots/ Dance. Rock guitar, electric fiddle, vocals.*
***Musicians' Union member***
**RAB** West Midlands Arts

## Firefrost

**Contact** Clunie Creative Enterprises
**Web** www.come.to/clunie
*4 piece band playing contemporary and traditional Scottish, Irish and N American folk with fiddle, guitar, vocals etc. Also storytelling*
**Agent** Clunie Creative Enterprises
**AC** Scotland

## Fish N' Taters Ceilidh Band

**Contact** Steve Earwicker
**Mail address** 3 Normanby Road, Wollaton, NOTTINGHAM, NG8 2TA
**Phone** 0115 928 2566
07710 099844
**Fax** 0115 916 2870
**Email** fish.n.taters@btinternet.com
**Web** www.earwicker.inetc.net/fish_n'taters.htm
**RAB** East Midlands Arts

## Fishing for Eels

**Contact** Dick Jones
**Mail address** 36 Cloisters Road, LETCHWORTH, Herts, SG6 3JS
**Phone** 01462 642820
07775 610159
**Fax** 01462 481578
**Email** patteran@ntlworld.com
*4 - 12 piece ceilidh/ world dance band.*
**RAB** East England Arts

## Five Furious Fish

**Contact** Adastra
**Web** www.adastra-music.com
*Roots dance band. Mix of Cajun, reggae, Celtic and funk*

## FKG Band

**Contact** Pam Bishop
**Mail address** 35 Waterloo Road, Kings Heath, BIRMINGHAM, B14 7SD
**Phone** 0121 2443513
**Email** pam@cabaret.free-online.co.uk
*Traditional music dance band. Concertina, guitar, sax, drums. Ceilidhs, barn dances, etc.*
***Musicians' Union member***
**RAB** West Midlands Arts

## Flaithri and Eoghan Neff (NeffBros)

**Contact** NeffBros
**Mail address** Boithrin Dearg, RATHPEACAIN, Corcaigh, Ireland
**Phone** +353 21 4308872
+353 87 4162515
**Email** neffbros@eircom.net
**Web** http://homepage.eircom.net/~teaghlach/index.html
**Email** teaghlach@eircom.net
*Traditional Irish & other Celtic music Uilleann pipes and fiddle duo. 5 piece also available.*
**RAB** Ireland

## Flaky Jake and The Steamin' Locos

**Contact** Matters Musical
*Roots band mixing Zydeco and Latin styles*

## Flatville Aces

**Contact** Jock Tyldesley
**Mail address** The North Star, Queen's Head, OSWESTRY, Shrops, SY11 4ED
**Phone/Fax** 01691 610128
**Phone** 07796 694191
**Email** jock.t@virgin.net
**Alt contact** Gavin Lewery
**Alt address** 2 Lower Elms Farm, Cross Lane, Minshull Bernon, CREWE, Cheshire, CW1 4RG
**Phone/Fax** 01270 522438
**Phone** 07714 266130
**Email** rosco@ukonline.co.uk
*Traditional Cajun music. 2-6 piece band available*
**Agent** Matters Musical, Swamp Music
**RAB** West Midlands Arts

## Flook!

**Contact** Sarah Allen
**Mail address** 33 Lemsford Road, ST ALBANS, Herts, AL1 3PP
**Phone/Fax** 01727 833863
**Email** info@flook.co.uk
**Web** www.flook.co.uk
*Popular Anglo-Irish 4 piece playing traditional and contemporary material. Twin flutes, accordion, guitar and bodhran*
**Agent** themusictree. (uk) ltd
***Musicians' Union member***
**RAB** London Arts

## Florida

**Contact** Tim Bull
**Mail address** Marsh End, Mill Lane, Frittenden, CRANBROOK, Kent, TN17 2DR
**Phone** 01580 852317
**Email** Tim.bull@saga.co.uk
**Web** http://ourworld.compuserve.com/homepages/rgoodwin/florida.htm
**Alt contact** Gavin Atkin
**Alt address** 10 Western Road, TUNBRIDGE WELLS, Kent, TN1 2JJ
**Phone** 01892 514177
**Email** gmatkin@clara.net
*Popular brass-led English style ceilidh band. Ceildhs, concerts & workshops*
**Agent** Matters Musical
**RAB** Southern Arts

## Fluff

**Contact** Clare Smith
**Mail address** 21 Wistaston Road, CREWE, Cheshire, CW2 7RA
**Phone** 01270 567750
01270 569780
**Email** fluff@tower-struck-down.freeserve.co.uk
*Freelance fiddle player & electric violinist. Classical and folk training. Session musician and workshop leader.*
***Musicians' Union member***
**RAB** North West Arts

## The Flying Toad Band

**Contact** Dave Shaw
**Mail address** 2 Shafto Cottage, Craghead, STANLEY, Co Durham, DH9 6DW
**Phone** 01207 231474
**Email** flyingtoad@daveshaw.co.uk
**Web** www.flyingtoad.oneuk.com
*Ceilidh/ concert band with Northumbrian pipes, melodeon, mandolin, fiddle.*
***Musicians' Union member***
**RAB** Northern Arts

## The Flying Toads

**Contact** Keith Whiddon
**Mail address** 6 Hill Mead, HORSHAM, West Sussex, RH12 2PU
**Phone** 07971 661615
**Email** mail@flyingtoads.co.uk
**Web** www.flyingtoads.co.uk
*Sussex based 3 piece traditional Irish music band. Concerts, ceilidhs, pubs & weddings.*
**RAB** South East Arts

## Foghorn Leghorn

**Contact** Matters Musical
**Web** www.mattersmusical.com
*Roots country bluegrass on fiddle, banjo and double bass etc*



*Artists in the main A-Z listing are mostly available for concert and club bookings.*

*See page 11 for details of other artist listings (Dance Display, Solo Musicians, Composers, Arrangers, Session Musicians, Band Deps. Lecturers, MCs, Tutors, Street Theatre, Children's Entertainers, Theatre Companies).*

*Agents section appears on pages 119-131.*

*Artists in the main A-Z listing are mostly available for concert and club bookings.*

*See page 11 for details of other artist listings (Dance Display, Solo Musicians, Composers, Arrangers, Session Musicians, Band Deps. Lecturers, MCs, Tutors, Street Theatre, Children's Entertainers, Theatre Companies).*

*Agents section appears on pages 119-131.*

## The Fold
**Contact** Jon Wood
**Mail address** 23 Harrington Villas, BRIGHTON, BN1 6RG
**Phone** 01273 564797
**Fax** 01273 540801
**Email** jon@Orangesky.demon.co.uk
**Web** www.thefold.co.uk
*6 piece folk rock band. Dual male/female vocals, fiddle, mandolin, flute, guitar, drums, percussion.*
**RAB** South East Arts

## Foni Mitchell
**Contact** Clive Witcombe
**Mail address** 22 Swarthmore Road, Selly Oak, BIRMINGHAM, B29 4JS
**Phone** 0121 2440878
07752 775756
**Email** fonimitchell@aol.com
**Web** www.fonimitchell.homepage.com
*5 piece Joni Mitchell tribute band.*
**RAB** West Midlands Arts

## Footloose
**Contact** Colin Baker
**Mail address** 16 The Charne, Otford, NR SEVENOAKS, Kent, TN14 5LS
**Phone** 01959 524437
*4 piece barn dance/ ceilidh band with or without caller.*
**RAB** Southern Arts

## Forrester
**Contact** John Forrester
Seaview Music, 88 Greenham Wood, BRACKNELL, RG12 7WH
**Phone** 07976 786403
**Fax** 07970 463497
**Email** seaview@lineone.net
**Web** www.forrester.uk.com
*Contemporary acoustic songwriter. Available solo, duo or with band.*
***Musicians' Union member***
**RAB** Southern Arts

## FOS Brothers
**Contact** OTB Productions
**Web** www.otbproductions.co.uk
*Irish 4 piece song, fiddle & drum band*

## Fox Amongst The Chickens
**Contact** Mike Longhurst
**Mail address** Briar Croft, The Square, HARROW BARROW, Cornwall PL17 8BA
**Phone** 01579 351201
**Email** mrlonghurst@talk21.com
**Web** member.tripod.com/fatc-hj
*English barn dance band with some French influence. Own caller.*
**RAB** South West Arts

## Fran McGillivray and Mike Burke
**Contact** Roland Kemp
**Mail address** Flat 2 , Mowbray Road, LONDON, SE19 2RN
**Phone/Fax** 020 8771 4557
**Email** roland.kemp@virgin.net
*Blues and orginal songs; vocals, guitar and bass. Founder members of 5 piece band "So Long Angel".*
**RAB** London Arts

## Fran O'Boyle
**Mail address** 5 Coronation Cottages, STIPERSTONES, Shropshire, SY5 0NA
**Phone** 01743 792993
*Storyteller and ballad singer*
**RAB** West Midlands Arts

## The Frances Doonan Band
**Contact** Mick Doonan
**Mail address** 51 Jacob's Well Lane, Wakefield WF1 3PB
**Phone** 01924 366126
**Email** mick@mdoonan.freeserve.co.uk
**Alt email** frankadoonan@hotmail.com
*8 piece electric band - Irish traditional dance display, rock, soul and ceilidh.*
**RAB** Yorkshire Arts

## Frances Oates
**Mail address** 76 Bosvean Gardens, Illogan, REDRUTH, Cornwall, TR16 4DH
**Phone** 01209 217918
01872 252717
**Email** frances.oates@rcht.swest.nhs.uk
*Caller for ceilidhs, barn and social dances.*
**RAB** South West Arts

## Frankie Armstrong
**Mail address** 45 Cecil Street, Roath, CARDIFF, CF2 1NW, Wales
**Phone** 029 2048 0429
*Celebrated unaccompanied singer. Voice workshops based on traditional styles of singing.*
**AC** Wales

## Frankie Gavin
**Contact** Stoneyport Agency
**Phone/Fax** 0131 5571050
**Email** dfrancis@musicscotland.com
**Web** home.att.net/frankiegavin/index.html
*Renowned Irish fiddle player. Leader of De Dannan.*

## Fraser Nimmo
**Contact** Elizabeth Jones Entertainments
**Web** www.bromyard.co.uk/ejones
*Singer songwriter with humour*
**RAB** London Arts

## The Fraser Sisters
**Contact** Well Groomed Management
**Web** www.freya.org.uk
*Quartet with the 2 Fraser sisters. Mix of traditional & contemporary tunes & songs. Fiddle, dulcimer, saxes, bazouki, concertina, bass, etc.*
***Musicians' Union member***
**RAB** East Midlands Arts

## Freddy Macha
**Mail address** Flat B, 12 Durley Road, LONDON, N16 5JS
**Phone** 07961 833040
020 7502 9814
**Fax** 020 7281 6677
**Email** fmacha@yahoo.com
*Performance poet & musician; multiple music/ poetry styles based on African & Brazilian roots. Regular promoter of world music events at Bar Lorca & various other clubs in London.*
***Musicians' Union member***
**RAB** London Arts

## Fred Morrison
**Mail address** The Old School House, Lochcarnan, ISLE OF SOUTH UIST, Outer Hebrides, HS8 5PD, Scotland
**Phone** 01870 610278
077 6986 2111
**Email** culla@hotmail.com
**Alt address** 141 Old Greenock Road, BISHOPTON, Renfrewshire, PA7 5DL, Scotland
**Phone** 01505 862275
*Solo and accompanied Highland pipes, Uillean pipes, Scottish border and small pipes & low whistle*
**Agent** Stoneyport Agency
***Musicians' Union member***
**AC** Scotland

## Free Range
**Contact** John Peel
**Mail address** Southby, Bielby, YORK, YO42 4JL
**Phone** 01759 318311
*Anglo/Celtic/European music duo on hurdy gurdy, bagpipes, bodhran, etc. Suitable for indoors or outdoors.*
***Musicians' Union member***
**RAB** Yorkshire Arts

## Freeland Barbour
**Mail address** 44 Beauchamp Road, EDINBURGH, EH16 6LU, Scotland
**Phone** 0131 6661024
**Fax** 0131 6661024
**Email** info@castlesound.co.uk
**Web** www.freelandbarbour.co.uk
*Accordion & piano player and teacher. Producer and composer.*
***Musicians' Union member***
**AC** Scotland

### Freya Federation
**Contact** Well Groomed Management
*6 piece band led by Jo Freya. Folk/ roots/Euro dance with saxes, guitar, cello, tabla, etc*
***Musicians' Union member***
**RAB** East Midlands Arts

### Freya/Locke
**Contact** Well Groomed Management
*Sax/ clarinet/ cello/ vocal duo, composers.*
***Musicians' Union member***
**RAB** East Midlands Arts

### The Friday Folk Band (of St Albans)
**Contact** Derek Gregory
**Mail address** 52 Oakhampton Road, Mill Hill, LONDON, NW7 1NH
**Phone/Fax** 020 8349 2893
**Email** dgregor@tesco.net
*Band for barn dances and ceildhs.*
**RAB** East England Arts

### Friday Street
**Contact** Matters Musical
**Web** www.mattersmusical.com
*3 to 6 piece English barn dance band with caller*

### Frolicking Pete and The Fumbling Fingers Ceilidh Band
**Contact** Peter F Crewe
**Mail address** 38 Chatburn Park Drive, BRIERFIELD, Lancs, BB9 5QA
**Phone** 01282 698455
07712 468327
**Email** pete@fumble67.freeserve.co.uk
**Web** www.fumble67.freeserve.co.uk
*Ceilidh/ barn dance band with caller. Concertina, melodeon, bouzouki, singing, etc.*
**RAB** North West Arts

### The Front Parlour Band
**Contact** Ben Farmer
**Mail address** 27 Regent Street, LANCASTER, LA1 1SQ
**Phone** 01524 847135
**Email** info@chouchenn.net
*A complete evening's entertainment including dancing, music, song & humour. Please include the word "Parlour" in any email.*
**RAB** North West Arts

### The Gaberlunzies
**Contact** Matt Armour
**Mail address** 99 Malletts Close, Stony Stratford, MILTON KEYNES, MK11 1DG
**Phone** 01908 566407
*Ceilidh band. Socials, weddings, etc.*
**RAB** Southern Arts

### Gabhru Panjabi De
**Contact** Access All Areas
*UK Punjab act*

### Gabriel Yacoub
**Contact** Adastra
**Web** www.adastra-music.com
*French singer and guitarist, traditional and new tunes. Solo or with trio.*

### Gaelstrom
**Contact** Angie Courtney
**Phone** 023 9267 2087
**Email** www.angcourtney@aol.com
*4-5 piece celtic band; vocals, fiddle, bodhran, mandolin, etc.*

### Gail Duff
**Mail address** Wynlic, Bull Lane, Lenham Heath, MAIDSTONE, Kent, ME17 2JA
**Phone** 01622 858460
0772 0592126
**Email** greenwillow@folkarts.fsnet.co.uk
*Ceilidh caller, singer (with Bing Lyle), teacher of Border Morris, song and songwriting, social dance and calling, traditional drama.*
**RAB** South East Arts

### The Gambit Jazzmen
**Contact** Matters Musical
**Web** www.mattersmusical.com
*6 piece New Orleans music on clarinet, banjo, sousaphone, etc*

### The Gander Band
**Contact** David Ledsam
**Mail address** 5 Market Place, Castle Donnington, DERBY, DE74 2JD
**Phone** 01332 810174
**Fax** 01332 810174
**Email** steve@gander.demon.co.uk
*Derbyshire based folk band.*
**RAB** East Midlands Arts

### Gary and Vera Aspey
**Contact** Gary Aspey
**Mail address** 29 Beech Walk, Pennington, LEIGH, Lancs, WN7 3LL
**Phone/Fax** 01942 671995
**Email** gv.aspey@tesco.net
*Guitar, accordion, concertina, Lancs clog. North-West traditions*
**RAB** North West Arts

### Gaye Anthony and Trish Norman
**Contact** Gaye Anthony
**Mail address** Dalherrick Croft, Sauchen, INVERURIE, Aberdeenshire, AB51 7RP
**Phone** 01330 833883
**Email** gaye.trish@talk21.com
*Scottish song duo, traditional and contemporary, NE Scots fishing songs. Unaccompanied and with guitars.*
***Musicians' Union member***
**AC** Scotland

### Geckoes
**Contact** Caroline Ritson
**Mail address** 31 Edward Street, ABINGDON, Oxon
**Phone/Fax** 01235 530346
**Email** jocar@tesco.net
**Web** www.hulot.demon.co.uk/ geckoes.htm
**Alt contact** Andy Cheyne
**Email** geckoes@hulot.demon.co.uk
*Popular English ceilidh band.*
**RAB** Southern Arts

### Geoff Higginbottom
**Mail address** 6 Whitehurst Road, Heaton Mersey, STOCKPORT, Cheshire, SK4 3NZ
**Phone** 0161 432 5083
07721 629621
*Solo singer, traditional/ contemporary, accompanied/ unaccompanied*
**RAB** North West Arts

### Geoff Muldaur
**Contact** Adastra
**Web** www.adastra-music.com
*Respected American folk & blues guitarist and singer*

### Georgia Shorrock, The Ceilidh Company
**Mail address** 2 The Barns, Low Hesket, CARLISLE, Cumbria, CA4 0EU
**Phone** 016974 73431
0771 239 7761
**Email** gshorrock@carlisle.ac.uk
**Email** lhgeorgia@aol.com
*Caller for ceilidhs, barn dances and dance workshops.*
**RAB** North West Arts

### Gerry Rafferty
**Contact** Asgard Promotions
*Celebrated songwriter, once of Stealers Wheel*

### Gesuino Deiana
**Contact** mARKO pOLO
**Web** www.markopolo.co.uk
*Sardinian traditional guitarist*



*Artists in the main A-Z listing are mostly available for concert and club bookings.*

*See page 11 for details of other artist listings (Dance Display, Solo Musicians, Composers, Arrangers, Session Musicians, Band Deps. Lecturers, MCs, Tutors, Street Theatre, Children's Entertainers, Theatre Companies).*

*Agents section appears on pages 119-131.*

**artists**

**g**

*Artists in the main A-Z listing are mostly available for concert and club bookings.*

*See page 11 for details of other artist listings (Dance Display, Solo Musicians, Composers, Arrangers, Session Musicians, Band Deps. Lecturers, MCs, Tutors, Street Theatre, Children's Entertainers, Theatre Companies).*

*Agents section appears on pages 119-131.*

## Gill Bowman
**Contact** Stockbridge Music
**Mail address** 3 Leslie Place, EDINBURGH, EH4 1NG, Scotland
**Phone/Fax** 0131 332 7067
**Email** johnbrown@stockbridgemusic.demon.co.uk
**Web** www.stoneyport.demon.co.uk/index.html
*Scottish singer*
**Agent** Stoneyport Agency
**AC** Scotland

## Gilly Darbey
**Contact** Karisma Music Management
**Web** www.karisma.net
*Singer, formerly with Waterfall*

## Gilly Hewitt
**Mail address** 21 Groathill Avenue, EDINBURGH, EH4 2LZ, Scotland
**Phone** 0131 3322788
07949 202843
**Fax** 0131 5384616
**Email** Gillian.Hewitt@florastevenson.edin.sch.uk
*Singer of Scottish and Irish, traditional and contemporary songs. Robert Burns specialist, accompaniment on 5 string banjo.*
**AC** Scotland

## Gina Le Faux
**Mail address** 359 Salterhebble Hill, HALIFAX, Yorks, HX3 0QA
**Phone** 01422 362634
0789 9773537
*Traditional and new dance music and songs on fiddle, viola and guitar. Baroque dance music on period instruments. Lectures/workshops on fiddle construction and playing. Fiddle maker. Ceilidh band with caller.*
**RAB** Yorkshire Arts

## Gina Mackey
**Mail address** 1 Cloister Road, LONDON, W3 0DE
**Phone/Fax** 020 8993 0639
**Phone** 07977 671056
**Web** www.jlvideo.co.uk/mackey.htm
*Singer and Celtic harpist; traditional & contemporary reportoire*
**Agent** Matters Musical
***Musicians' Union member***
**RAB** London Arts

## Gjallarhorn
**Contact** mARKO pOLO
**Web** www.gjallerhorn.com
*Young Finnish band playing world music rooted in the Swedish folk music of Finland*

## Glissando Steel Orchestra
**Contact** Matters Musical
**Web** www.mattersmusical.com
*British-Caribbean steel pan orchestra.Available for workshop and educational performances*

## Global Sound
**Contact** mARKO pOLO
**Web** www.markopolo.co.uk
*Jazz fusion band with musicians from US, Israel, Sweden, Denmark, Ghana, former Yugoslavia and Holland*

## The Gloworms
**Contact** Laurel Swift
**Mail address** 62 Eade Road, LONDON, N4 1DH
**Phone** 07855 389360
**Email** laurel@beam.freeserve.co.uk
**Alt contact** Jonathan Brenner
**Alt address** 24A Rathbone Place, Balham, LONDON, SW12
*3 piece budget price folk-swing ceilidh band! Fiddle, accordion and guitar.*
**RAB** London Arts

## Good Rockin' Dave and Zydeco Hot Rods
**Contact** Smalltown Promotions
*5 piece 50's/60's style zydeco rock n roll band*
**Agent** Smalltown Promotions, Swamp Music
**RAB** East Midlands Arts

## The Goose and Gridiron Band
**Contact** Steve Bryan
**Mail address** 124 Piggotshill Road, HARPENDEN, Herts, AL5 1LS
**Phone/Fax** 01582 762674 - eve
**Phone** 01908 205419 - day
**Email** swbryan@btinternet.com
**Web** www.btinternet.com/~swbryan/g&ginfo.htm
**Alt contact** Theo Thomas
**Alt address** 40 Osbourne Road, BARTON LE CLAY, Beds
**Phone** 01582 882831
**Email** trpthomas@aol.com
*4 piece English ceilidh band. Melodeon, dulcimer, bouzouki, concertina, bass, percussion.*
**RAB** East England Arts

## Gordon Giltrap
**Contact** Speaking Volumes
**Web** www.speakingvolumes.co.uk
*Recognised as one of the finest acoustic guitarists on the scene*
**Agent** Speaking Volumes
**RAB** West Midlands Arts

## Gordon Gunn Band
**Email** gordon.gunn@ntlworld.com
*Scottish fiddle, guitar and accordion/ percussion trio.*

## Gordon Potts
**Mail address** 124 Streatham Road, MITCHAM, Surrey
**Phone** 020 8769 4400
020 8640 4879
**Email** gordon.potts@cableinet.co.uk
*Popular ceilidh caller, a regular at major festivals.*
**RAB** South East Arts

## Gordon Tyrrall
**Mail address** 12 Nettleton Court, Whitkirk, LEEDS, Yorks, LS15 9AW
**Phone** 0113 225 6314
**Email** gordon@tyll.telinco.co.uk
*Traditional & new music and song with guitar and flute.*
**RAB** Yorkshire Arts

## Grae J Wall
**Mail address** Trashville, PO Box 272, ST ALBANS, Herts, AL1 5AJ
**Phone** 01727 761456
**Email** baytree@easynet.co.uk
**Web** www.trashville.co.uk
*Roots performer. Solo, duo with fiddle and melodica, or with bands The Young Trash Lovers and Los Chicos Muertos.*
**RAB** East England Arts

## Graham and Eileen Pratt
**Mail address** 20 Sharpe Avenue, SHEFFIELD, Yorks, S8 7SJ
**Phone** 0114 274 6330
**Email** graham.pratt@virgin.net
**Web** www.folkmusic.net/grahamandeileenpratt
*Traditional & self-penned songs, accompanied or unaccompanied*
**RAB** Yorkshire Arts

## The Grand Acoustic Roadshow
**Contact** TomCat Music
**Web** www.tomcatmusic.com
*Complete evening of traditional music & song from Pauline Cato, Tom McConville, Maggie Boyle & Clive Carroll*
***Musicians' Union member***
**RAB** Yorkshire Arts

## Grass Fire
**Contact** Matters Musical
**Web** www.mattersmusical.com
*Western square dance band featuring slide guitar and banjo*

## The Gravelly Hillbillies
**Contact** Richard Heath
**Mail address** Flat 1, 65 Mayfield Road, Moseley, BIRMINGHAM, B13 9HT
**Phone** 0121 684 2485
*Four piece skiffle band*
**Agent** Karisma Music Management
**RAB** West Midlands Arts

## Great Big Sea
**Contact** The Concert Clinic
**Web** www.concertclinic.com
*Canadian folk roots band*

## Gregori Scheichter's Klezmer Festival Band
**Contact** Elizabeth Jones Entertainments
**Web** www.bromyard.co.uk/ejones
*Klezmer music for large venues*
**Agent** Elizabeth Jones Entertainments

## The Grinnigogs
**Contact** Quentin Budworth
**Mail address** Molescroft Grange Farmhouse, BEVERLEY, Yorks, HU17 9RS
**Phone** 01482 865604
**Email** grinnigogs@pop3.poptel.org.uk
**Web** www.grinnigogs.co.uk
*Street theatre with historical themes and medieval music. Strolling minstrel up to multi-skilled ensemble. Also children's/ family show*
**Agent** Artists Connect, Matters Musical
**RAB** Yorkshire Arts

## Grumbling Old Men
**Contact** Dave Brown
**Mail address** 3 Fanshaw Way, WARMINSTER, Wilts, BA12 9QX
**Phone** 01985 847417
07788 143580
**Fax** 01985 219548
**Email** dave@dlbmusic.freeserve.co.uk
**Web** www.dlbmusic.freeserve.co.uk
**Alt contact** Alan Carhett
**Alt address** 14 Mill Lane, Netter Stawey, BRIDGWATER, Somerset, TA5 1NL
**Phone** 01278 732202
*Folk dance band playing for Playford, Contras, etc.*
**RAB** Southern Arts

## Grupo Folia
**Contact** Matters Musical
**Web** www.mattersmusical.com
*Up to 10 piece band, variety of Brazilian music*

## Guy Davis
**Contact** mARKO pOLO
**Web** www.markopolo.co.uk
*US acoustic blues singer and guitarist*

## Gwerinos
**Contact** Ywain Myfyr
**Mail address** Penybryn, DOLGELLAU, Gwynedd, LL40 1SP, Wales
**Phone** 01341 423355
**Email** myfyr@sesiwnfawr.demon.co.uk
*7 piece band playing traditional Welsh music*
**Agent** Access All Areas, mARKO pOLO
**AC** Wales

## Gyosei Taiko Drummers
**Contact** Matters Musical
**Web** www.mattersmusical.com
*British taiko drum ensemble. Perform in costume and feature the largest taiko drum in Britain. Run training for students in taiko drumming*

## Gypsy Duo
**Contact** Louise Appleby
**Mail address** Higher Larcombe, DIPTFORD, S Devon, TQ9 7PD
**Phone** 01548 821332
0778 8897884
*Clarinet & accordion duo. Eastern European folk and gypsy music. 5 piece band also available.*
**RAB** South West Arts

## Hackney Ramblers
**Contact** Tony Weathera l
**Mail address** 138 Longslow Road, MARKET DRAYTON, Shropshire, TF9 3QZ
**Phone/Fax** 01630 652034
**Email** Vines@tisbuts.supanet.com
*4 piece Cajun band. Accordion, fiddle, guitar, drums*
**Agent** Access All Areas, Matters Musical, Swamp Music
**RAB** North West Arts

## Hamish Curry
**Mail address** 27 Lombardy Drive, BERKHAMPSTEAD, Herts, HP4 2LQ
**Phone** 01442 872910
**Email** hamish@lombardy.clara.net/ hamishcurrie
**Web** www.lombardy.clara.net/ hamishcurrie
*Singer, guitarist & MC from Tudor Folk Club. Traditional & Modern songs*
**RAB** East England Arts

## Hammer and Tongues
**Contact** Steve Bryan
**Mail address** 124 Piggottshill Lane, HARPENDEN, Herts, AL5 1LS
**Phone** 07710 471862
01908 205419
**Email** scobryan@btinternet.com
**Web** www.btinternet.com/~swbryan/ jssbinfo.htm
**Alt contact** Janet Strapp
**Address** 143 Strathmore Avenue, LUTON, Beds, LU1 3QW
**Phone** 07850 163241
*Duo playing traditional music on hammered dulcimer, bouzouki, mandola, concertina.*
**RAB** South East Arts

## Handsel
**Contact** Brian Miller
**Mail address** 36 Greenhill Park, PENICUIK, Midlothian, EH26 9EX, Scotland
**Phone** 01968 678153
**Email** brian@horniegollach.com
**Web** www.horniegollach.com
*4 piece group playing new arrangements of traditional Scottish songs.*
***Musicians' Union member***
**AC** Scotland

## Hanging Johnny
**Contact** Mike Longhurst
**Mail address** Briar Croft, The Square, HARROW BARROW, Cornwall, PL17 8BA
**Phone** 01579 351201
**Email** mrlonghurst@talk21.com
**Web** members.tripod.com/fatc.htm
*Singers of shanties and traditional & modern sea songs. Accompanied & unaccompanied.*
**RAB** South West Arts

## Hank Wangford and The Lost Cowboys
**Contact** mARKO pOLO
**Web** www.markopolo.co.uk
*New Country music with attitude*

## Hans Theessink
**Contact** The Bechhofer Agency
*Holland. Also with Jon Sass*

## Harem Scarum
**Contact** Organic Arts
**Web** www.organicarts.co.uk
*5 piece Scottish band with Eilidh Shaw and Inge Thomson. Traditional and new Celtic songs & tunes*
***Musicians' Union member***
**AC** Scotland



*Artists in the main A-Z listing are mostly available for concert and club bookings.*

*See page 11 for details of other artist listings (Dance Display, Solo Musicians, Composers, Arrangers, Session Musicians, Band Deps. Lecturers, MCs, Tutors, Street Theatre, Children's Entertainers, Theatre Companies).*

*Agents section appears on pages 119-131.*

## artists
## h

*Artists in the main A-Z listing are mostly available for concert and club bookings.*

*See page 11 for details of other artist listings (Dance Display, Solo Musicians, Composers, Arrangers, Session Musicians, Band Deps. Lecturers, MCs, Tutors, Street Theatre, Children's Entertainers, Theatre Companies).*

*Agents section appears on pages 119-131.*

### The Harvesters
**Contact** Ian Hartland
**Mail address** 45 Mill Street, Harbury, LEAMINGTON SPA, Warks, CV33 9HR
**Phone** 01926 612734
**Email** ianhartland@compuserve.com
*Duo performing humorous and serious songs, accompanied on stringed instruments*
**Agent** Karisma Music Management
**RAB** East Midlands Arts

### Harvey Andrews
**Contact** Speaking Volumes
**Web** www.speakingvolumes.co.uk
*Established singer, songwriter, raconteur and guitarist*
***Musicians' Union member***
**RAB** West Midlands Arts

### The Harvs'
**Contact** Ian Harvey
**Email** ian1759@aol.com
**Web** www.theharvs.co.uk
*Father and son duo.*

### Hassan Erraji and Arabesque
**Contact** Adastra
**Web** www.adastra-music.com
*Moroccan musican offering a complete performance of Arabic music and song from North Africa. Available solo or with band. Workshops available*

### Heartfield
**Contact** Angela Williams
**Mail address** Blue Stack Music, 52 Abbott Avenue, LONDON, SW20 8SQ
**Phone/Fax** 020 8540 3350
**Email** bluestack@hotmail.com
**Web** www.countrymusic.org.uk/heartfield
*5 piece country rock band.*
**RAB** London Arts

### Hearts Of Oak
**Contact** Kathleen Davy - Booking Sec.
**Mail address** Bradicott House, Bradiford, BARNSTAPLE, Devon, EX31 4AW
**Phone** 01598 760354
**Email** jparker@bradicott.freeserve.co.uk
**Alt contact** John Parker - Group Leader
**Phone** 01271 374286
*Folk band.*
**RAB** South West Arts

### Heather Enid Wells
**Mail address** 48 Sprowston Road, NORWICH, NR3 4QN
**Phone** 01603 413509
07870 349 088
**Email** Heather.E.Wells@btinternet.com
**Web** www.blackcatmusic.org.uk
*Songwriter, fingerstyle guitarist & bassist. Teacher of guitar and bass .*
***Musicians' Union member***
**RAB** East England Arts

### Heather Hawthorn
**Mail address** 88 Clifton Road, Ruddington, NOTTINGHAM, NG11 6DE
**Phone** 0115 984 5052
07778 269048
**Email** heather@heathermixture.co.uk
**Web** www.heathermixture.co.uk
*Accordionist for wide variety of themed events.*
***Musicians' Union member***
**RAB** East Midlands Arts

### Heather Innes
**Contact** Clunie Creative Enterprises
**Web** www.come.to/clunie
*Unaccompanied traditional & contemporary folk singer*
***Musicians' Union member***
**AC** Scotland

### Heather Innes and Ciaran Dorris
**Contact** Clunie Creative Enterprises
**Web** www.come.to/clunie
*Singer/ songwriter and singer duo. Contemporary and traditional*
***Musicians' Union member***
**AC** Scotland

### Heather Mixture
**Contact** Heather Hawthorn
**Mail address** 88 Clifton Road, Ruddington, NOTTINGHAM, NG11 6DE
**Phone** 0115 984 5052
07778 269048
**Email** heather@heathermixture.co.uk
**Web** www.heathermixture.co.uk
*Folk dance band, Scottish, ballroom & old- time on accordion and drums. With caller.*
***Musicians' Union member***
**RAB** East Midlands Arts

### The Hedgehog's Skin
**Contact** David Oliver
**Mail address** 9a Tynedale Terrace, HEXHAM, Northumberland, NE46 3JE
**Phone** 01434 607432
07790 856307
**Email** david@hexham.globalnet.co.uk
*Northumbrian ceilidh band and caller. Accordion, bass, fiddles, whistles.*
***Musicians' Union member***
**RAB** Northern Arts

### Hegedos
**Contact** Elizabeth Jones Entertainments
**Web** www.bromyard.co.uk/ejones
*5-6 piece Hungarian folk music band*

### Helen Chadwick and Amar
**Contact** Helen Chadwick
**Mail address** Romaine Records, 11 John Campbell Road, LONDON, N16 8JY
**Phone/Fax** 020 7241 3152
**Email** romaine@helenchadwick.com
**Web** www.helenchadwick.com
*Solo singer/ songwriter. Acapella with Amar; 4 voice female group. Singing workshops available.*
***Musicians' Union member***
**RAB** London Arts

### Helen Watson
**Contact** Blue Moon Music
**Web** www.bluemoonmusic.co.uk
*Solo blues artist. Singer and guitarist*

### Hen Party
**Contact** Heather Bradford
**Mail address** 15 Harestock Road, WINCHESTER, SO22 6NS
**Phone** 01962 880714
07967 688674
**Email** hebradford@threemaids.fsnet.co.uk
**Alt contact** Sarah Morgan
**Alt address** 2 Southview Terrace, St Mary Bourne, ANDOVER, Hants, SD11 6BQ
**Phone** 01264 738629
**Email** sarah.bourne@andover.co.uk
*Female vocal trio. Harmony songs rooted in traditional style.*
**RAB** Southern Arts

### Henry Garfath
**Contact** ABDC Entertainments
**Web** www.abdc.co.uk
*Caller, dance teacher & choreographer of English (including playford), Scottish, American (square, contra and line) dance*
**RAB** Southern Arts

### Herb Boys
**Contact** Steve Harrison
**Mail address** Blakeclough, Shaw Lane, Slaithwaite, HUDDERSFIELD, Yorks, HD7 5XA
**Phone** 01484 844055
**Email** gamut@dial.pipex.com
**Alt contact** Vic Gammon
**Alt address** 12 Beechfield Road, HUDDERSFIELD, HD2 2XQ
**Phone** 01484 424465
**Email** gammon@dial.pipex.com
*Ceilidh/ barn dance band with caller. Mostly English tunes on melodeon, banjo, piano, etc.*
***Musicians' Union member***
**RAB** Yorkshire Arts

## Highly Strung

**Contact** Kay Tierney
**Mail address** 146 Fleeming Road, Walthamstow, LONDON, E17 5EU
**Phone** 020 8281 4051
07714 771889
**Alt contact** Gill Warnell
**Alt address** 47 Milton Crescent, ILFORD, Essex, IG2 6DN
**Phone** 020 8554 0727
**Email** g.warnell@virginnet.co.uk
*5 piece English folk music dance band playing traditional and new music. With/ without caller.*
**RAB** London Arts

## Hilary Spencer

**Mail address** 368 Manchester Road, Deepcar, SHEFFIELD, Yorks, S36 2RH
**Phone** 0114 283 0531
07974 300252
**Email** hilary@halpins.demon.co.uk
**Web** www.hilaryspencer.com
**Alt contact** Mike Halpin
**Email** mike@halpins.demon.co.uk
*Folk, jazz and contemporary singer.*
**RAB** Yorkshire Arts

## His Worship & The Pig

**Contact** Jeff Parton
**Mail address** 2 Birchgate Grove, Bucknall, STOKE ON TRENT, ST2 8JU
**Phone** 01782 266821
07980 839565
**Email** jeff@hisworshipandthepig.co.uk
**Web** www.hisworshipandthepig.co.uk
Singing & songwriting duo. Acoustic, folk based with comedy. Vocals with various stringy things.
**RAB** West Midlands Arts

## Hodmadoddery

**Contact** The Moonson Co
**Mail address** 5 Cleveland Row, BATH, Somerset, BA2 6QR
**Phone** 01225 446975
**Fax** 01225 480079
**Email** moonson@clark-kent.demon.co.uk
*Acoustic duo, guitars and vocals, emphasis on harmony. Traditional and contemporary songs.*
**RAB** South West Arts

## Holly Karlsen

**Mail address** c/o Widdacombe Cottage, Lewdown, OKEHAMPTON, Devon, EX20 4EA
**Phone** 07866 795942
*Unaccompanied singer, mostly traditional.*
***Musicians' Union member***
**RAB** South West Arts

## The Holmes Brothers

**Contact** mARKO pOLO
**Web** www.markopolo.co.uk
*Blues/ Gospel trio*

## Home Brew Country Dance Band

**Contact** Colin Andrews
**Mail address** Bonny Green, Morchard Bishop, CREDITON, Devon, EX17 6PG
**Phone/Fax** 01363 877216
**Email** colin@bonnygreen.co.uk
**Web** www.bonnygreen.co.uk
*3-5 piece folk dance band. Caller available.*
**RAB** South West Arts

## Hoogie

**Contact** Keith Smith
**Mail address** 35 Selwyn Gardens, CAMBRIDGE, CB3 9AY
**Fax** 01223 357703
**Web** www.hoogie.co.uk
*5 piece upbeat Scottish broadcast concert and ceilidh band.Traditional and new music and songs. Pipes, fiddle, percussion, etc.*
***Musicians' Union member***
**AC** Scotland

## Hoolie

**Contact** Teresa Maguire
**Phone** 020 8902 8385
**Email** teresa@hoolie99.freeserve.co.uk
*4 piece vocal and instrumental Irish influenced band.*
***Musicians' Union member***
**RAB** London Arts

## Hootenanny 3

**Contact** OTB Productions
**Web** www.otbproductions.co.uk
*Irish-American acoustic 3 piece band, members of Afterhours, Daily Planet and Madigan*

## Hoover The Dog

**Contact** Paul Hutchinson
**Mail address** Upper Celn-y-Pwll, Abermule, MONTGOMERY, Powys, SY15 6JN, Wales
**Phone/Fax** 01686 630419
**Email** welshpaul@lineone.net
**Web** www.hooverthedog.freeserve.co.uk
*Trio fusing Celtic/ jazz/ classical styles. Concerts and workshops (violin, accordion, bouzouki, guitar, vocals)*
**Agent** Matters Musical
**AC** Wales

## Horace X

**Contact** Matters Musical
**Web** www.horacex.co.uk
*Techno beats, Eastern European fiddle and jazz horn section plus bodysuit/ UV stage display*
***Musicians' Union member***

## Horner & Horn

**Contact** Sally Horner
**Phone** 020 7771 7533
**Email** sallyhorner@orange.net
*Sally Horner & Paul Taylor. Trombone & song duo. Folk, jazz, world & pop music.*
***Musicians' Union member***
**RAB** London Arts

## Hosepipe Band

**Contact** Val Haines
**Mail address** 33 Beaconsfield Avenue, COLCHESTER, Essex CO3 3DH
**Phone** 01206 547830
07778 869919
**Fax** 01206 572235
**Email** kan83@dial.pipex.com
**Web** www.hosepipe.dial.pipex.com
*Electric ceilidh band playing traditional and newly composed material, British and European influences.*
**RAB** East England Arts

## The Hot Club

**Contact** Stoneyport Agency
**Web** www.stoneyport.demon.co.uk

## The Hot Rats

**Contact** Doug Hudson
**Mail address** 182 Windmill Road, GILLINGHAM, Kent, ME7 5PE
**Phone/Fax** 01634 574837
**Phone** 07941 238377
**Email** doug.hudson@lineone.net
**Web** www.hotrats.net
*Celtic style world/ European music with violinist Ian Cutler and singer Doug Hudson.*
**RAB** South East Arts

## The Hot Tamales

**Contact** The Able Label
**Mail address** Red House Cottage, Botley Road, SHEDFIELD, Hants, SO32 2HN
**Phone/Fax** 01329 833359
**Email** gone@globalnet.co.uk
**Web** www.tamales.co.uk
*3 piece acoustic band; guitar, double bass & washboard. Mostly original songs of a good-timey disposition.*
**RAB** Southern Arts

## The Houghton Weavers

**Contact** Phil McGuiver
**Mail address** 20 Bradshaw Lane, Mawdesley, ORMSKIRK, Lancs L40 3SE
**Phone** 01257 473813
0374 680629
**Fax** 01257 473850
**Email** Hweavers@aol.com
**Web** www.houghtonweavers.com
*Traditional and contemporary folk and humour.*
**RAB** North West Arts

*Artists in the main A-Z listing are mostly available for concert and club bookings.*

*See page 11 for details of other artist listings (Dance Display, Solo Musicians, Composers, Arrangers, Session Musicians, Band Deps. Lecturers, MCs, Tutors, Street Theatre, Children's Entertainers, Theatre Companies).*

*Agents section appears on pages 119-131.*

*Artists in the main A-Z listing are mostly available for concert and club bookings.*

*See page 11 for details of other artist listings (Dance Display, Solo Musicians, Composers, Arrangers, Session Musicians, Band Deps. Lecturers, MCs, Tutors, Street Theatre, Children's Entertainers, Theatre Companies).*

*Agents section appears on pages 119-131.*

## Howling Wind
**Contact** Alan Hewson
**Mail address** 9 Listor Avenue, HITCHIN, Herts, SG4 9ES
**Phone** 01462 438373
**Fax** 01462 433395/ 421272
**Email** alan@questor-cp.demon.co.uk
**Web** www.questor-cp.demon.co.uk/ tamlin.htm
*Band playing traditional Irish music.*
***Musicians' Union member***
**RAB** East England Arts

## Hubert Sumlin and Sean Chambers
**Contact** mARKO pOLO
**Web** www.markopolo.co.uk
*Chicago and Delta Blues. Sumlin is Howlin' Wolf's guitarist*

## The Huckleberries
**Contact** OTB Productions
**Web** www.otbproductions.co.uk
*Goodtime band based on a mix of folk styles*

## Hughie Jones
**Contact** 31 Mornington Terrace, Upper Duke Street, LIVERPOOL, L1 9DY
**Phone** 0151 709 3336
*Maritime songs from former Spinner.*
**RAB** North West Arts

## Hukwe Zawose and Charles Zawose
**Contact** The Equator Company Ltd
**Web** www.equatorcompany.com
*Vocal and traditional music duo from Tanzania*

## The Hula Bluebirds
**Contact** Matters Musical
**Web** www.mattersmusical.com
*Male Hawaiian trio, close vocals, steel guitar, ukulele etc. Also swing, pre-war US comedy, blues & jazz*

## Hurry The Jug
**Contact** John Littler PO Box 408, BANBURY, Oxon, OX15 4PR
**Phone** 01295 721180 - day
01869 338659 - eve
**Fax** 01295 722916
**Email** 106200.667@compuserve.com
*Barn dance & ceilidh band.*
**RAB** Southern Arts

## Hybrid
**Contact** John Adams
**Mail address** 13 Chevin Road, BELPER, Derbys, DE56 2UW
**Phone** 01773 829602
07941 534968
**Email** hybrid@cothrecords.co.uk
**Web** www.cothrecords.co.uk
**Alt contact** Sarah Matthews
**Alt address** 10 Hamblin Crescent, BELPER, Derbys, DE24 9PL
**Phone** 07941 366319
01332 273383
**Email** sarah@folkspace.idps.co.uk
*5 piece band fusing English traditional tunes & songs with heavy metal.*
***Musicians' Union member***
**RAB** East Midlands Arts

## Iain Matthews
**Contact** UK Touring
**Web** www.uktouring.org.uk
*Renowned singer/ songwriter, founder of Matthews' Southern Comfort & Plainsong*

## Iain Matthews and Andy Roberts/Plainsong
**Mail address** UK Touring
**Web** www.ianmatthews.com
*Singer/ songwriter and multi-instrumentalist duo. See above*

## Ian Bruce
**Contact** Oscar Music Agency
*Popular Scottish contemporary singer songwriter*

## Ian Carr and Karen Tweed
**Contact** Brass Tacks
*Instrument duet of guitar and acordion. Both compose and are experienced teachers, known for collaborations with Kathryn Tickell, Roy Bailey, John McCusker, Liz Doherty, etc*
***Musicians' Union member***

## Ian Smith
**Contact** 1 Holme Road, MATLOCK BATH, Derbys, DE4 3NU
**Phone** 07976 206568
01629 57082
**Email** pregosmith@hotmail.com
**Web** www.pregomusic.co.uk
*Multi-instrumentalist, solo or with band. Melodeon, Galician pipes, percussion, bombarde. Also 'peoplesound.com':agent.*
***Musicians' Union member***
**RAB** East Midlands Arts

## Ian Wilson
**Mail address** 254 Oakdale Road, Carlton, NOTTINGHAM, NG4 1BQ
**Phone** 0115 9872770
0771 1180027
**Email** iwil@tesco.net
*Caller for ceilidhs/ barn dances. Freelance musician; fretted strings and free reeds.*
**RAB** East Midlands Arts

## Imbizo
**Contact The** Equator Company Ltd
**Web** www.equatorcompany.com
**Alt contact** Majahawodwa Ndlovu
*10 piece a capella performing arts group from Bulawayo, Zimbabwe*

## Imbongi and Albert Nyathi
**Contact** CTM UK
**Web** www.ctmuk.com
*10 piece Zimbabwean music, song and dance band. Available May-Sept 2001*

## The Incredible String Band
**Contact** Moneypenny
*Robin Williamson, Mike Heron and Clive Palmer in reformed legendary band of the 1960s/70s featuring founder members.*

## The Incredibly Strange Film Band
**Contact** Matters Musical
**Web** www.mattersmusical.com
*9 piece band playing 1960s-1990s film & TV themes. Costumes, wigs, brass & rhythm section*

## Indian Summer
**Contact** Jon Bamforth
**Mail address** 162 Alexandra Road, PETERBOROUGH, PE1 3DL
**Phone** 01733 310968
**Alt contact** Annie Bamforth
*Electric or acoustic folk trio. Costumed/ medieval events.*
***Musicians' Union member***
**RAB** East Midlands Arts

## Iris Dement
**Contact** Asgard Promotions
*High profile singer songwriter from Arkansas*

## Isla St Clair
**Contact** Speaking Volumes
**Web** www.speakingvolumes.co.uk
*Highly respected Scottish traditional singer*

### Itchy Feet
**Contact** Tony Roberts
**Mail address** 14 The Pippins, HALSTEAD, Essex, CO9 1JY
**Phone** 01787 479977
**Alt contact** Elaine Barker
**Phone** 01206 735606
*Barn dance/ ceilidh band with caller.*
**RAB** East England Arts

### Ivo Papasov and His Bulgarian Wedding Band
**Contact** mARKO pOLO
**Web** www.markopolo.co.uk
*Balkan gypsy jazz*

### Jabadaw
**Contact** Simon Dew
**Phone** 0795 898 4664
**Email** jabadaw@compuserve.com
**Web** www.jabadaw.com
**Alt contact** Martin Keates
**Phone** 0794 101 6561
**Email** martin@jabadaw.fsnet.co.uk
*5 piece band playing English & French music for Ceilidhs, Bals, Barn Dances, etc*
**Agent** Hemlock Music
**RAB** North West Arts

### Jack Evans
**Email** music@jackevans.net
**Web** www.jackevans.net
*Scottish guitarist & multi-instrumentalist./ producer. Member of Keltic Elektrik, Springwell, Cauld Blast Orchestra*
**Agent** Stoneyport Agency
***Musicians' Union member***
**AC** Scotland

### Jackie Leven
**Contact** Moneypenny
*Singer, also songwriter, raconteur & guitarist*
**Agent** Moneypenny, themusictree. (uk)

### Jacqueline Grant
**Mail address** Flat C, 122 Tressillian Road, LONDON, SE4 1XX
**Phone** 020 8694 1409
*Traditional Japanese tunes on shamisan and sanshin, UK/ US fingerstyle guitarist.*
***Musicians' Union member***
**RAB** London Arts

### Jacqueline Patten
**Mail address** Kerlistz , The Green, Morchard Bishop, CREDITON, Devon, EX17 6PD
**Phone** 01363 877503
**Email** patten@kerlistz.freeserve.co.uk
*Singer, workshop & project leader. Promoter of workshops & concerts.*
**RAB** South West Arts

### Jacqui McShee's Pentangle
**Contact** Park Promotions
**Web** www.folkcorp.co.uk/pent.welcome.htm
*Reworking of seminal 60's folk group, led by founder member*
**Agent** Park Promotions, themusictree.(uk)
**RAB** Southern Arts

### The Jaggamuffins
**Contact** mARKO pOLO
**Web** www.markopolo.co.uk
*Blues-Zydeco-Country outfit*

### Jah Wobble and the Invaders of the Heart
**Contact** Hemlock Music
**Web** www.hemlockmusic.demon.co.uk
*Jah Wobble plus members of Paris-based Molam Lao, playing Molam Dub (thousand year old Southern Laos musical tradition)*
**RAB** North West Arts

### Jah Wobble's Deep Space
**Contact** Hemlock Music
**Web** www.hemlockmusic.demon.co.uk
*4 piece playing a mix of trance, jazz and contemporary music with world influences. Bass, drums, woodwind*
**RAB** North West Arts

### Jambalaya
**Contact** Matters Musical
**Web** www.mattersmusical.com
*5 to 15 piece uniformed New Orleans marching band.*

### James Hunter Band
**Contact** Matters Musical
**Web** www.mattersmusical.com
*Soul singer and guitarist backed by twin saxophones, double bass and drums*

### James O'Hara's Detonators
**Contact** Matters Musical
**Web** www.mattersmusical.com
*5 piece high energy jazz led by blues guitar and vocals*

### Jane and Amanda Threlfall, Martin Ellison and Roger Edwards
**Contact** Roger Edwards
**Mail address** 199 Town Lane, Whittle le Woods, CHORLEY, Lancs, PR6 8AG
**Phone** 01257 276022
*English traditional song duo with guitar, melodeon, etc.*
**RAB** North West Arts

### Jansci Hosszu
**Contact** Matters Musical
**Web** www.mattersmusical.com
*Hungarian gypsy fiddler available with guitar and keyboard trio*

### Jaynes Red House
**Contact** Jayne Mursden
**Mail address** 68 Arthur Street, DERBY
**Phone** 01332 384516
*4 piece concert band drawing on Celtic/ English roots. Female lead singer, jazz/ roots/ blues feel.*
**RAB** East Midlands Arts

### Jazz Jamaica All Stars
**Contact** The Concert Clinic
**Web** www.concertclinic.com

### JazzIndo
**Contact** Matters Musical
**Web** www.mattersmusical.com
*Combines jazz and Indian classical music, featuring sitar player Punita Gupta. Also available for schools' workshops*

### Jean Redpath
**Email** info@jeanredpath.com
**Web** www.jeanredpath.com
*Scottish singer, mainly Robert Burns.*

### Jean-Pierre Rasle (and The Dancing Drones)
**Contact** Hemlock Music
**Web** www.hemlockmusic.demon.co.uk
*Costumed solo or group themed period concerts and workshops based around French bagpipes and other historical instruments*
**RAB** Southern Arts

### Jed Grimes
**Mail address** 37 Grosvenor Place, SOUTH SHIELDS, Tyne & Wear NE29 0NH
**Phone** 0191 290 2785
**Email** jed@franticprod.demon.co.uk
**Web** www.jedgrimes.co.uk
*Guitarist, composer, singer, producer, broadcaster and event compere. Trad./Celtic and contemporary*

### Jenna Monroe
**Contact** Elizabeth Jones Entertainments
**Web** www.bromyard.co.uk/ejones
*Singer & pianist*



*Artists in the main A-Z listing are mostly available for concert and club bookings.*

*See page 11 for details of other artist listings (Dance Display, Solo Musicians, Composers, Arrangers, Session Musicians, Band Deps. Lecturers, MCs, Tutors, Street Theatre, Children's Entertainers, Theatre Companies).*

*Agents section appears on pages 119-131.*

*Artists in the main A-Z listing are mostly available for concert and club bookings.*

*See page 11 for details of other artist listings (Dance Display, Solo Musicians, Composers, Arrangers, Session Musicians, Band Deps. Lecturers, MCs, Tutors, Street Theatre, Children's Entertainers, Theatre Companies).*

*Agents section appears on pages 119-131.*

## Jennifer & Hazel Wrigley
**Contact** JH Wrigley
**Mail address** PO Box 23280, EDINBURGH, EH8 9WJ
**Email** office@wrigleysisters.com
**Web** www.wrigleysisters.com
*Award winning fiddle & piano/guitar duo playing & recording their music from the Orkney Isles. UK representation by Stoneyport, other enquries direct*
**Agent** Stoneyport Agency
**AC** Scotland

## Jennifer Port
**Mail address** Woodlands, Woodland Way, GOLSPIE, Sutherland, KW10 6TU
**Phone/Fax** 01408 633900
**Email** jennifer_port@hotmail.com
*Clarsach/ Scottish harp player (Double National Gold Medallist). Singer with/without harp. Will travel.*
***Musicians' Union member***
**AC** Scotland

## Jenny Crook and Henry Sears
**Contact** The Other Agency
*Duo; vocals, harp, fiddle, whistle, etc. Traditional and new. Workshops on harp and fiddle*
**RAB** South West Arts

## Jenny Newman and Andy Glass
**Contact** Jenny Newman
**Mail address** 17 Bridge Road, Cosgrove, MILTON KEYNES, Bucks, MK19 7JH
**Phone/Fax** 01908 262098
**Phone** 07961 983483
**Email** new.glass@virgin.net
**Web** www.jennynewman.com
*Fiddle and guitar duo.*
**RAB** Southern Arts

## Jenny's Chickens
**Contact** Jenny Newman
**Mail address** 17 Bridge Road, Cosgrove, MILTON KEYNES, Bucks, MK19 7JH
**Phone/Fax** 01908 262098
**Phone** 07961 983483
**Email** new.glass@virgin.net
**Web** www.jennynewman.com
*Funky 4 or 5 piece ceilidh band with caller. Duo plus caller also available.*
**RAB** Southern Arts

## Jerry Cahill
**Contact** OTB Productions
**Web** www.otbproductions.co.uk
*Solo guitarist*

## Jerry Holland
**Contact** mARKO pOLO
**Web** www.markopolo.co.uk
*Highly respected Cape Breton fiddler, accompanied by pianist and guitarist*

## Jez Lowe
**Contact** Lowe Life Music
**Mail address** PO Box 25, PETERLEE, Co Durham, SR8 3SX
**Phone/Fax** 0191 586 1938
**Phone** 07770 793564
**Email** jez.lowe@lineone.net
**Web** www.jezlowe.com
*Popular North East singer and instrumentalist. Solo or with band. Respected songwriter.*
***Musicians' Union member***
**RAB** Northern Arts

## Jez Lowe and The Bad Pennies
**Contact** Lowe Life Music
**Mail address** PO Box 25, PETERLEE, Co Durham, SR8 3SX
**Phone/Fax** 0191 586 1938
**Phone** 07770 793564
**Email** jez.lowe@lineone.net
**Web** www.jezlowe.com
*4 piece instrumental/ vocal group performing traditional style orginal material*
**Agent** Emerging Music
***Musicians' Union member***
**RAB** Northern Arts

## Jezreels Ceilidh Band
**Contact** Doug Hudson
**Mail address** 182 Windmill Road, GILLINGHAM, Kent, ME7 5PE
**Fax** 01634 574837
**Phone** 07941 238377
**Email** doug.hudson@lineone.net
**Web** www.doughudson.com
*Ceilidh band with Doug Hudson, Chris Taylor, violin & bass. Resident band at Leeds Castle.*
**RAB** South East Arts

## Jezz Hall
**Mail address** 14A Burns Street, Radford, NOTTINGHAM, NG7 4DT
**Phone** 07944 710015
**Email** jezzhall@talk21.co.uk
*Acoustic guitarist, singer/ songwriter, performer of English & American traditional material.*
**RAB** East Midlands Arts

## Jienat
**Contact** mARKO pOLO
**Web** www.markopolo.co.uk
*Sami music with percussion*

## Jig For A Kiss
**Contact** Andy Bowdin
**Mail address** 19 Dobbin Hill, SHEFFIELD, S11 7JA
**Phone** 0114 2665197
**Email** slipjig@mcmail.com
**Alt address** 77 Hordean Road, Firvale, SHEFFIELD, S5 6UJ
**Phone** 0114 2435835
*4 piece Celtic folk band, English, Welsh and Greek song with flute, fiddle, guitar etc.*
**RAB** Yorkshire Arts

## Jiggerypipery
**Contact** Tony Bayliss
**Mail address** Upper Barn, Collihole Farm, Chagford, NEWTON ABBOT, Devon, TQ13 8DY
**Phone** 01647 433352
**Email** info@jiggerypipery.co.uk
**Web** www.jiggerypipery.co.uk
**Alt contact** Carl Allerfeldt
Hurston Farm, Chagford, NEWTON ABBOT, Devon, TQ13 8EF
**Phone** 01647 433390
**Email** carl@aller.idps.co.uk
*5 piece funky Highland pipe- led Celtic rock and roll. Caller availble for ceilidhs.*
**RAB** South West Arts

## Jim & Lynette Eldon
**Mail address** 129 Westcott Street, HULL, Yorks, HU8 8NB
**Phone** 01482 703261
*Songs and fiddle tunes learnt from source with champion clog dancer.*
**RAB** Yorkshire Arts

## Jim Couza
**Mail address** 7 Woodcroft Avenue, Whitehall, BRISTOL, BS5 9AS
**Phone** 0117 939 4249
0117 9394249
**Alt contact** Graham Bradshaw
**Alt address** 250 Earlsdon Avenue North, COVENTRY, CV5 6GX
**Phone** 024 7671 1935
**Fax** 024 7671 1191
**Email** rootsrecs@btclick.com
*Hammered dulcimer player, folklorist, singer. Workshop leader for song & Anglo-American traditional music.*
***Musicians' Union member***
**RAB** South West Arts

## Jim Hancock
**Mail address** 57 Lloyds Avenue, SCUNTHORPE, N Lincs, DN17 1BY
**Phone/Fax** 01724 844241
**Email** jim@guestlist.freeserve.co.uk
*Unaccompanied songs from the agricultural, industrial & maritime traditions. Solo or with the Roaring Forties or Clarty Sough.*
**RAB** Yorkshire Arts

## Jimmie Dale Gilmore
**Contact** Asgard Promotions
*Premier league Country singer, once with Flatlanders*

## Jimmy Crowley
**Contact** Stoneyport Agency
**Web** www.irishtrad.com/crowley
*Popular singer, songwriter and humorist from Cork*

## Jimmy Young
**Email** jimmy_rua@yahoo.com
**Web** www.geocities.com/jimmy_rua/jimmies.html
*Northumbrian piper, flute and whistle player.*

## Jive Wires
**Contact** mARKO pOLO
**Web** www.markopolo.co.uk
*Canadian 7-piece jump-jive band*

## Jo Freya
**Contact** Well Groomed Management
*Band leader, musician, singer, songwriter, composer, caller. Workshop leader*
***Musicians' Union member***
**RAB** East Midlands Arts

## Joan Baez
**Contact** Asgard Promotions
*"One of popular music's most distinctive voices."*

## Joan Gifford
**Mail address** 2 Denton's Terrace, Wivenhoe, COLCHESTER, CO7 9NE
**Phone** 01206 833087
*Singer, guitarist & banjo player. Humorous & serious songs.*
**RAB** South East Arts

## Jock Tamson's Bairns
**Contact** Norman Chalmers
**Phone** 0131 5567645
**Email** info@jtbairns
**Web** www.jtbairns.com
**Alt contact** Derek Hoy
**Phone** 0131 6697508
*5 piece Scottish music band.*
**AC** Scotland

## Jock Tyldesley and Gavin Lewery
**Contact** Jock Tyldesley
**Mail address** North Star, Queen's Head, OSWESTRY, Shrops, SY11 4ED
**Phone/Fax** 01691 610128
**Phone** 07796 694191
**Email** jock t@virgin.net
**Alt contact** Gavin Lewery
**Alt address** 2 Lower Elms Farm, Cross Lane, Minshull Vernon, CREWE, Cheshire, CW1 4RG
**Phone/Fax** 01270 522438
**Phone** 07714 266130
**Email** rosco@ukonline.co.uk
*Traditional Cajun music on accordeon and fiddle. See also Flatville Aces*
**Agent** Matters Musical, Swamp Music
**RAB** West Midlands Arts

## Joe Burke with Anne Conroy Burke
**Contact** The Bechhofer Agency
*Legendary Irish button accordeon duo*

## Joe Ely
**Contact** Asgard Promotions
*Top Texan songwriter*

## Joe Giltrap and Michael O'Rourke / Irish Mist
**Contact** Matters Musical
**Web** www.mattersmusical.com
*Irish music duo*

## Joe Le Taxi
**Contact** Swamp Music
**Web** www.swampmusic.co.uk
*British Zydeco outfit led by Rees Wesson*

## Joe O'Donnell
**Mail address** 5 Argyll Street, COVENTRY, CV2 4FJ
**Phone** 024 7627 5807
*Irish fiddler and singer. Traditional and contemporary. Solo, with trio or band. Tuition on violin and mandolin. Celtic composer*
**Agent** The Other Agency
**RAB** East Midlands Arts

## Joe Stead
**Mail address** Providence Place, SOWERBY BRIDGE, Yorks, HX6 1BA
**Phone** 01422 833659
07959 863479
**Fax** 01422 833628
**Email** banjostead@compuserve.com
**Web** www.joestead.com
*Long-established singer/banjo player with recently developed show on shanty theme*
**RAB** Yorkshire Arts

## John Alderslade
**Mail address** 54 Church Lane, MELKSHAM, Wilts, SN12 7EQ
**Phone/Fax** 01225 707346
**Email** john@aldersladej.fsnet.co.uk
**Web** www.alderslade.com
*Multi-instrumental folk entertainer: songs, jokes and audience participation.*
**RAB** Southern Arts

## John Conolly
**Mail address** 18 Scrivelsby Court, CLEETHORPES, Lincs, DN35 0HJ
**Phone** 01472 695836
**Web** www.folkmusic.net/johnconolly
*Singer/ songwriter with guitar & melodeon. Writer of 'Fiddler's Green' and others.*
**RAB** East Midlands Arts

## John Conolly and Robin Garside
**Contact** John Conolly
**Mail address** 18 Scrivelsby Court, CLEETHORPES, Lincs, DN35 0HJ
**Phone** 01472 695836
**Email** robin@robin-garside.freeserve.co.uk
**RAB** East Midlands Arts

## John Coy
**Mail address** The Hawthorns, Church Lane, Thornhill, DEWSBURY, WF12 0JZ
**Phone** 01924 515541
*Singer and guitarist, mainly traditional, some contemporary.*
**RAB** Yorkshire Arts

## John Dipper
**Mail address** West End House, HEYTESBURY, Wiltshire, BA12 0EA
**Phone** 01985 840516
07811 839997
**Email** johndipp@hotmail.com
*Fiddle and concertina player with Confluence, Patterson - Jordan - Dipper, Sofibacugo.*
**RAB** Southern Arts

## John Herald
**Contact** Active
*American acoustic artist with a Country edge*

## John Howarth
**Mail address** 13 Verney Road, Royton, OLDHAM, Lancs, OL2 6AZ
**Phone** 0161 624 0008
*Solo singer, mainly traditional Lancashire with guitar, 5 string banjo, concertina, whistle.*
***Musicians' Union member***
**RAB** North West Arts



*Artists in the main A-Z listing are mostly available for concert and club bookings.*

*See page 11 for details of other artist listings (Dance Display, Solo Musicians, Composers, Arrangers, Session Musicians, Band Deps. Lecturers, MCs, Tutors, Street Theatre, Children's Entertainers, Theatre Companies).*

*Agents section appears on pages 119-131.*

## artists
## j

*Artists in the main A-Z listing are mostly available for concert and club bookings.*

*See page 11 for details of other artist listings (Dance Display, Solo Musicians, Composers, Arrangers, Session Musicians, Band Deps. Lecturers, MCs, Tutors, Street Theatre, Children's Entertainers, Theatre Companies).*

*Agents section appears on pages 119-131.*

### John Hyland
**Mail address** 34 Rosary Road, OLDHAM, Lancs, OL8 2SL
**Phone** 0161 628 7481
*Caller for barn dances, etc.*
Musician; guitar and tenor banjo.
**RAB** Northern Arts

### John Kirkpatrick
**Contact** Speaking Volumes
**Web** www.speakingvolumes.co.uk
*Widely recognised as the UK's finest squeezebox exponent. Melodeon, concertina player and singer, songwriter, workshop leader*
**RAB** West Midlands Arts

### John Kirkpatrick Ceilidh Band
**Contact** Speaking Volumes
**Web** www.speakingvolumes.co.uk
*5 piece ceilidh band*
**RAB** West Midlands Arts

### John Maycraft
**Contact** Craftvert Digital
**Mail address** 8 Harwood Meadow, Harwood, BOLTON, BL22 3QP
**Phone** 01204 439444
0796 8669590
**Email** john.maycraft@btinternet.com
*Instrumental guitar music. Writer/ player/ recording.*
**RAB** North West Arts

### John Otway
**Contact** Matters Musical
**Web** www.mattersmusical.com
*Rock 'n roll's greatest failure! Solo to big band.*

### John Pearson
**Contact** Last Days Recording, PO Box 128, DOVER, Kent, CT6 2SX
**Phone** 01304 330375
**Phone/Fax** 01304 826119
**Email** johnpearsonblues@yahoo.com
**Web** www.blues4ever.com
*Solo blues singer and guitarist.*
***Musicians' Union member***
**RAB** South East Arts

### John Pearson's Blues and Beyond
**Contact** John Pearson
**Mail address** Last Day's Recording, PO Box 128, DOVER, CT16 2SX
**Phone** 01304 330375
**Phone/Fax** 01304 826119
**Email** johnpearsonblues@yahoo.com
**Web** www.blues4ever.com
*Blues rooted singer/ guitarist and band - duo to quintet.*
***Musicians' Union member***
**RAB** South East Arts

### John Perkins – Silversitarco
**Mail address** 3 Ashleigh Villas, Plymouth Road, TOTNES, Devon TQ9 5PG
**Phone/Fax** 01803 868687
**Phone** 07967 526887
**Email** john@silver-sitar-co.fsnet.co.uk
**Web** www.sitar.co.uk
*Concert performer of Indian Classical music on sitar*
**Agent** Matters Musical
***Musicians' Union member***
**RAB** South West Arts

### John Prine
**Contact** Asgard Promotions
*Highly popular and original American singer songwriter blending folk, country and rock*

### John Renbourn
**Contact** NEM Productions (UK)
**Web** www.nemproductions.com
*Influential fingerstyle acoustic guitarist*

### John Renbourn and Clive Carroll
**Contact** NEM Productions (UK)
**Web** www.nemproductions.com
*Acoustic guitar duo*

### The John Richards Acoustic Band
**Contact** Working Joe Music
**Web** www.workingjoe.co.uk
*Variable line-up led by, and performing mainly, John Richrds' songs.*
**RAB** West Midlands Arts

### The John Tams Band
**Contact** Adastra
**Web** www.adastra-music.com
*Much fêted award winning singer and songwriter with his band.*

### John Townsend
**Mail address** 54 Lambton Road, LONDON, SW20 0LP
**Phone** 020 8947 4693
0771 4705976
*Traditional and contemporary singer, guitarist and banjo player. Experienced festival compere.*
**RAB** London Arts

### John Ward
**Mail address** PO Box 59, LOWESTOFT, Suffolk, NR33 8EA
**Phone** 01502 588137
**Email** john.ward11@virgin.net
**Web** http://freespace.virgin.net/john.ward11/index.htm
*Own, traditional & standard songs with guitar, bodhran, harmonica. Solo or duo with violinist Mario Price.*
***Musicians' Union member***
**RAB** East England Arts

### John Wilson
**Mail address** 18 South Terrace, ESH WINNING, Co Durham, DH7 9PR
**Phone** 0191 3764616
**Email** john@lawsonstudio.supanet.com
*Solo singer and guitarist, mainly traditional.*
**RAB** Yorkshire Arts

### John Wood
**Mail address** 17 Balliol Avenue, Chingford, LONDON, E4 6LX
**Phone** 020 8926 7293
**Email** jswood@cwctv.net
*Caller; Playford to barn dance. Writes dances.*
**RAB** London Arts

### John Wright
**Contact** Oscar Music Agency
**Web** freespace.virgin.net/royhunter/wright.htm
*Singer. Available solo or with Kenny Spiers and Stuart Hardy*

### Johnny Collins
**Mail address** 22 Athol Gardens, PINNER, Middx, HA5 3XQ
**Phone** 020 8866 1635
07970 245440
**Email** jcpedlar.songs@virgin.net
**Web** www.shanty.co.uk
*Traditional and contemporary singer, mainly shanties & maritime songs. Unaccompanied and with guitar, concertina.*
***Musicians' Union member***
**RAB** London Arts

### Johnny Coppin
**Contact** Red Sky Records
**Mail address** PO Box 27, STROUD, Glos, GL6 0YQ
**Phone/Fax** 01453 836877
**Web** www.johnnycoppin.co.uk
**Fax** 01453 757376
**Email** crispin@ctmuk.freeserve.co.uk
*Singer/ songwriter, guitarist and pianist. Traditional and contemporary English songs. Solo or duo with Paul Burgess (fiddle).*
***Musicians' Union member***
**RAB** South West Arts

## Johnny Handle
**Mail address** 15-16 Wood Terrace, High Spen, ROWLANDS GILL, Tyne & Wear, NE39 2AQ
**Phone** 01207 543873
*Music, songs and recitations from the North East. Accordion and Northumbrian pipes.*
**RAB** Northern Arts

## Joji Hirota
**Contact** Matters Musical
**Web** www.mattersmusical.com
*Japanese taiko drummer. Also performs neo-classical pieces, own compositions and Japanese folk songs on shakukachi flute and voice*
**RAB** London Arts

## Jon Bickley
**Mail address** 70 The Meadow Way, HARROW WEALD, Middx, HA3 7BS
**Email** jcbickley@hotmail.com
**Web** www.jcbickley.com
*Blues, folk and country singer/ songwriter.*
**RAB** London Arts

## Jon Harvison
**Mail address** PO Box 138, KEIGHLEY, Yorks, BD20 6UX
**Phone** 01535 654836
**Email** jonharvison@lineone.net
**Web** www.drive-on.co.uk
**Email** jonharvison@drive-on.co.uk
*Singer/ songwriter*
**RAB** Yorkshire Arts

## Jonathan Loomes
**Mail address** 4 Wheatfield Drive, Ramsey, HUNTINGDON, Cambs, PE26 1SH
**Phone** 07879 844137
01487 812072
**Email** jonloomes@hotmail.com
**Web** www.jonloomes.com
*Young performer of English traditional music. Singer, fiddle, English concertina, fingerstyle guitarist.*
***Musicians' Union member***
**RAB** East England Arts

## Jonathan Shorland
**Phone** 029 2046 5639
**Fax** 029 2025 6168
**Email** jonathan.shorland@vizzavi.net
*Player of fluted, various bagpipes. Maker and workshop facilitator. Ex Bluehorses, Fernhill. Currently in Juice. Influences Breton, Irish, Welsh.*
***Musicians' Union member***

## Jonny Hardie
**Email** jonnyhardie@hotmail.com
**Web** www.scotlandcreates.com/jonnyhardie
*North East Scots fiddle player. Trio with Gavin Marwick playing mainly eighteenth century reportoire.*
**AC** Scotland

## Jook Joint
**Contact** Al Summers
**Mail address** 61 Bratton Road, WESTBURY, Wilts, BA13 3ES
**Phone** 01373 864721
**Email** gill.summers@virginnet.co.uk
**Web** www.jookjoint.co.uk
*Duo to 7 piece. Acoustic blues, folk, jazz band. Vocals, guitars, bottleneck, etc. Available for workshops/ education.*
***Musicians' Union member***
**RAB** South West Arts

## Jooks
**Contact** Keith Calton
**Mail address** 6 Grove Road, Ash, NR ALDERSHOT, Hants, GU12 5BD
**Phone/Fax** 01252 314300
**Email** keith@calton.fsbusiness.co.uk
*3 piece playing Old Timey, Rock 'n Roll/ Jive/ Comedy/ Jazz/ Bluegrass. Good time band.*
**RAB** South East Arts

## Joseph Porter
**Contact** Gary Hatcher
**Mail address** PO Box 255, HARROGATE, Yorks, HG2 7QJ
**Phone/Fax** 01423 532342
**Phone** 07901 898473
**Email** 56134@blythpower.co.uk
**Web** www.blythpower.co.uk
*Solo, performing original material.*
***Musicians' Union member***
**RAB** Yorkshire Arts

## The Joyce Gang
**Contact** John Redmond
**Mail address** 22 Smithery Meadows, Christow, EXETER, Devon, EX6 7LE
**Phone/Fax** 01647 252246
**Phone** 07970 655942
**Email** John@Joycegang.co.uk
**Web** joycegang@co.uk
*Band playing a mix of contemporary folk and jazz*
**Agent** Total Music Agency
***Musicians' Union member***
**RAB** South West Arts

## Juan Martin
**Contact** Adastra
**Web** www.adastra-music com
*Flamenco guitarist. Available solo or with band, combining Flamenco, Indian, Jewish and Arabic sounds*

## Judy Dunlop and Jon Scaife
**Contact** Elizabeth Jones Entertainments
**Web** www.bromyard.co.uk/ejones
*Former Albion Band singer with multi-instrumentalist*
**RAB** Yorkshire Arts

## Juice
**Contact** Danny Kilbride
**Mail address** 7 The Square, Llanharan, PONTYCLUN, Rhondda Cynon Taf, CF72 9NR, Wales
**Phone** 01443 224446
**Email** kilbride@baynet.co.uk
**Alt contact** Dean Ryan
**Alt address** Deri Cottage, Forrest Coalpit, ABERGAVENNY, Wales
**Phone** 01873 890154
**Email** dean@dericot.freeserve.co.uk
*Welsh ceilidh band playing everything from Django to death metal (sort of thing).*
***Musicians' Union member***
**AC** Wales

## Julian Goodacre
**Mail address** 4 Elcho Street, PEEBLES, EH45 8LQ, Scotland
**Phone** 01721 722539
**Email** goodacres@cwcom.net
**Web** www.goodacrepipes.mcmail.com
*Performer with the goodacre brothers English bagpipe trio. Bagpiper maker and repairer.*
**AC** Scotland

## Julie Ellison
**Mail address** 68 Brunswick Street, Thurnscoe, ROTHERHAM, S Yorks, S63 0HY
**Phone** 01709 881339
**Email** julieellison@zen01709.freeserve.co.uk
**Web** www.julieellison.uklinux.net
*Solo songwriter, singer and guitarist. Songwriting and guitar workshops. See Damn Heart.*
**RAB** Yorkshire Arts

## Julie Felix
**Contact** Speaking Volumes
**Web** www.speakingvolumes.co.uk
*Political/ spiritual folk singer, star of the 60s folk scene*

## Julie Murphy
**Contact** Beautiful Jo Records
**Phone** 01865 249194
**Fax** 01865 792765
**Alt Phone** 01559 384962
**Email** ceri.matho@btinternet.com
*Highly regarded singer of contemporary and traditional songs in Welsh and English.*
***Musicians' Union member***
**AC** Wales



*Artists in the main A-Z listing are mostly available for concert and club bookings.*

*See page 11 for details of other artist listings (Dance Display, Solo Musicians, Composers, Arrangers, Session Musicians, Band Deps. Lecturers, MCs, Tutors, Street Theatre, Children's Entertainers, Theatre Companies).*

*Agents section appears on pages 119-131.*

artists
j-k

*Artists in the main A-Z listing are mostly available for concert and club bookings.*

*See page 11 for details of other artist listings (Dance Display, Solo Musicians, Composers, Arrangers, Session Musicians, Band Deps. Lecturers, MCs, Tutors, Street Theatre, Children's Entertainers, Theatre Companies).*

*Agents section appears on pages 119-131.*

## Julio Cortez Salsa Band
**Contact** Latin Arts Services
**Web** www.lasgroup.com
**RAB** London Arts

## June Peters
**Mail address** 30 Dahomey Road, LONDON, SW16 6ND
**Phone** 020 8677 3803
07961 173157
**Email** june.pet@virgin.net
*Storyteller, singer, fiddler, harpist, mbira player. Multicultural traditional material, focusing on Celtic.*
**RAB** London Arts

## June Tabor
**Contact** NEM Productions (UK)
**Web** www.nemproductions.com
*'One of England's great interpreters of popular song' The Guardian*
**AC** Wales

## Juno
**Contact** Elizabeth Jones Entertainments
**Web** www.bromyard.co.uk/ejones
*Trio with singer/ songwriter*

## Kadugan Ceilidh Band
**Contact** Judith Linton
**Mail address** 1 Barnstorm Farm, Abbey-St-Bathans, DUNS, Berwickshire, TD11 3TX
**Phone/Fax** 01361 840238
**Phone** 07860 326171
**Email** judfiddle@aol.com
*Scottish ceilidh band.*
***Musicians' Union member***
**AC** Scotland

## Kafoozalum Country Dance Band
**Contact** Peter Jenkins
**Mail address** 20 Charles Street, HILLINGDON HEATH, Middlesex, UB10 OSY
**Phone/Fax** 020 8581 0359
0797 325 0918
**Email** peter@kafoozalum.co.uk
**Web** www.kafoozalum.co.uk
*Scottish country dance band with caller.*
***Musicians' Union member***
**RAB** London Arts

## Kalinka Vulcheva
**Contact** The Other Agency
*Bulgarian folk singer. Also works with Bulgarian group "Bisseri". Workshops in Bulgarian folksongs and harmony*

## Kangaroo Moon
**Contact** Total Music Agency
*Australian Celtic rock*

## Karen and Colin Cater
**Contact** Colin Cater
**Mail address** Sunnyside, Southey Green, SIBLE HEDINGHAM, Essex, CO9 3RN
**Phone** 01787 462731
**Fax** 01787 463393
**Email** cater@hedfair.demon.co.uk
*English traditional and modern songs in harmony and with concertina, melodeon, banjo and percussion. See also Hedingham Fair.*
**RAB** East England Arts

## Karan Casey
**Contact** Tom Sherlock Management
*Acclaimed Irish singer formerly with American based band Solas*

## Karen Marshalsay
**Mail address** c/o 20 Stoneleigh Road, GREENOAK, PA16 7TB, Scotland
**Phone** 07710 496730
*Traditional Scottish & Paraguayan harper and composer. Solo or with fiddle, vocals, guitar, etc. Commissions taken. Workshop leader.*
***Musicians' Union member***
**AC** Scotland

## Karen Tweed
**Mail address** PO Box 5009, DERBY, Derbys, DE1 9FQ
**Phone** 01332 677046
**Fax** 01332 677047
**Email** karen@kstweed.co.uk
*Accordionist, composer, arranger, teacher and producer of instrumental music with roots in Irish, British and Scandanavian traditions. See Poozies, Ian Carr, Two Duos Quartet, etc.*
***Musicians' Union member***
**RAB** East Midlands Arts

## Kasutima
**Contact** Tim Garland
**Mail address** 25 Baden Road, Evington, LEICESTER, LE5 5PA
**Phone** 0116 273 4453
*Dance music, tunes & songs from around the world. Concerts or ceildihs, with caller.*
**RAB** East Midlands Arts

## Kate & Anna McGarrigle
**Contact** Moneypenny
*World-famous Quebec sisters. Singers, songwriters and musicians*

## Kate Aldis
**Contact** Kathryn Aldis
**Mail address** 88 Lowestoft Road, Worlingham, BECCLES, Suffolk, NR34 7RD
**Phone** 01502 712160
**Email** katealdis@netscape.net
*Freelance melodeon player, specialising in English dance music.*
***Musicians' Union member***
**RAB** East England Arts

## Kate Bramley
**Mail address** 5 Lowfield Lane, Staveley, HARROGATE, N Yorks, HG5 9LB
**Phone** 07957 229045
01423 340415
**Email** Kate_bramley@hotmail.com
**Web** www.katebramley.com
*Singer, songwriter and fiddle player. Available solo, or in duo with Sam Pirt (422 accordionist).*
***Musicians' Union member***
**RAB** Yorkshire Arts

## Kate Rusby
**Contact** Steve Rusby
**Mail address** PO Box 174, SHEFFIELD, S36 9BY
**Phone** 01226 790536
**Email** steve@purerecords.demon.co.uk
**Web** www.purerecords.demon.co.uk
*Highly acclaimed young English traditional singer, accompanying herself on guitar & piano. Solo, trio with John McCusker and Andy Cutting or the Kate Rusby Band with the above plus Ian Carr, Michael McGoldrick and Andy Seward.*
***Musicians' Union member***
**RAB** Yorkshire Arts

## Kate Witney
**Mail address** 1 Church Cottages, LISSINGTON, Lincs, LN3 5AE
**Phone** 01673 885058
07974 934668
**Email** kate.witney@lineonenet
**Web** www.piper-kj.demon.co.uk
*Traditional unaccompanied songs from the British Isles, North America, Europe and Armenia.*
**RAB** East Midlands Arts

## Kathryn Nicoll and Sean O'Donnell
**Contact** Mesmerist Productions
**Web** www.mesmerist.com
*Champion traditional Scottish fiddle player and guitarist. Plays with Keltic Elektrik*
**AC** Scotland

## Kathryn Roberts and Sean Lakeman
**Contact** NEM Productions (UK)
**Web** www.nemproductions.com
*Young Tradition Award winning vocalist with guitarist*

## Kathryn Tickell Band
**Contact** Karen McWilliams
**Mail address** PO Box 130, MORPETH, Northumberland, NE65 7WD
**Phone/Fax** 01669 621886
**Email** karen@kathryntickell.co.uk
*Band led by award winning Northumbrian piper, fiddler and composer, Kathryn Tickell.*
***Musicians' Union member***
**RAB** Northern Arts

## Kathy Stewart
**Contact** Adastra
**Web** www.adastra-music.com
*US Singer/ songwriter*

## Katie Howson and Jeannie Harris
**Contact** Katie Howson
**Mail address** 44 Old Street, Haughley, STOWMARKET, Suffolk, IP14 3NX
**Phone** 01449 673695
**Email** katie@veteran.co.uk
*Melodeon duo; traditional music from Suffolk.*
***Musicians' Union member***
**RAB** East England Arts

## Katrina Rublowska
**Mail address** 1 Katherine Court, 70 Honor Oak Road, LONDON, SE23 3RS
**Phone** 020 8699 6646
**Email** katrina.rublowska@virgin.net
**Web** www.rublowska.co.uk
*Singer of traditional blues, contemporary folk & own songs with guitar or piano.*
***Musicians' Union member***
**RAB** London Arts

## Keeba
**Contact** Beyond
*Scottish Celtic pop band*

## The Keelers
**Contact** Peter Wood
**Mail address** 6 Welburn Close, OVINGHAM, Northumberland, NE42 6BD
**Phone** 01661 832705
0191 525 2514
**Email** peter.wood@sunderland.ac.uk
**Alt contact** Jim Mageean
**Alt address** 2 Marden Terrace, Cullercoats, NORTH SHIELDS, Tyne & Wear
**Phone** 0191 251 3847
*4 part unaccompanied male harmony group. Shanties, sea & NE songs.*
**RAB** Northern Arts

## Keep It Up
**Contact** Martin Coull Music Management
**Mail address** Studio 7, 6 New Street, EDINBURGH, EH8 8BH, Scotland
**Phone/Fax** 0131 557 5330
**Phone** 07803 137509
**Email** marticoull@aol com
**Web** www.tartantapes.com/keepitup
*Scottish traditional and new music band with Simon Thoumire, Eilidh Shaw, Malcolm Stitt, Kevin Mackenzie*
**Agent** Stoneyport Agency
**AC** Scotland

## Keith B Smith
**Mail address** 35 Selwyn Gardens, CAMBRIDGE, CB3 9AY
**Phone/Fax** 01223 357703
**Email** keith.smith@quista.net
**Web** www.hoogie.co.uk
*Scottish violinist, bagpiper and studio producer.*
***Musicians' Union member***
**RAB** East England Arts

## Keith Brown
**Mail address** 41 Eltham Road, Cantley, DONCASTER, DN4 6LQ
**Phone** 01302 533503
07780 734047
*Singer and guitar/concertina player, traditional plus some contemporary songs.*
**RAB** Yorkshire Arts

## Keith Davis
**Mail address** 6 North Street, Downend, BRISTOL, Avon, BS16 5SY
**Phone** 0117 957 0323
**Email** keithdavis@madasafish.com
*Solo acoustic blues singer/ guitarist.*
*Guitar teacher/ workshop leader.*
***Musicians' Union member***
**RAB** South West Arts

## Keith Hancock
**Mail address** Emerging Music
**Web** www.emerging.demon.co.uk
*Songwriter, singer and melodeon player*
**RAB** North West Arts

## Keith Hinchliffe
**Mail address** 23a Spring Hill, SHEFFIELD, S10 1ET
**Email** keith.hinchliffe@lineone.net
**Web** www.stirrings.co.uk/folkzone/artistes/keith.hinchliffe
*Solo acoustic guitarist/ singer of traditional English, Celtic, American contemporary songs. Workshop leader/ teacher for guitar arrangement and song accompaniment*
**Agent** Elizabeth Jones Entertainments
***Musicians' Union member***
**RAB** Yorkshire Arts

## Keith Kendrick
**Mail address** 88 Highfield Road, ASHBOURNE, Derbyshire, DE6 1DX
**Phone/Fax** 01335 345675
**Phone** 07885 345367
**Email** eyup@freeuk.com
**Web** www.eyuk.freeuk.com
*Mainly traditional English songs, music, dialect stories and humour. Concentinas & guitar. Workshops & schools projects.*
**RAB** East Midlands Arts

## Keith Kendrick and Lynne Heraud
**Contact** Keith Kendrick
**Mail address** 88 Highfield Road, ASHBOURNE, Derbys, DE6 1DX
**Phone/Fax** 01335 345675
**Phone** 07885 345367
**Email** eyup@freeuk.com
**Web** www.eyup.freeuk.com
**Alt contact** Lynne Heraud
**Alt address** 29 Cappell Lane, STANSTEAD ABBOTTS, Herts, SG12 8BU
**Phone** 01920 870558
01920 870027
**Email** lynneheraud@btinternet.com
*Mainly English traditional songs and ballads in harmony. Acappella/ with concertinas & whistles.*
**RAB** East Midlands Arts

## Keith Leech
**Mail address** 205 Priory Road, HASTINGS, Sussex, TN34 3JB
**Phone/Fax** 01424 716576
**Email** chiefbogie@hotmail.com
*Caller for English style ceilidhs. Also Punch and Judy. Folk animateur.*
**RAB** South East Arts



*Artists in the main A-Z listing are mostly available for concert and club bookings.*

*See page 11 for details of other artist listings (Dance Display, Solo Musicians, Composers, Arrangers, Session Musicians, Band Deps. Lecturers, MCs, Tutors, Street Theatre, Children's Entertainers, Theatre Companies).*

*Agents section appears on pages 119-131.*

*Artists in the main A-Z listing are mostly available for concert and club bookings.*

*See page 11 for details of other artist listings (Dance Display, Solo Musicians, Composers, Arrangers, Session Musicians, Band Deps. Lecturers, MCs, Tutors, Street Theatre, Children's Entertainers, Theatre Companies).*

*Agents section appears on pages 119-131.*

## Kellie While
**Contact** Blue Moon Music
**Web** www.bluemoonmusic.co.uk
*Singer with E2K and The Albion Band. Available solo. Roots/ pop, guitar & vocals*

## Kelly's Heroes
**Contact** Matters Musical
**Web** www.mattersmusical.com
*Traditional and contemporary Celtic songs*
**RAB** East Midlands Arts

## Kelter
**Contact** Fiona Taylor
**Mail address** 196 Simonside Terrace, Heaton, NEWCASTLE UPON TYNE, NE6 5DR
**Phone** 0191 224 1815
07967 737001
**Email** fionacattaylor@hotmail.com
**Alt address** 42 Wissage Lane, LICHFIELD, Staffs, WS13 6DF
**Phone** 01543 305779
*Lively 6 piece young anglo celtic band. Fiddles, cello, melodeon, dance, voice, crumhorn, pipes, percussion and bass. Concerts and workshops.*
***Musicians' Union member***
**RAB** Northern Arts

## Keltic Elektrik
**Contact** Stoneyport Agency
**Phone/Fax** 0131 5571050
**Email** dfrancis@musicscotland.com
**Web** www.jackevans.co.uk
*Scottish Celtic-dance act*
**AC** Scotland

## Ken Nicol
**Mail address** 298 Tag Lane, INGOL, Lancs, PR2 3UY
**Phone** 01772 510144
07909 991051
**Email** ken.nicol@virgin.net
*Guitarist and singer, styles include folk, blues, ragtime, ballads etc. Lead guitarist and singer with the Albion Band.*
**RAB** North West Arts

## Kenny Young and The Eggplants
**Contact** Stoneyport Agency
**Web** www.stoneyport.demon.co.uk

## Kerensa
**Contact** Kerensa Newman
**Mail address** 7 St. Aubyns Vean, TRURO, Cornwall TR1 2DX
**Phone** 01872 240475
07833 393928
**Email** kerensaay2k@supanet.com
*Player of hammered dulcimer, whistles, mandola, guitar & vocals. Traditional & contemporary folk music & song.*
**RAB** South West Arts

## Kettle Of Fish
**Contact** John Adams
**Mail address** 13 Chevin Road, BELPER, Derbys, DE56 2UW
**Phone** 01773 829602
07941 534968
**Email** jadams@cothrecords.co.uk
**Web** www.cothrecords.co.uk
**Alt contact** Sarah Matthews
**Alt address** 10 Hamblin Crescent, SINFIN, Derbys, DE24 9PL
**Phone** 07941 366319
01332 273383
**Email** sarah@folkspace.idps.co.uk
*4 piece ceilidh band, fiddle, melodeon, bass and drums. Caller available.*
***Musicians' Union member***
**RAB** East Midlands Arts

## Kevin Dempsey
**Contact** Karisma Music Management
**Web** www.karisma.net
*Available solo or with Tom Leary*

## Kevin MacLeod and Springwell
**Email** kev-chris.mcleod204@freeserve.co.uk
**Email** Kevindo@rcahms.gov.uk
*Banjo, bouzouki, guitar player etc. Also with Springwell with Tony Mcmanus and Jack Evans.*

## Kevin Rowsome
**Mail address** 3 Belton Park Villas, Donnycarney, DUBLIN 9, Ireland
**Phone** +353 1 8510031
+353 87 6994904
**Email** kevin-rowsome@esatclear.ie
**Web** www.kevinrowsome.ipfox.com/
*Acclaimed solo uilleann piper and duo with fiddle player, Lorraine Hickey.*
**AC** Ireland

## Kieron Means
**Mail address** c/o Sara Grey Ploughman's Cottage, EDINBANE, Isle of Skye, IV51 9PW, Scotland
**Phone** 01470 582254
**Email** saragrey@compuserve.com
*US/ UK singer and guitar player. Traditional and contemporary songs.*
**AC** Scotland

## Kila
**Mail address** The Concert Clinic
**Web** www.concertclinic.com
*Ancient & modern sounds fused into 'infectious dance style'. From Dublin*

## The KilBride Brothers
**Contact** Danny KilBride
**Mail address** 7 The Square, Llanharan, PONTYCLUN, Rhondda Cynon Taf, CF72 9NR, Wales
**Phone** 01443 224446
07809 063144
**Email** kilbride@baynet.co.uk
**Web** www.kilbridebros.com
*4 piece outfit playing music from Wales and the Atlantic seaboard. Workshop leaders.*
***Musicians' Union member***
**AC** Wales

## The Kimbara Brothers
**Contact** Matters Musical
**Web** www.mattersmusical.com
*Hot Club style band 2 guitars, fiddle and bass*

## Kimmo Pohjonen
**Contact** mARKO pOLO
**Web** www.markopolo.co.uk
*Experimental virtuoso Finnish traditional accordionist*

## Kingdom Choir
**Contact** Matters Musical
**Web** www.mattersmusical.com
*Young group of up to 20 singers from Pentecostal churches in London.*

## King's Lynn Waites
**Contact** Chris Gutteridge
**Mail address** The White Cottage, 58 Brow of the Hill, Leziate, KING'S LYNN, Norfolk, PE32 1EN
**Phone** 01553 630442
**Email** chiefwaite@lynnwaites.co.uk
**Web** www.lynnwaites.co.uk
*Traditional band of waites, playing and singing music from early music to mid- eighteenth century. Mainly wind instruments.*
**RAB** East England Arts

## Kinin
**Contact** Sarah Cheffins
**Mail address** Station House, Woodhead, GLOSSOP, Derbys, SK13 1JE
**Phone** 01457 762456
07752 323259
**Email** scheffins@pop3.poptel.org.uk
**Web** homepages.poptel.org.uk/scheffins.index.htm
*Duo, cittern, fiddle, vocals. Traditional and contemporary.*
***Musicians' Union member***
**RAB** North West Arts

## Kiranpal Singh
**Mail address** 16 Meadows Road, SOUTHALL, Middx, UB1 2JE
**Phone** 020 8574 3445
07971 199790
**Fax** 07951 601236
*Professional santoor player (100 stringed hammered dulcimer from Kashmir). Concerts, demonstrations, tuition. Also plays tabla.*
***Musicians' Union member***
**RAB** London Arts

## Kirsty Cotter
**Mail address** 23 Moorfield Rd, WOODBRIDGE, Suffolk, IP12 4JN
**Phone** 01394 388221
07796 184981
**Email** kirsty.cotter@btinternet.co.uk
*Player and teacher of Scottish traditional fiddle.*
**AC** Scotland

## Kit Packham's One Jump Ahead
**Contact** Matters Musical
**Web** www.mattersmusical.com
*Jump jive band led by vocalist, composer and saxophonist Kit Packham*

## The Kitchen Girls
**Contact** Shindy Arts
**Web** www.shindy.org.uk
*6 piece string band, Americana roots for ceilidhs and concerts*
**RAB** Southern Arts

## The Klezmatics
**Contact** Adastra
**Web** www.adastra-music.com
*New York based band playing Jewish roots music*

## Klezmer Festival Band
**Contact** Adastra
**Web** www.adastra-music.com
*Celebratory music from Jewish traditions*
**RAB** London Arts

## Klezmer Jazz Quartet
**Contact** Philip Clouts
**Mail address** 28A Portland Rise, LONDON, N4 2PP
**Phone** 020 8802 9688
*Jewish and other East Euroepan folk music with an element of jazz improvisation.*
***Musicians' Union member***
**RAB** London Arts

## Knotted Chord Folk Dance Band
**Contact** Philip Rowe
**Mail address** 24 Kingsley Drive, HARROGATE, N Yorks, HG1 4TJ
**Phone** 01423 540056
**Email** PhilipRowe@beeb.net
**Web** knottedchord.members.beeb.net
*Folk dance band for barn dances, ceilidhs, club dances, American contra dance, etc.*
**RAB** Yorkshire Arts

## K-Passa
**Contact** David McNicholas
**Mail address** 1 Bedford Street, DERBY, DE22 3PB
**Phone** 01332 291603
**Fax** 07092 291604
**Email** escapecom@lineone.net
**Web** www.k-passa.com
*Celtic roots rockers. 6 piece band.*
**RAB** East Midlands Arts

## Kristina Olsen and Peter Grayling
**Contact** Emerging Music
**Web** www.emerging.demon.co.uk
*American/ Australian song, guitar (acoustic and steel body slide) and cello duo*

## Krosfyah
**Contact** Adastra
**Web** www.adastra-music.com
*Caribbean band with influences of soca, calypso, soul, reggae and zouk*

## Kuljit Bhamra Band
**Contact** Matters Musical
**Web** www.mattersmusical.com
*Composer, tabla player and percussionist, fusing bhangra dance beats and Hindi film tunes into British-Asian pop. Band of up to 9 musicians*

## La Bottine Souriante
**Contact** Adastra
**Web** www.adastra-music.com
*Nine piece Quebecois band including accordion, fiddle, horns and rhythm section. 'The best band in the world."*

## La Boum!
**Contact** Stoneyport Agency
**Phone** 0131 6628358
07785 720987
**Email** hmac518996@aol.com
**Web** www.laboum.co.uk
*Mixture of Scots, African, jazz, latin and dub. Features brass & vocal sections, percussion and guitar*
**AC** Scotland

## La Cucina Trio
**Contact** Matters Musical
**Web** www.mattersmusical.com
*Traditional Neopolitan trio*

## La Sonera Calaveras
**Contact** Active
*Scottish 6 piece Latin act. Son with a contemporary edge*

## La Timbala
**Contact** Artists Connect
**Web** www.artistsconnect.com
*12 piece group playing Cuban music*

## La Volee d'Castors
**Contact** mARKO pOLO
**Web** www.markopolo.co.uk
*Young 6 piece Quebec band. Voted best New Folk Artists 1999-2000*

## Laoise Kelly
**Contact** Smallworld Music
*Irish harp player, solo or with The Bumblebees*
**AC** Northern Ireland

## Last Night's Fun
**Contact** The Event Shop
**Web** www.lastnightsfun.com
*Chris Sherburn, Denny Bartley & Nick Scott. Traditional music (mainly Irish) on concertina, pipes and guitar/ vocals plus lots of daft patter*
**RAB** Yorkshire Arts

## The Laurence Sisters
**Contact** Rachel & Miranda Laurence
39 Park Avenue, Histon, CAMBRIDGE, CB4 9JU
**Phone** 01223 237843
**Fax** 01223 237476
**Email** mirandalaurence@tinyonline.co.uk
*Young duo; two fiddles and voices. Exploring the fusion of many musical influences & the texture of voice & fiddle.*
**RAB** East England Arts



*Artists in the main A-Z listing are mostly available for concert and club bookings.*

*See page 11 for details of other artist listings (Dance Display, Solo Musicians, Composers, Arrangers, Session Musicians, Band Deps. Lecturers, MCs, Tutors, Street Theatre, Children's Entertainers, Theatre Companies).*

*Agents section appears on pages 119-131.*

Artists in the main A-Z listing are mostly available for concert and club bookings.

See page 11 for details of other artist listings (Dance Display, Solo Musicians, Composers, Arrangers, Session Musicians, Band Deps. Lecturers, MCs, Tutors, Street Theatre, Children's Entertainers, Theatre Companies).

Agents section appears on pages 119-131.

## Le Gop!
**Contact** Adastra
**Web** www.adastra-music.com
*French band fusing traditional music and modern dance rhythms*

## Le Rue
**Contact** Adastra
**Web** www.adastra-music.com
*Pierre Le Rue's band. New Orleans, Cajun, R&B, Jazz and Zydeco*

## Lee 'n Zach
**Mail address** c/o 139 Priory Road, St Denys, SOUTHAMPTON, SO17 2JS
**Phone** 023 8055 8460
023 8032 6812
**Email** folkmania@hotmail.com
**Web** www.folkmania.org.uk
**Alt Phone** 0771 8834 766
*Duo, multi-instrumental traditional and contemporary roots based music.*
**RAB** Southern Arts

## Lee Raymond
**Mail address** 139 Priory Road, St Denys, SOUTHAMPTON, SO17 2JS
**Phone** 023 8055 8460
023 8032 5704
**Email** folkmania@hotmail.com
**Web** www.folkmania.org.uk
**Alt Phone** 0771 8834 766
*Singer/ songwriter and instrumentalist. Traditional and contemporary roots based songs incl. shanties & blues.*
***Musicians' Union member***
**RAB** Southern Arts

## LeeZ Argonauts
**Mail address** 139 Priory Road, SOUTHAMPTON, SO17 2JS
**Phone** 023 8055 8460
023 8032 5704
**Email** folkmania@hotmail.com
**Web** www.folkmania.org.uk
**Phone** 0771 8834 766
*Contemporary roots based band, playing traditional and new Irish, blues, shanties and folk opera.*
***Musicians' Union member***
**RAB** Southern Arts

## Left Hand Drive
**Contact** P White - Management
**Mail address** 2 North Street, CROMFORD, Derby, DE4 3RG
**Phone** 07968 096382
**Email** lefthd@ukmusicnetwork.co.uk
**Web** www.ukmusicnetwork.co.uk/lhd
**Alt contact** S Ball
**Alt address** 87 Foljambe Road, CHESTERFIELD, Derbys, S40 1NJ
**Phone** 01246 558214
07748 322907
**Email** funkydoo100@hotmail.com
*3 piece acoustic roots influenced band.*
**RAB** East Midlands Arts

## Legacy
**Contact** Elizabeth Jones Entertainments
**Web** www.bromyard.co.uk/ejones
*4 piece Irish music/ song band*
**RAB** South East Arts

## Lennie Gallant
**Contact** Adastra
**Web** www.adastra-music.com
*Canadian singer/ songwriter*

## Leo McCann
**Mail address** PO Box 23341, EDINBURGH, EH1 3WQ, Scotland
**Phone** 0131 4764363
07780 608098
**Email** leo@mcccann.sol.co.uk
**Web** www.leomccann.musicscotland.com
*Button box and low whistle player. Tours with guitarist/ singer or four piece band. Instrumental workshops.*
***Musicians' Union member***
**AC** Scotland

## Leon Rosselson
**Mail address** 28 Park Chase, WEMBLEY PARK, Middlesex, HA9 8EH
**Phone** 020 8902 0655
**Fax** 020 8902 3829
**Email** rinar@dial.pipex.com
**Web** www.fishdesign.com/rosselson/leon.html
*Performs in the English chanson idiom. Respected writer of political songs*
**Agent** The Other Agency
***Musicians' Union member***
**RAB** London Arts

## Les Barker
**Contact** Emerging Music
**Web** www.mrsackroyd.com
*Popular writer and performer of strange poems.*
**RAB** North West Arts

## Les Batinses
**Contact** Adastra
**Web** www.adastra-music.com
*6 piece Quebec band with fiddle, vocal, bombard, percussion etc*

## Lester Simpson
**Mail address** 4 Golf Lane, Duffield, DERBY, Derbyshire, DE6 4EE
**Phone/Fax** 01332 840758
07850 108371
**Email** lestersimpson@hommelarts.fsnet.co.uk
**Web** www.coopeboyesandsimpson.co.uk
*Singer/songwriter, unaccompanied & playing melodeons or bagpipes*
**RAB** East Midlands Arts

## Life And Times
**Contact** Barry Goodman
**Mail address** 54 Ickleford Road, HITCHIN, Herts, SG5 1TR
**Phone** 01462 456811
**Email** barry.goodman1@ntlworld.com
**Web** www.good-man.freeserve.co.uk
*Duo, own songs/ tunes in folk idiom. Guitar, melodeon and concertina.*
***Musicians' Union member***
**RAB** East England Arts

## Lindisfarne
**Contact** Ray Laidlaw
**Mail address** Syncopation Ltd, 67 Hotspur Street, TYNEMOUTH, Tyne and Wear, NE30 4EL
**Phone** 0191 2965577
**Email** info@lindisfarne.co.uk
**Web** www.lindisfarne.co.uk
*Renowned North-East based folk rock band - "Fog on the Tyne"*
**Agent** Adastra
***Musicians' Union member***
**RAB** Northern Arts

## Lionel Lodge
**Contact** Clunie Creative Enterprises
**Web** www.come.to/clunie
*Austrian singer/songwriter/ guitarist, contemporary folk. Solo, duo & with band. Clunie are UK agents & European management*

## The Little Band
**Contact** Max Bradley
**Mail address** 23 Hardy's Road, CLEETHORPES, N Lincs, DN35 0DL
**Phone** 0850 838088
01472 694735
**Email** liam@thelittleband.fsnet.co.uk
**Web** www.thelittleband.fsnet.co.uk
*Ceilidh/ barn dance band with caller and PA. Fiddle, flute, melodeon and guitars.*
**RAB** Yorkshire Arts

## Little Johnny England
**Contact** PJ Wright
**Phone** 01604 660458
01327 260117
**Email** elljayee@hotmail.com
**Web** www.littlejohnnyengland.co.uk
*5 piece English folk rock band with Gareth Turner and others*
**Agent** Speaking Volumes
***Musicians' Union member***
**RAB** East Midlands Arts

## Liz Carroll
**Contact** themusictree. (uk) ltd
**Web** www.lizcarroll.com
*Celebrated American-Irish fiddle player. Occasional tours.*

## Liz Doherty
**Contact** Dunmore Productions
**Web** www.tartantapes.com/lizdoherty
*Irish fiddle player (solo or with her band), workshop leader and lecturer in traditional Irish, Scottish & Cape Breton music*
**AC** Ireland

## Llio Rhydderch
**Mail address** Gwenallt, Marian-Glas, YNYS MON, LL73 8PE, Wales
**Phone/Fax** 01248 853741
**Email** llio.rhydderch@freeuk.com
**Web** www.llio.rhydderch.freeuk.com
*Welsh triple harper of Welsh traditional music. Recording artist, solo performer and teacher. Director of young group of triple harpers "Telynwyr Llio".*
***Musicians' Union member***
**AC** Wales

## The London Community Gospel Choir
**Contact** Asgard Promotions, Matters Musical

## London Gallery Quire
**Contact** Francis Roads
**Mail address** 61 Malmesbury Road, South Woodford, LONDON, E18 2NL
**Phone** 020 85054381
**Email** francis@jfroads.demon.co.uk
*Lectures, concerts, services and workshops of West Gallery music.*
**RAB** London Arts

## The London Lasses and Pete Quinn
**Contact** Karen Ryan
**Mail address** 48 Louise White House, Pilgrims Way, LONDON, N19 3LU
**Phone** 020 7281 8837
07771 782384
**Email** london.lasses@virgin.net
**Web** www.londonlasses.net
*Traditional London Irish style all female band, flute, fiddles banjo and piano.*
**RAB** London Arts

## London Philharmonic Skiffle Orchestra
**Contact** Mike Martin
**Mail address** 30 Maple Springs, Upshire, WALTHAM ABBEY, Middx, EN9 3LL
**Phone** 01992 700287
**Email** lpso@lineone.net
**Web** http://website.lineone.net/~lpso
**Alt contact** Martyn Oram
**Phone** 01923 672520
07887 606214
*4 piece band combining country, folk, cajun and eastern music with skiffle.*
**RAB** London Arts

## The London Ragtime Orchestra
**Contact** Matters Musical
**Web** www.mattersmusical.com
*Ragtime orchestra*

## Loosehound Drifters
**Contact** Adastra
**Web** www.adastra-music.com
*Folk-rock band, Waterboys-esqe*

## Lorenna McKennitt
**Contact** Primary Talent

## Lorna Brooks
**Contact** Active

## Lorraine Jordan
**Contact** Unforgettable Music
**Mail address** PO Box 23316, EDINBURGH, EH7 5XQ, Scotland
**Phone/Fax** 0131 538 3473
**Phone** 07947 603683
**Email** lorrainejordan@unforgettable.com
**Web** www.musicscotland.com/lorrainejordan
*Singer and writer of songs reflecting a Celtic heritage and contemporary musical tastes*
**Agent** Mesmerist Productions
***Musicians' Union member***
**RAB** Northern Arts

## Lorraine Lee and Bennett Hammond
**Contact** The Bechhofer Agency
*Visiting American duo*

## Los Charros
**Contact** Matters Musical
**Web** www.mattersmusical.com
*Traditional songs and music from South America. Solo to 6 piece costumed band*

## Los Gringos
**Contact** Access All Areas
*10 piece Havana-style salsa band. Professional salsa dance instruction available*

## Los Mojados del Rio Tamesis
**Contact** Matters Musical
**Web** www.mattersmusical.com
*Mexican /Tex Mex fusion using both Mexican and European musicians*

## Los Pistoleros
**Contact** Matters Musical
**Web** www.mattersmusical.com
*Honky tonk band featuring Bobby Valentino on vocals and fiddle, withBJ Cole on steel guitar. Tex Mex, R&B, western swing and rockabilly*

## Los Soneros
**Contact** Matters Musical
**Web** www.mattersmusical.com
*Duo to full scale salsa band including vocal harmonies and acoustic guitar*

## Los Squideros
**Contact** Ian Smith
**Mail address** Trewadoc, GARWAY, Herefordshire, HR2
**Phone** 01600 750365
**Email** keneasy@lounge77.fsnet.co.uk
**Alt contact** Leo
**Alt address** 79 Holme Lacy Road, HEREFORD, HR2 6DF
**Phone** 01432 343217
*10 piece comedy Mexican tribute band.*
**RAB** West Midlands Arts

## Loscoe State Opera
**Contact** Kate Rounding
**Mail address** 17A Claremount Road, HEANOR, Derbys, DE75 7HS
**Phone** 01773 719104
07790 159249
**Email** Kate@mytempo.fsnet.co.uk
**Web** www.loscoestateopera.com
**Alt contact** Andy Martin
**Phone** 01773 744320
*7 piece contemporary/traditional folk rock band.*
***Musicians' Union member***
**RAB** East Midlands Arts

## Lou Marriott
**Mail address** 3 Carlthorpe Grove, High Green, SHEFFIELD, S35 4PL
**Phone** 0114 284 5922
*Singer /guitarist. Contemporary British & American song.*
**RAB** Yorkshire Arts

## Lough Swilly
**Contact** Matters Musical
**Web** www.mattersmusical.com
2-4 piece Celtic and country band, etc

## Lucinda Williams
**Contact** Asgard Promotions
*American contemporary singer songwriter. 'Supplies the missing link between Sheryl Crow and Neil Young.' The Times*

## Lucky Bags
**Contact** Emerging Music
**Web** www.emerging.demon.co.uk
*5 piece all female band; song, harp, fiddle, dulcimer etc*
**Agent** Emerging Music

## Luka Bloom
**Contact** Asgard Promotions
*Irish contemporary singer.*



*Artists in the main A-Z listing are mostly available for concert and club bookings.*

*See page 11 for details of other artist listings (Dance Display, Solo Musicians, Composers, Arrangers, Session Musicians, Band Deps. Lecturers MCs, Tutors, Street Theatre, Children's Entertainers, Theatre Companies).*

*Agents section appears on pages 119-131.*

artists
l-m

*Artists in the main A-Z listing are mostly available for concert and club bookings.*

*See page 11 for details of other artist listings (Dance Display, Solo Musicians, Composers, Arrangers, Session Musicians, Band Deps. Lecturers, MCs, Tutors, Street Theatre, Children's Entertainers, Theatre Companies).*

*Agents section appears on pages 119-131.*

## Lunasa
**Contact** The Concert Clinic
**Web** www.concertclinic.com
*Popular Irish traditional music band, flutes, fiddle, guitar and double bass*

## The Lush Rollers
**Contact** Nick Turner
**Mail address** Watercolour Music, ARDGOOR, PH33 7AH, Scotland
**Phone** 01855 841259
**Fax** 01855 841364
**Email** wcmmusic@cs.com
*4 piece new country/ Americana roots band*
**Agent** Beyond
***Musicians' Union member***
**AC** Scotland

## Lusty and Strong
**Contact** Castlelake Consultancy Castlelake, CASHEL, Co Tipperary, Irish Republic
**Phone** +353 62 62685
+353 87982 1916
**Fax** +353 62 62967
**Email** slaffey@iol.ie
**Web** www.iol.ie/~didly-didly
*Sea shanty group with Sean Laffey, Tony Canniffe, John Wall, etc. Mandolins, bodhran, concertina and striped pullovers!*

## M Yogeswaran – "Tamil Classics"
**Mail address** 10 Gledwood Crescent, HAYES, Middx, UB4 0AX
**Phone/Fax** 020 8573 1930
**Phone** 07979 891649
**Email** yoga.swara@talk21.com
**Web** www.yogaswara.co.uk
**Alt contact** Eva Skalla
**Phone** 020 8946 2147
*Classical Indian vocalist and multi-instrumentalist. Solo concerts, work-shops, lectures.*
**Agent** Global Heritage
***Musicians' Union member***
**RAB** Southern Arts

## macAlias
**Contact** Martin Coull Music Management
**Mail address** Studio 7, 6 New Street, EDINBURGH, EH8 8BH, Scotland
**Phone/Fax** 0131 557 5330
**Phone** 07803 137509
**Email** marticoull@aol.com
*Scottish duo: Gill Bowman and Karine Polwart*
**Agent** Stoneyport Agency
**AC** Scotland

## McManus, Evans, McLeod
**Contact** Stoneyport Agency
**Phone/Fax** 0131 5571050
**Email** dfrancis@musicscotland.com
*Three leading Scottish musicians*
**Agent** Stoneyport Agency
**AC** Scotland

## MacUmba
**Contact** Karen Gault
**Email** karen.gault@talk21.com
**Web** www.macumba.com
*Drum and Bagpipe band merging Brazilian and Carribbean rhythms with Scottish tunes.*
**AC** Scotland

## Mad Dogs and Englishmen
**Contact** Gary Hatcher
**Mail address** PO Box 225, HARROGATE, North Yorks, HG2 7QJ
**Phone** 01423 552342
07901 898473
**Email** 56134@blythpower.co.uk
**Web** www.whiskeypriests.co.uk/maddogs
*Acoustic trio, accordion, mandolin, guitars & vocals. New contemporary material*
**Agent** Whippet Promotions
***Musicians' Union member***
**RAB** Yorkshire Arts

## Mad Jocks and Englishmen
**Contact** Elizabeth Jones Entertainments
**Web** www.bromyard.co.uk/ejones
*Trio, comedy and songs*

## Mad Pudding
**Contact** Emerging Music
**Web** www.emerging.demon.co.uk
*Canadian 5 piece band, Celtic rock/folk/funk*

## Mad Rush (Den and Ned Couch)
**Contact** Den Couch
**Mail address** 10 Short Park Road, Peverell, PLYMOUTH, Devon, PL3 4PZ
**Phone/Fax** 01752 661367
**Phone** 0421 614547
**Email** deniuphillbooks@plymouth online.net
**Web** www.dbmasters.co.uk/artists.madrush.htm
*Songwriting duo, traditional & contemporary English & Celtic folk. Guitar, accordion, etc.*
***Musicians' Union member***
**RAB** South West Arts

## Maddy Prior
**Contact** Park Promotions
**Web** www.parkrecords.com
*Revered folk singer: "the voice of English music" and of Steeleye Span.*
**RAB** Southern Arts

## Madeline Milla
**Contact** Beautiful Enough Records
**Mail address** 38 Greenfields Close ST LEONARDS ON SEA, East Sussex TN37 7LP
**Phone** 01424 443735
**Email** made1@made1.fsnet.co.uk
**Web** www.madelinemilla.com
*Singer/ songwriter.*
**RAB** South East Arts

## Madigan
**Contact** Elizabeth Jones Entertainments
**Web** www.bromyard.co.uk/ejones
*4 piece fiddle, harp, drums, etc*
**RAB** South West Arts

## Maggie Boyle
**Mail address** 4 Victoria Street, Oakworth, KEIGHLEY, West Yorks, BD22 7HU
**Phone** 01535 647848
**Email** maggieboyle@hotmail.com
*Traditional singer, flute & bodhran player. Solo, duo, trio, with Grand Acosutic Roadshow and Grace Notes/ Gordon Tyrrall/ Clive Carroll.*
***Musicians' Union member***
**RAB** Yorkshire Arts

## Maggie Boyle and Clive Carroll
**Contact** Elizabeth Jones Entertainments
**Web** www.bromyard.co.uk/ejones
*Traditional singer and flute player with guitarist*

## Maggie Holland
**Phone** 0131 554 5776
**Email** maggie@dhenderson.rapidial.co.uk
*Solo singer of mostly modern songs accompanied on guitar and 5 string banjo.*
***Musicians' Union member***
**AC** Scotland

## Maggie MacInnes
**Mail address** Underwood Mains, Underwood, BY SYMINGTON, Ayrshire, KA1 5NG
**Fax** 01563 830006
**Email** maggie@maggiemacinnes.com
**Web** www.maggiemacinnes.com
*Singer of mostly Scottish Gaelic songs plus other traditional material. Clarsach player.*
**AC** Scotland

## Magna Carta
**Contact** Elizabeth Jones Entertainments
**Web** www.bromyard.co.uk/ejones
*Singer/ songwriter duo or band*
**Agents** Elizabeth Jones Entertainments, Karisma Music Management

### Magpie
**Contact** The Bechhofer Agency
*Visiting American duo*

### Magpie Lane
**Contact** Mat Green
**Mail address** 5 Mercury Court, BAMPTON, Oxon, OX18 2AJ
**Phone** 01993 850760
**Email** matthew.green@onmail.co.uk
**Web** http://homepages.tesco.net/~andy.ands/magpielane.htm
**Alt contact** Andy Turner
**Alt address** 37 Orwell Drive, DIDCOT, oxon, OX11 7RX
**Phone** 01235 811757
**Email** andyturner@britishlibrary.net
*6 piece concert band specialising in English traditional music and song.*
**RAB** Southern Arts

### Maighread and Triona Ni Dhomnaill
**Contact** Tom Sherlock Management
*Esteemed Irish singers*
**AC** Ireland

### Maire Clerkin
**Mail address** 40 Wakelin House, Sebbon Street, LONDON, N1 2EF
**Phone** 020 7359 1024
07940 547346
**Email** maire@clerkinworks.freeserve.co.uk
**Web** www.kickirishdance.co.uk
**Alt contact** KICK Irish Dance Theatre Co
**Alt address** Greenwich Dance Ag, The Borough Hall, Royal Hill, Greenwich, LONDON, SE10 8RE
**Phone** 07956 937461
**Email** donna@kickirishdance.co.uk
*Ceilidh caller. Irish dance specialist teacher/ performer. Director of KICK Irish Dance Theatre Co. (formerly Clerkinworks).*
**RAB** London Arts

### Máire Ní Chathasaigh and Chris Newman
**Contact** Kevin Martin
**Mail address** Old Bridge Music, PO Box 7, ILKLEY, W Yorks, LS29 9RY
**Phone/Fax** 01943 602203
**Phone** 07710 413548
**Email** mail@oldbridgemusic.com
**Web** www.oldbridgemusic.com
*Irish harp, acoustic guitar duo. Irish music from 17th to 21st centuries with diversions!*
***Musicians' Union member***
**RAB** Yorkshire Arts

### Mairi Campbell
**Mail address** 214 Portabello High Street, EDINBURGH, EH15 2AU
**Phone** 0131 664 8824
*Freelance fiddle and viola player, teacher of Scots fiddle and step dancing.*
***Musicians' Union member***
**AC** Scotland

### Mairtin O'Connor
**Contact** Adastra
**Web** www.adastra-music.com
*Renowned Irish button accordeonist*

### Mal Brown
**Mail address** Bryn Coed, Cruckmeole, Hanwood, SHREWSBURY, Shropshire, SY5 8JN
**Phone** 01743 861159
**Email** mal@onelorry.fsnet.co.uk
*Traditional singer/ songwriter and instrumentalist, performance poet, performer in education (schools, prisons, etc.).*
**RAB** West Midlands Arts

### Malinky
**Contact** Stoneyport Agency
**Web** www.stoneyport.demon.co.uk
*4 piece vocal-led Scottish group headed by Karine Polwart*
***Musicians' Union member***
**AC** Scotland

### Maman Roulaille
**Contact** Access All Areas
*French all female Cajun & Creole trio.*

### Mambo Jambo
**Contact** Oren Stone
**Mail address** 20 Richmond Gardens, SOUTHAMPTON, SO17 1RY
**Phone** 023 8059 2372
023 8039 2140
**Fax** 023 8059 3007
**Email** oms@soton.ac.uk
**Web** www.mambojambo.com
*Southampton based 14 piece Colombian tropical dance music band. Guitar, bass, 3 drummers, 5 saxes, 3 brass plus singer.*
**RAB** Southern Arts

### Mambo Jambo
**Phone** 07770 475278
**Email** mamboandjambo@hotmail.com
**Web** www.mambojambo.org.uk
*Acoustic duo playing world roots styles, rhythms and jazz. Spanish guitar, sax, clarinet, quatro and banjo*
**Agent** Adastra
**RAB** Yorkshire Arts

### Margaret Stewart
**Email** pogcd@aol.com
*Highly regarded traditional Gaelic singer.*
**AC** Scotland

### Marie Little
**Contact** Elizabeth Jones Entertainments
**Web** www.bromyard.co.uk/ejones
*Singer of traditional and contemporary songs*

### Mark Bazeley, Jason Rice and Robert Murch
**Contact** Mark Bazeley
**Mail address** Stoneley Cottage, South Zeal, OKEHAMPTON, Devon, EX20 2LA
**Phone** 01837 840775
**Email** mark4sarah@aol.com
**Alt contact** Jason Rice
**Alt address** 1 Porch Cottage, Copplestone, CREDITON, Devon
**Phone** 01367 84205
**Email** jason.rice@talk21.com
*Dartmoor traditional music on melodeon, accordion and banjo, plus Dartmoor step dancing and possible dance band.*
**RAB** South West Arts

### Maroon Town
**Contact** Access All Areas
*UK/West Indies reggae, ska and dub*

### The Marsh Warblers
**Contact** David Dedrick
**Mail address** 9 Knockwood Road, TENTERDEN, Kent, TN30 7AP
**Phone** 01580 763377
**Alt address** Zion Baptist Church, High Street, TENTERDEN, Kent, TN30 6LB
*West Gallery quire. 16 singers plus 4 piece band. Concerts and costumed presentations.*
**RAB** South East Arts

### Martin and Thornbory
**Contact** Matters Musical
**Web** www.mattersmusical.com
*Theme music duo, variety of styles including costumed medieval minstrels, sea shanties, folk, Victorian, Viking, etc*

### Martin Carthy
**Contact** Moneypenny
*Fine traditional singer and guitaist. "One of the giants of contemporary British music". Solo, duo with Norma Waterson, or with Waterson:Carthy. Also with Wood, Wilson, Carthy*
***Musicians' Union member***
**RAB** Yorkshire Arts

### Martin Dent
**Mail address** 12 Witley Green, LUTON, Beds, LU2 8TR
**Phone** 01582 727947
*Contemporary singer/ songwriter, spiritual, environmental, comical.*
**RAB** South East Arts



*Artists in the main A-Z listing are mostly available for concert and club bookings.*

*See page 11 for details of other artist listings (Dance Display, Solo Musicians, Composers, Arrangers, Session Musicians, Band Deps. Lecturers, MCs, Tutors, Street Theatre, Children's Entertainers, Theatre Companies).*

*Agents section appears on pages 119-131.*

*Artists in the main A-Z listing are mostly available for concert and club bookings.*

*See page 11 for details of other artist listings (Dance Display, Solo Musicians, Composers, Arrangers, Session Musicians, Band Deps. Lecturers, MCs, Tutors, Street Theatre, Children's Entertainers, Theatre Companies).*

*Agents section appears on pages 119-131.*

## Martin Hayes and Dennis Cahill
**Contact** Adastra
**Web** www.adastra-music.com
*Celebrated fiddle and guitar duo "traditional Irish music with jazz-blues approach"*
**AC** Ireland

## Martin Simpson
**Contact** Adastra
**Web** www.adastra-music.com
*Influential virtuoso guitarist and singer, based in US but regularly touring UK.*

## Martin Stephenson and The Daintees
**Contact** NEM Productions (UK)
**Web** www.nemproductions.com
*Singer songwriter and his band*

## Martyn Bennett
**Contact** Active
*Internationally respected favourite on festival circuit; pipes, fiddle and DJ skills combined.*

## Martyn Harvey
**Contact** 2 Airlie Villas, Gillinggate, KENDAL, Cumbria, LA9 4JD
**Phone** 01539 720551
0771 4506307
*Popular caller, frequently booked at major festivals. Workshop leader & compere.*
**RAB** Northern Arts

## Martyn Oram
**Mail address** Greensleeves, Verdure Close, WATFORD, WD25 9NJ
**Phone** 01923 672520
07887 606214
**Email** martyn.oram@yahoo.co.uk
**Web** www.martynoram.co.uk
*Solo singer with guitar and violin. Mostly new compositions in contemporary folk style.*
**RAB** South East Arts

## Martyn Wyndham-Read
**Mail address** PO Box 341, FARNHAM, Surrey, GL49 OYT
**Email** wyndham.read@btinternet.com
**Web** www.martynwyndhamread.com
*Established singer of contemporary and traditional songs, mostly on an Australian theme.*
**RAB** Southern Arts

## Mary Black
**Mail address** Asgard Promotions
*High profile Irish singer, now performing contemporary material*

## Mary Coughlan
**Mail address** themusictree. (uk) ltd
*Popular jazz/blues singer*
**Agents** Asgard Promotions, themusictree. (uk) ltd

## Mary Humphreys
**Mail address** 2 Belle Vue, Barkisland, HALIFAX, W Yorks, HX4 0DW
**Phone** 01422 825084
**Email** maryh@heddwch.u-net.com
**Web** www.heddwch.u-net.com/
*Solo singer of traditional British songs accompanied on English concertina & banjo.*
***Musicians' Union member***
**RAB** Yorkshire Arts

## Mary Macmaster
**Phone** 0131 664 5211
**Email** mymacmaster@hotmail.com
*Scottish small harp player and singer. Member of Sileas and Poozies, currently in Shine.*
***Musicians' Union member***
**AC** Scotland

## Mary MacNamara
**Contact** Kevin Costello
**Mail address** Main Street, TULLA, County Clare, Ireland
**Phone** +353 65 6835314
**Email** mary@marymacnamara.com
**Web** www.marymacnamara.com
*Irish anglo concertina player in the East Clare style.*
**AC** Ireland

## maSamba Samba School
**Contact** Sarah Walker
**Mail address** 30 Bayview Avenue, North Strand, DUBLIN 3, Ireland
**Phone** +353 87 2363813
+353 1 8551838
**Fax** +353 1 6770131
**Email** info@maSamba.com
**Web** www.masamba.com
*Irish 12 piece Latin American percussion group with vocalist. Parades, workshops, etc.*
**AC** Ireland

## Massif Village Orchestra
**Contact** Ian Clabburn
**Mail address** 6 Greyfriars Road, DAVENTRY, Northants, NN11 4RS
**Phone** 01327 705265
**Email** clabburn@sakbut.fsnet.co.uk
**Web** www.vickhast.demon.co.uk/mvohome.htm
*30-40 piece band, playing French dance music on bagpipes, hurdy gurdy, melodeon, etc. Concerts, dances, smaller ensembles, workshops in music and dance.*
**RAB** East England Arts

## Matchless Ceilidh Band
**Contact** Peter Cripps
**Mail address** 22 Severn Way, APPERLEY, Glos, GL19 4DA
**Phone** 01452 780401
**Web** www.geocities.com/broadway/1018
*Barn dance band with PA and callers.*
**RAB** South West Arts

## Matt Armour
**Mail address** 99 Malletts Close, Stony Stratford, MILTON KEYNES, MK11 1DG
**Phone** 01908 566407
*Singer songwriter in Scottish traditional idiom, fisherman's songs a speciality.*
**RAB** Southern Arts

## Matt Seattle
**Mail address** PO Box 13772, PEEBLES, EH45 8YE, Scotland
**Phone/Fax** 01721 724707
**Email** matt@dragonflymusic.co.uk
**Web** www.dragonflymusic.co.uk
*Traditional border piper. Available solo, with cittern player Nigel Richard, with the Border Directors or with Mr MacFall's String Quartet.*
***Musicians' Union member***
**AC** Scotland

## Maurice Dickson
**Mail address** PO Box 59, LISBURN, Co. Antrim, BT28 1FE, N Ireland
**Phone/Fax** 028 92 603296
*Irish singer songwriter and guitarist.*
**AC** Northern Ireland

## Maybug
**Contact** Martyn Oram
**Phone** 01923 672520
07887606214
**Email** maybugfolkrock@yahoo.com
**Web** www.maybug.de
**Alt contact** Walter F Diet
**Alt address** Eningerstrasse 11, 72555 METZINGEN, Germany
**Phone** +49 7123 20881
*5 piece folk rock group.Acoustic & electric guitars, violin, mandolin, bass & drums.*

## The McCalmans
**Contact** Stoneyport Agency
**Web** www.mccalmans.com
*Long-established Scottish group basing their style around 3-part vocal harmony, with & without instruments*
**AC** Scotland

## The McClusky Brothers
**Contact** Active
*Ken & Dave McClusky plus band*

## Mediaeval Baebes
**Contact** The Concert Clinic
**Web** www.concertclinic.com
*Early music with contemporary style*

## Meet On The Ledge
**Contact** Karisma Music Management
**Web** www.karisma.net
*Folk rock band*

## The Mellstock Band
**Contact** Dave Townsend
**Mail address** 22 Swinbourne Road, Littlemore, OXFORD, OX4 4PZ
**Phone** 01865 714778
07798 520552
**Fax** 01865 749428
**Email** mellstock@hotmail.com
*Music and songs of Hardy's Wessex. Concertina, fiddle, oboe, serpant, etc. Themed shows, concerts and dances*
**Agent** Speaking Volumes
***Musicians' Union member***
**RAB** Southern Arts

## Men-an-tol Project
**Contact** Richard C Barton
**Mail address** 2 Barfold, North Mymms, HATFIELD, Herts, AL9 7NG
**Phone** 01707 268923
**Email** menantol.project@talk21.com
*Soloist or band available. Songwriter and mandocello/ octave mandola player. Please contact via email if possible.*
***Musicians' Union member***
**RAB** South East Arts

## Merengada
**Contact** Nina Jaffa
**Mail address** 24B Colless Road, LONDON, N15 4NR
**Phone/Fax** 020 8808 4290
**Phone** 07956 395018
**Email** info@merengada.co.uk
**Web** www.merengada.co.uk
*10 piece merengue/salsa band (2 singers, 3 brass, 3 percussion etc). High energy, festival/ carnival style*
**Agent** mARKO pOLO, Matters Musical
***Musicians' Union member***
**RAB** London Arts

## Metalworks Gamelan
**Contact** Matters Musical
**Web** www.mattersmusical.com
*Mix of Indonesian pop, Sudanese nightclub hits, English church bellringing and new compositions. saxophone, latin percussion, klaxons and voice*

## The Metric Foot Band
**Contact** Sarah Graves
**Mail address** 52 Cross Road, MALDON, Essex, CM9 5EE
**Phone/Fax** 01621 853941
**Email** mickgraves@hotmail.com
*Ceilidh band with own caller, songs and step-clog display.*
**RAB** East England Arts

## Mic Spenceley
**Mail address** 35 Gudge Heath Lane, FAREHAM, Hants, PO15 5AB
**Phone** 01329 822657
**Fax** 01329 329895
**Email** mike-spenceley@lineone.net
*Caller for ceilidhs, barn dances, social dances.*
**RAB** Southern Arts

## Michael Barraclough
**Mail address** 21 Colbert Park, SWINDON, Wilts, SN2 3YJ
**Phone** 01793 700099
07710 806610
**Email** mab@tgis.co.uk
**Web** www.tgis.co.uk/home/mab
*Caller for ceilidhs and barn dances. Lectures and workshops on authentic 17th and 18th century English country dance.*
**RAB** Southern Arts

## Michael Burnham's World Music Ensemble
**Contact** Elizabeth Jones Entertainments
**Web** www.bromyard.co.uk/ejones
*Fiddle player with various outfits appropriate to venue*
**RAB** West Midlands Arts

## Michael Catovsky
**Contact** Hemlock Music
**Web** www.hemlockmusic demon.co.uk
*Caller for beginners to experienced dancers. Contra dances and dance/ calling workshops*
**RAB** London Arts

## Michael Chapman
**Contact** The Blues Line
**Web** www.bluesline.freeserve.co.uk
*Established blues guitarist and singer*

## Michael Hobson and Chris Bright
**Contact** Snapshot Productions
**Mail address** Number 5 , Rear of 32 Buxton Road, High Lane, STOCKPORT, SK6 8BH
**Phone/Fax** 01663 765860
**Phone** 07889 745594
**Email** a6-acts@mighty-micro.co.uk
**Web** www.snapshotproductions.co.uk
*Vocal, guitar and clarinet duo. Emphasis on humour and participation*
**Agent** The A6 Agency
**RAB** North West Arts

## Michael Marra
**Contact** Stoneyport Agency
**Web** www.innercitysound.com
*Scottish singer, with keyboard accompaniment, and writer of unusual poetic songs*

## Michael Raven
**Mail address** 126 Jug Bank, Ashley, MARKET DRAYTON, Shrops, TF9 4NJ
**Phone** 01630 672304
*Guitarist, composer and poet. Workshop leader.*
**RAB** West Midlands Arts

## Michael Roach
**Contact** GTA Music Agency
*Solo acoustic blues*
**Agents** The Blues Line, GTA Music Agency

## Micheal O Suilleabhain
**Contact** Asgard Promotions
*Celebrated composer.*

## Michelle Shocked
**Contact** Primary Talent
*Texan singer songwriter drawing on experiences of nomadic lifestyle*

## Mick Groves
**Mail address** 343 Topsham Road, Countess Wear, EXETER, EX2 6EY
**Phone** 01392 219469
*Solo singer, or with band, music written & collected by Ewan McColl.*
**RAB** South West Arts

## Mick Haywood
**Mail address** 3 Woodwarks Yard, Church Street, WHITBY, N Yorks, YO22 4DG
**Phone** 01947 601963
**Email** mick.angi@btinternet.com
*Traditional ballad monger. Unaccompanied Yorkshire, humorous, drinking and sea songs.*
**RAB** Yorkshire Arts

## Mick Peat
**Mail address** Woodland View, Kirkham Lane, FRITCHLEY, Derbys, DE56 2FS
**Phone** 01773 853428
**Fax** 01773 850000
*Dance caller, MC and workshop leader. Available full time.*
***Musicians' Union member***
**RAB** East Midlands Arts



*Artists in the main A-Z listing are mostly available for concert and club bookings.*


*See page 11 for details of other artist listings (Dance Display, Solo Musicians, Composers, Arrangers, Session Musicians, Band Deps. Lecturers, MCs, Tutors, Street Theatre, Children's Entertainers, Theatre Companies).*

*Agents section appears on pages 119-131.*

*Artists in the main A-Z listing are mostly available for concert and club bookings.*

*See page 11 for details of other artist listings (Dance Display, Solo Musicians, Composers, Arrangers, Session Musicians, Band Deps. Lecturers, MCs, Tutors, Street Theatre, Children's Entertainers, Theatre Companies).*

*Agents section appears on pages 119-131.*

## Mick Ryan and Pete Harris

**Contact** Pete Harris
**Mail address** 154A Locks Road, Locks Heath, SOUTHAMPTON, SO31 6LL
**Phone** 01489 600268
**Email** phas@aol.com
**Web** www.freenetpages.co.uk/hp/trg/scoff/ryhar.htm
**Alt contact** Mick Ryan
**Phone** 01202 392239
*Duo performing traditional and new songs, solo and harmony,with guitar and bouzouki. Available for songwriting workshops.*
**RAB** Southern Arts

## Mike Deavin

**Mail address** 4 Sylvan Court, 102 Holden Road, Woodside Park, LONDON, N12 7ED
**Phone** 020 8446 0718
07831 663660
**Fax** 020 8446 6922
**Email** m.deavin@virgin.net
*Singer, songwriter and guitarist.*
**RAB** London Arts

## Mike Freeman and Tania Opland

Contact The Lighthouse Music Agency
**Web** www.lighthouse-music.co.uk

## Mike Jackson

**Contact** Flying Wombat Music
**Mail address** 11 Margary Street, MOUNT GRAVATT, QLD 4122, Australia
**Phone** +61 7 3343 2423
+61 418 630290
**Fax** 0061 7 3343 2423
**Email** flyingwombatoz@hotmail.com
**Alt contact** c/o Mrs B Jackson
**Alt address** 18 Cromwell Avenue, WOODHALL SPA, Lincolnshire, LN10 6TH
**Phone** 01526 352934
*Entertainer/ educator. Player of 15 instruments, dance caller, juggler, string tricks. Performances & workshops for children & adults.*
***Musicians' Union member***

## Mike O'Connor

**Mail address** Lyngham House, St Ervan, WADEBRIDGE, Cornwall, PL27 7RT
**Phone** 01841 540042
**Email** mikeoconnor@ndirect.co.uk
**Web** www.ndirect.co.uk/~mikeoconnor
*Fiddle player, singer and storyteller. Accompanist and arranger.*
**RAB** South West Arts

## Mike O'Connor and Sarah Morgan

**Contact** Mike O'Connor
**Mail address** Lyngham House, St Ervan, WADEBRIDGE, Cornwall, PL27 7RT
**Phone** 01841 540042
**Email** mikeandsarah@angelfire.com
**Web** www.ahgelfire.com/ms/mikeandsarah
**Alt address** 2 South View Terrace, St Mary Bourne, ANDOVER, Hants, SP11 6BZ
*Traditional duo, 2 voices, fiddle and two concertinas.*
**RAB** South West Arts

## Mike Raven and Joan Mills

**Contact** Michael Raven
**Mail address** 126 Jug Bank, Ashley, MARKET DRAYTON, Shrops, TF9 4NJ
**Phone** 01630 672304
*Duo, vocals and guitar. Traditional and contemporary songs.*
**RAB** West Midlands Arts

## Mike Silver

**Mail address** Tredarrup, Warbstow, LAUNCESTON, Cornwall, PL15 8RL
**Phone** 01566 781667
0771 8116889
**Email** mikes@dial.pipex.co.uk
**Web** www.faymus.co.uk *or* www.gobmusic.co.uk
**Alt contact** Roddy Steele
**Alt address** Good Old Boy Music, 6 Chestnut Way, MEPAL, Cambs, CB6 2YR
**Phone** 01353 777553
**Fax** 01353 777349
**Email** Roddy@gobmusic.co.uk
*Singer, guitarist and songwriter. Session guitarist, vocalist and studio producer*
**Agent** Oscar Music Agency
***Musicians' Union member***
**RAB** South West Arts

## Mike Willoughby

**Mail address** 17 Sun Street, ULVERSTON, Cumbria, LA12 7BX
**Phone/Fax** 01229 588852
**Email** willoughbymj@aol.com
*Cumbrian based singer-songwriter, concerts and workshops. Artist in residence for Radio Cumbria.*
***Musicians' Union member***
**RAB** Northern Arts

## Millrace

**Contact** Alan Hewson
**Mail address** 9 Lister Avenue, HITCHIN, Herts, SG4 9ES
**Phone** 01462 438373
**Fax** 01462 433395/ 421272
**Email** alan@questor-cp.demon.co.uk
4 piece dance band for ceilidhs, barn dances, private functions etc. Caller available.
***Musicians' Union member***
**RAB** East England Arts

## Misericordia

**Contact** Steve Tyler
**Mail address** Brancepeth Castle, BRANCEPETH, Co Durham, DH7 8DE
**Phone** 0191 378 3836
**Email** misericordia@lineone.net
**Web** www.misericordia.netsystem.co.uk
*Medieval music and song, period instruments. Workshops available.*
***Musicians' Union member***
**RAB** Northern Arts

## Monkeydoyles

**Contact** Wendy Grady
**Mail address** Cambridge House, Wensley, MATLOCK, Derbys, DE4 2LH
**Phone** 01629 734793
**Fax** 07811 756809
**Email** wendygrady@hotmail.com
**Web** www.monkeydoyles.freeserve.co.uk
*6 piece band, new and traditional songs & tunes. Celtic folk to Parisian jazz via good time acoustic R 'n B.*
**RAB** East Midlands Arts

## Monkey's Orphan

**Contact** Shanty Jack
**Mail address** 16 The Kingsway, CLEETHORPES, NE Lincs, DN35 8QU
**Phone/Fax** 01472 696757
**Phone** 07970 651293
**Email** morphan@anchorage.f9.co.uk
*Trio specialising in sea songs and shanties. Acappella and with fidlle, mandolin and guitars. Shanty Jack, Robin Garside and Paul Gough.*
***Musicians' Union member***
**RAB** Yorkshire Arts

## Moon & Castle Band

**Contact** Julian Pilling
**Mail address** 126 Railway Street, NELSON, Lancs, BB9 9AL
**Phone** 01282 698366
*4 piece dance band for dances from 1650 to present, including ceili.*
**RAB** North West Arts

## MoonDance
**Contact** Hemlock Music
**Web** www.moondance.org.uk
*5 piece ceilidh band, fiddle, saxophone, bass, drums, guitar.*
**RAB** East England Arts

## Mor
**Contact** Jenny Newman
**Mail address** 17 Bridge Road, Cosgrove, MILTON KEYNES, Bucks, MK19 7JH
**Phone/Fax** 01908 262098
**Phone** 07961 983483
**Email** new.glass@virgin.net
**Web** www.jennynewman.com
*Crossover band; traditional and new tunes with contemporary grooves. Fiddles, guitars, percussion, bass.*
**RAB** East Midlands Arts

## Morris and Dexter Ardoin
**Contact** Access All Areas
*US fiddle and accordion, plus guitar. Cajun and 'Zarico' trio*

## Mo's Barn Dance Parties
**Contact** Maureen Waddington
**Mail address** Mill Cottage, Mill Lane, Weetwood, TARPORLEY, Cheshire, CW6 0NQ
**Phone** 01829 751667
**Web** www.familyband.co.uk
**Alt contact** The Family Band
**Phone** 01244 348473
*Barn dance caller. Musicians available. Also Playford caller.*
**RAB** North West Arts

## Mountain Ash Folk Dance Band
**Contact** Eric Storey
**Mail address** 133 Compass Road, Beverley Road, HULL, HU6 7AW
**Phone** 01482 804962
**Email** ericstorey@folknews.freeserve.co.uk
*Folk dance/ ceilidh band.*
***Musicians' Union member***
**RAB** Yorkshire Arts

## Mouse
**Contact** Martha Tilston
**Mail address** 6 Weston Court, Denmark Road, KINGSTON UPON THAMES, Surrey, KT1 2RX
**Phone** 07974 091012
**Email** mail@mouse.uk.co
**Web** www.mouse.uk.co
**Alt contact** Nick Marshall
**Alt address** 20 Riverside Close, KINGSTONE UPON THAMES, Surrey, KT1 2JF
**Phone** 0771 8762280
*Acoustic duo.*
**RAB** South East Arts

## Moussa Kouyate
**Contact** Meg Roberton
**Mail address** MMM Production Company, The Windmill, Aylesbury Road, WENDOVER, Bucks, HP22 6JJ
**Phone** 01296 620389
0780 3981586
**Fax** 01296 696536
**Email** mmmproduction@talk21.com
**Web** http://moussaweb.speedroad.net
*Senegalese master kora player based in The Gambia, UK tours. Performance, workshops & schools visits. Solo or with UK slide blues guitarist Kevin Brown.*
**RAB** Southern Arts

## The Mrs Ackroyd Band
**Contact** Emerging Music
**Web** www.emerging.demon.co.uk
*Les Barker's band with Chris Harvey, Alison Younger and Hilary Spencer*
**RAB** North West Arts

## Mugenkyo Taiko Drummers
**Contact** Neil Mackie
**Mail address** PO Box 5124, LANARK, ML11 0WA, Scotland
**Phone** 01357 522008
**Email** mail@mugenkyo.com
**Web** www.mugenkyo.com
*European Japanese Taiko group. Energetic, visual performance with choreographed moves*
**Agent** Matters Musical
***Musicians' Union member***
**AC** Scotland

## Mundy-Turner
**Contact** Jacey Bedford Tour Management
**Web** www.jacey-bedford.com
*Anglo-Australian contemporary duo, songwriting and instrumentals*

## Murphy's Marbles
**Contact** Kevin Sauntry
**Mail address** The Haven, Park Lane, CHEDDLETON, Staffs, ST13 7JS
**Phone** 01538 398553
**Alt contact** Dave Shaw
**Phone** 07884 180599
*5 piece Irish band. Flute, fiddle, etc. 5 part harmony.*
**RAB** West Midlands Arts

## Muscadin
**Contact** John Somerscales
**Mail address** 3 Fernhill Close, Kidlington, OXFORD, OX5 1BB
**Phone** 01865 375292
01865 512331
**Alt address** 8 Chestnut Road, Botley, OXFORD
**Phone** 01865 791607
*5 piece acoustic band playing instrumental music from Europe.*
**RAB** Southern Arts

## Music Magic
**Contact** Tim Manning
**Mail address** 12 Bath Road, FROME, Somerset, BA11 2HH
**Phone** 01373 465596
**Email** music.magic@virgin.net
**Web** www.homepage.virgin.net/music.magic
*Musical instrument maker; Hammered dulcimer player.*
**RAB** South West Arts

## Music & Memories
**Contact** Rowena Wilson
**Phone** 01273 772707
*Music & reminiscent performer, songs from 1880-1949 in period costume, working with over 60's, using ukulele, accordion and memorabilia. Sussex area only.*

## Muzsikas featuring Marta Sebestyn
**Contact** Moneypenny
*Hungarian band with acclaimed singer, as featured on the soundtrack to "The English Patient"*

## Myd Wynter Band
**Contact** Damian Clarke
**Mail address** 25 Kings Road, DORCHESTER, Dorset, DT1 1NH
**Phone/Fax** 01305 267510
**Email** mwb@voxpop.demon.co.uk
**Web** www.voxpop.demon.co.uk
*Winter songs and carols. Available December & January only.*
**RAB** South West Arts

## Mystery Juice
**Contact** Stoneyport Agency
**Phone** 0131 6628358
07785 720987
**Email** hmac518996@aol.com
**Web** audiophile.com/mysteryjuice
*Scottish Celtic rock band*
**AC** Scotland

## na Dorsa
**Contact** Paul Bradley
**Mail address** 2 Newtownsmith, GALWAY CITY, Ireland
**Phone** +353 87 6 102030
**Email** paulbradleyireland@yahoo.com
*6 piece Irish new traditional music band*
**Agent** Mutiny Music
**RAB** Ireland

## Nanci Griffiths
**Contact** Asgard Promotions
*Top Texan singer, songwriter crossing the boundaries between folk and country music*



*Artists in the main A-Z listing are mostly available for concert and club bookings.*

*See page 11 for details of other artist listings (Dance Display, Solo Musicians, Composers, Arrangers, Session Musicians, Band Deps. Lecturers, MCs, Tutors, Street Theatre, Children's Entertainers, Theatre Companies).*

*Agents section appears on pages 119-131.*

## artists
## n

*Artists in the main A-Z listing are mostly available for concert and club bookings.*

*See page 11 for details of other artist listings (Dance Display, Solo Musicians, Composers, Arrangers, Session Musicians, Band Deps. Lecturers, MCs, Tutors, Street Theatre, Children's Entertainers, Theatre Companies).*

*Agents section appears on pages 119-131.*

### Nancy Kerr and James Fagan with Tim Van Eyken
**Contact** Emerging Music
**Web** www.emerging.demon.co.uk
*Fiddle, flat-backed bouzouki and song duo, with Young Folk Award Winner, melodeon player and singer*

### Nancy Kerr and James Fagan
**Contact** Emerging Music
**Web** www.emerging.demon.co.uk
*Northumbrian-Australian song and fiddle/flat-backed bouzouki duo. Winners of BBC Folk Music Awards'"Best New Act on the Scene"*

### Napper, Le Faux and Boyle
**Contact** Tom Napper
**Mail address** Flat 2, 2 Woodland View, LEEDS, LS7 4QJ
**Phone** 0113 268 0963
*Fiddles and guitar, mandola, etc with All -Ireland bodhran player Cieran Boyle.*
**RAB** Yorkshire Arts

### Narinder Singh
**Contact** N Kambo
**Mail address** 113 Featherstone Road, SOUTHALL, Middx, UB2 5AQ
**Phone** 07989 355867
**Email** KAMBO121@hotmail.com
*Tabla player, with underground jazz band 'Blowpipe',and with other solo artists.*
**RAB** London Arts

### Natalie MacMaster Band
**Contact** Adastra
**Web** www.adastra-music.com
*Champion Cape Breton fiddler and step dancer with her band*

### Ned O'Grady
**Mail address** 158 Hinckley Road, Leicester Forest East, LEICESTER, LE3 3JT
**Phone** 0116 291 2121
0116 2689301
*Singer/ guitarist, Irish traditional & contemporary songs. Lively, with some ballads. Pubs, clubs, weddings, etc.*
**RAB** East Midlands Arts

### Neelam
**Contact** Neelam Blue Diamond
**Phone** 07946 236511
**Email** berry@neelu95.freeserve.co.uk
**Web** www.neelu95.freeserve.co.uk
*Indian female singer/songwriter. Writes Hindi/ Punjabi lyrics. TV, film, etc. production.Multi-cultural projects.*
***Musicians' Union member***
**RAB** London Arts

### Neil Mulligan
**Mail address** 2 Eachlann Ashington, BAILE ATHA CLIATH 7, Eire
**Phone** +353 1 882 1400
**Fax** +353 1 838 1094
**Email** neillidh@hotmail.com
**Web** http://neillidh.uilleann.nl/
**Email** neillidh@ireland.com
*Uilleann piper, singer and whistle player. Performs solo and in groups. Available for workshops and classes. Contact by email advised.*
**AC** Ireland

### The New House Band
**Contact** Adastra
**Web** www.adastra-music.com
*Well respected UK/USA five piece band, music and songs from celtic countries.*

### New Scorpion Band
**Contact** Tim Laycock
**Mail address** 9 Wingreen View, SHAFTESBURY, Dorset, SP7 8SR
**Email** enquiries@new-scorpion-band.com
**Web** www.new-scorpion-band.com
*5 piece acoustic band playing traditional/historical music and song from the British Isles.*
***Musicians' Union member***
**RAB** South West Arts

### The News of The Victory
**Contact** Derek Paice
**Mail address** 6 The Chase, Tilney St Lawrence, KING'S LYNN, Norfolk, PE34 4RD
**Phone** 01945 881072
07930 430752
**Email** notv@deepmusic.co.uk
*5 piece electric rock/ ceilidh band, including caller. Violin, guitar, bass, drums, percussion. Landline messages picked up throughout the day.*
**RAB** East England Arts

### Next Generation Steel Orchestra
**Contact** Artists Connect
**Web** www.artistsconnect.com
*Welsh steel pan group playing Caribbean tunes to pop songs*

### Niamh Parsons
**Contact** Emerging Music
**Web** www.emerging.demon.co.uk
*Irish singer who recently rediscovered her traditional roots, to great acclaim*

### Nick Harper
**Contact** themusictree. (uk) ltd
**Web** www.nickharper.com
*Fast rising young singer songwriter*
**RAB** London Arts

### Nick Pickett
**Email** nickpi9115@aol.com
*Contemporary singer, guitarist & harmonica player.*
**RAB** London Arts

### Nick Walden
**Phone** 020 7228 3285
*Popular ceilidh caller.*
**RAB** London Arts

### Nigel Close
**Mail address** 1 Beaulieu Cottages, High Street, Twyford, WINCHESTER, Hants, SO21 1RF
**Phone** 01962 714220
07866 837853
**Email** barndance@closetwyford.freeserve.co.uk
**Alt contact** Una Bolton
**Alt address** CONTACTABAND, 14 Portsdown Hill Road, BEDHAMPTON, Hants, PO9 3JY
**Phone** 023 9245 2770
*Caller for ceilidhs/ barn dances. Live or recorded music. Workshops for clubs & festivals in Manx, Welsh, Early English and display dance presentation.*
**RAB** Southern Arts

### Nigel Mazlyn Jones and Ellen Harvey
**Contact** OTB Productions
**Web** www.otbproductions.co.uk
*Classical pianist and 6 & 12 string guitar player/ percussionist duo. Show incorporating songs, poetry and visual projections*

### Nikki Hampson
**Mail address** 2 Towngate, Lepton, HUDDERSFIELD, W Yorks, HD8 0NR
**Phone** 01484 604704
**Email** bedlam@selwynmusic.co.uk
*Caller for ceilidhs and barn dances.*
**RAB** Yorkshire Arts

### No Worries
**Contact** Cliff Baylis
**Mail address** 77 Old Tovil Road, MAIDSTONE, Kent, ME15 6QE
**Phone** 01622 674725
07799 768725
**Email** cliff@folknet.co.uk
**Web** www.folknet.co.uk/noworries
*Trio performing songs and tunes on guitar, whistle, concertina, bodhran. Folk, blues, rags.*
**RAB** South East Arts

### Noel Murphy
**Mail address** The Bricks, MULLION, Cornwall, TR12 7HR
**Phone** 01326 241166
*Long-established folksinger, humorist & storyteller. Vocal and guitar.*
**RAB** South West Arts

## Noise of Minstrels
**Contact** Michael Sargeant
**Mail address** 19 Burke Street, HARROGATE, Yorks, HG1 4NR
**Phone/Fax** 01423 500351
**Phone** 0860 955347
**Email** anlu@globalnet.co.uk
**Web** www.noiseofminstrels.co.uk
**Alt contact** David Chatterley
**Alt address** 94 High Street, TRING, Herts, HP23 4AF
**Phone** 01442 825191
*Early and traditional music on bagpipes, hurdy gurdies, flutes, voices, shawm, percussion, etc. 2-6 players.*
***Musicians' Union member***
**RAB** Yorkshire Arts

## Norma Waterson
**Contact** Moneypenny
*Leading traditional English singer. BBC Radio 2 Folk Singer of the Year 2000. Also in duo with Martin Carthy and in Waterson:Carthy*

## Nostalgia Steel Orchestra
**Contact** Matters Musical
**Web** www.mattersmusical.com
*Formed and still run by Sterling Betancourt. Established 'pan round the neck' steel orchestra*

## Notts Alliance
**Contact** Phil Hardcastle
**Mail address** 31 Flaxfield Close, GROBY, Leics, LE6 0EZ
**Phone** 0116 287 6119
**Email** phil@flaxfield.demon.co.uk
**Web** www.flaxfield.demon.co.uk
**Alt contact** Sid Long
**Alt address** 31 Granville Street, LOUGHBOROUGH, Leics
**Phone** 01509 266103
*Four part all-male a capella group singing a wide range of folk material.*
**RAB** East Midlands Arts

## Nuduo
**Contact** Andy Caven
**Mail address** 20 Meyrick Crescent, COLCHESTER, Essex, CO2 7QY
**Phone** 01206 549582
**Email** andy@andycaven.freeserve.co.uk
**Web** www.andycaven.co.uk
**Alt contact** Robbie Gladwell
**Alt phone** 07785 316116
*Singer & guitarist duo - rock 'n roll, blues & love songs.*
**RAB** East England Arts

## Nuzha
**Contact** mARKO pOLO
**Web** www.markopolo.co.uk
*Vocal and instrumental Arab/Israeli tradition crossover*
**RAB** London Arts

## The O'Cajunal Playboys
**Contact** Elizabeth Jones Entertainments
**Web** www.bromyard.co.uk/ejones
*5 piece Irish/ Cajun band*

## The Occasionals
**Contact** Freeland Barbour
**Mail address** 44 Beauchamp Road, EDINBURGH, EH16 6LU, Scotland
**Phone/Fax** 0131 6661024
**Email** info@castlesound.co.uk
**Web** www.theoccasionals.co.uk
*Scottish ceilidh band. Ceilidhs and concerts, Scottish & Old time. Freeland Barbour, Ian Hardie and Kevin MacLeod.*
***Musicians' Union member***
**AC** Scotland

## Ock 'n' Dough
**Contact** Robin Hillman
**Mail address** 4 Saxon Rise, Earls Barton, NORTHANTS, NN6 0NY
**Phone** 01604 810896
**Email** hillmanimps@talk21.com
**Alt contact** Janis Zakis
**Alt address** 7 Broadlands, RAUNDS, Northants
**Phone** 01933 623172
01933 277717
**Fax** 01933 270277
*English and Latvian folk dance band with own caller. Concerts, including English/ Latvian songs; songs of East Northamptonshire for 'speciality' concerts. See also Doughboy Zydecajun.*
**RAB** East Midlands Arts

## The Oddsods
**Contact** Pete Willow
**Mail address** 57 Heath Lane, BRINKLOW, Warks, CV23 0NR
**Phone** 01788 832608
**Phone/Fax** 07887 552896
**Email** pete@karisma.net
**Web** www.brinklow-57.freeserve.co.uk
*5 piece band playing mainly Irish traditional songs and tunes.*
**RAB** West Midlands Arts

## Odetta
**Contact** mARKO pOLO
**Web** www.markopolo.co uk
*Renowned blues singer with pianist*

## Official Brawl
**Contact** Steve Harrison
**Mail address** Blakeclough, Shaw Lane, Slaithwaite, HUDDERSFIELD, Yorks, HD7 5XA
**Phone** 01484 844055
**Email** gamut@dial.pipex.com
*Ceilidh/ barn dance band with caller. Includes melodeon, pipes, horns, percussion, etc.*
**RAB** Yorkshire Arts

## Ogam
**Contact** Emyr Rhys
**Mail address** 12 Lon Arfon, CAERNARFON, Gwynedd, LL55 2ER
**Phone** 01286 677140
07787 543298
**Email** emyrrhys@onetel.net.uk
**Alt contact** Sianelen Pleming
**Alt address** Blwch y Mynydd, LLITHFAEN, Gwynedd
**Phone** 01758 750462
**Email** fsifan@kpleming.freeserve.co.uk
*5 piece Welsh folk group. Harp, guitar, fiddle, flute, vocals, etc.*
***Musicians' Union member***
**AC** Wales

## Old Blind Dogs
**Contact** Artistic Upstarts
**Web** members.xoom.com/oldblinddogs
*5 piece upbeat Scottish band*
**Agents** Artistic Upstarts, Stoneyport Agency
**AC** Scotland

## Old Friends
**Contact** Dave Illingworth
**Mail address** 87 Palmerston Road, Wimbledon, LONDON, SW19 1PB
**Phone** 020 8540 2919
*Vocal folk song duo plus some tunes.*
**RAB** London Arts

## Old Friends Ceilidh Band
**Contact** Mike Kermode
**Mail address** 60 Soutergate, Ulverston, Cumbria, LA12 7ES
**Phone** 01229 582704
**Email** Kmode@onetel.net.uk
*Band plays traditional Lake District and Cumbrian music.*
**RAB** Northern Arts

## Old Hat
**Contact** Katie Howson
**Mail address** 44 Old Street, Haughley, STOWMARKET, Suffolk, IP14 3NX
**Phone** 01449 673695
**Email** katie@veteran.co.uk
*7 piece English ceilidh band.*
***Musicians' Union member***
**RAB** East England Arts



*Artists in the main A-Z listing are mostly available for concert and club bookings.*

*See page 11 for details of other artist listings (Dance Display, Solo Musicians, Composers, Arrangers, Session Musicians, Band Deps. Lecturers, MCs, Tutors, Street Theatre, Children's Entertainers, Theatre Companies).*

*Agents section appears on pages 119-131.*

*Artists in the main A-Z listing are mostly available for concert and club bookings.*

*See page 11 for details of other artist listings (Dance Display, Solo Musicians, Composers, Arrangers, Session Musicians, Band Deps. Lecturers, MCs, Tutors, Street Theatre, Children's Entertainers, Theatre Companies).*

*Agents section appears on pages 119-131.*

## Old Parrot Band
**Contact** Penny Sykes
**Mail address** Emmanuel Cottage, Starlode Drove, West Pinchbeck, SPALDING, Lincs, PE11 3TD
**Phone** 01775 640476
**Email** john@jsykes.freeserve.co.uk
**Web** www.jsykes.freeserve.co.uk
**Alt contact** Paul Dickinson
**Phone** 01775 723026
**Email** deadparrot@clara.co.uk
*Ceilidh and song band. New tunes and mostly Lincs songs. Sax, keyboard, fiddle, etc.*
**RAB** East Midlands Arts

## Old Rope String Band
**Contact** Joe Scurfield
**Mail address** 2 Wellesley Terrace, NEWCASTLE UPON TYNE, Tyne & Wear
**Phone** 0191 272 3867
07867 805634
**Alt contact** Tim Dalling
**Alt address** 2 Stratford Grove, West Heaton, NEWCASTLE UPON TYNE, NE6 5BB
**Phone** 0191 2651708
**Email** annietimcd@hotmail.com
*Musical comedy trio combining traditional music and eccentric antics.*
**Agent** Adastra
***Musicians' Union member***
**RAB** Northern Arts

## The Old School Ceilidh Band
**Contact** Phil Armitage
**Mail address** 9 St Mary's Close, PRESTON, Lancs, PR1 4XN
**Phone** 01772 490579
*4 piece ceilidh band with caller.*
***Musicians' Union member***
**RAB** North West Arts

## Old Swan Band
**Contact** Jo Freya
**Mail address** 95 Laurie Avenue, Forest Fields, NOTTINGHAM, NG7 6PH
**Phone/Fax** 0115 9782642
**Phone** 07900 215419
**Email** freya@mcmail.com
**Alt contact** Fi Fraser
**Alt address** 10 Moor Rise, HOLBROOK, Derbys, DE56 0TR
**Phone** 01332 883472
**Email** fifraser@coopefamily.demon.co.uk
*8 piece band playing traditional and new tunes for dancing. Driven by 3 fiddles, 3 piece brass section and rhythm.*
***Musicians' Union member***
**RAB** East Midlands Arts

## The Oldham Tinkers
**Contact** John Howarth
**Mail address** 13 Verney Road, Royton, OLDHAM, Lancs, OL2 6AZ
**Phone** 0161 624 0008
*3 piece traditional folk group. Songs and poetry from Lancashire with classical guitar, banjo, mandolin concertina and whistle.*
***Musicians' Union member***
**RAB** North West Arts

## Orquesta Cache
**Contact** mARKO pOLO
**Web** www.markopolo.co.uk
*Salsa show, available from a trio to 10 piece*

## Orquesta Huracan
**Contact** Access All Areas
**Web** www.oh-latinmusic.com
*9 piece Latin orchestra with horn section. Salsa dance and percussion workshops available*

## Orquesta La Clave
**Contact** Matters Musical
**Web** www.mattersmusical.com
*11 piece Latin band including brass and 2 singers*

## Otra Vez
**Contact** Matters Musical
**Web** www.mattersmusical.com
*5 piece Latin American music incl. African drums and Iberian strings*

## Our Lady and The Apostles
**Contact** Paul Hutchinson
**Mail address** Upper Cefn-Y-Pwll, Abermule, MONTGOMERY, Powys, SY15 6JN, Wales
**Phone** 01686 630419
**Email** welshpaul@lineone.net
*Ceilidh band (Flos Headford, Alan Harris & Paul Hutchinson). Caller: Shelia Mainwaring.*
**AC** Wales

## The Oxford Waits
**Contact** Tim Healey
**Mail address** PO Box 1039, OXFORD, OX1 4UA
**Phone** 01865 249194
**Fax** 01865 792765
**Email** info@bejo.co.uk
**Web** www.bejo.co.uk
*1-8 piece 17th century costume band; lute, fiddle, pipes, hurdy-gurdy and more.*
**RAB** Southern Arts

## Oysterband
**Contact** The Concert Clinic
**Web** www.oysterband.co.uk
*Celebrated five piece folk rock band with large dedicated following. Mail order from runningman@oysterband.co.uk*

## Pamela Ward
**Mail address** Providence House, Brooks House, Brooks Road, RAUNDS, Northants, NN9 6NS
**Phone** 01933 624963
**Fax** 01933 625458
**Email** pam@pamelaward.co.uk
**Web** www.pamelaward.co.uk
*Singer/ guitarist, traditional and contemporary songs.*
**RAB** East Midlands Arts

## Papa Schnitzel
**Contact** Matters Musical
**Web** www.mattersmusical.com
*3 to 8 piece costumed Bavarian barn dance band*

## Paradise Steel Band
**Contact** Matters Musical
**Web** www.mattersmusical.com
*8 core members, expanding for venue. Traditional steel pan, electric backing group avaiable*

## Paris Moon
**Contact** Matters Musical
**Web** www.mattersmusical.com
*2-3 piece French café style band*

## Patricia Carron-Smith
**Mail address** 1 Ty Clwyta Cottages, Cross Inn, LLANTRISANT, Rhondda Cynon Taf, CF72 8AZ, Wales
**Phone/Fax** 01443 226892
**Email** patsmith@folkwales.org.uk
**Web** www.folkwales.org.uk
*Caller for Welsh dances. Available with Calennig and other bands.*
**AC** Wales

## Patrick Dunbar
**Mail address** Pengwern Fach, Penrherber, NEWCASTLE EMLYN, Carmarthenshire, SA38 9RL
**Phone** 01239 710098
**Email** DunbarClanUK@tesco.net
*Highland bagpiper. Also smallpipe player.*
***Musicians' Union member***
**AC** Wales

## Patrick Street
**Contact** Adastra
**Web** www.adastra-music.com
*Highly acclaimed four piece Irish band featuring Andy Irvine, Kevin Burke, Jackie Daly and Ged Foley.*
**AC** Ireland

## Pat Ryan
**Mail address** 45 Little Scotland, Blackrod, Bolton BL6 5LW
**Email** pat@littlescotland.freeserve.co.uk
*Fine singer of trad. & contemporary material.*

## Patterson - Jordan - Dipper
**Contact** James Patterson
**Mail address** 33 Burton Road, ASHBY DE LA ZOUCHE, Leics, LE65 2LF
**Phone** 01530 563245
**Email** jm.patterson@ntlworld.com
*Trio combining variety of traditional songs with contemporary material & range of European tunes. Roots & approach firmly in the English tradition*
**RAB** East Midlands Arts

## Paul Boizot
**Mail address** 9 Sturton Road, SHEFFIELD, S4 7DE
**Phone** 0114 256 1708
**Email** paulboizot@synergynet.co.uk
*Circle dance teacher. Session musician; vocals, bouzouki, drum. East European folk music/ circle dance band available.*
**RAB** Yorkshire Arts

## Paul Brady
**Contact** Asgard Promotions
*Celebrated Irish singer & songwriter*

## Paul Brennan Band
**Contact** Matters Musical
**Web** www.irishmusic.fsbusiness.co.uk
*Traditional Irish singer and uillean piper*

## Paul Culkin
**Mail address** 1 Granville Terrace, Lawrence Street, YORK, YO10 3DY
**Phone** 01904 416557
**Email** user@culkin.fsnet.co.uk
*Ukulele, voice, guitar, own compositions, music hall and ragtime.*
**RAB** Yorkshire Arts

## Paul Dickinson and Angela King
**Contact** Paul Dickinson
**Mail address** 26 Holland Road, SPALDING, Lincs, PE11 1UL
**Phone** 01775 723026
**Email** deadparrot@clara.co.uk
*Vocal harmony duo with guitar/ concertina. Traditional and contemporary.*
**RAB** East England Arts

## Paul Downes
**Contact** Elizabeth Jones Entertainments
**Web** www.bromyard.co.uk/ejones
*Singer/ songwriter*

## Paul Heron
**Contact** The Bechhofer Agency

## Paul James
**Mail address** 60 High Street, HUNGERFORD, Berks, RG17 0NE
**Phone** 01488 686039
07887 948853
**Email** info@pauljamesmusic.com
**Web** www.pauljamesmusic.com
*Musician, composer, arranger, playing British & European music. Saxophones, bagpipes and traditional woodwind/ reeds. Producer of traditional & contemporary music.*
**RAB** Southern Arts

## Paul Jones and Dave Kelly
**Contact** GTA Music Agency
*Acoustic blues duo*

## Paul Scourfield and Michael Davidson
**Contact** Paul Scourfield
**Mail address** 9 Victoria Road, HITCHIN, Herts, SG5 2LS
**Phone** 01462 458031
**Email** pscourfield@mac-river.co.uk
**Web** www.peoplesound.com/artist/ paulscourfieldmichaeldavidson
*Traditional & original tunes & songs from UK, France, etc. on melodeon, guitar and fiddle. Music workshops in schools*
**RAB** East England Arts

## Paula Smith
**Contact** Cauldron Music
**Mail address** Cahermakerla, LISDOONVARNA, County Clare, Ireland
**Phone** +353 65 707 4822
**Email** pauladsmith@eircom.net
**Web** www.cauldronmusic.com
**Alt contact** Paula Smith
**Alt address** White Lodge, 5 Bexmoor Way, OLD BASING, Hants, RG24 7BL
**Phone** 01256 810555
**Fax** 01256 323057
*Singer of Irish songs accompanied by Celtic harp. Also keyboards, guitar and woodwind.*
***Musicians' Union member***
**AC** Ireland

## Pauline Cato and Tom McConville
**Contact** Tomcat Music
**Mail address** PO Box 2100, SHEFFIELD, Yorks, S36 9BW
**Phone** 01535 658392
**Fax** 01226 370640
**Email** concerts@tomcatmusic.com
**Web** www.tomcatmusic.com
*Established duo playing Northumbrian pipes, fiddle and song. Traditional & contemporary reportoire.*
***Musicians' Union member***
**RAB** Yorkshire Arts

## Pavlov's Cat
**Contact** James Hibbins
**Mail address** 19 Priory Street, COLCHESTER, CO1 2QA
**Phone** 07798 752148
01206 514360
**Email** james@pavlovscat.net
**Web** www.pavlovscat.net
**Alt contact** Darren Tansley
**Alt address** 25 Mill Road, COLCHESTER
**Phone** 01206 510023
**Email** natureboy@ntlworld.com
*Contemporary folk band with English feel. Based around the songs of singer/ guitarist James Hibbins.*
**RAB** East England Arts

## PDP
**Contact** Kerry Fletcher
**Mail address** 80 Ryarsh Road, BIRLING, Kent, ME19 5JR
**Phone/Fax** 01732 849163
**Phone** 07703 639720
**Email** kerryfletcher@bigfoot.com
*3 piece percussion and step dance ensemble.*
**RAB** South East Arts

## The Peace Artistes
**Contact** Matters Musical
**Web** www.mattersmusical.com
*Street band blending African, salsa, folk and funk*

## The Pearlfishers
**Contact** Active
*Scottish pop.*

## Peatbog Faeries
**Contact** Martin Coull Music Management
*Danceable Scottish fusion from the Isle of Skye*

## Peeping Tom
**Contact** Ben Woodward
**Mail address** 76 Highland Road, Earlsdon, COVENTRY, CV5 6GR
**Phone** 024 7671 1924
024 7667 4491
**Fax** 024 7671 1191
**Email** peepingtom@btinternet.com
**Alt contact** Graham Bradshaw
**Alt address** 250 Earlsdon Avenue North, COVENTRY, CV5 6GX
**Phone** 024 7671 1935
**Email** rootsrecs@btclick.com
*Long established and popular five piece folk-rock ceilidh band. Melodeon led with keyboard, strings, drums, etc.*
**RAB** West Midlands Arts



*Artists in the main A-Z listing are mostly available for concert and club bookings.*

*See page 11 for details of other artist listings (Dance Display, Solo Musicians, Composers, Arrangers, Session Musicians, Band Deps. Lecturers, MCs, Tutors, Street Theatre, Children's Entertainers, Theatre Companies).*

*Agents section appears on pages 119-131.*

artists

p

Artists in the main A-Z listing are mostly available for concert and club bookings.

See page 11 for details of other artist listings (Dance Display, Solo Musicians, Composers, Arrangers, Session Musicians, Band Deps. Lecturers, MCs, Tutors, Street Theatre, Children's Entertainers, Theatre Companies).

Agents section appears on pages 119-131.

## Peggy Seeger
**Mail address** NEM Productions (UK)
**Web** www.nemproductions.com
*Renowned American songwriter, singer and activist*

## Penni Blythe
**Mail address** Alderhay, Fairclose, COMBE ST NICHOLAS, Somerset, TA20 3LU
**Phone/Fax** 01460 61969
**Email** penni@ccchange.clara.net
*Traditional solo unaccompanied singer.*
**RAB** South West Arts

## Penny & Stuart Mack
**Mail address** 4 Wellington Road, LOWESTOFT, Suffolk, NR33 7AL
**Phone** 07980 504739
*Contemporary and traditional songs with guitar and bodhran*

## Pesky
**Contact** Anna Tabbush
**Mail address** 70 Burnthill Road, Lower Bourne, FARNHAM, Surrey, GU103LN
**Phone/Fax** 01252 722938
**Phone** 07989 556164
**Email** pesky@treehugger.com
**Alt contact** Holly Sheldrake
**Alt address** 33 Pine Avenue, HASTINGS, E Sussex, TN34 3PP
**Phone** 020 8870 4757
07759 590951
*3 piece traditional concert & ceilidh band. Workshops in French dance, vocal harmony and percussion.*
**RAB** South East Arts

## Peta Webb and Ken Hall
**Contact** Peta Webb
**Mail address** 52 Cecile Park, LONDON, N8 9AS
**Phone** 020 8340 0530
**Email** petawebken@aol.com
*Traditional acapella duo, songs and duets from Britain, Ireland & America.*
**RAB** London Arts

## Peta Webb, Ken Hall and Simon Hindley
**Contact** Peta Webb
**Mail address** 52 Cecile Park, LONDON, N8 9AS
**Phone** 020 8340 0530
**Email** petawebken@aol.com
*Vocal duo plus blues guitarist/ singer. American country music, country blues and brother duets.*
***Musicians' Union member***
**RAB** London Arts

## Pete Berryman
**Mail address** Hill Cottage, Lanwithan Road, LOSTWITHIEL, Cornwall, PL22 0LA
**Phone** 01208 873904
*Guitarist, composer, singer, songwriter, arranger, Cornish traditional music. Guitar teacher. Solo, duo & band.*
***Musicians' Union member***
**RAB** South West Arts

## Pete Castle
**Mail address** 190 Burton Road, DERBY, DE1 1TQ
**Phone** 01332 346399
**Email** steelcarpet@lineone.net
**Web** www.folkmusic.net/petecastle
*Folk singer, storyteller & community musician. Mainly English traditional stories & songs with guitar. Available solo or as a duo with fiddler Lucy Castle.Workshop leader inc. schools.*
***Musicians' Union member***
**RAB** East Midlands Arts

## Pete Coe
**Mail address** 103 Oldham Road, RIPPONDEN, West Yorks, HX6 4EB
**Phone/Fax** 01422 822 569
**Email** petecoe@backshift.demon.co.uk
**Web** www.backshift.demon.co.uk/petehome.htm
*One man folk industry! Singer and bouzouki/ banjo/ melodeon/ feet/ dulcimer player. Dance caller & musician. Schools projects.*
***Musicians' Union member***
**RAB** Yorkshire Arts

## Pete Cooper
**Mail address** 3 Astra House, Mount Pleasant Villas, LONDON, N4 4HB
**Phone** 020 8340 7760
**Email** petecooperfiddle@hotmail.com
*Solo fiddle player and singer of traditional and new music. Workshop leader for fiddle (various styles).*
***Musicians' Union member***
**RAB** London Arts

## Pete Cooper and Richard Bolton
**Contact** Pete Cooper
**Mail address** 3 Astra House, Mount Pleasant Villas, LONDON, N4 4HB
**Phone** 020 8340 7760
**Email** petecooperfiddle@hotmail.com
*Performers of traditional and new acoustic music (incl song) on fiddle and cello.*
***Musicians' Union member***
**RAB** London Arts

## Pete Durber
**Contact** Peter Durber
**Mail address** 30 Spinney Drive, Kirby Grange, BOTCHESTON, Leics, LE9 9FG
**Phone/Fax** 01455 824125
07768 312199
**Email** pdurber@compuserve.com
*Caller for ceilidhs, barn dances and American squares*
**Agent** Midland Barndance Agency
**RAB** East Midlands Arts

## Pete Glyde
**Mail address** Hill House, 471 Burton Road, Midway, SWADLINCOTE, Derbys, DE11 7NB
**Phone** 01283 218233
**Email** peterglyde@moonrise.free-online.co.uk
**Web** www.peterglyde.co.uk
*Singer and guitarist. Traditional and unaccompanied.*
***Musicians' Union member***
**RAB** East Midlands Arts

## Pete Grassby
**Mail address** 22 Derwent Road, Whitmore Park, COVENTRY, W Midlands, CV6 2HB
**Phone** 024 7633 6740
07768 683015
*Folk dance caller, band available. Mainly traditional unaccompanied singer, melodeon and dulcimer player.*
**RAB** West Midlands Arts

## Pete Jennings
**Mail address** 12 Carleton Close, GT YELDHAM, Essex, CO9 4QJ
**Phone/Fax** 01787 238257
07778 366469
**Email** pete@gippeswic.demon.co.uk
**Web** www.gippeswic.demon.co.uk
**Alt address** BBC Radio Suffolk, St Matthews Street, IPSWICH, Suffolk, IP1 3EP
*Festival and concert compere. Sings & plays bones/ bodhran. Talks on folk traditions. Presents 'Suffolk Folk' for BBC Radio Suffolk.*
**RAB** East England Arts

## Pete Lockett
**Phone** 07976 426773
**Email** pete@perc.fsnet.co.uk
**Web** www.petelockett.com
*Percussionist:traditional drumming from cultures worldwide and contemporary styles. Live and studio.*

Artists in the main A-Z listing are mostly available for concert and club bookings.

See page 11 for details of other artist listings (Dance Display, Solo Musicians, Composers, Arrangers, Session Musicians, Band Deps. Lecturers, MCs, Tutors, Street Theatre, Children's Entertainers, Theatre Companies).

Agents section appears on pages 119-131.

## Pete Morton
**Contact** themusictree. (uk) ltd
**Web** www.rootsworld.com/harbourtown
*Solo singer and songwriter. Also traditional material, mainly English & Scottish*
***Musicians' Union member***
**RAB** East Midlands Arts

## Pete Oakley
**Mail address** 46 Station St, BURTON UPON TRENT, Staffs, DE14 1AX
**Phone** 01283 500366
07887 993838
**Fax** 01283 500365
**Email** pete@guitarsuperstore.com
**Web** www.peteoakley.com
*Folk/ Blues recording artist and performer. Guitar and vocals.*
**RAB** West Midlands Arts

## Pete Shaw
**Mail address** 35 Hartford Court, BEDLINGTON, Northumberland, NE22 6LP
**Phone** 01670 369905
07774 604585
**Fax** 0191 212 0033
**Email** mesymusic@hotmail.com
*Singer/songwriter with folk/blues influences*
**RAB** Northern Arts

## Pete Stanley and Brian Golbey
**Contact** Pete Stanley
**Mail address** 15 Torriano Avenue, LONDON, NW5 2SN
**Phone** 020 7916 4178
0115 922 5392
**Email** golbey@swamp-opera.freeserve.co.uk
**Web** www.swamp-opera.freeserve.co.uk
*Acoustic string band; Bluegrass and Old Time. Banjo, fiddle and guitar.*
**RAB** London Arts

## Peter Barnard
**Mail address** 1 Battle Green, Epworth, DONCASTER, DN9 1JT
**Phone** 01427 873937
**Email** peter_barnard.squeeze@virgin.net
*Folk dance caller.*
**RAB** East Midlands Arts

## Peter Buckley-Hill
**Mail address** 31 Fortess Road, LONDON, NW5 1AD
**Phone** 0207 267 8459
07421 463333
**Email** buckers@pbh.clara.net
**Web** www.pbh.clara.net
*Comic songs about small furry animals, wheelclampers, etc.*
**RAB** London Arts

## Peter Knight and Felicity Buirski
**Contact** Elizabeth Jones Entertainments
**Web** www.bromyard.co.uk/ejones
*Violinist/ keyboard player from Steeleye Span, with singer/ songwriter/ poet*

## Peter Mayes
**Mail address** 24b Bedford Grove, EASTBOURNE, Sussex, BN21 2DU
**Phone** 01323 642116
**Email** pjmayes@sniffout.com
**Email** letsmakemusic99@hotmail.com
*Caller, workshop leader for social, morris and sword dance. Band tutor.*
**RAB** South East Arts

## Peter Mulvey
**Contact** Young/Hunter Management (USA)
**Phone** 00 1 781 643 2773
**Email** carol@younghunter.com
**Web** www.petermulvey.com
*American singer songwriter with funk, folk and rock influences.*

## Peter Quinn
**Mail address** 205A Eltham High Street, LONDON, SE9 1TS
**Phone** 020 8480 8164
07953 543976
**Email** PeterQuinn@ireland.com
*Pianist/ keyboard player with traditional Irish group "The London Lasses". Also plays fiddle and bodhran.*
***Musicians' Union member***
**RAB** London Arts

## Peter Wood
**Mail address** 6 Welburn Close, OVINGHAM, Northumberland, NE42 6BD
**Phone** 01661 832705
0191 515 2514
**Email** peter.wood@sunderland.ac.uk
*Singer & musician, mostly traditional English concertina, fiddle & keyboard.*
**RAB** Northern Arts

## Peter Wyton
**Contact** The Blues Line
**Web** www.bluesline.freeserve.co.uk
*Performance poet*
**RAB** South West Arts

## Ph. B
**Contact** Matters Musical
**Web** www.mattersmusical.com
*Trio playing Celtic, jazz and blues on harmonica, fiddle and guitar*
**RAB** London Arts

## Phase Space
**Contact** Matters Musical
**Web** www.mattersmusical.com
*Jazz, East European, funk, Brazilian and Cuban fusion band*

## Phil Bates
**Contact** Elizabeth Jones Entertainments
**Web** www.bromyard.co.uk/ejones
*Ex ELO singer/ songwriter/ guitarist*
**Agent** Elizabeth Jones Entertainments, Karisma Music Management

## Phil Berthoud
**Mail address** 125 Exe Hill, TORQUAY, Devon, TQ2 7RG
**Phone** 01803 614978
**Email** phil@berthoudmusic.co.uk
*Fiddle/mandolin/guitar player. Mainly Celtic styles. Composer/ arranger and teacher of above instruments.*
***Musicians' Union member***
**RAB** South West Arts

## Phil Brown
**Contact** Big Whistle Music
**Mail address** PO Box 23, ACCRINGTON, Lancs, BB5 5GX
**Phone/Fax** 01254 397623
**Phone** 07976 809623
**Email** phil@bigwhistle.co.uk
**Web** www.bigwhistle.co.uk
*Player of high and low whistles. Specialist supplier of instruments & materials. Workshops.*
**RAB** North West Arts

## Philippe Barnes
**Mail address** 59 Wish Road, HOVE, Sussex, BN3 4LN
**Phone** 07989 950622
**Email** philippe@alljiggedout.co.uk
**Web** www.philippebarnes.co.uk
*Flute player, multi-instrumentalist and composer. Irish and other traditional music, flamenco-jazz.*
***Musicians' Union member***
**RAB** South East Arts

## The Picts
**Contact** Active
*Orginally a ceilidh act, now fusing modern celtic sounds with own material*

## Pied Piper Folk Dance Band
**Contact** Cyril Swales
**Mail address** 5 Osgodby Hall Road, SCARBOROUGH, Yorks, YO11 3PX
**Phone** 01723 582681
*4-6 piece barn dance band with caller.*
**RAB** Yorkshire Arts

## Pierre Bensusan
**Contact** NEM Productions (UK)
**Web** www.nemproductions.com
*Respected French guitarist*

*Artists in the main A-Z listing are mostly available for concert and club bookings.*

*See page 11 for details of other artist listings (Dance Display, Solo Musicians, Composers, Arrangers, Session Musicians, Band Deps. Lecturers, MCs, Tutors, Street Theatre, Children's Entertainers, Theatre Companies).*

*Agents section appears on pages 119-131.*

## Pierre Le Rue

**Contact** Adastra
**Web** www.adastra-music.com
*New Orleans, Cajun, R&B dance music, etc*
**Agent** Adastra, Swamp Music

## The Pierre Schryer Band

**Contact** Emerging Music
**Web** www.emerging.demon.co.uk
*All Canadian fiddle Champion and his band*

## Pierrot

**Contact** Peter Barnard
**Mail address**1 Battle Green, Epworth, DONCASTER, Yorks, DN9 1JT
**Phone** 01427 873937
**Email** peter_barnard.squeeze@virgin.net
*Band playing French and English folk dance music with caller. Workshops available.*
**RAB** East Midlands Arts

## Pigeon Toes Ceilidh Band

**Contact** Clive Tiarney
**Mail address**17 Windermere, Stukeley Meadows, HUNTINGDON, Cambs
**Phone** 01480 413347
*Ceilidh band with caller.*
***Musicians' Union member***
**RAB** East England Arts

## Pigs Might Fly

**Contact** Richard Mason
**Mail address** 3 Kingfisher Drive, EXETER, Devon, EX4 4SN
**Phone** 01392 213499
**Email** Richard_Mason@multilex.com
**Alt contact** Julie Spiller
**Email** jspiller@fire-stone.freeserve.co.uk
*Barn dance/ ceilidh and concert band. British, American, European tunes and songs.*
**RAB** South West Arts

## Pigyn Clust

**Contact** Idris M Jones
**Mail address** Benallt, Llanwnda, CAERNARFON, Gwynedd, LL54 5SD, Wales
**Phone** 01286 831762
01523 170898 - pager
**Email** info@pigyn-clust.co.uk
**Web** www.pigyn-clust.co.uk
**Alt contact** Cass Meurig
**Alt address**Allt Goch, Cwm Y Glo, LLANBERIS, Gwynedd, LL55 4DW
**Phone** 01286 871042
*5 piece band playing Welsh language songs & traditionaltunes. 2 fiddles, guitar & crwth.*
**AC** Wales

## Piotr Jordan

**Contact** Matters Musical
**Web** www.mattersmusical.com
*Violinist playing orchestral, baroque, country, Eastern European and Irish folk and jazz with piano, guitar, bass and female vocalist*

## Pomegranate

**Contact** Tara Mackenney
**Email** pomegranatefansite@hotmail.com
**Web** www.geocities.com/pomegranatefansite
*Solo singer and storyteller. Mouth Music for dancing, traditional ballads. Workshop leader.*
***Musicians' Union member***
**RAB** London Arts

## The Poozies

**Contact** Stoneyport Agency
**Web** www.stoneyport.demon.co.uk
*Very popular four piece female ensemble with harps, fiddle, accordion & close vocal harmony. Scots/ Irish with Scandanavian and English influences.*
***Musicians' Union member***

## Popa Chubby

**Contact** mARKO pOLO
**Web** www.markopolo.co.uk
*Blues guitarist with band*

## The Popes

**Contact** Moneypenny
*Raucous mix of Irish traditional and Indie music*

## Port and Brandy

**Contact** Pearl O'Neill
**Mail address** 31 Comet Way, Woodley, READING, Berks, RG5 4NZ
**Phone** 0118 944 8269
**Email** tonyandpearl@redadmiral.freeserve.com.uk
*Female vocal duo. Mainly contemporary songs in a traditional style.*
**RAB** Southern Arts

## The Posh Band

**Contact** Ken Lees
**Mail address** 100 Beech Hall Road, LONDON, E4 9NX
**Phone/Fax** 020 8527 8419
**Email** poshband@clara.co.uk
**Web** www.poshband.clara.net
**Alt contact** Simon Ritchie
**Alt address** Goldens Farm, Boyton End, THAXTED, Essex, CM6 2RB
**Phone** 01371 830804
**Email** simon.ritchie@btinternet.com
*Traditional style English country dance band for dances and concerts including songs, tunes and step dancing.*
**RAB** South East Arts

## Prego

**Contact** Ian Smith
**Mail address** 1 Holme Road, MATLOCK BATH, Derbys, DE4 3NU
**Phone** 07976 206568
01629 57082
**Email** pregosmith@hotmail.com
**Web** www.pregomusic.co.uk
*7 piece European/ global roots dance and concert band.Available from 3 piece up. Instrumental and dance workshops*
**Agent** Matters Musical
***Musicians' Union member***
**RAB** East Midlands Arts

## Pressgang

**Contact** Vox Pop
*Trad/contemporary, with songs*
**RAB** South West Arts

## Providence

**Contact** mARKO pOLO
**Web** www.markopolo.co.uk
*Dublin-based band including members of the Fallen Angels, Arcady and Sean Keane Band*
**AC** Ireland

## The Pugwash Band

**Contact** Bo Foaks
**Mail address** 18 The Glebe, Bidborough, TUNBRIDGE WELLS, Kent, TN3 0UR
**Phone** 01892 547660
**Email** pugwashband@folk.co.uk
**Web** www.folknet.co.uk/pugwashband.htm
**Alt contact** Cliff Baylis
**Alt address** 77 Old Tovil Road, MAIDSTONE, Kent, ME15 6QE
**Phone/Fax** 01622 674725
**Phone** 07799 768797
**Email** cliff@folknet.co.uk
*6 piece ceilidh band, based in the South East.*
**RAB** South East Arts

## Punita Gupta
**Contact** Matters Musical
**Web** www.mattersmusical.com
*Indian classical sitar player and vocalist, Punita has studied with Ravi Shankar for the past 24 years. Also teaches*

## Quicksilver
**Contact** Matters Musical
**Web** www.mattersmusical.com
*Barn dance and ceilidh band*
**RAB** Southern Arts

## Quimantu
**Contact** Rachel Pantin
**Mail address** 113 Ridley Road, LONDON, E8 2NH
**Phone/Fax** 020 7690 9128
**Email** rachel@rkpantin.freeserve.co.uk
*London based South American music group.*
***Musicians' Union member***
**RAB** London Arts

## R Cajun and The Zydeco Brothers
**Contact** Adastra
**Web** www.adastra-music.com
*7 piece long established major league Cajun band led by Chris Hall's accordion*
**Agents** Adastra, Matters Musical, Swamp Music
**RAB** East Midlands Arts

## Rab Noakes
**Contact** The Bechhofer Agency
*UK songwriter and performer*
***Musicians' Union member***

## Rachel and Common Ground
**Contact** Mark Heffer Manager
**Phone** 07771 925375
01872 276228
**Email** mark@commonground.fsbusiness.co.uk
**Web** www.rachelandcommonground.cjb.net
**Alt contact** Terry Wallwork - Songwriter
**Phone** 01872 241845
*5 piece folk rock band. Guitars, harp, bass, drums. Celtic/ world influences.*
***Musicians' Union member***
**RAB** South West Arts

## Rachel Laurence
**Mail address** 39 Park Avenue, Histon, CAMBRIDGE, CB4 9JU
**Phone** 01223 237843
**Email** rachellaurence@tinyonline.co.uk
*Teacher and performer of an eclectic mix of music for fiddle, viola and voice.*
**RAB** East England Arts

## Radio Sweethearts
**Contact** Active
*Scottish band playing a 'honky tonk country' and bluegrass blend*

## Rag Foundation
**Contact** Kaye Roncon Woollard
**Mail address** 555 Gower Road, Upper Killay, SWANSEA, SA2 7DR, Wales
**Phone/Fax** 01792 280759
**Phone** 07790 812175
**Email** ragfoundation@minka.freeserve.co.uk
**Web** www.ragfoundation.com
*5 piece South Wales band. Traditional ballads and contemporary songs from Swansea and Gower. Voice, fiddle, crwth, double bass, drums*
**Agent** mARKO pOLO
***Musicians' Union member***
**AC** Wales

## Ralph McTell
**Contact** Tickety-Boo
**Mail address** Boat House, Crabtree Lane, LONDON, SW6 6TY
**Phone** 020 7610 0122
**Fax** 020 7610 0133
**Email** tickety-boo@tickety-boo.com
**Web** www.tickety-boo.com
*Pre-eminent singer songwriter*

## Rampageri
**Contact** Keith Calton
**Mail address** 6 Grove Road, Ash, NR ALDERSHOT, Hants, GU12 5BD
**Phone/Fax** 01252 314300
**Email** keith@calton.fsbusiness.co.uk
*3 piece barn dance band with caller. English/Irish/ American & Scandanavian.*
**RAB** Southern Arts

## Ramsey and Vaan
**Contact** Neti Vann
**Mail address** 101 Mellitus Street, LONDON, W12 0AU
**Phone** 020 8735 0833
USA +504 895 8378
**Email** neti@ramseyvaan.com
**Web** www.ramseyvaan.com
**Alt contact** Mike Peters - Agent
**Alt address** 17 Virginia Road, WHITSTABLE, Kent, CT5 3HY
**Phone** 01227 264026
**Email** mike@muzikman.freeserve.co.uk
*Folk roots acoustic duo. Fiddle/ vocal/ guitar. UK from July to October plus short tours, otherwise New Orleans based.*
***Musicians' Union member***
**RAB** London Arts

## Random
**Contact** Hemlock Music
**Web** www.hemlockmusic.demon.co.uk
*6 piece electric ceilidh band. Features Saul Rose on melodeon, plus trombone, drums.*
**RAB** London Arts

## Rattling Gate Band
**Contact** John Littler
**Mail address** PO Box 408, BANBURY, Oxon, OX15 4PR
**Phone** 01295 721180 - day
01869 338659 - eve
**Fax** 01295 722916
**Email** 106200.667@compuserve.com
*Oxfordshire based Irish concert band.*
**RAB** Southern Arts

## RAVI
**Contact** JP Freeman
**Mail address** 46 Merle Avenue, HAREFIELD, Middx, UB9 6DG
**Phone** 07711 265011
**Email** info@ravi-art.co.uk
**Web** www.ravi-art.co.uk
*Musician, specialising in kora. Kora Colours with tablas, guitar & percussion. Workshops in world percussion and overtone singing.*
***Musicians' Union member***
**AC** Scotland

## Raymond Wright
**Mail address** 33 Griffon Close, Quedgeley, GLOUCESTER, GL2 4NQ
**Phone** 01452 721953
*Caller for barn dances and ceilidhs.*
**RAB** South West Arts

## RBB Band
**Contact** Bob Rushton - Bookings
**Mail address** 46 Church Street, Denby Village, RIPLEY, Derbys, DE5 8PH
**Phone** 01332 882857
07980 624457
**Email** bobruston@supanet.com
**Web** www.welocme.to/rbb
**Alt contact** Haydon Taylor - Publicity
**Alt address** 25 Northolme Avenue, Bulwell, NOTTINGHAM, NG6 9AP
**Phone** 0115 9276189
**Email** htaylor@eidosnet.co.uk
*Ceilidh band playing traditional French dance music. Available for bals, ceilidhs, etc.*
**RAB** East Midlands Arts

## The Real Macaws
**Contact** Artists Connect
**Web** www.artistsconnect.com
*Street band mixing carnival styles from around the world. Sax, sousaphone, trombone, accordion, steel pans etc*
**Agent** Artists Connect, Fool's Paradise



*Artists in the main A-Z listing are mostly available for concert and club bookings.*

*See page 11 for details of other artist listings (Dance Display, Solo Musicians, Composers, Arrangers, Session Musicians, Band Deps. Lecturers, MCs, Tutors, Street Theatre, Children's Entertainers, Theatre Companies).*

*Agents section appears on pages 119-131.*

# artists
## r

*Artists in the main A-Z listing are mostly available for concert and club bookings.*

*See page 11 for details of other artist listings (Dance Display, Solo Musicians, Composers, Arrangers, Session Musicians, Band Deps. Lecturers, MCs, Tutors, Street Theatre, Children's Entertainers, Theatre Companies).*

*Agents section appears on pages 119-131.*

### Reckless Elbow
**Contact** Phil McGivity
**Mail address** 7 Woburn Road, WALLASEY, Wirral, CH45 5DU
**Phone** 07973 886267
**Fax** 0151 6484148
**Email** band@reckless-elbow.com
**Web** www.reckless.elbow.com
*5 piece folk- roots band. Traditional and contemporary music.*
**RAB** North West Arts

### Red House
**Contact** Chris Beaumont
**Mail address** 30 Cudhall Street, Charlton Kings, CHELTENHAM, GL53 8HG
**Phone** 01242 571185
*English music dance band for celidhs and barn dances.*
**RAB** South West Arts

### Redhed
**Contact** Helene Hambrook
**Mail address** 64 Talbot Road, OLD ISLEWORTH, Middx, TW7 7HF
**Phone** 020 8891 0623
*4 piece electric fiddle led roots-rock band.*
**RAB** London Arts

### Rees Wesson
**MAil address** PO Box 55, WELSHPOOL, Powys, SY 21 9WA, Wales
**Phone** 01938 556438
**Email** rees@melodeons.com
**Web** www.melodeons.com
*Melodeon player and singer.*
***Musicians' Union member***
**AC** Wales

### Repercussion Street Band
**Contact** Artists Connect
**Web** www.artistsconnect.com
*12-15 piece street band. Samba, Samba-Reggae, etc*

### Rhyme and Blues
**Contact** The Blues Line
**Web** www.bluesline.freeserve.co.uk
*Rick Payne and Peter Wyton: performance poetry and music, mostly blues and American folk plus Spanish, Celtic etc*
**RAB** South West Arts

### The Rhythm Chaps
**Contact** Chris McShane
**Phone** 01226 765792
*Yorkshire based 3 -5 piece acoustic/electric ceilidh band with caller.*

### The Rhythm Doctors
**Contact** Fool's Paradise
**Web** www.foolsparadise.co.uk
*Trumpet and guitar jazz & comedy duo. Street show or walkabout*

### The Rhythm Kings
**Contact** Matters Musical
**Web** www.mattersmusical.com
*Dixieland jazz. 4 piece dinner jazz up to 8 piece marching band*

### Richard Grainger
**Contact** Jeanette
**Mail address** Klondike Music, 23 Derwent Street, Norton, STOCKTON ON TEES, TS20 2BZ
**Phone** 01642 861899
07970 228534
**Email** richard.grainger@onyxnet.co.uk
**Web** www.richardgrainger.co.uk
*Singer & guitar. Traditional & new songs, mainly of Cleveland.*
**RAB** Northern Arts

### Richard Heaney and Andrea Ingham
**Contact** The Bechhofer Agency

### Richard Thompson
**Contact** Primary Talent
*"One of the greatest singer/ songwriter/ guitarists alive" Rolling Stone.*
**RAB** London Arts

### Richard Wood
**Contact** mARKO pOLO
**Web** www.markopolo.co.uk
*Young dynamic Canadian fiddle and step dance champion, with band and stage show*

### Rick Christian
**Mail address** PO Box 4099, MALDON, Essex, CM9 4YQ
**Phone** 01621 859561
0771 302 1978
**Email** rickchristian@tinyonline.co.uk
**Web** www.redroad.co.uk/rickchristian
*Singer/ songwriter and 6 & 12 string guitarist.*
***Musicians' Union member***
**RAB** East England Arts

### Rick Payne
**Contact** The Blues Line
**Web** www.bluesline.freeserve.co.uk
*Blues singer/ slide guitarist. TV/ radio, workshops*
**RAB** South West Arts

### Rick Townend
**Mail address** 2 Fair View Cottages, Balaclava Lane, WADHURST, E Sussex, TN5 6EQ
**Phone** 01892 782412 - home
01732 458261 - some office hrs
**Fax** 01732 465788
**Email** banjos@supanet.com
*Bluegrass & Old Timey musician. 5-string banjo, guitar, fiddle, dobro, bass, etc.*
**RAB** South East Arts

### Ricky Cool
**Contact** Matters Musical
**Web** www.mattersmusical.com
*Blues style harmonica and saxophone*

### Ring O'Bells Ceilidh Band
**Contact** Derek Jones
**Mail address** 62 Beechwood Road, SOUTH CROYDON, Surrey, CR2 0AA
**Phone** 020 8657 2813
**Fax** 020 8651 6080
**Web** www.barn-dance.co.uk
*5 piece ceilidh band with caller. Fiddle, drums, bass, banjo. Barn dances, Playford, etc.*
***Musicians' Union member***
**RAB** South East Arts

### River Pickle Party Band
**Contact** Dave East & Doreen Lighter
**Mail address** 21 Fernthorpe Road, Streatham, LONDON, SW16 6DP
**Phone** 020 8677 9989
*4 piece concert & dance band. Fiddle, harp, whistle, guitar & song.*
**RAB** London Arts

### Roam
**Contact** The Event Shop
*4 piece band with songs written by Colin Rudd and singer Rachael Anne Davies. Viola, harp, bouzouki, whistle, etc*
**RAB** North West Arts

### Roaring Mary
**Contact** Matters Musical
**Web** www.mattersmusical.com
*Celtic tunes and songs, banjo, fiddle, etc*

### Rob Peters
**Mail address** PO Box 81, BIRMINGHAM, B30 2LF
**Phone** 0121 444 5887
07971 974108
**Email** robpeters@uk.packardbell.org
**Web** www.collective.co.uk/robpeters
*Singer/ songwriter.*
**RAB** West Midlands Arts

## Robb Johnson
**Mail address** PO Box 72, HOUNSLOW, Middlesex, TW5 0YB
**Phone** 07958 236103
**Email** irregular@moosemusic.co.uk
**Web** www.nightcafe.co.uk
*Radical songwriter, English chanson.*
***Musicians' Union member***
**RAB** London Arts

## Robb Johnson, Miranda Sykes and Saskia Tomkins
**Contact** The Other Agency
*Trio - singer/ songwriter with fiddle and double bass. Workshops in songwriting and fiddle*

## Robb Johnson's "Gentle Men"
**Contact** The Other Agency
*Song suite based on Robb's grandfathers' experiences in the First World War*

## Robert Greig
**Mail address** Tegfan, Llanfaelog, ANGLESEY, LL63 5ST, N Wales
**Phone** 01407 810511
**Fax** 01407 810073
**Email** gwyfynd@freeuk.com
**Web** www.gwyfyn.freeuk.com
*Solo singer/songwriter, plays guitar, bodhran, harmonica.*
**AC** Wales

## Robin Garside
**Mail address** 70 Marlcliffe Road, Wadsley, SHEFFIELD, S6 4AG
**Phone** 0114 2347143
07890 910653
**Email** robin@garside.f9.co.uk
**Web** www.robin-garside.freeserve.co.uk
*Singer (traditional), songwriter, guitarist, fiddler. Music workshops.*
**RAB** Yorkshire Arts

## Robin Huw Bowen
**Mail address** Nancy Carlin Associates
*A master of the music for Welsh triple harp*
**Agent** Nancy Carlin Associates
**AC** Wales

## Robin Laing
**Email** 100060.1000@compuserve.com
**Web** www.folkmusic.net/robinlaing
*Scottish folk-singer and songwriter. Traditional song classes in Lanarkshire.*
**AC** Scotland

## Robin Williamson
**Contact** Moneypenny
*Songwriter, interpreter of traditional song, published poet and novelist. Solo and with Martin Carthy*

## Robin Willow
**Mail address** PO Box 332, LONDON, NW2 5PQ
**Phone** 0845 3777031
**Fax** 020 8451 2590
**Email** robin@dragonar.co.uk
**Web** www.dragonar.co uk
*Songwriter, singer, guitarist. Own and traditional songs.*
***Musicians' Union member***
**RAB** London Arts

## Rock The Boat
**Contact** Shindy Arts
**Web** www.shindy.org.uk
*American-English percussive dance, music & song ensemble. Concerts, dances & workshops*
**RAB** East England Arts

## Rock, Salt & Nails
**Contact** Emerging Music
**Web** www.lismor.co.uk
*Shetland 5 piece group, traditional tunes and contemporary songs*

## Rocky Mountain Playboys
**Contact** Brian Peters
**Mail address** 72 Sheffield Road, GLOSSOP, Derbys, SK13 8QP
**Phone** 01457 862560
**Email** brian.peters@cwcom.net
**Alt contact** Graham Buckley
**Alt address** 17 Wood End Lane, HYDE, Cheshire, SK14 1DT
**Phone** 0161 3688769
**Email** big@bucks.u-net.com
*Good-time band playing old-time, blues, country, rock n roll. Fiddle, banjo, double bass, etc and 3 part vocals.*
**RAB** North West Arts

## Rod Clements
**Contact** Adastra
**Web** www.adastra-music.com
*Singer/ songwriter, originally wih Lindisfarne, Pentangle*
**Agent** Adastra, Blue Daisy Music
***Musicians' Union member***

## Rod Meredith
**Mail address** 7 West View, Langcliffe, SETTLE, North Yorks, BD24 9LZ
**Phone** 01729 825466
01729 823247
*Solo vocals, all styles, guitar accompaniment. Bass guitar/ vocals for ceilidh or jazz bands.*
***Musicians' Union member***
**RAB** Yorkshire Arts

## Rod Patterson
**Contact** The Bechhofer Agency
*Scottish solo singer & guitarist, also currently a member of Jock Tamson's Bairns*

## Rod Paul
**Contact** Greentrax
**Mail address** Cockenzie Business Centre, Edinburgh Road, COCKENZIE, East Lothian, EH32 0XL, Scotland
**Phone** 01875 814155
01875 815888
**Fax** 01875 813545
**Email** greentrax@aol.com
**Web** www.greentrax.com
*Ex Iron Horse guitar, mandolin, bodhran player etc*

## Rod Sinclair
**Mail address** Gravsgade 51, RIBE, 6760, Denmark
**Fax** +45 7542 2150
**Phone** +45 7688 2055
**Email** rod.sinclair@ribesem.dk
*Denmark based perfomer of Scots music and song. See also Sula*

## Roddy Campbell
**Email** jayare@iorram.co.uk
*Traditional singer from the Isle of Barra. Also player of bagpipe, flute and whistles.*

## Roger Downton and Corkscrew
**Contact** Roger Downton
**Mail address** 43 Pottery Road, Lower Parkstone, POOLE, Dorset, BH14 8RB
**Phone/Fax** 01202 740279
**Phone** 07767 366433
**Email** risotto_roger@hotmail.com
*2-4 piece barn dance band with caller. Mix of old timey, R&B, country folk rock and songs. Also Appalachian display.*
**RAB** South West Arts

## Roger Pugh/ Roger Pugh and The Orchestra of Wishes
**Contact** Roger Pugh
**Mail address** 47 Bulwer Road, LEICESTER, LE2 3BW
**Phone** 0116 270 1983
07779 694615
*Singer/ songwriter & guitar/mandola player. Solo or with 5 piece plus Celtic and eclectic folk rock band.*
**RAB** East Midlands Arts



*Artists in the main A-Z listing are mostly available for concert and club bookings.*

*See page 11 for details of other artist listings (Dance Display, Solo Musicians, Composers, Arrangers, Session Musicians. Band Deps. Lecturers, MCs, Tutors, Street Theatre, Children's Entertainers, Theatre Companies).*

*Agents section appears on pages 119-131.*

artists

r

*Artists in the main A-Z listing are mostly available for concert and club bookings.*

*See page 11 for details of other artist listings (Dance Display, Solo Musicians, Composers, Arrangers, Session Musicians, Band Deps. Lecturers, MCs, Tutors, Street Theatre, Children's Entertainers, Theatre Companies).*

*Agents section appears on pages 119-131.*

## Roger Wilson
**Mail address** 71 Lothair Road, LEICESTER, LE2 7QE
**Phone/Fax** 0116 2440528
**Phone** 07939 516551
**Email** roger@wilsongs.freeserve.co.uk
**Web** www.littlebackroom.co.uk
*Highly regarded folk singer, traditional and contemporary, with fiddle and guitar.*
***Musicians' Union member***
**RAB** East Midlands Arts

## Rogues Gallery
**Contact** Mick Peat
**Mail address** Woodland View, Kirkham Lane, FRITCHLEY, Derbys, DE56 2FS
**Phone** 01773 853428
*Ceilidh and barn dance band, own caller and PA.*
***Musicians' Union member***
**RAB** East Midlands Arts

## Rolling Forties
**Contact** Castlelake Consultancy
**Mail address** Castlelake, CASHEL, Co Tipperary, Irish Republic
**Phone** +353 62 62685
+353 87982 1916
**Fax** +353 62 62967
**Email** slaffey@iol.ie
**Web** www.iol.ie/~didly-didly
*Close harmony sextet. Sea shanties with an African-American accent. Led by Jack Harrison. Please give 8 weeks notice for availabilty*

## Ron Trueman-Border
**Mail address** 8 Sharon Court, 18 Hadlow Road, SIDCUP, Kent, DA14 4AE
**Phone** 020 8302 2537
**Web** www.folking.com/rontrueman border
**Alt contact** A Francis 56 Anerly Park, LONDON, SE20 8ND
**Phone** 020 8676 8724
*Contemporary folk singer/ songwriter.*
**RAB** South East Arts

## Root Chords
**Contact** Mick Green
**Mail address** Primrose Cottage, Chester Road, Kelsall, NR TARPORLY, Cheshire, CW6 0SJ
**Phone** 01829 752461
**Email** kmgrennie@hotmail.com
**Alt contact** Graham Bellinger 9 Ivy Mews, Hoole, CHESTER, CH2 3SA
**Phone** 01244 403782
**Email** bellinger@netlocal.co.uk
*4 piece band playing anything from rock n roll to folk. Also ceilidh band with expanded line up and caller.*
**RAB** North West Arts

## Roots Quartet
**Contact** Yvette Staelens
**Mail address** RQRecords, Higher Wrantage Farm, Wrantage, TAUNTON, Somerset, TA3 6DF
**Phone** 01823 481257
01823 456006
**Email** roots@dangermedia.com
**Web** http://rootsquartet.dangermedia.com
*Female vocal harmony duo. Traditional English/ Scottish & new songs. Also with Dave Vermond. Workshops in singing & harmony.*
***Musicians' Union member***
**RAB** South West Arts

## Rory Block
**Contact** NEM Productions (UK)
**Web** www.nemproductions.com
*American (Mississippi Delta) country blues singer/ songwriter/ guitarist*

## Rory Campbell and Malcolm Stitt
**Contact** Martin Coull Music Management
**Mail address** Studio 7, 6 New Street, EDINBURGH, EH8 8BH, Scotland
**Phone/Fax** 0131 557 5330
**Phone** 07803 137509
**Email** marticoull@aol.com
*Scottish smallpipes and guitar duo*
**Agent** Stoneyport Agency
**AC** Scotland

## Rory McLeod
**Contact** NEM Productions (UK)
**Web** www.nemproductions.com
*One man soul band, poet, songwriter & storyteller. Tap shoes, harmonica, song, trombone, spoons, guitar, etc*

## Rosie Upton and Pete MacGregor
**Contact** Rosie Upton
**Mail address** 24 Bearfield Buildings, BRADFORD ON AVON, Wilts, BA15 1RP
**Phone/Fax** 01225 865107
**Email** rosie@bearfld.demon.co.uk
*Traditional and contemporary song duo, some with guitar accompaniment.*
**RAB** Southern Arts

## Roy Bailey
**Contact** Brass Tacks
*Acknowledged as one of Britain's finest interpreters of contemporary songs.*
***Musicians' Union member***
**RAB** Yorkshire Arts

## Roy Clinging
**Mail address** 79 Panton Road, CHESTER, CH2 3HL
**Phone** 01244 319509
**Email** roy@motmove.freeserve.co.uk
**Web** www.folkmusic.net/royclinging
*Cheshire traditional songs and tunes.*
**RAB** North West Arts

## Roy Harris
**Mail address** 31 Carling Court, Haig Place, CARDIFF, CF5 4PH, Wales
**Phone** 029 2065 7311
**Fax** 029 2065 7312
**Email** reharris@ntlworld.com
*Admired solo unaccompanied singer, now part-time. Recording artist. Freelance writer & reviewer.*
**AC** Wales

## RSVP
**Contact** Sarah Holmes
**Mail address** St Edmunds Cottage, Brockley Corner, Culford, BURY ST EDMUNDS, Suffolk, IP28 6UA
**Phone** 01284 728297
**Email** rsvp@st-edmunds-cottage.freeserve.co.uk
**Web** www.st-edmunds-cottage.freeserve.co.uk
*4 piece ceilidh band: melodeons, hurdy gurdy, pipes, percussion, etc. 2 callers, bi-lingual singer. English, French and Spanish folk & dance music.*
**RAB** East England Arts

## Rude Knot To
**Contact** Jeff Davis
**Mail address** 114 Victoria Avenue, HASTINGS, East Sussex, TN55 5DT
**Phone** 01424 722371
01424 445028
**Email** jlaidlaw@dircon.co.uk
**Web** www.jlaidlaw.dircon.co.uk/rkt/rkt.html
*Folk roots trio; mandolin, vocals & guitar.*
***Musicians' Union member***
**RAB** Southern Arts

## Rue Bourbon
**Contact** Access All Areas
*USA Zydeco band*

## Rufus Wainwright
**Contact** Primary Talent

## Rum & Shrub Shantymen
**Contact** Colin Hawke
**Mail address** 2 Trenance Cottages, St Newlyn East, NEWQUAY, Cornwall, TR8 5HU
**Phone** 01872 510370
**Email** colin@rumandshrub.freeserve.co.uk
**Web** www.rubandshrub.co.uk
*8 piece vocal group singing shanties, sea songs and Cornish songs.*
**RAB** South West Arts

## Running on Empty
**Contact** Penni
**Phone** 01902 340844
**Email** penni@care4free.net
*3-6 piece barn dance/ ceilidh band.*
***Musicians' Union member***
**RAB** West Midlands Arts

## Russell's House
**Contact** Mesmerist Productions
**Web** www.mesmerist.com
*Edinburgh based folk band*
**AC** Scotland

## Russian Tornado
**Contact** Matters Musical
**Web** www.mattersmusical.com
*Led by Bibs Ekkel, show includes Russian instruments and 'balalaika juggling'*

## Sacaulait
**Contact** Access All Areas
*US traditional Cajun trio. Accordion/vocals, violin and guitar*

## Saffron Summerfield
**Contact** Mother Earth Agency
**Mail address** 25 Ferndale Road, LONDON, SE25 4QR
**Phone** 020 8406 7881
**Email** saffron@motherearthmusic.co.uk
**Web** mothearthmusic.co.uk
*Singer and guitarist, bouzouki and cuatro player. Own songs plus others from around the world. Voice and songwriting workshop tutor.*
***Musicians' Union member***
**RAB** London Arts

## Sally Barker
**Mail address** PO Box 8, LUTTERWORTH, Leics, LE17 4SN
**Phone** 01455 552592
**Email** sal@sallybarker.co.uk
**Web** www.sallybarker.co.uk
*Contemporary folk & blues singer/ songwriter. Solo or duo with Keith Richard Buck*
**Agent** Speaking Volumes
***Musicians' Union member***
**RAB** West Midlands Arts

## Sally Horner
**Phone** 020 7771 7533
**Email** sally.horner@orange.net
*Unaccompanied singer of traditional & original songs. Solo or duo with guitarist. plus see Horner & Horn.*
***Musicians' Union member***
**RAB** London Arts

## Salsa Celtica
**Contact** Active
**Web** www.salsaceltica.com
*9 piece Latin - Scottish roots band*
**Agents** Active, Adastra
**AC** Scotland

## Samba Gales
**Contact** Chris Girling
**Mail address** 41 Lansdowne Road, Canton, CARDIFF, CF5 1DQ, Wales
**Phone** 029 2034 5609
07773 947885
**Email** chrisjgirling@ukonline.co.uk
*30-40 piece percussion orchestra drawing on Brazilian, Cuban, African roots. Performance & workshops.*
***Musicians' Union member***
**AC** Wales

## Sam Pirt
**Mail address** 97 Hook Road, GOOLE, DN14 5JR
**Phone** 01405 769010
07718 950417
**Email** sampirt@folkmusic.freeserve.co.uk
**Web** www.sampirt.co.uk
*Accordion player. Member of 422 - 1999 winners of BBC Radio 2 Young Folk Award. Performs solo, duo and with 422. Workshop leader.*
***Musicians' Union member***
**RAB** Yorkshire Arts

## Sandra Kerr
**Mail address** 5 Heatherleazes, Warkworth, NR. ALNWICK, Northumberland, NE65 0TZ
**Phone/Fax** 01665 712488
**Email** sandra.kerr@which.net
*Singer, writer and musician, popular workshop leader & voice teacher.*
**RAB** Northern Arts

## Sandy Archer
**Mail address** 43 Pottery Road, Lower Parkstone, POOLE, Dorset, BH14 8RB
**Phone/Fax** 01202 740 279
**Phone** 07767 366433
**Email** yasminasar@hotmail.com
*Caller for ceilidhs and barn dances. Also offers dance display including Appalachian, Irish soft shoe, etc.*
**RAB** South West Arts

## The Sandy Brechin Band
**Contact** Sandy Brechin
**Mail address** 5 The Square, KIRKLISTON, West Lothian, EH29 9AX, Scotland
**Phone** 01783 253228
0131 333 3252
**Email** sandy@squeeze.demon.co.uk
**Web** www.squeeze.demon.co.uk or www.accordions.com/sandy
*4 piece accordion led folk group. Fast & furious. New/ traditional music.*
***Musicians' Union member***
**AC** Scotland

## Sandy Stanage
**Contact** Elma Harkins
**Mail address** 53 James Street, PITTENWEEM, Fife, KY10 2QN, Scotland
**Phone** 01333 312497
**Fax** 01334 462543
**Email** emh3@st-andrews.ac.uk
**Web** www.fokmusic.net/sandystanage
*Scottish guitarist; traditional, contemporary, jazz, classical. Noted for his arrangements.*
**AC** Scotland

## Sangeeta
**Contact** Matters Musical
**Web** www.mattersmusical.com
*Popular Indian female singer with a Bhangra/ Bollywood feel. Her band is led by Kuljit Bhamra*

## Sangsters
**Contact** Greentrax
**Mail address** Cockenzie Business Centre, Edinburgh Road, COCKENZIE, East Lothian, EH32 0XL, Scotland
**Phone** 01875 814155
01875 815888
**Fax** 01875 813545
**Email** greentrax@aol.com
**Web** www.greentrax.com
*Scottish song/ harmony group. Traditional, Burns and contemporary songs*

## Sara Grey
**Mail address** Ploughman's Cottage, EDINBANE, Isle Of Skye, IV51 9PW
**Phone** 01470 582254
**Email** saragrey@compuserve.com
*Scotland based American singer, banjo player and song collector.*
**AC** Scotland

## Sarah Allen and Chris Thompson
**Contact** Emerging Music
**Web** www.emerging.demon.co.uk
*Ex-Barely Works flute, accordion, song and banjo duo*
***Musicians' Union member***



*Artists in the main A-Z listing are mostly available for concert and club bookings.*

*See page 11 for details of other artist listings (Dance Display, Solo Musicians, Composers, Arrangers, Session Musicians, Band Deps. Lecturers, MCs, Tutors, Street Theatre, Children's Entertainers, Theatre Companies).*

*Agents section appears on pages 119-131.*

*Artists in the main A-Z listing are mostly available for concert and club bookings.*

*See page 11 for details of other artist listings (Dance Display, Solo Musicians, Composers, Arrangers, Session Musicians, Band Deps. Lecturers, MCs, Tutors, Street Theatre, Children's Entertainers, Theatre Companies).*

*Agents section appears on pages 119-131.*

## Sarah Crofts
**Mail address** 7 Northbrook Road, Lewisham, LONDON, SE13 5QT
**Phone** 020 8331 9153 - day
020 8852 6618 - eve
**Email** s.j.crofts@gre.ac.uk
*Anglo concertina player, mostly English traditional. Also step dancer.*
***Musicians' Union member***
**RAB** London Arts

## Savourna Stephenson's Scottish Women's String Quintet
**Contact** Emerging Music
**Web** www.emerging.demon.co.uk
*Instrumental music and song; Mairi Campbell, Wendy Weatherby, Anne Wood, Jenny Gardner & Savourna Stephenson*

## Savourna Stevenson
**Contact** Emerging Music
**Web** www.emerging.demon.co.uk
*Solo harpist/composer*
**Agent** Elaine Heron, Emerging Music
**AC** Scotland

## Savourna Stevenson and Les Barker
**Contact** Emerging Music
**Web** www.emerging.demon.co.uk
*Duo with Scottish harp player and Manchester poet*

## Scallywag
**Contact** Dave Wells
**Mail address** 'Fairview', Meare Green, Stoke St Gregory, TAUNTON, TA3 6HZ
**Phone** 01823 490764
**Email** dd.wells@btinternet.com
**Alt contact** Mark Halliwell 19 Stephen Street, TAUNTON, Somerset
**Phone** 01823 270409
**Email** mark@halliwell.eurobell.co.uk
*4 piece ceilidh/ barn dance band. Melodeon, guitar, bass, drums, etc. English & French with African/ Latin beats.*
**RAB** South West Arts

## Schooner Rigged
**Contact** Rick Hamilton
**Mail address** 8 Orwell Crescent, Titchfield Common, FAREHAM, Hants PO14 4JR
**Phone** 01489 589370
023 8059 6293
**Fax** 023 8059 6295
**Email** Rickhamilton61@hotmail.com
*Five piece folk band specialising in Irish, Scottish and English songs and songs of the sea.*
**RAB** Southern

## Scold's Bridle
**Contact** Sue Bousfield
**Mail address** 7 The Hermitage, CLEVELEYS, Lancs, FY5 2TH
**Phone** 01253 822089
07977 208524
**Email** scolds.bridle@ukgateway.net
**Alt contact** Liz Moore
**Alt address** 5 Cotswold Road, The Belfry, LYTHAM-ST-ANNES, Lancs
**Phone** 01253 738633
*Female duo, traditional and contemporary songs with guitar and concertina.*
**RAB** North West Arts

## Scotch The Rumour Ceilidh Band
**Contact** Matt Swindlehurst
**Mail address** 106 Oxley Moor Road, WOLVERHAMPTON, W Midlands, WV10 6TX
**Phone** 01902 785002
**Email** matt@lmsmusic.co.uk
**Web** www.lmsmusic.co.uk
*English ceilidh band with caller.*
***Musicians' Union member***
**RAB** West Midlands Arts

## The Scottish Stepdance Company
**Contact** Martin Coull Music Management
**Mail address** Studio 7, 6 New Street, EDINBURGH, EH8 8BH, Scotland
**Phone/Fax** 0131 557 5330
**Phone** 07803 137509
**Email** marticoull@aol.com
**Web** www.musicscotland.com/stepdance
*Group of top Scottish musicians and step dancers, mixing music, song & dance on stage*
**Agent** Stoneyport Agency
**AC** Scotland

## Scrap!
**Contact** mARKO pOLO
**Web** www.markopolo.co.uk
*Vancouver 5 piece multi-racial group playing instruments made from salvaged recycled junk*

## Sean Tyrrell
**Contact** The Bechhofer Agency
*Irish singer and guitarist*

## The Sedatives
**Contact** Dave Banks
**Mail address** 86 Holymoor Road, Holymoorside, CHESTERFIELD, Derbys, S42 7DX
**Phone/Fax** 01246 568433
**Email** david@holymoor.force9.co.uk
**Web** www.holymoor.force9.co.uk/sedatives.htm
*Songwriting duo. Anglo-Norwegian, guitar and bass, rock-folk.*
**RAB** East Midlands Arts

## Seize The Day
**Contact** Carol Smy
**Mail address** PO Box 23, 5 High St, GLASTONBURY, Somerset, BA6 9DP
**Phone** 01458 850955
07788 446109
**Email** seizetheday@thismoment.freeserve.co.uk
**Web** www.seizetheday.org
**Alt contact** Louise Somerville
**Alt address** Grace Cottage, 6 Longman's Lea, DITCHFEET, Somerset, BA6 6RT
**Phone** 01749 860689
*6 piece acoustic vocal and drum band, traditional roots, singing about current issues.*
***Musicians' Union member***
**RAB** South West Arts

## The Sensational Jimmy Shandrix Experience
**Contact** Sandy Brechin
**Mail address** 5 The Square, KIRKLISTON, West Lothian, EH29 9AX, Scotland
**Phone** 07831 253228
0131 333 3252
**Email** sandy@squeeze.demon.co.uk
**Web** www.accordions.com/sandy
*5 piece Scottish, wild electric ceilidh band with caller.*
***Musicians' Union member***
**AC** Scotland

## Serious Kitchen
**Contact** Vicki Swan
**Mail address** 23 North Road, BRENTWOOD, Essex, CM14 4XE
**Phone** 01277 260252
07721 519719
**Email** vix@muckle.demon.co.uk
**Web** www.seriouskitchen.co.uk
*3 piece folk band. Vocals, small pipes/ flute, guitar. Workshops available.*
***Musicians' Union member***
**RAB** East England Arts

## Shagpile
**Contact** Jacey Bedford Tour Management
**Web** www.jacey-bedford.com
**Alt contact** Dave Burland
**Alt address** 14 Longman Road, BARNSLEY, S Yorks, S70 2LD
**Alt email** s.burland14@aol.com
*Five-piece electric dance band featuring Dave Burland on vocals and guitars. Mix of traditional rock 'n' roll, R&B, Country. Also available with The Fraser Sisters saxophone section.*
**Agent** Jacey Bedford Tour Management

### Shake-A-Leg
**Contact** Big Whistle Music
**Mail address** PO Box 23, ACCRINGTON, Lancs, BB5 5GX
**Phone/Fax** 01254 397623
**Phone** 07976 809623
**Email** phil@bigwhistle.co.uk
**Web** www.bigwhistle.co.uk
*Rootsy English dance band for ceilidhs and barn dances. Brass, squeeze boxes, percussion, etc.*
**RAB** North West Arts

### Shane Brogan
**Mail address** 21D High Street, AYR, South Ayrshire, KA7 1LU, Scotland
**Phone** 07989 261247
**Email** broganshane@hotmil.com
*Accordionist, teacher, composer/ arranger, publisher/ copyist, recording artist.*
***Musicians' Union member***
**AC** Scotland

### The Shanty Crew
**Contact** Chris Roche
**Mail address** 6 Brafferton Road, CROYDON, Surrey, CR0 1AD
**Phone** 020 8688 3580
**Email** chrisroche@onet.co.uk
**Web** www.shantycrew.co.uk
*5 piece acapella sea-song and shanty group. Illustrated talks available*
**Agent** Matters Musical
**RAB** South East Arts

### Shanty Jack
**Contact** Pete Hayselden
**Mail address** 16 The Kingsway, CLEETHORPES, NE Lincs, DN35 8QU
**Phone/Fax** 01472 696757
**Phone** 07970 651293
**Email** shantyjack@anchorage.f9.co.uk
*Specialise in sea-songs & shanties*
***Musicians' Union member***
**RAB** Yorkshire Arts

### Sharon
**Contact** Sharon Fountain
**Mail address** 110 Worsbrough Road, Birdwell, BARNSLEY, Yorks, S70 5RG
**Phone** 01226 281106
07867 871613
**Email** sharon.fountain@ntlworld.com
*Singer/songwriter/guitarist, traditional & contemporary material.*
**RAB** Yorkshire Arts

### The Sharon King Band
**Contact** Organic Arts
**Web** www.organicarts.co.uk
*4 piece band fronted by Scottish singer-songwriter. Country folk blend*
***Musicians' Union member***
**AC** Scotland

### Sharon Shannon
**Contact** Asgard Promotions
*Hugely popular Irish button accordion and fiddle player.*

### Sheena Wellington
**Contact** M H Wellington
**Mail address** 6 St Andrews Road, Largoward, LEVEN, Fife, KY9 1HZ, Scotland
**Phone/Fax** 01334 840297
07711 828119
**Email** shesings@compuserve.com
*Traditional singer, unaccompanied or with guitarist.*
***Musicians' Union member***
**AC** Scotland

### Sheila Mainwaring
**Mail address** 1 Herbert Avenue, Wellington, TELFORD, Shropshire, TF1 2BT
**Phone** 01952 240989
**Email** mainwaring@enta.net
*Caller for ceilidhs & teacher of folk dances for all ages/ experiences.*
**RAB** West Midlands Arts

### Shep Woolley
**Contact** Jacey Bedford Tour Management
**Web** www.jacey-bedford.com
*Folk and roll comedian*
**RAB** Southern Arts

### Sheryl Cormier and The Cajun Sounds
**Contact** Access All Areas
*US Cajun accordionist plus her seven piece band*

### Shikisha
**Contact** Matters Musical
**Web** www.mattersmusical.com
*Women's group mixing traditional Zulu, Sotho, Xhosa and Shangaan dances, chants and drumming with electric sounds from South African townships. Workshop instructors in drumming, singing and dance etc*

### Shindig
**Contact** Brian & Carol Massen
**Mail address** 5 Laburnum Ave, Waltham, GRIMSBY, NE Lincs, DN37 0JT
**Phone** 01472 825309
07703 900875
**Email** brian.massen@btinternet.com
*Ceilidh band.*
**RAB** Yorkshire Arts

### Shine
**Contact** Alyth McCormack
**Phone** 0777 1787377
**Alt contact** Corrina Hewatt
**Phone** 07711 512692
**Email** shine@bachue.co.uk
*Scottish group blending 2 electro-harps and 3 voices. New and traditional songs in Scots, Gaelic and English. Alyth McCormack, Corrina Hewat and Mary Macmaster.*
***Musicians' Union member***
**AC** Scotland

### Shooglenifty
**Contact** Brass Tacks
**Web** www.shoogle.com
*Very popular six piece Scottish Celtic dance roots band*
**AC** Scotland

### Show of Hands
**Contact** Vaughan Pearce
**Mail address** Newhouse Farmhouse, Frog Lane, CLYST ST MARY, Devon EX5 1BX
**Phone** 01392 879458
07798 840203
**Email** info@showofhands.co.uk
**Web** www.showofhands.co.uk
*One of England's foremost acoustic groups, instrumentals combined with contemporary songwriting*
***Musicians' Union member***
**RAB** South West Arts

### Si Kahn
**Contact** Adastra
**Web** www.adastra-music.com
*Respected American writer and singer of political songs*

### Sian James
**Contact** Gwyn Jones
**Mail address** PO Box 56, WELSHPOOL, Powys, SY21 0WP, Wales
**Email** gwyn@sianjames.co.uk
**Web** www.sianjames.co.uk
*Traditional Welsh folk singer and harpist*
***Musicians' Union member***
**AC** Wales

### Sian Phillips
**Mail address** 27A Glebe Street, PENARTH, Vale of Glamorgan CF64 1EE
**Phone** 029 2063 9168
07720 019373
**Email** sianfiddle@hotmail.com
**Web** msnhomepages.talkcity.com/ lyricln/sianfiddle
*Traditional Welsh folk fiddle player.*
***Musicians' Union member***
**AC** Wales



*Artists in the main A-Z listing are mostly available for concert and club bookings.*

*See page 11 for details of other artist listings (Dance Display, Solo Musicians, Composers, Arrangers, Session Musicians, Band Deps. Lecturers, MCs, Tutors, Street Theatre, Children's Entertainers, Theatre Companies).*

*Agents section appears on pages 119-131.*

*Artists in the main A-Z listing are mostly available for concert and club bookings.*

*See page 11 for details of other artist listings (Dance Display, Solo Musicians, Composers, Arrangers, Session Musicians, Band Deps. Lecturers, MCs, Tutors, Street Theatre, Children's Entertainers, Theatre Companies).*

*Agents section appears on pages 119-131.*

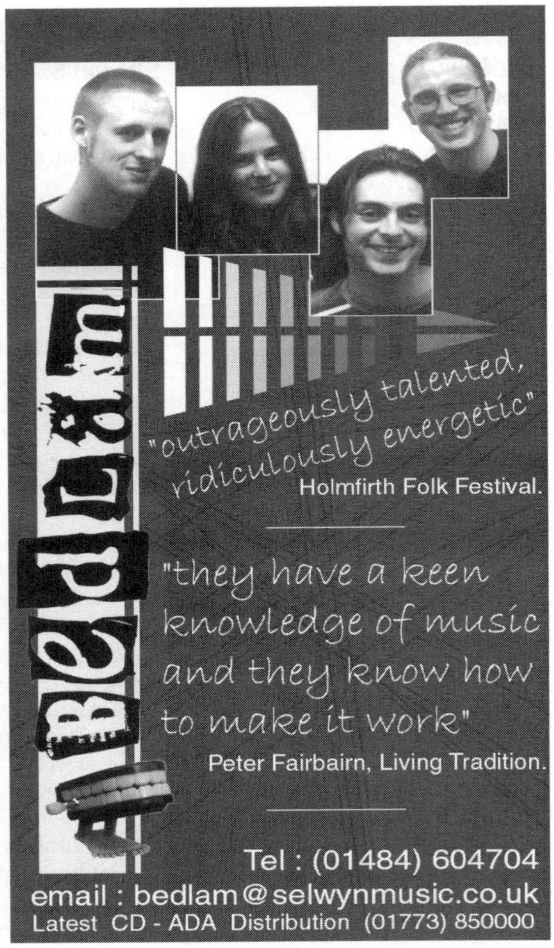

## Sid Griffin
**Contact** Pat McGarvey
**Mail address** 108A Acton Lane, LONDON, NW10 8TX
**Phone** 020 8838 0804
**Fax** 020 7794 9549
**Email** patmcgarvey@x-stream.co.uk
**Web** www.sidgriffin.com
*Acoustic folk and bluegrass music. Available solo, duo or trio.*
**RAB** London Arts

## Sid Kipper
**Contact** Elaine Cooper
**Mail address** 4 Ransomes Row, North Dalton, DRIFFIELD, YO25 9XA, W Yorks
**Phone/Fax** 01377 217080
*Singer, storyteller, author, multi-instrumentalist & broadcaster, in the Trunch tradition*
***Musicians' Union member***
**RAB** Yorkshire Arts

## Sileas
**Contact** Stoneyport Agency
**Web** www.stoneyport.demon.co.uk
*Scottish harp and vocal duo Mary MacMaster and Pasty Seddon*
**AC** Scotland

## Simon Haworth
**Mail address** 58 Eleventh Ave, Stobhill, MORPETH, Northumberland, NE61 2HT
**Phone** 01670 504531
**Email** simonh@morpeth61.freeserve.co.uk
**Web** www.morpeth61.freeserve.co.uk
*Singer, songwriter, guitarist, double bass and cittern player. Solo artist, accompanist & member of Jez Lowe and the Bad Pennies.*
**RAB** Northern Arts

## Simon Mayor and Hilary James
**Contact** The Other Agency
*Duo: mandolin, vocals, mandobass. Folk, blues, swing, etc. Workshops on singing, songwriting, mandolin*

## Simon Mayor's Mandolinquents
**Contact** The Other Agency
*Four piece modern mandolin quartet with vocals, playing a mixture of folk music*

## Simon Thoumire
**Contact** Elizabeth Hepburn
**Mail address** 17 Redford Drive, EDINBURGH, EH13 0BL
**Phone** 0131 4413135
07775 854572
**Email** sales@tartantapes.com
**Web** www.tartantapes.com/simonthoumire
*Award winning concertina player, composer and teacher.*
***Musicians' Union member***
**AC** Scotland

## Simon Thoumire and David Milligan
**Contact** Elizabeth Hepburn
**Mail address** 17 Redford Drive, EDINBURGH, EH13 0BL
**Phone** 0131 4413135
07775 854572
**Email** sales@tartantapes.com
**Web** www.tartantapes.com
*Concertina and piano duo. Traditional and 'weird' music.*
***Musicians' Union member***
**AC** Scotland

## Sin É
**Contact** The Concert Clinic
**Web** www.concertclinic.com
*UK based band mixing Celtic and world traditions. Pipes, fiddle, tabla, etc*
**Agents** The Concert Clinic, themusictree. (uk) ltd

## Sinead Lohan
**Contact** Primary Talent
*Popular young Irish singer/songwriter*

## Skillet
**Contact** Tony Weatherall
**Mail address** 138 Longslow Road, MARKET DRAYTON, Shrops, TF9 3QZ
**Phone/Fax** 01630 652034
**Email** Vines@tisbuts.supanet.com
*Barn dance band with twin melodeons, piano, double bass and drums. Own caller*
**RAB** West Midlands Arts

## Skiphire
**Contact** John Ward
**Mail address** PO Box 59, LOWESTOFT, Suffolk, NR33 8EA
**Phone** 01502 588137
**Email** john.ward11@virgin.net
**Web** http://freespace.virgin.net/john.ward11/index.htm
*Ceilidh band, own caller. Violin, guitar, bass, etc. UK & European tunes.*
***Musicians' Union member***
**RAB** East England Arts

## Slainte Mhath
**Contact** mARKO pOLO
**Web** www.markopolo.co.uk
*Popular young Cape Breton band with step dancing*

## Slim Panatella and The Mellow Virginians
**Contact** The Other Agency

## The Slip Jigolos
**Contact** Matters Musical
**Web** www.mattersmusical.com
*Irish vocal led band. Expandable three piece*

## Sofibacugo
**Contact** Laurel Swift
**Mail address** 62 Eade Road, LONDON, N4 1DH
**Phone** 07855 389360
**Email** laurel@beam.freeserve.co.uk
*Four piece young English music song and dance band. Concerts, ceilidhs and workshops.*
**RAB** East England Arts

## So Long Angel
**Contact** Roland Kemp
**Mail address** 14 Mowbray Road, LONDON, SE19 2RN
**Phone/Fax** 020 8771 4557
**Phone** 07860 237739
**Email** roland.kemp@virgin.net
*5 piece blues band. Female vocalist, bass, sax, harmonica, guitar, keyboards, drums. Traditional and new songs.*
**RAB** London Arts

## Solan
**Contact** Frances Wilkins
**Mail address** Mill Cottage, Marton, SHREWSBURY
**Phone** 07719 344789
**Email** solan@music.shetland.co.uk
**Web** www.music.shetland.co.uk
**Alt contact** Richard Chaff
**Phone** 07714 295035
**Email** solan@cds-studio.shetland.co.uk
*Shetland duo performing songs and tunes on concertinas, guitar & piano.*
**AC** Scotland

## Solid Steel Ambassadors
**Contact** Matters Musical
**Web** www.mattersmusical.com
*Steel pan ensemble, trio up to large orchestra*



*Artists in the main A-Z listing are mostly available for concert and club bookings.*

*See page 11 for details of other artist listings (Dance Display, Solo Musicians, Composers, Arrangers, Session Musicians, Band Deps. Lecturers, MCs, Tutors, Street Theatre, Children's Entertainers, Theatre Companies).*

*Agents section appears on pages 119-131.*

## artists

## S

*Artists in the main A-Z listing are mostly available for concert and club bookings.*

*See page 11 for details of other artist listings (Dance Display, Solo Musicians, Composers, Arrangers, Session Musicians, Band Deps. Lecturers, MCs, Tutors, Street Theatre, Children's Entertainers, Theatre Companies).*

*Agents section appears on pages 119-131.*

### The Somersham Popular Front
**Contact** Len Dee
**Mail address** Alpine Rose, Main Road, Somersham, NR IPSWICH, Suffolk, IP8 4PH
**Phone** 01473 832510
07979 590433
**Email** lendee@alpinerose.fsnet.co.uk
*Song & guitars/ mandolin/ harmonica duo. Modern, traditional & humorous folk style.*
**RAB** East England Arts

### Sonny Condell
**Contact** Elizabeth Jones Entertainments
**Web** www.bromyard.co.uk/ejones
*Irish singer/ songwriter, formly of Tir na Nog*

### Souls of Fire
**Contact** Nic Bradford
**Mail address** 37 Northbrook Road, SOUTHAMPTON, SO14 0BW
**Phone** 023 8022 7256
**Email** souls@meltingpot.org.uk
**Web** www.meltingpot.org.uk/sof
*Klezmer and Eastern dance grooves.*
**RAB** Southern Arts

### South African Gospel Choir
**Contact** Matters Musical
**Web** www.mattersmusical.com
*8 piece mixed choir backed by brass and rhythm section*

### Space Goats
**Contact** Mandala
**Web** www.mandala.mcmail.com
*Tribal folk/ rock band*
**RAB** London Arts

### Spartacus
**Contact** Matters Musical
**Web** www.mattersmusical.com
*3 - 5 piece Greek band. Also latin and salsa. Dancers and belly dancers available*

### The Spikedrivers
**Contact** Access All Areas
*UK/ USA Delta blues band, folk/ country influence. Vocals, guitar, bass and drums*

### Spinach for Norman
**Contact** Martin Henning
**Mail address** 1 Pittford Cottages, Wenbworthy, CHULMLEIGH, Devon, EX18 7QA
**Phone** 01837 83347
**Email** m.henning@talk21.com
**Web** www.flaxey-green.co.uk
**Alt contact** Joel Segal
**Alt address** 57 Fore Street, Topsham, EXETER, Devon
**Phone** 01392 875239
07974 068023
**Email** angelcast@aol.com
*4 piece ceilidh band with caller. Music from UK, Ireland, East Europe, US, etc. 2 fiddles, guitar and bass.*
***Musicians' Union member***
**RAB** South West Arts

### Spinning Jelly
**Contact** Kathleen Robertshaw
**Mail address** Yarnbury House, GRASSINGTON, N Yorks, BD23 5EQ
**Phone** 01756 753014
**Email** rshaw@daelnet.co.uk
**Web** www.sjelly.btinternet.co.uk
*English and Celtic music for ceilidhs and concerts. Multi-instrumental band with adaptable caller.*
**RAB** Yorkshire Arts

### Spiro
**Contact** Jane Harbour
**Mail address** Uncle Records, 58 Leighton Rd, Southville, BRISTOL, Avon, BS3 1NU
**Phone** 0117 902 1532
0117 966 1443
*4 piece band drawing from English repertoire, especially Northern tunes, with influences from classical to punk.*
**RAB** South West Arts

### Splendid Isolation
**Contact** Phil Mosley
**Mail address** PO Box 1157, WINDSOR, Berks
**Phone** 07759 474276
01753 833889
**Email** phil@splendidisolation.net
**Web** ww.splendidisolation.net
**Alt contact** Graham Crockford
**Phone** 07803 144014
**Email** graham@splendidisolation.net
*Song/guitar based duo, mix of traditional and contemporary songs.*
**RAB** Southern Arts

### Springer Sisters and Springer Surprise Band
**Contact** Pamela Wilson
**Mail address** Devils Dream Cottage, Colts Hill, Capel, TONBRIDGE, Kent, TN12 6SW
**Phone** 01892 835191
**Email** springers@springersmusic.co.uk
**Web** www.springersmusic.co.uk
*Barn dance/ ceilidh band and duo. Music from Tudor to present. Costumed events.*
**RAB** South East Arts

### Square Root Folk Dance Band
**Contact** Mic Spenceley
**Mail address** 35 Gudge Heath Lane, FAREHAM, Hants, PO15 5AB
**Phone** 01329 822657
**Fax** 01329 829895
**Email** mike-spenceley@lineone.net
*3-4 piece band for ceilidhs, barn dances & social dances.*
**RAB** Southern Arts

### Squeal Like A Pig
**Contact** Fool's Paradise
**Web** www.foolsparadise.co.uk
*Costumed comedy group playing Cajun music. Also as a straight Cajun band*

### Stafford Wells
**Contact** Brian Stafford
**Mail address** 21 Brighton Street, SKIPTON, N Yorks, BD23 1QQ
**Phone** 01756 798285
07968 826191
**Email** brian@stafford.uklinux.net
**Web** stafford.uklinux.net/sw/
*Trio with uillean pipes playing traditional & contemporary Irish and Scottish tunes and songs.*
***Musicians' Union member***
**RAB** Yorkshire Arts

### Stanley Accrington
**Mail address** Greenbank, Chamber Row, Shaw, OLDHAM, Manchester, OL2 7AR
**Phone** 01706 844264
07747 655403
*Solo singer with guitar. Satire, silly and serious songs.*
**RAB** North West Arts

### Steafan Hannigan
**Phone** 01908 225500
**Email** o-omusic@dircon.co.uk
*Solo pipes, multi-instrumentalist, producer and storyteller*
***Musicians' Union member***

## Steamchicken
**Contact** Andrew Sharpe
**Mail address** 18 Stoneleigh Road, KENILWORTH, Warks, CV8 2DG
**Phone** 01926 850648
*Ceilidh band.*
**RAB** West Midlands Arts

## Steeleye Span
**Contact** Park Promotions
**Web** www.parkrecords.com
*Doyens of English folk-rock*
**RAB** Southern Arts

## Step Rideau and the Zydeco Outlaws
**Contact** Access All Areas
*USA Zydeco group*

## Stephen Rees
**Mail address** Gwenlais, 8 Bron Arfon, LLANLLECHID, Gwynedd, LL57 3LW, Wales
**Phone/Fax** 01248 600247
**Phone** 07880 602897
**Email** stephen.rees@btinternet.com
*Performer, teacher & researcher specialising in Welsh traditional music plus European & American fiddle traditions.*
***Musicians' Union member***
**AC** Wales

## Steve Ashley
**Contact** Elizabeth Jones Entertainments
**Web** www.bromyard.co.uk/ejones
*Co-founder of the Albion Country Band*
**RAB** South West Arts

## Steve Ashley and Al Fenn
**Contact** Elizabeth Jones Entertainments
**Web** www.bromyard.co.uk/ejones
*Acoustic songwriting duo. Guitar & mandolin*

## Steve Cunio
**Mail address** 1 Lower Hyde Road, MONTACUTE, Somerset, TA15 6UR
**Phone** 01935 829050
**Email** steve@cunio-marsh.freeserve.co.uk
*Caller for barn dances and ceilidhs.*
**RAB** South West Arts

## Steve Gibbons/ The Steve Gibbons Band
**Contact** Iconic Music & Media
*Singer and guitarist. Own songs plus R&B standards/ Dylan covers. Solo or with 5 piece band, Rock n Roll, R&B, Blues/Soul classics*

## Steve Phillips
**Contact** Adastra
**Web** www.adastra-music.com
*Renowned blues guitarist. Also available with Yorkshire western swing band 'The Rough Diamonds'*

## Steve Tilston
**Mail address** 17 Station Rd, Oakworth, KEIGHLEY, W Yorks, BD22 0DU
**Phone** 01535 642988
**Email** mail@steve-tilston.co.uk
**Web** www.steve-tilson.co.uk
*Singer, songwriter & guitarist. Solo and with other combinations.*
***Musicians' Union member***
**RAB** Yorkshire Arts

## Stocai
**Contact** Chris Walshaw
**Mail address** 80 Ryarsh Road, BIRLING, Kent, ME19 5JR
**Phone/Fax** 01732 849163
**Email** C.Walshaw.gre.ac.uk
**Web** www.gre.ac.uk/~c.walshaw/stocai
**Alt contact** Kevin Adams
**Alt address** 5 Bullington End Road, Castlethorpe, MILTON KEYNES MK19 7ER
**Phone** 01908 511156
**Email** Kevin.Adams@care4free.net
*5 piece ceilidh band featuring bagpipes, melodeon, keyboards, bassoon, etc.*
**RAB** South East Arts

## Stomp
**Contact** Jeff Dent
**Mail address** 6 Riverside Walk, ISLEWORTH, Middx, TW7 6HW
**Phone** 020 8737 7307
*Rock-based English Country Dance band.*
**RAB** London Arts

## Stompin' Crawfish
**Contact** Access All Areas
*French Cajun band with Anne Ramande on sax*

## Stormy Weather Boys
**Contact** Richard Grainger
**Mail address** 23 Derwent Street, Norton, STOCKTON ON TEES TS20 2BZ
**Phone/Fax** 01642 861899
**Phone** 07970 228534
**Email** richard.grainger@onyxnet.co.uk
**Web** www.richardgrainger.co.uk
*Traditional style shanties and orginal songs. Un/ accompanied.*
**RAB** Northern Arts

## Stradivarious
**Contact** Howard Mitchell
**Mail address** 1 Bramblewick Drive, Littleover, DERBY, DE23 7YG
**Phone** 01332 514088
**Email** howard@stradivarious.co.uk
**Web** www.stradivarious.co.uk
*Live music for folk, Scottish, square, contra & country dances, festivals & workshops.*
**RAB** East Midlands Arts

## Strawhead
**Contact** Malc Gibbons
**Mail address** Stoneleigh, 2 Mornington Rd, Adlington, CHORLEY, Lancs PR6 9NX
**Phone** 01257 482737
**Web** www.strawhead.org.uk
*Popular music from 16th to 19th centuries.*
***Musicians' Union member***
**RAB** North West Arts

## Strawplaiters Folk Dance Band
**Contact** Brian Patrick
**Mail address** 15 Felstead Way, LUTON, Beds, LU2 7LH
**Phone** 01582 732656
*Band and caller for EFDSS style groups and barn dances.*
**RAB** East England Arts

## Street Beast
**Contact** Artists Connect
**Web** www.artistsconnect.com
*Afro-Brazilian dance & percussion group. 6 drummers, bass and keyboard, 6-12 dancers in full costume*
**AC** Wales

## Street Dance Union
**Contact** Artists Connect
**Web** www.artistsconnect.com
*12 piece Brazilian-Jazz-Hiphop dance group. Available street and indoors*
**AC** Wales

## Striding Edge
**Contact** Mike Willoughby
**Mail address** 17 Sun Street, ULVERSTON, Cumbria, LA12 7BX
**Phone/Fax** 01229 588852
**Email** info@striding-edge.org
**Web** www.striding-edge.org
**Alt contact** Carolyn Francis
**Phone/Fax** 01524 35391
*Roots rock band, Cumbrian based material. Concerts, ceilidhs, festivals & workshops.*
***Musicians' Union member***
**RAB** Northern Arts



*Artists in the main A-Z listing are mostly available for concert and club bookings.*

*See page 11 for details of other artist listings (Dance Display, Solo Musicians, Composers, Arrangers, Session Musicians, Band Deps. Lecturers, MCs, Tutors, Street Theatre, Children's Entertainers, Theatre Companies).*

*Agents section appears on pages 119-131.*

*Artists in the main A-Z listing are mostly available for concert and club bookings.*

*See page 11 for details of other artist listings (Dance Display, Solo Musicians, Composers, Arrangers, Session Musicians, Band Deps. Lecturers, MCs, Tutors, Street Theatre, Children's Entertainers, Theatre Companies).*

*Agents section appears on pages 119-131.*

## Strings
**Contact** Kiran Thakrar
**Mail address** 30 Westmorland Road, NORTH HARROW, Middlesex, HA1 4PL
**Phone** 07957 190680
020 8427 7952
**Email** kiran@strings-band.com
**Web** www.strings-band.com
*Indian folk music band.*
***Musicians' Union member***
**RAB** London Arts

## The Stubble Stompers
**Contact** Larry Freeman
**Mail address** The Mount, Church Bank, Temple Grafton, ALCESTER, Warks, B49 6NU
**Phone** 01789 773856
**Email** stubblestompers@aol.com
**Alt contact** John Tatlow
Grafton House Farm, Temple Grafton, ALCESTER, Warks, B49 6NS
**Phone** 01789 772289
*5 piece all male goodtime band. Skiffle, folk country, old pop, etc.*
**RAB** West Midlands Arts

## Sue Coe
**Mail address** 103 Oldham Road, Ripponden, SOWERBY BRIDGE, West Yorks, HX6 4EB
**Phone/Fax** 01422 822569
**Email** suecoe@backshift.demon.co.uk
*Dance caller.*
**RAB** Yorkshire Arts

## Sula
**Contact** Eskil Romme
**Mail address** Hedegaardsvej 10, Hallaer, 9240 NIBE, Denmark
**Phone** +45 9866 6476
**Email** eskilromme@hotmail.com
*Danish band playing Scots and Scandinavian folk music. Frequent UK tours*

## Sunhoney
**Contact** Aidan O'Rourke
**Mail address** 2/3 13 Church Street, Partick, GLASGOW, G11 5JP, Scotland
**Phone** 0141 581 6147
0777 9293527
**Email** aidanorourke@aol.com
*Celtic roots meet urban grooves. Aidan O'Rourke with Alyth McCormack, Fergus Mackenzie, Quee MacArthur, Kevin Mackenzie & Donald Hay.*
***Musicians' Union member***
**AC** Scotland

## The Sussex Pistols
**Contact** Vic and Tina Smith
**Mail address** 26 Ferrers Road, LEWES, East Sussex, BN7 1PZ
**Phone/Fax** 01273 478124
**Email** tinvic@globalnet.co.uk
**Web** www.users.globalnet.co.uk/~tinvic/pistols.htm
*Six-piece barn dance/ ceilidh band comprising accordion, 2 fiddles, hammered dulcimer, concertina, guitar, mandolo, bass.*
**RAB** South East Arts

## SWÅP
**Contact** Brass Tacks
*Anglo-Swedish ensemble presenting traditional and new material, drawing from Irish, British and Scandanavian roots. All are respected composers & workshop tutors*
***Musicians' Union member***

## Sweet Lorraine
**Contact** Artists Connect
**Web** www.artistsconnect.com
*Duo with guitar, vocals, sax etc. West African and English roots*

## Swervy World Theatre
**Contact** Artists Connect
**Web** www.artistsconnect.com
*Mix of music and theatre, jump jazz, skiffle, kitsch, jive, etc*

## Szapora
**Contact** Dave Kelbie
**Mail address** PO Box 26294, LONDON, W3 7GE
**Phone** 020 8992 0283
07967 728259
**Fax** 020 8932 4836
**Email** lejazztel@lejazztel.com
**Web** www.lejazztel.com
*UK based Balkan music multi-national collective. With Mirella & Tea Hodzic, Mirza Halilovic, Vanja Krawczyk and others*
**Agents** Adastra, Lejazzetal, Matters Musical, Triss Dickin
***Musicians' Union member***
**RAB** London Arts

## Tabache
**Contact** Aidan O'Rourke
**Phone** 0141 5816147
07779 293527
**Email** aidanorourke@aol.com
*Scottish-Irish traditional music trio. Clare Mann, Aidan O'Rourke & Ross Martin.*
**AC** Scotland

## The Tabs
**Contact** Elizabeth Jones Entertainments
**Web** www.bromyard.co.uk/ejones
*Folk-rock band*

## Tabuka
**Contact** Ben Farmer
**Mail address** 27 Regent Street, LANCASTER, LA1 1SQ
**Phone** 01524 847135
**Email** info@chouchenn.net
*Trio playing traditional & new tunes from Lancashire, Ireland, Europe and Israel, for ceilidhs and concerts.*
**RAB** North West Arts

## Taiko to Tabla
**Contact** mARKO pOLO
**Web** www.markopolo.co.uk
*Fusion of percussion from Japan, India and around the world. With Joji Hirota and Peter Lockett*
**Agent** mARKO pOLO, Matters Musical

## Taj Mahal
**Contact** Asgard Promotions
*Played a pivotal role in the mid-sixties Blues revival, and later made his mark in Rock, Soul, contemporary Blues & World Music*

## Tala
**Contact** Sarah Jones
**Mail address** The Forge, Goodrich, ROSS ON WYE, Herefordshire, HR9 6HY
**Phone/Fax** 01600 891284
**Phone** 07973 143950
**Email** sarah@bluebearmusic.demon.co.uk
**Web** www.bluebearmusic.demon.co.uk
*Acoustic based contemporary folk band. Original material.*
**RAB** West Midlands Arts

## Tall Stories
**Contact** Ken Howard
**Mail address** 45, Little Scotland, Blackrod, Bolton BL65LW
**Phone** 01942 832739
**Email** pat@littlescotland.freeserve.co.uk
**Web** www.littlescotland.freeerve.co.uk
*Traditional trio performing original & contemporary material, harmonies & arrangements. Malc Gibbons of Strawhead, Pat Ryan and Ken Howard.*

## Tam Lin
**Contact** Alan Hewson
**Mail address** 9 Lister Avenue, HITCHIN, Herts, SG4 9ES
**Phone** 01462 438373
**Fax** 01462 433395/ 421272
**Email** tamlin@questor-cp.demon.co.uk
**Web** www.questor-cp.demon.co.uk/tamlin.htm
*4 piece band playing traditional vocal and instrumental music from England, Ireland and Scotland.*
***Musicians' Union member***
**RAB** East England Arts

### Tam White and Brian Kellock
**Contact** Stoneyport Agency
**Web** www.stoneyport.demon.co.uk
*Jazz-blues duo*

### Tam White's Groove Connection
**Contact** Stoneyport Agency
**Web** www.stoneyport.demon.co.uk
*Eight-piece jazz-blues group*

### Tam White's Shoestring
**Contact** Stoneyport Agency
**Web** www.stoneyport.demon.co.uk
*Electro-acoustic blues-jazz trio*

### Tamarack
**Contact** Emerging Music
**Web** www.emerging.demon.co.uk
*Canadian trio, instrumental and vocal*

### Tan Tethera
**Contact** David Grabham
**Mail address** Poolside Cottage, Redbrook Street, Woodchurch, ASHFORD, Kent, TN26 3QR
**Phone** 01233 860789
*2/ 3 piece traditional & contemporary English & Irish folk.*
***Musicians' Union member***
**RAB** South East Arts

### Tanglefoot
**Contact** Jacey Bedford Tour Management
**Web** www.jacey-bedford.com
*Canadian 5 piece band. Canadian songs, 5 part harmony and instrumentals*
**Agent** Jacey Bedford Tour Management

### The Tango Band
**Contact** Martin Henning
**Mail address** 1 Pittford Cottages, Wenbworthy, CHULMLEIGH, Devon, EX18 7QA
**Phone** 01837 83347
**Email** m.henning@talk21.com
**Web** www.otherproductions.demon.co.uk
**Alt contact** Hugh Colvin
**Alt address** The Old School House, Llanfair Waterdine, KNIGTON, Powys
**Phone** 01547 520339
**Email** broadsheep@aol.com
*5/ 6 piece world music dance band with influences from East Europe, South America, Africa, Ireland and the UK*
**Agent** OTB Productions
***Musicians' Union member***
**RAB** South West Arts

### Tango Siempre
**Contact** Artists Connect
**Web** www.artistsconnect.com
*Quartet of violin, accordion, piano and double bass. A tango Argentina from 1920's-40's. Dancers available*
**RAB** South West Arts

### Tannahill Weavers
**Contact** Emerging Music
**Web** www.emerging.demon.co.uk
*Established Scottish 5 piece vocal and instrumental band*
**AC** Scotland

### Tarika
**Contact** The Concert Clinic
**Web** www.froots.demon co.uk/ tarika.html
*Madagascar's No. 1 Roots band. Regular UK/ European tours*

### Tarras
**Contact** Emerging Music
**Web** www.emerging.demon.co.uk
*Young Northumbrian band. Songs, fiddle, guitars, etc*

### Tartan Amoebas
**Contact** Active
*7 piece Celtic roots band. Bagpipes and brass*

### Tashbain
**Contact** Lindsay Aitkenhead
**Mail address** 19 Yeomans Road, SHEFFIELD, S6 3JD
**Phone** 0114 281 7614
**Email** lindsay.aitkenhead@newscientist.net
**Web** www.tashbain.f9.co.uk
*Jewish storytelling band*
**Agent** Elizabeth Jones Entertainments
**RAB** Yorkshire Arts

### Te Vaka
**Contact** mARKO pOLO
**Web** www.markopolo.co.uk
*Pacific Islands log drumming combined with the Maori tradition*

### Teddy Peiro's Tango
**Contact** Matters Musical
**Web** www.mattersmusical com
*UK based 5 piece tango band. Dancers available*

### Terry Mann
**Mail address** 35 Nottingham Road, Leyton, LONDON, E10 6BP
**Phone/Fax** 020 8556 7005
**Email** tmann@cwcom.net
*Composer, performer & workshop leader. Percussion, sax/ wind & guitar, community music. Recipient of George Butterworth Award 2000.*
***Musicians' Union member***
**RAB** London Arts

### Thee Na Shee
**Contact** Matters Musical
**Web** www.mattersmusical.com
*Celtic-world music*

### Thingumajig
**Phone** 01273 455202
**Email** pete@mcmail.demon.co.uk
**Web** www.hobgoblin.com/thingumajig
*Ceilidh/barn dance band.*

### This Way Up
**Contact** Richard Payne
**Mail address** Swn Yr Afon, Waterfall Street, LLANRHAEADR Y M, Powys, SY10 0JX
**Phone/Fax** 01691 780064
**Email** thiswayup@compuserve.com
**Web** members.madasafish.com/~this_way_up/
**Alt contact** Stuart Altman
**Alt address** 51 Trinity Street, Belle Vue, SHREWSBURY, Shrops
**Phone** 01743 242055
*6 piece folk rock and English ceilidh band with drums, bass, melodeons, saxs. Available for ceilidhs and concerts anywhere.*
**AC** Wales

### Three Sheets To The Wind
**Contact** Keith Kendrick
**Mail address** 88 Highfield Road, ASHBOURNE, Derbyshire, DE6 1DX
**Phone/Fax** 01335 345675
**Phone** 07885 345367
**Email** eyup@freeuk.com
**Web** www.eyuk.freeuk.com
*Mainly maritime songs/ shanties. Un/ Accompanied. Keith Kendrick, Geoff Higginbottom & Derek Gifford.*
**RAB** East Midlands Arts

### The Three Tenners
**Contact** UK Touring
**Web** www.uktouring.org.uk
*Walkabout a capella song street theatre trio.*

*Artists in the main A-Z listing are mostly available for concert and club bookings.*

*See page 11 for details of other artist listings (Dance Display, Solo Musicians, Composers, Arrangers, Session Musicians, Band Deps. Lecturers, MCs, Tutors, Street Theatre, Children's Entertainers, Theatre Companies).*

*Agents section appears on pages 119-131.*

# artists
## t

*Artists in the main A-Z listing are mostly available for concert and club bookings.*

*See page 11 for details of other artist listings (Dance Display, Solo Musicians, Composers, Arrangers, Session Musicians, Band Deps. Lecturers, MCs, Tutors, Street Theatre, Children's Entertainers, Theatre Companies).*

*Agents section appears on pages 119-131.*

### Three Tuns O' Grass
**Contact** David Hatfield
**Mail address** Willow Croft, Wagg Drove, Hulsh-Epislopi, NR LANGPORT, Somerset, TA10 9ER
**Phone/Fax** 01458 250317
**Phone** 01458 253838
**Email** david@changing-world.com
*5 piece Bluegrass and acoustic music band. Banjo, fiddle, guitar, mandolin, bass.*
**RAB** South West Arts

### The Thunderdog Ceilidh Band
**Contact** Iain E MacLachlan
**Mail address** 11 Scone Gardens, EDINBURGH, EH8 7DQ
**Phone** 0131 6611655
**Email** iain@thunderdog.co.uk
**Web** www.thunderdog.co.uk
*5 piece ceilidh band with caller. Fiddle, banjo, etc. Dances from Scotland and all over the world. Workshops, ceilidhs, weddings, etc.*
***Musicians' Union member***
**AC** Scotland

### Ti Jaz
**Contact** Adastra
**Web** www.adastra-music.com
*Breton dance music on bombarde, brass, etc*

### Tich Frier
**Mail address** 8 Rannoch Place, KINROSS, Tayside, KY13 8BQ, Scotland
**Phone** 01577 864164
**Email** tich@frier.demon.co.uk
*Solo Scottish song and guitar.*
**AC** Scotland

### The Tide
**Contact** Jim Bean
**Mail address** 64 Talbot Road, OLD ISLEWORTH, Middx, TW7 7HF
**Phone** 020 8891 0623
*Irish music acoustic quartet. Bazouki, fiddle, guitar, double bass.*
**RAB** London Arts

### Tiharea
**Contact** Adastra
**Web** www.adastra-music.com
*Female trio from Southern Madagascar*

### Tim Garland
**Mail address** 25 Baden Road, Evington, LEICESTER, LE5 5PA
**Phone** 0116 273 4453
*Solo singer of traditional and self written songs, with guitar, cittern, fiddle, saz and pipes.*
**RAB** East Midlands Arts

### Tim Kent
**Mail address** 2 Medway Court, Kingston Lane, SOUTHWICK, W Sussex, BN42 4SL
**Phone** 01273 595614
**Email** tktw@mistral.co.uk
**Web** www.uksoundcraft.com
*Singer/ songwriter/ entertainer. Guitar, dulcimer/ keyboards, contemporary and traditional songs. Solo or duo "Two & a Hat". Folk, pop, rock & blues.*
***Musicians' Union member***
**RAB** South East Arts

### Tim Laycock
**Mail address** 9 Wingreen View, SHAFTESBURY, Dorset, SP7 8SR
**Email** tim@new-scorpion-band.com
*Solo singer of mainly traditional English songs accompanied on concertina or melodeon.*
***Musicians' Union member***
**RAB** South West Arts

### Tim Lyons and Fintan Vallely
**Contact** The Bechhofer Agency
*Trad songs, tunes and humour.*
**AC** Ireland

### Tim O'Brien and Darrell Scott
**Contact** Adastra
**Web** www.adastra-music.com
*Grammy nominated American singers & musicians. Also 'The Crossing'*

### Tim van Eyken
**Contact** Appledore Music
**Mail address** Old Wells Road, SHEPTON MALLETT, Somerset, BA4 5XZ
**Phone** 07970 472725
**Fax** 07971 653883
**Email** appledore.music@ukonline.co.uk
**Web** www.timvaneyken.co.uk
*BBC 2 Young Folk Award winning accordeon player, singer and guitarist, mostly traditional English music. Solo, with Waterson:Carthy; James Fagan & Nancy Kerr; Robert Harbron & Dr Faustus*
**Agent** Access All Areas, Elizabeth Jones Entertainments
***Musicians' Union member***
**RAB** South West Arts

### Tim van Eyken and Robert Harbron
**Contact** Robert Harbron
**Mail address** 94 Roxeth Green Avenue, HARROW, Middx, HA2 8AQ
**Phone** 020 8357 3261
07973 717786
**Fax** 020 8537 8335
**Email** rob.harbron@virgin.net
**Web** www.robertharbron.co.uk
*English folk duo, concertina, melodeon, guitar, voice.*
**RAB** South East Arts

### Tim Willets
**Mail address** 21 Hambrook Close, WOLVERHAMPTON, WV6 0XA
**Phone** 01902 715235
**Email** tlw@redowa.co.uk
*Performer of traditional English dance music on meldeons, guitars, fiddle.*
***Musicians' Union member***
**RAB** West Midlands Arts

### Time Of Your Life
**Contact** Barry Goodman
**Mail address** 54 Ickleford Road, HITCHIN, Herts, SG5 1TR
**Phone** 01462 456811
**Email** barry.goodman1@ntlworld.com
**Web** www.good-man.freeserve.co.uk
*5 piece English ceilidh band with caller. Herts/ Beds based.*
**RAB** East England Arts

### Tinkers Bag
**Contact** Robert Berry
**Mail address** 19 Whistley Road, Potterne, DEVIZES, Wilts, SN10 5QY
**Phone** 01380 726597
07714 550990
**Email** potfolk@aol.com
*8 piece group performing themed concert shows plus various other song, music and dance.*
**RAB** Southern Arts

### Token Women
**Contact** Shindy Arts
**Web** www.freya.org.uk
*Popular 6 piece all female dance band. Fiddles, brass, percussion and keyboard*
***Musicians' Union member***
**RAB** East Midlands Arts

## Tollhouse Company
**Contact** Barbara Griffiths
**Mail address** 1 Station Cottages, Grunty Fen, WILBURTON, Cambs, CB6 3PZ
**Phone** 01353 740101
**Email** info@tollhouse.co.uk
**Web** www.tollhouse.co.uk
*History based musical theatre performances, traditional and original material for schools/ family audiences. English ceilidh band with caller.*
***Musicians' Union member***
**RAB** East England Arts

## Tom & Barbara Brown
**Contact** Tom Brown
**Mail address** Trafalgar House, Castle Street, COMBE MARTIN, N Devon, EX34 0JD
**Phone** 01271 882366
07977 914736
**Email** tom.brown1@virgin.net
*English traditional song; unaccompanied and with guitar, concertina, melodeon, mandola. Available full time.*
***Musicians' Union member***
**RAB** South West Arts

## Tom Ball and Kenny Sultan
**Contact** mARKO pOLO
**Web** www.markopolo.co.uk
*US acoustic blues guitar and harmonica duo*

## Tom Brown
**Mail address** Trafalgar House, Castle Street, COMBE MARTIN, N Devon, EX34 0JD
**Phone** 01271 882366
07977 914736
**Email** tom.brown1@virgin.net
*Caller for barn dances/ ceilidhs. English and Scottish dances. Solo or band available. Not records. Available full time.*
***Musicians' Union member***
**RAB** South West Arts

## Tom Leary and Kevin Dempsey
**Contact** Iconic Music & Media
*Guitar and fiddle duo; own compositions and traditional reportiore in the folk idiom*
**RAB** West Midlands Arts

## Tom Napper and Gina LeFaux
**Contact** Tom Napper
**Mail address** Flat 2, 2 Woodland View, LEEDS, Yorks, LS7 4QJ
**Phone** 0113 268 0963
**Alt Phone** 01422 362634
*Folk music and song on fiddle, viola, guitar, mandola, etc.*
***Musicians' Union member***
**RAB** Yorkshire Arts

## Tom Robinson
**Contact** Sue Brearley
**Mail address** Leporine Ltd, PO Box 3185, LONDON, SW18 3JG
**Phone** 020 8874 9607
**Fax** 020 8333 2468
**Email** siouxsie@bothways.com
**Web** www.tomrobinson.com
**Alt contact** Rob Stringer
**Alt address** CMP Concerts, 34 Market Street, SOUTHPORT, PR8 1HJ
**Phone** 01704 539746
**Fax** 01704 500709
**Email** cmpgigs@aol.com
*Songwriter, broadcaster, band leader & solo performer. Schools workshops on creative writing and live performance skills.*
***Musicians' Union member***
**RAB** Northern Arts

## Tom Walwyn
**Mail address** 1A East Brunton Farm Cottages, Brunton Lane, Gosforth, NEWCASTLE UPON TYNE, NE13 7NS
**Phone** 0191 2363082
07787 518281
**Email** tomwalwyn@hotmail.com
*Solo English half-long pipes and bamboo flutes. Irish, French, Spanish and Northumbrian music.*
**RAB** Northern Arts

## Tomas Lynch
**Contact** CTM UK
**Web** www.ctmuk.com
*Irish singer, guitarist and piper traditional & contemporary music*
**AC** Scotland

## Tommy Emmanuel
**Contact** NEM Productions (UK)
**Web** www.nemproductions.com
*Esteemed Ausvalian guitarist*

## Tommy Sands
**Contact** The Bechhofer Agency
*Highly regarded singer songwriter*
**AC** Northern Ireland

## Tony Backhouse
**Contact** New Earth Publishing
**Mail address** 83 Milton Lane, Walkden, Worsley, MANCHESTER, M28 0SZ
**Phone** 0161 799 9979
**Email** newearthpub@hotmail.com
**Web** www.ndirect.co.uk/chrisconway
*Guitar/ mandola player & vocalist*
**Agent** Elizabeth Jones Entertainments
***Musicians' Union member***
**RAB** North West Arts

## Tony Kelly
**Contact** 15 Langham Close, GODALMING, Surrey, GU7 1LE
**Phone** 01483 421965
07730 045122
**Email** info@tonykelly.net
**Web** www.tonykelly.net
Caller for barn dances.
**RAB** South East Arts

## Tony Kendall
**Contact** Stormforce Arts
**Mail address** 18 Edward Avenue, Chingford, LONDON, E4 9DN
**Phone** 020 8527 0574
*Researcher, lecturer and writer on all Essex traditions; song, dance, music, customs, rituals etc. Performer of Essex songs, tunes and stories.*
***Musicians' Union member***
**RAB** London Arts

## Tony McManus
**Contact** Denise Moore
**Mail address** Integral Music, 32 Bryson Road, Unit 13, EDINBURGH EH11 1DX Scotland
**Phone** 0131 3460519
**Email** denise@tonymcmanus.com
**Web** www.tonymcmanus.com
*Scottish guitar player. Solo, traditional music from Scotland and beyond*

## Tony O'Leary
**Contact** Angela Williams
**Mail address** 52 Abbott Avenue, LONDON, SW20 8SG
**Fax** 020 8540 3350
**Email** bluestack@hotmail.com
**Web** www.countrymusic.org.uk/heartfield
*Singer/ songwriter*
**RAB** London Arts

## Tony Rose
**Mail address** 13 Lower Odcombe, YEOVIL, Somerset, BA22 8TX
**Phone** 01935 862007
**Fax** 0870 0561678
**Email** boneshaker@bigfoot.com
*Eminent solo singer of mostly traditional songs with English concertina and guitar. Workshops on song, performance and accompaniment.*
**RAB** South West Arts



*Artists in the main A-Z listing are mostly available for concert and club bookings.*

*See page 11 for details of other artist listings (Dance Display, Solo Musicians, Composers, Arrangers, Session Musicians, Band Deps. Lecturers, MCs, Tutors, Street Theatre, Children's Entertainers, Theatre Companies)*

*Agents section appears on pages 119-131.*

# artists
## t-u

*Artists in the main A-Z listing are mostly available for concert and club bookings.*

*See page 11 for details of other artist listings (Dance Display, Solo Musicians, Composers, Arrangers, Session Musicians, Band Deps. Lecturers, MCs, Tutors, Street Theatre, Children's Entertainers, Theatre Companies).*

*Agents section appears on pages 119-131.*

### Tony Wilson
**Mail address** 27 Julian Street, SOUTH SHIELDS, Tyne & Wear, NE33 2EP
**Phone** 0191 4561803
0777 9945411
**Email** joat.ink@btinternet.com
**Web** http://freespace.virgin.net/joat.ink/tonywilson/
*Guitarist, mandola, banjo player, traditional singer, compere, storyteller. Storytelling workshops*
**Agent** Bogle Music, Elizabeth Jones Entertainments
**RAB** Northern Arts

### Tony Winn
**Mail address** 21 London Road, KELVEDON, Essex, CO5 9AR
**Phone** 01376 571775
**Fax** 01376 571722
**Email** tony.winn@btinternet.com
*Songwriter/ singer/ guitarist and traditional frailing banjo*
**Agent** Elizabeth Jones Entertainments
***Musicians' Union member***
**RAB** East England Arts

### Toque de Caixa
**Contact** Adastra
**Web** www.adastra-music.com
*Portuguese group*

### Tower Struck Down
**Contact** Clare Smith
**Mail address** 21 Wistaston Road, CREWE, Cheshire, CW2 7RA
**Phone** 01270 567750
01270 569780
**Email** fluff@tower-struck-down.freeserve.co.uk
*5 piece band playing a indie, folk, roots, punk and folk-rock mix.*
**RAB** North West Arts

### Township Express
**Contact** Matters Musical
**Web** www.mattersmusical.com
*Band led by vocals and South African guitar. Plus bass, saxophone, drums and percussion*

### Tragic Roundabout
**Contact** Sandy Cameron
**Mail address** 24 College Gardens, BRIGHTON, BN2 1HP
**Phone** 01273 606218
**Email** tragic@breathemail.net
**Web** www.tragicroundabout.freeserve.co.uk
*6 piece band playing klezmer, folk and jazz plus humour. Also street festivals and processions.*
**RAB** South East Arts

### The Transsylvanians
**Contact** mARKO pOLO
**Web** www.markopolo.co.uk
*Berlin based German, Hungarian and Russian musicians playing traditional-based music*

### Trevor Carter
**Mail address** 82 Uttoxeter Road, Blythe Bridge, STOKE ON TRENT, Staffs, ST11 9JG
**Phone** 01782 398657
**Email** carter@edgemusic.fsnet.co.uk
**Web** www.edgemusic.fsnet.co.uk
*Singer/ songwriter, guitar, keyboard, concertina.*
**RAB** West Midlands Arts

### Trevor James
**Mail address** 7 Park Close, Markyate, ST ALBANS, Herts, AL3 8RG
**Phone** 01582 842178
*Minstrel, playing folk/ celtic music on borderpipes, whistles, pipe and tabor, etc.*
***Musicians' Union member***
**RAB** Southern Arts

### Tricks Upon Travellers
**Contact** Dick Langford
**Mail address** PO Box 2693, BRIGHTON, BN1 5QL
**Phone** 01273 564692
07771 736802
**Email** dicklangford@pavilion.co.uk
**Web** www.tricksupontravellers.co.uk
*5 piece folk rock band.*
**RAB** South East Arts

### Trish Sweeney and Peta Webb
**Contact** Trish Sweeney
**Mail address** 166 Glenarm Road, LONDON, E5 0NB
**Phone** 020 8985 1556
**Email** petawebken@aol.com
**Alt contact** Peta Webb
**Alt address** 52 Cecile Park, LONDON, N8 9AS
**Phone** 020 8340 0530
*Vocal harmony duo with guitar, bodhran and fiddle accompaniment. Traditional Irish and American and contemporary political songs.*
***Musicians' Union member***
**RAB** London Arts

### Truss and Bucket Band
**Contact** Matters Musical
**Web** www.mattersmusical.com
*Ceilidh band including rock & roll vocalists*

### Tryckster
**Contact** David Camlin
**Mail address** Ghyll Cottage, Lamplugh Glen, WORKINGTON, Cumbria, CA14 4TY
**Phone** 01946 861080
01946 726013
**Email** tryckster@btinternet.com
**Web** www.comonecomputers.com
*6 piece folk rock band; fiddle, flute, mandolin, bouzouki, bass, drums, vocals.*
***Musicians' Union member***
**RAB** Northern Arts

### Tuesday Occasionals
**Contact** Dave & Ruth Cooper
**Mail address** 94 Pasture Road, Stapleford, NOTTINGHAM, NG9 8GL
**Phone** 0115 9399730
**Email** rcooper@stapleford-centre.org
**Web** www.wtsinfo.btinternet.co.uk/to
*20 strong group singing Sacred Harp, West Gallery, Gospel & folk music. Charity concerts, workshops, festivals, community events etc.*
**RAB** East Midlands Arts

### The Two Duos Quartet
**Contact** Brass Tacks
**Web** www.rufrecords.com
*4 piece English ensemble combining the compositions and arrangements of Chris Wood, Andy Cutting, Karen Tweed & Ian Carr. Known for their work as two duos*
***Musicians' Union member***
**RAB** East Midlands Arts

### Tziganarama
**Contact** Chris Haigh
**Mail address** 232 Sebert Road, Forest Gate, LONDON, E7 0NP
**Phone** 020 8534 3887
**Email** chris@fiddlingaround.co.uk
**Web** www.fiddlingaround.co.uk/tzig
*Trio playing Eastern European music on fiddle, accordion & double bass Matters Musical*
***Musicians' Union member***
**RAB** London Arts

### Uilliam Haicead
**Mail address** 10A Lefroy Street, COATBRIDGE, Lanarkshire, ML5 1PN, Scotland
**Phone** 01236 428947
020 7487 4739
**Email** liam.hackett@talk21.com
*Uillieann piper with full national dress (kilt, corbin, cloak etc). All-Scotland silver medal.*
***Musicians' Union member***
**AC** Scotland

### The Ukrainians
**Contact** Moneypenny

## Ulstersongs (John Moulden)
**Contact** John Moulden
**Mail address** 10 Apollo Walk, PORTRUSH, Co Antrim, BT56 8HQ, N Ireland
**Phone/Fax** 028 7082 5080
**Phone** 028 7082 5025
**Email** john@ulstersongs.com
**Web** www.ulstersongs.com
*Singer of unaccompanied (Northern) Irish songs, percussionist.*
**AC** Northern Ireland

## Used Notes
**Contact** Dan Quinn
**Mail address** 87 St Andrews Road, Portslade, BRIGHTON, Sussex, BN41 1DD
**Phone** 01273 881316
**Email** quinn@unisonfree.net
*4 piece English dance band featuring ex members of Gas Mark 5 and The Oyster band. Guitars, banjos, melodeon, bass.*
**RAB** South East Arts

## Vasmalom
**Contact** Adastra
**Web** www.adastra-music.com
*Hungarian band playing comtemporary and traditional music on traditional Hungarian instruments*

## Vera Bila & Kale
**Contact** mARKO pOLO
**Web** www.markopolo.co.uk
*Romany singer, latin-pop*

## Vice Bishops Blues Band
**Contact** Smalltown Promotions
*4 piece band; twin guitars, bass & drums*
**RAB** West Midlands Arts

## Vice Bishops of Uttoxeter
**Contact** Smalltown Promotions
*Multi instrumental duo & session musicians*
**RAB** West Midlands Arts

## Victor Hugo Salsa Show
**Contact** Latin Arts Services
**Web** www.victorhugosalsa.com
*Large Latin American Salsa show*
***Musicians' Union member***
**RAB** London Arts

## Vikki Clayton
**Mail address** 9 Fern Close, THURNBY, Leics, LE7 9QJ
**Phone** 0116 2433447
**Email** vikki@clara.co.uk
**Web** www.vikkiclayton.co.uk
*Singer & songwriter. Singer with Fairport Convention. Solo or with own band*
**Agent** Elizabeth Jones Entertainments, Speaking Volumes
***Musicians' Union member***
**RAB** East Midlands Arts

## The Vikki Clayton Band
**Contact** Elizabeth Jones Entertainments
**Web** www.bromyard.co.uk/ejones
*Singer/ songwriter and her band*

## Vin Garbutt
**Contact** Speaking Volumes
**Web** www.vingarbutt.com
*Very popular folk singer, songwriter, guitarist, humorist and whistle player.*

## Viramundo
**Contact** Matters Musical
**Web** www.mattersmusical.com
*6-8 piece Brazilian samba band. Dance troupe available*

## Viva Flamenco
**Contact** Matters Musical
**Web** www.mattersmusical.com
*International Flamenco guitar and dance group*

## Vladimir Asriev
**Contact** Matters Musical
**Web** www.mattersmusical.com
*Russian Gypsy fiddle player. Costumed Russian & East European duo or trio*

## Vocalzone
**Contact** Dave & Ruth Cooper
**Mail address** 94 Pasture Road, Stapleford, NOTTINGHAM, NG9 8GL
**Phone** 0115 9399730
**Email** rcooper@stapleford-centre.org
*4 part harmony vocal group with some accompaniment. English traditional, Sacred Harp, West Gallery, etc. Harmony workshops.*
**RAB** East Midlands Arts

## Voxy
**Contact** Roland Kemp
**Mail address** 14 Mowbray Road, LONDON, SE19 2RN
**Phone/Fax** 020 8771 4557
**Phone** 07860 237739
**Email** roland.kemp@virgin.net
*Female vocal duo. English & Irish folk songs, acapella and with guitar and violin.*
**RAB** London Arts

## Walker Family
**Contact** Brenda Walker
**Mail address** 12 High Street North, LANGLEY MOOR, Durham, DH7 8JG
**Phone** 0191 3784993
07939 517010
**Fax** 0191 3860714
**Email** brendaw@globalnet.co.uk
*Group including Clog dance team, Highland dance team and full band playing Northern English music. Workshops.*
**RAB** Northern Arts

## Warren Malone
**Contact** Elizabeth Jones Entertainments
**Web** www.bromyard.co.uk/ejones
*Singer/ songwriter*

## Waterson:Carthy
**Contact** Moneypenny
*First family of English folk music; Martin Carthy, Norma Waterson, Elzia Carthy and Tim van Eyken*

## The Watts Prophets
**Contact** mARKO pOLO
**Web** www.markopolo.co.uk
*Founders of West Coast Rap from LA and working with broken education systems, prisons, etc*

## Wavet
**Contact** Nina Jaffa
**Mail address** 24B Colless Road, LONDON, N15 4NR
**Phone** 020 8808 4290
07956 395018
**Email** info@salsadirect.co.uk
**Web** www.salsadirect.co.uk
*Uk based St Lucian soca/ calypso/ reggae carnival/ dance band. Fronted by Yvonne Curtis.*
***Musicians' Union member***
**RAB** London Arts

## Wayra de Los Andes
**Contact** Artists Connect
**Web** www.artistsconnect.com
*Group playing Andean panpies from Bolivia*

## Weapons of Sound
**Contact** Fool's Paradise
**Web** www.soundhouse.co.uk/wos
**Alt contact** Nicky Street
*10-14 piece drum group using instruments made from waste materials*
**RAB** Southern Arts

*Artists in the main A-Z listing are mostly available for concert and club bookings.*

*See page 11 for details of other artist listings (Dance Display, Solo Musicians, Composers, Arrangers, Session Musicians, Band Deps. Lecturers, MCs, Tutors, Street Theatre, Children's Entertainers, Theatre Companies).*

*Agents section appears on pages 119-131.*

## artists

## W

Artists in the main A-Z listing are mostly available for concert and club bookings.

See page 11 for details of other artist listings (Dance Display, Solo Musicians, Composers, Arrangers, Session Musicians, Band Deps. Lecturers, MCs, Tutors, Street Theatre, Children's Entertainers, Theatre Companies).

Agents section appears on pages 119-131.

### Wei Li Chinese Orchestra
**Contact** Matters Musical
**Web** www.mattersmusical.com
*Chinese musicians and dancers, performing on traditional instruments, led by Chinese soprano Wei Li.*

### The Wendigo
**Contact** Steve Tyler
**Mail address** Brancepeth Castle, BRANCEPETH, Co Durham, DH7 8DE
**Phone** 0191 378 3836/ 9321 07939 522675
**Email** amsummers@lineone.net
**Alt contact** Julian Sutton
**Alt address** 38 Ferne Avenue, Jesmond, NEWCASTLE UPON TYNE, NE2 2QX
**Phone** 0191 2720427
*Trio playing European, early music and traditional English/ Celtic music on pipes, hurdy-gurdy and melodeon Concert and dance band.*
***Musicians' Union member***
**RAB** Northern Arts

### West Country Dance Orchestra
**Contact** Chris Bartram
**Mail address** Granway House, 3 Coldharbour, Uffculme, CULLOMPTON, Devon, EX15 3EE
**Phone/Fax** 01884 841499
**Phone** 07968 193555
**Email** chris@chris-bartram.co.uk
**Web** www.westcountrydanceorchestra.org.uk
*Tunes, dances & songs from SW England performed on fiddles, flute, concertina, tuba & piano.*
**RAB** South West Arts

### Western Electric
**Contact** Pat McGarvey
**Mail address** 108A Acton Lane, LONDON, NW10 8TX
**Phone** 020 8838 0804
**Fax** 020 7794 9549
**Email** patmcgarvey@x-stream.co.uk
**Web** www.sidgriffin.com
*Alternative Country and psychadelic roots Rock n Roll. Led by ex-Long Ryder and Coal Porter frontman Sid Griffin.*
***Musicians' Union member***
**RAB** London Arts

### Whapweasel
**Contact** Brian Bell
**Phone** 01434 684 705
**Email** mail@whapweasel.com
**Web** www.whapweasel.com
Ceilidh band.
***Musicians' Union member***
**RAB** Northern Arts

### Wheelwrights Bane
**Contact** Rex Morrey
**Mail address** 333 Whitley Wood Lane, READING, Berks, RG2 8PX
**Phone** 0118 987 6734
**Email** rex.morrey@wheelwrights-bane.com
**Web** www.wheelwrights-bane.com
*Ceilidh/ barn dance band. Whistles, concertina, bass & drums, etc. UK music plus self penned with rock, jazz & blues elements.*
**RAB** Southern Arts

### While & Matthews
**Contact** Blue Moon Music
**Web** www.bluemoonmusic.co.uk
*Prolific acoustic roots duo. Female singer/songwriters and instrumentals.*

### The Whisky Priests
**Contact** Whippet Promotions
**Web www.**whiskypriests.co.uk
*5 piece folk-rooted band, own songwriting*
***Musicians' Union member***
**RAB** Yorkshire Arts

### Whistlebinkies
**Contact** Eddie McGuire
**Mail address** 13 Lawrence Street, GLASGOW, G11 5HH, Scotland
**Phone** 0141 334 8580
**Web** www.whistlebinkies.net
*Traditional and new Scottish music on bagpipes, clarsach, fiddle, flute, concertina, voice, drums. Orchestral collaborations, etc.*
***Musicians' Union member***
**AC** Scotland

### White Horse Band
**Contact** Colin Dipper
**Mail address** West End House, HEYTESBURY, Wilts, BA12 0EA
**Phone** 01985 849516
**Email** dipperconcertinas@hotmail.com
*Band for functions, weddings & barn dances, village dances & ceilidhs.*
**RAB** Southern Arts

### Whorticulture
**Contact** Hemlock Music
**Web** www.hemlockmusic.demon.co.uk
*4 piece band; English traditional a capella songs and instrumentals. Bagpipes, tuba, squeezeboxes, guitar, etc*
***Musicians' Union member***
**RAB** East England Arts

### Wild Cigarillos
**Contact** Bill Barclay
**Mail address** c/o 39 Shandon Crescent, EDINBURGH, EH11 1QF, Scotland
**Phone** 0131 3394279
**Email** bb003@almac.co.uk
*Ceilidh band with broad repertoire. Own PA, two callers*
**Agent** Stoneyport Agency
**AC** Scotland

### Wild Welsh Women
**Contact** Rob Morris
**Mail address** 63 High Street, AYLBURTON, Glos, GL15 6DE
**Phone** 01594 840152
**Fax** 01594 840251
**Email** robert.morris1@btinternet.com
**Web** www.powell168.freeserve.co.uk
*6 piece celtic/ roots vocal duo led band. Workshops in vocal technique and Welsh fiddle playing*
**Agent** Elizabeth Jones Entertainments
**RAB** South West Arts

### Wild Women
**Contact** Matters Musical
**Web** www.mattersmusical.com
*Vocal and bass guitar duo drawing from jazz/ blues, reggae and folk ballads*

### Will Duke and Dan Quinn
**Contact** Dan Quinn
**Mail address** 87 St Andrews Road, Portslade, BRIGHTON, Sussex, BN41 1DD
**Phone** 01273 881316
**Email** quinn@unisonfree.net
*Traditional songs and tunes (mainly Southern English) accompanied on melodeon and concertina.*
***Musicians' Union member***
**RAB** South East Arts

### William Crawford
**Mail address** Upper Leanassie, Kilmorack, BEAULY, Ross-shire, IV4 7AF, Scotland
**Phone** 01463 782153
**Fax** 01463 782366
**Email** highmusic@fsbdial.co.uk
**Alt address** Highlander Music, Unit 7D, Muir of Ord Ind. Est., Ross-shire, IV6 7UA
**Phone** 01463 871422
**Fax** 01463 871433
**Email** highlander.music@zetnet.co.uk
*Caller for ceilidhs, Scottish country dances and reel parties.*
**AC** Scotland

### William Pint and Felicia Dale
**Mail address** Jacey Bedford Tour Management
**Web** www.jacey-bedford.com
*American duo, sea songs with guitar, whistle, mandola and hurdy gurdy*

## Wiltshire Traditions
**Contact** Robert W Berry
**Mail address** 19 Whistley Road, Potterne, DEVIZES, Wilts, SN10 5QY
**Phone** 01380 726597
07714 550990
**Email** potfolk@aol.com
**Web**
http://hometown.aol.com/potfolk/myhomepages/business.html
*Research, collection. Collates and re-enacts traditional music, song, dance, customs and traditions of Wiltshire.*
**RAB** Southern Arts

## Wizz Jones
**Mail address** 38 Webbs Road, LONDON, SW11 6SF
**Phone** 07712 361430
**Web** www.rockinworld.com
*Respected acoustic guitarist, folk blues singer and songwriter.*
***Musicians' Union member***
**RAB** London Arts

## WOB
**Contact** Ian Williams
**Mail address** PO Box 2684, READING, Berks, RG2 7YD
**Phone** 07971 420043
**Email** wobonline@yahoo.co.uk
*Singer/ songwriter. Solo, duo and with band.*
***Musicians' Union member***
**RAB** Southern Arts

## Wood Wilson Carthy
**Contact** Chris Wood
**Mail address** 40 Whitstable Road, FAVERSHAM, Kent, ME13 8DL
**Phone** 01795 537906
**Email** cw@rurecords.com
**Web** www.rufrecords.com
*Trio of respected English muscians, songs, ballads and tunes. Martin Carthy with Chris Wood and Roger Wilson*
**Agent** Adastra
***Musicians' Union member***
**RAB** South East Arts

## Wood WorX
**Contact** The Other Agency
**Web** www.woodworx.org
**Alt contact** Steafan Hannigan
*Vocalist Toni Wood and guitarist Brian Heywood. Traditional folk with contemporary influences. Trio or full band*
***Musicians' Union member***
**RAB** East England Arts

## The Woodpecker Band
**Contact** Ali Smith
**Mail address** 34 Chestnut Avenue, Headington, OXFORD, OX3 9JH
**Phone** 01865 761219
07957 146511
**Email** wishingchair@tesco.net
**Web** www.woodpeckerband.co.uk
**Alt contact** Matthew Green
5 Mercury Close, BAMPTON, Oxon
**Phone** 01993 850760
07850 108938
**Email** jeff@thepieces.freeserve.co.uk
*Respected Oxfordshire high energy ceilidh band.*
**RAB** Southern Arts

## Woody Mann
**Contact** NEM Productions (UK)
**Web** www.nemproductions.com
*Fingerstyle guitarist and singer*

## Workhouse
**Contact** Hemlock Music
**Web** www.hemlockmusic.demon.co.uk
*Ceilidh band; European-Celtic dance music. Melodeon, fiddle, bass, keyboard, drums, etc*
**RAB** East England Arts

## Wraggle Taggle
**Contact** Mick Bailey
**Mail address** 18A Dunollie Road, LONDON, NW5 2XP
**Phone** 020 7267 7737
**Fax** 020 7267 7737
**Email** mbailey@belsizesquare.freeserve.co.uk
**Web** www.belsizesquare.freeserve.co.uk
*Band ranges from a duo to a 6 piece, acoustic/ amplified, caller available for ceilidhs*
**Agent** Matters Musical
***Musicians' Union member***
**RAB** London Arts

## Wrekin Havoc Mountain Boys
**Contact** Access All Areas
*Bluegrass band*
**RAB** West Midlands Arts

## Wysiwyg Acoustic
**Contact** Ged Pether - Secretary
**Mail address** Haven Cottage, Bottle Lane, SHEPTON BEAUCHAMP, Somerset, TA19 0LG
**Phone** 01460 241010
01460 68221
**Email** ged.pether@lineone.net
**Alt contact** F Alex Boydell - Bookings
**Alt address** Hillview, Salwayash, BRIDPORT, Dorset, DT6 5HU
**Phone** 01308 488456
**Email** alexboydell@hotmail.com
*Open group of 12-16 musicians playing folk, old time & light music. Includes singers and step dancers.*
**RAB** South West Arts

## Xeliba
**Contact** mARKO pOLO
**Web** www.markopolo.co.uk
*Spanish 6 piece band*

## Xenia Horne
**Contact** Musicmakers
**Mail address** 4 Springfield Terrace, Alburgh, HARLESTON, Norfolk, IP20 0DG
**Phone/Fax** 01986 788858
**Email** musicmakersuk@aol.com
**Web** www.musicmakers.uk.com
*Harpist, singer, songwriter, composer and arranger.*
***Musicians' Union member***
**RAB** East England Arts

## Xim
**Contact** Frank Vickers
**Mail address** 200 Unthank Road, NORWICH, Norfolk, NR2 2AH
**Phone** 01603 443942
**Email** info@xim.org.uk
**Web** www.xim.org.uk
*Dance band playing tunes based on the traditional dance rhythms of Central France. Ceilidhs, bals, concerts, workshops.*
***Musicians' Union member***
**RAB** East England Arts

## Yard of Ale
**Contact** Alistair McDougald
**Mail address** 41 Whitehall Gardens, MUSSELBURGH, East Lothian, EH21 6PH
**Phone** 0131 6655291
07693 615671
**Email** alistair@mcdougald.freeserve.co.uk
**Web** www.mcdougald.freeserve.co.uk
*3 part harmony trio. Traditional songs accompanied on guitar, banjo, fiddle, harmonica, etc.*
***Musicians' Union member***
**AC** Scotland

## Yat-Kha
**Contact** The Concert Clinic
**Web** www.concertclinic.com
*Tuvian group. Mongolian overtone singing - punk cross!*

## Yeah Jazz
**Contact** Smalltown Promotions
*Roots influneced pop band*
**RAB** East England Arts



*Artists in the main A-Z listing are mostly available for concert and club bookings.*

*See page 11 for details of other artist listings (Dance Display, Solo Musicians, Composers, Arrangers, Session Musicians, Band Deps. Lecturers, MCs, Tutors, Street Theatre, Children's Entertainers, Theatre Companies,.*

*Agents section appears on pages 119-131.*

*Artists in the main A-Z listing are mostly available for concert and club bookings.*

*See page 11 for details of other artist listings (Dance Display, Solo Musicians, Composers, Arrangers, Session Musicians, Band Deps. Lecturers, MCs, Tutors, Street Theatre, Children's Entertainers, Theatre Companies).*

*Agents section appears on pages 119-131.*

## The York Waits

**Contact** Ann Smith
**Mail address** 5 Parramatta Street, RAWTENSTALL, Lancs, BB4 6AF
**Phone** 01706 230084
**Email** annsmith@theyorkwaits.org.uk
**Web** www.theyorkwaits.org.uk
**Alt contact** James Merryweather
**Alt address** 6 Ingleborough Ave, Tanghall, YORK, YO10 3SA
**Phone** 01904 431328
**Email** james@theyorkwaits.org.uk
*6 piece renaissance band. Concerts, banquets, processions, workshops.*
***Musicians' Union member***
**RAB** Yorkshire Arts

## Zabumba Carnival Street Band

**Phone** 01270 760820
**Email** info@zabumba.org.uk
**Web** www.zambumba.org.uk
*Sandbach, Cheshire based street band. Music inspired by the music of Latin America & the Caribbean.*
**RAB** North West Arts

## Zambula

**Contact** Matters Musical
**Web** www.mattersmusical.com
*Afro-European dance band fronted by Ugandan percussionist/ singer Titus Muwanga-Sembatya. Demonstration and instruction in African dance, singing and percussion*

## Zephyrus

**Contact** Terry Mann
**Mail address** 35 Nottingham Road, Leyton, LONDON, E10 6BP
**Phone** 020 8556 7005
*Group of 6 border bagpipes and percussionist playing music composed by Jon Swayne and Terry Mann.*
***Musicians' Union member***
**RAB** London Arts

## Zigazag!

**Contact** Swamp Music
**Mail address** PO Box 94, DERBY, DE22 1XA
**Phone/Fax** 01332 332336
**Phone** 07702 564804 (mob)
**Email** chrishall@swampmusic.co.uk
**Web** www.swampmusic.co.uk
*Cajun band*

## Zuba

**Contact** Active
*Scottish band led by Jerry Boweh. Reggae, world and pop mix*

## Zubop

**Contact** Philip Clouts
**Mail address** 28A Portland Rise, LONDON, N4 2PP
**Phone** 020 8802 9688
**Email** duncan.noble@btinternet.com
**Web** www.zubop.com
*7 piece global dance band playing original material with range of influences includingjazz & world music*
**Agent** Matters Musical
***Musicians' Union member***
**RAB** London Arts

## Zvuk Bazaar

**Contact** Matters Musical
**Web** www.mattersmusical.com
*Ukrainian accordionist & vocalistand Polish fiddler. Klezmer, Macedonian, Turkish, etc. tunes and songs*

## Zydecoactive

**Contact** Access All Areas
*Zydeco band featuring Gavin Lewery*
**Agents** Access All Areas, Matters Musical, Swamp Music

## Zydecomotion

**Contact** Swamp Music
**Web** www.swampmusic.co.uk
*5 piece zydeco band mixing zydeco with blues, funk & other dance music*
**Agent** Matters Musical, Swamp Music

## Absolutely Legless
**Contact** Rachel Howitt
**Mail address** 53 Gledhow Wood Avenue, Roundhay, LEEDS, LS8 1NX
**Phone** 0113 266 8425
07989 063195
**Web** www.oblique-design.demon.co.uk/absolutelylegless
*Irish step dance company.*
**RAB** Yorkshire Arts

## Badejo Arts
**Contact** Peter Badejo - Artistic Director
**Mail address** Harmood Community Centre, 1 Forge Place, Ferdinand Street, LONDON, NW1 8DP
**Phone/Fax** 020 7482 4292
**Email** badejoarts@badejo.demon.co.uk
**Web** www.badejo.demon.co.uk
**Alt contact** Kerry Andrews - Administrator
*Contemporary African dance company. Performances, educational outreach, seminars and corporate work.*
**Musicians Union member**
**RAB** London Arts

## Bibs Ekkel's Tziganka
**Contact** Matters Musical
**Web** www.mattersmusical.com
*11 piece Russian folk music and dance group.*

## The Black Eagles
**Contact** Fool's Paradise
**Web** www.foolsparadise.co.uk
*Tanzanian acrobats. Series of acrobatic and dance routines set to African music, with fire and limbo dancing.*

## Bluefields
**Contact** Nick Pilley
**Mail address** 53 North Street, BRIDGWATER, Somerset, TA6 3PW
**Phone** 01278 450780
**Email** bluefields_appalachian@hotmail.com
**Web** www.bluefields.org.uk
*Appalachian dance team with band.*
**RAB** South West Arts

## Brandywine Cloggers
**Contact** Marie Beal
**Mail address** 6 Catalpa Close, Malpas, NEWPORT, Gwent, NP9 6JW, Wales
**Phone** 01633 856967
*Appalachain Dance Team.*
**AC** Wales

## Broken Ankles
**Contact** Penny Allen
**Mail address** 89 Hollingbury Park Avenue, BRIGHTON, BN1 7JQ
**Phone** 01273 541453
07951 663570
**Fax** 01273 554189
**Email** brokenankles@btinternet.com
**Web** www.brokenankles.btinternet.co.uk
*American/Appalachian percussive dance with band. Tutors for beginners through to advanced.*
**Agent** Shindy Arts
**RAB** South East Arts

## Caribbean Carnival Extravaganza
**Contact** mARKO pOLO
**Web** www.markopolo.co.uk
*Caribbean street carnival tradition, with spectacular costumes.*

## Celtic Feet
**Contact** Matters Musica
**Web** www.celticfeet.co.uk
*Irish dance troupe.*
**RAB** West Midlands Arts

## The Chase
**Contact** Kerry Fletcher
**Mail address** 80 Ryarsh Road, BIRLING, Kent ME19 5JR
**Phone/Fax** 01732 849163
**Phone** 07703 639720
**Email** TheChase@bigfoot.com
**Web** www.bigfoot.com/~thechase
*New music and dance performance based on European traditions. 5-7 performers, element of audience participation. Range of music and dance workshops.*
**Musicians Union member**

## Chinese Dragon and Lion Dancers
**Contact** Artists Connect
**Web** www.artistsconnect.com
*Dragon of 10 + dancers in one costume, lion of 2. Additional percussion and banner carriers.*

## City Clickers
**Contact** Julie Williams
**Mail address** 41 Linden Road, Westbury Park, BRISTOL, BS6 7RN
**Phone/Fax** 0117 9427051
**Email** city_clickers@hotmail.com
**Alt contact** Penny Sheard
**Alt address** 3 Frank Street, NEWPORT, NP9 7AF, Wales
**Phone** 01633 673695 - home
01633 817500- work
**Email** city_clickers@hotmail.com
*English Clog and Canadian stepping team with own musicians. Choreographed traditional steps.*
**RAB** South West Arts

## The Cossacks Dance Troupe
**Contact** Matters Musical
**Web** www.mattersmusical.com
*Cossack dance group and band.*

## Dalila Heath
**Mail address** 18 Calder Avenue, BROOKMANS PARK, Herts, AL9 7AQ
**Phone** 01707 642774
**Fax** 01707 665091
*Teacher and performer of Armenian folk dances.*
**RAB** London Arts

## Dance AV
**Contact** Shindy Arts
**Web** www.bigfoot.com/~danceav
*All male collective performing percussive dance from around the world. Shows, workshops and showcases*

## Dawnswyr Pen Y Bont
**Contact** Sandra Jones
**Mail address** 6 Walston Road, WENYOE, Vale of Glamorgan, CF5 6AU, Wales
**Phone** 029 2059 4248
**Email** dawnswyrp@twmpath.freeserve.co.uk
**Alt contact** Miss Angela Giddings
**Alt address** 14 Acland Road, BRIDGEND, CF31 1TF, Wales
*Welsh folk dance team. Caller and musicians available for twmpathau (Welsh barn dances).*
**AC** Wales

## Delphine Daigane
**Contact** Flamenco Producions
**Mail address** 4 Cormorant Rise, Lower Wick, WORCESTER, Worcs, WR2 4BA
**Phone** 01905 424083
*Flamenco dancer*
**RAB** West Midlands Arts

## Down Mexico Way
**Contact** Matters Musical
**Web** www.mattersmusical.com
*Mexican dance team covering folk dances from Mexico and central America.*
**Agent** Matters Musical

## Fiona & Rhiannon
**Contact** Rhiannon Taylor
**Mail address** 42 Wissage Lane, LICHFIELD, Staffs, WS13 6DF
**Phone** 01543 305779
07779 784123
**Email** tinybag@hotmail.com
*Irish dance duo. Arrangements of contemporary and traditional Irish dances. Musicians available.*
**RAB** West Midlands Arts



**Pages 91-94 include:**
- **Appalachian**
- **Irish**
- **Scottish**
- **Welsh**
- **Latin**
- **European**
- **World Dance**

*See Morris section on pages 179-215 for Dance Display Teams including Appalachian.*

*See Percussive Dance and Appalachian Clogging on pages 216-217*

# artists display

**Pages 91-94 include:**

- **Appalachian**
- **Irish**
- **Scottish**
- **Welsh**
- **Latin**
- **European**
- **World Dance**

*See Morris section on pages 179-215 for Dance Display Teams including Appalachian.*

*See Percussive Dance and Appalachian Clogging on pages 216-217*

## Firestone Percussive Dance Group

**Contact** Richard Mason
**Mail address** 3 Kingfisher Drive, EXETER, Devon, EX4 4SN
**Phone** 01392 213499
**Email** Richard_Mason@multilex.com
**Web** www.kyper.freeserve.co.uk/firestone
**Alt contact** Julie Spiller
**Email** jspiller@fire-stone.freeserve.co.uk
*Percussive dance group performing Appalachian, Irish and Canadian stepping. Workshop leaders. Dance classes in Exeter every Wednesday.*
**RAB** South West Arts

## Flashdance

**Contact** Matters Musical
**Web** www.mattersmusical.com
*Latin folk dance, salsa and mambo dance duo*

## Footworks

**Contact** Adastra
**Web** www.adastra-music.com
*USA percussive dance group. Native American dance to jazz tap.*

## Georgia Shorrock

**Contact** The Ceilidh Company
**Mail address** 2 The Barns, Low Hesket, CARLISLE, Cumbria, CA4 0EU
**Phone** 016974 73431
0771 239 7761
**Email** gshorrock@carlisle.ac.uk
**Email** lhgeorgia@aol.com
*Clog, step and hard shoe dancer.*
**RAB** North West Arts

## Ira Bernstein

**Mail address** 179 Flint Street, ASHEVILLE, NC 28801, USA
**Phone** +1 828 255 9393
**Fax** +1 828 255 9291
**Email** ira@tentoepercussion.com
**Web** www.tentoepercussion.com
*Solo percussive step dancing; appalachian, clog, rhythm tap, etc. With musicians including Trevor Stewart. Regular tours.*

## Jeannette Springer

**Contact** Matters Musical
**Web** www.mattersmusical.com
*British based female limbo dancer.*

## Kerry Fletcher

**Mail address** 80 Ryarsh Road, BIRLING, Kent, ME19 5JR
**Fax** 01732 849163
**Phone/fax** 07703 639720
**Email** kerryfletcher@bigfoot.com
*Teacher of Appalachian clogging, Swedish dance, warm up techniques. Performer with The Chase, etc.*
**RAB** South East Arts

## Lynch Irish Dance Troupe

**Contact** Matters Musical
**Web** www.mattersmusical.com
*Male & female Irish dance group. Traditional or 'Riverdance' dress.*

## Maire Clerkin

**Mail address** 40 Wakelin House, Sebbon Street, LONDON, N1 2EF
**Phone** 020 7359 1024
07940 547346
**Email** maire@clerkinworks.freeserve.co.uk
**Web** www.kickirishdance.co.uk
**Alt contact** KICK Irish Dance Theatre Co
**Alt address** Greenwich Dance Ag, The Borough Hall, Royal Hill, Greenwich, LONDON, SE10 8RE
**Phone** 07956 937461
**Email** donna@kickirishdance.co.uk
*Irish dance specialist teacher/performer. Director of KICK Irish Dance Theatre Co. (formerly Clerkinworks).*
**RAB** London Arts

## Mambo Jumbo

**Contact** Matters Musical
**Web** www.mattersmusical.com
*Limbo dancer, act includes flaming pole.*

## Otta Nye Moaz

**Contact** Karen Brown
**Mail address** 19 Polbreen Avenue, ST AGNES, Kernow, TR5 0TR
**Phone** 01872 553663
**Email** polbreen19@lineone.net
*Young Celtic dance team. Dance workshops, concerts/ shows & informal dance evenings.*
**RAB** South West Arts

## PDP

**Contact** Kerry Fletcher
**Mail address** 80 Ryarsh Road, BIRLING, Kent ME19 5JR
**Phone/Fax** 01732 849163
**Phone** 07703 639720
**Email** kerryfletcher@bigfoot.com
*3 piece percussion and step dance ensemble.*
**RAB** South East Arts

## Perree Bane

**Contact** John Dowling
**Mail address** 2 Balladbridson Park, BALLASALLA, Isle of Man, IM9 2ES
**Phone** 01624 823047
01624 821864
**Email** juanyd@mcb.net
*Traditional Manx music and dance group.*

## Rock The Boat

**Contact** Shindy Arts
**Web** www.shindy.org.uk
*American-English percussive dance, music & song ensemble. Concerts, dances & workshops.*
**RAB** East England Arts

## Ross Allen

**Contact** Shindy Arts
**Web** www.bigfoot.com/~danceav
*Performs and teaches range of percussive dance styles including flatfooting, clog, French-Canadian, rhythm tap.*

## Sandy Archer

**Mail address** 43 Pottery Road, Lower Parkstone, POOLE, Dorset, BH14 8RB
**Phone/Fax** 01202 740 279
**Phone** 07767 366433
**Email** yasminasar@hotmail.com
*Caller for ceilidhs and barn dances. Also offers dance display including Appalachian, Irish soft shoe, etc.*
**RAB** South West Arts

## The Scottish Stepdance Company

**Contact** Martin Coull Music Management
**Mail address** Studio 7, 6 New Street, EDINBURGH, EH8 8BH, Scotland
**Phone/Fax** 0131 557 5330
**Phone** 07803 137509
**Email** marticoull@aol.com
**Web** www.musicscotland.com/stepdance
*Group of top Scottish musicians and step dancers, mixing music, song & dance on stage.*
**Agent** Stoneyport Agency
**AC** Scotland

## Scrambled Leggs

**Contact** Jan Jones
**Mail address** 37 Sidwell Ave, SOUTH BENFLEET, Essex, SS7 1LF
**Phone** 01268 793905
**Email** jan@essexfolknews.co.uk
*Appalachian dancers with old time band.*
**RAB** East England Arts

## Shades of Black

**Contact** Matters Musical
**Web** www.mattersmusical.com
*UK Caribbean folk dance group, depicting the history of the Afro-Caribbean people.*

### Shoostring Appalachian Dancers
**Contact** Karen Price
**Mail address** Mount View, Waunfaur Park Road, CROSS KEYS, Gwent, Wales
**Phone** 01495 273220
*Own band and portable floor. Available for festivals, etc.*
**AC** Wales

### Sister Act
**Contact** Sara Marshall
**Mail address** 22 Flamborough Close, Lower Earley, READING, Berks, RG6 3XB
**Phone/Fax** 0118 9353382
**Phone** 07803 137354
**Email** sara_marshall@flatfoot.fsnet.co.uk
**Web** www.flatfoot.fsnet.co.uk
*Irish, Appalachian and percussive dance act.*
**RAB** Southern Arts

### Siyaya
**Contact** Equator Company Ltd
**Web** www.equatorcompany.com
*15 piece mixed theatre/ dance company from Bulawayo. Theatre work written and directed by Saimon Mbazo Phiri.*

### Slapdash
**Contact** Sue Hargreaves
**Mail address** 5 Church Street, Pinchbeck, SPALDING, Lincs PE11 3UA
**Phone** 01775 713598
**Email** SueHargreaves@hotmail.com
*South Lincs Appalachian dance team.*
**RAB** East England Arts

### Spank The Planks
**Contact** Jennet Lambert
**Mail address** 97 Suffolk Avenue, CHRISTCHURCH, Dorset, BH23 2TJ
**Phone** 01202 476631
07770 773320
**Email** jlambert@netcomuk.co.uk
**Alt contact** Jane Melauish
**Address** 70 Canford Bottom, Colehill, WIMBOURNE, Dorset
**Phone** 01202 882166
**Email** jonandjane@madasafish.com
*Choreographed routines, flat footing, acapella and French Canadian. Old Time band and bright costume.*
**RAB** South West Arts

### Stepback Project
**Contact** Anthony Allen
**Mail address** 89 Hollingbury Park Avenue, BRIGHTON, BN1 7JQ
**Phone** 01273 541453
07951 663570
**Fax** 01273 554189
**Email** brokenankles@btinternet.com
**Web** www.brokenankles.btinternet.co.uk
*Project teaching dance students through workshops, etc. Stage performances of traditional English based dance.*
**RAB** South East Arts

### Street Beast
**Contact** Artists Connect
**Web** www.artistsconnect.com
*Afro-Brazilian dance & percussion group. 6 drummers, bass and keyboard, 6-12 dancers in full costume.*
**AC** Wales

### Street Dance Union
**Contact** Artists Connect
**Web** www.artistsconnect.com
*12 piece Brazilian-Jazz-Hiphop dance group. Available street and indoors.*
**AC** Wales

### Sue Coe
**Mail address** 103 Oldham Road, Ripponden, SOWERBY BRIDGE, West Yorks, HX6 4EB
**Phone/Fax** 01422 822569
**Email** suecoe@backshift.demon.co.uk
*Dance caller, workshop leader in Appalachian flatfooting & longsword.*
**RAB** Yorkshire Arts

### Tiger Feet
**Contact** Robin Abel
**Mail address** 33 Cefn Coed Gardens, Cyncoed, CARDIFF, CF2 6AX, Wales
**Phone** 029 2075 8692
**Email** info@rubicondance.freeserve.co.uk
**Web** www.rubicondance.freeserve.co.uk
**Alt contact** Rubicon Dance
**Address** Nora Street, Adamsdown, CARDIFF, CF24 1ND, Wales
**Phone** 029 2049 1477
**Fax** 029 2047 2240
*Appalachian group.*
**AC** Wales

### Tonbridge Mummers & Hoodeners
**Contact** Geoff Doel
**Mail address** Owl House, 3 Charlton Terrace, TONBRIDGE, Kent, TN9 1PG
**Phone** 01732 366857
*Seasonal mummers play; Available for bookings at Halloween, Christmas/ New Year and May/ June. Song and music available.*
**RAB** South East Arts

### Touchwood Appalachian Dancers
**Contact** Steve Earwicker
**Mail address** 3 Normanby Rd, Wollaton, NOTTINGHAM, NG8 2TA
**Phone** 0115 928 2566
07710 099844
**Fax** 0115 916 2870
**Email** touchwood.dance@btinternet.com
**Web** earwicker.inetc.net/touchwood.htm
*Dance displays, Appalachian and Old Time music workshops, Old Time music band (Peach Bottom String Band).*
**RAB** East Midlands Arts

### Tribe featuring Karina Rebello
**Contact** Matters Musical
**Web** www.mattersmusical.com
*Latin dance company.*

### Volkovtsi Cossacks
**Contact** Matters Musical
**Web** www.mattersmusical.com
*Outstanding Ukranian Cossack dance troup including acrobatics. Live folk musicians avaiable.*

### The Walker Family
**Contact** Brenda Walker
**Mail address** 12 High Street North, LANGLEY MOOR, Durham, DH7 8JG
**Phone** 0191 3784993
07939 517010
**Fax** 0191 3860714
**Email** brendaw@globalnet.co.uk
*Group including Clog dance team, Highland dance team and full band playing Northern English music. Workshops.*
**RAB** Northern Arts



**Pages 91-94 include:**
- Appalachian
- Irish
- Scottish
- Welsh
- Latin
- European
- World Dance

*See Morris section on pages 179-215 for Dance Display Teams including Appalachian.*

*See Percussive Dance and Appalachian Clogging on pages 216-217*

**Pages 91-94 include:**

- **Appalachian**
- **Irish**
- **Scottish**
- **Welsh**
- **Latin**
- **European**
- **World Dance**

*See Morris section on pages 179-215 for Dance Display Teams including Appalachian.*

*See Percussive Dance and Appalachian Clogging on pages 216-217*

### Woodfidley

**Contact** Huw Francis
**Mail address** Flint Cottage, Shepherds Lane, Compton, WINCHESTER SO21 2AB
**Phone** 01962 715841
**Email** huw@woodfidley.org.uk
**Web** www.woodfidley.org.uk
**Alt contact** Geraldine Buchanan 29 Elm Road, WINCHESTER, SO22 5AG
**Phone** 01962 856787
**Email** geraldine@woodfidley.org.uk
*English social dance display team.*
**RAB** South East Arts

### Yasmin Asar

**Mail address** 43 Pottery Road, Lower Parkstone, POOLE, Dorset, BH14 8RB
**Phone/Fax** 01202 740279
**Email** yasminasar@hotmail.com
**Web** www.tonyandyasmin.co.uk
*Professional performer and teacher of Egyptian Belly Dancing, Arabic, Nubian & Turkish Gypsy dance.*
**RAB** South West Arts

### Yurupari Latin Dance Team

**Contact** Matters Musical
**Web** www.mattersmusical.com
*8 - 12 piece Latin dance team. Cover folklore and traditions from the whole Latin continent.*

**Pages 95-98 include:**
- Solo Musicians
- Composers
- Arrangers
- Session Musicians
- Band Deps.
- Lecturers
- MCs.

## Alex Debnam
**Mail address** 71 Millias Road, Itchen, SOUTHAMPTON, SO14 2FX
**Phone** 023 8044 0835
0771 235 7443
**Fax** 023 8034 6326
**Email** pauldrums@aol.com
**Web** www.pauldrums.com
*Musician; drums and bodhran.*
***Musicians' Union member***
**RAB** Southern Arts

## Alicia Davies
**Mail address** 282 Loughborough Park, Brixton, LONDON, SW9 8TD
**Phone** 020 7738 3817
07718 178682
*Percussion including djembe, balafon, bougarabom etc. Session work, performance, workshops and tuition.*
***Musicians' Union member***
**RAB** London Arts

## Alistair Gillies
**Mail address** 58 King Street, BROSELEY, Shropshire, TF12 5NA
**Phone** 01952 882909
07973 866198
**Email** alistair@agpstudio.demon.co.uk
*Musician; saxophone, hammered dulcimer, recorders. Member of All Blacked Up, available for other playing opportunities.*
**RAB** West Midlands Arts

## Andrew Cronshaw
**Contact** Cloud Valley Music
**Mail address** 51 Hainault Court, Forest Rise, LONDON, E17 3NW
**Phone/Fax** 020 8521 4649
**Email** cloudval@aol.com
**Web** http://members.aol.com/cloudval
*Multi-instrumentalist: zithers, wind instruments, etc. Producer and sound engineer.*
***Musicians' Union member***
**RAB** London Arts

## Anne Lorne Gillies
**Contact** Kevin Bree
**Email** kevinbree@bigfoot.com
**Email** annelornegillies@bigfoot.com
*Gaelic singer/ songwriter/ pianist. Teacher and writer of Gaelic and English books/ stories.*

## Becky Taylor
**Contact** Becky Speller
**Mail address** 10 Langton Street, Sowerby Bridge, HALIFAX, West Yorks HX6 2HD
**Phone** 01422 839262
07980 600476
**Email** rebecca.taylor@eu.interfaceinc.com
*Performer and teacher of Uilleann pipes, Northumbrian smallpipes, fiddle & whistles. Composer & arranger.*
**Agent** Artists Connect
**RAB** Yorkshire Arts

## Benny McHugh
**Mail address** 89 Croptend Avenue, GLASGOW, G44 5PE, Scotland
**Phone** 0141 569 3557
0141 4180585
**Alt Address** c/o 36 Kerrylemont Avenue, Toryglen, GLASGOW G42, Scotland
*Fiddle player, runs Sharkey's Session, Glasgow and The Jimmy McHugh Memorial Concert.*
**AC** Scotland

## Brian Heywood
**Mail address** Poke Records,
**Mail address** PO Box 649, DUNSTABLE, Beds, LU5 4XD
**Phone** 01582 475655
**Fax** 01582 475739
**Email** info@brianheywood.com
**Web** www.brianheywood.com
*Electric, acoustic, synthesised & bass guitarist, vocalist. Depping/ session work. Electric folk, ceilidh & barn dance.*
***Musicians' Union member***
**RAB** East Midlands Arts

## Charles Spicer
**Mail address** 3 The Square, Spencers Wood, READING, Berks, RG7 1BS
**Phone** 0118 988 4337
*Player of period and modern oboe and cor anglais, bagpipes, shawm. Musical arranger. Member of Mellstock band, Oxford Waits, Boka Halat. Workshop leader.*
***Musicians' Union member***
**RAB** Southern Arts

## Chris Bartram
**Mail address** Granway House, 3 Coldharbour, Uffculme, CULLOMPTON, Devon EX15 3EE
**Phone/Fax** 01884 841499
**Phone** 07968 193555
**Email** chris@chris-bartram.co.uk
**Web** www.chris-bartram.co.uk
*Southern English traditional fiddle player & singer. Workshop leader. Extensive research on English fiddle music.*
***Musicians' Union member***
**RAB** South West Arts

## Chris Sugden
**Mail address** 10 Perseverence Road, Queensbury, BRADFORD, W Yorks, BD13 1LY
**Phone** 01274 831745
*Performances, talks and workshops built around unaccompanied songs in English.*
***Musicians' Union member***
**RAB** Yorkshire Arts

## Chris Wood
**Mail address** 40 Whitstable Road, FAVERSHAM, Kent, ME13 8DL
**Phone** 01795 537906
**Email** cw@rurecords.com
**Web** www.rufrecords.com
*Musician, composer, arranger, producer & teacher. Violinist & singer.*
**RAB** South East Arts

## Cliff Stapleton
**Mail address** 31 Meynell Road, Hackney, LONDON, E9 7AP
**Phone** 020 8986 0531
**Email** j.stapleton@talk21.com
*Composer and hurdy-gurdy player, performer and teacher. Commissions to write music for dance, theme, song, ambience, etc.*
***Musicians' Union member***
**RAB** London Arts

## Dan Danford
**Mail address** 75 Annandale Road, Greenwich, LONDON, SE10 0DE
**Phone** 020 8853 0780,
07713 921555
**Email** drd1@breathemail.net
*Solo fiddle/ viola for Irish, English, Scottish, N American folk ensembles, ceilidh groups etc. Also tenor banjo and bodhran.*
***Musicians' Union member***
**RAB** London Arts

## artists
## miscellaneous

**Pages 95-98 include:**
- Solo Musicians
- Composers
- Arrangers
- Session Musicians
- Band Deps.
- Lecturers
- MCs.

### Dave Toussaint
**Mail address** 25 Grove Crescent Road, Stratford, LONDON, E15 1BJ
**Phone** 020 8555 3785
**Email** davetoussaint@hotmail.com
**Web** www.harmonica.boom.ru
*Harmonica player; sessions, deps and tuition.*
***Musicians' Union member***
**RAB** London Arts

### David Chatterley
**Mail address** 94 High Street, TRING, Herts, HP23 4AF
**Phone** 01442 825191
07720 734750
*Hurdy gurdy and percussion player; with ceilidh band 'Ode' and for French dance.*
***Musicians' Union member***
**RAB** Southern Arts

### David Thomas
**Mail address** 119 Kenilworth Road, EDGEWARE, Middx, HA8 8XB
**Phone** 020 8958 4947
*Instrumentalist specialising in most forms of folk, roots and related music on violin, mandolin and flute.*
***Musicians' Union member***
**RAB** London Arts

### Douglas Keir
**Mail address** 7 Pitfirrane Park, CROSSFORD, Fife, KY12 8NO, Scotland
**Phone** 01383 725359
*Teacher, conductor/ musical director & researcher.*
***Musicians' Union member***
**AC** Scotland

### DRQ DJ & Compere
**Contact** Quentin Budworth
**Mail address** Molescroft Grange Farmhouse, BEVERLEY, Yorks, HU17 9RS
**Phone** 01482 865604
**Email** grinnigogs@pop3.poptel.org.uk
*World music DJ and compere.*

### Fintan Vallely
**Mail address** 15 Castlewood Terrace, Rathmines, DUBLIN 6, Ireland
**Phone/Fax** +353 1 497 2979
**Phone** +353 86 603 9461
**Email** f@fidil.com
**Web** www.fidil.com
*Irish flute player and teacher. Writer and lecturer on flute and Irish traditional music.*
**Agent** Bechhofer Agency
**AC** Ireland

### Fluff
**Contact** Clare Smith
**Mail address** 21 Wistaston Road, CREWE, Cheshire, CW2 7RA
**Phone** 01270 567750
01270 569780
**Email** fluff@tower-struck-down.freeserve.co.uk
*Freelance fiddle player & electric violinist. Classicial and folk training. Session musician and workshop leader.*
***Musicians' Union member***
**RAB** North West Arts

### Fraser Fifield
**Mail address** 10 Linlithgow Terrace, Ormiston, TRANENT, E Lothian, EH35 5LJ
**Phone** 01875 612196
**Email** fraserfifield@onetel.net.uk
*Instrumentalist/ composer. Soprano sax, pipes (highland, border, small), whistles. Improvised, sight-reading and session player.*
***Musicians' Union member***
**AC** Scotland

### Freeland Barbour
**Mail address** 44 Beauchamp Road, EDINBURGH, EH16 6LU, Scotland
**Phone/Fax** 0131 6661024
**Email** info@castlesound.co.uk
**Web** www.freelandbarbour.co.uk
*Accordion & piano player and teacher. Producer and composer.*
***Musicians' Union member***
**AC** Scotland

### Geoff Doel
**Mail address** Owl House, 3 Charlton Terrace, TONBRIDGE, Kent, TN9 1PG
**Phone** 01732 366857
*Lecturer on traditional culture. Illustrated talks, university work, TV, etc.*
**RAB** South East Arts

### Ian Wilson
**Mail address** 254 Oakdale Road, Carlton, NOTTINGHAM, NG4 1BQ
**Phone** 0115 9872770
0771 1180027
**Email** iwil@tesco.net
*Freelance musician; fretted strings and free reeds.*
**RAB** East Midlands Arts

### Jane Lawrence
**Mail address** 6 Springfield Street, LANCASTER, LA1 4XL
**Phone** 01524 389967
07980 655945
**Email** jane.lawrence@lineone.net
*Fiddle and tabla player, music from from central France, Brittany, Sweden, Balkans & Klezmer. Community music workshop leader, member of Chochenn.*
**RAB** North West Arts

### Jed Grimes
**Mail address** 37 Grosvenor Place, SOUTH SHIELDS, Tyne and Wear, NE29 0NH
**Phone** 0191 290 2785
**Email** jed@franticprod.demon.co.uk
**Web** www.jedgrimes.co.uk
*Guitarist and singer of traditional/ Celtic and contemporary. Producer, broadcaster and event compere. TV and radio theme composer.*

### Jennie Hawes
**Mail address** 27 Viking Heights, Martlesham, WOODBRIDGE, Suffolk, IP12 4RT
**Phone** 01394 384356
07776 195849
**Email** jenniehawes@aol.com
*Workshop leader, especially youth music. Performer; oboe, whistles, fiddle.*
**RAB** East England Arts

### Jo Freya
**Contact** Well Groomed Management
*Band leader, musician, singer, songwriter, composer, caller. Workshop leader.*
***Musicians' Union member***
**RAB** East Midlands Arts

### John Adams
**Mail address** 13 Chevin Road, BELPER, Derbys, DE56 2UW
**Phone** 01773 829602
07941 534968
**Email** jadams@cothrecords.co.uk
**Web** www.cothrecords.co.uk
*Tuition in folk, blues and rock on acoustic/ electric guitar, bass & mandolin. Performance and recording.*
***Musicians' Union member***
**RAB** East Midlands Arts

### John Maycraft
**Contact** Craftvert Digital
**Mail address** 8 Harwood Meadow, Harwood, BOLTON, BL22 3QP
**Phone** 01204 439444
0796 8669590
**Email** john.maycraft@btinternet.com
*Instrumental guitar music. Writer/ player/ recording.*
**RAB** North West Arts

### John-Mark Addison
**Mail address** Squirrel's Haunt, Main Rd, Sibsey, BOSTON, Lincs PE22 0TN
**Phone** 01205 750753
07780 831385
**Fax** 01205 750753
**Email** mark@addisonfolk.freeserve.co.uk
*Electric & acoustic bass guitar and acoustic guitarist available for work in all folk & roots styles.*
***Musicians' Union member***
**RAB** East Midlands Arts

### Jon Bamforth
**Mail address** 162 Alexandra Road, PETERBOROUGH, Cambs PE1 3DL
**Phone** 01733 310968
*Session player of 4-6 string bass.*
***Musicians' Union member***
**RAB** East Midlands Arts

### Jonathan J Quick
**Mail address** 2 The Greenings, Buckland Brewer, BIDEFORD, Devon, EX39 5LR
**Phone** 01237 451033
07715 8499413
**Email** jonathan.quick@foxtrot.co.uk
**Web** www.foxtrot.co.uk
*Mandolin & guitar player. Available for deps, recordings, etc. Will travel.*
***Musicians' Union member***
**RAB** South West Arts

### Karen Tweed
**Mail address** PO Box 5009, DERBY, Derbys, DE1 9FQ
**Phone** 01332 677046
**Fax** 01332 677047
**Email** karen@kstweed.co.uk
*Accordionist, composer, arranger, teacher and producer of instrumental music with roots in Irish, British and Scandanavian traditions.*
***Musicians' Union member***
**RAB** East Midlands Arts

### Kevin Mackie
**Mail address** 104 John Finnie Street, KILMARNOCK KA1 1BB Scotland
**Phone** 07779 005516
01563 555999
**Fax** 01563 573365
**Email** info@theduallist com
*Drummer and percussionist.*
***Musicians' Union member***
**AC** Scotland

### Laurel Swift
**Mail address** 62 Eade Road, LONDON, N4 1DH
**Phone** 07855 389360
020 8211 8298
**Email** laurel@beam.freeserve.co.uk
*Double bassist, fiddler and dancer (morris and clog). Workshop leader for youth, band, dance and other workshops.*
**RAB** London Arts

### Mike O'Connor
**Mail address** Lyngham House, St Ervan, WADEBRIDGE, Cornwall, PL27 7RT
**Phone** 01841 540042
**Email** mikeoconnor@ndirect.co.uk
**Web** www.ndirect.co.uk/~ mikeoconnor
*Fiddle player, singer and storyteller. Accompanist and arranger.*
**RAB** South West Arts

### Narinder Singh
**Contact** N Kambo
**Mail address** 113 Featherstone Road, SOUTHALL, Middx, UB2 5AQ
**Phone** 07989 355867
**Email** KAMBO121@hotmail.com
*Tabla player, with underground jazz band 'Blowpipe', and with other solo artists.*
**RAB** London Arts

### Neelam Blue Diamond
**Phone** 07946 236511
**Email** berry@neelu95.freeserve.co.uk
**Web** www.neelu95.freeserve.co.uk
*Indian female singer/songwriter. Writes Hindi/ Punjabi lyrics. TV, film, etc. production.Multi-cultural projects.*
***Musicians' Union member***
**RAB** London Arts

### Paul Boizot
**Mail address** 9 Sturton Road, SHEFFIELD, S4 7DE
**Phone** 0114 256 1708
**Email** paulboizot@synergynet.co.uk
*Circle dance teacher. Session musician; vocals, bouzouki, drum. East European folk music/ circle dance band available.*
**RAB** Yorkshire Arts

### Paul James
**Mail address** 60 High Street, HUNGERFORD, Berks RG17 0NE
**Phone** 01488 686039
**Email** info@pauljamesmusic.com
**Web** www.pauljamesmusic.com
*Musician, composer, arranger, playing British & European music. Saxophones, bagpipes and traditional woodwind/ reeds. Producer of traditional & contemporary music.*
**RAB** Southern Arts

### Paul Sartin
**Mail address** May Cottage, WHERWELL, Hants, SP11 7JS
**Phone** 01264 860791
07711 485798
*Oboe and violin player, vocalist. Vocal and instrumental teacher, producer, composer/ arranger.*
**RAB** Southern Arts

### Paul Saunders
**Mail address** 6 Swan Meadow, MUCH WENLOCK, Shropshire, TF13 6JQ
**Phone/Fax** 01952 728283
**Email** ps@workingjo.co.uk
**Web** www.workingjoe.co.uk
*Multi-discipline animateur specialising in historical & environmental themes. Events, shows, workshops, MCing.*
***Musicians' Union member***
**RAB** West Midlands Arts

### Pete Jennings
**Mail address** 12 Carleton Close, GT YELDHAM, Essex, CO9 4QJ
**Phone** 01787 238257
07778 366469
**Fax** 01787 238257
**Email** pete@gippeswic.demon.co.uk
**Web** www.gippeswic.demon.co.uk
**Alt address** BBC Radio Suffolk, St Matthews Street, IPSWICH, Suffolk, IP1 3EP
*Festival and concert compere. Sings & plays bones/ bodhran. Talks on folk traditions. Presents 'Suffolk Folk' for BBC Radio Suffolk.*
**RAB** East England Arts

### Pete Lockett
**Phone** 07976 426773
**Email** pete@perc.fsnet.co.uk
**Web** www.petelockett.com
*Percussionist:traditional drumming from cultures worldwide and contemporary styles. Live and studio.*



**Pages 95-98 include:**
- **Solo Musicians**
- **Composers**
- **Arrangers**
- **Session Musicians**
- **Band Deps.**
- **Lecturers**
- **MCs.**

**Pages 95-98 include:**

- **Solo Musicians**
- **Composers**
- **Arrangers**
- **Session Musicians**
- **Band Deps.**
- **Lecturers**
- **MCs.**

## Phil Berthoud

**Mail address** 125 Exe Hill, TORQUAY, Devon, TQ2 7RG
**Phone** 01803 614978
**Email** phil@berthoudmusic.co.uk
*Fiddle/mandolin/guitar player. Mainly Celtic styles. Composer/ arranger and teacher of above instruments.*
***Musicians' Union member***
**RAB** South West Arts

## Philippe Barnes

**Mail address** 59 Wish Road, HOVE, Sussex, BN3 4LN
**Phone** 07989 950622
**Email** philippe@alljiggedout.co.uk
**Web** www.philippebarnes.co.uk
*Flute player, multi-instrumentalist and composer. Irish and other traditional music, flamenco-jazz.*
***Musicians' Union member***
**RAB** South East Arts

## Rod Meredith

**Mail address** 7 West View, Langcliffe, SETTLE, North Yorks, BD24 9LZ
**Phone** 01729 825466
01729 823247
*Solo vocals, all styles, guitar accompaniment. Bass guitar/ vocals for ceilidh or jazz bands.*
***Musicians' Union member***
**RAB** Yorkshire Arts

## Shane Brogan

**Mail address** 21D High Street, AYR, South Ayrshire, KA7 1LU, Scotland
**Phone** 07989 261247
**Email** broganshane@hotmil.com
*Accordionist, teacher, composer/ arranger, publisher/ copyist, recording artist.*
***Musicians' Union member***
**AC** Scotland

## Simon Thoumire

**Contact** Elizabeth Hepburn
**Mail address** 17 Redford Drive, EDINBURGH, EH13 0BL
**Phone** 0131 4413135
07775 854572
**Email** sales@tartantapes.com
**Web** www.tartantapes.com/ simonthoumire
*Award winning virtuoso concertina player, composer and teacher.*
***Musicians' Union member***
**AC** Scotland

## Stephen Rees

**Mail address** Gwenlais, 8 Bron Arfon, LLANLLECHID, Gwynedd, LL57 3LW, Wales
**Fax** 01248 600247
**Phone/Fax** 07880 602897
**Email** stephen.rees@btinternet.com
*Performer, teacher & researcher specialising in Welsh traditional music plus European & American fiddle traditions.*
***Musicians' Union member***
**AC** Wales

## Terry Mann

**Mail address** 35 Nottingham Road, Leyton, LONDON, E10 6BP
**Phone/Fax** 020 8556 7005
**Email** tmann@cwcom.net
*Composer, performer & workshop leader. Percussion, sax/ wind & guitar, community music. Recipient of George Butterworth Award 2000.*
**RAB** London Arts

## The Green Roadshow

**Contact** OTB Productions
**Web** www.otbproductions.co.uk
*A travelling roadshow dedicated tosustainable living.Includes electric vehicles, clowns, solar powered roundabouts and wind/ solar powered PA system and lighting rig plus engineer.*
**Mail to** OTB Productions

## Ulstersongs (John Moulden)

**Contact** John Moulden
**Mail address** 10 Apollo Walk, PORTRUSH, Co Antrim, BT56 8HQ, N Ireland
**Phone/Fax** 028 7082 5080
**Phone** 028 7082 5025
**Email** john@ulstersongs.com
**Web** www.ulstersongs.com
*Researcher; of North Irish song tradition, especailly of history in song. Lecturer on all aspects.*
**AC** Northern Ireland

## Wiltshire Traditions

**Contact** Robert W Berry
**Mail address** 19 Whistley Road, Potterne, DEVIZES, Wilts, SN10 5QY
**Phone** 01380 726597
07714 550990
**Email** potfolk@aol.com
**Web** http://hometown.aol.com/ potfolk/myhomepages/business.html
*Research, collection. Collates and re-enacts traditional music, song, dance, customs and traditions of Wiltshire.*
**RAB** Southern Arts

## Xenia Horne

**Contact** Musicmakers
**Mail address** 4 Springfield Terrace, Alburgh, HARLESTON, Norfolk, IP20
**Fax** 01986 788858
**Phone/Fax** 0336 778677
**Email** musicmakersuk@aol.com
**Web** www.musicmakers.uk.com
*Harpist, singer, songwriter, composer and arranger.*
***Musicians' Union member***
**RAB** East England Arts

**Alicia Davies**
**Mail address** 282 Loughborough Park, Brixton, LONDON, SW9 8TD
**Phone** 020 7738 3817
07718 178682
*Percussion including djembe, balafon, bougarabom etc. Session work, performance, workshops and tuition.*
***Musicians' Union member***
**RAB** London Arts

**Alistair Anderson**
**Mail address** Mount Hooley, Whittingham, ALNWICK, Northumberland, NE66 4RN
**Phone** 01665 574631
07720 451496
**Fax** 01665 574354
*Concertina and Northumbrian pipes player. Solo and workshop leader. Dance caller & band leader.*
***Musicians' Union member***
**RAB** Northern Arts

**Alyth McCormack**
**Phone** 0777 1787377
**Email** bratach2@aol.com
**Web** www.alyth.com
*Singer of mainly Gaelic song, with piano, guitar & fiddle accompanists. Available for workshops/ vocal coaching.*
***Musicians' Union member***
**AC** Scotland

**Andy Perkins**
**Mail address** 21 Stone Street, FAVERSHAM, Kent, ME13 8PU
**Phone** 01795 533864
01795 590374
**Email** andybanjo@aol.com
*Tenor banjo player, teacher and barn dance band leader.*
***Musicians' Union member***
**RAB** South East Arts

**Andy Thorburn**
**Phone** 01349 830132
**Email** andythorburn@madasafish
**Web** www.musicscotland.com/andy
*Scottish pianist, composer, musical director and teacher.*
**AC** Scotland

**Anne Lister**
**Mail address** 34 Nightingale House, Thomas More Street, LONDON, E1 9UA
**Phone** 020 7481 3619
**Email** anne.lister@virgin.net
**Web** http://freespace.virgin.net/anne.lister
*Singer-songwriter, storyteller, workshop leader.*
**RAB** London Arts

**Becky Taylor**
**Contact** Becky Speller
**Mail address** 10 Langton Street, Sowerby Bridge, HALIFAX, West Yorks, HX6 2HD
**Phone** 01422 839262
07980 600476
**Email** rebecca.taylor@eu.interfaceinc.com
*Performer and teacher of Uilleann pipes, Northumbrian smallpipes, fiddle & whistles.*
**Agent** Artists Connect
**RAB** Yorkshire Arts

**Black Umfolosi**
**Contact** Adastra
**Web** www.adastra-music.com
*Traditional Zimbabwean song and dance group. Workshops and community residencies available.*

**Bob Armstrong**
**Mail address** 6 Stanley Road, HORNCHURCH, Essex, RM12 4JN
**Phone** 01708 455276
**Email** masterclass@bobarmstrong.freeserve.co.uk
**Alt address** 51 Alexandra Road, East Ham, LONDON, E6
*Bodhran teacher/ workshop leader.*
**RAB** London Arts

**Boka Halat**
**Contact** Hemlock Music
**Web** www.hemlockmusic.demon.co.uk
*6 piece dance band fusing English tunes with rhythms from the Gambia, India, etc. Workshops on multicultural dance, percussion, improvisation, etc. Hemlock Music*
**RAB** Southern Arts

**Branco Stoysin**
**Mail address** 59A East Dulwich Grove, LONDON, SE22 8PR
**Phone/Fax** 020 8693 2398
*Guitarist, composer, tutor.*
***Musicians' Union member***
**RAB** London Arts

**Brenda Walker**
**Mail address** 12 High Street North, LANGLEY MOOR, Durham, DH7 8JG
**Phone** 0191 3784993
07939 517010
**Fax** 0191 3860714
**Email** brendaw@globalnet.co.uk
*Teacher of Northumberland & Durham clog dancing.*
**RAB** Northern Arts

**Brendan McGlinchey**
**Mail address** 50 Highfield Lane, Oving, CHICHESTER, W Sussex, PO20 6DL
**Phone** 01243 778845
**Email** McGlinchey100@hotmail.com
*Solo fiddle artist, workshop and masterclass leader. Examiner to Royal Irish Academy of Music, Dublin.*
**RAB** South East Arts

**Brian O hEadhra**
**Phone** 07802 433294
**Email** brian@anam.co.uk
**Web** www.brianoheadhra.com
*Singer, songwriter and teacher.*
***Musicians' Union member***
**AC** Scotland

**Bruce MacGregor & Friends**
**Contact** Bruce MacGregor
**Mail address** Holmburn, Essich Road, INVERNESS, IV2 6AH, Scotland
**Phone** 01463 238070
**Email** bruce.mac@virgin.net
*Tuition from founding member of Blazin Fiddles.*
**AC** Scotland

**Carolyn Francis**
**Mail address** 16 Hinde Street, LANCASTER, LA1 1DX
**Phone/Fax** 01524 35391
**Email** carolyn@striding-edge.demon.co.uk
*Performer; fiddle, vocals, trombone, percussion. Workshop leader; community & schools workshops, fiddle teacher.*
***Musicians' Union member***
**RAB** Northern Arts

**Carolyn Robson**
**Mail address** 70 Burnt Hill Rd, Lower Bourne, FARNHAM, Surrey, GU10 3LN
**Phone/Fax** 01252 722938
**Email** carolyn.robson@virgin.net
**Web** www.carolynrobson.com
*Solo singer of mostly traditional songs from NE England & Scotland. Workshops & schools.*
**RAB** South East Arts

**Cass Meurig**
**Mail address** Min Y Nant, Allt Goch, CWM-Y-GLO, Caernarfon, LL55 4DW
**Phone** 01286 871042
**Email** cassmeurig@aol.com
*Fiddler and Welsh Crwth player, mainly traditional Welsh music. Workshops in Welsh fiddle/Crwth, led in English or Welsh.*
***Musicians' Union member***
**AC** Wales



**Pages 99-107 include:**
- Instrumental
- Song
- Dance
- Community Arts

artists
tutors

Pages 99-107 include:

- Instrumental
- Song
- Dance
- Community Arts

## Cath James
**Phone** 0114 2680880
**Email** cath@sett.demon.co.uk
*Fiddle tuition. Private lessons or workshops for any age. Traditional music from the British Isles, music reading not essential.*
***Musicians' Union member***
**RAB** Yorkshire Arts

## Catriona MacDonald
**Contact** Peerie Angel Productions
**Web** www.peerieangel.demon.co.uk
*Scottish fiddle artist and teacher playing in the Shetland tradition.*
***Musicians' Union member***
**AC** Scotland

## Charles Bolton
**Mail address** 20 The Woodlands, Broom, BIGGLESWADE, Beds SG18 9NH
**Phone** 01767 312315
**Email** cboltbroom@aol.com
**Web** www.charles-bolton.co.uk
*Caller, teacher and composer of Playford and Playford-style dances.*
**RAB** East Midlands Arts

## Chris Bartram
**Mail address** Granway House, 3 Coldharbour, Uffculme, CULLOMPTON, Devon, EX15 3EE
**Phone/Fax** 01884 841499
**Phone** 07968 193555
**Email** chris@chris-bartram.co.uk
**Web** www.chris-bartram.co.uk
*Southern English traditional fiddle player & singer. Workshop leader. Extensive research on English fiddle music.*
***Musicians' Union member***
**RAB** South West Arts

## Chris Coe
**Mail address** 21 Halifax Road, Ripponden, SOWERBY BRIDGE HX6 4AH
**Phone** 01422 822413
07870 337603
**Email** chris.coe@tesco.net
*Solo traditional singer accompanied by dulcimers and concertina. Step dancer. Workshop leader for voice, traditional song and dance.*
**RAB** Yorkshire Arts

## Chris Haigh
**Mail address** 232 Sebert Road, Forest Gate, LONDON, E7 0NP
**Phone** 020 8534 3887
**Email** Chris@fiddlingaround.co.uk
**Web** www.fiddlingaround.co.uk
*Fiddle player (all styles). Tutor and workshop leader.*
***Musicians' Union member***
**RAB** London Arts

## Chris Hawes
**Mail address** 3 Roe's Close, Sawston, CAMBRIDGE, CB2 4TH
**Phone** 01223 834678
*Concertina (duet) and keyboard player. Workshop leader.*
**RAB** East England Arts

## Chris Turner
**Mail address** 9 Glendale Avenue, LONDON, N22 5HL
**Phone** 020 8889 0634
*Dance caller & teacher.*
***Musicians' Union member***
**RAB** London Arts

## Chris Wood
**Mail address** 40 Whitstable Road, FAVERSHAM, Kent, ME13 8DL
**Phone** 01795 537906
**Email** cw@rurecords.com
**Web** www.rufrecords.com
*Musician, composer, arranger, producer & teacher. Violinist & singer.*
**RAB** South East Arts

## Christine Kydd
**Contact** Stockbridge Music
**Mail address** 3 Leslie Place, EDINBURGH, EH4 1NG, Scotland
**Phone/Fax** 0131 332 7067
**Email** johnbrown@stockbridgemusic.demon.co.uk
**Web** www.musicscotland.com/kydd
*Scottish singer, respected interpreter of the Scots song tradition. Teacher of Scots song and voicework.*
**Agent** Stoneyport Agency
**AC** Scotland

## Cliff Stapleton
**Mail address** 31 Meynell Road, Hackney, LONDON, E9 7AP
**Phone** 020 8986 0531
**Email** j.stapleton@talk21.com
*Composer and hurdy-gurdy player, performer and teacher.*
***Musicians' Union member***
**RAB** London Arts

## cMc
**Contact** Stoneyport Agency
**Web** www.deafshepherd.com
*Scottish fiddle duo: Marianne Campbell and Clare McLaughlin. Respected workshop leaders.*
**Agent** Stoneyport Agency
**AC** Scotland

## Corrina Hewat
**Mail address** 11A Ettrick Road, SELKIRK, TD7 5AJ, Scotland
**Phone/Fax** 01750 22023
**Phone** 07711 512692
**Email** bachue@bachue.co.uk
**Web** www.corrinahewat.com
*Traditional Scottish harp player and singer (Scots and Gaelic). Teacher of harp & voice.*
***Musicians' Union member***
**AC** Scotland

## Cragg Vale Gamelan
**Contact** Jan Scott
**Mail address** 3 Regent Place, HEBDEN BRIDGE, W Yorks, HX7 7DF
**Phone** 01422 843315
07808 854664
**Email** jan.scott@u.genie.co.uk
**Web** www.craggvalegamelan.co.uk
*Wide reportoire of Indonesian inspired music, plus world influences. Educational workshops.*
**RAB** Yorkshire Arts

## Cyril Jones
**Mail address** 3 Uplands Way, Grange Park, LONDON, N21 1DH
**Email** cydorjones@aol.com
*MC & barn dance caller. Qualified EFDSS tutor for English country dance workshops.*
**RAB** London Arts

## Dalila Heath
**Mail address** 18 Calder Avenue, BROOKMANS PARK, Herts, AL9 7AQ
**Phone** 01707 642774
**Fax** 01707 665091
*Teacher and performer of Armenian folk dances.*
**RAB** London Arts

## Dana Robinson
**Contact** Other Agency
**Alt contact** Steafan Hannigan
*American singer, old-time fiddle, guitar, banjo. Workshops in old-time fiddle, flat-picking guitar styles.*

## Dansing Music
**Contact** Dan Evans
**Mail address** 61 Sillswood, OLNEY, Bucks, MK46 5PN
**Phone/Fax** 01234 241976
**Email** dansing.music@virgin.net
**Web** www.musiclink.co.uk/dansing
*Voice, performance skills, acoustic guitar & mountain dulcimer tuition.*
***Musicians' Union member***
**RAB** East England Arts

## Dave and Mike
**Contact** Mike Longhurst
**Mail address** Briat Croft, The Square, HARROW BARROW, Cornwall, PL17 8BA
**Phone** 01579 351201
**Email** mrlonghurst@talk21.com
*Workshops on "the great days of sailing" for schools (suits key stages)/ festivals.*
**RAB** South West Arts

## Dave Hunt
**Mail address** 74A King Street, Dawley, TELFORD, Shropshire, TF4 2AQ
**Phone** 01952 505073
**Email** davehunt@aol.com
*Workshops for adults & schools. Available full time.*
**RAB** West Midlands Arts

## Dave Shaw
**Mail address** 2 Shafto Cottage, Craghead, STANLEY, Durham, DH9 6DW
**Phone/Fax** 01207 231474
**Email** dave@daveshaw.co.uk
**Web** www.daveshaw.co.uk
*Northumbrian smallpipe maker and player. "Play in a day" workshops.*
***Musicians' Union member***
**RAB** Northern Arts

## Dave Toussaint
**Mail address** 25 Grove Crescent Road, Stratford, LONDON, E15 1BJ
**Phone** 020 8555 3785
**Email** davetoussaint@hotmail.com
**Web** www.harmonica.boom.ru
*Harmonica tutor.*
***Musicians' Union member***
**RAB** London Arts

## Dave Townsend
**Mail address** 22 Swinbourne Road, Littlemore, OXFORD, OX4 4PQ
**Phone** 01865 714778
07798 520552
**Fax** 01865 749428
**Email** mellstock@aol.com
*English traditional songs and music with concertina, fiddle and accordion. Workshop leader and dance caller.*
***Musicians' Union member***
**Agent** Speaking Volumes
**RAB** Southern Arts

## David Milner
**Mail address** 14a Rectory Close, BROADMAYNE, Dorset, DT2 8EQ
**Phone** 01305 852773
**Email** dmilner@thomas-hardye.dorset.sch.uk
*Leader of Breton dance workshops.*
**RAB** South West Arts

## Derek Gifford
**Mail address** 22 Stoney Brow, Roby Mill, UP HOLLAND, Lancs, WN8 0QE
**Phone** 01695 625097
**Email** derek.gifford@talk21.com
*Talks and workshops.*
***Musicians' Union member***
**RAB** North West Arts

## Donal Maguire
**Mail address** 5 Tor View, Haslingden, ROSSENDALE, Lancs, BB4 6PN
**Phone** 01706 214994
**Email** rossrecs@talk21.com
**Web** www.donalmaguire co.uk
*Seminars/ workshops in singing styles.*
**RAB** North West Arts

## Douglas Keir
**Mail address** 7 Pitfirrane Park, CROSSFORD, Fife, KY12 8NO, Scotland
**Phone** 01383 725359
*Teacher, conductor/ musical director & researcher.*
**AC** Scotland

## Earthworks
**Contact** Paul Saunders
**Mail address** 6 Swan Meadow, MUCH WENLOCK, Shrops, TF13 6JQ
**Phone** 01952 728283
**Email** earthworks@heypressco.com
**Alt contact** Dave Hunt
**Alt address** 74A King Street, Dawley, TELFORD, Shrops, TF4 2AQ
**Phone** 01952 505073
**Email** daverhunt@aol.com
*Home Office approved community artists; work with children. Music, song, dance, stories, drama, creative craft activities with historical and environmental themes.*
***Musicians' Union member***
**RAB** West Midlands Arts

## Elaine Barker
**Mail address** Holly Cottage, Lower Road, PELDON, Essex, CO5 7PR
**Phone** 01206 735606
*Guitar teacher and guitar tutor books.*
**RAB** East England Arts

## Elspeth Cowie
**Mail address** 3 Rockville Terrace, BONNYRIGG, Midlothian, EH19 2AG, Scotland
**Phone/Fax** 0131 6637647
**Email** elspeth@scotfolk.com
**Web** www.scotfolk.com/cowie
*Teacher of Scots song & bodhran.*
***Musicians' Union member***
**AC** Scotland

## Esyllt Harker
**Mail address** 7/1 Stryd Y Ffynon, Gerlan, BETHESDA, Gwynedd, LL57 3TN
**Phone** 01248 602033
*Workshops in voice & movement, led in English or Welsh.*
**AC** Wales

## Extra
**Contact** Hemlock Music
**Web** www.hemlockmusic.demon.co.uk
*Folk arts teaching group. Workshops include Morris (most styles), percussive dance, ceilidh dance, mummers plays, music & song.*
**RAB** London Arts

## The Faceless Company
**Contact** Cath Tyrrell/ Bev Adams
**Mail address** Wakefield Arts Mill, Bridge Street, WAKEFIELD, Yorks WF1 5JR
**Phone** 01924 215790
07770 933484
**Fax** 01924 215791
**Email** arts@facelessco.com
**Web** www.facelessco.com
*Community arts company, touring a wide range of participatory projects.*
**RAB** Yorkshire Arts

## Fine Tuning
**Contact** Tony Westran
**Phone/Fax** 01302 562875
**Phone** 07958 963417
**Email** fine-tuning@appleonline.net
*Maker and supplier of early & unusual musical instruments. Hands on fun & educational demonstrations for festivals, schools, colleges, etc.*
**RAB** Yorkshire Arts

## Fintan Vallely
**Mail address** 15 Castlewood Terrace, Rathmines, DUBLIN 6, Ireland
**Phone/Fax** +353 1 497 2979
**Phone** +353 86 603 9461
**Email** f@fidil.com
**Web** www.fidil.com
*Irish flute player and teacher. Writer and lecturer on flute and Irish traditional music.*
**Agent** Bechhofer Agency
**AC** Ireland

**Pages 99-107 include:**

- **Instrumental**
- **Song**
- **Dance**
- **Community Arts**

## Fiona MacKenzie
**Phone** 07802 433294
**Email** fiona@anam.co.uk
**Web** www.fionamackenzie.com
*Singer/ songwriter with the celtic group Anam. Solo singer in Gaelic and English. Gaelic song tutor.*
**AC** Scotland

## Fluff
**Contact** Clare Smith
**Mail address** 21 Wistaston Road, CREWE, Cheshire, CW2 7RA
**Phone** 01270 567750
01270 569780
**Email** fluff@tower-struck-down.freeserve.co.uk
*Freelance fiddle player & electric violinist. Classical and folk training. Session musician and workshop leader.*
***Musicians' Union member***
**RAB** North West Arts

## Francis Roads
**Mail address** 61 Malmesbury Road, South Woodford, LONDON, E18 2NL
**Phone** 020 85054381
**Email** francis@jfroads.demon.co.uk
*Workshops in West Gallery Church Music.*
**RAB** London Arts

## Frankie Armstrong
**Mail address** 45 Cecil Street, Roath, CARDIFF, CF2 1NW, Wales
**Phone** 029 2048 0429
*Unaccompanied singer. Voice workshops based on traditional styles of singing.*
**AC** Wales

## Freeland Barbour
**Mail address** 44 Beauchamp Road, EDINBURGH, EH16 6LU, Scotland
**Phone/Fax** 0131 6661024
**Email** info@castlesound.co.uk
**Web** www.freelandbarbour.co.uk
*Accordion & piano player and teacher.*
***Musicians' Union member***
**AC** Scotland

## Gail Duff
**Mail address** Wynlic, Bull Lane, Lenham Heath, MAIDSTONE, Kent, ME17 2JA
**Phone** 01622 858460
0772 0592126
**Email** greenwillow@folkarts.fsnet.co.uk
*Ceilidh caller, singer (with Bing Lyle), teacher of Border Morris, song and songwriting, social dance and calling, traditional drama.*
**RAB** South East Arts

## Gina Le Faux
**Mail address** 359 Salterhebble Hill, HALIFAX, Yorks, HX3 0QA
**Phone** 01422 362634
0789 9773537
*Lectures/ workshops on fiddle construction and playing. Fiddle maker.*
**RAB** Yorkshire Arts

## Heather Enid Wells
**Mail address** 48 Sprowston Road, NORWICH, NR3 4QN
**Phone** 01603 413509
07870 349 088
**Email** Heather.E.Wells@btinternet.com
**Web** www.blackcatmusic.org.uk
*Teacher of guitar and bass guitar.*
***Musicians' Union member***
**RAB** East England Arts

## Helen Chadwick and Amar
**Contact** Helen Chadwick
**Mail address** Romaine Records, 11 John Campbell Rd, LONDON N16 8JY
**Phone/Fax** 020 7241 3152
**Email** romaine@helenchadwick.com
**Web** www.helenchadwick.com
*Solo singer/ songwriter. Acapella with Amar; 4 voice female group. Singing workshops.*
***Musicians' Union member***
**RAB** London Arts

## Helen East and Rick Wilson
**Contact** Rick Wilson
**Mail address** 29 Gleneldon Road, Streatham, LONDON, SW16 2AX
**Phone/Fax** 020 8677 0352
**Email** suitablelanguage@hotmail.com
*Storytelling and drumming workshops.*
***Musicians' Union member***
**RAB** London Arts

## Henry Garfath
**Mail address** ABDC Entertainments
**Web** www.abdc.co.uk
*Caller, dance teacher & choreographer of English (including Playford), Scottish, American (square, contra and line) dance. ABDC Entertainments*
**RAB** Southern Arts

## HNC Musical Instrument Technology (Fretted Instrument Construction)
**Contact** David Lim
**Mail address** 5 Hazel Avenue, Whalley Range, MANCHESTER, M16 8DY
**Phone** 0161 881 2796
**Email** dlim@lineone.net
*Part-time 2 year course in construction of fretted instruments. Build 3 instruments during the course.*
**RAB** North West Arts

## Ian Clabburn
**Mail address** 6 Greyfriars Road, DAVENTRY, Northants, NN11 4RS
**Phone** 01327 705265
**Email** clabburn@sakbut.fsnet.co.uk
*Workshop leader: Scottish smallpipes for absolute beginners (instruments provided), also for hammered dulcimers.*
**RAB** East Midlands Arts

## Jane Lawrence
**Mail address** 6 Springfield Street, LANCASTER, LA1 4XL
**Phone** 01524 389967
07980 655945
**Email** jane.lawrence@lineone.net
*Community music workshop leader, member of Chochenn.*
**RAB** North West Arts

## Jennie Hawes
**Mail address** 27 Viking Heights, Martlesham, WOODBRIDGE, Suffolk, IP12 4RT
**Phone** 01394 384356
07776 195849
**Email** jenniehawes@aol.com
*Workshop leader, especially youth music. Performer; oboe, whistles, fiddle.*
**RAB** East England Arts

## Jennifer & Hazel Wrigley
**Contact** JH Wrigley
**Mail address** PO Box 23280, EDINBURGH, EH8 9WJ
**Email** office@wrigleysisters.com
**Web** www.wrigleysisters.com
*Award winning fiddle & piano/guitar duo from the Orkney Isles. UK representation by Stoneyport, other enquries direct.*
**Agent** Stoneyport Agency

### Jim Couza
**Mail address** 7 Woodcroft Avenue, Whitehall, BRISTOL, BS5 9AS
**Phone** 0117 939 4249
0117 9394249
**Alt contact** Graham Bradshaw
**Address** 250 Earlsdon Avenue North, COVENTRY, CV5 6GX
**Phone** 024 7671 1935
**Fax** 024 7671 1191
**Email** rootsrecs@btclick.com
*Hammer dulcimer player, folklorist, singer. Workshop leader for song & Anglo-American traditional music.*
***Musicians' Union member***
**RAB** South West Arts

### Jo Freya
**Contact** Well Groomed Management
*Band leader, musician, singer, songwriter, composer, caller. Workshop leader.*
***Musicians' Union member***
**RAB** East Midlands Arts

### Joe O'Donnell
**Mail address** 5 Argyll Street, COVENTRY, CV2 4FJ
**Phone** 024 7627 5807
*Irish fiddler and singer. Solo, with trio or band. Tuition on violin and mandolin.*
**Agent** The Other Agency
**RAB** East Midlands Arts

### John Adams
**Mail address** 13 Chevin Road, BELPER, Derbys, DE56 2UW
**Phone** 01773 829602
07941 534968
**Email** jadams@cothrecords.co.uk
**Web** www.cothrecords.co.uk
*Tuition in folk, blues and rock on acoustic/ electric guitar, bass & mandolin.*
***Musicians' Union member***
**RAB** East Midlands Arts

### John Kirkpatrick
**Contact** Speaking Volumes
**Web** www.speakingvolumes.co.uk
*Melodeon, concertina player and singer, songwriter, workshop leader. Masterclass video available.*
**Agent** Speaking Volumes

### Jon Bamforth
**Mail address** 162 Alexandra Road, PETERBOROUGH, Cambs, PE1 3DL
**Phone** 01733 310968
*Session bass player of 4-6 string bass. Tuition at all levels available.*
***Musicians' Union member***
**RAB** East Midlands Arts

### Julie Ellison
**Mail address** 68 Brunswick Street, Thurnscoe, ROTHERHAM, S Yorks S63 0HY
**Phone** 01709 881339
**Email** julieellison@zen01709.freeserve.co.uk
**Web** www.julieellison.uklinux.net
*Songwriting and guitar workshops.*
**RAB** Yorkshire Arts

### Karen Tweed
**Mail address** PO Box 5009, DERBY, Derbys, DE1 9FQ
**Phone** 01332 677046
**Fax** 01332 677047
**Email** karen@kstweed.co.uk
*Accordionist, composer, arranger, teacher of instrumental music with roots in Irish, British and Scandanavian traditions.*
***Musicians' Union member***
**RAB** East Midlands Arts

### Keith Davis
**Mail address** 6 North Street, Downend, BRISTOL, Avon, BS16 5SY
**Phone** 0117 957 0323
**Email** keithdavis@madasafish.com
*Guitar teacher/ workshop leader.*
***Musicians' Union member***
**RAB** South West Arts

### Keith Hinchliffe
**Mail address** 23a Spring Hill, SHEFFIELD, S10 1ET
**Email** keith.hinchliffe@lineone.net
**Web** www.stirrings.co.uk/folkzone/artistes/keith.hinchliffe
*Workshop leader/ teacher for guitar arrangement and song accompaniment.*
**Agent** Elizabeth Jones Entertainments
***Musicians' Union member***
**RAB** Yorkshire Arts

### Keith Jackman
**Mail address** 43 Wentworth Road, YORK, YO24 1DG
**Phone** 01904 632073
**Email** keithjackman@dairy-drum.freeserve.co.uk
*Hand drum, percussion and didgeridoo teacher. Available for workshops and schools.*
***Musicians' Union member***
**RAB** Yorkshire Arts

### Keith Kendrick
**Mail address** 88 Highfield Road, ASHBOURNE, Derbyshire, DE6 1DX
**Phone/Fax** 01335 345675
**Phone** 07885 345367
**Email** eyup@freeuk.com
**Web** www.eyuk.freeuk.com
*Mainly traditional English songs, music, dialect stories and humour. Concertinas & guitar. Workshops & schools projects.*
**RAB** East Midlands Arts

### Kerry Fletcher
**Mail address** 80 Ryarsh Road, BIRLING, Kent, ME19 5JR
**Phone/Fax** 01732 849163
**Phone** 07703 639720
**Email** kerryfletcher@bigfoot.com
*Teacher of Appalachian clogging, Swedish dance, warm up techniques.*
**RAB** South East Arts

### Kiranpal Singh
**Mail address** 16 Meadows Road, SOUTHALL, Middx, UB1 2JE
**Phone** 020 8574 3445
07971 199790
**Fax** 07951 601236
*Professional santoor player (100 stringed hammer dulcimer from Kashmir). Concerts, demonstrations, tuition.*
***Musicians' Union member***
**RAB** London Arts

### Kirsty Cotter
**Mail address** 23 Moorfield Rd, WOODBRIDGE, Suffolk, IP12 4JN
**Phone** 01394 388221
07796 184981
**Email** kirsty.cotter@btinternet.co.uk
*Player and teacher of Scottish traditional fiddle.*
**AC** Scotland

### Laurel Swift
**Mail address** 62 Eade Road, LONDON, N4 1DH
**Phone** 07855 389360
020 8211 8298
**Email** laurel@beam.freeserve.co.uk
*Workshop leader for youth, band, dance and other workshops.*
**RAB** London Arts

### Leo McCann
**Mail address** PO Box 23341, EDINBURGH, EH1 3WQ, Scotland
**Phone** 0131 4764363
07780 608098
**Email** leo@mcccann.sol.co.uk
**Web** www.leomccann.musicscotland.com
*Button box and low whistle workshops.*
***Musicians' Union member***
**AC** Scotland



**Pages 99-107 include:**
- **Instrumental**
- **Song**
- **Dance**
- **Community Arts**

artists tutors

Pages 99-107 include:

- Instrumental
- Song
- Dance
- Community Arts

## Liz Doherty

**Contact** Dunmore Productions
**Web** www.tartantapes.com/lizdoherty
*Irish fiddle player (solo or with her band), workshop leader and lecturer in traditional Irish, Scottish & Cape Breton music.*
**AC** Ireland

## Llio Rhydderch

**Mail address** Gwenallt, Marian-Glas, YNYS MON, LL73 8PE, Wales
**Phone/Fax** 01248 853741
**Email** llio.rhydderch@freeuk.com
**Web** www.llio.rhydderch.freeuk.com
*Welsh triple harp player and teacher of young group of triple harpers "Telynwyr Llio".*
***Musicians' Union member***
**AC** Wales

## M Yogeswaran – "Tamil Classics"

**Mail address** 10 Gledwood Crescent, HAYES, Middx, UB4 0AX
**Phone/Fax** 020 8573 1930
**Phone** 07979 891649
**Email** yoga.swara@talk21.com
**Web** www.yogaswara.co.uk
**Alt contact** Eva Skalla
**Phone** 020 8946 2147
*Classical Indian vocalist and multi-instrumentalist. Workshops, lectures.*
**Agent** Global Heritage
***Musicians' Union member***
**RAB** Southern Arts

## Maire Clerkin

**Mail address** 40 Wakelin House, Sebbon Street, LONDON, N1 2EF
**Phone** 020 7359 1024
07940 547346
**Email** maire@clerkinworks.freeserve.co.uk
**Web** www.kickirishdance.co.uk
**Alt contact** KICK Irish Dance Theatre Co
**Alt address** Greenwich Dance Ag, The Borough Hall, Royal Hill, Greenwich, LONDON, SE10 8RE
**Phone** 07956 937461
**Email** donna@kickirishdance.co.uk
*Ceilidh caller. Irish dance specialist teacher/ performer. Director of KICK Irish Dance Theatre Co. (formerly Clerkinworks).*
**RAB** London Arts

## Mairi Campbell

**Mail address** 214 Portabello High Street, EDINBURGH, EH15 2AU
**Phone** 0131 664 8824
*Freelance fiddle and viola player, teacher of Scots fiddle and step dancing.*
***Musicians' Union member***
**AC** Scotland

## Massif Village Orchestra

**Contact** Ian Clabburn
**Mail address** 6 Greyfriars Road, DAVENTRY, Northants, NN11 4RS
**Phone** 01327 705265
**Email** clabburn@sakbut.fsnet.co.uk
**Web** www.vickhast.demon.co.uk/mvohome.htm
*30-40 piece band, playing French dance music, workshops in music and dance.*
**RAB** East England Arts

## Michael Barraclough

**Mail address** 21 Colbert Park, SWINDON, Wilts, SN2 3YJ
**Phone** 01793 700099
07710 806610
**Email** mab@tgis.co.uk
**Web** www.tgis.co.uk/home/mab
*Caller for ceilidhs and barn dances. Lectures and workshops on authentic 17th and 18th century English country dance.*
**RAB** Southern Arts

## Mick Peat

**Mail address** Woodland View, Kirkham Lane, FRITCHLEY, Derbys, DE56 2FS
**Phone** 01773 853428
**Fax** 01773 850000
*Dance caller, MC and workshop leader. Available full time.*
***Musicians' Union member***
**RAB** East Midlands Arts

## Mike Gilpin Hurdy Gurdies

**Mail address** Hill Cottage, Heath Road, SWAFFHAM BULBECK, Cambs, CB5 0LS
**Phone** 01223 812378
**Email** mjgilpin@tesco.net
*Hurdy gurdy tutor.*
**RAB** East England Arts

## Mike Jackson

**Contact** Flying Wombat Music
**Mail address** 11 Margary Street, MOUNT GRAVATT, QLD 4122, Australia
**Phone** +61 7 3343 2423
+61 418 630290
**Fax** +61 7 3343 2423
**Email** flyingwombatoz@hotmail.com
**Alt contact** c/o Mrs B Jackson
**Alt address** 18 Cromwell Avenue, WOODHALL SPA, Lincolnshire LN10 6TH
**Phone** 01526 352934
*Entertainer/ educator. Player of 15 instruments, dance caller, juggler, string tricks. Performances & workshops for children & adults.*
***Musicians' Union member***

## Mike Willoughby

**Mail address** 17 Sun Street, ULVERSTON, Cumbria, LA12 7BX
**Fax** 01229 588852
**Email** willoughbymj@aol.com
*Cumbrian based singer-songwriter, concerts and workshops. Artist in residence for Radio Cumbria.*
***Musicians' Union member***
**RAB** Northern Arts

## Neil Mulligan

**Mail address** 2 Eachlann Ashington, BAILE ATHA CLIATH 7, Eire
**Phone** +353 1 882 1400
**Fax** +353 1 838 1094
**Email** neillidh@hotmail.com
neillidh@ireland.com
**Web** http://neillidh.uilleann.nl/
*Uilleann piper, singer and whistle player. Available for workshops and classes. Contact by email advised.*
**AC** Ireland

## Nigel Close

**Mail address** 1 Beaulieu Cottages, High Street, Twyford, WINCHESTER, Hants, SO21 1RF
**Phone** 01962 714220
07866 837853
**Email** barndance@closetwyford.freeserve.co.uk
**Alt contact** Una Bolton
**Address** CONTACTABAND, 14 Portsdown Hill Road, BEDHAMPTON, Hants, PO9 3JY
**Phone** 023 9245 2770
*Caller for ceilidhs/ barn dances. Workshops for clubs & festivals in Manx, Welsh, Early English and display dance presentation.*
**RAB** Southern Arts

## Paul Boizot

**Mail address** 9 Sturton Road, SHEFFIELD, S4 7DE
**Phone** 0114 256 1708
**Email** paulboizot@synergynet.co.uk
*Circle dance teacher.*
**RAB** Yorkshire Arts

## Paul Sartin

**Mail address** May Cottage, WHERWELL, Hants, SP11 7JS
**Phone** 01264 860791
07711 485798
*Oboe and violin player, vocalist. Vocal and instrumental teacher.*
**RAB** Southern Arts

**artists tutors**

Pages 99-107 include:
- Instrumental
- Song
- Dance
- Community Arts

### Paul Scourfield and Michael Davidson
**Contact** Paul Scourfield
**Mail address** 9 Victoria Road, HITCHIN, Herts, SG5 2LS
**Phone** 01462 458031
**Email** pscourfield@mad-river.co.uk
**Web** www.peoplesound.com/artist/paulscourfieldmichaeldavidson
*Music workshops in schools.*
**RAB** East England Arts

### Pesky
**Contact** Anna Tabbush
**Mail address** 70 Burnthill Road, Lower Bourne, FARNHAM, Surrey, GU103LN
**Phone/Fax** 01252 722938
**Phone** 07989 556164
**Email** pesky@treehugger.com
**Alt contact** Holly Sheldrake
**Alt address** 33 Pine Avenue, HASTINGS, E Sussex, TN34 3PP
**Phone** 020 8870 4757
07759 590951
*Workshops in French dance, vocal harmony and percussion.*
**RAB** South East Arts

### Pete Berryman
**Mail address** Hill Cottage, Lanwithan Road, LOSTWITHIEL, Cornwall PL22 0LA
**Phone** 01208 873904
*Guitar teacher.*
***Musicians' Union member***
**RAB** South West Arts

### Pete Castle
**Mail address** 190 Burton Road, DERBY, DE1 1TQ
**Phone** 01332 346399
**Email** steelcarpet@lineone.net
**Web** www.folkmusic.net/petecastle
*Folk singer, storyteller & community musician. Workshop leader inc. schools.*
***Musicians' Union member***
**RAB** East Midlands Arts

### Pete Coe
**Mail address** 103 Oldham Road, RIPPONDEN, West Yorks, HX6 4EB
**Phone/Fax** 01422 822 569
**Email** petecoe@backshift.demon.co.uk
**Web** www.backshift.demon.co.uk/petehome.htm
*One man folk industry! Singer and bouzouki/ banjo/ melodeon/ feet/ dulcimer player. Dance caller & musician. Schools projects.*
***Musicians' Union member***
**RAB** Yorkshire Arts

### Pete Cooper
**Mail address** 3 Astra House, Mount Pleasant Villas, LONDON, N4 4HB
**Phone** 020 8340 7760
**Email** petecooperfiddle@hotmail.com
*Solo fiddle player and singer of traditional and new music. Workshop leader for fiddle (various styles).*
***Musicians' Union member***
**RAB** London Arts

### Peter Mayes
**Mail address** 24b Bedford Grove, EASTBOURNE, Sussex, BN21 2DU
**Phone** 01323 642116
**Email** pjmayes@sniffout.com
**Email** letsmakemusic99@hotmail.com
*Caller, workshop leader for social, morris and sword dance. Band tutor.*
**RAB** South East Arts

### Phil Berthoud
**Mail address** 125 Exe Hill, TORQUAY, Devon, TQ2 7RG
**Phone** 01803 614978
**Email** phil@berthoudmusic.co.uk
*Fiddle/mandolin/guitar player. Mainly Celtic styles. Composer/ arranger and teacher of above instruments.*
***Musicians' Union member***
**RAB** South West Arts

### Phil Brown
**Contact** Big Whistle Music
**Mail address** PO Box 23, ACCRINGTON, Lancs, BB5 5GX
**Phone/Fax** 01254 397623
**Phone** 07976 809623
**Email** phil@bigwhistle.co.uk
**Web** www.bigwhistle.co.uk
*Player of high and low whistles. Workshops.*
**RAB** North West Arts

### Rachel Laurence
**Mail address** 39 Park Avenue, Histon, CAMBRIDGE, CB4 9JU
**Phone** 01223 237843
**Email** rachellaurence@tinyonline.co.uk
*Teacher and performer of an eclectic mix of music for fiddle, viola and voice.*
**RAB** East England Arts

### RAVI
**Contact** JP Freeman
**Mail address** 46 Merle Avenue, HAREFIELD, Middx, UB9 6DG
**Phone** 07711 265011
**Email** info@ravi-art.co.uk
**Web** www.ravi-art.co.uk
*Musician, specialising in kora. Kora Colours with tablas, guitar & percussion. Workshops in world percussion and overtone singing.*
***Musicians' Union member***
**AC** London Arts

### Robin Garside
**Mail address** 70 Marlcliffe Road, Wadsley, SHEFFIELD, S6 4AG
**Phone** 0114 2347143, 07890 910653
**Email** robin@garside.f9.co.uk
**Web** www.robin-garside.freeserve.co.uk
*Singer (traditional), songwriter, guitarist, fiddler. Music workshops.*
**RAB** Yorkshire Arts

### Robin Laing
**Email** 100060.1000@compuserve.com
**Web** www.folkmusic.net/robinlaing
*Scottish folk-singer and songwriter. Traditional song classes in Lanarkshire.*
**RAB** Scotland

### Rock The Boat
**Contact** Shindy Arts
**Web** www.shindy.org.uk
*American-English percussive dance, music & song ensemble. Concerts, dances & workshops.*
**RAB** East England Arts

### Roots Quartet
**Contact** Yvette Staelens
**Mail address** RQRecords, Higher Wrantage Farm, Wrantage, TAUNTON, Somerset, TA3 6DF
**Phone** 01823 481257
01823 456006
**Email** roots@dangermedia.com
**Web** http://rootsquartet.dangermedia.com
*Female vocal harmony duo. Workshops in singing & harmony.*
***Musicians' Union member***
**RAB** South West Arts

## Ryburn 3 Step
**Mail address** 103 Oldham Road, Ripponden, SOWERBY BRIDGE, W Yorks, HX6 4EB
**Phone/Fax** 01422 822569
**Email** ryburn3step@backshift.demon.co.uk
**Web** www.ryburn3step.org.uk
*Group of singers, dancers & musicians performing at & organising wide variety of folk events in W Yorks. Presentations, workshops and consultancy for schools and community organisiations.*
**RAB** Yorkshire Arts

## Saffron Summerfield
**Contact** Mother Earth Agency
**Mail address** 25 Ferndale Road, LONDON, SE25 4QR
**Phone** 020 8406 7881
**Email** saffron@motherearthmusic.co.uk
**Web** mothearthmusic.co.uk
*Voice and songwriting workshop tutor.*
***Musicians' Union member***
**RAB** London Arts

## Samba Gales
**Contact** Chris Girling
**Mail address** 41 Lansdowne Road, Canton, CARDIFF, CF5 1DQ, Wales
**Phone** 029 2034 5609
07773 947885
**Email** chrisjgirling@ukonline.co.uk
*30-40 piece percussion orchestra drawing on Brazilian, Cuban, African roots. Performance & workshops.*
***Musicians' Union member***
**AC** Wales

## Sandra Kerr
**Mail address** 5 Heatherleazes, Warkworth, NR. ALNWICK, Northumberland, NE65 0TZ
**Phone/Fax** 01665 712488
**Email** sandra.kerr@which.net
*Singer, writer and musician, popular workshop leader & voice teacher.*
**RAB** Northern Arts

## Sara Marshall
**Mail address** 22 Flamborough Close, Lower Earley, READING, Berks, RG6 3XB
**Phone/Fax** 0118 9353882
**Phone** 07803 137354
**Email** Sara_Marshall@flatfoot.fsnet.co.uk
**Web** www.flatfoot.fsnet.co.uk
*Appalachian dance instructor.*
**RAB** Southern Arts

## Sarah Matthews
**Mail address** 10 Hamblin Crescent, SINFIN, Derbys, DE24 9PL
**Phone** 07941 366319
01332 273382
**Email** sarah@folkspace.idps.co.uk
**Web** www.cothrecords.co.uk
*Tuition in folk fiddle, especially English and French traditions.*
***Musicians' Union member***
**RAB** East Midlands Arts

## Shane Brogan
**Mail address** 21D High Street, AYR, South Ayrshire, KA7 1LU, Scotland
**Phone** 07989 261247
**Email** broganshane@hotmil.com
*Accordionist, teacher.*
***Musicians' Union member***
**AC** Scotland

## Sheila Mainwaring
**Mail address** 1 Herbert Avenue, Wellington, TELFORD, Shropshire, TF1 2BT
**Phone** 01952 240989
**Email** mainwaring@enta.net
*Teacher of folk dances for all ages/experiences.*
**RAB** West Midlands Arts

## Simon Mayor and Hilary James
**Contact** Other Agency (The)
**Alt contact** Steafan Hannigan
*Workshops on singing, songwriting, mandolin.*

## Simon Thoumire
**Contact** Elizabeth Hepburn
**Mail address** 17 Redford Drive, EDINBURGH, EH13 0BL
**Phone** 0131 4413135
07775 854572
**Email** sales@tartantapes.com
**Web** www.tartantapes.com/simonthoumire
*Concertina player, composer and teacher.*
***Musicians' Union member***
**AC** Scotland

## Stepback Project
**Contact** Anthony Allen
**Mail address** 89 Hollingbury Park Avenue, BRIGHTON, BN1 7JQ
**Phone** 01273 541453
07951 663570
**Fax** 01273 554189
**Email** brokenankles@btinternet.com
**Web** www.brokenankles.btinternet.co.uk
*Project teaching dance students through workshops, etc. Stage performances of traditional English based dance.*
**RAB** South East Arts

## Stephen Rees
**Mail address** Gwenlais, 8 Bron Arfon, LLANLLECHID, Gwynedd, LL57 3LW, Wales
**Phone/Fax** 01248 600247
**Phone** 07880 602897
**Email** stephen.rees@btinternet.com
*Teacher & researcher specialising in Welsh traditional music.*
***Musicians' Union member***
**AC** Wales

## Steve Cunio & Jane Marsh
**Mail address** 1 Lower Hyde Road, MONTACUTE, Somerset, TA15 6UR
**Phone** 01935 829050
**Email** steve@cunio-marsh.freeserve.co.uk
*Morris workshop leaders. North-West and Border styles, for musicians and dancers.*
**RAB** South West Arts

## Sue Coe
**Mail address** 103 Oldham Road, Ripponden, SOWERBY BRIDGE, West Yorks, HX6 4EB
**Phone/Fax** 01422 822569
**Email** suecoe@backshift.demon.co.uk
*Workshop leader in Appalachian flatfooting & longsword.*
**RAB** Yorkshire Arts

## Terry Mann
**Mail address** 35 Nottingham Road, Leyton, LONDON, E10 6BP
**Phone/Fax** 020 8556 7005
**Email** tmann@cwcom.net
*Workshop leader. Percussion, sax/wind & guitar, community music.*
**RAB** London Arts

## Tim van Eyken
**Contact** Appledore Music
**Mail address** Old Wells Road, SHEPTON MALLETT, Somerset BA4 5XZ
**Phone** 07970 472725
**Fax** 07971 653883
**Email** appledore.music@ukonline.co.uk
**Web** www.timvaneyken.co.uk
*BBC 2 Young Folk Award winning accordeon player, singer and guitarist, mostly traditional English music.*
**Agent** Elizabeth Jones Entertainments
***Musicians' Union member***
**RAB** South West Arts

## Tom Robinson
**Contact** Sue Brearley
**Mail address** Leporine Ltd, PO Box 3185, LONDON, SW18 3JG
**Phone** 020 8874 9607
**Fax** 020 8333 2468
**Email** siouxsie@bothways.com
**Web** www.tomrobinson.com
**Alt contact** Rob Stringer
**Alt address** CMP Concerts, 34 Market Street, SOUTHPORT, PR8 1HJ
**Phone** 01704 539746
**Fax** 01704 500709
**Email** cmpgigs@aol.com

*Songwriter, broadcaster, band leader & solo performer. Schools workshops on creative writing and live performance skills. Session leader at Skyros Holistic Holidays see www.bothways.com/skyros.*

***Musicians' Union member***
**RAB** Northern Arts

## Tony Rose
**Mail address** 13 Lower Odcombe, YEOVIL, Somerset, BA22 8TX
**Phone** 01935 862007
**Fax** 0870 0561678
**Email** boneshaker@bigfoot.com

*Workshops on song, performance and accompaniment.*

**RAB** South West Arts

## Vocalzone
**Contact** Dave & Ruth Cooper
**Mail address** 94 Pasture Road, Stapleford, NOTTINGHAM, NG9 8GL
**Phone** 0115 9399730
**Email** rcooper@stapleford-centre.org

*4 part harmony vocal group. Harmony workshops.*

**RAB** East Midlands Arts

## Wild Welsh Women
**Contact** Rob Morris
**Mail address** 63 High Street, AYLBURTON, Glos, GL15 6DE
**Phone** 01594 840152
**Fax** 01594 840251
**Email** robert.morris1@btinternet.com
**Web** www.powell168.freeserve.co.uk

*Workshops in vocal technique and Welsh fiddle playing*

**Agent** Elizabeth Jones Entertainments
**RAB** South West Arts

## Wynndebagge The Piper
**Contact** Paul Saunders
**Mail address** 6 Swan Meadow, MUCH WENLOCK, Shropshire, TF13 6JQ
**Phone/Fax** 01952 728283
**Email** ps@workingjo.co.uk
**Web** www.workingjoe.co.uk

*14 -18th century costumed street style musician, family entertainer, MC & workshop leader. Music, dance, stories, song.*

***Musicians' Union member***
**RAB** West Midlands Arts

## Yasmin Asar
**Mail address** 43 Pottery Road, Lower Parkstone, POOLE, Dorset, BH14 8RB
**Phone/Fax** 01202 740279
**Email** yasminasar@hotmail.com
**Web** www.tonyandyasmin.co.uk

*Professional performer and teacher of Egyptian Belly Dancing, Arabic, Nubian & Turkish Gypsy dance.*

**RAB** South West Arts

artists entertainers

Pages 108-113 include:

- Street Theatre
- Children's Entertainers
- Theatre Companies

### Adrian Spendlow
**Contact** Bright Light Arts
*Performance poet & MC. Music collaborator with wide range of line ups. Poetry adventures for children, reminiscence work.*
**RAB** Yorkshire Arts

### Aksident
**Agent** Fool's Paradise
**Web** www.foolsparadise.co.uk
*Characterisation street theatre trio from Belgium.*

### Albert Alchemy
**Mail address** 5 Beech Avenue, Rawmarsh, ROTHERHAM, S Yorks, S62 5HH
**Phone/Fax** 01709 710780
**Email** albert@albertalchemy.com
**Web** www.albertalchemy.com
*Entertainer; fire-eating, escapology, court jester, medieval fool, etc.*
**RAB** Yorkshire Arts

### Alessandro, the Menace from Venice
**Contact** Fool's Paradise
**Web** www.foolsparadise.co.uk
*Solo musical comedy; Latin guitarist/singer with sudden hysterical laughter.*

### The Baggettes
**Contact** Paul Saunders
**Mail address** 6 Swan Meadow, MUCH WENLOCK, Shropshire, TF13 6JQ
**Phone/Fax** 01952 728283
**Email** ps@workingjo.co.uk
**Web** www.workingjoe.co.uk
*14-18th century costumed street band. Authentic sounds & sights. Medieval ceilidhs with caller.*
***Musicians' Union member***
**RAB** West Midlands Arts

### The Barrel Boys
**Contact** Quentin Budworth
**Mail address** Molescroft Grange Farmhouse, BEVERLEY, Yorks, HU17 9RS
**Phone** 01482 865604
**Email** grinnigogs@pop3.poptel.org.uk
*Traditional street theatre: juggling, fire eating, escapology and the beer barrel of death.*

### Bernie Bennett
**Contact** Fool's Paradise
**Web** www.foolsparadise.co.uk
*Street theatre tightrope act and 9ft, 3 headed alien.*

### The Better Halves
**Contact** Fool's Paradise
**Web** www.foolsparadise.co.uk
Street theatre/cabaret act, incorporating fire eating, juggling, stilts, living statue (concrete punk rocker and cleaning lady) etc.
**Agent** Artists Connect, Fool's Paradise

### Blaize
**Contact** Ellen Thorpe
**Mail address** Garsdale, Easby Drive, ILKLEY, W Yorks, LS29 9BE
**Phone** 01943 607030
**Email** thorpe_garsdale@compuserve.com
*Performance-based community arts company. Producers of large-scale events (Frost & Fire, Flashback), workshop- based projects, village touring, audio & video recordings.*
***Musicians' Union member***
**RAB** Yorkshire Arts

### Bob & Bob Jobbins
**Contact** Fool's Paradise
**Web** www.foolsparadise.co.uk
*Street theatre show or walkabout. Fireman, pirate or pilot with vehicles.*
**RAB** Southern Arts

### Bread & Butter Theatre Company
**Contact** Fool's Paradise
**Web** www.foolsparadise.co.uk
*Static street theatre show involving a giant television, or traditional circus skills. Various character walkabouts.*
**RAB** Northern Arts

### Chipolatas
**Contact** Tristan Glover
**Mail address** PO Box 160, CHELTENHAM, Glos, GL5 2ZQ
**Phone** 01242 577745
**Fax** 01242 577702
**Email** chipolatas@hotmail.com
**Web** www.chipolatas.com
*Street theatre - children's cabaret - trio or five piece.*
**Agents** Fool's Paradise, Hoodlum Productions
**RAB** South West Arts

### Circo Rum Ba Ba
**Contact** Fool's Paradise
**Web** www.foolsparadise.co.uk
*All women troupe with a range of costumed stilt walking shows, including Valkyrie Vikings and a 50ft sperm whale.*

### Circus Fudge
**Contact** Mick Chapman
**Mail address** 8 Weir Road, Milnrow, ROCHDALE, Lancs, OL16 3UX
**Phone** 01706 524228
07889 680787
**Email** fudge@circusfudge.co.uk
**Web** www.circusfudge.co.uk
*One-man kaleidoscope of circus, street theatre, music and comedy. Side-shows, street shows, workshops and walkabout.*
**RAB** North West Arts

### Clatterati
**Contact** Fool's Paradise
**Web** www.foolsparadise.co.uk
**Alt contact** Nicky Street
*Street theatre-style drumming group, who play dustbins and wear leather.*

### Cosmic Sausages
**Contact** Artists Connect
**Web** www.artistsconnect.com
*Streetfolk band, pop classics, theatre, circus, slapstick and crowd participation.*

### Cragg Vale Gamelan
**Contact** Jan Scott
**Mail address** 3 Regent Place, HEBDEN BRIDGE, W Yorks, HX7 7DF
**Phone** 01422 843315
07808 854664
**Email** jan.scott@u.genie.co.uk
**Web** www.craggvalegamelan.co.uk
*Wide reportoire of Indonesian inspired music. New street theatre & shadow play. Educational workshops.*
**RAB** Yorkshire Arts

### Dave Holder
**Contact** Fool's Paradise
**Web** www.foolsparadise.co.uk
*Escapologist and unicyclist. Static and walkabout city slicker with goose*

### David Jackson the Organ Grinder
**Contact** David Jackson
**Mail address** 9 Edward Street, KING'S LYNN, Norfolk, PE30 5QS
**Phone** 01553 768930
*Street organ player of popular and folk music. "Busker" presentation, themed events, etc.*
**RAB** East England Arts

### De Ramos Acrobats
**Contact** Fool's Paradise
**Web** www.foolsparadise.co.uk
*Brazilian/ UK street theatre; acrobatic stunts and knife diving. Outdoors or cabaret.*

## Doctor Sunshine
**Contact** Dave Hunt
**Mail address** 74A King Street, Dawley, TELFORD, Shropshire, TF4 2AQ
**Phone** 01952 505073
**Email** daverhunt@aol.com
*Children's entertainer/ educator. Songs, games, stories, creative craft workshops (giants, dragons, kites, banners, etc).* ***See*** *Earthworks.*
***Musicians' Union member***
**RAB** West Midlands Arts

## Dot Comedy
**Contact** Fool's Paradise
**Web** www.foolsparadise.co.uk
*Street theatre trio, various character shows.*

## Dr Bliss & Friends
**Contact** Dr Alan Bliss
**Phone** 01547 529700
**Email** enquiry@drbliss.org
**Web** www.drbliss.org
*Provide covered stage with crew. Circus skills, balloon modelling and theatre workshops*
**AC** Wales

## Dr Southall's Medicine Show
**Contact** Fool's Paradise
**Web** www.foolsparadise.co.uk
*Acrobatics, escapology and physical street theatre.*

## Enigmatic Eve
**Contact** Fool's Paradise
**Web** www.foolsparadise.co.uk
*Mime, puppetry, clowning and magic, exploring the world of film/ the human soul. Static and walkabout.*

## The Faceless Company
**Contact** Cath Tyrrell/ Bev Adams
**Mail address** Wakefield ArtsMill, Bridge Street, WAKEFIELD, Yorks WF1 5JR
**Phone** 01924 215790
07770 933484
**Fax** 01924 215791
**Email** arts@facelessco.com
**Web** www.facelessco.com
*Street performance and community arts company, touring a wide range ofparticipatory projects.*
**RAB** Yorkshire Arts

## Fair Play
**Contact** Fool's Paradise
**Web** www.foolsparadise.co.uk
*Street theatre duo based on mind-reading aliens riding children's cars, or dodgy East End lads.*

## Fairplay
**Contact** Artists Connect
**Web** www.artistsconnect.com
*Absurd street theatre. Acrobatics, clowning, song, dance, puppetry and mime. Available for street or stage and as walkabout characters.*
**AC** Scotland

## Feeding The Fish
**Contact** Fool's Paradise
**Web** www.foolsparadise.co.uk
*Choreographed juggling, with computer controlled lighted props. Static shows and walkabouts with glo balls, etc.*

## Golem Theatre
**Contact** Fool's Paradise
**Web** www.foolsparadise.co.uk
*Street theatre acts including singing monks, storytelling and puppetry.*
**RAB** Yorkshire Arts

## The Grand Theatre of Lemmings
**Contact** Fool's Paradise
**Web** www.foolsparadise.co.uk
*Street theatre; comic shows and stiltwalking.*

## The Great British Street Show
**Contact** Fool's Paradise
**Web** www.foolsparadise.co.uk
*Street theatre with dance, song, golfers etc. Shows and walkabout.*

## The Grinnigogs
**Contact** Quentin Budworth
**Mail address** Molescroft Grange Farmhouse, BEVERLEY, Yorks HU17 9RS
**Phone** 01482 865604
**Email** grinnigogs@pop3.pootel.org.uk
**Web** www.grinnigogs.co.uk
*Street theatre with historical themes and medieval music. Strolling minstrel up to multi-skilled ensemble. Also children's/ family show.*
**Agents** Artists Connect, Matters Musical
**RAB** Yorkshire Arts

## Half Human Video Theatre
**Contact** Fool's Paradise
**Web** www.foolsparadise.co.uk
*Indoor live theatre and digital video theatre show; folk singer accompanied by his own TV image.*

## Hand to Mouth Theatre
**Contact** Su Eaton
**Mail address** 51 Arnold Road, SOUTHAMPTON, SO17 1TF
**Phone** 023 8055 5392
**Email** htmtheatre@btinternet.com
**Web** www.handtomouth.com
**Alt contact** Martin Bridle
*Eccentric English theatre for all ages*
**RAB** Southern Arts

## Heir of Insanity
**Contact** Fool's Paradise
**Web** www.foolsparadise.co.uk
*Theatre/ street theatre act with trapeze, acrobatics, comic drama and an inflatable "fairy land" set.*

## Incandescence
**Contact** Fool's Paradise
**Web** www.foolsparadise.co.uk
*Contemporary visual theatre with dance and circus skills including fire shows. Static shows and walkabout.*

## Incomposmentis
**Contact** Artists Connect
**Web** www.artistsconnect.com
*Two stilt walking nutty grannies.*

## Indigo Moon
**Contact** Anna Ingleby
**Mail address** 29 Eagle Mansions, Salcombe Road, LONDON, N16 8AU
**Phone/Fax** 020 7241 6341
**Email** anna@indigomoontheatre.com
**Web** www.indigomoontheatre.com
*Puppet company; dancing puppets and tales using puppets from Asian countries. Workshops. Adults or children.*
**RAB** London Arts

## The Invisible Men
**Contact** Fool's Paradise
**Web** www.foolsparadise.co.uk
*Street theatre show; series of visual comedy/ audience interaction sketches, including the metamorphosis trunk.*

## Jason Maverick
**Contact** Fool's Paradise
**Web** www.foolsparadise.co.uk
*Street theatre or cabaret, featuring giant rabbit and fire swinging, crystal balls and living statues.*

## The Jelly Rollers
**Contact** Fool's Paradise
**Web** www.foolsparadise.co.uk
*Street theatre duo with a tricycle and brass instruments, etc. Shows and walkabouts.*

## John Teasdale
**Contact** Fool's Paradise
**Web** www.foolsparadise.co.uk
*Juggler and uni-cyclist. Outdoor and indoor.*

## Junction Jugglers/ Circus Berks
**Contact** Pete Wintercrane
**Mail address** 60 Orts Road, READING, Berks, RG1 3JS
**Phone/Fax** 0118 9660430
**Email** Pete@junctionjugglers.com
**Web** www.junctionjugglers.com
*Fleas to dragons, a selection of street theatre and circus performances and programming.*
**RAB** Southern Arts

## Keith Gregson "The Music Man"
**Mail address** 8 The Elms, SUNDERLAND, Tyne & Wear, SR2 7BZ
**Phone** 0191 510 9206
**Email** keith.gregson@talk21.com
*Singer/ songwriter & instrumentalist, specialising in children's entertainment.*
***Musicians' Union member***
**RAB** Northern Arts

## Keith Leech
**Mail address** 205 Priory Road, HASTINGS, Sussex, TN34 3JB
**Phone/Fax** 01424 716576
**Email** chiefbogie@hotmail.com
*Punch and Judy.*
**RAB** South East Arts

## Kwabana Lindsay
**Contact** Fool's Paradise
**Web** www.foolsparadise.co.uk
*"Slack rope trick" street theatre show.*

## Lighthouse Theatre
**Contact** Fool's Paradise
**Web** www.foolsparadise.co.uk
*Walkabout street theatre including a 10ft tall Victorian mother, nanny and animated baby and "Wide Nannies".*

## Mad Pash
**Contact** Fool's Paradise
**Web** www.foolsparadise.co.uk
*Opera singing theatre walkabout in a horse drawn chariot.*

## Makendoo
**Web** www.foolsparadise.co.uk
*Interactive art workshops for children.*

## Mario Morris
**Contact** Artists Connect
**Web** www.artistsconnect.com
*Magician, comic and street entertainer.*

## Maynard Flip Flap
**Contact** Fool's Paradise
**Web** www.foolsparadise.co.uk
*Clown and walkabout"living box". Fool's Paradise.*
**RAB** Yorkshire Arts

## Mike Hancock
**Contact** Fool's Paradise
**Web** www.foolsparadise.co.uk
*Street theatre character shows; static or walkabout.*

## mimbre
**Contact** Fool's Paradise
**Web** www.foolsparadise.co.uk
*Acrobatic trio. Performance using theatre, clown, breakdance, set to music.*
**RAB** London Arts

## Miniscule of Sound
**Contact** Fool's Paradise
**Web** www.foolsparadise.co.uk
*The world's smallest nightclub, with dance floor, dj, bouncers, and over-played records.*

## Mischief La Bas
**Contact** Fool's Paradise
**Web** www.foolsparadise.co.uk
*Interactive walkabout street theatre group of 5 -10 or more. Characters including the Elvis Cleaning Company and the Paparazzi.*

## Mistic Eggbox
**Contact** Artists Connect
**Web** www.artistsconnect.com
*Clown, storylines about absurd characters.*

## Moon Carrot
**Contact** Sarah Chard
**Mail address** 11 Prince Charles Close, RAGLAN, Monmouthshire, NP15 2HD, Wales
**Phone** 07778 615384
**Fax** 07785 896242
**Email** sarah@streetentertainers.co.uk
**Web** www.streetentertainers.co.uk
*Duo; puppets, magic, stilt walking, comedy characters. Workshop leaders. Agent for street performers.*
**AC** Wales

## Mr Winter
**Contact** Fool's Paradise
**Web** www.foolsparadise.co.uk
*Street theatre walkabout; rude old man with an umbrella on which it ispermenantly snowing.*

## Nakupelle
**Contact** Fool's Paradise
**Web** www.foolsparadise.co.uk
*US and Finnish theatre duo. Combines circus, mask, puppetry, mime, acrobatics, etc.*

## No Strings Puppet Theatre
**Contact** Alan Kirkpatrick, Sue Murphy
**Mail address** Archway House, Mansfield Road, EDWINSTOWE, Notts, NG21 9HF
**Phone** 01623 824210
*Indoor and outdoor performances using puppets and walkabout characters.*
**RAB** East Midlands Arts

## One Yellow World
**Contact** Artists Connect
**Web** www.artistsconnect.com
*Street humour with ballet, tai chi and mime, in ever changing colours.*

## The Onion Boys
**Contact** Ellen Thorpe
**Mail address** Garsdale, Easby Drive, ILKLEY, West Yorks, LS29 9BE
**Phone/Fax** 01943607030
**Email** thorpe_garsdale@compuserve.com
*Street theatre quartet mixing music & song with magic, illusion and comedy. Suitable for set shows and walkabout.*
***Musicians' Union member***
**RAB** Yorkshire Arts

## Original Mixture
**Contact** Fool's Paradise
**Web** www.foolsparadise.co.uk
*Walkabout animation theatre and a miniature touring circus.*

## Parachute Theatre
**Contact** Fool's Paradise
**Web** www.foolsparadise.co.uk
*Puppetry based on Japanese Bunraku puppets. Live animation, music and humour, 5 different shows.*

## Patti Bee and Ross Foley
**Contact** Fool's Paradise
**Web** www.foolsparadise.co.uk
*Walkabout street theatre acts including Fairy Snowflake & Norbert Gnome, Lady Christobel and her Butler.*

## Pete Lawless White's Suitcase Circus
**Contact** Pete White
**Mail address** 54 Melville Place, LEEDS, LS6 2LZ
**Phone** 0113 2939904
**Email** suitcase@snapsnap.demon.co.uk
*Street theatre, stage MC, stiltwalker, workshops.*
**RAB** Yorkshire Arts

## Peter Optical
**Mail address** 36 Oakleigh Park Drive, LEIGH ON SEA, Essex, SS9 1RP
**Phone/Fax** 01702 715882
**Phone** 07765 917291
**Email** peteroptical@the-storyteller.co.uk
**Web** www.peteroptical.co.uk
*Adult & children's entertainer; storyteller, poet, singer, musician, magician, stiltwalker, fire-eater, juggler. Workshops in circus skills, etc.*
**RAB** East England Arts

## Philip Spellacy
**Mail address** 19 Falkland Rise, LEEDS, Yorks, LS17 6JQ
**Phone/Fax** 0113 269 1228
*Puppetry performances, arts workshops - puppets, masks, murals.*
**RAB** Yorkshire Arts

## Poppet's Puppets
**Contact** Uncle Tacko!
**Mail address** 8 Ashdowne Place, Manningham, BRADFORD, West Yorks, BD8 8AL
**Phone** 01274 546177
**Email** gbbgbridgens666@hotmail.com
**Web** www.poppets-puppets.co.uk
*Traditional storytelling with a puppet booth. Folk tales, nursery rhymes, pantomine, nonsense & silliness.*
**RAB** Yorkshire Arts

## The Promenaders
**Contact** Artists Connect
**Web** www.artistsconnect.com
*Street act, slow moving figures in Victorian costume drama without words.*

## Pyromania
**Contact** Fool's Paradise
**Web** www.foolsparadise.co.uk
*Multi-media dance company. Electric dance, commedia del arte & lightwire son et lumiere theatre.*

## Rex Boyd
**Contact** Fool's Paradise
**Web** www.foolsparadise.co.uk
*Street theatre:various shows & characters, walkabout and static.*

## The Rhythm Doctors
**Contact** Fool's Paradise
**Web** www.foolsparadise.co.uk
*Trumpet and Guitar jazz & comedy duo. Street show or walkabout.*

## Risky In Pink
**Contact** Artists Connect
*Street theatre.*

## Roxy's Toolbox
**Contact** Fool's Paradise
**Web** www.foolsparadise.co.uk
*5 piece acoustic street/ stage act. Rock and roll with comedy.*

## The Singing Kettle
**Contact** David McQuillan
**Mail address** Post House, 26 Main Street, KINGSKETTLE, Fife, KY15 7PN, Scotland
**Phone** 01337 831121
07710 771078
**Fax** 01337 831374
**Email** info@singingkettle.com
**Web** www.singingkettle.com
*Children's musical theatre group.*
**AC** Scotland

## Skate Naked
**Contact** Fool's Paradise
**Web** www.foolsparadise.co.uk
*Acrobatic street theatre duo.*

## Skinning The Cat
**Contact** Aerial Theatre Company Ltd. Helen Fagelman - Admin
**Mail address** 163 Washington Street, Girlington, BRADFORD, BD8 9QP
**Phone** 01274 770300
07770 461642
**Fax** 01274 770352
**Email** skcats@globalnet.co.uk
**Alt contact** Becky Truman - Artistic Director
**Phone** 07767 387099
*Aerial theatre company providing a range of shows forindoor and outdoor festivals. Shows can be on outside trapeze rigs or on existing rigging points*
**RAB** Yorkshire Arts

## Skylarks
**Contact** Skylarks Theatre Company
**Mail address** 27 Causeway Head, PENZANCE, Kernow, TR18 2SP
**Phone** 01736 332569
07870 780552
**Email** paul@skylarks.net
**Web** www.skylarks.net
**Alt contact** Aerial Puppetry Foundation
**Alt address** 21 Taroveor Terrace, PENZANCE, Kernow, TR18 2SY
**Phone** 01736 365849
**Email** jacqui@aerialpuppetry com
*Aerial puppetry walkabout performance, dance, workshops.*
**RAB** South West Arts

## Slim & Slam
**Contact** Fool's Paradise
**Web** www.foolsparadise.co.uk
*Pyrotechnic show with household objects, trumpet and guitar. Static or musical walkabout with trumpet and banjo.*

## Smythe & Saucier
**Contact** mARKO pOLO
**Web** www.markopolo.co.uk
*Equilibrist, juggler, trick cyclist, acrobat and musician. Performs in English, French, silence or gibberish.*

## Snapshot Productions
**Contact** Michael Hobson
**Mail address** Number 5 , Rear of 32 Buxton Road, High Lane, STOCKPORT, SK6 8BH
**Phone/Fax** 01663 765860
**Phone** 07889 745594
**Email** a6-acts@mighty-micro.co.uk
**Web** www.snapshotproductions.co.uk
*Children's entertainment: music, magic, circus skills and Punch & Judy.*
**RAB** North West Arts

## Space Cadets
**Contact** Fool's Paradise
**Web** www.foolsparadise.co.uk
*Design and make large scale inflatable sculpture and live art.*
**RAB** North West Arts

## Sparky
**Contact** Fool's Paradise
**Web** www.foolsparadise.co.uk
*Street theatre walkabout: self-contained, radio controlled life size robot with video screen face.*

## The Splott Brothers
**Contact** Fool's Paradise
**Web** www.foolsparadise.co.uk
*Cabaret street theatre duo playing live cheesy piano music.*

## The Spores
**Contact** Artists Connect
**Web** www.artistsconnect.com
*Walkabout street theatre trio with bizarre costumes.*

## Squeal Like A Pig
**Contact** Fool's Paradise
**Web** www.foolsparadise.co.uk
*Costumed comedy group playing Cajun music. Also as a straight Cajun band.*

## Stickleback Plasticus
**Contact** Fool's Paradise
**Web** www.foolsparadise.co.uk
*Street theatre shows or walkabout ballroom dancing duo and more.*



**Pages 108-113 include:**
- **Street Theatre**
- **Children's Entertainers**
- **Theatre Companies**

**Pages 108-113 include:**

- Street Theatre
- Children's Entertainers
- Theatre Companies

## The Stiltoneers
**Contact** Fool's Paradise
**Web** www.foolsparadise.co.uk
*Stiltwalking 4 piece street band.*

## The Stockwell Puppet Theatre
**Contact** Alan Stockwell
**Mail address** Vesper Cottage, Smarden, ASHFORD, Kent, TN27 8NA
**Phone/Fax** 01233 770513
**Email** puppetshow@talk21.com
*Puppets for all occassions including a reportoire of dramatised folk tales.*
**RAB** South East Arts

## The Strangelings
**Contact** Fool's Paradise
**Web** www.foolsparadise.co.uk
*Creators of sculptural animations derived from orginal sculptures and historical figures.Solo to 5 piece.*

## Strawberry
**Contact** Fraser Hooper
**Mail address** The Flat, Chorleywood Town Post Office , Lower Road, CHORLEYWOOD, Herts, WD3 5LQ
**Phone/Fax** 01923 283920
**Phone** 07970 507371
**Email** comedy@fraserhooper.co.uk
**Web** www.fraserhooper.com
*Clown. Funny family show, suitable for stage or street.*
**RAB** London Arts

## Strung Out Puppet Company
**Contact** Artists Connect
**Web** www.artistsconnect.com
*Company of two foot high puppets.*

## Sue Arnold
**Contact** Fool's Paradise
**Web** www.foolsparadise.co.uk
*Walkabout singing and street theatre performer.*

## Surreal McCoy
**Contact** Fool's Paradise
**Web** www.foolsparadise.co.uk
*Giant street theatre characters, including Big Rory and Wee Malky.Solo to trio, with bagpipes, singing, magic and musical saws, etc.*

## Swank
**Contact** Fool's Paradise
**Web** www.foolsparadise.co.uk
*Street theatre duo - various daft female characters riding dragons, doing make-up and being Girl Guides.*

## Swervy World Theatre
**Contact** Artists Connect
**Web** www.artistsconnect.com
*Mix of music and theatre, jump jazz, skiffle, kitsch, jive, etc.*

## Theatre of Fruit
**Contact** Fool's Paradise
**Web** www.foolsparadise.co.uk
*2 person walkabout street theatre show, comdey and music from the land of "Norwiska".*

## The Three Tenners
**Contact** UK Touring
**Web** www.uktouring.org.uk
*Walkabout a capella song street theatre trio, looking for a concert hall, missing orchestra and British shoppers.*

## Ticklish Allsorts
**Contact** Gary Nunn
**Mail address** Cremyll, Marshmead Close, Clarendon, SALISBURY, Wilts, SP5 3DD
**Phone** 01722 711800
07721 992994
**Email** garynunn@x-stream.co.uk
**Web** www.ticklishallsorts.co.uk
*Children's performances, shows, workshops, ceilidh, medieval & street theatre. All UK.*
**RAB** Southern Arts

## Tollhouse Company
**Contact** Barbara Griffiths
**Mail address** 1 Station Cottages, Grunty Fen, WILBURTON, Cambs, CB6 3PZ
**Phone** 01353 740101
**Email** info@tollhouse.co.uk
**Web** www.tollhouse.co.uk
*History based musical theatre performances, traditional and original material for schools/ family audiences.*
***Musicians' Union member***
**RAB** East England Arts

## Tony and Yasmin Risotto
**Mail address** 43 Pottery Road, Lower Parkstone, POOLE, Dorset, BH14 8RB
**Phone/Fax** 01202 740279
**Phone** 07767 366433
**Email** risotto_roger@hotmail.com
**Web** www.tonyandyasmin.co.uk
*Comedy, magic and belly dancing duo.*
**RAB** South West Arts

## UK Chinese Acrobatic Company
**Contact** Matters Musical
**Web** www.mattersmusical.com
*From small ensemble up to full circus, live musicians and dancers available.*

## Weapons of Sound
**Contact** Fool's Paradise
**Web** www.foolsparadise.co.uk
*10-14 piece drum group using instruments made from waste materials.*
**RAB** Southern Arts

## Whalley Range All Stars
**Contact** Fool's Paradise
**Web** www.foolsparadise.co.uk
*Street theatre group, range of interactive shows, including "Head Quarters" and "Headcases".*
**RAB** North West Arts

## Wynndebagge The Piper
**Contact** Paul Saunders
**Mail address** 6 Swan Meadow, MUCH WENLOCK, Shropshire, TF13 6JQ
**Phone/Fax** 01952 728283
**Email** ps@workingjoe.co.uk
**Web** www.workingjoe.co.uk
*14 -18th century costumed street style musician, family entertainer, MC & workshop leader. Music, dance, stories, song.*
***Musicians' Union member***
**RAB** West Midlands Arts

## Zack Attack
**Contact** Fool's Paradise
**Web** www.foolsparadise.co.uk
*Ladder walking, acrobalancing and fire juggling.*

## Zoot
**Contact** Tim Byrom
**Mail address** 66 Machon Bank, Nether Edge, SHEFFIELD, S7 1GP
**Phone** 0114 2556289
07785 306812
**Email** tim@zootstuff.f9.co.uk
*Street theatre performer combining unicycling, clown, accordion, mime, etc. Energetic half hour show and 3 legged walkabout available.*
**RAB** Yorkshire Arts



**Pages 108-113 include:**
- Street Theatre
- Children's Entertainers
- Theatre Companies

agents section

# agents

agents
section

• **Agents - Why Use Them?** by **Chris Wade**

# Agents - Why use them? By Chris Wade

Artists engage agents to represent them since they prefer to have someone else arranging the business side of their work so that they can concentrate on performing - which is - after all what they are really wanting to do.

Some artists positively dislike having to ring up promoters trying to sell themselves and many just don't have the time, contacts or expertise to do this work.

The agent's role is to serve both the artists and the promoter, making the resulting event a success for all concerned. This involves making the best deal possible on behalf of the artist whilst at the same time trying to ensure that the promoter is able to present a successful show in terms of artistic quality, financial success and audience satisfaction.

Artists are often not available to answer the phone or to make calls due to the nature of their work, but since agents are office based, they should be on hand to answer queries at least 5 days a week during normal office hours. Most however, work longer hours as a matter of course but are often expected by promoters to be on hand virtually 24 hours a day, 7 days a week. A compromise needs to be made.

When an artist and agent first become a partnership, it is necessary to establish the worth or selling power of the former - in other words what sort of audience they can attract, hence the fee they can command. Artists very often are unaware of the tremendous competition they face in the real world and therefore it is the role of the agent to explain the severe pressures they may be faced with. The need for fees which are competitive but which at the same time will enable the artist to earn a modest (or high quality - hopefully) living must be established and at the same time, the artists must be prepared to make available suitable promotional material to enable the promoter to sell their show. The agent should understand both these points of view and therefore be the perfect intermediary to satisfy both parties.

ADASTRA attempts to ensure that the artists it represents are not only good quality in terms of performance value, but also behave and perform in a professional manner. It aims to supply the promoter with as professional a service as possible in negotiating and dealing with contracts and supplying the required information on the artist.

It is vital when negotiating a contract that both promoter and agent are satisfied with and aware of what they have agreed to. It is important that a contract is drawn up which clearly states everything that has been agreed and that this is signed by both parties to endorse this agreement. Some artists have a rider, which is supplementary but integral to the contract and will require careful reading by the promoter before signing and returning it with the contract.

It is the role of the agent to specify anything on the rider, during the negotiation stage, which may influence a promoter's decision to book the band. It is easy for the rider to be tagged on to a contract without having been discussed beforehand.

Agents differ in how much they are prepared to do on behalf of their artists and promoters, from just taking the bookings to arranging accommodation, travel, promotional material, obtaining Work Permits etc. The amount of back-up they are able or willing to provide to promoters needs to be established before a contract is made in order to guarantee that the service required will be provided. For example, ADASTRA produces a monthly media mailshot of tour dates, which is sent to nearly 300 press and media contacts, and these dates are also posted on our website. This is in addition to the provision of publicity material in the form of posters, photographs, press packs, CD's and promotional videos in some cases, plus tour adverts.

Where artists are based overseas, it is the role of the agents to ensure that the tax laws relating to non-residents are adhered to (via the Foreign Entertainers Unit - FEU). Agents are obliged to notify the FEU at least 30 days prior to a tour starting of all the income and expenditure that an artist will incur during the tour. Copies of all contracts made must be sent to the FEU along with the above mentioned figures. It will then be decided if and how much tax must be paid and whether the promoter should deduct it directly from the fee paid or whether the agent pays it on behalf of the artist. The forms relating to this tax often cause confusion amongst promoters and it is the role of the agent to ensure that the procedure is explained where necessary.

In addition, artists who are not residents of the European Union will be required to have Work Permits in order to perform in this country. They will not be allowed to enter the country without these, which must be obtained by the agent prior to the tour starting. Overseas nationals from certain countries will also be required to obtain Visas before attempting to enter the country. The agent should be responsible for dealing with all these items, which cannot be dealt with by the artist themselves and often not by the promoter either.

As an agent of 13 years standing, I have come to develop relationships with the promoters I have worked with over the years, and have made friends with many. Other agents will no doubt have found the same. I believe that it is vital for the agent, promoter and artist to be able to trust and respect one another if our music is to thrive in today's competitive world.

For the agent it can be a difficult job to keep both the artists and the promoters happy.

The agent has pressures in both directions - trying to obtain the best deal for their artists but at the same time trying not to push the promoter too hard. It is a very stressful role and requires a certain type of person to be able to achieve the best results - the most suitable judges of their success being the artists and the promoters.

Whilst it is important that the agent behaves in a fair and honest way, it is also the responsibility of the artist to honour the agreements made on their behalf, and the promoters to ensure that they adhere to all the conditions of the contract and rider and make every reasonable effort to publicise and promote the concert or event in a professional way.

If all these factors are taken into consideration, the Agent will prove to be an invaluable service in the circle of events and will help to ensure that artists' careers will develop and that promoters will prosper - hence the live music scene will continue to thrive.

**Chris Wade**
**Director, ADASTRA**

# Working with Agents By Alan Bearman

As someone who spends much of the working day booking and programming artists, I often prefer to work with agents than to contact artists direct. Some artists have proved impossible to tie down over the years until they've found the right agent. Sometimes the more impersonal contact through an agent can allow for exploration of ideas and possibilities without feeling the obligation to proceed if things don't turn out quite as one had hoped. The dynamics between the parties are different between booker and agent from those between booker and artist so potential benefits and problems should be considered in advance.

Agents vary considerably in the way that they work and it is useful to establish a way of working which improves the chances of the relationship being a fruitful one. The following suggestions may help:

**First call** - As a booker you may be making an enquiry about availability/ cost etc or may have already decided to make a definite booking before the call. This needs to be made clear to avoid misunderstandings. Are you window shopping, shopping around or buying ?

Everyone has their own negotiating style! I like to keep my options open as long as possible and rarely make a definite decision on the first call. The question of who wants the gig to happen most is always significant. Before the call it is useful to consider what "currencies" can be used to convince an artist / agent that the offer is viable. Good spots, exposure, prestige can be attractions on some occasions but not on others.

What needs to be covered on first or subsequent call ? This depends on the artist, agent, size and nature of event but some guidelines might include:

- Availability
- Fee
- Accommodation - what level, how many?
- PA- backline etc. Who provides?
- Hospitality, meals etc
- What other costs might be incurred?
- What sort of deal - straight fee, accommodation, tickets?
- What other performances in the area might the agent be looking at? Exclusion clauses may need to be considered.

If the artist is from overseas then there are tax implications to be considered. See the articles on Foreign Entertainers. Work permits and visas may also need to be considered. Discuss at an early stage whose responsibility this will be. If the agent is running a tour for overseas artists, the responsibilities should be theirs.

**Publicity – photos, blogs etc.** Check what is and what will be available. Some agents take a hands-on role with publicity, some devolve it to managers or record companies and some do the bare minimum. Decide what you need and ask where it will come from. Merchandising rights may be raised. Many agents will ask for sole rights but will know this is unlikely when dealing with festivals.

**Wrapping it up** Establish who is contracting and what the timescale for this is. I agree verbally, often long before issuing the festival's standard contract but there are sometimes cases when I prefer a contract to be issued very quickly. Some agents won't issue their own contract if there is a standard festival contract. I prefer to issue our own and receive the agent's own contract so I can check if there are any conflicting expectations.

At the end of the call, a check is useful. Are we agreed?- if so, what happens next? Can we publicise? Is it on hold? How long for? What happens if another gig comes in?

Then to contract ...

**Contract, Agreement or waste of paper?**

There are often questions asked about the legality and worth of such agreements and contracts. Some will claim they offer protection against dubious practices and can be fully tested in law. My experience is that they are extremely valuable tools but often won't be tightly enough drawn up to make a case stick in law.

I use such contracts in an effort to ensure that all those concerned have the same expectations of what is going to happen. As a booker you can use the contract to protect your interests. The agent's contract will be to protect their interests and those of their artist. So there may be clashes. Avoid some of these by carefu negotiations before contracting but look out for others before signing the agreement. Most differences can be sorted out provided they are discussed well before the performance day.

Put as much in your contract as makes you feel comfortable. Additional sheets can be useful to gather necessary information on P.A., accommodation requirements etc and to carry extra clauses. If contracts can be generated through a database you can put in the necessary clauses and drop ones that are not applicable to all artists. The less extraneous lines there are, the more likely it is that key points will be read.

Sidmouth International Festival's standard contract covers

- Artist name (as known)
- Nature of performance (e.g. concert set of 70 minutes)
- When? day/date
- Where- venue name and address if known
- Fee
- How paid? (cheque/cash/on the day/in advance/ currency where there may be doubt)
- Accommodation – specify type, dates
- Hospitality/ meals etc.
- Tickets/ Passes- numbers and days
- PA / Backline etc. Clarify who provides what and who has ultimate control of sound quality and levels
- Standard clause outlining that the work is offered on a self employed basis
- FEU / Work Permits etc. Clarify whose responsibility this is
- Publicity requirements
- Merchandising
- Confirm date when later details will follow
- Insurance indemnity
- Exclusion clause
- Cancellation clause

**What accompanies contract ?**

Sidmouth International Festival includes, as part of the contract:

- Accommodation rules and form for requirements
- PA requirements sheet
- Publicity requirements
- List for names needing passes
- Questionnaires - re programming

Agent,s contracts and riders can be a concern. I prefer to see the rider before verbally confirming but will often settle for an outline of what will be expected. By seeing the agent's contract and rider you can see the band's usual expectations. The agent might know it's a small folk festival so there's no crate of champagne but the artist might not. If there are bits of the rider that you don't like, then challenge them in advance, don't ignore them.

Overall then, working with agents should give you a wider range of possibilities, easier contact and good back up service. Sometimes it's preferable to talk direct to artists about their actual performance if you are looking for something more particular than just a straight concert. If you have a good relationship with the agent this is usually OK.

Building a relationship is the key to success in working with agents. It is no doubt easier to do this when you have plenty of work to offer at prestige events but even then there are always new areas to explore, new contacts to be made and new relationships to be built. Newcomers to event organisation may well be more comfortable with a limited number of personal contacts at first but there are agents working at most levels now. Shop around until you find a number of agents whose style suits you and then proceed with cautious optimism. It could just make your life easier.

**Alan Bearman**
Artistic Director, Sidmouth International Festival



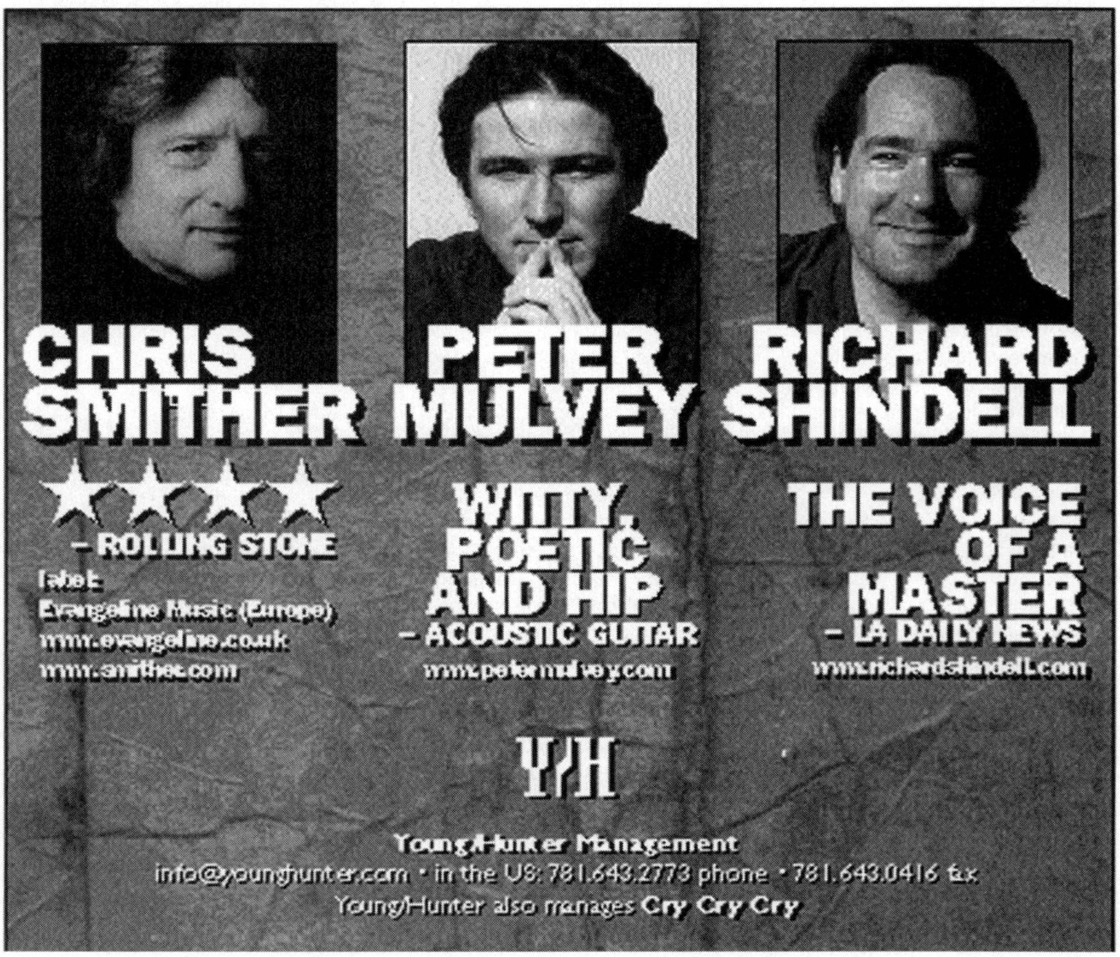

## The A6 Agency
**Contact** Michael Hobson
**Mail address** Number 5, Rear of 32 Buxton Road, High Lane, STOCKPORT, SK6 8BH
**Phone/Fax** 01663 765860
**Phone** 07889 745594
**Email** a6-acts@mighty-micro.co.uk
**Web** www.snapshotproductions.co.uk
**RAB** North West Arts
Representing
- *Snapshot Productions*
- *The Travelling Fun Band*
- *Colonel Custard*
- *Caught On The Hop*
- *Just Another Circus*
- *Michael Hobson & Chris Bright*

## ABDC Entertainments
**Contact** Henry Garfath
**Mail address** La Loma, 18 Halls Farm Close, WINCHESTER, Hants, SO22 6RE
**Phone** 01962 885628
0709 2035070
**Fax** 0845 3344981
**Email** anyact@abdc.co.uk
**Web** www.abdc.co.uk
**RAB** Southern Arts
*Entertainment agency and event management specialising in folk and traditional acts and artists.*
Representing
- *Aces High*
- *Banish Misfortune*
- *Bon Accord Ceilidh Band*
- *Boreen*
- *Henry Garfath*
- *Stars & Bars*

## Access All Areas
**Contact** Graham & Angie Breakwell
**Mail address** 44 Alexandra Avenue, Meole Brace, SHREWSBURY, SY3 9HS
**Phone/Fax** 01743 235384
**Phone** 07850 734182
**Email** cajunclub@btinternet.com
**Email** accessallareas2000@btinternet.com
**RAB** West Midlands Arts
*Represents world music acts including cajun, bhangra, latin, folk, blues, etc. Promote concerts at various venues including the Buttermarket, Shrewsbury.*
Representing
- *Achanak*
- *Allie Fox*
- *Arve Haland's Cajun Gumbo*
- *Baghdaddies*
- *Balfa Toujours*
- *Baton Rouge*
- *Bayou Seco*
- *Bob Everhart*
- *Cajun Aces*
- *Cajun Company*
- *Cajun Hurricane*
- *Cajun Pioneers*
- *Cajuns Denbo*
- *Connie Lush & Blues Shouter*
- *Cross O' Th Hands*
- *Daisy-Belle*
- *Dirk Powell*
- *Doughboy Zydecajun*
- *Eh, La-Bas! with Moise & Alida Viator*
- *Gabhru Panjabi De*
- *Gwerinos*
- *Hackney Ramblers*
- *Los Gringos*
- *Maman Roulaille*
- *Maroon Town*
- *Morris & Dexter Ardoin*
- *Orquesta Huracan*
- *Rue Bourbon*
- *Sacaulait*
- *Sheryl Cormier & The Cajun Sounds*
- *Skillet*
- *Spikedrivers*
- *Step Rideau amd the Zydeco Outlaws*
- *Stompin' Crawfish*
- *Tim van Eyken*
- *Wrekin Havoc Mountain Boys*
- *Zydecoactive*

## Active
**Contact** Lisa Whytock
**Mail address** 128 Elderslie Street, GLASGOW, G3 7AW, Scotland
**Phone** 0141 221 8408
**Fax** 0141 221 8410
**Email** active.events@virgin.net
**AC** Scotland
*Agency with 23 acts on roster, ranging from top Celtic Roots to Salsa . Event management, including programming Hogmanay celebrations in major Scottish towns.*
Representing
- *Big Sky*
- *Dean Owens*
- *Donnie Munro*
- *The Felsons*
- *John Herald*
- *La Sonera Calaveras*
- *Lorna Brooks*
- *Martyn Bennett*
- *The McClusky Brothers*
- *The Pearlfishers*
- *The Picts*
- *Radio Sweethearts*
- *Salsa Celtica*
- *Tartan Amoebas*
- *Zuba*

## Adastra
**Contact** Chris Wade
**Mail address** 2 Star Row, North Dalton, DRIFFIELD, East Yorkshire, YO25 9UR
**Phone** 01377 217662
07801 124264
**Fax** 01377 217754
**Email** adastra@adastey.demon.co.uk
**Web** www.adastra-music.com
**RAB** Yorkshire Arts
*Agent and manager for folk, roots, world and blues artists from Britain, Europe, North America etc. Education and artistic development projects.*
Representing
- *Abdul Teejay's Rokoto*
- *Acaysha*
- *Alain Genty Band*
- *Alan Stivell Band*
- *Aly Bain & Phil Cunningham*
- *Barachois*
- *Black Umfolosi*
- *Blazin' Fiddles*
- *Bleizi Ruz*
- *Bluehorses*
- *Brendan Croker*
- *The Burning Bush*
- *Carlos Sisters*
- *Celtic Fiddle Festival*
- *Dervish*
- *e2K*
- *East Of Ealing*
- *The Fairfield Four*
- *Five Furious Fish*
- *Footworks*
- *Gabriel Yacoub*
- *Gabriel Yacoub Trio*
- *Geoff Muldaur*
- *Hassan Erraji and Arabesque*
- *The John Tams Band*
- *Juan Martin*
- *Kathy Stewart*
- *The Klezmatics*
- *Klezmer Festival Band*
- *Krosfyah*
- *La Bottine Souriante*
- *Le Gop!*
- *Le Rue*
- *Lennie Gallant*
- *Les Batinses*
- *Lindisfarne*
- *Loosehound Drifters*
- *Mairtin O'Connor*
- *Mambo Jambo*
- *Martin Hayes & Dennis Cahill*
- *Martin Simpson*
- *Natalie MacMaster Band*
- *The New House Band*
- *Old Rope String Band*
- *Patrick Street*
- *Pierre Le Rue*
- *R Cajun & The Zydeco Brothers*
- *Rod Clements*
- *Salsa Celtica*
- *Si Kahn*
- *Steve Phillips*
- *Szapora*
- *Ti Jaz*
- *Tiharea*
- *Tim O'Brien and Darrell Scott*
- *Toque de Caixa*
- *Vasmalom*
- *Wood Wilson Carthy*



**Pages 119-130 include contact details of UK Agents and Managers with lists of their represented artists.**

**To find the artists listed under these Agents see pages below:**

# agents a-b

**Pages 119-130 include contact details of UK Agents and Managers with lists of their represented artists.**

**To find the artists listed under these Agents see pages below:**



## African Caribbean Asian Entertainment Agency
**Contact** Mr Sackey
**Mail address** Stars Building, 10 Silverhill Close, NOTTINGHAM, Notts, NG8 6QL
**Phone/Fax** 0115 9519864
**Phone** 07769 902420
**Email** acts@african-caribbean-ents.com
**Web** www.african-caribbean-ents.com
**RAB** East Midlands Arts

*Agency providing African Caribbean and Asian acts for events, festivals, etc.*

## Alan Robinson Management
**Contact** Alan Robinson
**Mail address** PO Box 177, NEW MALDEN, Surrey, KT3 3YT
**Phone** 020 8949 8885
**Fax** 020 8949 3558
**Email** arm5043@aol.com
**RAB** South East Arts

*Personal management service*

Representing
- *Eric Bibb*

## Artistic Upstarts
**Contact** Kresanna Aigner
**Mail address** Ground Floor, 23 Notting Hill, BELFAST, BT9 5NS, N Ireland
**Phone/Fax** 028 9066 8108
**Phone** 07050 229275
**Email** kresanna@artisticupstarts.demon. co.uk
**Web** www.artisticupstarts.demon.co.uk
**AC** Northern Ireland

*Management/ agent for Colin Reid, Old Blind Dogs and UK booking agent for Beginish. Associated with Stoneyport Agency.*

Representing
- *Beginish*
- *Colin Reid*
- *Old Blind Dogs*

## Artists Connect
**Contact** Adrian Wiggins
**Mail address** 35 Llandaff Road, CARDIFF, CF1 9NG, Wales
**Phone** 029 2025 8257
**Fax** 029 2030 4178
**Email** adrian@artistsconnect.com
**Web** www.artistsconnect.com
**AC** Wales

*Entertainment agency providing Jazz, Latin, Soul, Funk and non-music acts including all types of street theatre. Workshops available.*

Representing
- *The Adamant Band*
- *The Ambling Band*
- *Baton Rouge*
- *Becky Taylor*
- *The Better Halves*
- *The Bucket Band*
- *Calum Mor (pipe major)*
- *Celtarabia*
- *Chinese Dragon and Lion Dancers*
- *Cosmic Sausages*
- *Elephant Talk*
- *Fairplay*
- *The Grinnigogs*
- *Incomposmentis*
- *Jeanette Hodgson*
- *La Timbala*
- *Mario Morris*
- *Mistic Eggbox*
- *Next Generation Steel Orchestra*
- *One Yellow World*
- *The Promenaders*
- *The Real Macaws*
- *Repercussion Street Band*
- *Risky In Pink*
- *The Spores*
- *Street Beast*
- *Street Dance Union*
- *Strung Out Puppet Company*
- *Sweet Lorraine*
- *Swervy World Theatre*
- *Tango Siempre*
- *Wayra de Los Andes*

## Asgard Promotions
**Contact** Paul Charles
**Mail address** 125 Parkway, Regents Park, LONDON, NW1 7PS
**Phone** 020 7387 5090
**Fax** 020 7387 8740
**Email** info@asgard-uk.com
**RAB** London Arts

*Major agency representing many of the world's top folk, roots, country and blues artists including Tom Waites, James Taylor, Jackson Browne*

Representing
- *Altan*
- *Christine Collister*
- *Donal Lunny*
- *Emmylou Harris*
- *Eric Bibb*
- *Gerry Rafferty*
- *Hothouse Flowers*
- *Iris Dement*
- *Jimmie Dale Gilmore*
- *Joan Baez*
- *Joe Ely*
- *John Prine*
- *London Community Gospel Choir*
- *Lucinda Williams*
- *Luka Bloom*
- *Mary Black*
- *Mary Coughlan*
- *Micheal O Suilleabhain*
- *Nanci Griffiths*
- *Paul Brady*
- *Sharon Shannon*
- *Taj Mahal*

## Barn Dance & Line Dance Agency Ltd
**Contact** Derek Jones
**Mail address** 62 Beechwood Road, SOUTH CROYDON, Surrey, CR2 0AA
**Phone** 020 8657 8788
**Fax** 020 8651 6680
**RAB** South East Arts

*Agency with 900 barn dance/ ceilidh bands and 200 line dance callers/ bands. Whole country covered.*

## The Bechhofer Agency
**Contact** Frank Bechhofer
**Mail address** 51 Barnton Park View, EDINBURGH, EH4 6HH, Scotland
**Phone** 0131 339 4083
**Fax** 0131 339 9261
**Email** agency@bechhofer.demon.co.uk
**AC** Scotland

*Long established agency working with Scots, Irish & American acts.*

Representing
- *Andy Irvine*
- *Bobby Eaglesham*
- *Duck Baker*
- *Ed Miller*
- *Fintan Vallely*
- *Hans Theessink*
- *Joe Burke with Anne Conroy Burke*
- *Lorraine Lee & Bennett Hammond*
- *Magpie*
- *Paul Heron*
- *Rab Noakes*
- *Richard Heaney & Andrea Ingham*
- *Rod Patterson*
- *Sean Tyrrell*
- *Tim Lyons & Fintan Vallely*
- *Tommy Sands*

## Beyond
**Contact** Robert Hicks
**Mail address** 23 Market Street, ULLAPOOL, Wester Ross, IV26 2XE, Scotland
**Phone/Fax** 01854 613342
**Email** robertjhicks@hotmail.com
**AC** Scotland

*Agent for Celtic pop acts.*

Representing
- *Coinneach*
- *Keeba*
- *Lush Rollers*

## Big Whistle Music
**Contact** Phil Brown
**Mail address** PO Box 23, ACCRINGTON, Lancs, BB5 5GX
**Phone/Fax** 01254 397623
**Phone** 07976 809623
**Email** phil@bigwhistle.co.uk
**Web** www.bigwhistle.co.uk
**RAB** North West Arts

*Promoter and agent for acoustic and roots music.*

## Blackfriars Agency
**Contact** Willie Haines
**Mail address** 49 Blackfriars Street, Off The Royal Mile, EDINBURGH, EH1 1NB, Scotland
**Phone/Fax** 0131 557 3090
**Email** scotfolk@compuserve.com
**AC** Scotland

*Artists & performers for all types of Scottish occasions.*

## Blue Moon Music
**Contact** Jil Barke
**Mail address** 39 Chapel Street, Birdwell, BARNSLEY, S Yorks, S70 5UW
**Phone/Fax** 01226 746821
**Phone** 07973 463767
**Email** jil@bluemoonmusic.co.uk
**Web** www.bluemoonmusic.co.uk
**RAB** Yorkshire Arts
Representing
- *Helen Watson*
- *Kellie While*
- *While & Matthews*

## The Blues Line
**Contact** Linda Fisher
**Mail address** 14 Grisedale Close, LONGLEVENS, Glos, GL2 0EG
**Phone** 01452 532081
**Email** linda@bluesline.freeserve.co.uk
**Web** www.bluesline.freeserve.co.uk
**RAB** South West Arts

*Programmes the annual Gloucester Blues festival. Agency for blues artists including Perry Foster, Clarence Tex Walker.*

Representing
- *Dave Peabody*
- *Michael Chapman*
- *Michael Roach*
- *Peter Wyton*
- *Rhyme and Blues*
- *Rick Payne*

## Brass Tacks
**Contact** Kit Bailey
**Mail address** PO Box 1162, SHEFFIELD, Yorks, S8 9JY
**Phone** 0114 250 9124
07957 822642
**Fax** 0114 255 4973
**Email** brass250@aol.com
**RAB** Yorkshire Arts

*Agent and festival organiser, event co-ordinator and producer.*

Representing
- *Ian Carr & Karen Tweed*
- *Roy Bailey*
- *Snooglenifty*
- *SWÅP*
- *Two Duos Quartet*

## Brian Yeates Associates
**Contact** Ashley Yeates
**Mail address** Home Farm House, Canwell, SUTTON COLDFIELD, W Mids, B75 5SN
**Phone** 0121 3232200
**Fax** 0121 3232313
**Email** ashley@brianyeates.co.uk
**Web** www.brianyeates.co.uk
**RAB** West Midlands Arts

*Agent for various mainstream artists.*

## Bright Light Arts
**Contact** Adrian Spendlow
**Mail address** 23 Bright Street, YORK, Yorks, YO2 4XS
**Phone** 01904 647086
**Email** ade01@globalnet.co.uk
**RAB** Yorkshire Arts
Representing
- *Adrian Spendlow*
- *Damn Heart*

## Clunie Creative Enterprises
**Contact** Heather Ponting (Innes)
**Mail address** Auld of Clunie Farmhouse, BLAIRGOWIE, Perthshire, PH10 6RH, Scotland
**Phone** 01250 884265
**Fax** 01250 884748
**Email** clunieenterprise@talk21.com
**Web** www.come.to/clunie
**AC** Scotland

*Small UK agency and management for folk acts.*

Representing
- *Caim*
- *Dulaman*
- *Firefrost*
- *Heather Innes*
- *Heather Innes and Ciaran Dorris*
- *Lionel Lodge*

## The Concert Clinic
**Contact** Rob Challice
**Mail address** 35 Brittania Row, LONDON, N1 8QH
**Phone** 020 7354 8000
**Fax** 020 7704 8999
**Email** info@concertclinic.com
**Web** www.concertclinic.com
**RAB** London Arts

*International agency & tour producer. Work predominantly with dance, pop, rock, jazz, world and folk music acts. Artists include Andy Sheppard, Asian Dub Foundation, Dreadzone, Sneaker Pimps, etc.*

Representing
- *Cara Dillon*
- *Eliza Carthy Band*
- *Great Big Sea*
- *Jazz Jamaica All Stars*
- *Kila*
- *Lunasa*
- *Mediaeval Baebes*
- *Oysterband*
- *Sin E*
- *Tarika*
- *Yat-Kha*

## CTM UK/ Celtic Traditional Music
**Contact** Crispin Thomas
**Mail address** 4 The Retreat, Butterow STROUD, Glos, GL5 2LS
**Phone/Fax** 01453 757376
**Email** crispin@ctmuk.freeserve.co.uk
**Web** www.ctmuk.com
**RAB** South West Arts

*Tour agent for Celtic traditional music/folk, Irish/world roots, dance. UK Agency and European representation for folk acts.*

Representing
- *Anam*
- *Baghdaddies*
- *Bohinta*
- *Carmina*
- *Craobh Rua*
- *Drop The Box*
- *Imbongi & Albert Nyathi*
- *Tomas Lynch*

## Duende
**Contact** Yvonne Mara
**Mail address** 37 Oakshaw Road, LONDON, SW18 3BS
**Phone** 020 8877 3831
**Fax** 020 8870 7971
**Email** info@duendemusic.co.uk
**Web** www.duendemusic.co.uk
**RAB** London Arts

*Latin & world music agency offering quality artists for all occassions; weddings, corporate, festivals, etc. Acts include Salsa, Brazilian, Latin, Jazz, African, Flamenco, Carribean, etc.*

## Dunmore Productions
**Contact** Angela McLaughlin - Arts Manager
**Mail address** Glebe, Culdaff, INISHOWEN, Co Donegal, Ireland
**Phone** +353 77 79358
**Fax** +353 77 79235
**Email** mrsmac@eircom.net
**AC** Ireland

*Arts consultancy and project management. Clients include Liz Doherty, Earagail Arts Festival. Liz Doherty.*

## East Central One Agency
**Contact** Bob Paterson
**Mail address** 1 York Street, LONDON, W1H 1PZ
**Phone** 020 7272 8454
07946 038634
**Email** bob@eastcentralone.com
**Web** www.bobpaterson.com
**RAB** London Arts

*Live music booking agency, working within a record company. Not exclusive. Pop/ folk influenced bands.*



**Pages 119-130 include contact details of UK Agents and Managers with lists of their represented artists.**

**To find the artists listed under these Agents see pages below**

**agents section**

# EMERGING MUSIC

## REPRESENTING

Niamh Parsons (Ireland)
Rock Salt & Nails
Tarras
Clive Gregson
Boo Hewerdine
Tannahill Weavers
Savourna Stevenson's Scottish Women's String Quintet
Kristina Olsen & Peter Grayling (USA/Australia)
Jez Lowe & The Bad Pennies
Nancy Kerr & James Fagan (also with Tim Van Eyken)
Les Barker
Mad Pudding (Canada)
Dave Swarbrick & Alistair Hulett
The Mrs Ackroyd Band
Pierre Schryer Band (Canada)
Savourna Stevenson
Tamarack(Canada)
Keith Hancock
An evening with Savourna Stevenson & Les Barker
Sarah Allen & Chris Thompson

**Contact Sue or Ken on Tel /Fax**
**+44 (0)1228 670580**
email ken@emerging.demon.co.uk
email sue@emerging.demon.co.uk
www:emerging.demon.co.uk

# shindy::arts

www.shindy.org.uk

*Promoting the best in traditional music and dance...*

Token Women ✻ Asha
The Kitchen Girls

DanceAV ✻ The Fraser Sisters
Broken Ankles ✻ Rock the Boat
Ross Allen ✻ Bob Adams

In addition to representing the artists above we offer a range of corporate theme nights and village hall music and dance events.

For further info please visit *www.shindy.org.uk* or contact Jackie Allen direct.

jackie@shindy.org.uk
tel/fax/ansa: 01908 225681
34 Fosters Lane, Bradwell,
Milton Keynes MK13 9HZ, UK

# ACCESS ALL AREAS

representing

from the USA

**BALFA TOUJOURS**
**EH, LA-BAS!**
**SHERYL CORMIER**

from the UK

**BIG TOWN PLAYBOYS**
**ACHANAK**
**ORQUESTA HURACAN**
**MAROON TOWN**
**BAGHDADDIES**
**CONNIE LUSH & Blues Shouter**
**TIM VAN EYKEN**
**CAJUN COMPANY (NL)**
**ZYDECO ACTIVE . SKILLET**
**JOE LE TAXI . SWINGTHING**
**SPIKEDRIVERS . EAST OF EALING . BIG BOY BLOATER**
**GWERINOS . ALLIE FOX**

**Contact: Graham or Angie Breakwell**
Tel/Fax: 01743 235384 Mob: 07850 734182
accessallareas@bttinternet.com

## Elizabeth Jones Entertainments
**Contact** Elizabeth Jones
**Mail address** 3 Conifer Heights, Sunningdale, KNIGHTWICK, Worcs, WR6 5PP
**Phone/Fax** 01886 821931
**Email** ejonesents@talk21.com
**Web** www.bromyard.co.uk/ejones
**RAB** West Midlands Arts
*Booking agent for folk and roots performers.*
Representing
- *Adderstone*
- *Alan Woolley*
- *Allie Fox*
- *Altar Native*
- *Amazing Blondel*
- *Andy Guttridge*
- *Andy Smythe*
- *Anne Duggan*
- *Aranmore*
- *Band of Rack and Ruin*
- *Band Of Two*
- *Benji Kirkpatrick*
- *Beverley Martyn*
- *Budowitz*
- *Chris Conway*
- *Christian Laverick*
- *Dean Johnson*
- *Delyth Jenkins*
- *Elaine Samuels & Kindred Spirit*
- *Fraser Nimmo*
- *Gregori Scheichter's Klezmer Festival Band*
- *Hegedos*
- *Jenna Monroe*
- *Judy Dunlop & Jon Scaife*
- *Juno*
- *Keith Hinchliffe*
- *Legacy*
- *Mad Jocks & Englishmen*
- *Madigan*
- *Maggie Boyle & Clive Carroll*
- *Magna Carta*
- *Marie Little*
- *Michael Burnham's World Music Ensemble*
- *The O'Cajunal Playboys*
- *Paul Downes*
- *Peter Knight & Felicity Buirski*
- *Phil Bates*
- *Sonny Condell*
- *Steve Ashley*
- *Steve Ashley & Al Fenn*
- *The Tabs*
- *Tashbain*
- *Tim van Eyken*
- *Tony Backhouse*
- *Tony Wilson*
- *Tony Winn*
- *Vikki Clayton*
- *The Vikki Clayton Band*
- *Warren Malone*
- *Wild Welsh Women*

## Emergency Exit Arts
**Contact** Mark Allan
**Mail address** PO Box 570, LONDON, SE10 0EE
**Phone** 020 8853 4809
**Fax** 020 8858 2025
**Email** bollywood@eea.org.uk
**Web** www.eea.org.uk
**RAB** London Arts
*Agent for street music and bands.*
Representing
- *The Bollywood Brass Band*
- *Crocodile Style*

## Emerging Music
**Contact** Ken Bradburn
**Mail address** Burnbrook Cottage, Faugh, Heads Nook, BRAMPTON, Cumbria, CA8 9BS
**Phone/Fax** 01228 670580
**Email** ken@emerging.demon.co.uk
**Web** www.emerging.demon.co.uk
**RAB** Northern Arts
*Booking agent for folk acts, UK and overseas.*
Representing
- *April Verch Band*
- *Boo Hewerdine*
- *Clive Gregson*
- *Clive Gregson & Boo Hewerdine*
- *Dave Swarbrick and Alistair Hulett*
- *Jez Lowe and The Bad Pennies*
- *Keith Hancock*
- *Kristina Olsen and Peter Grayling*
- *Les Barker*
- *Lucky Bags*
- *Mad Pudding*
- *The Mrs Ackroyd Band*
- *Nancy Kerr & James Fagan with Tim Van Eyken*
- *Nancy Kerr and James Fagan*
- *Niamh Parsons*
- *The Pierre Schryer Band*
- *Rock, Salt & Nails*
- *Sarah Allen and Chris Thompson*
- *Savourna Stephenson's Scottish Women's String Quintet*
- *Savourna Stevenson*
- *Savourna Stevenson & Les Barker*
- *Tamarack*
- *Tannahill Weavers*
- *Tarras*

## The Equator Company Ltd
**Contact** Louise Harding
**Mail address** 54 Northload Street, GLASTONBURY, Somerset, BA6 9JP
**Phone/Fax** 01458 834177
**Phone** 01458 830240
**Email** email@equatorcompany.com
**Web** www.equatorcompany.com
**Alt contact** Majahawodwa Ndlovu
**RAB** South West Arts
*Promotion, marketing and tour management of world music groups, especially Zimbabwe and Africa.*
Representing
- *Albert Nyathi & Imbongi*
- *Hukwe Zawose & Charles Zawose*
- *Imbizo*
- *Siyaya*

## The Escape Committee
**Contact** David McNicholas
**Mail address** 1 Bedford Street, DERBY, DE22 3PB
**Phone/Fax** 01332 291603
**Email** escapecommittee@ukonline.co.uk
**Web** www.ukonline.co.uk/escapecommittee
**RAB** East Midlands Arts
*Management company.*

## The Event Shop
**Contact** Adrian McNally
**Mail address** 24 Lewisham Road, Slaithwaite, HUDDERSFIELD, HD7 5AL
**Phone** 01484 840369
07714 105091
**Email** theeventshop@netscape.net
**RAB** Yorkshire Arts
*Artist representation and event management, including corporate events & weddings. Specialise in Irish bands & ceilidhs.*
Representing
- *Alan Burke*
- *Davey Arthur*
- *Last Night's Fun*
- *Roam*

## Flamenco Productions
**Contact** James Peterson
**Mail address** 4 Cormorant Rise, Lower Wick, WORCESTER, WR2 4BA
**Phone** 01905 424083
**RAB** West Midlands Arts
*Provides Flamenco for all types of venues and media.*

## Fool's Paradise
**Contact** Jo Burgess
**Mail address** Sentry Farm, Exminster, EXETER, Devon, EX6 8DY
**Phone** 01392 832268
**Fax** 01392 833122
**Email** fools@foolsparadise.co.uk
**Web** www.foolsparadise.co.uk
**Alt contact** Nicky Street
**RAB** South West Arts
*Agency promoting and supporting outdoor theatre and cabaret.*
Representing
- *Aksident*
- *Alessandro, the Menace from Venice*
- *Bernie Bennett*
- *Better Halves*
- *Black Eagles*
- *Bob & Bob Jobbins*
- *Bread & Butter Theatre Company*
- *Chipolata 5*
- *Circo Rum Ba Ba*
- *Clatterati*
- *Dave Holder*
- *De Ramos Acrobats*
- *Dodger*
- *Dot Comedy*
- *Dr Southall's Medicine Show*



**Pages 119-130 include contact details of UK Agents and Managers with lists of their represented artists.**

**To find the artists listed under these Agents see pages below:**


- **Main Artist A-Z Listing** Artists in the main A-Z listing are mostly available for concert and club bookings. 13-90
- **Dance Display Listing** 91-94
- **Miscellaneous Listing** Solo Musicians, Composers, Arrangers, Session Musicians, Band Deps. Lecturers, MCs. 95-98
- **Tutors** Instrumental, Song, Dance, Community Arts 99-107
- **Entertainers Listing** Street Theatre, Children's Entertainers, Theatre Companies 108-113

agents
f-j

Pages 119-130 include contact details of UK Agents and Managers with lists of their represented artists.

To find the artists listed under these Agents see pages below:



- *The Dream Engine*
- *Enigmatic Eve*
- *Fair Play*
- *Feeding The Fish*
- *Golem Theatre*
- *Grand Theatre of Lemmings*
- *Great British Street Show*
- *Half Human Video Theatre*
- *Heir of Insanity*
- *Incandescence*
- *The Invisible Men*
- *Jason Maverick*
- *The Jelly Rollers*
- *John Teasdale*
- *Kwabana Lindsay*
- *Lighthouse Theatre*
- *Mad Pash*
- *Makendoo*
- *Maynard Flip Flap*
- *Mike Hancock*
- *mimbre*
- *Miniscule of Sound*
- *Mischief La Bas*
- *Mr Winter*
- *Nakupelle*
- *Original Mixture*
- *Parachute Theatre*
- *Patti Bee & Ross Foley*
- *Pyromania*
- *Ramon Kelvink*
- *Real Macaws*
- *Rex Boyd*
- *The Rhythm Doctors*
- *Roxy's Toolbox*
- *Skate Naked*
- *Slim & Slam*
- *Space Cadets*
- *Sparky*
- *The Splott Brothers*
- *Squeal Like A Pig*
- *Stickleback Plasticus*
- *Stiltoneers (The)*
- *Strangelings*
- *Sue Arnold*
- *Surreal McCoy*
- *Swank*
- *Theatre of Fruit*
- *Weapons of Sound*
- *Whalley Range All Stars*
- *Zack Attack*

## Georgia Shorrock

**Contact** The Ceilidh Company
**Mail address** 2 The Barns, Low Hesket, CARLISLE, Cumbria, CA4 0EU
**Phone** 016974 73431
0771 239 7761
**Email** gshorrock@carlisle.ac.uk
**Email** lhgeorgia@aol.com
**RAB** North West Arts

*Contact for several North West ceilidh bands.*

## Gordie Campbell

**Contact** Peerie Angel Productions
**Mail address** 1A Towedykeside, HAWICK, Scottish Borders, TD9 9EA
**Phone/Fax** 01450 372081
**Email** gordiecampbell@aol.com
**AC** Scotland

*Scotland based production/ tour management, festival organisation & artist relations. Previously based in Canada, now UK available.*

## GTA Music Agency and Consultants

**Contact** Dave Kelly
**Mail address** Navigator House, 60 High Street, HAMPTON WICK, Surrey, KT1 4DB
**Phone** 020 8943 9113
**Fax** 020 8943 9112
**Alt contact** Toni Weekes
**RAB** London Arts

*Agency for Blues acts. Additional bands and soloists to those listed including Paul Lamb & The Kingsnakes, Dana Gillespie, Dennis Locorriere, The Blazing Homesteads.*

Representing
- *Angela Brown & The Mighty 45s*
- *The Blues Band*
- *Bob Hall*
- *Cathryn Craig & Brian Willoughby*
- *Dave Kelly*
- *Eugene 'Hideaway' Bridges*
- *Michael Roach*
- *Paul Jones & Dave Kelly*

## Hemlock Music

**Contact** Michael Catovsky
**Mail address** PO Box 32515, LONDON, W3 0NS
**Phone/Fax** 020 8992 8691
**Email** office@hemlockmusic.co.uk
**Web** www.hemlockmusic.demon.co.uk
**RAB** London Arts

*Agency for ceilidh bands and other traditional music/ dance based acts. Take bookings for all kinds of events requiring a folk act.*

Representing
- *Boka Halat*
- *Cheap Jack*
- *Citizen Camembert*
- *Cock & Bull Band (The)*
- *Extra*
- *Jabadaw*
- *Jah Wobble and the Invaders of the Heart*
- *Jah Wobble's Deep Space*
- *Jean-Pierre Rasle (and The Dancing Drones)*
- *Michael Catovsky*
- *MoonDance*
- *Random*
- *Whorticulture*
- *Workhouse*

## Hoodlum Productions

**Contact** Tristan Glover
**Mail address** PO Box 160, CHELTENHAM, GL5 2ZQ
**Phone** 01242 577745
**Fax** 01242 577702
**Email** chipolatas@hotmail.com
**Web** www.chipolatas.com
**RAB** South West Arts

*The Chipolatas' production company, representing UK/ Australian acts.*

## Hot Promotions

**Contact** Hot Hole
**Mail address** PO Box TR69, LEEDS, LS12 5HE
**Phone** 0113 2566733
**Email** hotholesalsa@hotmail.com
**Web** www.magnificent.net/hothole or www.hothole.leedsnet.org
**RAB** Yorkshire Arts

*Event organisers, agency service for world music bands and dancers.*

## Iconic Music & Media

**Contact** Ms Stevie Horton
**Mail address** PO Box 1957, Eathorpe, LEAMINGTON SPA, Warks, CV33 9YG
**Phone/Fax** 01926 632946
**Phone** 07989 373698
**Email** iconicmusic@hotmail.com
**Alt phone** 01926 814111
**RAB** West Midlands Arts

*Small booking agency and publicist. Midlands based, covering the whole UK. Artists range from electric bands to acoustic soloists.*

Representing
- *Bob Fox*
- *Steve Gibbons*
- *The Steve Gibbons Band*
- *Tom Leary & Kevin Dempsey*

## Jacey Bedford Tour Management

**Contact** Jacey Bedford
**Mail address** 10 Park Head, Birdsedge, HUDDERSFIELD, Yorks, HD8 8XW
**Phone** 01484 606230
**Fax** 01484 606290
**Email** jacey@jacey-bedford.com
**Web** www.jacey-bedford.com
**RAB** Yorkshire Arts

*Small agency run by a touring musician for touring musicians. Mainly American, Australian & Canadian acts.*

Representing
- *Artisan*
- *Eileen McGann*
- *Mundy-Turner*
- *Shagpile*
- *Shep Woolley*
- *Tanglefoot*
- *William Pint & Felicia Dale*

## Karisma Music Management

**Contact** Pete Willow
**Mail address** 57 Heath Lane, Brinklow, NR RUGBY, CV23 0NR
**Phone/Fax** 01788 832608
**Phone** 07887 552896
**Email** pete@karisma.net
**Web** www.karisma.net
**RAB** West Midlands Arts

*Representation and promotion of a selection of contemporary folk artists. Organisation and promotion of events.*

Representing

- *Andy Guttridge & Martin Green*
- *Armpit Jug Band*
- *Cofa*
- *Derek Brimstone*
- *Gilly Darbey*
- *Gravelly Hillbillies*
- *Harvesters*
- *Kevin Dempsey*
- *Magna Carta*
- *Meet On The Ledge*
- *Phil Bates*

## Latin Arts Services

**Contact** Hector Rosquete
**Mail address** PO Box 14303, LONDON, SE26 4ZH
**Phone/Fax** 07000 472 572
**Email** latinarts@lasgroup.com
**Web** www.lasgroup.com
**Alt contact** Jo Courtney
**RAB** London Arts

*Promotion of Latin American artists and records to outlets worldwide.*

Representing

- *Julio Cortez Salsa Band*
- *Victor Hugo Salsa Show*

## Macmeanmna

**Contact** Arthur Cormack
**Mail address** Gladstone Buildings, Quay Brae, PORTREE, Isle of Skye, IV51 9DB, Scotland
**Phone** 01478 612990
**Fax** 01478 613263
**Email** arthur@gaelicmusic.com
**Web** www.gaelicmusic.com
**AC** Scotland

*Management and marketing company for Gaelic music artists and consultancies.*

Representing

- *Cliar*
- *Donnie Murdo MacLeod*
- *Kenna Campbell*

## mARKO pOLO

**Contact** Mark Ringwood
**Mail address** The Barn, Fordwater Lane, CHICHESTER, W Sussex, PO19 4PT
**Phone** 01243 789786
**Fax** 01243 789787
**Email** markringwood@btinternet.com
**Web** www.markopolo.co.uk
**RAB** South East Arts

*Large booking agency and tour management, representing blues & roots acts worldwide.*

Representing

- *Alkasalsa*
- *Barra MacNeils*
- *Beppe Gambetta*
- *Beppe Gambetta & Dan Crary*
- *Beware Of The Dog*
- *Big Bill Morganfield*
- *Big Nite Out*
- *Bisserov Sisters*
- *Calypso Rose, Mighty Shadow and Reasons Orchestra*
- *Caribbean Carnival Extravaganza*
- *Chris Thomas King*
- *Cordas et Cannas*
- *Dino Baptiste*
- *Gesuino Deiana*
- *Gjallarhorn*
- *Global Sound*
- *Guy Davis*
- *Gwerinos*
- *Hank Wangford & The Lost Cowboys*
- *The Holmes Brothers*
- *Hubert Sumlin & Sean Chambers*
- *Ivo Papasov & His Bulgarian Wedding Band*
- *The Jaggamuffins*
- *Jerry Holland*
- *Jienat*
- *Jive Wires*
- *Kimmo Pohjonen*
- *La Volee d'Castors*
- *Merengada*
- *Nuzha*
- *Odetta*
- *Orquesta Cache*
- *Popa Chubby*
- *Providence*
- *Rag Foundation*
- *Richard Wood*
- *Scrap!*
- *Slainte Mhath*
- *Smythe & Saucier*
- *Taiko to Tabla*
- *Te Vaka*
- *Tom Ball & Kenny Sultan*
- *The Transsylvanians*
- *Vera Bila & Kale*
- *The Watts Prophets*
- *Xeliba*

## Matters Musical

**Contact** Frank Warren
**Mail address** The Loft, Rear of 8 West Street, DORKING, Surrey, RH4 1BL
**Phone** 01306 741007
07790 014279
**Fax** 01306 741008
**Email** info@mattersmusical.com
**Web** www.mattersmusical.com
**RAB** South East Arts

*Well-established agent for huge range of acts offering "music from around the globe".*

Representing

- *Abana*
- *Abdelkader Saadoun*
- *Adel Salameh*
- *Afroshock*
- *Alexander D Great and The Great Band*
- *Amaru III*
- *Ana Leon Flamenco Group*
- *Andalus*
- *Apu*
- *Balalaika Orchestra*
- *Baluji Shrivastav*
- *Barnstorm*
- *Bearcat Trio*
- *The Bearcats*
- *Beyond The Pale*
- *Bhodan Chomenko*
- *Bibs Ekkel's Tziganka*
- *Boat Band*
- *Bobby Valentino*
- *Bucharest String Duo*
- *Café Aman*
- *Carrig*
- *Casa Latina Allstars*
- *The Casablanca Steps*
- *Celtarabia*
- *Celtic Feet*
- *Cheb Nacim*
- *Claudio Allodi Italian Orchestra*
- *The Coal Porters*
- *Coco Xpress*
- *The Cossacks Dance Troupe*
- *Coyotes*
- *The Dagmars*
- *Dalcassian*
- *Diego Brown and The Good Fairy*
- *Down Mexico Way*
- *Dragonsfire*
- *Durga Rising*
- *Ebony Steel Band*
- *El Adivino*
- *Electric Bluebirds*
- *Elephant Talk*
- *Elephant Talk featuring special guest Eddi Reader*
- *Eliot Mackrell*
- *Errol Linton's Blues Vibe*
- *Fantazia*
- *Fiddlin' Around*
- *Finality Jack*
- *Flaky Jake & The Steamin' Locos*
- *Flashdance*
- *Flatville Aces*
- *Florida*
- *Foghorn Leghorn*



**Pages 119-130 include contact details of UK Agents and Managers with lists of their represented artists.**

**To find the artists listed under these Agents see pages below:**

# agents

## m

**Pages 119-130 include contact details of UK Agents and Managers with lists of their represented artists.**

**To find the artists listed under these Agents see pages below:**



- *Friday Street*
- *Gambit Jazzmen*
- *Gina Mackey*
- *Glissando Steel Orchestra*
- *Grass Fire*
- *Grinnigogs*
- *Grupo Folia*
- *Gyosei Taiko Drummers*
- *Hackney Ramblers*
- *Hoover The Dog*
- *Horace X*
- *Hula Bluebirds*
- *Incredibly Strange Film Band*
- *Jambalaya*
- *James Hunter Band*
- *James O'Hara's Detonators*
- *Jansci Hosszu*
- *JazzIndo*
- *Jeannette Springer*
- *Jock Tyldesley & Gavin Lewery*
- *Joe Giltrap and Michael O'Rourke / Irish Mist*
- *John Otway*
- *John Perkins - Silversitarco*
- *Joji Hirota*
- *Jooks*
- *Kelly's Heroes*
- *The Kimbara Brothers*
- *Kingdom Choir*
- *Kit Packham's One Jump Ahead*
- *Kuljit Bhamra*
- *Kuljit Bhamra Band*
- *La Cucina Trio*
- *London Community Gospel Choir*
- *London Ragtime Orchestra*
- *Los Charros*
- *Los Mojados del Rio Tamesis*
- *Los Pistoleros*
- *Los Soneros*
- *Lough Swilly*
- *Lynch Irish Dance Troupe*
- *Mambo Jumbo (Limbo)*
- *Martin and Thornbory*
- *Merengada*
- *Metalworks Gamelan*
- *Mugenkyo Taiko Drummers*
- *Nostalgia Steel Orchestra*
- *Orquesta La Clave*
- *Otra Vez*
- *Papa Schnitzel*
- *Paradise Steel Band*
- *Paris Moon*
- *Paul Brennan Band*
- *Peace Artistes*
- *Ph. B*
- *Phase Space*
- *Piotr Jordan*
- *Prego*
- *Punita Gupta*
- *Quicksilver*
- *R Cajun & The Zydeco Brothers*
- *Rhythm Kings*
- *Ricky Cool*
- *Roaring Mary*
- *Russian Tornado*
- *Sangeeta*
- *Shades of Black*
- *Shanty Crew*
- *Shikisha*
- *The Slip Jigolos*
- *Solid Steel Ambassadors*
- *South African Gospel Choir*
- *Spartacus*
- *Szapora*
- *Taiko to Tabla*
- *Teddy Peiro's Tango*
- *Thee Na Shee*
- *Township Express*
- *Tribe featuring Karina Rebello*
- *Truss & Bucket Band*
- *Tziganarama*
- *UK Chinese Acrobatic Company*
- *Viramundo*
- *Viva Flamenco*
- *Vladimir Asriev*
- *Volkortsi Cossacks*
- *Wei Li Chinese Orchestra*
- *Wild Women*
- *Wraggle Taggle*
- *Yurupari Latin Dance Team*
- *Zambula*
- *Zubop*
- *Zvuk Bazaar*
- *Zydecoactive*
- *Zydecomotion*

## Mesmerist Productions
**Contact** Bill Nicoll
**Mail address** PO Box 2345, ABERDEEN, AB24 3XE, Scotland
**Phone/Fax** 01224 641400
**Phone** 07050 255902
**Email** info@mesmerist.com
**Web** www.mesmerist.com
**AC** Scotland

*Scotland based music agency.*

Representing
- *Boogalusa*
- *Carmen Higgins*
- *Cluanas*
- *Kathryn Nicoll & Sean O'Donnell*
- *Lorraine Jordan*
- *Russell's House*

## Midland Barndance Agency
**Contact** Peter Durber
**Mail address** 30 Spinney Drive, Kirby Grange, BOTCHESTON, Leics, LE9 9FG
**Phone/Fax** 01455 824125
**Email** pdurber@compuserve.com
**RAB** East Midlands Arts

*Agency for barn dance and ceilidh bands and callers.*

## Moneypenny
**Contact** Nigel Morton
**Mail address** The Stables, Westwood House, Main Street, N Dalton, DRIFFIELD, E Yorks, YO25 9XA
**Phone** 01377 217815
**Fax** 01377 217754
**Email** nigel@adastey.demon.co.uk
**RAB** Yorkshire Arts

*Agency and management company for top folk acts, mainly UK, some overseas.*

Representing
- *Angelou*
- *Damon & Naomi*
- *Eliza Carthy*
- *Incredible String Band*
- *Jackie Leven*
- *Kate & Anna McGarrigle*
- *Martin Carthy*
- *Muzsikas featuring Marta Sebestyn*
- *Norma Waterson*
- *The Popes*
- *Robin Williamson*
- *Ukrainians*
- *Waterson:Carthy*

## Moon Carrot
**Contact** Sarah Chard
**Mail address** 11 Prince Charles Close, RAGLAN, Monmouthshire, NP15 2HD, Wales
**Phone** 07778 615384
**Fax** 07785 896242
**Email** sarah@streetentertainers.co.uk
**Web** www.streetentertainers.co.uk
**AC** Wales

## Mrs Casey Music
**Contact** Steve Heap
**Mail address** PO Box 296, AYLESBURY, Bucks, HP19 9TL
**Phone** 01296 394411
**Fax** 01296 392300
**Email** office@mrscasey.co.uk
**Web** www.mrscasey.co.uk
**RAB** Southern Arts

*Festival & event organisers and consultants*

Representing
- *Brass Monkey*

## Music Matters
**Contact** Di Whitehead
**Mail address** Stag's Lodge, Main Street, WEST HAGBOURNE, Oxon, OX11 ONJ
**Phone/Fax** 01235 850781
**Phone** 07976 232115
**Email** dj@music-matters.uk.com
**Web** www.music-matters.uk.com
**RAB** Southern Arts

*Agents providing music and entertainment for all occasions; weddings, corporate, concerts.*

## Mutiny Music
**Contact** Tim Richardson
**Mail address** 51 Brunel Drive, Preston, WEYMOUTH, Dorset, DT3 6NY
**Phone** 01305 832447
**Email** tim@talkingheads.co.uk
**RAB** South West Arts

*Agent & management, all styles. Acts include traditional Irish and Acoustic Blues/ American.*

Representing
- *Broderick*
- *Devana*
- *na Dorsa*

## Nancy Carlin Associates
**Contact** Nancy Carlin
**Mail address** PO Box 6499, CONCORD, CA 94524, USA
**Phone** 925 686 5800
**Fax** 925 680 2582
**Email** nancyc@well.com

*California based folk agency representating Welsh acts in the UK. Representation in America & Canada for UK acts including Jez Lowe.*

Representing
- *Carreg Lafar*
- *Crasdant*
- *Robin Huw Bowen*
- *Sian James*

## NEM Productions (UK)
**Contact** Dave Smith
**Mail address** Priory House, 55 Lawe Road, SOUTH SHIELDS, Tyne and Wear, NE33 2AL
**Phone** 0191 427 6207
**Fax** 0191 427 6323
**Email** nemproductions@blueyonder.co.uk
**Web** www.nemproductions.com
**RAB** Northern Arts

*Agent for major acoustic music acts*

Representing
- *Bob Brozman*
- *Clive Carroll*
- *Dougie MacLean*
- *Equation*
- *John Renbourn*
- *John Renbourn & Clive Carroll*
- *June Tabor*
- *Kathryn Roberts & Sean Lakeman*
- *Martin Stephenson & The Daintees*
- *Peggy Seeger*
- *Pierre Bensusan*
- *Rory Block*
- *Rory McLeod*
- *Tommy Emmanuel*
- *Woody Mann*

## One Off Productions
**Contact** Doug Hudson
**Mail address** 182 Windmill Road, GILLINGHAM, Kent, ME7 5PE
**Phone/Fax** 01634 574837
**Phone** 07941 238377
**Email** doug.hudson@lineone.net
**Web** www.doughudson.com
**RAB** South East Arts

*Folk agency, plus organiser of Rochester Sweeps Festival, Gravesend World Music Day and the Medway Folk Cellar.*

## Organic Arts
**Contact** Alison Smith
**Mail address** 3 Mains of Dumbreck, Udny, ELLON, Aberdeenshire, AB41 7PJ, Scotland
**Phone** 01651 842838
**Fax** 01651 842133
**Email** bands@organicartsco.uk
**Web** www.organicarts.co.uk
**AC** Scotland

*Music agent and band management for North Scottish folk artists.*

Representing
- *Drop The Box*
- *Harem Scarum*
- *Sharon King Band*



**Pages 119-130 include contact details of UK Agents and Managers with lists of their represented artists.**

**To find the artists listed under these Agents see pages below:**

# agents
## O-S

**Pages 119-130 include contact details of UK Agents and Managers with lists of their represented artists.**

**To find the artists listed under these Agents see pages below:**



### OTB Productions
**Contact** Dave McCrory
**Mail address** OTB Productions, 5 Oldridge View, TEDBURN ST MARY, Devon, EX6 6AB
**Phone** 01647 61237
**Email** dave@otbproductions.co.uk
**Web** www.otbproductions.co.uk
**RAB** South West Arts
Representing
- *Alan Burke*
- *Baka Beyond*
- *FOS Brothers*
- *Green Roadshow*
- *Hootenanny 3*
- *Huckleberries*
- *Jerry Cahill*
- *Nigel Mazlyn Jones & Ellen Harvey*
- *Tango Band*

### The Other Agency
**Contact** Vivienne Bloomfield
**Mail address** 84 High Street, Potterspury, TOWCESTER, Northants, NN12 7PQ
**Phone** 01908 542894
**Fax** 01908 543913
**Email** vivienne@jvmb.powernet.co.uk
**Alt contact** Steafan Hannigan
**Alt address** 188 Church Street, Wolverton, MILTON KEYNES, MK12 3JG
**Phone** 01908 222966
**RAB** Southern Arts
*Booking agent, folk acts.*
Representing
- *Bob Fox*
- *Broderick*
- *Collen Gregory*
- *Dana Robinson*
- *Faye Rochelle*
- *Jenny Crook & Henry Sears*
- *Joe O'Donnell*
- *Kalinka Vulcheva*
- *Leon Rosselson*
- *Robb Johnson, Miranda Sykes & Saskia Tomkins*
- *Robb Johnson's "Gentle Men"*
- *Simon Mayor & Hilary James*
- *Simon Mayor's Mandolinquents*
- *Slim Panatella & The Mellow Virginians*
- *Wood WorX*

### Park Promotions
**Contact** John Dagnell
**Mail address** PO Box 651, OXFORD, OX2 9RB
**Phone** 01865 241717
**Fax** 01865 204556
**Email** parkrecords@cwcom.net
**Web** www.parkrecords.com
**RAB** Southern Arts
Representing
- *Jacqui McShee's Pentangle*
- *Maddy Prior*
- *Steeleye Span*

### Peerie Angel Productions
**Mail address** 1A Towedykeside, HAWICK, Scottish Borders, TD9 9EA
**Phone/Fax** 01450 372081
**Email** catriona@peerieangel.demon.co.uk
**Web** www.peerieangel.demon.co.uk
**AC** Scotland
Representing
- *Catriona MacDonald*

### Porthole Promotions
**Contact** Jim McLaughlin
**Mail address** Highfields, Sledgates, Fylingthorpe, WHITBY, Yorks, YO22 4TZ
**Phone** 01947 880962
0777 9861709
**Email** portholepromotions@ic24.net
**RAB** Yorkshire Arts
Representing
- *Banoffi*

### Primary Talent
**Contact** Nigel Hassler
**Mail address** 5th Floor, 2-12 Pentonville Road, LONDON, N1 9PL
**Phone** 020 7833 8998
**Fax** 020 7833 5992
**Email** nigel@primary.uk.com
**Alt contact** Andy Woolliscroft
**Email** andy@primary.uk.com
**RAB** London Arts
*Major London agency representing top artists both within & outside the folk genre, including Indigo Girls and The Proclaimers, Dar Williams, John Cale*
Representing
- *Afro Celt Sound System*
- *Angelique Kidjo*
- *Ani Difranco*
- *Capercaille*
- *Harlem Gospel Choir*
- *Janis Ian*
- *Lorenna McKennitt*
- *Michelle Shocked*
- *Richard Thompson*
- *Sinead Lohan*

### RAVI
**Contact** JP Freeman
**Mail address** 46 Merle Avenue, HAREFIELD, Middx, UB9 6DG
**Phone** 07711 265011
**Email** info@ravi-art.co.uk
**Web** www.ravi-art.co.uk
*Agent for ethnic & world musicians.*

### Rent-A-Band
**Mail address** Burnside House, 10 Burns Court, BIRSTALL, Yorks, WF17 9JB
**RAB** Yorkshire Arts
*Specialist band hiring contractors.*

### Salsa Direct
**Contact** Nina Jaffa
**Mail address** 24B Colless Road, LONDON, N15 4NR
**Phone** 020 8808 4290
07956 395018
**Email** info@salsadirect.co.uk
**Web** www.salsadirect.co.uk
**RAB** London Arts
*UK specialist contact for all styles of Latin music acts: bands, artists and dancers.*

### SASA Music Ltd
**Contact** David Flower
**Mail address** 309 Aberdeen House, 22-24 Highbury Grove, LONDON, N5 2EA
**Phone** 0207 359 9232
**Fax** 0207 359 9233
**Email** rab@sasa.demon.co.uk
**Alt contact** Leah Zakss
**RAB** London Arts
*Prominent world music promoter and agency. Artists represented include Buena Vista Social Club & Juan de Marcos.*

### Serious International Music Producers
**Contact** David Jones
**Mail address** Chapel House, 18 Hatton Place, LONDON, EC1N 8RN
**Phone** 020 7405 9900
**Email** david@serious.org.uk
**Web** www.serious.org.uk
**RAB** London Arts
*Major jazz and world music promoters.*

### Shindy Arts
**Contact** Jackie Allen
**Mail address** 34 Fosters Lane, Bradwell, MILTON KEYNES, MK13 9HZ
**Phone** 01908 225681
**Email** jackie@shindy.org.uk
**Web** www.shindy.org.uk
**RAB** Southern Arts
*Agent for folk bands and dance acts.*
Representing
- *Asha*
- *Bob Adams*
- *Broken Ankles*
- *DanceAV*
- *J P Jazz*
- *The Kitchen Girls*
- *Rock The Boat*
- *Ross Allen*
- *Token Women*

## Smalltown Promotions

**Contact** Fred Hopwood
**Mail address** 17 Colne Mount, UTTOXETER, Staffs, ST14 7QR
**Phone** 01889 563123
07989 669824
**RAB** West Midlands Arts

*Agent for Cajun, Zydeco, Blues, R & B and barn dance bands.*

Representing

- *Good Rockin' Dave & Zydeco Hot Rods*
- *Vice Bishops Blues Band*
- *Vice Bishops of Uttoxeter*
- *Yeah Jazz*

## Smallworld Music

**Contact** Becky Morris
**Mail address** PO Box 747, BELFAST, BT9 5ES, N Ireland
**Phone** 028 9038 2384
**Fax** 028 9029 5173
**Email** Becksworld@btinternet.com
**AC** Northern Ireland

Agency specialising in Irish music acts.

Representing

- *Alan Kelly*
- *The Bumblebees*
- *Cathal Hayden & Eamon McElholm*
- *Dezi Donnelly*
- *Laoise Kelly*

## Speaking Volumes

**Contact** Chris Jaeger
**Mail address** Huntingdon Hall, Crown Gate, WORCESTER, Worcs, WR1 3LD
**Phone** 01905 611323
07831 588780
**Fax** 01905 619958
**Email** chris@speakingvolumes.co.uk
**Web** www.speakingvolumes.co.uk
**RAB** West Midlands Arts

*Folk music agent, largely well known, mainly English, folk acts.*

Representing

- *The Albion Band*
- *Gordon Giltrap*
- *Harvey Andrews*
- *Isla St Clair*
- *John Kirkpatrick*
- *John Kirkpatrick Ceilidh Band*
- *Julie Felix*
- *Little Johnny England*
- *The Mellstock Band*
- *Sally Barker*
- *Vikki Clayton*
- *Vin Garbutt*

## Stoneyport Agency

**Contact** John Barrow
**Mail address** 39 Shandon Crescent, EDINBURGH, EH11 1QF, Scotland
**Phone** 0131 346 8237
**Fax** 0131 313 2083
**Email** jb@folkmus.demon.co.uk
**Web** www.stoneyport.demon.co.uk
**AC** Scotland

*Major Scottish agency for folk acts. This is the main contact, there are 8 agents working under the Stoneyport umbrella.*

Representing

- Allan Taylor
- *Amos Garrett*
- *Andy M Stewart & Gerry O'Beirne*
- *Bag O'Cats*
- *Beginish*
- *Bert Jansch*
- *Bill Barclay*
- *Blue Hyenas*
- *Burach*
- *The Cast*
- *Ceolbeg*
- *Christine Kydd*
- *cMc*
- *Croft No. Five*
- *De Dannan*
- *Deaf Shepherd*
- *Dick Gaughan*
- *Dick Gaughan & Brian McNeill*
- *Eric Bogle*
- *Fairport Convention*
- *Fiddlers' Bid*
- *Finlay MacDonald Band*
- *Frankie Gavin*
- *Fred Morrison*
- *Gill Bowman*
- *Hot Club*
- *Jack Evans*
- *Jennifer & Hazel Wrigley*
- *Jimmy Crowley*
- *Keep It Up*
- *Keltic Elektrik*
- *Kenny Young and The Eggplants*
- *La Boum!*
- *macAlias*
- *MacManus, Evans, McLeod*
- *Malinky*
- *The McCalmans*
- *Michael Marra*
- *Mystery Juice*
- *Old Blind Dogs*
- *The Poozies*
- *Rory Campbell & Malcolm Stitt*
- *The Scottish Stepdance Company*
- *Sileas*
- *Tam White and Brian Kellock*
- *Tam White's Groove Connection*
- *Tam White's Shoestring*
- *Wild Cigarillos*

## Stoneyport Agency

**Contact** Bill Barclay
**Phone/Fax** 0131 3394 279
**Email** bb003@almac.co.uk

*Arranges the agency's 'specials'... weddings, speakers, cabaret, etc.*

## Stoneyport Agency

**Contact** Kresanna Aigner
**Mail address** Ground Floor, 23 Notting Hill, BELFAST, BT9 5NS, N Ireland
**Phone/Fax** 028 9066 8108
**Phone** 07050 229275
**Email** kresanna@artisticupstarts.demon.co.uk
**Web** www.artisticupstarts.demon.co.uk

*Management/ agent for Colin Reid, Old Blind Dogs and UK booking agent for Beginish. See Artistic Upstarts.*

## Stoneyport Agency

**Contact** John Brown
**Phone/Fax** 0131 332 7067
**Email** johnbrown@stockbridgemusic.demon.co.uk

*Artists include Gill Bowman. See Stoneyport main entry.*

## Stoneyport Agency

**Contact** Jim Condie
**Mail address** 44 Queens Drive, GLASGOW, G42 8DD, Scotland
**Phone** 0141 4240280
0771 201 4248
**Fax** 0141 401 9741
**Email** jimcondie@aol.com
**Web** www.btinternet.com/~jimcondie
**AC** Scotland

*Section of Stoneyport Agency dealing with North American acts.*

## Stoneyport Agency

**Contact** Martin Coull Music Management
**Mail address** Studio 7, 6 New Street, EDINBURGH, EH8 8BH, Scotland
**Phone/Fax** 0131 557 5330
**Phone** 07803 137509
**Email** marticoull@aol.com
**AC** Scotland

Representing

- *Croft No 5*
- *Malinky*
- *macAlias*
- *Deaf Shepherd*
- *Finlay MacDonald.*

## Stoneyport Agency

**Contact** Heather MacLeod
**Phone** 0131 6628358
07785 720987
**Email** hmac518996@aol.com
**AC** Scotland

Representing

- *Mystery Juice*
- *La Boum!*

## Stoneyport Agency

**Contact** Dave Francis
**Phone/Fax** 0131 5571050
**Email** dfrancis@musicscotland.com
**AC** Scotland

Representing

- *Fiddler's Bid*
- *The Cast*
- *Ceolbeg*
- *De Dannan*
- *Frankie Gavin*
- *Keltic Elektrik*
- *McManus Evans McLeod.*



**Pages 119-130 include contact details of UK Agents and Managers with lists of their represented artists.**

**To find the artists listed under these Agents see pages below:**

## agents

### s-w

**Pages 119-130 include contact details of UK Agents and Managers with lists of their represented artists.**

**To find the artists listed under these Agents see pages below:**


- **Main Artist A-Z Listing** Artists in the main A-Z listing are mostly available for concert and club bookings. 13-90
- **Dance Display Listing** 91-94
- **Miscellaneous Listing** Solo Musicians, Composers, Arrangers, Session Musicians, Band Deps. Lecturers, MCs. 95-98
- **Tutors** Instrumental, Song, Dance, Community Arts 99-107
- **Entertainers Listing** Street Theatre, Children's Entertainers, Theatre Companies 108-113


### Swamp Music
**Contact** Chris Hall
**Mail address** PO Box 94, DERBY, DE22 1XA
**Phone/Fax** 01332 332336
**Phone** 07702 564804 (mob)
**Email** chrishall@swampmusic.co.uk
**Web** www.swampmusic.co.uk
**RAB** East Midlands Arts

*Agency representing many major Cajun & Zydeco acts including touring US artists.*

Representing
- *Bearcats*
- *Boat Band*
- *Bon Temps Playboys*
- *Flatville Aces*
- *Good Rockin' Dave & Zydeco Hot Rods*
- *Hackney Ramblers*
- *Jock Tyldesley & Gavin Lewery*
- *Joe Le Taxi*
- *Pierre Le Rue*
- *R Cajun & The Zydeco Brothers*
- *Zydecoactive*
- *Zydecomotion*

### themusictree. (uk) ltd
**Contact** Harry Farmer
**Mail address** Fish Factory, 1 & a half Disbrowe Road, LONDON, W6 8QG
**Phone** 020 7386 0696
**Fax** 020 7386 0695
**Email** themusictree@aol.com
**RAB** London Arts

Representing
- *Buddy Mondlock*
- *Colin Reid*
- *Danu*
- *Don Mescall*
- *Flook*
- *Jackie Leven*
- *Jacqui McShee's Pentangle*
- *Liz Carroll*
- *Mary Coughlan*
- *Nick Harper*
- *Pete Morton*
- *Sin É*
- *Susan McKeown*

### Three's Company
**Contact** Fay Hield
**Mail address** 63 Nelson Street, Cross Roads, KEIGHLEY, W Yorks, BD22 9EA
**Phone** 01535 643249
**Email** three_s_company@hotmail.com
**RAB** Yorkshire Arts

*Promoters of concerts ranging from world music to comedy to local audiences in West Yorks. Artist representation for*

Representing
- *Maggie Boyle*
- *Damien Barber*
- *Fay Hield*
- *Grace Notes.*

### Tickety-Boo
**Contact** Dee Whelan
**Mail address** Boat House, Crabtree Lane, LONDON, SW6 6TY
**Phone** 020 7610 0122
**Fax** 020 7610 0133
**Email** tickety-boo@tickety-boo.com
**Web** www.tickety-boo.com
**RAB** London Arts

*Artist management company, for artists including Ralph McTell.*

### Tom Sherlock Management
**Contact** Tom Sherlock
**Mail address** 71 Carysfort Avenue, BLACKROCK, Co Dublin, Ireland
**Phone** +353 1 2781090
**Fax** +353 1278 1093
**Email** sherlock@altan.ie
**AC** Ireland

*Irish management, agency and promotions work for traditional music.*

Representing
- *Altan*
- *Karan Casey*
- *Maighread & Triona Ni Dhomnaill*

### Total Music Agency
**Contact** Peter Wilson
**Mail address** BRIDPORT, Dorset, DT6 3DZ
**Phone/Fax** 01308 425713
**RAB** South West Arts

*Agency specialising in folk & roots.*

Representing
- *The Joyce Gang*
- *Kangaroo Moon*

### Triss Dickin
**Mail address** 26 North Villas, Camden, LONDON, NW1 9BL
**Email** triss101@hotmail.com
**RAB** London Arts

*Agent, representing artists of all types incl. East European, Arabic and Jazz.*

### UK Steel Bands Agency
**Phone** 0115 9762726
**Email** enquiries@uk-steel-bands-agency.com
**Web** www.uk-steel-bands-agency.com

*Agent for steel bands, retailers of a range of African, Caribbean, Latin and Asian World music.*

### UK Touring
**Contact** Adrian Mealing
**Mail address** The Croft, Old Church Road, COLWALL, Worcs, WR13 6EZ
**Phone/Fax** 01684 540366
**Email** adrian@uktouring.org.uk
**Web** www.uktouring.org.uk
**RAB** West Midlands Arts

Representing
- *The Big Hum*
- *Boneshaker*
- *Iain Matthews*
- *Iain Matthews & Andy Roberts/ Plainsong*
- *The Three Tenners*

### Vox Pop
**Contact** Damian Clarke
**Mail address** 25 Kings Road, DORCHESTER, Dorset, DT1 1NH
**Phone/Fax** 01305 267510
**Email** damian@voxpop.demon.co.uk
**Web** www.voxpop.demon.co.uk
**RAB** South West Arts

*UK management/ agency for European folk bands including Plommon from Sweden, Dinwall from Brittany and Lack of Limits fom Germany.*

Representing
- *Pressgang*

### Well Groomed Management
**Contact** Dave Groom
**Mail address** 80 Hood Street, NOTTINGHAM NG5 4AQ
**Phone/Fax** 0115 952 2638
**Email** wellgroomed@proweb.co.uk
**RAB** East Midlands Arts

*Artist & eveng management company.*

Representing
- *Jo Freya*
- *The Fraser Sisters*
- *Freya Federation*
- *Freya/Locke*

### Whippet Promotions
**Contact** Gary Miller
**Mail address** PO Box 72, YORK, YO31 1LD
**Phone/Fax** 01904 410038
**Phone** 01904 423060
**Email** gary@whippetpromotions.fsnet.co.uk
**Web** whiskypriests.co.uk
**RAB** Yorkshire Arts

*Booking agent & management.*

Representing
- *Mad Dogs and Englishmen*
- *The Whisky Priests*

## Whitewave Music

**Contact** John White
**Mail address** 19 Linicro, KILMUIR, Isle of Skye, IV51 9YN, Scotland
**Phone** 01470 542414
**Fax** 01470 542443
**Email** info@gaelic-song.com
**Web** www.whiteact.demon.co.uk
**AC** Scotland
Representing
- *Anne Martin*

## Willie Eckerslike Management

**Contact** Colin Jones
**Mail address** 20 Montague Road, LONDON, E8 2HW
**Phone** 020 7275 8292
07973 217878
**Fax** 020 75038034
**Email** angelstears@appleonline.net
**RAB** London Arts
*Artist management company.*

## Working Joe Music Ltd

**Contact** Paul Saunders
**Mail address** 6 Swan Meadow, MUCH WENLOCK, Shropshire, TF13 6JQ
**Phone/Fax** 01952 728283
**Email** ps@workingjoe.co.uk
**Web** www.workingjoe.co.uk
**RAB** West Midlands Arts
*Independent record label and agency representing & recording roots artists. Contemporary songwriters to medieval street bands.*
Representing
- *Bill Caddick*
- *Desperate Men*



**Pages 119-130 include contact details of UK Agents and Managers with lists of their represented artists.**

**To find the artists listed under these Agents see pages below:**

spotlight
section

# spotlight

# World Roots UK

By **Ian Anderson**, *Editor, fRoots Magazine*

Britain, like most islands, has always been a multi-cultural nation. Over the centuries, numerous immigrants have been absorbed and helped make our unique culture. Music has been part of that: witness the way that the polka is a traditional folk dance form all over these islands, though once it - like the waltz - was an early sighting of what we now call 'world music'.

With the apparent shrinking of the planet because of modern media, communications and travel, world music - local music, not from here - has been one of the most successful growth areas in the UK in the past two decades, boosted further in recent times by its local cousin, urban British multicultural music. Until the 1980s, world music had a small following restricted by the availability of recordings (hard to find outside specialised outlets like the long-lost Collett's) and the rarity of tours by roots artists from other parts of the globe. Similarly, although there have historically been many immigrant communities in Britain, music making had often been kept within those various cultures - a classic example of which would be the way that contemporary bhangra music evolved from the unique experience of the UK Asian population, but with little involvement from other communities in the country.

From the early 1980s, an escalating number of enthusiast-driven UK record labels and event organisers brought about an entirely different climate. Tours organised by Anne Hunt's **Arts Worldwide**, events in London funded by the GLC and the Commonwealth Institute, the founding of the **Womad** organisation, broadcasting by Radio 1 DJs **Alexis Korner**, **John Peel** and soon **Andy Kershaw**, and the birth of labels like **GlobeStyle**, **Stern's**, **World Circuit** and later **Real World** all contributed to this change. What was variously tagged 'international', 'ethnic', 'roots', 'tropical' or in America 'worldbeat' was off and running, though not without problems for record shops trying to work out where to put albums from such diverse artists as Bulgarian choirs, Pakistani qawwali groups, hot Latin bands, kora players from West Africa and jit-jivers from Zimbabwe.

In 1987, most of the key labels and activists got together above an Islington pub to instigate a cooperative campaign, the first task for which was to agree on an a unified genre name. For those interested in the 'who' and 'why' of that campaign, the minutes of the meetings and the names of all the culprits can be read at website *www.froots.demon.co.uk/features/world_music_history/minutes*. Regardless, it was one of the single most successful PR campaigns pound-per-column-inch in the history of the music business, and world music is now an accepted and broadly understood genre that fills record shop racks, the festival calendar and the programming of most respectable multi-arts venues alongside and of course crossing over with jazz or folk.

There are numerous artists and bands featuring UK-based immigrant musicians playing essentially unchanged music from their home countries, be they African, South American or Asian. But as all this music became a regular sub-plot to national listening habits, inevitably other British musicians were inspired to participate. All this coincided with the growth of accessible recording technology, club culture, and the burgeoning confidence of second and later generation musicians from immigrant communities.

Back in the 1960s, the adventurous explorations of local musicians like the **Incredible String Band**, **Davey Graham** and even the **Beatles** with their involvement with Indian players like **Ravi Shankar** were rare enough to be exceptional. Even in the '80s, the work of godfathers like the **3 Mustaphas 3** was ahead of its time. By the late '90s, however, you could probably describe multicultural music all over the UK as a 'movement', though the paricipants and the directions they come from (and are heading in) are so diverse as to defy categorisation. Just a few examples like **Edward II** (lately transformed into **e2K**), **Salsa Celtica**, the **Bollywood Brass Band**, **Baka Beyond**, **Fantazia**, **Talvin Singh**, **Bloco Vomit**, **Suns Of Arqa**, **Oi-Va-Voi**, **Afro-Celt Sound System**, **Transglobal Underground**, **La Boum**, **Natacha Atlas**, **MoMo**, **Zohar** and **Asian Dub Foundation** are the tip of the iceberg and give a clue to how widespread and varied all this has become.

Two things are for sure, though. Firstly, multi-cultural roots music making in the UK is going through an exciting phase that cannot help but have a long term effect on our mainstream. And perhaps most importantly of all, in a culture here that has almost entirely lost touch with its traditions as they have become obliterated by global (read American) corporate dominance, what could be more inspiring than the example of artists from countries where traditionally rooted artists are still the biggest popular stars?

## Resources

### Publications

#### fRoots

Established in 1979, **fRoots** magazine has been the UK's front-line reporter on the evolution of local and world roots music making. Since issue one their motto has been "inspiration to enthusiasm". The magazine's features, reviews and news of everything under the roots music umbrella - from Anglo trad to Zanzibar pop, via the great mixing desk in the sky - have laid down content parameters that have been the model for many subsequent magazines internationally. With its unbroken record of publishing every single issue on time, fRoots has invariably been the first to write about emerging artists and to document areas of "local music from out there", worldwide.

The fRoots team were amongst the prime movers and catalysts of the World Music explosion in the '80s, and with many of the leading experts among their writers, the magazine continues to be the monthly market leader in content and circulation. With more than a dozen features and 150 to 200 often hard-hitting reviews each month, a massive news coverage and a nose for controversy, fRoots is subscribed to worldwide, read by nearly everybody in the business, and the key advertising medium.

Two issues a year come with unique compilation CDs of hard-to-find music. The annual fRoots Critics' Poll uses a huge panel of experts to to make a definitive assessment of the albums of the year, whilst the April edition traditionally contains an exhaustive diary and supplement on the year's European roots, folk and world music festivals. Details of all these can be found on the fRoots web site along with many other resources.

fRoots have close sponsorship links with Sidmouth and Womad festivals and the annual Womex convention,

and at press date were working with BBC Radio 3 on establishing World Music Awards.
**Web** www.froots.demon.co.uk
**Phone** +44 (0)20 8340 9651 for subscription and advertising details.

The 2nd edition of the **Rough Guide To World Music**, published in 2000, is easily the most comprehensive background reference, contributed to by all the leading experts.

### *Radio*

Under new controller Roger Wright, BBC Radio 3 has become the main national channel on which you can find world and UK multicultural roots music. **Andy Kershaw** (Fridays), **Lucy Duran's World Routes** (Saturdays) and **Late Junction** (Monday to Thursday) guarantee some coverage 7 days a week. The growth of web-based broadcasting means that regional programmes like **Charlie Gillett** and **Gerry Lyseight** on BBC London Live are listened to nationally and internationally on the internet.

### *Records*

Among the leading UK-based labels with in-depth catalogues are **GlobeStyle (Ace)**, **Real World**, **Stern's**, **World Circuit**, **World Music Network Nascente (MCI)**

### Promoters

Among the main promoters of key events are **Serious**, **Como No** and **Multi Culti** in London, **World Unlimited** in the Midlands, the **Womad** organisation, **Asian Music Circuit**, **African & Caribbean Music Circuit.**

**Ian Anderson**

# World Music Resources

## *Publications*

### fRoots

**Mail address** PO Box 337, London N4 1TW
**Phone** 020 8340 9651
**Fax** 020 8348 5626
**Email** froots@froots.demon.co.uk
**Web** www.froots.demon.co.uk
*Content as described by editor Ian Anderson on page 134.*

### Songlines

**Songlines**, which is published quarterly, is dedicated to World Music. It reviews between 100 and 120 CDs each issue with features and news stories. Alongside these each issue has a Songlines Guide to a particular style of music and a Tools of the Trade feature on a musical instrument. There have been Songlines Guides to Cuban son, Algerian rai, Congolese soukous, South African Township music and Qawwali amongst others and Tools articles on the sitar, mbira, uilleann pipes, English melodeon, Native American flute and several more.

Each issue highlights 10 Top of the World discs, which are particularly recommended and to date each issue has come with a free CD usually presenting the output of a particular label. Last year tracks from the Top of the World discs of 2000 were compiled onto a Songlines CD, which was released by Manteca.

The magazine is aimed at those who are interested in world music, but are not necessarily experts and tries to be accessible and readable, but also accurate and authoritative. It costs £3.50 an issue or £14.00 per year by subscription in the UK.
**Subscriptions**
**Phone** 01795 414827
**Fax** 01795 414555.
**Email** songlines@galleon.co.uk

### Get Rhythm Music Magazine

**Mail address** PO Box 102, Forest Hall Newcastle upon Tyne, NE12 7WD
**Phone** 0191 245 3782
**Fax** 0191 245 3786
**Email** getrhythm@ukonline.co.uk
**Web** www.getrhythm.co.uk

### World Music: The Rough Guide

**(2 volumes)** ISBN 1-85828-635-2
**Mail address** Rough Guides Ltd 62-70 Shorts Gardens, London WC2H 9AB
**Web** www.roughguides.com
*Dist by Penguin £17.99 (UK)*

## *Organisations*

### African & Caribbean Music Circuit

*See Introduction to the African and Caribbean Circuit on page 143.*

### Asian Music Circuit

**Mail address** Ground Floor Unit E, West Point, 33/34 Warple Way, London W3 0RG
**Phone** 020 8742 9911
**Fax** 020 8749 3948
**Email** info@amc.org.uk
**Web** www.amc.org.uk
*See introduction to Asian Music Circuit on page 142.*

### Visiting Arts

**Mail address** 11 Portland Place, London W1N 4EJ
**Phone** 020 7389 3019
*See introduction to Visiting Arts on page 388.*

## *Promoters*

### Como No

**Web** www.comono.co.uk
**Email** info@comono.co.uk

### Serious International Music Producers

**Mail address** Chapel House 18 Hatton Place London EC1N 8RN
**Phone** 020 7405 9900
**Email** david@serious.org.uk
**Web** www.serious.org.uk

### WOMAD

**Mail address** Millside, Mill Lane, Box, Wilts SN13 8PN
**Phone** 01225 743188
**Fax** 01225 743481
**Email** womad@realworld.on.net
**Web** www.womad.org

### World Unlimited

**Web** www.worldunlimited.freekuk.com

### MultiCulti

**MultiCulti** is a London based company that presents a diverse array of traditional music and dance performances on the South Bank in London. Some of the artists have included **Zakir Hussain and the Masters of Percussion**, the **Whirling Dervishes of Damascus**, **Eleftheria Arvarritaki**, **Miriam Makeba**, **Misia**, **Vicente**, **Amigo** and many more.
**Contact** Kola Adefobe
**Mail address** MultiCulti, P.O. Box 8964, London, SE12 0ZA
**Phone** 020 8857 9512

## Record labels

### Claddagh Records
**Mail address** Dame House, Dame Street, Dublin 2, Ireland
**Email** claddagh@crl.ie
**Web** http://indigo.ie/~claddagh
*Irish label, largely traditional, established 40+ years*

### Discovery Records
**Mail address** Kings Corner, Pewsey, Wilts, SN9 5BS
**Phone** 01672 563931
**Fax** 01672 563934
**Email** discovery.records@virgin.net
*Largely compilations*

### Earthsongs
**Mail address** 2-3 Fitzroy Mews, London. W1P 5DQ
**Email** earthsongs@connoisseur collection. co.uk
*Zimbabwe & Native American*

### Flame Tree Music Ltd
**Mail address** PO Box 23024, London W11 2WA
*West African re-issues*

### Gael-Linn Records
**Mail address** 26 Merrion Square Dublin 2, Ireland
**Email** eolas@gaellinn.iol.ie
**Web** www.gael-linn.ie
*Irish traditional classics*

### Globestyle
**Mail address** 48-50 Steele Road, London NW10 7AS
**Email** info@acerecords.co.uk
**Web** www.acerecords.co.uk
*Established 20+ years; worldwide sources*

### Grapevine
**Mail address** 5-6 Lombard Street East, Dublin 2, Ireland
**Email** grape@iol.ie
*Ireland/USA/Canada*

### Hannibal
**Mail address** PO Box 2401, London W2 5SF
**Email** data@rykodisc.com
**Web** www.rykodisc.com
*Varied sources.*

### Harmonia Mundi
**Mail address** 19-21 Nile Street, London N1 7LL
**Phone** 020 7608 2787
**Fax** 020 7253 3237
**Email** info.uk@harmoniamundi.com
**Web** www.harmoniamundi.com
*French early & other world music*

### Hemisphere (EMI Records)
**Mail address** 43 Brook Green, London W6 7EF
*Mid-price compilations (Africa,Middle East etc). Recent high-profile signings*

### Interstate Music Ltd
**Mail address** 20 Endwell Road, Bexhill on Sea, E Sussex, TN40 1EA
*Europe/Latin/W Africa 78 remasters*

### M.E.L.T. 2000
**Mail address** 6c Littlehampton Road Worthing, W Sussex, BN13 1QE
**Phone** 01903 260033
**Fax** 01903 261133
**Email** info@melt2000.com
**Web** www.melt2000.com
*African, S African emphasis*

### Nascente
**Mail address** MCI Ltd, 72-74 Dean Street, London W1V 5HA
**Phone** 020 7470 6680
**Email** info@mcimusic.co.uk
**Web** www.nascente.co.uk
*Budget compilations, often Latin*

### Nation Records
**Mail address** 19 All Saints Road London , W11 1HE
**Email** aki@nationrecs.demon.co.uk
**Web** www.nationrecs.demon.co.uk
*Asian fusion*

### Nimbus Records
**Mail address** Wyastone Leys, Monmouth, NP25 3SR
**Phone** 01600 890682
**Fax** 01600 892119
**Web** www.nimbusrecords.com
*SE Asian/Indian + other traditions*

### Outcaste Records
**Mail address** Queens House, 1 Leicester Place, London, WC2H 7BP
**Email** info@outcaste.com
**Web** www.outcaste.com
*New Asian*

### Palm Pictures
**Mail address** 8 Kensington Park Road London W11 3BU
**Email** gerry@islandlife.co.uk
**Web** www.islandlife.com
*Successor to Island label*

### Rags Productions
**Mail address** 29 Abingdon Road London, W8 6AH
*Ethiopia/Eritrea/Sudan*

### RealWorld
**Mail address** Mill Lane, Box, Corsham Wilts, SN13 8PL
**Web** http://realworld.on.net/home. html
*WOMAD stable-mate*

### RetroAfric
**Mail address** PO Box 2977, London W11 2WL
**Web** www.hpd-online.demon.co.uk
*African dance re-issues*

### Rykodisc
**Mail address** PO Box 2401, London, W2 5SF
**Email** data@rykodisc.com
**Web** www.rykodisc.com
*Roots/jazz/rock & re-issue projects*

### Stern's
**Mail address** 74-75 Warren Street London, W1P 5PA
**Phone** 020 7388 5533
**Fax** 020 7388 2756
**Email** info@sternsmusic.com
**Web** www.sternsmusic.com
*Leading African label*

### Topic Records
**Mail address** 50 Stroud Green Road London, N4 3EF
*Leading British artists & 'Topic World'*

### Triple Earth
**Mail address** 24 Foley Street London, W1P 7LA
**Email** iain@triple-earth.co.uk
*Eclectic*

### World Circuit
**Mail address** 106 Cleveland Street London, W1P 5DP
**Email** post@worldcircuit.co.uk
**Web** www.worldcircuit.co.uk
*Largely Latin/African. 'Buena Vista Social Club'*

### World Music Network
**Mail address** 6 Abbeville Mews, 88 Clapham Park Road, London, SW4 7BX
**Email** wldmusic@dircon.co.uk
**Web** www.worldmusic.net
*Rough Guide compilations*

### ECM Records
**Mail address** New Note Electron House, Cray Avenue, Orpington, Kent BR5 3RJ
**Web** www.ecmrecords.com

### Jewish Music Heritage Recordings
**Mail address** PO Box 232, Harrow, Middlesex HA1 2NN
**Phone** 020 8909 2445
**Fax** 020 8909 1030

### Koch International
**Mail address** Charlotte House, 87 Little Ealing Lane, London W5 4EH
**Phone** 020 8832 1800
**Fax** 020 8832 1801

**Navras Records Ltd**
**Mail address** 22 Sherwood Road
London NW4 1AD
**Phone** 020 8203 2553
**Fax** 020 8203 2542
**Email** music@navrasrecords.com
**Web** www.navrasrecords.com

**Sona Rupa Ltd**
**Mail address** 103 Belgrave Road
Leicester LE4 6AS
**Phone** 0116 266 8181
**Fax** 0116 261 0336
**Email** music@sonarupa.co.uk

**Tibet Foundation**
**Mail address** 2 Bloomsbury Way
London WC1A 2SH
**Phone** 020 7404 2889
**Fax** 020 7404 2366

**Trehantiri**
**Mail address** 365-367 Green Lanes
London N4 1DY
**Phone/Fax** 020 8802 6530

**World Music Tours**
**Fax** 0870 052 7278
**Email** wmt@worldmusictours.com
**Web** www.worldmusictours.com

# Irish Traditional Music

**An overview of the current state and trends of Irish Traditional Music.** By **Alan O'Leary**

In 1910 when Chief O'Neill, head of the Chicago Police force published his book, "Irish Folk Music, A Fascinating Hobby", he was hoping to preserve what was left of a dying art. Interesting to note he included a reproduction of O'Farrell's "Treatise on the Irish or Union Pipes", (first published 1806), an instrument, which, like the music, was facing extinction.

As we look back from the beginning of this new century, it's interesting to muse how far Irish music has come.

With music of Irish influence having toured the world with successful dance shows like *Riverdance* and *Lord of the Dance* it is now almost compulsory for it to be included in any new movie.

Strangely enough, after the highpoint during the 70s when Irish groups made music which thrilled the world, I would cite the music of bands like **Planxty**, **The Bothy Band** and **Moving Hearts**, as being some of the most important music made in the previous decades, and their legacy is still an inspiration for much of the music being made today.

Sadly, I would suggest that there is no band of this calibre providing such influential music these days.

Sure **The Chieftains** still go on producing critically acclaimed albums but they are not ground breaking and not Irish in the main. **De Dannan** have celebrated their 25th year, but their music is hardly at the cutting edge.

Thankfully, **Patrick Street** still come up with great recordings and tour the UK every year, but seem unable to create the interest and approval their abilities and musicianship deserve. This band is as good as any of its predecessors. **Moving Cloud**, the band based in Clare, have produced two classic albums for their American recording label Green Linnet, but appearances in UK have been few mainly due to their semi-professional status The foremost band of the 90s were **Altan**, whose progress may be hindered by their exclusively Donegal music policy.

From America came groups like **Solas** who have 3 albums for Shanachie under their belt, but have not appeared in the UK enough, despite working very hard at raising their profile at home by touring the US extensively.

**Cherish the Ladies** have toured the UK annually for several years, but thus far have had little influence over here.

I would recommend the recordings of **Patrick Street**, **Moving Cloud**, **Danú**, **Martin Hayes** and **Trian** from America.

The current trend in recording Irish traditional music has been set by the companies who previously championed such recording. These are becoming eclipsed by their inability to handle any recording which won't sell thousands of copies mainly due to overheads like staff wages and the sky-high cost of promotion.

Another problem here is so little word space devoted to our music in the national and music press; it is a battle to get any coverage. The same can be said about current radio coverage, and this being hailed as the age of communication!

But I believe help is at hand via the Internet. If used correctly it will provide a new mode of communication, which will help minority music's to flourish and develop. You can now put your session on the Internet and reach an enormous worldwide audience. Thus will we break the stranglehold the majors have on our music.

The most innovative happening is a growing tendency for top flight musicians to produce their own CDs, initially for sales at their gigs, and then for licence to record companies. This is by far the most exciting trend and will prove the best way of getting the music out there.

Independent promotion companies are springing up, wanting to help the music and the musicians' profile with the general public. Utilising the level playing field of the Internet, this music is beginning to find its audience and a place in the market place. This is currently the most exciting area of activity in Irish traditional music. One of the reasons being that the major companies don't know how to sell traditional music.

These are usually solo recordings and this is a return to the roots of Irish traditional music which is essentially a solo music, i.e. a music the Irish workers would have played after their day's work to relieve tension and lift the spirits. It became a band thing when the larger halls were built to get the music out of the kitchens and dancers would drown out the music of the solo player. This was the beginning of the Ceili Band and amplification.

I would suggest that groups were a search for further acceptance outside the immediate audience. This is a personal opinion, but the endemic beauty and essence of Irish traditional music are so subtle that they pass most people by, and when adorned with guitars, bouzouki and didgeridoo, it's the accompaniment that most people are used to hearing and thus find it easier to identify with. This is not intended as a put down, just a thought to ponder.

The recording side proved the salvation of Irish traditional music earlier in the century especially the recordings of the masters, which filtered back to Ireland from America. The recordings of **Michael Coleman**, **James Morrison**, **Patsy Touhey**, **John McKenna** were marvelled at by the listeners back at home. I believe they frustrated as many as they inspired. But they were playing the bright music coming from the "New World".

I have often wondered what would

have been Michael Coleman's fate if he had remained at home like his brother Jimmy, also a master fiddler, who stayed at home in Sligo and died unrecorded and whose music is only remembered by a few old neighbours in Sligo. To quote that great man Chief O'Neill, "Irish indifference paralyses optimism and discourages effort".

Many of these recording have become readily available nowadays, and the genius of those early players can still only be marvelled at. It is strange that in these enlightened times with better recording facilities and better instruments and strings etc, many have tried to capture the musicianship and vibe of the music of earlier in this century but they have never been able to capture the feel of the music of those distant times. I feel this is true of other genres like jazz and blues.

I am old enough to remember the days when there were very few recordings of Irish traditional music available and we knew, and some could play, every tune on those records. Nowadays there are thousands of recordings available, and I wonder, do we know any more?

It's getting almost impossible to weed out the worthy recordings from the overpowering dross, which today is being hyped as Irish traditional music. Even some of Ireland's best traditional musicians have lost sight of their vocation and have diluted their undoubted talents and their music in pursuit of the bigger bucks.

So in the early part of the 21st Century, we find Irish traditional music everywhere but is it as healthy as it should be?

The area where most progress has been achieved is in live music; I would venture that there have never been more people playing and dancing and singing Irish traditional music. In almost every sizeable town in UK I would bet there is a session or a branch of **Comhaltas Ceoltoiri Eireann**, an organisation which promotes the culture and arts of Ireland, which despite its forbidding Gaelic title welcomes everyone.

There are over 29 branches throughout UK, many of which will run classes and sessions. They also run annual competitions for all ages on all instruments. The **All Britain Fleadh** is a movable feast and can be a great musical event. Many local councils also run tuition classes in Irish music and its appreciation.

In every city there are always Irish musicians of the highest calibre living and playing their music. In most cases, these are shy people who play for their own enjoyment and are not interested in furthering their careers. I recall with joy, the great musicians who cheered our lives and raised our emigrant spirits in London. The likes of the late **Darach O'Cathain**, who spent many years in Leeds, **Joe Heaney** in Southampton, the great fiddler **Jimmy McHugh**, who played his music for the Irish community in Glasgow, and died in January 2000. Also the wonderful fiddler **Des Donnelly** who warmed many a heart in Manchester during the 60s and 70s. Currently **Mike Hipkiss** a wonderful singer who has been a mainstay of song in Birmingham for over 30 years and musicians like **John Ferguson** in Leeds, **Lucy Farr** in Newbury and **Tony Corcoran**, in Newcastle. In London there are **John Bowe**, **Liam Farrell**, **Brian Rooney**, **Joe Whelan** and too many others to mention here. These are all great musicians and can be easily tracked down and they are only too happy to share their music with anyone who shows interest. This is how the music has survived everything from famine, war and even now, overkill. Word of mouth!

It also has the roots of life enhancement. By getting to know these musicians personally and thus coming to understand them and their motivation for playing the music, you will learn a lot about your own life, which is also a side effect of following all styles of folk music. One of the things that attracted me to Irish music is that you could get know and in most cases become friends with musicians of world renown. I still prize the friendships of **Paddy Taylor**, **Raymond Roland** and **Paddy Carty** who have long since left us for their eternal reward. Their music is still a constant source of enjoyment and to be marvelled at.

These musicians will invariably have a regular pub or club where they will play for a session.

We mentioned O'Neill's inclusion of O'Farrell's, "Treatise on Uilleann Pipes". I must document the work carried out by Na Piobairi Uilleann, which since its establishment in the 60s, as the dream child of Brendan Breathnach, has nurtured the explosion in interest in Uilleann piping and has a thriving branch in London and pockets of pipers all over UK. The piping family has grown from around 100 world wide in O'Neill's time to one of thousands scattered all over the world. Many of them annually turn up in Miltown Malbay, Co Clare for the Willie Clancy Summer School, which every year for the first full week of July, provides a meeting place and a reaffirmation of our love for the music and our love for each other, we who are bonded by our mutual love for Irish traditional music.

There will undoubtedly be a folk club in your locality, which will occasionally feature Irish musicians.

The major folk festivals like Sidmouth, Cambridge, Towersey, Wadebridge (now Cornwall), and The National Folk Festival usually have a representation of Irish music.

This is a big factor in America where Irish festivals are of enormous proportions, like **The Milwaukee Irish Festival**, which lasts for three days and generates its own village, **The San Francisco Irish Music Festival**, **The Celtic Gathering** at Swannanoa and **The Gaelic Roots Festival** at Boston College masterminded by Clare master fiddler, **Seamus Connolly**. **Washington DC Irish Festival** is on the first weekend of September, now in its new home at Montgomery County Fairgrounds and is the best pure traditional music festival. It is run by the **National Council for Traditional Arts**.

What does the future hold for Irish music? Well I believe the musical duet of **Martin Hayes and Denis Cahill** will continue to push back the barriers, (but always paying due respect to the music and musicians who inspired them, and inbred good musical taste). I love the idea of them appearing recently in the **London Jazz Festival**. Then there's Chicago fiddler and composer **Liz Carroll**, the multi talented **Lunasa**, the exciting burgeoning talent of Manchester's master fiddler, **Dezi Donnelly** and his musical pal, **Michael McGoldrick** and young Waterford based Irish band **Danú**, whose individual credentials are of the highest order. I look forward to the long awaited new recording from. Their CD *Think Before You Think* is making them many friends and gaining awards by the dozen. They recently won the prestigious BBC Radio 2 Folk Award as best band. In a group, which hosts some of Ireland's finest young musicians, it's very interesting that the singing of **Ciaran O Gealbhain** is receiving great critical acclaim.

So, after the closing of a century which witnessed the rebirth of interest in Irish traditional music, we see a music that is being played and enjoyed and studied by more people than ever before. It is easily accessible to anyone interested enough to seek it out.

More recordings are readily available than ever before. Thankfully it should never return to the days of Chief O'Neill's fears, but I feel that in this rush to become universally accepted (much as Ireland itself has) we are losing a lot of what made our music and culture so wonderful and universally admired.

**Alan O'Leary**
*Copperplate Distribution and Consultants*

## Resources

### Websites

**Na Piobairi Uilleann**
www.iol.ie/~npupipes/index.htm

**Ceolas**
www.ceolas.org/ceolas.html

**Musical Traditions Web Magazine**
www.mustrad.org.uk

**The Irish Traditional Music Archive**
www.itma.ie

**Copperplate Mail Order**
http://go.to/copperplate

### Organisations

**Comhaltas Ceoltoiri Eireann**
Belgrave Square, Monkstown, Co Dublin
**Phone** 00353 12800295
**Fax** 00353 12803759
**Web** www.comhaltas.com email
**Email** enquiries@comhaltas.com

**C.C.E.**
UK Provincial Secretary. Ann Kelly
14, Evans Road, Basford, Nottingham NE6 0QP
**Phone** 0115 970 2878
**Email** comhaltasUK@ic24.net

**Na Piobairi Uilleann**
15, Henrietta St, Dublin 1
**Phone** +353 1 8730093
**Email** npupipes@iol.ie

**Folk Music Society of Ireland,**
15 Henrietta St, Dublin 1

**The Irish Traditional Music Archives**
63, Merrion Square, Dublin 2
**Phone** +353 16619699
**Fax** +353 16624585

**Irish World Music Centre**
University of Limerick, Limerick
**Phone** +353 61 202917
**Fax** +353 61 202589
**Web** www.ul.ie/~iwmc
**Email** ellenbyrne@ul.ie

**Coleman Music Centre**
Gurteen, Co Sligo
**Phone** +353 7182599
**Web** www.colemanirishmusic.com

**Ceol**
Smithfield Village, Dublin 7
**Phone** 00353 18173820
**Fax** 00353 18173821
**Web** www.ceol.ie

**London Pipers Club**
Tim Dowd, 20, Holmdene Ave, North Harrow, Middx HA2 6HR

**South West Pipers Association**
Mr Edwin Spring, Street, Somerset, England

**Ossian Publications Ltd,**
PO Box 84, MacCurtain St. Cork
**Phone** +353 21502040

### Summer Schools and Festivals

**The Willie Clancy Summer School**
Miltown Malbay, Co, Clare
*First full week of July*
**Contact** Harry Hughes
**Phone** +353 658 4281

**The South Sligo Summer School**
Tubbercurry, Co Sligo
*Second full week of July*
**Contact** Rita Flannery
**Phone** +353 7185010

**The Joe Mooney Summer School**
Drumshambo, Co Leitrim
**Contact** Nancy Woods
**Phone** +353 7841213

**The Frankie Kennedy School**
Gweedore, Co Donegal
*Over the New Year period*
**Contact** Geariod O' Maonaigh
**Email** gearoidm@iol.ie

**The Joe Cooley/Kieran Collins Memorial Weekend**
Peterswell, Co Galway
*October*

**Aonach Paddy O'Brien**
Nenagh, Co Tipperary
*3rd week of August*
**Contact** Deirdre McSherry, Secretary
St Conlon's Rd, Nenagh, Co Tipperary
**Web** http://homepage.tinet.ie/~aonach

**Feakle, Co Clare Music Festival**
*First Weekend of August*
**Phone/Fax** +353 61924288

**Blas Summer School**
Irish World Music Centre, Limerick
*University 9th July - 20th 2001*

**Jimmy McHugh Memorial Weekend**
*13th January 2002. Glasgow*
**Phone** 0141 569 3557

**Coleman Traditional Festival**
Gurteen, Co Sligo
*29th Aug - 2nd September 2001*

**Cumar Gealic Arts Summer School**
Connamara, Co Galway. *Easter Week*
**Email** cic@iol.ie

**Fleadh Nua**
Ennis, Co Clare
*May 24-28*

**Fleadh Cheoil na hEireann**
Listowel, Co Kerry
*August 24-26*

**Celtic Roots**
Boston College, USA.
*17 - 23rd June 2,001*
**Web** www.bc.edu/gaelicroots

**Celtic Gathering**
Swannanoa, NC, USA.
Warren Wilson College, PO Box 9000, Asheville, NC 28815-9000
**Phone** 828 298 3434
**Fax** 828 2993326
**Email** gathering@warren-wilson.edu

**Milwaukee Irish Fest (USA)**
*17-20 Aug 2000*
**Phone** 414 476 3378
**Web** www.irishfest.com

**Celtic Colours**
Cape Breton Island, Canada
*October 5 –13.*
**Phone** 902 295 1414
**Email** info@celtic-colours.com
**Web** www.celtic-colours.com

### Stonehill Irish Festival
Boston. Mass.
*2nd weekend in June*

### Catskills Irish Arts Week
East Durham.
*2nd week in July*

### Augusta Heritage Week
Elkins, West Virginia.
*Last week of July*

### Copenhagen Irish Festival
*First weekend of November.*
**Web** www.ashplant.dk

## Record labels

### Hummingbird
35,Harcourt St, Dublin 2
**Phone** +353 1475 0867
**Fax** +353 14750869

### Chart
5/6, Lombard Street, Dublin 2

### Claddagh Records
Dame House, Dame St, Dublin 2
**Phone** +353 1677 8943
**Fax** +353 1679 3664
**Email** claddagh@crl.ie
**Web** http://indigo.ie/claddagh

### Gael Linn
26, Merrion Square, Dublin 2
**Phone** +353 1676 7283
**Fax** +353 1 6767030
Email eolas@gaellinn.iol.ie

### Clo Iar Chonnachta
Indreabhan, Connameara, Co Galway
**Phone** +353 91 593307
**Fax** +353 91 593362
**Email** cic@iol.ie

### Ossian
40, MacCurtain St, Cork, Ireland.
**Phone** +353 21 502040
**Fax** +353 21 502025

### Outlet Recording Co
15, Gordon St, Belfast BT1 2LG
**Phone** 01232 322826
**Fax** 01232 332671
**Web** www.outlet-music.com

### Shanachie
Moneystown North, Roundwood, Co Wicklow
**Phone** +353 404 45139
**Fax** +353 404 45146
**Web** www.shanachie.com

### Green Linnet
26, Millward Crescent, Hastings, East Sussex TN34 3RU
**Phone** 01424 713904
**Fax** 01424 461224
**Web** www.greenlinnet.com

### Topic Records
50, Stroud Green Rd, London N4 3EF
**Phone** 0171 263 1240
**Fax** 0171 281 5671

## Fleadh Cheoils

### London Regional Fleadh Cheoil
*Sunday April 1st.*
**Venue** Nicholas Breakspear School, St Albans
**Phone** 01727 823140
01582 564234
**Email** Ivan Anders@Aol.com

### Midlands Regional Fleadh Cheoil
*Sunday April 8th*
**Venue** Princethorpe College, Princethorpe, Rugby, Warwickshire
**Phone** 01223 514805
**Email** jc226@hermes.cam.ac.uk

### Scottish Regional Fleadh Cheoil
*Sunday May 13th*
**Venue** St Andrews College, Duntocher Road, Bearsden, Glasgow.
**Phone** 0141 558 7482
**Fax** 0709 211 40703
**Email** martinoneill@blueyonder.co.uk

### Northern Regional Fleadh Cheoil
*Sunday May 13th*
**Venue** Rochdale Town Hall
**Phone** 0161 866 9604
**Email** Desfarry@aol.com

### All Britain Fleadh Cheoil
*Saturday 23rd and Sunday 24th June*
**Venue** St Gregory's School, Donnington Road, Kenton, Middx
**Phone** 0207 263 9366
**Fax** 0207 916 8727
**Email** comhaltasUK@ic24.net

### Fleadh Cheoil na hEireann
Listowel, Co Kerry, Ireland
*August 24-26*

**Alan O'Leary**

# What is English Folk Music? By John Kirkpatrick

Anyone who loves English Folk Music has had to accept that they are part of a minority.

The most traditional thing about traditional English music is that most people in England, the British Isles and in the world at large neither know nor care what it is. Well, in case anyone out there is wondering how to find out, here's how you do it and it's dead easy.

In any region of the world it is the local dancing that gives the music its character – the steps, the rhythm, the tempo, the ebb and flow of the movements, the amount of energy expended – all these things affect the style of the music in that place. The more closely the accompaniment matches the pulse of the dance, the more distinctive a voice it will have and the more exotic and mysterious it will appear to foreign ears. If you ignore the needs of the dance, you just end up with a spineless blancmange of bland fusion styles with no roots in anything.

England can easily match any other country for the richness and diversity of its traditional dances. You can dance with sticks, handkerchiefs, swords that bend, swords that don't bend, poles, brooms, cotton slings, wooden coconuts, garlands, tobacco pipes and antlers that are a thousand years old. You can dance in couples, on your own, in sets of three or four, or six, or eight, or in townfulls. You can dance in shoes, or boots, or clogs; in your ordinary clothes, in the garb of a hero, in rags, in uniform, all in white, with a disguised face; or dressed as a horse, or as Robin Hood, or as someone of the opposite sex. You can dance in a straight line, in a circle, in a square, in a hey, round a tree, back and forth, up and down and you can tie yourself in knots. And all these dances have their own precise requirements that must be matched by the music.

So, if there's all this wonderful stuff lying around, why aren't we more aware of it as an everyday part of our national culture? Why aren't we all doing it and valuing it and treasuring it? Well, of course some of us are, but it is or was, mostly done, valued and treasured in the country. Folk music in all its forms has been preserved most tenaciously by the least privileged layers of society – that's part of the definition – because even if there's little in the way of material wealth or worldly possessions, at least you know who you are, and where you come from, and your place in your local community, because you re-affirm all these connections every time you do your local dance, or song, or custom, at the right time of the year, in the right way, to the right music. And the begging verses that so often occur aren't something quaint or curious stuck on to spoil things – they are a vital part of the survival of the custom and of those doing it – a chance to gather a few much-needed extra pennies.

As people moved more and more into towns, as well as leaving behind the physical setting of these customs, they also left behind the reason for keeping them up. If you work in town, indoors, you don't even need to be aware of the weather, let alone what time of year it is. Every day is the same. And the number of people around you all the time lessens the feeling of community, lessens the strong identification with the place where you live. And that in turn leads to the happy acceptance of any form of cultural stimulation, whatever its source, especially if your new-found urban wealth and sophistication makes you feel ashamed of what you got up to in the days of your poverty.

The Royal Family hasn't helped. Historically they've always been more inclined to look for spouses for their offspring from other royal families in Europe rather than from native English stock (we might never have had Christmas trees or maypole dancing in this country if Queen Victoria hadn't married a German). Even though the current royals are better about this than their forbears, their birthday bashes are still stuffed with all their foreign cousins and you can bet your life that they don't get up to any step dancing, or belt out 'Pleasant and Delightful', or do a Morris jig – not even 'Princess Royal'. And although Princess Margaret is the President of the English Folk Dance & Song Society, and has attended occasional functions, you only ever see the rest of the family doing the Scottish dancing, never English. A fine example!

The Glorious British Empire probably did as much to stamp out ethnic culture in England as it did everywhere else it crunched its mighty boots. Rule Britannia, Land of Hope and Glory and Jerusalem are brilliantly designed to whip up fervent patriotism and nationalist feelings but do so by smothering more local and parochial loyalties, in much the same way as Hymns Ancient & Modern and the church organ combined to smother and drive underground the old style and repertoire of the church bands. You can easily understand how the Scots, the Irish, and the Welsh have had cause to feel resentment against their London-based ruling classes, but so too have the English.

Cecil Sharp probably did the cause no good by getting the folk music he had been collecting (from adults) into the school curriculum in the early twentieth century. How many grown-ups do you see playing hopscotch or conkers or doing a nativity play or maypole dancing? It's OK to do these things at school, but you leave all that behind as an adult, don't you? I know I hated having to do country dancing at primary school myself, and I only changed my mind when the hormones kicked in, and holding hands with girls stopped being utterly embarrassing and actually became something rather desirable. But not everyone gets the chance to make that connection, and many would dismiss it all as kids' stuff.

If the story so far explains why we English are so reticent and unsure about our Englishness; then the final nail in the coffin must be the onslaught of American culture. We're swamped by it. Records, films, radio, television – it's everywhere. All the forms of popular music come from there – ragtime, jazz, blues, big bands, and gospel. Musicals, rock & roll, country music, pop music, rap – they all sing with an American voice. Pop music sounds ridiculous in an ordinary English accent and the singers in all these styles of music know it doesn't work because wherever they come from they always sing in American. It's so pervasive that you don't even notice it and the sad result is that when you do hear singing in a straightforward English voice, in classical music say, it sounds fabulously square and old-fashioned. At least punk bands tried to sing in English, but that's largely lost now.

But the worst contamination was yet to come, because America also had folk singers.

They were people with guitars who wrote their own songs. This was obviously the real thing, not those old fogeys singing songs they'd learned from their grandparents in the pub. I mean, they didn't even play anything! They didn't even think to use a microphone! For the cool and sophisticated, the way forward was to put our deepest thoughts into bland melodies over a bland guitar pattern and work through our angst in a sleepy American drawl.

But traditional music isn't cool and sophisticated, it isn't easy listening, it isn't quiet and introspective. It's simple and straightforward, it's full of life and lust, it's dark and dangerous, it's exotic and mysterious. It addresses the uncivilised part of human nature, it deals with epic themes in a way we can cope with, it channels our excess energy, it makes us feel we belong somewhere.

One aspect of English culture we'd all agree about is that we're bad at complaining, but let's start making our voices heard. Next time you see a singer-songwriter in a folk venue whispering away in a mid-Atlantic twang, ask them what's wrong with singing out in their own voice and accent. Next time you see parents putting in a pop video to keep their kid quiet, ask them if they know that singing them nursery rhymes would do far more good to the kids and themselves – it's the best possible introduction to live music, to learning speech patterns, and rhythm, how to match words and a tune. Next time you see a pub session that is non-stop reels at the speed of light, ask if they think anyone could ever dance at that speed, and ask them to play a nice steady jig– it's much harder! Next time you see a slovenly team of Morris dancers shuffling half-heartedly or half drunk through their routines, ask them if they think they are justifying their position as guardians of our shared national heritage.

The raw material of English traditional folk music is sensational. Let's do it justice, let's be proud of it, let's cherish it. Let's listen to all those field recordings of singers and musicians and wonder at their strangeness. Let's use our brains and our hearts and get out there and build up something unique to where we live, like they do in Allendale or Abbots Bromley or Bampton or Abingdon or Handsworth or Grenoside or Helston or Haxey. And if these names mean nothing to you then join the English Folk Dance & Song Society and support the work of The Vaughan Williams Memorial Library – one of the best folk music libraries in the world – and go there and find out.

**John Kirkpatrick**
*Morris dancer, singer, musician and Englishman.*

# Asian Music in the UK By Penny King

The popularity, scope and availability of the numerous diverse and beautiful forms of Asian music have grown enormously in the UK in recent years and are still on the increase. The Asian Music Circuit (AMC) is the national organisation for the promotion of Asian music, producing a year round programme of inspiring and innovative UK concert tours, events and education projects including an annual summer school, covering a wide range of Asian musical genres - classical, traditional and contemporary. Whilst specialising in touring visiting artists from across the Asian continent, the AMC also pioneers new contemporary music projects, many of which involve collaborations with musicians and composers from the UK.

Many forms of Asian classical and traditional music are well established in the UK - from Indian classical music (Hindustani and Carnatic) to Javanese and Balinese gamelan, Beijing opera, Thai classical music and Japanese drumming to name a few. The wealth of home grown talent in the UK is also particularly visible in the area of contemporary, pop and dance music. In addition to the well known names of Talvin Singh and Nitin Sawhney, record companies such as Outcaste and Nation Records are constantly developing and promoting a wide range of new talent from bands to DJs and rappers. There are also numerous folk and pop bhangra bands providing exhilarating entertainment across the country.

A number of centres offer regular practical and academic classes and courses in Asian music traditions including the School of African and Oriental Studies at the University of London, the Bharatiya Vidya Bhavan in London and the Leeds Centre for Indian Music and Dance, amongst others.

For further information on Asian music in the UK, please contact:

## Asian Music Circuit

Ground Floor Unit E
West Point, 33/34 Warple Way,
London W3 0RG
**Phone** 020 8742 9911
**Fax** 020 8749 3948
**Email** info@amc.org.uk
**Web** www.amc.org.uk

See **World Roots UK** for further Asian music resources.

**The Rough Guide to World Music Volume 1** has a section on Bhangra/Asian Beat. DJ Ritu, BBC radio presenter and co- founder of the Outcaste label, takes a journey through the new music of Asian Britain together with an introductory discography.

**www.sitar.co.uk** is designed as an educational resource rather than a commercial promotion.

Below are internet locations created this year. All offer hindustani classical CDs for sale with free downloadable sample tracks. Mp3.com pays a small playback royalty to the artist for each download.
**Web** www.sitar.co.uk
**Email** john@silver-sitar-co.fsnet.co.uk

Sites offering indian classical music, mp3 links, CDs and samples:

**www.mp3.com/Padma BhanSingh** sitar

**www.mp3.com/VijitSingh** sarod (velum fronted lute)

**www.mp3.com/arvindsingh** sitar

**www.mp3.com/johnsinclairperkins** sitar

**www.mp3.com/kailashnishad** tabla

**www.mp3.com/RajBhanSingh** surbahar

**www.mp3.com/swarasound** compilation cd

**www.mp3.com/ziamohudhindagar** rudra vina

**www.mp3.com/panditjasraj** hindustani classical vocal

**www.mp3.com/gajendragadkarvora** flute and tar-shenai (relative of the dilruba, a bowed instrument)

**www.mp3.com/drnrajam** hindustani classical violin

**www.mp3.com/rameshkhaladkar** Shehnai (a double reed instrument like the oboe)

**www.mp3.com/brijnarayan** sarod (velum fronted lute)

**www.mp3.com/usmankhan** sitar

**www.mp3.com/gangubaihangal** vocal

**www.mp3.com/abirsingh** esraj

**www.mp3.com/tablaShivShankar Misra**

**www.mp3.com/tabla** tabla solo passages from artists appearing elsewhere on silversitarco.

Sites offering world fusion music:

**www.mp3.com/silversitarco** John perkins indian classical and fusion music

**www.mp3.com/jeztimecycles** Jez and friends

**www.mp3.com/davereeves** Dave reeves and friends - peace on earth song

**www.mp3.com/sunsofarqa** just how much can you fuse

**www.mp3.com/bluesitar** blues with electric sitar lead

**www.mp3.com/NetaiNathSitars** interview with sitar maker

## Surdhwani National Arts Organisation

**Contact** Mrs Maitreyee Sarcar - Secretary
**Mail address** 3 Sherington Drive, Goldthorn Park, WOLVERHAMPTON, WV4 5DX
**Phone** 01902 658793
**Fax** 01902 830278
**Email** maitreyee@surdhwani.org.uk
**Web** www.surdhwani.org.uk
*National arts organisation dedicated to promoting Asian arts and culture in the UK.*
**RAB** West Midlands Arts

# The African and Caribbean Music Circuit Ltd

**The African and Caribbean Music Circuit** was set up as an in-house organisation of the Arts Council of England. The Music Circuit became autonomous in 1991 and continues to be an annual revenue client of the Arts Council.

The Music Circuit exists to raise standards in, and the quality of awareness of music, from African and Caribbean people, through tours and the provision of education and training activities within a variety of cultural settings.

The performances organised by the Music circuit currently reach a diverse cross-section of the community in England. With partners in the regions, the Music Circuit organises activities in schools and community centres as well as at festivals and commercial venues.

In London, the Music circuit has initiated a schools programme, and young peoples' activities in the build up to the Notting Hill Carnival.

**Some Of Our Tours**

Ali Hasan Kuban
Boukmans Experyans
Burning Spear
Byron Lee & the Dragoneers
Kanda Bongo Man
Kente
The Mighty Diamonds
The Mighty Sparrow
Roaring Lon
Papa Wemba
Shikamoo Jazz
Western Diamonds
Les Tetes Brulees
Thomas Mapfumo & The Blacks Unlimited
Vieja Trova Santiaguera
Lubumbashi Stars

**Education projects** include Caribbean Carnival Experience, Calypan - Steelpan and Calypso workshops and The Children of Yaa - a Carnival Arts and Performance Summer School funded by the National Lottery A4E.

**Recent collaborators** have been The Yaa Asantewa Arts and Community Centre, Paddington Arts, Tamarside Community College and Plymouth Heritage and Leisure Services.

**Contact** Charles Easmon (Artistic Director)
Unit 5 Ellerslie Square, Lyham Road
London SW2 5DZ
**Phone** 020 7733 8897
**Fax** 020 7733 2675

# Latin Links

There's been an explosion of Latin music and dance styles in the UK in recent years. This is not the place to document the thousands of Salsa classes throughout the country or even to enthuse about the major Latin stars to visit these shores. The latter is best served by **fROOTS** and **Songlines** magazines ( see Media and World Roots UK) and the former by a number of agencies and useful websites that have emerged to spread the word on Salsa, Meringue, Rumba, Afro Cuban, Brazilian, Flamenco, Latin-Jazz, Samba and all things Latin.

## Latin Arts Services

*A long established agency covering the full range of Latin styles.*
**Contact** Hector Rosquete
Mail address P.O. Box 14303, London, SE26 4ZH
**Phone/Fax** 07000 472572
**Email** latinarts@artquest.co.uk
**Web** www.latinartsgroup.com

## Duende Music

*A Latin and World Music agency offering artists in all Latin styles.*
**Contact** Yvonne Mara
**Mail address** 37 Oakshaw Road, London, SW18 3BS
**Phone** 020 8877 3831
**Email** info@duendemusic.co.uk
**Web** www.duendemusic.co.uk

## Salsa Direct

*UK specialist contact for all styles of Latin music acts.*
**Contact** Nina Jaffa
**Mail address** 24b Colless Road, **London** N15 4NR
**Phone** 020 8808 4290
**Email** info@salsadirect.co.uk
**Web** www.salsadirect.co.uk

## Sasa Music

*A major agency and promotions company working with premier league Latin artists.*
**Phone** 020 7359 9232

## Matters Musical

*A long established agency with links to all types of Latin music and dance. See Agents for full listing.*
**Phone** 01306 741007
**Web** www.mattersmusical.com

## Salsa World magazine

**Mail address** PO Box 406 Horsham, W. Sussex RH12 1BR
**Phone** 01403 249411
*Articles, Event listings and Regional Directory. Published by Club Salsa Ltd.*

**Latin Latest** *concentrates on event listings in Sussex.*
**Web** www.latinlatest.co.uk

## SalsaVibe

*A new website dedicated to expanding and promoting Latin Music and dance throughout the world.*
**Web** www.SalsaVibe.co.uk

## Sambistas

*Web site covering Samba in Britain and Ireland featuring news events and a comprehensive list of bands as part of a global network of Samba websites.*
**Web** www.sambistas.org.uk

**www.flamencoflamenco.com**
*A management agency of 150 flamenco artists. This page takes you to a Spanish language page. The English version is at* **www.flamencoflamenco.com/english/home.asp**

**www.dancematrix.com** and **www.salsajive.co.uk** for national Salsa and other Latin dance events

**www.lambadanews.co.uk** for news on lambada !

**www.salsaambiente.com/links.htm**
**www.clubcubana.com**

**Listed Latin Roots artists include:**

Alkasalsa
Casa Latina Allstars
Coco Xpress
El Adivino
Grupo Folia
Julio Cortez Salsa Band
La Sonera Calaveras
La Timbala
Los Charros
Los Gringos
Los Mojados del Rio Tamesis
Los Soneros
Los Squideros
Mambo Jambo
maSamba Samba School
Merengada
Orquesta Cache
Orquesta Huracan
Orquesta La Clave
Otra Vez
Salsa Celtica
Street Beast
Teddy Peiro's Tango
The Brasshoppers
Victor Hugo Salsa Show
Viramundo
Wavet.

spotlight

trad music and song

# Traditional Music and Song

By **Derek Schofield**

It is possible to make a distinction between 'traditional' singers and musicians, who are part of a continuing tradition and who learnt their music from family and / or the local community; and 'revival' singers and musicians, who consciously learnt from the folk revival, from recordings and publications and from sources which are removed in time and/or space.

Yet, as change affects the social conditions that allowed traditional music-making to prosper, then the number of singers and musicians in the former category inevitably declines. But also, the distinction between the two categories becomes less clear. In recent years the term 'tradition bearers' has been coined by The Living Tradition magazine to encompass singers who sing traditional songs in a traditional style, and who have been inspired by traditional singers. These singers also put some personal interpretation into the songs so that they are not slavish copiers. The phrase can be extended to include instrumentalists as well.

This section, therefore, focuses on this slightly wider definition of traditional singers and musicians and the songs and music they perform. There is information about where to hear the music and find out more about it, in terms of the historical and contemporary context, repertoire, style, genre and the major collectors and collections.

## *Festivals and Events*

The best way to appreciate traditional music and song is to hear it live. Some festivals concentrate on presenting traditional musicians and singers, whilst others make a point of including them in the programme.

**The National Folk Music Festival, Sutton Bonington, Leicestershire (April)** has its roots in the Keele Folk Festival and then the Loughborough Folk Festival and, over the last 35 years, these events have featured almost every traditional singer and musician from the British Isles who was able and willing to travel. The events are informal, and include talks and lectures from noted authorities on the music.
**Contact** John Heydon
**Mail address** 5 Church Street, Aylesbury, HP20 2QP
**Phone** 01296 415333
**Fax** 01296 397092
**Email** Johnh@fosterwiggins.co.uk

**Sidmouth International Festival, Devon (July/August)** always includes concerts and informal events, under the title 'In the Tradition', featuring singers and musicians from all over the British Isles.
**Contact** Sidmouth Festival Office
**Mail address** PO Box 296, Aylesbury, HP19 9TL
**Phone** 01296 433669
**Fax** 01296 392300
**Email** sidmouth@mrscasey.co.uk
**Web** www.mrscasey.co.uk/sidmouth

**Whitby Folk Week, Yorkshire (August)** features traditional singers and musicians in its events, most of which are in intimate venues.
**Contact** Malcolm Storey
**Mail address** PO Box 44, Selby, North Yorkshire, YO8 9YP
**Phone/Fax** 01757 708424
**Email** wfw@box44selbyfreeserve.co.uk

**The English Country Music Weekend (June)** is held in a different location each year - recent festivals have been in Gloucestershire, Yorkshire and Suffolk (2001).
The emphasis is on instrumental music, but song events are also held.
**Contact** Katie Howson
**Mail address** 44 Old Street, Haughley, Stowmarket, IP14 3NX
**Phone** 01449 673695
**Email** emw@veteran.co.uk
**Web** www.mustrad.org.uk/ecmw

**Sussex Singers Weekend, Seaford, East Sussex (February/March)** includes many singers and musicians from Sussex, but also performers from Scotland, Ireland and other parts of England.
**Contact** Barbara on 01323 490825 or Hazel 01323 490665
**Email** barbara@haycosh.freeserve.co.uk
**Web** www.users.globalnet.co.uk/~tinvic

**The Auchtermuchty Festival Traditional Music Weekend, Fife (August)** comes in the middle of a larger community festival. Most of the singers and instrumentalists are Scottish, and the programme includes concerts, workshops, informal sessions as well as competitions, dances and ceilidhs.
**Contact** Citty Finlayson
**Mail address** 17 High Street, Auchtermuchty, KY14 7AP
**Phone** 01337 828732
**Fax** 01337 828060
**Email** cittyfin@aol.com
**Web** www.auchtermuchty.co.uk

**Keith Festival, Grampian (June)** is organised by the local branch of the Traditional Music and Song Association of Scotland, and features informal music and song events, as well as competitions.
**Contact** Edith Lewis
**Mail address** 10 South Court, Darliston, Elgin, IV30 1ND
**Phone** 01343 540325
**Email** lewishugh@talk21.com or keithfestival@btinternet.com
**Web** www.keithfestival.btinternet.co.uk

**Cullerlie Traditional Singing Weekend, Aberdeenshire (July)** is a new festival held on Tom and Anne Reid's farm, and featuring traditional singers from England and Scotland, including the host, bothy singer Tom Reid.
**Contact** Anne Reid
**Mail address** Cullerlie Farm Park, Echt, Skene, Aberdeenshire, AB32 6XL
**Phone** 01330 860549
**Web** www.abdn.ac.uk/Elphinstone/

**Clare Festival of Traditional Singing in Ennistymon, Co. Clare, Ireland (June)** concentrates on Irish traditional singing.
**Contact** Tom Munnelly
**Mail address** Miltown Malbay, Co. Clare
**Phone/Fax** +353 65 708 4365
**Email** munnelly@eircom.net
**Alt contact** Roisin White
**Alt address** 4 The Crescent, Miltown Malbay, Co. Clare
**Phone** +353 65 708 4996
**Alt contact** Project Ennistymon
**Alt address** Parliament Street, Ennistymon, Co. Clare
**Phone/Fax** +353 65 707 2990
**Email** ennistymon@eircom.net

**Folksong and Ballad Seminar, Ballyliffen, Co. Donegal (March)** is a traditional singing weekend, often with a theme. It is organised by the Inishowen Traditional Singers' Circle. The concentration is on Irish song, although some of the guests are from other parts of the British Isles.
**Contact** Jimmy McBride
**Mail address** Dun Emir, Shore Road, Buncrana, Co. Donegal

**Phone** +353 77 61210
**Email** jimmymcb@iol.ie
**Web** http://sites.netscape.net/milnerconroy/inishowenseminar

**The Willie Clancy Summer School (Scoil Samhraidh Willie Clancy), Miltown Malbay, Co. Clare (July)** is Ireland's largest traditional music summer school, held annually since 1973 in memory of the piper Willie Clancy. The School includes daily classes taught by experts in Irish music and dance. In addition, a full programme of lectures, recitals, dances (céilithe) and exhibitions are run by the summer school.
**Contact** Harry Hughes (Administrative Director)
**Phone** +353 65 708 4281
**Web** www.setdancingnews.net/wcss/wcsst.htm

Other events that feature traditional music and song are more occasional - for details see the folk music press.

Several clubs regularly include traditional music and song in their programmes. These clubs include:

**Musical Traditions Club (London)** meets at The King and Queen, Foley Street, London W1, approximately monthly on Fridays, and features traditional singers and musicians from the British Isles.
**Contact** Peta Webb
**Phone** 020 8340 0530

**The Royal Oak Club, Lewes (East Sussex)** meets in the Royal Oak, Station Street, Lewes, East Sussex on Thursdays and features traditional singers as well as revival performers.
**Contact** Vic and Tina Smith
**Mail address** 26 Ferrers Road, Lewes, East Sussex, BN7 1PZ
**Phone/Fax** 01273 478124
**Email** tinvic@globalnet.co.uk
**Web** www.users.globalnet.co.uk/~tinvic

## *Recordings*

The next best thing to hearing the music live is to listen to it on recordings. Many excellent traditional singers and instrumentalists are no longer with us but fortunately they can be heard on CD.

**Topic Records** is the longest-established folk record label in the UK, and from the 1950s to the 1980s they were renowned for their recordings of traditional musicians and singers from the whole of the British Isles. Since CDs have replaced vinyl, some of those recordings have been repackaged. Pre-eminent amongst these CDs is *The Voice of the People* series of 20 CDs, edited by **Reg Hall** and **Tony Engle**: each CD comes with a very detailed booklet. Other important recordings from Topic include double CDs of **Harry Cox** and **Joe Heaney**, and single CDs of **Walter Pardon** and **Sam Larner**, the English Country Music CD, and recordings of Irish traditional musicians.
**Contact** Topic Records
**Mail address** 50 Stroud Green Road, London, N4 3ES
**Phone** 020 7263 1240
**Fax** 020 7281 5671
**Email** info@topicrecords.co.uk
**Web** http://topicrecords.co.uk

**Veteran** is a specialist traditional music label, run by **John Howson**. Originally concentrating on East Anglia, Veteran's catalogue has been extended to include other English singers (**Bob Lewis**, **Vic Legg** and **George Fradley**) and musicians (**Bob Cann** and **Mark Bazeley** and **Jason Rice**), as well as Scottish and Irish singers. Many of the earlier recordings were released on audiocassette but new releases, as well as the back catalogue, are now being issued on CD. Distributed directly - Veteran also has a mail order service for traditional music and song recordings from many sources.
**Contact** Veteran
**Mail address** 44 Old Street, Haughley, Stowmarket, Suffolk, IP14 3NX
**Phone/Fax** 01449 673695
**Email** mailorder@veteran.com
**Web** www.veteran.com

**Musical Traditions** is the recording branch of the on-line magazine of the same name. Using CDR format, short runs of recordings can be published. The recordings have included **Walter Pardon**, **Cyril Poacher**, **Daisy Chapman** and **Wiggy Smith and family**, as well as compilation CDs from Sussex. All the CDs come complete with detailed booklets. Distributed directly.
**Contact** Rod Stradling
**Mail address** 1 Castle Street, Stroud, Gloucestershire, GL5 2HP
**Phone** 01453 759475
**Email** rod@mustrad.org.uk
**Web** www.mustrad.org.uk

**Village Carols** specialises in the traditional Christmas Carols of Yorkshire and the Derbyshire Peak District, all resulting from **Ian Russell**'s extensive research in the region.

Some of the early recordings are available on audiocassette, whilst recent releases have been on CD - they are all accompanied by detailed booklets. Distributed directly.
**Contact** Ian Russell
**Mail address** 41 Osborne Place, Aberdeen, AB25 2BX
**Phone** 01224 645486
**Email** ian.russell@abdn.ac.uk

**Coppersongs** is the label dedicated to releases of the **Copper Family** from Sussex. After the EFDSS released the original *Coppersongs* CD in 1988, the family themselves have recorded and released *Coppersongs 2* and *Coppersongs 3*.
**Contact** Coppersongs
**Mail address** PO Box 21, Peacehaven, East Sussex, BN10 7TL

**The English Folk Dance and Song Society (EFDSS)** has published a small number of CDs - *A Century of Song* included cylinder recordings from the early 20th century, whilst *Absolutely Classic: The Music of William Kimber* was released to celebrate the centenary of Sharp's meeting with the musician. *Root and Branch* is a CD magazine - in addition to a CD, each issue has booklets, a poster and other printed material. The two issues so far released are *A New World* and *Everybody Swing*. Some of the audio cassettes released by the EFDSS's Vaughan Williams Memorial Library are still available.
**Contact** EFDSS
**Mail address** Cecil Sharp House, 2 Regent's Park Road, London, NW1 7AY
**Phone** 020 7485 2206
**Email** info@efdss.org
**Web** www.efdss.org

**Folktrax** releases recordings of traditional music, song, speech and customs made by **Peter Kennedy** and colleagues from the 1950s onwards.
**Contact** Peter Kennedy
**Mail address** 16 Brunswick Square, Gloucester, GL1 1UG
**Phone** 01452 415110
**Fax** 01452 503643
**Email** feedback@folktrax.freeserve.co.uk
**Web** www.folktrax.freeserve.co.uk

**Rounder Records** in the USA are engaged in an extensive project to make available the recordings of **Alan Lomax**. As Lomax spent several years in the UK in the early 1950s, British and Irish singers and musicians are included on many of these CDs. *The Portraits* series has included CDs of **Harry Cox**, **Jeannie Robertson** and **Margaret Barry**.

The renowned 10-volume Caedmon recordings, *The Folk Songs of Britain*, (re-released by Topic in the 1960s) are also being reissued in the Lomax series. *Classic Ballads of Britain and Ireland* (two volumes) and *Songs of Seduction* have already been published.

These recordings were edited by **Peter Kennedy**, although **Mike Yates** will be editing future releases.
**Contact** Rounder Records
**Mail address** 1 Camp Street, Cambridge, MA 02140, USA
**Phone** + 1 800 768 6337
**Web** www.rounder.com

**Smithsonian Folkways Recordings** are part of the Smithsonian Center for Folklife and Cultural Heritage in Washington DC, USA. Their releases have included CDs on Northumbrian music and Yorkshire carols.
**Contact** Smithsonian Folkways
**Mail address** Smithsonian Institution, Suite 4100, 750 9th Street, NW, Washington DC 20560-0953, USA
**Phone** +1 202 275 1150
**Fax** +1 202 275 1119
**Web** www.si.edu/folkways

**Greentrax Records** specialises in Scottish music recordings. The catalogue includes the Scottish Tradition series: the early recordings were originally released by Tangent in association with the School of Scottish Studies. These CDs include bothy ballads, piping and fiddle music, Gaelic psalms and waulking songs. Greentrax has also re-released some of Topic Records' Scottish music recordings on CD.
**Contact** Ian Green
**Mail address** Greentrax, Cockenzie Business Centre, Edinburgh Road, Cockenzie, East Lothian, EH32 0HL.
**Phone** 01875 814155
**Fax** 01875 813 545
**Email** andrew@greentrax.com
**Web** www.greentrax.com

**Springthyme Records** have released several CDs of traditional singers and musicians, including **Jock Duncan** and **Jane Turiff**.
**Contact** Springthyme Records
**Mail address** Balmalcolm House, Balmalcolm, Cupar, Fife, Scotland, KY15 7TJ
**Fax** 01337 831773
**Email** music@springthyme.co.uk
**Web** www.springthyme.co.uk

**Claddagh Records** is a long-established label specialising in Irish music and song. Featured musicians include **Leo Rowsome**, **Seamus Ennis** and **Tommy Potts**, and the singers include **Rita and Sarah Keane**. Claddagh also operate a mail order service for a wide range of CDs of traditional music and song.
**Contact** Claddagh Records
**Mail address** Dame House, Dame Street, Dublin 2
**Phone** +353 1 6778943
**Fax** +353 1 6793664
**Email** claddagh@crl.ie
**Web** http://indigo.ie/~claddagh

**Ossian Publications** produces a range of CDs of Irish traditional music and song, in some cases reissues of recordings released on vinyl by Topic Records and others. Ossian also produces tune books. Ossian products are sold at The Living Tradition music shop at the same address.
**Contact** Ossian Publications
**Mail address** PO Box 84, 40 MacCurtain Street, Cork, Ireland
**Phone** 00 353 21 4502040
**Fax** 00 353 21 4502025
**Email** ossian@iol.ie
**Web** www.ossian.ie

## Discographies

**The Musical Traditions** on-line magazine has two discographies - one is a complete Topic Records discography, whilst the other covers all other recordings, including deleted recordings.
**Contact** Rod Stradling
**Mail address** 1 Castle Street, Stroud, Gloucestershire, GL5 2HP
**Phone** 01453 759475
**Email** rod@mustrad.org.uk
**Web** www.mustrad.org.uk

## Periodicals

**The English Folk Dance and Song Society (EFDSS)** publishes two periodicals, both available free to members or through purchase. *English Dance and Song* is a quarterly magazine with a number of articles on traditional song and music. *Folk Music Journal* is an annual academic periodical with fully referenced and refereed articles, plus reviews.
**Contact** EFDSS
**Mail address** Cecil Sharp House, 2 Regent's Park Road, London, NW1 7AY
**Phone** 020 7485 2206
**Email** info@efdss.org
**Web** www.efdss.org

**Musical Traditions** is an on-line magazine that publishes articles, reviews, news and enthusiasms. The nature of Musical Traditions means that reviews are published very soon after the release date, the reviews can be very detailed and they often include sound clips. The accumulated contents are published on CD-ROM each year.
**Contact** Rod Stradling
**Mail address** 1 Castle Street, Stroud, Gloucestershire, GL5 2HP
**Phone** 01453 759475
**Email** rod@mustrad.org.uk
**Web** www.mustrad.org.uk

**fROOTS** includes a wide spectrum of music from around the world, including traditional music from the British Isles. The magazine's website includes an index of articles published.
**Contact** fROOTS
**Mail address** PO Box 337, London, N4 1TW
**Phone** 020 8340 9651
**Web** www.froots.demon.co.uk

**The Living Tradition** features music from all over the British Isles although there is a concentration on Scotland. This magazine coined the phrase 'tradition bearers' and has published CDs of several of these singers.
**Contact** The Living Tradition
**Mail address** PO Box 1026, Kilmarnock, Ayrshire, KA2 0LG
**Phone** 01563 571220
**Email** living.tradition@almac.co.uk
**Web** www.folkmusic.net

**Tocher and Scottish Studies** are two publications from the School of Scottish Studies of the University of Edinburgh - the former publishes brief articles on all aspects of folklife in Scotland, often including transcriptions of recordings and interviews. Scottish Studies is an annual academic journal on all aspects of Scottish folklife.
**Contact** School of Scottish Studies,
**Mail address** University of Edinburgh, 27-29 George Square, Edinburgh, EH8 9LD.
**Phone** 0131 650 4167
**Web** www.ed.ac.uk/SoSS/

**The British Journal of Ethnomusicology** is the annual periodical of the *British Forum for Ethnomusicology* (the UK national section of the international Council for Traditional Music). There is a concentration on the music of other countries, although it does not exclude music from the British Isles.
**Contact** Rosemary Dooley
**Mail address** Music Books, Crag House, Witherslack, Grange-over-Sands, Cumbria, LA11 6RW.
**Phone** 015395 52286
**Web** www.rdooley.demon.co.uk

**Welsh Music History** is the journal of the newly established Centre for Advanced Welsh Music Studies, part of the Welsh Music Institute being developed at the University of Wales, Bangor. It is a bilingual journal of musicology covering all aspects of Welsh music and music in Wales, including Welsh traditional and folk music.
**Contact** John Harper (Editor), Professor of Music
**Mail address** University of Wales, Bangor, Wales.

**Irish Folk Music Studies (Eigse Cheol Tire)** is the journal of **The Folk Music Society of Ireland**.
**Contact** Na Piobairi Uilleann
**Mail address** 15 Henrietta Street, Dublin 2, Ireland.
**Web** http://homepage.eircom.net/~shields/fmsi/index.htm

## Publications

**Atkinson, David**. *English Folk Song: An Introductory Bibliography.* (EFDSS, 1999). Second edition. This bibliography lists over 500 items on all aspects of English folk song. Most, if not all the items, are in the Vaughan Williams Memorial Library of the EFDSS.

**Lloyd, A L** *Folk Song in England.* (Lawrence & Wishart, 1967). This book is still the most influential book in the post-war English folk revival, in spite of recent critical assessment.

**Hall, Reg** *"I Never Played to Many Posh Dancers": Scan Tester, Sussex musician, 1887-1972.* (Musical Traditions, 1990). There are no comprehensive guides to instrumental music in England, but Reg Hall's book provides an in-depth study of a traditional musician.

**Vallely, Fintan** (ed) *The Companion to Irish Traditional Music,* (Cork University Press, 1999). This compendium covers themes and instruments, as well as individual singers and instrumentalists, traditional and revival.

## Organisations

**The English Folk Dance and Song Society (EFDSS)** has several objectives concerned with the preservation, promotion, encouragement of the practice of and research into folk music, dance and song. The Society publishes periodicals, CDs etc, maintains the Vaughan Williams Memorial Library and organises some events.
**Contact** EFDSS
**Mail address** Cecil Sharp House, 2 Regent's Park Road, London, NW1 7AY
**Phone** 020 7485 2206
**Email** info@efdss.org
**Web** www.efdss.org

**The Traditional Music and Song Association of Scotland (TMSA)** aims to promote, present and preserve the traditional music and song heritage of Scotland. TMSA provides information about traditional music events and workshops and maintains a database of performers of traditional music as well as of festivals and folk clubs. It also publishes books of tunes and songs, a newsletter and a festivals calendar.
**Contact** TMSA
**Mail address** 95-97 St Leonard's Street, Edinburgh, EH8 9QY.
**Phone** 0131 667 5587
**Email** tmsa@tmsa.demon.co.uk
**Web** www.tmsa.demon.co.uk

**The Elphinstone Institute** is part of the University of Aberdeen and exists to study, record and promote the cultural traditions and language of communities in the North of Scotland and, in particular, in the North East. In addition to its university teaching and research, a programme of fieldwork, research, outreach, collaborative projects and publication is being developed, including lectures and conferences. A CD-ROM has been produced: *Northern Folk: Living Traditions of North East Scotland.* The Director of the Institute is Ian Russell.
**Contact** The Elphinstone Institute
**Mail address** The University of Aberdeen (King's College), Old Aberdeen, AB24 3UB.
**Phone** 01224 272996
**Fax** 01224 272728
**Email** elphinstone@abdn.ac.uk
**Web** www.abdn.ac.uk/elphinstone

**Welsh Folk-Song Society.**
**Contact** Dr Rhidian Griffiths
**Mail address** Coed y Berllan, Ffordd Bryn-y-Mor, Aberystwyth, Ceredgion.
**Phone** 01970 610160.
**The Traditional Song Forum** aims to encourage research into, and dissemination of, traditional song and traditional singing in all its forms, and to provide channels of communication and mutual support between those interested in the field. The Forum organises a couple of meetings a year for members and guests, and the main means of communication is through their website.
**Contact** Martin Graebe
**Mail address** 100 Cheltenham Road, Gloucester, GL2 0LX
**Phone** 01452 523861
**Email** martin.graebe@btinternet.com
**Web** www.tradsong.freeserve.co.uk

**The British Forum for Ethnomusicology** is also the UK section of the International Council for Traditional Music. It organises an annual conference, other events and publishes a journal.
**Contact** British Forum for Ethnomusicology
**Mail address** Department of Music, SOAS, Thornhaugh Street, London, WC1H 0XG.
**Email** dh6@soas.ac.uk
**Web** www.shef.ac.uk/uni/academic/I-M/mus/staff/js/BFE.html

**The West Gallery Music Association** is an informal group of singers, instrumentalists and scholars. They all share an interest in the sacred music, psalmody and hymnody, and the secular music and dance of the men and women who performed from the west galleries of parish churches, in chapels, and around the towns and villages of England during the eighteenth and nineteenth centuries.
**Contact** Jackie Patten
**Mail address** Kerlistz, The Green, Morchard Bishop, Crediton, Devon, EX17 6PD.
**Phone** 01363 7503
**Email** patten@kerlistz.freeserve.co.uk
**Web** www.wgma.co.uk

## Resources

**The Vaughan Williams Memorial Library** of the English Folk Dance and Song Society (EFDSS) is the national archive and resource centre for folk music, dance and song in England, although its coverage includes the whole of the British Isles, as well as many other countries. It is a multi-media collection, which includes books, periodicals, manuscripts, records, tapes, CDs, photographic images, films, videos and artefacts. It contains the originals or copies of almost all the major fieldwork collections carried out in the last 100 years, either in manuscript or audio formats. The website includes bibliographies, which are also available in printed formats.
**Contact** The Librarian
**Mail address** EFDSS, Cecil Sharp House, 2 Regent's Park Road, London, NW1 7AY.
**Phone** 020 7485 2206
**Email** library@efdss.org
**Web** http://efdss.org

**The School of Scottish Studies** includes sound and manuscript archives covering traditional songs, tales, instrumental music and information on traditional and changing ways of life. The School continues to undertake systematic and extensive recording of folklore and ethnology in the field.
**Contact** School of Scottish Studies,
**Mail address** University of Edinburgh, 27-29 George Square, Edinburgh, EH8 9LD.
**Phone** 0131 650 4167
**Email** Scottish.Studies@ed.ac.uk
**Web** www.ed.ac.uk/SoSS/

**The Irish Traditional Music Archive** is a multi-media reference archive and resource centre for the traditional song, music and dance of Ireland. It includes sound recordings, books, photographs, videos, etc. for the appreciation and study of Irish traditional music. It covers the island of Ireland, areas of Irish settlement abroad (especially in Britain, North America and Australia), and non-Irish performers of Irish traditional music.
**Contact** ITMA
**Mail address** 63 Merrion Square, Dublin 2, Ireland.
**Web** www.itma.ie

**National Centre for English Cultural Tradition and Language (NATCECT)** is based at the University of Sheffield and includes a library of books, periodicals and other written material on folklore in general, including folk music and song.
**Contact** NATCECT
**Mail address** 9 Shearwood Road, University of Sheffield, S10 2TD
**Phone** 0114 222 6296
**Web** www.shef.ac.uk/~lib/libsites/cectal.html

**The Archive of Traditional Welsh Music** at the University of Wales, Bangor collects, preserves and provides direct access to sound recordings collected in many areas of Wales, both published and unpublished recordings. The Archive exists primarily as a research, teaching and training centre for the University's Ethnomusicology courses, although there is also access to the general public.
**Contact** Wyn Thomas
**Mail address** Archive of Traditional Welsh Music, Department of Music, University of Wales, Bangor, LL57 2DG
**Phone** 01248 382182
**Email** w.thomas@bangor.ac.uk
**Web** www.bangor.ac.uk/music/WMI/WMI.html

**The British Library National Sound Archive International Music Collection** includes collections of recordings of traditional, folk or world music. It comprises both published recordings as well as unpublished recordings, including the fieldwork collections of **Mike Yates**, **A L Lloyd** and others. The NSA is embarking on a project to acquire the originals or copies of unpublished traditional music recordings from the British Isles.
**Contact** International Music Collection
**Mail address** British Library National Sound Archive, 96 Euston Road, London, NW1 2DB.
**Phone** 020 7412 7427
**Fax** 020 7412 7441
**Email** NSA-IMC@bl.uk
**Web** www.bl.uk/collections/sound-archive
The NSA catalogue is available on-line at http://cadensa.bl.uk

**The Village Music Project** aims to locate and copy all available manuscript collections of traditional social dance music in England. This inevitably overlaps with religious music as well as military and town band music. The Project also aims to transcribe original material into more legible forms and publish it using the web, CD-ROM and printed methods, to aid research, comparison and performance.
**Contact** John Adams (Project Director)
**Mail address** Music, Media and Performance, University of Salford, Adelphi, Peru Street, Salford, M3 6EQ.
**Phone** 0161 295 6057
**Fax** 0161 295 6023
**Email** j.adams@salford.ac.uk
**Web** www.performance.salford.ac.uk/research/vmp/Index.htm

**The Charles Parker Archive** is dedicated to the recordings and work of the late **Charles Parker**, a radio producer who worked on, and recorded, traditional folk song. He is best known for The Radio Ballads. The Archive is held by the Birmingham City Archives in the city's Central Library. It consists of tapes, production books, papers, correspondence and scripts for most of the programmes Charles Parker produced and the organisations in which he was active.
**Contact** Birmingham Central Library,
**Mail address** Chamberlain Square, Birmingham, B3 3HQ
**Phone** 0121 303 4217
**Fax** 0121 464 1176
**Email** central.library@birmingham.gov.uk
**Web** www.birmingham.gov.uk/epislive/libpages.nsf/(exlinks)/Home?OpenDocument

**The Frank Kidson Collection** is held at the Mitchell Library in Glasgow. Born in Leeds, **Frank Kidson** (1855-1926) was a folksong collector, and an authority on English music, especially the pedigree of tunes. The collection includes the folksongs he collected, but also volumes of broadsides, tunes and songs from a wide variety of sources.

The collection is a Special

Collection in the Arts Department of the Library.
**Contact** The Mitchell Library
**Mail address** North Street, Glasgow, G3 7DN
**Phone** 0141 287 2934
**Email** arts@gcl.glasgow.gov.uk
**Web** www.mitchelllibrary.org

**The Roud Folk Song Index** is a computer database that seeks to index all the English language traditional songs collected in Britain and Ireland, North America and Australasia. It covers published books and recordings as well as unpublished collections. A new master-numbering system allows songs to be identified even if they are hidden under variant titles. A companion database, the Broadside Index, includes songs printed on broadsides and chap-books, sheet music, music hall and early commercial recordings. Both indexes stand at over 110,000 references, and continue to grow. They are available on subscription or in selected libraries, including the Vaughan Williams Memorial Library.
**Contact** Steve Roud
**Mail address** Southwood, Maresfield Court, High Street, Maresfield, East Sussex TN22 2EH
**Phone** 01825-766751
**Email** Roud@supanet.com

### Websites

**Musical Traditions**: see periodicals.

**English Folk Music and Traditional Music on the Internet: A Guide to Resources** is an extensive site, the contents of which include organisations, libraries, resources, events, artists, etc. The site is regularly updated by the owner, Martin Nail.
**Email** martin.nail@ukonline.co.uk
**Web** http://web.ukonline.co.uk/martin.nail/Folkmus.htm

**The Bodleian Library Broadside Ballad Project** has catalogued the Library's 30,000 broadside ballads and this catalogue is now available online. The web interface allows searches for, inter alia, song sheets, ballads or illustrations.
**Web** http://bodley.ox.ac.uk/ballads/

**The Baring-Gould Project** is a website dedicated to **Sabine Baring-Gould** and his folksong collecting in the south-west of England. The site includes biographical information, details of the song collections and writings by the site's author, **Martin Graebe**.
**Web** www.greenjack.btinternet.co.uk

**Roots of Folk** is a website dedicated to old English, Scottish and Irish songs and tunes. The site is maintained by **William Bruce Olson**.
**Email** olsonw@erols.com
**Web** http://users.erols.com/olsonw/

**The Traditional Ballad Index** is an annotated bibliography of the folksongs of the English-speaking world. A collaborative effort designed to help find reference information on folk ballads. It is not itself a source of song texts. It is compiled by **Robert B. Waltz** and **David G. Engel**.
**Web** www.csufresno.edu/folklore/BalladIndexTOC.html

**Sixteenth Century Ballads** is the title of a website that aims to produce a collection of pre-1600 ballads. The site belongs to **Greg Lindahl**.
**Email** lindahl@pbm.com
**Web** http://pbm.com/~lindahl/ballads/ballads.htm

**Digital Tradition Folksong Database** (Digitrad) is a collection of over 8000 songs accessed by search or browse. It is also possible to download a DOS based program of the database. **Digitrad** is part of **The Mudcat Café** on-line blues and folk magazine.
**Email** digitrad@world.std.com
**Web** www.mudcat.org

**Derek Schofield** *is a researcher of the Folk Revival and of Calendar Customs. Arena Dance Director at Sidmouth International Festival 1992-1996.*

# Traditional Music in England By John Howson

Here are my thoughts on what England has to offer in the way of genuine traditional music and singing at the beginning of this millennium. My criterion for what I see as real is simply music and singing which has been handed down by family or community without any initial influence from the folk song revival.

I will give you a 'musical' tour of where I see existing 'hot-beds' to be and who are the important names within these areas. This is a personal view and I am more than happy to hear of real traditional musicians and singers that I have missed!

Let's start with one of the best known 'hot-beds', where I now live in Suffolk. Certainly just about every parish in the county would have boasted a melodeon player and at least one 'old boy' who could stepdance. Not so now, but **Cyril Barber** of Felsham is still on great form both as a melodeon player and stepdancer. Other well-known local families for stepping were the **Whitings** and the **Wests**. **Lennie Whiting** of Brundish is holding up his family tradition while **Percy West** of Rickenhall continues his. Then if you're in the right pub at the right time you could catch one of the late **Font Watling**'s sons sparking the flags. Leiston's **Reg Reader** plays his family dulcimer bought by his great-grandfather for a pair of boots and passed on to Reg by his grandfather **Charlie Philpotts** who taught him to play. Reg is now a stalwart of Old Hat Music. Traditional singing in the area is continued by local farmer **Tony Harvey** of Tannington, **Hubert Freeman** of Bedfield and Essex man **Jack Tarling**.

Sussex has had a long and extensive singing tradition with the most famous exponents being the **Copper Family**. Led by eighty-five year old **Bob Copper** with his son John, daughter Jill and son-in-law Jon they have sung all over the country. Watch out for the increasing involvement of Bob's grandchildren Mark, Andy, Sean, Ben, Lucy and Tom. There are of course other continuing family traditions in the county. **Bob Lewis** of Peacehaven learned the vast majority of his songs from his mother and his lyrical singing style is certainly worth a listen. Since starting this, Horsham's dynamic **Gordon Hall** has sadly died. He must be one of the last century's greatest traditional singing discoveries. The folk song collector **Mike Yates** recorded Gordon's mother Mabs only to find that her son had quite a voice himself and the repertoire to match. Not forgetting before we leave this area the effervescent singing of **Louie Fuller** who now lives in Surrey.

Unusually there seems to have been little evidence of a continuation of a once strong instrumental music tradition in the South East corner, but along the coast in Hampshire is a fine single row melodeon player called **Stan Seaman** who comes from the sea-faring tradition at Buckler's Hard.

The West Country has several

## spotlight
## trad music

** At time of going to press we were sad to hear of the death of **Sam Sherry**. He will be sorely missed.*

excellent traditional performers. In Dorset, near Ilminster, is **George Withers** who comes from one of the singing communities that **Cecil Sharp** cut his collecting teeth on. Then on Dartmoor the local musical tradition has been handed down to **Bob Cann**'s grandson **Mark Bazeley** who has joined up with **Jason Rice**, the grandson of another local character, **Les Rice**. In North Devon around the village of Holsworthy is a large family of settled gypsies led by melodeon playing **Tom Orchard** who is one of the finest step-dancers you're likely to come across. His wife Jean learned her singing from her mother the great **Amy Birch**. North Cornwall is renowned for traditional singing and Bodmin's **Vic Legg** sings the songs that his travelling family sang on every occasion he can. Occasionally he will stray up to the coast to Padstow where, on Saturday night, it is not unusual to find a gathering of singers led by **Charlie Pitman** or fisherman **Johnny Murt**. Padstow is of course known for May Day and because of that there are probably more traditional melodeon players in that town than anywhere else in the country.

Coming back up country, Bampton in Oxfordshire is rightly famous for its morris dancing and the president of the traditional side **Francis Shergold** has many songs passed down through his community. Gloucestershire has many settled gypsy communities and one of their most accessible singers is **Wiggy Smith**. While in Shropshire lives England's archetypal traditional singer, the ever popular **Fred Jordan**. The West Midlands tradition of plectrum dulcimer playing is continued by fine performances from **Fred Woodley** of Solihull who makes his own dulcimers as his father did before him. Across the Midlands into rural Northamptonshire is the recently retired farmer **Jeff Wesley** who dispels the ill-founded myth that traditional singers are only worth listening to when they are old and often past their best.

The myth is also defeated by the great (in both stature and voice) South Yorkshire singer **Will Noble**, a dry stone waller who along with singing partner **John Cocking** occasionally visits the after-hunt singing sessions, possibly meeting up with another fine singer **Barry Bridgewater**. Love or loathe hunting, these gatherings can still be one of the bastions of traditional singing, as are the Christmas pub carol singing sessions of this region. There are still many pubs that uphold the tradition such as the Royal Hotel at Dungworth and the Blue Ball at Worrall with some great characters like **Billy Mills** leading the singing. Into North Yorkshire and up to Cleveland, the continuing tradition of Fishermen's Choirs is as vibrant as ever in Filey, Marske and (probably the most active) the small fishing village of Staithes. Of course not all their members are fishermen nowadays but then again colliery bands would now be hard pushed to fill every seat with working miners!

The ever-strong instrumental traditions of the North East of England have had more encouragement than many areas in recent years, particularly with the help of anglo-concertina player **Alistair Anderson**. He has built around the many fine traditional performers, and the one that needs special mention has to be the mouth organ wizard **Will Atkinson**. On the song side **Brian Watson** has an extensive Northumberland repertoire and is certainly the man to listen out for.

It is said that the Lake District sees much of its traditional singing at Shepherds' Meets and of course the famous Appleby Horse Fair where travellers from around the country gather. There is also a strong Music Hall tradition in the North West and this has crossed over with traditional music through the Lancaster clog dancer **Sam Sherry***. If you're in a Lancashire market listen out for busker **Harry Litherland** regaling the crowds on duet concertina. Then there are the old and strong Irish communities that have thrived in the North West, and in Liverpool **Sean McNamara** has carried the flag for traditional music for over forty years.

I'll finish back in the capital and London again has been renowned for Irish Music. Have a listen to **Liam Farrell**, **Joe Whelan** and **Reg Hall** and if you want to know about London Music Halls ask **John Foreman** and he'll probably sing you most of the songs that were performed in them!

So I started with the premise that the performers that I would call traditional had learned their craft from family or community without an initial influence from the folk revival. This is unlikely to be the case in the future with a folk scene which stretches back over forty years so what happens next? I would suggest that there are revivalists (for want of a better word) who have absorbed parts of the tradition, not always consciously and often by osmosis. My current nominations for this category would be **Bob Davenport**, **Norma Waterson**, **Dan Quinn & Will Duke**, **Jim Ward**, **Simon Ritchie**, **Jim Eldon**, **Taffy Thomas** and **Peta Webb**. What I have noticed is that they have enjoyed the company of traditional performers and probably more importantly the 'old boys' (and girls) have felt at ease with them.

**John Howson**
*Record Producer for Veteran, proprietor of Veteran Mail Order and musician with Old Hat.*

# An Introduction to English Ceilidh By Gordon Potts

English Ceilidh or eCeilidh as it is sometimes called, is one of the current versions of a type of folk dance called English Country Dancing. There was a "Book of Country Dances" listed in Queen Elizabeth I's house contents, but the earliest surviving book is John Playford's "The English Dancing Master", published in London in 1651. In one form or another, with continuous changes in style and continual bouts of rediscovery and re-interpretation, this way of dancing has been popular ever since.

The key to this success is flexibility. The dances, usually danced as couples in a group called a set, are made up of a fixed sequence of movements called figures which fit to the music, usually exactly. This has several implications. One is that once you have learnt the basic figures the work of a few moments, you can join in. Immediately. More or less instant participation!

Another less obvious but very significant implication is that because the figures only fix where you are and when, not how you dance to get there, the dances can in fact be done to just about any tune of the right number of bars in the right length phrases. This means that the music and arrangements can easily be made appropriate to era, culture and so forth. It is partly because of these characteristics that this style of dance spread so quickly and so far. It could be fitted to tunes that local musicians already knew, and almost anyone could join in more or less straight away.

Yet another implication of this kind of structure is that a complex architecture of figures can be put together to create intellectually challenging dances for people who like that kind of thing. As a rule, Ceilidh dancers don't like that kind of thing. They'd rather keep it simple, with space in the music to step it out and to improvise their own complexities – known technically as "messing around".

Ceilidh became recognised as a new, separate dance form sometime in the seventies, partly as a reaction against the American-accented dance styles left over from the square-dance boom of the late fifties & early sixties. Stepping, often borrowed from the Morris, was used for (mostly) traditional English dances and the dance tunes were often those recently collected from English traditional instrumentalists such as **Bob Cann**, **Scan Tester**, **Oscar Woods** and **Walter and Daisy Bulwer**.

The result was slow and very energetic, suiting the younger and more vigorous element of traditional dance; physically excluding those who felt more at home with the fast, flat dance walk inherited from square dance. The bands that specialised in this effectively new dance (including **The Rakes**, **The Old Swan Band** - still swanning after all these years, **Flowers and Frolics** - with a recent revival of a near original line-up and **The New Victory Band**), almost always had backgrounds in both folkdance and folksong ; unusual at the time, and were often actively involved in the collection of the music and dance of rural England.

The callers – dance teachers cum MCs - who fronted these bands included **Taffy Thomas**, **Hugh Rippon**, **Roy Dommett**, **Tubby Reynolds**, **Roger Watson** and **Eddie Upton**. And **John Kirkpatrick** could play, sing, call and dance all at the same time, if needed.

Hard on the heels of the first wave came a small avalanche of new bands, most significantly **The Albion Dance Band**. Formed by **Ashley Hutchings**, already a veteran of folk-rock originals **Fairport Convention**, **Steeleye Span** and the **Morris On!** project with **John Kirkpatrick**, the **Albions** presented an attractive and acceptable face for the English uprising, drawing in many fringe fans, and working as a kind of validation to the music media in general. English ceilidh on a major record label.

Later, the insistence on extreme slowness moderated. Stepping was still seen as important, but it sped up to a comfortable lope as more people wanted to dance, and ceilidh got very popular.

About this time a few bands, most particularly **Blowzabella**, now at home with their Englishness, started to add in music and dance from other countries and cultures and supplied another jolt of interest in the early 80s. This helped to push other bands into seeking their own distinctive repertoires and to make their own sounds distinct from other bands.

A few names (there've been so many): **Gas Mark 5**, **Ran Tan Band**, **Old Hat Band**, **The Oyster Ceilidh Band** (later **Oysterband!**), **Ram's Bottom**, **Late Night Band**, **Umps and Dumps**, **Banjax**, **Edward the Second and the Red Hot Polkas** (later **Ell**), **Feckless** and **Tiger Moth**.

Callers include **Dave Hunt**, **Martyn Harvey**, **Sheila Mainwaring**, **Mary Panton**, **Nick Walden**, **Mick Brooks**, and me, **Gordon Potts**. And loads more, just as good, many of whom played or called on their own patch for their own local crowd.

Nowadays, the ceilidh is danced in village halls, at PTAs and at weddings. There is a network of public dances all over the country where you pay your money and hit the floor. And there are the festivals. Almost every folk festival will have a ceilidh or two as part of the main programme nowadays, and at **Sidmouth**, **Whitby**, **Chippenham**, **Bromyard** and **Towersey** as well as a load of others, ceilidhs are central major events, often with over a thousand folks on the dance floor.

**How do you find them?**

Apart from checking your local folk guide, the absolute easiest way is to look on Martin Kiff's Webfeet website: **http://www.ftech.net/~webfeet/**

Martin Nail also runs a links site, which will help you find your way around folk music in general.

Its regional links are very useful. : **http://web.ukonline.co.uk/martin.nail/Folkmus.htm**

For anybody interested in camping as well as ceilidh and all other folk pastimes, the Folk Camps were and are a hotbed of activity. **http://www.folkcamp.clara.net/index.htm**

**Stomp**, **Stocai**, **Chalktown**, **The Committee Band**, **Whapweasel**, **Token Women**, **Bedlam**, **Bursledon Village Band**, **All Blacked Up**, **The Woodpecker Band**, **Tickled Pink**, **Cock and Bull Band**, **Michael Catovsky**, **Rachael Bearon**, **Andrew Swain**, **Chris Pitt**, **Sheena Masson** and **Paul Bain**. The list could just about be endless. So many bands and callers sounding so different, and yet part of the same dance. There is now no instantly identifiable sound that says English Ceilidh. It could be the rootsy drive of the **Bismarcks** or the **Posh Band**; the Status Quo-y folk rock of Coventry's **Peeping Tom**, or the buzzing of the hurdy-gurdy in **Jabadaw**, a young post-Blowzabella outfit from Manchester. Or **Florida**, (from Kent), sounding like a village brass band. Or **Hekety** or **Pepper In The Brandy** or any number of up and coming new, young bands with deep interest and knowledge. It's all very interesting, right now the scene is the most diverse it has ever been.

**Gordon Potts**
*Caller and Committee Band guitarist.*

spotlight

social dance

# Social Dance – English and American Country Dancing

By Chris Turner

Social Dance – a convenience label for a part of the English Folk Dance genre – thrives through a loosely connected network of clubs spread throughout the world from Helsinki to Melbourne and from Los Angeles to Dundee. The courtly idiosyncrasies of English Country Dancing are alive and well, often interspersed with the newest American Contras and Squares.

In the UK there are some 450 Dance Clubs running Saturday Night dances as well as regular, usually weekly, club nights. At most venues dances 'fresh off the Internet' are performed cheek by jowl with traditional and well-known English Country Dances from the earliest published sources. A few clubs specialise, dancing 'mostly Playford' or even 'Playford's dances only'. Much of the music used on club nights is pre recorded and many of the teachers are local club members, willing and varyingly able to give freely of their time and expertise. More expert callers, usually working with live music, are the usual fare on Saturday nights, with clubs often hiring a bigger hall and providing refreshments.

Unlike many other dance traditions, English social dance has no governing body or formal styructure to set standards or establish a plausible training programme. The Grand Union Structured Training Organisation (GUSTO) offers a modular system of teaching, a broad spread of dancing styles, five levels and dozens of trained tutors (Phone 01865 376584.)

Even more dancing is available at folk festivals. In the UK there are dedicated social dance programmes at the Sidmouth, Lichfield, Broadstairs, Whitby and Chippenham festivals. The Eastbourne and Southam festivals are entirely dedicated to Social Dance. At these festivals the Social Dance enthusiasts will be exposed to callers from all corners of the UK and frequently guest callers from overseas as well.

Festival organisers vie with each other to assemble the worthiest of musicians and the most able of these are in constant demand to spend their weekends travelling up and down the country to play for the devotees.

Many smaller one-day festivals are organised as well, such as Worcester and Bletchingley, and they have a dedicated Social Dance programme. In some areas clubs promote dance days, workshops and grand balls.

'Playford' balls are promoted at various splendid venues across the country, recreating the social 'Assemblies' of earlier times. These events are often enhanced by the dancers arriving in all manner of varyingly appropriate costume, sometimes of doubtful historical accuracy and often reflecting the eclectic stock at charity shops. At these events the repertoire is usually taken from Playford's "The Dancing Master" published originally in 1651 and regularly thereafter, and compulsively reinterpreted by academics, teachers, callers, musicians and dancers ever since.

Festival details and contact points for dance clubs can be found in a magazine called Set and Turn Single.

**Set and Turn Single** – an independent magazine for folk dancers – was launched as a London Area free sheet at the end of 1999, aimed at the dancing fraternity and intended as a listings service. It has grown rapidly into a 16-page magazine covering most of the UK and distributed in the USA, Finland, Italy, Hungry and Holland. For a free copy send a SAE to S & TS at 9 Glendale Avenue, London, N22 5HL or phone 020 8889 0634.

# Bubbling in the Cauldrons of Europe

By **Andrew Cronshaw**

Some European countries have been regular places of work for British roots performers, with local agents and promoters accepting of the fact that they probably don't speak the language and will need looking after, need the provision of hotels, meals, often transport and probably a native minder/tour manager, and where needed, the handling of any necessary documentation. In contrast Britain hasn't been an easy place for foreign musicians to get gigs or tour. Though it still isn't, and British fees aren't on a par with those in some European countries, at least the documentation aspect has diminished for some nationalities with the coming of the EU. And there are now a number of British agents regularly bringing performers to Britain, and some of them do the sort of complete job that's necessary for a stranger in a strange land - a promoter who wants to get a musician or band over here may find an agent of like mind who will attempt to find enough other interested parties and set up a tour.

I've been asked in this piece to attempt some pointers to what, where and who is currently hot in Europe, with particular reference to foreign-touring performers and bands, and give some starting points in the tracking down of information and contacts. That's a big brief, but I'll try to cover some of those countries and regions from which roots music is currently doing the most bursting out, or is about to. Of necessity it'll be brief and superficial - there's a reason why the **Rough Guide to World Music** has grown to two fat volumes, and even at that can be no more than an introduction - so this snippet of a couple of thousand words isn't going to get you through any exams, and no-one without Star-Trek instantaneous transit can have a complete, up-to-date, overview of what's happening in so many countries, but it and the contacts at the end might give you some leads.

This rambling tour of Europe begins with its southernmost mainland region, Iberia.

The penny is starting to drop in Britain that Spain has many musical cultures, that flamenco is just one of them, and that most don't even involve guitars. The north has been making particular waves over recent decades. Galicia and Asturias are the source of an extraordinary renaissance of gaita (bagpipe) music. Asturian gaiteiro Hevia's latest-but-one album Tierra de Nadie has sold nearly two million copies. Also well known internationally is **Carlos Núñez**, and coming up fast are fellow Galicians **Xosé Manuel Budiño**, **Susana Seivane**, and the band **Berrogüetto**. A hugely influential band in the Galician renaissance is the long-established **Milladoiro**, which has hardly ever played in Britain. Singing has been slower to reactivate, but currently Galician **Mercedes Peón** is changing all that with a powerful album and magnificent shows. Other fine performers are legion, particularly in Galicia: singer **Uxía**, pandeiretera vocal group **Leilía**, bands like **Os Cempés**, **Na Lúa** and **Camerata Meiga**, and from Asturias those regularly playing abroad include **Llan de Cubel**, **Tejedor**, **Felpeyu** and **the Asturiana Mining Company**.

Also on the north coast of Spain (and into south-west France) is Euskadi (the Basque country) whose very different traditions include trikitixa - dazzling diatonic accordion playing, traditionally accompanied by skittering tambourine and ululating yells (irrintziak). Best known trikitilari abroad is **Kepa**, and he is indeed a fine player with a sophisticated band, but actually it doesn't include a tambourine player and with it he rarely these days makes the classic raw trikitixa sound. **Tapia**, with tambourine-player Leturia, is the technical equal of Kepa and has maintained a strong connection with the wild exuberance of trikitixa, and Euskal singing (while Kepa is instrumental only), as well as being a prime mover in the evolution of young Euskal triki-pop bands. Also with a new lease of life in Euskadi and beginning to reach abroad is the playing of txalaparta - two or more planks hit with vertical sticks by a pair of musicians, creating interweaving patterns - a tradition far older than trikitixa which is establishing new connections with very modern musical forms.

The further south one goes in Spain the greater are the discernible links with Arabic music, and it's not surprising that Spanish musicians, such as the Madrid-based band **Radio Tarifa** and percussionist **Luís Delgado**, are making new music acknowledging that. Delgado has been involved with much other central and southern Spanish roots evolution, including a band well known for specialising in central Spanish music, **La Musgaña**, and singer **Manuel Luna**. Indeed, just as there are long-established connections between the countries with a north Atlantic seaboard, so there is musical continuity around and across the easily navigated Mediterranean. In Iberia, for example, Catalunya looks to the sea, to its Iberian hinterland and to nearby France, and these influences show in its traditional and new music. Amongst internationally performing Catalan musicians reflecting this is singer **Maria del Mar Bonet**. And of course the Arabic in the aforementioned flamenco, of which fine exponents both traditional and new-fusion are too legion to begin to mention here, is explicit in its musical structure, singing styles and oud-like guitar technique.

Just as the perception abroad of Spanish music was dominated by flamenco, so when Portugal is mentioned, even among the world music-savvy, the response is likely to be "oh, yes, I love fado". And, as with flamenco in Spain, fado and fado-influenced music is undergoing a rise in popularity. Current notable fado exports include **Mafalda Arnauth** and **Misia**, and blind triangle-playing Lisbon street singer **Dona Rosa** has recently been gaining acclaim abroad. The long-established band **Madredeus** uses fado and other influences in its elegant music, while **Amélia Muge**, **Dulce Pontes** and **Teresa Silva Carvalho** amongst others show strong fado influences while also (as did the late great **Amália Rodrigues**) exploring other styles. From the more instrumental-oriented fado style of Coimbra comes guitarrista **Pedro Caldeira Cabral**. But while fado is a music arising in the cities Portugal also has a wide variety of rural traditional musics, with much longer history than fado, and showing strong differences between the south and north. The only surviving pocket of a northern tradition, the music of the gaita de foles, the Portuguese bagpipe, is **Terra de Miranda**, and there is to be found the very fine and vibrant traditional gaita, percussion and vocal group **Galandum Galundaina**. Social and industrial change has removed the context of much of the old rural music, but as in

spotlight
europe

other countries musicians have sought out the dwindling old traditions and are evolving contemporary forms made for stage performance and touring, forms which usually draw on more than one regional tradition. Among them are the long-established and still strong **Brigada Victor Jara**, the bands **Realejo** and **Vai de Roda**, indigenous-fretted-instrument player **Júlio Pereira** and the exciting and exploratory **Gaiteiros de Lisboa** who, as their name suggests, do use bagpipes (a northern Portuguese tradition) but also draw on the polyphonic vocal sounds of the Alentejo, hefty percussion and a range of other instruments, some of them ingenious fruits of their own creation.

Just as Spanish culture reaches far afield into the Americas, so Portuguese music is a link into the whole Lusophone musical world, including the former colonies in South America and Africa and the Atlantic island groups - Cape Verde (not in Europe, but home of famous morna singer **Cesaria Evora**, and others including **Herminia** and roots band **Simentera**), the Azores and, nearer the mainland, the island of Madeira, which is showing signs of new roots-connected musical developments beginning to poke through its Saga Holidays resort surface, including the promising multifaceted band **Almma**.

Moving eastward, France has, like Iberia, a patchwork of regional musical cultures, with performers taking aspects of them abroad - for example, from the south and centre come Béarnais singer **Marilis Orionaa**, Massif Central fiddler **Jean-François Vrod** and hurdy-gurdy player **Valentin Clastrier**, from the hurdy-gurdy hotbed of Berry **Gilles Chabenat** and **Patrick Bouffard**, from Bourbon bagpipers such as **Jean Blanchard**. And of course in the north Brittany is the home of an intensely vibrant musical scene, of dance, song, bagpipes, bombardes, harps, fiddles and new evolutions, from long-established names and new - **Alan Stivell**, **Dan Ar Braz**, **Bagad Kemper**, **Gwerz**, **Erik Marchand**, fiddler **Jacky Molard**, his piper brother **Patrick Molard** and very many more. France is also the home of many leading African and North African bands, from Algerians to Madagascans, and also the place of fusion between European, North African, Gypsy and other musics - for example there's **Lo'Jo**, **Orchestre National de Barbès**, or the work of Spanish-born **Manu Chao**. Corsican polyphonic singing has become a phenomenon; much of it is male, but one of the best-known exemplars is the magnificent female group **Donnisulana**.

Neighbouring Sardinia also has moving polyphonic singing (try **Tenores di Bitti** - and of course the island also home to well-known female singer **Elena Ledda**). Indeed passionate vocal polyphony is a feature of several regions adjoining the northern Mediterranean coasts, including the trallaleri of the Genoa region of Italy (of which **La Squadra** is a touring exemplar) and the soaring interweaving of Albanian polyphony (for example **Ensemble Tirana**).

Lately the profile of Italian music has risen abroad, most recently with the band **Spaccanapoli** from Naples. Italy has a rainbow of regional styles; for example, the strident bagpipe-chanter-like piffaro (listen to **Stefano Valla**, who I encountered recently perched with accordionist **Franco Guglielmetti** on a table-top playing lively dance music at 3am in a tiny village in the hills above Milan, alternating with groups of trallaleri). A master of the Italian organetto (diatonic button accordion) is **Riccardo Tesi**, who has often performed with French mandolinist **Patrick Vaillant**. Italy has bagpipes, too - the zampogna - as used for example by Calabrian band **Re Niliu**.

Only a short hop east from the heel of Italy is Greece, yet another place whose musical riches have only relatively recently become apparent to foreigners through the smokescreen of hackneyed tourist-targeted images. Greece's position between the Mediterranean and the Balkans is reflected in the variety and intermingling of western European and oriental in its musics, which include the urban rembétika, songs of the countryside and islands, and not just the well-known and often brilliantly-played bouzouki but a wide range of instruments such as the exquisite yearning edginess of the three-stringed bowed lyra, bagpipes, clarinets, the Thracian kaváli, bagpipe, and the zournas, a strident shawm. As with other nationalities that have large exile communities in Britain, leading Greek and Cypriot musicians pass in and out of the UK regularly but unknown to the non-Greek population. However, lately **Eleftheria Arvanitaki**, with her large and splendid band, and British-born but Crete-resident multi-instrumentalist **Ross Daly** have played more widely advertised concerts, and there are likely to be more making the crossover.

The cultures of northern Greece are continuous with those of an area laden with thrilling vocal and instrumental music, full of the sparks of the meeting of west and east - the Balkans. Before the evaporation of the communist bloc the musics of Bulgaria, Romania, et al were the stuff of thin-sleeved state record label LP releases copied between excited westerners who felt like explorers of a new world, but one by one, or usually ensemble by ensemble, the magical singers and players of gaida, kaval, gadulka, cimbalom, violin, taragot, or various lutes showed up in the West, and now the demise of the state ensembles has made many to look west for work. The great Bulgarian singer **Kalinka Vulcheva**, a leading voice in those magical Bulgarian choral recordings, is married to, and works with, British musician **Martin Jenkins**, and brilliant Bulgarian gadulka player **Georgi Petrov** has lived in Britain while a member of the Riverdance band, and made albums with harmonica whizz **Brendan Power**.

Multi-instrumentalist **Nikola Parov**, Bulgarian-born but with strong Hungarian connections, has also been a Riverdance member, and earlier collaborated with **Andy Irvine** and other western musicians. Meanwhile Hungarian folk bands have of course been coming to Britain; the best known is probably **Muzsikás** with or without **Márta Sebestyén**, but there has been a tendency for western bookers to look no further, when there are a slew of other fine bands and performers combining deep roots with modern sensibilities, such as **Vasmalom** (regular visitors to the UK), singer **Kati Szvorák** (who has appeared here several times), **Ghymes**, **Lantos Banda**, or the zither-led **Gereben**.

There's more to the Balkans than Bulgaria, Romania and Hungary, of course; to the west are Macedonia, Serbia, Montenegro, Bosnia-Herzegovina, Croatia and Slovenia, from all of which comes fascinating music, traditional or roots-progressive, which is being increasingly heard abroad. Indeed the former iron curtain countries, through the Czech Republic, Slovakia, Poland, and those just re-emerging as entities from the Soviet bloc - Ukraine, Moldova, Belarus and the myriad peoples of Russia - are full of interesting musics; an enterprising booker would find there much to excite a UK audience, and musicians keen to play to that audience. Among what is likely to be a fast-growing field, Russian band **Farlanders** featuring singer-guitarist **Inna Zhelannaya** and singer multi-instrumentalist **Sergey Starostin** have recently stirred up considerable interest, as has Sarajevo-born **Goran Bregovic**'s varied, muscular work with Gypsy music and with Polish singer **Kayah**. And one of my own most surprising musical moments of the past year was the magical single unaccompanied folksong verse sung by a striking young East European Gypsy woman, who I'd love to trace and bring to a bigger stage, on a Piccadilly line tube train. There's much exotic music among the often remarkable people arriving, and sometimes being disregarded, here in Britain.

Gypsy music runs throughout European music, western and eastern, crossing political boundaries, taking local musical forms and twisting them into something exotic but also partly familiar. Lately a lot more attention has been paid to it on the world-music scene, with a stream of compilation CDs, and appearances in Britain by Gypsy stars from Iberia to Russia and, beyond Europe, right back to North India, including Gypsy-jazz from France, Germany, flamenco and rumba from Spain, dazzling Hungarian cimbalomist **Kálmán Balogh**, Romania's **Taraf de Haïdouks** and wild brass band **Fanfare Ciocarlia**, singers Macedonian **Esma Redzepova** and Bohemian **Vera Bila**.

Jewish Klezmer music has long been another strong thread in European music, and while it was a fundamental influence in American popular music of the 20th century, both there and back in Europe, there are many delving back into it and creating a new fine voluptuous music of reeds and violins; among particular hot names to be seen regularly in Britain is the Polish trio **Kroke**, while US exponents include the dazzling **Klezmatics**.

Heading northward, there has recently been an increase in roots activity in Germany and Austria, often involving rich multi-ethnic eclecticism - for example in Vienna's **Wiener Tschuschenkapelle** or Köln's **Schäl Sick Brass Band** - or cheerily black irony, as in Bavaria's **Hundsbuam Miserablige**.

Northward further gets us to the Nordic countries, and it's well-known that there's a lot of interesting music happening there, and after years of just occasional Nordic performers playing in Britain the gates are now opening wider, encouraged by an increased amount of UK airplay, particularly on Radio 3's *Late Junction*, and by considerable help from Nordic government bodies which, unlike in some countries, are wont to regard their countries' roots music as actually a significant aspect of their culture. Of the Finns, lately **Kimmo Pohjonen**'s extraordinary live-sampling accordion-wrestling solo show has made waves in Britain, high-energy Karelian-rooted **Värttinä**, Ostrobothnian fiddle band **JPP** and subtle accordionist **Maria Kalaniemi** have made several successful trips, and others such as kantele player **Minna Raskinen**, singer **Anna-Kaisa Liedes** and the band **Tallari** have appeared occasionally. At the time of writing this **Gjallarhorn** an exciting young band from Finland's 6% Swedish-speaking minority featuring twin fiddles, didgeridoo, percussion and **Jenny Wilhelms**' luminous microtonal vocals, are about to surprise British audiences, and a certain show including Wilhelms, kantele player **Hannu Saha** and extraordinary singer **Heikki Laitinen** will reach Britain in 2002.

Several leading Swedish performers and bands have already been to Britain - multi-instrumentalist **Ale Möller**, magnificent singer **Lena Willemark** and fiddler **Per Gudmundson** have all been here in various contexts; together they comprise the essential-to-experience trio **Frifot**. The long-established **Groupa**, featuring **Mats Edén**'s bowed strings with **Jonas Simonson**'s flutes, **Rickard Åström**'s keyboards and recently joined by lively vocalist **Sofia Karlsson** and Norwegian percussionist **Terje Isungset**, have made a few low-profile forays to the UK over the years. Even the mighty **Hedningarna** have played only a couple of shows here, at the time when their two Finnish vocalists were **Sanna Kurki-Suonio** and **Tellu Virkkala** (both of them now involved in a variety of interesting other projects); their stormingly powerful sound of rasping strings and meaty percussion hasn't made it to the UK since. Also in drone-roots rock territory, **Garmarna** appeared at Glasgow's Celtic Connections in 2001, as did the driving nyckelharpa-led polska of Uppland's **Väsen** and the brilliant quartet **SWÅP** comprising Swedish fiddlers **Ola Bäckström** and **Carina Normansson** with British accordionist **Karen Tweed** and guitarist **Ian Carr**, at the first of a three-year series of Nordic Nights weekends that are at last providing a focus for a stepping up of the Nordic invasion of the UK. There's much more back home - legions too numerous to mention of wonderful fiddlers, a rising tide of dazzling nyckelharpa players, bands acoustic and electric, and an increasing number of fine singers.

Norway is equally musically rich, with a particularly productive mutual respect between deep traditional musicians and those from jazz and rock, evolving a very distinctive clear bright open Norwegian sound of high hardanger-fiddle and ordinary-fiddle strings and spaciously luxurious ambiences. Again, too much to cover, but just a sampling of the names to notice, only a few of whom have played here, includes the hardanger/reeds/percussion trio **Utla**, fiddle queens **Annbjørg Lien** and **Susanne Lundeng** each with their magnificent bands, electric and acoustic guitarist **Knut Reiersrud**, with his band or deep-groove church organist **Iver Kleive**, and the unbelievably tight and eclectic **Farmer's Market**'s "speed-Balkan-boogie" which description goes no way to describe it.

The roots music scene in the southernmost Nordic country, Denmark, often a host to others' musics, has recently begun to take off in its own right with a growing range of high-achievers including techno-roots band **Sorten Muld**, full-blooded folk-rockers **Serras**, (both featuring fiddler **Harald Haugaard**, who also plays in a duo with guitarist **Morten Høirup**) and acoustic **Lang Linken**.

Just across the Baltic from Finland the three Baltic States are just emerging musically from the deadening influence of the Soviet Union, with musicians exploring traditional musics and also creating new evolutions. Examples include Estonian singer **Kirile Loo** working with techno ambiences, Latvian folk band **Ilgi** combining its traditional music with lessons learned as part of rock band **Jauns Meness**.

Finally, at the top of Europe, there are only about 75,000 Sámi, spread across the north ends of Norway, Sweden, Finland and north-western Russia, but they're making a lot of very impressive music, most of it revolving round the minimalism of joik, from traditional solo unaccompanied to ambient and techno; **Mari Boine**, **Wimme**, **Angelit**, **Transjoik**, **Ulla Pirttijärvi** might begin your investigations...

**Andrew Cronshaw**
*Musician and journalist*

# European Resources By Andrew Cronshaw

I've done my best to make what follows as up to date as possible, but addresses, phone numbers, emails and web sites are prone to change, and artists to change agencies or management. Furthermore, touring artists usually have to work through different agents in different countries.

No single agency gives you access to the full range of even a single country's music, and few countries have any kind of one-stop shop, nor even directory, for getting in touch with performers.

The contact list below is arranged in the same country order as in the text above. It covers as many as possible of the names I mentioned, but I've also included a some extra performers whom I couldn't fit into the text but who are well worth seeking out - and there are many more. Since I don't have direct or agent contact for all those mentioned, I've often included the label an artist records for, - they might be trackable down that way (but don't count on it - labels can evaporate too). And festivals and promoters in the relevant countries are likely to be good sources of contact info, too, but look for them in places like fRoots; the festival list is also on its website.

This is nothing like a comprehensive guide, just an introduction; it doesn't cover every country in Europe, and some countries are covered in greater detail than others, either because they noise abroad more information or simply because I know more people there!

Even so, it's taken quite a while to put together; let me know (via cloudval@aol.com) if it's helped you to plunge into Europe and book someone surprising.

## General contacts in the UK

### Magazines

Principal English-language magazines covering European roots musics; magazines in other languages are mentioned in the country listings that follow.

#### fRoots
PO Box 337, London N4 1TW
**Phone** (020)-8340-9651
**Email** froots@froots.demon.co.uk
**Web** www.froots.demon.co.uk
*Monthly world music magazine, with the greatest English-language coverage of European roots musics, performers and news.*

#### Songlines
Gramophone Publications
38-42 Hampton Road, Teddington
Middlesex, TW11 0JE
**Phone** +44 (0)20-8267-5124
**Fax** -8267-5844
**Email** songlines@haynet.com
**Subscriptions** PO Box 326, Sittingbourne, Kent ME9 8FA
*Quarterly magazine on world music including European.*

#### Dirty Linen
PO Box 66600, Baltimore, Maryland
MD 21239-6600, USA
**Phone** (410)-583-7973
**Fax** -337-6735
**Email** office@dirtylinen.com
**Web** www.dirtylinen.com
*US magazine, 6 issues p.a., with some coverage of European musics.*

### Books

**Rough Guide to World Music vol.1**
1999, ISBN 1-85828-635-2, published by Rough Guides, distributed by Penguin.
**Web** www.roughguides.com
*The logical next step to find out more about the music of most of the countries mentioned above.*

**Celtic Music** (ed. Kenny Mathieson)
2001, ISBN 0-87930-623-8, published by Backbeat Books.
**Web** www.backbeatbooks.com
*Includes chapters on musicians, music and recordings from Northern Iberia and Brittany as well as UK, Ireland and Cape Breton.*

### Webzines

**RootsWorld**
Box 1285, New Haven, Connecticut
CT 06505, USA
**Email** cliff@rootsworld.com
**Web** www.rootsworld.com/rw/
*Also has linked sites including a list of roots radio streaming on the Internet and a sales site.*

**www.worldmusicportal.com** is a substantial world music site with some useful European links and addresses, and also information about events and trade fairs.

### Radio

UK-wide programmes playing substantial amounts of European roots music:

**Late Junction** (presenters Fiona Talkington, Verity Sharp): BBC Radio 3 Mon, Tues, Wed, Thurs 10.15 pm - 12.05. Playlists with full label details at **Web** www.bbc.co.uk/radio3/playlists/latejunction.shtml

**Andy Kershaw**: BBC Radio 3 Fri 10.15 pm - 12.05

**World Routes** (presenter Lucy Duran): BBC Radio 3 Sat 1-2pm

### Organisations and conferences

**WOMEX**
c/o Piranha Records, Carmerstr.11
D-10623 Berlin, Germany
**Phone** (+49)-30-318-614-0
**Fax** -30-318-614-10
**Email** womex@womex.com
**Web** www.womex.com
*World music conference, with seminars, showcases and much informal networking. Its attendee list is a very useful international address book, too. In 2001 it's in Rotterdam, 25-28 Oct.*

**Strictly Mundial**
c/o Instituto Cultural Casa Via Magia
Rua Heriqueta Catarino 123 - Federação, 40220-180 Salvador, BA - Brasil
**Email** mercado@viamagia.com.br
**Phone** (+55)-(71)-247-0068
(71)-331-2198
**Fax** (+55)-(71)-245-3089
*World music conference, with seminars and showcases and particular emphasis on bookings for live events. First, in 2000, was in Zaragoza, Spain; in 2001 (4-9 Dec.) it will be in Bahia, Brazil.*

### Record retailers

The bigger branches of chains Virgin, HMV and Tower carry varying-sized ranges of European roots music in their world music sections. They're also to be found at many of the scattering of excellent specialist roots shops around Britain. Most of what they don't carry is available mail order, either direct from labels or through suppliers such as ADA, and via the internet; a little time spent on Google or another search engine, searching by artist name, will turn up plenty of sources and a whole lot of other interesting information.

### Agencies or organisations regularly bringing European roots performers to the UK

**Serious**
Chapel House, 18 Hatton Place
London EC1N 8RU
**Email** info@serious.org.uk
**Web** www.serious.org.uk

**Adastra**
2 Star Row, North Dalton, Driffield
E.Yorkshire YO25 9UR
**Phone** (01377) 217662
**Fax** (01377) 217754
**Email** adastra@adastey.demon.co.uk
**Web** www.adastra-music.co.uk

**mARKO pOLO**
**Phone** (01243) 789786

**Folkworks**
69 Westgate Road,
Newcastle-upon-Tyne NE1 1SG
**Phone** +44-(0)191-222-1717
**Fax** +44-(0)191-230-2484
**Email** folkworks@folkworks.co.uk
**Web** www.folkworks.co.uk

**¡Como No!**
34 Osnaburgh Street,
London NW1 3ND
**Phone** (020) 8916 5479
**Fax** 8916 5480
**Email** comono@btinternet.com
*Performers from Spanish and Portuguese-speaking countries*

**Portugal 600**
Palingswick House, 241 King Street,
London, W6 9LP
**Phone** (020) 8748 0884
**Fax** 8748-4187
**Email**
mail@portugal600.demon.co.uk
*The UK connection for the Gulbenkian Foundation, involved with Portuguese music and culture.*

## SPAIN

### Magazines

**World 1 Music**
C/. Valencia 54, entlo. 2ª
08015 Barcelona, Spain
**Phone** 93 226 64 77
**Fax** 226 94 04
**Email** pw1@menta.net, subscriptions
**Email** pw1@idgrup.ibernet.com
*Glossy world music magazine, 6 issues p.a.*

### Conferences/trade fairs

**Mercat de Música Viva de Vic**
Edificiel Sucre
C Ramon d'Abadal de Vinyals, 5 2a
08500 Vic, Spain
**Phone** (+34) 93 88 33 100
**Fax** -93-88-32-626
**Email** mmvv@osona.net
**Web** www.mmvv.impevic.net

### Organisations

**Iberian Ethnomusicology Association** (Sociedad Ibérica de Etnomusicología (SIbE)).
**E-mail** sibe@retemail.es
**Web** personal2.iddeo.es/sibe
*Research, publishing and preservation projects, and annual convention.*

### Record labels

**Resistencia**
c/ San Isidro Labrador N° 19
28005 Madrid, Spain
**Phone** (+34)-1-366-67-23
**Fax** -364-21-10
**Email** resistencia@edires.com

**Nubenegra**
Toledo 54, 2 iz., 28005 Madrid
Spain
**Phone** (+34)-91-365-82-34
**Fax** -364-02-29
**Email** nubenegra@nubenegra.com
**Web** www.nubenegra.com
(Nubenegra is linked with Intuition records, PO Box 270 126, 50508 Cologne, Germany,
**Email** intuition@intuition-music.com,
**Web** www.intuition-music.com)

**Discmedi**
Cardener 32-34, 08024 Barcelona
Spain
**Phone** (+34)-93-284-95-16
**Fax** -93-219-85-10
**Email** discmedi@discmedi.com

**Sonifolk**
C/ Fernández de los Rios 78,
28015 Madrid, Spain
**Phone** +34-(9)1-544-59-55
**Fax** -544-97-38
**Email** sonifolk@iv.eurociber.es
**Web** intervia.com.sonifolk

**Several Records**
Matilde Hernández 31
28019 Madrid, Spain
**Phone** (+34)-(1)-471-5613
**Fax** -(1)-471-4711
**Email** trading-records@flashnet.es
**Web** www.trading-records.com

## Galicia

### Agencies and managements

**Nordesía Productions**
Vía Sacra 3, 2°
15704 Santiago de Compostela
Galicia, Spain
**Phone** +34-(9)81-55-59-30
**Fax** -(9)81-55-72-76
**Email** nordesia@ctv.es
*Bookings for many of the leading roots performers: Berrogüetto, Os Cempés, Chouteira, Uxía, Leilía, Na Lúa, Susana Seivane, Xosé Manuel Budiño*

**Keltia Produccións, SL**
Marqués de Valladares, 12-3° Of.1
E-36201 Vigo (or Apartado de Correos 318, E-36201 Vigo)
Pontevedra, Galicia, Spain
**Phone/Fax** 34-(9)86-43060-41
**Email** keltiasl@arrakis.es
*Management of Carlos Núñez*

### Record labels

**Do Fol Edicións**
Boa Musica S.L., Hierro 9, Madrid
28045, Spain
**Phone** (+34)-(9)15-06-32-20
**Fax** -915-28-67-54
**Galicia office:** Elduayen 16 1ºA, Vigo 36202, Email vigo@boa-music.com
**Email** dofol@boa-music.com
boa@boa-music.com
**Web** www.boa-music.com
**Web** www.dofol.com
*Roots performers include Susan Seivane, Berrogüetto, Emilio Cao, Os Cempés, Chouteira, Na Lúa, Henrique Otero, Xistra de Coruxo, Rodrigo Romaní, Pancho Álvarez, Maite Dono et al. Distributed by Boa Music. Distributed in UK by ADA.*

**Xosé Manuel Budiño**
**Web** www.xosemanuelbudino.com
**Bookings** Nordesía (see above)
*Label of most recent CD: Virgin Records España, www.virgin-records.es*

european resources

### Artists

**Susana Seivane**
**Bookings** Nordesía (see above)
**Record label** Do Fol (see above)

**Milladoiro**
Label of most recent CD: Discmedi (see above)

**Mercedes Peón**
**Record label** Resistencia (see above)

**Berrogüetto**
**Bookings** Nordesía (see above)
**Record label** Do Fol (see above)

**Uxía**
**Bookings** Nordesía (see above)
**Record label** Do Fol (see above)

**Leilía**
**Bookings** Nordesía (see above)

**Os Cempés**
**Email** oscempes@terra.es
**Bookings** Nordesía (see above)
**Record label** Do Fol (see above)

**Na Lúa**
**Bookings** Nordesía (see above)
**Record label** Do Fol (see above)

**Chouteira**
**Bookings** Nordesía (see above)
**Record label** Do Fol (see above)

**Camerata Meiga**
**Phone** (+34)-988-23-72-11
**Email** gilope@arrakis.es
**Record label** Resistencia (see above)

**Luar Na Lubre**
**Bookings** Gin Tonic
**Phone** (+34)-943-40-14-18
**Record label** Warner Music Spain

**Emilio Cao** (Harpist/songwriter)
Cumios Produccións, Apartado 181
15700 Santiago de Compostela
Galicia, Spain
**Phone/Fax** (981)-58-83-83
**Record label** Do Fol (see above)

**Xistra de Coruxo**
Camiño do Ceán 48, Vigo 36331
Galicia, Spain
**Phone** +34-(9)86-49-04-69
**Fax** -86-46-07-63
**Record label** Do Fol (see above)

**Rodrigo Romaní**
(Harpist, recently left Milladoiro)
**Record label** Do Fol (see above)

## Asturias

### Organisations

**Música Tradicional Muyeres**
C/ Muñoz Degraín 14 - 9° C
33007 Oviedo - Uviéu, Asturies, Spain
**Phone** (+34)-98-523-6120
*Association of traditional female vocal groups, set up after the Muyeres vol.1 CD on FonoAstur; also contact for performing unit, Muyeres.*

### Record Label

**FonoAstur**
c/ Cardenal Cienfuegos 2, Escal.2,
baxu B, 33007 Uviéu/Oviedo,
Asturies
Spain
**Phone** (+34)-985-27-80-50
**Email** info@fonoastur.com
**Web** www.fonoastur.com

### Artists

**Hevia**
**Email** busindre@joseangelhevia.com
**Web** www.joseangelhhevia.com
**Management** Limac
Breton de los Herreros 31,
28003 Madrid, Spain
**Phone** (+34)-91-441-60-11
**Fax** (+34)-91-441-19-62
**Email** limac@wztech.com
**Record label** EMI-Odeón
**Web** www.emimusic-spain.com

**Llan de Cubel**
Apdo. 2127, 33013 Uviéu, Asturies
Spain
**Phone** (+34)-98-597-23-23
**Fax** (+34)-98-522-51-35
**Record label** FonoAstur (see above)

**Tejedor**
**Management** El Cohete Internacional
C/ Mendizábal 4, 1° Iz, Uvieu 33003
Asturies, Spain
**Phone** (+34)-985-20-53-96
**Fax** (+34)-985-20-54-81
**Email** cohete@interbook.net
**Record label** Resistencia (see above)

**Felpeyu**
**Record label** FonoAstur (see above)

**Asturiana Mining Co.**
**Record label** KRL/Lochshore Records,
9 Watt Rd., Hillington, Glasgow G52 4RY, Scotland
**Phone** (0141) 882 9060
(0141) 882 9986
**Fax** (0141) 883-3686
**Email** krl@krl.co.uk
**Web** www.krl.co.uk

**Xéliba**
Aptu.320, 33400 Avilés, Asturies,
Spain
**Phone** (+34)-649-07-82-07
**Email** info@xeliba.com
**Web** www.xeliba.com
**Record label** FonoAstur (see above)

## Cantabria

### Artists

**Atlántica**
Villasuso de Anievas, 39451
Cantabria, Spain
**Phone** (+34)-942-840-649
**Email** atlantica@interbook.net
**Web** www.interbook.net/personal/atlantica
**Record label** elTripulante
**Web** www.elTripulante.com

## Euskadi

### Agencies and managements

**Kap Produkzioak**
Francisco Maciá 11 - 6 piso / Dpt.5
48014 Bilbao, Euskadi, Bizkaia
Spain
**Phone** (+34) 94-447-88-40
**Fax** (+34) 94-447-22-39
**Email** kap_prod@teleline.es

**Elena Serrano**
2710 West 10th Ave., Vancouver
British Columbia, V6K 2J9, Canada
**Phone** (604)-730-8625
**Email** ebasque@axionet.com

### Record labels

**Elkarlanean**
Portuetxe kalea 88 bis, 20018
Donostia, Gipuzkoa, Euskadi, Spain
**Phone** (+34)-(9) 43-31-02-67
**Fax** (+34)-(9) 43-31-02-16
**Email** musika@elkarlanean.com
**Web** www.elkarlanean.com
*Most of the leading Euskal musicians have recorded for Elkarlanean*

**Gaztelupeko Hotsak**
94 p.k. , Soraluze 20590, Euskadi
Spain
**Phone** (+34)-943-75-30-16
**Fax** (+34) -943-75-01-39

**NO-CD**
Apdo 329, 20100 Orereta-Rentería
Euskadi
**Phone** (+34)-43-52-91-71
**Fax** (+34)-43-51-62-92
or
Apdo 18.041, 28080 Madrid
**Phone** (+34)-1-369-49-99
**Fax** (+34) -1-369-06-68

european resources

### Artists

**Kepa Junkera**
**Management** Kap Produkzioak (see above)
**Label of most recent CD** Resistencia (see above)

**Joseba Tapia/ Tapia eta Leturia**
**Email** tapi@euskalnet.net
**Most recent record labels**
(T&L): Elkarlanean (see above)
(Tapia): Gaztelupeko Hotzak (see above)

**Oskorri**
Loteria 4 - 4.ezk
**Phone/fax** (+34)-94-416-23-85
**Web** www.oskorri.com
**Management** Kap Produkzioak (see above)
**Record label** Elkarlanean (see above)
*Long established and very influential Euskal band*

**Hiru Truku**
**Record label** Nuevos Medios, Marqués del Duero 8, 28001 Madrid
*Traditional song trio of Joseba Tapia, guitarist Ruper Ordorika and Oskorri frets-player Bixente Martinez.*

**Amaia Zubiria**
**Label of most recent album**
Elkarlanean (see above)
*Singer*

**Alboka**
Pº Isasti 27, 20180 Oiartzun, Gipuzkoa
Euskadi, Spain
**Phone** (+34) 943-49-39-30
**Fax** (+34) 943-33-23-97
**Email** joxan@encomix.es
**Web** www.encomix.es/users/joxan
**Record label** Aztarna, Pol Lastaola 94, 20120 Hernani, Gipuzkoa

**Pomada**
**Phone** (+34) 93-310-38-34
(+34) 655-08-09-27
*Lively young trikitixa duo from the new wave of triki-pop; Catalans but singing in Euskara.*

## Central, south and other parts of Spain

### Organisations

**Centro Andaluz de Flamenco,**
Palacio de Pemartín, Plaza de San Juan I, 11403 Jerez de la Frontera
Cadiz, Spain
**Phone** (+34) 956-349-265
(+34) 321-602
(+34) 322-711
**Fax** (+34) 321-127
**Email** caf@cica.es

**Cristina Heeren Flamenco Foundation**
Casa de Pérez Comendador, Santa Cruz, Sevilla, Spain
**Web** www.servicom.es/heeren/english/Welcome.html

**Organización Cultural de Desarrollo Flamenco**
Pico de la Brújula 6, 1º, 28031 Madrid, Spain
**Phone** (+34)-91-3038573

**Centro Cultural Gitano "La Mina" (Gypsy Cultural Centre)**
Levante 1, bajo, San Adrián del Besos
Barcelona, Spain
**Phone** (+34)-93-3819504

### Agents and managements

**Anacrusa Producciones**
Apartado de Correos 195, 08810 Sant Pere de Ribes, Barcelona, Spain
**Phone** (+34)-93-896-18-62
**Fax** (+34)-93-896-17-43
**Email** anacrusa@anacrusa.com
*Represents tango artists and Catalan rumba*

**Batall**
Balmes 25, baixos 3, Apartado de Correos 45, 43800 Valls, Spain
**Phone** (+34) 977-613-339
**Fax** (+34) 977-613-134
**Email** batall@batall.com
**Web** www.batall.com
*Agency involved with music and theatre, managing Catalan rock, jazz and world music acts and producing concerts and events.*

**ICART**
C/. Carretas 14 - 5º - Pta. I-5
28012 Madrid, Spain
**Phone** (+34) 91-531-24-40
(+34) 91-531-13-21
**Fax** (+34) 91-531-59-36
**Email** icart@icart.es
*Represents some leading flamenco musicians and dancers, and world music artists.*

### Artists

**Radio Tarifa**
**Record label** World Circuit
**Web** www.worldcircuit.co.uk

**Luís Delgado**
**Record label** Intuition/Nubenegra (see above)

**La Musgaña**
**Record label** Resistencia (see above)

**Manuel Luna**
Producciones Trenti/Música de Raiz
Apartado 2133, 30080 Murcia
Spain
**Phone/Fax** (+34) (9)68-23-33-66
**Email** mluna1@arrakis.es
*Cantabrian-born singer, now living in the south; guests with La Musgaña.*

**Acetre**
C/ Sta Engracia 14, 06100 Olivenza (Badajoz), Spain
**Phone** (+34) 924-49-02-86
(+34) 639-780-031
(+34) 606-022-659
**Email** acetre@hotmail.com
**Web** www.acetre.com
*Extremadura roots band. CDs on own label.*

**Paco Díez**
Miguel Delibes 9, 47270 Cigales (Valladolid), Spain
**Phone/Fax** (+34)-983-58-68-49
*Singer, bagpiper, hurdy-gurdy player Diez is based at the Ethnographic Centre in Uruena (Valladolid); organises concerts & lectures on trad instruments. Traditional Iberian and Judeo-Spanish music.*
CDs on Several Records (see above)

**Eliseo Parra**
**Record label**
Música Sin Fin, c/ Corazón de María 2 - 6º 40, 28002 Madrid, Spain
**Phone/fax** (+34)-91-416-3380
**Email** musica.sin.fin@via.goya.es

## Catalunya

### Artists

**Maria del Mar Bonet**
Management Comunicamusic, Laforja 77, 08021 Barcelona
**Fax** (+34)-93-209-5389
**Email** comunica@mx3.redestdb.es
**Record label** Picap

european resources

# PORTUGAL

## Organisations

### Instituto de Etnomusicologia
Universidade Nova de Lisboa
Social and Human Sciences College
Av. de Berna 26-C, 1069-061 Lisboa
Portugal
**Phone** (+351) 21-793-3519
**Fax** (+351) 21-797-7759
**Email** iem@fcsh.unl.pt
**Web** www.fcsh.unl.pt/hp/UNIDADES/IE.HTM

*Research, promotion and preservation of music from Portugal and the Portuguese speaking countries.*

### Fundação Calouste Gulbenkian
Avenida de Berna 45
P-1093 Lisboa 45-A Codex, Portugal
**Phone** (+351) 1-793-5131
**Fax** (+351) 1-793-7296

## Agencies and management

### Vachier & Associados / Farol Música
R.de São Bento 672, 1250 223
Lisboa
Portugal
**Phone** (+351) 21-383-89-80
(+351) 01-383-05-74
**Fax** (+351) 01-387-55-93
(+351) 21-387-55-93
**Email** vachier@vachier-producao.pt

### Ocarina
Rua da Barroca 93, 1200-050
Lisbon,
Portugal
**Phone/Fax** (+351)-21-342-7087,
**Email** ocarina@ocarina-music.pt

*Traditional and contemporary rural or urban musicians from the Portuguese-speaking and Iberian countries, including Almma, Brigada Victor Jara, Toque de Caixa et al.*

### Etnia
Calçada Marquês de Abrantes, 10-3
Esq., P-1200 Lisboa, Portugal
**Phone** (+351) 1-395-1415
**Fax** (+351) 1-396-1355
**Email** etnia@esoterica.pt
**Web** www.terravista.pt/enseada/1465

## Record labels

### Movieplay
Rua Alfredo Guisado Nº 10 - 5º
1500 Lisboa, Portugal

## Artists

### Mafalda Arnauth
**Agent** Ocarina (see above)
**Record label** EMI

### Misia
**Management** Olivier Gluzman, les Visiteurs du Soir,
**Phone** +33-(1)-44-93-02-02
**Fax** +33-(1)-44-93-04-40
**Email** ogluzman@aol.fr
**Record label** Erato Detour
**Web** www.erato.com

### Dona Rosa
**Record label & agent** Jaro Medien GmbH, Bismarckstrasse 43, D-28203 Bremen, Germany.
**Phone** (+49) 421-78080
**Fax** (+49) 421-74066
**Email** mail@jaro.de
**Web** www.jaro.de

### Madredeus
**Web** www.madredeus.net
**Management** Antonio Cunha, União Lisboa, Casa Alvorada, Av. do Brasil 30, 2750-309 Cascais, Portugal.
**Phone** (+351) 21-4827-170
**Fax** (+351) 21-4827-174
**Email** antonio.cunha@gruporeuniao.pt
**Web** www.mind.pt/madredeus
**Record label** EMI-Valentim de Carvalho

### Amélia Muge
**Record label** Sony Portugal
(Also guests with Galician band Camerata Meiga, see above)

### Dulce Pontes
**Record label** Polydor/Universal

### Pedro Caldeira Cabral
**Record label** Network GmbH, Merianplatz 10, D-60316 Frankfurt, Germany
**Phone** (+49) 69-499-0040
**Fax** (+49) 69-499-0097
**Email** networkmedien@compuserve.com
**Web** www.networkmedien.de

### Galandum Galundaina
Fonte de Aldeia, 5210 Miranda do Douro, Portugal
**Phone** (+351) 933-426-1972
(+351) 931-924-507

### Realejo
**Agency** Ocarina (see above)
**Record label** Movieplay

*Multi-instrumental roots band*

### Gaiteiros de Lisboa
Ave Almirante Reis 70, 6° Esq.°
1150 Lisboa, Portugal
**Phone** (+351) 936-620-560
(+351) 931-218-369
**Fax** (+351) 1-814-7370
**Email** rui.vaz@ip.p
jsalg@clix.pt
**Management** O Grito, Praça da Igreja N° 18, 3°Dto. 2700 Lisboa, Portugal
**Phone** (+351) 1-49-32733
**Fax** (+351) 1-49-26613
**Agency** Ocarina (see above)
**Record label** Farol Música Ltda.

### Júlio Pereira
**Record label** Sony Portugal
**Representation** Vachier (see above)

### Brigada Victor Jara
Rua Eng., Canto Resende, 18
3030 Coimbra, Portugal
**Fax** (+351)-39-713-103
**Email** brigadavjara@mail.telepac.pt
**Agency** Ocarina (see above)
**Record label** Farol Música Ltda.

### Vai de Roda
R.Garcia de Orta 51
4435 Rio Tinto, Portugal
**Phone** (+351)-2-480-4311
**Record label** Alba

### Sergio Godinho
**Agent** Praça das Flores - Produção de Espectaculos, Lda
Rua da Imprensa Nacional 36
1250 Lisboa, Portugal
**Phone** (+351) 1-397-2389
**Fax** (+351) 1-397-2430
**Email** praca.das.flores@ip.pt
**Web** www.praca.das.flores.pt

*Much respected songwriter.*

# Azores

## Artists

### José Medeiros
**Agency** Ocarina (see above)

*Fine Azorean singer*

### Balada do Atlântico
**Agency** Ocarina (see above)

*Varied Azorean roots band - particularly interesting fiddler/vocalist*

european resources

## Madeira

### Organisations

**Almasud Records / Associação de Música Tradicional e Popular da Madeira**
João Maurício Marques
Apartado 677, 9008 Funchal
Madeira, Portugal
**Phone** (+351) 936-484-464
(+351) 936-989-964
**Email** almasud@almasud.com
jmarques@almasud.com
**Web** www.almasud.com

**Bis-Bis**
Gestão de Cultura, Lda.
R. Eng. Júlio Gomes da Silva 26-3º
2725 Algueirão, Portugal

### Artists

**Almma**
Record label & management Almasud (see above)
Agency Ocarina (see above)

## FRANCE

### Organisations

**French Music Bureau**
(Director Marie-Agnes Beau)
Institut Français, London
**Web** www.french-music.org
*Set up in 2001, "a joint venture between the French record industry and the French government, to put money and human resources behind French-based performers aiming to make an impact in Britain."*

### Magazines

**Trad Magazine**
BP 27, F-62350 Saint Venant, France
**Phone** (+33)-21-02-52-52
**Fax** (+33)-21-27-16-70
**Web** www.tradmagazine.com
*French roots & world music magazine*

**Musiques Traditionelles Rhône-Alpes**
(Editors Eric Montbel & Jean Blanchard)
Centre des Musiques Traditionelles Rhône-Alpes, 12, rue Gambetta
F-69190 Saint-Fons, France
**Phone** (+33) 4-78-70-81-75
**Fax** (+33) 4-78-70-81-85
**Email** cmtra@cmtra.org
**Web** www.cmtra.org
*Quarterly, covers both local music and incoming.*

### Record labels

**Auvidis**
47 av. P.Vaillant-Couturier
94250 Gentilly, France
**Phone** (+33)-(0)-1-46-15-88-00
**Fax** (+33)-(0)-1-47-40-36-85

**Ocora/Radio France**
116, avenue du président Kennedy
75016 Paris
**Phone** (+33)-(0)-1-42-30-15-45
**Fax** (+33)-(0)-1-42-30-49-49
Distributed by Harmonia Mundi

### Artists

**Marilis Orionaa**
**Record label** La Voce (address as Cinq Planètes, see below)

**Jean-François Vrod**
**Record label** Cinq Planètes, 10 rue Saint Sebastien, 75011 Paris
**Phone** (+33)-43-55-00-10
**Email** cinqpla@club-internet.fr
**Web** www.cinqplanetes.com

**Valentin Clastrier**
**Record label** Auvidis

**Gilles Chabenat**
**Record label** Ocora/AMTA

**Patrick Bouffard**
**Record label** Ackousteack, Boucherie Productions, 15bis, Rue du Plateau, F-75019 Paris
**Phone** (+33)-1-44-52-94-15

**Jean Blanchard**
Centre des Musiques Traditionelles Rhône-Alpes (see above)
Record labels Ocora, Auvidis/Silex (see above)

## Brittany

### Record labels

**Coop Breizh**
Kerangwen, 29540 Spezet, France
**Phone** (+33)-(0)-2-98-93-83-14
**Fax** (+33)-(0)-2-98-93-87-97
*Breizh distributes many Breton labels, including Escalibur, Gwerz Pladenn, and Arfolk, and also books*

**Keltia Musique**
1 Place au Beurre, 29000 Quimper
Breizh , France
**Phone** (+33)-2-9895-4582

### Artists

**Alan Stivell**
**Record label** Dreyfus

**Dan Ar Braz**
**Record label** Sony

**Bagad Kemper**
**Record label** Keltia (see above)

**Gwerz**
**Record label** Gwerz Pladenn (see above)

**Erik Marchand**
**Record label** Auvidis/Silex (see above)

**Jacky Molard**
Record label (with Archetype) Escalibur (see above)

**Patrick Molard**
Record label (with Jacky Molard in Triptyque, with Youenn Le Bihan and with Gwerz) Gwerz Pladenn, (with Pierre Crépillon & Laurent Bigot) Escalibur (see above)

**Lo'Jo**
**Record label** Emma Productions/Night & Day

**Orchestre National de Barbès**
Agency Samarkand, France
**Phone** (+33)-1-46-63-71-71
**Fax** (+33)-1-46-63-69-31
**Record label** Virgin France

**Manu Chao**
**Record label** Virgin France, Palm Pictures UK

## CORSICA

### Artists

**Donnisulana**
**Record label** Auvidis/Silex (see France above)

# ITALY

## Magazines

### FB - Folk Bulletin
**Editor** Roberto G. Sacchi
Cascina Pavarola 1, 27040 Borgo Priolo (PV), Italy
**Phone** (+39) (0) 0338-638-8859
(+39) (0) 0383-872-429
**Fax** (+39) (0) 0383-872-351
**Email** FB@docaware.it
**Web** www.docaware.it/FB

## Organisation/Agency/ Management

### EthnoSuoni
via Duomo 3, 15033 Casale Monferrato Al , Italy
**Phone** (+39)-(0)142-782182
**Fax** (+39)-(0)142-71389.
**Email** Ethno@Ethnosuoni.it, ethno@dialup.italnet.it

*Association devoted to the promotion of Italian traditional music. EthnoSuoni manages Italian roots bands such as B.E.V., Compagnons Roulants, Ensemble del Doppio Bordone, Epinfrai Lionetta, Tendach'nt and also produces an annual music festival, Folkermesse*

## Record labels

### CNI - Compagnia Nuove Indye
Via Luigi Luciani 7, 00197 Roma, Italy
**Phone** (+39) 06-326-511-77
**Fax** (+39) 06-3600-5827
(+39)-06-3265-6276
**Email** staff@cnimusic.it
cnimusic@alt.it
**Web** www.cnimusic.it

*Roots & new-roots bands Agricantus, Bagnoturco, Càlic, Novalia et al.*

### Robi Droli Records
Strada Roncaglia 16
15040 San Germano (AL), Italy
**Phone** (+39)-(0)142-50577
**Fax** (+39)-(0)142-50780
**Email** droli@inrete.alpcom.it
**Web** www.inrete.it/robidroli/home.html

# SARDINIA

## Artists

### Tenores de Bitti
**Record label** Real World (UK)
Try also Tenores de Oniferi (Kuntzertu records, UK dist. by Discovery)

### Elena Ledda
**Record label** Dunya

# MAINLAND ITALY

## Artists

### La Squadra
**Record label**
Buda Musique, 188 bd.Voltaire, 75011 Paris, France
**Fax** (+39) (0)1-40-24-04-27
**Email** buda@imaginet.fr
**Web** www.budamusique.com

### Spaccanapoli
**Record label** Real World (UK)
**Web** realworld.on.net

### Stefano Valla/Franco Guglielmetti
Both are also members of I Suonatori delle Quattro Province, & Valla is a member of La Squadra (see above)
**Record label** Robi Droli (see above)

### Riccardo Tesi
Skip Agency, Via Sivori 16/23
16136 Genova, Italy
**Phone** (+39) (0)10-272-45-88
**Fax** (+39) (0)10-21-98-57
**Email** skipagency@libero.it
**Record label** Dunya

### Re Niliu
**Record label** Pontesonoro

# GREECE

## Record labels

### Lyra/Kinisis/Misurgia Graeca
176 Alimou Ave. 16452 Athens, Greece
**Email** lyra@otenet.gr
**Web** www.lyra.gr
Distributed in UK by Trehantiri

### FM Records
7 Knossou str. 11146 Galatsi, Athens Greece
**Phone** (+30) (1) 222-2301/-3
(+30) (1) 213-0600/-6
**Fax** (+30) (1) 222-1603
**Email** fmrecord@acci.gr
**Web** www.acci.gr/~fmrecord

*Large catalogue of traditional and popular music. Also offices in Thessaloniki and Cyprus*

### Libra Music
26a Kersoundos str.
GR-157 71 Athens, Greece
**Phone** (+30) 1-7757-683
**Fax** (+30) 1-7750-119
**Email** libramusic@ath.forthnet.gr
**Web** www.forthnet.gr/libra-music

*CDs by Michalis Nikoloudis, Nor dar, Arto Tuncboyaciyan & Ara Dinkjian, Anastasia, Haig Yazdjian, Giorgos Maglaras et al.*
*One of the world's most comprehensive and helpful shops and mail order suppliers for Greek recordings, and a big range of Arabic too, is here in the UK*

### Trehantiri
365-367 Green Lanes, London N4 1DY
**Phone/Fax** (020)-8802-6530
**Email** email@trehantiri.com
**Web** www.trehantiri.com.

## Agencies/organisations

### Global Vision
Proussou 3 Zografou, 15773 Athens Greece
**Phone** (+30) (1) 748 0251
**Fax** (+30) (1) 778 8879
**Email** global@athens.mbn.gr
**Web** www.fora.gr/globalvision

## Artists

### Eleftheria Arvanitaki
**Web** www.arvanitaki.gr
**Record label** Mercury (PolyGram) Greece

### Ross Daly
Record labels Network Medien (Germany) (see above), Oriente Augustastrasse 20 B, D-12203 Berlin, Germany
**Phone** (+49)-30-833-6639
**Email** oriente@bln.de
**Web** www.oriente.de)

# BULGARIA

## Organisations

In Britain, the **Society for Friendship with Bulgaria** c/o Finsbury Library, 245 St. John Street, London EC1V 4NB
**Phone** 020 8837 2304 organises occasional concerts, and musical and dance trips to Bulgaria, including to the big National Folklore Festival in Koprivshtitsa, which happens every five years (the next should be in 2005)

## Artists

### Kalinka Vulcheva
**Record label** Offspring, PO Box 7028, Milton Keynes MK12 5ZH
**Phone** (01908) 542-894
**Fax** (01908) 225-5000
**Email** vivienne@offspringrecords.freeserve.co.uk

**Georgi Petrov**
Agent Jaro Medien GmbH, Bismarckstrasse 43, D-28203 Bremen, Germany.
**Phone** (+49) 421-78080
**Fax** (+49) 421-74066
**Email** mail@jaro.de
**Web** www.jaro.de

## HUNGARY

### Agencies and management

**Nikola Parov**
**Record label**
Hannibal, Rykodisc, 78 Stanley Gardens, London W3 7SZ,
**Email** rykoeuro@rykodisc.com
**Web** www.rykodisc.com

### Record labels

**Concert & Media / Kalaka International Folk Festival**
Csaba Lökös, Belgrád Rakpart 21
H-1056 Budapest, Hungary
**Phone** (+36)-1-266-8362
**Fax** (+36)-1-117-9228
**Mobile** (+36)-20-941-9930
**Email** conmedia@mail.matav.hu

**Fonó Records**
Sztregova utca 3, H-1116 Budapest
Hungary
**Phone** (+36)-1-203-1751
**Fax** (+36)-203-1752
**Web** www.fonorecords.hu
Also run the Fonó Music Hall.

**Etnofon Records**
Ferenc Kiss, Falk Miksa utca 16
1055 Budapest, Hungary
**Phone** (+36)-1-266-5091
**Fax** (+36)-1-429-0324
(+36)-1-266-5091
**Email** etnofon@mail.datanet.hu
**Web** www.w3.datanet.hu/~etnofon
Etnofon also has a shop and folk centre, at Dohány u.74, 1074 Budapest, tel/fax (+36-1)-351-3341

**Periferic Records/ Stereo Kft.**
Bartók Béla út 59, 1114 Budapest
Hungary
**Phone/Fax** (+36)-1-166-9674
(+36)-1-385-6343
**Email**
stereoperiferic@mail.datanet.hu
*A label and distribution organisation for several interesting labels, including releases by Vasmalom, Vujicsics and many more.*

**Hungaroton**
**Email** classic@mail.hungaroton.hu
**Web** www.hungaroton.hu
*Until post-communist changes Hungaroton was the only label in Hungary, and many fine traditional musicians recorded for it (as did Bulgarian musicians for their equivalent, Balkanton)*

### Artists

**Muzsikás/Marta Sebestyén**
Management Concert & Media (see above)
**Record label** Hannibal, Rykodisc, 78 Stanley Gardens, London W3 7SZ,
**Email** rykoeuro@rykodisc.com
**Web** www.rykodisc.com

**Vasmalom**
7 Dozsa St., 8419 Csesznek, Hungary
**Email** vasrgm@elender.hu

**Kati Szvorák**
Honvéd u.4, H-2009 Pilisszentlászló
Hungary
**Phone/Fax** (+36) 26-338-045
(+36) 26-392-224
**Email** szvorak@contarex.hu
**Web** www.contarex.hu/szvorak
**Record label** Etnofon (see above)

**Ghymes**
Monique Agency / Ghymes Group
Svätoplukova 1, 903 01 Senec
Slovakia
**Phone/Fax** (+42)-1-7-923-872
**Record label** Fonó (see above), Hungaroton (see above)

**Lantos Banda**
**Record label** Mélodie, France
**Web** www.melodie.fr

**Gereben**
**Record label** Pan Records, PO Box 155, 2300 AD Leiden, Netherlands,
**Phone** (+31-71)-521-9479
**Fax** (+31-71)-522-6869
**Email** paradox@dataweb.nl

**Vízöntö**
Budai Laszlo 14, 1024 Budapest, Hungary
**Phone/Fax** (+36) 1-316-9173
**Record label** Felmay/Dunya (see Robi Droli, Italy, above)

**Ökrös Ensemble**
Management Kálmán Magyar at Centrum Management
US agent Concerted Efforts Inc.
**Phone** (+1)-617-969-0810
**Email**
concerted@concertedefforts.com
**Web** www.concertedefforts.com
**Record label** Rounder (USA)
*Transylvanian village music from Gypsy Hungarian and Romanian traditions*

## MACEDONIA

### Artists

**Vujicsics**
Bogdányi u. 40, H-2000 Szentendre
Hungary
**Fax** (+36)-26-325-734
**Record label** e-Disc, distributed by Stereo Kft, (see above)
*Long-established band from the Serbo-Croatian minority in Hungary, often collaborating with Márta Sebestyén*

**dd Synthesis**
**Web** www.ddsynthesis.com.mk
**Management/label** Oliver Belopeta
Skopje Jazz Festival / SJF Records
Maksim Gorki 5, MAC-91000 Skopje
Republic of Macedonia
**Phone** (+389)-91-131-090
**Fax** (+389)-91-225-033
**Email** sjf@unet.com.mk
**Web** www.skopjejazzfest.com.mk
*Impressive evolutionary Macedonian roots ensemble with gaida, kaval, zurla, piano, trad percussion, three female singers.*

## SERBIA

Many interesting roots developments in Serbia are showcased on the CD Srbija Sounds Global, put together by Belgrade's Radio B92
**Contact** K.V.S./FreeB92, Svetozara Markovica 79, 11000 Beograd, Serbia,
Yugoslavia.
**Phone/Fax** (+381)-11-361-96-68
**Web** www.freeb92.net
It gives band and agency contacts in the booklet notes, too.

### Agencies

**Ring Ring Promotions**
Bogdan Djordjevic, Stojana Aralice 6/19, 11077 Belgrade
Yugoslavia
**Phone/Fax** (+381)-11-454-255
**Email** ringring@ptt.yu
**Web** www.cyberrex.org/ringring

**Take It Or Leave It**
Beograd (Belgrade), Yugoslavia
**Email** tioli@infosky.net

**Goran Bregovic**
**Record label** Zic-Zac/RCA Victor
**Web** www.bmg-poland.com.pl
**Management** Grzegorz Brzozowicz

### Artists

**Ognjen I Prijatelji**
**Phone** (+381)-13-43-183
*Clarinetist with band*

### Lajko Felix
**Phone** (+381)-24-22-962
*Influential violinist and sometimes zitherist, with various collaborations including with Boban Markovic's band*

### Boban Markovic Orkestar
**Agent** Ring Ring (see above)
*Gypsy brass band*

### Orkestar Milovana Mice Petrovica
**Agent** Take It Or Leave It (see above)
*Non-Gypsy village brass band*

### Drina
**Agent** Ring Ring (see above)
*Urban group finding and performing traditional songs.*

### Darko Macura
**Email** drina@eunet.yu
*Traditional multi-instrumentalist*

### Dragoslav Pavle Aksentijevic
**Phone** (+381)-11-184-206
*Singer*

### LaDaABa Orchest
**Agent** Ring Ring (see above)
*Band of clarinet, sax, accordion, bass, percussion.*

## CROATIA
### *Organisation*

### Croatian Musicians' Union
Zagreb, Croatia
**Email** mojimir.novakovic@st.tel.hr

## SLOVENIA
### *Record labels*

### Sraka International
Valanticevo 17, 68000 Novo Mesto
Slovenia
**Phone** (+386)-68-23-174
**Phone/Fax** (+386)-68-24-094

## ALBANIA
### *Artists*

### Ensemble Tirana
Agency Itinérance, 52 Rue Letort, 75018 Paris
**Phone** (+33)-(01)-42-54-78-33
**Fax** (+33)-(01)-42-23-92-57
**Email** soavi@club-internet.fr
**Record label** Iris Musique, 5 Passage Saint-Sébastien, 75011 Paris
**Email** iris@mservices.com
**Web** www.mservices.com/iris, distributed by Harmonia Mundi.

## CZECH REPUBLIC
### *Record label*

### Gnosis Brno
Rezkova 30, 602 00 Brno, Czech Republic
**Phone** (+420)-5-339-086
**Fax** (+420)-5-4321-5463
**Email** plocek@iach.cz
**Web** www.mujweb.cz/www/gnosis_brno
*Concentrates largely on music from Moravia. Label boss Jirí Plocek is also a very good bluegrass mandolinist in the band Teagrass (remember, the Dobro is a Czech invention!) which has recently, to surprisingly non-gross effect, combined bluegrass with traditional Moravian songs.*

## POLAND
### *Record labels*

### Polskie Radio S.A.
Kleszcz Wlodzimierz
Folk Radio Centre
Al. Niepodlegtosci 77/85
00-977 Warszawa, Poland
**Phone** (+48-22)-645-58-52
**Fax** (+48-22)-645-39-85
**Email** ludowa@radio.com.pl.

### Kamahuk World Music
**Web** www.soundpol.com
*Source of the excellent Pofolkuj Sobie! sampler CD of movers and shakers in new Polish roots music.*

### Orange World
ul. Wierzbowa 30/4, 81-558 Gdynia Poland
**Phone/Fax** (+48)-58-664-9966
**Email** orange@orange.com.pl
**Web** www.orange.com.pl
*Label and distributor supplying over 3000 titles of Polish and world music. Newsletter & radio programme too.*

### *Artists*

### Kayah
Management Impress Jot, Poland
**Record label** Zic-Zac/RCA Victor
**Web** www.bmg-poland.com.pl

### Orkiestra p.w. sw. Mikolaja (St.Nicholas Orchestra)
ACK UMCS "Chatka Zaka",
ul. Radziszewskiego 16,
20-031 Lublin, Poland
**Phone/Fax** (+48)-81-533-32-01 ext.114
**Fax** (+48)-81-537-51-02
(+48)-81-533-36-69
**Email** mikolaje@klio.umcs.lublin.pl
**Web** www.mikolaje.lublin.pl

### Trebunie Tutki
**Manager** Hanna Houszka
Gersona str.41/6
51-664 Wroclaw, Poland
**Phone/Fax** (+48)-71-345-1936

## RUSSIA
### *Artists*

### Farlanders / Inna Zhelannaya / Sergey Starostin
**Agent** Jaro Medien GmbH, Bismarckstrasse 43, D-28203 Bremen, Germany.
**Phone** (+49)-421-78080
**Fax** (+49)-421-74066
**Email** mail@jaro.de
**Web** www.jaro.de
**Contact** Greenwave International Prospect Vernadskogo 29, Suite 1901 RUS-117331 Moscow, Russia.
**Phone** (+7)-0951-382-874
**Fax** (+7)-0951-313-901
**Email** cheparukhin@greenwave.polus.ru

## GYPSY MUSIC from various countries
### *Agencies and management*

### Asphalt Tango Production
Fehrbelliner Strasse 24
D-10119 Berlin, Germany
**Phone** (+49)-30-2858528,
**Fax** (+49)-30-2858512
**Email** agency@asphalt-tango.de
**Web** www.asphalt-tango.de
*Agency and management company specialising in Gypsy music from Europe. Represents Fanfare Ciocarlia (Romania) worldwide, Rom Bengale (Romania) worldwide, Yuri Yunakov (Bulgaria) in Europe & Asia, Esma Redzepova (Macedonia) in Germany/Austria/Switzerland/ Canada & Asia, Kocani Orkestar (Macedonia) in Germany & Austria, Tekameli (France) in Germany & Austria.*

### *Artists*

### Vèra Bílá & Kale
**Manager** Jiri Smetana
Vinohradska 168, CZ-1300 Prague 3
Czech Republic
**Phone/Fax** (+42)-27-173-35-67

### Kálmán Balogh
**Record labels** Fonó, Hungary (see above), Rounder (USA)
**US agent** Concerted Efforts (see above for Ökrös Ensemble)

### Taraf de Haïdouks
**Record label** Crammed Discs

### Fanfare Ciocarlia
**Agency** Asphalt Tango (see above)
**Record label** Piranha, Germany (see above)

### Esma Redzepova
**Record label** World Connection, Schermerstraat 9 Rood, NL-2013 EP Haarlem, Netherlands
**Phone** (+31)-23-551-0854
**Fax** (+31)-23-551-0856
**Email** albert.nijmolen@capitolonline.nl

## KLEZMER
### Artists

### Kroke
**Record label** Oriente Musik, Germany,
**Phone** (+49)-30-833-66-39
(+49)-312-40-27
**Fax** (+49)-30-84-30-61-46
**Email** oriente@bln.de
**Web** www.oriente.de

## GERMANY
### Magazines

### Folker!
Postfach 1269, D-53582 Bad Honnef Germany
**Phone** (+49)-2224-76510
**Fax** (+49)-2224-71464
**Email** info@folker.de
**Web** www.folker.de

### Agencies

### Profolk
Rathausstrasse 9, D-10178 Berlin Germany
**Phone** (+49)-30-2472-2145
**Fax** (+49)-30-2472-1875
**Email** kontor@PROFOLK.de
**Web** www.PROFOLK.de

### Concert Idee
**Phone/Fax** (+49)-30-4-42-80-14

### Music Contact/ Akku Disk
Rainer Zellner, Saarstr. 8
D-72070 Tübingen, Germany
**Phone** (+49)-70-73-2250
**Fax** (+49)-70-73-2134
**Email** zellner@musiccontact.com
music.contact@real-net.de
**Web** musiccontact.com
*Mostly bringing foreign performers to Germany, but contact for Hoelderlin Express et al.*

### Artists

### Schäl Sick Brass Band
**Contact & record company** ACT Music + Vision, Seewiesstraße 1
D-82340 Feldafing, Germany
**Fax** (+49)-8157-922639
**Web** www.actmusic.com

### Hundsbuam Miserablige
**Record label** BMG/Lawine, Germany

### Hoelderlin Express
**Agency** Music Contact (see above)

## AUSTRIA
### Magazines

### Folkladen
Neustiflg. 1C, A-1070 Wien, Austria
**Phone/Fax** (+43)-(1)-522-37-27
**Email** othmar@folkladen.com

### Artists

### Wiener Tschuschenkapelle
Klimschgasse 20/5, A-1030 Wien Austria
**Phone/Fax** (+43)-(1)-714-74-86
**Email** wtkp@ins.at
**Web** www.tschuschenkapelle.at

## FINLAND
### Organisations

### Finnish Music Information Centre
Lauttasaarentie 1, FIN-00200 Helsinki Finland
**Phone** (+358)-(0)9-681-01-313
**Fax** (+358)-(0)9-682-07-70
**Email** info@mic.teosto.fi
**Web** www.fimic.fi
*Heavily involved with encouraging export of Finnish folk music, as well as other Finnish musics. Publishes annually Arctic Paradise, a CD sampler of Finnish roots music recordings and companion book, in English, containing artist information and label and organisation contacts.*

### The Folk Arts Centre
(Kansantaiteenkeskus)
PL 11, FIN-69601 Kaustinen, Finland
**Phone** (+358)-(0)-6-860-4111
**Fax** (+358)-(0)-6-860-4222
**Email** folk.art@kaustinen.inet.fi
*The high-tech national folk arts centre isn't in the capital, but in west central Finland in a rural area famous for its fiddlers and kantele players and its big folk music festival. the Centre houses the national Folk Music Institute (Kansanmusiikki-instituutti), the offices of Kaustinen International Folk Music Festival, a concert hall, recording studio, instrument collection, rehearsal spaces, shop, cafeteria etc.*

### Finland-Swedish Folk Music Institute
(Finlands Svenska Folkmusikinstitutet)
Handelsesplanaden 23 A
FIN-65100 Vaasa, Finland
**Phone** (+358)-6-324-2232
**Fax** (+358)-6-324-2209
**Email** fmi@vyi.fi

### Publications and magazines

### Friiti
Published by the Folk Music Institute
**Address** as Folk Arts Centre, see above.
*6 issues p.a. Covers Finnish traditional and new-roots and some world music, sometimes including compilation CD of new and pre-release Finnish roots recordings.*

### Arctic Paradise
See above, under Finnish Music Information Centre

### Agencies

### Hoedown
Phillip Page, Laivurinrinne 2
FIN-00120 Helsinki, Finland
**Phone** (+358) (0)9-666-375
**Fax** (+358) (0)9-628950
**Email** pap@hoedown.com
**Web** www.hoedown.com
*Agent/manager for Värttinä, JPP, Kimmo Pohjonen, Troka, Maria Kalaniemi. Laivurinrinne 2 is also the address of Digelius Music, a very well-stocked emporium of recordings from Norden and the world; it also sells mail order and via its English-language website.*
**Web** www.digelius.com

### RockAdillo
Tapio Korjus, Ilmarisenkatu 12 A 2
FIN-33500 Tampere, Finland
**Phone** (+358) (0)3-213-1260
**Fax** (+358) (0)3-213-1297
**Email** records@rock.pp.fi
*Record company and agent/manager for Wimme, Piirpauke, Slobo Horo.*

### Akombi
Susanna Salokannel, Hulluksentie 5 B 6, FIN-02430 Masala, Finland
**Phone/Fax** (+358)-9-298-0608
**Email** susanna.salokannel.akombi@kolumbus.fi
*Agent for Anna-Kaisa Liedes, Heikki Laitinen, Me Naiset, Helsinki Melodeon Ladies*

## Record labels

As with other countries, I'm just including those for which the listed artists record; for others see Arctic Paradise

### Kansanmusiikki-instituutti (Folk Music Institute)
(See above)

### RockAdillo
(See above)

### Olarin Musiikki
PO Box 20, FIN-00211 Espoo Finland
**Phone** (+358)-9-881-3227
**Fax** (+358)-9-804-3469

### NorthSide
530 North 3rd Street, Suite 230
Minneapolis, MN 55401, USA
**Phone** (+1) 612-375-0233
**Fax** (+1) 612-375-9580
**Email** chill@noside.com
**Web** www.noside.com
*Label specialising in licensed-release of leading Nordic roots albums in N.America. Also runs Nordic Roots festival in Minneapolis and books tours for the artists. Newsletter via email, and useful website.*

## Artists

### Kimmo Pohjonen
**Agency/management** Hoedown (see above)
**Record label** RockAdillo (see above)

### Värttinä
**Agency/management** Hoedown (see above)
**Record label** Wicklow (BMG)

### JPP
**Agency/management** Hoedown (see above)
**Record label** RockAdillo (NorthSide in US - see above)

### Maria Kalaniemi
**Agency/management** Hoedown (see above)
**Record label** RockAdillo (NorthSide in US - see above)

### Gjallarhorn
**Email** info@gjallarhorn.com
**Web** www.gjallarhorn.com
**Bookings** Martin Kantola, Lilltået 20, 65630 Karperö, Finland
**Phone** (+358)-500-564-858
**Fax** (+358)-6-359-1588
**Email** martin@gjallarhorn.com
**Record label** Ranarop, distributed by MNW, PO Box 845, 33101 Tampere, Finland
**Fax** (+358)-3-38-99-336
**Email** sami.juntunen@mnw.fi.
In US NorthSide (see above)

### Minna Raskinen
Keski-Pohjanmaan Konservatorio
Pitkänsillankatu 16
FIN-67100 Kokkola, Finland
**Phone** (+358)-6-831-5177
**Fax** (+358)-6-831-5386
**Email** minna.raskinen@cop.fi
**Record label** Olarin (see above)

### Anna-Kaisa Liedes
**Agency/management** Akombi (see above)
**Record label** Olarin (see above); Riverboat (UK)

### Hannu Saha
Folk Arts Centre, Kaustinen (see above)
**Record label** Folk Music Institute (see above)

### Heikki Laitinen
**Agency/management** Akombi (see above)
**Record label** HecRec

### Tallari
Folk Arts Centre, Kaustinen (see above)
**Record label** Folk Music Institute (see above)

### Sanna Kurki-Suonio
**Record label** Zen Garden, PO Box 76, FIN-00501 Helsinki
**Web** www.zengarden.fi

### Tellu
**Record label** Folk Music Institute (see above)

### Ottoset
Pirjo Palosaari-Penttilä
PL 47, FIN-69601 Kaustinen, Finland
**Phone** (+358)-40-504-6076
**Fax** (+358)-6-8612-363
**Email** pirjopa@kaustinen.kpnet.fi
*Remarkable young dance group, taking folk dance into new creative areas, with its own bands*

# SWEDEN

## Magazines

### Lira
Box 367, S-791 28 Falun, Sweden
**Phone** (+46)-23-63377
**Fax** (+46)-23--63388
**Email** lira@lira.se
*Swedish and world music magazine*

### Folklore Centrum
Izzy Young, Wollmar Yxkullsgatan 2
S-118 50 Stockholm, Sweden
**Phone/Fax** (+46)-8-643-46-27
*Small magazine with listings and ads for traditional and roots music events.*

## Conferences/trade fairs

### Nordic Lights (Norrsken)
c/o Falun Folkmusik Festival
Box 387, S-791 28 Falun, Sweden
**Phone** (+46)-23-383-90
**Fax** (+46)-23-83314
**Email** festivalen@falufolk.falun.se
**Web** www.falufolk.com
Annual conference/trade fair devoted to seminars, showcasing and networking of Nordic-rooted music from all the Nordic countries.

## Organisations

### Svenska Rikskonserter - the Swedish Concert Institute
Sten Sandahl, Nybrokajen 11
S-111 48 Stockholm, Sweden
**Phone** (+46)-8-407-1651
**Fax** (+46)-8-407-1648
**Email** sten.sandahl@srk.se
*For all music in Sweden, but strong support of roots music at home and abroad, including release of Folk Acts Sweden boxes of compilation CDs from the various labels. Runs Swedish and world music record label Caprice.*

### RFoD - Riksföreningen för Folkmusik och Dans
**(The Swedish Folkmusic and Dance Assn.)**
Lars Farago, Nybrokajen 11
S-111 48 Stockholm, Sweden
**Phone** (+46)-8-407-1732
**Fax** (+46)-8-407-1650
**Email** rfod@srk.se

## Eric Sahlströminstitutet
Bruksgatan 3, S-748 50 Tobo
Sweden
**Phone** (+46)-295-342-90
**Fax** (+46)-342-99
**Email** esitobo@algonet.se
*Sweden's first folk music institute. Opened 1998*

### Agencies and management

## Kario Kultur
Irma Kario, Brännkyrkagatan 41
S-118 22 Stockholm, Sweden
**Phone/Fax** (+46)-08-462-02-80
**Email** kario@bahnhof.se
*Management of Frifot and Ale Möller's Stockholm Folk Big Band.*

## KonTur (Kontaktnätet Turnéproduktion AB)
Hans Hjorth, Box 499, 701 49 Örebro
Sweden
**Phone** (+46)-70-59-242-59
**Fax** (+46)-70-610-42-59
**Email** hans.hjorth@kontur.se

## D-Tours
Ken Day, Box 67,
S-812 03 Kungsgården, Sweden
**Phone** (+46)-290-37082
**Fax** (+46)-290-37083
**Email** ken.day@ebox.tninet.se
**Web** www.dtours.org
*Agent for world music, with some Swedish, including Hoven Droven, Triakel.*

### Record labels

## Drone Music AB
Petterslundsgatan 11 A
S-753 28 Uppsala, Sweden
**Phone** (+46) 18 129 466
**Fax** (+46) 706 159 641
**Email** olle.paulsson@drone.se
**Web** www.drone.se
*Drone is also the contact for Folknet Sweden (***Web** *www.folknetsweden), a marketing collaboration between several independent labels involved in Swedish roots music*

## Giga records
Borsheden, Box 1107,
S-780 40 Mockfjärd, Sweden
**Phone** (+46) 241-20940
(+46) 241-200-80
**Fax** (+46) 241-210-70.
**Email** giga.folkmusik@giga.w.se
**Web** www.giga.w.se
*Respected label devoted to the leading players, past and present, of traditional music, largely unaccompanied solo or duetting fiddlers.*

## Xource / MNW
MNW Records Group
**Phone** (+46) 8-630-36-44
**Fax** (+46) 8-630-36-01
**Email** xource@mnw.se
**Web** www.mnw.se

## Amigo
Box 4113, S-102 62 Stockholm
Sweden
**Fax** (+46)-8-55-69-69-89
**Email** hq@amigo.se
**Web** www.amigo.se

### Artists

## Frifot (Ale Möller, Lena Willemark, Per Gudmundson)
Management Kario Kultur (see above)
**Record label** ECM, Postfach 600 331, 81203 München, Germany
**Web** www.ecmrecords.com

## Groupa
Rickard Åström, Uddevallaplatsen 16
S-416 70 Göteborg, Sweden
**Phone/Fax** (+46)-31-21-60-64
**Record label** Xource (see above); NorthSide in US (see above)

## Hedningarna
Visionen, Svärdsjögatan 13
S-791 31 Falun, Sweden
Tel/fax (+46)-23-278-60
Visionen is also contact for Boot.
**Management** for Hedningarna
Ulf Andersson, DMR, Sten Stureg. 8,
S-411 39 Göteborg, Sweden
**Phone** (+46)-31-16-57-75
(+46)-31-18-96-76
**Record label** Xource (see above); in US NorthSide (see above under Finland)

## Garmarna
**Email**
garmarna@massproduktion.y.se
**Management** Hans Hjorth - KonTur (see above)
**Record label** MNW (see above); in US NorthSide (see above under Finland)

## Väsen
**Management** Uno Hendrixon
Performing Arts Productions
St Eriksgatan 11, S-112 39
Stockholm
Sweden
**Phone** (+46)-8-651-02-65
**Fax** (+46)-8-709-220-416
**Email** uno@pap.a.se
**Record label** Xource (see above); in US NorthSide (see above under Finland)

## SWÅP
**Email** karen@kstweed.co.uk
**Web** www.cutting-tweed.demon.co.uk
**Record label** Amigo (see above); in US NorthSide (see above under Finland)

## Hurv
**Record label** Amigo (see above); in US NorthSide (see above under Finland)
*Powerful bowed-string duo of Magnus Stinnerbom & Daniel Sandén-Warg*

## Björn Ståbi & Kalle Almlöf
**Record label** Giga (see above)
*Two of the duetting great fiddlers.*

## Toxa
**Record label** Drone (see above)
*Tight fiddles & guitar trio*

## Nyckelharpa Orchestra
**Record label** Drone (see above); in US NorthSide (see above under Finland)
*Awesome wall of intricate keyed fiddle sound.*

# NORWAY

### Publications and magazines

## Folknett Norway - The Guide to Norwegian Folk Music
Jointly published in the late 1990s by the Norwegian record labels connected with folk music, this was a one-off but still useful free English-language introduction to the musics and artists, with contacts for labels, festivals and organisations and a discography. Should still be available (and its companion CD sampler) from record distributor **Musikkoperatørene**, Skippergata 28, N-0154 Oslo
**Phone** (+47)-22-33-03-09
**Fax** (+47)-22-41-2041
**Email** musikkop@notam.uio.no,
*or contact* **FONO**, the Norwegian Independent Record Producers' Association, Major Studio, P.b. 5949 Majorstua, N-0308 Oslo
**Phone** (+47)-22-46-22-99,
**Fax** (+47)-22-60-07-89
**Email** fono@online.no
**Web** www.fono.no/folknettnorway.

european resources

### Spelemannsbladet

Hellandstunet, N-3800 Bø-i-Telemark, Norway
**Phone** (+47)-35-06-15-45
**Fax** (+47)-06-15-46)
**Email** spelemannsbladet@folke musikk.no
**Web** www.folkemusikk.no

*The main Norwegian roots magazine, covering traditional and some new-roots. Published by LfS (see below). 8 issues p.a.*

## Organisations

### Landslaget for Spelemenn (LfS)

Tollbugata 28, N-0157 Oslo, Norway
**Phone** (+47)-22-42-45-30
**Fax** (+47)-22-42-55-07
**Email** lfs@folkemusikk.no
**Web** www.folkemusikk.no

*The national association of fiddle players, with about 150 member organisations. Run the annual Landskappleik, the national contest for traditional musicians and folk dance festival. Publishes Spelemannsbladet (see above)*

### NFD - Norsk Folkemusikk og Danselag - Norwegian Folk Music Association

Same address as LfS, above.
**Phone** (+47)-22-42-02-94
**Fax** (+47)-22-42-32-08
**Email** nfd@folkogdans.no
**Web** www.folkogdans.no

*Arranges concerts, courses, presents annual award to promising young performers & their teachers. Publishes Yearbook of Norwegian Folk Music & members' publication Kvinten. In process of founding Norwegian Folk Music Agency.*

### Rikskonsertene (The Norwegian Concert Institute)

Postbox 2835 Solli, N-0204 Oslo Norway
**Phone** (+47)-22-83-83-50
**Fax** (+47)-22-83-16-10
**Email** kari.diesen@rikskonsertene.no
**Web** www.rikskonsertene.no

*Government institution, under Ministry of Cultural Affairs. Produces concerts & organises promotional activities & provides economic support.*

### RFF - Rådet for folkemusikk og folkedans

RFF-sentret, N-7055 Dragvoll, Norway
**Phone** (+47)-73-59-65-76
**Fax** (+47)-73-59-65-73
**Email** bjorn.aksdal@hf.ntnu.no
**Web** www.hf.ntnu.no/rff

*Public foundation subsidised by Ministry of Cultural Affairs. Assists in relation to performers and government funding of Norwegian folk music, and is an advisory body to the Ministry.*

### Norwegian Music Information Centre

Same address as LfS and NFD above.
**Phone** (+47)-2242-9090
**Fax** (+47)-2242-9091
**Email** nmic@notam.uio.no
**Web** www.notam.uio.no/nmi

### Ole Bull Akademiet

Boks 443, N-5701 Voss, Norway
**Phone** (+47)-56-51-65-00
**Fax** (+47)-56-51-48-63
**Email** ole.bull@voss.online.no

*Traditional music school offering courses up to 2 years long in fiddling and singing taught by many leading folk music performers.*

## Agents and management

### PJP

Pål Gjersum, Boks 176, N-5601 Voss Norway
**Phone** (+47)-56-51-67-00
**Fax** (+47)-56-51-67-01
**Email** pjpaal@online.no

## Record labels

### Kirkelig Kulturverksted

**Phone** (+47)-22-99-34-60
**Fax** (+47)-22-99-34-51
**Email** kkv@kkv.no
**Web** www.kkv.no

### Grappa

Akersgata 7, 0158 Oslo
**Phone** (+47)-22-41-24-00
**Fax** (+47)-22-41-55-52
**Email** info@grappa.no

*Grappa also handles traditional label Heilo*

### NOR-CD

Kongens gate 16, N-0153 Oslo, Norway
**Phone** (+47)-22-33-41-44
**Fax** (+47)-22-33-41-43
**Email** norcd@online.no
**Web** home.sol.no/~norcd

## Artists

### Utla

Utla's Karl Seglem runs NOR-CD records (see above)

### Annbjørg Lien

**Record label** Grappa (see above); in US NorthSide (see above under Finland)

### Susanne Lundeng

**Agent** PJP (see above)
**Record label** Kirkelig Kulturverksted (see above)

### Knut Reiersrud / Iver Kleive

**Agent** PJP (see above)
**Email** pjpaal@online.no
**Record label** Kirkelig Kulturverksted (see above)

### Farmers Market

N-2074 Eidsvold Verk, Norway
**Phone/Fax** (+47)-63-95-14-65
**Record label** Winter & Winter (UK dist. by Harmonia Mundi)

### Knut Buen

Buen Kulturverkstad, N-3697 Tuddal Norway
**Phone/Fax** (+47)-35-02-40-15
**Record label** Buen Kuturverksted

*Famous player of hardingfele*

### Hallvard T. Bjørgum

Sylvartun, Nomeland, N-4692 Rysstad, Setesdal, Norway
**Phone** (+47)-37-93-63-06
**Fax** (+47)-37-93-63-05
**Email** hal-bjoe@online.no
**Record label** Sylvartun

*Another famous hardingfele player*

### Fliflet/Hamre

Gabriel Fliflet, Lahrmsteiner Elite records, Skjoldstølen 56, N-5236 Rådal, Norway
**Phone** (+47)-55-13-62-41
**Record label** Lahrmsteiner Elite

*Extraordinary and witty accordion/drums duo*

# DENMARK

## Magazines

### Folk & Musik - Folkemusik i Danmark

Folkemusikkens Fælles Sekretariat Graven 25 A, DK-8000 Århus C Denmark
**Phone** (+45)-86-76-11-41
**Fax** (+45)-86-76-11-47

*6 issues p.a.*

### Organisations

**Folkemusikkens Fælles Sekretariat - The Danish Folk Council**
Graven 25 A, DK-8000 Århus C
Denmark
**Phone** (+45)-86-76-11-41
**Fax** (+45)-86-76-11-47
**Email** ffs@folkmusik.dk
**Web** www.folkemusik.dk

*FFS formed in 1994 as a result of collaboration between Danish Music Council & the 3 national folk organisations. It's very active in promoting the whole range of Danish roots music, and is responsible in association with MXP (Danish Music Export & Promotion,* **Web** *www.mxp.dk) for the very useful annual Folk Music From Denmark compilation CD packages, which give contact information for the featured bands, agencies and record companies.*

### Agencies

**Roots Music Agency**
Christiansgade 29, 1tv
DK-8000 Århus C, Denmark
**Phone** (+45)-86-18-53-03
**Fax** (+45)-86-18-53-73
**Email** office@rootsmusicagency.com
**Web** www.rootsmusicagency.com

### Record labels

**Go' Danish Folk Music Distribution**
Ribe Landevej 190
DK-7100 Vejle, Denmark
**Phone** (+45)-75-72-24-86,
**Fax** (+45)-75-72-24-85
**Email** go@folkmusic.dk
**Web** www.folkmusic.dk

*For all Danish folk releases. Now a label too, with Haugaard & Høirup, Lang Linken, Phønix, Fenja Menja et al*

**Tutl Records**
Reynagøta 12, FR-100 Tórshavn,
Faroe Islands
**Phone** (+298)-14815
**Fax** (+298)-14825
**Email** tutl@olivant.fo
**Web** www.tutl.com

*The main Faroese label, owned by Kristian Blak, jazz and classical keyboardist, member of folk band Spælimenninir, and the main connection for things musical in the Faroes.*

### Artists

**Sorten Muld**
**Web** www.sortenmuld.dk
**Agency** Roots Music (see above)
**Record label** Pladecompagniet/Sony, **Phone** (+45)-33-76-03-00
**Fax** (+45)-33-76-03-33
**Web** www.sonymusic.dk

**Serras**
**Web** www.serras.dk
**Agency** Danartist
**Phone** (+45)-40-19-94-41
**Fax** (+45)-66-14-30-13
**Email** mail@danartist.dk
**Record label** Go' Danish (see above)

**Haugaard & Høirup**
**Agency** Roots Music (see above)
**Record label** Go'Danish (see above)

**Lang Linken**
CE Musik, Høgsholtvej 1
DK-5690 Tommerup, Denmark
**Phone** (+45)-64-76-17-34
**Email** carlerik@mail.dk
**Web** www.langlinken.dk
**Record label** Go'Danish (see above)

## ESTONIA

### Artists

**Kirile Loo**
**Record label** Erdenklang, In Der Habbecke 18, 59889 Eslohe, Germany

## LATVIA

### Record label

**UPE Recording Company**
Skanstes iela 13, Riga LV-1013
Latvia
**Phone** (+371)-7-362-222
**Fax** (+371)-7-821-457
**Email** upe@radioswh.lv
**Web** www.upe.parks.lv

### Artists

**Ilgi**
**Record label** Upe (see above)

## SÁMILAND

### Record labels

**DAT**
Pb 31, N-9520 Guovdageaidnu / Kautokeino, Norway
**Phone** (+47)-78-48-67-72
(+47) 91 79 25 26
**Fax** (+47) 78-48-67-88
**Email** dat@dat.net
**Web** www.dat.net

**Idut Records**
Iggaldas, N-9710 Indre Billefjord
Norway
**Phone** (+47)-78-46-47-49
**Fax** (+47) 78-46-47-67

### Artists

**Mari Boine**
**Agency** PJP (see above under Norway)

**Wimme**
**Agency** RockAdillo (see above under Finland)
**Record label** RockAdillo (in US NorthSide)

**Angelit**
**Management** Blue Buddha, Box 40, Tallberginkatu 1, FIN-00180 Helsinki, Finland
**Phone** (+358)-9-68-59-32-21
**Fax** (+358)-9-68-59-32-24
**Email** possi@kaktus.pp.fi
**Record label** Warner Finlandia Innovator, PO Box 169, Länsituulentie 1 A, 02101 Espoo, Finland,
**Phone** (+358)-(0)9-435-011
**Fax** (+358)-9-455-2352.

**Transjoik**
**Record label** Atrium
**Email** atrium@warnermusic.se

**Ulla Pirttijärvi**
**Record label** Atrium

**Jienat**
Postboks 65, 9615 Hammerfest
Norway
**Web** www.jienat.com

# French Music and Dance in the UK By Ayla Bedri

If you went to a ceilidh in the 1980s featuring top Eurodance band Blowzabella, as well as the Dorset 5-hand reel and the Stoke Golding Country Dance, you would have found yourself dancing a bourrée or a laridé. For many people, this band was the first to introduce them to the then, largely unfamiliar dances and music from France and Brittany. Founder members of Blowzabella had started out studying early music instrument-making and had gone on to discover the still rich tradition of bagpipe and hurdy-gurdy playing in Central France. They began teaching the dances they picked up, during their ceilidhs, as well as at their annual workshop weekends, to which they also invited French bands to play and teach.

When Blowzabella split up in the early 1990s, many people had already caught the French dancing bug, seduced by the all-night dancing found at French festivals and the infectious rhythms of the hurdy-gurdy and bagpipes. The workshop weekends, featuring authentic French and Breton bands, were carried on by the Hot Springs organisation in Bath, whose Grand Bal de Bath became a regular annual fixture in the UK French dancing calendar.

In March 1994, the monthly club On Bouge was set up by a group of London-based French music and dancing enthusiasts, with the aim of having somewhere to play and dance on a regular basis. Since then, the UK French music scene has gone from strength to strength. There are now regular French dance and music clubs and sessions up and down the country; major festivals like Sidmouth, consistently book French bands as well as running dance and music workshops, and if you go to a dance with the re-formed Blowzabella, you will find yourself dancing more French and European dances than English ones!

For people interested in getting more involved in French music and dancing there is now more opportunity than ever. Several regular events take place throughout the year and are a good starting point, featuring music and dance workshops as well as the chance to dance and listen to French bands.

**In the UK:**
**Folkbeat Weekend in Derby** (March)
**Contact** Chapel Lunch Productions,
**Phone** 01332 677046
**Fax** 01332 677047
**Email** Fiona@chapel-lunch.co.uk,
**Web** www.cutting-tweed.demon.co.uk/index.htm

**Thoresby Fest-Noz** (June)
**Email** arts@nottscc.gov.uk
**Web** www.nottscc.gov.uk/ARTS/INDEX.htm

**Yorkshire Dales Workshops**
(throughout the year - often do workshop weekends on Euro-dance and music styles including French)
**Contact** Yorkshire Dales Workshops,
**Mail address** 14 Oakburn Road, Ilkley, West Yorkshire, LS29 9NN
**Phone/Fax** 01943 609421,
**Email** ydw@btinternet.com
**Web** www.btinternet.com/~ydw

**MADE** events (throughout the year, usually at Kinnersley Castle)
**Contact** Bridgend Cottage, Forden,. SY21 8NR,
**Phone** 0151 644 8560,
**Email** patlindop@hotmail.com
**Web** www.made.fsnet.co.uk

**In FRANCE:**
**St Chartier** (July)
**Contact** Comité George Sand, 5 place du Marché, BP 136, 36400 La Châtre, France
**Phone** +33 (0) 254 060 996
**Fax** +33 (0) 254 482 129
**Email** info@saintchartier.com
**Web** www.saintchartier.com

**Le Grand Bal de L'Europe**
(Gennetines) (July)
**Contact** Les Gauthiers, 03400 Gennetines, France
**Phone** +33 (0) 470 421 442
**Fax** +33 (0) 470 421 442
**Email:** BalEurope.Gennetines@wanadoo.fr
**Web** gennetines.trad.org/

French artists to try and catch, who have toured the UK regularly, include **La Chavannée**, **Le Gop**, **Maubuissons**, **Ti Jaz**, **Trio Patrick Bouffard**, **Jean-Francois Vrod** (with Chris Wood). Additionally, there is an ever-growing group of UK musicians now playing music influenced by French and European music; names to look out for include: **Blowzabella**, **Continental Drift**, **Eelgrinders**, **Jabadaw**, **Xim** as well as the workshop-based **Massif Village Orchestra**.

Regular French music and dance clubs and sessions can be found around the country including:

**Birmingham:** Roger Dennis
**Phone** 0121 4445227
0410- 057608
**Web** www.btinternet.com/~radical/rdennis/home.html

**Cambridge:**
**Web** www.chiark.greenend.org.uk/mailman/listinfo/cam-french/

**Chippenham:** Brian Tilley
**Phone** 01225- 810268
**Email** briantilley@neston1.freeserve.co.uk
**Web** www.neston1.freeserve.co.uk/

**Leeds:** Yannick Minvielle-Debat,
**Phone** 01274 833473
**Email** yannick@frenchdanceleeds.co.uk
**Web** www.fortunecity.co.uk/mad chester/latin/336/

**London**: Ayla Bedri
**Phone** 020 8928 1884
**Email** islab@yahoo.co.uk
**Web** www.gre.ac.uk/~c.walshaw/Music/OnBouge.html

**Norwich:** Frank Vickers
**Phone** 01603 505910
**Email** frank@vickhast.demon.co.uk
**Web** www.vickhast.demon.co.uk/pieda.htm

**Ockbrook (near Derby)**: Keith
**Phone** 0115 9609057
**Email** J2ohn@bigfoot.com
**Web** earwicker.inetc.net/ockbrook.htm

For further information (UK), a good starting point on the net is the Webfeet site (**www.ftech.co.uk/~webfeet/index.html**), which is a mine of traditional dancing information, including French and European, listing clubs, classes, tour dates and more. There are also French and Breton sites for information on festivals and workshops in France: try Music Trad (**www.musictrad.org/accueil/index2.html**) and Bretagne Musiques On-Line (**www.bmol.infini.fr**).

**Ayla Bedri**
*On Bouge; French Traditional Dance and Music Club.*

# Blues in the UK By Linda Fisher

Blues in the UK has a very loyal and enthusiastic following and continues to thrive. There are so many styles, from finger picking Piedmont to blues-rock, via boogie-woogie, jump-jive, swing, jazz, soul and gospel, to mention just a few, that almost everyone can find some aspect which appeals to them.

There are many talented professional and semi-pro blues musicians in this country, some specialising in a particular style, others encompassing a variety of styles and yet more stamping their own identity onto the genre. A satisfying number of these regularly take their brand of the blues back to the USA and a number of American musicians have become resident in the UK.

Opportunities to listen to, or play the blues are many. Dedicated enthusiasts run successful Blues Clubs nation-wide, often giving their time freely for sheer love of the music. Most Arts centres include Blues in their programming and, of course, there are numerous pubs and restaurants ranging from those that offer local bands their first taste of performing in public to those attracting the top, established bands. General Arts festivals usually have blues acts on the agenda as do those which are dedicated to folk or jazz. Blues specific festivals abound, notably, those at Colne, Burnley, and Gloucester, each of which has been championing the cause on an annual basis for the past decade. The more recent, but now firmly established, Bishopstock Blues Festival is easily the biggest in terms of the star names it is able to present. **Ray Charles**, **Taj Mahal** and **Buddy Guy** are all on this year's' bill. There is much interest in the blues among the younger generation as a survey carried out at the 2000 Gloucester Blues Festival confirmed.

Bishopstock is committed to encouraging this new, young talent and together with the Blues Foundation are looking for 'Bishopstock Young Musician Of The Year'. The award is open to any musician under 25. The winner will be announced at the festival and will receive a trophy, an opportunity to enter the 'International Blues Challenge' in Memphis, cash and the chance to perform live on the Bishopstock stage next year.

Many musicians are keen to pass on their skills and offer lessons and workshops and there are residential courses where everyone from beginners to gigging musicians can learn with and from their peers and mentors.

A particularly good online workshop can be found at **www.acousticguitarworkshop.com**.

The tutor here is noted slide specialist **Rick Payne** who teaches guitar in schools, and at workshops in conjunction with gigs. His performances take him to prime time television, festivals, arts centres, theatres and on tour to Europe, Scandinavia and the USA. He also works very successfully with performance poet **Peter Wyton**. This collaboration has opened up the boundaries and taken the blues to some unlikely settings; literature festivals, poetry festivals and a classical music festival where they performed in a church, on stage after the English Symphony Orchestra.

**Blueprint magazine** is a major source of information about the UK blues scene. There are articles, reviews, festival details, tour guides and a very comprehensive gig list. They also bring out a CD each year showcasing the best of the unsigned British blues acts.

Their excellent web site has links to all that is best in blues in the UK and further afield.
**Contact** 10 Messaline Avenue, London, W3 6JS
**Phone** 020 8723 7376
**Fax** 020 8723 7380
**E-mail** t.goldstone@virgin.net
**Web** www.blueprint-blues.co.uk

**European Blues Foundation**
This is a non-profit making organisation and educational institute. Their aim is to be 'the resource' for their members and the general public who are interested in the historical past and the modern progression of the blues. They are dedicated to the appreciation and understanding of all aspects of the music and the African American culture from which it evolved. They organise residential weeks and workshops which offer the opportunity to learn about the blues and are planning a 'Blues -In -The- Schools' project.
**Contact** PO Box 347, Cheltenham, Glos., GL52 2YA
**Phone** 01242 701 765
**E-mail** info@euroblues.org

**Bishopstock Music Festival** takes place over the late May bank holiday weekend (delayed to August in 2001) in beautiful private grounds.
**Contact** Bishop's Court Palace, Clyst St. Mary, Exeter, Devon, EX5 1DH
**Phone** 01392 875 220
**Fax** 01392 876 528
**Email** helen@bishopstock.co.uk
**Web** www.bishopstock.co.uk

**Gloucester Blues And Heritage Festival** takes place over the first 10 days of August (3rd to 12th in '2001). There are acts in venues around the city centre culminating in major events on a number of outdoor stages on the final weekend. This festival has been running in various formats for over ten years and with the support of the Central Gloucester Initiative it is planned to expand it over the next few years. Almost everything is free entry.
**Phone** 01452 532081
**Email** linda@bluesline.freeserve.co.uk

**Colne The Great British R & B Festival** has also been running for over ten years and takes place over the August Bank holiday weekend.
**Contact** Colne Municipal Hall, Albert Road, Colne, Lancs.
**Phone** 01282 661 234
**Web** www.bluesfestival.co.uk

**Burnley Blues Festival**
Another long running festival which takes place over the Easter weekend.
**Contact** Burnley Mechanics, Manchester Road, Burnley, Lancs. BB11 1JA
**Phone** 01282 664 400
**Web** www.bluesinburnley.co.uk

**Edinburgh International Jazz and Blues Festival** is a major Scottish event taking place over 9 days at the beginning of August.
**Contact** Mike Hart, 29 St. Stephen Street, Edinburgh, EH3 5AN
**Phone** 0131 667 7776
**Fax** 0131 225 3321

**The Welsh R&B festival, 'Dragon Blues'** is a July event in Wrexham. The organiser also runs 'Hooker's Blues Club' in Wrexham.
**Phone** 01948 770215 between 7pm and 9pm ONLY.
**Email** Petevans@btinternet.com

**Bushey's Big Wheel Blues Festival**
Laxey, Nr. Douglas, Isle Of Man
**Phone** 01624 861 625
**Email** bridleco@hotmail.com
**Web** www.bluesit.com

*Continued from previous page.*

**Boogaloo Promotions** organise the **Farnham Festival** (November), run **Farnham's Blues & Boogie Club** and much more.
**Contact** Boogaloo Promotions, Boogaloo House, Forest Glade, Rowledge, Farnham, GU10 4DG
**Phone** 01252 793430
**Fax** 01252 794509
**Email** MEM.BOOGALOO@btinternet.com

***Blues Clubs include:***
**Bottleneck Blues Club**
**Contact** John Adams, Powerhouse Productions, PO Box 211, W. Malling, Maidstone, ME19 6JR
**Web** www.bottleneckblues.co.uk

**Crawley Blues Club**
**Web** www.crawleyblues.co.uk

**Dorchester Blues Club**
**Web** www.bluesnights.co.uk

***Band sites:***
**Contact** Eddie Martin, Blueblood Records, PO box 416, Bristol, BS99 2DE
**Phone** 01179 079358
**Fax** 01179 041726
**Email** info@eddiemartin.com
**Web** www.eddiemartin.com

**Sonny Black and the Dukes**
**Contact** Bluetrack Records, PO Box 1028, Oxford, OX3 8XX
**Email** bluetrack@bluesarchive.com,
**Web** www.bluesarchive.com

Various artists can be found at **www.bluesline.freeserve.co.uk**

**Linda Fisher**, *The Blues Line*

# Bluegrass Music in Britain

By **Rick Townend**

Bluegrass Music in Britain? Banjos finger-picking Kentucky-style in the garden of England? Yes indeed – bluegrass and 'old-time' American music has been played over here since the 1950s, and the scene has been growing, especially since the British Bluegrass Music Association started up in 1991. There are many excellent musicians and bands in the country. Players such as **Pete Stanley** are well known internationally and watch out for **A Band like Alice**, the **Acme Bluegrass Band**, and **Bluegrass Experience**. Musicians cross boundaries too – **Tim O'Brien** has been working with **Kate Rusby** and other UK folk artistes in '*The Crossing*', **Dave Arthur** is playing old-timey banjo and accordeon with the **'Doctor, Doctor' String Band**, and young bands like **Acaysha** include bluegrass music and influence in their performance.

Bluegrass festivals, clubs and 'picking-sessions' take place all over England, and in Scotland, Wales and Ireland. There are also occasional concerts by high-profile American artistes such as **Ricky Skaggs**, **Alison Krauss**, **Ralph Stanley** and **Jimmy Gaudreau**; also fairly regular visits by other U.S bands, and some of the outstanding European bands such as **Hot String Quintet** and **Lilly of the West**.

The British Bluegrass Music Association has a magazine *British Bluegrass News* with news of all these; they also have a network of Area Reps who can give advice about local sessions, finding a teacher, where to buy an instrument/a better instrument/strings/picks/records etc., and how to meet other players or fans.

**Membership Secretary** – 30 Six Acres, Hemel Hempstead, HP3 5HY, or see website **www.bbma.freeserve.co.uk** which has links to local sites all over the UK.

The European scene is covered by *Bluegrass Europe* magazine – Bloezenweg 17, CH-4133 Pratteln, Switzerland or see website **www.bluegrass-europe.com**

For **Friends of Old Time Music and Dance** see below.
**FOAOTMAD Membership Secretary**
64 Alma Terrace, York, YO10 4DJ
**Phone** 01904 632674

The dance associated with this music (Appalachian clogging/flat-foot) has also become popular, with sparkling dancers such as **Rosie Davis** and **Ross Allen**, and teams all over the country. There are also visits by stars such as **Ira Bernstein**, and **Chris Ginn**, whose amazing 'buck-dance' stole the show at Gainsborough in February 2001.

**Rick Townend** *has played Bluegrass and Old-timey Music since 1963. He is the South East Area Representative for the BBMA.*

# Friends of American Old-time Music and Dance

By **Keith Johnson**

The 'Friends Of American Old-time Music And Dance' is a Society that was formed after a Sara Grey Old-time Banjo Workshop at Ripponden in November 1993.

There were 25 people on the Old-time Banjo Workshop, and it seemed that 3 of these people came from the same town, and neither knew the other, and no one at the Workshop had much information on how or where to obtain Old-time tapes, CDs, or tabulature. It was suggested that we keep in touch and form an interest group, and possibly hold another meeting.

On arriving back at my hometown Gainsborough in Lincolnshire, I set about organising another meeting for the coming February. Fortunately I stumbled across a Mr David Popple, the Director at the Trinity Arts Centre in Gainsborough. David needed no converting to Old-time as he had been a fan for some years, and was keen to have a meeting at the Arts Centre in Gainsborough, and from this, the first meeting turned into the only dedicated Old-time Music And Dance Festival in the UK.

It was at this Festival that a Committee was elected and the Friends Of American Old-time Music And Dance was formed. The aims of the Society are to encourage and promote the music, we have around 300 Members and **Tom Paley** of the **New Lost City Ramblers** is our President. Every February we have our Festival at Gainsborough, an informal Weekend Camp in May and a 10 Day Summer Camp in August, mainly just sitting around picking and informal teaching. In November we arrange three-day Intensive Beginners and Intermediate Workshops often with American Tutors.

The Friends have four excellent Newsletters per year full of information on sessions, festivals, CD reviews, tablature, and forthcoming events, our website is now regularly updated, it includes forthcoming events, membership proposal form that can be downloaded, and lots of Old-time links.

Lots of our Membership frequent the Bluegrass Festivals, and arrange sessions in their local areas, many Members visit the Festivals in the States. Gainsborough Festival has featured **The Gandydancer String Band** (Gerry Milnes, Dave Bing, Ron Mullennex, Jim Martin, Mark Payne), **Jim Lloyd** and **Jim Costa**, **Dwight Diller**, **Kate Lissauer**, **The Konnorock Critters** ( Brian Grimm, Debbie Grimm, Al Firth, Riley Baugus and Dancer Kathleen O'Connell), **Bob Carlin**, **Debbie McClatchy**, **Bruce Molsky**, **The New Deal String Band** (Tom Paley, Joe Lockier, Ben Paley), **The Rough Deal String Band** from Dublin (Bill Whelan, Tim Rogers, Ben Keogh) and lots of UK talent such as **Cotswold Mountain Boys**, **Henhouse Allstars**, **Sensible Shoestring Band**, **Old Redeye**, **Ragged But Right** and many more.

It is without doubt, that were it not for the Society lots of our Membership would never have seen many of the Artists mentioned. The Society has in the last year produced a compilation CD called *Ripples Across The Pond* which has been very favourably reviewed by the Old-Time Herald. The CD gives a very broad array of Old-time Music and Dance including ballads, dance tunes and flatfooting.

Membership of the Friends is £12 per individual and £20 for Couples, Groups and Bands. For this you receive 4 Newsletters, discount to the Festival, cheap camping, concessions at some Festivals and all the information you are likely to require on Old-time in the UK.

# What is Cajun and Zydeco music?

By **Graham Breakwell**

Cajun music is one of America's great down-home musics, moulded inexorably by the harshness of Acadian history. The preserve of the French-speaking settlers of the South-West Louisiana bayous, the authentic Cajuns, it combines French folk traditions with German, Spanish, Irish and a host of other ethnic influences. The root sound of Cajun is more evident in the waltz numbers, much favoured by the older Cajuns, than in the livelier two-steps (or "specials"). On the other hand, the exhilaration of the two-step tunes appeals more to the younger generations and has increased the popularity far beyond the bounds of Louisiana, where the sound is more important than the linguistically challenging Cajun-French lyrics.

In its simplest form the music is an acoustic style driven by the fiddle and accordion, often combined with a rhythm guitar and percussion in the shape of a heavy triangle (or 'tit fer). A more contemporary sound is achieved by the addition of drums, electric guitar and bass. Either way, the music portrays the soul of the Cajun heritage and has enormous listening and dancing appeal to all ages.

Zydeco music combines Cajun styles and other Caribbean and Creole sources, in a mixture of fiddle, accordion and rub-board or "frottoir", together with electric and bass guitar, drums and sometimes even a brass section.

The sound was created by the black French-speaking people of the same region of Louisiana. The result is a relentless hard-driving rhythm, that ranges from Cajun through to blues and back again - sometimes in the same number!

While both Cajun and Zydeco have strong traditional roots they are both very much alive today. It's not hard to see why, as they say in Cajun country, "Laissez les bon temps roulez" - let the good times roll! Both musical forms enjoy a popular following in the UK and there are a reasonable number of excellent Cajun groups, a modest selection of Zydeco bands and several dance instructors based here. As with any specialised musical genre, however, the market is limited, so visits to the UK by authentic Louisiana-based Cajun and Zydeco bands are fairly scarce.

## Cajun and Zydeco Directory

### *Cajun Times*

An independent non-profit making quarterly magazine promoting Cajun and Zydeco music and dancing, providing information on Cajun events and culture and a forum for readers.
**Editor** Laraine Bridges, 20 Pensford Close, Crowthorne, Berks, RG45 6QR.
**Phone** 01344 776143
**Fax** 01344 750208
**Email** ouisas@aol.com
Available free from Cajun clubs or by sending 4 SAEs (A5 sized) to Laraine.

### *Cajun UK*

A Midlands-based group promoting Cajun and Zydeco music, running their own dances at Beeston, near Nottingham, leading dance workshops and supplying listings.
**Contacts** Mick Billings
**Phone** 01530 263421
or Jim Jeffery
**Phone** 0115 925 2460,
**Email** cajun.uk@btinternet.com,
**Web** www.cajun.freeserve.co.uk

### *Peterboro Folk*

Cajun and Folk Listings websites:
www.pborofolk.co.uk
www.btinternet.com/~pete.shaw/bayou.html

### *Access All Areas*

Music agents and promoters with a roster of World music artists, which includes the leading Louisiana, UK and European Cajun and Zydeco bands. Organisers of festivals, dances and concerts. Tours arranged for USA bands - **Balfa Toujours**, **Eh, La-Bas! featuring Moise and Alida Viator**, **Bayou Seco**, **Sheryl Cormier and the Sounds of Cajun**, **Step Rideau and the Zydeco Outlaws** and **Morris and Dexter Ardoin with Bobby Michot**. Also representing many UK based bands. See listing in Agents section.
**Contact** Graham and Angie Breakwell,
**Mail address** Access All Areas, 44 Alexandra Avenue, Meole Brace, Shrewsbury, SY3 9HS
**Phone/Fax** 01743 235384
**Mobile** 07850 734182
**Email** accessallareas@btinternet.com

### *Swamp Music*

Long-running Derby based agency representing UK acts including **R Cajun and Zydeco Brothers**, **Bearcats**, **Zydecomotion**, **Flatville Aces**, **Hackney Ramblers** and **Good Rocking Dave** and tours for US artists **Steve Riley**, **Charivari** and **Zydecool.**
Event management and planning, tour organisation, festivals, marketing and promotion of Cajun and Zydeco music.
**Contact** Chris Hall
**Mail address** PO Box 94, Derby, DE3 1XA
**Phone** 01332 332 336
**Email** chrishall@swampmusic.co.uk
**Web** www.swampmusic.co.uk

spotlight

cajun zydeco

*See main artist A-Z listing on pages 11-90 for cajun and zydeco bands.*

## *Matters Musical*

Frank Warren's agency has specialised in Cajun and Zydeco since its inception. The company was established on the knowledge acquired by Frank, who formed one of Britain's earliest Cajun/ Zydeco bands, **The Crayfish Five**.
**Contact** Matters Musical Ltd
**Mail address** The Loft, Rear of 8 West Street, Dorking, Surrey, RH4 1BL,
**Phone** 01306 741007
**Fax** 01306 741008
**Web** www.mattersmusical.com

## *Gary Hayman's Cajun and Zydeco Music and Dance page*

The best starting point on the Internet for all Cajun and Zydeco stuff. USA and International event coverage, lots of links, photo bank and the opportunity to sign up to regular comprehensive electronic newsletter.
**Web** www.erols.com/ghayman

### *Wesson Accordions*

Supplier of new and used Cajun and Zydeco accordions and melodeons.
**Contact** Rees Wesson
**Phone** 01938 850351
**Email** rees@wesson.ws
**Web** www.melodeons.com

## *Regular venues for Cajun and Zydeco*

**Nuit Cajun**, Lichfield Arts Centre, The Guildhall, Lichfield, Staffs.
First Saturday in the month, Cajun or Zydeco bands plus dance workshops.
Annual festival in June/July.
**Phone** Box Office 01543 262223.

**Cajun in Sheffield** at the Eccleshall Non-Political Club.
Usually third Thursday in the month.
**Contact** Bob Hazlewood
**Phone** 0114 273 8085

**File Gumbo Cajun Music Club** at Cecil Sharp House, 2 Regent's Park Road, London, NW1 7AY
First Friday in the month, Cajun bands plus dance workshops and sessions.
Tuesday nights, dance workshops.
Annual festival first weekend in November.
**Contact** Erling Hagland
**Phone** 01708 558128
or Tim Rutherford
**Phone** 020 7720 6580

**Oxford Cajun Club** at South Oxford Community Centre, Lake Street, Oxford.
Cajun bands last Saturday in alternate months. Dance classes occasional Wednesdays.
**Contact** Viv Peto
**Phone** 01865 510066
**Email** oxcajun@hotmail.com

**Bristol Cajun Club** at The Polish Club, 50 St Pauls Road, Clifton.
Cajun bands first Saturday in alternate months.
**Contact** Phillippa Woodcock
**Phone** 0117 960 4159
**Web** www.geocities.com/bristol_cajun

**Cajun Barn** at The Tudor Barn, Eltham in SE London.
Cajun bands approximately every six weeks on Sunday nights
**Contact** Steve and Lynne Lane
**Phone** 020 8850 2893
**Web** www.cajunbarn.co.uk

**Moor Cajun**, various venues in North Yorkshire.
Dance classes and occasional bands.
**Contact** Glyn Roberts
**Phone** 01439 788177 or 770184.

## *Festivals*

**Lichfield Annual Cajun and Zydeco Festival**. See Nuit Cajun above.

**File Gumbo, London**, see above.

**Gloucester Cajun and Zydeco Festival** Guildhall Arts Centre, Eastgate Street, Gloucester.
Last weekend in January.
**Contact** Box Office
**Phone** 01452 505089

**Bracknell Cajun Day** at South Hill Park Arts Centre, Bracknell.
Annual event, 28 April 2001.
**Contact** Box Office
**Phone** 01344 484123

**Bury International Cajun and Zydeco Festival** The Met, Bury, Lancs.
11th Annual Festival, 12-14 October 2001.
**Contact** Box Office
**Phone** 0161 761 2216

**Other UK Festivals with a regular Cajun/Zydeco content**
Sidmouth, Towersey, Trowbridge, Crawley, Broadstairs, White Horse in Hastings, Fylde, Middlewich, Nantwich, Stockton International Riverside, Cambridge, Nottingham Riverside, Abergavenny, Big Big Country in Glasgow, Belper, Wimborne, Gosport and Fareham, Shetland Isles and Celtic Connections in Glasgow.

## *UK tours of overseas Cajun bands in 2001/2002*

Contact Access All Areas for tour details.

**Eh, La-Bas! featuring Moise and Alida Viator**, 19 July - 5 August 2001.

**Balfa Toujours**, 11-28 October 2001

**The Cajun Company**, 18-21 October 2001

**Cory McCauley's Evangeline Aces**, provisionally early November.

**Bayou Seco**, January 2001 and summer 2002
**Web** www.btinternet.com/~pete.shaw/bayou.html

## *UK-based Cajun and Zydeco Bands include*

*Baton Rouge*
*Bayou Gumbo*
*Bearcats*
*Bellaroots*
*Boat Band*
*Bon Temp Playboys*
*Cajun Aces*
*Cajun Catfish*
*Cajun Cru*
*Cajuns Denbo*
*Cajun Specials*
*Doughboy Zydecajun*
*Elvis Fontenot and the Sugar Bees*
*Flatville Aces*
*Good Rockin' Dave*
*Gumbo Flyers*
*Hackney Ramblers*
*Joe Le Taxi*
*Joli Blon*
*K-Zee*
*La la Zydeco*
*m-c- Cajun*
*R Cajun and the Zydeco Bothers*
*Zarico*
*Ziga Zag!*
*Zydeco Active*
*Zydecomotion*

**Graham Breakwell**
*Promoter and Agent. Access All Areas (see above).*

# Music on the Streets

By **Mark Allan**

**Overview of the scene:**
The street band scene in the UK is extremely diverse both in quality and style. There are some professional bands, and many non-professional and community bands, which vary from virtually pro quality to very basic. There is no substitute for seeing a band before you book them.

Contact details (phone, email and website) are given with each mention below – a name in brackets means an agent, whose full contact details will be found at the end of the article.
I have not attempted to deal with the wealth of traditional brass, silver, pipe and marching bands that exist all over the country, nor with New Orleans style jazz bands.

## *Styles*

**Horns and drum bands**
The standard line-up includes brass, saxes and drums/percussion, playing world music (Latin, African, Indian), funk, jazz, film and TV themes etc. These are the current generation of a "New Wave" of alternative street bands from the 80's, initially playing on demos and community events, which has merged with the world of community and large scale spectacular arts. A more recent influx has been from the free festival scene. Professional bands include the **Bollywood Brass Band** and **Crocodile Style** (EEA), the **Brasshoppers**, the **Real Macaws**, **SALT the Band**, the **Baghdaddies**, the **Stiltoneers**, **Brassa Nova** (klezmer/ska) and **Tragic Roundabout**.

Leading non-professional and community bands include West Yorkshire's **Peace Artistes**, Newcastle's **Tenth Avenue Band**, Folkestone's **Busker Du**, Barrow's **Barracudas**, and Morecambe's **Bay Beat Judy**.

**Pipes and drums**
Aside from the many traditional pipe bands, there are at least two that are more unusual: **MacUmba** fuse Scottish pipes with Brazilian rhythms, while **The Pokey Hats**, also known as the **Gutty Slippers** are a small group of hard partying pipers and drummers who are as likely to throw in "Wild Thing" as a pibroch, and the similar **The Shooglies**.

**Vocals strings etc.**
Bands which (almost) look like a stage band, with vocals, guitars and other string instruments, often with a lot of comedy and audience participation. Usually immobile, and often with small battery powered amps. **Roxy's Toolbox** and **Cosmic Sausages**

**Percussion bands - samba schools and blocos.**
It's hard to believe indigenous samba drumming groups are only about 20 years old in this country, now every carnival procession has one. Samba schools derive from Rio, and blocos from Bahia in North East Brazil, but many UK groups play from both styles, as well as fusions with reggae, hiphop, drum and bass and everything else. Locating them is made easier by the excellent and well maintained website for Samba in UK and Ireland www.sambistas.org.uk (info@sambistas.org.uk), which lists more than 100 bands by name and region, and even has an archive for defunct bands.

Well established names include **Inner Sense** and **Sambangra** from Manchester, the **London School of Samba**, Brighton's **Carnival Collective**, and Scotland's **Bloco Vomit** and **MacUmba**.

**Dhol groups**
There are now numerous groups playing the thunderous double ended Punjabi drum, in styles varying from trad Bhangra to breakbeats. Pioneers
**The Dhol Foundation**
**Web** http://dhol.uv.net
**Phone** 020 8707 5858 have groups all over the country, with most other groups coming from the West Midlands and the London area, including the **Dhol Academy**
**Web** www.virdibrothers.com/dhol academy
**Ministry of Dhol**
**Web** www.punjab2000.co.uk/Ministry OfDhol.html
**Phone** 07074 64647879 and the **Dhol Blasters**. If you are looking for a very local group, contact your closest gurdwara (Sikh temple).

**African**
**Akwaaba** play West African drums, mainly djembe
**Imbizo** - Zimbabwean vocal group

**Other percussion**
Dan Fox from **Salt** also leads **Boneshaker**, a 4 piece percussion band on stilts with good performance and strong visual sense.
**Weapons of Sound** do batphones and other large junk percussion with a modern dance sensibility

**Steel pan bands** need little description. Some bands do "pan round de neck" so are able to process without needing a vehicle. The Arts Council of England's www.carnivalnet.org.uk gives links for 5 bands, and Complete Talent Agency has about 10 on its roster.

**Small Scale – duos** include **The Jellyrollers** provide costumed performances with "musical engines of distinction", and the **Rhythm Doctors.** One man band **Pete Moser** of More Music in Morecambe claims to be the fastest over 100m, and also organises an annual festival of one-man-bands
**Phone** 01524 831997
**Email** mormusic@hothouse.u-net.com

**Bands from outside the UK**
If you have enough budget you might want to bring in a band, or join in with a tour. There is no easy way of knowing who is planning to bring a band in, unless you are contacted by an agent - Visiting Arts (020 7389 3019) may be helpful. A key word here is fanfare, French for street band, and used widely on the continent. Top names on the European scene include Balkan brass bands **Fanfare Ciocarlia** and **Kocani Orkestar**; French bands like the 25 strong **Occidentale de Fanfare** featuring Breton pipes as well as horns and drums (Troisquatre), the theatrical **Les Brankignols** (http://brank.free.fr brank@free.fr) (Cie Azimuts) and **Uranus Bruyant**, the very funky saxes, drums and loudhailer rap of **Accoules Sax**, and excellent non-pro bands such as Rouen's **Mona Lisa Klaxon**. Other large and accomplished non-pro groups who often do a summer tour in a European country include the Dutch **Tegenwind** (www.tegenwind.nl) and **Fanfare van de Eerste Liefdesnacht** (www.xs4all.nl/~fan fare/eindex.htm), and Dortmund's unwieldyly named **schwarz/rot Atemgold09** (www.atemgold.de) Two useful websites for fanfares, both in French are http://cybodega.free.fr

and http://bozart.ctw.net/acceuil.html The French national organisation for street arts, **Hors les Murs** is reconstructing its website to include a large on-line database of street acts from France and elsewhere, including 80+ street bands (groupe musical de rue). Due in June 2001, until then this data is only in their publication Goliath (FFr 300) http://www.horslesmurs.asso.fr/ Tel +33 1 55 28 10 10, Fax +33 1 55 28 10 11

**Things to consider when booking**

- Some bands can play on both stage and street, so you may be able to programme them in both modes.
- Not all do parades, and some do them badly...
- Visual presentation varies enormously from tight movement to comedy to colourful chaotic energy.
- Some groups come with optional dancers eg many samba groups (**London School of Samba**), **Bollywood Brass Band** with 4x4 Bhangra Dancers
- Community bands vary from booking to booking depending on how many members can make it
- Many groups do workshops

**Care of artists**

All the normal needs of artists apply - even more so as street music groups are often large and doing several sets in a day, without a venue with dressing rooms etc.

- Look after them properly - they are not the second class citizens they often feel
- Make sure water is provided - on hot days they will go through litres
- Provide somewhere accessible but secure to store instruments in safe places when not playing and valuables while playing.

Apologies if these are obvious, but from experience, they often aren't...

**How to contact bands**

There is no contact point in UK for street bands as a whole, nor is there an online database, though this may change in the next year.
Professional bands and well organised non-pro bands can be found both directly and through agents; many are listed in this directory. Agents not listed here may be found elsewhere e.g. ads in fROOTS. Community bands are the hardest to find! Ask other festivals locally, or arts development officers.

There are 2 showcase festivals of street performance and theatre at the beginning of May – **x.trax** in Manchester, and **Streets of Brighton** further south. Some festivals have large annual street programmes – **Bradford**, **Stockton Riverside** in the UK, and the enormous street festivals in **Chalons sur Saone** and **Aurillac** in France.

## Agents

### Fools Paradise
**Contact** Jo Burgess
**Mail address** Sentry Farm, Exminster, EXETER, Devon EX6 8DY
**Phone** 01392 833122
**Email** fools@foolsparadise.co.uk
**Web** www.foolsparadise.co.uk

### Continental Drifts
**Contact** Chris Tofu
**Mail address** Hilton Grove, Hatherley Mews, LONDON E17 4QP
**Phone** 020 8509 9531
**Web** www.continentaldrifts.uk.com

### Adrian Mealing
**Mail address** The Croft, Old Church Road, Colwall, Worcs WR13 6EZ, UK
**Phone** 01684 540366

### Artists Connect
**Mail address** 35 Llandaff Rd, Cardiff CF1 9NG

### Complete Talent Agency
**Mail address** 200 London Road, Hadleigh, Benfleet, Essex SS7 2PD.
**Phone** 01702 427100 (10 lines)
**Fax** 01702 427109.
**Email** Info@entertainers.co.uk
**Web** www.entertainers.co.uk

### Troisquatre
**Mail address** Cie Azimuts, 55500 Le Bouchon s/Saulx
**Phone** +33 (0)3 29 78 66 60
**Email** brank@free.fr
**Web** http://brank.free.fr
www.troisquatre.com/eng/accueil.htm

### TMC
**Mail address** 40/12 Harden Green Business Park Dalhousie Rd Dalkeith, Scotland EH22 3NU
**Phone** 0131 654 1000
**Email** tmcspeak@aol.com
**Web** www.tmcentertainment.co.uk

### Tarby Davenport
**Mail address** The Cottage, Wetherden, Stowmarket, IP14 3JS,
**Phone** 01359 240 724
**Email** tarby@stowhundreds.freeserve.co.uk

**Mark Allan** *plays in and manages the Bollywood Brass Band and Crocodile Style. He is keen to develop a network of promoters interested in programming street music – contact him at mark.allan@eea.org.uk. Thanks to Anne Sanders of the Peace Artistes and Bradford Festival for help with this article – all opinions and errors remain Mark Allan's.*

morris section



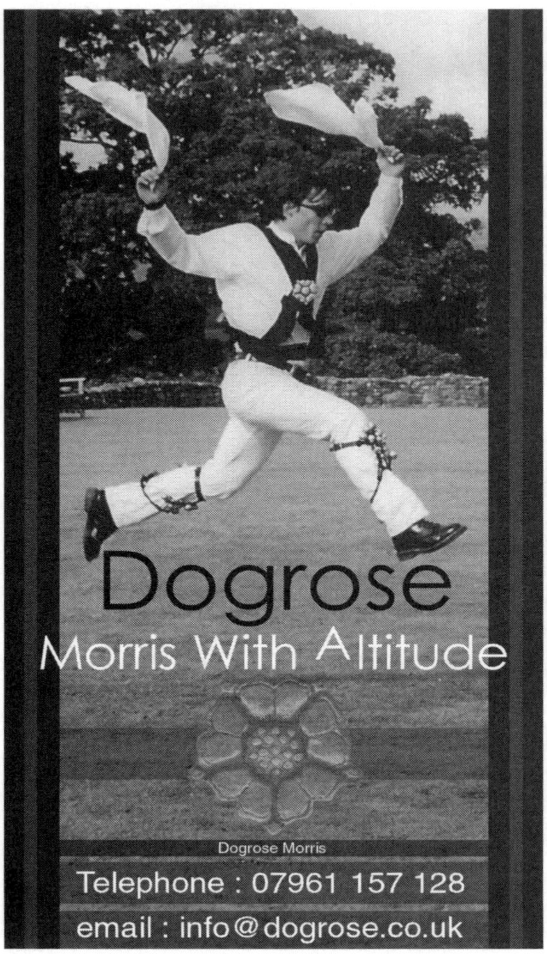


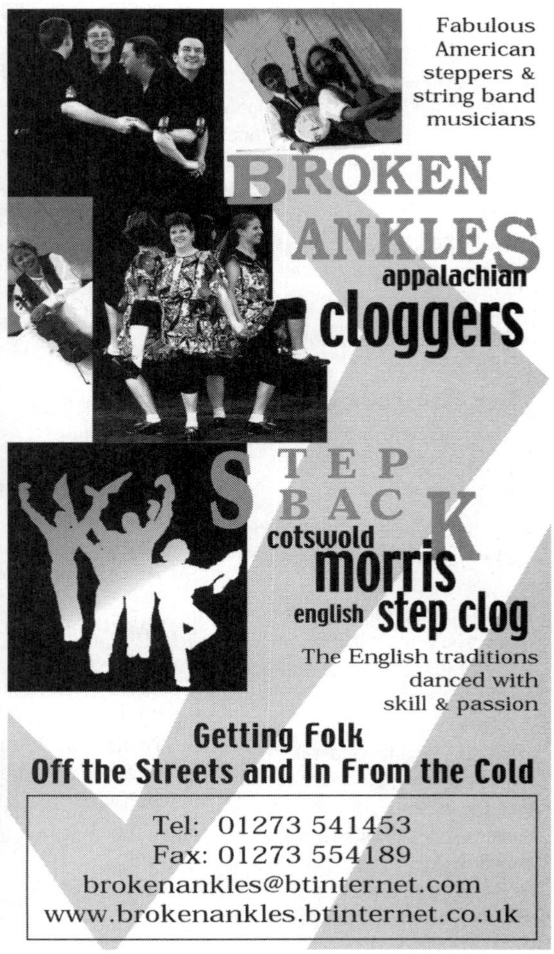

# morris
## & percussive dance



***See also Dance Display listings*** 91-94

# Morris, Sword Dancing and Mummers By Sue Swift

It is frequently imagined that all morris teams comprise six men waving hankies, a musician and a fool on the village green in front of the local pub. The purpose of this introduction is to briefly describe the wealth of English culture that is called morris dancing, sword dancing or mumming, and to give an insight into the ethos behind the wide variety of current teams and routes of accessibility.

**How teams are organised**
Morris dancers are grouped in teams or sides comprising 4 or more dancers, one or more musicians and sometimes a character and an announcer. An average team will have 20 or more active members, with 3 or more officers taking charge of team direction (squire or leader), teaching (foreman or dance leader) and finance (bagman/woman). Most teams finance themselves by subscription from the members to pay for the practice venue, a few teams are sponsored. Dance teams usually practise one night a week (2 hours) all year round, or use the practice night for outdoor performances (mostly pubs) in the summer. All teams are amateur but most charge expenses for travel and a small fee, which is comparatively cheap considering the number of people involved. The majority of teams belong to one of the three morris organisations and are covered for public liability insurance.

**Types of performance**
Duration and frequency of performances vary with each team and should be arranged individually. As a general guide, performances may range from 10 to 30 minutes and up to three dance spots with a break of up to an hour in between. The appearance of the team and performance varies considerably according to the dance type, the team style and attitude. The main dance types are as follows:

**Cotswold Morris** – the dancers frequently wear white clothes, bells and use sticks or handkerchiefs. They perform short (2-5 minutes) intricate dances involving 6 or 8 dancers (or 1-2 for jigs), 1-3 musicians and often have a fool or announcer.

**North West Morris** – the dancers wear bright colours and beads, clogs or hard shoes and use short sticks or slings. The dances are long (5-10 minutes) involving 8-16 dancers in processional formation. The musicians frequently comprise a band with a drum.

**Border Morris** – the dancers have black or disguised faces, wear rag jackets, a few bells and perform with much stick clashing, noise and a big band of musicians. The dances vary in difficulty and the number of dancers also varies but is usually between 4 and 12.

**Molly Dancers** – the costume varies from sashes to bright modern clothes. Many teams feature cross -dressing, wear hard soled boots, do not wear bells and have black or disguised faces. Dances normally involve 6 to 8 people (but can be many more) with a small band.

**Longsword Dancers** – the performance most frequently includes 6 to 8 dancers with rigid wooden or steel swords that are steadily interwoven into shapes accompanied by one, two or three musicians. Costume may be trousers with a jacket, waistcoat or ribbons. The repertoire of dances may be small.

**Rapper Sword Dancers** – the performance often comprises five dancers with flexible steel swords, one or more characters and one or two musicians. The repertoire may consist of many figures which are put together as a dance. It is fast and intricate.

**Mummers** – they often comprise a small group (up to ten) that may perform during a particular season or event. The assorted costume, characters and duration are dependent on the type of play performed and include Pace Egg, St George and Derby Tup plays.

**Suitable events**
Events suitable for the teams range from village fetes to TV game shows and persuading the team to perform is dependent on what exactly is on offer, whether they want to do it and availability of sufficient dancers for a full performance. For an outdoor venue, the dancing surface is very important in that grass may not be suitable and cobbles or uneven surfaces are dangerous.

The size of the arena is also important and most teams prefer to have their audience as close as possible so they can talk to them and show off the intricate movements. The musical instruments are not usually amplified and, particularly for the smaller teams, there needs to be sufficient quiet for them to be heard. Indoor performances can be central to an audience or on a stage of sufficient size for the team in question. The proximity of a bar and toilets may be requested.

**History**
Audiences frequently ask about the history of morris dancing and many teams have a leaflet containing a short description. Essentially the dances were noted in Europe (Spain and Portugal) in the 1100s and were recorded in England from the 1400s. There are some surviving pictures but very few dance notations. Interest in folk dance and song was widespread in the early 1900s when many of the dances were collected and notated. This resulted in morris and sword dancing being taught in schools and the establishment of many male morris dance clubs from the 1920s onwards. Women's teams became established in the 1970s, followed by mixed sex teams. Today, traditional teams with an unbroken existence spanning perhaps a hundred years dance alongside the more modern teams. There were clear regional variations between the dances when they were first written down. Some of this separation of type is maintained today although nearly all dance forms can now be found in every area.

**Booking a team**
Check the suitability of the event (see above). Decide what sort of team you want, what length of performance you need and what distance you can expect them to travel. Get in contact with one of the team officers, giving details of the event including date, time and suitability of the space for performance. The team may take several weeks to be able to give a definite answer so allow plenty of time.

**How to talk to morris people**
Team members are mostly ordinary people and include teachers, social workers, computer analysts, company directors, doctors, secretaries and almost anything else. They like you to watch the dances/plays and comment on how well they were performed, the precision of the stick clashing or clog stepping, the excitement and athleticism of the body movements or the integration of music and dance. Someone in the team often knows about the historical aspects and all dancers are usually willing to show you how to do difficult dance movements. While questions on why they do it are welcome, they are frequently unanswerable. Many of the longer established teams are male. The more recent teams, formed within the last 30 years, may be all male, all female or mixed sex. The women's teams frequently are told 'I thought only men did it' and all teams have heard 'pull the other one it's got bells on' a thousand times.

**Sue Swift**
*Morris Dancer, musician and Advisor to Sidmouth International Festival.*

# The Morris Ring

**Squire** Gerald Willey
29 Stratford Road, Warwick,
Warwickshire, CV34 6AS
**Phone** 01926 493674
**Email** msrep@snow.csv.warwick.ac.uk

**Bagman** John Frearson
7 Birch Grove, Sandy,
Bedfordshire, SG19 1NG
**Phone** 01767 681057
**Mobile** 07976 577723
**Email** frearsonj@rugbycement.co.uk
RingBagman@TheMorrisRing.org

**Treasurer** Steve Adamson
44,Whetley Close, Manningham,
Bradford, BD8 8HL
**Phone** 01274 773830
**Email** stephen@adamsonbfb.freeserve.co.uk
**Email** RingTreasurer@TheMorrisRing.org

The oldest of the national Morris Dance Organisations, The Morris Ring is an association of Men's Morris, Sword and Mummers Clubs and Teams.

The object of The Morris Ring is to encourage the performance of the morris, to maintain its traditions and to preserve its history; and to bring into contact all the men's Morris clubs or teams, which in all respects retain their independence.

A revival of morris dancing in England started at the turn of the last Century, and in 1934 the Cambridge Morris Men invited five other teams to join them in the formation of a national organisation. The six clubs - Cambridge, Letchworth, Thaxted, Oxford, East Surrey and Greensleeves met at Thaxted in Essex that year to inaugurate The Morris Ring.

The Morris Ring is run by a Squire, Bagman and Treasurer, and now has 246 members and associate teams, yet the clubs retain their independence and The Ring is basically still the simple organisation set up by the men at Cambridge in 1934.

There is an annual meeting at Thaxted on the weekend following the Spring Bank Holiday, and several other Ring meetings are organised by local morris teams during the year.

Today, morris dancers can be seen at local pubs in the summer, at school and village fêtes, in processions, and participating in festivals or trade show all over the world. The Morris has become a world wide dance form with over a thousand groups of dancers participating.

More details on The Morris Ring and its member clubs can be obtained from its web-site www/TheMorrisRing.org which provides the contact numbers and links to the web-sites of its members, or from the bagman:
**John Frearson**
7 Birch Grove, Sandy,
Bedfordshire, SG19 1NG
**Phone** 01767 681057
**Email** RingBagman@TheMorrisRing.org

**Contact details for Members and Associates of the Morris Ring are listed below. Practice day is given between contact phone number and address.**

### Abingdon Traditional Morris Dancers
**Contact** Stuart Jackson
**Email** Atmd@ifwtech.com
**Phone** 01235 527064
***Thursday***
34 Larkhill Road, Abingdon,
Oxfordshire OX14 1BL

### Adlington Morris Men
**Contact** Geoff Smith
**Email** geoffrey.w.smith@mcmail.com
**Phone** 0161 224 6356
***Tuesday***
21, Meredith Street, Ladybarn,
Manchester M14 6ST

### Aldbury Morris Men
**Contact** Bryan Daniels
**Phone** 01442 211854
***Thursday***
Tannenhof, Leighton Road, Northall,
Dunstable, Beds LU6 2HA

### Anker Morris Men
**Contact** Joe Oldaker
**Phone** 02476 372276
***Wednesday***
127, Hinckley Road, Nuneaton,
Warwicks CV11 6LJ

### Ashdown Forest Morris Men
**Contact** Bob Draper
**Email** Bob.draper@btinternet.com
**Phone** 01342 322653
***Wednesday***
56, Fairlawn Drive, East Grinstead,
West Sussex RH19 1NT

### Banchory-Ternan Morris Men
**Contact** Noel Pritchard
**Phone** 01330 811215
***Tuesday***
Forresters Cottage, Durris,
Kincardineshire AB31 3BD

### Barnsley Longsword Dancers
**Contact** Chris Davison
**Email** Chrisd324@yahoo.com
**Phone** 01642 823934
***Tuesday***
31, Ravenscroft Avenue, Linthorpe,
Middlesborough TS5 7QN

### Bathampton Morris Men
**Contact** Idris Roker
**Email** Bmm@rtdesign.com
**Phone** 01225 315660
***Thursday***
85, High Street, Weston, Bath, Avon
BA1 4DD

### Beaux of London City
**Contact** John Russell
**Phone** 01753 866001
***Tuesday***
2, Stuart Close, Windsor, Berks SL4 5NU

### Bedford Morris Men
**Contact** Keyth Richardson
**Email** Keyth@w-l-c.co.uk
**Phone** 01582 881642
***Wednesday***
8, Windsor Road, Barton-le-Cley,
Bedfordshire MK45 4LX

### Belchamp St Paul Morris Men
**Contact** Bary Hammond
**Email** Belchamp@btinternet.com
**Phone** 01440 785901
***Monday***
3, Bridge Cottages, Chapel Road,
Ridgewell, Essex CO9 4RQ

### Benfieldside Morris and Sword Dancers
**Contact** Brian Pollard
**Email** Bripol@cwcom.net
**Phone** 0191 3886834
***Wednesday***
9, Hawes Avenue, Chester-Le-Street,
Co. Durham DH2 3DX

### Boar's Head Morris Men
**Contact** Andy Fieldhouse
**Phone** 01535 645227
***Wednesday***
Ramsghyll, 10, Brook Row, Oakworth,
Keighley, West Yorks BD22 0EA

### Bourne River Morris Men
**Contact** Chris Mason
**Email** chris_mason@linekey.freeserve.co.uk
**Phone** 01202 553294
***Thursday***
20, Grand Marine Court, Durley Gdns, Bournemouth, Dorset BH2 5HS

### Brackley Morris Men
**Contact** Robin Stanley
**Email** stovepipehat@aol.com
**Phone** 01908 221205
***Thursday***
118, Crispin Road, Bradville, Milton Keynes, Buckinghamshire MK14 7BP

### Bristol Morris Men
**Contact** Phill Butler
**Email** Phillip.Butler@burohappold.com
**Phone** 01225 320600
***Thursday***
7, High Street, Saltford, Bristol BS31 3ED

### Britannia Coconut Dancers
**Contact** Tom Healey
**Email** tom@healeystarr.freeserve.co.uk
**Phone** 01706 875136
***Monday***
59 New Line, Bacup, Lancs OL13 9RN

### Broadstone Morris Men
**Contact** Nick Pal
**Email** Broadstone@incognito.demon.co.uk
**Phone** 01777 817241
***Monday***
The Old Smithy, Clayworth, Retford, Notts. DN22 9AA

### Broadwood Sword & Morris Men
**Contact** Bob Weddell
**Email** bob@rweddell.fsnet.co.uk
**Phone** 01293 536887
***Thursday***
30, Monksfield, Three Bridges, Crawley, West Sussex RH10 1PL

### Cam Valley Morris Men
**Contact** Simon Gordon-Walker
**Email** simongw@beeb.net
**Phone** 01285 652654
***Monday***
22, Shepherds Way, Cirencester, Gloucestershire GL7 2ET

### Cambridge Morris Men
**Contact** John Jenner
**Email** johnjenner1@compuserve.com
**Phone** 01763 242127
***Tuesday/Friday***
47, Spring Lane, Bassingbourn, Royston, Hertfordshire SG8 5HT

### Cardiff Morris Men
**Contact** Mike Angove
**Email** mike_angove@fsmail.net
**Phone** 029 2070 5256
***Tuesday***
2, Milton Road, Penarth, Vale of Glamorgan CF64 2SW

### Carn Brea Morris Men
**Contact** Peter Hurrell
**Phone** 01326 376071
***Monday***
10, Bodinar Road, Penryn, Cornwall TR10 8JD

### Castleford Sword Dancers
**Contact** Barry Green
**Email** jackie@townville.freeserve.co.uk
**Phone** 01977 510770
***Tuesday***
5, Hillcrest Close, Townville, Castleford, West Yorks WF10 3QS

### Chalice Morris Men
**Contact** Chris Franklin
**Email** chrisfranklin@franklin44.screaming.net
**Phone** 01278 780304
***Thursday***
25, St. Paul's Road, Burnham On Sea, Somerset TA8 2BH

### Chanctonbury Ring Morris Men
**Contact** Stuart Bown
**Email** stuart.bown@lineone.net
**Phone** 01903 526802
***Wednesday***
1, Archibald Road, Worthing, Sussex BN11 2SL

### Chapel-en-le-Frith Morris Men
**Contact** Philip Jupp
**Phone** 01663 735387
***Monday***
74, Buxton Road, Whaley Bridge, High Peak, Derbyshire SK23 7JE

### Chester City Morris Men
**Contact** Allan Jones
**Phone** 01244 316644
***Monday***
19, Boughton Hall Drive, Chester, Cheshire CH3 5QG

### City of Gloucester Mummers
**Contact** Chris Burge
**Phone** 01453 759921
12, Bath Road, Stroud, Glos GL5 3JG

### Claro Sword & Morris Men
**Contact** Robert Hart
**Email** harts@csma-netlink.co.uk
**Phone** 01423 865873
***Thursday***
Kintail, Brearton, Harrogate, HG3 3BX

### Colchester Morris Men
**Contact** Martin Theobald
**Phone** 01206 853500
***Friday***
49, Braiswick, Colchester, Essex CO4 5BQ

### Colne Royal Morris Men
**Contact** Julian Pilling
**Phone** 01282 698366
126, Railway Street, Nelson, Lancashire BB9 9AL

### Coventry Morris Men
**Contact** Martin Trewinnard
**Email** martin.trewinnard@coventry.gov.uk
**Phone** 02476 676991
***Tuesday***
78, Whoberley Avenue, Coventry, West Midlands CV5 8EQ

### Coventry Mummers
**Contact** John Havell
**Phone** 02476 672297
***Wednesday***
35, Belvedere Road, Earlsdon, Coventry, West Midlands CV5 6PG

### Cumberland Morris Men
**Contact** David Day
**Email** CumberlandMM@42abbey.freeserve.co.uk
**Phone** 01946 810867
***Tuesday***
210, Frizington Road, Frizington, Cumbria CA26 3QU

### Cup Hill Morris Men
**Contact** Dave Rush
**Email** df.rush@ntlworld.com
**Phone** 01252 518620
***Wednesday***
104a, Coleford Bridge Road, Mytchett, Camberley, Surrey GU16 6DT

### Darlington Mummers
**Contact** Jim Smith
**Phone** 01325 320806
34, Westwood Avenue, Heighinton Village, Newton Ayc, Co. Durham DL5 6SA

### Dartington Morris Men
**Contact** John Culf
**Email** johnculf@harbertondevon.co.uk
**Phone** 01803 863468
***Friday***
West Lodge, Tristford, Harberton, Totnes, South Devon TQ9 7RZ

### Datchet Morris Men
**Contact** Keith Walter (Squire)
**Phone** 01784 256537
***Monday***
3, Seaton Drive, Ashford, Middlesex PW15 3ET

## Derby Morris Men
**Contact** Peter Cave
**Email** dmm@writers-inc.ndirect.co.uk
**Phone** 0115 9323902
***Monday***
2, Little Hallam Hill, Ilkeston, Derbys DE7 4LY

## Dolphin Morrismen
**Contact** David Walters
**Email** david.walters@nottingham.ac.uk
**Phone** 0115 9140904
***Thursday***
90, Seymour Road, West Bridgford, Nottingham NG2 5EF

## Durham Rams Sword and Morris Men
**Contact** Stan Otterburn
**Email** joculator@btinternet.com
**Phone** 0191 3849052
***Tuesday***
35, The Avenue, Pity Me, Durham DH1 5DY

## Earlsdon Morris Men
**Contact** Martin Love
**Email** martin.love@virgin.net
**Phone** 024 7645 4958
***Tuesday***
146, Shakespeare Street, Stoke, Coventry CV2 4NF

## East Kent Morris Men
**Contact** Roger Bryan
**Phone** 01303 268290
***Wednesday***
Bluehouse Cottage, Bluehouse Lane, Saltwood, Kent CT21 4EN

## East Suffolk Morris Men
**Contact** Mike Palmer
**Email** mpalm@crickets11.freeserve.co.uk
**Phone** 01449 711627
***Monday***
Crickets, Stonham Road, Mickfield, Suffolk IP14 5LR

## East Surrey Morris Men
**Contact** Bob Davies
**Phone** 01372 720527
***Monday/Monday***
22, Meadway, Epsom, Surrey KT19 8JZ

## Escafeld Morris Men
**Contact** John Bowden
**Phone** 0114 2465317
***Monday***
163, Cross Hill, Ecclesfield, Sheffield, South Yorkshire S35 9WS

## Etcetera Morris Men
**Contact** Robert Malleson
**Email** RobertMalleson@rpm associates. freeserve.co.uk
**Email** 0208 3630289
***Monday***
18, Parsonage Gardens, Enfield, Middlesex EN2 6JR

## Ewell St Mary's Morris Men
**Contact** Mick Sargeant
**Email** jacksarg@care4free.net
**Phone** 020 8393 9640
***Thursday***
38, Station Avenue, West Ewell, Surrey KT19 9UH

## Exeter Morris Men
**Contact** Bob Higgs
**Email** Exetermm@eclipse.co.uk
**Phone** 01392 875438
***Thursday***
16, Major Field Road, Topsham, Devon EX3 0ES

## Faithful City Morris Men
**Contact** Ian Currie
**Email** ian_currie@compuserve.com
**Phone** 01531 670417
***Wednesday***
Nurses Cottage, Stretton Grandison, Herefordshire HR8 2TN

## First Sedgeley Morris Men
**Contact** Owen Jones
**Phone** 0121 6811433
***Thursday***
11, Oaklands Avenue, Harbourne, Birmingham B17 9TU

## Forest of Dean Morris Men
**Contact** Dave Evans
**Phone** 01594 563354
***Wednesday***
Fairview House, Little Drybrook, Clements End, Coleford, Glos. GL16 8LP

## Foresters Morris & Sword Dance Club
**Contact** Stephen Earwicker
**Email** Earwicker@btinternet.com
**Phone** 0115 9282566
***Monday***
3, Normanby Road, Wollaton Nottingham, Notts NG8 2TA

## Furness Morris Men
**Contact** Ian Boyle
**Email** jib68262@GlaxoWellcome.co.uk
**Phone** 01229 583658
***Friday***
32, Queen Street, Ulverston, Cumbria LA12 7AF

## Gloucestershire Morris Men
**Contact** Mike Hill
**Email** Hillsalive@fsmailtv.com
**Phone** 01242 674462
***Tuesday***
Alum Chine, Buschcombe Lane, Woodmancote, Gloucestershire GL52 4QQ

## Goathland Ploughstots
**Contact** Mike Cook
**Email** Mikecook@supanet.com
**Phone** 01653 694319
***Tuesday***
28, Chandlers Wharf, Castlegate, Malton, North Yorkshire YO17 7YL

## Grand Union Morris
**Contact** Lester Bailey
**Email** Lester.bailey@bigfoot.com
**Phone** 01296 582653
***Thursday***
13, Thornton Crescent, Wendover, Buckinghamshire HP22 6DG

## Green Ginger Morris Men
**Contact** Andrew Farrall
**Email** andrew@farrall.karoo.co.uk
**Phone** 0142 803199
***Tuesday***
3, Skidby Grove, Hull, East Yorkshire HU6 8PB

## Green Man's Morris and Sword Club
**Contact** Jim Pennells
**Email** anne_jim.pennells@breathemail.net
**Phone** 01827 714307
***Tuesday***
26, Nursery Road, Atherstone, Warwicks CV9 1PN

## Green Oak Morris Men
**Contact** Neil Dawson
**Phone** 01302 811076
***Wednesday***
10, Liverpool Ave, Wheatley, Doncaster, S Yorks DN2 4EX

## Greensleeves Morris Men
**Contact** Chris Benson
**Email** c.benson@wes.gdst.net
**Phone** 020 8224 3985
***Friday***
46, Thorndon Gardens, Stoneleigh, Epsom, Surrey KT19 0QW

## Grimsby Morris Men
**Contact** Steve Massen
**Phone** 01472 884656
***Tuesday***
25, Clarkson Drive, Stallingborough , N E Lincs DN41 8BQ

### Hageneth Morris Men
**Contact** Val Sutton-Smith
**Email** hageneth@talk21.com
**Phone** 01284 700680
***Wednesday***
45, Eastgate Street, Bury St. Edmunds, Suffolk IP33 1YW

### Handsworth Traditional Sword Dancers
**Contact** Donald Watts
**Email** family.watts@virgin.net
**Phone** 0114 2585283
***Wednesday***
54, Montgomery Road, Nether Edge, Sheffield, S.Yorkshire S7 1LQ

### Harthill Morris Men
**Contact** Brian Shutt
**Phone** 01909 773102
***Thursday***
10, Casson Drive, Harthill, Sheffield, South Yorkshire S26 7WA

### Hartley Morris Men
**Contact** Tony Tomlin
**Email** Hartleymen@aol.com
**Phone** 01622 685960
***Thursday***
139, Farleigh Hill, Tovil, Maidstone, Kent ME15 6RQ

### Harwich Morris Men
**Contact** Malcolm Batty
**Email** mrb@battym.freeserve.co.uk
**Phone** 01255 851399
***Monday***
24, Butchers Lane, Walton-on-the-Naze, Essex CO14 8QU

### Headington Quarry Morris Dancers
**Contact** Terry Phipps
**Email** HQMD@bigfoot.com
**Phone** 01865 765581
13, Larkfields, Headington, Oxford OX3 8PF

### Helier Morris Men
**Contact** Graeme Bennett
**Email** helier_morris@hotmail.com
**Phone** 01534 735886
***Monday***
Bas Terrain, St Clements Road, St Saviour, Jersey, Channel Islands JE2 7PX

### Helmond Morris Men
**Contact** Antony Heywood
**Email** antony@iae.nl
**Phone** 00 31 40 285 3337
***Friday***
Rietstraat 15, 5662 RA Geldrop, The Netherlands

### Herga Morris Men
**Contact** Bob Hawkes
**Phone** 01799 528046
***Wednesday***
109, Radwinter Road, Saffron Walden, Essex CB11 3HY

### Hoghton Rapper
**Contact** Thomas Calderbank
**Phone** 01772 731483
13, Daisey Croft, Lea Preston, Lancs PR2 1RU

### Horwich Prize Medal Morris Men
**Contact** Bob Bradley
**Email** horwichmorris@breathe.com
**Phone** 01204 840949
15, Shrewsbury Road, Bolton, Lancs BL1 4NW

### Icknield Way Morris Men
**Contact** Peter Ambidge
**Email** bagman@icknieldwaymorris men. org.uk
**Phone** 01367 820211
***Wednesday***
7, Craven Common, Uffington, Faringdon, Oxfordshire SN7 7RN

### Isca Morris Men
**Contact** Adrian Foss
**Email** Bagman@isca-morrismen.com
**Phone** 01633 664534
***Wednesday***
30, Brynhyfryd Road, Newport, South Wales NP9 4FX

### Jockey Morris Men
**Contact** Dick Franks
**Email** Administration@greatbarr. bham.sch.uk
**Phone** 0121 313 1732
***Friday***
1065, Chester Road, Erdington, Birmingham B24 0NR

### John O'Gaunt Morris (Lancaster)
**Contact** Rodney Briddon
**Email** rodney.briddon@bgtechnology. com
**Phone** 01995 600369
***Wednesday***
Roan House, 3, Lathom Way, Garstang, Lancashire PR3 1RX

### Kemp's Men of Norwich
**Contact** Peter Salt
**Phone** 01603 615066
***Wednesday***
7, Connaught Road, Norwich, Norfolk NR2 3BP

### Kennet Morris Men
**Contact** Jon Holmes
**Email** jon@jaholmes.demon.co.uk
**Phone** 0118 9471246
***Monday***
29, Highdown Avenue, Emmer Green, Reading, Berkshire RG4 8QT

### King John's Morris Men
**Contact** Malcolm Cope
**Phone** 02380 641182
***Monday/Thursday***
45, Mottisfont Road, Eastliegh, Hants SO50 4PN

### The King's Morris
David Jackson
**Phone** 01553 768930
***Tuesday***
9, Edward Street, Kings Lynn, Norfolk PE30 5QS

### Kinnerton Morris Men
**Contact** Terry Peach
**Email** Peach.Fam@btinternet.com
**Phone** 01244 325821
***Monday***
2, Leahurst Close, Off Hoole Road, Chester, Cheshire CH2 3NS

### Lassington Oak Morris Men
**Contact** Mike Firth
**Email** wingco.lassoak@tesco.net
**Phone** 01452 310699
***Wednesday***
5, Popes Meade, Highnam, Gloucester GL2 8LH

### Leeds Morris Men
**Contact** Moss Ambrose
**Phone** 01132 781202
***Thursday***
2, Kirkstall Avenue, Leeds LS5 3DN

### Leicester Morris Men
**Contact** Charlie Corcoran
**Email** charliecorcoran@nasuwt.net
**Phone** 01162 675654
***Wednesday***
70, Greengate Lane, Birstall, Leicester, Leics LE4 3DL

### Letchworth Morris Men
**Contact** Alan Creamer
**Email** alan.creamer@virgin.net
**Phone** 01582 724261
***Thursday***
66, Wychwood Avenue, Luton, Beds LU2 7HU

### Leyland Morris Men
**Contact** Len Daniels
**Phone** 01772 434458
***Monday***
Pleasant View, Ulnes, Walton Lane, Leyland, Preston, Lancs PR5 3LU

### Lichfield Morris Men
**Contact** Peter Cole
**Email** Peter.Cole@University-b.wmids.nhs.uk
**Phone** 01543 252758
***Tuesday***
204, Upper St. John Street, Lichfield, Staffordshire WS14 9EF

### Lincoln & Micklebarrow Morris Men
**Contact** Ian Thomson
**Phone** 01636 892951
***Monday***
Trevone, Low Street, Collingham, Newark, Notts NG23 7LS

### London Pride Morris Men
**Contact** Peter Judge
**Phone** 020 8674 6595
***Monday***
89, Upper Tulse Hill, Brixton, London SW2 2RA

### Long Man Morris Men
**Contact** David Rannie
**Email** thebagman@longman.org.uk
**Phone** 01323 520977
***Friday***
24, Ruskin Road, Eastbourne, East Sussex BN20 9AY

### Lord Conyers Morris Men
**Contact** John Ledbury
**Email** LordConyers@lineone.net
**Phone** 01332 799074
***Wednesday***
5, The Maltings, Shardlow, Derbyshire DE72 2HH

### Lutterworth Morris Men
**Contact** Bryan Higgs
**Phone** 01788 814098
***Sunday***
12, Trowbridge Walk, Rugby, Warwickshire CV22 7LP

### Malvern SwordsMen
**Contact** Anthony Lewis
**Phone** 01242 227103
15, Garden Road, Cheltenham, Gloucestershire GL53 8LT

### Manchester Morris Men
**Contact** Keith Ashman
**Email** Keith@manchester-morris.freeserve.co.uk
**Phone** 01565 653970
***Thursday***
52, Glebelands Road, Knutsford, Cheshire WA16 9DZ

### Manley Morris Men
**Contact** Derek Schofield
**Email** Derek@dschofield.demon.co.uk
**Phone** 01270 663041
***Monday***
2, Carrisbrooke Close, Wistaston, Crewe CW2 8JO

### Martlet Sword & Morris Men
**Contact** Michael McNamara M.B.E.
**Email** Mmmcn@waitrose.com
**Phone** 01903 263892
***Wednesday***
83, Offington Drive, Worthing, Sussex BN14 9PS

### Mayflower Morris Men
**Contact** Geoff Douglas
**Email** geoffdouglas@hotmail.com
**Phone** 01268 710709
***Thursday***
22, Carsey Close, Ramsden Heath, Billericay, Essex CM11 1PB

### Men of Wight Morris Men
**Contact** Martin Davis
**Phone** 01983 882143
***Thursday***
130, High Street, Wootton Bridge, Ryde, Isle of Wight PO33 4LZ

### Mendip Morris Men
**Contact** Chris Avery
**Email** cavery6843@aol.com
**Phone** 01934 833818
***Monday/Thursday***
Bridge Villa, 29, Pauls Causeway, Congresbury, North Somerset BS49 5DQ

### Mersey Morris Men
**Contact** Anthony Foard
**Email** bagman@merseymorrismen.com
**Phone** 0151 3344566
***Monday***
33, Cunningham Drive, Bromborough, Wirral, Merseyside L63 0JX

### Milton Morris Men
**Contact** David Jones
**Email** djones@rowans98.freeserve.co.uk
**Phone** 01223 441309
***Monday***
98, The Rowans, Milton, Cambridge, Cambs CB4 6YU

### Monkseaton Morris Men
**Contact** Peter Brown
**Phone** 01912 523022
***Monday***
59, Uplands, Monkseaton, Whitley Bay, Tyne & Wear NE25 9AG

### Mossley Morris Men
**Contact** Roy Blick
**Email** RoyBlick@lineone.net
**Phone** 0161 292 3794
77, Springfield Road, Droylsden, Manchester M43 7RD

### Moulton Morris Men
**Contact** Bob Ham
**Email** hamfamily@breathemail.net
**Phone** 01604 642884
***Thursday***
16, High Street, Moulton, Northants NN3 7SR

### Mount Bures Morris Men
**Contact** Sarah White
**Phone** 01621 817502
***Thursday***
9, Osbourne Cottages, School Road, Messing, Colchester, Essex CO5 9TJ

### North Wood Morris Men
**Contact** Jon Wimhurst
**Email** Northwood@dunmore.ndo.co.uk
**Phone** 020 8657 3859
***Thursday***
52, Belfield, Pixton Way, Croydon, Surrey CR0 9JX

### Northampton Morris Men
**Contact** Steve Bignell
**Phone** 01604 633326
***Monday***
117, Colwyn Road, Northampton, Northamptonshire NN1 3PU

### Oakworth Village Morris Men
**Contact** Phil Bartram
**Phone** 01274 497935
***Monday***
14, Woodland Cresent, Stoney Ridge, Bradford BD9 6PE

### Offley Morris Men
**Contact** Michael Pike
**Phone** 01462 634893
***Friday***
15, Netley Dell, Letchworth, Herts SG6 2TF

### Oxford City Morris Men
**Contact** Duncan Drummond
**Email** D.L.Drummond@rl.ac.uk
**Phone** 01235 528359
***Wednesday***
16, Borough Walk, Abingdon, Oxon OX14 1HW

### Oxford University Morris Men
**Contact** Peter Lund
**Email** Peter.lund@eng.ox.ac.uk
**Phone** 01865 248966
***Thursday***
The Old School House, Binsey, Oxford OX2 0NG

## Packington Morris Men
**Contact** Dave Johns
**Email** davidjohns@nasuwt.net
**Phone** 01530 270494
***Wednesday***
4, Silver Street, Oakthorpe, Swadlincote, Derbys DE12 7RA

## Peterborough Morris Men
**Contact** Alan Smalldridge
**Phone** 01778 348119
***Tuesday***
40, West End Road, Maxey, Peterborough, Cambs PE6 9EJ

## Pinewoods Morris Men
**Contact** Martin Graetz
**Email** jmgraetz@world.std.com
**Phone** 00 - 1 - 978 2636469
Alt Suns:Sept-Dec:Jan-April
49, Stow Street, Acton, Mass., USA Mass 01720

## Plymouth Morris Men
**Contact** Julian Kohler
**Phone** 01752 402841
***Wednesday***
47, Dean Hill, Plymstock, Plymouth, Devon PL9 9AF

## Ravensbourne Morris Men
**Contact** Ian Peretti
**Email** ravensbourne@ianperetti.in2home.co.uk
**Phone** 020 8643 3863
***Tuesday***
306, Carshalton Road, Carshalton, Surrey SM5 3QB

## Redcar Sword Dancers
**Contact** Brian Pearce
**Email** brian@pearce15.freeserve.co.uk
**Phone** 01642 454371
***Monday***
4, Normanby Road, Ormesby, Middlesborough, Cleveland TS7 9NS

## Richmond on Swale Morris Men
**Contact** Jim McCaffery
**Email** jim@dunelmcity.freeserve.co.uk
**Phone** 0191 3868149
***Thursday***
7, Hillcrest, Gilesgate, Durham City DH1 1RB

## Ripley Morris Men
**Contact** Michael Brittain
**Email** brittainmj@fsmail.net
**Phone** 01773 744923
***Thursday***
Sunshine Cottage, 16, Moss Lane, Ripley, Derbyshire DE5 3LY

## Royal Liberty Morris Men
**Contact** Kevin Frost
**Phone** 01708 700667
***Thursday***
305, Gorseway, Rush Green, Romford, Essex RM7 0SD

## Royal Preston Morris Dancers
**Contact** Alan Salter
**Email** alan.salter@tesco.net
**Phone** 01772 601259
***Wednesday***
Gable House, Highfield Road, Croston, Preston, Lancs PR5 7HH

## Rumford Morris
**Contact** David Bennett
**Phone** 01702 714328
***Thursday***
51, Kingswood Chase, Leigh-on-Sea, Essex SS9 3BB

## Rutland Morris Men
**Contact** Barry Mather
**Email** anne-barry@kingscliffe79.freeserve.co.uk 01780 470464
***Monday***
47, Park Street, King's Cliffe, Peterborough PE8 6XN

## Saddleworth Morris Men
**Contact** Richard Hankinson
**Email** rghankinson@hotmail.com
**Phone** 01457 834871
***Thursday***
31, Moorgate Drive, Carrbrook, Stalybridge, Cheshire SK15 3LX

## Shakespeare Morris Men
**Contact** Philip Taylor
**Email** smmjpt@aol.com
**Phone** 01789 268301
***Monday***
6, Hamilton Road, Tiddington, Stratford-upon-Avon, CV37 7DD

## Silkeborg Morris Men
**Contact** Bob Dickson
**Email** dickson@post.tele.dk
**Phone** 00 - 45 - 86812874
***Thursday***
Guldbergsdade 24, 8600 Silkeborg, Denmark

## Silurian Border Morris Men
**Contact** Roger Page
**Email** rogermpage@talk21.com
**Phone** 01531 660686
***Monday***
Stone Cottage, Rye Meadow, Much Marcle, Ledbury, Herefords HR8 2NB

## South Shropshire Morris Men
**Contact** Jim Logan
**Phone** 01584 856510
***Monday***
Garden House, Oakley Park, Bromfield, Ludlow, Salop SY8 2JW

## Southport Sword Dancers
**Contact** John Clarke
**Phone** 01704 574762
***Tuesday***
11 Dunster Road, Birkdale, Southport, Merseyside, PR8 3AG

## Spring Grove Morris Men
**Contact** Stephen Nash
**Email** nash@nationwideisp.net
**Phone** 020 8942 6176
***Monday***
18, Sandal Road, New Malden, Surrey KT3 5AP

## St Albans Morris Men
**Contact** John Beecham
**Email** morris@protem.net
**Phone** 01582 762913
***Monday***
53, Station Road, Harpenden, Hertfordshire AL5 4XE

## Stafford Morris Men
**Contact** Alan Dandy
**Email** 101713.3701@CompuServe.com
**Phone** 01952 810334
***Monday***
74, Wallshead Way, Church Aston, Nr Newport TF10 9LT

## Standon Morris Men
**Contact** Barry Warner
**Email** barry.warner.16@yahoo.com
**Phone** 01920 822341
***Thursday***
16, High Street, Standon, Ware, Hertfordshire SG11 1LA

## Stevenage Sword Dancers
**Contact** Mike Nye
**Email** mikenye@cwcom.net
**Phone** 01438 221518
***Tuesday***
37, Sish Lane, Stevenage, Herts SG1 3LS

## Stockton Morris Men
**Contact** Brian Padget
**Phone** 01642 583945
***Saturday***
23, Elton Grove, Stockton-on-Tees TS19 7RF

## Sweyn's Ey Morris and Sword Dancers (Men of)
**Contact** Keith Lascelles
**Email** Lascelles@argonet.co.uk
**Phone** 01792 843210
***Thursday***
755, Clydach Road, Ynystawe, Swansea, West Glamorgan SA6 5BA

## Sydney Morris Men
**Contact** John Milce
**Email** Jmilce@sherborne.com.au
**Phone** 00 - 61 - 298173529
25, Isler Street, Gladesville, N.S.W., Australia NSW 211

## Taunton Deane Morris Men
**Contact** Tim Wingfield
**Email** wingspan@tinyworld.co.uk
**Phone** 01823 251979
***Tuesday***
10, Wilton Grove, Taunton, Somerset TA1 4HA

## Thames Valley Morris Men
**Contact** John Elkins
**Email** Johnelkins@compuserve.com
**Phone** 020 8977 2096
***Tuesday***
1, Udney Park Road, Teddington, Middx TW11 9BB

## Thaxted Morris Men
**Contact** Richard Morgan
**Email** Richard@thaxted1.freeserve.co.uk
**Phone** 01371 830978
***Monday***
65, Newbiggen Street, Thaxted, Dunmow, Essex CM6 2QU

## Thelwall Morris Men
**Contact** James Berry
**Phone** 01925 601826
***Wednesday***
Ivy Cottage, Bell Lane, Thelwall, Cheshire WA4 2SY

## Towersey Morris Men
**Contact** Paul Dolman
**Phone** 01844 344255
***Monday***
5, Berryfield Road, Princes Risborough, Bucks HP27 0HF

## Traditional Bampton Morris Dancers
**Contact** Darren Lloyd
**Phone** 01993 851971
***Sunday***
17, St Mary's Court, Bampton, Oxon OX18 2HX

## Trigg Morris Men
**Contact** Roger Hancock
**Email** roger@hancock98.freeserve.co.uk
**Phone** 01208 73907
***Thursday***
10, Halgavor Road, Bodmin, Cornwall PL31 1BW

## Het Utrecht Morris Team
**Contact** Arnold Madderom
**Phone** 00 - 31 - 30 231 7360
Mgr.v.d. Weteringstraat 79, 3581 ED Utrecht, The Netherlands

## Uttoxeter Heart of Oak Morris Men
**Contact** Keith Hutchinson
**Phone** 01283 761088
***Thursday***
7, Warran Drive, Linton, Swadlincote, Derby DE12 6QP

## Vancouver Morris Men
**Contact** Graham Baldwin
**Email** Gbaldwin@info-mine.com
**Phone** 00 - 1 - 604 3225476
2211, Portside Court, Vancouver, BC Canada V5P 4T9

## Victory Morris Men
**Contact** Jim Seal
**Email** james_seal@tinyworld.co.uk
**Phone** 02392 798941
***Thursday***
34, Binstead Road, Portsmouth, Hants PO2 7PL

## Wgutteradard Morris Men
**Contact** Laurence Hodges
**Email** L_hodges@cix.co.uk
**Phone** 01959 573402
***Wednesday***
120, Sunningdale Avenue, Biggin Hill, Westerham, Kent TN16 3TN

## Wantsum Morris Men
**Contact** Peter Roberts
**Email** wantsum1@tinyworld.co.uk
**Phone** 01843 590048
***Sunday***
132, Dumpton Park Drive, Ramsgate, Kent CT11 8BP

## Wath upon Dearne Morris Men
**Contact** Alec Lowe
**Email** AlecLowe@yahoo.com
**Phone** 01709 878592
***Tuesday***
49, Fitzwilliam Street, Wath upon Dearne, Rotherham, South Yorks S63 7HG

## Wessex Morris Men
**Contact** Patrick Harries
**Email** pth1145@aol.com
**Phone** 01963 362863
***Monday***
21, Grosvenor Road, Stalbridge, Dorset DT10 2PL

## West Somerset Morris Men
**Contact** Malcolm Appleton
**Email** Bagman@westsomersetmorris.freeserve.co.uk
**Phone** 01643 862541
***Thursday***
Fairhaven, Bossington Lane, Porlock, Minehead, Somerset TA24 8HD

## Westminster Morris Men
**Contact** Philip Staker
**Email** WestminsterMM@staker.demon.co.uk
**Phone** 01371 830014
***Wednesday***
39, Mill End, Thaxted, Dunmow, Essex CM6 2LT

## Whitchurch Morris Men
**Contact** Leonard Pepper
**Email** bagman@whitchurchmorris.freeserve.co.uk
**Phone** 01865 766191
***Tuesday***
19, Gardiner Street, Oxford OX3 7AW

## White Hart Morris Men
**Contact** Keith Lovell
**Phone** 01527 60697
***Monday***
118, Vicarage Cresent, Redditch, Worcestershire B97 4RP

## White Horse Morris Men
**Contact** Reuben Chappell
**Phone** 01747 851097
***Wednesday***
4, Victoria Street, Shaftesbury, Dorset SP7 8AG

## White Rose
**Contact** David [Ned] Barstow
**Phone** 01484 660289
***Wednesday***
20, Station Approach, Honley, Huddersfield, West Yorks. HD7 2LD

## Winchester Morris Men
**Contact** Stroph Rayner
**Email** s.rayner@aepind.co.uk
**Phone** 02380 252112
***Wednesday***
16, Stourvale Gardens, Chandlers Ford, Eastleigh, Hants SO53 3NE

### Woodside Morris Men
**Contact** Roger Bangs
**Email** woodside@ungoliant.easynet.co.uk
**Phone** 01923 720143
***Wednesday***
130, Tudor Way, Rickmansworth, Hertfordshire WD3 2HL

### Wyre Forest Morris Men
**Contact** Nigel Cavendish
**Email** cavn@cavn.freeserve.co.uk
**Phone** 01562 67506
***Tuesday***
1, Redwing Court, Kidderminster, Worcs. DY10 4TR

### Wyvern Jubilee Morris Men
**Contact** Alan Cocker
**Email** bignose@onmail.co.uk
**Phone** 01963 440612
5, West View, South Cadbury, Somerset BA22 7EX

### Yateley Morris Men
**Contact** Paul Montague
**Email** yateleymorrismen@hotmail.com
**Phone** 01276 20817
***Tuesday***
22, Glassonby Walk, Heatherside, Camberley, Surrey GU15 1SD

## TRAVELLING SIDES

### Ancient Men (Oxford on Tour)
**Contact** Gerard Robinson
**Email** gerard.robinson@imsu.ox.ac.uk
**Phone** 01608 643279
48, Churchill Road, Chipping Norton, Oxfordshire OX7 5HP

### Travelling Morrice (Cambridge on Tour)
**Contact** John Jenner
**Email** johnjenner1@compuserve.com
**Phone** 01763 242127
47, Spring Lane, Bassingbourn, Royston, Hertfordshire SG8 5HT

### Adderbury Village Morris Men
**Contact** Donald McCombie
**Phone** 01789 450103
Farmcote Cottage, Wimpstone, Nr. Stratford on Avon, Warwickshire CV37 8NS

### Albion Morris Men
**Contact** Martin Long
**Phone** 01795 538238
***Monday***
2, Whitstable Road, Faversham, Kent ME13 8BD

### Anstey Morrismen (Everards Old Original)
**Contact** Phil Preen
**Email** Phil@thehat.free-online.co.uk
**Phone** 01509 212657
88, Sharpley Road, Loughborough, Leicestershire LE11 4PN

### Armitage Mummers
**Contact** Duncan Rippon
**Email** Duncan@Lichfield.safc.co.uk
**Phone** 01283 791303
***Tuesday***
Oaklands, Long Lane, Fradley, Lichfield, Staffordshire WS13 8NS

### Ashdown Mummers
**Contact** Adrian Norman
**Phone** 01483 502040
134, Guildford Park Avenue, Guildford, Surrey GU2 5NN

### Barnstaple Morris Men
**Contact** Pete Westcott
**Email** p.westcott@virgin.net
**Phone** 01271 375082
***Wednesday***
Lowercroft Cottage, Landkey Road, Barnstaple, North Devon EX32 9DH

### Blackheath Morris Men
**Contact** Stuart Conney
**Email** Conney@ukgateway.net
**Phone** 0208 316 7291
***Wednesday***
65, Heathwood Gardens, Charlton, London SE7 8ET

### Blackmore Morris Men
**Contact** Steve Delarre
**Email** steve.delarre@btinternet.com
**Phone** 01277 890519
***Wednesday***
4, Mill Lane, Moreton, Essex CM5 0DN

### Blue Anchor Morris
**Contact** Peter Reynolds
**Phone** 01326 573706
Glenside, Trevenen, Helston, Cornwall TR13 0ND

### Bovey Tracey Mummers
**Contact** Rod Wilkins
**Phone** 01803 812581
14, Dornafield Close, Ipplepen, Newton Abbot, Devon TQ12 5SN

### Buckland Shag Morris Men
**Contact** Rob Mayes
**Phone** 01883 717463
***Friday***
15, Hurst Green Road, Oxted, Surrey RH8 9BS

### Chameleonic Morris Men
**Contact** David Brewster
**Email** David_brewster@lineone.net
**Phone** 01245 420742
10, Chancery Place, Writtle, Chelmsford, Essex CM1 3DY

### Charlbury Morris
**Contact** Peter Smith
**Phone** 01608 811007
***Friday***
1, Mount Pleasant, Dances Hill, Charlbury, Oxon OX3 3RZ

### Chelmsford Morris Men
**Contact** Peter Bell
**Email** petebell3@aol.com
**Phone** 01371 850085
***Wednesday***
The Priest House, Rotten End, Wethersfield, Chelmsford CM7 4AL

### Chippenham Town Morris Men
**Contact** Richard Aylen
**Phone** 01249 814632
***Wednesday***
1, Redhill Close, Derry Hill, Calne, Wilts SN11 9NY

### Chipping Campden Morris Men
**Contact** David Hart
**Phone** 01386 840869
Trinder House, High Street, Chipping Campden, Glos GL55 6AG

### Churchwardens Morris Men
**Contact** Ian Morden
**Phone** 01803 550360
***Wednesday***
2, Park Lodge, Oldenburg Park, Paignton, Devon TQ3 2UA

### Coton Village Morris Men
**Contact** Andrew Blagbrough
**Phone** 01480 810756
***Thursday***
127, Mill Road, Buckden, Huntingdon, Cambs PE18 9SN

### Crendon Morris Men
**Contact** Pete Summerskill
**Email** Bagman@crendonmorris.co.uk
**Phone** 01844 291172
***Tuesday***
77, Churchway, Haddenham, Aylesbury, Buckinghamshire HP17 8DT

### Devil's Dyke Morris Men
**Contact** Nick Kerry
**Email** Nick@njkerry.freeserve.co.uk
**Phone** 01638 742116
***Thursday***
22, Newmarket Road, Burwell, Cambridge, Cambridgeshire CB5 0AE

**Dublin City Morris Dancers**
**Contact** Alan Corsini
**Phone** 00 - 3531 - 2985068
***Wednesday***
38, Meadow Mount, Dublin 16, Rep. of Ireland

**The Dunton Morris**
**Contact** Chris Rhodes
**Email** appletarts@dial.pipex.com
**Phone** 01767 315488
***Monday***
2, Horseshoe Close, Dunton, Biggleswade, Bedfordshire SG18 8RY

**Ebor Morris Men**
**Contact** Jonathan Brockbank
**Phone** 01904 659600
***Monday***
56, Dale Street, York YO23 1AE

**Frome Valley Morris Men**
**Contact** David Milner
**Email** Dmilner@Thomas-Hardye. Dorset.Sch.uk
**Phone** 01305 852773
***Thursday***
14a, Rectory Close, Broadmayne, Dorset DT2 8EQ

**Gallus Morris Men**
**Contact** Norman Peacock
**Email** nmjpeacock@yahoo.co.uk
**Phone** 01419 561183
***Tuesday***
16, Drumlin Drive, Milngavie, Glasgow G62 6LN

**Greenwich Morris Men**
**Contact** Ged Balmer
**Email** Ged.Balmer@btinternet.com
**Phone** 020 8857 2528
***Thursday***
54, Lavidge Road, Mottingham, London SE9 3NF

**Grenoside Traditional Sword Dancers**
**Contact** Ray Ellison
**Phone** 0114 2453361
***Thursday***
3, Greno Gate, Grenoside, Sheffield, South Yorks S30 3NY

**Hexham Morris Men**
**Contact** Paddy Docherty
**Phone** 01434 605048
***Thursday***
36, Millfield Terrace, Hexham, Northumberland NE46 3EF

**High Spen Blue Diamonds**
**Contact** Frederick Foster
**Phone** 01914 102157
***Tuesday***
12, Northumberland Place, Chester-le-Street, Co. Durham DH3 2AP

**Hinckley Bullockers**
**Contact** Tony Ashley
**Phone** 01455 239690
2nd+4th ***Monday*** Oct-Dec
4, Rannock Close, Hinckley, Leicestershire LE10 0UU

**Hoddesdon CrownsMen**
**Contact** Ken Arton
**Phone** 01279 723433
***Sunday***
26, Sayesbury Avenue, Sawbridgeworth, Herts CM21 0ED

**Ilmington Morris Men**
**Contact** Paul Bryan
**Email** Paul@bryans99.freeserve.co.uk
**Phone** 01608 662167
***Wednesday***
Whole Hey, 23, Gerrards Road, Shipston on Stour, Warks CV36 4HH

**Leominster Morris**
**Contact** Tony Locock
**Phone** 01544 388686
Steps House, Market Square, Pembridge, Herefordshire HR6 9DZ

**Lordsmere Longsword**
**Contact** Richard Hankinson
**Email** Rghankinson@hotmail.com
**Phone** 01457 834871
31, Moorgate Drive, Carrbrook, Stalybridge, Cheshire SK15 3LX

**Man Friday Morris Men**
**Contact** Ian Hubbard (F)
**Email** i.hubbard@ntlworld.com
**Phone** 0116 2209133
***Monday***
44, Deangate Avenue, Birstall, Leicester LE4 3GG

**MCMorris & the Knuckle Rappers**
**Contact** Graham Newson
**Email** Graham.r.newson@bankers trust.com
**Phone** 020 8661 1585
***1st & 3rd Monday***
6, Colston Avenue, Carshalton, Surrey SM5 2NU

**Merrie England Mummers**
**Contact** Clive Bennett
**Email** clivebennett.folk@virgin.net
**Phone** 01273 881226
48, Kingston Close, Hove, East Sussex BN3 8LE

**North Curry Mummers**
**Contact** David Lawrence
**Email** greenman@fromthegreenwood. com
**Phone** 01823 490007
Middle House, 5, Windmill Hill North, Curry, Taunton, Somerset TA3 6LY

**Oak Apple Mummers/ Mid Winter Mummers**
**Contact** Michael Schaschke
**Phone** 01733 750582
34, Mayor's Walk, Peterborough, Cambridgeshire PE3 6ES

**One Day's Wonder Travelling Morris**
**Contact** Tony Ashley
**Phone** 01455 239690
4, Rannoch Close, Hinckley, Leics LE10 0UU

**Pilgrim Morris Men**
**Contact** Geoff Balls
**Email** Bagman@Pilgrimmorrismen.org .uk
**Phone** 01483 823259
***Wednesday***
16, Ennismore Avenue, Guildford, Surrey GU1 1SP

**Plymouth Reunion Morris Men**
**Contact** Stephen Haswell
**Phone** 01482 876628
27, Hall Walk, Snuff Mill Lane, Cottingham, Humberside H16 4RL

**Priston Jubilee MorrisMen**
**Contact** Mark Swabey
**Email** Swabey@freewire.co.uk
**Phone** 01761 470305
***Monday***
1, Bell Close, Farmborough, Bath BA3 1AP

**Prize Old Mummers**
**Contact** Graham Wright
**Phone** 02392 831751
***Wednesday***
20, Bramshott Road, Southsea, Hants PO4 8AN

**Rose & Castle Morris Men**
**Contact** Brian Street
***Wednesday***
Whilton Locks, Daventry, Northamptonshire NN11 5NH

**Royal Borough Morris**
**Contact** Ray Collins
**Phone** 01892 653444
Wareham Lodge, Boar's Head, Crowborough, East Sussex TN6 3HE

**Royal Marine Morris**
**Contact** Gerald Rayner
**Email** Morris@waltonnaze.demon. co.uk
**Phone** 01255 673848
***Sunday***
20, Beaumont Close, Walton-on-the-Naze, Essex CO14 8TX

### Saint Bees Mummers
**Contact** Neil Bettinson
22, Main Street, St. Bees,
Cumbria CA27 0AA

### Sallyport Sword Dancers
**Contact** Vince Rutland
**Phone** 01609 780536
***Thursday***
37, Church View, Brompton,
Northallerton, North Yorks DL6 2QX

### Spen Valley Longsword Dancers
**Contact** John Browell
**Phone** 01274 681844
***Monday***
1, Moorlands, Birkenshaw, Bradford,
West Yorks BD11 2BH

### Stockport Morris Men
**Contact** Dave Johnson
**Phone** 0161 3082113
10, Westminster Way, Dukinfield,
Hyde, Cheshire SK16 5BQ

### Tarka Morris Men
**Contact** Keith Bowden
**Email** Keithbowden@callnetuk.com
**Phone** 01237 421812
3, Holt Cottages, Richmond Road,
Appledore, Bideford,
Devon EX39 1QN

### Thameside Mummers
**Contact** Derek J Oliver
**Email** Mummers@ravenswood.co.uk
**Phone** 01268 794556
148, Essex Way, South Benfleet,
Essex SS7 1LN

### Watling Street Mummers
**Contact** Mike O'Connor
**Phone** 01604 858764
9, Greenside, Blisworth,
Northampton, Northants NN7 3BY

### Weald of Kent Morris Men
**Contact** Tim Dwyer
**Email** timdwyer@wealdofkentmorris.org.uk
**Phone** 01424 240414
***Wednesday***
2, Joys Hill Cottages, Goudhurst Road,
Marden, Tonbridge, Kent TN12 9NB

### Welsh Border Morris Men
**Contact** Mike Finn
**Email** Mfinn@worcestershire.gov.uk
**Phone** 01905 422851
Stonecrop, Main Road, Hallow,
Worcestershire WR2 6PH

### White Star Sword Dancers
**Contact** Simon Evans
**Phone** 01622 812158
***Sunday***
2, Court Lodge Cottages, West
Peckham, Maidstone, Kent ME18 5JN

### Winster Morris Men
**Contact** David Mitchell
**Email** sheilamitch@supanet.com
**Phone** 01629 650220
The old Forge, Main Street, Winster,
Derbyshire DE4 2DJ

### Woodchurch Morris Men
**Contact** David Grabham
**Phone** 01233 860789
***Thursday***
Poolside Cottage, Redbrook St,
Woodchurch, Ashford, Kent TN26 3QR

# The Morris Federation

In 1975, the inaugural Annual General Meeting of the Women's Morris Federation was held in Bath. The founder member teams, according to Val Parker's exhaustive record-searching were Bath City, Bourne Bumpers, Cardiff, Earley, England's Glory, Holden's Goldens, Knots of May, (Ladies of) Green Willow, Maids of Barum, Meridian, New Esperance, Nutting Girls, Oxford, Phoenix, Queen of Hearts, Seven Sisters, Somerset Maids, Stag Hill, Teign, Water-cum-Jolly (who became Derby Crown) and Windsor. Maygog (sic), Exeter (?Glory of the West), Invicta, Strand on the Green and Whitty Pear were also around at about that time although it's not clear precisely when they joined.

The mood of the morris-dancing world then was one of resistance to women dancing, although the number of women's sides joining increased almost exponentially, and at the time of writing there are 148 women's teams, 51 men's teams, 181 mixed, 52 individual members, 5 Honorary Life Members and 2 Friends. In 1977 there was the first proposal to drop the word "women", however, it wasn't until 1980 that the constitution was changed to permit mixed sides. In 1982 Ripon City joined as the first men's team and the named changed to The Morris Federation in 1983, and since that time there has been a considerable lessening in the original antipathy.

Betty Reynolds, first President and Honorary Life Member, said, "We started the Federation to give out information on material to be had and from where, to give friendship and help and to have get-togethers to discuss problems AND dance". Today, the aims of the Federation are (a) to encourage and maintain interest in the practice of morris dancing by women and men of all ages, (b) to provide a channel of communication between member sides and (c) to encourage the improvement of standards of dancing among its members. Sounds good to me.

**Fee Lock**, Secretary
Hastings, April 2001

*With grateful thanks to Beth Neill, my predecessor, for extracts from Twenty One Years, 1975 – 1996, published by The Morris Federation.*

## THE MORRIS FEDERATION

*Group Members as at 1st March 2001*

### Acorn Morris
**Contact** Gina Brockbank
**Mail address** 15 Dale Street, York, North Yorkshire YO23 1AE
**Phone** 01904 659600
**Email** gina@brockbankg.freeserve.co.uk
**Web** www.d-n-a.net/users/dnetJjSc/acorn
**Practice** in York on Wed.
**Dance style** Border and Cotswold
**Gender** Female

### Adderbury Morris Men
**Web** www.btinternet.com/~Kickback/Adderbury.Morris/Adderbury.html
**Contact** Stephen Wass
**Mail address** 3 Chapel Row, Cropredy, Banbury, Oxfordshire OX17 1NS
**Phone** 01295 758222
**Email** StephenandVerna.Wass@btinternet.com
**Practice** in Adderbury on Wed.
**Dance style** Cotswold
**Gender** Male

### Adlington Morris Men
**Contact** Geoff Smith
**Mail address** 21 Meredith Street, Ladybarn, Manchester, Greater Manchester M14 6ST
**Phone** 0161 224 6356
**Email** geoffrey.w.smith@mcmail.com
**Practice** in Handforth on Tue.
**Dance style** Cotswold, Long Sword and Mumming
**Gender** Male

### Alive and Kicking
**Web** www.alive-and-kicking.org.uk
**Contact** Julie Page
**Mail address** Trelawney, Polson Hill, Morchard Bishop, Exeter, Devon EX17 6JD
**Email** enquiries@alive-and-kicking.org.uk
**Practice** in Exeter on Thu.
**Dance style** Appalachian
**Gender** Mixed

### Alive & Kicking - Maldon
**Contact** Angela Clarke
**Mail address** 31 Suffolk Road, Maldon, Essex CM9 6AX
**Phone** 01621 853680
**Practice** in Maldon on Wed.
**Dance style** North West Clog
**Gender** Female

### Alton Morris
**Web** www.opread.f9.co.uk/AltonMorris
**Contact** John Edgecombe
**Mail address** Holtwood, Stapley Lane, Ropley, Hampshire SO24 0EL
**Phone** 01962 772565
**Email** nsparkes@bigfoot.com
**Practice** in Alton on Fri.
**Dance style** Border
**Gender** Mixed

### Amersham Garland Dancers
**Contact** Mrs Phyllis Chapman
**Mail address** 20 The Drive, Amersham, Buckinghamshire HP7 9AA
**Phone** 01494 725962
**Practice** in Chesham Bois on Thu.
**Dance style** Garland and Stave
**Gender** Female

### Amounderness Ladies
**Contact** Alan Thwaites
**Mail address** 79 Woodplumpton Lane, Broughton, Preston, Lancs PR3 5JZ
**Phone** 01772 863073
**Practice** in Preston on Thu.
**Dance style** North West Clog and Garland
**Gender** Female

### Anstey Royale Chalfont
**Web** www.martinwildig.com/mwchalfont.htm
**Contact** Diane Kruge
**Mail address** 16 Bodicoat Close, Whetstone, Leicestershire LE8 6ZN
**Phone** 0116 284 9425
**Email** diane@kruge.freeserve.co.uk
**Practice** in Newton Linford on Tue.
**Dance style** North West Clog and Garland
**Gender** Female

### Antrobus Soulcakers
**Contact** Chris Eyres
**Mail address** Springwater, Cogshall Lane, Comberbach, Northwich, Cheshire CW9 6BS
**Phone** 01606 892027
quackdoctor@virgin.com
Practice location and day not known.
**Dance style** Mumming and Other/Own
**Gender** Male

## Appalachian Controlee
**Contact** Mrs S Hutchings
**Mail address** 72 Little Week Road, Dawlish, Devon EX7 0NL
**Phone** 01626 864232
**Practice** in Newton Abbot on Sun.
**Dance style** Appalachian
**Gender** Mixed

## Appleyard
**Contact** Mary Ward
**Mail address** 21 The Village, Powick, Worcester, Worcestershire WR2 4QR
**Phone** 01905 830285
**Email** powickfrog@aol.com
**Practice** in Earls Croome on Thu.
**Dance style** Border, Garland, North West Clog and Other/Own
**Gender** Female

## Applejacks Appalachian
**Contact** Martin Newman
**Mail address** 21 Kenmore Drive, Horfield, Bristol, Avon BS7 0TS
**Phone** 0117 969 0521
**Practice** in Almondsbury on Wed.
**Dance style** Appalachian
**Gender** Mixed

## Argameles Clog Team
**Contact** George Garside
**Mail address** 87 Gardner Road, Formby, Merseyside, West Midlands L37 8DE
**Phone** 01704 871430
**Email** george.garside@talk21.com
**Practice** in Formby on Tue.
**Dance style** Garland, North West Clog and Step
**Gender** Mixed

## Arrowhead Morris
**Contact** Lynda Sutton
**Mail address** 31 Beaufort Avenue, Fareham, Hampshire PO16 7PE
**Phone** 01329 220247
**Email** Dave_Sutton@pall.com
**Practice** in Fareham on Fri.
**Dance style** Border and Cotswold
**Gender** Mixed

## Arum Lords and Ladies
**Contact** Jan Guppy
**Mail address** Rookwoods Cottage, Yeldham Road, Sible Hedingham, Essex CO9 3QG
**Phone** 01787 460842
**Practice** in Belchamp on Wed.
**Dance style** North West Clog
**Gender** Mixed

## Ashvale Longsword
**Contact** Chris Higgs
**Mail address** 7 Ware Road, Tonwell, Ware, Hertfordshire SG12 0HN
**Phone** 01920 464395
**Practice** in Wareside on Tue.
**Dance style** Long Sword
**Gender** Mixed

## Aynho Apricots
**Contact** Jane Wills
**Mail address** 9 The Square, Aynho, Banbury, Oxfordshire OX17 3BL
**Phone** 01869 810179
**Practice** in Aynho on Wed.
**Dance style** Border, Cotswold and Long Sword
**Gender** Female

## Babylon
**Contact** Phil Workman
**Mail address** 3 Mitchelmore Road, Yeovil, Somerset BA21 4BA
**Phone** 01935 410773
**Email** Babylon@cunio-marsh.freeserve.co.uk
**Practice** in Corscombe on Wed.
**Dance style** Mumming and Other/Own
**Gender** Mixed

## Bakanalia Border Morris
**Contact** John Talbut
**Mail address** The Laurels, Berry Hill Lane, Donington le Heath, Coalville, Leicestershire E67 2FB
**Phone** 01530 836780
**Email** Bakanalia@dpets.demon.co.uk
**Practice** in Leicester on Mon.
**Dance style** Border and Mumming
**Gender** Mixed

## Baldock Midnight Morris
**Contact** Sarah Cass
**Mail address** 5 Hitchin Road, Arlesley, Bedfordshire SG15 6RR
**Phone** 01462 638401
**Email** molley97@hotmail.com
**Practice** in Baldock on Tue.
**Dance style** Cotswold
**Gender** Mixed

## Bare Bones Women's Morris
**Contact** Mel Harmer
**Mail address** 27 Leicester Rd, Shepshed, Loughborough, Leicestershire LE12 9DF
**Phone** 01509 503745
**Email** wendy.english@dtn.ntl.com
**Practice** in Loughborough on Wed.
**Dance style** Border
**Gender** Female

## Barley Break
**Contact** Sheryl Massen
**Mail address** 25 Clarkson Drive, Stallingborough, Lincolnshire DN41 8BQ
**Phone** 01472 884656
**Practice** in Grimsby on Thu.
**Dance style** North West Clog and Garland
**Gender** Female

## Basingclog
**Contact** Bill Hayes
**Mail address** 11 Oakley Lane, Oakley, Basingstoke, Hampshire RG23 7JZ
**Phone** 01256 781027
**Practice** in Basingstoke on Tue.
**Dance style** North West Clog
**Gender** Mixed

## Bedfordshire Lace
**Contact** Sonja Harbottle
**Mail address** 75 Station Road, Woburn Sands, Bedfordshire MK17 8SH
**Phone** 01908.582735
**Email** sonja.harbottle@lineone.net
**Practice** in Ampthill on Tue.
**Dance style** Cotswold
**Gender** Female

## Beetlecrushers
**Contact** Ann Smith
**Mail address** The Old Bakery, Anchor Rd, Coleford, Bath, Avon BA3 5PB
**Phone** 01373 812227
**Email** beetlecrushers@hotmail.com
**Practice** in Gurney Slade on Wed.
**Dance style** Step
**Gender** Mixed

## Beggars Oak Clog
**Web** freespace.virgin.net/tedwards.hednesford
**Contact** Mrs Trish Cadman
**Mail address** Elmhurst Hall Farm, Fox Lane, Lichfield, Staffordshire SW13 8HB
**Phone** 01543 253084
**Email** tedwards.hednesford@virgin.net
**Practice** in Armitage on Mon.
**Dance style** Garland and North West Clog
**Gender** Mixed

## Belle d'Vain
**Contact** Nicola McCrae
**Mail address** 36 St Laurence Way, Bidford-on-Avon, Warwickshire B50 4FF
**Phone** 01789 773008
**Email** Nicki.McCrae@barclayscorporate.com
**Practice** in Bretforton on Fri.
**Dance style** North West Clog
**Gender** Female

## Belles & Broomsticks
**Contact** Mrs Margaret Webster
**Mail address** L'Etacq, Goldcrest Avenue, Port Soif, Vale, Guernsey GY6 8HP
**Phone** 01481 53785
**Email** stuart@maggie70.freeserve.co.uk
**Practice** in St Peters on Mon.
**Dance style** Border and Cotswold
**Gender** Female

## Benskins Morris
**Web** www.freespace.virginnet.co.uk/benskins.Morris
**Contact** Ted Richards
**Mail address** 6 Woodview Cottages, The Vale Road, Chesham, Buckinghamshire HP6 3NT
**Phone** 0208 420 3612
**Email** ted.richards@baesystems.com
**Practice** in Watford on Mon.
**Dance style** North West Clog
**Gender** Mixed

## Berkshire Bedlam Morris
**Web** www.ariadnet.demon.co.uk
**Contact** Malcolm Major
**Mail address** 20 Chestnut Ave, Wokingham, Berkshire RG41 3HX
**Phone** 0118 977 1952
**Email** malcolmmajor@lineone.net
**Practice** in Wokingham on Thu.
**Dance style** Cotswold
**Gender** Male

## Betty Luptons Ladle Laikers
**Web** members.aol.com/teddods/betty.htm
**Contact** Kath Day
**Mail address** 86 Poplar Grove, Harrogate, North Yorkshire HG1 4PW
**Phone** 01423.563694
**Email** TedDods@aol.com
**Practice** in Harrogate on Wed.
**Dance style** Garland/North West Clog
**Gender** Female

## Beverley Garland
**Contact** Mrs A Smith
**Mail address** 149 Grovehill Rd, Beverley, East Yorkshire HU17 0ET
**Phone** 01482 867450
**Practice** in Beverley on Thu.
**Dance style** Garland/North West Clog
**Gender** Female

## Bideford Phoenix Morris
**Contact** Martin Boyles
**Mail address** 1 J H Taylor Drive, Northam, Bideford, Devon EX39 1TT
**Phone** 01237 423716
**Email** bagman@bidefordphoenix morris.fsnet.co.uk
**Practice** in Bideford on Wed.
**Dance style** Cotswold and Border
**Gender** Mixed

## Bishop Gundulf's Morris
**Contact** Josie Anstee
**Mail address** 23 Jefferson Drive, Rainham, Kent ME8 0DB
**Phone** 01634 260281
**Email** gundulf@compuserve.com
**Practice** in Chatham on Tue.
**Dance style** Long Sword and North West Clog
**Gender** Joint

## Black Adder Clog
**Contact** Ms Sue Vigers
**Mail address** 15 Breedon Road, Cotteridge, Birmingham, West Midlands B30 2HT
**Practice** in Cotteridge on Thu.
**Dance style** North West Clog and Other/Own
**Gender** Mixed

## Black Annis
**Contact** Lynn Goodall
**Mail address** 34 Bollington Road, Oadby, Leicester, Leicestershire LE2 4NB
**Phone** 0116 271 9728
**Email** lynn@lynngoodall.freeserve.co.uk
**Practice** in Leicester on Thu.
**Dance style** Cotswold and Molly
**Gender** Female

## Black Bess Border Morris
**Contact** Suzanne Lovell
**Mail address** 36 Fore Street, Kingskerswell, Newton Abbot, TQ12 5HZ
**Phone** 01803 873908
**Email** paul.lovell@reimsnet.com
**Practice** in Kingskerswell on Mon.
**Dance style** Border
**Gender** Female

## Black Boy Rapper
**Contact** Phil Merriott
**Mail address** 14 Kreswell Grove, Dovercourt, Essex CO12 3SZ
**Phone** 01255 502042
**Email** philmerriott@tinyworld.co.uk
**Practice** in Harwich on Wed.
**Dance style** Rapper
**Gender** Mixed

## Black Bull Clog
**Contact** Mrs Rosie Flint
**Mail address** 13 Orchard Lane, Pilgrims Hatch, Brentwood, Essex CM15 9RD
**Phone** 01277 374378
**Email** rosie@thebriars13.freeserve.co.uk
**Practice** in Moreton on Thu.
**Dance style** Garland and North West Clog
**Gender** Female

## Black Dog Molly
**Contact** Mary Adderley
**Mail address** 46 Pacific Road, Trentham, Stoke on Trent, Staffordshire ST4 8UD
**Phone** 01782 643348
**Practice** in Tunstall on Thu.
**Dance style** Border and Molly
**Gender** Mixed

## Black Horse and Standard NW
**Contact** Carol Selby
**Mail address** 63 Thorold Rd, Ilford, Essex IG1 4EU
**Phone** 0181 514 8771
**Email** carol.mcguinness@eulergroup.com
**Practice** in London, Walthamstow on Wed.
**Dance style** North West Clog
**Gender** Female

## Black Pig Border
**Web** members.aol.com/BlackPig1/BLACKPIG.html
**Contact** Yvonne Morley
**Mail address** 7 Sperry Close, Spelston, Nottinghamshire NE16 6BS
**Phone** 01773 781933
**Email** YMorley@aol.com
**Practice** in Giltbrook on Wed.
**Dance style** Mumming and Border
**Gender** Mixed

## Black Sheep Morris
**Contact** Andrew Bishop
**Mail address** 7 Startforth Park, Startforth, Barnard Castle, Co Durham DL12 9AL
**Phone** 01833 631025
**Email** andrew@bishop20.freeserve.co.uk
**Practice** in Barnard Castle on Wed.
**Dance style** Border
**Gender** Mixed

## Blackwater Morris
**Web** freespace.virgin.net/k.jeary/index.html
**Contact** Liz Jeary
**Mail address** 27 Austral Way, Althorne, Chelmsford, Essex CM3 6UP
**Phone** 01621 740978
**Email** liz.jeary@rmplc.co.uk
**Practice** in Maldon on Tue.
**Dance style** North West Clog
**Gender** Mixed

## Bloxham Morris
**Web** kickback.btinternet.co.uk/Bloxham.Morris/Bloxham/html
**Contact** Verna Wass
**Mail address** 3 Chapel Row, Cropredy, Banbury, Oxfordshire OX17 1NS
**Phone** 01295 758227
**Email** verna.wass@btinternet.com
**Practice** in Bloxham on Thu.
**Dance style** Cotswold
**Gender** Female

## Bluefields
**Web** www.bluefields.org.uk
**Contact** Nick Pilley
**Mail address** 53 North Street, Bridgwater, Somerset TA6 3PW
**Phone** 01278 450780
**Email** bluefields_appalachian@hotmail.com
**Practice** in Overstratton on Tue.
**Dance style** Appalachian
**Gender** Mixed

## Bog Hoppers & Bushbeaters
**Contact** Lydia Wills
**Mail address** 141 Everton Road, Hordle, Hampshire
**Phone** 01425 618314
**Email** boghoppersnewforest@paulwills.screaming.net
**Practice** in Milford-on-Sea on Mon.
**Dance style** North West Clog and Border
**Gender** Mixed

## Bon Accord Cloggies
**Contact** Sara Nicol
**Mail address** Cairncosh Cottage, Rullysessle, Alford, AB33 8AY
**Phone** 019755 63170
**Practice** in Aberdeen on Tue.
**Gender** Mixed

## Border Dash
**Contact** Barney Barnett
**Mail address** 26 Lodge Close, Benfleet, Essex SS7 3DA
**Practice** in Leigh on Sea on Fri.
**Dance style** Border
**Gender** Mixed

## Boughton Monchelsea
**Contact** Andrea Brooker
**Mail address** 32 Playstool Road, Newington, Sittingbourne, Kent ME9 7NE
**Phone** 01795 843331
**Email** trevandrea@supanet.com
**Practice** in Maidstone on Thu.
**Dance style** Cotswold and Border
**Gender** Mixed

## Bourne Borderers
**Web** lineone.net/~bourne_borderers
**Contact** Nicola Darby
**Mail address** 7 Lamport Close, Market Deeping, Peterborough, PE6 8BU
**Phone** 01778 342490
**Email** bourne_borderers@lineone.net
**Practice** in Edenham on Wed.
**Dance style** Border
**Gender** Mixed

## Bows 'n' Belles
**Contact** Sue Pratt
**Mail address** Westways, Halstead Rd, Aldham, Colchester, Essex
**Phone** 01206 240682
**Practice** in Colchester on Sun.
**Dance style** Garland, North West Clog and Step
**Gender** Female

## Brackets (Hong Kong)
**Contact** John Bacon
**Mail address** 57 East End Lane, Ditchling, Hassocks, East Sussex BN6 8UR
**Phone** 01273 843938
**Email** jandabacon@aol.com
**Practice** in a variety of locations on (some) Sundays.
**Dance style** Cotswold
**Gender** Mixed

## Bradshaw Mummers
**Contact** Mrs Krys Lyon
**Mail address** 4 Greenacres Grove, Shelf, Halifax, West Yorkshire HX3 7RN
**Phone** 01274 675985
**Email** krys@pklyon.fsnet.co.uk
**Practice** in Halifax on Wed.
**Dance style** Mumming
**Gender** Male

## Brighton Morris Men
**Web** www.blueanchor.demon.co.uk/brighton.htm
**Contact** Malcolm Smale
**Mail address** 44 Bannings Vale, Saltdean, Brighton, East Sussex BN2 8DB
**Phone** 01273 307175
**Email** rowansmale@mistral.co.uk
**Practice** in Brighton on Thu.
**Dance style** Cotswold
**Gender** Male

## Broken Ankles
**Web** www.brokenankles.btinternet.co.uk
**Contact** Penny Allen
**Mail address** 89 Hollingbury Park Ave, Brighton, East Sussex BN1 7JQ
**Phone** 01273 541453
**Email** brokenankles@btinternet.com
**Practice** in Brighton on Sun.
**Dance style** Appalachian, Cotswold and Step
**Gender** Mixed

## Bullnose Morris
**Contact** Glynis Candler
**Mail address** 79 Belfairs Park Drive, Leigh on Sea, Essex SS9 4TW
**Phone** 01702 525804
**Email** jjnew@easynet.co.uk
**Practice** in Pitsea on Tue.
**Dance style** Appalachian and Cotswold
**Gender** Mixed

## Calceto Morris
**Contact** Christine Sargent
**Mail address** 4 Whylands Crescent, Worthing, West Sussex
**Phone** 01903 264495
**Email** csargent@boffin-durrington-worthing.co.uk
**Practice** in Durrington on Tue.
**Dance style** Border, Cotswold and Garland
**Gender** Mixed

## Cardiff Ladies Morris
**Contact** Ruth Parton
**Mail address** 30 Heol Seddon, Danescourt, Cardiff, West Glamorgan CF5 2QX
**Phone** 02920 552632
**Email** monica@mehers.demon.co.uk
**Practice** in Llandaff on Tue.
**Dance style** Border and Cotswold
**Gender** Female

## Carlisle Sword Morris and Clog
**Contact** Frank Lee
**Mail address** Leafield, Market Place, Brampton, Cumbria CA8 1TL
**Phone** 016977 2649
**Practice** in Carlisle on Mon.
**Dance style** Border, Garland, Long Sword, Rapper, Step
**Gender** Joint

## Carnkie Cloggers
**Contact** Sylvia Penhaligon
**Mail address** 1 Ruby Terrace, Porkellis, Helston, Cornwall TR13 0LD
**Practice** in Redruth on Tue.
**Dance style** Border, Garland, Stave and North West Clog
**Gender** Female

## Carreg Las
**Contact** Lin Cram
**Mail address** Cnwc y Carreg, Hebron, Whitland, Carmarthenshire SA34 0JS
**Phone** 01994 419779
**Email** diane.copperl@btinternet.com
**Practice** in Abercych on Wed.
**Dance style** Border and Other/Own
**Gender** Mixed

## Charnwood Clog
**Web** www.radoyle.u-net.com/charnwoodclog.htm
**Contact** Islay Sayles
**Mail address** 82 The Meadows, Loughborough, Leicestershire LE12 9QN
**Phone** 01509 502064
**Email** robb@radoyle.u.net.com
**Practice** in Quorn on Mon.
**Dance style** Step
**Gender** Mixed

## Chelmsford Morris
**Contact** Lewis Conquer
**Mail address** 82 Health Drive, Chelmsford, Essex CM2 9HF
**Phone** 01245 492066
**Email** lewis.conquer@btinternet.com
**Practice** in Chelmsford; (Female on Tue; Male on Wed).
**Dance style** Cotswold and North West Clog
**Gender** Joint

## Cheshire Royal Morris Dancers
**Contact** Judith Parker
**Mail address** Stonechair House, Stonechair Lane, Scholar Green, Cheshire ST7 3JJ
**Phone** 01782 773287
**Practice** in Goostrey on Tue.
**Dance style** North West Clog
**Gender** Female

## Chesterfield Garland
**Contact** Janet Scott
**Mail address** 11 Park Lane, Newbold, Chesterfield, Derbyshire S41 8SQ
**Phone** 01246 206124
**Email** janetscott958@hotmail.com
**Practice** in Chesterfield on Tue.
**Dance style** North West Clog
**Gender** Female

## Chiltern Hundreds
**Web** www.morrisdancers.com
**Contact** Celia Smith
**Mail address** 26 Oxney Road, Watford, Hertfordshire WD1 4QQ
**Phone** 01923 221701
**Email** csmith@sunley.com
**Practice** in Watford on Tue.
**Dance style** North West Clog
**Gender** Mixed

## Chinewrde
**Contact** Dyan Hewett
**Mail address** The Cottage Garden, North Street, Marton, Warwickshire CV23 9RJ
**Phone** 01926 633243
**Email** dyan@marton01.freeserve.co.uk
**Practice** in Kenilworth on Wed.
**Dance style** North West Clog
**Gender** Female

## Chingford Morris Men
**Contact** Adrian Hilton
**Mail address** 53 Swanfield Road, Waltham Cross, Hertfordshire EN8 7JS
**Phone** 01992 622487
**Email** adrian.hilton@lbwf.gov.uk
**Practice** in London, Highams Park on Mon (for full details contact Adrian).
**Dance style** Cotswold and Other/Own
**Gender** Joint

## Chip Off The Old
**Web** homepage.dtn.ntl.com/p.benson/Chiphome.html
**Contact** Sue Smith
**Mail address** 86 Farneworth Road, Mickleover, Derbyshire DE3 5ES
**Phone** 01332 519170
**Email** b.m.gotheridge@derby.ac.uk
**Practice** in Derby on Wed
**Dance style** Cotswold
**Gender** Female

## Chobham Morris
**Contact** Tony Edie
**Mail address** 3 Back of High St, Chobham, Woking, Surrey GU24 8AE
**Phone** 01276 857656
**Email** johnm@ensigngeo.com
**Practice** in Chobham on Sun.
**Dance style** Cotswold and Other/Own
**Gender** Mixed

## Chorlton Green
**Web** ourworld.compuserve.com/homepages/opsis/chorlton.htm
**Contact** Lesley Blackshaw
**Mail address** 1 Kayswood Road, Marple, Cheshire SK6 6EW
**Phone** 0161 427 5705
**Email** lesley@kayswood.freeserve.co.uk
**Practice** in Chorlton on Mon.
**Dance style** North West Clog
**Gender** Female

## City Clickers
**Contact** Alison Meredith
**Mail address** 1 Marygold Leaze, Cadbury Heath, Bristol, BS30 8AS
**Phone** 0117 967 5320
**Email** A.K.Meredith@bath.ac.uk
**Practice** in Bishopston on Tue.
**Dance style** Step
**Gender** Mixed

## Clerical Error
**Web** www.millennas.force9.co.uk/clerical.htm
**Contact** Sam Jupp
**Mail address** Hen Efail y Glyn, Llanrhaedr, Denbigh, Denbighshire LL16 4NW
**Phone** 01745.815180
**Email** lawrencejupp@netscapeonline.co.uk
**Practice** in Ysceifiog on Thu.
**Dance style** Border and Mumming
**Gender** Mixed

## Clydeside Sword & Step
**Contact** Ranko Vrcelj
**Mail address** Flat 3R, 40 Springhill Gardens, Queens Park, Glasgow, Strathclyde G41 2EY
**Phone** 0141 632 4904
**Email** r.m.vrcelj@strath.ac.uk
**Practice** in Glasgow on Wed.
**Dance style** Step and Long Sword
**Gender** Mixed

## Cock & Magpie Morris
**Contact** Shirley Niblock
**Mail address** 338 Ashgate Rd, Chesterfield, Derbyshire S40 4BW
**Phone** 01246 207080
**Practice** in Chesterfield on Mon.
**Dance style** Border and Cotswold
**Gender** Mixed

## Cockleshell Clog
**Contact** Bill Delderfield
**Mail address** 145 Ramuz Drive, Westcliff on Sea, Essex SS0 9JN
**Phone** 01702 353020
**Email** cockleshellclog@freewebemail.com
**Practice** in Southend on Thu.
**Dance style** North West Clog and Other/Own
**Gender** Mixed

## Cogs & Wheels
**Contact** Mrs Shelagh Palmer
**Mail address** Seekings, 39 Lamb Park, Chagford, Devon TQ13 8DN
**Phone** 01647 433464
**Practice** in South Zeal on Thu.
**Dance style** Cotswold and Mumming
**Gender** Female

## Copperfield Clog
**Web** members.aol.com/copclog/Clog1.htm
**Contact** Mrs Louise Smith
**Mail address** 23 The Braes, Higham, Rochester, Kent ME3 7NA
**Phone** 01474 822148
**Email** themsmiths@excite.co.uk
**Practice** in Higham on Mon.
**Dance style** North West Clog
**Gender** Female

## Cottonmill Clog
**Web** www.cottonmillclog.supanet.com
**Contact** Mrs S Sanger
**Mail address** 298 Jeans Way, Dunstable, Bedfordshire LU5 4PT
**Phone** 01582 662276
**Email** su.sanger@btinternet.com
**Practice** in St Albans on Wed.
**Dance style** North West Clog
**Gender** Mixed

## Cry Havoc
**Contact** Susie Onions
**Mail address** 16 Westland Way, Woodstock, Oxfordshire OX20 1YF
**Phone** 01993.811865
**Email** malch@patrol.i-way.co.uk
**Practice** in Botley on Thu.
**Dance style** Cotswold
**Gender** Mixed

## Cuckoos Nest
**Contact** Mrs Carolyn Mears
**Mail address** 28 Chalkland Rise, Woodingdean, Brighton, East Sussex BN2 6RH
**Phone** 01273 302006
**Practice** in Brighton on Mon.
**Dance style** Cotswold
**Gender** Female

## Dacre
**Contact** Amy Philips
**Mail address** Flat 2, 17 Priory Hill, Dartford, Kent DA1 2BD
**Phone** 01322 294743
**Email** b.newman@aut.org.uk
**Practice** in London, Lewisham on Mon.
**Dance style** Cotswold
**Gender** Female

## Daisy Roots
**Web** www.btinternet.com/~daisy.roots
**Contact** Chris Milkins
**Mail address** 8 Gillsman's Drive, St Leonards on Sea, East Sussex TN38 9JF
**Phone** 01424 435147
**Email** daisy.roots@btinternet.com
**Practice** in Hastings on Thu.
**Dance style** Cotswold
**Gender** Female

## Danegeld Morris
**Contact** Brian Prettyman
**Mail address** 7 Nicolls Close, Ufford, Woodbridge, Suffolk
**Phone** 01394 460567
**Practice** in Bredfield on Tue.
**Dance style** North West Clog
**Gender** Mixed

## Dark Horse Morris
**Contact** Web www.dykech.freeuk.com
**Contact** Mike Watson
**Mail address** 3 Dykes Chase, Maldon, Essex CM9 6HP
**Phone** 01621 852941
**Email** mike@dykech.demon.co.uk
**Practice** in Maldon on Sun.
**Dance style** Border
**Gender** Mixed

## Datchet Border Morris
**Web** www.datchetbordermorris.fsnet.co.uk
**Contact** Keith Walter
**Mail address** 3 Seaton Drive, Ashford, Middlesex TW15 3ET
**Phone** 01932 561454
**Email** JohnWicking@aol.com
**Practice** in Datchet on Mon.
**Dance style** Border, Long Sword and Mumming
**Gender** Male

## Dead Horse Morris
**Contact** Chris Janes
**Mail address** 52 Cromwell Road, Whitstable, Kent CT5 1NN
**Phone** 01227 264851
**Email** alex.clifton-fearnside@ons.gov.uk
**Practice** in Whitstable on Mon.
**Dance style** Other/Own
**Gender** Male

## Ditchling Morris
**Contact** Annie Vail
**Mail address** Eastview, 10 East Gardens, Ditchling, East Sussex BN6 8ST
**Phone** 01273 844454
**Email** morrismatters@thevails.demon.co.uk
**Practice** in Ditchling on Thu.
**Dance style** Border and Cotswold
**Gender** Mixed

## Dorset Buttons
**Contact** Sian Salisbury
**Mail address** Flat 11, East Cliff Grange, 35 Knyveton Road, Bournemouth, Dorset BH1 3QJ
**Phone** 01202 395674
**Email** sian@salisbury199.freeserve.co.uk
**Practice** in Wareham on Wed.
**Dance style** North West Clog and Rapper
**Gender** Joint

## Dorset Knob Knockers
**Contact** Colin Shapter
**Mail address** Nutwood, 81C West End, Street, Somerset BA16 0LG
**Email** colin.shapter@ukonline.co.uk
**Practice** in Yarlington on Sun.
**Dance style** Stave
**Gender** Mixed

## Downes on Tour
**Contact** Mr Chris Callaghan
**Mail address** 24 Marjorie Grove, Battersea, London SW11 5SJ
**Phone** 0207 978 5585
**Email** c.callaghan@ucl.ac.uk
**Practice** in London, variable on Sat.
**Dance style** Cotswold
**Gender** Joint

## Dr Turberville's Morris
**Contact** Web www.bluefin-analysis.com/crewkerne/clubs/drt_Morris
**Contact** Alan Curtis
**Mail address** 7 Waverley, Somerton, Somerset TN11 6SH
**Phone** 01458 272062
**Email** alan_curtis@yahoo.com
**Practice** day and location not notified.
**Dance style** Cotswold
**Gender** Mixed

## Ducklington Morris
**Web** www.hulot.demon.co.uk/Duckindex.htm
**Contact** Peter West
**Mail address** 6 Beaufort Close, Bicester, Oxfordshire OX6 7XN
**Phone** 01869 601451
**Email** badger@ducklington.u-net.com
**Practice** in Ducklington on Tue.
**Dance style** Cotswold
**Gender** Mixed

## Duke's Dandy Clog
**Contact** Penny Smith
**Mail address** 48 Lime Tree Avenue Retford, Nottinghamshire DN22 7BA
**Phone** 01777 703837
**Practice** in Retsford on Wed.
**Dance style** Step
**Gender** Female

## East Saxon Sword
**Web** www.kibbler.demon.co.uk/ess
**Contact** Dave Law
**Mail address** 68 Rushden Gardens, Clayhall, Ilford, Essex, IG5 0BW
**Phone** 0208 550 0032
**Email** david.law@newham.gov.uk
**Practice** in London, Plaistow on Tue.
**Dance style** Long Sword and Rapper
**Gender** Male

## Elephant up a Pole
**Web** www.angelfire.com/co/bordermorriseuap
**Contact** Kate Balfour
**Mail address** 5 Bartlett Close, Warwick, Warwickshire CV34 4UY
**Phone** 01926 403059
**Email** ksb@balfour0.demon.co.uk
**Practice** in Coventry on Thu.
**Dance style** Border
**Gender** Mixed

### Ellington Morris
**Web** www.sjshaw.dircon.co.uk/ellington
**Contact** Brian Woodhead
**Mail address** 318 Marlow Bottom, Marlow, Buckinghamshire SL7 3QH
**Phone** 01628 485051
**Email** sjshaw@dircon.co.uk
**Practice** in Pinkneys Green on Wed.
**Dance style** Cotswold and Rapper
**Gender** Mixed

### Ely & Littleport Riot
**Contact** Rhiannon Williams
**Mail address** 20 Victoria Street, Ely, Cambridgeshire CB7 4BL
**Phone** 01353 664857
**Email** rhiannon@elycambs.free-online. co.uk
**Practice** in Ely on Fri.
**Dance style** Border
**Gender** Female

### Enfield Chasers
**Contact** Jackie Bolton
**Mail address** 1f South Road, Edmonton, London N9 6JJ
**Phone** 0208 804 3968
**Practice** in Enfield on Mon.
**Dance style** Garland and North West Clog
**Gender** Joint

### England's Glory Ladies' Morris
**Web** www.geocities.com/Broadway/1018
**Contact** Liz Humphries
**Mail address** 34 Ratcliffe Lawn, Southam, Cheltenham, Gloucestershire GL52 3NT
**Phone** 01242 221440
**Email** isabel.dedman@dial.pipex.com
**Practice** in Cheltenham on Mon.
**Dance style** Garland and Cotswold
**Gender** Female

### English Miscellany
**Web** www.btinternet.com/~english.miscellany
**Contact** Peter Lane
**Mail address** 20 Langdale Ave, Harpenden, Hertfordshire AL5 5QU
**Phone** 01582 764084
**Email** english.miscellany@btinternet.com
**Practice** in Harpenden on Sun.
**Dance style** Cotswold, Garland, North West Clog, Long Sword, Mumming, Stave, Step and Other/Own (phew!)
**Gender** Mixed

### Everards Old Original Anstey
**Web** homepages.go.com/~phil_the/anstey_morrismen
**Contact** Phil Preen
**Mail address** 88 Sharpley Road, Loughborough, Leicestershire LE11 4PN
**Phone** 01509 212657
**Email** anstey@thehat.free-online.co.uk
**Practice** in Anstey on Wed.
**Dance style** Cotswold
**Gender** Male

### Exmoor Border Morris
**Contact** Heather Murch
**Mail address** Mudds Tenement, Aclard Road, Landkey, Barnstaple, Devon EX32 0LA
**Phone** 01271 830769
**Email** Tony@Mason4.freeserve.co.uk
**Practice** in West Down (nr Ilfracombe) on Wed.
**Dance style** Border
**Gender** Mixed

### The Fabulous Fezheads
**Web** www.Fezheads.com
**Contact** Phil Long
**Mail address** 7 Swallow Rise, Princes Park, Chatham, Kent ME5 7QB
**Phone** 01634 862177
**Email** OurGloriousLeader@Fezheads.com
**Practice** in Camber, Kent on Wed.
**Dance style** Other/Own
**Gender** Male

### Famous Angel Morris Men
**Web** members.netscapeonline.co.uk/famousangels
**Contact** Timothy Lole
**Mail address** 8 Highbury Hill, London, N5 1LA
**Phone** 0207 354 2589
**Email** TimothyLole@nationwideisp.net
**Practice** in London, Islington on Wed.
**Dance style** Cotswold
**Gender** Joint

### Feet First
**Contact** Fran Ferner
**Mail address** 15 Shetland Road, Dronfield, Sheffield, South Yorkshire S18 1WB
**Phone** 01246 417359
**Email** john.fermer@care4free.net
**Practice** in Chesterfield on Wed.
**Dance style** Appalachian
**Gender** Mixed

### Festus Derriman
**Contact** Rosemary Massey
**Mail address** 36 St Anne's Road, Weymouth, Dorset DT4 9LW
**Phone** 01305 782966
**Practice** in Upsey on Wed.
**Dance style** Cotswold
**Gender** Mixed

### Fiddle 'n' Feet
**Contact** David Carr
**Mail address** 28 Rhodes Street, Saltaire, Shipley, West Yorkshire BD18 3JJ
**Phone** 01274 588276
**Practice** in East Morton on Tue.
**Dance style** Appalachian
**Gender** Mixed

### Fiddlesticks
**Web** www.members.aol.com/fiddlesticksclog
**Contact** Sue Holt
**Mail address** 9 Lavender Grove, Toftwood, Dereham, Norfolk NR19 1JZ
**Phone** 01362 693942
**Email** sue@skholt.fsnet.co.uk
**Practice** in Norwich on Mon.
**Dance style** North West Clog and Garland
**Gender** Female

### Fidlers Fancy Women's Morris
**Contact** Lesley Airey
**Mail address** 7 Cliston Walk, Hazel Grove, Stockport, Cheshire SK7 5QL
**Phone** 0161 456 9355
**Email** Lesley.Airey@simcar.co.uk
**Practice** in Stockport on Wed.
**Dance style** North West Clog
**Gender** Female

### First Class Stamp
**Contact** Joanne Lole
**Mail address** 33 Blackthorn Grove, Nuneaton, Warwickshire CV11 6UX
**Email** malcg@pipemedia.co.uk
**Practice** in Attleborough on Mon.
**Dance style** Appalachian
**Gender** Mixed

### Flag Crackers of Craven
**Web** www.flagcrackers.cjb.net
**Contact** Dave Banks
**Mail address** 8 Middleton, Cowling, Keighley, West Yorkshire BD22 0DQ
**Phone** 01535 634985
**Email** squire@flagcrackers.cjb.net
**Practice** in Farnhill on Wed.
**Dance style** Border
**Gender** Mixed

## Flag & Bone Gang
**Web** members.aol.com/teddods/flagand.htm
**Contact** Jeff Garner
**Mail address** 28 Scriven Road, Knaresborough, North Yorkshire HG5 9EJ
**Phone** 01423 865086
**Email** teddods@aol.com
**Practice** in Harrogate on Sun.
**Dance style** Other/Own
**Gender** Male

## Flash Company
**Web** www.snozz.co.uk/flashwebsite
**Contact** Dick Taylor
**Mail address** 74 Greenhead Road, Utley, Keighley, West Yorkshire BD21 2JP
**Phone** 01535 681865
**Practice** in Otley on Tue.
**Dance style** Molly, Border, Step and Appalachian
**Gender** Mixed

## Fleet Morris
**Contact** Mrs Wendy Morris
**Mail address** 6 Velmed Close, Fleet, Hampshire GU13 9LR
**Phone** 01252 644354
**Email** wendymorris@tinyonline.co.uk
**Practice** in Church Crookham on Tue.
**Dance style** Cotswold
**Gender** Female

## Fleur de Lys
**Web** www.kellis.demon.co.uk/FDLhomepage.html
**Contact** Jane Stickings
**Mail address** 8 Robin Hill, Godalming, Surrey GU7 2HL
**Phone** 01483.415349
**Email** jasjasjas@tinyworld.co.uk
**Practice** in Godalming on Thu.
**Dance style** Border, Stave, Other/Own and Cotswold
**Gender** Female

## Flying Tatters
**Contact** Helene Thomas
**Mail address** 47 St Mary's Road, Ipswich, Suffolk IP14 1LP
**Phone** 01449 616060
**Email** helenet@talk21.com
**Practice** in Ipswich on Thu.
**Dance style** Border and Molly
**Gender** Mixed

## Fox's Morris
**Contact** Martin de Vine
**Mail address** 22 Lindale Crescent, Brierley Hill, West Midlands DY5 2RL
**Phone** 01384 893800
**Email** m_de_vine@hotmail.com
**Practice** in Cookley (Kidderminster) on Thu.
**Dance style** Border
**Gender** Mixed

## Foxwhelp Morris
**Contact** Emma Harrington
**Mail address** Kingstreet Farm House, Ewyas Harold, Hereford, Herefordshire HR2 0HB
**Phone** 01981 240208
**Email** emmaharrington@care4free.net
**Practice** in Ewyas Harold on Thu.
**Dance style** Cotswold, Mumming and Border
**Gender** Mixed

## Frog Island Morris
**Contact** Trevor John
**Mail address** 95 Shepherds Lane, Dartford, Kent DA1 2PA
**Phone** 01322 225380
**Practice** in Gravesend on Mon.
**Dance style** Cotswold
**Gender** Male

## Full Moon Morris
**Web** www.convex.demon.co.uk/fullmoon/index.htm
**Contact** Lisa Patrick
**Mail address** 8 Squires Gate, Rogerstone, Newport, Gwent NP10 0BP
**Phone** 01633 897358
**Email** fullmoon_morris@hotmail.com
**Practice** in Pontypool on Sun.
**Dance style** Cotswold
**Gender** Mixed

## Furness Clog Dancers
**Contact** Josie Coombe
**Mail address** The Dell, Watery Lane, Kirkby in Furness, Cumbria LA17 7UW
**Phone** 01229 889592
**Practice** in Ulverston on Tue.
**Dance style** North West Clog and Step
**Gender** Mixed

## Fylde Coast Cloggers
**Contact** Jeanette Dickin
**Mail address** 52 Newbury Road, Lytham St Anne's, Lancashire FY8 1DY
**Phone** 01253 782131
**Email** jjdickin@fsbdial.co.uk
**Practice** in Lytham St Anne's on Thu.
**Dance style** North West Clog and Garland
**Gender** Female

## Gift Rapper
**Contact** Andrea Watts
**Mail address** 54 Montgomery Rd, Sheffield, South Yorkshire S7 1LQ
**Phone** 0114 258 5283
**Email** family.watts@virgin.net
**Practice** in Sheffield on Wed.
**Dance style** Long Sword and Rapper
**Gender** Female

## Glorishears of Brummagem
**Contact** Alison Simpson
**Mail address** 69 Norfolk Road, Erdington, Birmingham, West Midlands B23 6ND
**Phone** 0121 373 4654
**Practice** in Perry Barr on Sun.
**Dance style** Cotswold
**Gender** Female

## Glory of the West
**Contact** Carol Mantell
**Mail address** Beggars Roose, Higher Ashton, Exeter, Devon EX6 7QR
**Phone** 01647 252740
**Practice** in Exeter on Wed.
**Dance style** Cotswold
**Gender** Female

## Great Central Clog
**Contact** Lesley Robson
**Mail address** 40 Grasmere Close, Rugby, Warwickshire CV21 1LS
**Phone** 01788 562418
**Practice** in Rugby on Mon.
**Dance style** Step
**Gender** Female

## Great North Clog
**Web** www.greatnorthclog-morris.demon.co.uk
**Contact** Margaret Williams
**Mail address** 9 Friars Pardon, Hurworth on Tees, Darlington, Co Durham DL2 2EA
**Phone** 01325 720744
**Email** mwilliams@qeliz.ac.uk
**Practice** in Darlington on Mon.
**Dance style** North West Clog
**Gender** Mixed

## Great Western Morris
**Web** www.great-western.org.uk
**Contact Mail address** 1 Croft Cottage, Church Lane, Sheraton Bishop, Devon EX6 6JU
**Phone** 01647 24307
**Email** tcook@avimo.co.uk
**Practice** in Exeter on Mon.
**Dance style** Cotswold
**Gender** Male

## Green Dragon Morris
**Contact** Amanda Kingsnorth
**Mail address** 30 Jarman Close, Bury St Edmunds, Suffolk IP33 2PR
**Phone** 01284 760078
**Email** amanda.kingsnorth@clmr.cam.ac.uk
**Practice** in Bury St Edmunds on Mon.
**Dance style** Border
**Gender** Mixed

## Green Ginger Garland
**Contact** Helene Marks
**Mail address** 88 Summergangs Road, Hull, East Yorkshire HU8 8LP
**Phone** 01482 791350
**Practice** in Hull on Thu.
**Dance style** North West Clog and Garland
**Gender** Female

## Green Willow Clog
**Contact** John Skirton
**Mail address** The Linhay, Grimpston Leigh, East Allington, Totnes, Devon TQ9 7QH
**Phone** 01548 521287
**Email** john.skirton@virgin.net
**Practice** in Totnes on Thu.
**Dance style** North West Clog, Garland and Molly
**Gender** Female

## Greenwood Step Clog
**Contact** Tricia Gotheridge
**Mail address** Crantock, Moor lane, Ockbrook, Derby, Derbyshire DE72 3SA
**Phone** 01332 672204
**Email** b.m.gotheridge@derby.ac.uk
**Practice** in Nottingham on Mon.
**Dance style** Step
**Gender** Female

## Grimspound Border
**Contact** Don McMillan
**Mail address** Mapledurham, Kingsteignton, Newton Abbot, Devon TQ12 3BL
**Phone** 01626 207600
**Email** don.mcmillan@btinternet.com
**Practice** in Stokeinteignton on Mon.
**Dance style** Border
**Gender** Male

## Gyppeswyck Garland
**Contact** Mrs A Marriott
**Mail address** 3 Vicarage Close, Bramford, Ipswich, Suffolk IP8 4AF
**Phone** 01473 743568
**Email** adriennemarriott@hotmail.com
**Practice** in Ipswich on Wed.
**Dance style** Garland, Step and North West Clog
**Gender** Female

## Hammersmith Morris Men
**Contact** Andy Williams
**Mail address** 30 Cheltenham Road, Peckham, London SE15 3AQ
**Phone** 0207 639 2938
**Email** ydnaw@hotmail.com
**Practice** in London, Hammersmith on Tue.
**Dance style** Cotswold and Mumming
**Gender** Male

## Hampshire Garland
**Web** www.wellow84.freeserve.co.uk/hghome
**Contact** Hilary Turner
**Mail address** 35 Pirrie Close, Shirley, Southampton, Hampshire SO15 7QA
**Phone** 023 8036 0892
**Email** jhmturner@compuserve.com
**Practice** in Swaythling on Wed.
**Dance style** North West Clog and Garland
**Gender** Female

## Hands Around
**Contact** Ms June Wells
**Mail address** 610 Whitmore Way, Basildon, Essex SS14 2EP
**Phone** 01268 521645
**Practice** in Fobbing on Fri.
**Dance style** Cotswold
**Gender** Female

## Harberton Morris
**Contact** Dave Hewitt
**Mail address** 2 The Exchange, Church St, South Brent, Devon TQ10 9AE
**Phone** 01364 72972
**Practice** in Dartington on Tue.
**Dance style** Border and Cotswold
**Gender** Mixed

## Harberton Navy
**Contact** Nicky Gilhespy
**Mail address** Higher Cholwell, Harberton, Totnes, Devon TQ9 7RZ
**Phone** 01803 865204
**Email** nick@gilhespy.demon.co.uk
**Practice** in Harberton on Wed.
**Dance style** Cotswold and Other/Own
**Gender** Mixed

## Hart & Sole Clog Morris
**Web** http://members.tripcd.co.uk/hartandsole/hartsole.htm
**Contact** Jim Middlebrook
**Mail address** 4 Proctors Road, Wokingham, Berkshire RG40 1RP
**Phone** 0118 978 3436
**Email** jim.middlebrook@bigfoot.com
**Practice** in Sandhurst on Sun.
**Dance style** North West Clog
**Gender** Mixed

## Hartshead Morris
**Contact** Keith Binns
**Mail address** 70 West End Drive, Cleckheaton, West Yorkshire BD19 6JD
**Phone** 01274 873943
**Practice** in Cleckheaton on Thu.
**Dance style** North West Clog
**Gender** Mixed

## Haughley Hoofers
**Web** www.haughleyhoofers.co.uk
**Contact** Jill Manning
**Mail address** 98 Chalk Road, Bury St Edmonds, Suffolk IP33 3BW
**Phone** 01284 700280
**Email** haughleyhoofers@hotmail.com
**Practice** in Haughley on Sun.
**Dance style** Step and North West Clog
**Gender** Female

## Haverhill Harlots
**Web** homepages.force9.net/martin50
**Contact** Linda Leon
**Mail address** 110 Withersfield Road, Haverhill, Suffolk CB9 9HE
**Phone** 0140 708280
**Email** harlots@martin50.force9.co.uk
**Practice** in Haverhill on Fri.
**Dance style** Border, Other/Own and Cotswold
**Gender** Female

## Headcorn Morris
**Contact** Ned Gayner
**Mail address** High Barn Cottage, Charing Hill, Charing, Kent TN27 0NG
**Phone** 01233 714622
**Email** headcorn.morris@gayner.co.uk
**Practice** in Headcorn on Mon.
**Dance style** Other/Own and Cotswold
**Gender** Joint

## Heather & Gorse
**Contact** Maggie Anderson
**Mail address** Homefield, Liverton, Newton Abbot, Devon TQ12 6NH
**Phone** 01626 821664
**Email** maganderson@hotmail.com
**Practice** in Combeinteignhead on Wed.
**Dance style** North West Clog
**Gender** Female

## Hedge Betty
**Contact** Jacqui Worroll
**Mail address** 38 Layamon Walk, Stourport-on-Severn, Worcestershire
**Phone** 01299 829689
**Practice** in Kidderminster on Mon.
**Dance style** North West Clog
**Gender** Female

## Hell's Belles
*(Border side of* ***Belles & Broomsticks*** *- see their entry for details)*

## Hereburgh Morris
**Web** http://come.to/hereburgh
**Contact** Mike Putnam
**Mail address** Orchard House, Harbury, CV33 9HG
**Phone** 01926 613853
**Practice** in Harbury on Wed.
**Dance style** Border, Cotswold and Other/Own
**Gender** Mixed

## Hertfordshire Holly
**Contact** Barbara Jeffery
**Mail address** 21 Greenstead, Sawbridgeworth, Hertfordshire CM21 9NY
**Phone** 01279 723090
**Practice** in Albury on Thu.
**Dance style** Garland and North West Clog
**Gender** Female

## Hexhamshire Lasses
**Web** www.hexhamshirelasses.fsnet.co.uk
**Contact** Eileen Suckling
**Mail address** Deerwood, Boat Rd, Bellingham, Hexham
**Phone** 01434 220353
**Email** val@whapweasel.com
**Practice** in Corbridge on Mon.
**Dance style** Garland and North West Clog
**Gender** Female

## Hi Jinx
**Contact** Daphne Hawkins
**Mail address** 19 Lamberhurst Walk, Furnace Green, Crawley, West Sussex RH10 6SN
**Phone** 01293 413654
**Practice** in Horsham on Thu.
**Dance style** Appalachian
**Gender** Mixed

## Hips and Haws
**Contact** Jackie Midgley
**Mail address** 26 Corfe Crescent, Calne, Wiltshire SN11 9EB
**Phone** 01249 815816
**Practice** in Chippenham on Mon.
**Dance style** Garland, North West Clog, Step and Other/Own
**Gender** Female

## Holt Morris
**Contact** Ray Dixon
**Mail address** 285c Bradley Lane, Holt, Trowbridge, Wiltshire BA14 6QE
**Phone** 01225 782787
**Practice** in Bradford on Thu.
**Dance style** Cotswold
**Gender** Male

## Hook Eagle Morris Men
**Web** www.lanng.demon.co.uk/hookeagl.htm
**Contact** John Lambert
**Mail address** 1 Railway Cottages, Hook, Hampshire RG27 9HT
**Phone** 01256 763546
**Email** mike@lanng.demon.co.uk
**Practice** in Hook on Fri.
**Dance style** Border
**Gender** Male

## Hoxon Hundred
**Contact** Ron Ross
**Mail address** Southview, Common Rd, Shelfanger, Diss, Norfolk IP22 2DP
**Phone** 01379 643563
**Email** castleto@globalnet.co.uk
**Practice** in Hoxon on Wed.
**Dance style** Border, Cotswold, North West Clog and Long Sword
**Gender** Mixed

## Hurst Morris People (HuMP)
**Contact** Mary Esslemont
**Mail address** 4 Harsbourne Road, Earley, Reading, Berkshire RG6 5PY
**Phone** 0118 987 4346
**Email** mary@esslemontm.freeserve.co.uk
**Practice** in Hurst on Thu.
**Dance style** Cotswold
**Gender** Mixed

## Ilfracombe Red Petticoats
**Contact** Janet Ellis
**Mail address** 6 Pill Lane, Rumsam, Barnstable, Devon EX32 9EQ
**Phone** 01271 342351
**Email** jennyellis@onetel.net.uk
**Practice** in Ilfracombe on Thu.
**Dance style** Garland and North West Clog
**Gender** Female

## Inclognito
**Contact** Paul Hudson
**Mail address** Hill Top Farm Cottage, Winewall, Colne, Lancashire BB8 8BU
**Phone** 01282 868040
**Email** paul@inclognito.freeserve.co.uk
**Practice** in Winewall on Mon.
**Dance style** Step
**Gender** Mixed

## Insword
**Contact** Jill Griffiths
**Mail address** 37 Belmont Park Avenue, Maidenhead, Berkshire SL6 6JX
**Phone** 01628 419374
**Email** jill.griffiths@mcs.co.uk
**Practice** in Windsor on Sun.
**Dance style** Rapper
**Gender** Female

## Invicta Morris
**Web** www.invictamorris.org.uk
**Contact** Sheila Finn
**Mail address** 4A Kenilworth Road, Petts Wood, Orpington, Kent BR5 1DY
**Phone** 01689 825263
**Practice** in Otford on Mon.
**Dance style** Cotswold
**Gender** Female

## ISIS
**Contact** Fe Ambidge
**Mail address** 7 Craven Common, Uffington, Faringdon, Oxfordshire SN7 7RN
**Phone** 01367 820211
**Email** isis@theseed.net
**Practice** in Abingdon on Mon.
**Dance style** Step
**Gender** Female

## Jabberwocky
**Web** www.jabberwocky.org.uk
**Contact** Claire Groves
**Mail address** Waring Cottage, Stockleys Lane, Tingewick, Buckinghamshire MK18 4QX
**Phone** 01280.847130
**Email** adrian-groves@beeb.net
**Practice** in Chesterton on Thu.
**Dance style** North West Clog
**Gender** Mixed

## Jackstraws
**Web** www.tangwyn.clara.net/jackstraws
**Contact** Shirley Dixon
**Mail address** 23 Avondale Road, Fleet, Hampshire GU13 9BH
**Phone** 01252.628190
**Email** shirley.dixon@ntlworld.com
**Practice** in Farnborough on Mon.
**Dance style** Cotswold
**Gender** Female

## Jenny Geddes Clog Morris
**Contact** Lesley Spenceley
**Mail address** Prinlaws Ho, 12 Walkerton Drive, Leslie, Fife
**Phone** 01592 741378
**Practice** in Edinburgh on Tue.
**Dance style** North West Clog, Other/Own
**Gender** Mixed

## Jenny Pipes
**Web** www.jennypipes.axentronic.co.uk
**Contact** Teresa Cotterell
**Mail address** 7 Mill Close, Credenhill, Hereford HR4 7EQ
**Phone** 01432 760546
**Email** jennpipes@axentronic.co.uk
**Practice** on Thu in Stoke Prior.
**Dance style** Cotswold
**Gender** Female

## Jerusalem Jammers
**Contact** Mrs Margaret Osborne
**Mail address** 16 Spencer Street, Hinckley, Leicestershire LE10 1RB
**Phone** 01455 449956
**Practice** in Kirby Muxloe on Sat.
**Dance style** North West Clog and Garland
**Gender** Female

### Just William
**Contact** Peter Effer
**Mail address** 2a Jewel Road, Walthamstow, London E17 4QX
**Phone** 020 8521 2775
**Practice** in London, Walthamstow on Thu.
**Dance style** Border, Cotswold and North West Clog
**Gender** Mixed

### Kemp's Men
**Contact** Peter Salt
**Mail address** 7 Connaught Rd, Norwich, Norfolk NR2 3BP
**Phone** 01603 615066
**Practice** in Norwich on Wed.
**Dance style** Cotswold, Mumming and Other/Own
**Gender** Male

### Kent Korkers/ Pork Scratchins
**Contact** Sandra Woodfall
**Mail address** 93 Millfield Rd, West Kingsdown, Sevenoaks, Kent TN15 6BS
**Phone** 01474 853419
**Email** sandra.woodfall@medway.gov.uk
**Practice** in Dartford on Mon.
**Dance style** Border, North West Clog and Other/Own
**Gender** Joint

### Kern Morris
**Contact** Wendy Bradshaw
**Mail address** 32 Finchale Avenue, Brasside, Co Durham DH1 5SD
**Phone** 0191 386 0357
**Practice** in Durham on Wed.
**Dance style** Cotswold
**Gender** Mixed

### Kesteven Morris
**Web** www.endon-house.demon.co.uk/ kesteven.htm
**Contact** Val Smith
**Mail address** 56 High Street, Billinghay, Lincolnshire LN4 4ED
**Phone** 01526 861107
**Email** valcsmith@lineone.net
**Practice** in Sleaford on Tue.
**Dance style** Border. Cotswold, North West Clog and Long Sword
**Gender** Joint

### Kettlebridge Clogs
**Contact** Ian Sharp
**Mail address** Rowan Cottage, St Helens Lane, East Farleigh, Kent ME15 0JY
**Phone** 01622 721778
**Email** ian.sharp@joneslanglasalle.com
**Practice** in Maidstone on Tue.
**Dance style** North West Clog
**Gender** Female

### Kickin Alice
**Contact** Gill Lemon
**Mail address** 37 York Road, Bromyard, Herefordshire HR7 4BG
**Phone** 01885.486673
**Practice** in Leintwardine on Mon.
**Dance style** Appalachian
**Gender** not notified at time of compilation

### Kick the Cat Appalachian Dancers
**Contact** Charlotte Moon
**Mail address** 38A Morningside Park, Edinburgh, Midlothian EH10 5NA
**Phone** 0131 452 8463
**Email** C.Moon@ed.ac.uk
**Practice** in Edinburgh on Tue.
**Dance style** Appalachian
**Gender** Mixed

### Kick Start
**Contact** Sue Hartland
**Mail address** 45 Mill Street, Harbury, Leamington Spa, Warwickshire CV33 9HR
**Email** ianhartland@compuserve.com
**Practice** in Harbury on Sat.
**Dance style** Appalachian
**Gender** Mixed

### Kintbury May Maids Morris
**Contact** Penny Parker
**Mail address** 20 Meadow Close, Compton, Newbury, Berkshire RG20 6QQ
**Phone** 01635.578083
**Email** penny@20compton.freeserve.co.uk
**Practice** in Kintbury on Wed.
**Dance style** Border, Cotswold and Other/Own
**Gender** Female

### Kirkburton Rapier Dancers
**Contact** Roy Dyson
**Mail address** 22 Sheardale, Honley, Huddersfield, West Yorkshire HD7 2RU
**Phone** 01484 665365
**Email** roy@morganwolff.com
**Practice** in Kirkburton on Mon.
**Dance style** Cotswold and Long Sword
**Gender** Male

### Kitchen Taps Appalachian
**Contact** Janet Neve
**Mail address** Hyvinge, Burras Lane, Otley, West Yorkshire LS21 3ES
**Phone** 01943 465342
**Email** otleyneves@aol.com
**Practice** in Otley on Mon.
**Dance style** Appalachian
**Gender** Mixed

### Kits Coty Morris
**Contact** Betty Tuur
**Mail address** 'Haefen', 15 Veles Road, Snodland, Kent ME6 5RB
**Phone** 01634 244503
**Email** beandar@dial.pipex.com
**Practice** in E. Farleigh on Thu.
**Dance style** Cotswold
**Gender** Mixed

### Knaresborough Mummers
**Web** members.aol.com/teddods/knaresbo.htm
**Contact** Doug Child
**Mail address** White Cottage, Main Street, Great Ouseburn, North Yorkshire YO5 9RG
**Phone** 01423 330812
**Email** TedDods@aol.com
**Practice** in Knaresborough on Thu.
**Dance style** Mumming
**Gender** Male

### Knickerbocker Glory
**Contact** Lesley Wilkins
**Mail address** Silverlea, Paice Lane, Medstead, Alton, Hampshire GU34 5PT
**Phone** 01420 562471
**Email** lejwilkins@hotmail.com
**Practice** in Oakhanger, Alton on Mon.
**Dance style** Appalachian
**Gender** Mixed

### Knockhundred Shuttles
**Web** www.shuttles.freeserve.co.uk
**Contact** Tony Bennett
**Mail address** 93 St Michael's Grove, Fareham, Hampshire PO14 1T
**Phone** 01329 511023
**Email** benhopstep@madasafish.com
**Practice** in Midhurst on Mon.
**Dance style** North West Clog
**Gender** Mixed

### Knots of May
**Web** members.aol.com/suesteven/kom/kom.html
**Contact** Sue Stevens
**Mail address** 24 Oakroyd Close, Burgess Hill, East Sussex RH15 0QN
**Phone** 01444 242492
**Email** Suesteven@aol.com
**Practice** in Lewes on Tue.
**Dance style** Garland and North West Clog
**Gender** Female

### Ladies of Green Willow
**Contact** Ann Randall
**Mail address** 23 Mersey Rd, Bulkington, Bedworth, Warwickshire CV12 9QB
**Phone** 02476 345568
**Practice** in Nuneaton on Wed. Dance styled Garland and North West Clog
**Gender** Female

## Liddington Hall Morris
**Contact** Rosemary Mugford
**Mail address** 4 Fitzroy Road, Old Town, Swindon, Wiltshire SN1 4DU
**Phone** 01793 422217
**Email** Rosemary_Mugford@pparc.ac.uk
**Practice** in Swindon on Thu.
**Dance style** Cotswold
**Gender** Female

## Little Egypt Morris Men
**Web** web.ukonline.co.uk/stephen.clarke/contents.html
**Contact** Derek Southgate
**Mail address** 3 Kebble, Crownfield Road, Glemsford, Sudbury, Suffolk CO10 7UE
**Phone** 01787 281175
**Email** stephen.clarke@ukonline.co.uk
**Practice** in Glemsford on Tue.
**Dance style** Cotswold and Molly
**Gender** Male

## Lord Paget's Morris
**Contact** Christine Benner
**Mail address** 33 Bridge Road, Uxbridge, Middlesex UB8 2QP
**Phone** 01895 464982
**Practice** in Denham on Fri.
**Dance style** Border
**Gender** Female

## Mad Jack's Morris
**Web** http://ourworld.compuserve.com/homepages/David_Lock
**Contact** Mike Riley
**Mail address** 134 All Saints Street, Hastings, East Sussex TN34 3BG
**Phone** 01424 716840
**Email** keith.leech@britishlibrary.net
**Practice** in Hastings on Mon.
**Dance style** Cotswold
**Gender** Joint

## Maenads
**Web** www.compulab.co.uk/maenads
**Contact** Mrs T Payne
**Mail address** 1 Mill Cottages, Eastling, Faversham, Kent ME13 0BN
**Phone** 01795 890793
**Email** trish@champayne.co.uk
**Practice** in Lenham on Thu.
**Dance style** Mumming and Border
**Gender** Female

## Maisie Bloomers Morris
**Contact** Ian Dadswell
**Mail address** 54 Crews Park, Broseley Wood, Shropshire,
**Phone** 01952 882848
**Practice** in Shifnal on Wed.
**Dance style** Garland and North West Clog
**Gender** Mixed

## Maldon Greenjackets
**Web** www.dykech.demon.co.uk/mgj.htm
**Contact** Geoff Harris
**Mail address** 26 Granger Avenue, Maldon, Essex CM9 6AN
**Phone** 01621 858509
**Email** gordon@aubrey-jones.freeserve. co.uk
**Practice** in Maldon on Tue.
**Dance style** Cotswold
**Gender** Mixed

## Mandrake Morris
**Contact** Liz Bruce
**Mail address** 55 Station Street, Walton on Naze, Essex CO14 8DW
**Phone** 01255 676960
**Practice** in Holland on Sea on Fri.
**Dance style** Border, Other/Own, Step and North West Clog
**Gender** Mixed

## Manor Mill Morris
**Contact** Maxine Fay
**Mail address** 26 Redgate Rd, Girton, Cambridgeshire CB3 0PP
**Phone** 01223 564329
**Email** maxine.fay@cambridge.gov.uk
**Practice** in Cambridge on Mon.
**Dance style** North West Clog
**Gender** Female

## Mason's Apron
**Contact** Margaret Richardson
**Mail address** 20 Cherry Close, Kidlington, Oxford, Oxfordshire OX5 1ET
**Phone** 01865 371317169
**Email** msr@cherry20.freeserve.co.uk
**Practice** in Longhandborough on Mon.
**Dance style** North West Clog
**Gender** Mixed

## Maybe Morris
**Contact** May Littleton
**Mail address** 3 Howard Road, Horsham, West Sussex RH13 6AB
**Phone** 01403 268528
**Email** maybemorris@coneectfree.co.uk
**Practice** in Horsham, day unknown.
**Dance style** Cotswold, Border, Garland, North West Clog and Stave
**Gender** Unknown

## Mayflower Morris
**Contact** Joy Savastano
**Mail address** 40 Potley Hill Road, Yateley, Hampshire GU46 6AF
**Phone** 01252 877971
**Practice** in Aldershot on Mon.
**Dance style** North West Clog
**Gender** Female

## Merrydowners
**Contact** John Winkle
**Mail address** 553 Rayners Lane, Pinner, Middlesex HA5 5HP
**Phone** 0208 723 8276
**Email** jon.winkle@dial.pipex.com
**Practice** in North Harrow on Sun.
**Dance style** Cotswold, North West Clog and Long Sword
**Gender** Mixed

## Minden Rose
**Web** www.asimons.org.uk/Minden.Rose
**Contact** Imelda Simons
**Mail address** Ropley Manor Cottage, Petersfield Road, Ropley, Alresford, Hampshire SO24 0DX
**Phone** 01962 773487
**Email** squire@minden-rose.org.uk
**Practice** in Alton on Sun.
**Dance style** Garland and North West Clog
**Gender** Female

## Mockbeggar Morris
**Contact** Ruth Winterson
**Mail address** 28 Stanley Road, Haylake, Wirral CH47 1HP
**Phone** 0151 632 5195
**Practice** in Willaston on Thu.
**Dance style** North West Clog
**Gender** Female

## Mortimers
**Contact** Kathy Taylor
**Mail address** 25 Northolm Avenue, Bulwell, Nottingham, Nottinghamshire NG6 9AP
**Phone** 0115 927 6189
**Email** kathy_taylor9@hotmail.com
**Practice** in Nottingham on Sun.
**Dance style** North West Clog
**Gender** Female

## Motley Morris
**Web Contact** www.motley-morris.uk Sahra Smith
**Mail address** 20 Devonshire Road, Gravesend, Kent DA12 5AA
**Phone** 0780 378 6329 (mobile)
**Email** sahra.smith@globalmarinesystems.com
**Practice** in Dartfird on Wed.
**Dance style** Border
**Gender** Male

## Mr Leslie's Banbury Rapper
**Contact** Stephen Wass
**Mail address** 3 Chapel Row, Cropredy, Banbury, Oxfordshire OX17 1NS
**Phone** 01295 758222
**Practice** in Banbury on Sat.
**Dance style** Rapper
**Gender** Male

## Mr Wilkin's Shilling
**Contact** Ann Croft
**Mail address** 12A St Catherine's close, Bathwick, Bath,
**Phone** 01225 463497
**Practice** in Bath on Thu.
**Dance style** North West Clog
**Gender** Female

## Mythago
**Web** www.btinternet.com/~mythago
**Contact** Peter Luckin
**Mail address** Hamgate, Spatham Lane, Westmeston, Hassocks, West Sussex
**Phone** 01273 842569
**Email** peterluckin@pavilion.co.uk
**Practice** in Ashurst on Wed.
**Dance style** Border and Other/Own
**Gender** Mixed

## Nancy Butterfly
**Web** homepages.tesco.net/~sabrina/morris.htm
**Contact** Jenny Shufflebotham
**Mail address** 18 Burns Close, Headless Cross, Redditch, Worcestershire B97 5BS
**Phone** 01527 403656
**Email** nancybutterfly@tesco.net
**Practice** in Headless Cross on Mon.
**Dance style** Garland and North West Clog
**Gender** Female

## New Esperance Morris
**Contact** Hilda Dedic
**Mail address** 15 Belvue Rd, Northolt, Middlesex UB5 5HW
**Phone** 0208 933 6520
**Email** dedics@dircon.co.uk
**Practice** in London, Westminster on Wed.
**Dance style** Cotswold and Other/Own
**Gender** Female

## New Forest Meddlars
**Web** www.geocities.com/meddlarsmorris
**Contact** Bob Dodson
**Mail address** 4 Oaklands, South Wonston, Winchester, Hampshire SO21 3HZ
**Phone** 01962 886132
**Email** bob_dodson@hotmail.com
**Practice** in Lyndhurst on Tue.
**Dance style** Border and Cotswold
**Gender** Mixed

## New St George Morris
**Web** www.geocities.com/newstgeorge
**Contact** Steve Tunnicliff
**Mail address** The Homestead, East End, Long Clawson, Melton Mowbray, Leicestershire
**Phone** 01664 823041
**Email** newstgeorge@aol.com
**Practice** in Bottesford on Wed.
**Dance style** Cotswold
**Gender** Mixed

## Newburgh Morris
**Contact** Barbara Barclay
**Mail address** Badgers Rake, Vale Lane, Lathom, Lancashire L40 6JH
**Phone** 01695 723100
**Practice** in Newburgh on Tue.
**Dance style** North West Clog
**Gender** Female

## Newcastle Cloggies
**Contact** Jean Smith
**Mail address** 30 Ingleside Road, North Shields, Tyne & Wear NE29 9BP
**Phone** 0191 259 1349
**Email** jean@www.newcastlecloggies.org.uk
**Practice** in Newcastle on Thu.
**Dance style** Step
**Gender** Mixed

## Newton Bushel Morris Men
**Contact** Anthony Job
**Mail address** 29 Innerbrook Rd, Chelston, Torquay, Devon TQ2 6AG
**Phone** 01803 607987
**Email** dinglydell@hotmail.com
**Practice** in Torquay on Thu.
**Dance style** Cotswold
**Gender** Male

## No Mean Feet
**Contact** Angie Keating
**Mail address** Hamdon View, Over Stratton, South Petherton, Somerset TA13 5LE
**Phone** 01460 241089
**Practice** in Merriott on Tue.
**Dance style** Appalachian and Other/Own
**Gender** Mixed

## Noname
**Contact** Chris Dallimore
**Mail address** Edmores, Bristol Road, Whitminster, Gloucestershire GL2 7PB
**Phone** 01452 740096
**Practice** in Various (travelling side) on Sun.
**Dance style** Border
**Gender** Mixed

## Northgate Rapper
**Contact** Martin Hanley
**Mail address** 1 Pond Cottages, Faulkland, Somerset BA3 5XB
**Phone** 01373 834421
**Email** martin.hanley@newscientist.net
**Practice** in Bath on Wed.
**Dance style** Rapper
**Gender** Male

## Oast Ouse Oppers
**Contact** Eddie White
**Mail address** 412 Kingswear Gardens, Strood, Kent ME2 4QS
**Phone** 01634 719695
**Practice** in Rainham on Sun.
**Dance style** Other/Own
**Gender** Female

## OBJ Border
**Web** www.mulberries.freeserve.co.uk
**Contact** Colin & Christine Charman
**Mail address** 5 Southlands Close, Wokingham, Berkshire RG40 2HW
**Phone** 0118 989 0760
**Email** charmanc@mulberries.freeserve.co.uk
**Practice** in Bracknell on Tue.
**Dance style** Border
**Gender** Mixed

## Offcumduns
**Web** www.btinternet.com/~trevsworld/offcumduns/index.htm
**Contact** Dick Yarwood
**Mail address** 138 New Dover Road, Canterbury, Kent CT1 3EJ
**Phone** 01227 453077
**Email** Richard.Yarwood@questintl.com
**Practice** in Eastry on Tue.
**Dance style** North West Clog
**Gender** Mixed

## Off the Rails
**Contact** Derelys Rumble
**Mail address** The Ferns, 96 Whitworth Road, Swindon, Wiltshire SN2 3BH
**Phone** 01793 420945
**Dance style/Gender** No details known

## Old Glory
**Web** www.old-glory.co.uk
**Contact** David Woods
**Mail address** 11 Old Farm Rd, Carlton Colville, Lowestoft, Suffolk NR33 8RR
**Phone** 01502 518637
**Email** david@old-glory.co.uk
**Practice** in Rumburgh on Sun.
**Dance style** Molly
**Gender** Male

## Old Harry Morris (Purbeck)
**Contact** Stephen Parker
**Mail address** 14 Church Hill, Swanage, Dorset BH19 1HU
**Phone** 01929 427559
**Email** nareed@globalnet.co.uk
**Practice** in Harmonies Cross on Mon.
**Dance style** Cotswold and Mumming
**Gender** Male

## Old Meg
**Web** www.fishleys.demon.co.uk/oldmeg
**Contact** Mike Salter
**Mail address** Folly Cottage, 151 West Malvern Road, Malvern, Worcestershire WR14 4AY
**Phone** 01684 565211
**Email** oldmeg@fishleys.demon.co.uk
**Practice** in Malvern on Tue.
**Dance style** North West Clog
**Gender** Mixed

## Old Mother Redcaps
**Contact** Frances Thomas
**Mail address** 40 Wye Close, Bletchley, Milton Keynes, Buckinghamshire MK3 7PJ
**Phone** 01908 647394
**Email** Female.L.Thomas@open.ac.uk
**Practice** in Stony Stratford on Mon.
**Dance style** Garland and Other/Own
**Gender** Female

## Old Palace Clog
**Web** homepages.infoseek.com/~oldpalace/OldPalace.html
**Contact** Sue Bartell
**Mail address** 30 Nicholson Road, Croydon, Surrey CR0 6QS
**Phone** 020 8407.1074
**Email** suebartell@hotmail.com
**Practice** in London, South Norwood on Thu.
**Dance style** North West Clog
**Gender** Female

## Old Speckled Hen
**Contact** Duncan McIntosh
**Mail address** 7 Wormald Road, Wallingford, Oxfordshire OX10 9BD
**Phone** 01491 834730
**Practice** in Milton Heights on Thu.
**Dance style** North West Clog
**Gender** Mixed

## Old Star Morris
**Web** www.oldstarmorris.freeuk.com
**Contact** Curly Rayner
**Mail address** 170 Whitley Road, Eastbourne, East Sussex BN22 8LS
**Phone** 01323 640759
**Email** stuwalk@stuwalk@screaming.net
**Practice** in Eastbourne on Thu.
**Dance style** Border and Long Sword
**Gender** Mixed

## One Step Beyond
**Web** enquiries@onestepbeyond.fsnet.co.uk
**Contact** Margaret Daw
**Mail address** 32 Kineton Close, Matchborough West, Redditch, Worcestershire B98 0EU
**Phone** 01527 525773
**Email** drradaw@aol.com
**Practice** in Bromsgrove on Wed.
**Dance style** Appalachian
**Gender** Mixed

## Old Tanglefoot Clog
**Contact** Lesley Frostick
**Mail address** 15 Simpson Rd, Shipston on Stour, Warwickshire CV36 4JT
**Phone** 01608 662517
**Practice** in Shipston on Mon.
**Dance style** North West Clog
**Gender** Female

## Old Wrappers Morris
**Contact** Kate Allcock
**Mail address** Glenadder, Allanton Rd, Chirnside, Berwickshire TD11 3XJ
**Phone** 01890 818267
**Practice** in Allanton on Tue.
**Dance style** Cotswold, North West Clog and Border
**Gender** Mixed

## The Outside Capering Crew
**Web** www.capers.co.uk/crew
**Contact** Brian Mander
**Mail address** 8 Monmouth Close, Toddington, Bedfordshire LU5 6AQ
**Phone** 01525 872854
**Email** brian@mander.force9.co.uk
**Practice** in South Midands on Sun.
**Dance style** Other/Own
**Gender** Mixed

## Owlswick Morris
**Web** http://freespace.virgin.net/steve.wynn
**Contact** Mary Walter
**Mail address** 3 Routs Green, Bedlow Ridge, High Wycombe, Buckinghamshire HP14 4BB
**Phone** 01494 481459
**Email** bmtwalter@hotmail.com
**Practice** in Twyford on Tue.
**Dance style** Mumming, Cotswold, Rapper, Step and Appalachian
**Gender** Mixed

## Oyster Girls
**Contact** Ann Simpson
**Mail address** 13 Ward Close, Carisbrooke, Newport, Isle of Wight PO30 5SL
**Phone** 01983 529389
**Email** ann-m@simpsona12.fsnet.co.uk
**Practice** in Newport on Wed.
**Dance style** Garland, Other/Own and North West Clog
**Gender** Female

## Oyster Morris
**Web** www.hillside.co.uk/oyster
**Contact** Megan Taylor
**Mail address** 2 Rectory Farm Cottages, Drill Lane, Ickham, Canterbury, Kent CT3 1QL
**Phone** 01227 722332
**Email** megantaylor@beeb.net
**Practice** Men practice in Bridge on Mondays, the women in Bridge on.
**Dance style** Cotswold
**Gender** Joint

## Palatine Clog
**Contact** Carol Attwell
**Mail address** 8 Whickhope, Washington, Tyne & Wear NE38 8SH
**Phone** 0191 415 3506
**Practice** in Durham City on Wed.
**Dance style** Garland, Appalachian and North West Clog
**Gender** Female

## Pandemonium
**Web** members.aol.com/panstroud
**Contact** Mrs Sara Causon
**Mail address** 24 Freame Close, Chalford, Stroud, Gloucestershire GL6 8HG
**Phone** 01453 884489
**Email** PanStroud@aol.com
**Practice** in Stroud on Thu.
**Dance style** Border

## Paragon Pit Morris
**Contact** Eddie Strover
**Mail address** 6 Hillcrest Lane, Husbands Bosworth, Lutterworth, Leicestershire LE17 6LB
**Phone** 01858 880540
**Email** paragonpit@yahoo.com
**Practice** location and day not known.
**Dance style** Cotswold
**Gender** Mixed

## Pebworth Morris
**Contact** Kevin McLeish
**Mail address** The Old Bakery, Friday Street, Pebworth, Stratford on Avon, Worcestershire CV37 8XW
**Phone** 01789 720064
**Practice** in Bretforton on Fri.
**Dance style** Border and Cotswold
**Gender** Male

## Pennyroyal Garland Dancers
**Contact** Stephen Edkins
**Mail address** 11 Belsize, Lakeside, Tamworth, Leicestershire B77 2RB
**Phone** 01827 286001
**Email** stephen-edkins@supanet.com
**Practice** in Ashby de la Zouch on Wed.
**Dance style** Appalachian, Garland andNorth West Clog
**Gender** Female

## Persephone
**Contact** Carole Hall
**Mail address** 2 Parklands Crescent, Bramhope, Leeds, West Yorkshire LS15 9AQ
**Phone** 0113 284 2712
**Practice** in Bradford on Tue.
**Dance style** Garland and North West Clog
**Gender** Female

## Pigsty Morris
**Contact** Stephanie Walker
**Mail address** Greystone, Little Somerford, Chippenham, Wiltshire SN15 5JT
**Phone** 01666 822755
**Email** steph.walker@lineone.net
**Practice** in Bristol on Fri.
**Dance style** Cotswold
**Gender** Mixed

## Plain Capers
**Contact** Cathy Sharman
**Mail address** 7 Chipstead Park, Sevenoaks, Kent TN13 2SL
**Phone** 01732 455420
**Email** Cathy.Sharman@btinternet.com
**Practice** in Godden Green on Tue.
**Dance style** Cotswold
**Gender** Female

## Plum Jerkum
**Web** www.plum.jerkum.mcmail.com/index.htm
**Contact** Anthea Williams
**Mail address** 18 Cromwells Meadow, Burton Green, Lichfield, Staffordshire WS14 9EW
**Phone** 01543 262543
**Email** anthea.williams@ukgateway.net
**Practice** in Eathorpe on Mon.
**Dance style** Border
**Gender** Mixed

## Poacher Morris
**Contact** Susan Barter
**Mail address** 12 College Close, Newport, Lincoln, Lincolnshire LN1 3EA
**Phone** 01522 859579
**Practice** in Lincoln on Thu.
**Dance style** Border
**Gender** Mixed

## Point Devis
**Contact** Lin Barnes
**Mail address** Woodlands, Church Close, Kelsale, Saxmundham, Suffolk
**Phone** 01728 602416
**Email** reeldance@btinternet.com
**Practice** in Middleton on Wed.
**Dance style** Garland and North West Clog
**Gender** Mixed

## Poynton Jemmers
**Web** members.aol.com/PoyntonJem/private/JemR.htm
**Contact** S Chris Conway
**Mail address** 23 Newquay Drive, Bramall, Cheshire SK7 2HT
**Phone** 0161 469 6682
**Email** cbconway@cwctv.net
**Practice** in Poynton on Wed.
**Dance style** North West Clog
**Gender** Female

## Priory Morris
**Web** www.priory-morris.fsnet.co.uk
**Contact** Miriam Russell
**Mail address** 78 Clacton Road, St Osyth, Essex CO16 8PB
**Phone** 01255 822481
**Email** bagman@priory-morris.fsnet.co.uk
**Practice** in St Osyth on Sun.
**Dance style** Border
**Gender** Mixed

## Pump House Clog Morris
**Web** www.ph.watford.net/clogm.htm
**Contact** Jenny Geddes
**Mail address** 82 Townfield Rickmansworth, Hertfordshire WD3 7DD
**Phone** 01923 897384
**Email** jennibeal@yahoo.co.uk
**Practice** in Watford on Mon.
**Dance style** North West Clog
**Gender** Female

## Quayside Cloggies
**Contact** Chris Moore
**Mail address** 167 Ashley Road, Poole, Dorset BH14 9DL
**Phone** 01202 723745
**Email** ChristineMoore@Freenet.Co.Uk
**Practice** in Bournemouth on Mon.
**Dance style** North West Clog
**Gender** Female

## Queen Emma's
**Contact** Chris Clements
**Mail address** 224 Colwell Drive, Witney, Oxfordshire OX8 7LW
**Phone** 01993 200748
**Practice** in Witney on Wed.
**Dance style** Cotswold
**Gender** Female

## Queen's Oak Morris
**Contact** Mrs Male A Williamson
**Mail address** 9 Wakefield Way, Nether Hayford, Northamptonshire NN7 3LU
**Phone** 01327 340699
**Email** Lis@dancing.demon.co.uk
**Practice** in Yardley Gobion on Tue.
**Dance style** Border
**Gender** Female

## Raddon Hill Clog Morris
**Contact** Liz Alexander
**Mail address** 6 Chrystel Close, Tipton St John, Sidmouth, Devon EX10 0AY
**Phone** 01404 813787
**Email** lalexand@devon.gov.uk
**Practice** in Ide on Tue.
**Dance style** North West Clog
**Gender** Mixed

## Ragged and Old
**Contact** Jackie Thomas
**Mail address** Ashdown, Brownshill, Stroud, Gloucestershire GL6 8AP
**Phone** 01453 884805
**Email** jackie@thomas.freeserve.co.uk
**Practice** in Bussage on Wed.
**Dance style** Cotswold, Mumming and Step
**Gender** Mixed

## Ragged Heroes Mummers
**Web** www.crwldrvr.demon.co.uk/mumming.htm
**Contact** Colin Burge
**Mail address** 5 The Old Malthouse, Yatton Keynell, Chippenham, Wiltshire SN14 7EH
**Phone** 01249 782694
**Email** mike@crwldrvr.demon.co.uk
**Practice** in Chippenham on Sun.
**Dance style** Mumming
**Gender** Male

## Raggie Morrisons
**Contact** Ann Dutton
**Mail address** The Oaks, Bellwood Drive, Aboyne, Aberdeenshire AB34 5QG
**Phone** 01339 886791
**Email** av.comms@btinternet.com
**Practice** in Bieldside on Wed.
**Dance style** Garland and North West Clog
**Gender** Female

## Rainbow Morris
**Contact** Kay Sutcliffe
**Mail address** 51 St Pauls Rd, Shipley, West Yorkshire BD18 3EW
**Phone** 01274 592318
**Email** 100672.2135@compuserve.com
**Practice** in Shipley on Mon.
**Dance style** Garland, Appalachian and North West Clog
**Gender** Mixed

## Red Stags Morris
**Web** www.andrew.miller.clara.net/RedStags.html
**Contact** Christina Pritchard
**Mail address** 4 Westridge Road, Southampton, Hampshire SO17 2HQ
**Phone** 02380 583018
**Email** pd49@dial.pipex.com
**Practice** in Southampton on Thu.
**Dance style** Border
**Gender** Mixed

## Redbornstoke Morris
**Web** www.redbornstoke.freeserve.co.uk
**Contact** Barry Goodman
**Mail address** 54 Ickleford Rd, Hitchin, Hertfordshire SG5 1TR
**Phone** 01462 456811
**Email** barry@goodman.freeserve.co.uk
**Practice** in Ampthill on Mon.
**Dance style** Cotswold
**Gender** Male

## Ridgeway Revellers
**Contact** Joan Holloway
**Mail address** Coppersfield, Wildhern, Andover, Hampshire SP11 0JE
**Phone** 01264 735252
**Email** joan@ellenke.demon.co.uk
**Practice** in West Hendred on Mon.
**Dance style** Step
**Gender** Female

## Ripley Green Garters
**Contact** Mrs Ronda Sims
**Mail address** 5 Hawkins Drive, Ridgeway, Belper, Derbyshire DE56 2JN
**Phone** 01773 856040
**Email** sims_ronda@hotmail.com
**Practice** in Belper on Tue.
**Dance style** Garland/North West Clog
**Gender** Female

## Ripon City Morris Dancers
**Contact** Charlie Callis
**Mail address** 3 Kirkham Court, Knaresborough, North Yorkshire HG5 8LS
**Phone** 01423 865093
**Email** charliecallis@farming.co.uk
**Practice** in Bishop Monkton on Mon.
**Dance style** North West Clog
**Gender** Male

## Rivington Morris
**Web** www.personal.u-net.com/~rundall/home1.htm
**Contact** Hanneke van Dijk
**Mail address** 265 Chapeltown Rd, Turton, Bolton, Lancashire BL7 0HQ
**Phone** 01204 852632
**Email** hvandijk@textileinst.org.uk
**Practice** in Blackrod on Wed.
**Dance style** North West Clog
**Gender** Female

## Rockhopper Morris
**Contact** Julie Mabbett
**Mail address** Lilac Cottage, Long Wittenham Rd, North Moreton, Oxfordshire OX11 9AX
**Phone** 01235 811237
**Email** juliemabbet@hotmail.com
**Practice** in North Moreton on Sun.
**Dance style** Cotswold
**Gender** Mixed

## Rogue Morris
**Contact** Katie Moss
**Mail address** The Old Post Office, Weston Road, Bletchington, Oxfordshire OX5 3DH
**Phone** 01869 350219
**Email** heather.horner@physiol.ox.ac.uk
**Practice** in Oxford on Mon.
**Dance style** Border
**Gender** Female

## Rose & Castle Morris
**Contact** Brian Street
**Mail address** Whilton Marina, Whilton Locks, Daventry, Northamptonshire NN11 5NH
**Phone** 07850 672258
**Email** bstreet@ford.com
**Practice** in Stoke Bruerne on Wed.
**Dance style** North West Clog
**Gender** Male

## Roundhill Morris
**Contact** Sarah Heels
**Mail address** Corn Riggs, Mill Road, Steyning, West Sussex BN44 3LN
**Phone** 01903 814299
**Practice** in Steyning on Mon.
**Dance style** Border and Other/Own
**Gender** Mixed

## Royal Manor Morris
**Web** www.johnrnew.demon.co.uk/royman.htm
**Contact** Julie Matthews
**Mail address** 6 Spring Gardens, Portland, Dorset DT5 1JG
**Phone** 01305.821892
**Email** julie@matthews63.fsnet.co.uk
**Practice** in Portland on Wed.
**Dance style** Cotswold and Stave
**Gender** Female

## Royal Oak Morris
**Web** www.daventry-index.co.uk/eydon/morris.html
**Contact** Kevin Lodge
**Mail address** 18 High St, Eydon, Nr Daventry, Northamptonshire NN11 3PP
**Phone** 01327 261535
**Email** kevin.lodge@marconi.com
**Practice** in Eydon on Thu.
**Dance style** Cotswold
**Gender** Mixed

## Ryknild Rabble
**Web** www.risa.demon.co.uk
**Contact** Janet Hickman
**Mail address** 90 Upper St John's Street, Lichfield, Staffordshire WS14 9DX
**Phone** 01543 300178
**Email** chris@risa.demon.co.uk
**Practice** in Kings Bromley on Sun.
**Dance style** Border, North West Clog and Rapper
**Gender** Mixed

## Saddleworth Clog & Garland
**Contact** Josie Stott
**Mail address** 15 Juniper Close, Moorside, Oldham, Lancashire OL4 2NJ
**Phone** 0161 652 0003
**Email** josie.stott@tesco.net
**Practice** in Uppermill on Mon.
**Dance style** Garland and Step
**Gender** Female

## Saffron Maids
**Contact** Janet Ridley
**Mail address** Trenillocs, St Columb, Cornwall TR9 6JN
**Phone** 01637 880394
**Practice** in Wadebridge on Wed.
**Dance style** Garland/North West Clog
**Gender** Female

## Sarum Morris
**Contact** http://hometown.aol.com/chrisnlynn/myhomepage/club/html
**Contact** Graham Read
**Mail address** Matrons College Farmhouse, Castle Lane, Whaddon, Salisbury, Wiltshire SP5 3EQ
**Phone** 01722 710796
**Email** eggss@hotmail.com
**Practice** in Salisbury on Thu.
**Dance style** Mumming and Cotswold
**Gender** Mixed

## Scrambled Leggs
**Contact** Jan Jones
**Mail address** 37 Sidwell Avenue, Benfleet, Essex SS7 1LF
**Phone** 01268 793905
**Email** jjnew@easynet.co.uk
**Practice** in Basildon on Mon.
**Dance style** Appalachian
**Gender** Mixed

## Sergeant Musgrave's Dance
**Contact** Sharon Lee
**Mail address** 145 Derby Road, Sandiacre, Nottinghamshire NG10 5HL
**Phone** 0115 917 1496
**Email** shazelee@aol.com
**Practice** in Bramcote on Tue.
**Dance style** North West Clog
**Gender** Mixed

### Shalesbrook Morris
**Contact** Mrs Angela Lewis
**Mail address** Northwing, Richard Bertram House, Lewes Road, Danehill, West Sussex RH17 7HD
**Phone** 01825 790068
**Practice** in Forest Row on Thu.
**Dance style** Cotswold
**Gender** Female

### Sheffield City Morris Men
**Web** www.citymorris.f9.co.uk
**Contact** Derek Wood
**Mail address** 170 Springfield Road, Millfields, Sheffield, South Yorkshire S7 2RG
**Phone** 0114 236 5300
**Email** derek.p.wood@btinternet.com
**Practice** in Sheffield on Mon.
**Dance style** Other/Own and Cotswold
**Gender** Male

### Short Circuit
**Contact** Hazel Hall
**Mail address** 34 Springfield, Ovington, Northumberland NE42 6EH
**Phone** 01661 834400
**Email** hallhazel@hotmail.com
**Practice** in Ovington on Wed.
**Dance style** Step and Rapper
**Gender** Female

### Shrewsbury Morris Dancers
**Contact** Bev Langton
**Mail address** Lacon Hall, Lacon, Wem, Shropshire SY4 5RP
**Phone** 01939 233977
**Email** bev.langton@talk21.com
**Practice** in Shrewsbury on Thu.
**Dance style** Cotswold, North West Clog, Long Sword, Other/Own and Border
**Gender** Joint

### Shuffle the Deck
**Contact** Mrs H Palfrey
**Mail address** The Brambles, 18 Fallowfields, Totnes TQ9 5NG
**Phone** 01803 867999
**Practice** in Totnes on Wed.
**Dance style** Appalachian
**Gender** Mixed

### Sidmouth Steppers NW Morris
**Contact** Jean Salt
**Mail address** 81 Woolbrook Road, Sidmouth, Devon EX10 9XD
**Phone** 01395 516590
**Email** jeansalt@eurobell.co.uk
**Practice** in Sidmouth on Tue.
**Dance style** Garland and North West Clog
**Gender** Female

### Silhill Morris
**Web** http://ourworld.compuserve.com/homepages/JGlanville/silhill.htm
**Contact** Linda Glanville
**Mail address** 97 Purnells Way, Knowle, Solihull, West Midlands
**Phone** 01564 772373
**Email** linda.glanville@tesco.net
**Practice** in Whythall on Thu.
**Dance style** Border
**Gender** Mixed

### Singleton Cloggers
**Contact** Keith Walker
**Mail address** 32 Moorland Road, Poulton le Fylde, Lancashire FY6 7EU
**Phone** 01253 884217
**Practice** in Singleton on Mon.
**Dance style** North West Clog
**Gender** Mixed

### Slubbing Billy's
**Web** http://freespace.virgin.net/slubbing.billys
**Contact** Alex Bywaters
**Mail address** Wyncroft, Scholsmoor Road, Holmfirth, West Yorkshire HD7 1SR
**Phone** 01484 682083
**Email** a.bywaters@virgin.net
**Practice** in Slaithwaite on Tue.
**Dance style** North West Clog
**Gender** Mixed

### Soled Out
**Contact** Mike Knott
**Mail address** 9 Cromford Road, Wirksworth, Derbyshire DE4 4FH
**Phone** 01629 826075
**Practice** in Middleton-by-Wirksworth on Fri.
**Dance style** Appalachian
**Gender** Mixed

### Somerset Maids
**Web** wkweb4.cableinet.co.uk/wal/morris/maids.htm
**Contact** Julie Waldren
**Mail address** 3 Downs Cote Drive, Bristol, Somerset BS9 3TP
**Phone** 0117 985 2508
**Email** Somersetmaids@cableinet.co.uk
**Practice** in Marksbury on Thu.
**Dance style** Step and Cotswold
**Gender** Female

### Something's Afoot
**Web** www.btinternet.com/~scimitar.vc/afoot
**Contact** Geraldine Messenger
**Mail address** 34 Goylands Close, Howey, Llandrindod Wells, Powys LD1 5RB
**Phone** 01597 825390
**Email** somethingsafoot@bigfoot.com
**Practice** in Llanyre on Thu.
**Dance style** Appalachian
**Gender** Mixed

### Sompting Village
**Web** www.s-v-m.freeserve.co.uk
**Contact** Joe Curtis
**Mail address** 34 Rectory Farm Road, Sompting, West Sussex BN15 QED
**Phone** 01903 601351
**Email** s-v-m@bigfoot.com
**Practice** in Worthing on Wed.
**Dance style** North West Clog, Cotswold and Border
**Gender** Joint

### Southern Lights
**Contact** Marion Boxall
**Mail address** 106 Archery Grove, Woolston, Southampton, Hampshire SO19 9EU
**Phone** 01703 398830
**Practice** in Southampton on Wed.
**Dance style** Molly and Other/Own
**Gender** Female

### Southsea Belles
**Web** www.br2811.demon.co.uk/SSB.html
**Contact** Sue Walker
**Mail address** 1 Castle Gardens, Swan Street, Petersfield, Hampshire GU32 3AG
**Phone** 01730 261271
**Practice** in Portsmouth on Tue.
**Dance style** Cotswold
**Gender** Female

### Spank the Planks
**Contact** Jennet Lambert
**Mail address** 97 Suffolk Avenue, Christchurch, Dorset BH23 2TJ
**Phone** 01202 476631
**Practice** in Bournemouth on Tue.
**Dance style** Appalachian
**Gender** Mixed

### Spinning Jenny (Essex)
**Contact** Jan Jones
**Mail address** 37 Sidwell Avenue, South Benfleet, Essex SS7 1LF
**Phone** 01268 793905
**Practice** in Leigh on Sea on Wed.
**Dance style** Other/Own and Garland
**Gender** Female

### St Clement's Clogs
**Contact** Pat Osborne
**Mail address** 13 High Street, Swanscombe, Kent DA10 0AG
**Phone** 01322 385985
**Practice** in Gravesend on Thu.
**Dance style** North West Clog
**Gender** Female

## Standon Green N W Morris
**Contact** Sal Salloway
**Mail address** Rose End Cottage, 41 High Street, Standon, Ware, Hertfordshire SG11 1KA
**Phone** 01920 821785
**Email** sallo@aol.com
**Practice** in Standon on Tue.
**Dance style** Garland and North West Clog
**Gender** Female

## Stane Street Morris
**Contact** Roger Wilton
**Mail address** 54 Beech Road, Horsham, West Sussex RH12 4TU
**Phone** 01403 269126
**Email** quantox@compuserve.com
**Practice** in Horsham on Wed.
**Dance style** North West Clog
**Gender** Mixed

## Stone the Crows
**Contact** Brent Platt
**Mail address** 152 Chorley Old Road, Whittle le Wood, Chorley, Lancashire PR6 7NA
**Phone** 01257 263942
**Email** brent.platt@lineone.net
**Practice** in Leyland on Thu.
**Dance style** Border
**Gender** Mixed

## Stony Stratford Mummers
**Contact** Vicki Shakeshaft
**Mail address** 35 Wolverton Road, Stony Stratford, Milton Keynes, Buckinghamshire MK11 1EA
**Phone** 01908 562169
**Email** vicki@stratford.powernet.co.uk
Practice day and location not known.
**Dance style** Mumming
**Gender** Joint

## Stroud Morris Dancers
**Web** www.compulink.co.uk/~capers/stroud.html
**Contact** Jack Graham
**Mail address** The Laurels, Brimscombe Hill, Brimscombe, Stroud, Gloucestershire GL5 2QN
**Phone** 01453 885997
**Email** jack@meigh.demon.co.uk
**Practice** in Stroud on Mon.
**Dance style** Cotswold
**Gender** Joint

## Sussex Spinning Jenny
**Contact** Mrs Pat Sawyer
**Mail address** Flat 4, Boscobel, 53 Hastings Road, Bexhill on Sea, East Sussex TN40 2NH
**Phone**
**Email** t.sawyer@jonesbootmaker.com
**Practice** in Bexhill on Thu.
**Dance style** North West Clog
**Gender** Female

## Swanage Bay Morris
**Contact** Mrs Male C Tyrer
**Mail address** Bay Trees, 37 Bay Crescent, Swanage, Dorset BH19 1RB
**Phone** 01929 423234
**Email** Margaret.Tyrer@care4free.net
**Practice** in Swanage on Thu.
**Dance style** North West Clog
**Gender** Mixed

## Sweet Coppin
**Contact** Sarah Rudd
**Mail address** 16 Clifford Avenue, Taunton, Somerset TA2 6DJ
**Phone** 07977 825583
**Practice** in Taunton on Mon.
**Dance style** Step, Garland and Other/Own
**Gender** Female

## T'Gradely Lasses
**Contact** Sonia Atkin
**Mail address** 13 Rutland Ave, Pontefract, West Yorkshire WF8 3RD
**Phone** 01977 709992
**Email** sonia@atkinfam.freeserve.co.uk
**Practice** in Pontefract on Tue.
**Dance style** Other/Own
**Gender** Female

## Taeppas Tump
**Web** www.taeppastump.freeserve.co.uk
**Contact** Kay Carter
**Mail address** 59 Coulson Way, Burnham, SL1 7PL
**Phone** 01628 666763
**Practice** in Maidenhead on Tue.
**Dance style** North West Clog
**Gender** Female

## Tanglefoot Appalachian
**Web** homepages.go.com/~tanglefoot2/tanglefoot.html
**Contact** Bob Hawes
**Mail address** 29 Nuthatch, Longfield, Kent DA3 7NS
**Phone** 01474 704957
**Email** christine.bell@kcl.ac.uk
**Practice** in Hartley on Mon.
**Dance style** Appalachian
**Gender** Mixed

## Terpsichore
**Web** www.btinternet.com/~trip/terp
**Contact** Mrs J Green
**Mail address** 5 Hillcrest Close, Townville, Castleford, West Yorkshire WF10 3QS
**Phone** 01977 510770
**Email** jackie@townville.freeserve.co.uk
**Practice** in Castleford on Thu.
**Dance style** Garland and North West Clog
**Gender** Mixed

## Three Counties Garland Dancers
**Contact** Mrs Lisa Holden
**Mail address** 69 Craithie Road, Townmoor, Doncaster, South Yorkshire DN2 5EEE
**Phone** 01302 342037
**Practice** in Bawtrey on Fri.
**Dance style** North West Clog
**Gender** Female

## Three Shires
**Contact** Lesley Ellen
**Mail address** 7 Hudson Close, Harthill, Sheffield, South Yorkshire S23 7WB
**Phone** 01909 770129
**Email** L.Ellam@shu.ac.uk
**Practice** in Sheffield on Tue.
**Dance style** Step, Garland and North West Clog
**Gender** Female

## Three Spires Morris
**Contact** Catherine Carlisle
**Mail address** 21 Deerfold Crescent, Burntwood, Staffordshire WS7 9AX
**Phone** 01543 304489
**Email** stewart.carlisle@ntlworld.com
**Practice** in Lichfield on Thu.
**Dance style** Garland and North West Clog
**Gender** Female

## Tonbridge Morris
**Web** http://ds.dial.pipex.com/tonfolk
**Contact** Helen Crowle
**Mail address** 16 Bramley Road, East Peckham, Tonbridge, Kent TN12 5BW
**Phone** 01622 871951
**Email** helencrowle@aol.com
**Practice** in Tonbridge on Sun.
**Dance style** Border and Cotswold
**Gender** Mixed

## Tormohun Morris
**Contact** Frances Popley
**Mail address** 166 St Marychurch Road, Torquay, Devon TQ1 3HP
**Phone** 01803 322543
**Practice** in Torquay on Mon.
**Dance style** Cotswold
**Gender** Female

## Touchwood Appalachian
**Web** earwicker.inetc.net/touchwood.htm
**Contact** Steve Earwicker
**Mail address** 3 Normanby Road, Wollaton, Nottingham, Nottinghamshire NG8 2TA
**Phone** 0115 928 2566
**Email** touchwood.dance@btinternet.com
**Practice** in Castle Donington on Wed.
**Dance style** Appalachian
**Gender** Mixed

### Treacle Eater Clog
**Contact** Steve Cunio
**Mail address** 1 Lower Hyde Road, Montacute, Somerset TA15 6UR
**Phone** 01935 829050
**Email** TEC@cunio-marsh.freeserve.co.uk
**Practice** in Yeovil on Mon.
**Dance style** North West Clog
**Gender** Female

### Turnberrie Castle
**Contact** Mrs Denise Cooke
**Mail address** 7 Gillinstoll, Thornbury, Bristol, Avon BS35 2EG
**Phone** 01454 413004
**Email** cooke.family@care4free.net
**Practice** in Thornbury on Thu.
**Dance style** North West Clog, Border and Garland
**Gender** Mixed

### Wakefield Morris
**Contact** Liz Harwood
**Mail address** 108 Coxley View, Netherton, Wakefield, West Yorkshire WF4 4LY
**Phone** 01924 265229
**Email** harwoodliz@hotmail.com
**Practice** in Horbury on Mon.
**Dance style** North West Clog
**Gender** Mixed

### Weston
**Contact** Daryl Dawson
**Mail address** Trent Cottage, Kings Mills Lane, Weston on Trent, Derbyshire DE72 2BQ
**Phone** 01332 702386
**Email** daryldawson@hotmail.com
**Practice** in Weston on Tue.
**Dance style** Garland, Other/Own and North West Clog
**Gender** Female

### Westmorland Step and Garland
**Contact** Mrs Gillian Slater
**Mail address** Bracklyn, Silverdale Road, Arnside, Via Carnforth, Cumbria LA5 0DZ
**Phone** 01524 761576
**Email** gmslater@portables1.ngfl.gov.uk
**Practice** in Kendal on Mon.
**Dance style** Step and Garland
**Gender** Female

### Westrefelda
**Contact** Liz Whatling
**Mail address** 5 Borrowdale Ave, Ipswich, Suffolk IP4 2TN
**Phone** 01473 252098
**Email** lizwhatling@lineone.net
**Practice** in Westerfield on Mon.
**Dance style** Molly and Cotswold
**Gender** Mixed

### Whitethorn
**Contact** Susan Pearse
**Mail address** 2 Castle Meadow Close, Newport Pagnell, Buckinghamshire MK16 9EJ
**Phone** 01908 613644
**Email** suepearse@hotmail.com
**Practice** in Harrow on Thu.
**Dance style** North West Clog
**Gender** Female

### Whitty Pear
**Contact** Mrs Sue Gething
**Mail address** Bodiam, 16 Evertons Close, Droitwich, Worcestershire WR9 8AE
**Phone** 01905 774455
**Email** gordg@computerweekly.net
**Practice** in Kidderminster on Thu.
**Dance style** Border and Cotswold
**Gender** Female

### Wickham Morris
**Contact** http://www.geocities.com/wickham_Morris
**Contact** Yvonne Wheeler
**Mail address** Penshurst, Vicarage Lane, Swanmore, Southampton, Hampshire SO32 2PW
**Phone** 01489 892911
**Email** wheeler@totalise.co.uk
**Practice** in Wickham on Thu.
**Dance style** Border, Cotswold and Other/Own
**Gender** Mixed

### Wight Beaux & Belles
**Contact** Mrs Linda Williams
**Mail address** 5 Gordon Road, Newport, Isle of Wight PO30 2EU
**Phone** 01983 527442
**Email** petef@normanway.demon.co.uk
**Practice** in Newport on Thu.
**Dance style** Garland and North West Clog
**Gender** Female

### Wild Hunt
**Web** www.cuddly.demon.co.uk/wildhunt/wildhunt.htm
**Contact** Jacky Lowles
**Mail address** 28 Ownsted Hill, New Addington, Croydon, Surrey CR0 0JQ
**Phone** 0181 240 9511
**Email** jax@ying-yang.fsnet.co.uk
**Practice** in Croydon on Tue.
**Dance style** Border and Other/Own
**Gender** Mixed

### Windsor Morris
**Contact Contact** Sarah O'Neill
**Mail address** 341 Chartridge Lane, Chesham, Buckinghamshire HP5 2SH
**Phone** 01494 782240
**Email** sarah.o'neil@aspextec net
**Practice** in Windsor on Wed.
**Dance style** Cotswold
**Gender** Female

### Winkleigh Morris
**Contact** Anne Bendix
**Mail address** 18 Clinton Gardens, Merton, Oakhampton, Devon EX20 3DP
**Phone** 01805 603599
**Practice** in Winkleigh on Tue.
**Dance style** Border and Cotswold
**Gender** Mixed

### Winterbourn Down
**Contact** Mrs L Harley
**Mail address** 17 Oakwood Road, Henleaze, Bristol, Avon BS9 4NP
**Phone** 0117 962 2111
**Email** rharley@waitrose.com
**Practice** in Winterbourn on Mon.
**Dance style** Mumming and Border
**Gender** Mixed

### Witchmen
**Contact** Terry Dix
**Mail address** 7 Thomas Road, Kettering, Northamptonshire NN15 6HD
**Phone** 01536 521100
**Email** witchmen@hotmail.com
**Practice** in Isham on Sun.
**Dance style** Other/Own and Border
**Gender** Male

### Withy Morris
**Web** www.withymorris.org.uk
**Contact** Susan Mew
**Mail address** Mayhiull, Woodland Close, Carhampton, Minehead, Somerset TA24 6LY
**Phone** 01643 821209
**Email** susan@mayhill2000.fsnetco.uk
**Practice** in Wellington on Thu.
**Dance style** Cotswold and Border
**Gender** Mixed

### Woad Works Morris
**Contact** Mick Dale
**Mail address** 50 Oxford Street, Wolverton, Milton Keynes, MK12 5HP
**Phone** 01908 225439
**Email** woad_works_bag@yahoo.com
**Practice** in Cosgrove on Mon.
**Dance style** Molly and Border
**Gender** Mixed

### Wolfshead & Vixen Morris
**Web** www.hugin.demon.co.uk/wolfshead.html
**Contact** Kevin Shewan
**Mail address** 9 Kings Avenue, Rochester, Kent ME1 3DS
**Phone** 01634 404906
**Email** wolfshead@shewan.com
**Practice** in Rochester on Wed.
**Dance style** Border
**Gender** Joint

### Women on the Wold
**Contact** Mrs L Dickenson
**Mail address** Cleeve Cloud, Nutters Wood, Gloucestershire GL52 3PZ
**Phone** 01242 678323
**Email** g.heatley@ucas.ac.uk
**Practice** in Cheltenham on Wed.
**Dance style** North West Clog
**Gender** Female

### Wreckers
**Contact** Polly Leigh
**Mail address** Furslow Bungalow, Blunts, Saltash, Cornwall PL12 5AS
**Phone** 01752 851990
**Practice** in Saltash on Thu.
**Dance style** Border
**Gender** Mixed

### Wyvern Jubilee Morris Men
**Contact** Brian Baldwyn
**Mail address** 18 Henning Way, Milborne Port, Sherborne, Dorset DT9 5HN
**Phone** 01963 251163
Practice day and location not noted.
**Dance style** Cotswold
**Gender** Male

### Yorkshire Chandelier
**Mail address** 43 Tom Lane, Sheffield, South Yorkshire S10 3PA
**Phone** 0114 230 1423
**Practice** in Sheffield on Thu.
**Dance style** North West Clog
**Gender** Female

## Useful Addresses

### EFDSS
**Mail address** Cecil Sharp House, 2 Regents Park Road, London NW1 7AY
**Phone** 020 7485 2206

### The Morris Ring
**Contact** John Frearson
**Mail address** 7 Birch Grove, Sandy, Bedfordshire SG19 1NG
**Phone** 01767 681057
Email
RingBagman@TheMorrisRing.org

### Open Morris
**Contact** Tracey Good
**Mail address** 36 Hawthorne Avenue, Louth, Lincolnshire LN11 0LD
**Phone** 01507 608364
Email goodtracey@hotmail.com

### Morris Matters
**Contact** Beth Neill
**Mail address** 27 Nortoft Road, Chalfont St Peter, Buckinghamshire SL9 0LA
**Phone** 01494 871465

### American Morris Newsletter
**Contact** Jocelyn Reynolds
**Mail address** 2586 36th Avenue, San Francisco CA 94116 USA
**Email** joss@periodpieces.com

### New Zealand Morris Sphere
**Contact** Wendy Collings
**Mail address** PO Box 11, 509 Manners Street, Wellington, NZ

### Australasian Morris Ring
**Contact** Don Barnes
**Mail address** 31 Tidworth Crescent, Colonel Light Gardens, South Australia, Australia

# Open Morris

***A brief history***
Open Morris began in 1979 as a loose organisation of East Anglian dancers, following efforts by one of the (then) few mixed Morris sides in the country to find local friends and sympathisers.

Interest in Open Morris began to spread further afield and the organisation now has about 100 member sides from all over Britain, as well as a few from overseas and a number of individual members.

***About open morris***
What we stand for: Morris dancing for all! Open Morris is open to any group or individual involved in the performance of morris dancing or allied activities. All sides are welcome - mixed, male or female, as are dancers or musicians who wish to become individual members.

Morris should be FUN! We believe our members should enjoy their dancing.

***What we offer***
We arrange activities to bring members together, including instructional sessions covering aspects of morris such as different styles and traditions of dancing. Additionally, there are workshops for musicians, fools, animals and so on.

- *Dancing On* the Open Morris magazine is published approx. three times a year. In this light-hearted magazine members and non-members too get a chance to air their views and grievances relating to morris matters.
- *The Secretary's Newsletter* comes out at intervals during the year to publicise events and to keep members up-to-date with Open Morris matters.
- *Open Morris members* are automatically entitled to public liability insurance, which gives cover up to £5,000,000. Membership currently costs £24 per year for groups, £7 for individuals and children's teams are entitled to all the benefits of membership for the affordable subscription of only £5.

***Joining open morris***
If you or your side are interested in becoming members of Open Morris, please contact
**Secretary** Tracey Good
**Phone** 01507 608364
**Email** goodtracey@hotmail.com

See our web site at
**www.open-morris.com**

### Alford Morris
**Area** Lincs
**Contact** Patrick Purves
**Phone** 01507 605385
**Gender** mixed
**Dance types** Cotswold, Border
**Practice day** Sunday

### Allington Morris
**Area** Lincs
**Contact** M. McKinlay
**Phone** 01400 281671
**Gender** Mixed
**Dance types** Cotswold

### Annie's Fantasies
**Area** Essex
**Contact** Alice Luikinga
**Phone** 01206 853146
**Gender** Mixed
**Dance types** Northwest
**Practice day** Sunday

### Ashley's Rise
**Area** Bristol
**Contact** Rebecca Woodward
**Phone** 0117 940 1566
**E-mail** ashleyrisemorris@aol.com
**Gender** Mixed junior
**Dance types** Border
**Practice day** Tuesday

### Black Adder Clog Morris
**Contact** Jackie Burch
**Gender** Mixed
**Dance types** Northwest, Border and Mummers
**Practice day** Thursday

### Black Pig Border Morris
**Area** Notts
**Contact** Catherine Brooking
**Phone** 01773 852358
**Gender** Mixed
**Dance types** Border, Mummers
**Practice day** Wednesday

### Bollin Morris
**Contact** Brian Corrigan
**Phone** 01565 654014
**Gender** Mixed
**Dance types** North West

### Boston Morris Stumpers
**Area** Lincs
**Contact** Ria Maddy
**Phone** 01205 365250
**Gender** Mixed
**Dance types** Cotswold
**Practice day** Monday

### Bourne Borderers Morris
**Area** Peterborough
**Contact** Nicola Darby
**Phone** 01778 342490,
**E-mail** bourne_borderers@lineone.net
**Gender** Mixed, Juniors
**Dance types** Border, Molly
**Practice day** Wednesday

### Braybrooke Morris
**Area** Leics
**Contact** Geoff Pitcher
**Phone** 01858 467450
**Gender** Mixed
**Dance types** Cotswold, Border
**Practice day** Monday

### Brazenose Morris
**Area** Stamford
**Contact** Audrey Evans
**Phone** 01778 380791
**Gender** Mixed
**Dance types** Cotswold
**Practice day** Thursday

### Briggate Morris
**Area** Halifax
**Contact** Sharon Kirk
**Phone** 0422 378345
**E-mail** amathews@wakefield.gov.uk
**Gender** Female
**Dance types** North West
**Practice day** Monday

### Broomstick Womens Morris
**Area** Sheffield
**Contact** Lisa Bellamy
**Phone** 0114 258 7046
**Gender** Female
**Dance types** Cotswold, Border
**Practice day** Tuesday

### Bury Fair Women's Morris
**Area** Suffolk
**Contact** Celia Nicol
**Phone** 01284 830052,
**Email** ceal@hotmail.com
**Gender** Women
**Dance types** Cotswold
**Practice day** Wednesday

### Celtica
**Contact** Julie Cross
**Phone** 01270 211491
**Email** julie.cross@libertysurf.co.uk
**Dance types** Other (Irish)
**Practice day** Tuesday

### Charlton Cherries
**Contact** David Morgan
**Phone** 01295 811404
**Email** morgan@cartwright-rd.freeserve.co.uk
**Gender** Mixed junior
**Dance types** Maypole, other
**Practice day** alt Tuesdays

### Chelmsford Morris
**Area** Essex
**Dance types** Joint /Cotswold, North West
**Practice day** Tues (women), Wednesday (men)

## Cockleshell Clog
**Area** Southend on Sea, Essex
**Contact** Meg Thomas
**Email** cloggermt@hotmail.com
**Contact** Bill Delderfield
**Email** cockleshellclog@freewebEmail.com
**Gender** Mixed
**Dance types** North West Clog

## Commoners Morris
**Area** W.Mids
**Contact** John Eynon
**Phone** 01902 454457
**Gender** Mixed
**Dance types** Border
**Practice day** Tuesday

## Conwy Morris
**Area** N.Wales
**Contact** Sue Walmsley
**Phone** 01492 583834
**Email** c.a.appleton@talk21.com
**Gender** Mixed
**Dance types** Border, North West
**Practice day** Wednesday

## Coton Village Morris Men
**Area** Cambs
**Contact** A. Blagbrough
**Phone** 01480 810756
**Gender** Male
**Dance types** Cotswold, Border
**Practice day** Monday

## Crompton Nook Morris
**Area** Lancs
**Contact** Freda Taylor
**Phone** 01706 849561
**Gender** Mixed
**Dance types** North West
**Practice day** Friday

## Crosskey Clog
**Area** Cambs
**Contact** Christine Stevenson
**Phone** 01733 391506
**Gender** Mixed
**Dance types** North West
**Practice day** Wednesday

## Datchet Morris
**Area** Middlesex
**Contact** John Wicking
**Phone** 01932 560869
**Gender** Men
**Dance types** Border, Other
**Practice day** Monday

## Devils Jumps Clog
**Area** Hants
**Contact** Clare Mach
**Phone** 023 9278 7478
**Email** brian@br2811.demon.co.uk
**Gender** Mixed
**Dance types** Step, Clog
**Practice day** Thursday

## Dr Turbervilles Morris
**Area** Somerset
**Contact** Kath Saint
**Phone** 01460 57524
**E-mail** david.easeman@bluefin-analysis. co.uk
**Gender** Mixed
**Dance types** Cotswold
**Practice day** Tuesday

## Earl of Stamford Morris
**Area** Warrington
**Contact** Cindy Dunn
**Phone** 01606 891145
**Email** cindy.dunn@talk21.com
**Gender** Mixed
**Dance types** Cotswold, Border
**Practice day** Tuesday

## Eken Morris Dancers
**Area** Sweden
**Contact** Richard Kumlien
**Email** rickard.kumlien@aga.se
**Gender** Mixed
**Dance types** Cotswold
**Practice day** Thursday

## Eryri Morris
**Area** Gwynedd
**Contact** Gill Bilsborough
**Phone** 01248 681860
**Gender** Mixed
**Dance types** Cotswold, Border
**Practice day** Monday

## Fendance/Pig Dyke Molly
**Area** Peterborough
**Contact** Mandy Buckenham
**Phone** 01480 384538
**Email** abuckenham@aol.com
**Gender** Mixed
**Dance types** Cotswold, Border, Molly
**Practice day** Monday

## Fenstanton Morris
**Area** Cambs
**Contact** Robin James
**Phone** 01480 350575
**Email** robin.james@zetnet.co.uk
**Gender** Mixed
**Dance types** Cotswold
**Practice day** Monday

## Fiddlers Brook
**Area** Herts
**Contact** Gill Munro
**Phone** 01279 723707
**Email** Neil.Munro@tesco.net
**Gender** Mixed
**Dance types** North West, Border
**Practice day** Tuesday

## Flying Tatters
**Area** Suffolk
**Contact** Molly Gratten
**Phone** 01473 424348
**Gender** Mixed
**Dance types** Border
**Practice day** Thursday

## Freaks in The Peaks
**Area** travelling
**Contact** Val Huzzard
**Phone** 0114 281 0870
**Email** valerie.huzzard@virgin.net
**Gender** Mixed
**Dance types** Border
**Practice day** Occasional

## Gog Magog Molly
**Area** Cambs
**Contact** Rachel Bearon
**Phone** 01223 363779
**Email** R.N.Bearon@damtp.cam.ac.uk
**Gender** Mixed
**Dance types** Molly
**Practice day** Tuesday

## Golden Star Morris
**Area** Norfolk
**Contact** Mark Jones
**Phone** 01603 712169
**Gender** Mixed
**Dance types** Cotswold
**Practice day** Sunday

## Granta Morris
**Area** Cambridge
**Gender** Mixed
**Dance types** Cotswold, Border

## Heartsease
**Area** Beds
**Contact** Patti Pitt
**Phone** 01234 376278
**Gender** Female
**Dance types** North West and others
**Practice day** Thursday

## Helsinki Morrisers
**Area** Finland
**Contact** Anthony Shaw
**Email** tonyshaw@clinet.fi
**Gender** Mixed
**Dance types** Cotswold, Border
**Practice day** Friday

## Heptonstall Pace Eggers
**Area** W. Yorks
**Contact** David Burnop
**Phone** 01422 846277
**Dance types** Good Friday Mummers play

## Hobby Bobbies
**Area** Portsmouth
**Contact** Eve Flewin
**Phone** (023) 92793769
**Gender** Mixed
**Dance types** Cotswold
**Practice day** Wednesday

## Hurst Morris People
**Contact** Mike Russell
**Phone** 01494 520282
**Gender** Mixed
**Dance types** Cotswold
**Practice day** Thursday

## Kajelus
**Area** Bristol
**Contact** Nick Johansen
**Phone** 01453 821443
**Email** Nick.Johansen@motionmedia.co.uk
**Gender** Mixed
**Dance types** Border
**Practice day** Tuesday

## Kenninghall Morris
**Area** Norfolk
**Contact** Pete Osborne
**Phone** 01953 888291
**Email** Positive@compuserve.com
(Kenninghall Rural Artistic Performers)

**Kern Morris**
**Area** Durham
**Contact** Helen Kendall
**Phone** 0191 384 6050
**Gender** Mixed
**Dance types** Cotswold
**Practice day** Wednesday

**Lady Bay Revellers**
**Area** Notts
**Contact** Michelene Harris
**Phone** 0115 9821292
**Gender** Mixed
**Dance types** Cotswold, other
**Practice day** Wednesday

**Lagabag Morris**
**Area** Suffolk
**Contact** Elizabeth Woolnough
**Phone** 01473 601961
**Gender** Mixed
**Dance types** Cotswold
**Practice day** Monday

**Leggin' It**
**Area** Bucks
**Contact** Wendy Roberts
**Phone** 0118 940 3092
**Gender** Mixed
**Dance types** Appalachian
**Practice day** Thursday

**Lizzie Dripping**
**Area** Sheffield
**Contact** Brenda Johns
**Phone** 0114 231 4596
**Email** b.a.johns@sheffield.ac.uk
**Gender** Female
**Dance types** Own, Step
**Practice day** Thursday

**Lobster Potties**
**Area** Norfolk
**Contact** Clive Rayment
**Phone** 01263 822302
**Email** Rayment@Globalnet.co.uk
**Gender** Mixed
**Dance types** North West, Other
**Practice day** Tuesday

**Longshore and First Light**
**Area** Suffolk
**Contact** Elaine MeLean
**Phone** 01502 516515
**Email** mcleans@clava.net
**Gender** Mixed
**Dance types** Cotswold, North West
**Practice day** Thursday

**Madcap Morris**
**Area** Worcs
**Contact** Mike Salter
**Phone** 01684 565211
**Gender** Mixed
**Dance types** Border
**Practice day** Occasional

**Mary Rose and Royal George Street Dancers**
**Area** Hants.
**Gender** Mixed
**Dance types** Other
**Practice day** Wednesday

**Mercheford Morris**
**Area** Cambs
**Contact** Roger & Angela Watson
**Phone** 01354 680705
**Gender** Mixed
**Dance types** Cotswold
**Practice day** Wednesday (monthly)

**Merrydale Morris**
**Area** W.Midlands
**Contact** John Shirley
**Email** merrydalemorris@yahoo.co.uk
**Gender** Mixed
**Dance types** Cotswold, Border
**Practice day** Monday

**Milltown Cloggies**
**Area** Derby
**Contact** John Morrison
**Phone** 01457 863764
**Gender** Female
**Dance types** North West
**Practice day** Monday

**Mind The Step Appalachian Dancers**
**Area** Cheshire
**Contact** Margaret Carroll
**Phone** 0161 748 1274
**Gender** Mixed
**Dance types** Appalachian
**Practice day** Sunday

**Miss Demeanour's Morris**
**Contact** Pete Humble
**Phone** 020 8684 0020
**Email** peet@dircon.co.uk
**Dance types** Cotswold, Border, North West
**Practice day** 1st Sunday of the month

**Moonraker Morris**
**Area** Wilts.
**Contact** Sue Sims
**Phone** 01249 461295,
**Email** moonraker_morris@yahoo.com
**Gender** Mixed
**Dance types** Cotswold
**Practice day** Sunday

**Morris in The Maze**
**Area** Essex
**Contact** Ilse Pedlar
**Phone** 01799 541880
**Email** Ipedler@Compuserve.com
**Gender** Mixed
**Dance types** Cotswold
**Practice day** Thursday

**Mosely Morris**
**Area** Birmingham
**Contact** Brian Cooper
**Phone** 0121 440 3981
**Gender** Mixed
**Dance types** North West
**Practice day** Thursday

**Mr Baker's Dozen**
**Area** Isle of Wight
**Contact** Steve Baker
**Phone** 01983 730113,
**Email** sbaker@iwpartnership. com
**Gender** Mixed
**Dance types** Playford, English traditional
**Practice day** Monday

**Mr Fox**
**Area** South Yorks
**Contact** Mr Fox
**Phone** 0114 288 1673,
**Email** Mr.Fox@btinternet.com
**Gender** Mixed
**Dance type** Langsett Fox Dance
**Practice day** Occasional

**Mucky Mountains Morris**
**Area** Merseyside
**Contact** Jenni Bedford
**Phone** 01925 825948
**Gender** Mixed
**Dance types** Border, Cotswold
**Practice day** Thursday

**Northstow Mummers**
**Area** Cambs
**Contact** Nigel Pennick
**Phone** 01954 789751
**Gender** Mixed
**Dance types** Mummers Plays

**Noroc**
**Area** West Yorks
**Contact** Sharon Kirk
**Phone** 01422 378345
**Email** sckirk@talk21.com
**Gender** Mixed
**Dance types** Step Clog
**Practice day** Wednesday

**Oakworth Mixed Morris**
**Area** West Yorks
**Contact** Anne Billinge
**Phone** 01925 221416
**Email** anneb@heis.co.uk
**Gender** Mixed
**Dance types** North West

**Ouse Washes Molly**
**Area** Norfolk
**Contact** David Boddy
**Phone** 01603 630331
**Email** dboddy@wsatkins.co.uk
**Gender** Mixed
**Dance types** Molly
**Practice day** Monday

**Phoenix Morris**
**Area** Herts
**Contact** Sue Stimpson
**Phone** 01923 770425
01923 775825
**Email** SSTIMPSON@AOC.COM
**Gender** Mixed
**Dance types** Cotswold
**Practice day** Wednesday

**Platypus Appalachian**
**Area** Essex
**Contact** Christine Fen
**Phone** 01206 570826
**Gender** Female
**Dance types** Appalachian
**Practice day** Wednesday

**Plymouth Maids**
**Contact** Barbara Allen
**Phone** 01752 780599
**Gender** Female
**Dance types** North West
**Practice day** Thursday

**Pretty Grim Morris**
**Area** Ipswich
**Contact** Chris Sills
**Phone** 01394 383329
**Gender** Mixed
**Dance types** Border
**Practice day** Tuesday

## Rag Morris
**Area** Bristol
**Contact** Gavin Skinner
**Phone** 0117 953 2159
**Gender** Mixed
**Dance types** Cotswold, Border, Other
**Practice day** Thursday

## Rampant Rooster
**Area** Surrey
**Contact** Ray Henderson
**Phone** 01737 842780
**Email** 106141.3466@compuserve. com
**Gender** Mixed
**Dance types** Cotswold, Border, Other
**Practice day** Tuesday

## Ramrugge Clogg Morris
**Area** Herts
**Contact** Jenny McCann
**Phone** 01707 322233
**Gender** Mixed
**Dance types** North West
**Practice day** Wednesday

## Ram's Head Morris
**Area** W.Yorks
**Contact** Fred J. Knights
**Phone** 01422 831896
**Gender** Mixed
**Dance types** Border
**Practice day** Monday, Thursday

## Ringheye Morris
**Area** Cheshire
**Contact** Susan Ellis
**Phone** 01565 873277
**Gender** Mixed
**Dance types** North West
**Practice day** Wednesday

## Rochdale Morris
**Area** Lancs
**Contact** Judith Armstrong
**Phone** 01706 874176
**Gender** Mixed
**Dance types** North West, Female Mummers
**Practice day** Wednesday

## Rumworth Morris of Bolton
**Area** Lancs
**Contact** Norma Bearon
**Phone** 01695 422971
**Email** beronjn@ptc.pilkington.co.uk
North West
**Practice day** Thursday

## Ryburn 3 Step
**Area** W.Yorks.
**Contact** Liz Abbot
**Phone** 01422 823957
**Gender** Mixed
**Dance types** Longsword, Appalachian **Practice day** Sunday (L), Tuesday (A)

## Sandgate Morris
**Area** W.Yorks.
**Contact** Sylvia Armstrong
**Gender** Female
**Dance types** North West
**Practice day** Thursday

## Scragenz Morris/ Bunnies From Hell
**Area** travelling
**Contact** Phil Watson
**Phone** 01223 570378
**Gender** Mixed
**Dance types** Cotswold and Others

## Seven Stars Sword and Step Dancers
**Area** Merseyside
**Contact** John Kelly
**Phone** 01744 884931
**Gender** Mixed
**Dance types** Longsword, Step, Clog and others
**Practice day** Thursday

## Shepley Higlers Morris
**Area** W.Yorks
**Contact** Ann Ellis
**Phone** 01484 846611
**Gender** Female
**Dance types** North West

## Shinfield Shambles
**Area** Berks
**Contact** Hilary Mortimer
**Phone** 01734 696926
**Email** H.F.Mortimer@reading.ac.uk
**Gender** Female
**Dance types** Border
**Practice day** Monday

## Sowerby Bridge Morris Dancers
**Area** North West
**Practice day** Thursday

## Spinners
**Area** Norfolk
**Contact** Neville Lee
**Phone** 01629 402581
**Gender** Mixed
**Dance types** Cotswold
**Practice day** Thursday

## Spithead Morris
**Area** Hants
**Contact** Brian Haxby and Netty Chipperfield
**Phone** 01705 830152
**Gender** Mixed
**Dance types** Border, Cotswold
**Practice day** Friday

## Sullivan's Sword
**Area** Nottingham
**Contact** Brian Hobby
**Phone** 0115 930 6457
**Email** isolatedsystems@ndirect.co.uk
**Gender** Male
**Dance types** Longsword, Other
**Practice day** Tuesday

## Sutton Stomp
**Area** Cambs
**Gender** Mixed
**Dance types** Cotswold, North West, Other
**Practice day** Monday

## Tap & Sync Co
**Area** Peterborough
**Contact** Annie Fox
**Phone** 01733 752242
**Gender** Mixed
**Dance types** Appalachian
**Practice day** Thursday

## Tatterfoals Morris
**Area** Lincs
**Contact** Pam Cook
**Phone** 01724 846382
**Gender** Mixed
**Dance types** North West
**Practice day** Thursday

## Thakeham Morris
**Area** West Sussex
**Contact** Chris West
**Phone** 01903 744571
**Email** chrisjwest@LineOne.net
**Gender** Mixed
**Dance types** Cotswold

## Tynebridge Morris
**Area** Newcastle upon Tyne
**Contact** Brenda Boyd
**Phone** 0191 266 1103
0191 292 0291
**Gender** Female
**Dance types** Garland, North West, Other
**Practice day** Thursday

## Upstreet Morris
**Area** Essex
**Contact** Suzanne Eccleston
**Phone** 020 8550 2470
**Email** SuzanneEcclestone@LineOne.net
**Gender** Mixed
**Dance types** Cotswold, North West, Other
**Practice day** alt. Sunday

## Watling Street Mummers
**Contact** Mike O'Connor
**Phone** 01604 858764
**Dance types** Mummers

## Weavers Morris
**Area** Norfolk
**Contact** Matthew Burrell
**Phone** 01692 403538
**Gender** Mixed
**Dance types** Cotswold
**Practice day** Monday

## Wharfedale Wayzgoose
**Area** W.Yorks
**Contact** Jennie Hooper
**Phone** 01943 463334
**Email** jenniewayzgoose@fsmail.net
**Gender** Mixed
**Dance types** Border
**Practice day** Tuesday

## Wicked Stix
**Contact** Rick Prentice
**Phone** 0114 236 0139
**Email** rickp@btinternet.com
**Gender** Mixed
**Dance types** Border
**Practice day** Monday

## Wicket Brood
**Contact** Anne Bailey
**Phone** 01442 214998
**Gender** Mixed
**Dance types** Border
**Practice day** alt. Tuesday

## Withy Morris
**Area** Somerset
**Contact** Susan Mew
**Phone** 01643 821209
**Gender** Mixed
**Dance types** Cotswold, Border
**Practice day** Thursday

## Woad Works Morris
**Area** Northants
**Contact** Mike Dale
**Phone** 01908 225439
**Email** woad_works_bag@yahoo.com
**Gender** Mixed
**Dance types** Border
**Practice day** Monday

### Woodland Morris
**Area** Cheshire
**Contact** Rod Scotney
**Phone** 01925 418678
**Email** rod.scotney@autoglass.co.uk
**Gender** Junior Mixed
**Dance types** Own Style (NW Influenced)
**Practice day** Thursday

### Wype Doles Longsword
**Area** Peterborough
**Contact** Coral Cornell
**Phone** 01733 204343
**Email** ppcornell@swinternet.co.uk
**Gender** Male
**Dance types** Longsword
**Practice day** Tuesday

### Yare Valley Morris
**Area** Norwich
**Contact** Union of UEA Students
**Email** yvmorris@stu.uea.ac.uk
**Gender** Mixed
**Dance types** Border, Molly, Cotswold
**Practice day** Monday

### Yorkshire Coast Morris
**Area** Scarborough
**Contact** Wendy Bostock
**Phone** 01723 375773
**Email** wbostock@mistral.co.uk
**Gender** Mixed
**Dance types** Cotswold, Border
**Practice day** Thursday

***These Morris teams are additional to, or have additional contact details to, those listed by The Morris Federation, The Morris Ring and Open Morris.***

### Adlington Morris Men
**Contact** Duncan Broomhead
**Mail address** Butley Cottage, Well Lane, Butley Town, Macclesfield. SK10 4DZ
**Phone** 01625 827988
**Practice** in NE Cheshire
**Dance Style** Cotswold
**Gender** Male

### Bullnose Morris
**Contact** John New
**Mail address** 37 Sidwell Avenue, South Benfleet, Essex. SS7 1LF
**Phone** 01268 793905
**Email** john@essexfolknews.co.uk
**Practice** in Pitsea, Essex
**Dance Style** Cotswold
**Gender** Mixed

### Dacre Morris
**Contact** Sarah Crofts
**Mail address** 7 Northbrook Road, Lewisham, London. SE13 5QT
**Phone** 020 8852 6618
**Email** s.j.crofts@gre.ac.uk
**Web** www.gre.ac.uk/~cs02/index.htm
**Practice** in Lewisham, London
**Dance Style** Cotswold
**Gender** Female

### Dogrose Morris
**Contact** Ross McKinlay
**Mail address** 59 Buckingham Road, Aylesbury, Bucks. HP19 9PT
**Phone** 07961 157128
**Email** ross@dogrose.co.uk
**Practice** in Huddersfield
**Dance Style** Cotswold
**Gender** Male

### East Saxon Sword Dancers
**Contact** Paul Draper
**Mail address** 82 Boundary Road, London. E13 9QG
**Phone** 020 8548 1941
020 7369 2754
**Email** pdraper@gaum.co uk; paul_draper@ukgateway.net
**Web** www.kibbler.demon.co.uk/ess/index.htm
**Practice** in East London
**Dance Style** Longsword & Rapper
**Gender** Male

### The Ironmen
**Contact** Chris Hall
**Mail address** 31 Blakeway Close, Broseley, Shropshire. TF12 5SS
**Phone** 01952 884269
**Email** irongilder@bigfoot.com
**Web** www.bigfoot.com/~irongilder
**Practice** in Ironbridge, Shropshire
**Dance Style** Border
**Gender** Male
*Associated with Severn Gilders.*

### Ryburn Longsword Dancers
**Contact** Sue Coe
**Mail address** 103 Oldham Road, Ripponden, West Yorks. HX6 4EB
**Phone** 01422 822569
**Email** suecoe@backshift.demon.co.uk
**Web** www.ryburn3step.org.uk
**Practice** in Yorkshire
**Dance Style** Longsword
**Gender** Mixed

### Severn Gilders
**Contact** Chris Hall
**Mail address** 31 Blakeway Close, Broseley, Shropshire. TF12 5SS
**Phone** 01952 884269
**Email** irongilder@bigfoot.com
**Web** www.bigfoot.com/~irongilder
**Practice** in Ironbridge, Shropshire
**Dance Style** North West
**Gender** Female
*Associated with The Ironmen.*

### Stroud Morris Dancers
**Contact** Mark Rogers
**Mail address** 4 Castlemead Road, Stroud, Glos. GL5 3SF
**Phone** 01453 762752
01453 731715
**Email** mark@capers.co.uk
**Web** www.capers.co.uk
**Practice** in Gloucestershire
**Dance Style**
**Gender** Mixed

### Winkleigh Morris
**Contact** Colin Andrews
**Mail address** Bonny Green, Morchard Bishop, Crediton, Devon. EX17 6PG
**Phone** 01363 877216
**Email** morrisman@connectfree.co.uk
**Web** www.bonnygreen.co.uk
**Practice** in Winkleigh, Devon
**Dance Style** Cotswold & Border
**Gender** Mixed

# Percussive Dance – a global phenomenon

By **Ross Allen**

Percussive dance is the umbrella term used to refer to the astounding variety of different styles of dance which have developed and travelled all over the world. Loosely speaking percussive dance is where the primary element is the rhythm sounded-out by the feet – often also called step-dancing. Typically the dancing is lively and high-spirited, often based around personal creativity and improvisation and continues to evolve, absorbing influences left, right and centre.

The British Isles are home to many traditional styles such as English clog and Irish hard-shoe dancing which have between them had a significant influence in shaping the percussive dance styles popular in Canada and America today - most famously Appalachian clogging and tap dancing. There are also, however, strong and vibrant traditions elsewhere in the world which are not off-shoots of this tree such as India' s Kathak which is danced in bare feet, Spain' s flamenco, Mexico' s zapateado and Argentina' s malambo.

Percussive dance is undergoing a welcome renaissance. Once an important part of every-day leisure - socially, in performance and in competition - the move away from live entertainment took a heavy toll. Then, in 1994 *Riverdance* fired the public' s imagination as part of the Eurovision Song Contest. The subsequent productions have toured extensively to packed audiences world-wide, establishing Irish dance firmly on the world 'stage' and signalling a resurgence of interest. **Dein Perry' s Tap Dogs** built on **Hot Shoe Shuffle**'s success for tap, **Joaquim Cortez** did the same for flamenco, and **Gumboots** brought boot dancing from the diamond miners of South-Africa to the mainstream. Numerous other stage shows, displays, classes and other events of all sizes have followed up on this revival, moving percussive dance forward and getting more and more people involved.

So where can you try your feet? In the UK, the opportunities to see and try these types of dancing has steadily increased due to support from the Arts establishment and further education, and the many display groups from the folk tradition who are broadening their repertoire. Festivals and other dance events are excellent places at which to have a ' taste' and this directory will give you the contact information you need. You don' t normally need more than a pair of comfortable leather shoes to get started and anyone can have a go. So get dancing!

**Ross Allen** *has been performing various percussive styles for over fourteen years. He is a solo performer, Artistic Director of DanceAV and performs with Broken Ankles.*

***Percussive Dance performers detailed in the Display Listings on pages 91-94 include Absolutely Legless, Lynch Irish Dance Troupe, Maire Clerkin and The Scottish Step Dance Company.***

***English Clog and Step Dancers detailed in the Display Listings on pages 91-94 include The Walker Family, Georgia Shorrock and Chris Coe.***

# Tapping the Web

**tapdance.org** This is the business ... includes EVENTS, Who's Who in Tap, Tap in film, History, Resources, News etc. etc.
**Web** www.tapdance.org

**tapuk** - amateur tap dance association in the UK - quality and varied teaching at day and weekend festivals, small magazine sent to members etc.
**Web** www.tapuk.freeserve.co.uk

**Tony Curtis' timestep** site - more history plus downloadable videos of the greats in action.
**Web** www.ukjtd.force9.co.uk/Timestepsite

### *ENGLISH CLOG*

**Ossy Cloggers** - includes brief history and information on Ossy Cloggers and Clogology.
**Web** www.cougar01.freeserve.co.uk/

**Reading Cloggies** - some basic info on Reading Cloggies plus link to Reading Clog Day.
**Web** http://freespace.virgin.net/anne.garrison/Reading%20Cloggies.htm

**www.gre.ac.uk/~cs02/step.htm**
Sarah Crofts' clog page which lists clog dance homepages and printed resources.

**www.nicholware.fsnet.co.uk/cloggies/**
Newcastle Cloggies homepage, includes a list of UK clog makers.

**www.inclognito.freeserve.co.uk**
Home page of innovative West Yorks clog group, Inclognito.

**http://freespace.virgin.net/anne.garrison/festival.htm**
Homepage for the annual Reading Tradition Clog and Step Dance Festival.

### *IRISH*

**Anne's Place** - Irish Dance - History / FAQ / Links.
**Web**
http://aerobin.www7.50megs.com/irdance/index.html

### *FRENCH-CANADIAN*

**Pierre Chartrand** - note that the site is in French.
**Web** www.danse.qc.ca

# Appalachian Clogging

Appalachian clogging has many diverse roots, with English, Irish, Scottish, African rhythms and native American influences. It became very popular in the UK in the late eighties and the following decade. There are still many thriving teams in the UK and Appalachian events at many major festivals.

Appalachian teams detailed in the DISPLAY LISTING include **Bluefields**, **Brandywine Cloggers**, **Broken Ankles**, **City Clickers**, **DanceAV**, **Firestone Percussive Dance Group**, **Scrambled Leggs**, **Shoostring Appalachian Dancers**, **Slapdash**, **Spank The Planks**, **Tiger Feet** and **Touchwood Appalachian Dancers**. Individual performers and teachers include **Kerry Fletcher**, **Ross Allen**, **Sandy Archer**, **Sue Coe** and **Sister Act**. Also see the **Morris Federation** and **Open Morris** listings for more teams.

## Publications

Various books and videos are available from **Ira Bernstein**
**Mail address** Ten Toe Percussion, 179 Flint Street, Asheville. NC 28801 USA
**Phone** +1 828 255-9393
**Fax** +1 828 255 9291
**Email** IraTenToe@aol.com
**Web** www.tentoepercussion.com
**Publications** available include

- Appalachian Clogging and Flatfooting Steps (1992)
- Flatfooting Workshop - Instruction video with Ira Bernstein
- Ira Bernstein Live!
- Ten Toe Percussion Ensemble
- Mountain Legacy - A Celebration of Southern Appalachian Dance & Music.

**A Compilation of American Clogging Steps.** *Penny, Anthony & Ross Allen.* (1989) Book. £8 incl.p&p
**Available from** 89, Hollingbury Park Avenue, Brighton.BN1 7JQ
**Phone** 01273 541453
**Web** www.brokenankles.btinternet.co.uk

**Step into Appalachian Clogging.** *Rosie Davis.* Cassette & Booklet
**Available from** 2, Fairview Cottages, Balaclava Lane, Wadhurst, E. Sussex. TN5 6EQ
**Phone** 01892 782412

## Magazines

**Old Times News**
*The magazine of The Friends of American Old Time Music & Dance.*
**Contact** Fiona Cameron
**Mail address** Bridge Cottage, Netherside, Bradwell, Derbyshire, S33 9JL
**Phone** 01433 623343
**Email** oldtimenews@neilart.force9.co.uk
**Web** www.pillard.demon.co.uk/foaotmad

**The Double Toe Times**
*Information on the American Precision Clogging scene.*
**Contact** The Editor
**Mail address** Double Toe Times, P.O. Box 1352, St. Albans, WV 25177-1352
**Phone** +1 304 727-9357
**Fax** +1 304 727-9568

## Festivals and Events

There is currently no large dedicated Appalachian dance festival, however Appalachian dances teams perform and run workshops at many other festivals.

Events to watch out for include:
**A1 Festival of Music & Dance**, (End of June) nr Peterborough. Music & dance festival with a strong emphasis on American, Old Time and Appalachian.
**Web** http://members.aol.com/A1Festival/Sacrewell.index.htm

**Sue Coe** hosts a one week intensive course with ace dancer and visiting tutor Ira Bernstein, every October. Further information is available by phoning Sue
**Phone** 01422 822569
**Web** www.ryburn3step.org.uk

**Reading Tradition Clog and Step Dance Festival** happens every October (21st October, 2001) in Maidenhead, Berkshire. The workshops and performances are mainly English clog styles and usually include Appalachian, French Canadian or Cape Breton.
**Contact** Anne Garrison
**Email** anne.garrison@virgin.net
**Web** http://freespace.virgin.net/anne.garrison/festival.htm

**Haddenham Ceilidhs** sometimes have Appalachian teams performing plus occasional workshops before the ceilidh. See Southern region
**Web** www.haddenhamceilidhs.co.uk

**Stanchester Old Timers (Music & Dance Group)** is an informal weekend of Old Time Music & Dance, with a number of items of interest to cloggers, as well as the opportunity to freestyle to some of the best Oldtime musicians in the U.K.
**Web** www.oldtime.fsnet.co.uk

Many of the festivals that book Morris dance sides also feature Appalachian teams and workshops. These include **Sidmouth International Festival** (1st week of August), **Towersey Village Festival** (August Bank Holiday) and **Stroud Fringe festival**. (Early September). See the festivals listing for more details of all the mentioned events.

## Websites

**www.brokenankles.btinternet.co.uk**
*Broken Ankles website, including links to other UK teams and US sites.*

**www.gre.ac.uk~cs02/step.htm**
*Sarah Crofts' website of step dance resources, including Appalachian clogging. Links to many UK teams.*

**www.thebuck.de**
**The Buck**, *a bimonthly, bilingual (German/English) magazine. The website's many sections include Appalachian clogging. It has extensive links to clogging sites in the US and beyond.*

**www.pillard.demon.co.uk/foaotmad**
*The Friends of American Old Time Music and Dance's website includes details, of festivals, summer camps and links.*

**www.tentoepercussion.com**
*Ira Bernstein's site which has plenty about him. Books and videos are available from this site.*

**www.cdss.org**
*Website of the country dance and song society (USA) with links to other American organisations.*
**Contact** Country Dance and Song Society
**Mail address** 132 Main St, PO Box 338 Haydenville, MA 01039-0338
**Phone** +1 413-268-7426
**Fax** +1 413-268-7471
**Email** office@cdss.org

- ***Thanks to Penny Allen of Broken Ankles for the above information.***

# folk arts

folk arts
customs

# Customs

By **Derek Schofield**

## *Calendar Customs*

Each one of us takes part in customs that depend upon the time of year - Valentine's cards, Easter eggs, bonfires and Christmas trees.

**Calendar customs** - events that take place at a specific time of year, usually annually - include these 'national' occasions (often with local or family peculiarities), but they also include events that are unique to a particular location. Such events often have obscure or uncertain origins, but most of them have taken place and evolved over many generations. They are community celebrations.

These customs often involve instrumental music, song, drama or dance; the participants often adopt special or distinctive clothes; and there is often some sort of performance aspect. Some of the events have achieved national prominence, whilst others remain very local, almost private events.

There has always been an interest in these calendar customs within the folk music and dance revival, and the revival has frequently drawn inspiration from these events.

**Customs which have gained national prominence** include Up-Helly-Aa in Lerwick (Shetland) and the Helston Furry Dance (Cornwall).

**Customs that involve dance** include the Morris dance traditions in Bampton, Headington Quarry and Abingdon (Oxfordshire) and Chipping Campden (Gloucestershire), and the sword dance traditions in Handsworth and Grenoside (Sheffield), Flamborough (East Yorkshire) and Goathland (North Yorkshire). The Britannia Coco-nut Dancers from Bacup (Lancashire) and the Abbots Bromley Horn Dance (Staffordshire) are unique. Other customs involving dance include the Helston Furry Dance (Cornwall), Groveley Forest Rights in Wishford Magna (Wiltshire), Castleton Garland (Derbyshire) and Knutsford Royal May Day (Cheshire).

**Customs involving song** include the Wassailing traditions of Carhampton (Somerset) and Bodmin (Cornwall), as well as the Christmas carol singing in and around Sheffield and the Derbyshire Peak District, and Haxey Hood (Lincolnshire).

**Customs that feature instrumental music** include all the dance customs given above, plus the Padstow 'Obby 'Oss (Cornwall) and the Minehead Hobby Horse (Somerset).

**Customs that feature drama** include the mummers' plays in Antrobus (Cheshire), Symmondsbury (Dorset), Midgley (West Yorkshire) and Uttoxeter (Staffordshire).

The recent interest in choral singing within the folk music revival, including the interest in West Gallery music, has been inspired in part by the traditional Christmas carol singing in Sheffield. Fire customs such as Ottery St Mary Tar Barrels (Devon), Allendale Fire Ceremony (Northumberland) and Up-Helly-Aa (Shetland) have had their influence on community arts celebrations.

Amongst **other notable customs** not previously mentioned are the football games in Ashbourne (Derbyshire), Alnwick (Northumberland) and Kirkwall (Orkney), well-dressing in Derbyshire (Tissington and many other villages) and the Cliffe Bonfire in Lewes (Sussex).

Other cultures have brought their customs into the UK with Chinese New Year celebrations in major cities such as London, Manchester and Liverpool, the Notting Hill Carnival (London) and religious festivals such as Diwali.

## *Sources of Information*

**Publications**

**Folklore** (the journal of The Folklore Society) often features articles on customs, as does the Society's Newsletter.
**Contact** The Folklore Society, The Warburg Institute, Woburn Square, London, WC1H 0AB

**Folk Music Journal** and **English Dance and Song** are the two periodicals of the **English Folk Dance and Song Society**. Both publications include articles on customs.
**Contact** EFDSS, Cecil Sharp House, 2 Regent's Park Road, London, NW1 7AY
**Phone** 020 7485 2206

**Books on calendar customs** include the following (some of them are out of print but available in libraries):

**Shuel, Brian**. *The National Trust Guide to Traditional Customs of Britain* (Webb and Bower, 1985). Shuel is the best-known photographer of folk customs and folk musicians and singers. Unlike many of the writers on customs, Shuel has visited most of the customs described.

**Sykes, Homer**. *One a Year: Some Traditional British Customs* (Gordon Fraser, 1977). A professional photographer, Sykes photographed and described a selection of customs for this publication.

**Kightly, Charles**. *The Customs and Ceremonies of Britain* (Thames and Hudson, 1986). Described as an encyclopaedia of living traditions.

**Day, Brian**. *A Chronicle of Folk Customs* (Hamlyn, 1998). A day-to-day guide to folk traditions - the descriptions are brief but the coverage extensive.

**Cooper, Quentin and Sullivan, Paul**. *Maypoles, Martyrs and Mayhem* (Bloomsbury, 1994). Descriptions of British customs, myths and eccentricities.

**Simpson, Jacqueline and Roud, Steve**. *A Dictionary of English Folklore* (Oxford University Press, 2000). This dictionary includes a number of calendar customs.

*The Pitkin Guide: Customs and Traditions in Britain* (Pitkin, 2000). Largely comprising photographs, this publication also includes brief descriptions of a selection of customs.

The following books are historical surveys:

**Wright, AR and Lones, TE**. *British Calendar Customs: England*. Three volumes (William Glaisher for the Folk-Lore Society, 1936, 1938 and 1940). A compilation of many references and descriptions. The three volumes cover movable festivals and fixed festivals - January to May and June to December.

**Macleod Banks, Mrs M**. *British Calendar Customs: Scotland*. Three volumes (William Glaisher for the Folk-Lore Society, 1937, 1939 and 1941). The three volumes cover the same three areas as the English volumes.

**Owen, Trefor M**. *Welsh Folk Customs* (National Museum of Wales, first edition 1959, third edition 1974).

**Owen, Trefor M**. *A Pocket Guide: The Customs and Traditions of Wales*. (University of Wales Press, 1991).

Many books have been written on individual calendar customs - some of these are historical in perspective, whilst others are contemporary accounts with photographs. Some of the books have been written by folklorists, whilst others have been written by participants. Amongst the best are:

**Brown, Callum G**. *Up-Helly-Aa: Custom, Culture and Community in Shetland* (Manchester University Press, 1998).

**Morison, John and Daisley, Peter**. *Hallaton, Hare Pie Scrambling and Bottle Kicking: facts and folklore of an ancient custom* (Hallaton Museum Press, 2000).

**Etherington, Jim**. *Lewes Bonfire Night: A Short History of the Guy Fawkes Celebrations* (SB Publications, 1993).

Many calendar customs have produced their own booklets or guides, which are available locally.

## Websites

A major new website featuring calendar customs in the UK is being launched in the summer of 2001.
**Email** derek@dschofield.demon.co.uk

A number of customs are featured on websites. Some sites are dedicated to individual customs, others include local customs in their coverage of local events. Many local authority or tourist board websites include sections on local customs. Some websites to look for are:
Ashbourne Shrovetide Football (Derbyshire)
**Web** www.shrovetide.com

Ottery St Mary Tar Barrels (Devon)
**Web** www.tarbarrels.co.uk

Abingdon Traditional Morris Dancers and Election of Mayor of Ock Street
**Web** www.chris-bartram.co.uk/ATMD.htm

Up-Helly-Aa (Shetland)
**Web** www.up-helly-aa.com

Well Dressing in Derbyshire and elsewhere
**Web** www.welldressing.com

Maypoles (but not the ones with ribbons)
**Web** www.maypole2000.freeserve.co.uk

## Further Research

For detailed research into individual customs, the reader is advised to make use of the following libraries and archives:

**English Folk Dance and Song Society's Vaughan Williams Memorial Library**.
Extensive collection of books, periodicals and other printed materials, manuscripts, photographs and films/videos. Access is free to members and non-members pay a small fee.
**Contact** Vaughan Williams Memorial Library
**Mail address** Cecil Sharp House, 2 Regent's Park Road, London, NW1 7AY
**Phone** 020 7485 2206
**Email** library@efdss.org
**Web** www.efdss.org

**The Folklore Society**'s Library is currently split between The Warburg Institute and University College London. Many books are in store but available within 24 hours.
**Contact** The Folklore Society
**Mail address** The Warburg Institute, Woburn Square, London, WC1H 0AB
**Phone** 020 7862 8562
**Web** www.folklore-society.com

**School of Scottish Studies** contains extensive archives on all aspects of Scottish folk culture.
**Contact** School of Scottish Studies
**Mail address** University of Edinburgh, 27 George Square, Edinburgh, EH8 9LD
**Phone** 0131 650 4167.
**Web** www.sss.ed.ac.uk
The website gives a link to the archives, and also to PEARL (Providing Ethnological Archives for Research and Learning) which is an on-line accession database
**Web** www.pearl.arts.ed.ac.uk

**The Museum of Welsh Life** at St Fagans is part of the National Museums and Galleries of Wales. The museum includes archives on folklife and folklore.
**Contact** Museum of Welsh Life
**Mail address** St Fagans, Cardiff, CF5 6XB
**Phone** 01222 569441
**Web** www.nmgw.ac.uk/mwl/index.en

The author would be pleased to receive information about UK calendar customs.
**Contact** Derek Schofield
**Email** derek@dschofield.demon.co.uk

**Derek Schofield** *is a researcher of the Folk Revival and of Calendar Customs. Arena Dance Director at Sidmouth International Festival 1992-1996.*

# Community Arts

By **Mike Bettison**

In the late 1970s the Arts Council first acknowledged the existence of community arts. These were organisations and individuals that encouraged participation in the arts through sharing skills and opportunities. At first many projects were multi-disciplined, but over the years there has developed a range of movements such as community plays, community music, community print shops and the like.

There is a common premise behind both the community arts philosophy and the folk music revival. The belief that anyone can have a go and should be encouraged to do so is fundamental. Both camps however acknowledge that people do like to sit and watch, enjoy and admire excellence in the work of others.

Many folk festivals combine these two strands admirably, but may wish to look further afield towards those in the community arts arena to expand the workshop activities.

Processions are often used by festivals to promote the event and add excitement to the public face of the festival. There are a number of community artists who take influences from international processions - carnival, Mardi Gras etc. and augment the visual and aural effect.

Some street theatre companies seek to do similar. These can be seen at arts festivals but could greatly enhance the impact of many folk festivals.

The last fifteen years has seen a burgeoning of the rural touring schemes, encouraging and supporting professional performances in village halls and similar rural non-theatrical spaces. Drama, dance and opera companies, music ensembles of various genres, singers, storytellers, poets, puppeteers and pipers have created work that can be accommodated in a variety of spaces. The folk arts encompass all the general arts disciplines - music, dance, drama, literature, visual arts etc. and have always fed into the mainstream activities. However, there is a now a wider range of individuals and companies that could give additional energy to folk events.

## *Resources*

Probably a first port of call for contacts in this field is your local Regional Arts Board. They should have a database available of all sorts of artists in their area. You will probably have to define your field a little. You should also check to see if your local authority has an arts development officer as they should also have a list of good contacts.

There is a bi-monthly magazine called Mailout, sub-titled 'the national magazine for developing participation in the arts'.
You can contact them on
**Phone** 01246 207070
**Email** info@e-mailout.org.
Lots of information and contacts listed.

Street theatre is best seen in situ i.e. on the streets, so you should go and see people perform. There are a number of events which feature numerous acts, specifically the
**Stockton International Festival**
**Phone** 0191 276 9911

**X-Trax** in Manchester
**Phone** 0161 224 0020
**Email** mia@streetsahead.org.uk

**The Brighton Festival**
**Phone** 01273 821588.

There are also some showcase events run by agents such as **Fools Paradise**. If you are interested in village hall touring schemes try and find your local one first (probably again through RABs or your local authority), but you could get further information from the
**National Rural Touring Forum**
**Phone** 01759 303624
**Email** mail@nrtf.org.uk

**Mike Bettison**
*Artistic Director of Blaize. Director of events and projects, actor and musician.*

# Storytelling and The Folk Scene

By **Patrick Ryan**

The past few years saw increased interest and activity in storytelling. Some call this a revival. Others believe storytelling never died out and so can't be revived. In any case, there's a clear expansion of storytelling going on, both in traditional venues and new contexts. Many folk festivals always featured storytelling. In the late 1970s and throughout the '80s and '90s these festivals began to feature storytelling even more than previously.

**Early Developments**

Interest in storytelling rose and fell over the past century, alongside folk revivals. Within recent memory, prior to the 1980s, a great deal of storytelling for children occurred in schools and libraries. Storytelling for adults did take place within traditional contexts and a few folk clubs and festivals. Some involved during this period included **Eileen Colwell**, **Grace Hallworth**, **Janet Hill**, **John Mansfield**, **Packie Manus Byrne**, **Ruth Tongu**e, **Katherine Briggs**, **Seamus Ennis**, **Jim Carroll and Pat McKenzie**, **Charles Parker**, **the Stewarts of Blairgowrie**, and **Hamish Henderson**.

**The Late 1980s**

The latter half of the 80s saw the first clubs and festivals devoted entirely to storytelling. Some lasted, others provided models for festivals and clubs thriving now. **Ben Haggarty**, an influential storyteller, developed the first festivals and club (**The Crick Crack Club**) in London. At the same time, clubs sprang up in other parts of England, such as **Storytelling at the Edge** in Shropshire and the **Bit of Crack** in Newcastle-upon-Tyne. In Scotland, **Donald Smith** helped Scots tellers direct the first **Scottish International Storytelling Festival** and the first club (**The Guid Craic**). **Liz Weir**, in Northern Ireland, started the popular **Yarnspinners** and initiated the first festival in Ireland (**The Ulster Storytelling Festival**).

Those actively encouraging storytelling on the folk scene at this time included **Taffy Thomas**, **Jim Eldon**, **Sara Grey**, **Richard Walker (Mogsy)**, **Rosie Cross**, **the Kippers**, **Les Barker**, **Mike Rust**, **Duncan Williamson**, **Betsy White**, **Sheila Stewart**, **Packie Manus Byrne**, **John Campbell** and **Patrick Ryan**. Some also took part in the storytelling festivals and clubs, providing crossover between both scenes.

**The 1990s**
The number of clubs and festivals grew rapidly. **Festival at the Edge** in Shropshire established itself as the major storytelling festival in England, the Scottish festival continued in Edinburgh, and new ones appeared on Skye and elsewhere. **St. Donat's International Storytelling Festival** in Wales grew to be the biggest in Britain and Ireland, attracting thousands with tellers from many parts of the world. Festivals in Northern Ireland expanded too, and to these were added **Scéalta Shamhna**, **Beal Oscailte** and **Cape Clear Storytelling Festival** in Dublin, Mayo and Cork, respectively.

Storytelling manifested itself in other areas. Besides storytelling for children, projects appeared with tellers working with all ages and groups. Most significantly, various organisations and centres formed to support and promote storytelling and bring people interested in storytelling together.

**Storytelling Today**
Storytelling thrives. There is much lively discussion about storytelling, similar to debates about folk music, song and dance in previous generations. There are many cross-overs between folk, storytelling, community and literature festivals and projects. Tellers from overseas such as **Dan Keding**, **Jim May**, **David Holt** and **Dovie Thomason** from America, **Sharon Aviv** from Israel, and **Eddie Lenihan** from Ireland feature regularly at all these.

Many who raised the profile of storytelling within the folk scene continue working there. **Taffy Thomas**, **Patrick Ryan**, **Jim Eldon**, **Les Barker**, **Mike Rust**, **Duncan Williamson**, **Sheila Stewart**, **Stanley Robertson**, **Sara Grey**, and **John Campbell** feature regularly. So too, now, do **Liz Weir**, **Billy Teare**, **Eddie Lenihan**, **Bob Pegg**, **Joan Barr** (often working with musician **Brian Peters**), **Hugh Lupton**, **Amy Douglas**, and **Derek and Pippa Reid**. Tellers invited to one or two folk clubs or festivals and showing great promise for appearances at others include **Arti Prashar**, **Carol Russell**, **Linda Cotterill**, **Helen East and Rick Wilson**, **Carol Mason**, **Mike Wilson**, **Michael Harvey**, **David Campbell**, **George MacPherson**, **Alison Millen** and **Paraig MacNeill**, **Pat Speight**, **Sheila Quigley**, **Mick Quinn**, **Linda Bandelier**, **Vaiyu Naidu**, **Godfrey Duncan Tuup**, **Paddy O'Brien**, **Kate Corkery**, and **Winston Nzgania**.

Storytelling and other folk arts have great potential for working together. With storytelling, folk events find new audiences, linking communities and generations not involved with the folk scene. Folk performers and organisers of folk events have skills and knowledge that can benefit tellers. In terms of arts funding and commercial sponsorship, storytelling and folk arts make ideal partnerships. Storytelling falls under literature, folk music and dance under performance or traditional arts; bringing together different disciplines and cultural backgrounds for new projects appeals to funders.

## *Resources*

**Organisations**
The following organise events, courses, and provide publications:

**The Society for Storytelling**
PO Box 2344, Reading,
Berkshire, RG6 TFG
**Phone** 0118 935 1381
**Email** sfs@fairbruk.demon.co.uk
**Web** www.sfs.org.uk

**Tall Tales at The Web/**
**The Storytelling Diary/**
**The Storytelling Notice Board**
**Web** www.mcs.surrey.ac.uk/Personal/csxljw/talltales/

**The Scottish Storytelling Forum**
The Scottish Storytelling Centre,
Netherbow Arts Centre,
43-45 High Street, Edinburgh,
EH1 1SR,
**Phone** 0131 557 5724
**Email** netherbow-storytelling@dial.pipex.com
**Web** www.storytellingcentre org.uk

**The Verbal Arts Centre**
Mall Wall, Stable Lane,
Bishops Street, Londonderry, BT48,
**Phone** 01504 266 946
**Fax** 01504 263 368
**Web** www.verbart.demon.co.uk

**The Writers Museum/Writers Centre**
Parnell Square, Dublin 2,
Republic of Ireland

**The Storytelling Foundation**
International and The National Storytelling Network,
116 1/2 West Main Street,
Jonesborough, TN 37659, USA
**Phone** 001 800 525 4514
**Fax** 001 423 753 9331
**Email** nsn@naxs.net
**Web** www.storynet.org

*Note:* Many other countries, such as France, Belgium, Denmark, Norway, Holland, Argentina, Japan, Australia, New Zealand and Canada, have storytelling organisations to give advice and support storytelling. Information on these organisations can be obtained by searching the web, or by contacting one of the above organisations, who have details on storytelling in other countries.

## *Research Facilities*

Some sources for finding out about storytelling and stories to tell:

**The Folk-Lore Society**
The Warburg Institute, Woburn Square, London, WC1H 0AB
**Phone** 020 7862 8562

**The Vaughan Williams Memorial Library**
English Folk Dance and Song Society,
Cecil Sharp House,
2 Regent's Park Road,
London, NW1 7AY

**The School of Scottish Studies**
University of Edinburgh,
27-29 George Square,
Edinburgh, EH8 9LD

**The Museum of Welsh Life**
St. Fagans, Cardiff, CF5 6XB

**The Ulster Folk and Transport Museum**
Cultra, near Bangor,
County Down, Northern Ireland

**The Department of Folklore**
University College Dublin

**Centre for English Cultural Tradition and Language (CECTAL)**

*Note:* Don't forget to start at your local public library. Ask children's librarians, especially, who often have an expertise in storytelling.
Also be sure to check research libraries such as the British Library, the Library of Congress, The National Sound Archives, your local university library and so on.

## *Publications*

**Traditional Storytelling Today**
**Facts and Fiction**
**The Storytelling Diary**

## *Festivals*

- Festival at the Edge
- St. Donat's Storytelling Festival
- The North Pennines Storytelling Festival

- The Milton Keynes Storytelling Festival
- The Ogresses Storytelling Festival
- The Scottish International Storytelling Festival
- The Skye Storytelling Festival
- The Seacat Storytelling Festival at Cultra, the Ulster Folk and Transport Museum
- The Seacat Irish American Storytelling Festival, at the Ulster American Folk Park, Omagh
- To Shorten the Road, the Derry International Storytelling Festival
- So What's the Story, the Dublin International Storytelling Festival
- The Cape Clear Storytelling Festival
- The Kiltimagh Storytelling Festival
- The Kerry Storytelling Festival
- The West Cork Storytelling Festival
- The Wexford Storytelling Festival

### Folk Festivals and Arts Festivals often featuring storytelling

- The National Folk Festival
- The Word: The London Festival of Literature
- Chippenham Folk Festival
- Cleethorpes Folk Festival
- Isle of Arran Festival
- Galway Arts Festival
- Warwick Folk Festival
- Sidmouth International Festival
- Dartmoor Festival
- Auchtermuchty Festival
- The Edinburgh Festival
- Whitby Folk Week
- Towersey Village Festival
- Cornwall Folk Festival
- Bromyard Folk Festival
- The Cheltenham Literature Festival
- The Hay on Wye Literature Festival
- The Ilkley Literature Festival

### Clubs

New clubs are always appearing, and some clubs fade away or change names and venues. The Society for Storytelling, the Storytelling Diary and the Scottish Storytelling Centre have current information about clubs and festivals.

**Patrick Ryan**
*Storyteller*

## Storytellers and Poets

### Anne Lister
**Mail address** 34 Nightingale House, Thomas More Street, LONDON, E1 9UA
**Phone** 020 7481 3619
**Email** anne.lister@virgin.net
**Web** http://freespace.virgin.net/anne.lister
*Singer-songwriter, storyteller, workshop leader.*
**RAB** London Arts

### Bernard Wrigley
**Mail address** 'Brewin', 1a Ansdell Rd, Horwich, BOLTON, Lancs, BL6 7HJ
**Phone** 01204 697716
**Email** loofyman@aol.com
**Web** www.bernardwrigley.com
*Storyteller, singer and instrumentalist. Solo or sea song, fiddle and concertina duo with Wilf Darlington.*
**RAB** North West Arts

### Chris Cole – Creator of Memories
**Mail address** 29 Ashcombe Drive, BEXHILL, East Sussex, TN 39 3UL
**Phone** 01424 845605 evenings
**Email** colesy@zoom.co.uk
*Teller of English and American stories. Plus folk music.*
**RAB** South East Arts

### Christine Michael (The Singing Poet)
**Mail address** 54 Kingswood Road, West Bridgford, NOTTINGHAM NG2 7HS
**Phone** 0115 9819397
07973 296444
**Email** christinemichael@yahoo.com
**Web** homepages.ntlworld.com/christine.michael
**Alt address** PO Box 30, South PDO, NOTTINGHAM NG2 7JP
**Email** expansionspress@yahoo.co.uk
*Singer & 12 string guitarist, trad. & contemporary. Storyteller (adults and children), poetry readings.*
**RAB** East Midlands Arts

### Des Charnley
**Mail address** 2 Lake View Villas, BOWNESS ON WINDERMERE, Cumbria, LA23 3BP
**Phone** 01539 443252
*Storyteller, uses puppets and props. Arts centres, schools, museums, etc.*
**RAB** Northern Arts

### Dorothy Dearnley
**Mail address** Eleven North Drive, Heswall, WIRRAL, Merseyside CH60 0BB
**Phone** 0151 342 4490
*Singer/ storyteller of Lancashire and Cheshire material.*
***Musicians' Union member***
**RAB** North West Arts

### Esyllt Harker
**Mail address** 7/1 Stryd Y Ffynon, Gerlan, BETHESDA, Gwynedd, LL57 3TN
**Phone** 01248 602033
*Teller of Welsh and other stories, singer & actor. Workshops in voice & movement, led in English or Welsh.*
**AC** Wales

### Fiona Collins
**Mail address** 161 Lyham Road, LONDON, SW2 5PY
**Phone/Fax** 020 8674 4713
**Phone** 07941 918159
*Storyteller, traditional tales from around the world, suitable for adults, children and family audiences.*
**RAB** London Arts

### Freddy Macha
**Mail address** Flat B, 12 Durley Road, LONDON, N16 5JS
**Phone** 07961 833040
020 7502 9814
**Fax** 020 7281 6677
**Email** fmacha@yahoo.com
*Performance poet & musician; multiple music/ poetry styles based on African & Brazilian roots. Regular promoter of world music events at Bar Lorca & various other clubs in London.*
***Musicians' Union member***
**RAB** London Arts

## Graham Langley
**Mail address** 3 Mount Pleasant, Cromford, MATLOCK, Derbys, DE4 3QF
**Phone** 01629 826939
07020 910774
**Fax** 0870 055 4683
**Email** graham@stories.demon.co.uk
**Web** www.stories.demon.co.uk
*Storyteller. Workshops and special projects for all ages/ abilities.*
**RAB** East Midlands Arts

## Hand and Word Storytellers
**Contact** David Brown
**Mail address** 26 Hill Clough Grove, Laycock, NR KEIGHLEY, West Yorks, BD22 0PT
**Phone** 01535 680712
*Storyteller, accompaniment on celtic harp and African drum available.*
**RAB** Yorkshire Arts

## Heather Sharpe
**Mail address** 19 Broomfield Crescent, LEEDS, LS6 3DD
**Phone** 0113 2741015
**Email** heather@sharpemurply.freeserve.co.uk
*Storyteller, adults and children.*
**RAB** Yorkshire Arts

## Helen East and Rick Wilson
**Contact** Rick Wilson
**Mail address** 29 Gleneldon Road, Streatham, LONDON, SW16 2AX
**Phone/Fax** 020 8677 0352
**Email** suitablelanguage@hotmail.com
*Traditional storytelling and music. Worldwide repertoire, adults and children. Storytelling and drumming workshops.*
***Musicians' Union member***
**RAB** London Arts

## Jan Williams
**Mail address** 83 High Street, BRIGHTLINGSEA, Essex, CO7 0EG
**Phone** 01206 305630
**Fax** 01206 304242
*Welsh storyteller, adults and children.*
**RAB** South East Arts

## Jeanette Hodgson
**Contact** Artists Connect
**Web** www.artistsconnect.com
*Storyteller, children and adults.*

## June Peters
**Mail address** 30 Dahomey Road, LONDON, SW16 6ND
**Phone** 020 8677 3803
07961 173157
**Email** june.pet@virgin.net
*Storyteller, singer, fiddler, harpist, mbira player. Multicultural traditional material, focusing on Celtic.*
**RAB** London Arts

## Les Barker
**Contact** Emerging Music
**Web** www.mrsackroyd com
*Writer and performer of strange poems.*
**Agent** Emerging Music
**RAB** North West Arts

## Patrick Ryan
**Mail address** 72A Huxley Road, LONDON, E10 5QU
**Phone/Fax** 020 8558 0915
**Email** patryan@telltale.dircon.co.uk
*Highly regarded storyteller and workshop leader. Organiser of storytelling events.*
**RAB** London Arts

## Raymond Greenoaken
**Mail address** 11 Ratcliffe Road, SHEFFIELD, S11 8YA
**Phone** 0114 2661158
**Email** greenr@taproot.demon.co.uk
*Storyteller with musical accompaniment.*
**RAB** Yorkshire Arts

## Sally Pomme Clayton - The Company of Storytellers
**Contact** Sally Pomme Clayton
**Mail address** 7 Westcott Road, Kennington, LONDON, SE17 3QY
**Phone** 020 7582 3832
*Writer and traditional storyteller for adults and children.*
**RAB** London Arts

## Steve Manning Storytelling
**Mail address** 3 Roseland Crescent, Heavitree, EXETER, EX1 2TH
**Phone** 01392 272496
07932 002274
**Email** smanning@lineone.net
*Storyteller. Works with the National Trust, Devon Library services and runs training sessions for heritage organisations.*
**RAB** South West Arts

## Tashbain
**Contact** Lindsay Aitkenhead
**Mail address** 19 Yeomans Road, SHEFFIELD, S6 3JD
**Phone** 0114 281 7614
**Email** lindsay.aitkenhead@newscientist.net
**Web** www.tashbain.f9.co.uk
*Jewish storytelling band.*
**Agent** Elizabeth Jones Entertainments
**RAB** Yorkshire Arts

## Tony Morris
**Mail address** Heworth Moor House, 56 Heworth Green, YORK YO31 7TQ
**Phone/Fax** 01904 413381
**Email** morrishmh@themail.co.uk
*Poet, performer and improvising musician. Accompanies spoken word on a range on instruments. Funeral and memorial poetry.*
**RAB** Yorkshire Arts

## Tony Wilson
**Mail address** 27 Julian Street, SOUTH SHIELDS, Tyne & Wear NE33 2EP
**Phone** 0191 4561803
0777 9945411
**Email** joat.ink@btinternet.com
**Web** http://freespace.virgin.net/joat.ink/tonywilson/
*Traditional singer and storyteller with guitar/banjo. Storytelling workshops.*
**Agent** Elizabeth Jones Entertainments
**RAB** Northern Arts

# festivals

## uk festivals

### june 2001

***The festivals listed here appear alphabetically within date order beginning at 1st June 2001 through to 30th June 2002. Some 2002 dates are yet to be confirmed.***

**1 to 2 June 2001**
### Off The Tracks Spring Festival
**Location** Castle Donington
**Contact** Off The Tracks
**Mail address** PO Box 68, DERBY, DE1 3XY
**Phone** 01332 384518
01332 833673
**Email** andy@offthetracks.co.uk
**Web** www.offthetracks.co.uk
*Green Field site folk & roots festival.*
**RAB** East Midlands Arts

**1 to 3 June 2001**
### Stanchester Old Timers (Music & Dance Group)
**Location** Somerset
**Contact** Nick Pilley
**Mail address** 53 North Street, BRIDGWATER, Somerset, TA6 3PW
**Phone** 01278 450780
**Email** oldtimesouthwest@hotmail.com
**Alt contact** Fred Budden
**Address** Stanchester Community School, NR YEOVIL, Somerset
**Phone** 01460 240422
*Informal weekend promoting Old Time American music and dance.*
**RAB** South West Arts

**2 June to 20 August 2001**
### Sounds In The Round
**Location** Birmingham
**Contact** Dorothy Wilson
**Mail address** mac, Cannon Hill Park, BIRMINGHAM, B12 9QH
**Phone** 0121 4404221
**Fax** 0121 4464372
**Email** enquiries@mac birmingham.org.uk
*Outdoor music festival - open air Arena Theatre. Early June to Mid August. Broad range of acts.*
**RAB** West Midlands Arts

**3 June 2001**
**2 June 2002**
### Watling Festival
**Location** London
**Contact** Pattie Skeats
**Mail address** 13 Storksmead Road, EDGWARE, Middx, HA8 0JW
**Phone/Fax** 020 8959 8595
**Email** festival@waitrose.com
**Web** www.watlingfestival.co.uk
*Local festival with a variety of displays and music.*
**RAB** London Arts

**3 to 10 June 2001**
### The Tommy Makem International School of Song
**Location** Co. Armagh
**Contact** Peter Makem
**Mail address** 67 Armagh Road, NEWRY, Co Down, BT35 6PW, Northern Ireland
**Phone** 028 302 67517
**Email** peter@pmakem.freeserve.co.uk
**AC** Northern Ireland

**7 to 10 June 2001**
### Arran Folk Festival
**Location** Scotland
**Contact** Iain Frame
**Mail address** 29 Alma Park, BRODICK, Isle of Arran, KA27 8AT
**Phone** 01770 302623
**Fax** 01770 600719
**Email** info@arranfolkfestival.org
**Web** www.arranfolkfestival.com
*Concerts, workshops, school events.*
**AC** Scotland

**8 to 10 June 2001**
### Clitheroe Great Days Festival
**Location** Lancs.
**Contact** Barry Phillips
**Mail address** PO Box 33, CLITHEROE, Lancs, BB7 1GP
**Phone** 01200 425316
**Email** festival@great-days.co.uk
**Web** www.great-days.co.uk
**Alt contact** Steve Ragnall
**Email** email@greatdays.freeserve.co.uk
*Weekend of music, dance and street theatre in the Ribble Valley.*
**RAB** North West Arts

**8 to 10 June 2001**
### Gower Folk Festival
**Location** South Wales
**Contact** Joy Toole
**Mail address** Blue Anchor Cottage, Blue Anchor, Penclawdd, SWANSEA, SA4 3JQ, Wales
**Phone** 01792 850803
**Email** joy.toole@gowerfolkfestival.co.uk
**Web** www.gowerfolkfestival.co.uk
**AC** Wales

**8 to 10 June 2001**
### Keith Festival
**Location** Scotland
**Contact** Edith Lewis
**Mail address** 10 South Court, Darliston, ELGIN, Moray, Scotland
**Phone** 01343 540325
**Email** lewishugh@talk21.com
**Email** keithfestival@btinternet.com
*Formal and informal music, song and competitions.*
**AC** Scotland

**8 to 10 June 2001**
### Kirtlington Lamb Ale Morris Festival
**Location** Oxon
**Contact** Steve Hanley
**Mail address** PO Box 1281, East Oxford DO, OXFORD, OX4 3GJ
**Phone/Fax** 01865 396963
**Phone** 07780 993396
**Email** steve_hanley@lineone.net
**Web** www.kirtlington-morris.org.uk
*Morris festival with dancing around the village, barn dance on Saturday evening and craft fair on Sunday.*
**RAB** Southern Arts

**8 to 10 June 2001**
### Mersey International Shanty Festival
**Location** Liverpool
**Contact** Jack Coutts
**Mail address** 7 Thomas Lane, LIVERPOOL, L14 5NR
**Phone** 0151 2200152
**Email** merseyshantyfestival@zyworld.com
**Web** www.merseyshantyfestival.fsnet.co.uk
**Alt contact** Liverpool Direct
**Phone** 0151 233 3000
*Concerts, sessions & workshops.*
**RAB** North West Arts

**8 to 10 June 2001**
### Robin Hoods Bay Folk Weekend
**Location** N. Yorks
**Contact** Jim Foster
**Mail address** Coralline, Silver Street, ROBIN HOOD'S BAY, N Yorks YO22 4SB
**Phone** 01947 880660
01947 880390
**Email** folk@bayfair.co.uk
**Web** www.bayfair.co.uk
*Free weekend of Music sessions & singarounds around the town. Plus folk club, afternoon concert & dance event.*
**RAB** Yorkshire Arts

8 to 10 June 2001
## Stamford Folk & Blues Guitar Festival
**Location** Lincs
**Contact** David Popple
**Mail address** Stamford Arts Centre, 27 St Mary's Street, STAMFORD, Lincs, PE9 2DL
**Phone** 01780 763203
**Fax** 01780 766690
**Email** boxoffice@stamfordartscentre.com
**RAB** East England Arts

8 to 10 June 2001
7 to 9 June 2002
## Thoresby Fest Noz
**Location** Ollerton, Notts
**Contact** Dave Groom
**Mail address** Wellgroomed Management, 80 Hood Street, NOTTINGHAM, NG5 4AQ
**Phone/Fax** 0115 952 2638
**Email** tfestnoz@hotmail.com
**Web** www.thoresbyfestnoz.com
*Based on the traditional Breton Fez Noz, a weekend festival of European (mainly Breton) music and dancing. Grounds of country estate.*
**RAB** East Midlands Arts

8 to 10 June 2001
## Wimborne Folk Festival
**Contact** Linda Wild
**Location** Dorset
**Mail address** 32a Seaview Road, Upton, POOLE, Dorset, BH16 5NG
**Phone** 01202 623740
**Email** lwildwimborne@zoom.co.uk
**Web** www.wimbornefolkfestival.co.uk
**Alt contact** Brian Bisp
**Address** 32 Shillito Road, Parkstone, POOLE, Dorset
**Phone** 01202 743465
**Email** brian.bisp@wimbornefolkfestival.co.uk
*Weekend of Morris Dancing, concerts, ceilidhs,etc.*
**RAB** South West Arts

9 to 24 June 2001
## North Devon Festival
**Contact** Festival Hotline
**Phone** 01271 324242
**RAB** South West Arts

14 to 24 June 2001
20 to 30 June 2002
## Golowan Festival
**Location** Penzance, Cornwall
**Contact** Stephen Hall - Director
**Mail address** The Barbican, Battery Road, PENZANCE, Cornwall, TR18 4EF
**Phone** 01736 332211
01736 331933
**Fax** 01736 333332
**Email** admin@golowan.com
**Web** www.golowan.com
**Alt contact** Stephanie Hayward - Administration
**Email** steph@golowan.com
*Community festival with strong traditional roots. World music, street theatre, serpent dance, giant imagery, Mazey Day.*
**RAB** South West Arts

15 to 17 June 2001
21 to 23 June 2002
## Beverley and East Riding Folk Festival
**Location** E. Yorks
**Contact** Chris Wade - Artistic Director
**Mail address** 2 Star Row, North Dalton, DRIFFIELD, E Yorks, YO25 9UR
**Phone** 01377 217662
01377 217569
**Fax** 01377 217754
**Email** chris@adastey.demon.co.uk
**Web** www.adastey.demon.co.uk
**Alt contact** Julia Allsopp - General Enquiries
**Email** julia@adastey.demon.co.uk
*Weekend of music, dance, street shows, workshops etc. Range of major artists.*
**RAB** Yorkshire Arts

15 to 17 June 2001
## Caversham Folk Festival
**Location** Reading
**Contact** Mike Tierney
**Mail address** 81 Hadrian Walk East, READING, Berks, RG2 7TZ
**Phone** 0118 9751016
**Email** chris.smyth@ntlworld.com
**Alt contact** Chris Smyth
**Address** 44 Starlings Drive, Tilehurst, READING, Berks, RG31 4SU
**Phone** 0118 9615436
*Weekend folk music festival with blues and bluegrass fringe events. Free entry, charity collections taken.*
**RAB** South East Arts

15 to 17 June 2001
21 to 23 June 2002
## Lichfield Folk Festival
**Location** Staffs
**Contact** Penny McLennan - Dance
**Mail address** 123 Greenheath Road, HEDNESFORD, Staffs, WS12 4AU
**Phone** 01543 424292
**Alt contact** Sandra Robinson - Song
**Address** Tudor Rose Cottage, 55 Coleshill Road, SUTTON COLDFIELD, B72 1SH
**Phone** 0121 3544234
*Weekend of traditional dance and music workshops, Playford & American dances plus concert.*
**RAB** West Midlands Arts

15 to 17 June 2001 (Cancelled)
14 to 16 June 2002
## Middlewich Folk & Boat Festival
**Location** Cheshire
**Contact** Dave Thompson
**Mail address** 33 Manor Crescent, MIDDLEWICH, Cheshire, CW10 0EW
**Phone** 01606 836896 - after 6pm
**Email** peter@peterjohncox.freeserve.co.uk
**Web** www.middlewichfolkandboatfestival.com
*Music & dance, poetry, sessions/ singarounds. 15 venues, 2 main stages (world/ roots/dance concerts). Plus children's festival.*
**RAB** North West Arts

15 to 23 June 2001
## Sandwell Arts Festival
**Location** Shropshire
**Contact** Mal Salisbury
**Mail address** 9 St Lukes Road, Doseley, TELFORD, TF4 3BE
**Phone** 01952 505565
07710 409004
**Fax** 01952 507297
**Email** info@ironbridgefest.enta.net
*9 days of combined arts activities; music, theatre, dance, street festival.*
**RAB** West Midlands Arts

16 June 2001
## Folkworks Absolute Beginners' Workout
**Location** Tyne & Wear
**Contact** Pam Hobson
**Mail address** Folkworks, 69 Westgate Road, NEWCASTLE UPON TYNE NE1 1SG
**Phone** 0191 222 1717
**Fax** 0191 230 2484
**Email** folkworks@folkworks.co.uk
**Web** www.folkworks.co.uk
*Day of learning folk instruments, singing & dancing for absolute beginners.*
**RAB** Northern Arts



***The festivals listed here appear alphabetically within date order beginning at 1st June 2001 through to 30th June 2002. Some 2002 dates are yet to be confirmed.***

## uk festivals

### june 2001

*The festivals listed here appear alphabetically within date order beginning at 1st June 2001 through to 30th June 2002. Some 2002 dates are yet to be confirmed.*

**16 to 17 June 2001**
### Leamington Peace Festival
**Location** Warwicks
**Contact** Steff Hutchinson
**Mail address** PO Box 213, LEAMINGTON SPA, Warks, CV31 1ZP
**Phone** 01926 421830
**Email** mainstage@peacefestival.org.uk
**Web** www.peacefestival.org.uk
**Alt contact** Lucinda Tower
**Alt address** 2 Chapel Court, Murcott Road East, Whitnash, LEAMINGTON SPA, Warks CV31 2HZ
**Phone** 01926 330385
**Email** workshops@peacefestival.org.uk
*Free festival, 2 entertainment areas. Workshops, arts, kids' events, over 100 stalls. No camping.*
**RAB** West Midlands Arts

**21 to 23 June 2001**
### Mid Summer Song
**Location** Co. Durham
**Contact** Fred Brierley
**Mail address** The Wayfarer, HASWELL, Co Durham
**Phone** 0191 517 1274
*Weekend of song. Themed sessions plus evening singarounds.*
**RAB** Northern Arts

**22 to 24 June 2001**
### Alcester & Arden Folk Festival
**Location** Nr. Stratford on Avon
**Contact** Marje Stanley
**Mail address** 144 Easemore Road, Riverside, REDDITCH, Worcs, B98 8HH
**Phone** 01527 69390
**Email** marje.stanley@lineone.net
**Web** www.alcesterfolkfestival.co.uk
**Alt contact** Dave James
**Email** dave.alcester@ukonline.co.uk
*Concerts, singarounds, sessions, street dancing, beer festival, young musicians' contest. Campsite with Moor & Coast catering.*
**RAB** West Midlands Arts

**22 to 24 June 2001**
### English Country Music Weekend
**Location** Stowmarket, Suffolk
**Contact** Katie Howson
**Mail address** 44 Old Street, Haughley, STOWMARKET, Suffolk, IP14 3NX
**Phone** 01449 673695
**Email** emw@veteran.co.uk
**Web** www.mustrad.org.uk
*An informal weekend based on English dance music. Based in a different region each year.*
**RAB** East England Arts

**22 to 24 June 2001**
### Gwyl Ifan
**Location** Cardiff
**Contact** Dai James
**Mail address** 50 Prospect Drive, Llandaf, CAERDYDD, CF5 2HN, Wales
**Phone** 029 2056 3989
**Email** gwyl.ifan@ntlworld.com
**Web** www.gwylifano@uk
**AC** Wales

**22 to 24 June 2001**
**21 to 23 June 2002**
### Highland Traditional Music Festival
**Location** Ross-shire, Scotland
**Contact** Rob Gibson
**Mail address** Tir nan Oran, 8 Culcairn Road, EVANTON, Ross-shire, IV16 9YT, Scotland
**Phone** 01349 830388
**Fax** 01349 830599
**Email** robgibson@sol.co.uk
**Web** www.htmf.co.uk
*Ceilidhs, concerts, singarounds, workshops, street music and sessions.*
**AC** Scotland

**22 to 24 June 2001**
**28 to 30 June 2002**
### Leigh Folk Festival
**Location** Essex
**Contact** Sean Wyer
**Mail address** 235 Westborough Road, WESTCLIFF ON SEA, Essex, SS0 9PS
**Phone** 01702 390454
**Email** folk@priority1.demon.co.uk
**Web** www.folkfestival.org.uk
**Alt contact** Tony Prior
**Alt address** 60 The Ridgeway, WESTCLIFF ON SEA, Essex, SS0 8NU
**Phone** 01702 715111
**Fax** 01702 713984
*Free folk festival in seaside town, with over 600 performers.*
**RAB** East England Arts

**22 to 24 June 2001**
### National Forest Folk Festival
**Location** Moira, Leics
**Contact** Nina Szifris
**Mail address** 50 Brendan Close, Coleshill, BIRMINGHAM, B46 3EF
**Phone** 01675 465002
07881 558158
**Email** festival@affc.demon.co.uk
**Web** www.affc.demon.co.uk
*3 day festival with large concerts, singarounds, workshops and crafts.*
**RAB** East Midlands Arts

**22 to 24 June 2001**
**21 to 23 June 2002**
### Teignmouth Mid-Summer Folk Festival
**Location** South Devon
**Contact** Anne Gill
**Mail address** Maleth, 11 Cleveland Road, TORQUAY, Devon, TQ2 5BD
**Phone** 01803 290427
**Email** annemgill@dial.pipex.co.uk
**Web** www.flaxey-green.co.uk
**Alt contact** Martin Gosling
**Phone** 01626 335258
**Email** marting@goslingm.freeserve.co.uk
*Concerts, ceilidh, dance display & sessions.*
**RAB** South West Arts

**23 June to 1 July 2001**
**29 June to 7 July 2002**
### Beaminster Festival
**Location** Dorset
**Contact** Ronald Emett
**Mail address** 2 The Square, BEAMINSTER, Dorset, DT8 3AS
**Phone** 01308 862219
**Fax** 01308 863000
**Email** beamfest.ukonline.co.uk
*Festival of art and music, mostly classical, with some folk based events, including a folk fiddle day in 2001.*
**RAB** South West Arts

**27 June to 7 July 2001**
### Bradford Festival
**Location** W. Yorks
**Contact** Mark Fielding
**Mail address** The Wool Exchange, Hustlergate, BRADFORD, W Yorks BD1 1RE
**Phone** 01274 309199
**Fax** 01274 724213
**Email** info@bradfordfestival.yorks.com
**Web** www.bradfordfestival.yorks.com
*Large cross arts festival, featuring some folk & roots acts.*
**RAB** Yorkshire Arts

**28 June to 1 July 2001**
**27 to 30 June 2002**
## Blues On The Farm
**Location** Chichester, W. Sussex
**Contact** Julian Moores
**Mail address** Pump Bottom Farm, Birdham Road, Appledram, CHICHESTER, W Sussex, PO20 7EH
**Phone** 01243 773828
01243 539072
**Fax** 01243 773828
**Email** bluespumpbottomfarm@argonet.co.uk
**Web** www.pumpbottomfarm.co.uk/blues/index/htm
*Blues festival on secure site near Chichester. Friendly, party atmosphere with accent on the blues UK and USA plus world music and alternative attractions.*
**RAB** South East Arts

**29 to 30 June 2001**
## Nailers Folk Moot
**Location** Belper, Derbys
**Contact** Marianne Elliot
**Mail address** 101 Holbrook Road, BELPER, Derbys, DE56 8PB
**Email** mariel@iowbay.demon.co.uk
**Alt contact** Geoff Deighton
**Alt address** 15 Ashover Road, Old Tupton, CHESTERFIELD, Derbys, S42 6HH
*Weekend with concerts, ceilidh,folk club and workshops.*
**RAB** East Midlands Arts

**29 June to 1 July 2001**
## A1 Festival of Music & Dance
**Location** Peterborough
**Contact** Gill Barham
**Mail address** 58 Wood Road, Kings Cliffe, PETEBOROUGH, PE8 6XF
**Phone** 01780 470852
**Email** a1festival@aol.com
**Web** http://members.aol.com/a1festival/sacrewell.index.htm
**RAB** East Midlands Arts

**29 June to 1 July 2001**
## Christchurch Festival
**Location** Dorset
**Contact** Paul Cole
**Mail address** 87 Rodney Drive, Mudeford, CHRISTCHURCH, Dorset
**Phone** 01202 480209
**RAB** South West Arts

**29 June to 1 July 2001**
**28 to 30 June 2002**
## Crawley Folk Festival
**Location** W. Sussex
**Contact** Liz Hart
**Mail address** The Hawth, Hawth Avenue, CRAWLEY, W Sussex RH10 6YZ
**Phone** 01293 552941
**Fax** 01293 533362
**Email** liz.hart@crawley.gov.uk
**Web** www.hawth.co.uk/folk
*Weekend of folk, traditional, acoustic and roots music from Britain, Ireland and North America. 5 stages, stalls, CAMRA tent, workshops, etc.*
**RAB** South East Arts

**29 June to 1 July 2001**
**28 to 30 June 2002**
## Four Fools Folk Festival
**Location** Chorley, Lancs
**Contact** Angie & Ken Bladen
**Mail address** 36 The Oaks, Eaves Green, CHORLEY, Lancs, PR7 3QU
**Phone** 01257 263678
**Email** four.fools@virgin.net
**Web** www.four-fools.co.uk
*Small & friendly singers festival. All under one roof with the campsite at the back door!*
**RAB** North West Arts

**29 June to 1 July 2001**
**5 to 7 July 2002**
## Newcastleton Traditional Music Festival
**Location** Scottish Borders
**Contact** Malcolm McEwen
**Mail address** Shankend Station, HAWICK, Scottish Borders, TD9 9UA, Scotland
**Phone/Fax** 01450 377165
**Email** shankmac@aol.com
**Web** www.newcastleton.com
*Traditionally based on competitions, ceilidhs, concerts, sessions and workshops.*
**AC** Scotland

**29 June to 1 July 2001**
## The Vale Folk & Real Ale Festival
**Location** Evesham, Worcs
**Contact** Rob Hopkins
**Mail address** The Vauxhall Inn, Abbey Road, EVESHAM, Worcs, WR11 4BL
**Phone** 01386 446333
**RAB** West Midlands Arts

**29 June to 8 July 2001**
## Ashbourne Arts Festival
**Location** Derbys
**Mail address** PO Box 5552, ASHBOURNE, Derbys, DE6 2ZR
**Phone** 01335 348707
**RAB** East Midlands Arts

**30 June to 1 July 2001**
## The Moreton Midsummer Festival
**Location** Essex
**Contact** Jayne De Larre
**Phone** 01277 890519
**Web** www.blackbullclog.freeserve.co.uk
*Festival of traditional dance & music. Dancing around the village and pub sessions.*
**RAB** East England Arts

**30 June to 15 July 2001**
**6 to 21 July 2002**
## Cheltenham Festival Fringe
**Location** Glos
**Contact** Tim Hulse
**Mail address** Cheltenham Town Hall, Imperial Square, CHELTENHAM, Glos, GL50 1QA
**Phone** 01242 521621
**Fax** 01242 573902
**Email** timhu@cheltenham.gov.uk
**Web** www.cheltenhamfestivals.co.uk
**Alt contact** Sue Bird
**Email** suebi@cheltenham.gov.uk
*A summer festival with a diverse programme of concerts and gigs, theatre and comedy, street entertainment and family fun.*
**RAB** South West Arts

**1 to 4 July 2001**
## JMI KlezFest
**Location** London
**Mail address** Jewish Music Institute SOAS, University of London, Thornhaugh St, Russell Square, LONDON, WC1H 0XG
**Phone** 020 8909 2445 - tickets
**Fax** 020 8909 1030
**Email** jewishmusic@jmi.org.uk
**Web** www.jmi.org.uk
*4 day course of masterclasses, workshops & performances. Literature, culture, history & folklore.*
**RAB** London Arts

**1 to 7 July 2001**
**30 June to 6 July 2002**
## Tinto Summer School
**Location** Biggar, Scotland
**Contact** Clare McLaughlin- Trad Music Officer
**Mail address** South Lanarkshire Council, East Kilbride Arts Centre, EAST KILBRIDE, South Lanarkshire, G74 4DU, Scotland
**Phone** 01355 261000
**Fax** 01355 261280
*Traditional music residential summer school for secondary school pupils.*
**AC** Scotland



***The festivals listed here appear alphabetically within date order beginning at 1st June 2001 through to 30th June 2002. Some 2002 dates are yet to be confirmed.***

*The festivals listed here appear alphabetically within date order beginning at 1st June 2001 through to 30th June 2002. Some 2002 dates are yet to be confirmed.*

**1 to 31 July 2001**
**1 to 31 July 2002**

## Swale Festival

**Location** Kent
**Contact** Mrs Jan West - Arts & Facilities
**Mail address** Council Offices, Trinity Road, SHEERNESS, Kent, ME12 2PG
**Phone** 01795 585601
01795 585600
**Fax** 01795 669097
**Email** janwest@swale.gov.uk
**Alt contact** Christine Heathfield - Events
**Phone** 01795 585609
**Email** christineheathfield@swale.gov.uk

*Annual festival during July featuring music, theatre, art exhibitions, craft fayres and entertainment for everyone.*

**RAB** South East Arts

**4 July 2001**
**3 July 2002**

## St Michael's Street Folk Evening

**Location** St. Albans, Herts
**Contact** Trevor Adams
**Mail address** 76 Hillcrest, HATFIELD, Herts
**Phone** 01707 883476
**Email** ptadams@ntlworld.com
**Web** www.stalbans.gov.uk\events

*1st Wednesday in July, 8pm. Dancing in St Michael's Street plus music and song in its 4 pubs.*

**RAB** East England Arts

**4 to 6 July 2001**

## Larmer Tree Music Festival

**Location** Salisbury, Wilts
**Contact** Julia Safe
**Mail address** PO Box 1790, SALISBURY, Wilts, SP1 3WR
**Phone** 01722 415223
**Fax** 01722 413670
**Email** info@larmertree.demon.co.uk
**Web** www.larmertree.demon.co.uk

*World and folk roots music, 4 stages in 11 acres of Victorian gardens.*

**RAB** South East Arts

**6 to 7 July 2001**

## East Barnet Community Festival

**Location** Herts
**Contact** Michael Young - Press & PR
**Mail address** The Homecare Centre, 14 Church Hill Road, EAST BARNET, Herts, EN4 8TB
**Phone** 07071 781745
020 8449 8263
**Fax** 020 8840 8215
**Email** eastbarnetfestival@btinternet.com
**Web** www.eastbarnetfestival.org
**Alt contact** JJ Dunne - Music Programme
**Alt address** 128 Woodville Road, BARNET, Herts, EN5

*Annual community festival featuring music, sport, performance arts, family entertainment. Run by volunteers to support charities.*

**RAB** London Arts

**6 to 8 July 2001**

## Americana International

**Location** Newark, Notts
**Contact** Chris R Jackson
**Mail address** Jacksonville, 1 Middle Orchard St, STAPLEFORD, Notts, NG9 8DD
**Phone** 0115 939 0595
**Fax** 0115 949 0856
**Email** chris@americana-promotions.co.uk
**Web** www.americana-promotions.co.uk
**Email** silvereagleuk@aol.com

*Music festival and classic American auto, 40+ artists from the USA & UK performing Country, Cajun, Hillbilly, Rockabilly, Celtic, R&B. Camping available.*

**RAB** East Midlands Arts

**6 to 8 July 2001**
**5 to 7 July 2002**

## Beyond The Border Storytelling Festival

**Location** Glamorgan, Wales
**Contact** David Pepworth
**Mail address** St Donats Arts Centre, ST DONATS CASTLE, Vale of Glamorgan, CF61 1WF, Wales
**Phone** 01446 799096
01446 799104
**Fax** 01446 799101
**Email** marketing@stdonats.com
**Web** www.beyondtheborder.com

*Performers from around the world. Also features folk and world music programme.*

**AC** Wales

**6 to 8 July 2001**
**5 to 7 July 2002**

## Cleckheaton Folk Festival

**Location** Yorkshire
**Contact** Geoff Pickles
**Mail address** 7 Listerdale, Littletown, LIVERSEDGE, W Yorks, WF15 8ED
**Phone** 01924 404346
**Email** cleckheaton.folk@virgin.net
**Web** www.cleckheatonfolkfestival.co.uk

*Weekend festival of contemporary folk song, music & dance. Includes concerts, ceilidhs, singarounds, sessions, workshops, children's events, street theatre, etc.*

**RAB** Yorkshire Arts

**6 to 8 July 2001**

## Folk On The Farm Free Festival

**Location** Wolverhampton
**Contact** Matt Swindlehurst
**Mail address** 106 Oxley Moor Road, WOLVERHAMPTON, W Midlands, WV10 6TX
**Phone** 01902 785002
**Email** matt@lmsmusic.co.uk
**Web** www.lmsmusic.co.uk

*Free festival, literally on a farm!*

**RAB** West Midlands Arts

**6 to 8 July 2001**

## Priddy Folk Fayre

**Location** Wells, Somerset
**Contact** Peter Arnold
**Mail address** New House, The Green, PRIDDY, Somerset, BA5 3BB
**Phone** 01749 675562
**Fax** 01749 670771
**Email** hilaryra@aol.com
**Web** www.priddy.inuk.com

*Concerts, ceilidhs, dance festival, craft fayre, children's festival, all day folk club, workshops.*

**RAB** South West Arts

**6 to 8 July 2001**

## Traditional Singing Weekend at Cullerlie

**Location** Aberdeenshire
**Contact** Tom & Anne Reid
**Mail address** Cullerlie Farm Park, Echt, SKENE, Aberdeenshire, AB32 6XL, Scotland
**Phone** 01330 860549
**Email** elphinstone@abdn.ac.uk
**Web** www.abdn.ac.uk/elphinstone/
**Alt contact** Ian Russell
**Address** Elphinstone Institute, University of Aberdeen, 24 High St, ABERDEEN, Scotland
**Phone** 01224 272386
**Email** ian.russell@abdn.ac.uk

*Celebration of the singing traditions of North East Scotland, Orkney, England and Ireland, in rural Aberdeenshire setting.*

**AC** Scotland

**6 to 15 July 2001**
**5 to 14 July 2002**
## Birmingham International Jazz Festival
**Contact** Big Bear Music Agency
**Mail address** PO Box 944, Edgbaston, BIRMINGHAM, B16 8UT
**Phone** 0121 4547020
**Fax** 0121 4549996
**Email** bigbearmusic@compuserve.com
**Web** www.bigbearmusic.com
*Annual 10 day festival of Jazz, Blues and associated music in 70 venues. 90% free admission. Big Bear Music is the sole booking agent for the festival.*
**RAB** West Midlands Arts

**6 to 15 July 2001**
## Greenwich & Dockland International Festival
**Location** London
**Contact** Mathew Russell
**Mail address** 6 College Approach, Greenwich, LONDON, SE10 9HY
**Phone** 020 8305 1818
**Fax** 020 8305 1188
**Email** mathew@festival.org
**Web** www.festival.org
**RAB** London Arts

**7 July 2001**
## Global Bandstand
**Location** Canterbury, Kent
**Contact** Tom Andrews
**Mail address** Music for Change, 27 Watling Street, CANTERBURY, Kent, CT1 2UD
**Phone** 01227 459243
**Fax** 01227 455662
**Email** music.forchange@virgin.net
**Web** www.musicforchange.org
*Free festival of music from around the world, based in the heart of Cantebury.*
**RAB** South East Arts

**7 July 2001**
## One World Festival, Leicester
**Contact** Richard Haswell
**Mail address** De Montfort Hall, Granville Road, LEICESTER, Leics
**Phone** 0116 233 3149
0116 233 3111 - box office
**Fax** 0116 233 3182
**Email** haswr001@leicester.gov.uk
**Web** www.demontforthall.co.uk
**Alt contact** Alvin Hargreaves
**Phone** 0116 233 3138
**Email** harga001@leicester.gov.uk
*World music event. Worldwide main acts performing on outdoor stage to 5000 capacity. Indoor stage with mainly local artists.*
**RAB** East Midlands Arts

**7 July 2001**
**6 July 2002**
## Rainham Beer & Folk Festival
**Location** Kent
**Contact** Maz & Dan Hobday
**Mail address** 39 Brown Street, RAINHAM, Kent, ME8 7JN
**Phone** 01634 372048
*1st Saturday in July, 12 noon-11pm. Real ale tent, barbecueand live music. Open singers list plus guest artists.*
**RAB** South East Arts

**7 to 8 July 2001**
**6 to 7 July 2002**
## Lobster Potties Morris & Folk Festival
**Location** Norfolk
**Contact** Matthew Warnes
**Mail address** 14 Weynor Gardens, WELLING, Norfolk, NR 25 7EQ
**Phone** 01263 588074
**Alt contact** Clive Raynent
**Address** 10 Heath Road, SHERINGHAM, Norfolk
**Phone** 01263 822302
*Festival of morris, folk dancing and performers, run by morris team.*
**RAB** East England Arts

**7 to 8 July 2001**
## Shaw & Crompton Rushbearing & Dance Festival
**Location** Oldham, Lancs
**Contact** Phelyp Bennett
**Mail address** Croft House, 128 Beal Lane, Crompton, OLDHAM, Lancs, OL2 8PH
**Phone** 07808 107865
01706 847630
**RAB** North West Arts

**7 to 8 July 2001**
**6 to 7 July 2002**
## Sunderland International Kite Festival
**Location** Tyne & Wear
**Contact** Folkworks
**Mail address** 69 Westgate Road, NEWCASTLE UPON TYNE, NE1 1SG
**Phone** 0191 222 1717
**Email** folkworks@folkworks.co.uk
**Web** www.folkworks.co.uk
**Alt contact** Sunderland Arts Development Unit
**Address** Central Library, 28-30 Fawcett Street, SUNDERLAND, SR1 1RE
**Phone** 0191 514 8406
**Fax** 0191 514 8444
*Internationally renowned festival of kite flying with 2 days of free folk and world music programmed by Folkworks. Contact Sunderland for any non-music related enquiries.*
**RAB** Northern Arts

**8 to 14 July 2001**
## Gwyl Werin Y Cnapan
**Location** Ceredigion, Wales
**Contact** Emyr Hywel
**Mail address** Cnwc Yr Onnen, Blaenporth, ABERTEIFI, Ceredigion, SA43 2BD, WALES
**Phone** 01239 810045
**Fax** 01239 811433
**Email** emhywel@netscapeonline.co.uk
**AC** Wales

**9 to 15 July 2001**
**8 to 14 July 2002**
## Black Horse
**Location** Nr. Wrotham, Kent
**Contact** Ian Duncan
**Phone** 01732 822355
*Pub with regular sessions and annual festival. 2nd Sunday, lunchtime onwards, Irish traditional session. 4th Thursday, 8pm, traditional folk session. Festival of traditional music and morris dancing.*
**RAB** South East Arts

**10 to 20 July 2001**
**9 to 19 July 2002**
## Feis An Eilein - The Skye Festival
**Contact** Duncan McInnes
**Mail address** Ostaig House, ISLE OF SKYE, IV44 8RQ
**Phone** 01471 844207
**Fax** 01471 844411
**Email** feis@cali.co.uk
**Web** www.feisaneilein.com or www.skyefestival.com
*11 day feast of music, song, dance, theatre & film from Gaelic traditions and beyond.*
**AC** Scotland

**11 to 14 July 2001**
## Hebridean Celtic Festival
**Location** Isle of Lewis
**Contact** Caroline MacLennan
**Mail address** PO Box 9909, STORNOWAY, Isle of Lewis, HS2 9DW, Scotland
**Phone** 07001 878787
**Fax** 01851 710325
**Email** caroline@hebceltfest.com
**Web** www.hebceltfest.com
*4 day summer festival with concerts, workshops, sessions, fringe events, etc.*
**AC** Scotland



***The festivals listed here appear alphabetically within date order beginning at 1st June 2001 through to 30th June 2002. Some 2002 dates are yet to be confirmed.***

# uk festivals

## july 2001

***The festivals listed here appear alphabetically within date order beginning at 1st June 2001 through to 30th June 2002. Some 2002 dates are yet to be confirmed.***

**13 to 14 July 2001**
### Kirkby Blues 'n Rock Festival
**Location** Notts
**Contact** Jackie Knowles
**Mail address** 29 Forest Street, KIRKBY IN ASHFIELD, Notts, NG17 7DT
**Phone** 01623 753336
**Fax** 01246 819571
**Email** knowlespromotions@currantbun.com
**RAB** East Midlands Arts

**13 to 14 July 2001**
**12 to 13 July 2002**
### Romsey Beggars Fair
**Location** Hants
**Contact** Tony Dawes
**Mail address** 8 Peel Close, ROMSEY, Hants, SO51 7UQ
**Phone** 01794 501484
**Email** tony@beggarsfair.org.uk
**Web** www.beggarsfair.org.uk
*Free music, dance and street entertaiment.*
**RAB** Southern Arts

**13 to 15 July 2001**
### Chalgrove Live Music Festival
**Location** Oxon
**Contact** Julian Hawes
**Mail address** 40 Cronshaw Close, DIDCOT, Oxon, OX11 7JU
**Phone** 01235 810865
**Email** julian-hawes@talk21.com
**RAB** Southern Arts

**13 to 15 July 2001**
### Feis Eige
**Location** Isle of Eige, Scotland
**Contact** Camille Dressler
**Mail address** C/o Secretary, ISLE OF EIGG, Inverness-shire, Scotland
**Phone** 01687 482410
**Fax** 01687 482486
**Email** camille.d@talk21.com
**AC** Scotland

**13 to 15 July 2001**
### Furness Tradition
**Location** Cumbria
**Contact** M Kermode
**Mail address** 60 Soutergate, ULVERSTON, Cumbria, LA12 7ES
**Phone** 01229 582704
**Fax** 01229 588290
**Email** kmode@onetel.net.uk
**Web** www.rootsworld.com/harbourtown
*Year round events focusing on Furness & South Lakeland traditions. Schools & educational workshops. Festival weekend in Ulverston.*
**RAB** Northern Arts

**13 to 15 July 2001**
**12 to 14 July 2002**
### International Dance & Music Festival, Belton House
**Location** Grantham, Lincs
**Contact** Iona Sadler
**Mail address** South Kesteven District Council, St Peters Hill, GRANTHAM, Lincs, NG31 6PZ
**Phone** 01476 406155
07712 199082
**Fax** 01476 406011
**Email** i.sadler@skdc.com
**Web** www.skdc.com
**Alt contact** Lisa Pexton
**Address** Belton House, NR GRANTHAM, Lincs
**Phone** 01476 406157
**Email** l.pexton@skdc.com
*Family friendly festival with concerts, dances and workshops, children's events, food, drink and crafts.*
**RAB** East Midlands Arts

**13 to 15 July 2001**
### Roots, Hoots & Boots @ Bradninch
**Location** Devon
**Contact** Dik Banovich
**Mail address** 32 Hele Road, BRADNINCH, Devon, EX5 4QX
**Phone** 01392 881304
**Email** dik-banovich@bigfoot.com
**RAB** South West Arts

**13 to 15 July 2001**
### Rothbury Traditional Music Festival
**Location** Morpeth, Northumberland
**Contact** Mary Bathgate
**Mail address** Garleigh House, Rothbury, MORPETH, Northumberland, NE65 7RB
**Phone** 01669 620718
**Email** marybathgate@euphony.net
**Alt contact** Val Miller Brough Cottage, Thropton, MORPETH, Northumberland
**Phone** 01669 620419
*Ceilidhs, concerts, dances, competitions, outdoor displays, sessions, workshops.*
**RAB** Northern Arts

**13 to 15 July 2001**
### Stonehaven Folk Festival
**Location** Aberdeenshire
**Contact** Trudi Clayton
**Mail address** 14 Westfield Court, STONEHAVEN, Kincardineshire, AB39 2JW, Scotland
**Phone** 01569 767666
**Email** trudi.clayton@virgin.net
*Concerts, ceilidhs, workshops, sessions, kids concert, paper & comb championship.*
**AC** Scotland

**14 July 2001**
**13 July 2002**
### Birdsedge Village Festival
**Location** W. Yorks
**Contact** Jacey Bedford
**Mail address** 10 Park Head, Birdsedge, HUDDERSFIELD, Yorks, HD8 8XW
**Phone** 01494 606230
**Fax** 01494 606290
**Email** artisan@artifact.demon.co.uk
**Web** www.birdsedge.uk.com
*Mixed arts, community & music event with a bias towards folk. Stalls, music, fun and fundraising plus ticketed evening concert.*
**RAB** Yorkshire Arts

**14 to 15 July 2001**
### Rhythms of the World
**Location** Hitchin, Herts
**Contact** Hilary Ide
**Mail address** C/o The Harvest Moon Centre, 36 Bucklersbury, HITCHIN, Herts, SG5 1BG
**Phone** 01462 459020
**RAB** East England Arts

**14 to 15 July 2001**
### Tolpuddle Martyrs Festival
**Location** Nr. Dorchester, Dorset
**Contact** Nigel Costley
**Mail address** SWTUC, Church House, Church Road, FILTON, Glos, BS34 7BD
**Phone** 0117 947 0521
**Fax** 0117 947 0523
**Email** southwest@tuc.org.uk
**RAB** South West Arts

**14 to 16 July 2001**
### Lichfield Free Festival in The Park
**Location** Staffs
**Contact** Brian Pretty
**Mail address** LDAA, Donegal House, Bore Street, LICHFIELD, Staffs, WS13 6NE
**Phone** 01543 262223
**Web** www.lichfield.gov.uk
*New festival catering for a wide variety of music and children's workshops.*
**RAB** West Midlands Arts

**15 July 2001**
### Stafford Castle Festival of Folk & Blues
**Contact** Richard Musgrave
**Mail address** Stafford Castle Visitor Centre, Newport Road, STAFFORD, ST16 1DJ
**Phone** 01785 257698
*Free community based festival with main stage and acoustic tent.*
**RAB** West Midlands Arts

***The festivals listed here appear alphabetically within date order beginning at 1st June 2001 through to 30th June 2002. Some 2002 dates are yet to be confirmed.***

**15 to 20 July 2001**
## Feis Nan Garbh Chriochan
**Location** Argyle, Scotland
**Contact** Mary Lamont
**Mail address** The Barn, Salen, ACHARACLE, Argyll, PH36 4JN, Scotland
**Phone** 01967 431766
**Email** mary.lamont@lineone.net
**AC** Scotland

**18 to 28 July 2001**
**19 to 29 July 2002**
## Caerphilly International Festival
**Location** Wales
**Contact** Paul Hudson
**Mail address** Caerphilly County Borough Council, Nelson Rd, Tredomen, HENGOED, CF82 7WF, Wales
**Phone** 01443 864223
**Fax** 01443 864228
**Email** tourism@caerphilly.gov.uk
**Web** www.caerphilly.gov.uk
*Programme of events organised by local authority tourism department.*
**AC** Wales

**20 to 22 July 2001**
**19 to 21 July 2002**
## Brampton Live
**Location** Cumbria
**Contact** Ken & Sue Bradburn - Programming
**Mail address** Burncrook Cottage, Faugh, Heads Nook, BRAMPTON, Cumbria, CA8 9BS
**Phone/Fax** 01228 670580
**Email** ken@emerging.demon.co.uk
**Alt contact** Mick North - Promotion
**Address** Carlisle City Council Arts Unit, Tullie House Museum & Art G, CARLISLE, Cumbria, CA3 8TP
**Phone** 01228 534781 x244
**Fax** 01228 810249
**Email** mickn@carlisle-city.gov.uk
*Folk and roots festival booking top UK and overseas acts. 2 main stages and club stage.*
**RAB** Northern Arts

**20 to 22 July 2001**
## Customs House International Guitar Festival
**Location** Tyne & Wear
**Contact** Customs House, Mill Dam, SOUTH SHIELDS, Tyne and Wear
**Phone** 0191 4541234 - box office
**Web** www.nemproductions.com
**Alt contact** Dave Smith - NEM Productions
**Email** DaveSmithNEM@cs.com
*Concerts etc, with major UK/ International artists.*
**RAB** Northern Arts

**20 to 22 July 2001**
**19 to 21 July 2002**
## Festival At The Edge
**Location** Much Wenlock, Shropshire
**Contact** Ali Quarrell
**Mail address** Mythstories, 19-21 Hills Lane, SHREWSBURY, Shrops, SY1 1QU
**Phone** 01743 357140
**Email** info@festivalattheedge.org
**Web** www.festivalattheedge.org
**Alt contact** Chris Lambert
**Alt address** St. Christopher's, Weston Avenue, OSWESTRY, Shrops SY11 1BJ
**Phone** 01691 662981
*Storytelling festival with related arts and children's festival, on greenfield site.*
**RAB** West Midlands Arts

**20 to 22 July 2001**
## Saddleworth Folk Festival
**Location** Uppermill, Lancs
**Contact** Ali O'Brien - Enquries
**Mail address** 18 Queensway, Greenfield, OLDHAM, Lancs, OL3 7AH
**Phone** 01457 870391, 07711 214191
**Email** aobrien@nspcc.org.uk
**Web** www.btinternet.com/~saddleworthfolkfestival
**Alt contact** Jo Holden - Tickets
**Address** Sunnyside, Huddersfield Road, Scouthead, OLDHAM, OL4 4AS
**Phone** 0161 6248377
*Friendly festival in picturesque area with concerts, dance displays, workshops, singarounds, etc.*
**RAB** North West Arts

**20 to 22 July 2001**
**19 to 21 July 2002**
## Seafest
**Location** Scarborough, W. Yorks
**Contact** Richard Grainger
**Mail address** 23 Derwent Street, Derwent, STOCKTON ON TEES, TS20 2BZ
**Phone/Fax** 01642 861899
**Phone** 07970 228534
**Email** richard.grainger@onyxnet.co.uk
**Web** www.richardgrainger.co.uk
*Maritime, folk & world music, a celebration of the Yorkshire Coast fishing heritage. Artist submissions by mail please.*
**RAB** Yorkshire Arts

**20 to 22 July 2001**
## Sesiwn Fawr Dolgellau
**Location** Dolgellau, Wales
**Contact** Ywain Myfyr
**Mail address** Penybryn, DOLGELLAU, Gwynedd, LL40 1SP, Wales
**Phone/Fax** 01341 423355
**Email** myfyr@sesiwnfawr.demon.co.uk
**Web** www.sesiwnfawr.demon.co.uk
*Free music festival*
**AC** Wales

**20 to 22 July 2001**
**19 to 21 July 2002**
## Stainsby Folk Festival
**Location** Derbyshire
**Contact** Information Office
**Mail address** 46 John Street, Brampton, CHESTERFIELD, Derbys, S40 1DF
**Phone** 01246 559036
**Web** www.stainsbyfestival.org.uk
**Alt contact** Box Office
**Address** 65/67 Strettea Lane, Higham, ALFRETON, Derbys, DE55 6EJ
**Phone** 01773 834421
*Green field festival.*
**RAB** East Midlands Arts

**20 to 22 July 2001**
**19 to 21 July 2002**
## Trowbridge Village Pump Festival
**Location** Wiltshire
**Contact** Alan Briars - Artists & tickets
**Mail address** Romsey Oak Farmhouse, Bradford Road, Wingfield, TROWBRIDGE, Wilts, BA14 9LS
**Phone** 01225 769132
01225 762233
**Fax** 01225 753950
**Email** alan.briars@virgin.net
**Web** www.trowbridgefestival.co.uk
**Alt contact** Dave Newman- Site & trade
**Address** Dilley Brook Farm, Wingfield, TROWBRIDGE, Wilts
**Phone** 01373 830110
*Roots and world music; concerts, dances, workshops. Trade stall enquiries to Glen Wiscombe 01225 755239*
**RAB** Southern Arts

**20 to 23 July 2001**
## Isle Of Bute Festival
**Contact** Gillie Banks
**Mail address** 1 St Blane's Terrace, KILCHATTAN BAY, Isle of Bute, PA20 9NN, Scotland
**Phone** 01700 831614
**Fax** 01700 841342
**Email** gillie@butefolk.freeserve.co.uk
*Scottish & Irish folk music. World ceilidh band championships, ceilidhs, workshops, concerts, barn dances and sessions.*
**AC** Scotland

# uk festivals

## july 2001

***The festivals listed here appear alphabetically within date order beginning at 1st June 2001 through to 30th June 2002. Some 2002 dates are yet to be confirmed.***

**21 to 24 July 2001**
### Lichfield Real Ale, Jazz & Blues Festival
**Location** Staffs
**Contact** Brian Pretty
**Mail address** LDAA, Donegal House, Bore Street, LICHFIELD, Staffs, WS13 6NE
**Phone** 01543 262223
**Web** www.lichfieldarts.org.uk
*Mainly jazz festival with some world music and blues.*
**RAB** West Midlands Arts

**21 to 28 July 2001**
### Joe Mooney Summer School of Traditional Music, Song & Dance
**Location** Co. Leitrim
**Contact** Nancy Woods
**Mail address** Joe Mooney Summer School, DRUMSHANBO, Co Leitrim, Irish Republic
**Phone** +353 78 41213
**Email** nwoods@lol.ie
**Alt contact** Mary Doyle
**Phone** 00353 78 41426
*Daily classes/ workshops in traditional Irish music; flute, fiddle, harp, uilleann pipes, accordion, banjo, mandolin, whistle, concertina, bodhran, set dancing, song.*
**AC** Ireland

**21 to 28 July 2001**
### Yn Chruinnaght
**Location** Isle of Man
**Contact** Muriel Atkin
**Mail address** 3 Maycroft, May Hill, RAMSEY, Isle Of Man
**Phone** 01624 814559
**Email** atkin@magicaldesk.com

**22 to 29 July 2001**
### Fiddler's Green Festival
**Location** Co. Down, N. Ireland
**Contact** Kate Murphy
**Mail address** 5 Cherry Hill, ROSTREVOR, Co Down, BT34 3BD, N Ireland
**Phone** 028 4173 8819
**Fax** 028 4173 8738
**Email** fiddlers.green@dnet.co.uk
**Web** www.fiddlersgreenfestival.com
**Alt contact** Mairin McConville
**Address** 12A Greendale Crescent, ROSTREVOR, Co Down, BT34
*Celebration of Irish and International folk music and the cultural arts.*
**AC** Northern Ireland

**23 to 28 July 2001**
### Folkworks Adult Summer School
**Location** Durham
**Contact** Pam Hobson
**Mail address** Folkworks, 69 Westgate Road, NEWCASTLE UPON TYNE, NE1 1SG
**Phone** 0191 222 1717
**Fax** 0191 230 2484
**Email** folkworks@folkworks.co.uk
**Web** www.folkworks.co.uk
*5 days of instrument, song & dance workshops plus ensemble playing. Sessions, concerts and performance opportunuites. Ages 20+.*
**RAB** Northern Arts

**23 to 28 July 2001**
### Folkworks Youth Summer School
**Location** Durham
**Contact** Pam Hobson
**Mail address** Folkworks, 69 Westgate Road, NEWCASTLE UPON TYNE, NE1 1SG
**Phone** 0191 222 1717
**Fax** 0191 230 2484
**Email** folkworks@folkworks.co.uk
**Web** www.folkworks.co.uk
*5 days of workshops in song, a range of instruments, plus ensemble playing. Sessions, concerts, ceilidhs, performance opportunities. Ages 12-25.*
**RAB** Northern Arts

**25 to 29 July 2001**
### African Celtic Experience
**Location** Carms, Wales
**Contact** ACE Promotions
Pencraig Uchaf, Cwm Bach, WHITLAND, Carms, SA34 0DT, Wales
**Phone** 01994 484708
**Fax** 01994 484294
**AC** Wales

**25 to 29 July 2001**
### The North Atlantic Fiddle Convention: Crossing Boundaries
**Location** Aberdeen
**Contact** The Elphinstone Institute
**Mail address** University of Aberdeen, 24 High Street, ABERDEEN, AB24 3EB
**Phone** 01224 272996
**Fax** 01224 272728
**Email** elphinstone@abdn.ac.uk
**Web** www.abdn.ac.uk/elphinstone/
*British gathering dedicated to international traditional fiddle music, International guests from Ireland, Norway, Sweden, Cape Breton, UK. Range of concerts, workshops, recitals, sessions, street music.*
**AC** Scotland

**26 to 28 July 2001**
### Folkworks Durham Gathering
**Contact** Pam Hobson
**Mail address** Folkworks, 69 Westgate Road, NEWCASTLE UPON TYNE, NE1 1SG
**Phone** 0191 222 1717
**Fax** 0191 230 2484
**Email** folkworks@folkworks.co.uk
**Web** www.folkworks.co.uk
*Festival of evening concerts and a free folk picnic on Saturday, drawing on the 250 students and tutors of the Folkworks Summer Schools.*
**RAB** Northern Arts

**26 to 29 July 2001**
### Charles Wells Cambridge Folk Festival
**Contact** Eddie Barcan
**Mail address** Marketing & Promotions, The Guildhall, CAMBRIDGE, CB2 3QJ
**Phone** 01223 457515
01223 457512
**Fax** 01223 457529
**Web** www.cam-folkfest.co.uk
*High-profile festival of major concerts, largely featuring top names from Europe/US/Canada*
**RAB** East England Arts

**27 to 28 July 2001**
### Lewes International Guitar Festival
**Location** E. Sussex
**Contact** Laurence Hill
**Mail address** 5 Lancaster Street, LEWES, E Sussex, BN7 2PX
**Phone/Fax** 01273 476118
**Email** lorenzok1@yahoo.com
**Web** www.lewesguitarfestival.co.uk
**Alt contact** Mr S Hill
**Address** 5 Mount Pleasant, LEWES, E Sussex
*Acoustic, classical, flamenco, folk, blues & singer-songwriters. Concerts plus workshops, masterclasses, exhibition, children's events.*
**RAB** South East Arts

***The festivals listed here appear alphabetically within date order beginning at 1st June 2001 through to 30th June 2002. Some 2002 dates are yet to be confirmed.***

**6 to 28 July 2001**
**27 to 29 July 2002**
## Durham Folk Party
**Contact** Ian McCulloch
**Mail address** 166 Devonshire Road, Belmont, DURHAM, DH1 2BL
**Phone** 0191 384 4160
**Email** ian.mcculloch@virgin.net
**Alt contact** Colin Ryder
**Address** 29 Windsor Terrace, HEXHAM, Northumberland, NE46 3JR
**Phone** 01434 604152
**Email** colin.es@talk21.com
*Informal celebration of folk music & dance. Venues throughout Durham.*
**RAB** Northern Arts

**27 to 29 July 2001**
## Lomond Folk Festival
**Location** Balloch, Scotland
**Contact** Stewart Davidson
**Mail address** 45 Inchfad Road, BALLOCH, G83 8SY, Scotland
**Phone** 01389 757561
**Email** ssbdavidson@aol.com
*Concerts, workshops, competitions, sessions, folkcruise, open stage, children's entertainment.*
**AC** Scotland

**27 to 29 July 2001**
**26 to 28 July 2002**
## Warwick Folk Festival
**Contact** Dick Dixon
**Mail address** Festival Office, PO Box 429, COVENTRY, CV5 6SZ
**Phone** 024 7667 8738
**Email** warwick.folk.festival@iname.com
**Web** www.warfolk.demon.co.uk
**Alt contact** Jenny Freeman
**Address** Box Office, PO Box 1533, HARBURY, Warks, CV33 9ZU
**Phone** 01926 614932
**Email** BoxOffice@aol.com
*Music and dance festival. Mostly traditional music with some jazz & blues, concerts, ceilidhs, workshops, street entertainment.*
**RAB** West Midlands Arts

**27 to 29 July 2001**
## WOMAD Festival
**Location** Reading
**Mail address** WOMAD, Millside, Mill Lane, Box, CORSHAM, Wilts, SN13 8PN
**Phone** 01225 743188
01225 744494 - recorded info
**Fax** 01225 743481
**Email** womad@realworld.on.net
**Web** www.womad.org
*Major world music festival.*
**RAB** Southern Arts

**28 to 29 July 2001**
**27 to 28 July 2002**
## The Big Cheese
**Location** Caerphilly, Wales
**Contact** MJ Cawley
**Mail address** Ty Newydd, 1 Owen Street, PEMBROKE DOCK, Pembrokeshire, SA72 6SL, Wales
**Phone** 01646 682692, 07773 994514
**Email** sd@mjcawley.freeuk.com
*Set in Caerphilly Castle, celebrating the town's past as a cheese market, with Welsh music & dance, street entertainers, falconry, craft/ cuisine demonstrations, fun fair, etc.*
**AC** Wales

**28 July to 4 August 2001**
## Dartington International Summer School - Folk Fiddle with Pete Cooper
**Location** Totnes, Devon
**Contact** The Registrar
**Mail address** The Barn, Dartington Hall, TOTNES, Devon, TQ9 6DE
**Phone** 01803 847077
**Fax** 01803 847087
**Email** info@dartingtonsummerschool.co.uk
**Web** www.dartingtonsummerschool.co.uk
*Course focusing mainly on English, Irish and Scottish fiddle traditions. Part of the month-long summer school at Dartington.*
**RAB** South West Arts

**28 July to 5 August 2001**
**27 July to 4 August 2002**
## The Splore - Scottish Traditional Music School
**Location** Aberdeen
**Contact** Emily Prowse
**Mail address** 3 Nutborn House, Clifton Road, LONDON, SW19 4QT
**Phone** 020 8946 2995
**Fax** 020 8944 6507
**Email** admin@aiyf.org
**Web** www.aiyf.org
*Residential summer school for traditional musicins aged 16-25. Intensive course offering individual sessions and ensemble playing for fiddle, Scots song, clarsach, whistle, guitar and piano. Part of the annual Aberdeen International Youth Festival*
**AC** Scotland

**30 July to 3 August 2001**
## The English Acoustic Collective String School
**Location** Nailsworth, Glos
**Contact** Chris Wood
**Mail address** 40 Whitstable Road, FAVERSHAM, Kent, ME13 8DL
**Phone** 01795 537906
**Email** cw@rurecords.com
**Web** www.rufrecords.com
*Directed by Chris Wood, with a focus on individual development based on the best of our tradition. Annual summer school, last week of July plus other events during the year.*

**3 to 5 August 2001**
## Guildford Live 2001
**Location** Surrey
**Contact** Tony Scott
**Mail address** 54 Haydon Place, GUILDFORD, Surrey, GU1 4NE
**Phone** 01483 536270
**Fax** 01483 306551
**Web** www.guildford-live.co.uk
**RAB** South East Arts

**3 to 10 August 2001**
**2 to 9 August 2002**
## Sidmouth International Festival
**Location** E. Devon
**Contact** Festival Office
**Mail address** PO Box 296, AYLESBURY, Bucks, HP19 9TL
**Phone** 01296 433669 - box
01296 393293
**Fax** 01296 392300
**Email** sidmouth@mrscasey.co.uk
**Web** www.mrscasey.co.uk/sidmouth
*600 events over 8 days, including international folk, roots and world music and dance spectaculars, concerts, ceilidhs, dances, workshops, processions, street theatre, craft fair. Full children's and youth programmes.*
**RAB** South West Arts

**3 to 12 August 2001**
## Gloucester Blues Trail
**Contact** L Fisher
**Mail address** The Blues Line, 14 Grisedale Close, Longlevens, GLOUCESTER, GL2 0EG
**Phone** 01452 532081
**Email** linda@bluesline.freeserve.co.uk
**Web** www.bluesline.freeserve.co.uk
*10 day blues festival. Most events free, various venues in city centre.*
**RAB** South West Arts

***The festivals listed here appear alphabetically within date order beginning at 1st June 2001 through to 30th June 2002. Some 2002 dates are yet to be confirmed.***

**4 August 2001**
## Rhuddlan Folk Day
**Location** Denbighshire, Wales
**Contact** Vicki Williams
**Mail address** 15 Wynne Close, RHUDDLAN, Denbighshire, LL18 5RR
**Phone** 01745 591008
**Email** vicki.williams@talk21.com
*Traditional & contemporary folk music based in the community centre and the pub. Broad range of folk music.*
**AC** Wales

**4 to 5 August 2001**
**3 to 4 August 2002**
## Nottingham Riverside Festival
**Contact** Paul Morgan
**Mail address** Nottingham City Council, Arts & Events, 55 Castle Gate, NOTTINGHAM, NG1 6AF
**Phone** 0115 915 3595
**Fax** 0115 9153508
*World/roots based music festival. Run by local authority Arts & Events unit. Also occasional small scale events; see Roots In The City.*
**RAB** East Midlands Arts

**4 to 11 August 2001**
**3 to 10 August 2002**
## Alnwick International Music Festival
**Location** Northumberland
**Contact** Jim Thompson - co-ordinator
**Mail address** 119 Allerburn Lea, ALNWICK, Northumberland, NE66 2QP
**Phone** 01665 510417
**Email** jim@alnwick0.demon.co.uk
**Web** www.alnwickfestival.com and www.alnwickfestival.co.uk
**Phone** 01665 606033 (Press & Publicity)
*8 days of international music, song and dance. 300 entertainers from 10 countries. Free daily concerts in the market place, craft fair, themed evening concerts at the Playhouse.*
**RAB** Northern Arts

**4 to 25 August 2001**
## Guinness Live World Music
**Location** Belfast
**Contact** Smallworld Music
**Mail address** PO Box 747, BELFAST, BT9 5ES, N Ireland
**Phone** 028 9038 2384
**Fax** 028 9029 5173
**Email** Becksworld@btinternet.com
*Movies and music with a world music bias in al fresco setting adjacent to River Lagan. Weekends in August.*
**AC** Northern Ireland

**8 to 12 August 2001**
## African Arts Village
**Location** Tawd Vale, Lancs
**Contact** Anni
**Mail address** 84 Bank Side Street, LEEDS, LS8 5AD
**Phone** 0113 248 6746
**Fax** 0113 248 6746
**Email** drum.call@virgin.net
**Web** www.drumcall.co.uk
**RAB** Yorkshire Arts

**9 to 11 August 2001**
**8 to 10 August 2002**
## Cropredy Festival
**Location** Oxon
**Contact** Christine Pegg
**Mail address** PO Box 37, BANBURY, Oxon, OX16 8YN
**Fax** 01869 337142
**Web** www.fairportconvention.co.uk
*Large open air festival featuring Fairport Convention and other top acts. Please contact by post or fax only.*
**RAB** Southern Arts

**9 to 12 August 2001**
## Gosport Summer Festival
**Location** Hants
**Contact** Peter Chegwyn
**Mail address** 51 Russell Street, GOSPORT, Hants, PO12 3JD
**Phone/Fax** 023 92 528017
**Email** chegwyn@talk21.com
*Folk and roots festival.*
**RAB** Southern Arts

**10 to 12 August 2001**
## Auchtermuchty Traditional Music Weekend
**Location** Fife, Scotland
**Contact** Citty Finlayson
**Mail address** 17 High Street, AUCHTERMUCHTY, Fife, KY14 7AP, Scotland
**Phone** 01337 828732
**Fax** 01337 828060
**Email** cittyfin@aol.com
**Web** www.auchtermuchty.freeserve.co.uk
*Concerts, ceilidhs, TMSA competitions, workshops, open air events.*
**AC** Scotland

**10 to 12 August 2001**
## Dartmoor Folk Festival
**Location** South Zeal, Devon
**Contact** Mrs Jane White
**Mail address** Sunnyhill, Zeal Hard, South Zeal, OKEHAMPTON, Devon, EX20 2JL
**Phone** 01837 840162
*Small successful festival with a traditional emphasis.*
**RAB** South West Arts

**10 to 12 August 2001**
## Saltburn International Festival of Folk Music Dance & Song
**Location** Cleveland
**Contact** John Taylor
**Mail address** Fern Cottage, Dalehouse, STAITHES, Cleveland, TS13 5DT
**Phone** 01947 840928
**RAB** Northern Arts

**10 to 17 August 2001**
**9 to 16 August 2002**
## Broadstairs Folk Week
**Location** Kent
**Contact** Jane de Rose - Director
**Alt contact** Kim Headley - Artistic Director
**Mail address** Pierremont Hall, BROADSTAIRS, Kent, CT10 1JX
**Phone** 01843 604080
**Fax** 01843 866048
**Email** info@folk-week.demon.co.uk
**Web** www.broadstairsfolkweek.com
*Week festival promoting all aspects of music, song and dance. Concerts, workshops, street theatre, torchlight processions, children's programme.*
**RAB** South East Arts

**11 to 18 August 2001**
**10 to 17 August 2002**
## Billingham International Folklore Festival
**Location** Teesside
**Contact** Joe Maloney
**Mail address** Stockton Business Centre, 70 Brunswick Street, STOCKTON ON TEES, TS18 1DW
**Phone** 01642 651050
01642 553220
**Fax** 01642 602839
**Email** billingham.festival@virgin.net
**Web** www.billinghamfestival.co.uk
*8 days of International music and dance. CIOFF Member.*
**RAB** Northern Arts

**11 to 18 August 2001**
## Morland Folk Dance Week
**Location** Penrith, Cumbria
**Contact** David Jones
**Mail address** Newby End Farm, Newby, PENRITH, Cumbria, CA10 3EX
**Phone** 01931 714338
**Email** davidjonesnewby@ukonline.co.uk
**RAB** Northern Arts

**15 to 19 August 2001**
## Malborough Festival
**Location** S. Devon
**Contact** Jim Carr
**Mail address** The Royal Oak, Higher Town, Malborough, KINGSBRIDGE, Devon, TQ7 3RL
**Phone** 01548 562088
**Fax** 01548 560386
**Email** malborough.festival@ukonline.co.uk
**Web** www.malborough.fsbusiness.co.uk
**RAB** South West Arts

**16 to 27 August 2001**
## Ross on Wye International Festival
**Location** Herefordshire
**Contact** Helen Wragg - Director
**Mail address** Performance Related, The Mews, MITCHELDEAN, Glos, GL17 0SL
**Phone** 01594 544446
**Fax** 01594 544448
**Web** www.rossfest.wynet.co.uk
**RAB** West Midlands Arts

**17 to 19 August 2001**
## Burntwood Folk Festival
**Location** Staffs
**Contact** Margaret Porter
**Mail address** 431 Sutton Road, WALSALL, W Midlands, WS5 3AS
**Phone** 01992 625981
**Web** www.burntwoodfolkfestival.co.uk
*Mainly English folk acts, crafts, singarounds, childrens entertainment.*
**RAB** West Midlands Arts

**17 to 19 August 2001**
## Mull Of Kintyre Music Festival
**Location** Argyle, Scotland
**Contact** Anne Leith - secretary
**Mail address** 2d Meadowburn Place, CAMPBELTOWN, Argyll, PA28 6ST, Scotland
**Phone** 01586 551053
**Fax** 01586 554972
*Irish & Scottish music, pub sessions, ceilidhs and kids events.*
**AC** Scotland

**17 to 19 August 2001**
**16 to 18 August 2002**
## Nantwich Folk & Roots Festival
**Location** Cheshire
**Contact** Clare Smith
**Mail address** 21 Wistaston Road, CREWE, Cheshire, CW2 7RA
**Phone** 01270 567750
07803 209233
**Email** fluff@tower-struck-down.freeserve.co uk
**Web** www.folk-roots.co.uk
**Alt contact** Zoe Johnson
**Alt address** 80 Edleston Road, CREWE, Cheshire
**Phone** 01270 214779
**Fax** 01270 610871
**Email** nantwich.roots@excite.com
*Green field site festival with fringe events in the town's many pubs. Family event. Folk & roots music. Emphasis on young people.*
**RAB** North West Arts

**17 to 19 August 2001**
## Pontardawe Festival
**Location** S. Wales
**Contact** Helen Matthews
**Mail address** Pontardawe Inn, 12 Herbert Street, PONTARDAWE, W Glamorgan, SA8 4ED, Wales
**Phone** 01792 830200 - eve
**Fax** 01792 830649
**Email** pontardawe.festival@eclipse.co.uk
**Web** www.pontardawefestival.org.uk
*Festival of world music and dance, large craft market, children's festival.*
**AC** Wales

**17 to 19 August 2001**
## White Horse Folk Festival
**Location** Oxon
**Contact** Dave & Kate Guest
**Mail address** 1 Membury Way, Grove, WANTAGE, Oxon, OX12 0BP
**Phone** 01235 765445
**RAB** Southern Arts

**17 to 26 August 2001**
## Langholme & Eskdale Music & Arts Festival
**Location** Dumfrieshire, Scotland
**Contact** Jim Muir
**Mail address** Festival Office, 1st Floor Town Hall, LANGHOLME, Dumfrieshire, DG13 0JQ, Scotland
**Phone** 01387 380272
**Fax** 01387 380265
**Email** office@langholmefestival.co.uk
**Web** www.langholmefestival.co.uk
**Alt contact** Alan Weatherstone
**Phone** 01387 380912
*Eclectic festival covering all arts and music.Various venues in Langholme, giving as wide a choice as possible to audiences. TMSA.*
**AC** Scotland

**18 to 24 August 2001**
**17 to 23 August 2002**
## Whitby Folk Week
**Location** N. Yorks
**Contact** Malcolm Storey
**Mail address** PO Box 44, SELBY, N Yorks, YO8 9YP
**Phone** 01757 708424
**Fax** 01757 708424
**Email** wfw@box44selby.freeserve.co.uk
*Week long festival of traditional British & Irish folk music and dance. Indoor and outdoor venues throughout Whitby.*
**RAB** Yorkshire Arts

**23 to 26 August 2001**
## Marymass Folk Festival
**Location** Ayrshire, Scotland
**Contact** Joyce Hodge
**Mail address** 7 Machrie Place, KILWINNIG, Ayrshire, KA13 6RW, Scotland
**Phone** 01294 551047
**Email** joyceifc@aol.com
**Web** www.members.xoom.com/jimbarr/irvine.htm
*Local and visiting performers; concerts, sessions, schools events.*
**AC** Scotland

**23 to 27 August 2001**
**22 to 26 August 2002**
## Towersey Village Festival
**Location** Oxon
**Contact** Festival Office
**Mail address** PO Box 296, AYLESBURY, Bucks, HP19 9TL
**Phone** 01296 394411
**Fax** 01296 392300
**Email** towersey@mrscasey.co.uk
**Web** www.mrscasey.co.uk/towersey
*Strong community festival with folk/roots music, dance & song, now in 37th year.*
**RAB** Southern Arts

**24 to 26 August 2001**
## Bridgnorth Folk Festival
**Location** Shropshire
**Contact** Alan & Sandra Surtees
**Mail address** PO Box 1568, BRIDGNORTH, Shropshire, WV15 6YJ
**Phone/Fax** 01746 768813
**Email** alan.surtees@btinternet.com
*Concerts, ceilidhs, children's events, pub sessions, workshops, morris dancing, singarounds.*
**RAB** West Midlands Arts



***The festivals listed here appear alphabetically within date order beginning at 1st June 2001 through to 30th June 2002. Some 2002 dates are yet to be confirmed.***

***The festivals listed here appear alphabetically within date order beginning at 1st June 2001 through to 30th June 2002. Some 2002 dates are yet to be confirmed.***

**24 to 26 August 2001**
## The Wombwell Free Folk Festival
**Location** Barnsley
**Contact** Hedley Jones
**Mail address** 5A Aldham Crescent, Wombwell, BARNSLEY, S73 8ES
**Phone** 01226 752901
07773 072744
**Email** barleysheaf.folk@virgin.net
**Web** www.come.to/thebarleysheaf
*Free 3 day folk festival held in a big top marquee. Concerts, ceilidh, singarounds, Irish & Appalachian dancers.*
**RAB** Yorkshire Arts

**24 to 27 August 2001**
## B.B.'s Blues Club/ B.B.'s Unplugged
**Location** London
**Contact** Bob Brunning
**Mail address** 56 Cavendish Road, Colliers Wood, LONDON, SW19
**Phone** 020 8540 6652
**Alt contact** Wheel House Productions Merton Abbey Mills, Merantun Way, Colliers Wood, LONDON, SW19
**Phone** 020 8542 6644
*Thursday, acoustic blues guests. Sunday, electric blues guests. August Bank holiday festival with over 20 acoustic blues acts.*
**RAB** London Arts

**24 to 27 August 2001**
**23 to 26 August 2001**
## Cornwall Folk Festival
**Location** Wadebridge
**Contact** Eileen Conn
**Mail address** 11 Smithfield Drive, Latchbrook, SALTASH, Cornwall, PL12 4TW
**Phone** 01752 843510
**Alt contact** Clare Wilson
**Address** 3 Bossiney Grange, Bossiney, TINTAGEL, Cornwall, PL34 0AX
**Phone** 01840 770946
**Fax** 01840 770887
*Music, dance and song events throughout Wadebridge*
**RAB** South West Arts

**24 to 27 August 2001**
## Great British Rhythm & Blues Festival
**Location** Colne, Lancs
**Contact** Katy Mills
**Mail address** Pendle Leisure Ltd, Bank House, 61 Albert Road, COLNE, Lancs, BB8 0BP
**Phone** 01282 661233
**Fax** 01282 661221
**Email** kmills@leisureinpendle.co.uk
**Web** www.bluesfestival.co.uk
**Alt contact** Gary Hood
**Address** Colne Municipal Hall, Albert Road, COLNE, Lancs, BB8 0BP
**Phone** 01282 661220
**Email** ghood@leisureinpendle.co.uk
*Annual festival, August Bank Holiday weekend.*
**RAB** North West Arts

**24 to 27 August 2001**
## Haswell Do
**Location** Co. Durham
**Contact** Fred Brierley
**Mail address** The Wayfarer, HASWELL, Co Durham
**Phone** 0191 517 1274
*Charity weekend. Sessions hosted by Haswell folk club plus opportunity for spots.*
**RAB** Northern Arts

**25 to 27 August 2001**
## Bishopstock Music Festival
**Location** Exeter, Devon
**Contact** Julie Millard
**Mail address** Bishops Court Palace, Clyst St Mary, EXETER, Devon, EX5 1DH
**Phone** 01392 875 220
**Email** production@bishopstock.com
**Web** www.bishopstock.com
*Major Blues festival. Usually May, delayed to August this year.*
**RAB** South West Arts

**27 August 2001**
## Chapeltown Free Folk Day
**Location** Sheffield
**Contact** Lou Marriott
**Mail address** 3 Carlthorpe Grove, High Green, SHEFFIELD, S35 4PL
**Phone** 0114 284 5922
**Venue** The Commercial, Station Road, Chapeltown, SHEFFIELD
**Phone** 0114 2469066
*Noon - 11pm singaround, spots and music session.*
**RAB** Yorkshire Arts

**27 August 2001**
**26 August 2002**
## Kentucky To Kent UK
**Location** Sevenoaks, Kent
**Contact** Rick Townend
**Mail address** St Julians Club, St Julians Road, SEVENOAKS, Kent, TN15 0OX
**Phone** 01732 458261
01892 782412
**Fax** 01732 465788
**Email** banjos@supanet.com
**Web** www.stjulians.co.uk
*Bluegrass festival, music, song & dance workshops, instrument clinic, concerts and barndance. Set in old country house & grounds.*
**RAB** South East Arts

**31 August to 2 September 2001**
## Baggeridge Folk Festival
**Location** West Midlands
**Contact** Matt Swindlehurst
**Mail address** 106 Oxley Moor Road, WOLVERHAMPTON, WV10 6TX
**Phone** 01902 785002
**Email** matt@lmsmusic.co.uk
**Web** www.lmsmusic.co.uk
**Venue** Baggeridge Country Park, Gospel End, DUDLEY, West Mids
*Free festival*
**RAB** West Midlands Arts

**31 August to 2 September 2001**
**30 August to 1 September 2002**
## Fylde Folk Festival
**Location** Fleetwood, Lancs
**Contact** Alan Bell
**Mail address** 55 The Strand, Rossall, FLEETWOOD, Lancs, FY7 8NP
**Phone** 01253 872317
**Fax** 01253 878382
**Email** alanbell@fylde-folk-fest.demon.co.uk
**Web** www.fylde-folk-festival.com
**Alt contact** Eddie Sreen
**Address** The Lavendep, 33 Dowbridge, Kirkham, PRESTON, Lancs
**Phone** 01772 683027
*Northern folk festival celebrating traditional & contemporary folk song, music and dance. Concerts, sessions, morris teams, etc.*
**RAB** North West Arts

**31 August to 2 September 2001**
## Off The Tracks
**Location** Castle Donington, Derbys
**Contact** Andy Cooper
**Mail address** PO Box 68, DERBY, DE1 3XY
**Phone** 01332 384518
01332 833673
**Email** andy@offthetracks.co.uk
**Web** www.offthetracks.co.uk
*Greenfield site folk & roots festival.*
**RAB** East Midlands Arts

**31 August to 2 September 2001**
## Southsea Folk Festival
**Location** Hants
**Contact** Southsea Folk Festival Office
**Mail address** Kylebrack House, 41 Festing Grove, SOUTHSEA, Hants, PO4 9QB
**Email** barkingspidermusic@btinternet.com

*Weekend folk festival, mostly English traditional with concerts, Morris teams, sessions, etc.*

**RAB** Southern Arts

**1 to 2 September 2001**
## Faversham International Hop Festival
**Location** Kent
**Contact** Jan West - Arts & Facilities
**Mail address** Council Offices, Trinity Road, SHEERNESS, Kent, ME12 2PG
**Phone** 01795 585601
01795 585600
**Fax** 01795 669097
**Email** janwest@swale.gov.uk
**Alt contact** Christine Heathfield - Events
**Phone** 01795 585609
**Email** christineheathfield@swale.gov.uk

*2 day festival held in Faversham Town Centre, to celebrate the old days of hop picking. Music, dancing and entertainment for the whole family.*

**RAB** South East Arts

**1 to 2 September 2001**
## Sowerby Bridge Rushbearing Festival
**Location** W. Yorks
**Contact** Michael Bojczuk
**Mail address** Fairhaven, Tuel Lane, SOWERBY BRIDGE, W Yorks
**Phone** 01422 839076
**Fax** 01422 836067
**Email** mrbojczuk@hotmail.com
**RAB** Yorkshire Arts

**1 to 16 September 2001**
## Rye Festival
**Location** E. Sussex
**Contact** PO Box 33, RYE, E Sussex, TN31 7YD
**Phone** 01797 224442
**Email** ryefestival@yahoo.com
**RAB** South East Arts

**5 to 9 September 2001**
## Stroud Fringe Festival
**Location** Glos
**Contact** Sue Torres
**Mail address** PO Box 3016, SOUTH GLOUCESTER, GL2 7YJ
**Fax** 01452 741522 - info
**Phone/Fax** 01453 760900 - box
**Email** stroudfest@suetorres.demon.co.uk
**Web** www.stroudfestival.co.uk
**RAB** South West Arts

**7 to 9 September 2001**
**6 to 8 September 2002**
## Aberdare Folk Festival
**Location** Wales
**Contact** Steve Chandler
**Phone** 01685 877322

*Festival in country park. Popular concert acts.*

**AC** Wales

**7 to 9 September 2001**
## Dawlish Folk & Blues Festival
**Location** Devon
**Contact** Judy Forrow
**Mail address** Dol-Coth, Longlands, DAWLISH, Devon, EX7 9NE
**Fax** 01626 864042
**Email** martinfenton@eclipse.co.uk
**Web** www.eclipse.co.uk/dawlishfolkfest
**Alt contact** Martin Fenton

*West Country weekend festival with Blues emphasis.*

**RAB** South West Arts

**7 to 9 September 2001**
**6 to 8 September 2002**
## Donisthorpe Music Weekend
**Location** Derbys
**Contact** Lynne Tann-Watson
**Mail address** 49 Moira Road, DONISTHORPE, Derbys, DE12 7QD
**Phone** 01530 272835
07950 630410
**Email** lynne.tann-watson@virgin.net
**Alt contact** Sharon Moorcroft
**Venue** The Masons Arms, DONISTHORPE, Derbys
**Phone** 01530 270378

*Informal song/music festival for all. No booked guests, no admission charge, free camping available.*

**RAB** East Midlands Arts

**7 to 9 September 2001**
## Le Grand Bal De Bath
**Location** Avon
**Contact** Nicki Cawthorne
**Mail address** 119 Locksbrook Road, BATH, BA1 3EN
**Phone** 01225 332025
**Email** stephen.day@virgin.net
**RAB** South West Arts

**7 to 9 September 2001**
## Linlithgow Folk Festival
**Location** Lothian, Scotland
**Contact** Grace McClure
**Phone** 01506 844392
**Email** LFFA_enquiries@hotmail.com

*Sessions, workshops, concert, family ceilidh, open stage, street entertainment, crafts, etc.*

**AC** Scotland

**7 to 9 September 2001**
## Portpatrick Folk Festival
**Location** Dumfries and Galloway
**Contact** Glen Murray
**Mail address** Portpatrick Events, 45 Main Street, Portpatrick, STRANRAER, Dumfries & Galloway, DG9 8JJ, Scotland
**Phone/Fax** 01776 810717
**Phone** 01776 702151 ext 61344
**Email** info@portpatrickevents.php247.net

*Concerts, pub gigs, sessions, workshops, ceilidh, street events and children's events.*

**AC** Scotland

**7 to 9 September 2001**
**6 to 8 September 2002**
## Swanage Folk Festival
**Location** Dorset
**Contact** Mr Steve Parker
**Mail address** 14 Church Hill, SWANAGE, Dorset, BH19 1HU
**Phone** 01929 427559
**Web** come.to/swanage.folk.festival
**Alt contact** Swanage Tourism
**Address** Shore Road, SWANAGE, Dorset, BH19 2QG
**Phone** 01929 422885

*Music, dance, theatre and craft fair. Many free events.*

**RAB** South West Arts

**7 to 9 September 2001**
## Walton On The Naze Folk Festival
**Location** Essex
**Contact** Jon & Pam Fitzgerald
**Mail address** 21 Connaught Avenue, FRINTON-ON-SEA, Essex, CO13 9PN
**Phone** 01255 679232
**Email** festinfo@thrift-music.com
**Web** www.keme.co.uk/~bloor/walton/index.htm
**RAB** East England Arts



***The festivals listed here appear alphabetically within date order beginning at 1st June 2001 through to 30th June 2002. Some 2002 dates are yet to be confirmed.***

uk festivals

sept 2001

***The festivals listed here appear alphabetically within date order beginning at 1st June 2001 through to 30th June 2002. Some 2002 dates are yet to be confirmed.***

**8 to 15 September 2001**
**28 October to 2 November 2001**
**10 to 15 March 2002**
**29 April to 3 May 2002**
**29 September to 4 October 2001**

## English Country Dance Holidays

**Contact** Cyril Jones
**Mail address** 3 Uplands Way, Grange Park, LONDON, N21 1DH
**Email** cydorjones@aol.com
*Workshops in English Country Dance led by Cyril Jones.*
**RAB** London Arts

**8 September 2001**

## Dunstable Folk & Dance Festival

**Location** Beds
**Contact** Michele Alexander
**Mail address** c/o Grove House, 76 High Street North, DUNSTABLE, Beds, LU6 1NF
**Phone** 01582 607895
**Email** promotions.dunstable@towns.bedfordshire.gov.uk
*4 different bands & dance groups, 6-11pm.*
**RAB** East England Arts

**8 to 9 September 2001**

## Rotherham Folk & Jazz Festival

**Location** S. Yorks
**Contact** Judy Dalton
**Mail address** 213 Nursery Road, Dinnington, SHEFFIELD, S25 2QU
**Phone** 01909 569481
**Fax** 0703 1152002
**Email** judy@jdalton.easynet.co.uk
**Web** www.syfolk.co.uk/rotherhamfolkandjazz/
*Folk and jazz concerts in the park.*
**RAB** Yorkshire Arts

**8 to 22 September 2001**

## St Ives September Festival

**Location** Cornwall
**Contact** Cassiel Dennis
**Alt contact** Marion Stevens
**Mail address** Festival Office, Lower Stennack, ST IVES, Cornwall, TR26 1QG
**Phone** 01736 796888
01736 798721
**Email** festival@st-ives-cornwall.co.uk
**Web** www/penwith.com/september festival
*Festival of music and the arts. Jazz, blues, folk, contemporary and world music. Poetry & literature, open studios, guided tours, cinemas, exhibitions and more.*
**RAB** South West Arts

**9 September 2001**
**8 September 2002**

## Massed Morris Dancing In Thornham

**Location** Norfolk
**Contact** David Jackson
**Mail address** 9 Edward Street, KING'S LYNN, Norfolk, PE30 5QS
**Phone** 01553 768930
**Alt contact** Ian Heighton
**Email** thekingsmorris@waitrose.com
*Massed display of Cotswold Morris, hosted by The King's Morris with other male guest teams. Folllowed by music sessions.*
**RAB** East England Arts

**14 to 16 September 2001**
**13 to 15 September 2002**

## Exeter Set Dancing Weekend

**Location** Devon
**Contact** John Earle
**Mail address** 20 Dunvegan Close, EXETER, Devon, EX4 4AF
**Phone** 01392 420219
07714 122009
**Fax** 01392 662921
**Email** john@set-dancing.org
**Web** www.set-dancing.org
*Irish set dancing workshops and ceilis with visiting Irish teachers & musicians.*
**RAB** South West Arts

**14 to 16 September 2001**

## Gig 'n the Bann: Traditional Irish & Ulster-Scots Festival

**Location** Co. Antrim, N. Ireland
**Phone** 028 2582 1333
028 25 820832
**AC** Northern Ireland

**14 to 16 September 2001**

## Gwyl Bibau Pencader Pipes Festival

**Location** Carms, Wales
**Contact** John Tose
**Mail address** Ty'r Tose, CRYMYCH, Pembs, SA41 3SG
**Phone** 01239 831517
**Email** johntose@tyrbwlch.freeserve.co.uk
**Web** www.btinternet.com/~ceri.matho/index.html/pibau/index.htm
*Small friendly bagpipe festival including concerts, pub sessions and workshops. Quality guest artists.*
**AC** Wales

**1 to 3 June 2001**
**14 to 16 September 2001**

## Music in the Church at Aust

**Location** Sth. Glos
**Contact** Peter Dobbins
**Phone** 01454 632306
0117 918 8056
**Fax** 0117 918 8400
*Monthly concerts of traditional and early music, plus occasional weekend festivals with concerts in the church and workshops around the village. Policy of booking rarely heard Pan-European performers.*
**RAB** South West Arts

**14 to 17 September 2001**

## The Voice Weekend

**Location** Keighley, W. Yorkshire
**Contact** Yorkshire Dales Workshops
**Mail address** 14 Oakburn Road, ILKLEY, Yorks, LS29 9NN
**Fax** 01943 609421
**Phone/Fax** 07760 287384
**Email** ydw@ydw.btinternet.co.uk
**Web** www.ydw.btinternet.co.uk
*Weekend of voice workshops and concerts.*
**RAB** Yorkshire Arts

**15 to 16 September 2001**

## East Anglian Storytelling Festival

**Location** Harwich, Essex
**Contact** Jan Williams
**Mail address** 83 The High Street, Brightlingsea, NR COLCHESTER, Essex, CO7 0EG
**Phone** 01206 305630
**Fax** 01206 304242
**Alt contact** Carl Merry
**Address** 10 Larkswood Walk, WICKFORD, Essex, SS12 9BY
**Phone** 01268 76770
*Biennial festival for adults & children. Workshops, lectures & sessions.*
**RAB** East England Arts

**15 to 22 September 2001**

## Moving On Music Festival

**Location** Belfast
**Contact** Paul Brown
**Mail address** Moving On Music Ltd, 7 University Road, BELFAST, BT7 1NA, Northern Ireland
**Fax** 028 9024 8818
**Web** www.movingonmusic.co.uk
*Various loctions around Belfast.*
**AC** Northern Ireland

**16 September 2001**
**15 September 2002**
### Keyboard Sunday
**Location** Co. Durham
**Contact** Fred Brierley
**Mail address** The Wayfarer, HASWELL, Co Durham
**Phone** 0191 517 1274
*Day of tuition, workshops & performance. Beginners welcome.*
**RAB** Northern Arts

**21 to 23 September 2001**
### Bromyard Folk Festival
**Location** Worcs
**Contact** Annie Jones
**Mail address** PO Box 6, LEDBURY, Herefordshire, HR8 2YJ
**Fax** 01531 670593
**Email** info@bromyard-folk-festival.org.uk
**Web** www.bromyard-folk-festival.org.uk
*Long established festival, pub sessions, concerts, dances and morris teams, children's events.*
**RAB** West Midlands Arts

**21 to 23 September 2001**
**20 to 22 September 2002**
### Hairth O' Knokrach
**Location** Galloway, Scotland
**Contact** Liz Holmes
**Mail address** Knochengorroch Farm, Carsphairn, CASTLE DOUGLAS, Kirkcudbrightshire, DG7 3TJ, Scotland
**Fax** 01644 460662
**Email** goduha@ecosse.net
*Open air Celtic music festival set in the Galloway uplands. Promotes traditional/ roots music and rural regeneration. Concerts, workshops, artworks and demonstrations.*
**AC** Scotland

**21 to 23 September 2001**
### Otley Black Sheep Folk Festival
**Location** W. Yorks
**Contact** Steve Fairholme
**Mail address** PO Box 55, OTLEY, W Yorks, LS21 1XP
**Fax** 01943 464858
**Phone/Fax** 01943 467189
**Email** steve@otley-folkfest.demon.co.uk
**Web** www.otley-folkfest.demon.co.uk
**RAB** Yorkshire Arts

**28 to 29 September 2001**
### Hubble Bubble Festival
**Location** Islington, London
**Mail address** Union Chapel, Compton Avenue, Islington, LONDON, N1 2XD
**Phone** 020 7226 1686
**RAB** London Arts

**28 to 30 September 2001**
**27 to 29 September 2001**
### Dunbar Belhaven Best Traditional Music Festival
**Location** East Lothian, Scotland
**Contact** Bill Crookston - Secretary
**Mail address** Bonard House, Belhaven Road, DUNBAR, East Lothian, EH42 1NW, Scotland
**Phone** 01368 863301
**Alt contact** Andy Stephen - Treasurer
**Address** 31 Warrender Crescent, DUNBAR, East Lothian, EH42 1LU
**Phone** 01368 862731
*Weekend festival in hotels, halls and pubs in Dunbar. Traditional singers and musicians.*
**AC** Scotland

**28 to 30 September 2001**
### The Linking of the Chain Festival
**Location** Kendal, Cumbria
**Contact** Chrissy Thomas
**Mail address** Dancetales, Beech Cottage, Langdale Road, GRASMERE, Cumbria, LA22 9SU
**Phone** 015394 35641
**Fax** 015394 33441
**Email** taffy@dancetales.co.uk
**Web** www.dancetales.co.uk
*Storytelling and related arts.*
**RAB** Northern Arts

**29 September 2001**
### Traditions 2001
**Location** Halifax
**Contact** Pete Coe - Artists
**Mail address** 103 Oldham Road, RIPPONDEN, W Yorks, HX6 4EB
**Phone** 01422 822569
**Email** petecoe@backshift.demon.co.uk
**Web** www.ryburn3step.org.uk
**Alt contact** Sarah Cartlidge - Public enquires
**Address** Centre Management Office, 30 Woolshops, HALIFAX, HX1 1RU
**Phone** 01422 345277
**Fax** 01422 430500
**Email** woolshops@lasalle.com
*Street festival wih dance teams, street musicians and pavement performers.*
**RAB** Yorkshire Arts

**29 to 30 September 2001**
### Concertinas At Witney
**Location** Oxon
**Contact** Hands on Music Weekends
**Mail address** PO Box 1162, EAST OXFORD DO, OX4 4WS
**Phone** 01865 714778
07798 520552
**Fax** 01865 749428
**Email** homweekend@aol.com
*Concertina workshop & concert weekend.*
**RAB** Southern Arts

**4 to 7 October 2001**
### Ards Guitar Festival
**Location** Co. Down, N. Ireland
**Contact** 249 Cavehill Road, BELFAST, BT15 5BS, Northern Ireland
**Phone** 028 9096 2706
**Email** info@ardsguitarfestival.com
**Web** www.geocities.com/ards.geo/
**AC** Northern Ireland

**4 to 7 October 2001**
### Jersey Festival of World Music
**Contact** John Eeles
**Mail address** Orchard House, Hartpury, GLOUCESTER, GL14 3BG
**Fax** 01452 700736
**Email** jerseyworldfest@aol.com
**Web** www.jerseyworldfestival.co.uk

**5 to 7 October 2001**
### Penicuik Folk Festival
**Location** Midlothian, Scotland
**Contact** Brian Miller
**Mail address** 36 Greenhill Park, PENICUIK, Midlothian, EH26 9EX, Scotland
**Phone** 01968 678153
**Email** brian@horniegollach.com
**Web** www.horniegollach.com
*Concerts, ceilidhs and competitions.*
**AC** Scotland

**5 to 7 October 2001**
**4 to 6 October 2002**
### Tenterden Folk Festival
**Location** Kent
**Contact** Folk Spots
**Mail address** 15 Repton Manor Road, ASHFORD, Kent, TN23 3HA
**Phone** 01233 626805
**Email** folkspots@btinternet.com
**Web** www.folkspots.btinternet.com
*Town centre festival, emphasis on traditional English folk song and dance, especially from Kent and Sussex.*
**RAB** South East Arts

**5 to 7 October 2001**
### Ugie Folk Club Festival
**Location** Aberdeenshire
**Contact** Bill Buchan
**Phone** 01346 582081
**Email** ugiefolk@bigfoot.com
**AC** Scotland

**11 to 20 October 2001**
### Tyneside Irish Festival
**Location** Newcastle
**Contact** Tony Corcoran
**Fax** 0191 222 0398
**Email** irishfest@artsociety.net
**RAB** Northern Arts Board



***The festivals listed here appear alphabetically within date order beginning at 1st June 2001 through to 30th June 2002. Some 2002 dates are yet to be confirmed.***

***The festivals listed here appear alphabetically within date order beginning at 1st June 2001 through to 30th June 2002. Some 2002 dates are yet to be confirmed.***

**12 to 14 October 2001**
## Banbury's Folk n'Good Music Day
**Location** Oxon
**Contact** Ride a Cock Horse Folk Club
**Mail address** Just William, Fenny Marina, Wharf Road, FENNY COMPTON, Warks, CV47 2XD
**Phone** 01295 770952
**Email** derek/mary@rideacockhorsefolk.freeserve.co.uk
**Web** www.rideacockhorse.co.uk
**RAB** Southern Arts

**12 to 14 October 2001**
## Both Sides of the Tweed
**Location** Kelso, Scottish Borders
**Contact** Hector Christie
**Phone** 01750 23100
**Email** hectorc@freenetname.co.uk
*The big party to end the festival year!*
**AC** Scotland

**13 October 2001**
## Buzz Dance
**Location** Stockport, Cheshire
**Contact** Milly Chadband
**Mail address** 62 Ridge Crescent, Hawk Green, Marple, STOCKPORT SK6 7JA
**Phone** 0161 427 4430
**Email** bill@chadband.freeserve.co.uk
**Alt contact** Pauline Rutter
**Address** 14A Hillside Grove, Marple Bridge, STOCKPORT
**Phone** 0161 427 6075
*Day of dance.*
**RAB** North West Arts

**13 October 2001**
## Market Drayton Folk Festival
**Location** Shropshire
**Contact** Michael Raven
**Mail address** 126 Jug Bank, Ashley, MARKET DRAYTON, Shropshire, TF9 4NJ
**Phone** 01630 672304
**Email** michaelraven@freefolk.com
**Web** www.freefolk.com
*Festival of Welsh border songs, dances and stories.*
**RAB** West Midlands Arts

**13 to 27 October 2001**
## Canterbury Festival
**Location** Kent
**Contact** Jo Tuffs
**Mail address** Festival Office, Christchurch Gate, The Precincts, CANTERBURY, Kent, CT1 2EE
**Phone** 01227 452853
**Fax** 01227 781830
**Email** jo@canterburyfestival.co.uk
**RAB** South East Arts

**18 to 21 October 2001**
## Lowender Peran Celtic Festival
**Location** Perranporth, Cornwall
**Contact** Merv Davey
**Mail address** Meneghyjy, Withifc, BODMIN, Cornwall, PL30 5NN
**Phone** 01208 831642
**Email** merv@pybyor.freeserve.co.uk
**Alt contact** Gerald Morris
**Address** Ponsmere Hotel, PERRANPORTH, Cornwall
**Phone** 01872 553413
*Celtic music & dance and associated traditions.*
**RAB** South West Arts

**19 to 21 October 2001**
## Gainsborough Folk Fest
**Location** Lincs
**Contact** Sue Dewsbury
**Mail address** 46 Middle Street, Corringham, GAINSBOROUGH, Lincs, DN21 5QS
**Phone** 01427 838726
**Email** mandsd@yahoo.com
**Web** www.angelfire.com/folk/gainsboroughfolk
*General folk festival. Venues include medieval manor house, arts centre, real ale pub and the market place.*
**RAB** East Midlands Arts

**19 to 21 October 2001**
## Musicport World & Acoustic Music Festival
**Location** Whitby, N. Yorks
**Contact** Jim McLaughlin
**Mail address** 4 Park Terrace, WHITBY, N Yorks, YO21 1PN
**Phone** 01947 603475
**Email** musicport@email.com
*Please note: date changed from original announcement.*
**RAB** Yorkshire Arts

**19 to 28 October 2001**
**18 to 27 October 2002**
## Captain Cook Maritime Festival
**Location** N. Yorks
**Contact** Richard Grainger
**Mail address** 23 Derwent Street, Norton, STOCKTON ON TEES, TS20 2BZ
**Fax** 01642 861899
**Phone/Fax** 07970 228534
**Email** cookseafest@onyxnet.co.uk
**Web** www.richardgrainger.co.uk
*Maritime, folk & world music & dance. Artist submissions by post please.*
**RAB** Yorkshire Arts

**20 October 2001**
## Day Of Dance
**Location** Saltaire, W. Yorks
**Contact** Louise Eaton
**Mail address** 43 Tower Road, SHIPLEY, W Yorks, BD18 4BP
**Fax** 01274 775161
**Email** alex-louise@43tr.fsnet.co.uk
*Day of dance events, fundraising for Oxfam & Yorkshire CND.*
**RAB** Yorkshire Arts

**20 October 2001**
## Hastings Borough Bonfire Society
**Location** E. Sussex
**Contact** Keith Leech
**Mail address** 205 Priory Road, HASTINGS, E Sussex, TN34 3JB
**Phone** 01424 716576
**Email** chiefbogie@hotmail.com
*Sussex tradition with costumed torchlit procession (1066 torches), enormous bonfire and flaming effigies. Massive firework display.*
**RAB** South East Arts

**20 October 2001**
## PregoFest
**Location** Matlock Bath, Derbys
**Contact** Ian Smith - Programme Director
**Mail address** 1 Holme Road, MATLOCK BATH, Derbyshire, DE4 3NU
**Phone** 01629 57082
07976 206568
**Email** pregosmith@hotmail.com
**Web** www.pregomusic.co.uk
**Alt contact** Peter Gray - Admin
**Address** 39 Ardsley Road, CHESTERFIELD, Derbys
*Eclectic roots dance-based one day festival. Workshops, concert and dance.*
**RAB** East Midlands Arts

**20 to 21 October 2001**
## Fiddles At Witney
**Location** Oxon
**Contact** Hands on Music Weekends
**Mail address** PO Box 1162, EAST OXFORD DO, OX4 4WS
**Phone** 01865 714778
07798 520552
**Fax** 01865 749428
**Email** homweekend@aol.com
*Weekend of fiddle workshops, sessions & concerts.*
**RAB** Southern Arts

**20 to 30 October 2001**
**21 October to 1 November 2002**
## Big Big World
**Location** Glasgow
**Contact** Billy Kelly
**Mail address** 101 Ballantrae Cres, GLASGOW, G11 5TX, Scotland
**Phone** 0141 2210359
**Fax** 0141 2218609
**Email** billykelly@soundsfine.co.uk
*International festival of world music, various venues throughout Glasgow.*
**AC** Scotland

**22 to 26 October 2001**
**26 to 28 October 2002**
## Baring-Gould Folk Festival & Study Break
**Location** Okehampton, Devon
**Contact** Chris Foster
**Mail address** The Wren Trust, 1 St James Street, OKEHAMPTON, Devon, EX20 1DW
**Phone** 01837 53754
**Fax** 01837 55924
**Email** sbg@wrentrust.co.uk
**Web** www.wrentrust.co.uk
**Email** wrentrust@eclipse.co.uk
*5 day study break and weekend festival,based on traditional song and songs growing from tradition.*
**RAB** South West Arts

**26 to 28 October 2001**
## Folkworks Workout Weekend
**Location** Darlington
**Contact** Pam Hobson
**Mail address** Folkworks, 69 Westgate Road, NEWCASTLE-UPON-TYNE, NE1 1SG
**Phone** 0191 222 1717
**Fax** 0191 230 2484
**Email** folkworks@folkworks.co.uk
**Web** www.folkworks.co.uk
*Workshops in a variety of instruments and song plus ensemble playing for beginners and experienced players. Age 16 upwards.*
**RAB** Northern Arts

**26 to 28 October 2001**
**25 to 27 October 2002**
## Lancaster Clocks Back Festival
**Contact** Clocksback
**Mail address** 27 Regent Street, LANCASTER, LA1 1SQ
**Phone** 01524 847135
**Email** ben@farmerboymusic.fsnet.co.uk
**Web** www.beulah.demon.co.uk/clocksback.html
*Festival of music, dance and song from Europe, Ireland and the UK. Includes sessions and workshops.*
**RAB** North West Arts

**26 October to 4 November 2001**
## Return To Camden Town Festival
**Location** London
**Contact** Karen Ryan
**Mail address** 48 Louise White House, Pilgrims Way, LONDON, N19 3LU
**Phone** 020 7281 8837
07771 782384
**Email** k.ryan@virgin.net
**Alt contact** Geoff Holland
**Address** 85C Carlton Road, LONDON, N7 0EZ
**Phone** 020 7607 8396
**Email** contactgeoff@hotmail.com
*Ten day festival of Irish traditional music, song and dance. Please contact by email.*
**RAB** London Arts

**26 October to 4 November 2001**
## Scottish International Storytelling Festival
**Location** Edinburgh & Lothians
**Contact** Joanna Bremner
**Mail address** The Netherbow, 43-45 High Street, EDINBURGH, EH1 1SR, Scotland
**Phone** 0131 557 5724
**Fax** 0131 557 5224
**Web** www.storytellingcentre.org.uk
**AC** Scotland

**26 October 2001 to 11 November 2001**
## Belfast Festival at Queen's
**Contact** Margaret McKee
**Mail address** 25 College Gardens, BELFAST, BT9 6BS, Northern Ireland
**Phone** 028 9066 7687
**Fax** 028 9066 3733
**Email** festival@qub.ac.uk
**AC** Northern Ireland

**29 October to 4 November 2001**
## Folk In The Fall
**Location** London
**Contact** Steve Heap
**Mail address** PO Box 296, AYLESBURY, Bucks, HP19 9TL
**Phone** 01296 394411
**Fax** 01296 392300
**Email** sbank@mrscasey.co.uk
**Web** www.mrscasey.co.uk/sbank
*Packed autumn concert and free event series celebrating the rich diversity of folk and roots music.*
**RAB** London Arts

**2 to 4 November 2001**
**1 to 3 November 2002**
## The Flanders Experience
**Contact** Bob Hambleton
**Mail address** 17 Juniper Avenue, BRICKET WOOD, Herts, AL2 3LR
**Phone** 01923 672590
**Fax** 01923 404310 (phone first)
**Email** flanders@kestrel-folk.demon.co.uk
*Weekend event, taking folk enthusiasts over to WW1 battlefields, cemeteries, memorials and museums.*
**RAB** East England Arts

**2 to 4 November 2001**
## Folk South West's West Country Christmas Carols Workout
**Location** Glos
**Contact** Eddie Upton
**Mail address** Folk South West, The Stables, Montacute House, MONTACUTE, Somerset, TA15 6XP
**Phone** 01935 822911
**Fax** 01935 822024
**Email** folksw@folksw.org.uk
**RAB** South West Arts

**2 to 4 November 2001**
## Temple Harp Weekend
**Location** Midlothian, Scotland
**Contact** Temple Records
**Mail address** Shillinghill, TEMPLE, Midlothian, EH23 4SH, Scotland
**Phone** 01875 830328
**Fax** 01875 830392
**Email** robin@templerecords.co.uk
**Web** www.templerecords.co.uk
*Tuition in traditional Scottish harp music with Alison Kinnaird & Christine Primrose.*
**AC** Scotland

**16 to 18 November 2001**
## Raise Your Banners
**Location** Sheffield
**Mail address** 100 Leader Road, SHEFFIELD, S6 4GH
**Fax** 0114 233 0525
**Email** nigel@ryb.org.uk
**Web** www.ryb.org.uk
**Address** PO Box 44, SHEFFIELD S4 7RN
**Phone** 0114 249 5185
**Email** info@ryb.org.uk
*Biennial festival of political song.*
**RAB** Yorkshire Arts



***The festivals listed here appear alphabetically within date order beginning at 1st June 2001 through to 30th June 2002. Some 2002 dates are yet to be confirmed.***

*The festivals listed here appear alphabetically within date order beginning at 1st June 2001 through to 30th June 2002. Some 2002 dates are yet to be confirmed.*

**17 to 18 November 2001**
### Melodeons At Witney
**Location** Oxon
**Contact** Hands on Music Weekends
**Mail address** PO Box 1162, EAST OXFORD DO, OX4 4WS
**Phone** 01865 714778
07798 520552
**Fax** 01865 749428
**Email** homweekend@aol.com
*Weekend of melodeon workshops, sessions & concerts.*
**RAB** Southern Arts

**23 to 25 November 2001**
**22 to 24 November 2002**
### Fiddle 2001
**Location** Edinburgh
**Contact** Adult Learning Project (ALP)
**Mail address** 184 Dalry Road, EDINBURGH, EH11 2EP, Scotland
**Phone** 0131 3375442
0131 3460977
**Fax** 0131 3379316
**Email** scots-fiddle@lineone.net
**Web** www.musicscotland.com/fiddle2000
*Concerts, masterclasses, sessions, workshops, talks, stalls, etc*
**AC** Scotland

**24 to 26 November 2001**
### Bedworth Folk Festival
**Location** Warwicks
**Contact** Malc Gurnham
**Mail address** 22 Juliet Close, NUNEATON, Warks, CV11 6NS
**Phone** 024 7634 5568
**Email** festival@folkfax.net
**Web** www.folkfax.net/folkday
*3 day festival run in conjunction with Nuneaton & Bedworth Borough Council.*
**RAB** West Midlands Arts

**1 December 2001**
**6 December 2002**
### Haddenham Festival & Craft Fayre
**Location** Bucks
**Contact** John Heydon
**Mail address** 3/5 Church Street, AYLESBURY, Bucks, HP20 2QP
**Phone** 01296 415333
**Fax** 01296 397092
**Email** johnh@fosterwiggins.co.uk
**Web** www.haddenhamceilidhs.co.uk
**Venue** Haddenham Village Hall, Haddenham, AYLESBURY, Bucks
*One day festival and craft fair.*
**RAB** Southern Arts

**24 December 2001**
### Carols in the Pub
**Location** Co. Durham
**Contact** Fred Brierley
**Mail address** The Wayfarer, HASWELL, Co Durham
**Phone** 0191 517 1274
*Books provided, just bring voices.*
**RAB** Northern Arts

**12 January 2002**
### The Jimmy McHugh Memorial Concert
**Location** Glasgow
**Contact** Benny McHugh
**Mail address** 89 Croptend Avenue, GLASGOW, G44 5PE, Scotland
**Phone** 0141 569 3557
0141 4180585
*Weekend of music, in memory of Benny's late father, Jimmy McHugh.*
**AC** Scotland

**12 January 2002**
**11 January 2003**
### Whittlesea Straw Bear
**Location** Cambs
**Contact** Brian Kell
**Mail address** 119 Eastrea Road, WHITTLESEY, Cambs, PE7 2AJ
**Phone** 01733 208245
**Email** strawbear@btinternet.com
**Web** www.strawbear.org.uk
*One day event with appearances from the Whittlesea Straw Bear, a procession and morris dancing.*
**RAB** East England Arts

**16 January to 3 Febuary 2002**
### Celtic Connections
**Location** Glasgow
**Contact** Ian Bone
**Mail address** Press Dept, Glasgow Royal Concert Hall, 2 Sauchiehall Street, GLASGOW, G2 3NY, Scotland
**Phone** 0141 332 6633
**Fax** 0141 333 9123
**Web** www.grch.com
*3 weeks celebration of Celtic music from all the Celtic nations. Concerts, community projects, recitals, talks, workshops, dances and the legendary/ infamous early morning festival club.*
**AC** Scotland

**18 to 27 January 2002**
### Winter Ale Festival & Do
**Location** Co. Durham
**Contact** Fred Brierley
**Mail address** The Wayfarer, HASWELL, Co Durham
**Phone** 0191 517 1274
*Cask beer festival with concerts & singaround. Free & open. Charities contact re fundraising.*
**RAB** Northern Arts

**26 to 28 January 2002**
### Norwich 01
**Mail address** Folk Norfolk, 200 Unthank Road, NORWICH, NR2 2AH
**Phone** 01603 443942
**Email** n1@vickhast.demon.co.uk
**Web** www.vickhast.demon.co.uk/n1home.htm
*Workshops, concerts and dances.*
**RAB** East England Arts

**2 to 3 Febuary 2002**
### Strings & Bows at Witney
**Location** Oxon
**Contact** Hands on Music Weekends
**Mail address** PO Box 1162, EAST OXFORD DO, OX4 4WS
**Phone** 01865 714778
07798 520552
**Fax** 01865 749428
**Email** homweekend@aol.com
*Workshops, sessions & concerts for fiddle, cello and bass.*
**RAB** Southern Arts

**8 to 10 Febuary 2002**
### Cheltenham Folk Festival
**Location** Glos
**Contact** Tim Hulse
**Mail address** Cheltenham Town Hall, Imperial Square, CHELTENHAM, Glos, GL50 1QA
**Phone** 01242 521621
**Fax** 01242 573902
**Email** timhu@cheltenham.gov.uk
**Web** www.cheltenhamfestivals.co.uk
**Alt contact** John Shorter
**Address** 6 Postlip Hill, Winchcombe, CHELTENHAM, GL54 5AQ
**Phone** 01242 603187
**Email** john@shorterj.freeseve.co.uk
*A winter weekend of traditional folk music, song and dance. Workshops, children's events, sessions, ceilidhs and concerts.*
**RAB** South West Arts

15 to 17 Febuary 2002
## Old Time Music & Dance Festival
**Location** Gainsborough, Lincs
**Contact** Keith Johnson
**Mail address** 15 Walkerith Road, Morton, GAINSBOROUGH, DN21 3DA
**Phone** 01427 613643
**Fax** 01427 677441
**Email** keith@pillard.co.uk
**Alt contact** Jim Allen
**Address** Sycamores, Bockleton, TENBURY WELLS, Worcs, WR15 8PU
**Phone** 01568 750546
*Organised by the Friends of Old Time Music & Dance, who also run a newsletter, summer camps and CDs.*
**RAB** East England Arts

16 to 17 Febuary 2002
## Accordions at Witney
**Location** Oxon
**Contact** Hands on Music Weekends
**Mail address** PO Box 1162, EAST OXFORD DO, OX4 4WS
**Phone** 01865 714778
07798 520552
**Fax** 01865 749428
**Email** homweekend@aol.com
*Accordion workshops, sessions & concerts.*
**RAB** Southern Arts

2 to 3 March 2002
## Winds at Witney
**Location** Oxon
**Contact** Hands on Music Weekends
**Mail address** PO Box 1162, EAST OXFORD DO, OX4 4WS
**Phone** 01865 714778
07798 520552
**Fax** 01865 749428
**Email** homweekend@aol.com
*Weekend of workshops, sessions & concerts for wind instruments.*
**RAB** Southern Arts

2 to 4 March 2002
## Inter Varsity Folk Dance Festival
**Location** St. Andrews (2002)
**Contact** Steven Brockbank
**Mail address** 3 2F3 Newton Street, EDINBURGH, Scotland
**Phone** 07713 756483
**Email** ivfdf200W@bigfoot.com
*Ceilidhs and dance workshops, different University town each year.*

8 to 10 March 2002
## Milnathort Cracin' Ceilidh Weekend
**Location** Kinross-shire, Scotland
**Contact** Andy Ramage
**Mail address** 2 Gwendoline Row, Drunzie, GLENFARG, Perthshire, PH2 9QU
**Phone** 01577 830435
**Email** ramageandy@aol.com
**Alt contact** Robin Watson
**Address** The Haven, Greenbank Road, GLENFARG, Perthshire, Scotland
**Phone** 01577 830355
**Email** robin@gaberlunzie.com
*Ceilidh dances, concerts, pub sessions, Orwell Giro Championship. Small intimate venues and real Scottish hospitality.*
**AC** Scotland

14 to 17 March 2002
## Spring Thing Festival
**Location** Darlington
**Contact** Tom Hughes
**Mail address** Darlington Arts Centre, 111d Vane Terrace, DARLINGON, Co Durham, DL3 7AX
**Phone** 01325 261179
01325 486555
**Fax** 01325 365794
*Concerts, ceilidhs, singarounds, dance teams, crafts, children's workshop. Family emphasis.*
**RAB** Northern Arts

14 to 16 September 2001
15 to 17 March 2002
## Exeter Weekend Of Irish Set Dancing
**Contact** John Earle
**Mail address** 20 Dunvegan Close, EXETER, Devon, EX4 4AF
**Phone** 01392 420219
07714 122009
**Email** john@set-dancing.org
**Web** www.set-dancing.org
**RAB** South West Arts

15 to 17 March 2002
## Folkbeat Derby
**Contact** Karen Tweed
**Mail address** PO Box 5009, DERBY, DE1 9FQ
**Phone** 01332 677046
**Fax** 01332 677047
**Email** karen@kstweed.co.uk
**Web** www.cutting-tweed.demon.co.uk
**Email** kstweed@yahoo.com
*Festival of interactive music, song & dance, mainly British/ Irish/ European/ Scandanavian. Concerts, workshops, dances. Education work is a large part of the festival.*
**RAB** East Midlands Arts

16 to 17 March 2002
## Welcome to Heaven
**Location** Oxon
**Contact** Hands on Music Weekends
**Mail address** PO Box 1162, EAST OXFORD DO, OX4 4WS
**Phone** 01865 714778
07798 520552
**Fax** 01865 749428
**Email** homweekend@aol.com
*Weekend of workshops, sessions & concerts for strummed, plucked & hammered strings.*
**RAB** Southern Arts

22 to 31 March 2002
## Gatehouse Of Fleet Festival
**Location** Dumfries and Galloway
**Contact** George McCulloch
**Mail address** 4 Carney's Corner, GATEHOUSE OF FLEET, Dumfries & Galloway, DG7 2HW, Scotland
**Phone/Fax** 01557 814030
**Email** george.mcculloch@virgin.net
**Web** www.ednet.co.uk/~russell/gatehouse.htm
**Email** festival@gatehouseoffleet.ndirect.co.uk
*Small family folk festival with traditional music, plus arts & crafts exhibitions. Various venues.*
**AC** Scotland

23 to 24 March 2002
## String Plucking Weekend
**Location** Co. Durham
**Contact** Fred Brierley
**Mail address** The Wayfarer, HASWELL, Co Durham
**Phone** 0191 517 1274
*Workshops, sessions & evening performances. Beginners & players welcome.*
**RAB** Northern Arts

24 to 25 March 2002 tbc
## Crediton Folk Weekend
**Location** Devon
**Contact** P Lister
**Mail address** 32 Mill Street, CREDITON, Devon, EX17 1EZ
**Phone** 01363 775695
**RAB** South West Arts



***The festivals listed here appear alphabetically within date order beginning at 1st June 2001 through to 30th June 2002. Some 2002 dates are yet to be confirmed.***

***The festivals listed here appear alphabetically within date order beginning at 1st June 2001 through to 30th June 2002. Some 2002 dates are yet to be confirmed.***

**25 to 6 March 2002**
## Oxford Storytelling and Music Festival
**Contact** Jon Bennett
**Mail address** 84 Sandfield Road, OXFORD, OX3 7RL
**Phone** 01865 769206
**Email** jon.bennett@dial.pipex.com
**Alt contact** Chris Smith
**Address** 15 Holley Crescent, OXFORD, OX3 8AW
**Phone** 01865 452862
*International festival for storytellers and roots musicians. No unrequested mailings please.*
**RAB** Southern Arts

**29 to 30 March 2002**
## Lancaster Clocks Forward Festival
**Contact** Clocksback
**Mail address** 27 Regent Street, LANCASTER, LA1 1SQ
**Phone** 01524 847135
**Email** ben@farmerboymusic.fsnet.co.uk
**Web** www.beulah.demon.co.uk/clocksback.html
*Festival of music, dance and song from Europe, Ireland and the UK. Includes sessions and workshops.*
**RAB** North West Arts

**29 March to 1 April 2002 tbc**
## Burnley National Blues Festival
**Location** Lancs
**Contact** Jacqui Livesey
**Mail address** Burnley Mechanics, Manchester Road, BURNLEY, Lancs, BB11 1JA
**Phone** 01282 664400
**Fax** 01282 664431
**Email** tmcevoy@burnley.gov.uk
**Web** www.bluesinburnley.co.uk
*10 stages, day & night concerts, food & drink, craft & music stalls, fringe events.*
**RAB** North West Arts

**29 March to 1 April 2002 tbc**
## Lancaster Easter Maritime Festival
**Contact** David Wright Lancaster
**Mail address** Tourism Services, 29 Castle Hill, LANCASTER, LA1 1YN
**Phone** 01524 582395
**Fax** 01524 847472
*Gathering of sea-song & shanty singers plus talks and related workshops/ events.*
**RAB** North West Arts

**29 March to 1 April 2002 tbc**
## Miskin At Easter
**Location** Llantrisant
**Contact** Andy Jackson
**Mail address** 52 Llantrisant Road, PONTYCLUN, CF72 9DQ, Wales
**Phone** 01443 223053
**Email** andy.jackson@tesco.net
**Web** www.homepages.tesco.net/Andy.jackson/miskinfolk
*Moved to November 2001. Normally at Easter.*
**AC** Wales

**29 March 2002 to 1 Apr tbc**
## Music in Argyll
**Contact** Lorna Dewar
**Fax** 01292 313205
*Weekend of folk music and outdoor activities.*
**AC** Scotland

**30 March 2002**
## The 2002 International Fig and Date Fayre
**Location** Chippenham
**Contact** The Fabulous Fezheads
**Email** fezheads@hotmail.com
**Web** www.fezheads.com
**Alt contact** The Landlord
*A day of exotic games featuring figs and dates followed by an evening with the Fabulous Fezheads.*
**RAB** South East Arts

**30 to 31 March 2002 tbc**
## Lincoln Folk Festival
**Contact** Andy Watkins - info
**Phone** 01522 569434
**Email** recreation@lincoln.gov.uk
**Alt contact** The Box Office - tickets Waterside Centre, LINCOLN
**Phone** 01522 523000 (box)
01522 529828 (tourist info)
*Concerts, dance displays, sessions, childrens events, workshops.*
**RAB** East Midlands Arts

**30 to 31 March 2002**
## Witney Harmony Weekend
**Location** Oxon
**Contact** Hands on Music Weekends
**Mail address** PO Box 1162, EAST OXFORD DO, OX4 4WS
**Phone** 01865 714778
07798 520552
**Fax** 01865 749428
**Email** homweekend@aol.com
*Weekend of vocal workshops & concerts.*
**RAB** Southern Arts

**30 March to 3 April 2002**
## Gosport & Fareham Easter Festival
**Location** Hants
**Contact** Peter Chegwyn
**Mail address** 51 Russell Street, GOSPORT, Hants, PO12 3JD
**Phone/Fax** 023 9252 8017
**Email** chegwyn@talk21.com
**Web** www.gosportfestival.com
**Phone** 01329 231942 (venue)
*Indoor folk festival, mainly top Celtic acts. Concerts, workshops and late night festival club.*
**RAB** Southern Arts

**1 April 2002**
## Conradski
**Location** Unst, Shetland
**Contact** Conrad Ivitsky
**Mail address** 23 St Leonards Bank, EDINBURGH, EH8 9SQ
**Phone** 0131 6674484
**Email** conradski@hotmail.com
**Web** www.conradski.com
*Event combining dance and music. Check website for details!*
**AC** Scotland

**1 to 5 April 2002**
## Sore Fingers Summer Schools
**Location** Oxon
**Contact** Andrea Gauden
**Mail address** 12 Waterford Road, Ashley, NEW MILTON, Hants, BH25 5BH
**Phone** 01425 618286
01676 813590
**Fax** 01425 280905
**Email** Andrea@sorefingers.co.uk
**Web** www.sorefingers.co.uk
**Alt contact** John Wirtz
**Address** Park Farm, Buckland Down, NR FROME, Somerset, BA11 2RG
**Phone** 01373 813590
**Email** john@sorefingers.co.uk
*5 day Easter school in the Cotswolds. Bluegrass & Old Time music, with top American and English tutors.*
**RAB** Southern Arts

**5 to 10 Apr tbc**
## Edinburgh Harp Festival
**Contact** David G Mieras
**Mail address** 87 Swanston Avenue, EDINBURGH, EH10 7DA, Scotland
**Fax** 0131 445 2022
**Email** administrator@harpfestival.co.uk
**Web** www.harpfestival.co.uk
*Annual harp festival.Concerts, classes, workshops, ceilidhs, covering many forms & styles of harping, with focus on the clarsach.*
**AC** Scotland

**6 April 2002 tbc**
## Mansfield Beer & Cider Festival
**Location** Notts
**Contact** David Eyre
**Mail address** 10 Lindhurst Lane, MANSFIELD, Notts, NG18 4SE
**Phone** 01623 468980
**Email** jeyre51649@aol.com
**RAB** East Midlands Arts

**9 to 13 April 2002 tbc**
## Rootin' Aboot
**Location** Aberdeen
**Contact** Shona Powell
**Mail address** The LemonTree, 5 West North Street, ABERDEEN, AB24 5AT, Scotland
**Phone** 01224 647999 - admin
01224 642230 - box
**Email** shona@lemontree.org
**Web** www.lemontree.org
*Workshops, free luncntime concerts, children/ family events, evening concerts and club (chill room/ dance scene). Wide range of music genres.*
**AC** Scotland

**12 to 14 April 2002 tbc**
## Glenfarg Folk Feast
**Location** Perthshire
**Contact** Graham Brotherston - Info
**Mail address** 9 Fairways, DUNFERMLINE, Fife, KY12 0DU
**Phone** 01383 738 922 - info
07884 000840
**Email** graham@aqcgb.freeserve.co.uk
**Web** www.glenfargvillagefolkclub.freeserve.co.uk
**Alt contact** Bill Gillan - Tickets
**Address** 6 Old Town, GATESIDE, Fife, KY14 5SY
**Phone** 01337 860577 (tickets), 07971 179252
**Email** bill.gillan@virgin.net
*Traditional based folk festival.*
**AC** Scotland

**12 to 14 April 2002 tbc**
## Morpeth Northumbrian Gathering
**Contact** Kim Bibby-Wilson
**Mail address** Westgate House, Dogger Bank, MORPETH, Northumberland, NE61 1RF
**Phone** 01670 513308
**Web** www.northumbriana.org.uk
*Concerts, competitions, etc.*
**RAB** Northern Arts

**12 to 14 April 2002**
## National Folk Music Festival
**Location** Sutton Bornington, Leics
**Contact** John Heydon
**Mail address** 3/4 Church Street, AYLESBURY, Bucks, HP20 2QP
**Phone** 01296 415333
**Fax** 01296 397092
**Email** johnh@fosterwiggins.co.uk
*Festival of traditional song, music and dance with an emphasis on straight traditional song and music.*
**RAB** East Midlands Arts Board

**20 April 2002 tbc**
## Woodworks
**Location** Bishop's Stortford, Herts
**Contact** Jon & Elaine Dean
**Mail address** 18 Colney Green, SAWBRIDGEWORTH, Herts, CM21 0DA
**Phone** 01279 722326
**Fax** 01279 833484
**Email** info@woodworks-music.co.uk
**Web** www.woodworks-music.co.uk
*Annual event with music/ song/ dance workshops and concert.*
**RAB** East England Arts

**20 to 28 April 2002 tbc**
## Nailsworth Festival
**Location** Glos
**Contact** Sue Reed
**Mail address** Sesame House, Watledge, NAILSWORTH, Glos, GL6 0AU
**Phone** 01453 833472
**Email** sue_reed@hotmail.com
**RAB** South West Arts

**25 to 28 April 2002 tbc**
## Shetland Folk Festival
**Contact** Maria Strachan
**Mail address** 5 Burns Lane, LERWICK, Shetland, ZE1 CEL, Scotland
**Phone** 01595 694757
**Fax** 01595 695381
**Email** info@sffs.shetland.co.uk
**Web** www.users.zetnet.co.uk/sffs/
**AC** Scotland

**27 April 2002 tbc**
## Sturminster Newton Traditional Music Day
**Location** Devon
**Contact** Mike Preston
**Mail address** Waterloo Cottage, The Row, STURMINSTER NEWTON, Dorset, DT10 1AU
**Phone/Fax** 01258 471368
**Fax** 0831 279290
**Email** mike@stur1.demon.co.uk
*One day festival of traditional music.*
**RAB** South West Arts

**1st May 2002**
## Fowler's Troop Jack in the Green
**Contact** Sarah Crofts
**Mail address** 7 Northbrook Road, Lewisham, LONDON, SE13 5QT
**Phone** 020 8331 9153 - day
020 8852 6618 - eve
**Email** s.j.crofts@gre.ac.uk
**Web** www.gre.ac.uk/~cs02/index.htm
*May day (1st of May) tour of London with the Deptford Jack in the Green. Ring near the event for times. Musicians Union member*
**RAB** London Arts

**1 May 2002**
## Jack In The Green Awakening
**Location** Bluebell Hill, Kent
**Contact** Gordon Newton
**Mail address** 24 Kings Acre, Otham, MAIDSTONE, Kent, ME15 8UP
**Phone** 01622 721077
**Fax** 01622 720066
**RAB** South East Arts

**1 May 2002**
## King's Lynn May Garland Procession
**Location** Norfolk
**Contact** David Jackson
**Mail address** 9 Edward Street, KINGS LYNN, Norfolk, PE30 5QS
**Phone** 01553 768930
**Web** www.users@waitrose.com/~thekingsmorris
**Alt contact** Ian Heighton
**Email** thekingsmorris@waitrose.com
*Traditional May Day (1st) event. Floral garland is carried through the town, accompanied by blowing ox-horns. Presented by The King's Morris.*
**RAB** East England Arts

**1 to 6 May 2002 tbc**
## Cheltenham International Jazz Festival
**Location** Glos
**Contact** Jim Smith - Director
**Mail address** Performance Related, 6/11 The Mews, MITCHELDEAN, Glos, GL17 0SL
**Phone** 01594 544446
01242 227979
**Fax** 01594 544448
**Email** jim@festival.org,uk
**Web** www.cheltenhamfestivals.co.uk
**Venue** Cheltenham Town Hall, Imperial Square, CHELTENHAM, Glos, GL17 0SL
**Phone** 01242 521621
**Fax** 01242 573902
*Week of jazz - various genres.*
**RAB** South West Arts



***The festivals listed here appear alphabetically within date order beginning at 1st June 2001 through to 30th June 2002. Some 2002 dates are yet to be confirmed.***

***The festivals listed here appear alphabetically within date order beginning at 1st June 2001 through to 30th June 2002. Some 2002 dates are yet to be confirmed.***

**3 to 5 May 2002 tbc**
### Girvan Traditional Folk Festival
**Location** Scotland
**Contact** Robert Jardine - tickets/ accomodation
**Mail address** Westcliffe Hotel, Louisa Drive, GIRVAN, KA26 9AH, Scotland
**Phone** 01465 712128
**Email** seaayr@ntlworld.com
**Web** www.welcome.to/girvan
**Alt contact** Maggie Macrae- info
**Phone** 01560 321102
*Traditional family oriented festival. Concerts, ceilidhs, workshops, competitions, children's events, sessions, etc.*
**AC** Scotland

**3 to 5 May 2002 tbc**
### Moor & Coast Festival of Traditional Music, Song, Dance & Arts
**Location** Whitby, N.Yorks
**Contact** Glen Rogers
**Mail address** 9 Windsor Terrace, WHITBY, N Yorks, YO21 1ET
**Phone/Fax** 01947 820408
**Fax** 01947 821873
**Email** moorcoast@yahoo.com
**Web** www.moorandcoast.co.uk
*May Bank Holiday festival. Concerts, ceilidhs, workshops, singarounds, sessions, campsite, craft fair, ghost walks, real ale, etc.*
**RAB** Yorkshire Arts

**3 to 6 May 2002**
### Eastbourne International Folk Festival
**Location** E. Sussex
**Contact** Julian Burton
**Mail address** 180 Willingdon Road, EASTBOURNE, E Sussex, BN21 1TT
**Phone** 01323 641501
07976 572417
**Fax** 07092 252139
**Email** julian@eiff.org.uk
**Web** www.eiff.org.uk
**Alt contact** EIFF Bookings
**Address** Hurstpierpoint College, HASSOCKS, W Sussex, BN6 9JS
**Phone** 01273 835759
**Email** info@eiff.org.uk
*English, American and International Folk Dance festival. Venues local schools, within easy walking distance.*
**RAB** South East Arts

**3 to 6 May 2002**
### Manchester x.trax street festival
**Contact** Anne Tucker
**Mail address** 3 Birch Polygon, MANCHESTER, M14 5HX
**Phone** 0161 224 0020
**Fax** 0161 248 9331
**Email** mia@streetsahead.org.uk
**Web** www.streetsahead.org.uk
*Large, free street festival. Over 100 performers across the city centre. Street music, world music, street theatre, dance, circus, puppets, parades, visual installations, fireworks. See also x.trax (festival)*
**RAB** North West Arts

**3 to 6 May 2002 tbc**
### Scandanavian Festival
**Location** Settle, N. Yorks
**Contact** Yorkshire Dales Workshops
**Mail address** 14 Oakburn Road, ILKLEY, Yorks, LS29 9NN
**Phone/Fax** 01943 609421
**Fax** 07760 287384
**Email** ydw@ydw.btinternet.co.uk
**Web** www.ydw.btinternet.co.uk
*Fiddle & dance workshops, concert and sessions.*

**3 to 6 May 2002 tbc**
### The Teesdale Thrash
**Location** Co. Durham
**Contact** Roy Tranter
**Mail address** 49 Victoria Road, BARNARD CASTLE, Co Durham, DL12 8HR
**Phone** 01833 638288
*Ceilidh & concert.*
**RAB** Northern Arts

**3 to 6 May 2002**
### Wath Festival
**Location** Sth. Yorkshire
**Contact** Ruth Wells
**Phone** 01709 878361
**Email** ragwells@dialstart.net
**Web** http://freespace.virgin.net/wath.folk
**RAB** Yorkshire Arts

**3 to 6 May 2002**
### x.trax
**Location** Manchester
**Contact** Maggie Clarke
**Mail address** The Green Room, 54-56 Whitworth Street, MANCHESTER, M1 5WW
**Phone** 0161 2887273
**Fax** 0161 2885243
**Email** maggie@xtrax.org.uk
**Web** www.xtrax.org.uk
*International cross artform performance including diverse music programme on the streets and in music venues on the city. Also see Manchester x-trax street festival.*
**RAB** North West Arts

**4 May 2002 tbc**
### Cream of the Craic Storytelling Festival
**Location** Norfolk
**Contact** Magda Russell
**Mail address** 179 Dereham Road, NORWICH, Norfolk, NR2 3TB
**Phone** 01603 613177
**Email** magdaruss@aol.com
**RAB** East England Arts

**4 to 6 May 2002**
### The Border Gaitherin
**Location** Coldstream, Borders
**Contact** Liz Marroni
**Mail address** 15 Inch Park, KELSO, Scottish Borders, TD5 7EQ, Scotland
**Phone** 01573 224920
**Email** lizmarroni@argonet.co.uk
**Web** www.bordergaitherin.music scotland.com
*Celebrates the traditional music of the Borders of Scotland through tuition, recitals, concerts, ceilidhs, demonstrations, lectures and sessions. Emphasis on young singers/ players.*
**AC** Scotland

**4 to 6 May 2002 tbc**
### Feis Rois Inbhich
**Location** Ross-shire
**Contact** Rita Hunter
**Mail address** Feis Rois Ltd, Highland Council Offices, DINGWALL, Ross-shire, IV15 9QN, Scotland
**Phone** 01349 862600
**Email** rita@feisrois.freeserve.co.uk
*Adult feis rois. Tuition festival.*
**AC** Scotland

**4 to 6 May 2002**
### Hastings Traditional Jack In The Green
**Location** E. Sussex
**Contact** Keith Leech
**Mail address** 205 Priory Road, HASTINGS, E Sussex, TN34 3JB
**Phone** 01424 716576
**Email** jitg@talk21.com
**Web** www.jack-in-the-green.com
**Alt contact** Fee Lock
**Address** 28 Fairstone Close, HASTINGS, E Sussex, TN3 5EZ
**Email** Feelock@hotmail.com
*May celebration. Morris festival with ceilidhs and concerts, May Day procession and release of the Jack in the Green.*
**RAB** South East Arts

## uk festivals

may 2002

***The festivals listed here appear alphabetically within date order beginning at 1st June 2001 through to 30th June 2002. Some 2002 dates are yet to be confirmed.***

**4 to 6 May 2002**
### May Day Weekend with the Wayfarer Folk Club
**Location** Co. Durham
**Contact** Fred Brierley
**Phone** 0191 517 1274
*Afternoon workshops, session & concert. Free & open.*
**RAB** Northern Arts

**4 to 6 May 2002**
### Rochester Sweeps Festival
**Location** Kent
**Contact** Doug Hudson
**Mail address** 182 Windmill Road, GILLINGHAM, Kent, ME7 5PE
**Phone/Fax** 01634 574837
**Fax** 07941 238377
**Email** doug.hudson@lineone.net
**Alt contact** Events Office Medway Council, Civic Centre, STROOD, Kent, ME2 2AB
**Phone** 01634 332064
**Email** suejaycock@medway.gov.uk
*Big Morris Dance festival, incorporating amusic programme in the high street pubs.*
**RAB** South East Arts

**5 to 6 May 2002 tbc**
### Mayfest
**Location** Sheffield
**Contact** Martin Jones
**Mail address** Kelham Island Industrial Museum, Alma Street, SHEFFIELD, S3 8RY
**Phone** 0114 2722106
**Fax** 0114 2757847
**Email** postmaster@simt.co.uk
*Music, dance, song and Jack in The Green.*
**RAB** Yorkshire Arts

**6 May 2002**
### Chesterfield TUC May Day Festival
**Location** Derbyshire
**Contact** Ian Smith - Programmer
**Mail address** 1 Holme Road, MATLOCK BATH, Derbys, DE4 3NU
**Phone** 07976 206568
01629 57082
**Email** pregosmith@hotmail.com
*TUC rally and free, open air music/ street event.Dance/ roots orientated bands (no solo/ duo).*
**RAB** East Midlands Arts

**10 to 12 May 2002 tbc**
### Edward Bunting International Irish Harp & Traditional Singing Festival
**Location** Armagh, N. Ireland
**Contact** Patricia Daly
**Phone** 048 3755 1087
**Email** patricia@armaghharpers.freeserve.co.uk
**AC** Northern Ireland

**10 to 12 May 2002 tbc**
### Folk On The Pier
**Location** Cromer, Norfolk
**Contact** Scott Butler
**Mail address** Pavilion Theatre, CROMER, Norfolk, NR27 9HE
**Phone** 01263 579715
01263 512495 - box office
**Fax** 01263 515113- box office
**Email** media@north-norfolk.gov.uk
**Web** www.north-norfolk.gov.uk/leisure/folkonthepier
*Concerts, bops, ceilidhs, free events and workshops, real ale and club marquee.*
**RAB** East England Arts

**10 to 12 May 2002**
### Fox & Hounds Weekend of Song
**Location** Devon
**Contact** Jon Heslop & Kathy Wallis
**Mail address** 3 Durbar Villas, Station Road, Kelly Bray, CALLINGTON, Cornwall, PL17 8ES
**Phone** 01579 383794
**Email** redherring@unisonfree.net
*Relaxed weekend of singing in pub on edge of Dartmoor. Very friendly landlord, camping, caravanning & bunkhouse. Book with the pub.*
**RAB** South West Arts

**10 to 12 May 2002**
### Holmfirth Folk Festival
**Location** W. Yorks
**Contact** Linda Rice - Tickets & info 114 Dunford Road, HOLMFIRTH, West Yorks
**Phone** 01484 686792
**Email** linda@riceholm.demon.co.uk
**Web** www.riceholm.demon.co.uk
**Alt contact** Kate Atkinson - Artists & press
**Address** 70 Station Road, Shepley, HUDDERSFIELD, W Yorks, HD8 8DU
**Phone** 01484 605059
*Weekend of concerts, ceilidhs, workshops, street entertainment, crafts. International, traditional and new folk acts.*
**RAB** Yorkshire Arts

**10 to 12 May 2002 tbc**
### St Neots Folk Festival
**Location** Cambs
**Contact** Roger Pitt
**Mail address** The Mill House, Bolnhurst, BEDFORD, Beds, MK44 2ER
**Phone** 01234 376278
**Email** stneotsfolkclub@aol.com
**Web** www.users.zetnet.co.uk/rjames/festival.htm
**RAB** East England Arts

**10 to 12 May 2002 tbc**
### Strathspey In May
**Location** Scotland
**Contact** John Jackson
**Mail address** Canisp, Rhuarden Court, GRANTOWN ON SPEY, Scotland
**Phone** 01479 872546
**Email** john@bothybodhrans.com
*Sessions, recitals, ceilidh, workshops.*
**AC** Scotland

**10 to 12 May 2002**
### Tredegar House Dance Festival
**Location** Newport, wales
**Contact** Steve Lion
**Phone** 01633 612261
**Fax** 01633 601206
**Email** lion@celtic.co.uk
*Concerts & ceilidhs, workshops, storytelling, crafts with International & local dance artists.*
**AC** Wales

**10 to 26 May 2002**
### Bury St Edmunds Festival
**Location** Suffolk
**Contact** Nick Wells
**Mail address** Borough Office, Angel Hill, BURY ST EDMUNDS, Suffolk, IP33 1XB
**Phone** 01284 757630
**Fax** 01284 757931
**Email** nick.wells@stedsbc.gov.uk
**Web** www.stedmundsbury.gov.uk/buryfest
*17 day all Arts festival including music, comedy, theatre, dance, exhibitions and more.*
**RAB** East England Arts

**13 to 18 May 2002 tbc**
### A Little Festival
**Location** Penzance, Cornwall
**Contact** Martin Val Baker
**Mail address** Rainyday Gallery, 36 Market Jew Street, PENZANCE, Cornwall
**Phone** 01736 366077
**RAB** South West Arts

**17 to 18 May 2002 tbc**
### Brigg Fiddle Fest
**Location** Lincs
**Contact** Russell Coggle
**Phone** 01507 603049
**Alt contact** Sue Garner
**Phone** 01472 590102
*Weekend celebration of traditional fiddle music.*
**RAB** East Midlands Arts

*The festivals listed here appear alphabetically within date order beginning at 1st June 2001 through to 30th June 2002. Some 2002 dates are yet to be confirmed.*

**17 to 19 May 2002 tbc**
## Bushey's Big Wheel Blues Festival
**Location** Isle of Man
**Contact** Dave Wade
**Mail address** Bridle Cottage, Packhorse Lane, Baldrine, LONAN, Isle of Man, IM4 6EB
**Phone** 01624 861625
**Email** bridleco@hotmail.com
**Web** www.bluesit.com

**17 to 19 May 2002**
## Ceilidh Gall Gallowa
**Location** Dumfries and Galloway
**Contact** Liz Holmes
**Mail address** Knockengorroch Farm, CARSPHAIRN, Kirkcudbrightshire, DG7 3TJ, Scotland
**Phone/Fax** 01644 460662
**Email** goduha@ecosse.net
*Open air Celtic music festivalset in the Galloway uplands. Promotes traditional/ roots music and rural regeneration. Concerts, workshops, artworks and demonstrations.*
**AC** Scotland

**17 to 19 May 2002 tbc**
## Lancashire Folk & Clog Festival
**Contact** Cathy Tattersall
**Mail address** Accrington Info Centre, Town Hall, Blackburn Rd, ACCRINGTON, Lancs, BB5 1LA
**Phone** 01254 872595
01254 380293
**RAB** North West Arts

**17 to 19 May 2002**
## Moulton Village Festival
**Location** Northants
**Contact** Barry Care
**Mail address** Rooty Hill Cottage, 8 Chater Street, MOULTON, Northants, NN3 7UD
**Phone** 01604 646818
**Fax** 01604 493260
**Email** barrycare@lineone.net
*Small friendly festival held in a village setting. Folk song & dance plus traditional May Queen procession.*
**RAB** East Midlands Arts

**17 to 19 May 2002 tbc**
## Wheaton Aston Festival
**Location** Staffs
**Contact** Hilary Holton 10 Long Street, WHEATON ASTON, Staffs, ST19 9NF
**Phone** 01785 840010
**Email** wheatonastonfestival@supanet.com
**Web** www.wheatonastonfestival.supanet.com
*Broad based music, song and dance. Policy to encourage young talent besides nuturing established acts.*
**RAB** West Midlands Arts

**17 to 19 May 2002**
## Winchester Folk Festival
**Location** Hants
**Email** information@winchfolk.org.uk
**Web** www.winchfolk.org.uk
*Traditional folk dance, music & song. Dancing in the streets of Winchester and in the great hall. Concerts in pubs, churches, community halls, etc.*
**RAB** Southern Arts

**18 May 2002 tbc**
## Bletchingley Folk Festival
**Location** Surrey
**Contact** Les Vince
**Mail address** 81 Court Avenue, OLD COULSDON, Surrey, CR5 1HJ
**Phone** 01737 557497
**RAB** South East Arts

**18 to 19 May 2002**
## Fiddles At Fowey
**Location** Cornwall
**Contact** Mike O'Connor
**Mail address** Lyngham House, St Ervan, WADEBRIDGE, Cornwall, PL27 7RT
**Phone** 01841 540042
**Email** mikeoconnor@ndirect.co.uk
**Web** www.ndirect.co.uk/~mikeoconnor
**Alt contact** Chris Bartram
**Alt address** Gramway House, 3 Colharbour, Uffculme, Cullompton, Devon
**Phone** 01884 841499
*Instructional weekend for fiddle players focusing on music of Cornwall & the West of England with Mike O'Connor & Chris Bartram.*
**RAB** South West Arts

**23 to 26 May 2002 tbc**
## Orkney Folk Festival
**Contact** Johnny Mowat
**Mail address** Folk Festival Office, Town House Annexe, Victoria Street, STROMNESS, Orkney, KW16 5AA, Scotland
**Phone** 01856 851331
**Fax** 01856 851636
**Email** orkneyfolkfestival@btinternet.com
**Web** www.orkney.com/folkfestival
*Traditional music based festival based around Stromness with events in rural areas and smaller islands.*
**AC** Scotland

**24 to 9 May 2002 tbc**
## Bath Fringe Festival
**Contact** Bath Fringe Ltd
c/o 103 Walcot Street, BATH, Somerset, BA1 5BW
**Phone/Fax** 01225 480079
**Email** admin@bathfringe.co.uk
**Web** www.bathfringe.co.uk
*17 day festival including British and World Roots concerts, free gigs, etc.*
**RAB** South West Arts

**24 to 26 May 2002 tbc**
## Bluegrass & Old Time Music Festival
**Location** Devon
**Contact** Phil
**Phone** 01364 652725
**RAB** South West Arts

**24 to 26 May 2002 tbc**
## Gwyl Werin Abergwaun Fishguard Folk Festival
**Phone** 01348 872514
**Email** meddyg@stdavids.co.uk
**AC** Wales

**24 to 26 May 2002 tbc**
## The Hexham Gathering - Folkworks Youth Folk Festival
**Location** Northumberland
**Contact** Sharon Durant
**Mail address** Folkworks, 69 Westgate Raod, NEWCASTLE UPON TYNE, Tyne & Wear, NE1 1SG
**Phone** 0191 222 1717
**Fax** 0191 230 2484
**Email** sharon.durant@folkworks.co.uk
**Web** www.folkworks.co.uk
*Festival aimed primarily at young people with performance opportunities for singers, dancers and musicians (solo to band) plus concerts, sessions, ceilidhs.*
**RAB** Northern Arts

**24 to 26 May 2002 tbc**

## Isle Of Wight Folk Weekend

**Contact** Vic King
**Mail address** Palmers Forge, Newport Road, Niton, VENTNOR, Isle of Wight, PO38 2DB
**Phone** 01983 730930
**Email** vic-k@iowrock.net
**RAB** Southern Arts

**24 to 26 May 2002 tbc**

## Kirkmichael International Guitar Festival

**Location** Ayrshire
**Mail address** PO Box 8403, MAYBOLE, Ayrshire, KA19 7YB, Scotland
**Phone** 01292 61122
**Email** les.hannah@ntlworld.com
**AC** Scotland

**24 to 26 May 2002 tbc**

## Port William Folk Festival

**Location** Galloway, Scotland
**Contact** George Butterworth
**Phone** 01988 500771
**AC** Scotland

**24 to 27 May 2002 tbc**

## Chard Festival Of Women In Music

**Location** Somerset
**Mail address** 3 Howards Row, CHARD, Somerset, TA20 1PH
**Phone** 01460 66115
**Fax** 01460 66048
**Email** chardfest@cs.com
**Web** ourworld.cs.com/chardfest

*Promotes music written/ created by women, for everyone. Plus concerts, workshops and day of song.*

**RAB** South West Arts

**to 27 May 2002 tbc**

## Chester Folk Festival

**Contact** Cheryl Hunt
**Mail address** 21 Dee Fords Avenue, CHESTER, Cheshire, CH3 5UP
**Phone** 01244 320424
**Email** festival@chesterfolk.freeserve.co.uk
**Web** www.chesterfolk.freeserve.co.uk
**Address** The Morris Dancer, Kelsall, CHESTER, Cheshire

*General folk festival with children's events & crafts*

**RAB** North West Arts

**24 to 27 May 2002 tbc**

## Cleethorpes Folk Festival

**Location** Lincs
**Contact** Martin Campbell
**Mail address** 7 Collingwood Crescent, Laceby Acres, GRIMSBY, Lincs, DN34 5RG
**Phone** 01472 752852
**Email** clee.folk.robin-white@telinco.co.uk
**Web** www.telinco.co.uk/cleethorpes-folk-festival
**Alt contact** Mary White
**Address** The Rectory, Station Road, WILLOUGHBY, Lincs, LN13 9NA
**Phone** 01507 462045
**RAB** East Midlands Arts

**25 to 27 May 2002 tbc**

## Orange WOW

**Location** Tyne & Wear
**Contact** Carol Alevroyianni
**Mail address** 7 Northumberland Square, NORTH SHIELDS, Tyne & Wear, NE30 1QQ
**Phone** 0191 200 5164
07967 463012
**Fax** 0191 200 5798
**Email** carol.alevroyianni@northtyneside.gov.uk
**Web** www.orangewow.co.uk

*Large free international music festival, focused on World, Roots, Folk & Blues and new talent. 4 outdoor stages, exhibitions, crafts, food, fairground, etc.*

**RAB** Northern Arts

**27 to 31 May 2002 tbc**

## West End Words

**Location** Shrewsbury
**Contact** Mythstories, Museum Of Myth & Fable
**Phone** 01743 357140
**Email** dez@mythstories.com
**Web** www.mythstories.com
**Alt contact** Ali Quarrell
**Address** Rose Cottage, Church Road, WELSHPOOL, Powys, SY21 7LN
**Phone** 01938 554428
**Email** ali@mythstories.com

*Verbal arts street festival.*

**RAB** West Midlands Arts

**3 Jun to 6 May 2002**

## Upton Riverside Folk Festival

**Contact** Roger Davies
**Mail address** 6 Longfields, UPTON UPON SEVERN, Worcs
**Phone** 01684 593663
**RAB** West Midlands Arts

**10 to 17 June 2001**
**9 to 16 May 2002**

## Stony Live

**Contact** Matt Armour
**Mail address** 99 Malletts Close, Stony Stratford, MILTON KEYNES, MK11 1DG
**Phone** 01908 566407

*Community celebration of performing and visual arts.*

**RAB** Southern Arts

**Not happening in 2001, but announcing its appearance in October 2002**

## PeakBeat

**Contact** Ian Smith
**Mail address** 1 Holme Road, MATLOCK BATH, Derbys, DE4 3NU
**Phone** 01629 57082
07976 206568
**Email** ian@peakbeat.com
**Web** www.peakbeat.com
**Alt contact** Dave Wheeler
**Alt address** 1 Blind Lane, Hackney, MATLOCK, Derbys, DE4 2QE
**Phone** 01629 734517
**Email** dave@peakbeat.com

*Eclectic music & dance festival, jointly organised by Footloose Festival and Pregofest. Concerts all year round.*

**RAB** East Midlands Arts



***The festivals listed here appear alphabetically within date order beginning at 1st June 2001 through to 30th June 2002. Some 2002 dates are yet to be confirmed.***

# Association of Irish Festival Events (AOIFE)

**Association of Irish Festival Events (AOIFE)** Formed in March 1993, the Association of Irish Festival Events (AOIFE) is a voluntary organisation which aims to bring together the organisers of festivals and events in Ireland, to act as a forum for the sharing of ideas and to endeavour to resolve a number of common areas of concern. Since its inception, over 350 festivals and events have affiliated, ranging from prestigious international events to a host of smaller town and village festivals throughout the thirty-two counties of Ireland.

- The **AOIFE Public Liability Insurance Scheme**, administered by PJT Insurance Services, Dublin, is a package designed specifically for festivals and events. For the majority of AOIFE members the scheme offers substantial savings on premiums.
- The 8th issue of the **AOIFE Yearbook** was published early in 2001 - a publication which is now recognised as the essential reference book for festival and event organisers in Ireland. Designed to prove mutually beneficial to both organisers and those involved in the service, supply and entertainment industries, the Yearbook contains listings of acts, agencies, street entertainers, marquee and PA suppliers, comprehensive details of all AOIFE member festivals and events, a useful reference section with tips on many issues and lots more.
- The **AOIFE Advisory Council**, launched in February 1998, is a free hands-on advice service for members. If your event has a difficulty this service may very well be your answer.
- AOIFE also publishes a bi-monthly members' newsletter – **'Shenanigans'** - which provides invaluable information on the festival industry and an ideal forum for idea-sharing.
- **Corporate Membership** is open to companies, groups or individuals involved or interested in the event industry who do not actually organise an event (suppliers, agencies, acts, promoters etc)
- AOIFE has established strong links with a large number of arts, music, tourism and community development organisations at home and abroad. AOI FE is also in close contact with the **Association of Festival Organisers (AFO), the British Arts Festivals Association (BAFA)**, **Festivals of Wales**, **IFEA-Europe** and other European Festival Organisations. Links have also been established with **NOEA**, **TESA** and the **PSA** in the UK.
- AOIFE organises an **Annual Conference** with an agenda including presentations, seminars and workshops on a variety of relevant topics including funding, marketing, insurance, health and safety and sponsorship. The 2000 event was held in the Falls Hotel, Ennistymon, Co Clare from 10-12 November.
- AOIFE was instrumental in initiating the first ever "Showman's Show in Ireland" in the R.D.S., Dublin in October 1997. This valuable trade show event, which is organised in association with Lance Publications, is incorporated into the Conference each year.
- AOIFE is currently involved with Co-Operation Ireland in a "Community Festivals Networking Programme" which aims to foster relationships between festivals on both sides of the border.
- AOIFE is in the process of undertaking the first ever major piece of research into the economic, tourism and employment benefits of the festival industry in Ireland.
- Other projects include the production of a range of guidelines and codes of practice which will endeavour to raise the standard of good practice at festivals in Ireland. The first of these, "Happy Children" featuring the Child Protection issue, was launched in April 2000.

**Web** www.AOIFEonline.com
The AOIFE website which was launched at Conference 2000.

- Membership of AOIFE costs IR£75.00 per annum.

## Useful contacts in Ireland for Festival and Event Organisers

### Association of Irish Festival Events (AOIFE)
**Contact** Elizabeth Mc Loughlin
**Mail address** 1 Upper Main Street, Arklow, Co. Wicklow
**Phone** 0402-32732
**Fax** 0402-91030
**Email** aoifeireland@eircom.net
**Web** www.AOIFEonline.com

### PJT Insurance Services
**Contact** Peter Thomas
**Mail address** 39 Main Street, Santry Village, Dublin 9
**Phone** 01-842 5813
**Fax** 01-842 3830
**Email** pjtins@iol.ie

### Ireland's Festivals and Events
**Contact** Deirdre Connolly
**Mail address** 6-8 Garville Lane, Rathgar, Dublin 6
**Phone** 01-497 4037
**Fax** 01-497 4602
**Email** kst@tinet.ie

### The Arts Council
**Contact** The Festivals Officer
**Mail address** 70 Merrion Square, Dublin 2
**Phone** 01-661 1840
1850 392 492
**Fax** 01-676 1302
**Email** info@artscouncil.ie
**Web** www.artscouncil.ie

### The Arts Council of Northern Ireland
**Contact** Francis Murphy, Development Officer
**Mail address** Mac Neice House, 77 Malone Road, Belfast BT1 6AQ
**Phone** 028-903 85200
**Fax** 028-902 40960
**Email** info@artscouncil-ni.org
**Web** www.artscouncil-ni.org

### Bord Fáilte
**Mail address** Baggot Street Bridge, Dublin 2
**Phone** 01-602 4157
**Fax** 01-676 4764
**Web** www.ireland.travel.ie

*Note: This information is largely for the use of organisers in Ireland. Phone numbers have therefore been left as received from AOIFE.*

### Northern Ireland Tourist Board
**Contact** Hilary Cooke, Events Manager
**Mail address** St. Anne's Court, 59 North Street, Belfast BT1 1NB
**Phone** 028-902 31221
**Fax** 028-902 40960
**Web** www.ni-tourism.com

### Department of Tourism, Sport and Recreation
**Contact** Dr. James McDaid TD, Minister
**Mail address** Kildare Street, Dublin 2
**Phone** 01-662 1444
**Fax** 01-678 5906

### Department of Arts, Heritage and The Islands
**Contact** Sile De Valera TD, Minister
**Mail address** 43/49 Mespil Road, Dublin 4.
**Phone** 01-667 0788
**Fax** 01-667 0827

### Co-Operation Ireland
**Contact** Nuala McNally, Project Leader
**Mail address** 7 Botanic Avenue, Belfast BT7 1JG
**Phone** 028-903 21462
**Fax** 028-902 47522
**Email** info@co-operation.nireland.com
**Web** www.co-operation-ireland.ie

### Business2Arts
**(Formerly COTHU)**
**Contact** Brigid Roden, Chief Executive
**Mail address** 44 East Sussex Street, Temple Bar, Dublin 2
**Phone** 01-6766966
**Fax** 01-6766997
**Email** info@business2arts.ie
**Web** www.business2arts.ie

### Music Network
**Mail address** The Coach House, Dublin Castle, Dublin 2
**Phone** 01-671 9429
**Fax** 01-671 9230
**Email** info@musicnetwork.ie
**Web** www.musicnetwork.ie

### Contemporary Music Centre
**Mail address** 19 Fishamble Street, Temple Bar, Dublin 8
**Phone** 01-6731922
**Fax** 01-6489100
**Email** info@cmc.ie
**Web** www.cmc.ie

### Crafts Council of Ireland
**Mail address** Castle Yard, Kilkenny
**Phone** 056-61804
**Fax** 059-63754

### Irish Music Net
**Contact** Fergal McKay
**Mail address** 28 South Frederick Street, Dublin 2
**Phone** 01-671 3664
**Fax** 01-670 6889

### Association of Artists in Ireland
**Contact** Stella Coffey, Director
**Mail address** Art House, 43 Temple Bar, Dublin 2
**Phone** 01-874 0529
**Fax** 01-677 1585
**Email** artbulletin@artistsireland.com

### Event Guide
**Mail address** Eustace Street, Dublin 2
**Phone** 01-671 3377
**Fax** 01-671 0502

## *Health and Safety issues*

### Health and Safety Authority (HSA)
**Mail address** 10 Hogan Place, Dublin 2
**Phone** 01-614 7000
**Fax** 01-614 7020
**Email** infotel@hsa.ie
**Web** www.hsa.ie

### National Irish Safety Organisation (NISO)
**Mail address** Trident House, Main Street, Blackrock, Co Dublin
**Phone** 01-215 9266
**Fax** 01-215 9269
**Email** niso@iol.ie

### Health & Safety Executive – Northern Ireland
**Mail address** 83 Ladas Drive, Belfast BT6 9FR, Northern Ireland
**Phone** 028-9024-3249
**Fax** 028-9023-5383
**Email** hseni@detini.gov.uk
**Web** www.hse-ni.org.uk

## *Marketing contacts on the web*

Many AOIFE member festivals and events may be missing out on the opportunity of free marketing on the internet through a variety of festival and event websites, many of which offer you an opportunity of inserting your festival's details free of charge. There are also some which offer you the opportunity of linking to their sites if you already have a website yourself.

Check out the following:

**people.a2000.nl/rrspaans/euro fest.html#ireland**

**www.entertainmentireland.ie/festival/index.htm**

**www.imn.ie/midi/festivals. html**

**ifeaeurope.com**

**ifea.com**

**festivals.com**

**festpass.com**

**wow.ie**

Many local authorities also have websites, and the majority feature an events listing.

Make use of these services when they are provided free of charge.

It is also worth bearing in mind that the tourism authorities host websites and you may be able to link to these. Have a look at:

**www.ireland.travel.ie/home/index.asp**

**www.ni-tourism.com/index.asp**

**www.shannon-dev.ie**

It is anticipated that AOIFE itself will have a website up and running in the future and we hope to be in a position to offer linking opportunities. News on this front will be featured in the regular newsletter – AOIFE UPDATE.

## *Festival Organisations*

Association of Festival Organisers (AFO) **www.mrscasey.co.uk/afo**

British Arts Festivals Association (BAFA) **www.artsfestivals.co.uk**

British Federation of Festivals **www.festivals.demon.co.uk**

European Festivals Association (EFA) **www.euro-festival.net**

Festival Network Online (USA) **www.festivalnet.com**

Festivals of North America **www.festivalfinder.com**

Festpass **www.festpass.com**

International Festivals and Events Association – Europe **www.ifeaeurope.com**

International Festivals and Events Association – USA **www.ifea.com**

Local Ireland (Arts and Culture – Festivals) **www.local.ie/arts_and_culture/festivals**

## *Arts Councils*

Arts Council of Ireland **www.artscouncil.ie**

Arts Council of Northern Ireland **www.artscouncil-ni.org**

Arts Council of England **www.artscouncil.org.uk**

Arts Council of Scotland **www.sac.org.uk**

Arts Council of Wales **www.ccc-acw.org.uk**

## Health and Safety

Health and Safety Authority (HAS) **www.hsa.ie**

Health and Safety Executive – Northern Ireland **www.hse-ni.org.uk**

Health and Safety Executive (HSE – UK) **www.open.gov.uk/hse**

Production Services Association (PSA) **www.psa.org.uk**

## Government and Statutory Bodies

Department of Arts, Culture, Heritage and the Islands **www.irlgov.ie/ealga**

Department of Tourism, Sport and Recreation **www.irlgov.ie/tourism-sport**

Bord Failte (Irish Tourist Board) **www.ireland.travel.ie**

Northern Ireland Tourist Board (NITB) **www.ni-tourism.com**

## General Interest Sites

Charities Aid Foundation **www.cafonline.org**

Charity Commission (UK) **www.charity-commission.gov.uk**

Directory of Social Change **www.d-s-c.demon.co.uk**

Effective Meetings.com **www.effectivemeetings.com**

National Council for Voluntary Organisations (NCVO) **www.ncvo-vol.org.uk**

NICVA **www.nicva.org**

Volunteer Development Agency **www.volunteering-ni.org**

Voluntary Arts Network (VAN) **www.voluntaryarts.org**

# Festivals and Events 2001/2002

*Thanks to fRoots and A.O.I.F.E for the following information.*

**June 1-4 2001**

### Mick Carr Memorial Traditional Music Weekend, Co Donegal

**Contact** Rory O'Donnell, Meenancary, Carrick, Co Donegal.
**Phone/Fax** +353 73 39009

**June 3-10 2001**

### The Tommy Makem International School of Song

**Contact** Peter Makem
67 Armagh Road, NEWRY, Co Down, BT35 6PW, Northern Ireland
**Phone** 028 302 67517
**Email** peter@pmakem.freeserve.co.uk

**July 1-7 2001**

### Dr Douglas Hyde Summer School of Traditional Irish Music and Dance

Ballaghadereen, Co Roscommon, Eire
**Phone** +353 907 60013
+353 907 60136.
**Fax** +353 907 60765.
**Email** ocall@iol.ie
**Web** www.ballaghaderreen.com

**July 7-15 2001**

### Scoil Samhraidh Willie Clancy

Miltown-Maybay, Co Clare, Eire.
**Phone** +353 65 7084148
+353 65 7084 281.

**July 9-20 2001**

### BLAS 2001

Blas Summer School, Irish World Music Centre, University of Limerick, Limerick, Eire
**Phone** +353 61 202917.
**Fax** +353 61 202589.
**Email** ellen.byrne@ul.ie
**Web** http://ul.ie/~iwmc/blas

**July 15-21 2001**

### South Sligo

Tubbercurry, Co Sligo, Eire.
**Phone** +353 71 20912
+353 71 85010
+353 71 82151

**July 21-28 2001**

### Joe Mooney Summer School

Drumshanbo, Co Leitrim, Eire.
**Contact** Nancy Woods
**Phone** +353 78 41213 NW
**Alt contact** Mary Doyle
**Phone** +353 78 41426 MD.

**July 22 to 29 2001**

### Fiddler's Green Festival

**Contact** Kate Murphy, 5 Cherry Hill, Rostrevor, Co Down, BT34 3BD, N Ireland
**Phone** 028 4173 8819
**Fax** 028 4173 8738
**Email** fiddlers.green@dnet.co.uk
**Alt contact** Mairin McConville, 12A Greendale Crescent, Rostrevor, Co Down, BT34
**Web** www.fiddlersgreenfestival.com

**July 25-29**

### Feile Iorras: International Folk Arts Festival

Belmullet, Co Mayo, Eire.
Liam Mac Aindriu, Priomh Sraid, Beal An Mhuirthead, Co Mayo
**Phone** +353 97 81051
**Email** feileiorras@eircom.net
**Alt contact** Tony Conway Tallaghanbawn, Geesala, Ballina, Co Mayo
**Phone** +353 97 86941
**Web** www.feileiorras.org

**July 29-August 5 2001**

### Ardoyne Fleadh Cheoil

Co Antrim, Northern Ireland.
**Contact** Philip McTeggart, Ardoyne Fleadh Cheoil Office, 43 Herbert Street, Belfast. BT14 7LZ
**Phone** 028 9075 1056
**Fax** 028 9075 1055
**Email** philipmctaggert@irelandclick.com

**August 3-5 2001**

### Ballyshannon Music Festival

Donegal, Eire.
**Contact** Ray Gaughan
**Phone** +353 72 51088.
**Fax** +353 72 52832.
**Email** diceys@tinet.ie
**Web** www.donegalbay.ie

**August 3-5 2001**

### Cahersiveen Celtic Music Festival

Cahersiveen, Ring of Kerry, Eire.
**Contact** Shane O'Driscoll, 30 Church St, Cahersiveen, Co Kerry, Eire
**Phone** +353 87 222 4166.
**Fax** +353 66 947 3262.
**Email** info@celticmusicfestival.com
**Web** www.celticmusicfestival.com

August 3-6 2001
**O'Carolan Harp and Tradtitional Music Festival**
Co Roscommon
**Contact** Paraic Noone, Keadue, Co Roscommon
**Phone** +353 78 47204
**Fax** +353 78 47511
**Email** o'carolan@eircom.net

August 4 to 25 2001
**Guinness Live World Music**
**Contact** Smallworld Music, PO Box 747, Belfast, BT9 5ES, N Ireland
**Phone** 028 9038 2384
**Fax** 028 9029 5173
**Email** Becksworld@btinternet.com

August 9-13 2001
**Feakle International Traditional Music Festival**
Co Clare, Eire.
**Contact** Gary Pepper
**Phone** +353 61 924 322.
**Fax** +353 61 924 322.
**Web** www.iol.ie/~feakle

August 12-18 2001
**Fonn 2001 Traditional Music Summer School**
Galway, Eire.
**Contact** The Galway School of Irish Traditional Music, 6 Mainguard St, Galway, EIRE
**Phone** +353 91 562099.
**Email** gsitm@indigo.ie

August 16-19 2001
**Éigse Mrs Crotty**
Kilrush, Co Clare.
**Contact** Rebecca Brew, Market St, Kilrush, Co Clare, Eire
**Phone** +353 65 905 2470.
**Email** eigsemrscrotty@eircom.net
**Web** www.clare.local.ie

August 16-20 2001
**Aonach Paddy O'Brien**
Nenagh, Co Tipperary, Eire.
**Contact** Eileen O'Brien
**Phone** +353 87 244 5848
**Alt contact** Michael Scanlon
**Alt Phone** +353 86 810 4861
**Fax** +353 67 42900
**Email** eminogue@eircom.net

August 17-19 2001
**Michael Shanley Traditional Weekend**
Co Leitrim
**Contact** Frank Fox, Glenfarne Road, Kiltyclogher, Co Leitrim
**Phone** +353 72 54222
**Fax** +353 72 54044

August 30-September 2 2001
**Cork Folk Festival**
**Contact** William Hammond, 17 Victoria Avenue, Ballinlough, Co Cork
**Phone Fax** +353 21 431 7271
**Email** whammond@oceanfree.net

September 14 to 16 2001
**Gig 'N The Bann: Traditional Irish and Ulster-Scots Festival**
**Phone** 028 2582 1333
028 2582 0832

September 15 to 22 2001
**Moving On Music Festival**
**Contact** Paul Brown, Moving On Music Ltd, 7 University Road, Belfast, BT7 1NA, Northern Ireland
**Phone/Fax** 028 9024 8318
**Web** www.movingonmusic.co.uk

October 5-6 2001
**Mid Ulster Folk Festival**
Co Derry.
**Contact** Lorna Niven, Woodvale Cottage, Springhill Road, Moneymore, Londonderry BT45 7NH.
**Phone/Fax** 028 8674 8396

October 26 to November 11 2001
**Belfast Festival at Queens**
**Contact** Margaret McKee, 25 College Gardens, Belfast, BT9 6BS, Northern Ireland
**Phone** 028 9066 7687
**Fax** 028 9066 3733
**Email** festival@qub.ac.uk

October 4 to 7 2001
**Ards Guitar Festival**
**Contact** 249 Cavehill Road, Belfast, BT15 5BS, Northern Ireland
**Phone** 028 9096 2706
**Email** info@ardsguitarfestival.com
**Web** www.geocities.com/ards.geo/

April 2-6 2002 tbc
**Pan Celtic International Festival**
Co Kerry
**Contact** Margaret Maunsell, Feile Phan-Cheilteach Halla Thomas, Aghas, Tra-Li, Co Kerry
**Phone** +353 66 718 0050
**Fax** +353 66 713 9449
**Email** panceltic@tinet.ie
**Web** www.panceltic.com

May 3-5 2002 tbc
**Féile Na Ndéise Traditional Music Festival**
Dungarvan, Co Waterford, Eire.
**Phone** +353 58 41741
+353 58 45273

May 9 to 11 2002 tbc
**Edward Bunting International Irish Harp and Traditional Singing Festival**
**Contact** Patricia Daly
**Phone** 048 3755 1087
**Email** patricia@armaghharpers.freeserve.co.uk

# Festivals in Mainland Europe 2001

*Thanks to fRoots for the following information.*

## BELGIUM

### June

*June 29-1 July*
**COULEUR CAFÉ, Brussels, Belgium**
4 Avenue E Claes
B-1140 Brussels, Belgium
**Phone** +32 2 672 49 12
**Fax** +32 2 672 12 91
**Email** festival@couleurcafe.org

### July

*July 6-8*
**FEESTIVAL GOOIK, Gooik, Belgium**
Herman Dewit, Volkmuziekgilde,
Dorpsstraat 67, 1755 Gooik, Belgium
**Phone** +32 2532 2838
**Fax** +32 2532 2838
**Email** volksmuziekgilde@planet internet.be

*July 6-8*
**LATIN DANCE BEATS FESTIVAL, Paradiso, Melkweg, & Vondelpark, Amsterdam**

*July 6-14*
**WORLD FESTIVAL OF FOLKLORE, Schoten, Belgium**
Patrick Beauquesne,
Zwanebloemlaan 23,
2900 Schoten, Belgium
**Phone** +32 3 6850069
**Fax** +32 3 6581399
**Email** pbeauquesne@freegates.be/ wfs.schoten@ping.be

*July 14-15*
**BROSELLA FOLK & JAZZ, Brussels, Belgium**
Henri Vandenberghe,
Onze Lieve Vrouwstraat 15,
1850 Grimbergen, Belgium
**Phone** +32 2 270 98 56
**Fax** +32 2 270 98 56
**Email** henri.vandenberghe@pandora.be

*July 20-22*
**BELGIUM RHYTHM 'N' BLUES FESTIVAL, Peer, Belgium**
C C 't Poorthuis, Break-away vzw,
PO Box 42, B-3990 Peer, Belgium
**Phone** +32 11 610 720
**Fax** +32 11 611 126
**Email** brbf@break-away.be

*July 26-29*
**SFINKS FESTIVAL**
**Boechout, Belgium**
Patrick De Groote,
Jan Franks Willemsstraat 10a,
B-2530 Boechout, Belgium
**Phone** +32 3455 69 44
**Fax** +32 3454 11 62
**Email** info@sfinks.be

### August

*Aug 3-5*
**DRANOUTER FOLK FESTIVAL**
**Belgium**
Marnique Deswarte,
Dikkebusstraat 234,
B-8950 Loker, Belgium
**Phone** +32 57 44 69 33
**Fax** +32 57 44 62 43
**Email** mdeswarte@unicall.be

*Aug 10-11*
**ANTILLIAANSE FEESTEN/ CARIBBEAN FESTIVAL**
**Hoogstraten Belgium**
Louis Verschueren, Klinketstraat 17,
2323 Hoogstraten, Belgium
**Phone** +32 3 3143732
**Fax** +32 3 3148656
**Email** lo@antilliaansefeesten.be

*Aug 18*
**AFRO CARIBBEAN FESTIVAL**
**Bredene, Belgium**
De heer Hubert Schmitt,
Dienst voor toerisme Bredene,
Kapellestraat 70,
8450 Bredene, Belgium
**Phone** +32 59 32 09 98
**Fax** +32 59 33 19 80
**Email** Toerisme@Bredene.be

*Aug 18-20*
**DEERLYCKE FOLKFESTIVAL**
**Deerlijk, Belgium**
Rik Couchez, Schragenstraat 38,
8540 Deerlijk, Belgium
**Phone** +32 56 77 2315
**Fax** +32 56 77 2315
**Email** rik.couchez@pi.be

### September

*Sep 29*
**FOLKSTAGEFESTIVAL**
**Hasselt, Belgium**
Rik Schreurs, J V Oostenrijkstr 42,
3500 Hasselt, Belgium
**Phone** +32 11 87 34 55
**Fax** +32 11 87 34 55
**Email** folkstage@hotmail.com

### October

*Oct 2-7*
**INTERNATIONAL FOLKDANCING FESTIVAL, Tournai, Belgium**
Guy Desablens, Chemin de Maire 29,
Ere, 7500 Tournai, Belgium
**Phone** +32 69 22 06 80
**Fax** +32 69 22 06 80
**Email** festi.tournai@infonie.be

### June

*June 8-10*
**FESTIVAL OF ROSES**
**Kazanluk, Bulgaria**
Sirma Nedeva, 44 Pop Bogomil Str,
1202 Sofia, Bulgaria
**Phone** +359 2 9833322
**Fax** +358 2 9832371
**Email** alextour@omega.bg

### July

*July 14-27*
**BALKANFOLK 2001**
**Pamporovo, Bulgaria**
Emil Genov, 74 Opalchenska Str.,
1303 Sofia, Bulgaria
**Phone** +359 2 322010
**Fax** +359 2 333284
**Email** workshop2001@balkanfolk.com

## CZECH REPUBLIC

### June

*June 16-17*
**RESPECT FESTIVAL OF ETHNIC & WORLD MUSIC**
**Prague, Czech Republic**
Klara Kollarova, Tydenik RESPEKT,
Kemencova 10, 110 00 Prague 1,
Czech Republic
**Phone** +420 2 2493 0999
+420 6 0329 6560
**Fax** +420 2 2491 9274
**Email** festival@respekt.cz

### August

*Aug 1-12*
**SUMMER FOLK DANCE WEEK, Náchod & Piest'any, Czech Republic**
Dvorana, Spanielova 1275, 163 00
Praha 6, Czech Republic
**Phone** +420 2 302 13 30
+420 2 301 82 79
**Fax** +420 2 301 82 67
**Email** dvorana@mbox.vol.cz

*Aug 19-26*
**PRAGUE & ISTANBUL VINTAGE DANCE WEEKS**
**Prague, Czech Republic**
Dvorana, Spanielova 1275,
163 00 Praha 6, Czech Republic
**Phone** +420 2 302 13 30/
+420 2 301 82 79
**Fax** +420-2 301 82 67
**Email** dvorana@mbox.vol.cz

### September

*Sep 14-16*
**WOMAD, Prague, Czech Republic**
WOMAD Ltd, Millside, Mill Lane, Box,
Wilts SN13 8PN
**Phone** 01225 744494
**Fax** 01225 743481
**Email** womad@realworld.on.net

## DENMARK

### DENMARK

### June

*June 1-3*
**TARM VISEFESTIVAL, Denmark**
Bjarne Lund, Vinkelvej 11, DK 6880, Tarm, Denmark
**Phone** +45 97373337
**Fax** +45 97373317
**Email** info@vvf.dk

*June 28-1 July*
**ROSKILDE FESTIVAL, Denmark**
Jette Hansen, Havsteenavej 11, DK-4000 Roskilde, Denmark
**Phone** +45 46 36 66 13
**Fax** +45 46 32 14 99
**Email** bigbox@roskilde-festival.dk

*June 28-1 July*
**SKAGEN FESTIVAL, Denmark**
Peer Légsted Andersen, PO Box 33, 9990 Skagen, Denmark
**Phone** +45 98 44 49 69
**Fax** +45 98 44 63 77
**Email** peer.andersen@wanadoo.dk

### August

*Aug 23-26*
**TØNDER FESTIVAL, Denmark**
Carsten Panduro, Vestergade 80, 6270 Tønder, Denmark
**Phone** +45 74 72 46 10
**Fax** +45 74 72 01 23

## ESTONIA

### July

*July13-15*
**PAIDE SHANTY, Paide, Estonia**
Jaan Arvola, Järvamaa Maakond, Roosna-Alliku, Pärna 7, 73201, Estonia
**Phone** +372 50 45 592
**Fax** +372 38 95396
**Email** jaan.arvola@estpak.ee

*July 26-29*
**VILJANDI FOLK MUSIC FESTIVAL Estonia**
Andri Maimets, Posti 1, 71004 Viljandi, Estonia
**Phone** +372 52 75 161
**Fax** +372 43 55 258
**Email** folk@folk.ee

## FINLAND

### July

*July 14-22*
**KAUSTINEN FOLK MUSIC FESTIVAL Finland**
Festival Office, PO Box 24, FIN-69601 Kaustinen, Finland
**Phone** +358 6 8604111
**Fax** +358 6 8604222
**Email** folk.art@kaustinen.inet.fi

## FRANCE

### FRANCE

### June

*June 23-15 July*
**FESTIVAL DES HAUTS DE GARONNE, Bordeaux, a.o., France**
Patrick Duval, BP 42, F-33326 Eysines Cedex, France
**Phone** +33 5 56 28 57 14
**Fax** +33 5 56 57 56 30
**Email** mdn@free.fr

### July

*July 3-7*
**MUSIQUES SUR L'ILE, Nantes, Loire Atlantique, France**
M. Georgeault, Association NFIATP, Porte St Pierre, Rue de l'Évêché, F-44000 Nantes, France
**Phone** +33 2 40 08 01 00
**Fax** +33 2 40 48 12 64
**Email** contact@festival-ete-nantes.asso.fr

*July 12-15*
**INTERNATIONAL GATHERING OF INSTRUMENT MAKERS & MASTER-PIPERS, Saint-Chartier, France**
Rencontres de Saint-Chartier, BP 137, 36400 La Chatre, France
**Phone** +33 2 54 06 09 96
**Fax** +33 2 54 48 21 29
**Email** infos@saintchartier.com

*July 13-15*
**RENCONTRES INTERNATIONALES DE HARPE CELTIQUE, Dinan, Brittany, France**
Elisabeth, CRIHC, La Galerie, F-22490 Plouer sur Rance, France
**Phone** +33 2 96 86 84 94
**Fax** +33 2 96 86 89 40
**Email** harp@wanadoo.fr

### August

*Aug 3-12*
**FESTIVAL INTERCELTIQUE DE LORIENT, Brittany, France**
2 Rue Paul Bert 56100 Lorient, Brittany, France
**Phone** +33 2 97 21 24 29
**Fax** +33 2 97 64 34 13
**Email** festival@festival.interceltique.com

*Aug 19*
**NUIT DU FOLK Kerlouan, Brittany, France**
Anne Marie Riou Office du Tourisme, 29890 Kerlouan, Brittany, France
**Phone** +33 6 86 64 72 44
**Email** a.marie.riou@wanadoo.fr

### December

*Dec 22-25*
**AFRICOLOR, Paris, France**
Philippe Conrath, 145 Rue De Menilmontant, F-75020 Paris, France
**Phone** +33 1 47 97 69 99
**Fax** +33 1 47 97 65 44
**Email** africolor@africolor.com

## GERMANY

### June

*June 1-4*
**AFRICA FESTIVAL Würzburg, Germany**
Roland Gemeinder, Afro Project e.v., Kaiserstr. 16, D-97070 Würzburg, Germany
**Phone** +49 931 15060
**Fax** +49 931 15080
**Email** mondo-de@t-online.de

*June 1-4*
**KARNEVAL DER KULTUREN Berlin, Germany**
Werkstatt der Kulturen, Wissmannstrasse 32, 12049 Berlin, Germany
**Phone** +49 30 622 20 24
**Fax** +49 30 622 35 19
**Email** info@karneval-berlin.de

*June 3*
**DIE LANGE NACHT DER SOUNDSYSTEMS, Berlin, Germany**
Michael
**Phone** +49 30 318 614 0
**Fax** +49 30 318 614 10
**Email** events@piranha.de

*June 8-24*
**MASALA WORLD-BEAT FESTIVAL, Hanover, Germany**
Christoph Sure, Lister Meile 4, D-30161 Hannover, Germany
**Phone** +49 511 344 558
**Fax** +49 511 318 0615
**Email** masala@pavillon-hannover.de

### July

*July 6-8*
**TANZ & FOLKFEST Rudolstadt, Germany**
Peter Uhlmann, Stadt Rudolstadt, Dezernat Kultur, Markt 7, D-07407 Rudolstadt, Germany
**Phone** +49 3672 41 26 51
**Fax** +49 3672 41 27 96
**Email** tffrudolstadt@saale-net.de

*July 6-29*
**STIMMEN, Lörrach, Germany**
Marcel Falk, Burghof GmbH, Herrenstr. 5, D-79539 Lörrach, Germany
**Phone** +49 76 21 940 89 44
**Fax** +49 76 21 940 89 24
**Email** stimmen@burghof.com

festivals europe

*July 11-26 Aug*
**HEIMATKLÄNGE - SOUL & SOUL, Berlin, Germany**
Michael
**Phone** +49 303 186 140
**Fax** +49 303 186 14 10
**Email** events@piranha.de

*July 27-29*
**BARDENTREFFEN NÜRNBERG, Germany**
Karl-Heinz Fischer, Stadt Nürnberg, Bardentreffen, D-90317 Nürnberg, Germany
**Phone** +49 911 231 3410
**Fax** +49 911 231 3411
**Email** info@bardentreffen.de

### September

*Sep 15*
**5TH FESTIVAL KULTUREN DER WELT, Lohmar, Germany**
Check Web site for details

## GREECE

### August

*Aug 5-17*
**TRADITIONAL GREEK DANCE SEMINAR, Lake Prespes, Macedonia, Greece**
Maryse Fabre, 2 rue Coysevox, 75018 Paris, France
**Phone** +33 1 46 27 92 04
+33 1 47 68 06 21
**Fax** +33 1 53 56 52 20
**Email** maryse.fabre@eu.rhodia.com

### September

*Sep 6-8*
**GAIA FESTIVAL Thessaloniki, Greece**
Mrs Teresa Kerasides, 56 Andreou Georgiou St, GR-546 27 Thessaloniki, Greece
**Phone** +30 31 551 836
**Fax** +30 31 551 837
**Email** mylos@mylos.gr

## HUNGARY

### July

*July 5-9*
**KALAKA FOLK FESTIVAL, Miskolc, Hungary**
Lajos Fogarasi, Kalàka Foundation, Petöfi Hall, Zichy Mihaly ut 14, H-1146 Budapest, Hungary
**Phone** +36 1 343 4327
**Fax** +36 1 351 8455
**Email** biomusic@mentha.hu

## ITALY

### June

*June 14-29 July*
**FESTIVAL LATINOAMERICANO, Viareggio, Italy**
Juan José Fabiana Zignago, Viale Baracca 40, 28041 Arona Novara, Italy
**Phone** +39 03 22 47 679
**Fax** +39 03 22 24 03 97
**Email** latinamericando@pn.itnet.it

*June 30-1 July*
**VILLA SERRA FOLK, Genova, Italy**
Loris Bohm, Via Cresta di San Rocco 9, 16167 Genova, Italy
**Email** info@etnobazar.it

## NETHERLANDS

### June

*June 4*
**INTERNATIONAL GIPSY FESTIVAL, Tilburg, Netherlands**
Telefoonstraat 16, 5038 DM Tilburg, Netherlands
**Phone** +31 13 580 14 24
+31 13 580 14 11

*June 15-24*
**AMSTERDAM ROOTS FESTIVAL, Netherlands**
Anna John, Rootsfest @ Melkweg, Lijnbaansgracht 234A, 1017 PH Amsterdam, Netherlands
**Phone** +31 20 531 81 81
**Fax** +31 20 531 81 18
**Email** rootsfest@melkweg.nl

*June 30-1 July*
**INTERNATIONALE STRAATTHEATER FESTIVAL NOORDWIJK, Noordwijk, Netherlands**
Arno Bos, Postbus 126, 2200 AC Nordwijk, Netherlands
**Phone** +31 71 3618636
**Fax** +31 71 3620631
**Email** straattheater.noordwijk@wxs.nl

### October

*Oct 24-28*
**WOMEX, Rotterdam, Netherlands**
Michael v. Petrykowski, c/o Piranha Kultur, Carmerstr. 11, D-10623 Berlin, Germany
**Phone** +49 30 318 614 0
**Fax** +49 30 318 614 10
**Email** womex@womex.de

### November

*Nov 2-4*
**MUSIC MEETING NIJMEGEN, Netherlands**
Frans Cuypers, Music Meeting, PO Box 1535, NL-6501 BM Nijmegen, Netherlands
**Phone** +31 24 360 8813
**Fax** +31 24 360 6720
**Email** seeyou@music-meeting.nl

### January 2002

*Jan 23-27*
**INTERNATIONAL FOLK FESTIVAL, Tilburg, Netherlands**
International Folk Festival, Telefoonstraat 16, 5038 DM Tilburg, Netherlands
**Phone** +31 13 580 14 24
+31 13 580 14 11
**Fax** +31 13 580 14 25
**Email** info@folkfestival.nl

## NORWAY

### July

*July 5-8*
**FØRDE FOLK MUSIC FESTIVAL Norway**
Hilde Bjorkum, PO Box 395, N-6801 Førde, Norway
**Phone** +47 57 72 1940
**Fax** +47 57 72 1941
**Email** fordefolk@prodat.no

### August

*Aug 2-5*
**TELEMARK FOLK FESTIVAL, Bø i Telemark, Norway**
Øysten Akselberg, Telemarkfestivalen, Gullbringvegen 34, N-3800 Bø, Norway
**Phone** +47 3595 1919
+47 906 38 453 m
**Fax** +47 3595 3546
**Email** post@telemarkfestivalen.no

### October

*Oct 28-4 Nov*
**VERDEN I NORDEN, Oslo, Norway**
Anne Moberg, Rikskinsertene, PO Box 2835 Solli, N-0204 Oslo, Norway
**Phone** +47 2201 5500
**Fax** +47 2283 1610
**Email** post@rikskonsertene.no

## POLAND

### June

*June 29-1 July*
**FOLK FIESTA, Zabkowice, Poland**
Gregory Kurczynski, Rynek 24, PL-57-200 Zabkowice, Slaskie, Poland
**Phone** +48 748 152 896
**Fax** +48 748 151 381
**Email** zok@netgate.com.pl

## PORTUGAL

*June 29-1 July*
**WOMAD, Sintra, Portugal**
WOMAD Ltd, Millside, Mill Lane, Box, Wiltshire, SN13 8PN
**Phone** 01225 744494
**Fax** 01225 743481
**Email** womad@realworld.on.net

## SERBIA

### August

*Aug 24-26*
**SABOR TRUBACA/TRUMPET SUMMIT: FESTIVAL OF TRADITIONAL BRASS MUSIC, Guca, Serbia**
Mr Ilija Stankovic
**Phone** +381 11 625273
**Fax** +381 11 624 638
**Email** ilij@music.com

## SICILY

### August

*Aug 16-20*
**WOMAD, Palermo, Sicily**
WOMAD Ltd, Millside, Mill Lane, Box, Wiltshire, SN13 8PN
**Phone** 01225 744494
**Fax** 01225 743481
**Email** womad@realworld.on.net

## SLOVENIA

### June

*June 1-9*
**DRUGA GODBA, Ljubljana, Slovenia**
Bogdan Benigar, Kersnikova 4, SI-1000 Ljubljana, Slovenia
**Phone** +386 14 13 81 580
**Fax** +386 14 13 81 5885
**Email** bogdan.benigar@kiss.uni-lj.si

## SPAIN

### July

*July 6-28*
**PIRINEOS SUR, Lanuza, Huesca, Spain**
Luis Calvo, Porches de Galicia 4, E-22002 Huesca, Spain
**Phone** +34 974 29 41 51
**Fax** +34 974 29 41 50
**Email** pirineos-sur@dphuesca.es

*July 6-29*
**LA MAR DE MUSICAS Cartagena, Spain**
Francisco Martin Peña, c/ Jacinto Benevente 7-2a, E-30203 Cartagena, Spain
**Phone** +34 968 12 88 13
**Fax** +34 968 12 89 05
**Email** imusicas@ayto-cartagena.es

*July 20-22*
**ETNOSUR, Alcala la Real Jaen, Andalucia, Spain**
Pedro Melguizo
**Phone** +34 953 220299
**Fax** +34 953 220299
**Email** pedromelguizo@etnosur.com

*July 29-26*
**FESTIVAL FOLKLORICO INTERNACIONAL JUVENIL DEL 'BIDASOA', Bidasoa, Spain**
Oscar Lucas Gainza, c/ Mara Juncal Labandibar, n10-2D, 20305 Irn, Basque Country, Spain
**Phone** +34 943 628932
**Email** eraiki.zal@euskalnet.net

### September

*Sep 5-9*
**FOLK GETXO, Getxo, Bizkaia, Basque Country, Spain**
Marta Herrera, Aula de Cultura de Getxo, Urgul s/n 1a, E-48990 Algorta-Getxo, Spain
**Phone** +34 94 491 4080
**Fax** +34 94 491 2139
**Email** infocultur@getxo.net

*Sep 7-9*
**ETNOHELMATICA 2001 Salamanca, Spain**
Ismael Torres, C/ Torres Villarroel, 33, 8*A, E-37006 Salamanca, Spain
**Phone** +34 923 33 02 84
**Fax** +34 923 33 02 84
**Email** PMARTINP37@smail1.ocenf.org

*Sep 13-16*
**MERCAT DE MUSICA VIVA DE VIC Vic, Spain**
Carles Sala, Historiador R. d'Abadal I de Vinyals, 5, 2a Plta, E-08500 Vic, Spain
**Phone** +34 93 883 31 00
**Fax** +34 93 883 26 26
**Email** mmvv@aivic.es

### November

*Nov 9-11*
**WOMAD CANARIAS, Gran Canaria**
WOMAD Ltd, Millside, Mill Lane, Box, Wilts, SN13 8PN
**Phone** 01225 744494
**Fax** 01225 743481
**Email** womad@realworld.on.net

## SWEDEN

### July

*July 5-12*
**ETHNO 2001, Falun, Sweden**
PO Box 387, SE-79128 Falun, Sweden
**Phone** +46 23 83090
**Fax** +46 23 83314
**Email** festivalen@falufolk.falun.se

*July 11-14*
**FALUN FOLKMUSIC FESTIVAL Sweden**
Hans Hjorth, PO Box 387, S-79128 Falun, Sweden
**Phone** +46 23 83090
**Fax** +46 23 83314
**Email** festivalen@falufolk.falun.se

### August

*Aug 2-5*
**URKULT MUSIC & CULTURE FESTIVAL, Näsåker, Sweden**
Mia Tejle, PL 940, 881 95 Undrom, Sweden
**Phone** +46 0612 60199
**Fax** +46 0612 60156
**Email** urkult@hotmail.com

## SWITZERLAND

### June

*June 24-1 July*
**MUSIC OF THE WORLD Basel, Switzerland**
Thomas Kayser, Augustinergasse 4 / Postfach, CH-4001 Basel, Switzerland
**Phone** +41 61 266 56 45
**Fax** +41 61 266 56 44
**Email** musik.der.welt@bluewin.ch

### September

*Sep 7-9*
**AFRIKANISCHES KULTURFESTIVAL INTEGRATION, Zürich, Switzerland**
Louis Mombu, Verein Africa Freemon, Schaffhauserstr 408, CH-8050 Zürich, Switzerland
**Phone** +41 1 302 51 82
**Fax** +41 1 251 24 64
**Email** picaflor@freesurf.ch

## TURKEY

### August

*Aug 27-31*
**PRAGUE & ISTANBUL VINTAGE DANCE WEEKS, Istanbul, Turkey**
Dvorana, Spanielova 1275, 163 00 Praha 6, Czech Republic
**Phone** +420 2 302 13 30
+420 2 301 82 79
**Fax** +420-2 301 82 67
**Email** dvorana@mbox.vol.cz

# Association of Festival Organisers (AFO)

**working for and with festival & event organisers, supporting live music, dance, song, arts, crafts and theatre.**

The Association of Festival Organisers (AFO) was formed in 1987 to provide a channel of communication between festivals and events of all kinds.

Bringing together a group of festival organisers from the folk world in the early days, the AFO soon expanded to incorporate events in early music, bluegrass, jazz, cajun, step & clog, dance, world music, the folk arts and many other acoustic style music events. The list now forms the core of what is currently a membership of over 150 festivals and events.

The AFO has links with similar organisations and festivals overseas including:

**The Association of Irish Festivals and Events (AIOFE)**

**The International Festivals and Events Association of Europe (IFEA)**

**The International Council for Folklore Festivals (CIOFF)**

The AFO also works closely with a variety of UK based arts organisations, unions and associations:

**Folk Arts Network (FAN)**

**Musicians' Union (MU)**

**The Arts Council of England (ACE)**

In addition, the AFO is regarded as a leading partner in the events industry with such associations as:

**The Events Services Association (TESA)**

**The Mobile Outside Caterers Association (MOCA)**

**National Outdoor Events Association (NOEA)**

**Production Services Association (PSA)**

The AFO is also represented at many local and national Government levels, has links to all the English Regional Arts Boards along with Scottish, Welsh, Northern Ireland and English Arts Councils and has collaborated with the Health & Safety Executive in writing special chapters in the Event Safety Guide.

The AFO regularly consults with other organisations such as:

**The Core Cities Group**

**The Association of Local Government Officers**

**Health & Safety Executive (H&SE)**

**Performing Right Society (PRS)**

and many others.

Membership of AFO is open to any festival or event, with Associate Membership normally taken up by services and people who work closely with the festival and event industry.

The AFO's work is currently funded by the Arts Council of England and offers a channel of communication for events and festivals of all sizes. It also assists with the ups and downs of festival management, provides information, data, links and contacts, help and advice in the challenge to present the arts in a professional, popular and safe production to a wider audience.

**Membership includes:**

- A special rate for a very popular annual Conference
- Several newsletters per year
- Access to a specially devised insurance scheme

It also offers a source of useful information, reference books, a link to other festivals, a way in for non-members, new festivals and other national bodies. But perhaps most strong of all is the knowledge that within the AFO a member is with colleagues who can share festival management and offer mutual support.

A ticket swap system is in place where members offer complimentary tickets or discounted prices to other AFO members giving the organisers the opportunity to visit one another's festivals and events. There, they can learn more and improve by example and enthusiasm rather than just rules and regulations.

AFO member festivals annually play to approximately a third of a million people in a host of events throughout the spring, summer and autumn each year.

See also web page **www.mrscasey.co.uk/afo**

# Useful contacts for festival organisers

By **Steve Heap - Association of Festival Organisers**

There are several excellent guides and manuals available to the Events Industry and most can be purchased direct, some are available from the **Association of Festival Organisers'** Library to members, and others are available in public libraries. Some are for members of other associations and can be easily acquired through membership or often web pages.
The largest and perhaps most useful of these is **The White Book**, published by Inside Communications. The same organisation is responsible for publication of **Access All Areas**, a monthly newspaper for the Events Industry bringing news, views and comments about the industry, about legislation and delivering contacts old and new for infrastructure, catering and marketing.

**Catering**
Without doubt the best and most comprehensive list of caterers, and recommended by AFO as probably the safest route, is **MOCA (The Mobile Outside Caterers Association)**. The association registers mobile outdoor caterers and so provides them with good public liability cover and a code of practice on health & safety and hygiene. MOCA produces an annual reference handbook, which can either be purchased for £20 or comes free to members of AFO, TESA and of course MOCA.

**Publicity**
To gain more publicity for your festival there are all the usual festival guides in folk, roots and acoustic music magazines both regional and national. See the Media section for full listings. Some of these include **fRoots**, **Living Tradition**, **Joe Smith's Midlands Guide**, **Folk Directory** (EFDSS) and many others available on web sites. See Internet section.

However, the more general Events Industry is also happy to list your events. For instance you could be listed in:

**The Showman's Directory** published by Lance Publications. Originally started by Stephen Lance as a directory and advertising guide to the industry in general but especially for agricultural shows, it now covers a vast array of equipment and listings of equipment and events.

**Advance Show Dates** is also published by Lance Publications as a supplement to the Showman's Directory.

**The Event Industry Member Profile** is the handbook for the members of TESA, The Event Services Association. It publishes a comprehensive list of event industry suppliers (see also **The White Book**).

**British Federation of Festivals Year Book**

**International Events Guide**

**Corporate Event Services** - reference source for businesses in the events industry.

**Finding the Artist**
Within the folk, roots and traditional music scene there are several full time and part time agencies - see Agencies. Occasionally sliding outside of the folk scene you may find such books as **Showcase International Music Book** and **The White Book** useful.

**Your Audience**
Knowing the target audience for a festival or event is part of the battle. Produce publicity by all means, but know for whom you have published it and know how many to print by knowing whom you want to send it to. A useful guide to this area is **The Market Research Society (MRS)** who publish **Occupation Groupings**, the job dictionary.

It is also useful to understand who came to your event and why and so to undertake market research. The AFO recommends to its members a book by **Paul Hague and Peter Jackson** known as *Do Your Own Market Research*.

**Funding**
Then of course you may need some help with finding some funds. Obviously there is your own local authority, whose budget may well have dwindled for arts in recent years but some funding is still available from most District Councils. Festivals need more than arts funding and it may be more appropriate for you to approach a Leisure and Amenities officer to discuss what is available. Your next port of call should be your Regional Arts Board. See RAB's section for listings, and again there you will find several different angles to which you the Festival Organiser can apply.

In addition, there is European funding and AFO recommends the **Directory of Social Change** for a whole raft of books to assist with funding. In particular they publish **European Union Funding for the Voluntary Sector**.

A publication from the **Gulbenkian Foundation** called *Crossing the Line* may also be useful. The book, edited by **John Harland and Kay Kinder** raises awareness of access for young people, and points organisers in the right direction for facilitating young people's involvement in the arts, and recommends funding sources.

After grant funding one can turn to commercial sponsors and again the **Directory of Social Change** offers *Finding Company Sponsors for Good Causes* by **Chris Wells**.

Finally from the same source, **John Smyth and Dave Cassen** have edited the *Guide to UK Company Giving*. Updated regularly, the guide lists simply and easily in alphabetical order hundreds and hundreds of companies that reside in the UK and give charitable donations to the arts and sport.

## *Festival and Events Industry Associations*

In Ireland, **AOIFE - The Association of Irish Festivals and Events**
**British Federation of Festivals**

In England, **AFO - Association of Festival Organisers**
**TESA - The Events Services Association**
**MOCA - The Mobile Outside Caterers Association**
**NOEA - National Outdoor Event Association**
**PSA - Production Services Association**
**CIOFF - The International Association of Folklore Festivals**

Should the reader be an established festival or event organiser then any one of these associations can help improve knowledge, contacts and general information. If you are a new festival organiser on the folk and roots music scene then of course we would recommend contacting the AFO.

## Organisations, Publications etc.

### The White Book
**Contact** Sarah Hutchinson (Editor)
**Mail address** Inside Communications Ltd, 1st Floor, Bank House, 23 Warwick Road, Coventry CV1 2EW
**Phone** 024 7655 9590
**Fax** 024 7663 1185
**Email** Sarah_Hutchinson@mrn.co.uk
**Web** www.whitebook.co.uk

### Access All Areas
**Contact** Mike Gartside (Editor)
**Mail address** Inside Communications Ltd, 1st Floor, Bank House, 23 Warwick Road, Coventry CV1 2EW
**Phone** 024 7655 9590
**Fax** 024 7663 1185
**Email** mike_gartside@mrn.co.uk
**Web** www.access-aa.co.uk

### International Events Guide
**Mail address** Business Media Services, Centre Court, 1301 Stratford Road, Hall Green, Birmingham B28 9HH
**Phone** 0121 693 7000
**Fax** 0121 693 7100
**Web** www.eventsbook.co.uk

### The Showman's Directory
**Mail address** Lance Publications, Park House, Park Road, Petersfield, Hampshire, GU32 3DL
**Phone** 01730 266624
**Fax** 01730 260117
**Web** www.showmans-directory.co.uk

### British Federation of Festivals Year Book
(ISBN 090153241X)
**Mail address** Festivals House, 198 Park Lane, Macclesfield, Cheshire, SK11 6UD
**Phone** 01625 428297
**Fax** 01625 503229
**Web** www.festivals.demon.co.uk

### Corporate Event Services
(ISBN 095 284558X)
**Mail address** Showcase Publications, 38c The Broadway, Crouch End, London, N8 9SU,
**Phone** 020 8348 2332
**Fax** 020 8340 3750
**Web** www.cesbook.co.uk
*Reference source for businesses in the events industry.*

### Showcase International Music Book
**Mail address** Showcase Publications, 38c The Broadway, Crouch End, London, N8 9SU,
**Phone** 020 8348 2332
**Fax** 020 8340 3750
**Web** www.showcase-music.com

### The Market Research Society (MRS)
**Mail address** The Market Research Society, 15 North Burgh Street, London, EC1V 0AH.
*Publish "Occupation Groupings", the job dictionary*

### "Do Your Own Market Research"
**by Paul Hague and Peter Jackson**
(ISBN 0-7494-2652-7)
**Mail address** Kogan Page (Publishers), 120 Pentonville Road, London, N1 9JN

### Directory of Social Change
**Mail address** 24 Stephenson Way, London, NW1 2DP
**Phone** 020 7209 5151
**Fax** 020 7209 5049
**Email** info@dsc.org.uk
*"European Union Funding for the Voluntary Sector", "Finding Company Sponsors for Good Causes" by Chris Wells and the "Guide to UK Company Giving" edited by John Smyth and Dave Cassen are all published by the Directory of Social Change.*

### The Gulbenkian Foundation
*"Crossing the Line" edited by John Harland and Kay Kinder" is published by The Gulbenkian Foundation.*

### British Arts Festivals Association (BAFA)
**Contact** Gwyn Rhydderch
**Mail address** 77 Whitechapel High Street, London E1 7QX
**Phone** 020 7247 4667
**Fax** 020 7247 5010
**Email** bafa@netcomuk.co.uk
**Web** www.artsfestivals.co.uk

### The Event Services Association (TESA)
**Mail address** Centre Court, 1301 Stratford Road, Hall Green, Birmingham B28 9HH
**Phone** 0121 693 7000
**Fax** 0121 693 7100
**Email** enq@tesa.org.uk
**Web** www.tesa.org.uk

### The Production Services Association (PSA)
**Mail address** Centre Court, 1301 Stratford Road, Hall Green, Birmingham B28 9HH
**Phone** 0121 693 7127
**Fax** 0121 693 7100
**Email** twobob@psa.org.uk
**Web** www.psa.org.uk

### National Outdoor Events Association (NOEA)
**Mail address** 7 Hamilton Way, Wallingdon, Surrey SM6 9NJ
**Phone** 020 8669 8121
**Fax** 020 8647 1128
**Email** secretary@noea.org.uk
**Web** www.noea.org.uk

### Mobile & Outside Caterers Association (MOCA)
**Contact** Bob Fox
**Mail address** Centre Court, 1301 Stratford Road, Hall Green, Birmingham B28 9HH
**Phone** 0121 693 7000
**Fax** 0121 693 7100
**Email** enq@moca.org.uk
**Web** www.moca.org.uk

### Voluntary Arts Network
**Mail address** P O Box 200 Cardiff CF5 1YH, Wales
**Phone** 02920 395395
**Fax** 02920 297297
**Email** info@voluntaryarts.org
**Web** www.voluntaryarts.org

### Event Organiser
**Contact** Simon Ambrose (Publishing Director)
**Mail address** 8 Home Farm, Ardington, Oxfordshire OX12 8PN
**Phone** 01235 863008
**Fax** 01235 862288
**Email** editorial@papa.org.uk

### Events 2001 (Events Directory)
**Mail address** Business Media Services Ltd, Centre Court, 1301 Stratford Road, Hall Green, Birmingham B28 9HH
**Phone** 0121 693 7116
**Fax** 0121 693 7100
**Email** enq@bmsltd.co.uk

### Events Specialist
**Contact** Mark Peters (Editor)
**Mail address** Angelo Publishing Ltd 8 Old Printing House Arcade, Tarrant Street, Arundel, West Sussex BN18 9DG
**Phone** 01903 885252
**Fax** 01903 885617
**Email** angelo@pavilion.co.uk
**Web** www.angelo.uk.com

## Arts Business Magazine
**Mail address** PO Box 957, Cottenham Cambridge, CB4 8AB
**Phone/Fax** 01954 250600

## Health & Safety Executive (UK)
**Mail address 1** HSE Information Centre, Broad Lane, Sheffield S3 7HQ
**Phone** 0151 951 4000
**Mail address 2** Rose Court, 2 Southwark Bridge Road, London SE1 9HJ
**Phone** 020 7717 6104
**Fax** 020 7717 6134
**HSE Info line** 08701 545500
**Web** www.open.gov.uk/hse

## HSE Books Mail Order
**Mail address** PO Box 1999 Sudbury, Suffolk, CO10 2WA
**Phone** 01787 881165
**Fax** 01787 313995

## International Festivals & Events Association - (IFEA) Europe
**Contact** Evelien Winkel
**Mail address** C/O Netherlands Board of Tourism, P.O.Box 458, 2260 MG Leidschendam, The Netherlands.
**Phone** +31(0) 70 3705 296
**Fax** +31(0) 70 320 1654
**Email** ifea@nbt.nl
**Web** www.ifeaeurope.com

## European Festivals Association
**Contact** Tamas Klenjanszky
**Mail address** 120B rue de Lausanne CH-1202 Geneva, Switzerland
**Phone** +41 22 738 6873
**Fax** +41 22 738 4012
**Email** geneva@euro-festival.net
**Web** www.euro-festival.net

## Festpass
**Mail address** Le Clos du Gravillas, 34360 St. Jean de Minervois, France
**Phone** +33 (4) 673 809 01
**Fax** +33 (4) 673 809 03
**Email** efn@festpass.com
**Web** www.festpass.com

## Association of Music Industry Accountants (AMIA)
**Contact** Julie Hogarth
**Mail address** Unity House, 205 Euston Road, London, NW1 2AY
**Phone** 020 7383 9200
**Fax** 020 7383 9201
**Email** jules.hogarth@ga-lon.demon.co.uk

## Concert Promoters Association (CPA)
**Contact** Carole Smith
**Mail address** 6 St Mark's Road, Henley-on-Thames, Oxon. RG9 1LJ
**Phone** 01491 575 060
**Fax** 01491 414 082
**Email** carolesmith.cpa@virgin.net

## European Forum of Worldwide Music Festivals (EFWMF)
**Contact** Kathleen Jespers
**Mail address** JF Willemsstraat 10a B-2530 Boechout, Belgium
**Phone** +32 3 455 6944
**Fax** +32 3 454 1162
**Email** efwmf@sfinks.be

## National Union of Students (NUS) Ents. Division
**Contact** Jonathan Emmins
**Mail address** 45 Underwood Street, London N1 7LG
**Phone** 020 7490 0946
**Fax** 020 7490 1026
**Email** info@makingwaves.co.uk

## Made-Up Textiles Association (MUTA)
**Mail address** 42 Heath Street, Tamworth, Staffordshire B79 7JH,
**Phone** 01827 52337
**Fax** 01827 310827
**Email** association@muta.org.uk
**Web** www.muta.org.uk

## Regional Promoters Association (RPA)
**Contact** Josh Dean - Concorde Brighton
**Phone** 01273 207241
**Email** info@concorde2.co.uk

## The Agents Association (Great Britain)
**Contact** Bob James
**Mail address** 54 Keyes House, Dolphin Square, London SW1V 3NA
**Phone** 020 7834 0515
**Fax** 020 7821 0261
**Email** bob@artsworld.freeserve.co.uk

## National Campaign for The Arts (NCA)
**Mail address** Pegasus House, 37-43 Sackville Street, London, W15 3EH
**Phone** 020 7 333 0375
**Fax** 020 7333 0660
**Email** nca@artscampaign.org.uk
**Web** www.artscampaign.org.uk

## Local Government Association
**Contact** Roger Sykes
**Mail address** Smith Square London SW1P 3HZ
**Phone** 020 7664 3267
020 7664 3299
**Fax** 020 7664 3210
**Email** roger.sykes@lga.gov.uk

## Arts Fundraising Consultancy
**Phone** 01843 600586
**Email** Artsconsultancy@aol.com

## Arts Marketing Association
**Mail address** Bolton's Warehouse 23 Tenison Rd, Cambridge CB1 2DG
**Web** www.a-m-a.co.uk

## Association of British Theatre Technicians
**Contact** Exec. Director Howard Bird
**Phone** 020 7403 3778
**Email** abtt@pgen.net

## Awards for All
**Mail address** c/o National Lottery Charities Board
**Phone** 0845 6002040
**Web** www.nlbc.org.uk

## Department of Culture, Media and Sport
**Mail address** 2-4 Cockspur Street, London SW1Y 5DH
**Web** www.culture.gov.uk

## Funderfinder
**Phone** 0113 243 3008
**Web** www.funderfinder.org.uk

## Data Protection Register Home Page
**Mail address** Wycliffe House, Water Lane, Wilmslow, Cheshire, SK9 5AF
**Phone** 01625 545700
**Fax** 01625 524510
**Email** mail@dataprotection.gov.uk
**Web** www.dataprotection.gov.uk

## Foundation for Sports and The Arts
**Phone** 0151 259 5505

## National Council for Voluntary Organisers
**Mail address** Regents Wharf, 8 All Saints Street, London, N1 9RL
**Phone** 020 7713 6161
**Email** ncvo@ncvo-vol.org.uk

# CIOFF UK

## The Council of International Organisations of Folklore Festivals and Folk Arts

**The Council of International Organisations of Folklore Festivals and Folk Arts (CIOFF)** was formed in 1970.

Its aims are to promote the intangible heritage through such forms of expression as dance, music, games, rituals, customs and other arts; to serve the objectives of UNESCO (CIOFF has status B at UNESCO); to support the activities of its members and of non-governmental organisations working in the areas of folklore and cultural heritage; to serve the cause of peace through the above objectives.

Membership of CIOFF UK is open to: festivals, organisations, groups and individuals who are based in the UK, who are engaged in the field of folklore, and who support the aims of CIOFF UK.

**Membership Benefits** are:

**CIOFF Annual calendar**
All members shall receive copies of the annual CIOFF Calendar containing a detailed list of CIOFF International festivals around the World and National CIOFF Contacts. Members of CIOFF UK will be listed in the International CIOFF Calendar.

**International Folklore Directory**
All the Members shall receive a free detailed entry in the International Folklore Directory on the Internet. Contact: www.folkloredirectory.com

**CIOFF UK Web-site**
All the members will be listed on the CIOFF UK Web-site with a direct connection to their entry in the International Folklore Directory.
**www.folkloredirectory.com/cioff-uk**

**Invitations from CIOFF World Festivals**
All the members shall receive details of invitations to UK dance and music groups from International CIOFF festivals in other countries both directly and using members password on CIOFF UK Web-site.

**Application from the International Groups**
All the members shall receive details of overseas dance groups willing to take part in UK Festivals.

**Support and advice**
Where possible the members can receive initial contact support and advice from CIOFF UK on their trips abroad or visits of the international groups. At present CIOFF UK is not in a position to give financial support to individual organisations and groups.

**CIOFF UK AGM**
All the members have a right to attend the CIOFF UK Annual General Meetings, but only full members of CIOFF UK are entitled to vote at the AGM.

**Membership Fees**
Annual full membership is £250; associate membership ranges from £100 for festivals to £30 for organisations, groups and individuals.

**Joe Maloney** - Gen. Secretary CIOFF UK

**Olga Maloney** - Treasurer CIOFF UK

**CIOFF UK**, Stockton Business Centre, 70 Brunswick Street, Stockton on Tees, TS18 1DW
**Phone** 01642 651060
**Fax** 01642 602839
**Email** cioff@folkloredirectory.com
**Web** www.folkloredirectory.com

# Youth – A Different Kind of Folk

**Attracting the Youth to Folk, Roots and Traditional events** by **Ross McKinlay**

Young audiences can bring a lot of much needed excitement and enthusiasm to your events and festivals. The Government definition of a 'Youth' is a 13 to 19 year old, but I prefer not to classify them as a certain age.

I believe 'Youth' refers to an independent group of young people who are capable of making their own decisions. Being a 'Youth' is about making decisions concerning life, the clothes you choose to wear, the music you choose to listen to and the events you attend. Most people have an image of the 'Youth of Today' being open-minded and into all sorts of different types of music, but Youth's tastes are as diverse or as conservative as anyone else's.

I have spent a great deal of time trying to recognise common qualities, in any type of event, that attract a Youth audience and found it is easier to pin point the things that discourage them, but that would lead to a very negative article! I have also been to lots of events where there have been hoards of young supporters. The promoter may not have planned to appeal to a young audience; it's just that they have never been discouraged.

Here are a couple of ideas you could use as a way forward when creating or expanding your Youth audience.

- Involve Youth in the planning of your event at a number of different levels. They may be able to help you with the planning; they may like to steward at the event; help to distribute the publicity; run a music session; a workshop or even compere a concert.
- If possible have a ticketing structure so they are not paying as much as the adults. Most Youths are in full time education and you are competing with 'student priced' events.
- When they actually come to your event, talk to them informally and get as much information out of them as you can. If this is your target audience you want to know how they found out about it, if they would ever consider bringing their friends and if they are having a good time. You may even get them to join a mailing list so you can tell them about future events.
- If you do get any details from them, make sure you get their email address. Youths tend to move around from home to home especially if they are students. Email is a great way of keeping them in touch with your future plans.
- If creating a new event aimed at a Youth audience don't bill it as a Youth event, try and be a bit subtle. However, you may need to bill it as a Youth event if you feel this will help to keep an older audience away, for example if it is an established Youth event.
- Bands that you can dance or 'bop' to seem to be an excellent pull for a young audience. This doesn't however mean that a concert, workshop, session or a chance to perform will not equally attract them.
- Think of new places you can display your publicity, where Youths spend a lot of time. It is possible to get your posters and flyers into the local colleges and universities especially if you can enlist the help of friendly students that attend them.
- When planning try a different format to the event. You could have a session that starts at 11pm or include a world/jazz DJ in the gaps between bands.
- Lay the room out in a different way. Does it look inviting as you walk though the door? Is there room to dance if anyone decides to? Good lights and lighting effects add significantly to the overall atmosphere of the night and needn't be expensive.
- If starting an event from scratch choose a good venue that will appeal to the 'Youth', ideally use one that the 'Youth' are already familiar with.
- Children's events will not attract a Youth audience. If including a Youth element as part of a larger event it helps to exclude children as well as adults. Give it a separate identity.
- Young bands don't necessarily attract a young audience, however this could be a good way of introducing Youths to your event. Young bands love performing to young listeners - people that are their own age. Equally, a young audience is very supportive of a young band.

These are some ways you can actively entice 'Youth' to your events, the most important thing being not to discourage them. A new generation of ticket holders, organisers and performers is needed to bring a new level of excitement and passion to your events and festivals.

**Ross McKinlay** *is a musician, Morris dancer and a folk/roots administrator.*

# Children's and Family Entertainment

By **Ray and Bev Langton**

Many events that take place, either festivals or one-day events, attract audiences, which include children. Event organisers should consider whether they aim to provide specific activities for children or not. The programming of specific children's and family activities can often provide a more appropriate setting for children, which may then make the overall event more attractive to adult and family audiences. It is also possible that events that do not cater for children, still find children present who can then spoil the event for other adults. There are also many other reasons why event organisers may decide to promote children's events and activities. Early planning needs to identify priorities so budgets and financial considerations can be included.

Children's entertainers can be quite costly. Venue hire, artists and other needs may not always be covered by ticket revenue. Free, outside family entertainment can attract huge audiences and may be helpful in maintaining good public relations within the community: pro-active collections may help with covering costs. Thought needs to be given to ticket pricing policies, collections and sources of income. Sometimes educational type activities may be eligible for local grants and funding.

For all events involving children, safety is paramount. Consideration must be given to venues, access, equipment and adult supervision. For good, sound advice consult Chapter 22 of **The Event Safety Guide** published by the **Health & Safety Executive**. Advice is given on such areas as: planning and liaison, caring and activities for children within venues and events, facilities and space required and child protection issues. There is also help for considering activities suitable for children of differing ages. It is good practice for any event to have a lost children's policy.

Children's activities involving children 8 years and under, that run for more than 2 hours per day, for 6 or more days of the year are governed by the **1989 Children Act** and will require registration. Details will be available from the Registration and Inspection Unit of the local authority social services department. Even where the Children Act does not apply, the Act provides sound guidelines regarding adult:child ratios and space standards for premises.

Event organisers should ensure that their insurance cover includes the provision they have for children, also that those people working with children are covered by an appropriate insurance.

Children's entertainment covers a wide variety of events and activities. Before booking artists it is often helpful to define the aims of the events. Is the aim to entertain, provide learning opportunities or to occupy children whilst adults enjoy other activities? Entertainment is often well suited to family audiences, learning often means that age groups need to be considered and occupying unaccompanied children for long periods of times may have safety and legislation restrictions.

Children like to be entertained, but it is important to check that any entertainers provide a "clean act" without use of inappropriate language, will not frighten younger children and will not encourage children to try out dangerous activities at home.

Some street entertainment is well suited to outside venues but concerts may need to be programmed within halls or marquees.

Children also like to be actively involved and enjoy learning outside the bounds of the traditional classroom. However, workshop type activities are more suitable for daytime than evening. Children's concentration lessens as the day goes on. If activities for young children last more than an hour organisers need to consider the provision of suitable refreshments. Activities such as singing, dancing, drama and playing instruments are enjoyable and craft based or making things type activities are extremely popular. These latter activities need not cost very much as there are many suppliers of recycled or junk materials that will provide excellent scope for children to develop their imaginative skills. For details investigate local scrap-stores, recycling sections of Yellow Pages or contact local councils. "Making things" activities may well lead to a procession or display of what has been achieved. Such culmination can often be programmed into another part of the event.

There are many excellent potential workshop leaders available who will frequently organise sessions for little financial gain; try local contacts such as dance teams, bands etc. It is often more appropriate to organise learning activities into specific age groups e.g. 5-8 years and 8-11 years. This may then also need to be reflected in ticket pricing policies.

When planning events for children consider the suitability of the venue for the event. Workshops may need tables and chairs, or flooring within marquees. Noisy musical workshops must not conflict with quiet adult events and likewise amplified music from nearby concerts may conflict with quiet storytelling for children. Some activities may need specific equipment e.g. power supplies, water, lighting etc. and some activities are not so easy to organise within marquees as others are. Special considerations must be given to childcare facilities for pre-school children.

Children and families enjoy stories and there are many good storytellers available. Storytelling is often an attractive family event so long as artists are aware of the target audience.

Puppets are massively popular with all ages and many puppeteers can provide more than just the traditional Punch and Judy shows. Promoters would be well advised to ask puppeteers about the range of both indoor and outdoor shows that they can offer. Many excellent puppeteers belong to **The Midlands Puppet Forum**. Prices of puppeteers vary widely, however often quality is reflected in price. Many puppeteers do have specific technical requirements based on their own experience; promoters should take care to consult on these in advance.

Places to see a wide variety of entertainers and activities for children and families include **Chippenham Folk Festival**, **Festival At The Edge**, **Sidmouth International Festival**, **Stroud Fringe Festival**, **The Larmer Tree Festival** and **Towersey Village Festival**.

Some of the well-known and popular artists who have appeared at the above festivals include **Albert the Clown**, **Beresford Puppets**, **Brog Puppets**, **Caz**, **Colonel Custard**, **Dr Sunshine**, **Mick Scott's Hurly Burly Theatre**, **Martin Bridle The Puppet Man**, **Mike Jackson**, **No Strings Theatre**, **Pete White's Suitcase Circus**, **Pekkos Puppets**, **Poppets Puppets**, **Strawberry the Clown** and **Ticklish Allsorts**.

Most of these can provide a variety of activities including both performance and workshops. Fees vary according to what is taking place and wherever possible organisers are advised to view the acts themselves or follow up trusted references.

Organisers may also consider if any artists booked for the main event can contribute to the Children's Programme e.g. **Chris Foster**, **Colum Sands**, **Mike Fenton**, **Patrick Ryan**, **Pete Coe**, **Roy Atkinson (Colonel Custard)** and **The Chipolatas** have a variety of activities for both adult and children.

For events offering family ceilidhs, consider the choice of caller and suitability of the band. An event that caters well for children may well inspire enthusiasm for other events, but those that do not can easily have the opposite effect.

## *Contacts*

**The Event Safety Guide**
**HSE Info Phone** 0541 545500

**The Midlands Puppet Forum**
**Phone** 0121 441 5694

**Ray and Bev Langton**
*Children's Festival Producers at Sidmouth International Festival*
**Phone** 01939 233977
**Email** bev.langton@talk21.com

## ADA DISTRIBUTION & mail order specialists

PO Box 800 Belper Derby DE56 2ZA

ADA stocks most British Labels, including some of the harder to find titles, with a great selection of music from USA, Canada, France, Italy, Latvia, Sweden, Finland, Norway, Spain and other world music.

ADA is open 10 am - 5 pm Mon-Fri
Free catalogue on request
Compare our prices

ADA are the largest independent mail order CD specialists in the UK

Orders and Enquiries
Phone or Fax

**01773 850000**

e-mail adamailorder@aol.com
http://members.aol.com/adamailorder

Remember - ADA is just a phone call away!

## Oisín Studios

## Wolverton

*A compact, friendly and comfortable studio, only 55 miles from London with good road, rail and canal links to all parts of the country.*
*We specialize in acoustic music but are also able to offer state of the art computer composition and editing under the watchful eyes and ears of Steáfán Hannigan, Producer and Engineer.*

*Contact us:*
*o-omusic@dircon.co.uk*
*vivienne@jvmb.powernet.co.uk*
*01908 225500 (Studio)*

## The Music Room

Britain's centre of excellence for traditional musical instruments

**Covering all your traditional music needs...**

CLECKHEATON
YORKSHIRE HEAD OFFICE
SALES · ENQUIRIES · REPAIRS · WORLDWIDE MAIL ORDER
35 Bradford Road · Cleckheaton · West Yorkshire · BD19 3JN
Tel. 01274 879768 · Fax. 01274 852280

NOTTINGHAM – SALES · ENQUIRIES · REPAIRS
Tel. 0115 947 6911 · Fax. 0115 947 3179

OXFORD – SALES · ENQUIRIES · REPAIRS
Tel/Fax. 01865 249292

**WORLDWIDE MAIL ORDER +44 (0)1274 852020**
please visit our huge web site with secure shopping cart
**the-music-room.com**
E mail: info@the-music-room.com

## The Other Agency Session Fixing

If you need an unusual instrument to complete your recording, or a complete session solution for your album, **try us.**

We offer a huge range of unusual instruments from a wide variety of ethnic sources.

All kinds of Woodwind, Strings, Percussion, Brass
**Just ask**

String sections
Rhythm sections
in a wide variety of styles.

Clients have included Uriah Heep, Beth Orton, Gary Barlow, Loreena McKennett, Jackie Leven, Broderick, No masters, V2, Oysterband, Lionhead

01908 542 894
01908 22 55 00

# services

services
event

- Event Management
- Instrument Makers, Repairers and Retailers

## Event management

### All Sorted Event Management
**Contact** Graham Bradshaw
**Mail address** 250 Earlsdon Avenue North, COVENTRY, CV5 6GX
**Phone** 024 7671 1616
**Fax** 024 76 711191
**Email** rootsrecs@btclick.com
**Alt contact** Dick Dixon
**Phone** 024 7671 1616
**Email** dick.dixon@warfolk.demon.co.uk
*Event organisers and infrastructure providers for festivals, local authorities, corporate events.*
**RAB** West Midlands Arts

### Brass Tacks
**Contact** Kit Bailey
**Mail address** PO Box 1162, SHEFFIELD, Yorks, S8 9JY
**Phone** 0114 250 9124
07957 822642
**Fax** 0114 255 4973
**Email** brass250@aol.com
*Event co-ordinator and producer.*
**RAB** Yorkshire Arts

### Continental Drifts
**Contact** Chris Tofu
**Mail address** Hilton Grove, Hatherley Mews, LONDON, E17 4QP
**Phone** 020 8509 3353
**Fax** 020 8509 9531
**Web** www.continentaldrifts.uk.com
**Alt address** Chats Palace, Brooksbys Walk, LONDON, E8
*Agency working with new global dance music; organise festivals. Deal with music beyond the folk/ roots mainstream.*
**RAB** London Arts

### Gordie Campbell
**Contact** Peerie Angel Productions
**Mail address** 1A Towedykeside, HAWICK, Scottish Borders, TD9 9EA
**Phone** 01450 372081
**Email** gordiecampbell@aol.com
*Scotland based production/ tour management, festival organisation & artist relations. Previously based in Canada, now UK available.*
**AC** Scotland

### Heypressco
**Contact** Paul Saunders
**Mail address** 6 Swan Meadow, MUCH WENLOCK, Shropshire, TF13 6JQ
**Phone** 01952 728283
**Email** ps@workingjoe.co.uk
**Web** www.heypressco.com
*Event management for roots, historic music and related arts.*
***Musicians' Union member***
**RAB** West Midlands Arts

### Hot Promotions
**Contact** The Hot Hole
**Mail address** PO Box TR69, LEEDS, LS12 5HE
**Phone** 0113 2566733
**Email** hotholesalsa@hotmail.com
**Web** www.magnificent.net/hothole or www.hothole.leedsnet.org
*Event organisers, agency service for world music bands and dancers.*
**RAB** Yorkshire Arts

### Mrs Casey Music
**Contact** Steve Heap
**Mail address** PO Box 296, AYLESBURY, Bucks, HP19 9TL
**Phone** 01296 394411
**Fax** 01296 392300
**Email** office@mrscasey.co.uk
**Web** www.mrscasey.co.uk
*Festival & event organisers and consultants.*
**RAB** Southern Arts

### Roy Morley
**Mail address** 57 Ealing Park Mansions, South Ealing Road, LONDON, W5 4QH
**Phone** 020 8566 3142
07850 726735
**Fax** 020 85797584
**Email** roymorley@eventlogistics.demon.co.uk
*Site & event logistics; site management, licensing, health & safety, risk assessment, event safety plans, production.*
**RAB** London Arts

### Shanty Jack Consultancy
**Contact** Pete Hayselden
**Mail address** 16 The Kingsway, CLEETHORPES, Lincs, DN35 8QU
**Phone/Fax** 01472 696757
**Phone** 07970 651293
**Email** shantyjack@anchorage.f9.co.uk
*Consultancy services for promoters and organisers of maritime events/ events incorporating maritime elements. NB not an agency, works on behalf of the organiser.*
***Musicians' Union member***
**RAB** Yorkshire Arts

### Well Groomed Management
**Contact** Dave Groom
**Mail address** 80 Hood Street, NOTTINGHAM, NG5 4AQ
**Phone** 0115 952 2638
**Email** wellgroomed@proweb.co.uk
*Festival organisation, artist management, event management.*
**RAB** East Midlands Arts

## Instrument services

### A C Norman & Co
**Contact** Andrew Norman
**Mail address** Old Stables, Nursery Lane, NUTLEY, E Sussex, TN22 3NR
**Phone** 01825 713551
**Email** acnorman@btinternet.com
**Web** www.acnorman.co.uk
*Concertina manufacturer and restorer. Antique free reed specialist. Please call during office hours.*
**RAB** South East Arts

### Alan Edgar
**Mail address** 43 Beverley Road, HESSLE, E Yorks, HU13 9AE
**Phone** 01482 640330
*Maker of small harps and wood & brass music stands.*
**RAB** Yorkshire Arts

### Andy Perkins Traditional Instruments
**Contact** Andy Perkins
**Mail address** Apple Craft Centre, Selling Road, FAVERSHAM, Kent, ME13 8XF
**Phone** 01795 590374
01795 533864
**Email** andybanjo@aol.com
**Web** www.andybanjo.com
*Specialist banjo maker, dealer and repairer.*
***Musicians' Union member***
**RAB** South East Arts

### The Bagpipe Centre
**Contact** Willie Haines
**Mail address** 49 Blackfriars Street, Off The Royal Mile, EDINBURGH, EH1 1NB
**Phone** 0131 557 3090
**Email** scotfolk@compuserve.com
*Retailer of smallpipes and highland pipes, books, CDs and accessories.*
**AC** Scotland

### Bedroom Acoustic Music
**Mail address** 94 Dunstable Street, Ampthill, Beds. MK45 2JB
**Phone** 01525 404304
*Retailer of acoustic musical instruments; guitars, mandolins, whistles, melodeons, concertinas, etc. Open every day except Tuesday.*
**RAB** East England Arts

### Beverley Music Centre
**Contact** Rosalind Willoughby
**Mail address** 14 Norwood, BEVERLEY, East Yorks, HU17 9EZ
**Phone** 01482 881584
**Fax** 01482 867653
**Email** shop@beverleymusiccentre.co.uk
**Web** www.beverleymusiccentre.co.uk
*Music shop selling, repairing & valuing violins/ string instruments & accessories. Also sheet music & other instruments.*
**RAB** Yorkshire Arts

### Blackfriars Music
**Contact** Willie Haines
**Mail address** 49 Blackfriars Street, Off The Royal Mile, EDINBURGH, EH1 1NB, Scotland
**Phone** 0131 557 3090
**Email** scotfolk@compuserve.com
**Web** www.blackfriarsmusic.com
*Retailer of musical instruments and books.*
**AC** Scotland

### Brian Rathmill
**Mail address** 15 Belfairs Close, ASHTON UNDER LYME, Lancs, OL7 9TE
**Phone/Fax** 0161 330 4555
**Phone** 0161 447 1886
**Email** brian@briarmill.co.uk
**Web** www.briarmill.co.uk
*Producer of table mounted supports for guitars and fiddles & bow. Mail Order.*
**RAB** North West Arts

### Bridge Instruments Ltd
**Contact** Paul Bridgewater
**Mail address** Units 11-12, The Hoplands Business Centre, Boston Road, SLEAFORD, Lincs, NG34 7LZ
**Phone** 01529 415372
**Email** bridgeinst@aol.com
**Web** www.electricviolins.com/ www.bridgeinstruments.com
*Makers of violins and electric violins, violas, (inc 5 strings), cellos & double basses.*
**RAB** East Midlands Arts

### C & R Dipper
**Contact** Colin & Rosalie Dipper
**Mail address** West End House, High Street, Heytesbury, WARMINSTER, Wilts, BA12 0EA
**Phone** 01985 849516
**Email** dipperconcertinas@hotmail.com
*Concertina makers, restorers, repairers, designers, valuations, tuning, new & old systems. Anything concertina!*
**RAB** Southern Arts

### C Wheatstone & Co
**Contact** Steve Dickinson
**Mail address** 21 Bridge Street, STOWMARKET, Suffolk, IP14 1BP
**Phone** 01449 615523
**Email** concertinas@wheatstone.co.uk
**Web** www.wheatstone.co.uk
*Manufacturer of Wheatstone Concertinas. All instruments are handmade to order. Spares and repairs also available.*
**RAB** East England Arts

### Colchester Strings
**Contact** Mark Surridge
**Mail address** Unit 36A The Cowdray Centre, Cowdray Avenue, COLCHESTER, CO1 1BH
**Phone** 01206 543359
*Violin, mandolin, banjo repairs; bow rehairing and repair; violin sales.*
**RAB** East England Arts

### Colin Thompson Woodwind and String Repairs
**Mail address** 80 Dorchester Road, MAIDEN NEWTON, Dorset, DT2 0BG
**Phone** 01300 320558
*Repair, servicing & restoration of string & woodwind musical instruments.*
***Musicians' Union member***
**RAB** South West Arts

### Concertina Research and Resources
**Contact** Neil Wayne
**Mail address** The Cedars BELPER, Derbys, DE56 1DP
**Phone** 01773 824157
**Email** concertinas@free-reed.co.uk
**Web** www.come.to/concertinas
*Research, advice and publications on all aspects of the concertina and other free reed instruments.*
**RAB** East Midlands Arts

### Crehan Musical Instruments Ltd
**Mail address** 6 Carberry Road, Drumcondra, DUBLIN 9, Ireland
**Email** niall@crehans.com
**Web** www.crehans.com
**Email** ncrehan@eircom.net
*Violin makers & repairers. Accessories.*
**AC** Ireland

### Dave Shaw
**Mail address** 2 Shafto Cottage, Craghead, STANLEY, Durham, DH9 6DW
**Phone** 01207 231474
**Email** dave@daveshaw.co.uk
**Web** www.daveshaw.co.uk
*Northumbrian smallpipe maker and player. "Play in a day" workshops.*
***Musicians' Union member***
**RAB** Northern Arts

### David Thomas, Luthier
**Contact** David Thomas
**Mail address** 119 Kenilworth Road, EDGEWARE, Middx, HA8 8XB
**Phone** 020 8958 4947
*Maker of violins, violas and mandolins.*
***Musicians' Union member***
**RAB** London Arts

### DM Guitars
**Contact** Dan MacPherson
**Mail address** 179 Stornaway Road, SOUTHEND ON SEA, Essex, SS2 4NJ
**Phone** 01702 469301
07956 333527
*Luthier, stringed instrument maker and repairer. Polyester finishing specialist.*
**RAB** East England Arts

### Fine Tuning
**Contact** Tony Westran
**Phone/Fax** 01302 562875
**Phone** 07958 963417
**Email** fine-tuning@appleonline.net
*Maker and supplier of early & unusual musicial instruments. Hands on fun & educational demonstrations for festivals, schools, colleges, etc.*
**RAB** Yorkshire Arts

### Gerhard Kress @ Gurt Mint Drums
**Contact** Gerhard Kress
**Mail address** 6 Maycliffe Park, Ashley Down, BRISTOL, BS6 5JH
**Phone** 0117 954 2351
**Email** gurtmint@fsmail.net
*Maker and repairer of bodhrans, maker of long drums & morris bell pads.*
**RAB** South West Arts

### Gina Le Faux
**Mail address** 359 Salterhebble Hill, HALIFAX, Yorks, HX3 0QA
**Phone** 01422 362634
0789 9773537
*Fiddle/viola maker.*
**RAB** Yorkshire Arts

### The Guitar Doctor
**Contact** Alan Dumbleton
**Mail address** The Shambles, 1 Eastfield Road, BARTON UPON HUMBER, N Lincs, DN18 6AN
**Phone** 01652 636300
*Luthier, acoustic and fretted instruments made, repaired and refurbished.*
**RAB** Yorkshire Arts

### Highly Strung
**Contact** Nigel Thornbory
**Mail address** PO Box 90, WANTAGE, Oxon, OX12 9YT
**Phone** 01235 762000
**Email** nigel@highlystrung.co.uk
**Web** www.highlystrung.co.uk
*Online guitar store; sales of guitar accessories, strings, books & videos.*
**RAB** Southern Arts

### Hobgoblin Music
**Contact** Pete McClelland
**Mail address** PO Box 2522, HENFIELD, Sussex, BN5 9SN
**Phone** 07000 462462 - mail order
**Fax** 01273 419923
**Email** post@hobgoblin.co.uk
**Web** www.hobgoblin.com
*Chain of folk instrument & music shops. Branches throughout England.*
**RAB** South East Arts
***See Introduction to Hobgoblin***

### Hobgoblin Music (Bristol)
**Mail address** 30 College Green, BRISTOL, BS1 5TB
**Phone** 0117 929 0902
**Email** bristol@hobgoblin.co.uk
**RAB** South West Arts

### Hobgoblin Music (Crawley)
**Mail address** 17 The Parade, Northgate, CRAWLEY, W Sussex, RH10 2DT
**Phone** 01293 515858
**Email** crawley@hobgoblin.co.uk
**RAB** South East Arts

### Hobgoblin Music (Leeds)
**Mail address** 39 Call Lane, LEEDS, LS1 7BT
**Phone** 0113 245 3311
**Email** leeds@hobgoblin.co.uk
**RAB** Yorkshire Arts

### Hobgoblin Music (London)
**Mail address** 24 Rathbone Place, LONDON, W1T 1JA
**Phone** 020 7323 9040
**Email** london@hobgoblin.co.uk
**RAB** London Arts

### Hobgoblin Music (Manchester)
**Mail address** 123 Oxford Road, All Saints, MANCHESTER, M1 7DU
**Phone** 0161 273 1000
**Email** manchester@hobgoblin.co.uk
**RAB** North West Arts

### Hobgoblin Music (Nottingham)
**Mail address** 58 Derby Road, NOTTINGHAM, NG1 5FD
**Phone** 0115 911 9440
**Email** nottingham@hobgoblin.co.uk
**RAB** East Midlands Arts

### John Dike Violins
**Contact** John Dike
**Mail address** Westbury, SHERBORNE, Dorset, DT9 3EJ
**Phone** 01935 389070
*Violin maker and restorer. Violins, violas and cellos for sale. Bow rehairs. Repairs to stringed instruments and fiddle accessories.*
***Musicians' Union member***
**RAB** South West Arts

### Jonathan Shortland
**Phone** 029 2046 5639
**Fax** 029 2025 6168
**Email** jonathan.shortland@vizzavi.net
*Maker and player of flutes, various bagpipes, pastoral oboes, pibgorn, etc.*
***Musicians' Union member***
**AC** Wales

### Julian Goodacre Bagpipe Maker
**Mail address** 4 Elcho Street, PEEBLES, EH45 8LQ, Scotland
**Phone** 01721 722539
**Email** goodacres@cwcom.net
**Web** www.goodacrepipes.mcmail.com
*Bagpiper maker and repairer. Publisher of tunebooks and CDs of English piping. Performer with the Goodacre Brothers English bagpipe trio.*
**AC** Scotland

### Kai Toenjes
**Mail address** 4 Grovehurst Ave, SITTINGBOURNE, Kent, ME10 2RL
**Phone** 01795 423399
**Web** www.kai-toenjes.de
*Handmade instruments to customer's requirements; Irish bouzouki, citterns, mandolins, violins, violas, viola d'amore.*
**RAB** South East Arts

### Kathleen Robertshaw
**Mail address** Yarnbury House, GRASSINGTON, North Yorks, BD23 5EQ
**Phone** 01756 753014
**Email** rshaw@daelnet.co.uk
*Professional string repair and renovation. Maker of handmade guitars and fretted folk instruments.*
**RAB** Yorkshire Arts

### Knock On Wood
**Contact** Andy Wilson - Mail Order
**Mail address** Glasshouses Mill, HARROGATE, HG3 5QN
**Phone** 01423 712712
**Email** kow@globalnet.co.uk
**Web** www.knockonwood.co.uk
**Alt contact** Shop
**Alt address** 13 Eastgate, LEEDS, Yorks, LS2 7LY
**Phone** 0113 242 9146
**Fax** 0113 245 9878
*Retail, mail order and internet supplier of instruments, books and recordings from around the world. Specialist in Brazilian, African and Latin percussion.*
**RAB** Yorkshire Arts

### The Living Tradition (Retail)
**Contact** Tony O Flaherty
**Mail address** 40 Mac Curtain Street, CORK, Ireland
**Phone** +353 21 4502564
**Email** info@thelivingtradition.com
**Web** www.thelivingtradition.com
*Specialist traditional music shop. Irish & world music CDs, traditional musical instruments.*
**AC** Ireland

### Luton Accordion Centre
**Contact** Joe MacCarney
**Phone** 01582 402324
*Accordion & melodeon retailer. Tuning, repair & midi. Straps & accessories.*
**RAB** East England Arts

### MAC Distribution
**Contact** Derek Moir
**Mail address** 1 The Stables Yard, 1103 Argyle Street, GLASGOW, G3 8ND
**Phone/Fax** 0141 2215200
**Email** derek@macdistribution.com
**Web** www.macdistribution.com
**Alt contact** Steve Dunn
**Email** steve@macdistribution.com
*Music distribution to all major chains and the indie/ specialist sector.*
**AC** Scotland

### Mannings Musicals
**Contact** Malcolm Manning
**Mail address** 75 Westgate, BRADFORD, W Yorks, BD1 2RD
**Phone** 01274 723539
**Email** malcolm@mannings-musicals.force9.co.uk
**Web** www.mannings-musicals.force9.co.uk
*Retailer of old & unusual musical instruments.*
**RAB** Yorkshire Arts

### The Melodeon Repairer
**Contact** Pete Grassby
**Mail address** 22 Derwent Road, COVENTRY, W Mids, CV6 2HB
**Phone** 024 7633 6740
07768 683015
*Melodeon, concertin, accordion, bodhran repairs. Dealer in books, new/ used/ restored instruments.*
**RAB** West Midlands Arts

### Mick McConway Handmade Guitars
**Contact** Mick McConway
**Mail address** 4 Grosvenor Gardens, Jesmond, NEWCASTLE, NE2 1HQ
**Phone** 0191 281 1610
*Maker of acoustic & some electric guitars (not kits). Repairs & refrets. Also folk harps.*
**RAB** Northern Arts

### Mike Gilpin Hurdy Gurdies
**Mail address** Hill Cottage, Heath Road, SWAFFHAM BULBECK, Cambs, CB5 0LS
**Phone** 01223 812378
**Email** mjgilpin@tesco.net
*Hurdy gurdy maker; Bosch, 19th century French guitar bodied, 19th century French lute back. Also tuition.*
**RAB** East England Arts

### Moon Guitars
**Contact** Joan Moon
**Mail address** 974 Pollockshaws Road, Shawlands, GLASGOW, G41 2HA, Scotland
**Phone** 0141 6329526
**Fax** 0141 6324928
**Email** moonguitars@btinternet.com
**Web** www.moonguitars.co.uk
*Makers of acoustic and electric guitars, mandolins, bouzoukis, mandolas and citterns.*
**AC** Scotland

### Music Magic
**Contact** Tim Manning
**Mail address** 12 Bath Road, FROME, Somerset, BA11 2HH
**Phone** 01373 465596
**Email** music.magic@virgin.net
**Web** www.homepage.virgin.net/music.magic
*Musical instrument maker; construction and renovation of instruments including hammered dulcimer, lyre, cymbalom, aeolian harp, tongue drum, etc. Hammered dulcimer player.*
**RAB** South West Arts

### The Music Room
**Mail address** 35 Bradford Road, CLECKHEATON, W Yorks, BD19 3JN
**Phone** 01274 879768
01274 852020 - mail order
**Fax** 01274 852280
**Email** info@the-music-room.com
**Web** www.the-music-room.com
*Retailers and repairers of musical instruments, books, tutors, etc. Melodeon specialists.*
**RAB** Yorkshire Arts

### The Music Room (Nottingham Branch)
**Mail address** 123-125 Mansfield Road, NOTTINGHAM, NG1 3FQ
**Phone** 0115 9476911
**Fax** 0115 9473179
**Email** info@the-music-room.com
**Web** www.the-music-room.com
*Retailers and repairers of musical instruments, books, tutors, etc. Melodeon specialists.*
**RAB** East Midlands Arts

### The Music Room (Oxford Branch)
**Mail address** 27 Park End Street, Holly Bush Row Entrance, OXFORD, OX1 1HU
**Phone** 01865 249292
**Email** info@the-music-room.com
**Web** www.the-music-room.com
*Retailers and repairers of musical instruments, books, tutors, etc. Free reed specialists.*
**RAB** Southern Arts

### Oakwood Instruments
**Contact** Martyn Banks
**Mail address** 8 Ladywood Road, LEEDS, LS8 2ZF
**Phone** 0113 2658585
**Fax** 0113 2933011
**Email** workshop@oakwoodinstruments.co.uk
**Web** www.oakwoodinstruments.co.uk
*Makers of hand-made musical instruments; fretted strings, hammered dulcimers, harps andelectric instruments.*
**RAB** Yorkshire Arts

### P G Bleazey
**Contact** Phil Bleazey
**Mail address** 62 Chestnut Drive, New Ollerton, NEWARK, Notts, NG22 9SJ
**Phone** 01623 836814
**Email** phil@bleazey.co.uk
**Web** www.bleazey.co.uk
*Maker of wooden flutes, recorders, whistles & drums*
**RAB** East Midlands Arts

### Pat Stones
**Mail address** 22 Fairford Avenue, LUTON, Beds, LU2 7ER
**Phone** 01582 459585
**Email** patstones@clara.co.uk
*Maker of uilleann pipes. Please leave messages in the day for evening reply.*
**RAB** East Midlands Arts

### Paul Hathway
**Mail address** 47 Langley Drive, Wanstead, LONDON, E11 2LN
**Phone** 020 8530 4317
**Fax** 020 8925 9879
*Musical instrument maker & repairer. Mandolins, mandolas, bouzoukis, guitars, etc.*
**RAB** London Arts

### Pete Oakley Music
**Contact** Pete Oakley
**Mail address** 46 Station Street, BURTON ON TRENT, Staffs, DE65 5GU
**Phone** 01283 500366
01283 500365
**Email** pete@guitarsuperstore.com
**Web** www.guitarsuperstore.com or www.musicbooksonline.com
*Musical instrument retailer; guitar & folk instruments, sheet music/ books, repair & tuition. Online shop.*
**RAB** West Midlands Arts

### Peter Barton (Guitars)
**Mail address** 36 Main Street, Addingham, ILKLEY, West Yorks, LS29 0PL
**Phone** 01943 830447
**Email** pete@pbarton.dabsol.co.uk
**Alt contact** Barton - Workshop
**Alt address** 2 Bolton Road, Addingham, ILKLEY, W Yorks, LS29 0NR
**Phone** 01943 831749
*Acoustic guitar maker and repairer.*
**RAB** Yorkshire Arts

### Phil Brown
**Contact** Big Whistle Music
**Mail address** PO Box 23, ACCRINGTON, Lancs, BB5 5GX
**Phone/Fax** 01254 397623
**Phone** 07976 809623
**Email** phil@bigwhistle.co.uk
**Web** www.bigwhistle.co.uk
*Player of high and low whistles. Specialist supplier of instruments & materials. Workshops.*
**RAB** North West Arts

- **Instrument Makers, Repairers and Retailers**
- **PA & Lighting** (inc sound engineers, PA hire, pickup systems etc.)

### Rainbow Violin Co Ltd
**Contact** Emma Newton
**Mail address** 16 High Street, Merstham, SURREY, RH1 3EA
**Phone** 01737 645065
**Fax** 01737 645808
**Email** rainbowviolins@yahoo.co.uk
*Sales and service of acoustic and electric violins, violas, cellos, pickups, acoustic amps and accessories.*
**RAB** South East Arts

### S & E M Turner Violins
**Contact** S & E M Turner
**Mail address** 1-5 Lily Grove, Beeston, NOTTINGHAM, Notts, NG9 1QL
**Phone** 0115 943 0333
**Fax** 0115 943 0444
**Web** www.turnerviolins.co.uk
*Fiddles, violins, violas, cellos, double basses and bows.*
**RAB** East Midlands Arts

### Soar Valley Music
**Contact** David Ledsam
**Mail address** 3 Waldron Court, Prince William Road, LOUGHBOROUGH, Leics, LE11 5GU
**Phone** 01509 269629
**Fax** 01509 269206
**Email** info@soarmusic.demon.co.uk
**Web** www.soarmusic.demon.co.uk
*Supplier of traditional musical instruments plus African, Celtic and samba percussion.*
**RAB** East Midlands Arts

### Springers Music
**Contact** Pamela Wilson
**Mail address** Devils Dream Cottage, Colts Hill, Capel, TONBRIDGE, Kent, TN12 6SW
**Phone** 01892 835191
**Email** springers@springersmusic.co.uk
**Web** www.springersmusic.co.uk
*Musical instrument sales and repairs.*
**RAB** South East Arts

### Starfish Designs
**Contact** Mike Anderson
**Phone** 01855 821429
**Fax** 01855 821062
**Email** mike@starfishdesigns.co.uk
**Web** www.starfishdesigns.co.uk
**Alt contact** Dave Shepton
**Email** dave@starfishdesigns.co.uk
*Makers of a range of celtic harps, electric violins, cellos, violas and basses.*
**AC** Scotland

### Ted Brewer Violins
**Contact** Ted Brewer
**Mail address** 3 Lymington Lane, Treeton, ROTHERHAM, S60 5UG
**Phone/Fax** 0114 2691518
**Phone** 01554 231109
**Email** violin@lineone.net
*Maker of acrylic electric violins.*
**RAB** Yorkshire Arts

### The Violin Shop
**Contact** Ray Daniel
**Mail address** 11 Blackie Street, GLASGOW, G3 8TN, Scotland
**Phone** 0141 339 8078
**Email** rayandbill@theviolinshop-glasgow.co.uk
**Web** www.theviolinshop-glasgow. co.uk
**Alt contact** Bill McKenzie
*Retailers, repairers and makers of stringed instruments including violins, violas, cellos, double basses & accessories.*
**AC** Scotland

### Tim Phillips Violin Maker
**Contact** Tim Phillips
**Mail address** The Mill, Mochdre, NEWTOWN, Powys, SY16 4JL, Wales
**Phone** 01686 624536
**Email** timsviolins@supanet.com
**Web** www.timsviolins.supanet.com
*Maker of violins, 5 string violins, octave violins and 5 string violas, including unusual designs. Plus cases, bows, strings, etc.*
**AC** Wales

### Totnes School of Guitar Making
**Contact** Norman Reed
**Mail address** Collins Road, TOTNES, Devon, TQ9 5PJ
**Phone** 01803 865255
**Email** info@totnesschoolofguitarmaking.co.uk
**Web** www.totnesschoolofguitarmaking.co.uk
**Alt contact** James Huxley/Phill Messer
*Offer a 12 week course on making any kind of guitar or related instrument. Runs Sep - Dec, Jan - Mar and May - July every year.*
**RAB** South West Arts

### Wesson Accordion Co
**Contact** Rees Wesson
**Mail address** PO Box 55, WELSHPOOL, SY21 9WA, Wales
**Phone** 01938 556438
07980 258038
**Email** rees@melodeons.com
**Web** www.melodeons.com
*Melodeon sales. Main UK importer and stockist of Castagnari melodeons.*
***Musicians' Union member***
**AC** Wales

### Woodwind by De Witt
**Contact** Andrew De Witt
**Mail address** 51a Station Road, BARNET, Herts, EN5 1PR
**Phone** 020 8364 8090
**Email** kad_info@compuserve.com
**Web** http://ourworld.compuserve.com/homepages/kad_info
*Maker of all-wooden Irish whistles, custom voiced.*
**RAB** London Arts

## Lighting and PA

### ADPA
**Contact** Adie Bolton
**Mail address** 13 Drummond Street, EDINBURGH, EH8 9TU, Scotland
**Phone/Fax** 0131 557 6157
**Phone** 07711 574133
**Email** adie@adpa.co.uk
**Web** www.adpa.co.uk
*PA & transportation company, specialising in acoustic folk music.*
**AC** Scotland

### Amplification Services
**Contact** Roy Kavanagh
**Phone** 01563 850976
07703 530301
**Web** www.ampserv.freeserve.co.uk
*PA & lighting company. .*
**AC** Scotland

### Andrew Cronshaw
**Contact** Cloud Valley Music
**Mail address** 51 Hainault Court, Forest Rise, LONDON, E17 3NW
**Phone** 020 8521 4649
**Email** cloudval@aol.com
**Web** http://members.aol.com/cloudval
*Sound engineer.*
***Musicians' Union member***
**RAB** London Arts

### Angel Sound Systems
**Contact** John Henry
**Mail address** Lucton Court, Lucton, LEOMINSTER, Herefordshire, HR6 9PQ
**Phone** 01568 780534
**Fax** 01568 780996
*PA hire company.*
**RAB** West Midlands Arts

### Bluebear PA Hire
**Contact** Sarah Jones
**Mail address** The Forge , Goodrich, ROSS ON WYE, Herefordshire, HR9 6HY
**Phone/Fax** 01600 891284
**Phone** 07973 143950
**Email** sarah@bluebearmusic.demon.co.uk
**Web** www.bluebearmusic.demon.co.uk
*1 KW front of house, foldback, etc. Run by musicians, for small to medium venues.*
**RAB** West Midlands Arts

**C V Audio**
**Contact** Graham Bradshaw
**Mail address** 250 Earlsdon Avenue North, COVENTRY, CV5 6GX
**Phone** 024 7671 1935
**Fax** 024 7671 1191
*Sound hire, specialising in folk music.*
**RAB** West Midlands Arts

**Calton Acoustics**
Keith Calton
**Mail address** 6 Grove Road, Ash, NR ALDERSHOT, Hants, GU12 5BD
**Phone** 01252 314300
**Email** keith@calton.fsbusiness.co.uk
*600 Watt to 2500 Watt PA system for acoustic music, 12-16 channel desks. References available.*
**RAB** South East Arts

**Dansing Music**
**Contact** Dan Evans
**Mail address** 61 Sillswood, OLNEY, Bucks, MK46 5PN
**Phone** 01234 241976
**Fax** 01234 241976
**Email** dansing.music@virgin.net
**Web** www.musiclink.co.uk/dansing
*Acoustic PA service for small/ medium sized venues.*
***Musicians' Union member***
**RAB** East England Arts

**Gaelforce Productions**
**Contact** David Town
**Mail address** Unit 41, Queenslie Business Centre, GLASGOW, G33 4AN, Scotland
**Phone** 0141 774 5120
07973 688121
**Fax** 07973 688123
**Email** davetown@breathe.com
**Web** www.gaelforce-productions.co.uk
*Comprehensive sound hire facility with leaning towards roots, folk and acoustic music. Regular clients include Peatbog Faeries, Fiddlers Bid, Celtic Connections festival.*
**AC** Scotland

**Headway Electronics Partners**
**Contact** John Littler
**Mail address** PO Box 408, BANBURY, Oxon, OX15 4XU
**Phone** 01295 721180
**Fax** 01295 722916
**Email** 106200.667@compuserve.com
**Web** www.bigfoot.com/~headway electronics
**Alt contact** Steve Head
**Alt address** PO Box 12043, LONDON, E4 6YJ
**Phone** 020 8923 6390
020 8524 1855
**Fax** 020 8524 6414
*Makers of pickup systems to amplify musical instruments.*
**RAB** Southern Arts

**Hipposound**
**Contact** John Wirtz
**Mail address** Park Farm, Buckland Down, FROME, Somerset, BA11 2RG
**Phone** 01373 813590
**Fax** 01373 813518
**Email** John.wirtz@hipposound.co.uk
*PA Hire services*
**RAB** South West Arts

**Jake Loveday**
**Mail address** 3 Mains of Dumbreck, Undy, ELLON, Aberdeenshire, AB41 7PJ
**Phone** 07803 020850
**Email** jaketekkie@aol.com
*Sound engineer. Works with many different types of music, venues and festivals. Can arrange PA hire.*
**AC** Scotland

**JRP Sound Engineering**
**Contact** Jim Rolley-Parnell
**Mail address** c/o 75 Coopes Way, CHADDESDEN, Derby, DE21 4NU
**Phone** 07967 806547
**Fax** 01332 231563
**Email** jimrp@jrpsound.co.uk
**Web** www.jrpsound.co.uk
**RAB** East Midlands Arts

**London Musicians' Collective**
**Contact** Ed Baxter
**Mail address** 3-6 Lafone House, 11-13 Leathermarket Street, LONDON, SE1 3HN
**Phone** 020 7403 1922
**Fax** 020 7403 1880
**Email** lmc@lmcltd.demon.co.uk
**Web** www.l-m-c.org.uk
**Alt contact** Mick Ritchie
**Alt address** LMC Sound Studio, 130 Brixton Hill, LONDON, SW2
**Phone** 020 8671 6767
**Email** lmcsound@superorg.demon.co.uk
*PA for hire; contact studio..*
**RAB** London Arts

**MB Sound & Lights**
**Contact** Mark Butchers
**Mail address** 20 Meyrick Crescent, COLCHESTER, Essex, CO2 7QY
**Phone** 07930 545590
*3000 watts of PA equipment inc effects & sub-bass. Assorted lights. Disco decks & mixers. Sound & lighting engineer.*
**RAB** East England Arts

**Microvox**
**Contact** Alan Hughes
**Mail address** 19C Thorp Heys, Back Lane, HOLMFIRTH, W Yorks, HD9 1HG
**Phone/Fax** 01484 684049
**Phone** 0777 1934612
**Email** alan@microvox.demon.co.uk
**Web** www.microvox.co.uk
*Manufacturer of microphone systems for acoustic instruments.*
**RAB** Yorkshire Arts

**Microvox (distributors)**
**Contact** Andrew Mullins
**Mail address** West Field music, Belgrave Mount, WAKEFIELD, W Yorks, WF1 3SB
**Phone** 01924 361550
**Email** andrew@westf.demon.co.uk
**Web** www.westf.demon.co.uk
*Distributors of Microvox microphones, PA etc. Mail order and festival retail service.*
**RAB** Yorkshire Arts

**Panda Sound**
**Contact** Oliver Knight
**Mail address** Norman Hurst, Mount Pleasant North, Robin Hoods Bay, WHITBY, N Yorks, YO 22 4RE
**Phone** 01947 880067
07765 201399
**Fax** 01947 881073
*Live and studio freelance sound engineer specialising in folk and acoustic music. Recording studio.*
**RAB** Yorkshire Arts

**Paul Sparrow Sound**
**Contact** Paul Sparrow
**Mail address** 16 Donnington Grove, SOUTHAMPTON, SO17 1RW
**Phone** 023 8055 6622
07956 430887
**Fax** 023 8090 4198
**Email** sound@paulsparrow.demon. co.uk
*PA system plus engineers for rental to small & medium scale venues in the South of England. Clients include Bath International Music Festival, June Tabor, Arts Council, etc. Advice available.*
**RAB** Southern Arts

**Peter Wilson PA**
**Mail address** BRIDPORT, Dorset, DT6 3DZ
**Phone** 01308 425713
*PA hire with engineers. Specialise in folk, roots & acoustic music.*
**RAB** South West Arts

### The Pure Group Ltd
**Contact** Jeremy Millins
**Mail address** Unit F4, Chaucer Business Park, Kemsing, SEVENOAKS, Kent, TN15 6PL
**Phone** 01732 764800
**Fax** 01732 764801
**Email** info@pure.co.uk
**Web** www.puregroup.com
*Suppliers of lighting, sound, staging, temporary structures for all events, festivals & concerts.*
**RAB** South East Arts Board

### Shock Productions
**Contact** Andy Shaw
**Mail address** 8 New Farm Lane, NORTHWOOD, Middx, HA6 1HD
**Phone/Fax** 01923 841684
**Phone** 07941 558891
**Email** info@shockproductions.co.uk
**Web** www.shockproductions.co.uk
*PA hire and recording, "acoustic friendly".*
***Musicians' Union member***
**RAB** London Arts

### Sound Sense Pro PA Hire
**Contact** John Weatherby
**Mail address** Mid Forth Farm, 56 Manse Road, FORTH, ML11 8AJ, Scotland
**Phone** 01555 812009
07860 375183
**Fax** 01555 812009
**Email** sales@soundsensepa.co.uk
**Web** www.soundsensepa.co.uk
*Provision of PA for acoustic music events.*
**AC** Scotland

## Professional services

### Foster Wiggins
**Contact** John Heydon
**Mail address** 3/5 Church Street, AYLESBURY, Bucks, HP20 2QP
**Phone** 01296 485995
**Fax** 01296 397092
**Email** johnh@fosterwiggins.co.uk
**Web** www.fosterwiggins.co.uk
*Accountancy, taxation & business advisors looking after the affairs of singers, musicians, festivals, instrument makers, etc.*
**RAB** Southern Arts

### Golden Valley Insurance
**Contact** Sharron L O'Gorman
**Mail address** The Olde Shoppe, EWYAS HAROLD, Herefordshire, HR2 0ES
**Phone** 0800 015 4484
01981 241062
**Fax** 01981 240451
**Email** goldenvalleyins@cwcom.net
**Web** www.golden-valley-insurance.co.uk
*Insurance of all musical and electronic instruments and accessories. Designed by a musician to provide wide cover at home, at gigs and in transit.*
**RAB** West Midlands Arts

### JR Dunbar & Co
**Contact** Julian Dunbar
**Mail address** Leycester House, Farmer Ward Road, KENILWORTH, CV8 2DH
**Phone** 01926 511185
*Specialist insurance cover for makers and players of musical instruments, arranged by trained makers and players.*
**RAB** West Midlands Arts

## Promoters

### Access All Areas
**Contact** Graham & Angie Breakwell
**Mail address** 44 Alexandra Avenue, Meole Brace, SHREWSBURY, SY3 9HS
**Phone/Fax** 01743 235384
**Phone** 07850 734182
**Email** cajunclub@btinternet.com
**Email** accessallareas2000@btinternet.com
*Promote concerts at various venues including the Buttermarket, Shrewsbury.*
**RAB** West Midlands Arts

### The American Experience
**Contact** ABDC Entertainments
**Mail address** La Loma, 18 Halls Farm Close, WINCHESTER, Hants, SO22 6RE
**Phone** 01962 885628
0709 2035070
**Fax** 0845 3344981
**Email** anyact@abdc.co.uk
**Web** members.tripod.co.uk/abdc/americanexperience.html
*Arrangers of bespoke Western events.*
**RAB** Southern Arts

### Arts Alive
**Mail address** Further Up, Long Row, Lower Down, LYBURY NORTH, Shrops, SY7 8BB
**Phone** 01588 680388
**Fax** 01588 680398
**Email** info@artsalive.co.uk
**Web** www.artsalive.co.uk
*Rural touring scheme promoting live events in Shropshire and Herefordshire.*
**RAB** West Midlands Arts

### Asian Music Circuit
**Mail address** Ground Floor Unit E, West Point, 33/34 Warple Way, LONDON, W3 0RG
**Phone** 020 8742 9911
**Fax** 020 8749 3948
**Email** info@amc.org.uk
**Web** www.amc.org.uk
*National organisation for the promotion of Asian music. Touring, concerts, workshops and education programme.*
**RAB** London Arts

### Be@tts Inc
**Contact** Phil Plunkett
**Mail address** Loch Lomond Studio, Unt 20 Griffon Cn., Vale of Leven Ind E, DUMBARTON, G82 3PD, Scotland
**Phone** 01389 750555
**Email** phil@beattsinc.co.uk
**Web** www.beattsinc.co.uk
**Alt contact** Stuart Beattie/ Richy Plunkett
**Email** info@beattsinc.co.uk
*Local talent promotion, community learning, education service & tuition. MU discounts.*
***Musicians' Union member***
**AC** Scotland

### Big Whistle Music
**Contact** Phil Brown
**Mail address** PO Box 23, ACCRINGTON, Lancs, BB5 5GX
**Phone/Fax** 01254 397623
**Phone** 07976 809623
**Email** phil@bigwhistle.co.uk
**Web** www.bigwhistle.co.uk
*Promoter and agent for acoustic and roots music.*
**RAB** North West Arts

### Black Cat Music (Norwich)
**Contact** Simon Black
**Phone** 01603 483382
**Email** simonblack181@netscapeonline.co.uk
**Web** wwwblackcatmusic.org.uk
*Organiser of acoustic music events in the Norwich area. Encompasses the folk traditions and contemporary variations.*
**RAB** East England Arts

### Blues in the City
**Contact** Paul Morgan
**Mail address** Nottingham City Council, Arts & Events, 55 Castle Gate, NOTTINGHAM, NG1 6AF
**Phone** 0115 915 3595
**Fax** 0115 945 3508
*American blues concerts, once a month in the autumn and spring.*
**RAB** East Midlands Arts

### Celtic Spirit
Adrian Harman
**Mail address** 12 Sancreed Road, Parkstone, POOLE, Dorset, BH12 4DZ
**Phone** 01202 730111
**Email** celtic.spirit@virgin.net
**Web** www.celticspirit.org.uk
*Promoter of Celtic music at 300 capacity Wimbourne venue.*
**RAB** Southern Arts

### C.M.P.
**Contact** Chas Cole
**Contact** Market Place, 34 Market Street, Southport, Merseyside PR8 1HJ
**Phone** 01704 539746
**Fax** 01704 500709
**Email** cmpgigs@aol.com
*Major concert promoter.*
**RAB** North West

### Cornish Music Project
**Contact** Hilary Coleman
**Mail address** 24 Valley Close, Newbridge, TRURO, Cornwall, TR1 3UN
**Phone** 01842 275058
**Web** www.cmp.kernow.eu.org
**Alt contact** Frances Bennett
**Email** sfbennett@aol.com
*Cornish music organisation aiming to nurture a sense of pride of place through a variety of music projects covering 4 areas - education, networking, celebration and research. Workshops, concerts and publications.*
***Musicians' Union member***
**RAB** South West Arts

### Easington and District Music Festival
**Contact** Fred Brierley
**Phone** 0191 517 1274
**Alt contact** Dave Clarke, Easington & District Council
**Phone** 0191 527 0501
*Promotes a series of concerts at the Wayfarer.*
**RAB** Northern Arts

### Elaine Barker
**Mail address** Holly Cottage, Lower Road, PELDON, Essex, CO5 7PR
**Phone** 01206 735606
*Promoter of folk events and parties.*
**RAB** East England Arts

### The Equator Company Ltd
**Contact** Louise Harding
**Mail address** 54 Northload Street, GLASTONBURY, Somerset, BA6 9JP
**Phone/Fax** 01458 834177
**Phone** 01458 830240
**Email** email@equatorcompany.com
**Web** www.equatorcompany.com
**Alt contact** Majahawodwa Ndlovu
*Promotion, marketing and tour management of world music groups, especially Zimbabwe and Africa.*
**RAB** South West Arts

### Folk South-East
**Contact** John Smedley
**Mail address** 8 Bayham Road, SEVENOAKS, Kent, TN13 3XA
**Phone** 01732 460171
**Fax** 01732 460171
**Email** info@folksoutheast.org.uk
**Web** www.folksoutheast.org.uk
*The South-East's all-year-round folk festival. More than 30 concerts per year with a broad range of leading folk artists at various venues in Kent and Sussex.*
***Musicians' Union member***
**RAB** South East Arts

### Freddy Macha
**Mail address** Flat B, 12 Curley Road, LONDON, N16 5JS
**Phone** 07961 833040
020 7502 9814
**Fax** 020 7281 6677
**Email** fmacha@yahoo.com
*Performance poet & musician; multiple music/ poetry styles based on African & Brazilian roots. Regular promoter of world music events at Bar Lorca & various other clubs in London.*
***Musicians' Union member***
**RAB** London Arts

### The Hawth Theatre and Arts Centre
**Contact** Dave Watmore
**Mail address** Hawth Avenue, Crawley, West Sussex RH10 6YZ
**Phone** 01293 552941
**Fax** 01293 533362
**Web** www.hawth.co.uk
*Local authority venue programming regular folk & roots music as part of mixed arts policy. The Hawth (855), The Hawth Studio (147) & Crawley Leisure Centre (1600-2400).*
**RAB** South East Arts

### Heart of England Music
**Contact** Stevie Horton
**Mail address** PO Box 1957, EATHORPE, Warks, CV33 9YG
**Phone/Fax** 01926 632946
**Phone** 07989 373698
**Email** mayhem.design@cwcom.net
**Web** www.heartofenglandmusic.co.uk
*Independent Midlands based non-profit initiative, supporting charities by publishing compilation albums and staging benefit concerts. Works mainly with folk and folk-rock artists.*
**RAB** West Midlands Arts

### Hirio Events
**Contact** Arianna Fioretti
**Mail address** Via Don Caustico 123, 10095 Grugliasco (TO), ITALY
**Phone** +39 11 4159524
+39 335 5915186
**Fax** +39 114059700
**Email** hirio@hirio.com
**Web** www.hirio.com
*Italian company organisers and promoting all traditional music, mainly from Celtic areas, working all over Italy.*

### Irregular Records
**Contact** Robb Johnson
**Mail address** PO Box 72, HOUNSLOW, Middx, TW5 0YB
**Phone** 07958 236103
**Email** irregular@moosemusic.co.uk
*Record & management company, promoter for series "The Magnificent 7" series of English song concerts at Bread & Roses.*
***Musicians' Union member***
**RAB** Southern Arts

### Jacqueline Patten
**Mail address** Kerlistz , The Green, Morchard Bishop, CREDITON, Devon, EX17 6PD
**Phone** 01363 877503
**Email** patten@kerlistz.freeserve.co.uk
*Promoter of workshops & concerts.*
**RAB** South West Arts

### Karisma Music Management
**Contact** Pete Willow
**Mail address** 57 Heath Lane, Brinklow, NR RUGBY, CV23 0NR
**Phone/Fax** 01788 832608
**Phone** 07887 552896
**Email** pete@karisma.net
**Web** www.karisma.net
*Organisation and promotion of events.*
**RAB** West Midlands Arts

### Manchester International Arts
**Contact** Anne Tucker & Jeremy Shine
**Mail address** 3 Birch Polygon, MANCHESTER, M14 5HX
**Phone** 0161 224 0020
**Fax** 0161 248 9331
**Email** mia@streetsahead.org.uk
**Web** www.streetsahead.org.uk
*Promoter of a range of events including outdoor street festivals, international theatre, music and dance, world music events and special projects. Organisers of x.trax street festival.*
**RAB** North West Arts

### Money Pitt Promotions
**Phone** 01943 468133 - eve
0113 239 7274 - day
**Email** moneypitt@richardson.leeds.co.uk
*Promoter of folk concerts.*
**RAB** Yorkshire Arts

### Nightjar Music/ The Music Pool
**Contact** Rob Strawson
**Mail address** The Courtyard, Edgar Street, HEREFORD, HR4 9JR
**Phone** 01432 278118
**Fax** 01432 356238
**Email** muspool@globalnet.co.uk
**Web** www.musicpool.org.uk
*Promotion of folk/ roots/ world music events with accompanying education programme.*
**RAB** West Midlands Arts

### North Shropshire Folk
**Contact** Howard Prince
**Mail address** Braisty, Heathwood Road, Higher Heath, WHITCHURCH, Shrops, SY3 2HG
**Phone** 01948 840408
*Group of enthusiasts promoting folk concerts with local & national acts in the Whitchurch area.*
**RAB** West Midlands Arts

### One Off Productions
**Contact** Doug Hudson
**Mail address** 182 Windmill Road, GILLINGHAM, Kent, ME7 5PE
**Phone/Fax** 01634 574837
**Phone** 07941 238377
**Email** doug.hudson@lineone.net
**Web** www.doughudson.com
*Organiser of Rochester Sweeps Festival, Gravesend World Music Day and the Medway Folk Cellar.*
**RAB** South East Arts

### Peak Arts
**Contact** Mick Peat
**Mail address** PO Box 200, BELPER, Derbys, DE56 2ZL
**Phone** 01773 853428
**Fax** 01773 850000
*Promoter of folk concerts at venues in Derbyshire.*
***Musicians' Union member***
**RAB** East Midlands Arts

### Pilot Promotions
**Contact** Chris Roddy
**Mail address** The Menagerie, 130 University Street, BELFAST BT7 8HH, Northern Ireland
**Phone** 028 9023 5678
**Fax** 028 9029 5173
**Email** Becksworld@btinternet.com
*Promoter of folk, traditional and world music in Belfast.*
**RAB** Northern Ireland

### Porthole Promotions
**Contact** Jim McLaughlin
**Mail address** Highfields, Sledgates, Fylingthorpe, WHITBY, Yorks, YO22 4TZ
**Phone** 01947 880962
0777 9861709
**Email** portholepromotions@ic24.net
**RAB** Yorkshire Arts

### Rattan & Rush
**Contact** Penny or Paul
**Mail address** 39-41 Market Street, KIRKBY STEPHEN, Cumbria, CA17 4QN
**Phone** 01768 372123
**Email** rattanandrush@cs.com
*Promoter.*
**RAB** North West Arts

### Ryburn 3 Step
**Mail address** 103 Oldham Road, Ripponden, SOWERBY BRIDGE, W Yorks, HX6 4EB
**Phone** 01422 822569
**Email** ryburn3step@backshift.demon.co.uk
**Web** www.ryburn3step.org.uk
*Group of singers, dancers & musicians performing at & organising wide variety of folk events in W Yorks. Presentations, workshops and consultancy for schools and community organisiations.*
**RAB** Yorkshire Arts

### Slipped Discs
**Conatct** MJ Cawley
**Mail address** Ty Newydd, 1 Owen Street, PEMBROKE DOCK, Pembrokeshire, SA72 6SL, Wales
**Phone** 01646 682692
07773 994514
**Email** sd@mjcawley.freeuk.com
*Promoter of roots, world and acoustic music in W & S Wales to print and radio. Producers of The Big Cheese Festival and smaller community festivals.*
**AC** Wales

### South East Music Schemes and Spotlight South East
**Contact** Alison Maconochie
**Mail address** PO Box 2790, EASTBOURNE, BN20 7WF
**Phone** 01323 431283
**Email** sems@ukgateway.net
**Web** www.semusic.org
*Promotion of groups and individuals working in non-classical forms of music through an annual award scheme. Support includes subsized concerts/ bookings and administrative and marketing assistance.*
**RAB**South East Arts

### St Albans Folk Music
**Contact** Alison Macfarlane
**Mail address** 40 Warwick Street, ST ALBANS, Herts, AL1 4DL
**Phone** 01727 852111
**Email** alison.macfarlane@lineone.net
*Occasional concerts and workshops at various venues in St Albans.*
***Musicians' Union member***
**RAB** East England Arts

### Three's Company
**Contact** Fay Hield
**Mail address** 63 Nelson Street, Cross Roads, KEIGHLEY, W Yorks, BD22 9EA
**Phone** 01535 643249
**Email** three_s_company@hotmail.com
*Promoters of concerts ranging from world music to comedy to local audiences in West Yorks.*
**RAB** Yorkshire Arts

### Valley Roots
**Mail address** The Marketing Office, Theatr Brycheinog, Canal Wharf, BRECON, LD3 7EW
**Phone** 01874 622838
01495 224425
*Promoters of concerts with top national acts at 4 venues in South Wales.*

### Village Pump Presents
**Contact** John Alderslade
**Mail address** 54 Church Lane, MELKSHAM, Wilts, SN12 7EQ
**Phone/Fax** 01225 707346
**Email** john@aldersladej.fsnet.co.uk
**Web** www.alderslade.com
**Alt contact** Alan Briars
**Alt address** Romsey Oak Farmhouse, Bradford Road, Wingfield, TROWBRIDGE, Wilts, BA14 9LS
**Phone** 01225 769132
**Email** alanbriars@virgin.net
*Live folk & roots concerts at various venues in the West Country.*
**RAB**South West Arts

### Whitby Musicport
**Contact** Jim McLaughlin
**Mail address** 4 Park Terrace, WHITBY, N Yorks, YO21 1PN
**Phone/Fax** 01947 603475
**Phone** 07779 861709
**Email** musicport@email.com
**Web** www.musicport.fsnet.co.uk
*Concert promotion, workshops, october festival (see Whiby Musicport 2001).*
**RAB** Yorkshire Arts

### YaD Arts
**Conatct** Josephine Burton
**Mail address** 49 Basildon Court, 28 Devonshire Street, LONDON, W1G 6PR
**Phone** 020 7486 5627
07775 656775
**Fax** 020 8944 6143
**Email** josephine@yadarts.com
**Web** www.yadarts.com
**Alt contact** Johnathan Walton
**Email** johnathan@yadarts.com
*Promotion of contemporary Jewish arts in Britain. Encouagement of dialogue between ethnic communities through live collaborative projects and multi-media events.*
**RAB** London Arts

## Publicity and Marketing

### Andrew Cleal Photography
**Contact** Andrew Cleal
**Phone** 01206 751661
**Email** andrew@pukkaplanet.co.uk
**Web** www.pukkaplanet.co.uk
*Band/ festival/ press photographer.*
**RAB** East England Arts

### Annie Windley
**Mail address** 3 Palace Road, Crouch End, LONDON, N8 8QH
**Phone** 020 8342 9360
07931 718876
**Email** annie.windley@virgin.net
*PR for folk and acoustic artists. Freelance journalist.*
**RAB** London Arts

### B B Skone
**Contact** MJ Cawley
**Mail address** Ty Newydd, 1 Owen Street, PEMBROKE DOCK, Pembrokeshire, SA72 6SL, Wales
**Phone** 01646 682692
07773 994514
**Email** sd@mjcawley.freeuk.com
**Web** www.
*News, reviews and previews service of live and recorded music, based in West Wales. Plus full PR service. Festivals, events, acts.*
**AC** Wales

### Castlelake Consultancy
Sean Laffey
**Mail address** Castlelake, CASHEL, Co Tipperary, Irish Republic
**Phone** +353 62 62685
+353 87982 1916
**Fax** +353 62 62967
**Email** slaffey@iol.ie
**Web** www.iol.ie/~didly-didly
*Photography, journalism, editorial, design and representation services. Contact by email or phone preferred. No pictures on email please.*
**AC** Ireland

### Cool4Sure
**Contact** Ian Smith
**Mail address** 1 Holme Road, MATLOCK BATH, Derbys, DE4 3NU
**Phone** 07976 206568, 01629 57082
**Email** pregosmith@hotmail.com
**Web** www.cool4sure.com/co.uk
*Multimedia design company including e commerce consultation & general roots music business advice.*
***Musicians' Union member***
**RAB** East Midlands Arts

### Copperplate Consultants
**Contact** Alan O'Leary
**Mail address** 68 Belleville Road, LONDON, SW11 6PP
**Phone** 020 7585 0357
**Email** copperplate2000@yahoo.com
**Web** go.to/copperplate
*Promotion of good music to media, public and the retail trade.*
**RAB** London Arts

### Davelle Communications Ltd
**Contact** David Caren
**Mail address** 3rd Floor, 9 Parliament Street, Temple Bar, DUBLIN 2, Ireland
**Phone** +353 2 6719643
**Email** davelle@eircom.net
**Alt contact** Ellen O'Hea
*PR & marketing company specialising in promotion of traditional & folk music in Ireland. Clients include Solas, Danu, Cran, Iarla O'Lionaird (Afro Celt Sound System) and Tim Goulding (Doctor Strangley Strange).*
**AC** Ireland

### Fivetrees
**Contact** Steve Fairhead
**Mail address** 36 Livingstone House, HOVE, E Sussex, BN3 3WP
**Phone** 01273 706215
**Fax** 01273 774203
**Email** info@fivetrees.com
**Web** www.fivetrees.com
*Company serving independent musicians & labels. Recording to CD manufacture, marketing assistance, artist management. Reliable UNIX server, full website development, to suit artist's needs & pocket. Developing internet radio.*
**RAB** South East Arts

### Folksound Records
**Contact** Graham Bradshaw
**Mail address** 250 Earlsdon Avenue North, COVENTRY, CV5 6GX
**Phone** 024 7671 1935
**Fax** 024 7671 1191
**Email** rootsrecs@btclick.com
*Record label and production company, marketing & promotion.*
**RAB** West Midlands Arts

### Frantic Productions
**Contact** Jed Grimes
**Phone** 0191 290 2785
**Email** jed@franticprod.demon.co.uk
**Web** www.franticprod.demon.co.uk
*Complete PR package – press releases/ posters/ flyers/ CD sleeves/ video shoot and editing to custom websites including sound and animation features.*

### Gig Pix
**Mail address** Castlelake Consultancy Castlelake, CASHEL, Co Tipperary, Irish Republic
**Phone** +353 62 62685
+353 87982 1916
**Fax** +353 62 62967
**Email** slaffey@iol.ie
**Web** www.iol.ie/~didly-didly
*Photographic service of Castlelake Consultancy. Design service for websites, CD covers, press kits and music merchandise.*

### Glass Ceiling PR
**Contact** Harriet Simms
**Mail address** 50 Stroud Green Road, LONDON, N4 3EF
**Phone** 020 7263 1240
**Fax** 020 7281 5671
**Email** promo@glassceilingpr.com
**Web** www.glassceilingpr.com
**Alt contact** Sarah Wells
*Press and radio PR agency representing a variety of non-mainstream artists/ record companies/ venues to national & regional media.*
**RAB** London Arts

### Heavy Entertainment Ltd
**Contact** Nick St George
**Mail address** 222 Kensal Road, LONDON, W10 5BN
**Phone** 020 8960 9001/2
**Fax** 020 8960 9003
**Email** nick@heavy-entertainment.com
**Web** www.heavy-entertainment.com
**Alt contact** David Rover
*TV and radio production company; producers of broadcast programmes, promo audio and video, commercials and showreels. Audio studio available for hire. Music and arts specialists; BBC commissions include many world/ trad music series.*
**RAB** London Arts

### Heypressco
**Contact** Paul Saunders
**Mail address** 6 Swan Meadow, MUCH WENLOCK, Shropshire, TF13 6JQ
**Phone** 01952 728283
**Email** ps@workingjoe.co.uk
**Web** www.heypressco.com
*Specialist marketing, press, PR/ media services for roots, historic music and related arts.*
***Musicians' Union member***
**RAB** West Midlands Arts

### Iconic Music & Media
**Contact** Ms Stevie Horton
**Mail address** PO Box 1957, Eathorpe, LEAMINGTON SPA, Warks, CV33 9YG
**Phone/Fax** 01926 632946
**Phone** 07989 373698
**Email** iconicmusic@hotmail.com
**Phone** 01926 814111
*Small booking agency and publicist. Midlands based, covering the whole UK. Artists range from electric bands to acoustic soloists.*
**RAB** West Midlands Arts

### John Crosby Press/ Promotions
**Contact** John Crosby
**Mail address** 26 Milward Crescent, HASTINGS, East Sussex, TN34 3RU
**Phone** 01424 713904
07939 027786
**Fax** 01424 461224
**Email** johncrosby@pressproms.demon.co.uk
**Web** www.pressproms.demon.co.uk
*Folk (and acoustic related) music publicity*
**RAB** South East Arts

### Keith Hudson
**Mail address** 182 Broadway, Roath, CARDIFF, CF24 1QJ
**Phone** 029 2049 9759
07974 093514
**Fax** 029 2048 4882
*Photographer: performance, publicity, event coverage, album sleeves, etc.*
**AC** Wales

### Latin Arts Services
**Contact** Hector Rosquete
**Mail address** PO Box 14303, LONDON, SE26 4ZH
**Phone/Fax** 07000 472 572
**Email** latinarts@lasgroup.com
**Web** www.lasgroup.com
**Alt contact** Jo Courtney
*Promotion of Latin American artists and records to outlets worldwide.*
**RAB** London Arts

### Ledgard Jepson Ltd
**Contact** Bryan Ledgard
**Mail address** Mortimer Heights, Cubley, Penistone, SHEFFIELD, S36 9UY
**Phone** 01226 766608
**Fax** 01226 766619
**Email** studio@ledgardjepson.com
**Web** www.ledgardjepson.com
**Alt contacts** David Exley - Design,
Wayne Gilbert - Production
Lynne Lawton - Ad space
*Leading creative design, advertising and marketing company producing a wide range of print-based and web-based solutions; exhibition, display & signage; multimedia.*
*Specialists in CD sleeve artwork, print and manufacture; press advertising; promotional print from flyers to catalogues, music books to newsletters. Portfolio of music packaging and promotion for many top folk and roots artists.*
*Studio and loction photography.*

### Macmeanmna
**Contact** Arthur Cormack
**Mail address** Gladstone Buildings, Quay Brae, PORTREE, Isle of Skye, IV51 9DB, Scotland
**Phone** 01478 612990
**Fax** 01478 613263
**Email** arthur@gaelicmusic.com
**Web** www.gaelicmusic.com
*Management and marketing company for Gaelic music artists and consultancies.*
***Musicians' Union member***
**AC** Scotland

### Richard Wootton Publicity
**Contact** Claire Horton
**Mail address** 120 Kingston Road, LONDON, SW19 1LY
**Phone** 020 8542 8101
**Fax** 020 8540 0691
**Email** richard@rwpublicity.com
*Major publicist working with folk, world, country & blues artists plus Cambridge Festival.*
**RAB** London Arts

### Sally Burford Photography
**Contact** Sally Burford
**Mail address** PO Box 160, CHELTENHAM, Glos, GL50 4YE
**Phone** 01242 577997
**Fax** 01242 577745
**Email** chipolatas@cwcom.net
*Event photographer, photography for publicity, advertising and promotion.*
**RAB** South West Arts

### Slipped Discs
**Conatct** MJ Cawley
**Mail address** Ty Newydd, 1 Owen Street, PEMBROKE DOCK, Pembrokeshire, SA72 6SL, Wales
**Phone** 01646 682692
07773 994514
**Email** sd@mjcawley.freeuk.com
**Web** www.
*Publicists for acts, venues and organisiations throughout the region.*
**AC** Wales

## Publishers

### Accolade Music (Publishing)
**Contact** Graham Bradshaw
**Mail address** 250 Earlsdon Avenue North, COVENTRY, CV5 6GX
**Phone** 024 7671 1935
**Fax** 024 7671 1191
**Email** rootsrecs@btclick.com
*Music publishers, royalty collection services. Member of PRS, MCPS, PPL.*
**RAB** West Midlands Arts

### Anglo-American Dance Service (AADS)
**Mail address** Resedastraat 8, B-9920 LOVENDEGEM, Belgium
**Phone** +32 9 3729635
**Fax** +32 9 37229635
**Email** aads@village.uunet.be
**Web** http://gallery.uunet.be
*Promotors of Anglo-American dance in Western Europe. Dance courses and weekends, publishers and retailers of dance material and folk dance music.*

### Barn Dance Publications Ltd
**Contact** D L Jones
**Mail address** 62 Beechwood Road, CROYDON, Surrey, CR2 0AA
**Phone** 020 8651 2911
**Fax** 020 9651 6080
**Web** www.barn-dance.co.uk
*Supplier of barn dance and community dance books, tapes, CDs. Send for catalogue.*
***Musicians' Union member***
**RAB** South East Arts

### Blue Stack Music and Blue Stack Records
**Contact** Angela Williams
**Mail address** 52 Abbott Avenue, LONDON, SW20 8SG
**Phone** 020 8540 3350
**Email** bluestck@hotmail.com
**Web** www.countrymusic.org,uk/heartfield
*Country & Rock label and publisher.*
**RAB** London Arts

### Circuit Music
**Contact** Chris Euesden
**Mail address** 1 Holly Terrace, YORK YO1 4DS
**Phone** 01904 610899
*Music publisher.*

### Cloud Valley Music
**Mail address** 51 Hainault Court, Forest Rise, LONDON, E17 3NW
**Phone** 020 8521 4649
**Email** cloudval@aol.com
**Web** http://members.aol.com/cloudval
*Record company and publisher.*
**RAB** London Arts

### The Hardie Press
**Contact** Mary Hardie
**Mail address** 17 Harrison Gardens, EDINBURGH, EH11 1SE, Scotland
**Phone** 0131 3131383
**Fax** 0131 3131388
**Email** admin@hardiepress.co.uk
**Web** www.hardiepress.co.uk
*Publisher of Scottish traditional music for fiddle, guitar and voice; books on Scottish music and recordings.*
***Musicians' Union member***
**AC** Scotland

### ISA Music
**Contact** Bob McDowell
**Mail address** 27-29 Carnoustie Place, Scotland Street, GLASGOW, G5 8PH, Scotland
**Phone** 0141 4201881
**Fax** 0141 4201892
**Email** bob@isa-music.com
**Alt contact** Ronnie Simpson
*Music publishers, including books of mostly traditional style music and song. MCPS/PRS.*
**AC** Scotland

### Kid Menthal Music
**Contact** Andrew Caven-Atack
**Mail address** 20 Meyrick Crescent, COLCHESTER, Essex, CO2 7QY
**Phone** 01206 549582
**Email** KM@andycaven.freeserve.co.uk
**Web** www.kidmenthal.freeserve.co.uk
*Publish songs and tunes written by folk, jazz & blues performers. Music tutor books. Recordings on KM records.*
**RAB** East England Arts

### Kinmor Music
**Contact** Robin Morton
**Mail address** Shillinghill, TEMPLE, Midlothian, EH23 4SH
**Phone** 01875 830328
**Fax** 01875 830392
**Web** www.templerecords.co.uk
*Publisher of Scottish & Irish music plus some instrumental tutors.*
**AC** Scotland

### mally.com
**Contact** Dave Mallinson
**Mail address** 3 East View, Moorside, CLECKHEATON, West Yorks, BD19 6LD
**Phone** 01274 876388
**Fax** 01274 865208
**Email** mally@mally.com
**Web** www.mally.com
*Traditional music publishing, distribution and mail order.*
***Musicians' Union member***
**RAB** Yorkshire Arts

### Michael Raven Publications
**Contact** Michael Raven
**Mail address** 126 Jug Bank, Ashley, MARKET DRAYTON, Shrops, TF9 4NJ
**Phone** 01630 672304
*Publisher of guitar music, folksongs and country dance tunes.*
**RAB** West Midlands Arts

### Mick Tems
**Mail address** 1 Ty Clwyta Cottages, Cross Inn, LLANTRISANT, Rhondda Cynon Taf, CF72 8AZ, Wales
**Phone/Fax** 01443 226892
**Phone**07773 075962
**Email** micktems@folkwales.org.uk
**Web** www.folkwales.org.uk
*Print & internet writer & designer specialising in the traditional arts in Wales & beyond.*
**AC** Wales

### No Masters Co-operative Limited
**Mail address** 78 Moorgate Road, ROTHERHAM, S. Yorks, S60 2AY
**Phone** 01709 375063
**Email** georgina@nomasters.freeserve.co.uk
**Web** www.nomasters.co.uk
**Alt email** jim@nomasters.co.uk
*Northern-based recording, writing and publishing co-operative specialising in music grown out of traditional roots. Founded in 1990 by John Tams and Jim Boyes.*
**RAB** Yorkshire Arts

### Taigh Na Teud Music
**Contact** Christine Martin
**Mail address** 13 Upper Breakish, ISLE OF SKYE, IV42 8PY, Scotland
**Phone** 01471 822528
**Fax** 01471 822811
**Email** Christine@scotlandsmusic.com
**Web** www.scotlandsmusic.com
*Publishers of Scottish and Gaelic music, including collections for fiddle/ pipes etc., books for ensemble work, young players and reprints of early manuscripts. Mail orderbooks and CDs.*
**AC** Scotland

### Twah!/Freakline Publishing
**Contact** Kent Nielsen
**Mail address** Muhlenstrasse 8, LUBECK, D-23552, Germany
**Phone** 049 451 813 1491
**Fax** 049 451 8131098
**Email** twahrecs@aol.com
**Web** www.twah.com
*Roots label and affiliated publishing company.*

services section

# Direct mail orders and trade enquiries welcome


records@mrscasey.co.uk

Tel: 01296 394411

Fax: 01296 392300

Mrs Casey Records

Mrs Casey Records
PO Box 296
Aylesbury
Bucks, HP19 9TL


**www.mrscasey.co.uk/mcrecords**

## 3 New Releases for 2001

Whether you want one copy or one hundred copies, all our catalogue can be purchased by mail order from Mrs Casey Records at the contact details above.

***On Reflection***
**Eliza Carthy & Nancy Kerr**
MCRCD1003
Collection from 2 previous albums, plus some individual new material.

***How to Play English Melodeon Volume 3***
**John Kirkpatrick**
MCRV1004
Volume 3 elaborates on previous volumes with further exploration of the melodeon keyboard. John introduces new tunes and illustrates new techniques appealing to the more experienced player and those who wish to gain more experience from 'The Master of the Buttons'.

***Evolving Tradition 3***
*Unearthing the next generation*
MCRCD1002
Acaysha - 422 - NeffBros - Cara Dillon - Broderick - Oisín Mac Diarmada, Brian Fitzgerald & Micheál Ó Ruanaigh - Clive Carroll - Bedlam - The Black Cat Theory - Ola - Brolum - Chris Armstrong - Talei Edwards & Emma Reid - Kieron Means - Philippe Barnes & Tim Edey - Malinky -Dr Faustus - Phamie Gow

## Past Catalogue

***Eliza Carthy & Nancy Kerr***
MCRCD3991
"Sometimes it takes the freshness of youth to re-educate us to the glories of our own tradition The boldness and lack of self-consciousness with which these two women attack this album is revelatory.."

***Shape of Scrape***
**Eliza Carthy & Nancy Kerr**
MCRCD5992
"Second outing by the ethno-youth revivalists manages to even surpass their excellent debut..."

***Pumped Up & Loaded***
**Cock & Bull Band**
MCRCD6992
"...reaffirms the band as one of the most contemporary and progressive folk acts in the world..."

***Encore du Vingt***
**Cock & Bull Band**
MCRCD9993
Celebrating their 20th anniversary - a delicious brand of French & English electropipingstringdrum'n'basstechno music! A CD for dancing!

***Evolving Tradition***
*A celebration of the flourishing traditions in the british isles*
MCRCD5991
Kings of Calicutt - Ingrid & Allan Henderson - Luke Daniels Trio - Oige - Dan Plews & Cath James - Chris Sherburn & Denny Bartley - Bohinta - Eliza Carthy & Nancy Kerr - Shetland's Young Heritage - Kate Rusby & Kathryn Roberts - Rajan & Rakhi Sood - Catriona Macdonald & Ian Lowthian - The Hedgerows - Simon Thoumire & Ian Carr - Jennifer & Hazel Wrigley - Gavin Lewery & Jock Tyldesley - The Lakeman Brothers - Tim Van Eyken & Kerensa Wragg -
The Chipolata 5 - Carlene Anglim & Simon Howarth - Cythara

***Evolving Tradition 2***
*A fresh new generation of Britfolk perfomers*
MCRCD6991
Tabache - Ian Lowthian & Luke Daniels - Eliza Carthy - Richard Wood - Catriona Macdonald, Annbjørg Lien & Roger Tallroth - Robert Harbron - Kings of Calicutt - Céile - Cordelia's Dad - Brian Finnegan & Austin Maguire - Ben Paley - Michael McGoldrick - Seelyhoo - Oliver Bootle - Kate Rusby - John McCusker - Brothers Uhlmann

***How to Play English Melodeon Volume 1***
**John Kirkpatrick**
MCRV9991 (82mins)
"My playing advanced fifteen years in three months by listening to John K. The man is a virtuoso." Andy Cutting
Opens for the absolute beginner but quickly goes on to rise well above the basics. You may think you know all there is to know and skip past the first half hour. But can you risk it?

***How to Play English Melodeon Volume 2***
**John Kirkpatrick**
MCRV9992 (60mins)
Reveals more of those secrets whilst fully exploring the musical potential of the 1 and 2 row Melodeon system.

## Village Carols
**Contact** Ian Russell
**Mail address** PO Box 2099, SHEFFIELD, S35 0XU
**Phone** 01224 645486
**Fax** 01224 272728
**Email** ian.russell@abdn.ac.uk
**Web** www.sgpublishing.co.uk/gm/vc/vcabout.html/
*Non-profit making organisation recording and promoting local carol singing traditions. Fieldwork & research, collection of source material and promotion of local carol singing. Publisher and retailer of CDs, books and tapes.*
**RAB** Yorkshire Arts

# CDs – Recording to Retail

## ADA Distribution and Mail Order
**Mail address** PO Box 800, BELPER, Derbys, DE56 2ZA
**Phone** 01773 850000
**Email** adamailorder@aol.com
**Web** http://members@aol.com/adamailorder
*Folk music specialist; distribution and mail order.*
***Musicians' Union member***
**RAB** East Midlands Arts

## AGP Studio
**Mail address** 58 King Studio, BROSELEY, Shropshire, TF12 5NA
**Phone** 01952 882909
07973 866198
**Email** alistair@agpstudio.demon.co.uk
*Folk friendly recording/ editing studio based on Soundscape digital recorder & yamaha digital mixer. Sleeve design service.*
**RAB** West Midlands Arts

## Andrew Cronshaw
**Contact** Cloud Valley Music
**Mail address** 51 Hainault Court, Forest Rise, LONDON, E17 3NW
**Phone** 020 8521 4649
**Email** cloudval@aol.com
**Web** http://members.aol.com/cloudval
*Producer and sound engineer.*
***Musicians' Union member***
**RAB** London Arts

## Aran Productions
**Contact** Emyr Rhys
**Mail address** 12 Lon Arfon, CAERNARFON, Gwynedd, LL55 2ER, Wales
**Phone** 01286 677140
07787 543298
**Email** emyrrhys@onetel.net.uk
*Producer, specialising in folk material. All digital studio, housed ina converted chapel in Snowdonia.*
***Musicians' Union member***
**AC** Wales

## The Audio Loft
**Contact** Ron Angus
**Mail address** 28 Bourn Lea, HOUGHTON LE SPRING, Tyne and Wear, DH4 4PG
**Phone** 0191 3855351
**Email** info@audioloft.co.uk
**Web** www.audioloft.co.uk
*Digital mastering, remasters and transfers. CD duplication service.*
**RAB** Northern Arts

## Beautiful Jo Records
**Contact** Tim Healey
**Mail address** PO Box 1039, OXFORD, OX1 4UA
**Phone** 01865 249194
**Fax** 01865 792765
**Email** info@bejo.co.uk
**Web** www.bejo.co.uk
*Record label specialising in folk, roots, new acoustic and period music.*
**RAB** Southern Arts

## Blackfriars Music
**Contact** Willie Haines
**Mail address** 49 Blackfriars Street, Off The Royal Mile, EDINBURGH, EH1 1NB, Scotland
**Phone** 0131 557 3090
**Email** scotfolk@compuserve.com
**Web** www.blackfriarsmusic.com
*Retailer of CDs, instruments and books.*
**AC** Scotland

## Blue Stack Music and Blue Stack Records
**Contact** Angela Williams
**Mail address** 52 Abbott Avenue, LONDON, SW20 8SG
**Phone** 020 8540 3350
**Email** bluestck@hotmail.com
**Web** www.countrymusic.org,uk/heartfield
*Country & Rock label and publisher.*
**RAB** London Arts

## Brechin All Records
**Contact** Sandy Brechin
**Mail address** 5 The Square, KIRKLISTON, W Lothian, EH29 9AX, Scotland
**Phone** 01783 253228
0131 333 3252
**Email** sandy@squeeze.demon.co.uk
**Web** www.accordions.com/sandy
*Record label*
***Musicians' Union member***
**AC** Scotland

## Castlesound Studios
**Contact** Freeland Barbour
**Mail address** The Old School, Park View, PENCAITLAND, East Lothian, EH34 5DW, Scotland
**Phone/Fax** 0131 666 1024
**Phone** 01875 340143
**Email** info@castlesound.co.uk
**Web** www.castlesound.co.uk
*Professional recording studio. 48 track Tr Hard Disk/ 72 Ch. NEVE/ ProTools/ Sound-Picture. Large recording area & grand piano.*
**AC** Scotland

## Cloud Valley Music
**Mail address** 51 Hainault Court, Forest Rise, LONDON, E17 3NW
**Phone** 020 8521 4649
**Email** cloudval@aol.com
**Web** http://members.aol.com/cloudval
*Record company and publisher.*
**RAB** London Arts

## Coda Music
**Web** www.codamusic.co.uk
*Retailer of folk, traditional, Scottish and classical music CDs, videos and sheet music. Knowledgable staff, no mail order postage charge.*
**AC** Scotland

## Copperplate Distribution
**Mail address** 68 Belleville Road, LONDON, SW11 6PP
**Phone** 020 7585 0357
**Email** copperplate2000@yahoo.com
**Web** go.to/copperplate
*Distribution of reel Irish traditional music.*
**RAB** London Arts

## Copperplate Mail Order
**Mail address** 68 Belleville Road, LONDON, SW11 6PP
**Phone** 020 7585 0357
**Email** copperplate2000@yahoo.com
*Irish music CDs sold directly to the public, including those difficult to get hold of. Mail order.*
**RAB** London Arts

## Cottage Industry
**Contact** Peter Aston
**Mail address** Orchard End, Gaunts Common, WIMBOURNE, Dorset, BH21 4JR
**Phone** 01258 840844
01929 557221
**Email** cottageindustry@hotmail.com
*Recording studio.*
***Musicians' Union member***
**RAB** South West Arts

- **CDs – from Recording to Retail** (inc. Studio Services, Record Labels, Producers, CD/Cassette Duplication, Distribution, Mail Order, Retail.)

### DJC Records
**Contact** Dave Clague
**Mail address** 104 Constitution Hill, NORWICH, NR3 4BB
**Phone** 01603 403052
**Email** clague@paston.co.uk
**Web** www.jacana.demon.co.uk/djc
*Independent record label specialising in folk/contemporary jazz/rock plus 70's retro. Artists include Damien Barber, Hamilton Camp, Malarky.*
**RAB** East England Arts

### Dragon Records
**Contact** John Heydon
**Mail address** 3/ 5 Church Street, AYLESBURY, Bucks, HP20 2QP
**Phone** 01296 415333
**Fax** 01296 397092
**Email** johnh@fosterwiggins.co.uk
*CD retail sales at events and folk music festivals.*
**RAB** Southern Arts

### Faymus Productions
**Contact** David J Tong
**Mail address** PO Box 748, LUTON, Beds, LU1 5ZA
**Phone** 01582 481222
07740 213622
**Fax** 01582 481222
**Email** faymus@dial.pipex.co.uk
**Web** www.faymus.co.uk
**Alt contact** Mike Silver
**Alt address** Tredarrup, Warbstow, LAUNCASTON, Cornwall, PL15 8RL
**Phone** 01566 781667, 0771 8116889
**Email** mikes@dial.pipex.co.uk
*Principally but not exclusively sale and promotion of Mike Silver's recordings & songs. Solicited material only please.*
**RAB** East Midlands Arts

### Fellside Recordings
**Contact** Paul Adams
**Mail address** PO Box 40, WORKINGTON, Cumbria, CA14 3GJ
**Phone** 01900 61556
**Fax** 01900 61585
**Email** info@fellsidecom
**Web** www.fellside.com
*Leading independent record company specialising in folk and jazz.*
**RAB** Northern Arts

### Fflach
**Contact** Richard Jones
**Phone** 01239 614691
**Fax** 01239 614680
**Email** info@fflach.co.uk
**Web** www.fflach.co.uk
*Welsh recording company. 24 track analogue & digital*
**AC** Wales

### Fish Records
**Contact** Neil Pearson
**Mail address** PO Box 148, SHREWSBURY, Shropshire, SY3 5WQ
**Phone** 01743 231546
**Fax** 01743 354354
**Email** neil@fishrecords.co.uk
**Web** www.fishrecords.co.uk
*Suppliers of folk, singer/songwriter and acoustic music.*
**RAB** West Midlands Arts

### Fivetrees
**Contact** Steve Fairhead
**Mail address** The Bothy Bakehouse, Aish, Nr. Stoke Gabriel, Devon, TQ9 6PS
**Phone** 01273 706215
**Email** info@fivetrees.com
**Web** www.fivetrees.com
*Company serving the needs of independent musicians & labels. Recording to CD manufacture, marketing assistance, artist management. Reliable UNIX server, full website development, to suit artist's needs and pocket. Developing internet radio.*
**RAB** South East Arts

### Folk & World Tradition
**Mail address** PO Box 413, EAST GRINSTEAD, W Sussex, RH19 2XA
**Phone** 01342 305413
**Fax** 01342 305155
**Email** www.folkandworldtradition@hotmail.com
**Web** www.folkandworldtradition.com
*Folk and World music mail order.*
**RAB** South East Arts

### Folk Sales
**Contact** Derek & Ann Appleing
**Mail address** 55 Arle Road, CHELTENHAM, Glos, GL51 8LA
**Phone** 01242 692243
**Email** derek-ann@folksales.freeserve.co.uk
*Retailers of printed folk material plus recorded music for dance. Mail order/ catalogue available.*
**RAB** South West Arts

### Folksound Records
**Contact** Graham Bradshaw
**Mail address** 250 Earlsdon Avenue North, COVENTRY, CV5 6GX
**Phone** 024 7671 1935
**Fax** 024 7671 1191
**Email** rootsrecs@btclick.com
*Record label and production company, recording, tape/ CD duplication, marketing & promotion services.*
**RAB** West Midlands Arts

### Forest Tracks
**Contact** John Mann
**Mail address** Cecil Flat House, 27 Garfield Road, SOUTHAMPTON, Hants, SO19 4DA
**Phone** 023 8023 1805
**Alt contact** Paul Marsh
**Alt address** Elder Cottage, 30 Brambridge, NR EASTLEIGH, SO5 7HZ
**Phone** 019 6271 3608
*Recorded traditional music of Hampshire and Dorset.*
**RAB** Southern Arts

### Free Reed Records and Music
**Contact** Neil Wayne
**Mail address** The Cedars, BELPER, Derbys, DE56 1DD
**Phone** 01773 824157
**Fax** 01773 825573
**Email** neil.wayne@free-reed.co.uk
**Web** www.free-reed.co.uk
*Research and documentation of the music and history of the folk revival through the release of the "Revival Masters" series of CDs.*
**RAB** East Midlands Arts

### Freeland Barbour
**Mail address** 44 Beauchamp Road, EDINBURGH, EH16 6LU, Scotland
**Phone** 0131 6661024
**Fax** 0131 6661024
**Email** info@castlesound.co.uk
**Web** www.freelandbarbour.co.uk
*Producer and composer.*
***Musicians' Union member***
**AC** Scotland

### G8INA Studios
**Web** www.g8ina.enta.net
*Small mobile recording studio. All live to minidisc and mastered in software. Low rates. Discounts for MU and CCE members.*
***Musicians' Union member***
**RAB** West Midlands Arts

### Glade Recording
**Contact** Alistair Russell
**Phone** 0113 226 9209
**Email** soundout@clara.net
**Web** http://home.clara.net/soundout
*Acoustic recording facilities, static or mobile CD mastering, editing.*
***Musicians' Union member***
**RAB** Yorkshire Arts

### Green Fingers Music
**Contact** Penny or Stuart
**Mail address** 4 Wellington Road, LOWESTOFT, Suffolk, NR33 7AL
**Phone** 07980 504739
*Label specialising in folk and acoustic music. Cassette and CD duplication, labels and inlays. Live and studio recording.*
**RAB** East England Arts

### Greentrax
**Contact** Ian Green
**Mail address** Cockenzie Business Centre, Edinburgh Road, COCKENZIE, East Lothian, EH32 0XL, Scotland
**Phone** 01875 814155, 01875 815888
**Fax** 01875 813545
**Email** greentrax@aol.com
**Web** www.greentrax.com
**Alt contact** Brenda McCulloch
*Leading Scots label featuring Scottish and Gaelic traditions.*
**AC** Scotland

### Harbourtown Records
**Contact** Gordon Jones
**Mail address** PO Box 25, ULVERSTON, Cumbria, LA12 7UN
**Phone** 01229 588920
**Email** records@hartown.demon.co.uk
**Web** www.rootsworld.com/harbourtown
*Established independent record label.*
**RAB** Northern Arts

### Hat Records
**Contact** Tim Kent
**Mail address** 2 Medway Court, Kingston Lane, SOUTHWICK, W Sussex, BN42 4SL
**Phone** 01273 595614
**Email** tktw@mistral.co.uk
**Web** www.uksoundcraft.com
*Recording of folk clubs and local folk artists. Mobile 8 track digital mini disc studio. Service includes CD production, design & duplication.*
***Musicians' Union member***
**RAB** South West Arts

### Heart of England Music
**Contact** Stevie Horton
**Mail address** PO Box 1957, EATHORPE, Warks, CV33 9YG
**Phone/Fax** 01926 632946
**Phone** 07989 373698
**Email** mayhem.design@cwcom.net
**Web** www.heartofenglandmusic.co.uk
*Independent Midlands based non-profit initiative, supporting charities by publishing compilation albums and staging benefit concerts. Works mainly with folk and folk-rock artists.*
**RAB** West Midlands Arts

### Heavy Entertainment Ltd
**Contact** Nick St George
**Mail address** 222 Kensal Road, LONDON, W10 5BN
**Phone** 020 8960 9001/2
**Fax** 020 8960 9003
**Email** nick@heavy-entertainment.com
**Web** www.heavy-entertainment.com
**Alt contact** David Rover
*TV and radio production company; producers of broadcast programmes, promo audio and video, commercials and showreels. CD mastering and duplication. Audio studio available for hire. Music and arts specialists; BBC commissions include many world/ trad music series.*
**RAB** London Arts

### Highlander Music
**Contact** William Crawford
**Mail address** Unit 7D, Muir Of Ord Industrial Estate, Ross-shire, IV6 7UA, Scotland
**Phone** 01463 871422
01463 782153
**Fax** 01463 871433
**Email** highlander.music@zetnet.co.uk
**Alt address** PO Box 422, BEAULY, IV4 7WE, Scotland
*Distribution for record labels and music book publishers of Celtic and related music. Small record label for Scottish traditional music.*
**AC** Scotland

### Hobgoblin Music
**Contact** Pete McClelland
**Mail address** PO Box 2522, HENFIELD, Sussex, BN5 9SN
**Phone** 07000 462462 - mail order
**Fax** 01273 419923
**Email** post@hobgoblin.co.uk
**Web** www.hobgoblin.com
*Chain of folk instrument & music shops. Branches throughout England.*
**RAB** South East Arts

### Hobgoblin Music (Bristol)
**Mail address** 30 College Green, BRISTOL, BS1 5TB
**Phone** 0117 929 0902
**Email** bristol@hobgoblin.co.uk
**RAB** South West Arts

### Hobgoblin Music (Crawley)
**Mail address** 17 The Parade, Northgate, CRAWLEY, W Sussex, RH10 2DT
**Phone** 01293 515858
**Email** crawley@hobgoblin.co.uk
**RAB** South East Arts

### Hobgoblin Music (Leeds)
**Mail address** 39 Call Lane, LEEDS, LS1 7BT
**Phone** 0113 245 3311
**Email** leeds@hobgoblin.co.uk
**RAB** Yorkshire Arts

### Hobgoblin Music (London)
**Mail address** 24 Rathbone Place, LONDON, W1T 1JA
**Phone** 020 7323 9040
**Email** london@hobgoblin.co.uk
**RAB** London Arts

### Hobgoblin Music (Manchester)
**Mail address** 123 Oxford Road, All Saints, MANCHESTER, M1 7DU
**Phone** 0161 273 1000
**Email** manchester@hobgoblin.co.uk
**RAB** North West Arts

### Hobgoblin Music (Nottingham)
**Mail address** 58 Derby Road, NOTTINGHAM, NG1 5FD
**Phone** 0115 911 9440
**Email** nottingham@hobgoblin.co.uk
**RAB** East Midlands Arts

### Hurler Records
**Contact** Chris Ridley
**Mail address** Trenillocs, ST COLUMB, Cornwall, TR9 6JN
**Phone** 01637 880394
*Record label for Warm Gold's CD "A Taste of Cornwall". £8 inc. p&p.*
***Musicians' Union member***
**RAB** South West Arts

### Irregular Records
**Contact** Robb Johnson
**Mail address** PO Box 72, HOUNSLOW, Middx, TW5 0YB
**Phone** 07958 236103
**Email** irregular@moosemusic.co.uk
*Record & management company.*
***Musicians' Union member***
**RAB** Southern Arts

### Karen Tweed
**Mail address** PO Box 5009, DERBY, Derbys, DE1 9FQ
**Phone** 01332 677046
**Fax** 01332 677047
**Email** karen@kstweed.co.uk
*Accordionist, composer, arranger, teacher and producer of instrumental music with roots in Irish, British and Scandanavian traditions.*
***Musicians' Union member***
**RAB** East Midlands Arts

- **CDs - from Recording to Retail** (inc. Studio Services, Record Labels, Producers, CD/Cassette Duplication, Distribution, Mail Order, Retail.)

### Keith B Smith
**Mail address** 35 Selwyn Gardens, CAMBRIDGE, CB3 9AY
**Phone** 01223 357703
**Email** keith.smith@quista.net
**Web** www.hoogie.co.uk
*Scottish violinist, bagpiper and studio producer.*
***Musicians' Union member***
**RAB** East England Arts

### Klang Records
**Contact** Christopher Wagner
**Mail address** Clonan House, Midgehole Road, HEBDEN BRIDGE, Yorks, HX7 7AA
**Phone** 01422 842212
**Email** info@klang-records.co.uk
**Web** www.klang-records.co.uk
*Distributor of the German Trikont label.*
**RAB** Yorkshire Arts

### Knock On Wood
**Contact** Andy Wilson - Mail Order
**Mail address** Glasshouses Mill, HARROGATE, HG3 5QN
**Phone** 01423 712712
**Email** kow@globalnet.co.uk
**Web** www.knockonwood.co.uk
**Alt contact** Shop
**Alt address** 13 Eastgate, LEEDS, Yorks, LS2 7LY
**Phone** 0113 242 9146
**Fax** 0113 245 9878
*Retail, mail order and internet supplier of instruments, books and recordings from around the world. Specialist in Brazilian, African and Latin percussion.*
**RAB** Yorkshire Arts

### KRL
**Contact** Gus McDonald
**Mail address** 9 Watt Road, Hillington, GLASGOW, G52 4RY, Scotland
**Phone** 0141 882 9060
**Fax** 0141 883 3686
**Email** krl@krl.co.uk
**Web** www.lochshore.com
*Record Company.*
**AC** Scotland

### Lancashire Voices
**Contact** Derek Gifford
**Mail address** 22 Stoney Brow, Roby Mill, UP HOLLAND, Lancs, WN8 0PE
**Phone** 01695 625097
**Email** derek.gifford@talk21.com
**Alt contact** Christopher Harvey
**Alt address** Cock Robin Music, 8/9 Cock Robin Cottages, High Field Road, CROSTON, Lancs, PR5 7HG
**Phone** 01772 601060
**Email** c.h.poll@btinternet.com
*Recording, archiving and promotion of contemporary Lancashire singers and poets.*
***Musicians' Union member***
**RAB** North West Arts

### Linn Records
**Contact** Jennie Gardner -Press and Marketing
**Mail address** 257 Drakemuir Drive, GLASGOW, G45 9SZ, Scotland
**Phone** 0141 3035027
**Fax** 0141 6311485
**Email** jennie.gardner.linn.co.uk
**Web** www.linnrecords.com
**Alt contact** Philip Hobbs -Product Development
**Phone** 0141 3035026
**Email** philip.hobbs@linn.co.uk
*Independent record label, recording jazz, folk and classical music.*
**AC** Scotland

### Lismor Recordings
**Contact** Ronnie Simpson
**Mail address** 27-29 Carnoustie Place, Scotland Street, GLASGOW, G5 8PH, Scotland
**Phone** 0141 420 1881
**Fax** 0141 420 1892
**Email** lismor@lismor.com
**Web** www.lismor.com
**Alt contact** Kate Kenna
*Traditional music record company.*
**AC** Scotland

### Little Pot Stove Records
**Contact** John Dalton
**Mail address** 213 Nursery Road, Dinnington, SHEFFIELD, Yorks, S25 2QU
**Phone** 01909 569481
**Fax** 0703 1152002
**Email** johndalton@littlepotstove.co.uk
**Web** www.littlepotstove.co.uk
*CD stall for festivals. Internet sales of new & used CDs and collectors' vinyl.*
**RAB** Yorkshire Arts

### London Musicians' Collective
**Contact** Ed Baxter
**Mail address** 3-6 Lafone House, 11-13 Leathermarket Street, LONDON, SE1 3HN
**Phone** 020 7403 1922
**Fax** 020 7403 1880
**Email** lmc@lmcltd.demon.co.uk
**Web** www.l-m-c.org.uk
**Alt contact** Mick Ritchie
**Alt address** LMC Sound Studio, 130 Brixton Hill, LONDON, SW2
**Phone** 020 8671 6767
**Email** lmcsound@superorg.demon.co.uk
*Contact studio. Also documentation and post production.*
**RAB** London Arts

### MAC Distribution
**Contact** Derek Moir
**Mail address** 1 The Stables Yard, 1103 Argyle Street, GLASGOW, G3 8ND
**Phone** 0141 2212500
**Fax** 0141 2215200
**Email** derek@macdistribution.com
**Web** www.macdistribution.com
**Alt contact** Steve Dunn
**Email** steve@macdistribution.com
*Music distribution to all major chains and the indie/ specialist sector.*
**AC** Scotland

### Macmeanmna
**Contact** Arthur Cormack
**Mail address** Gladstone Buildings, Quay Brae, PORTREE, Isle of Skye, IV51 9DB, Scotland
**Phone** 01478 612990
**Fax** 01478 613263
**Email** arthur@gaelicmusic.com
**Web** www.gaelicmusic.com
*Record label specialising in Gaelic music.*
***Musicians' Union member***
**AC** Scotland

### Magnet Records
**Contact** Brian Healey
**Mail address** 28 Grafton Terrace, LONDON, NW5 4JJ
**Phone** 020 7424 0027
**Fax** 020 7267 2457
**Email** tmm@tradmusic.demon.co.uk
**Web** www.tradmusic.net
*Publishers of traditional music albums.*
**RAB** London Arts

**Malgamu Music**
**Contact** Paul Kelly
**Mail address** 5 Main Street, TALLLAGHT, Dublin 24, Ireland
**Phone** +353 1 4515765
**Email** malgamu@indigo.ie
**Web** www.malgamu.com
*Irish record company producing Irish traditional and acoustic music.*
**AC** Ireland

**Market Square Records**
**Contact** Peter Muir
**Mail address** Market House, Market Square, WINSLOW, Bucks, ML18 3AF
**Phone** 01296 715228
**Fax** 01296 715486
**Email** pete@marketsquarerecords.co.uk
**Web** www.marketsquarerecords.co.uk
*Independent label with key interest in folk and related releases.*
**RAB** East Midlands Arts

**Mike Silver**
**Mail address** Tredarrup, Warbstow, LAUNCESTON, Cornwall, PL15 8RL
**Phone** 01566 781667, 0771 8116889
**Email** mikes@dial.pipex.co.uk
**Web** www.faymus.co.uk
www.gobmusic.co.uk
**Alt contact** Roddy Steele
**Alt address** Good Old Boy Music, 6 Chestnut Way, MEPAL, Cambs, CB6 2YR
**Phone** 01353 777553
**Fax** 01353 777349
**Email** Roddy@gobmusic.co.uk
*Studio producer.*
***Musicians' Union member***
**RAB** South West Arts

**Mother Earth Music**
**Contact** Jeannette Yeoell
**Mail address** 25 Ferndale Road, LONDON, SE25 4QR
**Phone** 020 8406 7881
**Email** jy@motherearthmusic.co.uk
**Web** www.motherearthmusic.co.uk
*Record label for contemporary and traditional folk and world music.*
**RAB** London Arts

**Mrs Casey Records**
**Contact** Steve Heap
**Mail address** PO Box 296, AYLESBURY, Bucks, HP19 9TL
**Phone** 01296 394411
**Fax** 01296 392300
**Email** mcrecords@mrscasey.co.uk
**Web** www.mrscasey.co.uk/mcrecords
*Record label producing various CD series including "Evolving Tradition", Eliza Carthy's first albums and John Kirkpatrick's video "How To Play The English Melodeon".*
**RAB** Southern Arts

**Musical Traditions Records**
**Contact** Rod Stradling
**Mail address** 1 Castle Street, STROUD, Glos, GL5 2HP
**Phone** 01453 759475
**Email** rod@mustrad.org.uk
**Web** www.mustrad.org.uk
*Record company dedicated exclusively to the production of CDs of real traditional singers and musicians. Extensive notes with CDs.*
**RAB** South West Arts

**No Masters Co-operative Limited**
**Mail address** 78 Moorgate Road, ROTHERHAM S. Yorks, S60 2AY
**Phone** 01709 375063
**Email** georgina@nomasters.freeserve.co.uk
**Web** www.nomasters.cc.uk
**Alt email** jim@nomasters.co.uk
*Northern-based recording, writing and publishing co-operative specialising in music grown out of traditional roots. Founded in 1990 by John Tams and Jim Boyes.*
**RAB** Yorkshire Arts

**Offspring Records**
**Contact** Vivienne Bloomfield
**Mail address** PO Box 7028, MILTON KEYNES, MK12 5ZH
**Phone** 01908 542894
**Fax** 01908 543913
**Email** vivienne@offspringrecords.freeserve.co.uk
*Record label specialising in folk and acoustic music.*
**RAB** Southern Arts

**Oisin Studios**
**Contact** Steafan Hannigan
**Mail address** 84 High Street, Potterspury, TOWCESTER, Northants, NN12 7PQ
**Phone** 01908 225500
**Fax** 01908 225566
**Email** o-omusic@dircon.co.uk
**Alt contact** Vivienne Bloomfield
**Phone** 01908 542894
**Fax** 01908 543913
**Email** vivienne@jumb.powernet.co.uk
*Recording studio, specialists in acoustic and ethnic music.*
**RAB** Southern Arts

**Panda Sound**
**Contact** Oliver Knight
**Mail address** Norman Hurst, Mount Pleasant North, Robin Hoods Bay, WHITBY, N Yorks, YO 22 4RE
**Phone** 01947 880067
07765 201399
**Fax** 01947 881073
*Live and studio freelance sound engineer specialising in folk and acoustic music. Recording studio.*
**RAB** Yorkshire Arts

**Park Promotions**
**Contact** John Dagnell
**Mail address** PO Box 651, OXFORD, OX2 9RB
**Phone** 01865 241717
**Fax** 01865 204556
**Email** parkrecords@cwcom.net
**Web** www.parkrecords.com
**RAB** Southern Arts

**Paul James**
**Mail address** 60 High Street, HUNGERFORD, Berks, RG17 0NE
**Phone** 01488 686039
07887 948853
**Email** info@pauljamesmusic.com
**Web** www.pauljamesmusic.com
*Producer of traditional & contemporary music.*
**RAB** Southern Arts

**Paul Sartin**
**Mail address** May Cottage, WHERWELL, Hants, SP11 7JS
**Phone** 01264 860791
07711 485798
*Producer, composer/ arranger.*
**RAB** Southern Arts

**Pendle Hawk Music Distribution**
**Contact** Adrian Melling
**Mail address** 2nd Floor, 11 New Market Street, COLNE, Lancashire, BB8 9BJ
**Phone** 01282 866317
**Email** sales@pendlehawkmusic.co.uk
**Web** www.pendlehawkmusic.co.uk
*Music distributors with over 50 labels, especially American imports.*
**RAB** North West Arts

**Plant Records**
**Phone** 01282 866317
*Specialist retailer of folk, jazz, blues, country. 2000 new titles, deleted vinyl and used CDs.*
**RAB** North West Arts

**The Point**
**Mail address** PO Box 649, DUNSTABLE, Beds, LU5 4XD
**Phone** 01582 673002
**Fax** 01582 475739
**Email** point@poke.ltd.uk
**Web** www.poke.ltd.uk
*Small digital production/ recording facility specialising in acoustic & electric folk and acoustic music.*
***Musicians' Union member***
**RAB** East England Arts



- **CDs – from Recording to Retail** (inc. Studio Services, Record Labels, Producers CD/Cassette Duplication, Distribution, Mail Order Retail.)

services
section

# Veteran
*the traditional folk music label*

If you think we're still called Veteran Tapes then check out our CD catalogue below!

## Compilations

**VTC1CD 'Stepping it Out!'** Music, songs & dances from England

**VTC4CD 'Down in the fields'** An anthology of traditional folk music from Rural England

**VTC5CD 'When the wind blows'** An anthology of traditional folk music from Coastal England

## West Country

**VT119CD 'Catch me if you Can'** Songs from Cornish Travellers - **Betsy & Charlotte Renals** and **Sophie Legg**

**VT129CD 'I've come to sing a song'** Cornish Family Songs from one of England's most popular singers - **Vic Legg**

**VT138CD 'Proper Job'** Dartmoor melodeon playing recorded 1952-1988. One of England's greatest players! - **Bob Cann**

**VT139CD 'Moor Music'** The essence of real English country dance music today played by the grandsons of Bob Cann and Jack Rice - **Mark Bazeley & Jason Rice**

## Northern Ireland

**VT126CD 'The First of my Rambles'** Folk songs from Ulster sung by a festival favourite - **Roisin White**

**VT134CD 'Linkin' o'er the Lea'** Traditional folk songs and ballads from Tempo, County Fermanagh - **Maggy Murphy**

**VT137CD 'The Girls along the Road'** Traditional songs, ballads and whistle tunes from County Antrim - **John Kennedy**

## Suffolk

**VTC2CD 'Songs Sung in Suffolk'** Popular folk songs, old songs and ballads sung by **traditional singers from Suffolk**

**VTC3CD 'Comic Songs Sung in Suffolk'** Comic songs, music hall songs and parodies sung by **traditional singers from Suffolk**

**VT130CD 'Who owns the game?'** Songs and melodeon tunes from Central Suffolk - **Dolly Curtis, Cecil Pearl, Cyril Barber, Roy Last, Charlie Stringer** and **Fred Whiting**

**VT140CD 'Good Order'** Traditional singing & music from The Eel's Foot, Eastbridge recorded in the 1930s and 40s, including: **Velvet Brightwell, Jumbo Brightwell, Jack Clark, Edgar Button, 'Diddy' Cook,** and **Jack 'Dot' Button**

## Classic Singing

**VT136CD 'The Yellow Handkerchief'** England's greatest gypsy singer - **Phoebe Smith**

**VT131CD 'When the May is all in Bloom'** Traditional singing from the S. E. of England - **Bob Copper, John Copper, Gordon Hall, Bob Lewis, Ron Spicer** and **Louie Fuller**

## New Releases

**VT141CD Liam Farrell, Joe Whelan, James Carty** and **Reg Hall** Vibrant music from the current London Irish scene

**VT142CD 'Pass The Jug Round'** Lively pub recordings of Cumberland songs and music made in 1953

**VT143CD Phil Tanner** The complete recordings of classic traditional singing and mouth-music from the Gower Nightingale

**VT144CD The Rice Family** Traditional music and stepdancing from the 'other' legendary Dartmoor family

*Available from good record shops via* PROPER

*Or mail order from:* **Veteran Mail Order**, 44 Old Street, Haughley, Stowmarket, Suffolk 1P14 3NX
tel. 01449 673695 www.veteran.co.uk

VISA EUROCARD MasterCard

*Are you on our mailing list?*

### The Practice Pad Studios and The Foundary
**Contact** Hugh Carter
**Mail address** Unit B1, Glasgow Media Park, 24 Craigmount Street, GLASGOW, G20 9BT, Scotland
**Phone** 0141 9467656
**Email** hughcarter@thepracticepad.com
**Web** www.thepracticepad.com
**Alt contact** Colin Johnson at The Foundary
**Phone** 0141 4031556
*Folk & roots music a speciality. Four well equipped rehersal rooms, 48 track recording studio. Mastering facilities, café.*
**AC** Scotland

### The Premises
**Mail address** 20 Hackney Road, LONDON, E2 8JL
**Phone** 020 77297593
**Fax** 020 7739 5600
**Email** info@premises.demon.co.uk
**Web** www.premises.demon.co.uk
*Recording and rehearsals studios and café. Open 7 days a week, 10am - 11pm.*
**RAB** London Arts

### Prima Records Ltd
**Contact** Pat McGarvey
**Mail address** 108A Acton Lane, LONDON, NW10 8TX
**Phone** 020 8838 0804
**Fax** 020 7794 9549
**Email** patmcgarvey@x-stream.co.uk
**Web** www.sidgriffin.com
*Sid Griffin's record label.*
**RAB** London Arts

### Proper Music Distribution
**Contact** Richard Porter
**Mail address** The Powerhouse, Cricket Lane, BECKENHAM, Kent, BR3 1LW
**Phone** 0870 4440800
**Fax** 0870 444 0801
**Email** sales@proper.uk.com
**Web** www.proper.uk.com
*Distribution of CDs (& vinyl) to stores in the UK and for export.*
**RAB** South East Arts

### Purple Studios
**Contact** Richard Hammerton
**Mail address** The Old Parish Hall, Trowse, NORWICH, NR14 8SX
**Phone** 01603 622550
**Email** info@purplestudios.co.uk
**Web** www.purplestudios.co.uk
*Residential 32 track recording studio. CD manufacturing and duplication facilities.*
**RAB** East England Arts

### RAVI
**Contact** JP Freeman
**Mail address** 46 Merle Avenue, HAREFIELD, Middx, UB9 6DG
**Phone** 07711 265011
**Email** info@ravi-art.co.uk
**Web** www.ravi-art.co.uk
*Digital studio (can be mobile) specialising in acoustic music.*
***Musicians' Union member***
**AC** Scotland

### Ray's Jazz Shop
**Contact** Mike Gavin
**Mail address** 180 Shaftesbury Avenue, LONDON, WC2H 8JS
**Phone** 020 7240 3969
**Email** rays.jazz@dial.pipex.com
*Long established shop (orginally trading as Colletts), selling jazz, blues, folk & world music on LP, CD, cassette. New & second hand. Also books, mags, videos etc.*
**RAB** London Arts

### Remarkable Records
**Contact** Nigel Franks
**Mail address** 201 Town Street, Middleton, LEEDS, LS10 3SN
**Phone** 0113 271 8418
**Email** Nigel_Franks@compuserve.com
**Web** www.remarkable.freeserve.co.uk
*Record company, publishing, promotion.*
**RAB** Yorkshire Arts

### Repeat Performance
**Mail address** 6 Grand Union Centre, West Row, LONDON, W10 5AS
**Phone** 020 8960 7222
**Fax** 020 8968 1378
**Email** info@repeat-performance.co.uk
**Web** www.repeat-performance.co.uk
*Cassette, audio & enhanced CD mastering and duplication, booklet/inlay printing.*
**RAB** London Arts

### Rhiannon Records
**Contact** Colin Jones
**Mail address** 20 Montague Road, LONDON, E8 2HW
**Phone** 020 7275 8292
07973 217878
**Fax** 020 7503 8034
**Email** rhiannonmusic@appleonline.net
**Web** www.rhiannonrecords.co.uk
*Record label and music publishers.*
**RAB** London Arts

### Ridiculous Music Productions
**Mail address** Stars Building, 10 Silverhill Close, NOTTINGHAM, NG8 6QL
**Phone** 0115 9762726
**Fax** 0115 9519874
**Email** info@lidiculous-music-productions.com
**Web** www.ridiculous-music-productions.com
*Produce and release funny songs. Hilife, Dance, R&B, Pop, Soul, Hip, Garage, etc.*
**RAB** East Midlands Arts

### Robert Harbron
**Mail address** 94 Roxeth Green Avenue, HARROW, Middx, HA2 8AQ
**Phone** 020 8357 3261
07973 717786
**Fax** 020 8537 8335
**Email** rob.harbron@virgin.net
**Web** www.robertharbron.co.uk
*Location & studio recording, mixing, digital editing, live sound.*
**RAB** London Arts

### Rocking Chair Merchandising
**Contact** Mrs Casey Music
**Mail address** PO Box 296, AYLESBURY, Bucks, HP19 9TL
**Phone** 01296 394411
**Fax** 01296 392300
**Email** office@mrscasey.co.uk
**Web** www.mrscasey.co.uk/rockingchair
*Provider of record stalls at Sidmouth and Towersey festivals.*
**RAB** Southern Arts

### Rogue Productions
**Contact** PO Box 337, LONDON, N4 1TW
**Phone** 020 8340 9651
**Fax** 020 8348 5626
**Email** rogue@froots.demon.co.uk
**Web** www.froots.demon.co.uk/beatnik.html
*Record production and label.*
**RAB** London Arts

### Rollercoaster Records
**Mail address** Rock House, London Rock, St Mary's, CHALFORD, Glos, GL6 8PU
**Phone** 01453 886252
**Fax** 01453 885361
**Web** www.rollercoasterrecords.com
*Re-issue label for rock & roll and roots music.*
**RAB** South West Arts

When it comes to press and marketing, it's a jungle out there.
Whether you are big or small, we can help you make your mark.

Order our FREE Survivor's Marketing Guide
Call us on 01952 728283 or visit the website www.heypressco.com

## The Bodhrán – the Pulse of Irish Music

One of Ireland's oldest products is the Bodhran (Irish Drum), pronounced 'Bow-rawn' meaning deaf or haunting. It probably originated as a skin tray on the bogs for cutting turf (peat). Guaranteed genuine goatskin and native Irish beech, the skin is also glued on. Most of the traditional musicians worldwide use our Bodhran which is hand-crafted with care in Connemara. Treatment wax and hardwood beater included.

Goatskin Bodhrans

| | |
|---|---|
| 18" Plain – solid beech rim | IR£59.00 |
| 18" decorated – Celtic design, name, logo etc | IR£69.00 |
| 18" Deluxe – very Heavy goatskin | IR£79.00 |
| 18" Deluxe with Celtic Design | IR£89.00 |
| 18" Deluxe 4_ins. Deeper rim | IR£99.00 |
| 18"tuneable – very Heavy goatskin | IR£159.00 |
| 18"tuneable 4_ins. Deeper rim | IR£189.00 |

Mail Order
Despatch 2 to 3 days from order. Payment by cheque secured cred t card or PO. Price includes P&P in Irl./UK. and tutor book (English, French & German). P&P to Europe +IR£12.00 USA/Can. + IR£19.00

"I Kneel in Prayer Towards Roundstone" **Christy Moore**

**New Book! "Wallup! – Humour and Lore of Bodhran Making." £5.99**

Music and Craft shop open 7 Days.
6 days in winter.

Malachy Kearns
Roundstone Music
Connemara Co. Galway

Tel. 095 35875
Fax. 095 35980
Email. Bodhran@iol.ie
www.bodhran.com (secure ordering)
Please see our website or contact us for $ prices

Ireland's Master Bodhran Makers.®
For 25 years
Makers of Bodhrans and drums for Riverdance

**£11.95 each.**

**"Highly Recommended" in "GUITARIST" Jan. 2001 Issue.**

# Pub Prop

**Fastens to Tables and Holds Necked Instruments Upright.**

For: Guitar, Bouzouki, Cittern, 5str. Banjo, Octave Mandola, Mandolin, Fiddle+Bow.

**Packs flat into Pocket-sized Case.**

**Please send cheque, £11.95 m/o to 'Briarmill', with your Name, Address, & Phone No. to: PO Box 35, Ashton-u-Lyne, Lancs. OL7 9FJ
Tel/Fax 0161 330 4555 www.pubprop.co.uk**

## BRANCO STOYSIN

**CD'S ON SUN RECORDINGS
CRITICALLY HIGHLY ACCLAIMED**

***"Something between the Sea and the Sky" BS-SR 24597/1***
***"Amber" BS-SR 24597/2***

***"A truly individual voice on the instrument. He is a real find, a definitive original style laced with melodic and enthralling Eastern European Folk. Beautiful... Marvellous" CHRISSIE MURRAY - "JAZZ WISE"***

***"Peaceful, melodic originals in which each note is there for a reason. He also sounds like nobody but himself, a rarity in this copycat age" JACK MASSARIK - EVENING STANDARD"***

**DETAILS: BRANCO STOYSIN TRIO/DUET
INFO & BOOKINGS CALL SUN RECORDINGS TEL/FAX: 020 8693 2398**

## Roots Music
**Contact** Bob Clay - Mail Order
**Mail address** Butts House, 15 The Butts, Stanhope, BISHOP AUCKLAND, Co Durham, DL13 2UQ
**Phone** 01388 526688
**Fax** 01388 526370
**Email** enquiries@roots-music.co.uk
**Web** www.roots-music.co.uk
**Alt contact** Shop
**Alt address** 67B Westgate Road, NEWCASTLE UPON TYNE, NE1 1SG
**Phone** 0191 2302500
*Specialist CD retailer. Mail order, shop, website & stalls at events.*
**RAB** Northern Arts

## Roots Records
**Contact** Graham Bradshaw
**Mail address** 250 Earlsdon Avenue North, COVENTRY, CV5 6GX
**Phone** 024 7671 1935
**Fax** 024 7671 1191
**Email** rootsrecs@btclick.com
*Supplier of folk and roots recordings, mail order, trade distribution, festival merchandising.*
**RAB** West Midlands Arts

## RUF Records
**Contact** Chris Wood
**Mail address** 40 Whitstable Road, FAVERSHAM, Kent ME13 8DL
**Phone/Fax** 01795 537906
**Email** cw@rufrecords.com
*Record label for Chris Wood projects including work with Martin Carthy, Andy Cutting, Jean-Francois Vrod.*

## Rus Music Productions
**Contact** Rob Van Sante
**Phone** 0113 2752472
0780 1707413
**Fax** 0870 1328331
**Email** inforusmp@aol.com
*24 track, G4 Applemac and Protools based recording studio.*
***Musicians' Union member***
**RAB** Yorkshire Arts

## Sakay
**Contact** Rogue Productions
**Mail address** PO Box 337, LONDON, N4 1TW
**Phone** 020 8340 9651
**Fax** 020 8348 5626
**Email** rogue@froots.demon.co.uk
**Web** www.froots.demon.co.uk/beatnik.html
*Record label for Tarika.*
**RAB** London Arts

## Scottish-Irish.com
**Email** info@scottish-irish.com
**Web** www.scottish-irish.com
*Internet mail order of Celtic & traditional CD/ DVD.*
**AC** Scotland

## Shetland Music Distribution Ltd
**Contact** Ronald Jamieson
**Mail address** Griesta, TINGWALL, Shetland, ZE2 9SB
**Phone** 01595 840670
**Fax** 01595 840671
**Email** smd.ltd@zetnet.co.uk
**Web** www.shetlandmusicdistribution.co.uk
**Alt contact** Denise Morrison
*Distribution of Shetland music: traditional, contemporary, folk, rock & country CDs, cassettes and sheet music.*
***Musicians' Union member***
**AC** Scotland

## Shock Productions
**Contact** Andy Shaw
**Mail address** 8 New Farm Lane, NORTHWOOD, Middx, HA6 1HD
**Phone/Fax** 01923 841684
**Phone** 07941 558891
**Email** info@shockproductions.co.uk
**Web** www.shockproductions.co.uk
*PA hire and recording, "acoustic friendly".*
***Musicians' Union member***
**RAB** London Arts

## Short Audio Cassette Tapes
**Contact** Keith Orchard
**Mail address** 32 Myton Crescent, WARWICK, CV34 6QA
**Phone** 01926 490897
*C10 (5 mins/side) or C20 (10 mins/side) with cases and labels. £8 per 10, quantity discount. Postage £2-£15.*
**RAB** West Midlands Arts

## Smalltown Records
**Mail address** 17 Colne Mount, UTTOXETER, Staffs, ST14 7QR
**Phone** 01889 563123
07989 669824
*Record company, loosely rootsy. Artists include Zydeco Hot Rods, Vice Bishops, Yeah Jazz, etc.*
**RAB** West Midlands Arts

## The Sound Joint
**Contact** Barnaby Smith
**Mail address** 10 Parade Mews, Tulse Hill, LONDON, SE27 9AX
**Phone** 020 8678 1404
**Fax** 020 8671 0380
*32 track recording studio - live room, 400 sq foot. Good pre-amps and mics.*
**RAB** London Arts

## Stormforce Arts
**Contact** Tony & Carole Kendall
**Mail address** 18 Edward Avenue, Chingford, LONDON, E4 9DN
**Phone** 020 8527 0574
*Folk music record label, publishers and event organisers. Also royalty administration.*
**RAB** London Arts

## Tartan Tapes/ Foot Stompin' Records
**Contact** Elizabeth Hepburn
**Mail address** 17 Redford Drive, EDINBURGH, EH13 0BL
**Phone** 0131 4413135
07775 854572
**Email** sales@tartantapes.com
**Web** www.tartantapes.com
**Alt contact** Simon Thoumire
*Publishers of traditional and contemporary folk music CDs, with accent on young stars of the Celtic scene.*
***Musicians' Union member***
**AC** Scotland

## Temple Records
**Contact** Robin Morton
**Mail address** Shillinghill, TEMPLE, Midlothian, EH23 4SH, Scotland
**Phone** 01875 830328
**Fax** 01875 830392
**Email** robin@templerecords.co.uk
**Web** www.templerecords.co.uk
*Major Scottish record company.*
**AC** Scotland

## Touchwood Audio Productions
**Contact** Bruce Wood
**Mail address** 6 Hyde Park Terrace, LEEDS, LS6 1BJ
**Phone** 0113 278 7180
**Email** bruce.w@appleonline.net
*Recording studio specialising in acoustic live music.*
**RAB** Yorkshire Arts

## Twah!/Freakline Publishing
**Contact** Kent Nielsen
**Mail address** Muhlenstrasse 8, LUBECK, D-23552, Germany
**Phone** 049 451 813 1491
**Fax** 049 451 8131098
**Email** twahrecs@aol.com
**Web** www.twah.com
*Roots label and affiliated publishing company. Acts as press office for other labels.*

- **CDs – from Recording to Retail** (inc. Studio Services, Record Labels, Producers, CD/Cassette Duplication, Distribution, Mail Order, Retail.)

## Ulstersongs
**Contact** John Moulden
**Mail address** 10 Apollo Walk, PORTRUSH, Co Antrim, BT56 8HQ, N Ireland
**Phone/Fax** 028 7082 5080
**Phone** 028 7082 5025
**Email** john@ulstersongs.com
**Web** www.ulstersongs.com
*Retailer of books & recordings of unaccompanied songs from Ireland and of solo Northern Irish music. Mail order service.*
**AC** Northern Ireland

## Veteran
**Mail address** 44 Old Street, Haughley, STOWMARKET, Suffolk, IP14 3NX
**Phone** 01449 673695
**Email** info@veteran.co.uk
**Web** www.veteran.co.uk
*Record label specialising in traditional English & Irish music and song, particularly from East Anglia, the West Country and Northern Ireland.*
**RAB** East England Arts

## Veteran Mail Order
**Mail address** 44 Old Street, Haughley, STOWMARKET, Suffolk, IP14 3NX
**Phone** 01449 673695
**Email** mail@veteran.co.uk
**Web** www.veteran.co.uk
*Mail order company specialising in English, Irish & Scottish traditional music and singing from esoteric labels including Veteran.*
**RAB** East England Arts

## Wafer Thin
**Contact** Rob Peters
**Mail address** PO Box 81, BIRMINGHAM, B30 2LF
**Phone** 0121 444 5887
07971 974108
**Email** robpeters@uk.packardbell.org
**Web** www.collective.co.uk/robpeters
*Record company and recording studio.*
**RAB** West Midlands Arts

## Wall of Sound
**Mail address** Units 40 & 41, The Colonnade, Piecehall, HALIFAX
**Phone** 01422 343660
*Records, Tapes, CDs bought, sold & exchanged. Large folk, etc. selection. Open Wed - Sun.*
**RAB** Yorkshire Arts

## Weekend Beatnik
**Contact** Rogue Productions
**Mail address** PO Box 337, LONDON, N4 1TW
**Phone** 020 8340 9651
**Fax** 020 8348 5626
**Email** rogue@froots.demon.co.uk
**Web** www.froots.demon.co.uk/beatnik.html
*Record label specialising in mid-price re-issues.*
**RAB** London Arts

## Whippet Records
**Contact** Gary Miller
**Mail address** PO Box 72, YORK, YO31 1LD
**Phone/Fax** 01904 410038
**Phone** 01904 423060
**Email** gary@whippetpromotions.fsnet.co.uk
*Independent record company releasing material worldwide. Artists include the Whisky Priests.*
***Musicians' Union member***
**RAB** Yorkshire Arts

## The Whole Wide World
**Contact** Dave Longly
**Mail address** 27 Market Street, CREWKERNE, Somerset, TA18 7JU
**Phone** 01460 77748
**Email** info@thewholewideworld.freeserve.co.uk
**Web** www.thewholewideworld.co.uk
*Specialist retail, mail order & festival sales of Folk, Blues and World Music on CD.*
**RAB** South West Arts

## Wildgoose Records
**Contact** Doug Bailey
**Mail address** May Cottage, WHERWELL, Hants, SP11 7JS
**Phone** 01264 860569
**Email** wgoose@attglobal.net
**Web** www.wildgoose.co.uk
**Alt contact** Sue Bailey
**Phone** 01264 860818
*Record label with own recording studio. Specialise in folk music.*
**RAB** Southern Arts

## Wildwood Acoustic
**Contact** Bill Lloyd
**Mail address** PO Box 12, CARNFORTH, Lancs, LA5 9PD
**Phone** 01524 735873
**Fax** 01524 736448
**Email** wildwood@dnet.co.uk
**Web** www.wildwood-records.co.uk
*Record label specialising in acoustic music. Artists include Seize the Day, New Deal String Band and Chouchenn.*
**RAB** North West Arts

## Women's Revolutions Per Minute (WRPM)
**Contact** Hilary Friend
**Mail address** 7 Thornbridge Avenue, Chorlton, MANCHESTER, M21 9DN
**Phone** 0161 861 8727
**Fax** 0870 056 1726
**Email** wrpm@appleonline.net
**Web** www.wrpm.org.uk
*Sales & distribution of music performed & composed by women. Folk/ traditional & world. CDs, tapes and books. Mail order and festivals. Free 30 page catolgue.*
**RAB** North West Arts

### Woodworm Studios
**Contact** Dave Pegg
**Mail address** PO Box 37, BANBURY, Oxon, OX16 8YN
**Phone** 01869 338853
**Fax** 01869 337142
**Web** www.fairportconvention.com
*24 track analogue and digital recording studio with accomodation, specialising in roots, folk and acoustic music.*
***Musicians' Union member***
**RAB** Southern Arts

### Working Joe Music Ltd
**Contact** Paul Saunders
**Mail address** 6 Swan Meadow, MUCH WENLOCK, Shropshire, TF13 6JQ
**Phone** 01952 728283
**Email** ps@workingjoe.co.uk
**Web** www.workingjoe.co.uk
*Independent record label and agency representing & recording roots artists. Contemporary songwriters to medieval street bands.*
**RAB** West Midlands Arts

## Other Services

### Andrea
**Contact** Audrey Miller
**Mail address** 76 Burlington Ave, KEW, Middx, TW9 4DH
**Phone** 020 8876 6441
**Email** AudreyMiller@waitrose.com
*Painter in Canal Art style. Demonstrations, lectures and teaching. Information leaflets and decorated objects for sale. Author of craft books.*
**RAB** London Arts

### Be@tts Inc
**Contact** Phil Plunkett
**Mail address** Loch Lomond Studio, Unt 20 Griffon Cn., Vale of Leven Ind E, DUMBARTON, G82 3PD, Scotland
**Phone** 01389 750555
**Email** phil@beattsinc.co.uk
**Web** www.beattsinc.co.uk
**Alt contact** Stuart Beattie/ Richy Plunkett
**Email** info@beattsinc.co.uk
*Custom built, fully sound-proofed rehearsal/ tuition studio rooms, 3 miles from Loch Lomond.*
***Musicians' Union member***
**AC** Scotland

### Centre for Creative Change
**Contact** Penni Blythe
**Mail address** Alderhay, Fairclose, COMBE ST NICHOLAS, Somerset, TA20 3LU
**Phone** 01460 61969
**Email** penni@ccchange.clara.net
*Development & support for folk organisations and individuals. Development of skills, teams & vision; skills for education & training. Personal & professional life training.*
**RAB** South West Arts

### Derek Schofield
**Mail address** 2 Carisbrocke Close, Wistaston, CREWE, Cheshire, CW2 8JD
**Phone** 01270 663041
**Email** derek@dschofield.demon.co.uk
*Photographer: large collection of photos of folk customs, folk dancers, musicians, etc.*
**RAB** North West Arts

### Glade Recording
**Contact** Alistair Russell
**Phone** 0113 226 9209
**Email** soundout@clara.net
**Web** http://home.clara.net/soundout
*International road/ tour managment, fluent in several European languages.*
***Musicians' Union member***
**RAB** Yorkshire Arts

### Hedingham Fair
**Contact** Karen & Colin Cater
**Mail address** Sunnyside, Southey Green, SIBLE HEDINGHAM, Essex, CO9 3RN
**Phone** 01787 462731
**Fax** 01787 463393
**Email** cater@hedfair.demon.co.uk
*T-shirts, greetings cards, calendars, glassware, designed by Karen Cater and depicting English mystical heritage, traditional customs, music & dance. Trade and mail order catalogues and commissions available*
**RAB** East England Arts

### Roy Palmer
**Mail address** The Corner House, Greenway, DYMOCK, Glos, GL18 2DT
**Phone** 01531 890412
*Folklorist - songs & social history, song traditions etc. Gives lectures and workshops.*
**RAB** South West Arts

### Video Services
**Contact** Michael Raven
**Mail address** 126 Jug Bank, Ashley, MARKET DRAYTON, Shrops, TF9 4NJ
**Phone** 01630 672304
*Video filming of festivals and clubs, professional digital equipment.*
**RAB** West Midlands Arts

# Proper Music Distribution

**Proper Music Distribution** is the principle music distribution company in the UK for roots music (Folk, country, blues, bluegrass, singer-songwriter, reggae, world) as well as distributing other music genres such as rock, jazz etc .

Proper Music Distribution's role is to sell and market roots music to record stores in the UK. This takes the form of selling to chainstores such as Andys, Our Price, HMV, Virgin, Tower, Borders, MVC etc and to over 1500 independent stores which stock roots music in some shape or form. Proper Music Distribution also exports CDs all over the world.

Proper Music Mail Order has recently been set up to market directly to music fans who may not be able or desire to visit a record store. To develop these sales we are advertising in all relevant magazines and media. Marketing directly to customers via festivals, concerts etc. (See advert on inside back cover.)

Some of the key roots labels we distribute.... **A New Day**, **Arhoolie**, **A Recordings**, **Aughrim**, **Beautiful Jo**, **Bedspring**, **Blackburst**, **Boys of the Lough**, **Caber**, **Claddagh**, **Cloud Valley**, **Cuillin**, **Culburnie**, **Dunkeld**, **Fellside**, **Fledg'ling**, **Free Reed**, **Fuse**, **Green Linnet**, **Greentrax**, **Home Roots**, **Hypertension**, **Irregular**, **Leola**, **Lochshore**, **Lunasa**, **Monarch**, **Mooncrest**, **Mother**, **Mrs Ackroyd**, **Mrs Casey**, **No Masters Co-op**, **Old Bridge**, **Once Bitten**, **Osmosys**, **Peerie Angel**, **Pier**, **Pig's Whisker**, **Proper**, **Pure**, **Quinlan Road**, **R.U.F**, **Rebel**, **Rel**, **Resistencia**, **Road Goes On Forever**, **Rounder**, **Sain**, **Science Friction**, **Shanachie**, **Smallworld**, **Sugar Hill**, **Talkative**, **Tartan**, **Temple**, **Terra Nova**, **Topic**, **Tumi**, **Ulftone**, **Veesik**, **Vertical**, **Wayward Whirlie**, **Woodworm**.....

**Proper Music Imports** also sources thousands of releases which are not domestically released in the UK.

**Folk and roots music is distributed by several companies. Here are some of the key ones.**

## 3MV
City Network House, 81-83 Weston Street, London SE1 3RS
**Phone** 020 7378 8866
**Fax** 020 7378 8855
**Web** www.3mvmusic.com

## 33jazz Records
33 Guildford Street, Luton, Bedfordshire LU1 2NQ
**Phone** 01582 419584
**Web** www.jazz33.f9.co.uk

## ADA
P.O. Box 800, Belper, Derbyshire DE56 2ZA
**Phone/Fax** 01773 850000

## ARC Music Distribution
P.O. Box 111, East Grinstead, West Sussex RH19 4FZ
**Phone** 01342 312161
**Fax** 01342 325209
**Web** www.arcmusic.co.uk

## Arion
36 Avenue Hoche, 75008 Paris, France
**Phone** 00 33 1 45 63 76 70
**Fax** 00 33 1 45 63 79 54
**Web** www.arion-music.com

## BMG Distribution
Lyng Lane, West Bromwich, West Midlands B70 7ST
**Phone** 0121 500 5678
**Fax** 0121 553 6880
**Web** www.bmg.com

## Changing World
Willow Croft, Wagg Drove, Huish Episcopi, Langport, Somerset TA10 9ER
**Phone** 01458 253838
**Fax** 01458 250317

## Copperplate Distribution
68 Belleville Road, London SW11 6PP
**Phone** 020 7585 0357
**Web** www.go.to/copperplate

## Delta/BMG
**Phone** 01689 888888
**Fax** 01689 888800

## Demon Music Group
76 Dean Street, London W1V 5HA
**Phone** 020 7396 8899
**Fax** 020 7396 8903

## Discord Distribution
P. O. Box 50, Tunbridge Wells, Kent TN3 9ZP
**Phone** 01892 863888
**Fax** 01892 863808
**Web** www.discord.co.uk

## Discovery Records Ltd.
Nursteed Road, Devizes SN10 3DY
**Phone** 01380 728 000

## EMI Sales and Distribution
Hermes Close, Tachbrook Park, Leamington Spa, Warwickshire CV34 6RP
**Phone** 01926 888888
**Fax** 01926 466321
**Web** www.emigroup.com

## English Folk Dance and Song Society
Cecil Sharp House, 2 Regent's Park Road, London NW1 7AY
**Phone** 020 7485 2206
**Fax** 020 7284 0534
**Web** www.efdss.org

## Etnisk Musikklubb
Masovngata 20, N-3616 Kongsberg Norway
**Phone** +47 32 73 56 60
**Fax** +47 32 73 56 61
**Email** etnisk-musikklubb@pc-cons.no

## FMR Records
10 Baddow Road, Chelmsford, Essex CM2 0DG
**Phone** 01245 353878
**Web** www.fmr-records.com

## Greentrax
Cockenzie Business Centre, Edinburgh Road, Cockenzie, East Lothian EH32 0HL
**Phone** 01875 814155
**Fax** 01875 813545
**Web** www.greentrax.com

## Harmonia Mundi Distribution
19-21 Nile Street, London N1 7LL
**Phone** 020 7253 0865
**Fax** 020 7253 3237
**Web** www.harmoniamundi.com

## Hot Records
P.O. Box 333, Brighton, East Sussex, BN1 2EH
**Phone** 01903 779443/859559
**Fax** 01903 779442

## International Records/ Passion Music
37 Red Lion Lane, Overton RG25 3HH
**Phone/Fax** 01256 770747
**Web** www.passion-music.co.uk

**Kemp Town Books**
91 St. George's Road, Brighton
BN2 1EE
**Phone** 01273 682110

**Koch International**
Charlotte House, 87 Little Ealing Lane
London W5 4EH
**Phone** 020 8832 1817
**Fax** 020 8832 1813
**Web** www.kochuk.com

**Layali El Sharq Music, UK**
19 Cranley Gardens, London N10 3AA
**Phone/Fax** 020 8444 4229

**Lusafrica**
Hoche Building, 13, rue Auger
93500 Pantin, France
**Email** lusafrica@lusafrica.com
**Web** www.lusafrica.com

**Mac Two**
Truman Brewery Building, Brick Lane
London E1 6QB
**Phone** 020 7377 6515
**Fax** 020 7377 5841

**Magda**
21 Sheinkin Street, Tel Aviv 65232,
Israel
**Phone** +972 3 528 6106
**Fax** +972 3 528 3413
**Web** www.magda.co.il

**Musical Traditions Records**
**Phone** 020 7263 1240
**Web** www.mustrad.org.uk/records

**Navras**
33 Sherwood Road, London NW4 1AD
**Phone** 020 8203 2553
**Fax** 020 8203 2542
**Web** www.navrasrecords.com

**New Note**
(dealers should contact **Pinnacle**)
Electron House, Cray Avenue, St Mary
Cray, Orpington, Kent BR5 3RJ
**Phone** 01689 877884
**Fax** 01689 877891
**Web** www.newnote.com

**Nimbus**
Wyastone Leys, Monmouth, Gwent
NP5 3SR
**Phone** 01600 890682
**Fax** 01600 890779
**Web** www.classic.cz/katalogy/
nimbus/nimbusset

**Ninaad Music and Marketing PVT Ltd.**
5/16 Vrindavan, Tarun Bharat Society
Andheri (East), Mumbai 400 099
**Email** ninaad@bom3.vsnl.net.in

**Oxford University Press Distribution Services**
Saxon Way West, Corby, Northants
NN18 9ES
**Phone** +44 (0) 1536 741519
**Fax** 01536 746337
**Web** www.oup.com

**Pinnacle/Pinnacle Imports**
Osprey House, New Mill Road
Orpington, Kent BR5 3QG
**Phone** 01689 870622
**Fax** 01689 878269
**Web** www.pinnacle-records.co.uk

**Proper**
Powerhouse, Cricket Lane
Beckenham, Kent, BR3 1LW
**Phone** 0870 444 0800
**Fax** 0870 444 0801
**Web** www.proper-records.co.uk

**Red Hedgehog Music**
Brooklyn House, Brook Street,
Shepshed, Leicestershire LE12 9RG
**Phone** 01509 829301
**Fax** 01509 829302
**Web** www.red-hedgehog.co.uk

**Resistencia**
San Isidro Labrador 19, 28005
Madrid, Spain
**Phone** +34 91 366 53 46
**Fax** +34 91 364 00 36
**Email** resistencia@edires.com

**RMG**
33-35 Wembley Hill Road, Wembley,
HA9 8RT
**Phone** 020 8903 0360
**Fax** 020 8782 4706
**Web** www.rmgplc.com/distribution

**Select**
34 Holmethorpe Avenue,
Holmethorpe Estate, Redhill, Surrey
RH1 2NN
**Phone** 01737 760020
**Fax** 01737 766316
**Web** www.selectmusic.co.uk

**Silva Screen**
3 Prowse Place, London NW1 9PH
**Phone** 020 7428 5500
**Fax** 020 7482 2385
**Web** www.silvascreen.co.uk

**Sona Rupa**
103 Belgrave Road, Leicester LE4
6AS
**Phone** 0116 266 8181
**Fax** 0116 261 0336
**Web** www.sonarupa.co.uk

**Sony**
10 Great Marlborough Street,
London W1V 2LP
**Phone** 020 7911 8200
**Fax** 020 7911 8600
**Web** www.sonymusic.com

**Stern's**
74/75 Warren Street, London
W1P 5PA
**Phone** 020 7388 5533
**Fax** 020 7388 2756
**Web** www1.sternsmusic.com

**Trehantiri**
365-367 Green Lanes, London N4
1DY
**Phone/Fax** 020 8802 6530
**Web** www.trehantiri.com

**Union Square Music**
Unit 2, The Grand Union Office Park,
Packet Boat Lane, Cowley, Uxbridge
UB8 2GH
**Phone** 01895 458515
**Fax** 01895 458516
**Web** www.unionsquaremusic.co.uk

**Universal**
22 St Peters Square, London W6 9NW
**Phone** 020 8910 5000
**Fax** 020 8910 3132
**Web** www.umusic.com

**Virgin Records**
Kensal House, 553-579 Harrow Road,
London W10 4RH
**Phone** 020 8964 6000
**Fax** 020 8964 6073
**Web** www.virginrecords.com

**Vital**
338a Ladbroke Grove, London
W10 5AH
**Phone** 020 8324 2400
**Fax** 020 8324 0003

**Warner**
P.O. Box 59, Alperton Lane,
Wembley HA0 1FJ
**Phone** 020 8998 8844
**Fax** 020 8998 3429
**Web** www.wbr.com

**Wood Productions**
PO Box 131, 00141 Helsinki, Finland
**Email** woodprod@hotmail.com
**Web** www.members.tripod.com/
~woodproduc

**World Music Network**
6 Abbeville Mews, 88 Clapham Park
Road, London SW4 7BX
**Phone** 020 7498 5252
**Fax** 020 7498 5353
**Web** www.worldmusic.net

## A Guide to Making your Own CDs

**Malcolm Creese** has written an extensive document on this subject. It was produced by Jazz Services with the financial assistance of the Arts Council of England and the Musicians' Union.

Free copies of this document are available by sending an A5 stamped addressed envelope (2 x 1st or 2nd class). It covers:

**Preparation**
- Business
- Costing
- Raising Money
- Album Concept
- Live or Studio
- Choosing a Studio
- The Producer

**Recording**
- Setting Up
- Recording
- Mixing

**Post Production**
- Mastering, Compiling and PQ Encoding
- Choosing a Manufacturer
- MCPS Licence
- Artwork/Printing

**Marketing**
- Production
- Sales and Distribution

**New Technology**
- Super Audio CD
- Selling CDs via the Internet.
- Digital Distribution

### *Useful Contacts*

**Mechanical Copyright Protection Society (MCPS)**
Elgar House, 41 Streatham High Road, London, SW16 1ER
**Phone** 020 8664 4400

**Article Number Association (ANA)**
11 Kingsway, London, WC2B 6AR
**Phone** 020 7240 2912

**Performing Right Society (PRS)**
29-33 Berners Street, London, W1P 4AA
**Phone** 020 7580 5544

**British Phonographic Institute (BPI)**
25 Savile Row, London, W1X 1AA
**Phone** 020 7287 4422

**Phonographic Performance Ltd (PPL)**
Ganton House, 14-22 Ganton Street, London, W1V 1LB
**Phone** 020 7437 0311

**Jazz Services Ltd**
**Email** admin@jazzservices.org.uk
**Web** www.jazzservices.org.uk

## The DIY CD – some points to consider.

By **Bryan Ledgard**

As a designer of many print-based items of literature, including the 'paper parts' necessary to identify a CD, I have become involved in the processes that occur at either end of the 'performance to product' chain. Firstly, it may be useful to outline, in layman's terms, what happens to your recording after you have spent those many long hours recording and mixing.

As studio technology has developed, your recording will probably end up as a fully mixed, mastered and encoded CDR. At a suitable pressing plant this CDR is digitally transferred to a Glass Master, which then goes through a type of electroplating process, dissolving the glass master and leaving two chromed metal 'stampers'. These are fitted to a machine which literally sandwiches a blob of liquid plastic flattening it into a CD. (Okay, a simplistic description, but enough to get the picture.) The discs are then subjected to a screen printing process to imprint the disc design 'on-body'.

Let's move on to your packaging. Design is a very subjective issue, but it's important to be guided by some very basic rules. Never forget that your packaging is your shop window. The sleeve is always seen before the music is heard, and is often used as reference for titles, lyrics, timings, publishing details etc.

If it's your first album, perhaps the CD-buying public may want to see what you look like - putting a face to the name helps. Portraiture can often be quite an unappealing prospect for the performer, (and often for the public!) so choose a photographer with whom you enjoy working. Having a laugh, playing or listening to music during the shoot can produce natural and characterful pictures. Photographs taken at live events can be used to good effect if the photographer has access to the stage or surrounding area.

Your final album may be racked up in the stores and stalls either forwards or sideways, so make sure your name and title are visible and clear on the front and the left-hand spine.

Legibility is an issue, especially for the vision impaired, so try to avoid cramming all your lyrics onto a small booklet. A quart will not fit into a pint pot, no matter how much you squash and squeeze your text.

If your album is destined for the shops, a barcode is important for in-store stock control. Many designers and artwork producers are members of the Article Number Association (ANA) and are authorised to provide a unique number and the barcode itself.

Copyright and publishing details should never be overlooked. "A Guide to Making your Own CDs" by Malcolm Creese (see above) provides a guide to working with the licensing authorities (MCPS, PPL, PRS etc.).

Along with your mastered CDR, most pressing plants will print all the 'paper parts' and will accept your artwork in a variety of formats – on disc, Zip, via an ISDN line etc. – but it's always worth asking your designer to quote on producing the separated films needed to make the printing plates as costs can vary dramatically.

Separated films are a set of four pieces of acetate carrying information for each of the four process colour, cyan, yellow, magenta and black. When four plates are made from each of these films and printed one on top of the other, your full colour images are recreated.

You will need to design a booklet, in multipes of four pages – 4, 8, 12, 16 and so on, or a folding sheet, remembering, of course, that a thick booklet is difficult to fit into the case. You also need a tray liner to fit behind the CD in the case and a design for the on-body print.

When deciding on the quantity to have pressed, consider how you will sell them. From the stage on gigs? Through a recognised distributor? Your new album is little use to you in boxes under the bed.

It's usual for artists to put aside a number of CDs to send out as promotional copies for review or airplay. But be selective! Radio presenters, magazine editors and record companies are inundated with CDs daily, so choose a few contacts with whom you can be certain of some response. Compiling a 'press pack' with your CD, including biog, promo photo and press cuttings, will provide vital backround for reviewers.

**Bryan Ledgard**
*Senior designer consultant and photographer for Ledgard Jepson Ltd.*

## Choosing a Violin

By **Tim Phillips**

My gut reaction to the question of what to look for when buying a violin is 'buy one YOU like'. Let's face it, it's you who has to live with it! Not your teacher, or your friend, or your Mum, it's YOU!! But here are a few things to check for that may help save you from buying a 'lemon'.

**Overall condition**

Splits in the back, especially if they run under the sound post, are seriously bad news.

Look at the front for splits too, again if they run over the post or under the bridge feet they could be costly. Carefully look at the neck joint and button. Weakness or botched repairs here can cause serious neck angle problems.

Check the neck is straight and that the fingerboard is not warped. Scan the ribs for cracks and bulges, especially down by the chinrest and tailpiece button. If the ribs are coming away from the front or back, don't worry, get it fixed.

**Fittings**

Bridge, soundpost, tailpiece and chinrest are all easily replaced but do test the pegs to make sure they work properly before you hand over your money or you might get a nasty surprise!

**Testing**

Play some boring old scales over the whole range you're going to use, listening for any seriously dodgy notes that may occur before you launch into your latest party piece, and then if you still love it.....it's up to you.

Of course, if you buy new you can concentrate entirely on sound, feel and looks without the worry but cheap instruments will still need setting up properly.

**Tim Phillips**
**Web** www.timsviolins.supanet.com

## Hobgoblin Music - Britain's Leading Folk Music Retailer

By **Pete McClelland** (Partner)

Music is the longest established and largest retailer in the UK specialising in Acoustic and Folk and World music instruments. There are Hobgoblin shops in Crawley, London, Bristol, Leeds, Manchester, Nottingham and Wadebridge, all the staff are actively involved in traditional music making, and experts in helping customers. There is also a direct sales operation through the website **www.hobgoblin.com**, and a mail order service. During 2001 Hobgoblin are celebrating 25 successful years in business!

**Hobgoblin's Aims**

We want to give beginners a chance to take up a folk instrument as well as to provide the best for those who already play. We aim to encourage more people to discover and enjoy English, Irish, Scottish & Welsh traditional music. Everyone at Hobgoblin is involved in folk music, we provide employment to a growing number of folk musicians, makers and repairers. We want to help keep music live, by making real acoustic instruments widely available.

We always encourage people to make music themselves, by taking up a musical instrument. You are never too young or too old to start!

**Hobgoblin History**

Hobgoblin Music was founded in 1976, and is still run by Pete and Mannie McClelland. The early market stall and barn were quickly outgrown, and the Crawley shop was first opened in 1977.

In 1992 a period of expansion started, and the company grew from a single shop to seven shops and counting in 2001. An increasingly wide range of instruments, books and accessories for many styles of music is now on offer. Each summer since 1976 Hobgoblin staff have set up shop at folk festivals all around Britain, and occasionally overseas too. This has always proved a great opportunity for meeting customers, and keeping in touch with what is wanted and the new trends in folk music.

**Hobgoblin Music**
PO Box 2522, Henfield, BN5 9SN, UK
**Fax** 01273 491123
**Web** www.hobgoblin.com

## The Music Room – Britain's Centre of Excellence for Traditional Musical Instruments

By **John Turner**

How many times have you gone into a shop and been greeted by a friendly smile?

'The kettle's on, do you fancy a tea or coffee?" Even before "Sounds Interesting", the Leeds based squeezebox specialists, bought Dave Mallinson Music and subsequently became The Music Room, our commitment to total customer care and satisfaction was well known throughout the world of traditional music.

The Music Room experience is so much more than simply buying something from us.

Together, the partners and staff have far too many years worth of experience to count; our expert advice is readily available and free of charge. We use this collective experience and technical knowledge to search the world over and bring to you the finest quality musical instruments that truly represent value for money. We back up these products with service, repairs and mail order departments that are second to none and remember we are never beaten on price. Find the same product in stock and cheaper elsewhere and we refund the difference. We have a stunning FREE mail order catalogue available from all our outlets, ask for yours today.

Our commitment to traditional music does not end there. We are all musicians at The Music Room and help and encourage other musicians of all ages and abilities to get involved. We are the proud suppliers of all the musical instruments that go to make up the **Folkworks** instrument-lending bank: the leading initiative in encouraging young people in taking up traditional music and dance in the North of England. We also sponsor places for young people at the **Hands On** music weekends together with sponsoring the beginners workshops at the **Karen Tweed** and **Andy Cutting** organised **Folk Beat** festival. The melodeon playing competition at the **Sidmouth International Festival** is another Music Room project.

To come on board and start to enjoy The Music Room experience either visit one of our shops at Cleckheaton (West Yorkshire), Nottingham or Oxford. Or look up our secure shopping website at www.the-music-room.com. Alternatively why not come and say hello at one of the many UK festivals we set up shop at each year. We don't always have a kettle at outdoor festivals but the welcome is just as warm.

**The Music Room**
35 Bradford Road, CLECKHEATON,
W Yorks, BD19 3JN
**Phone** 01274 879768
01274 852020 - mail order
**Fax** 01274 852280
**Email** info@the-music-room.com
**Web** www.the-music-room.com

## The Music Room Guide to choosing a Folk Instrument

The next best thing to listening to traditional music is making traditional music. How do you begin to make that first all-important purchase that may not only introduce you to a completely new hobby but also a totally new way of life? The suggestions we make here are as a result of years of involvement in traditional music and encouraging hundreds of newcomers on the road to play traditional music.

## Melodeon, Button Accordion & Piano Accordion

**What kind of instrument do you want to play?**
These instruments come in all different shapes and sizes, suited to all types of music. If you want to play Irish, Scottish or English dance music (jigs, reels and the like) or morris dance music, or European folk music, or Cajun music, or even song accompaniment, there is a squeezebox for you. So here is our advice about squeezeboxes, along with the uses you might put them to.

**Melodeon or Button Accordion?** - It's all a question of geography.
There is a lot of confusion around as to when we should call one instrument a melodeon or another a button accordion, or indeed whether we should spell the word accordeon instead. As a rule of thumb, in Ireland, an instrument with 1 row of treble buttons and 2 bass is usually called a melodeon, while all other button instruments (with the exception of the concertina and bandoneon) are known as button accordions.
In England both 1 row and 2 row instruments would be classified as melodeons. The 2 row variety is further divided according to keys into diatonic (D/G, G/C, C/F and A/D) and chromatic (B/C and C#/D being the most popular).

Accordions with buttons are then further divided into those instruments which

(a) play different notes on the push and the pull of the bellows, usually with 8 but sometimes 4, 12, 14, 16 or 18 bass buttons, and are known as button accordions, and

(b) have buttons that play a different note in to out on the right hand and the same notes in to out on the left hand or bass end. These are known as button accordions (note the spelling) and are often referred to as British chromatics, magnificent in the hands of maestros such as **Jimmy Shand** and **John Kirkpatrick**.

A third instrument within the same branch of this squeezable family is the continental chromatic button accordeon, recognised by having anywhere from 3 to 5 rows of treble buttons and 2 to 6 rows of bass buttons. These play the same note on any given button regardless of the direction of the bellows.

If you want to play traditional English music, a 2 row diatonic instrument is usually best to start on. Don't make the mistake of thinking a 1 row instrument is easier to play. They are specialist instruments that do sound wonderful in the right hands but are not advised as a starting instrument.

Their limitations far outweigh their advantages, especially when it comes to joining in with other musicians at sessions etc. In England, D/G is the most popular tuning, whilst G/C and to a lesser extent C/F are the preferred keys in the rest of Europe. And don't think that a D/G is limited to those keys. It is possible to play to a greater or lesser extent in D, G, A, E minor, B minor and C, although the really good players can find more.

Very cheap instruments are available as starting instruments, but most people can see just how quickly these are put together. If possible you would always be better spending that little bit extra on say a **Hohner Pokerwork** than some of the cheaper alternatives. The Pokerwork is still the preferred choice of many musicians, notably **John Kirkpatrick** who firmly recommends this as the best instrument for English music.

You may prefer traditional Irish music! As a point of interest, it is a commonly held belief that it is easier to play Irish music on a D/G than it is to play English style on a B/C. It is perfectly possible to play Irish Traditional Music to a very high standard on the D/G diatonic melodeon; in fact until the 1940s and early 1950s the D/G and 1 rows were highly favoured. If you want to sound like one of the older traditionalists, a diatonic is the one to choose.

It wasn't until players like **Paddy O'Brien** came along that the modern Irish accordion style developed. They realised that switching to the B/C system had several advantages. Firstly, the fact that the C row comprises of all natural notes and the B row is all sharps and flats. By using a combination of notes from each row and playing across the rows, more keys were available and a smoother bellows action achieved. Secondly, the grace notes, triplets, runs and fills etc. which are characteristic of modern Irish music are more readily available and fall to hand easier than on a diatonic. Another difference is in the bass work. This differs from the English bouncy rhythmic style, which depends on changing bellows direction to play notes in the same direction of the bellows as their accompanying chords. Irish music on the other hand has very little bass accompaniment, placing more importance on the melody notes and ornamentations, rather than making sure these notes fall in a particular direction to make the basses fit.

The Irish style is still evolving and other keys are finding favour, especially C#/D, with exponents such as **Jackie Daly** popularising this tuning. Basically, the aim is to be able to play in the main fiddle keys of D, G and A and relative minors.

Using the C#/D allows you to play more or less up and down 1 row for most of the time, generating a more rhythmic effect. To start playing Irish music we would recommend a **Hohner Double Ray**.

Make sure the basses have been altered to suit Irish music at the time of purchase.

These well-proportioned instruments are easy to maintain and tend to hold more of their original value. A good second-hand Hohner would also give you good value for money.

The hottest-selling Irish style box in this country at the present time is the **Saltarelle Irish Bouëbe**.

More expensive than the Hohner, but a very useful mid-priced instrument featuring a flat enclosed fingerboard with a very fast action.

You can learn Cajun music on any diatonic box, but really a 1 row 4-stop is needed in the most popular Cajun key of C. The same instrument will also allow you to play in G in much the same way as a blues harmonica player would use the second position to get G from a C instrument.

A great deal of myth and folklore surrounds this type of instrument, ranging from the type of woods used in the construction to the direction the reeds are laid in. A genuine Louisiana box would in fact have 2 of its 4 reeds laid flat on the soundboard and 2 upright on a block. The best value for money entry-level instrument we have come across is the Italian made

**Acadia**. Available in different keys and tunings, a great box at a great price. This, together with the video by **Dirk Powell** "Learn to play Cajun Accordion - Starting Out" is all you really need to make a success of things.

G/C and C/F are the most popular tunings for European music, and incidentally these are also among the best keys to use when singing. **Hohner** supply the **Pokerwork** in G/C and C/F, but the more authentic instrument is the **Le Bouëbe** by the French Company **Saltarelle**. The UK does not have a wealth of tuition material, but 'Musique pour la Danse Bretonne' is useful.

#### Glossary of 'Squeezebox' Terms

**Voices** - refers to the number of reeds sounding e.g. 1 voice = 1 reed, 2 voices = 2 reeds, 3 voices = 3 reeds etc.

**Stops/Registers** - these are knobs or switches to allow certain reeds to be switched on and off.

**Dry** - when one reed is tuned in concert pitch and the second is tuned to the same pitch.

**Wet or Tremolo** - when one reed is tuned in concert pitch and the other is tuned very sharp - far enough to set up a fast beat between the reeds.

**Swing** - when one reed is tuned in concert pitch and the other is tuned slightly sharp, somewhere between wet and dry.

#### Manufacturers

Here is a list of some of the most highly regarded today.

**Hohner** - Once the market leaders but still producing good entry level instruments to suit all styles of playing.

**Saltarelle** - 'Faster than your fingers' A French company offering a range of instruments with some having had been specially designed for the British market.

**Dino Baffetti** - 'Quality at your fingertips'. Baffetti makes brilliant boxes especially useful for morris musicians and dance band work.

**Castagnari** is a family-run firm producing instruments in Italy to the highest quality - all of them named after members of the Castagnari family.

## Piano Accordion

The Piano Accordion is enjoying something of a revival. Once more it has become a popular instrument appealing as it does to a broad cross-section of musical styles. It is a very important instrument in traditional Scottish, Irish, English and classical music. Generally speaking, piano accordions are classified according to the number of basses they have and are available in bass sizes from 8 right up to the full 120 basses. Different models have the ability to play from 2 reeds at once up to 5 reeds at once. In the main the most useful size accordions for playing traditional music are the 48, 60 or the 72 bass model. Don't be fooled into buying a big 120 bass instrument as your first instrument. These can be acquired relatively cheaply but you will be buying facilities that you may hardly ever use and you may find the extra weight too off putting to want to practise a great deal.

The "action" of the piano accordion refers to how responsive the fingerboard is. A good action together with reeds which "speak" or play easily are signs of a good accordion. Instruments are available from makers from all over the world. Here are just a few.

**Primo** - A range of entry level instruments from the world famous accordion company of St Petersburg.

**Pigini** - 'Quality, sound, tradition'. Pigini are a leading Castelfidardo family in accordion manufacture. Many professional players choose Pigini for their quality and reliability, recently including piano accordion virtuosos **Karen Tweed, Chris Parkinson, Sam Pirt** and many others.

**Dino Baffetti** - Built in Castelfidardo, Italy to a very high quality specification. Baffetti accordions offer exceptional value for money.

## The Concertina

Basically there are 3 major systems - the Anglo system, the English System and the Duet system.

In the main the duet system has become less popular in recent years, with the Anglo gathering more favour with Irish style players, and the English systems with English style players. In brief the Anglo produces a different note on the push to the pull of the bellows on any given button.

Both 20 and 30 button instruments are available and are usually found in the keys of G/C or D/G.

Modern Italian instruments made by a company called **Stagi** are good beginners' instruments.

The English system instruments are characterised by having the same note on the push and pull of the bellows. 48 buttons is a very useful size allowing the player to play just about any tune in the world. Again **Stagi** make a 48 button entry-level instrument.

Please note that it is still possible to buy a vintage concertina. However these instruments are no longer manufactured today and are becoming ever more rare. They are a specialist purchase and can cost a considerable amount of money. Before purchasing any second-hand instrument please make sure you have contacted a specialist in the field to get the proper advice you need.

## The Guitar Family

If any instrument symbolises the freedom of choice that happened in popular and folk music from the 1950s onwards, it's the guitar.

The guitar's versatility makes it a great idea for someone who doesn't yet know exactly what they want to specialise in. Solo classical music, flamenco, song accompaniment, lead melody playing, dance music accompaniment - there's a guitar for all those jobs.

Acoustic guitars can be fairly easily categorised. There are nylon-strung (also known as classical, flamenco or Spanish) and steel-strung. There are purely acoustic, or electro-acoustic (with pickups). There are laminate-topped instruments, and solid-topped instruments, and guitars made of solid timber throughout. There are various body shapes and sizes, conventional and with cutaway (to let you get up to the top frets, otherwise known as 'the dusty end'.

Generally, the cheaper guitars have laminate tops, as they are quicker and easier to make.

The way they sound on the day of purchase will be the way they will sound all through their lives.

Many are great sounding and value for money. Solid tops, on the other hand, cost more to make as the choice of pieces of wood is crucial and the construction has to be more accurate to stop the top bending. But they generally sound far more resonant and exciting - and as the wood matures, the sound matures too! About 90% of the sound of a guitar comes from the top, so we often find solid tops and laminate back and sides. This is a good compromise between price and sound quality.

Modestly priced beginners' guitars of various makes, including smaller sizes for children are generally available. These are of the classical guitar shape with a wide, flat fingerboard. They are easier on the fingers than steel-stringed instruments, although the wider fingerboard can mean more stretching. The wide string spacing and nylon strings make these instruments especially suitable for solo melody finger picking styles - finger picking is where the tips of the fingers, or the fingernails, play one or more strings at a time, rather than strumming all strings at once.

**Nylon-Strung Classical Guitars**
Moving up the price range, we find guitars of the same style as the above but better made, perhaps with solid tops or even solid timbers throughout. Some are hand-made in Spain itself; reputable makers include **Rodriguez** and **Alvira**.

**Steel-Strung Acoustic Guitars**
A steel-strung guitar nearly always has a larger body than a nylon-strung, is well suited to strumming or picking with a plectrum, and has a narrower neck for fast chord changes. These are the guitars mostly used for folk, pop, country and jazz music.

**Beginners' Models And Better-Quality Laminate Top Guitars**
In the absolute lowest price range, but still full-sized instruments and definitely not toys, a variety of makes are generally available. A step up from these beginners' models is the better-quality laminate top guitars such as the **Tonewood TJ-10**.

**Solid Top Guitars** A few short years ago, solid top instruments were produced in small numbers in the USA and Europe and were beyond the means of the hobby guitarist. But a host of new companies, first in Japan then throughout the Far East, changed all that. Now there is an enormous selection of excellently constructed, affordable, great-sounding solid tops at good prices.

**All Solid Timber Guitars** From hand-crafted British made instruments like **Oakwood** and **Fylde**, through to the American legends like **Martin**, **Guild** and **Taylor**, these "thoroughbred" instruments can only grow to sound better with age, and even to appreciate in value in the long term - although you should buy for playing rather than investment! The arrival of **Taylor** on the top-class guitar scene, with their amazing consistency of quality and modern manufacturing techniques, galvanised all the other top makers into action.

**Electro-Acoustic Guitars** Some steel-strung guitars, and a few nylon-strung too, are supplied ready-fitted with various pickup systems so you can plug into an amplifier or PA system and get a louder, but still acoustic, sound. They will often come with a cutaway, because increased volume means they can be used as lead instruments in true rock 'n' roll fashion. You'll find electro-acoustics at all price levels. You can also buy a purely acoustic guitar, then have it adapted for amplification in various ways.

**Martin** C F Martin & Co. stands alone as the oldest surviving maker of guitars in the world. Through each of the six generations of family members that have managed the company, the Martin name has been held in high esteem as a symbol of enduring craftsmanship and quality.

**Taylor** "Hand built in the USA" Hand built in El Cajun, California, USA. Bob Taylor and Kurt Listug began building Taylor guitars in Lemon Grove, California in 1973. Their designs, choice of materials and quality of build has put them in the super league of USA luthiers.

**Simon & Patrick** Simon and Patrick luthier guitars are hand built in Canada to a very high standard using timbers from 900-year-old trees.

**Seagull** The Seagull Concept - the idea of the Seagull guitar was to place the emphasis on the creation of a quality musical instrument.

**Norman** Norman guitars were the original hand crafted instruments made in La Patrie, Quebec, Canada from mature North American trees.

## The Mandolin Family

Choosing and learning to play an instrument from the mandolin family.

**The Mandolin** Mandolin strings are tuned in unison pairs as follows: 'G' 4th pair, 'D' 3rd pair, 'A' 2nd pair and 'E' 1st pair - exactly the same tuning and fingering as the violin. When fiddle players choose to play a mandolin they just have to master the use of a plectrum.

You can start by learning half a dozen simple chords (these can be played using two fingers) and progress from there with simple scales and polka type tunes. If you have already played guitar or any other stringed instrument, it's even easier. The mandolin is mainly chosen for playing tunes and is picked with a plectrum. The most popular types are the 'flat-back' models which the **Gibson 'A' style** is the most popular. The **Gibson 'F' style** is the one with 'scroll' type shoulders; you see many bluegrass mandolin players using this style. The round back 'Neapolitan' mandolins, however nice sounding, are more difficult to hold (they slide away from your body). They are less popular today.

**The Octave Mandola** This instrument is a larger version of the standard mandolin. The most popular way to tune it is in unison pairs: 'G' 4th pair, 'D' 3rd pair, 'A' 2nd pair and 'E' 1st pair (this is the same tuning as the mandolin above but an octave below). The octave mandola is a good compromise between mandolin and bouzouki.

**The Bouzouki** The string length of the bouzouki is even longer than the octave mandola. It's much harder to play tunes on this instrument so the most popular use is for chord work and accompaniment.

**The Cittern** Has a scale similar in length to the octave mandola but usually with ten strings, not eight, and tuned modally (to a chord or drone). Strictly speaking, modern citterns are a remake of a medieval predecessor of the guitar, but musically they really belong in this group of instruments here.

It's usually tuned to some kind of open chord either GCGCG (C chord) or GDGDG (G chord) and is mostly used to play an accompaniment of melodic runs along with a bagpipe-type drone.

Its ten strings make it very versatile for chord work or for melody playing. The strings are usually tuned in pairs, but sometimes each pair will comprise of two strings an octave apart, like the bottom four strings of a twelve-string guitar.

**The Tenor Mandolin** This instrument has a scale length longer than the mandolin but shorter than the octave mandola.

It is normally tuned in unison pairs as follows: 'C' 4th pair, 'G' 3rd pair, 'D' 2nd pair and 'A' 1st pair.

## The Banjo Family

You may ask "what kind of banjo do I need?" Here is a description of the most common banjos used today, and a simple explanation of the music they are chosen for.

In the early 1900s the Tenor Banjo was designed and made for playing jazz music. It was tuned C4, G3, D2, A1 and either picked or strummed. This is the banjo that has been adapted for playing tunes in Irish and traditional music.

The earliest banjos that came from America (even earlier, from Africa!) reached maturity around the late 1800s. Many fine open back five-string banjos from this period can still be found today.

The most popular five-string models today have heavy tone rings and are fitted with a resonator.

These banjos are chosen for playing bluegrass, folk and general banjo music.

The Plectrum Banjo has a neck as long as the five-string banjo but is fitted with only four strings.

The instrument is ideal for chord work. You can 'pick' or 'strum' using a plectrum.

## Bodhráns and Percussion

Lots of people get into folk music, and especially Irish music, through the bodhrán, that well-known Irish hand drum. To be in a pub full of enthusiastic session musicians makes it almost irresistible to join in, and for someone with no previous musical knowledge, but a reasonable sense of rhythm, the bodhrán is the ideal starter instrument. But beware - lots of musicians spend years honing their talents. You enjoy listening to them. They're very welcoming people, or else they wouldn't be playing folk music in the pub, and they want you to join in. But please remember you have to walk before you run - buying a tutor book or video along with your bodhrán will let you get over the initial stages at home, so you'll get a genuine welcome when you turn up at the session!

You can get a reasonable starter bodhrán and beater for around £30. Prices then go up through various stages to around £200. As with all instruments, you get what you pay for. Move up slightly from the lowest price and you get into bodhráns with Celtic decoration. These will be of similar quality, but nicer-looking. Then we move up to £50 plus, and you're into the cheapest of the genuine Irish made goatskin bodhráns. A bit more money gets you a hand-made drum, which has had its skin carefully selected and processed. All the bodhrans up to this point will be of a simple construction, with the skin (usually goatskin) stretched over a simple hoop. Climatic conditions will affect the tension of the skin, so that on a cold, damp day you'll need to warm up the skin to get it to sound right, or, on a hot dry day you'll have to damp down the skin with a few drops of water to stop it 'pinging". But move a bit further up the price range, between £100 and £200, and you can get a tuneable bodhrán. These have a system, sometimes using a key, sometimes a cam wheel adjuster, which lets you tighten up and slacken off the skin mechanically. "Tuneable" can mean tuning to a note - but the nature of the drum and its reaction to the atmosphere would make it drift off the note fairly quickly. By "tuneable" we really mean "adjustable", so that you can easily get the skin to the right tension. And by the way, if you go for a tuneable bodhrán, a good tip is never to slacken it off fully after you've played. Continually taking the tension up and down puts too much stress on the skin - it's much better to keep your skin at a reasonable tension at all times.

A bodhrán is an organic instrument that needs a little bit of care and attention.

As mentioned above, we can't stress strongly enough that you should buy a basic bodhrán book and/or video to help you get the most out of your instrument.

## Flutes and Whistles

The penny whistle derives its name through buskers getting a penny for playing it, rather than that being how much they once were to buy. There are tons to choose from. In the main you can get a good entry level high whistle such as the **Generation** or the USA built **Susato** for a few pounds.

More expensive hand built whistles are available like **Overton**, **Howard**, **Shaw** or **Chieftain**.

The fingering you use on say a D whistle is transposable onto any other key whistle. In other words to change key when playing your whistle, pick up another whistle rather than learn new fingering.

The simple system D flute is the most commonly used flute in traditional music. Side blown it requires the same finger patterns as the D whistle. A good entry-level instrument is commonly made from plastic such as the **Acoustica Celtic Black**; ideal as a first side blown student instrument.

regional section

# rooting in the regions



# focus on Scotland



# focus on Ireland



# focus on Wales

## English Regional Arts Boards

By **Carolyn Nixson**, Administrator

**Mail address** 5 City Road, Winchester, SO23 8SD
**Phone** 01962 851063
**Fax** 01962 842033
**Email** info@erab.org.uk
**Web** www.arts.org.uk

The 10 English Regional Arts Boards (RABs) are each limited companies with charitable status.

They are partners with the Arts Council of England (ACE), now merged with the Crafts Council, the Film Council and the local authorities in developing, sustaining and promoting the arts in England.

They work as arts development agencies in the broadest sense, identifying needs and formulating strategies for arts provision in conjunction with their key partners, with government departments (e.g. in relation to EU Structural Funds, social inclusion and SRB), the private sector (including regional media and broadcasters) and Higher Education.

At the time of going to press, the Arts Council of England was in consultation with the Regional Arts Boards of England with regard to a complete restructuring of the systems and procedures for support and funding of the arts throughout England. Some Regional Arts Boards were to remain the same under the new proposals and Southern Arts was to be split between the South East and South West regions. The proposals suggest that after consultation, new systems would be in place in the near future. For the purposes of this publication we recognise the Regional Arts Boards and their boundaries as of March 31st 2001.

**Financial Support**

The RABs provide financial support for professional theatre companies, dance and mime companies, music ensembles, literature, film, and art and new media centres, galleries, community projects, arts education and training and a wide range of local arts bodies which promote arts events. The greater part of RAB funding is allocated to the professional sector, largely because of the greater expenses of professional arts companies and because amateur activities are more generally seen as the responsibility of local rather than regional authorities. Nevertheless, some assistance is provided to support high quality amateur work. Changes in Lottery distribution rules and greater decentralisation is also expanding the possibilities for supporting participation. Each RAB establishes its own priorities from year to year, in line with a strategy agreed with the Arts Council and with the Film Council. Generally, RABs are concerned to develop ventures in areas where provision is poor.

**The Lottery**

The RABs act as agents for the ACE in the assessment of applications for awards. RABs are also able to help potential applicants with advice and discussion of their Lottery bids before applications are formally made. As a result of the 1998 Lottery Act RABs are now delegated Lottery distributors of the ACE. Owing to the scale of existing committed projects, Lottery capital funding will be more difficult to access than hitherto. RABs now handle the decisions on all capital bids up to £100,000 and support development work at regional level through the Regional Arts Lottery Programme.

Further details on all RAB funding programmes can be found on the Website www.arts.org.uk

**Wales** and **Scotland** do not have regional boards but work directly through the Arts Council of Wales and Scottish Arts Council.

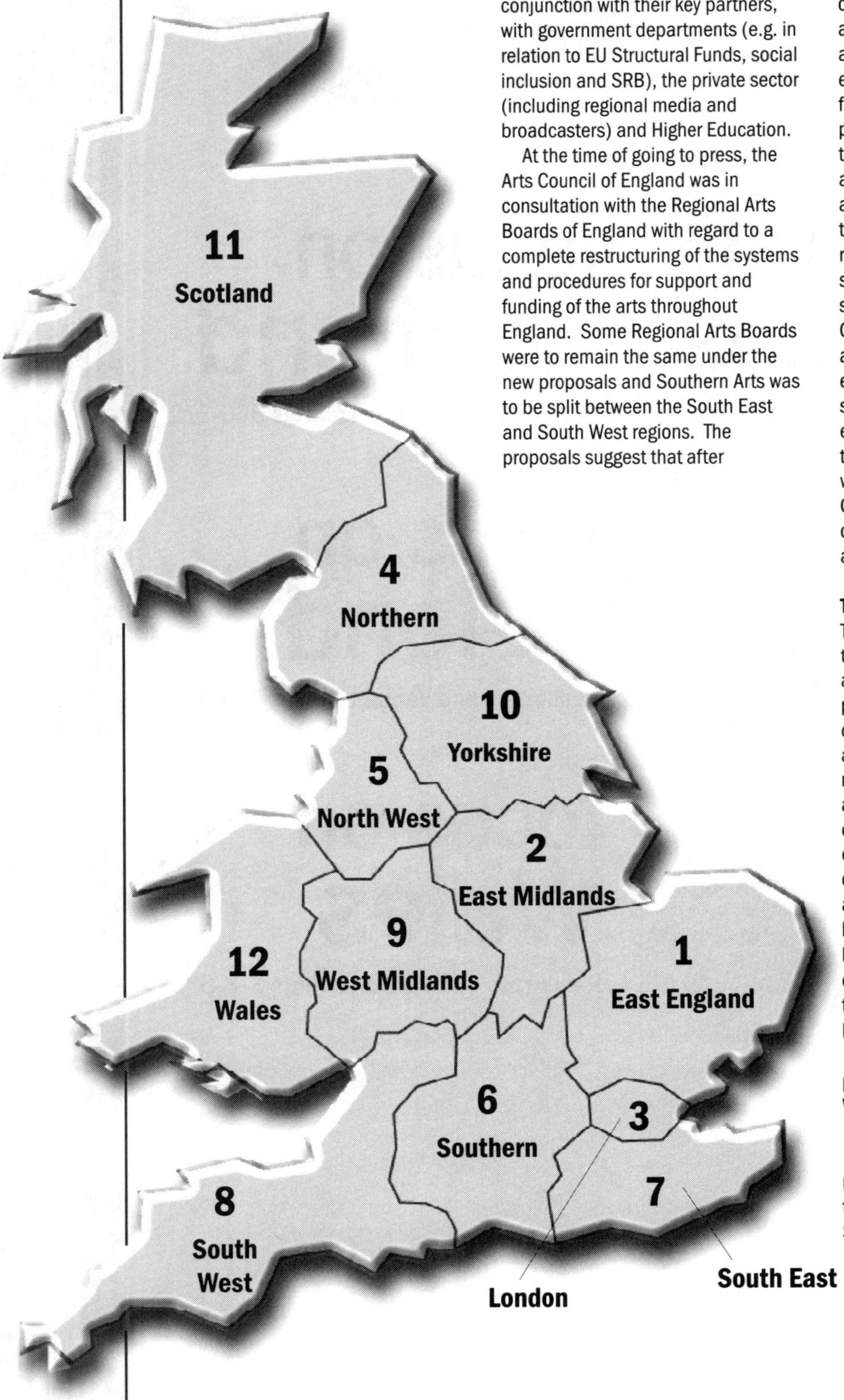

## Rooting around the regions

**Websites** by **Kevin Sheils**

In this section I am concentrating on web sites for local organisations and clubs in the English regions, based on those covered by the Regional Arts Boards. Similar listings for Scotland, Wales and Ireland will be covered under the appropriate "Artistic Area".

I have listed the web site for the appropriate Regional Arts Board, although be aware that they will cover all aspects of the arts and may not have anything relevant to your specific interests at the time you visit. Following that will be some web sites giving general regional information (such as a web version of a local listings magazine) followed by clubs/sessions that I know have web sites.

Some of the listings sites will cover areas across regional boundaries. I've tried to place these in the most appropriate region but if checking for clubs in, say, the Hampshire area (Southern by the Regional Arts Boards) it may be worth checking links in the adjacent South East and South West regions also.

At the time of writing I've checked if a web site was still live, and if so whether the information was current before including it here. I have not listed sites that are still live on the web but where there is no indication that any event has taken place since Cecil Sharp popped by to note a few songs. Since there is no easy way to be sure any are still active, it's always best to check with organisers before travelling.

Some regions seem to have more listings than others. This doesn't necessarily indicate a more active scene but simply a more obvious web presence. Sites I'm not aware of may well appear in the classified listings or by following links from other web sites.

**Kevin Sheils**
*Direct Roots Internet Researcher*

**See pages 398-399 for internet information**

## From Folk Clubs to the Albert Hall and Back again!

By **Chris Jaeger**

My first live 'Roots' experience was in 1973 - **Steeleye Span** supported by **Horslips** at the **Albert Hall**. I guess you might as well start at the top, although some folk veterans may not acknowledge that it was a Roots experience at all. It did bring me to the Folk genre, however, and I have been an unrepentant addict ever since. Over the years, I have watched hundreds of acts in a great variety of venues. Both acts and venues have varied enormously in quality!

Folk clubs for many years traditionally took place in smoky pub rooms, great for atmosphere, not necessarily for singers' voices (**Dick Gaughan** excepted!) Many of these clubs still exist, and form a vitally important part of the Roots world, though thankfully many of them have adopted a no-smoking policy. (Don't you just hate a reformed smoker!) However, there is as much variety in where you can see Roots music in Britain today as in the music itself, and this choice must be healthy for the business.

Folk clubs exist in many forms, from small rooms holding 40 people, to giants like **Nettlebed** and **The Red Lion**, Birmingham, which can get in 200+ people and book most of the major acts on the folk scene. The first winner of the **Radio 2 Folk Awards 'Club of the Year'** in 2000 was **Westhoughton**, which is held in a golf club. Many village halls stage concerts, both as part of rural touring schemes, and promotions by individuals who just like the act they are putting on.

As we move up capacity, many of the arts centres have wonderful character: **St. Mary in the Castle** in Hastings, **The Mill** at Banbury, **The Brewhouse** at Burton on Trent to name three. These are fine examples of buildings that did not start life as music venues; indeed my own venue is a converted Methodist chapel. There are many large civic centres and theatres which stage Roots, and indeed venues like **Symphony Hall**, Birmingham have been known to 'dip a toe in the water'.

The important thing is to see your music in a venue where you are comfortable. I am no longer a great lover of the smoky room with added bar noise, but that is purely a matter of personal taste (and asthma!). You need to feel comfortable in your favoured environment - you know the music will be great, just go somewhere you will really enjoy hearing it. Maybe **Show of Hands** have got the right idea. They have just finished a folk club tour, they are doing a major Arts Centre tour later in the year, and in between ... a sellout concert at the **Albert Hall**. You pays your money and you takes your choice.

**Chris Jaeger** *is Director of Huntingdon Hall in Worcester*

**The English Regions**
*These are based on Regional Arts Board representation with some variation. We have kept all of Derbyshire and Lincolnshire in the East Midlands. The RAB definitions are used here as a generally helpful way of splitting up England for a more detailed look at local resources. Also check sections for neighbouring regions for the band, caller or venue you are looking for. Contributors and magazine listings often mention venues and services based in adjacent regions.*

east england

region

**The English Regions**
*These are based on Regional Arts Board representation with some variation. We have kept all of Derbyshire and Lincolnshire in the East Midlands. The RAB definitions are used here as a generally helpful way of splitting up England for a more detailed look at local resources. Also check sections for neighbouring regions for the band, caller or venue you are looking for. Contributors and magazine listings often mention venues and services based in adjacent regions.*

# East England

**Bedfordshire, Cambridgeshire, Essex, Hertfordshire, Norfolk, Suffolk, Luton, Peterborough, Southend-on-Sea, Thurrock**

## Organisations

### East England Arts Board

**Mail address** Cherry Hinton Hall, Cherry Hinton Hall, Cambridge, CB1 4DW
**Phone** 01223 215355
**Fax** 01223 248075
**Web** www.eab.org.uk

East England Arts Board produce a list of venues, mostly Arts Centres and Theatres. Those regularly hosting folk related performances include **King's Lynn Corn Exchange**, **Harlow Playhouse**, **Norwich Arts Centre**, **Colchester Arts Centre** and **Cambridge Corn Exchange**.

**The East Anglian Traditional Music Trust** was founded in June 2000 by co-directors Katie and John Howson, with the aim of promoting the performance and appreciation of the traditional folk music, song, dance and customs of East Anglia.

EAMT runs events, organises projects, and manages research and archiving, as well as acting as an advocate for traditional music at local, regional and national levels.

Recent projects include community events, instrumental workshops and exhibitions. EATMT currently works mainly within Suffolk and Norfolk, but plans to extend its activities across East Anglia. Details of events and developments are available in a quarterly newsletter.
**East Anglian Traditional Music Trust**,
**Mail address** 44 Old Street, Haughley, Stowmarket, Suffolk IP14 3NX
**Answerphone/Fax** 01449 673695
**Email** EATMT@veteran.co.uk

**Essex Folk Association**
**Contact** John New
**Mail address** 37 Sidwell Avenue, Benfleet, Essex SS7 1LF
**Phone** 01268 793905
**Email** john@essexfolknews.co.uk

**Hertfordshire Folk Association**
**Contact** Roger Barnes
**Mail address** 40 Battlefield Road, St. Albans AL1 4DD
**Phone** 01727 851987
**Fax** 01727 853581
Clubs and projects including an annual dance festival at Hatfield House.

## Magazines

**Mardles** is the regional folk magazine covering Suffolk and surrounding counties. It is published three times a year. The magazine is available by subscription, by sale through clubs and at some folk shops.

It contains articles and gossip of local interest, reviews of recordings and live events, directories of local clubs, bands and callers, listing of forthcoming events, separate Gig Guide for Suffolk and separate Morris Diary.

Price: £1 (or £6 subscription for postal delivery of 4 issues)
**Contact** John Halliwell (Editor)
**Phone** 01394 279753
**Email** halliwell@btinternet.com
**Alt contact** Gloria Helliwell (subsciptions)
**Mail address** 320 Sidegate Lane, Ipswich, Suffolk IP4 3DW
**Phone** 01473 401439

***Editor's Note*** *The listings section is very comprehensive and each issue has reviews and articles of local and national relevance.*

**efn magazine** (formerly Essex Folk News).
Published quarterly since 1973.
*The* folk/roots listings for Essex & East London. Available through clubs or by subscription - £2.60 for four issues -
**Phone** 01268 793905
**Email** john@essexfolknews.co.uk
Further details, club guide, changes & late entries to the current issue available at:
**Web** www.essexfolknews.co.uk

***Editor's Note*** *Good listings and lots of useful contacts. The website has a Stop Press facility which is excellent for updates and changes.*

**Unicorn Magazine**
Quarterly folk magazine for Beds. Herts. and Bucks. Includes morris diary, sessions listings, club index and diary. Also club focus, Cajun news and CD reviews.
**Contact** Alan Creamer
**Mail address** 6 Dudley Street, Luton, LU2 0NT
**Phone** 01582 733113
**Email** alan.creamer@virgin.net

**Puddingstone**
Hertfordshire Folk Magazine produced by Herts Folk Association (Affiliated to EFDSS). Folk Dance Diary and News.
**Contact** Roger Swaine
**Mail address** 29 Turmore Dale, Welwyn Garden City, AL8 6HT

**Norfolk Folk List**
Regular sessions and dance groups, events diary, bands and callers list. 3 issues per year.
**The Norfolk Folk Association**
**Contact** Tony Gomme
**Mail address** Woodpeckers, Hunstead Lane, Brooke, Norwich, NR15 1JP

**Step in Time**
Community based musicians, promoting traditional English music and dance to children through music, dance and craft workshops.
**Contact** Kathryn Aldis
**Mail address** 88 Lowestoft Road, Worlingham, Beccles, Suffolk NR34 7RD
**Phone** 01502 712160
**Email** katealdis@netscape.net

## Radio

**Suffolk Folk on BBC Radio Suffolk** (103.9FM East, 104.6 FM West and 95.5FM) Saturdays 6-7pm. Presented by Pete Jennings.
**Contact** Brian Mann
**Mail address** BBC Radio Suffolk, Broadcasting House, St Matthew's Street, Ipswich, IP1 3EP
**Phone** 01473 250000
brian.mann@bbc.co.uk
**Alt contact** Pete Jennings
**Email** pete@gippeswic.demon.co.uk

**Folktracks on BBC Radio Cambridge**
Presented by Mandy Morton.
**Mail address** Broadcasting House, 104 Hills Road, Cambridge CB2 1LD
**Phone** 01223 259696
**Email** mandy.morton@bbc.co.uk

## Festivals

The major Eastern festival is the **Charles Wells Cambridge Folk Festival** which is usually the last weekend in July. See *www.cam-folkfest.co.uk* **Leigh Folk Festival** is a free event taking place at the end of June and **Folk on the Pier** is in Cromer mid May. The **St Albans Festival** is biennial (next one in 2002) and includes a folk element. Festivals in Suffolk include the **English Country Music Weekend** in Stowmarket late June.

## East England Highlights

**Reel Dance Ceilidhs** take place monthly in Saxmundham, Suffolk with national bands. **St Albans Folk Music** organise various concerts, workshops and "New Roots", an annual competition (April) for young folk musicians & singers. Major clubs in the region, with national guests include **Hitchin Folk Club**, Herts, **Colchester Folk Club**, **Hoy at Anchor**, Benfleet, Essex, **Everyman Folk Club**, Saxmundham, Suffolk & **Mad Nanny! Folk Club**, Letchworth, Herts. **The Portland Arms**, Cambridge is home to several established clubs including **Cambridge Folk Club** and **Mayflower Folk Club**. For sessions, try **The Orange Tree**, Chelmsford (Tuesday) or the **Rose & Crown**, St Albans (Thursday).

● ***Thanks to Katie Howson, John New, efn magazine, John Halliwell and Mardles for assistance with the above information.***

## efn magazine Dance Band Listings

### Finisterre
**Contact** Dave Andrews
**Phone** 01255 428579

### Stömp
**Contact** Martin Appleby
**Phone** 0208 527 8742

### Legacy
**Contact** Steve Atterton
**Phone** 01375 383350

### Economy Seven
**Contact** Elaine Barker
**Phone** 01206 735606

### Famous Potatoes
**Contact** Keith Baxter
**Phone** 01702 341889

### Jig and a Half
**Contact** Paddy Beadle
**Phone** 01702 348883

### Belchamp Morris Ceilidh Band
**Contact** Brian Bird
**Phone** 01787 277271

### Childgrove
**Contact** Paul Butcher
**Phone** 01245 325223

### Bullnose Morris/ Rat on a Stick
**Contact** Glynis Candler
**Phone** 01702 525804

### The Redbridge Folk Band
**Contact** Margaret Caton
**Phone** 01371 830751

### Scampering Rouges
**Contact** Sue Collins
**Phone** 01371 830457

### Barnacles
**Contact** Barry Cook
**Phone** 01206 330805

### Paisley Hat Band
**Contact** Liz Davies
**Phone** 01708 553361

### Knapfoot Country Dance Band
**Contact** Steve De Larre
**Phone** 01277 890519

### Slow Loris
**Contact** Terry Docherty
**Phone** 01702 351544

### Upstreet Irregulars
**Contact** Suzanne Eccleston
**Phone** 0208 550 2470

### Blue Jays
**Contact** Jim English
**Phone** 01268 755722

### Iceni Folk
**Contact** Jenny Firth
**Phone** 01206 863791

### The Old Court Ceilidh Band
**Contact** Cathy Fitzgerald
**Phone** 01206 548571

### Band Of Two
**Contact** Pete Fyfe
**Phone** 0208 680 4302

### Wayzgoose
**Contact** Colin & Di Garret
**Phone** 01708 225107

### Liz & Friends
**Contact** Liz Giddings
**Phone** 01245 231423

### Metric Foot
**Contact** Mick & Sarah Graves
**Phone** 01621 853941

### Hosepipe Band/ Bass Instincts
**Contact** Simon Haines
**Phone** 01206 547830

### Blackwater Scratch Band
**Contact** John Haste
**Phone** 01245 601934

### Tam Lin, Howling Wind and Millrace
**Contact** Alan Hewson
**Phone** 01462 438373

### J.C.B.
**Contact** Mike Jols
**Phone** 0208 286 2549

### Bushes & Briars
**Contact** Paul Kiff
**Phone** 01621 868219

### Last Resort
**Contact** Mike Last
**Phone** 01206 271668

### Duck and Dive / Fir na.
**Contact** John / Yvonne Layton
**Phone** 01255 850812

### Posh Band
**Contact** Ken Lees
**Phone** 0208 527 8419

### Hurry the Jug Band & The Rattle The Jug
**Contact** John Littler
**Phone** 0208 524 1855

### Wiccamen Ceilidh Band
**Contact** Cynthia Miller
**Phone** 01245 495321

### Finisterre
**Contact** Alan Moody
**Phone** 01277 633271

### Tyros
**Contact** John Morgan
**Phone** 01702 203695

### Garlic Spread
**Contact** Jim Murphy
**Phone** 01268 747869

### Blackwaterford
**Contact** John New
**Phone** 01268 793905

### Jig And a Half / Celtic Mix.
**Contact** Roy Nichols
**Phone** 01702 474952

### The Exiles
**Contact** Joe O'Connor
**Phone** 01702 582336

### Mayflower Ceilidh Band
**Contact** Mike Oxenham
**Phone** 01277 654532

### Legacy
**Contact** Les & Sandra Potts
**Phone** 01621 740983

## east england region

The bands on this page are ceilidh and social dance bands based in the East England region.

Bands in our full listings include **All Hands Around**, **Ancillary Folk Dance Band**, **Bushes & Briars**, **Chalktown**, **Fishing for Eels**, **Hoogie**, **Hosepipe Band**, **Itchy Feet**, **Millrace**, **MoonDance**, **Old Hat**, **Pigeon Toes Ceilidh Band**, **RSVP**, **Skiphire**, **The Famous Potatoes**, **The Goose and Gridiron Band**, **The Metric Foot Band**, **The News of The Victory**, **The Posh Band**, **Time Of Your Life**, **Tollhouse Company**, **Workhouse** and **Xim**.

Listed dance callers include **Alan Simpson**, **Barry Goodman**, **Charles Bolton** and **Elaine Barker**.

**The English Regions**
*These are based on Regional Arts Board representation with some variation. We have kept all of Derbyshire and Lincolnshire in the East Midlands. The RAB definitions are used here as a generally helpful way of splitting up England for a more detailed look at local resources. Also check sections for neighbouring regions for the band, caller or venue you are looking for. Contributors and magazine listings often mention venues and services based in adjacent regions.*

## east england region

The bands on this page are ceilidh and social dance bands based in the East England region.

Bands in our full listings include **All Hands Around**, **Ancillary Folk Dance Band**, **Bushes & Briars**, **Chalktown**, **Fishing for Eels**, **Hoogie**, **Hosepipe Band**, **Itchy Feet**, **Millrace**, **MoonDance**, **Old Hat**, **Pigeon Toes Ceilidh Band**, **RSVP**, **Skiphire**, **The Famous Potatoes**, **The Goose and Gridiron Band**, **The Metric Foot Band**, **The News of The Victory**, **The Posh Band**, **Time Of Your Life**, **Tollhouse Company**, **Workhouse** and **Xim**.

Listed dance callers include **Alan Simpson**, **Barry Goodman**, **Charles Bolton** and **Elaine Barker**.

**The English Regions**
*These are based on Regional Arts Board representation with some variation. We have kept all of Derbyshire and Lincolnshire in the East Midlands. The RAB definitions are used here as a generally helpful way of splitting up England for a more detailed look at local resources. Also check sections for neighbouring regions for the band, caller or venue you are looking for. Contributors and magazine listings often mention venues and services based in adjacent regions.*

### Elastic Band
**Contact** John Puddick
**Phone** 01702 587314

### Galliard
**Contact** Gay Reay
**Phone** 01622 756772

### All Stars
**Contact** Peter Redman
**Phone** 01268 753374

### Proud Aardvark
**Contact** Annette Stedman
**Contact** 0207 241 1351

### Ancillary Folk Dance Band
**Phone** Ann Steward
**Contact** 01353 778655

### Bonny Green Garters Band
**Contact** Maureen Taylor
**Phone** 01255 675682

### Nameste / Legacy
**Contact** Barry White
**Phone** 01268 490155

### Off The Rails
**Contact** Nick Whiteley
**Phone** 01245 233429

### Neck of the Wood
**Contact** Terry & Pauline Wisker
**Phone** 01279 305070

### Cockleshell Clog Ceilidh Band
**Contact** Malcolm & Olive Woods
**Phone** 01702 618097

### Nanci & the Wolves
**Contact** Nanci Goodman
**Phone** 01268 779159

### Side of the Plate
**Contact** Steve Hurrell
**Phone** 01702 466009

### Jims Band
**Contact** Steve Morris
**Phone** 01245 351552

### Serious Kitchen (formerly Muckle Flugga)
**Contact** Vicki Swan
**Phone** 01277 260252

### Bucket Band
**Contact** Colin O'Neal
**Phone** 01708 728994

### Strayaways
**Contact** John Smith
**Phone** 01255 551764

### BOPP !!
**Contact** Johnathan Potts
**Phone** 01621 842943

### Suntrap
**Contact** Paul Hoad
**Phone** 0207 635 8669

### Hot 'n Cold Ceilidh Band
**Contact** Olga & Noel Jackson
**Phone** 01327 359140

### Hosepipe Band / Bass Instincts
**Contact** Simon Haines
**Phone** 01206 547830

### Highly Strung Gillian Warnell
**Phone** 0208 554 0727
**Contact** Ola Michael Jary
**Phone** 07710 389607

*Thanks to efn magazine for permission to print this list.*

## Rooting around East England

### *Organisations, Listings etc.*

**www.essexfolknews.co.uk**
*Essex Folk News (also covers East London)*

**www.btinternet.com/~pete.shaw/index.html**
*Peterborough Folk Diary*

**www.gippeswic.demon.co.uk/musiclubgigweb.htm**
*Suffolk Folk Guide*

### *Clubs etc.*

**stortfolk.homepage.com**
*Bishop's Stortford, Stortfolk Music Club*

**www.cambridgefolkclub.com**
*Cambridge Folk Club*

**www.wheatstone.co.uk/EFChome.htm**
*Saxmundham, Everyman Folk Club*

**www.hoyatanchor.co.uk**
*Leigh-on-Sea, Hoy at Anchor Folk Club*

**www.hitchinfolkclub.org.uk**
*Hitchin Folk Club*

**www.questor-cp.demon.co.uk/mad.htm**
*Letchworth, Mad Nanny Folk Club*

**www.users.zetnet.co.uk/rjames/folkclub.htm**
*St Neots Folk Club*

## East England venues

### Barnet Folk Club
The Bull Arts Centre, 68 High Street, BARNET, Herts
**Contact** J J Dunne
**Phone** 020 8441 3620
*Traditional and contemporary folk.*

### Bedford Folk Music Club
The Kings Arms, 24 St Mary's Street, BEDFORD
**Contact** Mike Blair
**Phone** 01525 404513
01234 354494
*Every Thursday, 8.30pm. Singers nights with guests every 5-6 weeks.*

### Blackmore Folk Club
The Bull, BLACKMORE, Essex
**Contact** Sue Cubbin
**Phone** 01277 221123
*Monday, 9pm. Singers club.*

### The Boat Race
170 East Road, CAMBRIDGE, CB1 1DB
**Contact** Stan Engel
**Phone** 01223 508533
**Email** stan@boatrace.cambsnet.co.uk
**Web** www.boat-race.co.uk
*Respected venue, regular folk & blues.*

### Cambridge Corn Exchange
3 Parsons Court, Wheeler Street, CAMBRIDGE, CB1 2AX
**Contact** Neil Jones - Mktg Manager
**Phone** 01223 457555
01223 357851
**Fax** 01223 457559
**Email** admin.cornex@cambridge.gov.uk
**Web** www.cornex.co.uk
*Multi-purpose entertainment venue.*

### Cambridge Folk Club
Portland Arms, 129 Chesterton Road, CAMBRIDGE
**Contact** Anne Ryan
**Phone** 01223 262775
**Email** cambridgefolkclub@ryanne.freeserve.co.uk
**Web** www.cambridge.f9.co.uk
*Friday, 8pm. Alternate open stage, guest artists & feature nights.*

### Campton Sessions
The White Hart, Campton, NR SHEFFORD, Beds
**Contact** Jerry Cannon
**Phone** 01462 812657
*Wednesday, 8.30pm. Singaround, traditional English, Irish & Scottish folk plus some Blues.*

### The Cannon Live
The Cannon, 50 The High Street, NEWPORT PAGNELL, Herts
**Contact** Pat Mason
**Phone** 01908 610919
**Email** patmason@supanet.com
**Web** www.cannonlive.org.uk
**Alt contact** Paul Alexander
**Phone** 01908 611025
*Last Friday, 8.30pm. Guests*

## Castle Acre Folk Club
The Ostrich Inn, Castle Acre
Nr Swatham, NORWICH
**Contact** Jenny Cunningham
**Phone** 01362 668224
*Last Wednesday, 8.30pm, free. All kinds of acoustic music, song, stories and poetry. Featuring guests.*

## Clap 'n' Smile Music Club
The Half Moon, 30 North Street, BISHOP'S STORTFORD, Herts
**Phone** 01279 654978 - pub
**Contact** Karen Johnson
**Phone** 01279 658524
**Web** www.splodgeweb.co.uk/clapnsmile
*Tuesday 8.15pm. Concert based club with top quality folk acts.*

## Colchester Arts Centre
St Mary At The Walls, Church Street, COLCHESTER, Essex CO1 1NF
**Phone** 01206 500900
**Contact** Elaine Barker
**Phone/Fax** 01206 500187
**Email** colchester.artcentre@virgin.net
**Web** www.colchester-artscentre.co.uk
*Venue for Colchester Folk Club. National & international folk artists weekly.*

## Colchester Folk Club
**Address** Colchester Arts Centre
Church Street, COLCHESTER, Essex CO1 1NF
**Contact** Elaine Barker
**Phone** 01206 500900
*Monday nights. National and international guest artists.*

## Cross Folk Club
The Cross Pub, Ardleigh Road
GREAT BROMLEY, Essex
**Contact** Dick Spanner
**Phone** 01206 241936
*4th Wednesday, 8.30pm. Acoustic music encompassing traditional and modern folk. Forum for performers. Occasional guests.*

## Croxley Acoustic Music Club
'The Shed', The Sportsman,
2 Scots Hill, Croxley Green,
RICKMANSWORTH, Herts
**Contact** Mary Emerson
**Phone** 01923 443360
**Email** sportsman.croxley@barbox.net
*1st Thursday, 8.30pm. Singaround & instrumental music - all types. 3rd Sunday, 2.30pm. Traditional folk jam.*

## Dereham Folk Club
The King's Head Hotel, Norwich Road, DEREHAM, Norfolk
**Contact** Rob King
**Phone** 01362 695947
*3rd Wednesday, 8.30pm. Singers/acoustic club.*

## Ely Folk Club
**Contact** Ruth Bramley
**Mail address** 10 The Green, Haddenham, ELY, Cambs, CB6 3TA
**Phone** 01353 740999
**Email** ruthie@cellar.free-online.co.uk
**Web** www.ely.org.uk/folk.htm
*Occasional folk club in various venues around Ely.*
**RAB** East England Arts

## Everyman Folk Club
The Queens Head, High Street
SAXMUNDHAM, Suffolk
**Contact** Mary & Steve Dickenson
**Address** 21 Bridge Street
STOWMARKET, Suffolk IP14 1BP
**Phone** 01449 615523
**Email** everyman@wheatstone.co.uk
**Web** www.wheatstone.co.uk/efchome.htm
*Last Friday (Sept - May). Guest artist, residents and floor singers. New performers and audience welcome.*

## Fretless & Fancy Free
**Address** University of Luton
Park Square, LUTON, Beds, LU1 3JU
**Contact** Joan Drage
**Phone** 01582 489213
**Email** joan.drage@luton.ac.uk
**Alt contact** Hilary Ward
**Phone** 01582 734111 ext 2206
**Email** hilary.ward@luton.ac.uk
*Alternate Saturday mornings. Folk music workshop for singers and instrumentalists. Play with others, gain confidence, improve technique in a supportive atmosphere.*

## Hitchin Folk Club
The Sun Hotel, Sun Street, HITCHIN Herts
**Contact** Maureen Jones
**Address** Holly Court
Off High St., PIRTON, Herts SG5 3PS
**Phone** 01462 711164
**Email** goodmusic@hitchinfolkclub.org.uk
**Web** www.hitchinfolkclub.org.uk
*Sunday, 8.15pm. National guests. Capacity 200.*

## Hollybush Folk Club
The Hollybush, Church End,
REDBOURN, Herts AL3 7DU
**Contact** Steve Bryan
**Address** 124 Piggottshill Lane
HARPENDEN, Herts AL5 1LS
**Phone** 07710 471862, 01908 205419
**Email** swbryan@btinternet.com
**Web** www.btinternet.com/~swbryan/hollybushfc.htm
**Alt contact** Janet Strapp
143 Strathmore Ave, LUTON, Beds LU1 3QW
**Phone** 07850 163241
*Thursday 8.15pm. Small, friendly club, traditional & contemporary folk & blues. Guests & singers' nights.*

## Hoy At Anchor Folk Club
The Ship Public House, New Road
LEIGH ON SEA, Essex
**Contact** Tony Prior
**Phone** 01702 715111
**Email** hoy@priority1.demon.co.uk
**Web** www.hoyatanchor.co.uk
**Alt contact** Kath Levey
**Phone** 01268 792160
*Tuesday, 8.15pm. National/international guests plus open nights.*

## Jingling Gate Folk Club
Pitsea Leisure Centre, PITSEA, Essex
**Contact** Mick Spooner
**Phone** 01268 280351
*1st Saturday, 8.30pm. Singers club, mainly traditional, occasional guests.*

## King's Lynn Corn Exchange
Tuesday Market Place
KINGS LYNN, Norfolk PE30 5JW
**Phone** 01553 764864 - box office
*Venue promoting events including monthly concerts with national folk acts.*

## The Leather Bottle Folk Session
The Leather Bottle, Pleshy,
CHELMSFORD, Essex
**Contact** Fred Field
**Phone** 01245 380179
*Last Monday, 9pm. Open session, mainly English & Irish traditional folk.*

## Mad Nanny! Folk Club
The Place, Leys Avenue
LETCHWORTH, Herts
**Contact** Alan & Sue Hewson
**Address** 9 Lister Avenue
HITCHIN, Herts SG4 9ES
**Phone** 01462 438373
**Fax** 01462 433395/ 421272
**Email** nmin@questor-cp.co.uk
**Web** www.questor-cp.co.uk/madnanny.htm
*4th Friday, guest artists, primarily focusing on traditional music. 100 capacity. Call re disabled access.*



***See Folk London listing on page 322.***

**The English Regions**
*These are based on Regional Arts Board representation with some variation. We have kept all of Derbyshire and Lincolnshire in the East Midlands. The RAB definitions are used here as a generally helpful way of splitting up England for a more detailed look at local resources. Also check sections for neighbouring regions for the band, caller or venue you are looking for. Contributors and magazine listings often mention venues and services based in adjacent regions.*

**The English Regions**
*These are based on Regional Arts Board representation with some variation. We have kept all of Derbyshire and Lincolnshire in the East Midlands. The RAB definitions are used here as a generally helpful way of splitting up England for a more detailed look at local resources. Also check sections for neighbouring regions for the band, caller or venue you are looking for. Contributors and magazine listings often mention venues and services based in adjacent regions.*

## Norwich Arts Centre
Reeves Yard, St Benedicts Street, NORWICH, NR2 4PG
**Contact** Pam Reekie
**Phone** 01603 660352
**Fax** 01603 664806
**Email** pamreekie@norwichartscentre.co.uk
**Web** www.norwichartscentre.co.uk
*Arts venue promoting a wide variety of music.*

## The Orange Tree Folk Session
The Orange Tree Pub, Lower Anchor Street, CHELSMFORD, Essex
**Contact** Fred Field
**Phone** 01245 380179
*Tuesday, 9pm. Open session. Tends towards English & Irish traditional folk.*

## Red Lion Folk Club
**Address** Red Lion Hotel, Station Road WHITTLESFORD, Cambs CB2 4NL
**Contact** Alan Collins
**Address** 68 Station Road Steeple Morden, ROYSTON Herts SG8 0NS
**Phone** 01763 852446
**Email** alan@qdconsult.co.uk
**Web** www.qdconsult.co.uk/folk.
*Friday. Acoustic song and music session*

## Reel Dance Ceilidhs
Saxmundham Middle School Seaman Avenue, SAXMUNDHAM Suffolk
**Contact** Shirley Harry
**Address** 2 Bruisyard Road, Rendham, SAXMUNDHAM, Suffolk, IP17 2AG
**Phone** 01728 663286
**Email** shharry@reeldancer.fsnet.co.uk
**Web** www.reeldanceceilidhs.co.uk
**Alt contact** Lin Barnes
**Address** Woodlands, Church Close, Kelsale, , SAXMUNDHAM, Suffolk, IP17 2AG
**Phone** 01728 602416
**Email** reeldance@btinternet.co.uk
*1st Saturday, 8pm. Ceilidh series.*

## Romford Folk Club
The Sun, 47 London Road, ROMFORD, Essex RM7 9QA
**Contact** Monni Aldous
**Address** 21 Catherine Close Pilgrims Hatch, BRENTWOOD Essex CM15 9RJ
**Phone** 01277 373471
**Email** romfolk@tesco.net
*Wednesday 8.30 pm. Performance club for singers, musicians, poets, etc.*

## Sutton Folk Club
Sutton Village Hall, Sutton, NR SANDY, Beds
**Contact** Les Ivall
**Phone** 01767 260377
**Alt contact** Phil Lane
**Phone** 01767 260041
**Email** thelanes@lineone.net
*2nd Saturday, 8pm. Mix of acoustic music, including traditional English, Irish & Scottish plus American.*

## Romford & Brentwood Folk Dance Group
151 Havering Road, ROMFORD, Essex RM1 4RD
**Contact** K Pollard
**Address** 4 Nelmes Way, HORNCHURCH Essex RM11 2QZ
**Phone** 01708 473646
**Email** kpolrm11@aol.com
**Alt contact** M Bryan
**Alt address** Chadwick Room St Michaels Church, Main Road Gidea Park, ROMFORD, Essex
**Phone** 01708 752057
*Most Wednesdays 8pm. Social folk dance group. Plus annual day of demonstrations and dancing party.*

## The Round
Wesley Church, Christ's Pieces, CAMBRIDGE
**Contact** Hugh Stewart
**Address** 14 Silverwood Close CAMBRIDGE CB1 3HA
**Phone** 01223 368641 - home
01223 371593 - work
*Thursday, 8pm (term time). University English country dance club.*

## The Round Ceilidhs
New Hall College, Huntingdon Road, CAMBRIDGE
**Contact** Hugh Stewart
**Address** 14 Silverwood Close CAMBRIDGE CB1 3HA
**Phone** 01223 368641 - home
01223 371593 - work
*Saturday Ceilidh series, 8pm, monthly during term time.*

## Royal Oak Folk Club, Essex
**Address** The Royal Oak, High Street CHIPPING ONGAR, Essex
**Contact** Terry Butcher
**Phone** 01277 363893
*Alternate Tuesdays, 8.30pm. All types of music, singers and musicians welcome.*

## St Albans Traditional Music Session
**Address** Rose & Crown St Michaels Street, ST ALBANS, Herts
**Contact** Alison Macfarlene
**Address** 40 Warwick Road ST ALBANS, Herts AL1 4DL
**Phone/Fax** 01727 852111
**Email** alison.macfarlene@lineone.net
*Thursday 9pm. Informal session, mainly English and Irish traditional.*

## The Swan Inn Folk Session
The Swan Inn, Hatfield Peverel, CHELMSFORD, Essex
**Contact** Fred Field
**Phone** 01245 380179
*1st Sunday, 9pm. Open session. Variable, English & Irish folk.*

## Travellers Rest Folk Club
The Rising Sun, Twitton Lane, OTFORD, Essex
**Contact** Jon & Pam Fitzgerald
**Phone** 01255 679232
*2nd Thursday, 8.30pm. Guests, singers welcome.*

## Unicorn Ceilidhs
Hitchin Town Hall, HITCHIN, Herts
**Contact** Dave Eppy
**Address** 4 Ruskin Lane HITCHIN, Herts SG4 0PN
**Phone** 01462 622724
**Email** dave.eppy@ntlworld.com
**Alt contact** Alan Creamer
**Phone** 01582 733113
*Last Friday, 8pm. Ceilidh series. 200 dancing capacity, sprung floor, real ale bar. Not Summer.*

## Upstairs at The Red Lion
The Red Lion, South Street, MANNINGTREE, Essex
**Contact** Andy Dyer
**Phone** 01206 395649
*Monthly Saturdays, 7.45pm. Intimate acoustic music venue. Folk, blues and world music. Also stage plays and spoken word.*

## White Hart
White Hart, MORETON, Essex
**Contact** Jim
**Phone** 01277 890228
*Friday, musicians, singers. Real ale. Home of the Steve Monk Step dancing competition.*

## Wivenhoe Folk Club
The Greyhound, High Street WIVENHOE, Essex
**Contact** Joan Gifford
**Address** 2 Dentons Terrace Wivenhoe, COLCHESTER CO7 9NE
**Phone** 01206 822087
*1st Thursday, 8pm. Wide range of music. Guests plus occasional singarounds.*

# East Midlands

**Derbyshire, Leicestershire, Lincolnshire, Northamptonshire, Nottinghamshire, Derby, Leicester, Nottingham and Rutland**

## ORGANISATIONS

### East Midland Arts

**Mail address** Mountfields House, Epinal Way, Loughborough, LE11 0QE
**Phone** 01223 215355
**Fax** 01223 248075
**Web** www.arts.org.uk/directory/regions/eastmid/index.html

## Magazines and websites

### Leicester Folk Diary

*A web based diary of folk events in and around Leicestershire with links to other folk resources.*
**Web** http://members.tripod.co.uk/LeicesterFolk

### Spire Folk website

*Based in Chesterfield and provides news of folk, roots and world music from "the heart of England".*
**Web** www.spirefolk.org.uk

### Folktalk

*A magazine and website covering Lincolnshire and East Yorkshire. In its printed format, Folktalk is published and distributed free of charge at folk clubs, arts centres and other venues providing information on folk music in the region and festivals beyond.*
**Contact** Jim Hancock
**Mail address** 57 Lloyds Avenue, Scunthorpe, North Lincs. DI7 1BY
**Phone** 01724 844241
**Web** www.folktalk.co.uk

### Sounds Alive

*A website guide to Folk, Blues, Country and Roots in Leicestershire. The magazine version is distributed free.*
**Contact** John Fletcher
**Mail address** 27 Westview Avenue, Glen Parva, Leicester LE2 9JU
**Phone** 0116 278 5926
**Email** john@fletcher50.freeserve.co.uk
**Web** http://website.lineone.net/~soundsalive

### Richard Ashe's East Midlands Folk Pages

*provide information on folk activities in Derbyshire, Leicestershire, Nottinghamshire, Staffordshire and Warwickshire. Its Yellow Pages provide listings of local services (Instrument makers, repairers and accessories, PA, CD production and retail, agents and promoters, artists, callers and bands). The Folk Club listings are extensive and are linked to maps.*
**Web** www.emfp.co.uk

### FIZGIG

*An On-line guide to Folk music and gigs in Lincolnshire and the East Midlands, with artist profiles, news and links. Free listings service.*
**Web** http://users.tinyonline.co.uk/fizgig-tom/folk.htm
**Contact** Tom and Ali Beaumont
**Mail address** 11 Fortescue Close, Tattershall, Lincoln, LN4 4LN
**Phone** 01526 343989
**Email** fizgigmusic@tinyonline.co.uk

### What's On Midland Folk Diary

*Published monthly and carries details of most clubs throughout the East and West midlands.*
**Contact** Joe Smith
**Mail address** 121 Morris Avenue, COVENTRY CV2 5GS
**Phone** 024 7644 4405

## Leicester Links

**The Leicester Mercury** has a 'music listings' on a Friday containing all the folk events and venues.

The most prominent venues in Leicester for national and international acts include **De Montfort Hall**, which regularly programme roots events and also runs the **One World Festival** at the start of July. **The Phoenix Theatre** presents free folk music every Sunday lunchtime and receives touring folk acts. **Swan Folk** and the **Packhorse Folk Club** in Loughborough both have national guest acts fortnightly. For sessions, the first port of call is **Molly O'Grady's**, which has an Irish session on Tuesdays.

## Radio

### Folkwaves

*A two hour radio show on BBC in the Midlands. BBC Radio Derby (94.2 FM/104.5FM,1116MW), BBC Radio Lincolnshire(1368 MW, 94.9 (Lincoln), 104.7FM (Grantham) Nottingham, Leicester Mondays 7.05pm*
**Producer** Mick Peat
**Presenters** Lester Simpson/Mick Peat
**Mail address** Folkwaves, BBC in the Midlands, PO Box 104.5, Derby
**Phone** 01773 853428
**Email** radioderby@bbc.co.uk

## Derbyshire in Folkus

By **Ian Smith**

Derbyshire is relatively fortunate in its resource base, its location (central, excellent rail and road links) and local authority support for the folk arts. There are a number of significant promoters in the area as well as the work of authorities such as **Amber Valley Borough Council**, **Derbyshire Dales District Council** and **Erewash Borough Council**. Events such as the Illuminations now include some roots music and Derbyshire have recently appointed an Arts Officer.

It is however, the district councils which have the most positive attitude to outside help and influence in programming often because of the presence of local activists such as **Mick Peat** and **Dick Watson** in Amber Valley and **Alan Wooley** and **Chris Hall** among others in Derby City. **Andy Cooper** and **Andy Borys** of **Off The Tracks Festivals** now run two very successful festivals at Castle Donnington each year.

In Mid Derbyshire, my own role as artist, organiser of **Chesterfield's TUC May Day event** and a previous job at Chesterfield Arts Centre has enabled networking of contacts. This may result in the near future in a festival/promoter ring of organisers who have a broadly similar outlook in the way festivals are run. Notable events include **Stainsby Festival** and **Erewash Council's "Our Roots are Showing"** a series of folk and roots events over a five week period in summer and **Amber Valley's "Larks in the Parks"** at Belper River Gardens.

In Mid Derbyshire there are two very significant pub based venues that regularly promote live music several times a week with a broad music policy. These are **The Fishpond** in Matlock Bath and **The Flowerpot** in Derby.

Mention must be made of the prevalence of young performers playing in a roots based idiom. Recently 30 different bands played at The Fishpond all of which were of school age and mostly playing in a folk or roots form.

There is a small arts centre circuit in the area including **The Brewhouse** at Burton, **Chesterfield Arts Centre** and the **Regal Arts Centre**. Chesterfield has an excellent venue in **The Winding Wheel**; a refurbished cinema. Owned by the borough council its folk

## east midlands region

Listed ceilidh and social dance bands in the East Midlands include **Akmed's Camel**, **Fish N' Taters Ceilidh Band**, **Heather Mixture**, **Kasutima**, **Kettle Of Fish**, **Ock 'n' Dough**, **Old Parrot Band**, **Old Swan Band**, **RBB Band**, **Rogues Gallery**, **Stradivarious**, **Strawplaiters Folk Dance Band**, **The Broadside Ceilidh Band**, **The East Kent Hoppers**, **The Gander Band**, **The Little Band** and **Token Women**.

Listed dance callers include **Ian Wilson**, **Jo Freya**, **Mick Peat** and **Pete Durber**.

***The listed magazines and websites also provide useful band details.***

**The English Regions**
*These are based on Regional Arts Board representation with some variation. We have kept all of Derbyshire and Lincolnshire in the East Midlands. The RAB definitions are used here as a generally helpful way of splitting up England for a more detailed look at local resources. Also check sections for neighbouring regions for the band, caller or venue you are looking for. Contributors and magazine listings often mention venues and services based in adjacent regions.*

# east midlands venues

Listed ceilidh and social dance bands in the East Midlands include **Akmed's Camel**, **Fish N' Taters Ceilidh Band**, **Heather Mixture**, **Kasutima**, **Kettle Of Fish**, **Ock 'n' Dough**, **Old Parrot Band**, **Old Swan Band**, **RBB Band**, **Rogues Gallery**, **Stradivarious**, **Strawplaiters Folk Dance Band**, **The Broadside Ceilidh Band**, **The East Kent Hoppers**, **The Gander Band**, **The Little Band** and **Token Women**.

Listed dance callers include **Ian Wilson**, **Jo Freya**, **Mick Peat** and **Pete Durber**.

***The listed magazines and websites also provide useful band details.***

**The English Regions**
*These are based on Regional Arts Board representation with some variation. We have kept all of Derbyshire and Lincolnshire in the East Midlands. The RAB definitions are used here as a generally helpful way of splitting up England for a more detailed look at local resources. Also check sections for neighbouring regions for the band, caller or venue you are looking for. Contributors and magazine listings often mention venues and services based in adjacent regions.*

programming tends to be dominated by the likes of Fairport Convention and Steeleye Span.

Specialist enclaves still exist with French and Cajun music evident and Salsa burgeoning in Ashbourne and surrounding area. There are of course various Morris teams and the well travelled **Feet First Appalachian Cloggers** from Chesterfield.

Overall there are plenty of opportunities in events terms and a massive potential audience. There are numerous opportunities to perform and promote and many experienced activists to lead the way.

**Ian Smith**
*Musician and promoter*

## Local promoters

### Ian Smith
**Mail address** 1 Holme Road, Matlock Bath, Derbys, DE4 3NU
**Phone** 07976 206568
01629 57082
**Email** pregosmith@hotmail.com
**Web** www.pregomusic.co.uk

### Dave Wheeler
**Mail address** 1 Blind Lane, Hackney, Matlock, Derbys DE4 2QE
**Phone** 01629 734517
**Email** dave@peakbeat.com
**Web** www.peakbeat.com

### Andy Cooper
**Address** PO Box 68, Derby DE1 3XY
**Phone** 01332 384518
01332 833673
**Email** andy@offthetracks.co.uk
**Web** www.offthetracks.co.uk

### Dave Groom
**Address** 80 Hood Street, Nottingham NG5 4AQ
**Phone/Fax** 0115 952 2638
**Email** wellgroomed@proweb.co.uk

### Mick Peat
**Address** Woodland View, Kirkham Lane, Fritchley, Derbys DE56 2FS
**Phone** 01773 853428
**Fax** 01773 850000

### Chris Hall
**Address** PO Box 94, Derby, DE22 1XA
**Phone/Fax** 01332 332336
**Email** chrishall@swampmusic.co.uk
**Web** www.swampmusic.co.uk

- ***Thanks to Sue Swift, Richard Ashe, Mick Peat, Jim Hancock's Folk Talk and Ian Smith for assistance with the above information.***

## Rooting around the East Midlands

### *Organisations/Listings*

**www.folkspace.free-online.co.uk/main/sessions.htm**
*Folk Sessions in and around Derbyshire*

**www.folktalk.co.uk**
*Folk Talk, A magazine for Lincolnshire and East Yorkshire*

**members.tripod.co.uk/LeicesterFolk/lfd.html**
*Leicester Folk Diary*

**www.spirefolk.org.uk**
*Spire Folk, Chesterfield Area*

### *Clubs*

**www.affc.demon.co.uk/index.html**
*Ashby de la Zouch, National Forest Folk Club*

**www.folk.cwc.net/DBmark4.htm**
*Dunton Bassett Folk Club (Leics)*

**www.performing.at/gainsboroughfolk**
*Gainsborough Folk Club*

**www.browncow74.freeserve.co.uk**
*Mansfield, Brown Cow Folk club*

**www.rabidelephant.freeserve.co.uk/greatkn.htm**
*Northampton, Great Knight Folk Club*

**www.btinternet.com/~geoff.white/carlton.htm**
*Nottingham, Carlton Folk Club*

**members.tripod.co.uk/LeicesterFolk/Rose/rose.html**
*Thurnby (Leics), Rose and Crown Folk Club*

## East Midland venues

### 4 in a Bar Folk Club
The Belper Arms, NEWTON BURGOLAND, Leics
**Contact** Chris
**Phone** 01530 456191
*Traditional and contemporary folk based music.*

### The Arts Centre
Chesterfield College, Sheffield Road, CHESTERFIELD, Derbys S41 7LL
**Contact** Bernie Hayter - Co-ordinator
**Phone/Fax** 01246 500578
*Venue promoting live music concerts, band nights, theatre, dance, children's events, film.*

### The Assembly Rooms
Market Place, DERBY DE1 3AH
**Phone** 01332 255800
**Contact** Alf Fullerton - Gen.Manager
**Phone** 01332 255441
**Email** alf.fullerton@derby.gov.uk
**Web** www.derby.gov.uk
**Alt contact** Heather Errington - Hiring
**Phone** 01332 255442
**Email** heather.errington@derby.gov.uk
*Multi purpose venue.*

### The Attic, Chesterfield
Tullamore Hotel, Springbank Road, CHESTERFIELD, Derbys
**Contact** David Davidson
**Phone** 01246 277591
*Monthly Saturday, 8pm. Concerts with national guests plus local support.*

### Awaken Village Interest in Dance (AVID)
**Contact** Peter Barnard
**Address** 1 Battle Green, Epworth, NR DONCASTER, DN9 1JT
**Phone** 01427 873937
**Email** peter_barnard.squeeze@virgin.net
*Informal session ceilidhs in village halls in North Lincs and North Notts every 2nd Tuesday or Wednesday of the month.*

### Barley Mow
The Barley Mow, Bonsall, MATLOCK, Derbys
**Contact** Alan Webster
**Phone** 01629 825685
*Every Saturday, 9pm. All types of music.*

### Belper Folk Club
Old Kings Head, 1 Days Lane, BELPER, Derbys
**Contact** Marianne Elliott
**Phone** 01773 880877
*Tuesday, 8.30pm. Singers nights plus monthly guests.*

### Bingham Folk Club
The Fire Station Social Club, Long Acre, BINGHAM, Notts
**Contact** Chris Trivett
**Phone** 01949 875685
**Alt contact** George Davidson
**Phone** 01949 838564
*Friday, 8.30pm. Wide variety of music; singers and guests.*

**The English Regions**
*These are based on Regional Arts Board representation with some variation. We have kept all of Derbyshire and Lincolnshire in the East Midlands. The RAB definitions are used here as a generally helpful way of splitting up England for a more detailed look at local resources. Also check sections for neighbouring regions for the band, caller or venue you are looking for. Contributors and magazine listings often mention venues and services based in adjacent regions.*

### Blues in the City
Various mainly: The Old Vic, Fletcher Gate, NOTTINGHAM
**Contact** Paul Morgan
Nottingham City Council
Arts & Events, 55 Castle Gate
NOTTINGHAM NG1 6AF
**Phone** 0115 915 3595
**Fax** 0115 945 3508
*American blues concerts, once a month in the autumn and spring.*

### Buxton Opera House
Water Street, BUXTON, Derbyshire
**Contact** Andrew Aughton
**Phone** 01298 72190 - box office, 01298 72050 - admin
**Fax** 01298 27563
*Venue programming folk concerts.*

### De Montfort Hall
De Montfort Hall
Granville Road, LEICESTER LE1 7RU
**Contact** Richard Haswell
**Phone** 0116 233 3149
**Fax** 0116 233 3182
**Email** haswr001@leicester.gov.uk
**Web** www.demontforthall.co.uk
**Alt contact** Alvin Hargreaves
**Phone** 0116 233 3138
**Email** harga001@leicester.gov.uk
*Leicester's major venue, broad range of concerts and shows including regular roots & world events.Also see One World Leicester festival.*

### Dunton Bassett Folk Club
Red Admiral, 163 Station Road, Broughton Astley, Leics LE9 6PU
**Contact** John Eaves
**Phone** 01455 286708
**Web** freespace.virgin.net/john.patterson/dbmark4.htm
**Alt contact** Paul Tebbutt
**Phone** 01455 202246
*Thursday, 8.15pm. Friendly singers club starting with music session. Occasional guests.*

### The Fishpond
MATLOCK BATH, Derbys
**Phone** 01629 581000
**Contact** John Gill - Music Director
**Web** www.fishpond.co.uk
*Live music several times each week including free gigs and headline acts in 200 capacity ballroom.*

### Fox In The Box
The Old Cherrytree Inn
GREAT HOUGHTON, Northants
**Contact** Dave Jolly
**Email** jolly.box@virgin.net
*3rd Monday, 8pm. Singaround & session. All types of music.*

### Gainsborough Folk Club
8 Jolly Brewers
Ship Court, GAINSBOROUGH, Lincs
**Contact** Sue Dewsbury
46 Middle Street, Coveringham, NR GAINSBOROUGH
Lincs DN21 5QS
**Phone** 01427 838726
**Email** mandsd@yahoo.com
**Web** www.angelfire.com/folk/gainsboroughfolk
*Alternate Fridays, 8.30pm. All types of music, occasional guests.*

### Great kNight Folk Club
Old Black Lion, Marefair
NORTHAMPTON
**Contact** Andy Wintersgil
**Phone** 01604 642075
**Web** www.rabidelephant.freeserve.co.uk/greatkn.htm
**Alt contact** Steve Holden
**Phone** 01604 845026
*Fortnightly guests; mixture of local and national acts.*

### The Green Room
South Street, CHESTERFIELD
Derbys S40 1QX
**Phone** 01246 208105
**Contact** David Ashcroft
*General music venue. Live events Thurs & Sun, DJs Fri/ Sat, 1am licence. Creative booking policy.*

### Gretton Folk Club
The Hatton Arms, Arnhill Road, GRETTON, Northants
**Contact** Andy Butterworth
**Phone** 01536 770302
*Alternate Tuesdays, 8.30pm. Traditional folk/ all types of music. Singers & players welcome.*

### Grimsby Folk Club
Leaking Boot Hotel,
Grimsby Road, CLEETHORPES, Lincs
**Contact** Sue Houston
**Address** 37 Abbey Road, GRIMSBY, Lincs, DN32 0HQ
**Phone** 01472 322094
**Web** www.beehive.thisisgrimsby.co.uk/grimsbyfolkclub
**Alt contact** Mary White
**Address** The Rectory, Station Road, WILLOUGHBY, Lincs, LN13 9NA
**Fax** 01507 462045
**Email** grimsby.folkclub@tel nco.co.uk
*Sunday, 8pm. Alternate Guests andsingers' & musicians' nights. Closed during August.*

### Heart of Lincolnshire Folk, Roots & Blues Club
Eagle Lodge Hotel, The Broadway, WOODHALL SPA, Lincs
**Contact** Tom & Ali Beaumont
11 Fortescue Close
Tattershall, LINCOLN LN4 4LN
**Phone** 01526 343989 and 01526 353231
**Email** fizgigmusic@tinyonline.co.uk
**Web** users.tinyonline.co.uk/fizgig-tom/hol.htm
*Monthly guest nights, 50 capacity. Normal nights either Tuesday, Thursday or Friday, floor singers welcome.*

### Lift Global Music Club
The Globe, High Street West
GLOSSOP, High Peak, Derbys
**Contact** Rick & Chris
**Phone** 01457 853821
**Email** liftrick@aol.com
**Web** www.thelift@glossop.com
*Alternate Saturdays, 8.30pm til late. Live world music, covering whole range of genres inc. folk, African, Reggae, drum n bass, hip hop. Also workshops in local schools/ community centres.*

### Live Acoustic Special
The Priory, Nanpanton Road
LOUGHBOROUGH, Leics
**Contact** Howard Coleman
**Phone** 01509 829462
**Email** howard@coleman.globalnet.co.uk
*Tuesday, 8.30pm. Acoustic folk, roots, blues, jazz. All music welcome. Proceeds to Oxfam.*

### Louth Folk Club
White Swan, Eastgate, LOUTH, Lincs
**Contact** Ray Donnelly
**Phone** 01507 327741
*2nd & 4th Tuesday, 8pm. Traditional Irish, American & English folk, blues, sea shanties, poetry.*

### Lubenham Folk Club
The Coach & Horses, Lubenham, NR MARKET HARBOROUGH, Leics
**Contact** Bill Hewitt
**Phone** 01536 761043
**Alt contact** Richard Leach
**Phone** 01858 462892
*4th Sunday, 8.30 pm. Acoustic folk singers' and musicians' night.*

east midlands
venues

**The English Regions**
*These are based on Regional Arts Board representation with some variation. We have kept all of Derbyshire and Lincolnshire in the East Midlands. The RAB definitions are used here as a generally helpful way of splitting up England for a more detailed look at local resources. Also check sections for neighbouring regions for the band, caller or venue you are looking for. Contributors and magazine listings often mention venues and services based in adjacent regions.*

### National Forest Folk Club
Moira Miner's Welfare, Bath Lane, Moira, ASHBY DE LA ZOUCHE, Leics
**Contact** Nina Szifris
50 Brendan Close
Coleshill, BIRMINGHAM B46 2EF
**Phone** 01675 465002
07881 558158
**Email** club@affc.demon.co.uk
**Web** www.affc.demon.co.uk
**Email** club@affc.demon.co.uk
*Monthly music venue, mainly folk-based, featuring major artists.*

### Packhorse Folk Club
The Old Packhorse, Woodgate, LOUGHBOROUGH, Leics
**Contact** Frank Marmion
The White House, 2A Caldwell Street, LOUGHBOROUGH, LE11 3BB
**Phone** 01509 214292
**Web** www.loughborough.co.uk/folk-club
*Friday, 8.30pm. Alternate singers' & guest nights. Full range of traditional folk.*

### Regal Centre
Carlton Road, WORKSOP, Notts S80 1PD
**Phone** 01909 482896
**Contact** Julie Lawrence
*Venue promoting theatre, cinema & music. Fortnightly folk concerts with national acts.*

### Robin Hood Folk Club
The Star, Middle Street, Beeston, NOTTINGHAM
**Contact** Dave & Ruth Cooper
94 Pasture Road
Stapleford, NOTTINGHAM NG9 8GL
**Phone** 0115 939 9730
**Email** rcooper@stapleford-centre.org
**Web** www.musicmann.freeserve.co.uk/robinhood.htm
*Saturday, 8pm. A largely traditional singers' club with a diverse national/ international guest booking policy. 75 Capacity.*

### Roots In The City
Various mainly: The Old Vic
Fletcher Gate, NOTTINGHAM
**Contact** Paul Morgan
Arts & Events, 55 Castle Gate
NOTTINGHAM NG1 6AF
**Phone** 0115 915 3595
**Fax** 0115 915 3508
*Events througout the year. World/roots music with a bias towards music of Black origin.*

### Run of The Mill Folk Dance Club
Florence Nightingale Memorial Hall, Holloway, NR MATLOCK
Derbys
**Contact** David Skelton
**Address** 37 Chapel St Holbrook
BELPER, Derbys DE56 0TQ
**Phone** 01332 881221
**Email** skellybogs@dskelton.freeseve.co.uk
**Web** www.runmilldance.cwc.net
**Alt contact** Ted Roadhouse
**Alt address** 1C Laund Nook
BELPER, Derbys
**Phone** 01773 828269
**Email** tedroadhouse@cwcom.net
*2nd, 4th & 5th Wednesday, 7.30pm.*

### Scanlons Folk Nights
The Nelthorpe Arms, Bridge Street, BRIGG, Lincs
**Contact** Jim Hancock
**Address** 57 Lloyd Avenue
SCUNTHORPE, Lincs DN17 1BY
**Phone** 01724 844241
**Email** jim@guestlist.freeserve.co.uk
**Web** www.folktalk.co.uk
*2nd Wednesday. Informal singers' & musicians' night. Free.*

### Second Sunday Folk Club
The Angel Hotel, Market Place
BOURNE, Lincs
**Contact** Len Rout
**Phone** 01778 422456
*2nd Sunday, 8pm. Singers' club.*

### Spalding Folk Club
The Lincoln Arms
Bridge Street, SPALDING., Lincs
**Contact** Elizabeth Padgett
**Address** 24 Stonegate
Cowbit, SPALDING, Lincs PE12 6AH
**Phone** 01406 380100
*1st Wedneday, 8.15pm.*

### Spalding Singaround
Spalding Yacht Club
Cradge Bank, SPALDING, Lincs
**Contact** Paul Dickinson
**Address** 26 Holland Road
SPALDING, Lincs PE11 1UL
**Phone** 01775 723026
**Email** deadparrot@clara.co.uk
**Web** www.
*3rd Thursday, 8.15pm. Free singaround, no rules!*

### Swan Folk
The Swan in the Rushes
LOUGHBOROUGH, Leics
**Contact** Chris Flint
**Phone** 01664 569224
*Alternate Sundays, 8pm. Guest plus resident band & floor singers. Contemporary & traditional music. Not July & August.*

### Trinity Arts Centre
Trinity Street, GAINSBOROUGH, Lincs DN21 2AL
**Phone** 01427 810710 - box office
**Contact** Shona McLean - Marketing
**Phone** 01427 810298
*200 capacity arts venue. Extensive programme of English/ Celtic Folk & Roots music throughout the year.*

### Waterfront Folk Music Sessions
Waterfront, West Stockwith
NR GAINSBOROUGH, Notts
**Contact** Jerry Oakes
**Phone** 01427 890151
**Email** jerry@stockwith.freeserve.co.uk
**Phone** 01427 891223 (venue)
*3rd Wednesday, informal folk music session.*

# London

## London Arts Board

**Mail address** 2 Pear Tree Court
London EC1R 0DS
**Phone** 020 7608 6100
**Fax** 020 7608 4100

## Roots Music in London

by **John Crosby**

Roots music continues to flourish in the capital in a way unmatched by any other British city. On average each week there is a staggering ninety roots events for the metropolitan "live" music fan to choose from and enjoy. These include everything from folk clubs to Irish sessions, major concerts to arts centre performances, free foyer music to festivals.

The significant changes these past ten years have been demographic and generational. The folk clubs (and there are many fine ones - **The Cellar**, **Islington FC** and the **Croydon Folksong Club**) no longer attract the younger audiences they once did. **Peta Webb** of another fine venue the **Musical Traditions Club** at the King & Queen, W.1, confirms that, in spite of the youth of such performers as **Kate Rusby** and **Bill Jones**, audiences rarely include people under forty and some members are now in their seventies. To find out where the young audience has gone, you need to visit such establishments as the **12-Bar Club**, **Kashmir Klub**, **Bohemian Voices** (at the Lately Night Club) and the **Troubadour**. At these venues, such older singers and musicians as **John Renbourn**, **Wizz Jones** and visiting American **John Stewart** rub shoulders with the upcoming talent of **Jason McNiff**, **The Hank Dogs** and **Karen Westerhout**.

***Editor's Note*** *The growing new "Acoustic Music" scene is well covered by Acoustic London at* www.csed.demon.co.uk/aclon

The club that has notably come to the fore this past year is the **Borderline** (situated on the Charing Cross Road near Centrepoint). Since Barry Everitt took over the management reins in early 2000, a failing club has turned into one of the best in London. His eclectic music policy has ensured there is always something of interest worth catching and the central London location is ideal for public transport. Among the many artists recently appearing there have been **Danú**, **Dave Alvin**, **Kim Richey**, **Slaid Cleaves**, **Jacqui McShee's Pentangle**, **Roy Rogers & Shana Morrison** (Van's daughter) and **John Tams**.

If **The Forum**, one of the bigger venues of the 1980s and early '90s, does not currently host as many roots gigs as it once did, the **South Bank complex** (**Royal Festival Hall**, **Queen Elizabeth Hall** and **Purcell Room**) certainly has expanded its involvement. Along with numerous individual concerts (**Martin Hayes**, **June Tabor**), there are annual festivals plus a parade of free foyer music (always worth checking out on a weekend afternoon or early evening before attending a main performance). **Blackheath Concert Halls** and **The Barbican** both have similar comprehensive music programmes.

Some of the best weekly music, however, remains in the pubs and much of it is Irish. Traditional music sessions at **The Swan** in Stockwell and the **Kilkenny Tavern** have the kind of magic that the London Irish scene has always been renowned for (though if you're visiting the Swan, check in advance what's happening as some of their seven nights of music are devoted to other kinds of sounds).

To find out where to go and what's on offer, the following is a list of weekly or daily information sources for London events:

- **Time Out** - weekly magazine (plus, if you are visiting from another area,check the website at www.timeout.com)
- **London Evening Standard** - a daily 'Going Out' column and weekly 'Hot Tickets' listings magazine
- **Metro** - free London daily paper with extensive listings section,available from its own stands at railway stations.
- **Charlie Gillett** - highly respected show with strong world music content. Saturday Nights from 8-10pm on BBC London Live 94.9 FM and worldwide on www.bbc.co.uk/londonlive You can email charlie.gillett@bbc.co.uk for a playlist.
- **Spyda Internet Radio** - broadcast on website www.virtuetv.com Its *Folk Roots* show *The Guest List* is hosted by Irish flautist Alan O'Leary and goes out Thursdays from 7-10pm GMT. The stations other roots shows are presented by Bob Paterson and others.

Finally, to ensure a good night out, always ring a venue to check the performance you wish to attend is still happening (especially if you are travelling a long distance to be there).

**John Crosby**
*TIME OUT Folk and Roots Music Critic*

**Folk London** is the bimonthly listings magazine for folk clubs and events in and around London and the Home Counties. It publishes news, gossip, songs, reviews, adverts for events and individual performers, as well as the essential day-by-day diary of clubs, guests and folk events in and around London, from pub sessions in Kent to the Royal Albert Hall!
**Web** www.grove-cottage.demon.co.uk/folklon
**Editor** Sheila Finn
**Mail address** 4a Kenilworth Road, Petts Wood, Kent, BR5 1DY
**Phone/Fax** 01689 825 263
**Email** sheila@folklon.fsnet.co.uk
**Distribution** Gerry Milne
**Address** Grove Cottage, Amyand Park Road, Twickenham, Middx. TW1 3HG
**Phone** 020 8892 4621
**Email** gerry@grove-cottage.demon.co.uk/folklon/

***Editor's Note*** Folk London *provides a useful News page, a comprehensive diary of regular and weekly events and a clear venues page. Also Morris listings of teams within the M25 area and lots of useful adverts.*

## Ceilidhs in London

By **Michael Catovsky**

Flicking through the pages of **Time Out**, the sheer breadth and variety of dances and classes available in London can only be marvelled at. Everything from Salsa in Shadwell, Tango in Tooting, Egyptian in Eastcote to Funky flavas in Finchley, as well as a plethora of other moves and grooves, can be enjoyed up and down the capital. Odd then that traditional British dances are so hard to locate. Although there's a smattering of folk dance clubs around there are few places hosting ceilidhs. **The Knees Ups** at **Cecil Sharp House** are the longest running series of monthly ceilidhs, with the only other being **Reeling** in Ealing. **Scotch Mist** run some Scottish ceilidhs at Cecil Sharp every couple of months, and **Ripe** run Scottish ceilidhs in Ealing Town Hall three or four times a year. In addition, there are a couple of places to dance Irish-style ceilis, mostly in externally funded cultural centres.

London has the lowest number of

## london region

Listed ceilidh and social dance bands in London include **Cheap Jack**, **The Committee Band**, **Dropping Clangers**, **Fiddlin' Around**, **The Gloworms**, **Highly Strung**, **Kafoozalum Country Dance Band**, **Stomp** and **Wraggle Taggle**.

Listed dance callers include **Chris Turner**, **Cyril Jones**, **Dave Evans**, **Derek Gregory**, **John Wood**, **Maire Clerkin**, **Michael Catovsky** and **Nick Walden**.

See **efn magazine** list in East England section for other local bands.

**The English Regions**
*These are based on Regional Arts Board representation with some variation. We have kept all of Derbyshire and Lincolnshire in the East Midlands. The RAB definitions are used here as a generally helpful way of splitting up England for a more detailed look at local resources. Also check sections for neighbouring regions for the band, caller or venue you are looking for. Contributors and magazine listings often mention venues and services based in adjacent regions.*

# london region

Listed ceilidh and social dance bands in London include **Cheap Jack**, **The Committee Band**, **Dropping Clangers**, **Fiddlin' Around**, **The Gloworms**, **Highly Strung**, **Kafoozalum Country Dance Band**, **Stomp** and **Wraggle Taggle**.

Listed dance callers include **Chris Turner**, **Cyril Jones**, **Dave Evans**, **Derek Gregory**, **John Wood**, **Maire Clerkin**, **Michael Catovsky** and **Nick Walden**.

See **efn magazine** list in East England section for other local bands.

**The English Regions**
*These are based on Regional Arts Board representation with some variation. We have kept all of Derbyshire and Lincolnshire in the East Midlands. The RAB definitions are used here as a generally helpful way of splitting up England for a more detailed look at local resources. Also check sections for neighbouring regions for the band, caller or venue you are looking for. Contributors and magazine listings often mention venues and services based in adjacent regions.*

public ceilidhs per capita in the UK; whereas it has the highest number of other forms of public dance such as nightclubs, jive jamborees and the like. Recent attempts to re-invigorate the ceilidh scene have included Walthamstow council's attempt at restarting their monthly ceilidhs in the **Lloyd Park Theatre** (which may or may not continue) and Hemlock Music's **Beckenham Hops**, which looked promising initially, but soon collapsed under the weight of the capital's arcane travel infrastructure.

The capital's dance scene suffers from parochialism; it's a massive city and people are unwilling to travel too far. Most Londoners are keener to go out somewhere within walking distance, than face the hassle of changing tube lines to get to a specific event. They enjoy whatever is close. Public transport closes early, so using it to get to a ceilidh usually means leaving before the end. Driving is expensive, the roads are always gridlocked, and some people would consider drinking at a ceilidh as important as dancing. Promoters need to locate their ceilidhs in the suburbs, like the salsa phenomenon has done, and make sure it is around plenty of good public transport.

Ealing is notable in that it boasts not only the **Reeling in Ealing** English-style ceilidhs, but also the **Ripe Scottish ceilidhs**, as well as a folk dance club. The Town Hall is close to buses, two tube lines and over ground trains. **Reeling in Ealing** draws heavily on the local community as well as on people from the Home Counties. The locals enjoy a social activity near them, and ceilidh fanatics are delighted with the standard of music. With careful planning, similar series could be established in other London boroughs, and succeed if advertised both locally and London-wide. They could run once a month, each on different nights or weeks, giving touring bands different events at which to play, each with a different local audience.

Decent-sized halls in good locations in London come with an astounding price tag. It would not be uncommon to pay over £500 for a Saturday night. Add on the cost of a top band (£500,) caller (£75,) lighting, press releases, listings and advertising (£150,) and you need to charge at least £10 per head to break even. People usually pay half this outside London, but this is how much any other sort of night out in the capital costs. You are not just watching, but taking part, and can converse with other people. Many Londoners crave for any sort of community– most of us do not even greet our neighbours any more.

Ealing has the advantage of a legacy of ceilidhs in the area. **Herga Morris** used to stage ceilidhs, and out of town ceilidhs like **Haddenham**, **Oxfolk** and **Godalming** are not too far away. Additionally, a lot of work has been done making the borough aware of what ceilidhs are, and how much fun they can be. If a few people try it, like it, and come back, they bring their friends. Local singles groups come along en masse. Walthamstow also has a history of ceilidhs, and they could work again in the area, so long as the council realise that both beginners and the extant folk scene need to be targeted. Too many experienced dancers can put beginners off, but equally they should be interested in making the event successful, and try to help out the newcomers.

Other areas of London have no legacy of ceilidhs in the area. Although it may seem like climbing a mountain, with the correct kind of promotion, ceilidhs can work, and enter the local consciousness as a good night out. With a fresh crowd of dances, a new breed of London ceilidh could be created, which reflect and celebrate the capital. The new ceilidhs can be close, fast, sweaty and dark, more like nightclubs than country-dances, yet still allowing people to feel part of a community. If marketed correctly, the alienated populace will flood to them.

## The Vaughan Williams Memorial Library (VWML)

**THE LIBRARY AND ARCHIVE OF THE ENGLISH FOLK DANCE AND SONG SOCIETY**

**Phone** 0207 485 2206
**Fax** 0207 284 0523

The **Vaughan Williams Memorial Library** is internationally recognised as one of the world's principal sources of information about the folk arts. It offers a multi-media library and archive comprising printed, manuscript, visual and audio-visual materials, together with a small collection of artefacts.

Here you can look at Cecil Sharp's manuscripts, his photographs of the singers and dancers he met, and even listen to phonograph recordings dating from the first decade of the twentieth century. Or watch videos of the most recent celebrations in Padstow on May Day, recorded by modern day fieldworkers such as **Doc Rowe**.

No other collection in England offers such a comprehensive range of materials in one location, fully accessible through detailed catalogues and indexes. Living and growing, VWML is at the hub of all current research and fieldwork .

Access is free to members of the **English Folk Dance and Song Society**, who can also borrow some of the printed materials, either in person or by post. Non-members are charged a daily fee for reference access. Colleges of higher education and arts bodies are invited to join the Library Subscription Scheme. Please contact the librarian for details or visit the EFDSS website at www.efdss.org.

## Folk Clubs in London

by **Martin Nail**

The London folk song club scene seems to be in a fairly healthy state. There are by no means as many clubs as there were in the heyday of the folk revival, but there are now may more folk and world music events in other sort of venues, such as arts centres (both in local centres such as the **Watermans**, **Brentford**, and in national/regional centres such as the **Barbican**). There are probably about two dozen clubs in Greater London, plus a number in the parallel acoustic music (singer-songwriter) scene. Most meet weekly, though some are fortnightly or monthly, and have booked guests all or most weeks. Many of the clubs have been running for twenty years or more (**Herga** for almost forty). Recommended clubs include the **Cellar Upstairs** (Camden Town, Saturdays except in the summer), **Court Sessions** (Balham, Fridays), **Croydon** (Mondays), **Herga** (Harrow, Mondays), **Hale End** (Chingford, Thursdays), **Islington** (Thursdays), **Sharp's** (Camden Town, Tuesdays). **The Musical Traditions Club** (Fitzrovia, Fridays monthly) deserves a special mention on account of its policy of booking traditional source singers and revivalists with a compatible outlook. In addition there are a number of English music sessions in pubs such as the **Cricketers** in Greenwich (Tuesdays) and the **Wheatsheaf** (Borough Market, Sundays monthly), not to mention numerous sessions for other specific styles of music, such as American Old Time, Swedish, French, and of course Irish.

**Sources of information:** in print the main sources of information are the general listings magazines, in particular **Time Out** and the specialist bimonthly magazine **Folk London** (available in folk clubs or from 4a Kenilworth Road, Orpington, BR5 1DY). Online the primary source is the **Folk London web site**: http://www.grove-cottage.demon.co.uk/folklon/.

**Martin Nail's Folk and traditional music** in specific areas of England page http://web.ukonline.co.uk/martin.nail/regional.htm lists club which have their own webpages, which include most of those mentioned above. Information about the acoustic music scene is at **Acoustic London** www.csed.demon.co.uk/aclon.

● ***Thanks to John Crosby, Martin Nail, Sheila Finn and Gerry Milne of Folk London, Michael Catovsky and Kevin Sheils for their assistance with the above information.***

## Rooting around in London

**www.arts.org.uk/directory/regions/london/index.html**
*The Regional Arts Board*

### *Organisations, Listings etc*

**www.csed.demon.co.uk/aclon/**
*Acoustic London*

**www.efdss.org**
*Cecil Sharp House/Vaughan Williams Memorial Library*

**www.grove-cottage.demon.co.uk/folklon/**
*Folk London, Listings Magazine*

### *Clubs etc.*

**perso.libertysurf.co.uk/steve.jennings/index.html**
*Bromley, Orpington Folk Club*

**web.ukonline.co.uk/martin.nail/MTCintro.htm**
*Camden, The Musical Traditions Club (Fitzrovia)*

**web.ukonline.co.uk/martin.nail/SFCintro.htm**
*Camden, Sharp's Folk Club*

**www.croydonfolksongclub.org.uk**
*Croydon Folk Song Club*

**www.deptfordnet.org.uk/folkclub/index.html**
*Greenwich, Folk and Blues at The White Swan (Deptford)*

**ds.dial.pipex.com/mcp/herga**
*Harrow, Herga Folk Club (Wealdstone)*

**web.ukonline.co.uk/martin.nail/IFCintro.htm**
*Islington Folk Club (Clerkenwell)*

**www.sutton-acoustic.co.uk**
*Merton, Sutton Acoustic Club*

**web.ukonline.co.uk/martin.nail/Borosess.htm**
*Southwark, Borough Market English Music Session*

**www.btinternet.com/~haleend/prog.htm**
*Waltham Forest, Hale End Folk Club*

## London venues

### B.B.'s Blues Club/ B.B.'s Unplugged
Merton Abbey Mills, Merantun Way, Colliers Wood, LONDON SW19
**Contact** Bob Brunning
**Address** 56 Cavendish Road Colliers Wood, LONDON SW19
**Phone** 020 8540 6652
**Alt contact** Wheel House Productions
**Alt Address** Merton Abbey Mills Merantun Way, Colliers Wood, LONDON SW19
**Phone** 020 8542 6644
*Thursday, acoustic blues guests. Sunday, electric blues guests. August Bank holiday festival with over 20 acoustic blues acts.*

### Bar Lorca - World Music Events
175 Stoke Newington High St, LONDON N16
**Phone** 020 7275 8659 (venue)
**Contact** Freddy Macha
**Address** Flat B, 12 Durley Road LONDON N16 5JS
**Phone** 07961 833040
020 7502 9814
**Fax** 020 7281 6677
**Email** fmacha@yahoo.com
*Regular world music events.*

### Bar Lorca Brixton
261 Brixton Road, Brixton, LONDON SW9
**Contact** Freddy Macha
**Address** Flat B, 12 Durley Road LONDON N16 5JS
**Phone** 07961 833040
020 7502 9814
**Fax** 020 7281 6677
**Email** fmacha@yahoo.com
**Web** www.bouncerdan.com/freddy/gig.htm
*Sunday, world music events.*

### Blackheath Concert Halls
23 Lee Road, LONDON SE3 9RQ
**Contact** Karl Chapman
**Phone** 020 8318 9758
020 8463 0100
**Fax** 0208852 5154
**Email** karl@blackheathhalls.com
**Web** www.blackheathhalls.com
**Alt contact** Pamela McCormick
**Email** info@blackheathhalls.com
*Important South London venue, 2 halls. Programme includes regular folk & world concerts with national & international acts.*

### The Borderline
Orange Yard, Off Manette Street, LONDON W1V 5LB
**Phone** 020 7734 2095 - box office
**Contact** Barry Everitt
**Phone** 020 7434 1698 - promoters
**Email** barry.borderline@virgin.net
**Web** www.borderline.co.uk
*Leading alternative London venue. Concerts Mon-Sat. Programme includes rock, acoustic, world & roots music.*

### Borough Music Session
The Wheatsheaf, 6 Stoney Street, LONDON SE1 9AA
**Contact** Martin Nail
**Address** 14 Leighton Place LONDON NW5 2QL
**Phone** 020 7485 2459
**Email** martin.nail@ukonline.co.uk
**Web** http://ukonline.co.uk/martin.nail/borosess.htm
*1st Sunday, 12.30-3pm. English music session, loosely interpreted as Southern English style, i.e. with tunes from all over. All musicians welcome.*

### Cellar Upstairs Folk Club
The Golden Lion, 88 Royal College Street, LONDON NW1
**Contact** Sheila Miller
**Address** 55 Moray Road LONDON, N4 3LD
**Phone** 020 7281 7700
**Web** http://hometown.aol.co.uk/cellarupstairs/myhomepage/newsletter.html
*Saturday, 8pm. Guests, mainly traditional.*

Listed ceilidh and social dance bands in London include **Cheap Jack**, **The Committee Band**, **Dropping Clangers**, **Fiddlin' Around**, **The Gloworms**, **Highly Strung**, **Kafoozalum Country Dance Band**, **Stomp** and **Wraggle Taggle**.

Listed dance callers include **Chris Turner**, **Cyril Jones**, **Dave Evans** **Derek Gregory**, **John Wood**, **Maire Clerkin**, **Michael Catovsky** and **Nick Walden**.

See **efn magazine** list in East England section for other local bands.

**The English Regions**
*These are based on Regional Arts Board representation with some variation. We have kept all of Derbyshire and Lincolnshire in the East Midlands. The RAB definitions are used here as a generally helpful way of splitting up England for a more detailed look at local resources. Also check sections for neighbouring regions for the band, caller or venue you are looking for. Contributors and magazine listings often mention venues and services based in adjacent regions.*

# london venues

**The English Regions**
*These are based on Regional Arts Board representation with some variation. We have kept all of Derbyshire and Lincolnshire in the East Midlands. The RAB definitions are used here as a generally helpful way of splitting up England for a more detailed look at local resources. Also check sections for neighbouring regions for the band, caller or venue you are looking for. Contributors and magazine listings often mention venues and services based in adjacent regions.*

## Chats Palace Arts Centre
Chats Palace Arts Centre,
42-44 Brooksby's Walk, Hackney
LONDON E9 6DF
**Contact** Nick Reed
**Phone** 020 8533 0227
020 8986 6714
**Fax** 020 8785 6878
**Email** ChatsPal@aol.com
**Web** www.chatspalace.towp.co.uk
*80 capacity bar with small PA. Acoustic music incl. blues, folk, jazz. Occasional world music events in main hall (200 capacity)*

## Court Sessions
St. Boniface Social Club, Mitcham Road, Amen Corner, Tooting, LONDON SW17
**Contact** Dave East & Doreen Lighter
**Phone** 020 8677 9989
*Traditional music & song. Guests and singers nights. Venue may change September 2001.*

## Croydon Folksong Club
Ruskin House, 23 Coombe Road,
CROYDON, Surrey CR0 1BD
**Contact** Brian Dalton
**Address** 39 Overdown Road
Bellingham, LONDON SE6 3ES
**Phone** 020 8698 5322
0770 3210795
**Email** croydonfolkclub@aol.com
**Web** www.croydonfolksongclub.org.uk
*Most Mondays, 8pm.Folk song and music from the British tradition. Concerts, singarounds & barn dances.*

## East London Acoustic Music Workshop
45 Coldharbour, Poplar, LONDON E14
**Contact** Dave Toussaint
**Address** 25 Grove Crescent Road
Stratford, LONDON E15 1BJ
**Phone** 020 8555 3785
**Email** davetoussaint@hotmail.com
**Web** www.harmonica.boom.ru
*Thursday. Music co-op. Sessions, skills/ ideas exchange, etc. Occasional free workshops.*

## File Gumbo
Cecil Sharp House, 2 Regents Park Road, LONDON NW1 7AY
**Phone** 020 74852206 (venue)
**Contact** Tim Rutherford
**Phone** 01708 558128
**Web** www.londoncajun.co.uk
*Monthly Cajun dance with top national bands. Also dance workshop, jam session and Cajun food.*

## Folk on Platform One
"Platform One", Churchfield Road,
Acton, LONDON W3
**Contact** Hemlock Music
**Address** PO Box 32515,
LONDON W3 0NS
**Fax** 020 8992 8691
**Email** office@hemlockmusic.co.uk
**Web** www.hemlockmusic.demon.co.uk/platform1.html
*Monthly Sunday folk/roots concerts in Acton, London. Support slots welcome.*

## Gannets
Gannets Vegetarian Restaurant,
458 Hoe Street, Walthamstow,
LONDON E17
**Contact** Max Reid
**Address** 34 Quebec Road
ILFORD, Essex IG1 4TT
**Phone** 020 8554 2553
*2nd Tuesday, mainly instrumental English folk dance music session.*

## GAYA (Global Music For Dancing)
West Central Basement
Lisle Street, Chinatown, LONDON WC2
**Contact** Dubin G Murray
**Phone** 07790 698134
**Email** clubgaya@hotmail.com
**Web** www.lagaya.org
*Alternate Thursdays, 10.30pm. Lesbian and gay world music club night.*

## Hale End Folk Club
County Arms, 420 Hale End Road,
Highams Park, LONDON E4
**Contact** Frankie & Terry Cleeve
**Address** 142 The Avenue
Highams Park, LONDON E4 9RD
**Phone** 020 8523 2242
**Email** frankiecleeve@btinternet.com
**Web** www.btinternet.com/~haleend
*Thursday, members club featuring national guests and floor spots. Free membership, call Ann 01992 622487, 48 hrs in advance.*

## Hammersmith & Fulham Irish Centre
296 Blacks Road, LONDON, W6 9DT
**Phone** 020 8563 8232
**Contact** Ross Scanlon
**Phone** 020 8741 4590
**Fax** 020 8563 8233
**Email** irishcentre@ukgateway.net
**Web** www.ibhf.gov.uk/irishcentre
*London's focal centre for Irish Arts. Concerts, ceili's, theatre, classes, etc. Extensive programme of top Irish & Irish music acts. 250 capacity, bar, PA.*

## Herga Folk Club
The Royal Oak, Peel Road,
WEALDSTONE, Middx
**Contact** Bob Hambleton
**Address** 17 Juniper Avenue
Bricket Wood, ST ALBANS AL2 3LR
**Phone** 01923 672590
**Fax** 01923 404310 (phone first)
**Email** herga@kestrel-folk.demon.co.uk
**Web** http://ds.dial.pipex.com/mcp/herga
*Monday, 8.30pm. Singers' & musicians nights (open evenings) plus monthly guests.*

## Islington Folk Club
The Horseshoe, 24 Clerkenwell Close,
LONDON EC1R 0AG
**Contact** Bernard Puckett
**Address** 67 Waldeck Road
LONDON N15 3EL
**Phone** 020 8881 0828
**Web** http://web.ukonline.co.uk/martin.nail/ifcintro.htm
**Alt contact** Martin Nail
**Phone** 020 7485 2459
**Email** martin.nail@ukonline.co.uk
*Thursday, 8pm. Guests artists from fiercely traditional to frankly ecentric. Support by house band and resident singers. Not summer.*

## Knees Up Cecil Sharp Ceilidhs
Cecil Sharp House,2 Regents Park Road, LONDON NW1 7AY
**Phone** 020 7485 2206
**Contact** Mary Panton
**Address** 206 Victoria Park Road
LONDON E9 7HD
**Fax** 020 8986 8834
**Email** mary.panton@virgin.net
**Web** ukonline.co.uk/martin.nail/kucsintr.htm
**Alt contact** Martin Nail
**Email** martin.nail@ukonline.co.uk
*3rd Friday (usually), 8pm. Ceilidh series with top national and new bands & callers in the energetic English ceilidh style. New & experienced dancers welcome.*

## London Barndance Company
Cecil Sharp House, 2 Regents Park Road, LONDON NW1 7AY
**Phone** 020 7485 2206
**Contact** Andrew & Jane
**Phone** 01628 633962
**Email** home@barndance.org
**Web** www.barndance.org
*Monthly barndance (usually 3rd Saturday) with top national bands.*

**The English Regions**
*These are based on Regional Arts Board representation with some variation. We have kept all of Derbyshire and Lincolnshire in the East Midlands. The RAB definitions are used here as a generally helpful way of splitting up England for a more detailed look at local resources. Also check sections for neighbouring regions for the band, caller or venue you are looking for. Contributors and magazine listings often mention venues and services based in adjacent regions.*

### Musical Traditions Club
King & Queen, 1 Foley Street
LONDON W1
**Contact** Peta Webb
**Address** 52 Cecile Park
LONDON N8 9AS
**Phone** 020 8340 0530
**Email** petawebken@aol.com
*Monthly Friday folk club with guest singers/ performers in the oral tradition. Floorsingers welcome. For membership, please leave name and address on answer machine 48 hrs in advance.*

### On Bouge
London Welsh Centre, 157 Grays Inn Road, LONDON, WC1
**Contact** Ayla Bedri
**Phone** 020 8928 1884
07774 219769
**Email** islab@yahoo.co.uk
**Web** www.gre.ac.uk/~c.walshaw/music/onbouge.html
**Alt contact** Simon Moore
**Phone** 020 7485 0499
**Email** OnBouge@SimonMoore.com
*3rd Monday, 8pm. French music and dance (mainly Central France & Brittany). Short workshop followed by general playing & dancing. Some guest bands.*

### Reeling in Ealing
Queen's Hall, Ealing Town Hall
New Broadway, LONDON W5 2BY
**Contact** Hemlock Music
**Address** PO Box 32515, LONDON W3 0NS
**Phone/Fax** 020 8992 8691
**Email** office@hemlockmusic.co.uk
**Web** www.hemlockmusic.co.uk/reeling.html
*Monthly dance with top ceilidh bands and callers. Usually last Saturday.*

### Sharp's Folk Club
Cecil Sharp House, 2 Regents Park Road, LONDON NW1 7AY
**Phone** 020 7485 2206
**Contact** Shelia Finn
**Address** 4a Kenilworth Road, Petts Wood, ORPINGTON, Kent BR5 1DY
**Fax** 01689 825263
**Email** sheila@folklon.fsnet.co.uk
**Web** ukonline.co.uk/martin.nail/sfcintro.htm
**Alt contact** Martin Nail
**Email** martin.nail@ukonline.co.uk
*Tuesdays, 8pm. Singers' nights, all welcome to sing, play, stories, etc. Guest artist monthly. Closed in August*

### The Spitz
109 Commercial Street, LONDON E1 6BG
**Contact** T Dickin
**Phone** 020 7392 9032
**Fax** 020 7377 8915
**Email** mail@spitz.co.uk
**Web** www.spitz.co.uk
*London alternative venue, roots & world music included in programme.230 capacity*

### Staines Folk and Blues Club
The Three Tuns, 63 London Road, STAINES, Middx
**Contact** Geraldine Hurst
**Phone** 020 8897 9227
**Web** www.stainesfolkandblues.org.uk
*Monday, 8pm. Singers nights with monthly guests.*

### The Stomp Club
The Turks Head, Winchester Road, St Margarets, TWICKENHAM
Middx TW1 1LF
**Contact** Jim Bean
**Address** 64 Talbot Road OLD ISLEWORTH, Middx TW7 7HF
**Phone/Fax** 020 8891 0523
**Email** info@stompclub.fsnet.co.uk
**Web** www.stompclub.fsnet.co.uk
**Phone** 020 8892 1972 (venue)
*Bi-monthly world/ roots music club. Energetic and orginal dance music.*

### Teddington's Premier Folk Club
The Railway, Victoria Road
TEDDINGTON, Middx
**Contact** Peter Middlehurst
**Address** 1 Railway Approach
TWICKENHAM, Middx TW1 4LG
**Phone** 020 8892 8635
020 7343 4939
*Last Friday.*

### The Troubadour Folk & Blues Club
265 Old Brompton Road
Earl's Court, LONDON SW5
**Contact** Rodney
**Phone** 020 7737 0600
*Friday, 8.30pm. Mixture of folk, blues & more.*

### Twickenham Folk & Singers Club
The Cabbage Patch, 67 London Road, TWICKENHAM, Middx
**Phone** 020 8866 2621
*Sunday, 8pm. Alternate singers nights and guests.*

### Union Chapel
The Vestry, Compton Avenue, Islington, LONDON N1 2XD
**Contact** Julia Farrington
**Phone** 020 7226 3750
**Fax** 020 7354 8343
**Email** arts@unionchapel.org.uk
**Web** www.unionchapel.org.uk
*Community venue with full range of international & contemporary performers. Welcomes performances by culturally diverse & marginalised/ disadvantaged communities. Space for hire, 3 halls (150 to 1000 cap), bar.*

### Winchmore Folk Dance Club
St Pauls Centre, 102 Church Street, ENFIELD, Middx
**Contact** Lilian Noor
**Address** 2B The Chine, Grange Park
LONDON N21 2EB
**Phone** 020 8360 8784
**Alt contact** Cyril Jones
**Alt address** 3 Uplands Way, Grange Park, LONDON N21 1DH
**Phone** 020 8360 1968
**Fax** 020 8967 3561
**Email** cydorjones@aol.com
*Wednesday, 8pm and 2nd Saturday, 7.30pm. Dance club promoting all interest in English folk dance.*

### The South Bank Centre
Belvedere Road, London, SE1 8XX
**Phone** 020 7921 0600
**Fax** 020 7928 0063
**Web** www.sbc.org.uk
**Box Office** 020 7960 4242
**Email** boxoffice@rfh.org.uk

### Royal Festival Hall
**Contact** Neil Darlison - Head of Hall Programme Planning
**Phone** 020 7921 0843
**Fax** 020 7928 2049
**Email** ndarlison@rfh.org.uk

### Queen Elizabeth Hall
**Contact** Pam Chowhan - Queen Elizabeth Hall Planning Manager
**Phone** 020 7921 0815
**Fax** 020 7928 2049
**Email** pchowhan@rfh.org.uk

### Purcell Room
**Contact** Vanessa Casey - Purcell Room Planning Manager
**Phone** 020 7921 0952
**Fax** 020 7928 2049
**Email** vcasey@rfh.org.uk

### The Barbican Centre
Silk Street, London, EC2Y 8DS
**Phone** 020 7382 7036
020 7638 8891 – box office
**Fax** 020 7256 8580
**Web** www.barbican.org.uk

# london venues

**The English Regions**

*These are based on Regional Arts Board representation with some variation. We have kept all of Derbyshire and Lincolnshire in the East Midlands. The RAB definitions are used here as a generally helpful way of splitting up England for a more detailed look at local resources. Also check sections for neighbouring regions for the band, caller or venue you are looking for. Contributors and magazine listings often mention venues and services based in adjacent regions.*

## Folk London's Venues Listings

These are the addresses of venues listed in **Folk London's Regular events and Monthly** diaries.

ANCHOR FOLK CLUB: Blue Anchor, High Rd, Byfleet, Surrey. (01483 476715 or email Mike)

CECIL SHARP HOUSE: 2 Regents Park Rd, NW1 7AY. (020 7485 2206)

- Balkan Plus (01992 582717 Brian)
- Ceilidh Club (020 7243 4633 Ed)
- Friday Feet (020 8340 4683 Caspar)
- Hellzapoppin Jive Club (020 8444 9623 Christine)
- International Dance - (020 8340 4683 Caspar)
- Monday musicians (01628 486461 Maggie)
- Quadrille Club (01689 600768 or email Chris)
- Society for International Folk Dancing (020 7701 3785 George)

CHESHAM TUDOR: White Hill Centre, Chesham, Bucks. (01494 562093 Andy)

CHIPPENHAM: The Old Road Tavern, The Old Road, Chippenham, Wilts. (01225 810 268 Brian)

COURT SESSIONS: The Grove, Oldridge Rd, Balham, SW12. (020 8767 4185)

CROYDON: Ruskin House, 23 Coombe Rd, Croydon, Surrey. (020 8698 5322 Brian or Jenny)

DARTFORD: Dartford Working Mens Club, Essex Rd, Dartford, Kent. (01322 222 553)

FLEET FOLK CLUB: Fox & Hounds, Crookham Rd, Fleet. (01252 614866)

FOLK SOUTH EAST: (General enquiries: 01732 460171 John)

- FOLK SOUTH EAST CHEQUER MEAD: Chequer Mead Arts Centre, De La War Rd, East Grinstead, W Sussex. (Venue: 01342 302000.)
- FOLK SOUTH EAST CORN EXCHANGE: Maidstone. (Venue: 01622 758611.)
- FOLK SOUTH EAST MAIDSTONE: Pizza Express, Maidstone, Kent. (Venue: 01622 683548.)
- FOLK SOUTHEAST STAG THEATRE: Sevenoaks, Kent. (Box Office: 01732 450175.)
- FOLK SOUTH EAST TRINITY: Trinity Arts Centre, Church Rd, Tonbridge Wells, Kent. (Venue: 01892 678678.)

HADDENHAM: Village Hall, Haddenham, Bucks. (01296 415333 John Heydon)

HALE END: County Arms Tavern, Hale End Rd, E4. (020 8503 3484)

HERGA: Royal Oak, Peel Rd, Wealdstone, Middx. (01923 250640 Dorothy)

ISLINGTON: The Horseshoe, 24, Clerkenwell Close, London EC1R 0AG. (01233 820960 Dave)

KNEES UP CECIL SHARP: Cecil Sharp House (see above). (020 8986 8834 Mary)

LEIGH ON SEA: Hoy at Anchor, The Ship, New Rd, Leigh, Essex. (01268 792160 Kath)

LEWES ARMS, EAST SUSSEX: Lewes Arms, Mount Place, Lewes, East Sussex. (Valmai 01273 476757)

LONDON BARNDANCE COMPANY: Cecil Sharp House (see above). (01628 633 962 Andrew)

MAD NANNY FOLK CLUB: The Place, Leys Ave, Letchworth, Herts. (01462 438 373 or email Alan)

MAIDSTONE The F Word, The Soul Cafe, Week St, Maidstone, Kent.

MUSICAL TRADITIONS: King & Queen, 1 Foley St, W1 (020 8340 0530 Peta)

ORPINGTON SONG: White Hart, High St, Orpington, Kent. (01959 532 754 Steve.)

RAM CLAYGATE: Ram Club, Foley Arms, Hare Lane, Claygate, Surrey. (01372 467208)

REELING IN EALING: Queen's Hall, Ealing Town Hall, New Broadway, Ealing, London W5 2BY. (020 8992 8691 Michael).

ROYAL OAK, LEWES: Royal Oak, Station St, Lewes, East Sussex. (01273 478124 Vic & Tina)

SHARPS: Greene King Bar, Cecil Sharp House (see above)(01689 825263 Sheila)

STAINES: The Three Tuns, 63 London Rd, Staines TW18 4BN (020 8897 9227 Geraldine)

SUTTON ACOUSTIC KINGS HEAD: The Kings Head, Merton High St, London SW19. (020 8642 8341)

SUTTON ACOUSTIC SECOMBE CENTRE: The Secombe Centre, Cheam Road, Sutton, Surrey.

UXBRIDGE: The Crown and Treaty, Oxford Rd, Uxbridge. (01923 672590 Bob)

WALTHAM FOREST, O'NEILLS: O'Neills Irish Bar, 762 High Road, Leytonstone, London E11. (020 8521 7111)

WALTHAM FOREST THEATRE: The Theatre, Lloyd Park, Forest Rd, Walthamstow, London E17. (020 8521 7111)

WALTHAMSTOW ASSEMBLY HALL: Forest Rd, Walthamstow, London E17. (020 8521 7111)

WALTHAMSTOW BARN DANCE: Walthamstow Theatre, Lloyd Park, Forest Rd, E17. (020 8521 7111)

WHEATSHEAF BOROUGH: 6 Stoney St, SE1. (020 7485 2459 Martin)

● ***Reproduced by kind permission of Folk London.***

***Editor's Notes***

*There doesn't seem to be any activity at* O'Neills *and* Walthamstow Barn Dances *but they may reactivate during the year.*

*Folk clubs can close or change venue with little or no notice. If you haven't been to a particular club before, please check before setting out.*

*Many of these venues are listed in other regional sections; Southern, South East and East England.*

# Northern

**Cleveland, Cumbria, Durham, Northumberland, Newcastle, Gateshead, N. Tyneside, South Tyneside and Sunderland.**

**Northern Arts**, Central Square, Forth Street, Newcastle upon Tyne, NE1 3PJ
**Email** info@northernarts.org.uk
**Web** www.arts.org.uk/directory/regions/northern/index.html
*Northern Arts publish a comprehensive list of venues and promoters in the region.*

**Folk Roundabout** is the folk magazine for North East England. It has loads of club news and adverts, a large diary section and lots of performer news and reviews.
**Contact** Trevor Lister (Editor)
**Mail address** 24 Ambleside Grove, Acklam, Middlesbrough, Cleveland TS5 7DQ
**Phone** 01642 821776.
**Email** trevorl@ntlworld.com
*Quarterly. Annual subscription £6*

**Folkwords** is a Newsletter published five times a year by Folkworks. (see details below). It carries a substantial What's On Section with daily event listings, workshop and festival information and news of initiatives in the region.

## The performance of folk music and song in North East England

By **Eddie Walker**

It was the large and widespread folk club movement in North East England, enduring today more than 40 years since its inception, that provided the bedrock for the music's development and undoubted popularity in the region. That, and the emergence of such numbers of local players, singers and writers of great ability and influence . The late 1950's saw the establishment of the 'ballad and blues' clubs where enthusiastic amateurs sought to emulate their new-found musical heroes and great names from the past like **Billy Pigg** and **Tommy Armstrong**, became recognised once again alongside the new crop of contemporary writers creating in both modern and traditional style. A pop-chart phenomena called Skiffle, with its roots in American folk culture, had a bearing on performance attitudes demonstrating that anybody might 'give it a go', and this ethos, undoubtedly with both strengths and weaknesses, is the basis on which most clubs run today.

Arguably the strongest identifiable musical style comes from **Northumberland**, with its unique small pipes tradition, but fiddle, concertina, mouth organ and even penny whistle all claim a place. Tyneside Music Hall songs have come to be known the world over, and local coal mining ballads and maritime songs sit side by side with a wealth of contemporary and traditional song, both locally created or discovered by word-of-mouth, sound recordings or radio. Most everything is tolerated and accepted as a performers choice of expression, though some individual clubs choose to be categorised as to their preferred style. Unaccompanied singing, encouraging chorus participation, is a big feature in the area but traditional Folk Blues, for instance, has always had a very strong following especially around Tyneside while Teesside has, for close on 30 years, had clubs and events devoted specifically to Bluegrass and American Old Time and Traditional Country Music.

The concert-going public still remains well served with theatre and large hall events. Arts venues with a strong affinity for folk, can be found in **Newcastle**, **Gateshead**, **Stockton**, **Hartlepool** and **Wallsend**. **Washington** and **Darlington Arts Centres**, have formidable ongoing folk programmes, continuing with exceptional success. Festivals from **Rothbury** in the North to **Saltburn** and **Whitby** in the South are revivalist style summer events whilst more contemporary developments have emerged at riverside sites in **Stockton-on-Tees** and on **Tyneside**, featuring broader elements of Folk, Roots and World music. Community events like the **Washington Kite Festival** have always featured folk as their central musical theme.

The most significant achievement in the region during the last decade has been the establishment of **Folkworks**, (www.folkworks.co.uk). Based in Newcastle-upon-Tyne it's an agency working in development and education, especially encouraging young people to learn through musical tuition, participation and performance programmes reaching far beyond our regional boundary. And an exciting new ground-breaking project will be the opening of the £70m Music Centre in **Gateshead** during 2003. The spectacular development will provide a focus for musical education and performance for communities in the North and will become the home of **Folkworks** as well as **Northern Symphonia**. (www.gatesheadquays.com)

In partnership with **Northern Arts**, **Folkworks** publish a bi-monthly news and feature service called **Folkwords**. Another source of information is the quarterly publication **Folk Roundabout**, (email trevor@ntlworld.com) providing as it does extensive coverage of what is going on especially in the clubs.

## Folkworks

**Folkworks** was established in 1988, by Ros Rigby and Alistair Anderson with support from Northern Arts. Its aim is to develop interest and, wherever possible, practical involvement in traditional music, song and dance, from the North of England, the rest of the UK and beyond. From the outset their approach has been to reach out to people who may not have come across this genre of music before and excite them with events of the highest quality using top flight performers from round the world. These events are linked to opportunities to learn and participate so that the initial momentum generated by exposure to the experienced performers is converted into a desire to get stuck in and have a go. Of course the more people participate the more they want to hear good performers and then the more they are inspired to participate. Building on this general principle Folkworks has developed a very wide range of performance and participative events.

- Workshops and courses.
  One day workouts, weekly classes, weekend courses, and two week long Summer Schools, one for adults and one for young people, held in Durham.
- Schools and Colleges.
  Both long term and "one off" projects focussing on instrumental skills, songwriting, instrument making, storytelling, dance and other areas of folk arts. Plus major in-service training projects for teachers with linked festivals for youngsters from their schools.
- International work -
  Establishing links with similar organisations and with artists in Europe, North America and

## northern region

Listed ceilidh and social dance bands the Northern region include **Alistair Anderson**, **Angels Of The North**, **Fiddler's Elbow**, **Old Friends Ceilidh Band**, **Striding Edge**, **The Border Directors**, **The Flying Toad Band**, **The Hedgehog's Skin** and **Whapweasel**.

Listed dance callers include **Alistair Anderson**, **Martyn Harvey**, **Georgia Shorrock**, **The Ceilidh Company** and **Deborah Kermode**.

**The English Regions**
*These are based on Regional Arts Board representation with some variation. We have kept all of Derbyshire and Lincolnshire in the East Midlands. The RAB definitions are used here as a generally helpful way of splitting up England for a more detailed look at local resources. Also check sections for neighbouring regions for the band, caller or venue you are looking for. Contributors and magazine listings often mention venues and services based in adjacent regions.*

# northern region

Listed ceilidh and social dance bands the Northern region include **Alistair Anderson, Angels Of The North, Fiddler's Elbow, Old Friends Ceilidh Band, Striding Edge, The Border Directors, The Flying Toad Band, The Hedgehog's Skin** and **Whapweasel**.

Listed dance callers include **Alistair Anderson, Martyn Harvey, Georgia Shorrock, The Ceilidh Company** and **Deborah Kermode**.

**The English Regions**
*These are based on Regional Arts Board representation with some variation. We have kept all of Derbyshire and Lincolnshire in the East Midlands. The RAB definitions are used here as a generally helpful way of splitting up England for a more detailed look at local resources. Also check sections for neighbouring regions for the band, caller or venue you are looking for. Contributors and magazine listings often mention venues and services based in adjacent regions.*

elsewhere, and running international education projects such as Making Music on the Line.

- Consultancy
  Organising festivals and performances for other organisations, sucha as the International Kite Festival at Washington and a World Music weekend at the Bath International Music Festival.
- Tours
  By outstanding artists from both the UK and abroad, visiting venues throughout the northern region and nationwide.

Folkworks has also been successful in gaining two major Arts Lottery awards; one for its Training and Youth Project and one for The Folkworks Instrument Bank. Folkworks is also a partner in the development of the Music Centre Gateshead set to open on the south bank of the Tyne in 2003
**Contact** Folkworks, 69 Westgate Road, Newcastle-on-Tyne, NE1 1SG.
**Phone** 0191 222 1717
**Fax** 0191 230 2484
**Email** folkworks@folkworks.co.uk
**Web** www.folkworks.co.uk

## Radio

### Northern Folk

**A new radio show presented by Alistair Anderson.**
**BBC Radio Newcastle**, Cumbria and Cleveland Sundays 9 - 10pm

**Folkworks** is behind a new folk radio show which will go out weekly over the whole of the North East and Cumbria each Sunday from 9 - 10pm.

**Northern Folk** will be presented by the world renowned concertina player and composer Alistair Anderson, who is also Co-Director of Folkworks, and will include interviews with performers who are passing through the region and hopefully some live music along with a range of range of recorded material from the latest CD's to some classic tracks from the days of the LP.

There will also be a weekly diary round up with information about gigs,folk clubs and more.

Northern Folk will be broadcast on Sundays from 9 to 10 pm on Radio Newcastle (95.4FM, or 96FM in Northumberland), Radio Cumbria (95.6, 96.1,95.2, 104.1 or 104.2FM) and Radio Cleveland (95FM).

Information should be sent to Northern Folk, Folkworks, 69 Westgate Rd, Newcastle on Tyne NE1 1SG
**Fax** 0191 230 2484
**Email** folkworks@folkworks.co.uk.

## Magazines

**Get Rhythm Magazine** began life as a regional magazine based in the North East covering a wide range of music. It's now gone National. For more info or to subscribe to Get Rhythm Magazine call:
**Phone** 0191 245 3782 /3/4
**Web** www.getrhythm.co.uk

**Rock 'n' Reel** is a music magazine covering roots, rock, blues & beyond. There is a free CD with each issue. The magazine has national coverage and its base is in Cumbria.
**Contact** Sean McGhee PO Box 6, EGREMONT, Cumbria CA25 5GA
**Phone** 01946 812496
**Fax** 01946 813415
**Email** rocknreel@zetnet.co.uk
**Web** www.rocknreel.co.uk

## Clubs, festivals and events

The North East is a region rich in traditional music and has many clubs, festivals and events. There are good clubs in most towns, see listings. For current folk club programmes, get hold of a copy of Folk Roundabout (see above).

Major venues, clubs and arts centres in the region with regular folk programming include:
**The Playhouse**, Alnwick, a leading traditional music venue, **the Maltings Arts Centre**, Berwick Upon Tweed and **Queens Hall Arts Centre**, Hexham. **Northumbrian Music Nights** promote live music every weekend in the North Pennines. Further south, there is a folk club and regular events at **Darlington Arts Centre. South Shields' Customs House** hosts the **International Guitar Festival** in July plus other folk concerts. **Priory Promotions** programme events at **Buddle Arts Centre**, Wallsend. In Hartlepool, try **The Studio**, Tower Street for the **Sunday Night Roots** series. **The Davy Lamp Folk Club**, based at **Washington Arts Centre** won the Best Folk Club Award at the BBC Folk Awards in February 2001. (0191 416 6999). **The Wayfarer**, Haswell hosts many informal events including festivals, classes and a club. Major venues in Newcastle itself include **Tyneside Irish Centre** which has music and dance classes and traditional arts events. **Caedmon Hall**, Gateshead has weekly classes and some concerts. Recommended clubs and venues in Cumbria include **Carlisle Folk and Blues Club**, **Brewery Arts Centre**, Kendall, **Cockermouth Unplugged** (01900 824653), **Penrith Plug and Play** (01768 862695) at Penrith Playhouse, **Carnegie Theatre**, Workington, **The Rosehill Theatre** at Moresby and **Stanwix Arts Centre**, Carlisle (01228 534781).

Check the Festival List for:
**Brampton Live** 20,21,22 July 2001 is now one of the premier festivals in the country with this year's headliners including **Suzanne Vega**, **Lonnie Donegan** and **Mary Coughlan**.
**Contact** 01228 670580

**Furness Tradition Festival** runs 13-15 July in Ulverston. Furness Tradition promote year round events and educational workshops focussing on Furness and South Lakeland traditions.
**Contact** 01229 582704.

**Darlington Spring Thing**
**Morpeth Gathering** - April
**Teesdale Thrash** - May
**Orange WOW - Window on the World in North Shields** - late May.
**Folkworks Hexham Gathering** - youth folk festival - late May.
**Alnwick Fair** – has some folk elements
**Sunderland International Kite Festival** - free festival with substantial folk element – early July
**Rothbury Festival** - July
**Stockton International Riverside Festival** - free festival with folk and world music– July (www.festival.co.uk)
**Durham Folk Party** – late July
**Durham Gathering** (finale of Folkworks Summer Schools) – late July
**Alnwick International Festival** - wide range of folk and folkloric performers from Europe and beyond – early August
**Saltburn International Festival** - August
**Tyneside Irish Festival** - October
**Alnwick Gathering** – long established traditional music event - started in 1948 by Billy Pigg.

**Northumberland Traditional Music Festival** is a marketing umbrella helping to promote various events round Northumberland.
**Web** www.nlandmusicfest.co.uk

● ***Thanks to Eddie Walker, Alistair Anderson, Folkworks, Ken and Sue Bradburn and Folk Roundabout for their assistance with the above information.***

## Rooting around the net in the North

### Organisations, Listings etc:

**www.folkworks.co.uk**
Folkworks

**www.folknorthwest.co.uk**
North West Federation of Folk Clubs covers Cumbria. See North West section for full details.

**www.btinternet.com/~banjo.bill/len.htm**
Banjo Bill's Home Page with North East Listings etc.

**www.northumberland.gov.uk/vg/music.html**
Northumberland County Council's Music Pages

**www.folknorthwest.co.uk**
North West Federation of Folk Clubs (also covers Cumbria)

**www.getrhythm.co.uk**
Get Rhythm Magazine

**www.rocknreel.co.uk**
Rock 'n' Reel Magazine

### Clubs, Venues etc.

**www.breweryarts.co.uk**
Brewery Arts Centre, Kendall

**www.btinternet.com/~banjo.bill/bridge.htm**
The Bridge Folk Club, Newcastle

**www.talus.force9.co.uk/ssfc**
South Shields Folk club

**www.davylampfolkclub.co.uk**
Washington, Davy Lamp Folk Club

## Northern venues

### Acoustic Wednesday
The Beamish Mary, No Place, BEAMISH, Co Durham
**Contact** Mike Ollier
**Phone** 0191 510 3147
*Wednesday, 8.30pm. Folk, blues, country, jazz, calypso, hosted by 'Hit The Bottle Band'. Monthly guests.*

### ARC
Dovecot Street, STOCKTON ON TEES, TS18 1LL
**Phone** 01642 666600 - box
**Contact** Claire Munroe
**Phone** 01642 666669
*Arts and entertainment venue, regular music events.*

### The Barrels Alehouse
59-61 Bridge Street, BERWICK UPON TWEED, Northumberland, TA15 1ES
**Contact** Mark Dixon
**Phone** 01289 308013
01289 331307
**Alt contact** Steve Daggitt
*Small venue for singer/songwriters. Americana, etc.*

### Billingham Forum Theatre
Town Centre, BILLINGHAM, TS23 2LJ
**Contact** Derek Cooper
**Phone** 01642 551389
**Fax** 01642 360656
*Mid scale venue with professional programming & marketing. Co-productions & promotions with commerical & funded performing arts.*

### Birtley Folk Song Club
The Charles Perkins RACB Club, Sydney House, Birtley Lane, BIRTLEY, Tyne and Wear
**Contact** Mrs Pat Elliott
**Address** 8 Alwin, Rickleton Village, WASHINGTON, Tyne and Wear NE38 9EL
**Phone** 0191 4175266
07879 687345
*Wednesday, 8.30pm. Singaround, all welcome. Please ring for details 7pm weekdays.*

### Bishop Auckland Town Hall
Market Place, BISHOP AUCKLAND, Co Durham, DL14 7NP
**Contact** Gillian Wales
**Phone** 01388 602610
**Fax** 01388 604960
*Mixed programme of professional & amateur work.*

### Blyth Valley Music Workshops
Ridley Park Hotel, Wensleydale Terace, BLYTH, Northumberland
**Contact** A Lawrence
**Phone** 01670 360319
**Email** blyth_valley_music@yahoo.co.uk
*Sunday, 6.30-8.30pm. Traditional & folk music workshops.*

### Brewery Arts Centre
122A Highgate, KENDAL, Cumbria, LA9 4HE
**Contact** Stuart Johnson
**Phone** 01539 722833
*Arts centre with professional programming & marketing. Programme includes folk/ roots music & workshops.*

### Brewery Fiddlers
Brewery Arts Centre, KENDAL, Cumbria
**Contact** Carolyn Francis
**Address** 16 Hinde Street, LANCASTER, LA1 1DX
**Phone/Fax** 01524 35391
**Email** carolyn@striding-edge.demon.co.uk
*Mixed ability group of fiddlers, playing shared reportoire, including many local tunes. Beginners contact Carolyn for private lessons first.*

### Caedmon Hall
Central Library, Prince Consort Road, GATESHEAD, NE8 4LN
**Phone** 0191 433 3000
**Phone** 0191 4773478 - box office,
0191 478 2060 - text phone
**Fax** 0191 477 7475
**Email** enquiries@libarts.gatesheadmbc.gov.uk
**Web** www.gateshead.gov.uk
*Tuesday, 6.30pm Folkworks workshops. Monthly ceilidh, regular folk concerts. Full disabled access, 250 capacity.*

### Carlisle Folk & Blues Club
Coach House, Heads Nook, BRAMPTON, Cumbria
**Contact** Ken & Sue Bradburn
**Address** Burnbrook Cottage, Faugh, Heads Nook, BRAMPTON, Cumbria, CA8 9BS
**Phone/Fax** 01228 670580
**Email** ken@emerging.demon.co.uk
*Alternate Fridays, 8pm.*

### Coronation Hall
County Square, ULVERSTON, Cumbria, LA12 7LZ
**Contact** Janet Rydal
**Phone** 01229 582610
**Fax** 01229 588994
*Multi purpose venue, broad programming policy.*



**The English Regions**
*These are based on Regional Arts Board representation with some variation. We have kept all of Derbyshire and Lincolnshire in the East Midlands. The RAB definitions are used here as a generally helpful way of splitting up England for a more detailed look at local resources. Also check sections for neighbouring regions for the band, caller or venue you are looking for. Contributors and magazine listings often mention venues and services based in adjacent regions.*

**The English Regions**
*These are based on Regional Arts Board representation with some variation. We have kept all of Derbyshire and Lincolnshire in the East Midlands. The RAB definitions are used here as a generally helpful way of splitting up England for a more detailed look at local resources. Also check sections for neighbouring regions for the band, caller or venue you are looking for. Contributors and magazine listings often mention venues and services based in adjacent regions.*

## Cramlington Folk Club
Comrades Club, Church Street, CRAMLINGTON, Northumberland
**Contact** R K Taylor
**Address** 21 Lochcraig Place, Beaconhill, CRAMLINGTON, Northumberland, NE23 8DA
**Phone** 01670 715106
07831 890905
**Email** taylor@lochcraig.freeserve.co.uk
**Alt contact** L Smith (not publicity)
**Phone** 01670 715929
*Thursday, 8pm. 2 guest artists per month, other nights are singers' nights.*

## Cumby Arms Folk Evenings
The Cumby Arms, Heighington, NR DARLINGTON
**Contact** Dave Hutchinson
**Phone** 01325 315117, 07803 757184
*1st Thursday, 8 pm. Singers/ performers always welcome.*

## Darlington Arts Centre
Vane Terrace, DARLINGTON, Co Durham, DL3 7AX
**Phone** 01325 483168 - box office
**Contact** Lynda Winstanley
**Phone** 01325 483271
**Fax** 01325 365794
*Professional programming & marketing, range of events including regular folk/roots. See Darlington Folk Club, Spring Thing Festival.*

## Darlington Folk Club
The Arts Centre, Vane Terrace, DARLINGTON, Co Durham, DL3 7AX
**Phone** 01325 483271
**Contact** Tom Hughes
**Phone** 01325 261179
**Fax** 01325 365794
**Email** darlingtonfolkclub@darlington arts.co.uk
*Thursday, 8pm. Caters for broad folk music taste; best in traditional & contemporary acts plus up & coming young people.*

## Davy Lamp Folk Club
Washington Arts Centre, Biddick Lane, Fatfield, WASHINGTON, Tyne and Wear
**Contact** Terri Freeman
**Phone** 0191 416 6999
0191 416 6440
**Fax** 0191 416 6999
**Web** www.davylampfolkclub.co.uk
*Saturday, session from 7.30pm. Guest nights, plus singers night last Saturday. Singers welcome. 2001 BBC Folk Awards recipient.*

## Durham City Folk Club
Colpitts Hotel, Hawthorn Terrace, DURHAM
**Contact** Ian McCulloch
**Address** 166 Devonshire Road, Belmont, DURHAM, DH1 2BL
**Phone** 0191 3844160
**Email** ian.mcculloch@virgin.net
*Thursday, cheery singaround!*

## Forum 28
28 Duke Street, BARROW IN FURNESS, Cumbria, LA14 1HH
**Contact** Doe Brannon
**Phone** 01229 820000
**Fax** 01229 894942
*Venue with professional programming & marketing. Presents a wide range of performing arts.*

## Furness Community Band
Lanternhouse, The Ellers, ULVERSTON, Cumbria
**Contact** Carolyn Francis
**Address** 16 Hinde Street, LANCASTER, LA1 1DX
**Fax** 01524 35391
**Email** carolyn@striding-edge.demon. co.uk
*1st & 3rd Wednesdays. Mixed ability band, all acoustic instruments welcome, playing tunes from Furness traditions session (same night).*

## Guisborough Folk Club
Rugby Club, Belmangate, GUISBOROUGH, Cleveland, TS14 7BB
**Contact** Ralph Dolby
**Address** 93 Gunnergate Lane, MIDDLESBOROUGH, TS7 8JA
**Phone** 01642 278032
**Email** ralph@dolbyco.com
**Alt contact** Brain Prior
**Phone** 01642 475471
**Email** banjo.bill@mail.btinternet.com
*Sunday, 8pm. Alternate guests & singers'/musicians' nights. All welcome.*

## Maltings Arts Centre
Eastern Lane, BERWICK UPON TWEED, Northumberland, TD15 1DT
**Contact** Anne Plenderleith
**Phone** 01289 330661
**Fax** 01289 331367
*Mixed professional programming and film.*

## Middlesborough Theatre
The Avenue, Linthorpe, MIDDLESBOROUGH, TS5 6SA
**Contact** David Lindsey
**Phone** 01642 815181
**Fax** 01642 818947
*Mid scale venue with professional programming & marketing. Co-productions & promotions with commerical & funded performing arts.*

## North Pennine Highlights
Lazonby Village Hall, Lazonby, PENRITH, Cumbria
**Contact** Shelia Fletcher
**Phone** 01768 898804
01768 353954
*Village hall, occasional folk concerts.*

## Northumbrian Music Nights
The King's Head, Market Square, Allendale, HEXHAM, Northumberland, NE47 9UT
**Contact** Larry Winger
**Phone** 01434 685179
**Web** www.cserw.org
*Live music promotions every weekend in the North Pennines, eclecticmix of traditional, blues & participative musical entertainment featuring professional & nationally known bands & local performers.*

## Northumbrian Pipers' Society
Morpeth Chantry Bagpipe Museum, Bridge Street, MORPETH, Northumberland, NE61 1PJ
**Contact** Jim Richmond
**Address** 7 Halton Drive, Wideofen, NEWCASTLE UPON TYNE, NE13 6AA
**Phone** 0191 236 5724
**Email** seamus@richmond77.freeserve. co.uk
**Web** www.nspipes.co.uk/nps
**Alt contact** Colin Ross
**Address** 5 Denebank, Monkseaton, WHITLEY BAY, NE25 9AE
**Phone** 0191 252 6585
**Email** rosspipes@aol.com
*1st Monday, 7.30pm; 3rd Sunday 2.30pm. Society promoting the playing of Northumbrian smallpipes. Concert and competitions in October.*

## The Playhouse
Bondgate Without, ALNWICK, Northumberland, NE66 1PQ
**Contact** Steve Cowton
**Phone** 01665 510785
**Fax** 01665 605692
*Leading venue for traditional music in Northumberland.*

### Priory Promotions/ Buddle Arts Centre
Buddle Arts Centre, Wallsend, NEWCASTLE UPON TYNE
**Phone** 0191 2007132 (venue)
0191 2007141
**Web** www.nemproductions.com
**Contact** Dave Smith - NEM Productions
**Email** DaveSmithNEM@cs.com
*Regular folk concert series with top national acts.*

### Queen's Hall Arts Centre
Beaumont Street, HEXHAM, Northumberland, NE46 3LS
**Contact** Geof Keys
**Phone** 01434 606787
**Fax** 01434 606043
*Wide range of performing arts events.*

### Rosehill Theatre
Moresby, WHITEHAVEN, Cumbria, CA28 6SE
**Phone** 01946 694039 - box office
**Contact** Chris Lloyd - Director
*Wide programme including film, drama, dance, music (classical, folk, jazz), etc.*

### Ryton Village Folk Club
The Half Moon, RYTON VILLAGE, Tyne & Wear
**Contact** Danny McLeod
**Phone** 0191 4131584
**Email** djmcl@btinternet.com
*Thursday, 8.30pm. Guests, mainly traditional song. Free admission.*

### South Shields Folk Club
The Old Ship, Sunderland Rd, Harton, SOUTH SHIELDS, Tyne and Wear
**Contact** Penny Kennedy
**Phone** 0191 567 1617
**Email** keithcunningham@talus3.plus.com
**Web** www.talus.f9.co.uk/ssfc
**Alt contact** Bill Redhead
**Phone** 0191 4564450
*Sunday nights. Guests plus singers/ musicians nights.*

### Stanley Civic Theatre
Front Street, STANLEY, Co Durham, DH9 0NA
**Contact** Martin Weston
**Phone** 01207 218899
**Fax** 01207 284035
*Mixed programme venue.*

### Theatre by the Lake
Lakeside, KESWICK, Cumbria, CA12 5DJ
**Contact** Patrick Gilchrist
**Phone** 017687 72282
**Fax** 017687 74698
*New purpose built professional theatre. Own programme plus occasional touring performing arts.*

### Tyneside Irish Centre
43 Gallowgate
NEWCASTLE UPON TYNE NE1 4SG
**Contact** J O'Neill
**Phone** 0191 261 0384
*Venue with 400 capacity (200 dancing). Dance and music lessons weekly, plus live music/ dances Thursday to Sunday. Traditional & Country music.*

### The Wayfarer
Front Street, HASWELL, Co Durham
**Contact** Fred Brierley
**Phone** 0191 514 1274
*Pub with lots of folk music; 1st Wednesday singalong, 2nd Wednesday Irish session, last Wednesday trad jazz, 3rd Thursday string plucking plus.*

### Wayfarer Folk Club and Haswell
The Wayfarer, HASWELL
Co Durham
**Contact** Fred Brierley
**Phone** 0191 5171274
*Friday, 8pm. Singaround with occasional guests, wide interpretation of folk music. Many other events at this venue.*



**The English Regions**
*These are based on Regional Arts Board representation with some variation. We have kept all of Derbyshire and Lincolnshire in the East Midlands. The RAB definitions are used here as a generally helpful way of splitting up England for a more detailed look at local resources. Also check sections for neighbouring regions for the band, caller or venue you are looking for. Contributors and magazine listings often mention venues and services based in adjacent regions.*

North West / South

# north west region

**The English Regions**
*These are based on Regional Arts Board representation with some variation. We have kept all of Derbyshire and Lincolnshire in the East Midlands. The RAB definitions are used here as a generally helpful way of splitting up England for a more detailed look at local resources. Also check sections for neighbouring regions for the band, caller or venue you are looking for. Contributors and magazine listings often mention venues and services based in adjacent regions.*

## North West

**Cheshire, Lancashire, Blackburn with Darwen, Blackpool, Halton, Warrington, Bolton, Bury, Knowsley, Liverpool, Manchester, Oldham, Rochdale, St. Helens, Salford, Sefton, Stockport, Tameside, Trafford, Wigan and Wirral.**

### Organisations

**North West Arts**
**Contact** Debra King - Music Officer
**Mail address** Manchester House, 22 Bridge Street, Manchester, M3 3AB
**Phone** 0161 834 6644
**Fax** 0161 834 6969. :
**Web** www.arts.org.uk/directory/regions/north_west/index.html

**North West Arts Board's Information Unit** produce pamphlets including Small and Middle scale venues in the North West which also lists a number of promoters and organisations, mostly dance and cross arts.

**North West Federation of Folk Clubs**
**Contact** Dave Jones - Chairman
**Mail address** 4 Kingfisher Close, Swallowfield, Pleckgate Blackburn, Lancs, BB1 8NS
**Phone/Fax** 01254 54877
**Web** www.folknorthwest.co.uk

**Folkus Folk Arts** network for the North West
**Contact** Alan Bell - Chairman
**Mail address** 55 The Strand, Fleetwood, Lancs, FY7 8NP
**Phone** 01253 872317
**Fax** 01253 878382
One day workshops and touring groups throughout Lancashire.

**Clocksback** is an organisation running workshops for adults and children in the Lancaster/ Morecombe area, a folk club and other community folk projects. **Lancaster Clocksforward** and **Lancaster Clocksback Festivals** happen in March and October respectively.

### Magazines and websites

**The North West Federation of Folk Clubs' *Folk North West* magazine** is published 4 times a year. Articles, features, reviews, folk club listings. See organisations.

**Folk Buzz** covers the North West, North Midlands and overlaps into immediately adjacent areas. Incorporates **Scans Folk** magazine (South Cheshire and North Staffs)
**Web** http://website.lineone.net/~folkbuzz folkbuzz@lineone.net
**Subscriptions** Jason Hill
**Mail address** 54 Prince Street, Burslem, Stoke on Trent ST6 4EN
**Phone** 01782 813 401
**Email** jason@burslem.demon.co.uk
**Advertising** Dave Godwin
**Mail address** 15 Mount View, Uppermill, Saddleworth, Lancs.
**Phone** 01457 872494
**Email** dave.godwin@btinternet.com
Event diary, ceilidh band & callers listings, social dance lists and news, song club and session lists, Morris news and contact lists by county, reviews, news and features.

**Lancashire Wakes** magazine carries EFDSS news, dance events and clubs. Contact list of local bands and callers, folk song clubs, clog and step teams and classes.
**Contact** Roy Smith - Editor
**Mail address** Southgate, Fulwood, Preston, Lancs, PR2 3HX
**Phone** 01772 716772

**Wirral and Chester** activities are covered by Peter Massey's website and email newsletter Musica@plmassey.free.online.co.uk

Cheshire folk activities are covered in **Manchester Evening News** folk listings (Fridays) and **Evening Sentinel** (Stoke) which carries listings with occasional folk column (Folk Tales) written by **Eric Cox** (also Fridays).

**Irish Traditional music in NW England**
**Web** www.talented.fsnet.co.uk/links.htm contains links to artists, organisations, media, retail outlets, and Manchester and Liverpool music sites.

**www.clubcheoil.org.uk/contfram.htm** Club Cheoil's historical archive website of material about development of traditional Irish music in Manchester. Includes a good links selection.

### Radio

**Folkscene**
**BBC Radio Merseyside**
FM 95.8, MW 1485
*Thursday 6-7pm presented by Geoff Speed.*
**Email** geoffspeed@compuserve.com
**Email** radio.merseyside@bbc.co.uk

**Lancashire Drift**
**BBC Radio Lancashire**
FM 95.5, 103.9, 104.5
*Thursday 8-9pm.*

**Genevieve Tudor's Folk Music**
**BBC Radio Shropshire & BBC Radio Stoke**
*See West Midlands for details.*
**Email** genevieve.tudor@bbc.co.uk

**http://pages.unisonfree.net/folkimages/RAD.htm** is a listing of folk radio shows crossing the north generally. It also includes the Midlands.

### Venues within the region

Cheshire clubs and venues include **Biddulph Folk Club** and its off-shoot **Congleton Celtic & Acoustic Concerts** (01782 514896), **Northwich Folk Club** at the Harlequin Theatre, **Railway Folk Club**, Lymm, **Parkgate Folk Club**, **Porkies Folk Club**, Poynton. There are well established folk dance clubs in Neston (Wirral) and Adlington (Stockport) and the occasional Sandbach Ceildihs.

Merseyside's clubs include the **Bothy Folk Club** in Southport with national guests, related dance display sides, concerts and ceilidhs. Others such as **Albion Folk Club** have monthly guests. **The Citadel Arts Centre**, St Helens is a newly rebuilt arts centre with a broad programme including folk events. **The Irish Centre** is a focus for Irish music in the city. Occasional concerts take place at **Liverpool's Philharmonic Hall** and **Southport Arts Centre**.

Manchester's major venues all include varying amounts folk, roots & world music in their programming. Venues include **Band on the Wall**, the **University** and the **Academy**, **Lowry Centre**, Salford, **MANCAT**, **O'Sheas**, **Bridgewater Hall** and **Labatt's Apollo**. Sessions mainly centre around the Irish theme pubs. **Club Cheoil** are a big part of traditional Irish music in Manchester. See their website for project details, *www.clubcheoil.org.uk/contfram.htm* Events include sessions and concerts with visiting Irish performers.

In Greater Manchester and Lancashire the most popular ceilidh venue is the monthly **Knees Up North** at Ince in

Makerfield near Wigan. For national and international acts, **The Met Arts Centre**, Bury, **Playhouse 2**, Oldham, **The Platform**, Morecambe and **Burnley Mechanics Institute** include substantial folk and roots series as part of their programming. Clubs with national guests include **Station Buffet Bar**, Stalybridge, **Cross Keys Folk Club**, Saddleworth and **Fleetwood Folk**. **Westhoughton Folk Club** received BBC Radio 2 Folk Awards - Best Club in February 2000.

## Festivals in the region

These range from traditional style events such as **Fylde Folk Festival** (weekend following August bank holiday), **Saddleworth Folk Festival** (July) to festivals encompassing a wider definition of the folk scene including **Chester Folk Festival** (late May bank holiday), **Middlewich Folk and Boat Festival** (mid June but cancelled 2001 due to FMD), **Clitheroe Great Days of Folk** (June), **Nantwich Folk and Roots Festival** (August), **Nantwich Jazz and Blues Festival** (Easter) plus smaller events such as **Four Fools Folk Festival**, Chorley (late August) and **Lancashire Clog and Folk Festival** (May). Manchester's **x-trax** is a large multi art form festival including street arts and roots elements. There two major shanty festivals; **Lancaster Easter Maritime Festival** and **Mersey International Shanty Festival** (June).

● ***Thanks to Derek Schofield, Alan Bell, Folkus, North West Folk Federation and Folk Buzz for aasistance with the information above.***

## Rooting around the North West

### *Organisations/Listings etc.*

**www.fyldefolk.freeserve.co.uk/fatf/index.html**
*Folk in and around The Fylde Coast with folk links*

**website.lineone.net/~folkbuzz/index.htm**
*Folk Buzz Magazine*

**www.brightbell.com/folk**
*Folk Club Diary (Warrington and North Cheshire)*

**freespace.virgin.net/p.hood/folky.htm**
*Folky Stuff (Stockport, Manchester and Cheshire)*

**www.funforall.co.uk/lancashirefolk**
*Lancashire Folk Organisation*

**www.folknorthwest.co.uk**
*North West Federation of Folk Clubs*

**www.btinternet.com/~troubleatmill/whatson.htm**
*Trouble at' Mill, What's on in Lancashire*

**http://pages.unisonfree.net/folkimages/RAD.htm**
*is a listing of folk radio shows crossing the north generally. It also includes the Midlands.*

### *Clubs*

**www.seelie.freeserve.co.uk/index.htm** *Chester, Raven Folk club*

**www.gonline.demon.co.uk/opendoor**
*Manchester, Open Door Folk Club (Failsworth)*

**members.netscapeonline.co.uk/johnboothagain** *Northwich Folk Club*

**www.westhoughton.demon.co.uk**
*Westhoughton Folk Club, Lancs won the Best Folk Club Award at the first BBC Folk Awards in February 2000.*

## North West venues

### Albion Folk Club
The Albion Hotel, Albion Street, NEW BRIGHTON, Merseyside
**Contact** Roger Parker
**Phone** 0151 638 1987
*Sunday, 8.30 pm. Singers nights plus monthly guest night.*

### Alison Arms Folk Club
The Alison Arms, Preston Road, Coppull Moor, NR CHORLEY, Lancs
**Contact** Hilda Foy
**Phone** 01257 792246
*Wednesday, 8.45pm Storytelling, poetry, all music plus occasional dancing.*

### Band on the Wall
Swan Street, MANCHESTER
**Contact** Ian Croal
**Phone** 0161 8326625
**Alt contact** Gavin Sharp
*Major central Manchester alternative venue. Roots/jazz/regular folk acts.*

### Bhurtpore Inn Session
Wrenbury Road, Aston, NANTWICH, Cheshire
**Contact** Pete Hall
**Phone** 01630 661429
*3rd Tuesday, 9pm. Mainly Irish music session.*

### Blackburn Folk Club
The Fleece Inn, Penny Street, BLACKBURN, Lancs
**Contact** Brian Kirkham
**Phone** 01254 720745
*Wednesday, 8.30pm. All kinds of music and poetry.*

### Bollington Folk Club
The Dog & Partridge, Palmerston Street, BOLLINGTON Cheshire
**Contact** Arthur Wakefield
**Phone** 01625 573596
*Friday, 8.30pm, all year round. 'The best of traditional & contemporary folk music'.*

### Bothy Folksong Club
The Blundell Arms, 34 Upper Aughton Road, Birkdale, SOUTHPORT, PR8 5ND
**Contact** Clive Pownceby
**Address** 3 Brookfield Avenue, Great Crosby, LIVERPOOL, L23 3DN
**Phone** 0151 924 5078, 0151 8012723
**Fax** 0151 8012725
**Email** bothyfolkclub@8m.com
**Web** www.bothyfolkclub.8m.com
*Sunday, 8pm. Broad-based acoustic club. National guests alternating with singers' nights.*

### Broken Token Folk Club
The Globe Inn, 94 High Street, Standish, NR WIGAN, Lancs
**Contact** Angie & Ken Bladen
**Address** 36 The Oaks, Eaves Green, CHORLEY, Lancs, PR7 3QU
**Phone** 01257 263678
**Email** four.fools@virgin.net
**Web** www.four-fools.co.uk
*Monday, 815pm. Singers nights plus guests approx. monthly. All welcome.*

### Burnley Folk Club
The Waggon & Horses Inn, Colne Road, Brierfield, BURNLEY, Lancs
**Contact** Phyl Watson
**Phone** 01282 774 077
*Wednesday, 8.30pm. Mostly informal musicians and singers nights, all types of music welcome.*

### Burnley Mechanics
Manchester Road, BURNLEY, Lancs, BB11 1JA
**Contact** David Peirce
**Phone** 01282 664411
**Fax** 01282 664431
**Email** dpierce@burnley.co.uk
*Arts centre with a diverse programme including folk concerts with national artists. 427 capacity, disabled access.*



## north west region

Listed ceilidh and social dance bands in the North West include **Beehive Band**, **Boat Band**, **Carousel Ceilidh**, **Frolicking Pete & The Fumbling Fingers Ceilidh Band**, **Jabadaw**, **Moon & Castle Band**, **Old Friends Ceilidh Band**, **Root Chords**, **Shake-A-Leg**, **Tabuka** and **The Old School Ceilidh Band**.

Listed dance callers include **Deborah Kermode**, **John Hyland** and **Mo's Barn Dance Parties**.

Listed magazines (**Folk Buzz**, **Lancashire Wakes** and **Folk North West**) have useful contact lists.

Look also in neighbouring regions, particularly Northern, for Cumbrian based bands and callers.

**The English Regions**
*These are based on Regional Arts Board representation with some variation. We have kept all of Derbyshire and Lincolnshire in the East Midlands. The RAB definitions are used here as a generally helpful way of splitting up England for a more detailed look at local resources. Also check sections for neighbouring regions for the band, caller or venue you are looking for. Contributors and magazine listings often mention venues and services based in adjacent regions.*

north west
venues

**The English Regions**
*These are based on Regional Arts Board representation with some variation. We have kept all of Derbyshire and Lincolnshire in the East Midlands. The RAB definitions are used here as a generally helpful way of splitting up England for a more detailed look at local resources. Also check sections for neighbouring regions for the band, caller or venue you are looking for. Contributors and magazine listings often mention venues and services based in adjacent regions.*

## Buskers Ball
The Cross Guns, Bolton Road, Egerton, BOLTON, Lancs
**Contact** Alec Martin
**Email** busker@freeuk.com
**Web** www.busker.freeuk.com
*Every Sunday afternoon 4-8 pm. Email to book a spot or just turn up. Free, all welcome.*

## Cadillac Ranch
Parkside Social Club, Midland Road, Bramhall, STOCKPORT, Cheshire
**Contact** Ged & Jean
**Phone** 0161 494 6804
*Last Saturday, 8pm. Country and Western club. No mail to venue, please.*

## Chew Valley Country Music Club
Boarshurst Band Club, Greenbridge Lane, Greenfield, NR OLDHAM, Lancs
**Contact** Keith & Glenys Thompson
**Phone** 01457 865936
*Penultimate Saturday, 8.30pm. Live bands and artists.*

## Chorley Acoustic Music Club
Inn on The Park, Astley Village, CHORLEY, Lancs
**Contact** Steve Clifford
**Phone** 01257 268116
**Alt contact** John Joyce
**Phone** 01257 241536
*2nd & 4th Tuesday, 8.30pm. Platform for local musicians, poets, singers and dancers.*

## Citadel Arts Centre
Waterloo Street, ST HELENS, Merseyside, WA10 1PX
**Phone** 01744 735436
**Web** www.citadel.org.uk
*Venue promoting music events including folk, blues, rock, pop & world music and theatre.*

## Colne Municipal Hall
Pendle Leisure Ltd, Bank House, 61 Albert Road, COLNE, Lancs BB8 0BP
**Contact** Katy Mills
**Phone** 01282 661233
**Fax** 01282 661221
**Email** kmills@leisureinpendle.co.uk
**Alt contact** Gary Hood
**Phone** 01282 661220
**Email** ghood@leisureinpendle.co.uk
*Varied entertainment programme including hosting the annual Great British Rhythm & Blues Festival.*

## Cross Keys Folk Club
Cross Keys, Running Hill Gate, Upper Mill, SADDLEWORTH, Lancs
**Contact** Jim Schofield
**Address** 4 Ash Hill Drive, Mossley, ASHTON UNDER LYME, OL5 9PW
**Phone** 01457 833897
*Wednesday, 9pm. Guest artists. Singers club on Sunday at the Cross Keys.*

## Dabbers Folk Club
The Three Pigeons, Welsh Row, NANTWICH, Cheshire, CW5
**Contact** Lynne Barnes - Secretary
**Address** 68 The Beeches, NANTWICH, Cheshire, CW5 5YP
**Phone** 01270 628041, 07790 082523
**Email** a_mandalynne@yahoo.com
**Alt contact** Eddie Kerrin - Artist Booking
**Address** Shrewbridge Rd, NANTWICH, Cheshire, CW5
**Phone** 01270 628583
*Wednesday, 8.30pm. Song, music, stories, etc. All welcome. Occasional Friday night guest artists, annual Folk Ball. Easy boaters' access from Shrops Union Canal.*

## Edgeworth Folk Music Session
The Black Bull, Bolton Road, Edgeworth, Turton, NR BOLTON, Lancs
**Contact** Brian Frew
**Address** 14 Lower Meadow, Edgeworth, Turton, NR BOLTON, Lancs, BL7 0DQ
**Phone** 01204 852989
**Email** BrianDFrew@tinyonline.co.uk
**Web** www11.ewebcity.com/brianfrew/blackbull.html
*1st Monday, 8.45pm. Informal session, mainly traditional, some new. 50/50 songs and tunes.*

## Falcon Folk Club
Falcon Hotel, Church Street, Littleborough, NR ROCHDALE, Lancs
**Contact** Joan Barker
**Phone** 01706 342655
*Tuesday, 9pm. Free acoustic club with all types of music & poetry.*

## Fleetwood Folk
The Steamer Hotel, Queens Terrace, FLEETWOOD, Lancs
**Contact** David Ryan
**Address** 9 Fir Close, FLEETWOOD, Lancs, FY7 8QS
**Phone** 01253 876 351
*Thursday 8.30pm. Regular guest nights. All types of acoustic music, mainly folk.*

## The Folk Music Workshop
University of Salford, Refectory Rm, Maxwell Building, The Crescent, SALFORD, Greater Manchester
**Contact** Denise Doyle
**Phone** 0161 799 3923
**Alt contact** Doreen Shaw
**Phone** 0161 7364097
*1st Friday, 7.45pm. Workshops run by members and guest leaders. UK & American tunes & dance tunes. All welcome.*

## Folk Upstairs at the Railway
The Railway, Lumb Lane, Droylsden, MANCHESTER
**Contact** Christine
**Phone** 0161 370 6587
**Alt contact** Brenda
**Phone** 0161 432 4830
*1st & 3rd Thursday, 8.45pm. Folk and acoustic music, guests.*

## Hale & Hearty Folk Club
The Kings Arms, Hale, NR MILNTHORPE, Cumbria
**Contact** Frank Lewis
**Address** 9 Leapers View, Over Kellet, CARNFORTH, Lancs, LA6 1HL
**Phone** 01524 734440
**Email** franklewis@ballad.freeserve.co.uk
*1st & 3rd Friday, 8.30pm. Singaround.*

## Harlequin Theatre
Queen Street, NORTHWICH, Cheshire, CW9 5JN
**Contact** Gerry Harris
**Phone** 01606 76889
*Venue for Northwich folk club. Regular concerts with national & local guests.*

## Jim's Café
New Market Street, COLNE, Lancs
**Phone** 01282 866317 - tickets
*Concerts, occasional weekday evenings, 7.30pm. 60 capacity. Tickets from Plant Records/ venue.*

## Knees Up North
Ince Public Hall, Ince Green Lane, Ince-in-Makerfield, WIGAN, Lancs
**Contact** Peter Bearon
**Address** 14 Church Street, Westhoughton, BOLTON, Lancs BL5 3RS
**Phone** 01942 816569
**Fax** 0870 1259506
**Email** kneesupnorth@btinternet.com
**Web** www.btinternet.com/~kneesupnorth
*Monthly ceilidhs with top national bands. Usually 2nd Friday, 8pm. Other occasional dances and concerts.*

## Lancashire Band Workshop
**Contact** Chris Rowland
**Address** 17 Granville Street, Adlington, CHORLEY, Lancs, PR6 9PY
**Phone** 01257 482928
**Alt contact** Roy Hordley
**Address** 53 Heyes Avenue, Rainford, ST HELENS, Lancs, WA11 8AW
**Phone** 01744 882895

*2nd Sunday. Workshops for musicians wishing to learn English & Scottish dance music.*

## Last Thursday Live
The Boarhound, Brook Street, MACCLESFIELD, Cheshire
**Contact** Sue Capper
**Address** 6 Tarvin Close, MACCLESFIELD, Cheshire, SK11 7JJ
**Phone** 01625 614791

*Last Thursday. Mainly singers' club, occasional guests.*

## Leyland Accordion Club
The Priory Club, Broadfield Drive, LEYLAND, Lancs
**Contact** David Batty
**Address** 39 Wray Crescent, Ulnes Walton, LEYLAND, Lancs, PR26 8NH
**Phone** 01772 454328
**Email** david@accordionclub.co.uk
**Web** www.accordionclub.co.uk

*Practice night fortnighly, concert 3rd Wednesday. Accordion tuition, promotion, etc.*

## Liverpool Singaround
The Ship & Mitre, Dale Street, LIVERPOOL
**Contact** Helen Hebden
**Phone** 0151 727 0088

*Tuesday, 9pm. Acoustic songs and instrumental music. Friendly club.*

## The Met Arts Centre
Derby Hall, Market Street, BURY, Lancs, BL9 0BW
**Phone** 0161 761 2216 - box office
**Contact** Jed Kelly - Director
**Phone** 0161 7617107
**Fax** 0161 7635056

*Venue promoting all art forms. Folk & roots music at core of policy. 225 Capacity, disabled access, bar.*

## Ormskirk Folk Dance Club
Emmanuel Church, Derby Street, ORMSKIRK, Lancs
**Contact** Margaret McFarlane - Secretary
**Address** 4 Ledson Grove, Aughton, ORMSKIRK, Lancs, L39 6TB
**Phone** 01695 423882

*Every Monday, 8.15pm. Country, Playford and square social dance. All ages and abilities welcome.*

## The Parkgate Folk Club
The Boathouse, 1 The Parade, PARKGATE, Cheshire
**Contact** Eddie Morris
**Phone** 0151 677 1840

*Last Thursday, 8.15pm. Guests, mainly contemporary folk music.*

## The Platform
Station Buildings, Central Promenade, MORECAMBE BAY, Lancs, LA4 4DB
**Phone** 01524 582803 - box office
**Contact** Kirk Worley
**Phone** 01524 582815
01524 582803
**Email** kworley@lancaster.gov.uk

*Venue presenting mainly music, plus other performance. Roots & alternative bias.*

## Playhouse 2
Newton Street, Shaw, OLDHAM, Lancs, OL2 8NX
**Phone** 01706 847281
**Contact** Barrie Cottam - Artistic Director
**Address** 73 Charlotte Street, ROCHDALE, Lancs, OL16 4TN
**Phone** 01706 665649
07931 550661
**Email** info@playhouse2.com
**Web** www.playhouse2.com

*156 seater theatre: series of folk/ roots concerts - 10 per year. Policy is to present nationally known folk/ roots artists, supported by local performers.*

## Porkies Folk Club
Royal British Legion, Georges Street West, POYNTON, Cheshire
**Contact** Judy Hancock
**Phone** 01260 252633
**Alt contact** Dave Hughes
**Phone** 01625 873120

*1st Friday, 8.30pm. National/ international guests plus residents the Sad Pig Band. Contemporary folk.*

## Prospect Folk Club
Prospect Inn, Weston Road, Weston Village, RUNCORN, Cheshire
**Contact** Roger Hanslip
**Address** 14 School Lane, FRODSHAM, Cheshire, WA6 6AF
**Phone** 01928 731567

*Monday, 8.30pm. Traditional & contemporary folk music. Singers' nights with monthly guests.*

## Railway Folk Club
The Railway Hotel, Mill Lane, Heatley, LYMM, Cheshire
**Contact** Don Davies
**Phone** 0161 432 4317
**Web** www.railwayfolkclub.co.uk

*Thursday, 8.30pm. Alternate singers' and guests' nights. All types of music and poetry welcome.*

## The Roadhouse
8 Newton Street, Piccadilly, MANCHESTER, M1 2AN
**Phone** 0161 237 9789
**Contact** Natasha Young
**Email** live@theroadhouse.u-net.com
**Web** www.theroadhouse.u-net.com

*Central Manchester live music venue. 250 capacity. Predominatly Indie & Rock, but all styles considered. Alternate Sundays; singer/ songwriter night.*

## SAFRA
Masonic Lodge, UPPERMILL, Yorks
**Contact** Alison O'Brian or Jeff Miller
**Phone** 01457 870391

*2nd Friday, 8.30 pm. Singaround.*

## Sandbach Ceilidhs
Sandbach High School, Middlewich Road, SANDBACH, Cheshire
**Phone** 01270 765376
**Phone** 01270 766975

*Saturday, 8pm. 3 a year (Jan, April, Oct). Ceilidhs with top national bands, run for the whole family by non-profit community organisation.*

## Shroppie Fly Session
The Shroppie Fly, Audlem Wharf, Shropshire Street, AUDLEM, Cheshire
**Contact** Pete Hall
**Phone** 01630 661429

*4th Tuesday, 9pm-ish. Irish traditional music session.*

## St Annes Acoustic Roots Club
Kitty's Bar, The Bedford Hotel, 307-311 Clifton Drive South, ST ANNES ON SEA, Lancs FY8 1JE
**Contact** Sue Arrow & John Gibney
**Address** 61 Lightburn Avenue, ST ANNES, Lancs, FY8 1JE
**Phone** 01253 721503
**Email** susanna_arrow@hotmail.com
**Email** jtgibney@hotmail.com

*Tuesday, 8.30pm. Open session/ singaround with monthly guest artist and occasional workshops.*

## St Helens Folk Dance Club
**Contact** Ron Kells - Secretary
**Address** 49 St Georges Way, ST HELENS, Merseyside, WA10 4JX
**Phone** 01744 754810
**Alt contact** Keith Lyon - Tresurer
**Alt Address** 208 Woodlands Road, ST HELENS, Merseyside, WA11 9EB
**Phone** 01744 730066

*Wednesday. English country dancing. Annual dance with live music.*



**The English Regions**
*These are based on Regional Arts Board representation with some variation. We have kept all of Derbyshire and Lincolnshire in the East Midlands. The RAB definitions are used here as a generally helpful way of splitting up England for a more detailed look at local resources. Also check sections for neighbouring regions for the band, caller or venue you are looking for. Contributors and magazine listings often mention venues and services based in adjacent regions*

north west

venues

**The English Regions**

*These are based on Regional Arts Board representation with some variation. We have kept all of Derbyshire and Lincolnshire in the East Midlands. The RAB definitions are used here as a generally helpful way of splitting up England for a more detailed look at local resources. Also check sections for neighbouring regions for the band, caller or venue you are looking for. Contributors and magazine listings often mention venues and services based in adjacent regions.*

### Station Buffet Bar Folk Club
The Station Buffet Bar, The Railway Station, STALYBRIDGE, Greater Manchester
**Contact** Jim Schofield
**Address** 4 Ash Hill Drive, Mossley, ASHTON UNDER LYME, OL5 9PW
**Phone** 01457 833897
*Saturday, 9pm. Singers & guests, no charge.*

### Stockton Heath Country Dance Club
St Thomas's School, Parkgate Road, Stockton Heath, WARRINGTON, Cheshire
**Contact** Keith Williams
**Address** 8 Cloverfield, Norton Cross, RUNCORN, Cheshire, WA7 6SN
**Phone** 01928 713180
*Monday, 8-10pm*

### Sun Inn Folk Club
The Sun Inn, Old Mill Lane, MACCLESFIELD, Cheshire
**Contact** Tim Woodhouse
**Address** 9 Ryle Street, MACCLESFIELD, Cheshire, SK11 8BQ
**Phone** 01625 502749

### Triton Folk Club
Aigburth People's Hall, Aigburth, LIVERPOOL, Merseyside
**Phone** 0151 727 3357
**Contact** Barry Meyer
**Phone** 0151 7334159
*Monday, 8.30pm. Wide ranging song, poetry & music club. Mainly traditional folk, all welcome.*

### Tuesday Unplugged at Alexanders
Alexanders Jazz Theatre, Rufus Court, Northgate Street, CHESTER, CH1 2JW
**Contact** Graham Bellinger
**Address** 9 Ivy Mews, Hoole, CHESTER, CH2 3SA
**Phone** 01244 403782
**Email** bellinger@netlocal.co.uk
**Web** www.alexandersjazz.com
**Alt contact** Mick Green
**Alt Address** Primrose Cottage, Chester Road, Kelsall, CHESTER, CW6 0SJ
**Phone** 01829 752461
*Tuesday, open mike club night run by local folk & acoustic musicians for singing, playing and listening.*

### Walton Folk Club
County Ward Labour Club, 39 Hale Road, Walton, LIVERPOOL L4 3RS
**Contact** Lillian French
**Address** 42A Abingdon Grove, LIVERPOOL, L4 9XB
**Phone** 0151 474 0979
**Alt contact** Andrew Hesford Booth
**Address** 3 Geneva Road, Elm Park, LIVERPOOL, L6 3AS
**Phone** 0151 260 0536
**Email** Andrew.Hesfordbooth@btinternet.co.uk
*Friday, 8.30pm. Mainly acoustic folk, countrry & bluegrass. Musicians and singers. Sunday, 8.45pm as above plus Irish music.*

### Westhoughton Folk Club
Westhoughton Golf Club, Long Island, WESTHOUGHTON, Lancs
**Contact** Pat Batty
**Address** 332 Wigan Road, WESTHOUGHTON, Bolton, Lancs, BL5 2AR
**Phone** 01942 812301
**Email** wfc@folkclub.org.uk
**Web** www.folkclub.org.uk
**Alt contact** Ian Austen
**Address** 21 Dobb Brow, WESTHOUGHTON, Bolton, Lancs, BL5 2AY
**Phone** 01942 816531
07989 404802
**Email** ian@ianausten.net
*Friday, 8.15pm. Guests. Song club for all types of music. Sept to April.*

### The Witchwood
152 Old Street, ASHTON-UNDER-LYME, Lancs, OL6 7SF
**Phone** 0161 330 5028
0161 344 0321
**Contact** Pod
**Email** pod@arcmusic.freeserve.co.uk
**Web** www.witchwood-live.com
*200 capacity venue with broad booking policy.*

## The North West Folk Federation Folk Clubs

### Accrington Town Hall
7.30pm Sunday
Blackburn Road, Accrington
**Phone** 01254 380293 Box Office

### Albion
8.30pm Sunday
Albion Hotel, Albion Street, New Brighton
**Contact** Roger Parker
**Phone** 0151 638 1987

### Beer Engine
8.30pm Sunday
The Beer Engine, Poolstock Lane, Wigan
**Contact** Lawrence Hoy
**Phone** 01942 709 736

### Bothy
8.00pm Sunday
Blundell Arms, Upper Aughton Road, Birkdale, Southport
**Contact** Clive Pownceby
**Phone** 0151 924 5078

### Walton
8.45pm Sunday
**Contact** County Ward Labour Club, 39 Hale Road, Walton, Liverpool
**Contact** Lilian French
**Phone** 0151 474 0979

### Wooden Horse
8.30pm Sunday
The Junction, News Lane, Rainford
**Contact** Jim Coan
**Phone** 01772 452782

### Bridge
8.30pm Monday
The Bridge Inn, Georges Road, Stockport
**Contact** Peter Hood
**Phone** 0161 432 4142

### Broken Token
8.15pm Monday
The Globe Inn, High Street, Standish
**Contact** Ken & Angie Bladen
**Phone** 01257 263678

### Conwy
8.30pm Monday
The Malt Loaf, Rosehill Street, Conwy
**Contact** Denis Bennett
**Phone** 01492 877324

### Prospect
8.30pm Monday
The Prospect Inn, Weston Road, Weston Village, Runcorn
**Contact** Roger Hanslip
**Phone** 01928 731567

### Swinton
8.30pm Monday
The White Lion, 242 Manchester Road, Swinton
**Contact** Ged Todd
**Phone** 01942 811527

**The Shippons**
9.00pm Monday
The Shippons Inn, Irby Village, Wirral
**Contact** Alison Parker
**Phone** 0151 648 4444

**Triton**
8.30pm Monday
Aigburth Peoples Hall, Aigburth Vale, Liverpool
**Contact** Barry Meyer
**Phone** 0151 7334159

**Verse & Worse**
8.30pm Monday
Silverwell, Darlington Street East, Wigan
**Contact** Sheila Mellor-Bames
**Phone** 01942 741 220

**Folk at The Inn on the Park**
8.30pm Tuesday
The Inn on the Park, Astley Village, Chorley
**Contact** Steve Clifford
**Phone** 01257 268116

**Furness**
8.30pm Tuesday
The Cavendish Arms, Market Street, Dalton-in-Furness, Cumbria
**Contact** Graham Atkinson
**Phone** 01229 832354

**Howcroft Inn**
8.30pm Tuesday
The Howcroft Inn, 36 Pool Street, Bolton
**Contact** Ron Callow
**Phone** 01204 381956

**Jacqui's Folk Club**
8.30pm Tuesday
Sefton Park Cricket Club, Croxteth Drive (Sefton Park), Liverpool
**Contact** Jacqui McDonald
**Phone** 01244 300 576

**Johnson's Acoustic Circus**
7.00pm Tuesday
Red Triangle Boxing Club, Everton Road, Liverpool
**Contact** Roy Johnson
**Phone** 0151 286 2974

**Liverpool**
8.30pm Tuesday
The Ship & Mitre, Dale Street, Liverpool
**Contact** Helen Hebden
**Phone** 0151 727 0088

**Maghull**
8.30pm Tuesday
Hare & Hounds, Liverpool Road North, Maghull
**Contact** Tony Gibbons
**Phone** 01695 424327

**Ring 'O' Bells**
8.30pm Tuesday
Ring 'O' Bells, Farnworth Street, Widnes, Cheshire
**Contact** Iris Bickerstaffe
**Phone** 0151 424 7072

**Urmston Acoustics**
8.30pm Tuesday
The Nag's Head, Davyhulme Circle, Urmston
**Contact** Martin Kavanagh
**Phone** 0161 748 5497

**Wigan (Royal Oak)**
9.00pm Tuesday
Royal Oak, Wigan Lane, Wigan
**Contact** Joan Blackburn
**Phone** 01942 321 223

**Alison Arms**
8.30pm Wednesday
The Alison Arms, Preston Road, Coppull Moor, Nr Chorley
**Contact** Hilda Foy
**Phone** 01257 792 246

**Blackburn**
8.30pm Wednesday
Fleece Inn, Penny Street, Blackburn
**Contact** Brian Kirkham
**Phone** 01254 720 745

**Burnley**
8.30pm Wednesday
Waggon & Horses Inn, Colne Road, Brierfield
**Contact** Phyl Watson
**Phone** 01282 774 077

**Castle**
8.30pm Wednesday
Castle Hotel, Halton Village, Runcorn
**Contact** Bob O'Callaghan
**Phone** 0151 424 5367

**Deeside**
8.30pm Wednesday
The Jug and Bottle, Mount Avenue, Heswall, Wirral
**Contact** Alison Parker
**Phone** 0151 648 4444

**Hole in One**
8.30pm Wednesday
Hole in One, Forest Drive, South Park, Lytham, FY8 4QF
**Contact** Ann Green
**Phone** 01772 683027

**Jacqui's British Legion Club**
8.30pm Wednesday
British Legion, Heath Road, Upton-by-Chester
**Contact** Jacqui McDonald
**Phone** 01244 300 576

**St Annes Acoustic Roots Club**
8.30pm Wednesday
The Bedford Hotel, Clifton Drive South, St Annes on Sea
**Contact** Sue Arrow
**Phone** 01253 721 503

**The Falcon**
9.00pm Wednesday
The Falcon Hotel, Hardhom Way, Poulton-le-Fylde
**Contact** Pete Skinner
**Phone** 01253 301 483

**The Kings Arms**
8.30pm Wednesday
The Kings Arms, Delph Lane, Haskayne
**Contact** Sue Howard
**Phone** 0151 526 9927

**The Red Bull**
8.30pm Wednesday
The Red Bull, Hillgate, Stockport
**Contact** Peter Hood
**Phone** 0161 432 4142

**Biddulph**
8.15pm Thursday
The Biddulph Arms, Congleton Road, Biddulph, Stoke-on-Trent
**Contact** Eric Cox
**Phone** 01782 514 896

**Fleetwood**
8.30pm Thursday
Steamer Hotel, Queens Terrace, Fleetwood
**Contact** Dave Ryan
**Phone** 01253 876351

**Gregson Lane**
8.30pm Thursday
Gregson Lane Sports & Social Club, Gregson Lane, Hoghton
**Contact** Graham Dixon
**Phone** 01254 853 929

**Parkgate**
8.15pm Thursday
The Boathouse, 1 The Parade, Parkgate, Wirral
**Contact** Eddie Morris
**Phone** 0151 677 1840

**Railway**
8.30pm Thursday
Railway Hotel, Heatley, Lymm
**Contact** Don Davies
**Phone** 0161 432 4317



**The English Regions**
*These are based on Regional Arts Board representation with some variation. We have kept all of Derbyshire and Lincolnshire in the East Midlands. The RAB definitions are used here as a generally helpful way of splitting up England for a more detailed look at local resources. Also check sections for neighbouring regions for the band caller or venue you are looking for. Contributors and magazine listings often mention venues and services based in adjacent regions*

## north west venues

**The English Regions**
*These are based on Regional Arts Board representation with some variation. We have kept all of Derbyshire and Lincolnshire in the East Midlands. The RAB definitions are used here as a generally helpful way of splitting up England for a more detailed look at local resources. Also check sections for neighbouring regions for the band, caller or venue you are looking for. Contributors and magazine listings often mention venues and services based in adjacent regions.*

### Ruthin Acoustic Music
8.30pm Thursday
Castle Hotel, St Peter's Square, Ruthin, Denbighshire
**Contact** Campbell Finney
**Phone** 01824 750730

### The Greyhound
8.30pm Thursday
The Greyhound, Bodwen Street, Off King Street, Edgeley, Stockport
**Contact** Kieron & Mary Hartley
**Phone** 0161 480 4993

### Wigan (7 Stars)
9.00pm Thursday
Seven Stars Hotel, Seven Stars Bridge, Walgate, Wigan
**Contact** Joan Blackburn
**Phone** 01942 321223

### Wrexham Folk & Acoustic
8.30pm Thursday
Nags Head Inn, Mount Street, Wrexham
**Contact** Ian Chesterman
**Phone** 01978 357 307

### Bollington
8.30pm Friday
Dog & Partridge, Palmerston Street, Bollington, Nr Macclesfield
**Contact** Arthur Wakefield
**Phone** 01625 573 596

### Carlisle Folk & Blues
8.00pm Friday
The Coach House, Heads Nook, Carlisle
**Contact** Ken & Sue Bradburn
**Phone** 01228 670 580

### Hale & Hearty
8.00pm Friday
The Kings Arms, Hale, Cumbria
**Contact** Frank Lewis
**Phone** 01524 734 440

### Northwich
8.30pm Friday
Harlequin Theatre, Queen Street, Northwich
**Contact** John Booth
**Phone** 01606 793 56

### Porkies
8.30pm Friday
Royal British Legion, Georges Road, Poynton
**Contact** Judy Hancock
**Phone** 01260 252 633

### Preston
8.30pm Friday
Moorbrook Inn, North Road, Preston
**Contact** Rob Malaney
**Phone** 01257 231 463

### Rhyl
8.30pm Friday
Costigan's Pub, Bodfor Street, Rhyl
**Contact** Darryl Moorley
**Phone** 01745 353 859

### The Big Sing (SAFRA)
8.30pm Friday
Safra Club, Masonic Lodge, High Street, Uppermill, Saddleworth
**Contact** Ali O'Brien
**Phone** 01457 870 391

### Walton
8.30pm Friday
County Ward labour Club, 39 Hale Road, Walton, Liverpool
**Contact** Lilian French
**Phone** 0151 474 0979

### Westhoughton
8.15pm Friday
Westhoughton Golf Club, Long Island, Westhoughton
**Contact** Pat Batty
**Phone** 01942 812 301

### Brewery Arts
8.30pm Saturday
Brewery Arts Centre, 122a Highgate, Kendal
**Contact** Box Office
**Phone** 01539 725 133

### Citadel Arts Centre
8.30pm Saturday
Waterloo Street, St Helens, WA10 1PX
**Contact** Box Office
**Phone** 01744 735 436

### Hazel Pear
8.30pm Saturday
Hazel Pear Inn, Hill Top Road, Acton bridge, Nr Northwich
**Contact** Mike Price
**Phone** 01606 854 871

### Mr Kite Benefits
8.00pm Saturday
Worden Arts Centre, Worden Park, Leyland
**Contact** Steve Henderson
**Phone** 01772 621411

### Oswaldtwistle
8.30pm Saturday
St Mary's Parish Centre, Lock Street, Oswaldtwistle
**Contact** Dylan Owen
**Phone** 01254 390 391

### Playhouse 2
8.30pm Saturday
Newtown Street, Shaw, Oldham
**Contact** Barrie Cottam
**Phone** 01706 847 494

### Standish
8.15pm Saturday
St Wilfrid's Parish Centre, Standish, Nr. Wigan
**Contact** David Jones
**Phone** 01254 54877

### The Platform
8.00pm Saturday
The Platform, Station Buildings, Central Promenade, Morecambe
**Contact** Box Office
**Phone** 01524 582 803

- ***Reproduced by kind permission of Folk North West***

# Southern

**Berkshire, Buckinghamshire, Hampshire, Oxfordshire, Wiltshire, Bournemouth, Bracknell Forest, Isle of Wight, Milton Keynes, Poole, Portsmouth, Reading, Slough, Southampton, Swindon, West Berkshire, Windsor and Maidenhead**

## Organisations

**Southern Arts**
**Mail address** 13 Clement Street, Winchester, SO23 9DQ
**Phone** 01962 855099
**Fax** 01962 861186
**Web** www.arts.org.uk/directory/regions/southern/index.html

**Traditional Arts Projects TAPS**
Traditional Arts Projects is in its tenth year of operation as an independent company, core funded by Southern Arts, Hampshire County Council, Lloyds TSB and Test Valley Borough Council. Oxfordshire County Council Music Services also provide funding for extensive education work.

TAPS has worked in all parts of the Southern Arts Region, from Milton Keynes to the Isle of Wight and from Slough to Bradford-on-Avon. Projects have also been carried out in other regions and TAPS' touring bands have worked all over England, including Festival appearances at Sidmouth and Towersey. Links have also been established with Chile, Norway, France, India and the Gambia.

The main points of TAPS's artistic policy are as follows:

- Tradition does not only concern the past; we strive for continuity, rather than stasis; the evolutionary process of tradition is equal in importance to the material.
- The participatory nature of the traditional arts makes them an ideal vehicle for community and education work and makes community and education work a vital part of their development.
- Our work strives to be inter-cultural, with the traditional arts of England playing a major role in all collaborations.

From initial beginnings as a one-person operation, TAPS now employs four permanent staff and also has an African musician-in-residence; Musa Mboob, for 2001 - 2002.

Artists are booked to staff individual projects. These are mainly musicians, singers and dancers, but also include storytellers and circus-skills workers. Projects range from a short workshop session, using one artist, to complex programmes of workshop and performance, involving several professional artists and numbers of community volunteers and/or students. Clients include local authorities, community groups, regional, national and international organisations and schools, colleges and universities

Projects are funded from a number of sources and we work with clients, where necessary, to help identify possible funding sources. The organisation does not hold a reserve of project funding: core funding is less than core expenditure and an administrative charge is added to the costs of artists, venues, materials and other project expenditure. Project funding has been received in the past from the Arts Council of England, the Calouste Gulbenkian Foundation, Royal Mail and other trusts and sponsors, as well as local authorities.

**Roger Watson** is the Artistic Director. Founder of the organisation in 1989, he devises and leads many of the projects.
**Mail address** TAPS, The Heritage Site The Fairground, Weyhill, Andover Hants, SP10 0QN
**Phone** 01753 858577 (Artistic Director)
**Phone** 01264 773317 01264 772570 (Admin/ Finance)
**Phone** 01865 712134 (Education and Training)
**Fax** 0870 734 6005 (All Departments)
**Email** taps@dmac.co.uk
**Web** www.tradarts.co.uk

TAPS' partners in projects in the Southern Region have included the Southern Counties Folk Federation, Wiltshire Music Centre, The Anvil (Basingstoke), Asian Arts Access, and, on a national basis, the African & Caribbean Music Circuit and the Asian Music Circuit. TAPS is a member of the Folk Arts Network, the European Network of Traditional Music and Dance, Sound Sense and the Southern Counties Folk Federation.

**Southern Counties Folk Federation (SCoFF)** is a loose confederation of Folk Clubs, several Arts Centres and other bodies with an interest in promoting Folk and related acoustic music in the Southern Counties. The Federation is in effect a talking shop where members may not only sort out any problems and possible clashes of interest but also agree to back co-operative ventures like Festivals, Awards and Recordings which would be difficult for any one member to organise or fund. The Federation is happy to co-operate with and support any Folk projects in the area, either formally through the Committee or informally through the participation of members. The Federation also offers insurance cover to paid up members for Folk events and has a high-quality financially and editorially independent quarterly magazine Folk on Tap. See above.

The Federation covers most of Southern England, ranging east/west from East Sussex/Kent to Somerset and north/south from Bucks/Oxon/Berks to the Channel Islands; including Dorset, Hampshire, Sussex, Wiltshire and Surrey.
ScoFF has a list of members at *www.freenetpages.co.uk/hp/trg/ScoFF/members.htm*

**Trevor Gilson** of SCoFF has assembled a Southern Counties Folk Artistes database at *www.freenetpages.co.uk/hp/trg/ScoFF/artistes.htm* with a separate section for bands.

Trevor's Web Art pages *www.freenetpages.co.uk/hp/trg* include Viewpoint Arts Online with comprehensive Arts index for the Southampton area, **Fo'c'sle Folk Club**, **SCoFF**, **Solent Waves** (see below), **M27 Megabops Barn dances**, and more.

## Magazines and websites

### Folk On Tap

**Folk on Tap** is the leading quarterly folk music magazine of the South of England. The magazine was established in 1979, and is now in its 22nd year. It is published four times a year on 1st January, 1st April, 1st July and 1st October.

- features on local, national and international artistes
- articles on topical and other interesting issues
- sections on blues, world music and other genres
- regular columns written by national artistes
- reviews and previews of festivals and live gigs
- an artiste's tour guide
- diary listings of venues in the South

## southern region

Listed ceilidh and social dance bands in the Southern region include **Aces High**, **Asha**, **Atlantic Bridge**, **Banish Misfortune**, **Belshazzar's Feast**, **Boka Halat**, **Bon Accord Ceilidh Band**, **Boreen**, **Contradition**, **Dr Faustus**, **Florida**, **Geckoes**, **Grumbling Old Men**, **Hurry The Jug**, **Jenny's Chickens**, **Muscadin**, **Quicksilver**, **Rampageri**, **Random**, **Square Root Folk Dance Band**, **Stars & Bars**, **The Cock & Bull Band**, **The Gaberlunzies**, **The Kitchen Girls**, **The Mellstock Band**, **Wheelwrights Band**, **White Horse Band** and **The Woodpecker Band**.

Listed dance callers include **Andy Stafford**, **Bob Adams**, **Dave Townsend**, **Henry Garfath**, **Mic Spenceley**, **Michael Barraclough** and **Nigel Close**.

***See SCoFF band listings on this page.***

**The English Regions**
*These are based on Regional Arts Board representation with some variation. We have kept all of Derbyshire and Lincolnshire in the East Midlands. The RAB definitions are used here as a generally helpful way of splitting up England for a more detailed look at local resources. Also check sections for neighbouring regions for the band, caller or venue you are looking for. Contributors and magazine listings often mention venues and services based in adjacent regions.*

# southern region

**The English Regions**

*These are based on Regional Arts Board representation with some variation. We have kept all of Derbyshire and Lincolnshire in the East Midlands. The RAB definitions are used here as a generally helpful way of splitting up England for a more detailed look at local resources. Also check sections for neighbouring regions for the band, caller or venue you are looking for. Contributors and magazine listings often mention venues and services based in adjacent regions.*

- reviews of the latest album releases

The magazine is on sale in various venues in 14 counties in the south of England from Cornwall (W) to Kent (E) and from Buckinghamshire (N) to the Channel Isles (S), and by annual subscription (we have nationwide subscribers). For a free introductory copy of a recent back-issue, send a C4 size s.a.e stamped for 350gm (currently 87p).

Cover price for single issue £2.40 Annual subscription (4 issues inc. p&p) £9.50

**Contact** Sam Satyanadhan (Editor)
**Mail address** 3 Cranbury Road, Woolston, Southampton, Hants. SO19 2HZ
**Phone** 023 8057 0082
**Fax** 023 8043 7150
**Email** editor@folkontap.co.uk
**Web** www.folkontap.co.uk (under construction at present)

**Shirefolk** is a regional folk magazine covering the South East Midlands. It carries information on Oxfordshire, Buckinghamshire, Berkshire and neighbouring counties. Diary listings, Sessions, Dance Directory of local Display teams and News and Reviews.

**Contact** Chris Mills (Editor)
**Mail address** 5 Gladstone Road, Headington, Oxford, OX3 8LL
**Phone** 01865 769366
**Email** millses@btinternet.com

**Solent Waves** is the Newsletter of the Folk Association of South Hants, carrying listings of events at folk clubs, arts centres, dance clubs and contact numbers for local dance display teams.

The articles, club lists and event diaries can be found at www.freenetpages.co.uk/hp/trg/sw

**Contact** David Roberts (Editor)
**Mail address** 'Symposia', Bishops Sutton, Alresford, SO24 0AL
**Phone** 01962 735202
**Email** sw@symposia.freeserve.co.uk

## Venues

There are significant venues promoting folk & roots events in most of the major Southern towns.

The **Talking Heads**, Southampton is home of the **Southampton Celtic Music Club** and much Folk/ Roots music. **The Gantry Arts Centre** is an important venue while the **Fo'c'sle Folk Club** promotes concerts every Friday. In Fareham both the **Ashcroft Arts Centre** and **Cabaret Caff** (Ferneham Hall) host folk acts. **The Tower Arts Centre**, Winchester hosts many major groups as does **The Anvil**, Basingstoke. The **F Word Acoustic Club**, at the **Soul Café** in Maidenhead is a new venture with top folk & roots acts. In Reading, **21 South Street Arts Centre** has folk & roots concerts. **The Mill** at Banbury has a folk series and both **Forest Arts**, New Milton, Hants and **West End Centre** Aldershot are relevant venues.

There are 3 major ceilidh series: **Haddenham Ceilidhs**, Bucks, **M27 Megabops**, Southampton and **Oxfolk ceilidhs**, Oxford. In addition the regular series **Reeling** in Ealing and Godalming's **eCeilidh** are near the area.

## Festivals

The South hosts a diverse variety of festivals. Main events include **Gosport & Fareham Easter Festival**, featuring many top Celtic music acts. **WOMAD** is a massive roots and world music festival based in Reading in mid July. Major folk festivals in the region include **Chippenham**, Wilts (late May bank holiday) and **Towersey**, Oxon (August bank holiday). **Cropredy Festival** in July features **Fairport Convention** and their guests, **Trowbridge Village Pump Festival** has a diverse music policy and is also mid July. There are many other festivals incl;uding Banbury's **Folk 'n' Good Music Day** (October) and a large number of Morris dance events, most notably the festivities at Bampton, Oxon on Whit Monday (see the customs section for more details). Folk music courses include Dave Townsend's popular **Hands On Music Weekends in Witney**. See festival listings.

*Thanks to Folk On Tap, SCoFF, Peter Chegwyn, Trevor Gilson and mARKO pOLO for the above information*

## Rooting around the South

### Organisations/Listings etc.

**www.biclab.co.uk/efdbucks/Bucks**
*District EFDSS*

**users.comlab.ox.ac.uk/ian.page/music/folk.html**
*Listings in and Around Oxford*

**www.freenetpages.co.uk/hp/trg/SCoFF**
*Southern Counties Folk Federation*

**www.southfolkmusicnetwork.bigstep.com**
*South Folk Music Network*

**www.freenetpages.co.uk/hp/trg/sw**
*Solent Waves, South Hants*

### Clubs etc.

**www.csclarke.clara.net/fleet**
*Fleet Folk and Good Music Club*

**hambledon.parish.hants.gov.uk/spotfolk.htm**
*Hambledon Folk Club*

**www.dorl.freeserve.co.uk/wycombefolkclub.htm**
*High Wycombe, Wycombe Folk Club*

**www.redadmiral.freeserve.co.uk**
*Maidenhead Folk Club (Cookham)*

**www.nettlebed.freeserve.co.uk**
*Nettlebed Folk Club*

**ourworld.compuserve.com/homepages/rmb/homepage.htm**
*Newport (Isle of Wight), Live Music Club*

**members.aol.com/OxfordFolkClub**
*Oxford Folk Club*

**www.freenetpages.co.uk/hp/trg/focsle**
*Southampton, Fo'c'sle Folk Club*

**www.folkmania.org.uk/StDenysClub.htm**
*Southampton, St Denys Folk and Blues Club*

**www.users.waitrose.com/~pjntrish/railway-folk-club.doc-(2)/odyframe.htm**
*Southsea, Railway Folk Club*

**www.tudorfolkclub.org.uk**
*Chesham, Tudor Folk Club*

### 101 Club
The Song Loft, Cock Hotel, Stony Stratford, MILTON KEYNES
**Contact** Matt Armour
**Phone** 01908 566407
*Alternate Fridays, 8.30pm. All music types.*

### 21 South Street Arts Centre
21 South Street, READING, RG1 4QR
**Contact** Matthew Linley
**Phone** 0118 9015234
**Fax** 0118 9015235
**Email** matthew.linley@reading.gov.uk
**Web** www.readingarts.gov
*Arts centre with folk & traditional music programme.*

### Alton Community Chior
Quaker Meeting House, ALTON, Hants.
**Contact** Carolyn Robson
**Phone** 01252 722938
**Email** carolyn.robson@virgin.net
*Thursdays 8-9.30pm. All welcome.*

### The Anvil
Churchill Way, BASINGSTOKE, Hants, RG21 7QR
**Contact** Ann Dickson - Programme Manager
**Phone** 01256 819797
**Fax** 01256 331733
**Email** ann.dickson@theanvil.org.uk
**Web** www.theanvil.org
**Alt contact** Matthew Cleaver - Marketing Director
*Major music venue with up to 1400 seats and good acoustics. Regular Sunday lunchtime folk/ roots gigs in the foyer (150 capacity).*

### Ashcroft Arts Centre
Osborn Road, FAREHAM, Hants, PO16 7DX
**Contact** Genevieve Wilk
**Phone** 01329 235161
**Fax** 01329 825661
**Email** asharts@globalnet.co.uk
**Web** www.users.globalnet.co.uk/~asharts/ashcroft.htm
**Alt contact** Steve Rowley
*Varied programme of music, including folk & roots series, plus theatre, comedy, film, etc. 120-150 capacity, theatre & studio/ bar.*

### The Bowl
Quarry Road, Old Town, SWINDON, Wilts
**Contact** Tony Rathbone
**Address** Premier House, Station Road, SWINDON, SN1 1TZ
**Phone** 01793 466522
**Fax** 01793 466484
**Email** trathbone@swindon.gov.uk
**Web** www.swindon.gov.uk
*Saturdays in June & July. Ticketed world music concerts at 850 capacity outdoor venue. Salsa, African, Cajun and Afro-Caribbean events.*

### Cosgrove Fiddles
Cosgrove Village Hall, MILTON KEYNES, Bucks
**Contact** Jenny Newman
**Address** 17 Bridge Road, Cosgrove, MILTON KEYNES, Bucks, MK19 7JH
**Phone/Fax** 01908 262098
**Phone** 07961 983483
**Email** new.glass@virgin.net
**Web** www.jennynewman.com
*Sundays monthly, 11-4pm. Workshops on various styles & aspects of traditional fiddle playing. Weekly courses & private tuition available.*

### Daisy Roots Music Club
The Blue Boar Inn, Market Close, POOLE, Dorset
**Contact** Paul Burke
**Address** The Jays, Horton Road, RINGWOOD, Hants, BH24 2EJ
**Email** paulburke@cwcom.net
*Local performers club.*

### Durley Outlaws
Memorial Hall, Durley Brook Road, DURLEY, Hants
**Contact** ABDC Entertainments
**Address** La Loma, 18 Halls Farm Close, WINCHESTER, Hants, SO22 6RE
**Phone** 01962 885628
0709 2035070
**Fax** 0845 3344981
**Email** anyact@abdc.co.uk
**Web** www.abdc.freeserve.co.uk/dancer.html
*Monday morning & alternate Thursday evenings. Western line dance club.*

### Fleet Folk Club
The Fox & Hounds, Crookham Road, FLEET, Hants, GU13 0NP
**Contact** Chris Clarke
**Address** 21 Lancaster House, South Lynn Crescent, BRACKNELL, Berks, RG12 7JY
**Phone** 01344 440401, 01344 855610
**Email** fleet@csclarke.clara.net
**Web** www.csclarke.clara.net/fleet
**Alt contact** Caroline Neuberg
**Address** 5 Vivian Close, Church Crookham, FLEET, Hants, GU52 6AJ
**Phone** 01252 614866
*Tuesday, 8.30pm. Alternate guest and singers nights. Traditional and contemporary folk. 50 capacity.*

### Fo'c'sle Folk Club
The Duke of Wellington, Bugle Street, SOUTHAMPTON
**Contact** Trevor Gilson & Jane Allison
**Address** 3 Manchester Road, Netley Abbey, SOUTHAMPTON, SO31 5DB
**Phone** 023 8045 6337
**Email** trg@freenet.co.uk
**Web** http://scoff.welcome.to/focsle
*Friday, 8pm. Folk club and concert promotions.*

### Folk Workshop
The Vaults Bar, The Bull Hotel, High St, Stoney Stratford, MILTON KEYNES
**Contact** Matt Armour
**Address** 99 Mallets Close, Stony Stratford, MILTON KEYNES, MK11 1DG
**Phone** 01908 566407
*Sundays, 12.30pm. Song & tune swap/ singaround.*

### Forest Arts
Old Milton Road, NEW MILTON, Hants, BH25 6DS
**Phone** 01425 612393
*Arts centre promoting, folk, roots, jazz and world music.*

### The Gantry - Southampton Arts Centre
Off Blechynden Terrace, SOUTHAMPTON, SO15 1GW
**Phone** 023 8022 9319 - box office
**Email** boxoffice@gantry.org.uk
**Web** www.gantry.org.uk
Major arts venue also promoting regular world, roots & folk concerts.



**The English Regions**
*These are based on Regional Arts Board representation with some variation. We have kept all of Derbyshire and Lincolnshire in the East Midlands. The RAB definitions are used here as a generally helpful way of splitting up England for a more detailed look at local resources. Also check sections for neighbouring regions for the band, caller or venue you are looking for. Contributors and magazine listings often mention venues and services based in adjacent regions.*

**The English Regions**
*These are based on Regional Arts Board representation with some variation. We have kept all of Derbyshire and Lincolnshire in the East Midlands. The RAB definitions are used here as a generally helpful way of splitting up England for a more detailed look at local resources. Also check sections for neighbouring regions for the band, caller or venue you are looking for. Contributors and magazine listings often mention venues and services based in adjacent regions.*

## Haddenham Ceilidhs
Haddenham Village Hall
Haddenham, AYLESBURY, Bucks
**Contact** John Heydon
**Address** 3/5 Church Street, AYLESBURY, Bucks, HP20 2QP
**Phone** 01296 415333
**Fax** 01296 397092
**Email** Johnh@fosterwiggins.co.uk
**Web** www.haddenhamceilidhs.co.uk
*First Saturday, 8pm. Monthly ceilidhs October to June.*

## Hale Music Club
Hale Village Hall, HALE, Hants
**Contact** Roy Watts
**Phone** 01725 510718
*Various local music/ dance groups: Wednesday 7.30pm, Clog Stepping; Thursday 7.30pm, Choir; Sunday 3pm, Barn Dance Band; Sunday 5pm Classical Ensemble.*

## Hambledon Folk Club
Youth Club, The Vine, West Street, HAMBLEDON
**Contact** Steve Harrison
**Address** White Gables, East Street, HAMBLEDON, Hants, PO7 4RX
**Phone** 023 9263 2812
*2nd Wednesday, 8pm. Mainly acoustic traditional, other music welcome.*

## Limelight
Limelight Theatre, Queen's Park Arts Centre, Queen's Park, AYLESBURY, Bucks, HP21 7RT
**Phone** 01296 424332
**Contact** Amanda Eels
**Phone** 01296 431272
*1st Saturday, 8pm. Open mic. 120 capacity theatre venue for hire or box office spilt. Disabled access & rehearsal space. Policy: affordable, accessible music, theatre, dance for the local community.*

## M27 Megabops
The Eastpoint Centre, Burgoyne Road, SOUTHAMPTON, **Contact** John Connell - tickets
**Phone** 01489 690233
**Email** johncon@briony99.freeserve.co.uk
**Web** www.freenetpages.co.uk/hp/trg/megabops/
**Alt contact** Gill Redmond & Pete Gritton -info
**Phone** 01425 476350
*Monthly Saturday ceilidhs with national and local bands.*

## Maidenhead Folk Club
The Ferry, Sutton Road, COOKHAM, Berks
**Contact** Tony & Pearl O'Neill
**Address** 31 Comet Way, Woodley, READING, RG5 4NZ
**Phone** 0118 9448269
**Email** tonyandpearl@redadmiral.freeserve.co.uk
**Web** www.redadmiral.freeserve.co.uk
*Thursday 8.15pm. Mostly traditional. 30-40 capacity, disabled facilities.*

## Mill Arms Skittle Alley Folk Club
The Mill Arms, DUNBRIDGE, Hants
**Phone** 01794 340401
*1st Thursday,8pm. Traditional folk music; musicians & singers welcome.*

## The Mill Arts Centre
Spiceball Park, BANBURY, Oxon, OX16 8QE
**Phone** 01295 252050
**Contact** Deborah Clarke
**Alt contact** John Dickie
*Venue programming folk, acoustic, world, blues, pop and rock music.*

## Nettlebed Folk Song Club
The Village Club, High Street, Nettlebed, NR HENLEY-ON-THAMES, Oxon, RG9 5DD
**Contact** The Secretary - NFC
**Address** 3 Arlington Close, MAIDENHEAD, Berks, SL8 5JT
**Phone** 01628 636620 - Not before 10am/ after 9pm please
**Web** www.nettlebed.freeserve.co.uk
*Monday, 8pm. Folk concerts with wide range of national and local guests. Send SAE for programme.*

## Old Road Tavern
Old Road, CHIPPENHAM, Wilts, SN15 6UN
**Contact** Christine E France
**Phone** 01249 652094
**Alt contact** Torquil McInnes
**Address** 30 Marshfield Road, CHIPPENHAM, Wilts
**Phone** 01249 650450
*Pub with function room, beer garden and food 11am - 2 pm. Concerts during the year and events during Chippenham festival. French session 2nd Sunday, Irish/ English session 1st & 3rd Sunday.*

## Oxfolk
Exeter Hall, Oxford Road, KIDLINGTON, Oxon
**Contact** Annie Stockford/ Pete Welpy
**Phone** 01993 868140
**Alt contact** Barbara & Mike Honour
**Phone** 01865 374836
*1st Saturday, 8-11.30pm. Barn dances from October - May.*

## Oxford Fiddle Group
Headington Quarry Methodist Churh Hall, Headington, OXFORD
**Contact** Jed Mugford
**Address** 4 Lee Close, Kidlington, OXFORD OX5 2XZ
**Phone** 01865 374624
**Email** jed@fiddleon.co.uk
**Web** www.oxfordshire.gov.uk/groups
*Tuesday, 8.00pm.*

## Oxford Folk Club
Port Mahon, St Clements, OXFORD
**Contact** Pam Cooper
**Phone** 01865 768128
01865 761110
**Email** pamcooper@hotmail.com
**Web** www.members.aol.com/oxfordfolkclub
*Friday, 8.30pm. Alternate guest concerts and open nights.*

## The Railway Inn
3 St Pauls Hill, WINCHESTER, Hants, SO22 5AE
**Contact** Vic Toms
**Phone** 01962 867795 - 1pm-11pm
**Alt contact** Fred Eynon
*Monday, Roots night.Venue caters for all forms of music incl. roots, indie, rock, dance & punk.*

## Readifolk Folksong Club
The Lion, Great Knollys Road, READING, Berks
**Contact** Anne Bingham
**Address** 57 Brunswick Street, READING, Berks, RG1 6NY
**Phone** 0118 9613586
**Email** steven.bingham1@ntlworld.com
**Web** www.roots.net/readifolk
*Sunday. Regular guest evenings, theme nights and singers' nights.*

## Rhythm, Roots & Blues Roadshow
The Old House At Home, Locksway Road, Milton, PORTSMOUTH
**Contact** Roger Courtney
**Phone** 023 9267 2087
**Email** rog.courtney@aol.com
**Web** www.thursdaymusic.co.uk
*Thursday, 8.30pm. Venue for musicians & singers of all talents & ages.*

## Royal Oak Folk Club
Langstone High Street, HAVANT, Hants
**Contact** Sandy & Sam Satyanadhan
**Address** 3 Cranbury Road, Woolston, SOUTHAMPTON, Hants, SO19 2HZ
**Phone** 023 8043 4209
**Email** sandy@woolston-folk.co.uk
*3rd Sunday, 7.30pm. Alternate guests & singers/ musicians evenings.*

## Shep Woolley's Cabaret Caff
Ferneham Hall, Osbourne Road, FAREHAM, Hants, PO16 7DB
**Phone** 01329 824 864 - box office
*Monthly Sundays, 7pm. Concerts with national guests plus local support.*

## The Song Loft
The Cock Hotel, 72 High Street, Stony Stratford, MILTON KEYNES
**Contact** Matt Armour
**Address** 99 Mallets Close, Stony Stratford, MILTON KEYNES, MK11 1DG
**Phone** 01908 566407
*Alternate Fridays. Folksong venue, guest artists.*

## South Hill Park Arts Centre
BRACKNELL, Berks, RG12 7PA
**Phone** 01344 484123 - box
**Contact** Simon Chatterton - Arts Officer
**Phone** 01344 484858
**Fax** 01344 411427
**Email** simon.chatterton@southhillpark.org.uk
*Arts centre, also producing Bracknell festival (none in 2001).*

## St Denys Folk & Blues Club
St Denys Hotel, 1 Aberdeen Road, St Denys, SOUTHAMPTON
**Mail address** 139 Priory Road, St Denys, SOUTHAMPTON, SO17 2JS
**Phone** 023 8055 8460
023 8032 5704
**Email** folkmania@hotmail.com
**Web** www.folkmania.org.uk
*Thursday. Monthly feature night of local performers.*

## Stonesfield Folk Dance Group
Stonesfield Village Hall, STONEFIELD, Oxon
**Contact** Paul Davis
**Address** 43 Nicholson Road, New Martson, OXFORD, OX3 OHW
**Phone** 01865 283414
01865 727158
**Email** paul.davis@oucs.ox.ac.uk
*Wednesday.*

## Swindon Folksingers Club
Penhill Royal British Legion Club, Downton Road, Off Penhill, SWINDON, Wilts
**Contact** Ted Poole
**Phone** 01793 722335
**Alt contact** Eric Stott
**Phone** 01793 521301
*Friday, 8.15pm. Traditional & contemporary singers & musicians club. Regular guests.*

## The Telescope Club
The Herschel Arms, Herschel Street, SLOUGH, Berks
**Contact** Steve Hunt
**Email** telescopeclub@talk21.com
*Alternate Thursdays, 8.30pm. Quality acoustic music to an enthusiastic audience. Different guests each time, no floorspots/ singarounds. Regular sessions & Irish music performances at the Herschel Arms.*

## Tower Arts Centre
Romsey Road, WINCHESTER, SO22 5PW
**Contact** John Tellet
**Phone** 01962 867986
**Fax** 01962 849337
**Email** tac@towerarts.co.uk
**Web** www.towerarts.co.uk
*Major venue promoting concerts with top folk & roots acts.*

## Tudor Folk Club
White Hill Centre, CHESHAM, Bucks, HP5 1AH
**Contact** Jeff Dawson
**Address** 50 Deanway, CHALFONT ST GILES, Bucks, HP8 4JS
**Phone** 01494 872859
**Email** tudor@tudorfolkclub.org.uk
**Web** www.tudorfolkclub.org.uk
**Alt contact** Mike Stephenson
**Phone** 01442 875127
*Monday, 8.15pm. Alternate guest and sing-a-round nights.*

## The Village Folk Club
The Limes Hotel, Catisfield Lane, Catisfield, NR FAREHAM, Hants
**Contact** Frank Hall
**Address** 22 Churcher Close, Alverstoke, GOSPORT Hants, PO12 2SL
**Phone** 023 9252 2500
**Email** frank-hall@supanet.com
*1st Saturday, 8pm. Some guests, some sing/ play around nights (jug collection). Relaxed club, mix of tastes catered for. Bar meals.*

## White Horse Folk Club
The Fox Inn, Swindon Street, Highworth, NR SWINDON, Wilts
**Contact** Bill Bailey
**Phone** 01793 762835
*1st& 3rd Wednesday, 8.15pm. Folk singaround plus occasional guests.*

## Wiltshire Traditions Folk Club
The George and Dragon, High Street, Potterne, DEVIZES, Wilts
**Contact** Bob & Gill Berry
**Address** 19 Whistley Lane, Potterne, DEVIZES, Wilts, SN10 5QY
**Phone** 01380 726597
07714 550990
**Email** potfolk@aol.com
**Web** http://hometown.aol.co.uk/potfolk/myhomepage/business.html
*Monday, traditional folk club. Cellar location in a pub. Good beer & food.*

## Wycombe Folk Club
The Harrow, Quarrenden Road, Hughenden Valley, HIGH WYCOMBE, Bucks
**Contact** Karen & Paul
**Phone** 01494 520375
01494 438512
**Email** karen@dorl.freeserve.co.uk
**Web** www.dorl.freeserve.co.uk/wycombefolkclub.html
*Wednesday, 8.30pm. Singers nights plus monthly guest night & music session.*

## The Wyvern Theatre
Theatre Square, SWINDON, Wilts, SN1 1QN
**Phone** 01793 524481 - box office
**Contact** Jamie Walker - Marketing Dept.
**Phone** 01793 535534
**Fax** 01793 480278
**Email** jamie.walker@sfx.com
**Web** www.swindonguide.com/wyvern
*Theatre presenting range of music, comedy, musical, big band, plays, ballet, dance.*



***See Folk London listings on page 322 for more venues.***

**The English Regions**
*These are based on Regional Arts Board representation with some variation. We have kept all of Derbyshire and Lincolnshire in the East Midlands. The RAB definitions are used here as a generally helpful way of splitting up England for a more detailed look at local resources. Also check sections for neighbouring regions for the band, caller or venue you are looking for. Contributors and magazine listings often mention venues and services based in adjacent regions.*

## southern venues

**The English Regions**
*These are based on Regional Arts Board representation with some variation. We have kept all of Derbyshire and Lincolnshire in the East Midlands. The RAB definitions are used here as a generally helpful way of splitting up England for a more detailed look at local resources. Also check sections for neighbouring regions for the band, caller or venue you are looking for. Contributors and magazine listings often mention venues and services based in adjacent regions.*

**Additional venue information for the Southern region has been provided by Folk On Tap.**

PORTSMOUTH
### The Railway Folk Club
Rear Function Room, The Alma Arms
139 Highland Road, Southsea
**Contact** Sooty Broughton
**Phone** 01243 377499
**Email** Sooty.Broughton@tesco.net
*Every Monday at 8.00pm*

CHIPPING NORTON
### Chipping Norton Folk Club
The Fox Hotel, Market Place, Chipping Norton, Oxon
**Contact** Bill and Heather Long
**Phone** 01993 823797
**Email** billlong@no1ox184bg.swinternet.co.uk
*Monthly singarounds, SECOND Monday of Month. Occasional Guests. No Smoking venue, Start 8.30pm prompt.*

NORTH BOARHUNT
### Forest Folk
North Boarhunt Social Club,
Trampers Lane,
North Boarhunt, Nr Wickham
**Contact** Charles Gale
**Phone** 01329 237698
**Phone** Janet Wiles 023 9226 4288
**Email** forest.folk@virgin.net
*1st & 3rd Monday of the month. 8pm - 11pm. Informal singarounds, free with jug collections. Occasional guest nights £3*

RINGWOOD
### Ringwood Folk Club
Elm Tree Inn, Hightown, Ringwood from A31 follow signs to Owl Sanctuary
**Contact** Rod Biggs
**Phone** (eve) 01425 673713
**Phone** (day) 01202 782579
**Email** biggsra@aol.com
*8.30 to 11.15pm. No Smoking Venue. from A31 dual carriageway, turn off at Hightown, follow signs to Owl Sanctuary*

BRACKNELL
### Bracknell Folk Club
The Cellar Bar, South Hill Park Arts Centre, Bracknell, Berks
**Contact** Neil Corbett
**Phone** 01344 451947
*8.30pm start. Weekly singarounds, 2nd Wednesday includes a tune session*

PORTSMOUTH
### The Broadside Folk Club
The Old House at Home, Locksway Road, Milton, Portsmouth
**Contact** Paul Hawkins
**Phone** 01329 315889
*Weekly singarounds. Very occasional guests.*

BISHOP'S WALTHAM
### Nonsuch Folk Club
The White Swan, Bishop's Waltham
**Contact** Keith Ray
**Phone** 01489 891110
**Contact** Ann Baker
**Phone** 01489 893486
**Email** nonsuch@keithray.screaming.net
*Weekly singarounds. Monthly Guest.*

WHERWELL
### The White Lion Folk Club
The Lion's Den, The White Lion, Wherwell, Hants
**Contact** Steve Jordan
**Phone** 01264 738629
*2 days notice please for Song & Supper. Song & Supper with Guest - 1st Thursday of month. Singaround - 3rd Thursday of Month*

SOUTHAMPTON
### Southampton Celtic Music Club
The Talking Heads, Portswood Road, Southampton
**Contact** Peter Chegwyn
**Phone** 023 9252 8017
**Contact** Talking Heads
**Phone** 023 8055 5899
**Email** chegwyn@talk21.com
*Usually Second and Fourth Friday of month. Phone for details.*

SOUTHAMPTON
### Woolston Folk Club
The Obelisk, Obelisk Road, Woolston, Southampton
**Contact** Sandy Satyanadhan
**Phone** 023 8043 4209
**Email** sandy@woolston-folk.co.uk
**Website** www.woolston-folk.co.uk
*8.15pm - 11.15pm. Friendly club, all welcome. Jug collection. Guest nights - usually £3 (conc £2)*

BOURNEMOUTH
### New Xpress Folk Club
The Portman Arms, Ashley Road, Boscombe, Bournemouth
**Contact** Mo Hamill & Ed Mortimer
**Phone** 01202 428455
**Email** ednmo@tesco.net
*Club now starts at 8.00pm*
*Open Floor = singers/musicians/ poets/ raconteurs*

ISLE OF WIGHT
### Live Acoustic Music Club
St David's Church Hall, Connaught Road, East Cowes
**Contact** Russell Bave
**Phone** 01983 297058
**Email** rmb@compuserve.com
*2nd Saturday of the month, 8.30 - 11pm. Singarounds (folk, jazz, blues & acoustic rock)*

SOUTHMOOR
### Village Folk Concerts
Southmoor Village Hall,
Southmoor, Near Abingdon
**Contact** Paul Weaving
**Phone** 01865 820381
**Email** newblenheim@farmersweekly.net
**Website** www.laststraw-group.co.uk
*All concerts start at 8.00pm. Doors open 7.15pm. Monthly concerts. Phone for tickets.*

ALDERSHOT
### West End Centre
Queens Road, Aldershot
**Contact** Box Office
**Phone** 01252 330040
**Website** www.westendcentre.co.uk
*All concerts start at 8pm. Prices from £6*

PORTSMOUTH
### The New Theatre Royal
Guildhall Walk, Portsmouth
**Contact** Box Office
**Phone** 023 9264 9000
*All concerts start at 7.45pm, unless stated otherwise*

HAVANT
### Havant Arts Active
East Street, Havant
**Contact** Box Office
**Phone** 023 9248 0113
**Website** www.havarts.dircon.co.uk
*All concerts start at 8.15pm, unless stated otherwise*

HAMBLEDON
### Hambledon Hall Folk
Hambledon, Hants
**Contact** Colin Gordon
**Phone** 023 9263 2418
**Email** gordon@gordonc14.freeserve.co.uk
*Monthly concert nights.*

# South East

**Kent, Surrey, East Sussex and West Sussex**

## Organisations

**South East Arts**
**Mail address** 13 Clement Street, Winchester, S023 9DQ
**Phone** 01962 855099,
**Fax** 01962 861186
**Web** www.arts.org.uk/directory/regions/south_east/index.html

**TRADS** has been the folk development agency for Kent, East Sussex, West Sussex and Surrey for the past eight years. It is not core funded by South East Arts, but works independently on project money.

TRADS puts the traditional performing arts back into the community to which they belong, so they can develop a relevance to the present day and be taken forward into the future.

Music, song, dance, drama and storytelling provide a base for workshops, performances and community events in schools, community centres, youth centres, prisons, village halls and adult education centres and in centres for older people and those with special needs.

The work of TRADS extends from a single session to a series of themed workshops leading up to a combined arts performance that can involve all ages and all abilities.

TRADS is run by Gail Duff, with considerable input from Bing Lyle. Others who have worked on a variety of projects include Ben Paley, Chris Wood, Pete Castle, Keith Kendrick and community artist Deborah Robinson.
**Contact** Gail Duff
**Mail address** Wynlic, Bull Lane, Lenham Heath, Maidstone, Kent, ME17 2JA
**Phone** 01622 858460
**Email** greenwillow@folkarts.fsnet.co.uk

**West Surrey Folk Association**
**Contact** David and Christine Sansom
**Mail address** 27 Crofton Close, Ottershaw, Surrey KT16 0LR
**Phone** 01932 872617

**South East Music Schemes** promotes groups and individuals working in non-classical forms of music through an annual award scheme.
**Contact** Alison Maconochie
**Mail address** SENS, PO Box 2790, Eastbourne, BN20 7WF
**Phone** 01323 431283
**Email** sems@ukgateway.net
**Web** www.semusic.org

**Stepback Project** is an educational project based in Brighton, teaching dance students through workshops and project opportunities stage performances of traditional English based dance.
**Contact** Anthony Allen
**Mail address** 89 Hollingbury Park Avenue, Brighton, East Sussex BN1 7JQ
**Phone** 01273 541453
**Email** brokenankles@btinternet.com
**Web** www.brokenankles.btinternet.co.uk

**Folk South East** promotes events in Arts Centres and Theatres in Kent and Sussex.
**Contact** John Smedley
**Mail address** 8 Baynham Road, Seven Oaks, Kent, TN13 3XA
**Phone** 01732 460171
**Email** info@folksoutheast.org.uk
**Web** www.folksoutheast.org.uk

## Magazines and websites

**The Folk Diary** is a free bi-monthly guide to all the folk dance and song events in and around the Sussex area, plus album reviews, and adverts for folk music services. Now in its 32nd year of publication under the same editors. Send a s.a.e for current issue.
**Conact** Vic Smith
**Mail address** 26 Ferrers Road, Lewes, East Sussex BN7 1BZ
**Phone** 01273 478124
**Email** tinvic@globalnet.co.uk or folk@brighton.co.uk
**Alt contact** Jim Marshall
**Alt address** 3 Chester Terrace, Brighton, East Sussex BN1 6GB
**Phone** 01273 559750
**Email** james.marshall@bigfoot.com
**Web** www.users.globalnet.co.uk/~tinvic

**The Sussex Folk Guide** website carries extensive listings of events in and around Sussex.
**Web** http://whatson.brighton.co.uk/folk

**Folk in Kent** is a quarterly magazine giving information on Folk song and dance activities in Kent. Includes EFDSS news, dance club listings, magazine listing and adverts.
**Contact** Eddie Crook
**Mail address** 33 Chapel Street, East Malling, Kent, ME19 6AP.
**Phone** 01732 841178
**Email** folkinkent@cableinet.co.uk

**What's On Folks – A Guide to Folk Music in and Around Kent** is bi-monthly magazine covering Kent and bordering areas.
**Contact** Julia Winn
**Mail address** The Paw House, 30 Snoll Hatch Road, East Peckham, Tonbridge, Kent TN12 5ED
**Phone** 01622 873142

**The Latest** is a Brighton based cross arts listings magazine with a folk, roots and acoustic section.
**Contact** Gloucester House, 45 Gloucester Street, Brighton, BN1 4EW
**Phone** 01273 818150
**Email** latest@thelatest.co.uk

**Surrey Folk News**
**Contact** 125 Brabletyre Park Road, Redhill, Surrey, RH1 6EJ.
**Phone** 01737 760492
**Email** bobkeeble@lineone.net

**Folk London** also covers Kent and Surrey venues. See London section for details.

## Venues

Alongside the Folk South East concert series, there are several venues promoting top folk acts, notably **The Hawth**, Crawley and **The Electric Theatre**, Guildford. Other prominent venues booking folk, roots & world music include **Assembly Hall**, Tunbridge Wells, **The Pit**, Crondall, Surrey and **The Maltings**, Farnham. There are several significant series of concerts including **Footlights**, West Chiltington, West Sussex, **The F Word Club Acoustic Music Club** at The **Soul Café**, Maidstone and **Folk & Acoustic Music @ Komedia**, Brighton. **Worthing Theatres** promote concerts with top folk rock & roots acts at four venues in Worthing.

Major clubs in the area include **Lewes Arms Folk Club**, Lewes, running concerts with British folk & traditional guest acts plus instrumental workshops and English tune sessions and **The Royal Oak**, Lewes who host traditional and folk music & song and some sessions. Guests appear weekly

**south east region**

***See Folk London listings on page 322 for more venues.***

**The English Regions**
*These are based on Regional Arts Board representation with some variation. We have kept all of Derbyshire and Lincolnshire in the East Midlands. The RAB definitions are used here as a generally helpful way of splitting up England for a more detailed look at local resources. Also check sections for neighbouring regions for the band, caller or venue you are looking for. Contributors and magazine listings often mention venues and services based in adjacent regions.*

# south east region

Listed ceilidh and social dance bands in the South East include **Band B Band**, **Band Of Two**, **Blackthorn**, **Chris Taylor**, **Citizen Camembert**, **Footloose**, **Jezreels Ceilidh Band**, **Pesky**, **Ring O'Bells Ceilidh Band**, **Springer Sisters** and **Springer Surprise Band**, **Stocai**, **The Flying Toads**, **The Friday Folk Band (of St Albans)**, **The Pugwash Band**, **The Sussex Pistols**, **Thingumajig** and **Used Notes**.

Listed dance callers inlcude **Fee Lock**, **Gail Duff**, **Gordon Potts**, **Keith Leech**, **Peter Mayes** and **Tony Kelly**.

**The English Regions**
*These are based on Regional Arts Board representation with some variation. We have kept all of Derbyshire and Lincolnshire in the East Midlands. The RAB definitions are used here as a generally helpful way of splitting up England for a more detailed look at local resources. Also check sections for neighbouring regions for the band, caller or venue you are looking for. Contributors and magazine listings often mention venues and services based in adjacent regions.*

at **Dartford Folk Club**, **Faversham Folk Club** and **The Wellington**, Seaford, Sussex. Clubs with monthly guests include **Trident Folk Club**, Broadstairs, **Red Lion Folk Club**, Turners Hill, Sussex, **Bromley Acoustic Music Club**, **The Harbour Sessions**, Southwick, West Sussex, **Lamb Folk Club**, Eastbourne. The region also is home of the **Famous Willows Folk Club** and the **Black Horse Pub**, Wrotham, Kent, which has regular sessions and an annual festival.

There is a monthly dance series, **eCeilidh**, at Godalming Borough Hall.

## Festivals

**Broadstairs Folk Week** (August) is the largest summer folk festival in the South East. There are 2 major May Day celebrations in the region; **Rochester Sweeps Festival** and **Hastings Traditional Jack in the Green**. Other festivals throughout the area include **Crawley Folk Festival** at The Hawth, Crawley (late June), **Larmer Tree Music Festival** (July) - mainly world and folk roots music and **Tenterden Folk Festival**, Kent (October). **Blues On The Farm** near Chichester (June) encompasses world music, **Kentucky To Kent UK** (August) is a Bluegrass festival and **Eastbourne International Folk Festival** (May) is an event for English, American and international folk dance. Free festivals include **Global Bandstand** (July) in the heart of Canterbury. Both **Swale Festival**, Kent (July) and **Guildford Live** (August) feature folk, roots & world music in their programme. **Hastings Borough Bonfire** (October) is a Sussex tradition with a costumed torchlit procession, an enormous bonfire and flaming effigies.

*Thanks to TRADS, Gail Duff, Sussex Folk Diary, Folk On Tap and Peter Chegwyn for assistance with the above information.*

## Rooting around the South East

### Organisations/Listings etc.

**www.folksoutheast.org.uk**
*Folk South East Organisation*

**www.southfolkmusicnetwork.bigstep.com**
*Covers a wide area including the South East, plus areas from Cornwall to Essex.*

**kentfolk.freehosting.net/Kent Folk**
**whatson.brighton.co.uk/folk**
*Sussex Folk Guide*

### Clubs etc.

**ourworld.compuserve.com/homepages/MarKerr**
*Chichester Folk Song Club*

**web.ukonline.co.uk/graham.gurrin/ram**
*Claygate, Ram Folk Club*

**ourworld.compuserve.com/homepages/PaulHomer/dfc.htm**
*Dartford Folk Club*

**www.lambfolkclub.freeuk.com**
*Eastbourne, Lamb Folk Club*

**homepage.ntlworld.com/borodance/goodo.htm**
*Farncombe, Good Old Way Folk Club*

**homepage.ntlworld.com/borodance/evhome.htm**
*Guildford, Electric Voices*

**home.clara.net/gmgough/horsham.htm**
*Horsham Folk Club*

**members.aol.com/lewesarmsfolk**
*Lewes Arms Folk Club*

**www.users.globalnet.co.uk/~tinvic**
*Lewes, Folk at the Royal Oak*

**www.seaford4folk.fsnet.co.uk**
*Seaford Folk Song Club*

**www.btinternet.com/~folkspots/bells/eight.htm**
*Tenterden, Eight Bells Folk Club*

**www.folking.com/anchorfolk**
*West Byfleet, Anchor Folk Club*

**www.footlights.freeuk.com**
*West Chiltington, Footlights*

**www.stainesfolkandblues.org.uk**
*Staines Folk and Blues Club*

**www.csclarke.clara.net/windmill**
*Ewshott, The Windmill Acoustic Music Club*

### Acoustic Open Mic Night
The Evening Star, Surrey Street, BRIGHTON
**Contact** Janine Garrott
**Phone** 01273 328931
*Monday, 9pm, open mic. Plus live music on Sundays.*

### The Anchor Folk Club
The Blue Anchor, High Road, Byfleet, NR WEYBRIDGE, Surrey
**Contact** Mike Peach
**Address** 33 Herbert Crescent, Knaphill, WOKING, Surrey, GU21 2BZ
**Phone** 01483 476715, 07971 198412
**Email** anchorfolk@talk21.com
**Web** www.folking.com/anchorfolk
*Thursday.*

### Assembly Hall
The Assembly Hall Theatre
TUNBRIDGE WELLS, KENT
**Phone** 01892 530613 - box office
01892 532072
*Venue including concerts with top folk artists.*

### The Beacon Folk Club
The Beacon, Tea Garden Lane, TUNBRIDGE WELLS, Kent
**Contact** Peter
**Phone** 01892 782326
**Fax** 01892 784503
**Email** beacon.folk@btinternet.com
*2nd Monday, guests; 4th Monday, song & music session.*

### The Black Horse
The Black Horse, Stanstead, NR WROTHAM, Kent, TN15 7PR
**Contact** Ian Duncan
**Phone** 01732 822355
*Pub with regular sessions and annual festival. 2nd Sunday, lunchtime onwards, Irish traditional session. 4th Thursday, 8pm, traditional folk session. Festival of traditional music and morris dancing.*

### Bromley Acoustic Music Club
The Pavillion, Leisure Centre, Kentish Way, BROMLEY, Kent
**Phone** 020 83139911 (box office)
*1st Sunday, 7.30pm. Concerts.*

### Dartford Folk Club
Dartford Working Men's Club, Essex Road, DARTFORD, Kent
**Contact** Pam Colls
**Phone** 01322 222533
**Web** http://ourworld.compuserve.com/homepages/paulhomer/dfc.htm
*Tuesday, 8.30pm. Weekly guests, floor singers welcome.*

## eCeilidh
The Borough Hall, Bridge Street, GODALMING, Surrey
**Contact** L Heath
**Address** 6 Dunsdon Avenue, GUILDFORD, Surrey, GU2 5NX
**Phone** 01483 828452
**Email** borodance@ntlworld.com
*Saturdays, 8pm, monthly. Barn dances with top national bands.*

## Eight Bells
The Eight Bells, 43 High Street, TENTERDEN, Kent
**Contact** Alan Castle
**Address** Folk Spots, 15 Repton Manor Road, ASHFORD, Kent, TN23 3HA
**Phone** 01233 626805
**Email** bells@folkspots.btinternet.com
**Web** www.btinternet.com/~folkspots
*2nd Tuesday. Folk song & music singaround.*

## The Electric Theatre
Onslow Street, GUILDFORD, Surrey, GU1 4SZ
**Phone** 01483 444789
**Fax** 01483 563913
**Web** www.electrictheatre.co.uk
*180 capacity venue, broad mixed programme including folk music concerts.*

## Elsie's
The Queens Arms, Cowden Pound, NR EDENBRIDGE, Kent
**Contact** DaveWatt
**Phone** 01732 862862
*Monthly Saturdays, 8.45pm. Ring to confirm. Song and music session; all types of traditional music. Residents: Elsie's band.*

## F Word Club
The Soul Café, 110 Week Street, MAIDSTONE, Kent ME14 1RH
**Phone** 01622 751415 - venue
**Fax** 01622 751415 - venue
**Contact** Rick Clarke
**Address** Manor Farm, Easterfileds, East Malling, Kent, ME19 6BE
**Phone** 01732 871020 (info & tickets)
**Email** waterboy@talk21.com
*Monthly concerts, top folk/roots acts.*

## Faversham Folk Club
The Chimney Boy, Preston Street, FAVERSHAM, Kent
**Contact** Alan Cole (information)
**Phone** 01795 531649 - info
**Alt contact** Mary Henderson (bookings)
**Phone** 01795 534368
*Wednesday, 8.30pm. National guests plus singers nights.*

## Folk & Acoustic Music @ Komedia
Komedia, Gardner Street, BRIGHTON
**Phone** 01273 647100 - box office
**Phone** 07946 385415 - info
*Venue promoting concerts with major folk acts.*

## Folk at The Barge
The Barge, Layfield Road, GILLINGHAM, Kent
**Phone** 01634 850485
*Monday. Mainly local guests.*

## Folk at The Falcon
The Falcon, Malborough Road, GILLINGHAM, Kent
**Phone** 01634 860614
*Tuesday, 9pm. Free music, real ale.*

## Folk at The Horse, Sussex
The White Horse Inn, Bodle Street Green, NR HERSTMONCEUX, East Sussex
**Contact** Dave Hosie
**Fax** 01323 833243
**Alt contact** Dave Dyke
**Phone** 01435 812201
*Alternate Mondays, 8.30pm. Acoustic traditional & contemporary folk, bluegrass, singer-songwriters, etc. All welcome. Occasional guests.*

## Footlights
West Chiltington Village Hall, WEST CHILTINGTON, West Sussex
**Contact** Lynne Page
**Address** Winterwood, Nyetimber Copse, WEST CHILTINGTON, West Sussex, RH20 2NE
**Phone** 01798 812661
**Email** footlights@freeuk.com
**Web** www.footlights.freeuk.com
*Usually 1st Saturday, 7.30pm. Monthly series of folk concerts with national acts.*

## Fordwich Folk
The Fordwich Arms, King Street, Fordwich, CANTEBURY, Kent
**Phone** 01227 710444 - pub
**Contact** Susan
**Phone** 01227 712577
**Alt contact** Chris
**Phone** 01227 454070
*1st and 3rd Sundays. Folk evening - no admission fee.*

## Friday Folk
Liberal Club, 7 Station Road, ORPINGTON, Kent, BR6 0RZ
**Contact** Sue Tuckey
**Address** 49 Zelah Road, ORPINGTON, Kent, BR5 4JU
**Phone** 01689 838077
**Email** silly.monkey@ondigital.com
*Friday. Live music gathering, some guests, some singers nights. No email attatchments please.*

## Grey Horse Folk Club
The Grey Horse, 46 Richmond Road, KINGSTON UPON THAMES, Surrey, KT2 5EE
**Contact** Anna Tabbush
**Phone** 07989 556164
**Email** annatabbush@freeuk.com
**Web** www.grey-horse.co.uk
**Address** 70 Burnthill Road, Lower Bourne, FARNHAM, Surrey, GU10 3LN
**Fax** 01252 722938
*1st & 3rd Thursday. 1st; free session. 3rd; guest acts and open mic spot.*

## The Harbour Sessions
The Schooner Inn, SOUTHWICK, W Sussex
**Phone** 01273 592252
**Contact** John Collyer
**Phone** 01273 881582
**Web** www.uksoundcraft.com
**Alt contact** Tim Kent
**Address** 2 Meadway Court, Kingston Lane, SOUTHWICK, W Sussex BN42 4SL
**Phone** 01273 595614
**Email** tktw@mistral.co.uk
*1st Tuesday, 8pm. Floor spots followed by guests. 60 capacity, downstairs room.*

## Hardcore Troubadour
The Gordon Hotel, High Street, ROCHESTER, Kent
**Contact** John Matthews
**Phone** 01634 405552
*Wednesday, 8.30pm. Singers night plus some guests. Promotion of local artists.*

## The Hawth Theatre and Arts Centre
Hawth Avenue, CRAWLEY, West Sussex, RH10 6YZ
**Phone** 01293 552941
**Contact** Dave Watmore
**Web** www.hawth.co.uk
*Local authority venue programming regular folk & roots music as part of mixed arts policy. The Hawth (855), The Hawth Studio (147) & Crawley Leisure Centre (1600-2400).*

## Hazlitt Folk
The Old House at Home, Pudding Lane, MAIDSTONE, Kent
**Contact** Jacqui
**Phone** 01474 822010
**Web** www.hazlittfolk.co.uk
**Alt contact** Don
**Phone** 01634 244213
*Monday, 8.30pm. Singers nights, plus occasional guests. Range of music, host of local talent.*



**The English Regions**
*These are based on Regional Arts Board representation with some variation. We have kept all of Derbyshire and Lincolnshire in the East Midlands. The RAB definitions are used here as a generally helpful way of splitting up England for a more detailed look at local resources. Also check sections for neighbouring regions for the band, caller or venue you are booking for. Contributors and magazine listings often mention venues and services based in adjacent regions.*

## south east venues

*See Folk London listings on page 322 for more venues.*

**The English Regions**
*These are based on Regional Arts Board representation with some variation. We have kept all of Derbyshire and Lincolnshire in the East Midlands. The RAB definitions are used here as a generally helpful way of splitting up England for a more detailed look at local resources. Also check sections for neighbouring regions for the band, caller or venue you are looking for. Contributors and magazine listings often mention venues and services based in adjacent regions.*

### Horsham Folk Club
Horsham Cricket Club, Cricketfield Road, HORSHAM, Sussex
**Contact** Lawrence Long
**Phone** 01342 719624
*Sunday, 8pm. Alternate singers or song & dance nights and guest nights.*

### Lamb Folk Club
The Lamb Inn, High Street, EASTBOURNE, Sussex
**Contact** Nick Westcott
**Phone** 01323 728268
**Email** lambfolkclub@freeuk.com
**Web** www.lambfolkclub.freeuk.com
**Alt contact** Terry Fougere
**Phone** 01323 638811
*1st & 3rd Wednesday, 8.30pm. All forms of acoustic roots music, all welcome. Guests at least monthly.*

### Lewes Arms Folk Club
Mount Place, LEWES, Sussex
**Contact** Valmai Goodyear
**Address** 20 St John's Terrace, LEWES, East Sussex, BN7 2DL
**Phone** 01273 476757 - 24 hr ansaphone
**Email** vipgood@atlas.co.uk
**Web** http://members.aol.com/lewesarmsfolk/
*Saturday, except August. British traditional guest acts. 50 capacity. No smoking, steep stairs into club. Also, instrumental workshops with top performers. Plus English tune sessions.*

### Long Drop Small Music Club
The Royal Oak, BEARSTED GREEN, Kent
**Contact** Bob Piggott
**Phone** 01622 736661
**Email** rwpiggott@bun.com
*1st Tuesday, 8.30pm. Performers club, all types of music welcome; book a 15 min slot with the organiser. Occasional guests. Not August.*

### The Maltings, Farnham
Bridge Square, FARNHAM, Surrey, GU9 7QR
**Phone** 01252 726234 - box office
**Web** www.farnhammaltings.com

### Moore or Less Folk Club
The Three Mariners, Lower Rainham Road, RAINHAM, Kent
**Phone** 01634 231137 - pub
**Contact** Derek Moore
**Phone** 01634 376072
*Monthly singers nights plus occasional guest. Non smoking venue.*

### Music on Sundays
Chichester Centre of Arts, CHICHESTER, West Sussex
**Contact** Brian Walton
**Email** bjwalton@aol.com
**Web** www.musiconsundays.co.uk
*Last Sunday. Concerts & illustrated talks on mainly classical music with some jazz and folk.*

### Orpington Folk Club (Orpington Folk Music and Song Club)
The White Hart, High Street, ORPINGTON, Kent
**Phone** 01689 837778 (venue)
**Contact** Steve Jennings
**Address** 5 Johnsons Avenue, Badgers Mount, SEVENOAKS, Kent, TN14 7AX
**Phone** 01959 532754
**Email** orpingtonfolkclub@hotmail.com
**Web** www.orpingtonfolkclub.fsnet. co.uk
**Alt contact** Ivan North - Bookings
**Alt address** 87 Dyke Way, ORPINGTON, Kent
**Phone** 01689 870197
**Email** inorth@hotmail.com
*Thursday 8.15pm. Guest performers, singers' nights & singarounds. Please contact Ivan initiallyvia email. Not August.*

### The Phoenix Folk Club
The Social Club, 36 High Street, Green Street Green, ORPINGTON, Kent
**Contact** Maddie Brittain
**Phone** 01689 859625
*Alternate Mondays, 8.15pm. Floor singers welcome, monthly guests.*

### The Pit
Itchel Lane, CRONDALL, Surrey, GU10 5PU
**Phone** 01252 850789
*Venue programming monthly Blues/ Roots artists.*

### Rainham Folk Club
The Three Mariners, Lower Rainham Road, RAINHAM, Kent
**Contact** Maz & Dan Hobday
**Address** 39 Brown Street, RAINHAM, Kent, ME8 7JN
**Phone** 01634 372048
*1st & 3rd Fridays. Acoustic singers club with occasional guests.*

### Red Lion Folk Club
The Red Lion, TURNERS HILL, Sussex
**Phone** 01342 810291
*Fridays, 8pm. Alternate guest & singers nights.*

### Riverside Folk Club
The Fighting Cocks, The Street, HORTON KIRBY, Kent
**Phone** 01322 862299
*Sunday, 8pm. Open mic club, all styles, all welcome. Good beer, genial banjo-picking landlord!*

### Royal Oak
Station Street, LEWES, East Sussex
**Contact** Vic & Tina Smith
**Address** 26 Ferrers Road, LEWES, East Sussex, BN7 1PZ
**Phone** 01273 478124
**Fax** 01273 478124
**Email** tinvic@globalnet.co.uk
**Web** www.users.globalnet.co.uk/~tinvic
**Alt contact** Dan Quinn
**Address** 87 St Andrews Road, PORTSLADE, East Sussex
**Phone** 01273 881316
**Email** folk@brighton.co.uk
*Thursday, 8pm. Traditional and folk music and song.*
*Last Sunday, 3-5.30pm. Song and tune session.*

### Tonbridge Folk Club ("Nellie's")
The Medway Room, Rose & Crown Hotel, High Street, TONBRIDGE, Kent
**Contact** Geoff Doel
**Address** Owl House, 3 Charlton Terrace, TONBRIDGE, Kent, TN9 1PG
**Phone** 01732 366857
**Alt contact** Bob Kenward
**Address** 151 Stephens Road, TUNBRIDGE WELLS, Kent, TN4 9QT
*1st Sunday, 8pm. Traditional singers and musicians welcome. Small club; guests are booked for hat collection only.*

### Trident Folk Club
The Neptunes Hall , Habour Street, BROADSTAIRS, Kent
**Phone** 01843 603242 - info
**Email** trident.folkclub@virgin.net
**Web** www.tridentfolkclub.co.uk
**Phone** 01843 868225 - bookings
*Fornightly club, alternate guests & singaounds.*

### The Wellington
Steyne Road, SEAFORD, Sussex
**Email** folkclub@seaford4folk.fsnet.co.uk
**Web** www.seaford4folk.fsnet.co.uk
*Friday, 8pm. Local & national guests plus residents.*

### Wheatsheaf
The Wheatsheaf, BOUGH BEECH, Kent, TN8 7RU
**Contact** Pete Curry
**Phone** 01732 700254
*Wednesday, 8.30pm. Come all ye with Skinners Rats, Ian Petrie or Laing & Petrie.*

### Worthing Theatres
The Pavilion Theatre, WORTHING, Sussex
**Phone** 01903 206206 - box office
*Concerts with top folk rock & roots acts at 4 venues in Worthing.*

# South West Arts

**Cornwall, Devon, Dorset, Gloucestershire, Somerset Bath, Plymouth and Torbay**

## Organisations

**South West Arts**
**Mail address** Bradninch Place, Gandy Street, Exeter, EX4 3LS
**Phone** 01392 218188
**Fax** 01392 413554
**Web** www.swa.co.uk

**South West Arts** publishes various information sheets including a list of Theatre Companies in the region.

**Folk South West** is the regional development agency for the South West of England. It covers the counties of Cornwall, Devon, Dorset, Somerset and Gloucestershire and the unitary authorities within that area. Folk South West was founded in 1992 by Eddie Upton and Wendy Lutley and became a registered charity in 1994.

Folk South West's mission is to stimulate participation, enjoyment and creativity in the music, song, dance and traditions of the South West. The main areas of work include: education and training; recordings and publications; local projects; work with folk enthusiasts; an information and advisory service and a twice yearly newsletter - Folk in the South West
**Mail address** The Stables, Montacute House, Montacute, Somerset, TA15 6XP
**Phone** 01935 822911
**Fax** 01935 822024
**Email** folksw@folksw.org.uk
**Web** www.folksw.org.uk
**Director** Eddie Upton
**Administrator & Project Co-ordinator** Vanessa Williams
**Education & Training Co-ordinator** Philippa Toulson.

**The Wren Trust** is a professional community folk arts organisation, founded by co-directors Paul Wilson and Marilyn Tucker in 1983. Based in Okehampton, the Trust works with groups of people of all ages and abilities in urban and rural communities throughout Devon.

Wren aims to stimulate active participation in and enjoyment of traditional music and related arts and by this means to enable people to discover their own creativity and address issue which are important to them. While having a basis in traditional English folk music, Wren is not prescriptive and uses many different manifestations of popular culture as starting points for creative activity. Traditional music and customs along with oral history are augmented by new forms of popular expression, contemporary artistic practice and the potential of new technologies.

Wren's work is based on a belief in constantly evolving and plural traditions, but it also believes in preserving the roots of our traditions, like seed corn to allow for future evolution and growth.

*Wren Performances:* Striking vocal harmonies, instrumental variety and a wide repertoire combine in Paul and Marilyn to make compelling, accessible performances with wide appeal. Wren are welcome visitors in village halls, arts centres and folk clubs alike. A Wren show will adjust to any audience of any age, blending and balancing participation with listening, song with story. Firmly routed in the Devon tradition, the old songs are complemented by powerful new songs written by both of them. Marilyn and Paul can be joined by other musicians for special occasion, and a P.A. system and lights are available.

*Community Arts Programme*: A village's history, a neighbourhood's old and young affirming their identity, all of these things and more can make a Wren Trust Community Project. The Wren team will work with a group of people to help design a project, and then get as many people working creatively to express the themes in a community play, pageant or procession, using a variety of artistic forms, particularly music and song, but also involving textiles, sculpture, drama and puppets.

The Wren community arts programme aims for sustainability, and after the Wren input the community is invited to join the Wren Network, receive a newsletter and invitations to take part in training events.

*Lifelong Learning*: Wren has a commitment to lifelong learning in all it's forms, from formal provision through informal and social education, linking where possible with other areas of the curriculum. Whilst in the informal sector Wren takes a broad interpretation of folk music to working, for example, with all ages in a range of settings, from youth clubs to lunch clubs, and community folk choirs. Wren has two permanent choirs in Exeter, Voices in Common for adults, and Hocus Pocus Harmony for young people.

*Heritage:* Wren Trust's programme is backed by a collection of folk song and music and oral reminiscences, often themselves products of a community programme. A recent addition to the archive is Sabine Baring-Gould's entire folk song collection on micro-fiche. The Baring-Gould Heritage project is an integral part of the Wren's programme, aiming to put into the public domain the material from the Baring-Gould collection, to raise awareness of traditional music among local people, and to raise awareness of the significance of Baring-Gould and West Devon. The main Baring-Gould Heritage Project event of the year is the annual Folk Festival and Study Break held in October.

**The Baring-Gould Heritage project** is based in West Devon where Baring-Gould spent his last forty-three years. The project has three main aims:

1. To use live performance, recordings and publications to bring the material in the Baring-Gould archives into the public domain locally, nationally and internationally. To relate the cultural traditions of this corner of rural England to folk music traditions elsewhere and in particular to places which have historic links with Devon.
2. To raise awareness of the folk and vernacular traditions of the area among local people and, using a range of media including the songs in the Baring-Gould archives, to set up new community arts based projects which reflect contemporary experience and are relevant in today's world.
3. To raise awareness of the significance of Baring-Gould's role in recording the folklore and cultural history of the area and to help to develop appropriate initiatives to bring his work to the attention of tourists who visit the area.

As well as celebrating the folk song collection, this project takes the legacy of Baring-Gould's work and uses it as a platform for new, locally distinctive work for the social and cultural context of today, rather than focusing solely on Baring-Gould as a personality.
**Contact** Paul Wilson
**Mail address** The Wren Trust, 1 St James Street, Okehampton, Devon EX20 1DW
**Phone/Fax** 01837 53754
**Email** wrentrust@eclipse.co.uk
**Web** www.wrentrust.co.uk

## south west region

Listed ceilidh and social dance bands in the South West include **Big Bad Contra**, **Captain Thunderbolt**, **Cottage Industry**, **Fox Amongst The Chickens**, **Home Brew Country Dance Band**, **Jiggerypipery**, **Mark Bazeley, Jason Rice & Robert Murch**, **Matchless Ceilidh Band**, **Pigs Might Fly**, **Pressgang**, **Red House**, **Roger Downton and Corkscrew**, **Scallywag**, **Spinach for Norman**, **The Eel Grinders**, **The English Country Dance Band** and **Wysiwyg Acoustic**

Listed dance callers in the region include **Colin Andrews**, **David Milner**, **Frances Oates**, **Raymond Wright**, **Sandy Archer**, **Steve Cunio** and **Tom Brown**.

***Listed magazines and websites offer further band information.***

**The English Regions**
*These are based on Regional Arts Board representation with some variation. We have kept all of Derbyshire and Lincolnshire in the East Midlands. The RAB definitions are used here as a generally helpful way of splitting up England for a more detailed look at local resources. Also check sections for neighbouring regions for the band, caller or venue you are looking for. Contributors and magazine listings often mention venues and services based in adjacent regions*

# south west region

Listed ceilidh and social dance bands in the South West include **Big Bad Contra**, **Captain Thunderbolt**, **Cottage Industry**, **Fox Amongst The Chickens**, **Home Brew Country Dance Band**, **Jiggerypipery**, **Mark Bazeley**, **Jason Rice & Robert Murch**, **Matchless Ceilidh Band**, **Pigs Might Fly**, **Pressgang**, **Red House**, **Roger Downton and Corkscrew**, **Scallywag**, **Spinach for Norman**, **The Eel Grinders**, **The English Country Dance Band** and **Wysiwyg Acoustic**.

Listed dance callers in the region include **Colin Andrews**, **David Milner**, **Frances Oates**, **Raymond Wright**, **Sandy Archer**, **Steve Cunio** and **Tom Brown**.

***Listed magazines and websites offer further band information.***

**The English Regions**
*These are based on Regional Arts Board representation with some variation. We have kept all of Derbyshire and Lincolnshire in the East Midlands. The RAB definitions are used here as a generally helpful way of splitting up England for a more detailed look at local resources. Also check sections for neighbouring regions for the band, caller or venue you are looking for. Contributors and magazine listings often mention venues and services based in adjacent regions.*

**Acoustic Youth 2000**
Folk arts organisation run by young people for young people. Workshops, concerts and other youth events at festivals and venues across the country. Quarterly magazine AY2K
**Contact** Kerensa Newman
**Mail address** 7 St. Aubyn's Vean, TRURO, Cornwall TR1 2DX
**Phone** 01872 240475
07833 393928
**Email** kerensaay2k@supanet.com
**Web** www.acousticyouth.org

**Somerset Dance Connections**
**Mail address** 11/13 Castle Street, Bridgwater, Somerset, TA6 3DD
**Phone** 01278 446409
**Fax** 01278 447402
**Email** somdanceco.@aol.com
**Connect** is the magazine of Somerset Dance Connections. Its covers a broad range of dance styles including Salsa, Irish Step, Appalachian, Scottish Country, Middle Eastern.

## Magazines

**Folkwrite** is the quarterly folk magazine for Gloucestershire and environs. Articles, reviews, events, organisations and contacts lists.. £4.60 pa

Folkwrite was started 17 years ago by Pat Scrase. After the shock of her sudden death last year, her many friends thought it would be a shame to let all her hard work evaporate, so Folkwrite is now continued as a collaborative quarterly publication with kind financial backing from Glosfolk. With the departure for Poland of Charles Menteith, editorship fell to Flos Headford. Now a 52-page A5 booklet, it covers Gloucestershire and the nearer parts of surrounding counties. It contains lists of contacts for all sorts of folk organisations, a dates diary, reports and reviews of events, publications and recordings as well as articles. It is available at folk clubs in the area, and by post from Clive Brooks, 7 Pikes Pool Lane, Burcot, Bromsgrove. Contributions, adverts, queries and complaints should be sent to Flos.
**Contact** Flos Headford - Editor
**Mail address** 38 Upton Street, Tredworth Gloucester GL1 4LA
**Phone** 01592 240989
01452 310372
**Emails** flos@madasafish.com
flosthefiddle@netscapeonline.co.uk
**Web** www.folkwrite.org.uk

**What's Afoot** is the magazine of EFDSS Devon District Folk Committee. Useful contacts lists include social dance clubs and events, display dance groups, bands, callers, festivals and song clubs. Also news, reviews and articles.
**Contact** Colin Andrews (Editor)
**Mail address** Bonny Green, Morchard Bishop, Crediton, EX17 6PG
**Phone/Fax** 01363 877216
**Email** whatsafoot@bonnygreen.co.uk
**Web** www.bonnygreen.co.uk
**Advertising** Dick Little, Collaton Grange, Malborough, Kingsbridge, Devon, TQ7 3DJ
**Adv. Phone** 01548 561352

## Venues

See the Focus on Cornwall for details of its venues, clubs & festivals. Elsewhere in the South West...

**Guildhall Arts Centre**, Gloucester has world music events fortnightly plus annual Cajun & Zydeco and Blues festivals. **Brewhouse**, Taunton regularly programmes an extensive folk season. **Roses Theatre**, Tewkesbury programmes a mix of folk roots and folk rock plus has occasional folk club nights. **Music & Theatre at St Clare's**, Seaton, Devon has blues and folk acts fortnightly and **Brewery Arts Theatre**, Cirencester presents a mixed programme with emphasis on folk/ blues/ world music. In South Gloucestershire, **Music in the Church at Aust**, has monthly folk & early music concerts plus occasional weekends of concerts and workshops. Other arts centres presenting folk, roots & world music concerts include **Bridgwater Arts Centre**, Somerset and **Merlin Theatre**, Frome. **Halsway Manor**, Crowcombe, Somerset is a centre for dance & song weekends and other folk events (01984 618274)

**The Albert Hole**, Bristol has concerts with national & international guests. Many clubs have a mixture of informal sessions or singarounds with guest acts fortnightly, monthly or occasionally. These include **Ritz Acoustic Club**, Burnham on Sea, Somerset, **Folk on The Moor**, Plymouth, **Nailsea Folk Club**, Somerset, **Dragon Folk Club**, Shortwood, South Gloucestershire, **Torquay Folk Club**, Square & Compass, Worth Matravers, Swanage (01929 439229), **Hyde Folk Club**, Plymouth and **Fringe Folk Club**, Bridport, Dorset.

**Bridport Bull Ceilidhs** Bridport, Dorset is an occasional ceilidh series with top national bands. For 'FAB' ceilidhs in Bristol, see the Folk Around Bristol. **Web** www.folkaroundbristol.co.uk/cei.htm

## Festivals

**Sidmouth International Festival** (August) is one of the countries leading festivals. It has over 700 events including concerts and dances with many top folk & roots acts, a massive workshop programme and much more. Other prominent festivals include **Dartmoor Folk Festival** (August) a small successful festival with a traditional emphasis, **Cornwall Folk Festival**, Wadebridge (August), **Wimborne Folk Festival** (June) and **Cheltenham Folk Festival** (February) a weekend of folk music, song and dance based at the Town Hall.

Prominent arts festivals encompassing folk, roots & world music include **Bishopstock Music Festival** (Usually May, postponed to August in 2001 due to FMD); a major Blues festival, **Bath International Music Festival** (May) which has a World Music Weekend, **Bath Fringe Festival** (May) a 17 day festival including British and World roots concerts, free gigs, etc. **Cheltenham Festival Fringe** (June), a summer festival with a diverse programme of concerts, theatre, street entertainment, etc. **Stroud Fringe Festival**, Gloucestershire (September) and **Chard Festival Of Women In Music** (May).

Other smaller but significant festivals include **Le Grand Bal De Bath** (September), **Dawlish Folk & Blues Festival**, Devon (September), **Crediton Folk Weekend** (March, cancelled in 2001 due to FMD), **Teignmouth Mid-Summer Folk Festival** (June), **Lowender Peran Celtic Festival** (October), **Swanage Folk Festival** (September), **Priddy Folk Fayre** (July) and **Tolpuddle Martyrs Festival** (July).

**Capers Folk Activity Holidays** (also known as folk camps) are folk music, dance and song based activity holidays, incorporating workshops, ceilidhs and sessions. Based in the South West, the holidays happen at various locations throughout the UK and Europe. Each location has its own character and programme of events.

**Cornish Music Project** runs a variety of music projects covering 4 areas- education, networking, celebration and research through workshops, concerts and publications.
**Contact** Hilary Coleman
**Mail address** 24 Valley Close, Newbridge, Truro, Cornwall TR1 3UN
**Phone** 01842 275058
**Alt contact** Frances Bennett
**Email** sfbennett@aol.com

• ***Thanks to Mike O'Connor, Kernow Folk, Folkwrite and Wren Trust for assistance with the above information.***

## south west region

**The English Regions**

*These are based on Regional Arts Board representation with some variation. We have kept all of Derbyshire and Lincolnshire in the East Midlands. The RAB definitions are used here as a generally helpful way of splitting up England for a more detailed look at local resources. Also check sections for neighbouring regions for the band, caller or venue you are looking for. Contributors and magazine listings often mention venues and services based in adjacent regions.*

## Folk in Cornwall

By **Mike O'Connor**

Cornwall has a lively folk scene - one that has been growing slowly but steadily over the last 5 years. It's a scene that has very definitely evolved since the hey-day of the 60s and 70s. There are two very good folk clubs, countless sessions, and an enthusiastic Cornish music and dance scene that has evolved in the last 30 years as material has been discovered and researched.

**Kernowfolk** is the web incarnation of a (roughly) quarterly broadsheet called **FolkNews Kernow** which is collated from about 20 local (Cornish) sources by local singer/box player Chris Ridley - musician with Trigg Morris.

Folk News Kernow/Kernowfolk is the only such publication in Cornwall. It's supported by donations from clubs and venues and is distributed free to local folk clubs, TICs, town halls etc. There is no Cornish folk magazine as such. Regular users are invited to subscribe, details are on the website.

Kernowfolk duplicates the Broadsheet's calendar information, and adds anything else useful. Consequently it acts as a data magnet and has a database of directory information, relevant local links, info about performers and sessions etc. That said, it's a fluid scene. New sessions spring up, old ones die. The club and dance info is comprehensive and reliable.

**Contact** Chris Ridley
**Mail address** Trenillocs, St Columb, Cornwall
**Phone** 01637 880394
**Web** www.angelfire.com/mo/kernowfolk

**Administration** The area's Regional Arts Board is South West Arts. A major contribution of SWA is the funding of Folk South West. But of course Cornwall is only a small part of the FSW area and their activity in Cornwall in recent years has been resource limited. Over the border in Okehampton the Wren Trust is well respected, but it's just a small organisation. However, their work on Baring Gould and North Devon carols extends into North Cornwall.

### Websites

There are two Cornish websites that provide significant resources - **Kernowfolk** a diary / directory and **Ilow Kernow** (there's a link from Kernowfolk) which provides an excellent music database and sales facilities for Cornish Folk CDs etc. Other sites (also linked from Kernowfolk) are relevant to specific groups, bands, clubs, etc.

**Touring Artists** often do Bodmin on Friday, St Ives on Saturday, and Folk on the Moor on Sunday. The current club booking secretaries are used to working together to help put a series of viable gigs together. It is also possible to do Bideford Club on Thursday, but they take guests less frequently than the other clubs mentioned.

### Festivals

**Cornwall** (Wadebridge Late August bank holiday week-end)
**Lowender Peran** (Perranporth mid-October)

**Baring Gould: Lewtrenchard** October, in Devon but only just!

**Fiddles at Fowey:** late May, Cornish instructional fiddle weekend at Penquite House

**Golant Fowey.** Run by Mike O'Connor and Chris Bartram.

**Racca Day** Cornish musicians get together and dance, Bodmin Public Rooms, mid-February.

Two **Cultural Festivals** with significant folk elements are **Golowan** (Penzance midSummer), **St Ives** (mid-September), and there is a small folk element in the **Du Maurier festival** in Fowey (late May)

### Radio

**Fish on Folk**, is hosted by John the Fish for BBC Radio Cornwall on Sunday Evenings. Generally Radio Cornwall is very positive and regularly uses folk feeds and plugs folk events as long as the organisers get it together. Presenters like Ted Gundry and Chris Blount are friendly and helpful.

### Organisations

There isn't a Cornish Folk Alliance. But there are a number of organisations which happily work alongside each other: the Cornish Dance Society, Cowethas Ilow Kernow (the Cornish Music league), Cornish Music Projects, the North Cornwall Traditional Arts Project, and Cornwall Songwriters.

**Major clubs:** Bodmin, St Ives (also near are Bideford (Devon) and Folk on the Moor (near Plymouth))

**Other Venues known to book folk acts:** Hall for Cornwall (Truro) - big names only, Acorn Theatre (Penzance) See the Kernowfolk Website for contact info and/or links for just about all the above.

**Cornish Music and Dance** It's worth pointing out that because of its (relative) isolation and past contact with Brittany, Cornish folk music and dance is an interesting mix of material. Some would like it to be a clone of the Irish or Scots Celtic scene - but it isn't. Some deny there's any Celtic element at all - but there is! But these are mostly political stances. The truth is there's a significant minority of Cornish material that is definitely different, and all of it is worth celebrating and enjoying.

**Mike O'Connor**
*Musicologist, Member of Cornwall Songwriters, t/a Lyngham House Music (Cornish music books and CDs), Kernowfolk Webmaster.*

***Editors Note:*** *Cornish music sessions can be found at the Portreath Arms, Redruth and Porters Pub, St Agnes. There's also a regular session at The Cove Inn, Cadgwith. See listings for details.*

## Rooting around the South West

### *Organisations, Listings etc.*

**www.adop05.care4free.net/clubs.html**
*Devon Folk Club Listings*

**www.flaxey-green.co.uk**
*Flaxey Green Listings*

**www.folkaroundbristol.co.uk/main.htm**
*Folk Around Bristol (includes Avon Folk Diary)*

**www.angelfire.com/mo/kernowfolk/index.html**
*Kernow Folk (Cornwall)*

**www.wrentrust.co.uk/second.htm**
*The Wren Trust Organisation*

### *Clubs etc.*

**www.newrenaissance.ibs.ee/halsway_manor**
*Halsway Manor Folk Centre*

**www.btinternet.com/~John.W.B/moorfolk_html**
*Dousland, Folk on the Moor*

## south west venues

**The English Regions**
*These are based on Regional Arts Board representation with some variation. We have kept all of Derbyshire and Lincolnshire in the East Midlands. The RAB definitions are used here as a generally helpful way of splitting up England for a more detailed look at local resources. Also check sections for neighbouring regions for the band, caller or venue you are looking for. Contributors and magazine listings often mention venues and services based in adjacent regions.*

### The Acorn Theatre
Parade Street, PENZANCE, Cornwall, TR18 4BU
**Contact** Julia Twomlow
*Arts venue.*

### The Albert Hole
The Albert Inn, West Street, Bedminster, BRISTOL, BS3 3NN
**Contact** Lorraine Carpenter
**Address** 1 West Street, Bedminster, BRISTOL, BS3 3NN
**Phone** 0117 9661968
**Email** enquiries@thealberthole.co.uk
*Wednesday. Concert/ folk club, national & international guests. 50 capacity, in house PA.*

### Bodmin Folk Club
The Garland Ox Clubroom, Higher Bore Street, BODMIN, Cornwall
**Contact** Chris Ridley
**Address** Trenillocs, ST COLUMB, Cornwall, TR9 6JN
**Phone** 01637 880394
**Web** www.bodminfolk.freeserve.co.uk
**Alt contact** Jim Bassett
**Address** 17 Glynn Road, PADSTOW, Cornwall, PL28 8EF
**Phone** 01841 532469
*Every Friday 8.15pm. Alternates guest nights with "Open House" evenings.*

### Brewery Arts Theatre
Brewery Court, CIRENCESTER, Glos, GL7 1JH
**Phone** 01285 655522 (box)
**Contact** Sara Jennings - Theatre Administrator
**Phone** 01285 657181 - admin
**Fax** 01285 644060
**Email** admin@breweryarts.freeserve.co.uk
*Receiving venue, presenting a mixed programme with emphasis on folk/ blues/ world music. Capacity 120. Stage 4m x 4.5m.*

### Brewhouse
Coal Orchard, TAUNTON, Somerset, TA1 1JL
**Phone** 01823 283244 - box office
**Contact** Deb Richardson
**Phone** 01823 274608
**Fax** 01823 323116
**Email** brewhouse@btconnect.com
**Web** www.brewhouse-theatre.co.uk
*Welcoming, accessible arts centre venue, regularly programs an extensive folk season.*

### Bridport Bull Ceilidhs
The Bull Hotel, East Street, BRIDPORT, Dorset
**Contact** Hemlock Music
**Address** PO Box 32515 LONDON, W3 0NS
**Fax** 020 8992 8691
**Email** office@hemlockmusic.co.uk
**Web** www.hemlockmusic.demon.co.uk
*Occasional ceilidh series, top national bands.*

### Cadgwith Folk Club
The Cove Inn, CADGWITH, Cornwall
**Contact** Dave Leggett
**Phone** 01326 290812
*Tuesday, 8.30pm. Music & song session.*

### Dragon Folk Club
The Bridge Inn, Main Road, SHORTWOOD, S Glos
**Contact** Maggie Starkey
**Phone** 01454 321943
*Friday 8.15 pm Traditional & contemporary folk music.*

### Folk on The Moor
The Moorland Hotel, Wotter, PLYMOUTH, Devon, PL7 5HP
**Contact** Anton Horwich - Info
**Address** 3 Woodside Cottages, Milton Coombe, YELVERTON, Devon, PL20 6HQ
**Phone** 01822 853620
01752 261669
**Fax** 01752 221108
**Email** anton@healthypulses.co.uk
**Web** www.btinternet.com/~john.w.b/moorfolk_html
**Alt contact** Ben Campbell - Bookings
**Address** 51 Burnham Park Road, Peverell, PLYMOUTH, Devon, PL3 5QB
**Phone** 01752 708770
**Email** bencamp@ic24.net
*Sundays, 8pm. Alternating singers and guest nights. All types of music. Capacity 100.*

### Fringe Folk Club
The Bull's Head Hotel, BRIDPORT, Dorset
**Contact** Peter Wilson
**Phone** 01308 425713
*Alternate Tuesdays, 8pm. Regular jam session with occasional guests.*

### Guildhall Arts Centre
23 Eastgate Street, GLOUCESTER, GL1 1NS
**Contact** Julian Barr
**Phone** 01452 396389
**Fax** 01452 384734
**Email** julian.barr@glos-city.gov.uk
**Web** www.mylife.gloucester.gov.uk
**Alt contact** Andrew Mitchel-Stead
**Phone** 01452 396388
**Email** ams@glos-city.gov.uk
*Roots Café; world music events fornightly. Music Lab; local talent open stage & showcase fortnightly. Annual Cajun & Zydeco and Blues festivals.*

### Hyde Folk Club
Hyde Park Hotel, PLYMOUTH
**Contact** Den Couch
**Address** 10 Short Park Road, Peverell, PLYMOUTH, Devon, PL3 4PZ
**Phone/Fax** 01752 661367
**Phone** 0421 614547
**Email** deniuphillbooks@plymouth online.net
*Every Monday, 8pm. £1 admission. Folk & blues, floor singers welcome, occasional guests.*

### Merlin Theatre
Bath Road, FROME, Somerset, BA11 2HG
**Fax** 01373 461360
**Contact** Paula Hammond - Director
**Alt contact** Alan Moody - Admin & Finance
*240 seat performing arts theatre.*

### Music & Theatre at St Clare's
St Clare's, Fore Street, SEATON, Devon
**Contact** Pat Trezise
**Fax** 01297 20679
**Web** www.stclares.demon.co.uk
*Twice monthly venue for blues and folk acts. Salsa & Cajun dance bands, groups from UK + beyond, touring theatres. Small, acousticly 'perfect' venue.*

### Nailsea Folk Club
Ring O Bells, Whiteoak Way, NAILSEA
**Contact** Dave Francis & Val Broomhead
**Phone** 01275 855738

### Porters Session
The Porters Pub, ST AGNES, Cornwall
**Contact** Neil Davey
**Phone** 01209 219011
**Alt contact** Francis Bennett
**Phone** 01872 275058
*Wednesday, 8.30pm. Traditional Cornish music session.*

**Portreath Arms Folk Session**
Portreath Arms, The Square, Portreath, REDRUTH, Cornwall
**Contact** Chris James
**Address** Lanherch Bridge, REDRUTH, Cornwall, TR16 4QE
**Phone** 01209 843299, 07788 136089
**Email** chris@celtic-arts.co.uk
**Web** www.celtic-arts.co.uk
*Last Wednesday, 8pm. Emphasis on traditional Cornish material.*

**Ritz Acoustic Club**
The Ritz , Victoria Street, BURNHAM ON SEA, Somerset
**Contact** Dave Neville
**Phone** 01278 789376
**Email** ritzacousticclub@freeserve.co.uk
**Web** www.ritzacousticclub.ac.uk
**Alt contact** GC Music - Concert tickets
**Phone** 01278 794434
*Thursday, 8pm: open mic night. Plus regular Friday night concerts with national guests & local support.*

**Roses Theatre Tewkesbury**
The Roses Theatre, Sun Street, TEWKESBURY, Glos, GL20 5NX
**Contact** Robert Hamlin - Director
**Phone** 01684 290732
**Email** arts@rosestheatre.org
*Venue programming mix of folk roots & folk rock in the main house. Occasional folk club nights. 370 capcity, bar & disabled access.*

**The Square Folk Dance Club**
Witcombe Village Hall, Witcombe, NR GLOUCESTER
**Contact** Ann Appleing - Secretary
**Address** 55 Arle Road, CHELTENHAM, Glos, GL51 8LA
**Fax** 01242 692243
**Email** Derek-Ann@folksales.freeserve.co.uk
*Alternate Wednesdays, 8pm. Dance club for Country, Playford, Square & American contras with live music and various callers.*

**St Ives Folk Club**
The Star Inn, Fore St, Goldsithney, PENZANCE, Cornwall
**Contact** Johnathan Ryan
**Phone** 01736 711743
**Email** stivesfolkclub@aol.com
**Web** www.stivesfolk.freeserve.co.uk
**Alt contact** John Heath
**Phone** 01326 240182
*Saturday, 8.15pm. Small friendly club, all welcome. Traditional & contemporary folk. Alternate guests & open house.*

**Stroud Singers Session**
The Woolpack, Slad, STROUD, Glos
**Contact** Bob Bray
**Phone** 01453 764885
01453 765545
*1st & 3rd Tuesday, 8-11pm. Songs, stories & music in traditional style.*

**Torquay Folk Club**
The Crown and Sceptre, 2 Petitor Road, St Marychurch, TORQUAY, Devon
**Contact** Anne & Steve Gill
**Address** Maleth, 11 Cleveland Road, TORQUAY, Devon, TQ2 5BD
**Phone** 01803 290427
**Email** annemgill@dial.pipex.co.uk
**Web** www.flaxey-green.co.uk
*2nd Thursday. Singers nights with occasional guests.*



**The English Regions**
*These are based on Regional Arts Board representation with some variation. We have kept all of Derbyshire and Lincolnshire in the East Midlands. The RAB definitions are used here as a generally helpful way of splitting up England for a more detailed look at local resources. Also check sections for neighbouring regions for the band, caller or venue you are looking for. Contributors and magazine listings often mention venues and services based in adjacent regions.*

## west midlands region

Listed ceilidh and social dance bands in the West Midlands include **Aardvark Ceilidh Band**, **Alf Alfalfa & The Wild Oats**, **All Blacked Up**, **Amaryllis**, **Captain Swing**, **Claret**, **Cornfield Perambulation**, **Cuckoo's Nest**, **FKG Band**, **John Kirkpatrick Ceilidh Band**, **Peeping Tom**, **Running on Empty**, **Scotch The Rumour Ceilidh Band**, **Skillet**, **Steamchicken**, **The Baggettes**, **The Cat's Whiskers** and **The Cuckoo Ale Band**.

Listed dance callers include **Dave Hunt** and **Pete Grassby.**

***Listed magazines and websites offer further band information.***

**The English Regions**
*These are based on Regional Arts Board representation with some variation. We have kept all of Derbyshire and Lincolnshire in the East Midlands. The RAB definitions are used here as a generally helpful way of splitting up England for a more detailed look at local resources. Also check sections for neighbouring regions for the band, caller or venue you are looking for. Contributors and magazine listings often mention venues and services based in adjacent regions.*

# West Midlands

**Worcester, Shropshire, Staffordshire, Warwickshire, Herefordshire, Stoke on Trent, Telford and Wrekin, Birmingham, Coventry, Dudley, Sandwell, Solihull, Walsall and Wolverhampton**

## Regional organisations

**West Midlands Arts**
**Mail address** 82 Granville Street, Birmingham, B1 2LH
**Phone** 0121 631 3121
**Fax** 0121 643 7239
**Web** www.arts.org.uk/directory/regions/west_mid/index.html

**West Midlands Arts** produce information sheets including lists of music promoters and venues in the region.

**West Midlands Folk Federation**
An organisation comprising over 60 member organisations including festivals, folk song clubs, club/concert performers, ceilidh bands and dance display sides. WMFF exists to promote and support folk throughout the region by providing links between clubs, PR, advice and acting as a contact point.
**Web** www.collicutforce9.co.uk

## Local organisations

**Arts Alive** is a Rural Touring Scheme promoting live events in Shropshire and Herefordshire. See Organisations section.

**Heart of England Music** is an Independent Midlands based non-profit initiative which supports charities by publishing compilation albums and staging benefit concerts. See Organisations section.

**Mythstories Museum of Myth and Fable**, Shrewsbury is an educational charity promoting literacy & literature through storytelling and related artforms. Please note the venue is due to move Sept 2001. Also hosts Storytelling Café
**Phone** 01743 357140
**Web** www.mythstories.com

**North Shropshire Folk** is a group of enthusiasts promoting folk concerts in Whitchurch.
**Contact** Howard Prince
**Phone** 01948 840408

**Warwickshire Trad Arts** organise and co-ordinate folk & traditional arts activities in Warwickshire (incl. Coventry).
**Contact** Graham Bradshaw
**Phone** 024 7371 1616

## Magazines

**What's On – A Diary of Folk Events in the Midlands** comprises mostly adverts for a large number of folk clubs and concerts across the Midlands. 11 issues a year. Subscription £11 per year.
**Contact** Joe Smith (Editor)
**Mail address** 121 Morris Avenue, Coventry, CV2 5GS
**Phone** 024 76 444405

**In Touch** magazine provides a guide to folk and traditional music and arts in the Coventry/Warwickshire/West Midlands area. Distributed free around clubs.
**Contact** 28 Columbia Gardens, Bedworth, Warwickshire, CV12 9EF.
**Phone** 024 76310877
**Email** in_touch34@hotmail.com

**Shreds and Patches** covers Shropshire and bordering counties includes articles, reviews, previews, listings of festivals, workshops, song clubs and dance clubs, sessions and dance display sides.
**Contact** 1 Herbert Avenue, Wellington, Telford, Shropshire, TF1 2BT
**Phone** 01952 240989
**Email** mainwaring@enta.net

**Folk Buzz** (incorporating Scans folk magazine) covers the North West, North Midlands and overlaps into immediately adjacent areas. See North West Region for full contact details.
**Web** http://website.lineone.net/~folkbuzz

**The Folk Mag** is a web based folk magazine for Shropshire, Staffordshire, West Midlands, Warwickshire, Worcestershire and Herefordshire with news, reviews, articles, resources, song and dance diaries, contacts and music.
**Web** www.thefolkmag.co.uk

**Somers Folklife** is a membership based voluntary group providing information about all aspects of folk via publications.
**Web** www.somers-folklife.com

**The Evening Sentinel**, Stoke has music listings on Fridays including folk and has an occasional folk column (Folk Tales) written by Eric Cox.

## Radio

**Genevieve Tudor's Sunday Folk** is broadcast on BBC Radio Shropshire, BBC Hereford and Worcester and BBC Radio Stoke. The programme is two hours of music, interviews and chat. Sundays 8-10pm 94.6, 94.7,95,96, 104, 104.6 FM
BBC Radio Shropshire, PO Box 96, Shropshire, SY1 3WW
**Phone** 01743 248484
**Fax** 01743 271702
**Email** genevieve.tudor@bbc.co.uk
**Web** www.bbc.co.uk/england/radioshropshire/folk.shtml
**Radio Shropshire** also gives coverage of events through What's On type announcements.

**Fretwork** is a folk radio show going out on Radio Stoke 94.0 FM and Radio Hereford and Worcester 94.7, 104, 104.6 FM. Thursdays, 7pm.
**Presenter** Nonny James
**Mail address** BBC Radio Stoke, Cheapside, Hanley, Stoke on Trent ST1 1JJ
**Phone** 01782 208002
**Email** nonny.james@bbc.co.uk

**http://pages.unisonfree.net/folkimages/RAD.htm** is a listing of folk radio shows across the north and includes some West (and East) Midlands programs.

## Venues

There are various arts centres regularly presenting folk, roots and world acts throughout the regions and a growing number of local promoters.

Arts centres with a good folk concert series include **Oakengates Theatre**,Telford, **Lichfield Arts Centre**, **The Brewhouse Arts Centre**, Burton on Trent, **Old Chapel at Hollymoor**, Birmingham, **Stafford Gatehouse Theatre**, **Bridgehouse Theatre Concerts**, Warwick (programmed by Warkwickshire Trad Arts). Other venues regularly programming folk concerts include **Huntingdon Hall**, Worcester, **Courtyard Arts Centre**, Hereford, **mac**, Cannon Hill Park, Birmingham. **Ronnie Scott's**, Birmingham, **The Assembly Rooms**, Ludlow (01584 878141 and www.lar.co.uk) and the **Buttermarket**, Shrewsbury.

# west midlands region

Listed ceilidh and social dance bands in the West Midlands include **Aardvark Ceilidh Band**, **Alf Alfalfa & The Wild Oats**, **Al Blacked Up**, **Amaryllis**, **Captain Swing**, **Claret**, **Cornfield Perambulation**, **Cuckoo's Nest**, **FKG Band**, **John Kirkpatrick Ceilidh Band**, **Peeping Tom**, **Running on Empty**, **Scotch The Rumour Ceilidh Band**, **Skillet**, **Steamchicken**, **The Baggettes**, **The Cat's Whiskers** and **The Cuckoo Ale Band**.

Listed dance callers include **Dave Hunt** and **Pete Grassby**.

***Listed magazines and websites offer further band information.***

**The English Regions**
*These are based on Regional Arts Board representation with some variation. We have kept all of Derbyshire and Lincolnshire in the East Midlands. The RAB definitions are used here as a generally helpful way of splitting up England for a more detailed look at local resources. Also check sections for neighbouring regions for the band, caller or venue you are looking for. Contributors and magazine listings often mention venues and services based in adjacent regions*

**Solihull Folk & Acoustic Music Club** runs acoustic music concerts weekly and **The Newhampton Acoustic Music Club**, Wolverhampton alternate club nights with concerts. **Dove Valley Blues & Roots Club** nr Uttoxeter has blues, cajun, zydeco, soul, folk & Irish music. Monthly events are found throughout the region. **Folk on The Fosse** promote established contemporary folk acts, Roots & Blues at **The Dovehouse Theatre**, Solihull have top roots & blues and **Potteries Folk Club**, Stoke On Trent present mainly traditional music & song. **Food & Folk**, Worcester promote folk concerts monthly and **Folk in Goodrich**, Herefordshire run eight per year. There are both guest nights and singers nights at **Brew Town Folk Club**, Burton-On-Trent, the **Oak Room Music Club,** Warwick, **Unicorn Folk Club**, Tong, near Shifnal, and at **Cheque Mates Folk 'n' Roots Club**, nr Tamworth.

**Mythstories** (Museum of myth and fable) in Shrewsbury has regular storytelling events and a permanent display. (See above)

**Peeping Tom Ceilidhs**, Coventry are monthly with **Peeping Tom** and guest callers. **Shrewsbury Morris Dancers** organise a series of regular ceilidhs in Shrewsbury (01939 233977). See **Shreds & Patches** (details above) for other dances in the area .

## Festivals

The established festivals in the West Midlands region include **Warwick Folk Festival** (July) which has range of acts & events across the genre, a substantial Morris dance element, childrens & street events, **Bridgnorth Folk Festival** (August) and **Bromyard Folk Festival** (September), are also successful events with similar emphasis. **Festival At The Edge** (July) is a storytelling and related arts festival, **Market Drayton Folk Festival** (October) celebrates Welsh border songs, dances and stories and **Bedworth Folk Festival** (November) is a three day festival run in conjunction with Nuneaton & Bedworth Borough Council. **Lichfield Folk Festival** (July) is a dance based festival, followed by **Lichfield Real Ale, Jazz & Blues Festival** which has a world music element and by **Lichfield Cajun & Zydeco Festival**. **Sounds In The Round** at **mac**, Birmingham is an open air music festival running from early June to mid August. Free festivals include **Stafford Castle Festival of Folk & Blues** (July), **Baggeridge Folk Festival**, Dudley (late August) and **Lichfield Free Festival in The Park** (July). **Birmingham International Jazz Festival** (July) presents jazz, blues and associated music around the city with 90% free admission. Other events include **Sandwell Arts Festival** (June) - music, theatre, dance, street festival, **Burntwood Folk Festival** (August) - English folk acts, plus children's & informal events and **Wheaton Aston Festival** (May) - music, song & dance with a policy to encourage young talent.

● ***Thanks to Derek Schofield, Sheila Mainwaring, Shreda and Patches, Ray and Bev Langton, In Touch and The Folk Mag for assistance with the above information.***

## Rooting around the West Midlands

### Organisations/Listings etc.

**www.thefolkmag.co.uk**
*The Folk Mag*

**www.angelfire.com/mt/folkofax**
*Folkofax*

**www.cmarge.demon.co.uk/glosfolk.htm**
*Gloucestershire Folk Organisation*

**members.aol.com/mwpioneer/Home.htm**
*Mike Walton's Page (Worcester)*

**www.collicut.force9.co.uk**
*The West Midlands folk Federation*

### Clubs etc.

**www.btinternet.com/~folkfax/swan/index.htm**
*Bedworth, Folk at the Swan*

**www.thefolkmag.co.uk/diamond**
*Birmingham, Black Diamond Folk Song Club*

**www.thefolkmag.co.uk/btmc**
*Birmingham Traditional Music Club*

**www.wurzelbush.co.uk**
*Brinklow, Wurzel Bush Folk Club*

**members.aol.com/Bazyat/folk.html**
*Burntwood, Chase Folk Club*

**members.aol.com/jehill1/brewtown**
*Burton on Trent, Brewtown Folk Club*

**www.folkonthefosse.co.uk**
*Eathorpe, Folk on the Fosse*

**www.ennerdale.freeserve.co.uk/home.htm**
*Kingswinford, Woodman Folk Club*

**www.cuckoosnestleek.freeserve.co.uk**
*Leek, Cuckoo's Nest Folk Club*

**www.katiefitzgeralds.co.uk**
*Stourbridge, Katie Fitzgerald's*

**www.folkplus.freeserve.co.uk**
*Walsall, Folk Plus*

**www.somerstfc.org.uk**
*Worcester, Somers Traditional Folk Club*

**The English Regions**
*These are based on Regional Arts Board representation with some variation. We have kept all of Derbyshire and Lincolnshire in the East Midlands. The RAB definitions are used here as a generally helpful way of splitting up England for a more detailed look at local resources. Also check sections for neighbouring regions for the band, caller or venue you are looking for. Contributors and magazine listings often mention venues and services based in adjacent regions.*

### A People's Cabaret
Hare & Hounds, King's Heath High Street, BIRMINGHAM
**Contact** Pam Bishop
**Address** 35 Waterloo Road, Kings Heath, BIRMINGHAM, B14 7SD
**Phone** 0121 2443513
**Email** pam@cabaret.free-online.co.uk
**Web** www.cabaret.free-online.co.uk
*2nd Sunday, 8pm. Celebration of traditional performance arts, issue-based or benefit events. 80-100 capacity.*

### Alcester Folk Dance Club
Baptist Church Hall
ALCESTER, Warks
**Contact** David Pattenden
**Address** 10 Wordsley Close, REDDITCH, Worcs, B98 8RT
**Phone** 01527 65483
*Club running weekly social folk dances for members and visitors.*

### Alton Folk Club
Peakstone Inn, Cheadle Road, ALTON, Staffs
**Contact** Margaret Slinn
**Phone** 01538 755776
*1st Tuesday, 8pm. Acoustic players welcome.*

### Black Diamond Folk Club
The Turk's Head, Lawson Street, BIRMINGHAM
**Contact** Paul Ryan
**Address** 748 Walsall Road, Great Barr, BIRMINGHAM, B42 1EX
**Phone** 0121 358 2665
**Email** paulryan@bigfoot.com
**Web** www.thefolkmag.co.uk/diamond
*Fridays, some singers, some guest nights.*

### Blues & Ballad Club
The Rising Sun, Shraley Brook, Audley, NEWCASTLE UNDER LYME, Staffs
**Phone** 01782 629155
*Occasional Saturdays, 8pm. Blues, ballad, folk.*

### Brew Town Folk Club
Star and Garter, Grange Street, West Corner, BURTON-ON-TRENT, Staffs
**Contact** Carol Worker
**Address** 107 Hillside Road, LINTON, Derbys, DE12 6RB
**Phone** 01283 760575
**Web** members.aol.com/jehill1/brewtown
**Alt contact** Sam Scotney
**Address** 36 Balfour Street, BURTON UPON TRENT, Staffs, DE13 OTS
**Phone** 01283 532787
*Friday, 8.30pm. Alternate guest nights and singarounds. Floor spots on guest nights with 2 weeks notice.*

### Brewers Droop Free Folk Club
The Brewers Droop, Wolverhampton Street, WILLENHALL, West Midlands
**Contact** Bonny & Eddie
**Phone** 01922 722424
*Thursday, 8.30pm. Traditional & contemporary folk plus blues and acoustic. Small room (no drums!).*

### The Brewhouse Arts Centre
Union Street, BURTON UPON TRENT, Staffs, DE14 1EB
**Phone** 01283 567720 - admin, 01283 516030 - box
**Web** www.brewhouse.co.uk
*Monthly folk events. Large auditorium (seated or standing), plus smaller events in bar.*

### Bridgehouse Theatre Concerts
Warwick Grammar School, Mytom Road, WARWICK
**Contact** Graham Bradshaw
**Address** 250 Earlsdon Avenue North, COVENTRY, CV5 6GX
**Phone** 024 7671 1616
**Fax** 024 7671 1191
**Email** rootsrecs@brclick.com
**Alt contact** Dick Dixon
**Phone** 07831 890905
**Email** dick.dixon@warfolk.demon.co.uk
*Regular concerts with top national guests. 300 capacity, good acoustics.*

### Chase Folk Club
Bridge Cross Sports & Social Club, Bridge Cross Rd, Chase Te, BURNTWOOD, Staffs, WS7 8BX
**Contact** Barry Yates
**Phone** 01543 271269
*Friday, 9pm. Resident band; The Staffordshire Men. Irish, Scots, Australian, Bluegrass. Traditional & contemporary.*

### Cheque Mates Folk 'n' Roots Club
Coton and Hopwas Social Club and Institute, School Lane, Hopwas, NR TAMWORTH, Staffs
**Contact** Sandra Robinson
**Phone** 0121 354 4234
*Thursday, 8pm. Singers and musicians nights; wide range of folk. Guests at least once a month.*

### Club Accord
Catshill Working Men's Club, Meadow Road, Catshill, BROMSGROVE, Worcs
**Contact** Tracey Middleton
**Phone** 0121 7436637
*2nd Monday, 8pm. Piano accordion club. National/ international guest artists bi-monthly.*

### Common Folk
Free Trade Inn, Wood Lane, Pelsall, WALSALL, West Mids
**Contact** Steve Pickersgill
**Address** 67 Chapel Street, Pelsall, NR WALSALL, W Mids, WS3 4LW
**Phone** 01922 685568
07989 117020
**Email** comfolk@hotmail.com
*Thursday, 8.30pm. Mainly 'acoustic' performers nights, with occasional/ monthly guests. 75 capacity.*

### Coventry Folk Club
Malt Shovel, Spon End, COVENTRY, Warks
**Contact** Dick Dixon
**Address** 26 Spencer Avenue, Earlsdon, COVENTRY, CV5 6NP
**Phone** 024 7667 8738
**Email** dixon@warfolk.demon.co.uk
*2nd Thursday. Singers & musicians welcome.*

### Crystal Folk
The Old Dial, 17 Audnham St, Amblecote, STOURBRIDGE, West Mids
**Contact** Ann & Bob Adams
**Phone** 0121 559 8607
*Wednesday, 8.30pm. All forms of acoustic music welcome. Occasional guests.*

### Dove Valley Blues and Roots Club
Doveridge Village Club, NR UTTOXETER, Staffs
**Contact** Fred Hopwood
**Address** 17 Colne Mount, UTTOXETER, Staffs, ST14 7QR
**Phone** 01889 563123
07989 669824
*Venue for Blues bands, plus some Cajun, Zydeco, Soul, Folk & Irish.*

### Falconer's Country Dance Club
The Leisure Centre, Cruxwell Street, BROMYARD, Herefordshire
**Contact** Barbara Tyler
**Address** 48 Landsdowne Crescent, Bayston Hill, SHREWSBURY, SY3 OJD
**Phone** 01743 872182
*Alternate Sundays, September to May. English & American country dancing to live music from the Falconer's Band.*

## Folk in Goodrich
Goodrich Village Hall, GOODRICH, Herefordshire, HR9 6HY
**Contact** Sarah Jones
**Address** The Forge, Goodrich, ROSS ON WYE, Herefordshire, HR9 6HY
**Fax** 01600 891284
**Phone/Fax** 07973 143950
**Email** sarah@bluebearmusic.demon.co.uk
**Web** www.bluebearmusic.demon.co.uk
*Concerts with good quality acoustic acts. Approx 8 per year.*

## Folk on The Fosse
**Contact** Stevie Horton
**Address** PO Box 1957, Eathorpe, LEAMINGTON SPA, Warks, CV33 9YG
**Phone** 01926 632946
**Email** stevie@folkonthefosse.co.uk
**Web** www.folkonthefosse.co.uk
**Alt contact** Richard Barnes
**Phone** 01788 567338
**Email** richard@folkonthefosse.co.uk
*Last Tuesday. Top contemporary folk music guest acts. 120 capacity.*

## Food & Folk
Rushwick Village Hall, WORCESTER
**Contact** John Phillips
**Phone** 01905 640857
*2nd Saturday, 8pm. Guest acts, all types of folk music. £3, including light supper. Not August.*

## Harbury Folk Club
The Dog Inn, Harbury
NR LEAMINGTON SPA, Warks
**Contact** Peter MacDonald
**Phone** 01926 613730
**Email** harburyfolkclub@welcome.to
**Web** welcome.to/harburyfolkclub
*1st Thursday, 8.30pm. Primarily singers' club, all types of music, readings & dance welcome. Free entry.*

## The Hunter Folk Club
The Hunter, Saverley Green, Cresswell, BLYTHE BRIDGE, Staffs
**Phone** 01782 392067 - pub
**Contact** Lin and Ted
**Phone** 01782 395304
*3rd Tuesday, 8.30pm. Mainly folk singaround, all welcome.*

## Huntingdon Hall
Crowngate, WORCESTER, WR1 3LD
**Phone** 01905 611427 - box office
**Contact** Chris Jaeger
**Phone** 01905 23428
**Fax** 01905 619958
*Folk concert venue.*

## Lichfield Arts Centre
The Guildhall, Bore Street, LICHFIELD, WS13 6NE
**Contact** Brian Petty
**Address** Lichfield District Arts Assoc. , Donegal House, Bore Street, LICHFIELD, Staffs, WS13 6NE
**Phone** 01543 262223
**Fax** 01543 417308
**Email** bookings@lichfieldarts.org.uk
**Web** www.lichfieldarts.org.uk
*Arts centre regularly programming top folk, roots & blues acts.*

## mac
Cannnon Hill Park, BIRMINGHAM, B12 9QH
**Phone** 0121 440 3838 - box office
**Contact** Dorothy Wilson
**Phone** 0121 4404221
**Fax** 0121 4464372
**Email** enquiries@mac-birmingham.org.uk
**Web** www.mac.birmingham.co.uk
*Regular folk, roots, acoustic, world and singer/songwriter concerts. See also Sounds in The Round.*

## Millers Arms Folknight
The Millers Arms, Bridge Street, PERSHORE, Hereford
**Phone** 01386 553864
**Contact** Jim Richardson
**Phone** 01386 556992
*1st Wednesday, 8.30pm. Singaround; acoustic. all types of music.*

## The Newhampton Acoustic Music Club
The Newhampton Inn, Riches Street, WOLVERHAMPTON, West Mids
**Contact** Dave Brookes
**Phone** 01902 745773
**Email** dave@uppen-penn.freeserve.co.uk
**Email** david.j.brookes@talk21.com
*Alternate Saturdays, 8.30pm. Concert club featuring a broad range of acoustic roots and folk music.*

## Oak Room Music Club
The Oak Room, Globe Hotel, Theatre Street, WARWICK
**Contact** Pam Johnathan
**Phone** 01926 499178
*Monday, 8.30pm.Alternating singers nights, guest nights & session nights.*

## Oakengates Theatre
Limes Walk, Oakengates, TELFORD, Shrops, TF2 6EP
**Phone** 01952 619020 - box office
**Contact** Sarah Russell
**Phone** 01952 610163
**Fax** 01952 610164
**Email** oakthea@wrekin.gov.uk
**Web** www.oakengates-theatre.co.uk
*Venue promoting regular variety of folk & roots music. 650 capacity, bar, disabled facilities.L*

## Old Chapel at Hollymoor
Old Chapel, Hollymoor Centre, Manor Park Grove, Northfield, BIRMINGHAM, B31 5EX
**Phone** 0121 683 1834 (box)
**Contact** Alun Gunter
**Phone** 0121 303 9881
0121 303 9880
**Fax** 0121 3039889
**Email** bheag.al@virgin.net
**Alt contact** Suzzanne Cooper
**Phone** 0121 683 1836
**Fax** 0121 683 1837
*Venue promoting wide range of roots music.*

## Peeping Tom Ceilidhs
Massey Ferguson Social Club, Broad Lane, COVENTRY
**Contact** Ben Woodward
**Address** 76 Highland Road, Earlsdon, COVENTRY, CV5 6GX
**Phone** 024 7671 1924
024 7667 4491
**Fax** 024 7671 1191
**Email** peeping.tom@btinternet.com
**Alt contact** Graham Bradshaw
**Address** 250 Earlsdon Avenue North, COVENTRY, CV5 6GX
**Phone** 024 7671 1935
**Email** rootsrecs@btclick.com
*1st Thursday, 8pm. Monthly ceilidh series with Peeping Tom plus guest callers.*

## Potteries Folk Club
Rising Sun, Knowle Bank Road, Shraleybrook, Audley, STOKE ON TRENT, ST7 8DS
**Contact** Jason Hill
**Address** 54 Prince Street, Burslem, STOKE ON TRENT, Staffs, ST6 4EN
**Phone** 01782 813401
07778 913528
**Email** Jason@burslem.demon.co.uk
**Web** http://potteriesfolk.com
**Alt contact** Lorna Davies
**Address** Koinonia, Cheddleton Heath Road, Cheddleton, LEEK, Staffs, ST13 7DX
**Phone** 01538 360256
*2nd & 5th Friday. Mainly traditional. 60 capacity.*



**The English Regions**
*These are based on Regional Arts Board representation with some variation. We have kept all of Derbyshire and Lincolnshire in the East Midlands. The RAB definitions are used here as a generally helpful way of splitting up England for a more detailed look at local resources. Also check sections for neighbouring regions for the band, caller or venue you are looking for. Contributors and magazine listings often mention venues and services based in adjacent regions.*

**The English Regions**
*These are based on Regional Arts Board representation with some variation. We have kept all of Derbyshire and Lincolnshire in the East Midlands. The RAB definitions are used here as a generally helpful way of splitting up England for a more detailed look at local resources. Also check sections for neighbouring regions for the band, caller or venue you are looking for. Contributors and magazine listings often mention venues and services based in adjacent regions.*

## Ronnie Scott's (Birmingham)
258 Broad Street, BIRMINGHAM, B1 2HF
**Phone** 0121 643 4525
**Fax** 0121 643 8086
**Email** info@ronniescotts.demon.co.uk
**Web** www.bigbearmusic.com/ronnie scotts
**Alt contact** Big Bear Music Agency
**Address** PO Box 944, Edgbaston, BIRMINGHAM, B16 8UT
**Phone** 0121 4547020
**Fax** 0121 4549996
**Email** bigbearmusic@compuserve.com
*Live music 7 days a week. Venue/ bar/ restaurant. 300 capacity. Available for private promotions, all enquiries to Big Bear Music.*

## Roots & Blues at The Dovehouse Theatre
Dovehouse Theatre, Langlet Arts &Sports Centre, Kineton Green Road, SOLIHULL, B92 7ER
**Phone** 0121 7067139 (box)
**Contact** Transmusic
**Address** PO Box 8342, BIRMINGHAM, B9 4EZ
**Phone** 0121 680 7723
07940 354178
**Web** www.transmusic.co.uk
*Last Tuesday, 8pm. A variety of top roots & blues.*

## Solihull Folk & Acoustic Music Club
Damson Park, Damson Parkway, SOLIHULL, West Mids, B91 2PP
**Contact** Transmusic
**Address** PO Box 8342, BIRMINGHAM, B9 4EZ
**Phone** 0121 680 7723
07940 354178
**Web** www.transmusic.co.uk
*Monday, 8.30pm. Acoustic music concerts. 200 capacity, part seated. Children welcome, disabled access.*

## Stafford Gatehouse Theatre
Eastgate Street, STAFFORD, ST16 2LT
**Phone** 254653 - box office
**Contact** Daniel Shaw - Manager
**Phone** 01785 253595 - admin
**Fax** 01785 225622
*Venue promoting national folk & roots acts.Spring season in 98 capacity studio, autumn concerts in 506 capacity theatre.*

## Storytelling Café
Mythstories, Museum Of Myth & Fable, 1st Floor, 19/21 Hills Lane, SHREWSBURY, SY1 1QU
**Phone** 01743 357140
**Email** dez@mythstories.com
**Web** www.mythstories.com
**Alt contact** Ali Quarrell
**Address** Rose Cottage, Church Road, WELSHPOOL, Powys, SY21 7LN
**Phone** 01938 554428
**Email** ali@mythstories.com
*1st Monday. Storytelling club. Events at same venue other Mondays.*

## Unicorn Folk Club
The Bell Inn, Tong, NR SHIFNAL, Shropshire
**Phone** 01952 850210 - pub
**Contact** Vicky Evans
**Phone** 01952 810355
*Friday night, 8.45pm. Some singers nights, some guest nights.*

# Yorkshire

**North Yorkshire**
**East Riding, Kingston upon Hull, N and NE Lincolnshire, York, Barnsley, Bradford, Calderdale, Doncaster, Kirklees, Leeds, Rotherham, Sheffield and Wakefield**

## Organisations

**Yorkshire Arts**
**Mail address** 21 Bond Street, Dewsbury, WF 13 1AX
**Web** www.arts.org.uk/directory/regions/york/index.html

**Yorkshire Dales Workshops** is a traditional folk arts development company working in Yorkshire working to promote participation in folk arts through organising workshops, courses, concerts and dances for people of all ages. These workshops are mainly small-scale events and offer opportunities for developing skills in a small group situation and also in larger groups. YDW aim to provide for people of all ages and abilities, operating in the rural areas of North Yorkshire as well as the urban areas of Keighley, Bingley, Bradford and Leeds and surrounding districts. Residential weekends provide the added bonus of a day or two in the beautiful Yorkshire Dales. In addition to promoting workshops, courses and performances YDW provide opportunities in folk arts for school, taking visiting artists into schools for workshops and performances.

Song, fiddle traditions, Scandinavian Music and dance, Celtic traditions and local Yorkshire traditions all feature strongly in the regular programme. By providing resource materials at many of the workshops and courses and by publishing a small range of books on dance, music and the directory of folk and related arts in Yorkshire YDW offer the chance of further learning. YDW also produces CDs in relation to published music and dance books.

Yorkshire Dales Workshops has a membership of 14 at the moment, including professional performers, dancers, tutors, band members, administrators, photographers, a playwright, singer/songwriters. YDW try to collaborate with other Yorkshire Arts organisations both within and outside the folk world in the timing of events and sharing information and helping with each others marketing. It is not a for profit organisation and depend on voluntary labour. YDW are always pleased to hear from anyone keen on getting involved or wishing to contribute ideas.
**Contact** Geoff & Liz Bowen
**Mail address** Yorkshire Dales Workshops, 14 Oakburn Rd, ILKLEY, West Yorkshire LS29 9NN
**Phone/Fax** 01943 609421
**Phone** 01943 609393
**Email** ydw@ydw.btinternet.co.uk
**Web** www.ydw.btinternet.co.uk

**South Riding Folk Network** is a voluntary group of active folk musicians and artists supporting, promoting and raising the profile of the folk arts.
**Contact** May Cheadle (Chairperson)
**Phone** 01433 631352
**Email** chair@folk-network.com
**Alt contact** Cath James (Secretary)
**Phone** 0114 268 0880
**Email** secretary@folk-network.com

**Ryburn 3 Step** are singers, dancers and instrumentalists who perform and organise a wide variety of folk events in West Yorkshire including presentations, workshops and consultancy for schools and community organisations.
**Mail address** 103 Oldham Road, Ripponden, West Yorkshire HX6 4EB
**Phone/Fax** 01422 822 569
**Email** ryburn3step@backshift.demon.co.uk
**Web** www.ryburn3step.org.uk

**Village Carols** is a non-profit making organisation which exists to record and promote local carol traditions.
**Contact** Ian Russell
**Mail address** P.O. Box 2099 Sheffield, S35 0XU
**Phone** 01224 645486
**Fax** 01224 272728
**Email** ian.Russell@abdn.ac.uk
**Web** www.sgpublishing.co.uk/gm/vc/vcabout.html

## Magazines

**Filofolk** provides a three month diary listings and a club guide listing venue addresses and contact phone numbers.
**Web** www.tabbytail.freeserve.co.uk/filofolk.htm

**Spire Folk** is a web site covering folk and roots music in the heart of England. Centred around Chesterfield but includes club listings in South Yorkshire.
**Web** www.spirefolk.org.uk

**Folk News** in North and East Yorkshire is a magazine published quarterly by the North and East Yorkshire District of EFDSS. It has News, reviews, listings diary for Song Clubs, Musicians' Clubs, Sessions, Ritual Dance Clubs and Social Dance Clubs.
**Contact** Eric Storey (Editor)
**Mail address** 133 Compass Road, Hull, HU6 7AW
**Phone** 01482 804962
**Email** ericstorey@folknews.freeserve.co.uk

**Tykes News** magazine covers activities in and around Yorkshire. It is published quarterly by Tykes News association. Subscriptions by post- £5.25 for four issues.
**Mail address** 408 Skipton Road, Utley, Keighley, West Yorkshire, BD20 6HP
**Phone** 01535 606939
**Fax** 01535 211947
**Email** tykes@woodtyke.force9.co.uk

***Editor's note*** *This is a substantial publication full of news items, reviews, articles and song club adverts.*

**Stirrings** magazine covers folk, roots and acoustic music in South Yorkshire and beyond. Subscriptions £5.00 for four issues (inc p&p)
**Contact** Raymond Greenoaken (Editor)
**Mail address** 11 Ratcliffe Road, Sheffield S11 8YA
**Phone** 0114 266 1158
**Email** stirrings@taproot.demon.co.uk
**Web** www.stirrings.co.uk

***Editor's Note*** *With new editor, Raymond Greenoaken, Stirrings has gone glossy. It has plenty of news snippets, CD and live reviews and a variety of articles. The Make a Date section is a diary listing backed up by the Sessions and Club and Concert Venues sections which give full details.*

**South Riding Folk Network Web Directory** covers regional and national organisations, publications, events and provides useful links.
www.folk-network.com/directory

**South Riding Folk Network News** is a quarterly newsletter aimed at the general public as well as the folk community. It includes listings, articles and news.
**Contact** Paul Davenport
**Mail address** 6 Thompson Close, Maltby, South Yorkshire S66 8QG
**Phone** 01709 813862
**Email** paul.davenport@virgin.net

**South Yorkshire Folk** has current listings and information about music clubs, events and festivals in and around South Yorkshire.
**Web** www.syfolk.co.uk

## yorkshire region

Listed ceilidh and social dance bands in Yorkshire include **Bedlam**, **Black Sheep Ceilidh Band**, **Bracken Rigg Band**, **Ceili House**, **Gina Le Faux**, **Herb Boys**, **Knotted Chord Folk Dance Band**, **Mountain Ash Folk Dance Band**, **Official Brawl**, **Pied Piper Folk Dance Band**, **Pierrot**, **The Rhythm Chaps**, **Shindig** and **Spinning Jelly**.

Listed dance callers include **Nikki Hampson**, **Pete Coe**, **Peter Barnard** and **Sue Coe**.

***Listed magazines and websites offer further band information.***

**The English Regions**
*These are based on Regional Arts Board representation with some variation. We have kept all of Derbyshire and Lincolnshire in the East Midlands. The RAB definitions are used here as a generally helpful way of splitting up England for a more detailed look at local resources. Also check sections for neighbouring regions for the band, caller or venue you are looking for. Contributors and magazine listings often mention venues and services based in adjacent regions.*

NORTH WEST SOUTH

# yorkshire region

**The English Regions**
*These are based on Regional Arts Board representation with some variation. We have kept all of Derbyshire and Lincolnshire in the East Midlands. The RAB definitions are used here as a generally helpful way of splitting up England for a more detailed look at local resources. Also check sections for neighbouring regions for the band, caller or venue you are looking for. Contributors and magazine listings often mention venues and services based in adjacent regions.*

## Venues and Clubs

West Yorkshire has a large number of clubs plus a range of events run by organisations such as **Yorkshire Dales Workshops** and **Ryburn 3 Step**. Venues promoting folk and roots events include the **Trades Club**, Hebden Bridge (folk, jazz, rock & world music Thursdays to Sunday), **Slaithwaite Civic Hall**, Huddersfield and **Square Chapel Centre** for the Arts, Halifax. **Leeds Irish Centre** has concerts at weekends plus classes in Irish traditional music and dance. **Birdsedge Live Music** promote occasional concerts during Spring and Autumn in Birdsedge near Huddersfield.

Several clubs have guest artists most weeks including **Topic Folk Club**, Bradford (international guests), **Folk at The Grove**, (mainly singers), **Shoddy Doggie Folk Club**, Dewsbury and **Ryburn Folk Club**, near Ripponden (range of traditional based residents plus national & international guests).

Clubs with a mix of singers nights and guest nights include **Otley Folk Club**, **Skipton Folk Club**, **The Famous Bacca Pipes Folk Club**, Keighley and **The General Ludd Folk Club**, Huddersfield. **Croppers Folk Club**, Cleckheaton has occasional guests.

Regular dance events include **Ryburn Barn Dances** which are monthly in Mytholmroyd, near Halifax and **Les Panards Dansants**, Leeds for French music & dance.

In York itself, the **Black Swan Folk Club** has guests every week plus a monthly singers' night. Sessions can be found most nights of the week at various pubs in the city. **Friday 13th Folk Club**, Harrogate has both guests and singers & musicians nights. Sessions in Harrogate happen at the **Tap & Spile**, Tower St. **Ripon Folk Club** has singarounds plus a monthly guest night. **The Railway Tavern**, Hensell also has monthly, mainly traditional, folk guests. Yorkshire Coast clubs include **Whitby Folk Club**, **Whitby Session** at The Endeavour, **Bayfolk** at The Dolphin Hotel, Robin Hood's Bay and **Scarborough Folk**. **Whitby Musicport** promote events including concerts & workshops in Whitby, see ww.musicport.fsnet.co.uk

Across in East Yorkshire, **Driffield Live** is a series of monthly concerts, including folk, roots and comedy. **2nd Wednesday Folk Club**, Driffield is a singaround with occasional guests, the club also runs some concerts in Weaverthorpe village hall. There are guest nights at **Grimsby Folk Club** and the **White Horse Folk Club**, Beverley.

Focusing on Sheffield, Doncaster and Southern Yorkshire, the **Rockingham Arms**, Wentworth, near Rotherham, has very regular concerts with national and international folk artists. **Bob Hazelwood's Blues Folk & Roots Concert Lounge**, Sheffield has concerts weekly with top folk, blues & roots guests. **Penistone Paramount**, Penistone, near Sheffield, has many live events, including folk concerts. **Blaxton Live** promote monthly concerts with top national/ international guests in Blaxton and at other venues. **The Red House**, Solly Street, Sheffield has music every night of the week including sessions and workshops. **The Lion**, Wath Upon Dearne also has a session, singers nights and regular guests (Live @ The Lion). **Bay Horse Folk Club**, Doncaster, **Beehive Folk Club**, Harthill Village and **Wortley Arms Folk Club**, Sheffield have guests monthly, **Barley Sheaf Friday Folk**, Barnsley has both guest artists & open mic nights while **Booit Straps Folk Club**, Sheffield has floor spots and feature nights. **Doncaster Folk Club** is mainly a singers' club with occasional guests.

## Festivals

Popular and established festivals in Yorkshire include **Whitby Folk Week** (August), **Beverley & East Riding Folk Festival** (June), **Holmfirth Folk Festival** (May), **Otley Black Sheep Folk Festival** (September) and **Cleckheaton Folk Festival** (July). **Bradford Festival** (June) is a large cross arts festival, including free concerts featuring top folk & roots acts. Festivals associated with the sea include **Seafest**, Scarborough (July) and **Captain Cook Maritime Festival** (October). Other folk festivals, many with strong informal elements include **Robin Hoods Bay Folk Weekend** (June), **Moor & Coast Festival of Traditional Music, Song, Dance & Arts**, Whitby (early May) and **Musicport World & Acoustic Music Festival**, Whitby (October). **Traditions 2001**, Halifax (September) is a street festival with dance teams and street performers. In South Yorkshire, **Rotherham Folk & Jazz Festival** (September) features folk and jazz concerts in the park and **The Wombwell Free Folk Festival**, Barnsley (August) happens in a big top marquee. In the West, **Birdsedge Village Festival** (July) is a local mixed arts, community & music event with a bias towards folk, **Sowerby Bridge Rushbearing Festival** (September) is a traditional event and Yorkshire Dales Workshops' run several tuition based festivals including the **Fiddler's Meet** (November), **Scandinavian Festival** (May), plus voice and family weekends.

*Thanks to Pete Coe, Ryburn 3 Step, Yorkshire Dales Workshops, Jacey Bedford, Tykes News, South Riding Folk Network and Stirrings for assistance with the above information.*

## Rooting around in Yorkshire

### Organisations, Listings etc.

**www.stirrings.co.uk/folkzone/stirrings/index.html**
*Stirrings regional magazine*

**www.tabbytail.freeserve.co.uk/filofolk.htm**
*Filofolk (from Tykes News Magazine)*

**www.folk-network.com**
*South Riding Folk Network*

**www.syfolk.co.uk**
*South Yorkshire Folk*

**www.ryburn3step.org.uk**
*Ryburn 3 Step*

### Clubs etc.

**www.hammonda.fsnet.co.uk**
*Cottingham Live www.cottingham-live.co.uk*

**www.driffieldfolkclub.co.uk**
*Driffield Folk Club*

**www.users.globalnet.co.uk/~moxey/BeeHive.html**
*Harthill, Beehive Folk Club*

**www.syfolk.co.uk/anstonfolk**
*South Anston, Anston Folk Club*

**freespace.virgin.net/wath.folk**
*Wath-on-Dearne, Wath Folk Club*

**www.soft.net.uk/10sg/nellies.htm**
*Beverley, White Horse Folk Club*

**2nd Wednesday Folk Club**
The Ship Inn, Langtoft, DRIFFIELD, East Yorks
**Contact** Jim Clarke
**Address** Red Worms, Helperthorpe, MALTON, North Yorks, YO14 8TQ
**Phone** 01944 738422
*Monthly singaround with occasional guests plus some concerts in Weaverthorpe village hall.*

**Ackworth Folk Club**
The Mason's Arms, Bell Lane, ACKWORTH, W Yorks
**Contact** Ben May
**Phone** 01977 617758
*Monday (except Bank Holidays). Singaround and musicians club.*

**Anston Folk Club**
The Loyal Trooper, South Anston, NR SHEFFIELD
**Contact** Judy Dalton
**Address** 213 Nursery Road, Dinnington, SHEFFIELD, S25 2QU
**Phone** 01909 569481
**Fax** 0703 1552002
**Email** judy.dalton@btinternet.com
**Web** www.syfolk.co.uk/anstonfolk/
*3rd Thursday. Singers club with occasional guests.*

**Barley Sheaf Friday Folk**
The Barley Sheaf, Aldham House Lane, Wombwell, BARNSLEY, S Yorks
**Contact** Hedley Jones
**Address** 5A Aldham Crescent, Wombwell, BARNSLEY, S Yorks, S73 8ES
**Phone** 01226 752901, 07773 072744
**Email** barleysheaf.folk@virgin.net
**Web** www.come.to/thebarleysheaf
*Friday, 9pm. Folk/ acoustic evening with guest artists & open mic nights. Capacity 100.*

**Barnsley Folk Club**
The Shaw Inn, Shaw Street, BARNSLEY, Yorks
**Contact** Linda Harris
**Phone** 01226 246582
01226 242849
*Monday 8.45pm. Traditional folk.*

**Bay Horse Folk Club**
The Bay Horse, Chapel Street Bentley, DONCASTER
**Contact** Graham Hudson
**Phone** 01302 349329
**Web** www.bayhorsefolk.freeserve.co.uk
*Monthly, Saturdays (last), 8.30pm. Folk music guests.*

**Beehive Folk Club**
The Beehive Public House, HARTHILL VILLAGE, South Yorks
**Contact** Ken Atkinson
**Phone** 0114 266 4206
**Web** www.users.globalnet.co.uk/~moxey/beehive.html
**Alt contact** Pete Garratt
**Phone** 0114 2352850
*1st Friday (usual.), 8.30pm. Guests.*

**Birdsedge Live Music**
Birdsedge Village Hall, Penistone Road, Birdsedge
NR HUDDERSFIELD, W Yorks
**Contact** Jacey Bedford
**Address** 10 Park Head, Birdsedge, HUDDERSFIELD, HD8 8XW
**Phone** 01484 606230
**Fax** 01484 606290
**Email** artisan@artifact.demon.co.uk
**Web** www.birdsedge.uk.com
**Alt contact** Tim King - Tickets
**Phone** 01484 688350
*Concerts on occasional Saturdays & Sundays during Spring and Autumn.*

**Black Swan Folk Club**
The Black Swan Inn, Peasholme Green, YORK, YO1 2PR
**Contact** Ro and Walls
**Address** 50 St Olaves Road, YORK, YO3 7AL
**Phone** 01904 632922
*Thursday, 8pm. Guests, plus monthly singers' night. All folk styles. 60 capacity. No smoking.*

**Blaxton Live**
**Contact** Andy, Jacquie & Katie
**Phone** 01302 771354
**Web** www.btinternet.com/~blaxton.vh
*Saturdays, Monthly concerts with top national/ international guests. Various venues.*

**Bob Hazelwood's Blues Folk & Roots Concert Lounge**
The Ecclesall Non-Political Club, 509 Ecclesall Road, SHEFFIELD, S11
**Contact** Bob Hazelwood
**Phone** 0114 273 8085
**Web** http://my.genie.co.uk/bob.hazelwood
*Thursday evenings. Top national folk, blues & roots guests.*

**Booit Straps Folk Club**
**Address** The Commercial, Station Road, Chapeltown, SHEFFIELD
**Contact** Lou Marriott
**Address** 3 Carlthorpe Grove, High Green, SHEFFIELD, S35 4PL
**Phone** 0114 284 5922
**Web** freespace.virgin.net/wath.folk/booit-straps.html/
**Phone** 0114 2469066 (venue)
*Monday 8pm. Floor spots and feature spots. 40 capacity.*

**City Varieties Music Hall**
Swan Street, LEEDS, LS1 6LW
**Contact** Peter Sandeman
**Phone** 0113 2430808
**Alt contact** Richard Paddison
*Yorkshire's premier variety venue.*

**Croppers Folk Club**
The Priory, Whitechapel, CLECKHEATON, W Yorks
**Contact** Fran & Russ Hughes
**Phone** 0113 2605896
*Friday, 9pm. Singers club plus occasional guests. Non-smoking, all welcome.*

**Doncaster Folk Club**
The Railway, West Street, DONCASTER, Yorks
**Contact** Sue Knowles
**Phone** 01302 361985
*Tuesday, 8.30pm. Mainly singers' club, occasional guests.*

**Driffield Live**
The Bell Hotel, Market Place, DRIFFIELD, East Yorkshire
**Contact** David Allan
**Address** 6 West Garth, Kilham, DRIFFIELD, YO25 4RD
**Phone** 01262 420040
**Email** dsa@givendale.freeserve.co.uk
*Monthly concerts, 3rd Thursday. Folk, roots and comedy. 300 capacity. Monthly open mic nights, 1st Thursday.*

**Ep'th Folk Club**
The Red Lion, Epworth, NR DONCASTER, Yorks
**Contact** Eric Payne
**Phone** 01427 872010
*Alternate Mondays, 8.30pm. Acoustic club; traditional & contemporary folk, blues, classical guitar & humour.*

**The Famous Bacca Pipes Folk Club**
Ukrainian Club, Mayfield Road, off Spring Gardens Lane, KEIGHLEY, West Yorks
**Contact** Jenny Scott
**Phone** 01535 605310
*Friday, 8.30pm. Singers nights with monthly guests. Venue change possible call Jim 01535 664634.*

**Folk at The Grove**
**Address** The Grove Inn, Back Row, Holbeck, LEEDS, L11
**Phone** 0113 2439254 - pub
**Phone** 0113 258 7073
*Friday, 8.30pm. Guests, mainly singers.*



**The English Regions**
*These are based on Regional Arts Board representation with some variation. We have kept all of Derbyshire and Lincolnshire in the East Midlands. The RAB definitions are used here as a generally helpful way of splitting up England for a more detailed look at local resources. Also check sections for neighbouring regions for the band, caller or venue you are looking for. Contributors and magazine listings often mention venues and services based in adjacent regions.*

## yorkshire venues

**The English Regions**
*These are based on Regional Arts Board representation with some variation. We have kept all of Derbyshire and Lincolnshire in the East Midlands. The RAB definitions are used here as a generally helpful way of splitting up England for a more detailed look at local resources. Also check sections for neighbouring regions for the band, caller or venue you are looking for. Contributors and magazine listings often mention venues and services based in adjacent regions.*

### Folk Evenings at Tocket's Mill
The Stable Bar, Tockets Mill,
NR SKELTON, N Yorks
**Phone** 01947 840928
*Friday, 8pm. Monthly folk concerts.*

### Friday 13th Folk Club
The Knox Arms, Knox Lane,
HARROGATE, Yorks
**Contact** Ray Black
**Address** 49 Electric Avenue, HARROGATE, Yorks, HG1 2BB
**Phone** 01423 502875
**Email** blackmale@talk21.com
**Alt contact** Roy Hardacre
**Phone** 01423 505647
*Friday, 8.30pm. Guests and singers & musicians nights. Plus Tuesday, 8.30pm at the Tap & Spile, Tower St, Harrogate, instrumental session.*

### General Ludd Folk Club
The Wheel Inn, James Street , Golcar,
HUDDERSFIELD
**Contact** Dave Ellis
**Phone** 01484 846611
**Alt contact** Tony Taffinder - Bookings
**Phone** 01484 4621124
*Friday, 8.30pm. Live acoustic music, all welcome. Guests approx. monthly.*

### The Hot Hole
**Contact** Rachel Anstis
**Address** PO Box TR69, LEEDS LS12 5HE
**Fax** 0113 2566733
**Email** hotholesalsa@hotmail.com
**Web** www.magnificent.net/hothole or www.hothole.leedsnet.org
*Salsa classes and global music events.*

### Kiveton Park Folk Club
Kiveton Park Colliery Cricket Club,
Stone Close, Kiveton Park
SHEFFIELD
**Contact** Andy Ducker
**Phone** 0114 287 9592
*Tuesday, 8.45pm. Mainly traditional music & song, bimonthly guests. Friendly atmosphere.*

### Leeds CeilidhE Club
Civil Service Club, Newton Road,
Chapel Allerton, LEEDS
**Contact** Grahame Binless
**Phone** 0113 269 4764
*2nd Thursday, 8pm. Modern ceilidhE through to Playford. Singers welcome.*

### Leeds Irish Centre
York Road, LEEDS
**Phone** 0113 2480613
**Phone** 0113 2480887
**Fax** 0113 2489179
*Traditional Irish music, classes, etc. Dancing classes Monday, Music classes Saturday. Concerts Friday & Sunday.*

### Les Panards Dansants
Burnley Lodge Centre, 42-46 Burnley Lodge Road, Burnley, LEEDS
**Contact** Yannick Minvielle-Debat
**Phone** 01274 833473
**Web** www.frenchdanceleeds.co.uk
*3rd Monday, 7.30pm. French music & dance club. Plus other French dance events.*

### Live @ The Lion
The Red Lion, High Street, WATH UPON DEARNE, S Yorks
**Contact** Ruth Wells
**Phone** 01709 878361
07751 516611
**Email** ragwells@btinternet.com
**Web** www.syfolk.co.uk/lion
*Sundays, 8pm singers nights and regular guests. Plus Wednesday night jam session.*

### Mill Folk
Pool Mills Sports & Social Club,
Otley Road, POOL IN WHARFDALE,
West Yorks
**Contact** Mark Longster
**Phone** 01423 868632
**Email** marklongster@supanet.com
**Web** www.marklongster.supanet.com/
**Alt contact** Iain
**Phone** 01423 340113
07943 875971 (Anne)
*Monthly concerts. Free singarounds every Thursday plus free live music every Sunday.*

### No Smoke Folke
Commercial Inn, Station Road,
Chapeltown, SHEFFIELD
**Contact** Pete Swift
**Address** 20 Penistone Road, Grenoside, SHEFFIELD, S35 8QG
**Phone** 0114 2455442
*Friday, 8.30pm. Singers club. One of the first no smoking clubs.*

### Ossett Singers Club
Brewers Pride, Healey Road, OSSETT,
West Yorks
**Contact** Geoff Pyke
**Address** 17 Spring View, OSSETT, West Yorks, WF5 0QB
**Phone** 01924 279206
**Email** Geoff@pyke42.freeserve.co.uk
*Thursday 8.45 pm. Singers session for all types of music. Free entry.*

### Otley Folk Club
Three Horseshoes,
Bridge Street, OTLEY, West Yorks
**Contact** Steve Fairholme
**Phone** 01943 467189
01943 464858
**Email** steve.fairholme@otley-folkfest.demon.co.uk
*Wednesday. Singers nights plus fortnightly guests, mainly traditional.*

### Penistone Paramount
Shrewsbury Road, Penistone,
SHEFFIELD, S36 6DY
**Contact** Steve Tales
**Phone** 01226 767532
**Web** www.penistoneparamount.co.uk
**Alt contact** Wendy or Brenda
**Phone** 01226 370088
*348 capacity venue with events 7 days a week, including music, theatre, concerts, opera, films, community projects.*

### The Piece Hall
HALIFAX HX1 1RE
**Phone** 01422 358087
**Contact** Mark Humphreys
**Email** mark.humphreys@calderdale.gov.uk
**Web** www.calerdale.gov.uk
**Alt contact** Geraldine Robertson-Brown
*Grade 1 listed building, 3 floors of galleries surrounding a large courtyard. 7,500 capacity. Location for "Traditions 2001".*

### Play On
The Shakespeare Hotel,
Gibraltar Street, SHEFFIELD
**Contact** Andy Bowdin
**Address** 19 Dobbin Hill, SHEFFIELD, S11 7JA
**Phone** 0114 2665197
**Email** slipjig@mcmail.com
**Alt contact** Stella Davies
**Address** 77 Horndean Road, Firvale, SHEFFIELD, S5 6UJ
**Phone** 0114 2435835
*1st Friday, 8.30 pm. All types of performance welcome, hosted by "Jig for a Kiss".*

### Pot & Glass Folk Club
The Pot & Glass, Egglescliffe Village,
NR YARM ON TEES, N Yorks
**Contact** Fiona Harley
**Phone** 01642 786318
**Alt contact** Martyn Littlefair
**Phone** 07880 885627
*3rd Wednesday, 8.30pm. Floor singers & musicians welcome.*

### Railway Tavern
The Railway Tavern, Station Road,
HENSELL, Yorks
**Phone** 01977 661478 - pub
**Contact** Rod Calvert
**Phone** 01924 242205
*1st Saturday, 9.15pm. Mainly traditional folk. Guests plus floor singers.*

### Red House
168 Solly Street, SHEFFIELD, S1 4BB
**Phone** 0114 2727926
**Contact** Linda Greatorex
*Music every night of the week. Sessions, workshops, etc.*

### Ripon Folk Club
Black-A-Moor Inn, RIPON, Yorks
**Contact** Norman Garbutt
**Phone** 01765 606995
**Alt contact** Jeff Wright
**Phone** 01423 340571
*Sunday, 8.30pm singaround. Thursday, monthly guest night.*

### Rivelin Folk Club
Rivelin Inn, Tofts Lane, Stannington, SHEFFIELD
**Contact** Ian Gregg
**Phone** 0114 266 5638
**Alt contact** Betty Hemmings
**Phone** 0114 2348448
*Wednesday, 8.30pm. Monthly guests.*

### Rockingham Arms
8 Main Street, Wentworth, ROTHERHAM, South Yorks
**Contact** Rob Shaw
**Address** 3 King Street, Swinton, ROTHERHAM, South Yorks, S64 8ND
**Fax** 01709 585977
**Email** rob.shaw.rock.uk@faxvia.net
*Regular concerts with national and international guest artists.*

### Ryburn Barn Dances
Mytholmroyd Community Centre, Mytholmroyd, NR HALIFAX, West Yorks
**Contact** Johnny Adams
**Address** 21 Halifax Road, Ripponden, SOWERBY BRIDGE, W Yorks, HX6 4AH
**Phone** 01422 822413
**Email** j.adams@salford.ac.uk
**Web** www.ryburn3step.org.uk
*3rd Saturday, (Sept-June). Monthly barn dances with local and national bands and callers.*

### Ryburn Folk Club
The Royal Hotel, Oldham Road, Rishworth, NR RIPPONDEN, West Yorks
**Contact** Pete Coe
**Address** 103 Oldham Road, RIPPONDEN, West Yorks, HX6 4EB
**Fax** 01422 822 569
**Email** petecoe@backshift.demon.co.uk
**Web** www.backshift.demon.co.uk/petehome.htm
*Last Tuesday, 8pm. (Sept-June). Wide range of traditional based residents plus national/ international guests. Occasional special events.*

### Scarborough Folk
The Tap & Spile, Falsgrave Road, SCARBOROUGH, Yorks
**Contact** Val Russell
**Phone** 01723 870801
*Every Monday, 8.30pm. Session/ songs. No guests at present. Very small room.*

### Shoddy Doggie Folk Club
Station Hotel, Crackenedge Lane, DEWSBURY, West Yorks
**Phone** 01924 450727
**Contact** Lionel - bookings
**Phone** 01924 441606
**Alt contact** Anne - publicity
**Phone** 0113 257 4658
*Saturday, 8.30pm. Guests plus some singers nights. Info from Deanna on 01924 518753.*

### Silsden Singers
Cobbydale Social Club, Silsden, KEIGHLEY, W Yorks
**Contact** Janet Russell
**Phone** 01535 656877
*Tuesday evening. Group of 30+ singers exploring their voices & singing with others in a supportive atmosphere. All welcome.*

### Skipton Folk Club
Lock Stock & Barrel, Coach Street, SKIPTON, West Yorks
**Contact** Sheila
**Phone** 01535 665889
**Alt contact** Paul
**Phone** 01282 426859
*Tuesday, 8.30pm. Alternate guests and singers nights.*

### Slaithwaite Civic Hall
Slaithwaite, HUDDERSFIELD, W Yorks
**Contact** Colne Valley Trust - tickets
**Address** Canal Side, Civic Hall, Slaithwaite, HUDDERSFIELD, HD7 5AB
**Phone** 01484 847790
*Alternate Thursdays, 7pm. Concerts with local and national folk/ roots acts.*

### Square Chapel Centre for the Arts
10 Square Road, HALIFAX, HX1 1QG
**Contact** Sally Martin
**Phone** 01422 353073, 01422 349422 - box office
**Fax** 01422 347928
**Email** info@sq-chapel-arts.demon.co.uk
**Web** www.sq-chapel-arts.com.co.uk
*Community arts centre, venue for professional touring theatre, classical & world music, amateur groups and workshops.*

### Station Folk Club
Station Hotel, Boroughbridge Road, NORTHALLERTON, Yorks
**Contact** Harvey Blogg
**Phone** 01677 423272
**Alt contact** Clair Boyd
**Phone** 01609 773316
*Friday, 7.30pm.Mainly acoustic live music with bias towards folk. All welcome. Not August.*

### Topic Folk Club
Melborn Hotel, White Abbey Road, BRADFORD, Yorks
**Contact** Finola Hingston
**Phone** 01274 834837
*Thursday, 8.30pm. National/ International guests, mainly singers plus some singers/ musicians nights.*

### Trades Club
Holme Street, HEBDEN BRIDGE, W Yorks, HX7 8EE
**Contact** David Parry
**Phone** 01422 845265
**Alt contact** Duncan Smethurst
**Phone** 01422 845265
**Fax** 01422 845599
*Venue promoting folk, jazz, rock & world music. Thursdays, Fridays, Saturdays 9pm, Sundays 1pm.200 capacity & bar.*

### Whitby Folk Club
The Plough, Baxtergate, WHITBY, N Yorks
**Contact** Mick & Angie Haywood
**Address** 3 Woodwarks Yard, Church Street, WHITBY, Yorks, YO22 4DG
**Phone** 01947 601963
**Email** mick.angi@btinternet.com
*Wednesday, 8.30pm. Singaround with musical interludes.*

### White Horse Folk Club
The White Horse Inn, Hengate, BEVERLEY, East Yorks
**Contact** Richard Wastling
**Address** 58 Newtondale, Sutton Park, HULL, East Yorks, HU7 4BH
**Phone** 01482 823 743
**Web** www.soft.net.uk/10sg/nellies.htm
*Every Monday, 8.30pm. Guests 1/3 weeks, singers & musicians nights 2/3 weeks. Traditional and contemporary music, all welcome.*

### Wortley Arms Folk Club
Wortley Arms, Wortley, SHEFFIELD
**Contact** Trevor Wasteney
**Phone** 0114 245 5126
**Alt contact** David Atkin
**Phone** 0114 284 7190
**Email** davewortleyfolk.aol.com
*3rd Saturday, 8.30pm. Guests.*



**The English Regions**
*These are based on Regional Arts Board representation with some variation. We have kept all of Derbyshire and Lincolnshire in the East Midlands. The RAB definitions are used here as a generally helpful way of splitting up England for a more detailed look at local resources. Also check sections for neighbouring regions for the band, caller or venue you are booking for. Contributors and magazine listings often mention venues and services based in adjacent regions.*

# Focus on Scotland

**The Scottish Arts Council**
**Mail address** 12 Manor Place, Edinburgh EH3 7DD
**Phone** 0131 226 6051
**Fax** 0131 225 9833
**Emails** administrator@scottisharts.org.uk (general)
help.desk@scottisharts.org.uk (enquiries)
press.office@scottisharts.org.uk (press and media enquiries)
**Web** www.sac.org.uk

The emphasis in this section is to provide routes to more information about the huge amount of folk music, song and dance throughout Scotland. Scottish artists, agents, festivals, record labels and all manner of services are prominent through all the sections of **Direct Roots**. Rather than group them altogether here, we have tried to signpost the access points to more specific information. Many thanks to the **TMSA** for their generosity in providing the Festival and Club listings and to the **Scottish Folk Arts Group** for their support.

**The Traditional Music and Song Association of Scotland (TMSA)**
**Mail address** 95-97 St Leonard's Street, Edinburgh EH8 9QY
**Phone** 0131 667 5587
**Fax** 0131 662 9153
**Email** info@tmsa.demon.co.uk
**Web** www.tmsa.demon.co.uk

The TMSA was founded in 1966 to sustain and develop awareness of Scotland's traditions of music and song. This it does through working in collaboration and consultation with many other organisations, always seeking to position the music at the heart of Scottish cultural life. The Scottish Arts Council provides financial support.

The TMSA is an association of members with a national committee, network of branches and national office - base for our national organiser and administrative assistant. National office is a clearinghouse for queries from all over the world. Regular publications include information leaflets, listings, newsletters, fact sheets and an annual festival calendar.

The TMSA actively promotes Scottish traditional music at festivals, ceilidhs, and concerts, particularly through the efforts of Branch committees who organise local events. In addition the education programme offers workshops in schools and communities.

**The Scottish Music Information Centre** exists to document and promote Scottish Music. It has a large library of music, some available for sale and hire. It has an extensive database of musicians, festivals, promoters, agents, services etc covering all genres.
**Contact** Caitle Faulas
**Mail address** S.M.I.C., Bowmont Gardens, Glasgow, G12 9LR
**Phone** 0141 334 6393
**Email** info@smic.org.uk
**Web** www.smic.org.uk

**The Scottish Folk Arts Group**
The objectives of The Scottish Folk Arts Group (SFAG) are the collection, presentation and dissemination of contact and activity information relating to folk music and folk arts within Scotland through means of hard copy publications and associated world wide web sites.

SFAG publish the **Scottish Folk Directory**, which is currently in its 32nd year. This is now online at www.scottishfolkdirectory.com and lists thousands of contacts for performers, events and services associated with folk music and folk arts in Scotland. There is also a constantly updated, day by day listing of clubs, concerts, festivals and other events.

The group also publishes **Folk Around the Forth**, a leaflet showing events around the Edinburgh area, and another publication, **A Pocket Guide to Folk Events Around Scotland** listing festivals and other activities.

SFAG have access to an email database of over 5000 contacts worldwide which is used for promoting tours and new releases.

SFAG and The Folk Directory are based at Blackfriars Music, a specialist folk music shop in Edinburgh.
**Mail address** 49 Blackfriars Street, Edinburgh, EH1 1NB, Scotland.
**Phone/Fax** 0131 557 3090
**Email** sfag@scotfolk.org
**Web** www.scottishfolkdirectory.com

**The Living Tradition** magazine is well established as a significant voice on behalf of traditional music. Based in Scotland since its inception in 1993, it has covered the music across Britain and Ireland but has accepted that this has led to a Scottish bias in its content. The March / April 2001 edition heralded the opening of an office in the North East of England with a view to widening the scope of its coverage. Alongside this development it can be expected to remain a major source of information and debate on Scottish matters.

The Living Tradition has also launched the concept of **The Tradition Bearers**, a series of CDs dedicated to traditional songs.
**Contact** Pete Heywood (Editor)
**Mail address** The Living Tradition, P.O. Box 1026, Kilmarnock, Ayrshire KA2 0LG.
**Phone** 01563 571220
**Email** living.tradition@almac.co.uk
**Web** www.folkmusic.net is a spin off from the magazine with many of the published articles there.

## BBC Radio Scotland

**Mail address** Broadcasting House, Queen Margaret Drive, Glasgow G12 8DG
**Phone** 0141 339 8844

**Iain Anderson's Fine Tunes**
*FM92.4-94.7 MW 810*
*Monday- Friday 2.30-4.00pm*

**Celtic Connections**
*Tuesday 7.00-9.00pm*
*Repeated Saturday 10.00-12.00*
Presented by Anne-Marie Middleton

**Travelling Folk**
*Thursday 7.00-9.00pm*
*Repeated Saturday 8.00-10.00pm*
Presented by Archie Fisher

**Take the Floor**
*Saturday 6.30-8.00pm*
Presented by Robbie Shepherd

**The Reel Blend**
*Sunday 10.00am-12noon*
Presented by Robbie Shepherd

**Pipeline**
*Sunday 4.30-5.30pm*
Presented by Iain MacInnes

**Feisean nan Gaidheal- The National Association of Gaelic Arts Youth Tuition Festivals**. Feis is the gaelic word for a festival. Over the last few years the word has become firmly associated with the highly successful movement comprising of a series of gaelic arts tuition festivals mostly aimed at young people, which now take place throughout the Highlands and Islands and in Scotland's major cities. For details of Feisean 2001 and the work of Feisean nan Gaidheal:
**Contact** The Director
**Phone** 01478 613355
**Web** www.feisean.org

## Websites

**Celtic Roots**
**Web** www.bbc.co.uk/celticroots
*The first extensive traditional/ celtic music site to appear on BBC Scotland was launched on Tuesday 24th April with a live webcast of Shooglenifty, Alyth McCormack and James Grant! This interactive web site will take in all of BBC Scotland's traditional and celtic output with links to Archie Fisher's 'Travelling Folk', Robbie Shepherd's 'Take the Floor' and 'Reel Blend', 'Pipeline', 'Celtic Connections' and Iain Anderson as well as relevant TV programmes.*
**Email** celticroots@bbc.co.uk
For more information:
**Contact** Sophie Pragnell
**Phone** 0141 338 3162
**Email** sophie.pragnell@bbc.co.uk

**www.gigguide.co.uk**
Live music listings and information about bands and venues in Edinburgh, Glasgow and Aberdeen.

**www.musicinscotland.com**
Listings, band biogs and on-line shop for Scottish music.

**www.skyelive.com**
Information about Scottish folk bands, tour dates etc.

**www.highland-music.com**
Information about the music industry in the Highlands. Also info on bands, venues and festivals.

**www.shetland-music.com**
Shetland music - fiddle legends plus contemporary bands.

- ***Thanks to Alison Smith of Organic Arts for her website recommendations.***

## TMSA 2001 Scottish Traditional Music Festival Calendar

**Email** festivals@tmsa.demon.co.uk

**7th-10th June 2001**

### 13th Isle of Arran Folk Festival

*A long weekend commencing on the Thursday night, throughout the island. Concerts, workshops, school events - great festival!*
**Contact** Iain/Maggie Frame
**Phone** 01770 302 623
**Web** www.arranfolkfestival.org
Camp site at Brodick
**Accommodation** Isle of Arran Tourist Board
**Phone** 01770 302140

**8th-10th June 2001**

### 26th Keith Festival

*Enjoyable mixture of formal and informal music, song and competitions organised by the local TMSA branch. The town of Keith comes alive with music whether in the evening ceilidhs or the pub sessions*
**Events contact** Edith Lewis
**Mail address** 10 South Court, Darliston, Elgin IV30 1ND
**Phone** 01343 540325
**Email** lewishugh@talk21.com or keithfestival@btinternet.com
**Web** www.keithfestival.btinternet.co.uk **Accommodation** Lona Thomson
**Mail address** 13 Cuthel Road, Keith AB55 5AS
**Phone** 01542 882278

**16th-18th June 2001**

### 7th Killin Traditional Music & Dance Festival

*Award winning festival featuring top quality artistes in three concerts, two ceilidh dances, and workshops. Family events, special guest sessions, storytelling, folklore tales, and numerous evening sessions. TMSA senior, junior & chorus cup competitions. Craft fair and local art society exhibition. Camp site available (pre booking only)*
**Contact** Lesley Syme
**Mail address** Lochtay Cottage, Main Street, Killin FK21 8UH
**Phone** 01567 820424
**Alt contact** A. Stewart, Artistic Co-ordinator
**Mail address** 2 Dochart Road, Killin FK21 8SN
**Phone** 01567 820224
**Accommodation** Tourist Board
**Phone** 01567 820254

**22nd-24th June 2001**

### 20th Highland Traditional Music Festival

*Rooted in the Highlands, broadly in the Celtic tradition, based in Dingwall. Ceilidh dance, concerts, singarounds, workshops, street music and pub sessions.*
**Contact** Rob Gibson
**Mail address** Tir nan Oran, 8 Culcairn Road, Evanton
**Phone** 01349 830388
**Fax** 01349 830599
Free camping.
**Accommodation** Highland Tourist Board
**Phone** 01463 731505
Tickets from Maitland Music
**Phone** 01349 863191.

**29th, 30th June-1st July**

### North Fife Family Festival

*A unique family friendly festival featuring mainstream Scottish traditions and ethnic minority cultures*
**Contact** Douglas Dawson
**Mail address** Roadside Cottage, West Flisk, Newburgh, Fife. (SAE please)
**Phone** 01337 870319
**Email** ddawson@ecvg.ndo.co.uk
**Accommodation** Tourist Information Office
**Phone** 01334 472021

**29th/30th-1st July**

### 31st Newcastleton Traditional Music Festival

*"The friendly festival". Traditionally based on competitions, ceilidhs, concerts, continuous sessions and workshops*
**Contact** Malcolm McEwan
**Mail address** Shankend Station, Hawick, Borders TD9 9UA
**Phone** 01450 377165
**Email** shankmac@aol.com
Supervised campsite and caravans. Free riverside camping. Village Hall, No. 8 Club

**June/July/August**

### Scottish Summer Schools

*Week/weekend/day courses in: Scottish singing, accordian, fiddle, bagpipe, clarsach, guitar, dancing-highland, old-time, Scottish country, step, Gaelic song/language, Scottish literature, history*
**Contact** Margery Stirling, Summer School Organiser
**Mail address** Airthrey Castle, University of Stirling, FK9 4LA
**Phone** 01786 467951
**Email** m.f.stirling@stir.ac.uk
**Web** www.stir.ac.uk/daice/suschool

July/August
## Summer Festival of Music, Inverness
*Balnain House open 7 days. Ceilidh dances every Wednesday 9pm. Concerts/sessions Tues/Thurs evenings. Traditional music every lunchtime in the Cafe from 1pm - 1.30pm. Sessions in the evening in the Cafe Bar. Come along and listen or join in with a song or a tune. Good food, great craic!*
**Contact** Caroline Hewat
**Mail address** Balnain House, 40 Huntly Street, Inverness
**Phone** 01463 715757

6th-8th July
## Cullerlie Traditional Singing Weekend
*A celebration of the singing traditions of North-East Scotland, England & Ireland in the unique setting of Cullerlie farm in rural Aberdeenshire. Singing sessions & workshops. Limited tickets*
**Contact** Anne Reid
**Mail address** Cullerlie Farm Park, Echt, Skene, Aberdeenshire, AB32 6XL
**Phone** 01330 860549
Camping/Caravan can be booked free of charge
**Accommodation** Tourist Information Banchory
**Phone** 01330 822000
01224 632727

10th-20th July
## Feis an Eilein/Skye and Lochalsh Festival
*Celtic based concerts, ceilidhs & workshops, spiced with World music, theatre and occasional surprises, in the brand new Gaelic college, alongside the separately run fiddle and dance summer school*
**Contact** Duncan MacInnes
**Mail address** Seall Community Arts, Ostaig House, Teangue, Isle of Skye IV44 8RS
**Phone** 01471 844207
**Email** dm@cali.co.uk
**Accommodation** Tourist Board
**Phone** 01478 612137 or camping.

11th-14th July
## Hebridean Celtic Festival
*From intimate early evening events to the late night party atmosphere in the festival tent, with workshops, pub sessions plus a rich variety of fringe events - the Festival offers something for everyone, reflecting the amazing diversity found within the current scene*
**Contact** Caroline MacLennan
**Mail address** PO Box 9909, Stornoway, Isle of Lewis H52 9DW
**Phone** 07001 878787
**Email** caroline@hebceltfest.com
**Web** www.hebceltfest.com
**Accommodation** Western Isles Tourist Board. Festival Tent, Castle Grounds, Stornoway

13th-15th July
## Stonehaven Folk Festival
*Concerts, ceilidhs, Traditional Concert, kids concerts, aqua ceilidh*
**Contact** Trudi Clayton, Festival Organiser
**Mail address** 14 Westfield Court, Stonehaven, AB39 2JW
**Phone** 01569 767666
**Email** trudi.clayton@virgin.net

14th July
## Folk in the Orchard – Falkland Palace
*From 12 - 12, a day long event of traditional music in the historic setting of Falkland Palace*
**Contact** Judith Fisken
**Phone** 01337 857397
**Accomodation** Kingdom of Fife Tourist Board
**Phone** 01592 750066

20th-23rd July
## Lossiemouth Folk Festival
*Small traditional festival, all events and camping within precincts of Beach Bar. Concerts each night, singarounds, sessions, children's entertainment and competitions. Events are FREE*
**Contact** Alison Simpson
**Mail address** 21 King Street, Lossiemouth
**Phone** 01343 814036 or Beach Bar 01343 813164
**Web** www.users.zetnet.co.uk/lossiefolkclub

20th-23rd July
## Isle of Bute Festival
*Predominantly Scottish/Irish folk music. World Ceilidh Band Championships, ceilidhs, workshops, concerts, barn dance and sessions. Children's Festival*
**Contact** Gillie Banks
**Mail address** 1 St Blane's Terrace, Kilchattan Bay, Isle of Bute PA20 9NN
**Phone** 01700 831614
**Email** gillie@butefolk.freeserve.co.uk
**Camping/accommodation** Tourist Office
**Phone** 01700 502151

27th-29th July
## Lomond Folk Festival, Balloch
*Featuring traditional/contemporary Celtic music. Sessions will play a major role in this year's festival, which will also include concerts, folk cruise, open stage etc*
**Contact** Stewart Davidson
**Mail address** 45 Inchfad Road, Balloch, Dunbartonshire. G83 8SY
**Phone** 01389 757561
01389 753838
**Accommodation** (Camping available), Tourist Information Centre
**Mail address** Old Station House, Balloch Road, Balloch, G83 8LQ
**Phone** 01389 753533
**Travel** 0141 2264826

28th July - 5th August
## The Splore - Scottish Traditional Music School
*Part of the Aberdeen International Youth Festival - Intensive course for young musicians aged 16 - 25, offers individual sessions, ensemble playing & master classes. Tutors this year include: Alistair Hardie (fiddle); Mairi Campbell (fiddle); Corrina Hewat (clarsach); Norman Kennedy (Scots song); Hazel Wrigley (guitar, accompaniment)*
**Contact** Dave Francis, Course Director
**Phone** 0208 9462995.

August
## Scots Fiddle School
The Scots Fiddle School, St Andrews, will not take place in 2001, but will return in 2002. Please check the 2002 Calendar for details when available.

2nd-5th August
### 6th Speyfest (Fochabers)
*Pan Celtic Festival of music, dance, workshops and visual arts*
**Contact** Cath Collins
**Mail address** 28 Institution Road, Fochabers IV32 7DZ
**Phone** 01343 821974
**Web** www.speyfest.com
**Email** cathy.collins@moray-edunet.gov.uk
**Accommodation** Elgin Tourist Board
**Phone** 01343 542666
01343 820362 (caravan site)

10th-12th August
### Auchtermuchty Festival TMSA Traditional Music Weekend
*The Traditional Music Weekend run by the local TMSA branch concludes the Community Festival. Concerts, ceilidhs, dances, competitions, work-shops, sessions and open air events.*
**Festival contact** Citty Finlayson
**Mail address** 17 High Street, Auchtermuchty, KY14 7AP
**Phone** 01337 828732
**Fax** 01337 828060
**Email** cittyfin@aol.com
**Web** www.auchtermuchty.co.uk
Camping & caravan sites available.
Community Centre/Victoria Hall.

12th August
### The Border Gathering
*Border life past and present. Historic re-enactments, traditional games (tossing the caber etc). Border & Northumbrian pipes and drums. Young Piper competition.*
**Contact** May McKerrell
**Mail address** Magdalene House, Lochmaben Dumfries DG11 1PD
**Phone** 01387 810439
**Camping** Traditional/folk music of the Borders

17th-19th August
### Mull of Kintyre Music Festival
*The best in Scottish/Irish music, pub sessions, ceilidhs, kids events*
**Contact** Anne Leith
**Mail address** 2d, Meadowburn Place, Campbeltown
**Phone** 01586 551053
**Alt contact** Iain Johnston
**Phone** 01586 552034
Free camping.

17th-26th August
### Langholm & Eskdale Music &Arts Festival
*Eclectic festival - traditional, classical and contemporary music, in various venues*
**Contact** Jim Muir/Alan Weatherstone
**Phone** 01387 380914
**Fax** 01387 381316
**Accommodation** Tourist Information Centre
**Phone** 01387 253862
01387 380976

19th August
### Culzean Castle & Country Park Scottish Music & Dance Festival
*1230 - 1630 Fountain Court. Music, song and dance in the Scottish tradition. pipers, highland dancing, folk group. Open air Country Dancing*
**Contact** Jonathan Carcale
**Mail address** Culzean Castle and Country Park, Maybole, Ayrshire.
**Phone** 01655 884455
**Accommodation** Camping/caravan
**Phone** 01655 760627

23rd-26th August
### Marymass Folk Festival
*Traditional music in Ayrshire. A mix of local and visiting performers, concerts, sessions, schools events*
**Contact** Joyce Hodge
**Mail address** 7 Machrie Place, Kilwinning
**Phone** 01294 551047
**Accommodation** Tourist Information, Rivergate, Irvine
**Phone** 01294 313 886.
Campsite available.

31st August - 2nd September
### Tinto Festival
*Festival set in rural Lanarkshire at the foot of Tinto Hill. Enjoy three days of music, song and dance in this unique self contained site*
**Contact** Meg or Gil
**Mail address** Wiston Lodge, Wiston, Nr. Biggar ML12 6HT
**Phone** 01899 850228
**Alt contact** Katherine
**Alt phone** 01864 502497
**Email** wiston@zetnet.co.uk
**Web** www/users.zetnet.co.uk/wiston

September/October
### Highland Harp Festival
*Concerts, classes & workshops by top players. All abilities catered for. Dates of the festival are to be confirmed.*
**Contact** Caroline Hewat
**Mail address** Balnain House, 40 Huntly Street, Inverness
**Phone** 01463 715757.
Seat lift from ground floor to cafe/assistance provided.

1st September
### Braemar Night (Blairgowrie)
*Street Fair with traditional entertainment, music, song and dance*
**Contact** Joyce Scott
**Mail address** Tourist Information Centre, 26 Wellmeadow, Blairgowrie. PH10 6AS
**Phone** 01250 872960

7th - 9th September
### 20th TMSA Kirriemuir Festival
*Provisional dates for a friendly traditional Scottish music festival in the birthplace of J M Barrie, - ceilidhs, concerts, dancing, singarounds, sessions, competitions and Kirk service. Street entertainment*
**Contact** Pat Newman
**Phone** 01575 540261
**Alt contact** Helen Gardiner
**Alt phone** 01307 462176
Town Hall, phone for other venues
Campsite facilities

7th-9th September
### Portpatrick Folk Festival
*Friendly festival in beautiful harbour village looking across the North Channel to Ireland. Concerts, pub gigs, sessions, workshops, family ceilidhs, street entertainment and lots of children's events. Established names and new talent mingle in a very congenial setting*
**Contact** Glen Murray
**Mail address** Portpatrick Events, 45 Main Street, Portpatrick, Stranraer, DG9 8JW
**Phone/Fax** 01776 810717
**Email** info@portpatrickevents.php247.net

7th - 9th September
## Linlithgow Folk Festival
Friendly festival with sessions, workshops, concert, family ceilidh, open stage, singaround, pub gigs, street entertainers, craft fair, children's events & more. All welcome
**Contact** Grace McClure, 10 Avon Place, Strawberry Bank, Linlithgow EH49 6BL
**Phone** 01506 844392
Most Venues.

7th - 9th September
## "Heart of Scotland" Festival Aberfeldy
*Autumnal festival bringing together Scots, Irish and Celtic arts, music and performers. Prominent artistes mingling with some of the most exciting up and coming performers around. Concerts, arts, family events, ceilidhs & sessions*
**Contact** Sandy Goodyear
**Phone** 01887 820956

21st - 22nd September
## Northlands Festival
*These are provisional dates for a celebration of music, dance, drama, writing, visual arts and films from Scotland and the Nordic countries.*
**Contact** Rebecca Lloyd
**Mail address** Northlands Festival Office. Whitechapel Road, Wick KW1 7EA
**Phone** 01955 606660
**Web** www.northlands.org
**Email** infor@northlands.org

21st-23rd September
## Hairth O'Knokrach
*Unique, small, friendly festival set on a remote greenfield site in the Galloway Hills. Some of the best traditional musicians perform from an open-air stage, plus sessions, open stage, workshops and other arts events*
**Contact** Liz Holmes
**Mail address** Garths of Deagh, Upland Heritage Association, Knockengorroch, Carsphairn, Castle Douglas DG7 3TJ
**Phone** 01644 460662
**Accommodation** Dumfries and Galloway Tourist Board
**Phone** 01387 253862 or Ayrshire and Arran Tourist Board
**Phone** 01292 288688.
Free camping on festival site or adjacent field contact Liz Holmes (as above).

28th-30th September
## 13th Annual Dunbar Belhaven Best Traditional Music Festival
*Informal, friendly weekend with sessions, concerts, dances, ceilidhs and formal competitions*
**Contact** Bill Crookston
**Mail address** Bonard House, Belhaven Road, Dunbar EH42 1NW
**Phone** 01368 863301 (home).

6th October
## Ayrshire Scottish Music Association (ASMA)
*Accordion and Fiddle Competitions, Magnum Centre, Irvine. Accent on encouragement and enjoyment*
**Contact** Derek Hamilton
**Mail address** 22 Blair Street, Galston, Ayrshire
**Phone** 01563 820635.

5th-7th October
## Penicuik Folk Festival
*Small, friendly festival including TMSA events. Concerts, ceilidhs and competitions in Navaar House Hotel Penicuik. Brochure available May*
**Contact** Brian Miller
**Mail address** 36 Greenhill Park, Penicuik
**Phone** 01968 678153
**Email** brian@horniegollach.com

5th-21st October
## The Doric Festival
*A rich programme of events in Aberdeenshire to celebrate great North East of Scotland traditions*
**Contact** Sandy Stronach
**Mail address** North Skelmanae, Strichen, Aberdeenshire, AB43 6SE
**Phone** 01771 653320.

26th - 28th October
## Kilmarnock Folk Weekend
*Traditional concerts, singers work-shop, musician sessions/ schools ceilidhs (Cumnock Primaries).*
**Contact** Maggie Macrae
**Mail address** 2 Mairs Road, Darvel, Ayrshire KA17 OLA
**Phone** 01560 321102

26th-4th November
## Scottish International Storytelling Festival
*Festival of traditional & contemporary storytelling with music & song interspersed. Based in the Netherbow Centre.*
**Contact** Joanna Bremner
**Mail address** The Netherbow, 43-45 High Street, Edinburgh
**Phone** 0131 557 5724

23rd-25th November
## ALP/Scots Music Group Fiddle 2001
*Scotland's Fiddle Festival: concerts, masterclasses, workshops, talks, recitals, sessions, stalls. The Assembly Rooms, Edinburgh. The place to be for fiddlers of all ages & abilities*
**Contact** ALP
**Mail address** 184 Dalry Road, Edinburgh EH11 2EP
**Phone** 0131 337 5442
0131 346 0977

***There are currently no festivals organised in December***

January 16th – February 3rd 2002
## Celtic Connections
*Glasgow Events in Glasgow Royal Concert Hall & other venues in the city centre. Community workshops, concerts and events. TMSA concerts & competitions.*
**Phone** 0141 353 4137
**Tickets** 0141 287 5511

***NB: The dates for the following are unconfirmed and likely to remain so until October 2001.***

28 January - 9th February 2002
## Inverclyde & Renfrew Music Festival
*Competitive festival (jnrs/snrs) music, speech & dance. (Competition entries closed October 2000.) Classes incl: Scots song - solo, all age groups; & choir; Scots fiddle; Scots dialect; Scottish country dance*
**Contact** Mr. A. Cockle
**Mail address** 123 Newton Street, Greenock, PA16 8SJ
**Phone** 01475 721024

13th February - 2nd March 2002
## Inverness Music Festival
*Competitive music festival - traditional and classical music, various venues. Concerts in Eden Court Theatre*
**Contact** The Festival Office
**Mail address** 9-11 Kenneth Street, Inverness. IV3 5NR
**Phone** 01463 716616

26th February - 3rd March
## Whuppity Scoorie Storytelling Festival - Lanark
*Courses and workshops, events for children and families, pub sessions for adult tellers and listeners. Supported by TMSA Lanarkshire Branch*
**Contact** Colin McAllister, Arts Officer
**Mail address** East Kilbride Arts Centre, Old Coach Road, East Kilbride, G74 4DU
**Phone** 01355 261000

8th -10th March 2002
## Milnathort Crackin' Ceilidh Weekend
*Concerts, ceilidhs and informal pub sessions. Orwell Gird Championship*
**Contact** Robin Watson
**Mail address** "The Haven", Greenbank Rd, Glenfarg
**Phone** 01577 830355
**Alt contact** Andy Ramage
**Alt address** 2 Gwendoline Row, Drunzie, Glenfarg, Perthshire, PH2 9QU
**Phone** 01577 830435.

22nd-23rd March
## Crawfordjohn Spring Fling
*Two day celebration of local culture ending two months of workshops in music, oral traditions, crafts. Friday/Saturday also culminate a week long programme of events including visiting artists*
**Contact** Billy Stewart
**Mail address** Upper Callender, Overtown, Lanarkshire ML2 ORS
**Phone** 01698 359326
**Accommodation & Travel** Clyde Valley Tourist Board
**Phone** 01555 662544

30th March
## 'Terr' in the Terraces Stirling Folk Club
*Day of music & song, evening concert, Terraces Hotel, Melville Terrace, Stirling. Singers/Musicians rooms, Bar, Host Musician's Stage! Fun Starts 1pm 'till 1am!*
**Contact** Isobel Methven (Stirling Folk Club)
**Phone** 01259 218521
01786 47226 (Hotel)

April
## Edinburgh Harp Festival
*This always takes place the weekend before Easter check with contact. Concerts, workshops, courses and ceilidhs for all ages.*
**Venue** Merchiston Castle School, Colinton Road, Edinburgh
**Contact** David Mieras
**Mail address** 87 Swanston Avenue, Edinburgh. EH10 7DA
**Phone/Fax** 0131 4452022
**Email** harpfest@scotweb.co.uk

5th-14th April
## Gatehouse of Fleet Festival
*A compact small, interesting family festival of traditional music, arts and crafts, children's events, sessions, singalongs, competitions, festival party and concerts.*
**Mail address** 4 Carney's Corner, Gatehouse of Fleet, Dumfries and Galloway DG7 2HW
**Phone/Fax** 01557 814030
**Email** george.mcculloch@virgin.net
**Web** www.ednet.co.uk/-russell/gatehous.htm
**Accommodation** Information from George McCulloch
Access most venues.

8th-13th April
## Aberdeen - Rootin' Aboot
*Broad ranging folk, roots & acoustic festival based in and promoted by the Lemon Tree. Evening concerts, free lunchtime performances, kids shows, workshops and packed weekend programme*
**Contact** The Lemon Tree
**Mail address** 5 West North Street, Aberdeen AB24 5AT
**Phone** 01224 6479999
**Fax** 01224 630888
**Accommodation** Aberdeen Tourist Office

12th-14th April
## The 23rd Glenfarg Folk Feast
*Fun, games and music to suit all tastes. Competitions, concerts and singarounds*
**Contact** Graham Brotherston
**Mail address** 9 Fairways, Dunfermline, KY12 0DU
**Phone** 01383 738922
**Email** graham@a9cgb.freeserve.co.uk
**Web** www.glenfargvillagefolkclub.freeserve.co.uk
**Accommodation** Free campsite at Wallace Park. Access at Glenfarg Hotel and Village Hall.

19th-21st April
## Moffat Folk Festival
*Main concert, workshops, ceilidhs. Also some free events.*
**Contact** Phil Munton
**Mail address** Hole House Cottage, Annanwater, Moffat, DG10 9LS
**Phone** 01683 221235
**Accommodation** Moffat Tourist Information Centre, Churchgate, Moffat, DG10 9EG
**Phone** 01683 220620

25th - 28th April
## Shetland Folk Festival
*International community festival various venues throughout the islands*
**Contact** Maria Strachan
**Mail address** 5 Burns Lane, Lerwick, Shetland, ZE1 0EL
**Phone** 01595 694757
**Fax** 01595 695381
**Email** sffs@zetnet.co.uk/sffs/
**Accommodation** Tourist Information Centre,Lerwick
**Phone** 01595 693434

3rd - 5th May
## Girvan Festival
*Traditional family oriented festival. Concerts, ceilidhs, workshops, competitions, children's events, sessions.*
**Accommodation** Robt Jardine
**Mail address** Westclyffe Hotel, Girvan
**Phone** 01465 712128
01465 714950
(Girvan Tourist Info)
01560 321102 (Other info.)
Free campsite

4th - 6th May
## The Border Gatherin' (Coldstream)
*A new event celebrating the richness of Scottish traditional music, all in a fine setting on the banks of the Tweed. Workshops, concerts, recitals & demonstrations, family ceilidhs, sessions and singarounds*
**Contact** Liz/Martin Marroni
**Phone** 01573 224920
**Email** lizmarroni@argonet.co.uk

11th May
## Banchory Festival of Scottish Music
*Competitions for fiddle, accordion, piano. Winners' concert in evening.*
**Contact** Fiona Kenneth
**Mail address** 49 Balmoral Place, Aberdeen
**Phone** 01224 580 929
Town Hall

17th-19th May
### Ceilidh Gall Gallowa'
*Unique, small, friendly festival set on a remote greenfield site in the Galloway Hills. Some of the best "purist," and "crossover," traditional musicians perform from an open-air stage, plus sessions, open stage facility, workshops, demos and other arts events*
**Contact** Liz Holmes
**Mail address** Garths of Deagh, Upland Heritage Association, Knockengorroch, Carsphairn, Castle Douglas, Kirkuidbrightshire, DG7 3TJ
**Phone** 01644 460662
**Accommodation** Dumfries and Galloway Tourist Board
**Phone** 01387 253862 or Ayrshire and Arran Tourist Board
**Phone** 01292 288688. Free camping on festival site or adjacent field contact Liz Holmes (as above).

17th-19th May
### Buchan Heritage Festival
*Celebration of the richness of north east culture. Dance, competitions, ceilidhs, concerts*
**Contact** Evelyn Mundie
**Mail address** 28 School Place, New Pitsligo, Fraserburgh AB43 6NJ
**Phone** 01771 653761
Caravans can be parked at Ritchie Hall.

23rd -26th May
### Orkney Folk Festival
*Traditional music festival based around Stromness with events in rural areas and smaller islands. Concerts, ceilidhs, workshops, Fiddlers' Rally, sessions*
**Contact** Johnny Mowat
**Mail address** Folk Festival Office, Town House Annexe, Victoria Street, Stromness, Orkney, KW16 3AA
**Phone** 01856 851331
**Fax** 01856 851636
**Accommodation** Orkney Tourist Board
**Phone** 01856 872856
01856 850716

24th-26th May
### The 8th Doune and Dunblane Fling
*Ceilidhs, concerts, sessions, shows and games, workshops, free open air festival by the river Allan, drama, dance, poetry, craft fair plus dungeon storytelling at Doune Castle. A friendly festival in a lovely setting, everyone very welcome.*
**Contact** John Lord
**Phone** 01786 824519
**Accommodation** B&Bs in Dunblane, campsite nearby.

24th-8th June
### The Highland Festival
*Celebration of arts and culture in spectacular locations throughout the Highlands and Islands*
**Contact** Alastair McDonald
**Mail address** 40 Huntly Street, Inverness IV3 5HR
**Phone** 01463 711112
**Fax** 01463 716777
**Web** www.highlandfestival.org.uk

The 2002 Festival Calendar will be available in December 2001. To ensure you receive your copy early why not become a member of the TMSA. Email your name and address and we'll send you the membership form *membership@tmsa.demon.co.uk*

If you are a festival organiser please send details for 2002 by October 6th 2001. Similarly if your festival was not included this year, please email details to *festivals@tmsa.demon.co.uk* or send details to the national office
**Mail address** TMSA, 95-97 St Leonard's Street, Edinburgh EH8 9QY
**Phone** 0131 667 5587
**Fax** 0131 662 9153

## TMSA Traditional Music Listings
**Events featuring traditional and folk music in Scotland**

**These listings have been generously provided by TMSA.** They are drawn from their quarterly listings which carry diary dates as well as the general information on venues and events. These listings are produced quarterly in hard copy for the tourist information service of the Scottish Tourist Board. The web service updates information more regularly and will eventually carry more than just the quarterly information.

Please note that some events may be cancelled at short notice given the current foot and mouth restrictions. Please check with contacts beforehand.

Listings are for the whole of Scotland by Area Tourist Board (ATB) in alphabetical order. Within each ATB section the information is categorised under Sessions, Folk Clubs, and Other Concerts.

Folk Clubs fall broadly into two categories. The first is an informal gathering of people who meet to exchange songs, play tunes etc, often called a singers and/or musicians' night. The second is more of a concert setting with guest artists booked to perform for the evening. There is usually a door charge varying from £1/£2 for the first type to £4/5 or more for the concert style. It is not necessary to be a member of a club to attend, everyone is welcome. Most clubs are run by volunteers and exist to promote traditional and general folk music. They tend to take place in the same venue and on the same day each week or fortnight. Visitors may come across a variety of musical forms. In a folk club setting audience members are expected to be quiet during performances.

Accordion and Fiddle Clubs meet monthly in most instances and many take a break during from May to August. There are guest artists, monthly socials, workshops and dances and these vary from club to club. Clubs are only listed when a meeting is scheduled.

Concerts usually run along similar lines to folk clubs in that you are expected to be quiet during performances. Concerts will usually be held in village halls or local function rooms. There will be admission charges for concerts.

## *Aberdeen and Grampian Folk Clubs*

### Aberdeen Folk Club
**Mail address** The Loft, O'Donaghues, Justice Mill Lane, Aberdeen
*Meets Mondays 8.30pm Guest artists occasionally.*
**Email** Aberdeenfolkclub@hotmail.com
**Phone** 01224 575040 (venue)

### Fyvie Folk Club
**Venue** Vale Hotel, Fyvie
*1st Wed each month is club night 2nd Wed is short committee meeting then session!*
**Contact** Mike Rogers
**Phone** 01651 891797

### Huntly Folk and Blues Night
*Every 3rd Wednesday in the month. 8.30pm - Midnight. FREE. Singers, players, listeners always welcome*
**Venue** The Auld Pit (Rose and Thistle) Duke Street, Huntly.
**Contact** Keith Cockburn
**Phone** 01466 792780
01466 793808

### Lossiemouth Folk Club
*Meets Tuesdays, informal, all singers and players welcome.*
**Venue** Beach Bar, Lossiemouth
**Phone** 01343 813164

## Ugie Folk Club
*Meets 1st Friday in the month 8pm FREE. Singers, players, listeners always welcome*
**Venue** Crichie Arms, Stuartfield

## Stonehaven Folk Club
*Meets Fridays 8pm, informal sessions, singarounds and occasional guest artists.*
**Venue** Crichie Arms, Stuartfield. St Leonard's Hotel, Stonehaven
**Contact** Trudi Clayton
**Phone** 01569 767666

# *Aberdeen and Grampian Accordion and Fiddle Clubs*

## Turriff and District Accordion & Fiddle Club
*1st Thurs every month 7.30pm - 11pm £2.50 & £1.50 Guest artists.*
**Venue** Royal Oak, Turriff
**Contact** Mrs Wilson
**Phone** 01888 544381

# *Aberdeen and Grampian Sessions*

**Sunday**
## Prince of Wales
**Venue** St Nicholas Lane, ABERDEEN

**Tuesday**
## The Scottish Culture and Traditions (ScaT) session
**Venue** The Globe, North Silver Street, ABERDEEN
*3rd Tuesday in the month TMSA Aberdeen Branch sessions, at 8pm*

## British Legion
**Venue** Mugiemoss Road, Bucksburn, ABERDEEN
*All musicians welcome*

**Wednesday**
## Crescent Hotel
**Venue** Bon Accord Crescent, Union Street, ABERDEEN

**Friday**
## Waterwheel Inn
**Venue** Bieldside, ABERDEEN

## "Ship Inn Session"
Ship Inn, BANFF
*1st Thurs every month 8.30pm till late. All welcome, anything goes!*
**Contact** Ian and Moira McLennan
**Phone** 01261 812620

## Vale Hotel, FYVIE
*2nd Wednesday in the month*
**Contact** Mike Rogers
**Phone** 01651 891797

## The Beach Bar, LOSSIEMOUTH
*Weekly on Tuesdays*
**Phone** 01343 813164

## Fife Arms Hotel, KEITH
*Fridays*
**Contact** Rab Verth
**Phone** 01542 882351

## The White Horse STRICHEN
*Every Tuesday - 8pm till late Expect any sort of music!*

## Aberdeen Arms Hotel, TARVES
Last Sunday every month, 8pm-11pm
**Contact** Dick and Maggie Tricky
**Phone** 01358 761374

# *Angus and City of Dundee Folk Clubs*

## Montrose Folk Club
Corner House Hotel, High Street, Montrose
*Meets fortnightly on Tuesdays 8.30pm. Ticket price varies.*
**Contact** Ken Bruce
**Phone** 01674 830658
**Alt contact** Andy Webster
**Phone** 01241 828345

# *Angus and City of Dundee Sessions*

## The Foundry Bar
East St Mary, Arbroath
*Wednesdays and Fridays 9pm - midnight*
**Phone** 01241 872524

## Broughty Ferry
Fisherman's Tavern, Fort Street
*10pm - 1am every Thursday*

## Carnoustie
Almondbank Hotel
*Wednesdays 9pm - midnight. Good mix of singing and instrumental*

## Collieston Inn
Collieston, by Arbroath
*Most Mondays 9pm - 11.30pm. Strict tempo dance music accordions, fiddles, piano and bass.*

## The Campbeltown Bar
271 Hawkhill, Dundee
*Tues apart from the last Tues in the month. 8.30-11pm*

## Bay Horse
Pole Park Road, Dundee
*2nd Sunday every month 2.30pm - 5pm Mainly instrumental*
**Contact** Paul Blackburn
**Phone** 01382 542826

## Railway Hotel, Friockheim
*Mondays 9pm - midnight. Dance band based repertoire.*

# *Angus and City of Dundee Accordion and Fiddle Clubs*

## Montrose Accordion and Fiddle Club
Viewfield Hotel, Arbroath
*Meets 1st Sunday in month at 7.30pm Members £1.50, Visitors £2, Musicians FREE*
**Contact** Sheona Smith
**Phone** 01674 820200
**Email** Ssbolshan@btinternet.com

# *Argyll, The Isles, Loch Lomond, Stirling and Trossachs Folk Clubs*

## Falkirk Folk Club
Polish Club, Arnott Street Falkirk
*Meets Thursdays 8.30pm. Guest performers each week.*
**Contact** Moira Anderson
**Phone** 01324 613395

## Lomond Folk Club
Lomond Hotel, Balloch
*Meets every Wednesday in Argyll Bar Alexandria from 9pm and last Friday of the month 8pm. Usually singer and musician nights. Everyone welcome to come along and join in*
**Contact** Stewart Davidson
**Phone** 01389 757561
**Alt contact** Peter Parlane
**Phone** 01389 753838 .

## Stirling Folk Club
The Terraces Hotel, Melville Terrace, Stirling
*Meets Mondays 8pm*
**Contact** Isobel Methven
**Phone** 01259 218521
**Web** www.stirling-folk.freeserve.co.uk

# *Argyll, The Isles, Loch Lomond, Stirling and Trossachs Sessions*

## Stirling Arms Hotel, Dunblane
*Sundays 9pm - midnight. Mix of singing and instrumental. Every 2nd Wed 9pm - midnight The Village Bar & Bistro*

## The Tollbooth Bar, Falkirk
*Tuesday nights 9.45pm to midnight fiddle music.*



Listed ceilidh and social dance bands in Scotland include **Bella MacNab's Dance Band**, **Douglas Keir & The Bluebell Scottish Dance Band**, **Julian Goodacre**, **Kadugan Ceilidh Band**, **The Occasionals**, **The Sensational Jimmy Shandrix Experience**, **The Thunderdog Ceilidh Band** and **Wild Cigarillos**.

***Listed magazines and websites on pages 360-361 offer further band information.***

**Whistlebinkies**
St Mary's Wynd, Stirling
*Sunday Nights from 8.30pm All singers and musicians welcome*
**Contact** Gav
**Phone** 01786 811242 after 7pm.

### *Argyll, The Isles, Loch Lomond, Stirling and Trossachs Other Concerts*

**Clachaig Inn**, Glencoe, Argyll
**Phone** 01855 811252
**Web** www.glencoe-scotland.co.uk
**Email** inn@glencoe-scotland.co.uk

**The Coach House Hotel**, Killin
*Occasional gigs on Friday/ Saturday nights*
**Phone** 01567 820349.

### *Argyll, The Isles, Loch Lomond, Stirling and Trossachs Summer Schools*

**Stirling University**
*Beginning in June through July and August. Week/weekend/day courses in all aspects of Scottish culture at Stirling University campus.*
**Contact** Margery Stirling
**Phone** 01786 467951
**Email** m.f.stirling@stir.ac.uk
**Web** www.stir.ac.uk/daice/suschool

### *Ayrshire and Arran Folk Clubs*

**Irvine Folk Club**
Redburn Hotel, Kilwinning Road
*Meets every second Wednesday*
**Contact** Joyce Hodge
**Phone** 01294 602615

**Kilmarnock Folk Club**
The Hunting Lodge, Kilmarnock.
*Thursdays 8pm*
**Contact** Maggie Macrae
**Phone** 01560 321102

**Music at the Manor**
**(formerly the Symington Folk Club)**
Manor Park Hotel, Monkton
*Fridays 8pm. Restricted Smoking Policy*
**Contact** Dave and Lorna Dewar on
**Phone** 01292 313205

### *Ayrshire and Arran Sessions*

**The Wellington Bar**, Ayr
*Sunday and Wednesday*

**Queen's Hotel**, Girvan
*Fridays 9pm*

**Marina Inn**, Irvine
*Tuesday*

**Maggie's Singaround**
The Hunting Lodge, Kilmarnock
*Last Saturday in month*

### *Dumfries and Galloway Folk Clubs*

**Dalbeattie Folk Club**
Kings Arms Hotel, High Street, Dalbeattie
*Fortnightly on Thursdays*
**Contact** Phyllis Martin
**Phone** 01566 612306

**Stranraer Folk Club**
The Swan Inn, 17 Sheuchan Street Stranraer.
*Meets every Wednesday. Mixture of guest nights and sessions*
**Phone** 01776 703487

### *Dumfries and Galloway Sessions*

**Crown Hotel**, Castle Douglas
*Friday, fortnightly,*

**The Burnbank**
Twynholm, Kirkcudbright
*Friday, fortnightly,*

### *Edinburgh and Lothians Folk Clubs*

**Edinburgh Folk Club**
The Pleasance, Edinburgh
*Meets Wednesdays at 8pm. All tickets £6/£5 conc unless marked Doors open at 7.30pm*
**Contact** Frank Bechofer
**Phone** 0131 339 4083

**The Wee Folk Club**
Royal Oak, Infirmary Street, Edinburgh
*Meets Sundays 8.30pm (nb: very small venue (30 seats) call ahead to save disappointment). Tickets £3*
**Phone** 0131 557 2976

**Haddington**
The Victoria Inn, Haddington
*Meets Wednesdays 8.30pm Occasional guests, other nights singers/musicians.*
**Contact** Gordon Pearson
**Phone** 01620 822925

**Nitten Folk Club**
Dean Tavern, Newtongrange, Midlothian
*Meets Thursday, 8pm. Singarounds with occasional guests*
**Contact** Dennis Wilson
**Phone** 0131 660 3025

**Penicuik Folk Club**
Navaar House Hotel, Penicuik
*Meets Tuesdays 8pm Guest artist 2nd Tuesday in month singers/musicians other nights. Ticket prices vary.*
**Contact** Brian Miller
**Phone** 01968 678153

### *Edinburgh and Lothians Sessions*

**Sandy Bell's**, Forest Road, EDINBURGH
*Nightly 9pm*
**Phone** 0131 225 2751

**Royal Oak**, Infirmary St, EDINBURGH
*Tues - Sunday 9pm*
**Phone** 0131 557 2976

**Ensign Ewart**, Lawnmarket, EDINBURGH
*Tues, Thurs, Fri & Sat 9pm*
**Phone** 0131 225 7440

**The Castle Bar**, Johnston Terrace
*Tues singers Wed instrumental 9pm*
**Phone** 0131 225 7432

**The Tass**, Royal Mile
*Wednesday 8.30pm*
**Phone** 0131 556 6338

**The Harbour Inn**
Fishmarket Square, Newhaven (opp Harry Ramsden's)
*Sundays 3pm*

**The Central Bar**, 7-9 Leith Walk
*Hosted by Leo McCann and Chris Drever all welcome*
**Phone** 0131 467 3925

**Shetland Fiddlers**, Edinburgh
*Meet 1st and 3rd Sunday in month*

**Royal Scots Club**
29/31 Abercromby Place, Edinburgh
*All ages all instruments welcome.*
**Phone** 0131 554 1097

### The Harrow, Dalkeith
*A 'guitar class' every Thursday from 8pm to midnight, and has occasional' open nights', roughly monthly, generally on a Friday.*

### Laird and Dog, Lasswade
*Sessions 1st Saturday in month 8.30pm*

### Leadburn Inn, Leadburn
*3rd Sat in the month 8.30pm. There is a playable piano in the bar.*

### Mason's Arms (aka Paddy's) Loanhead
*2nd Friday in the month 8.30pm*

### Roslin Glen Hotel, Roslin
*4th Saturday each month.*

## Glasgow and Clyde Valley Folk Clubs

### Frisky Whisky 13th Note Club
Clyde Street, Glasgow
*3rd Wednesday of the month.*
**Contact** Donald Lindsay
**Phone** 0141 636 9287

### Live at the Star
The Riverside Club, Fox Street, Glasgow
*Thursdays 8pm. Guest information unavailable please check with contact.*
**Contact** Liz Clark
**Phone** 0141 569 7287

### Chapelton Inn Folk Club
**(Old Glassford Folk Club)**
Chapelton by Strathaven
*Meets Every Tuesday.Guests most weeks.*
**Contact** Liz McIntyre
**Phone** 01357 520528

### Clydesdale Folk Club
Elphinstone Hotel, Biggar
*Meets last Thursday in the month*
**Contact** Chris McCosh
**Phone** 01899 221663
**Email** crisscross@zetnet.co.uk

### Stonehouse Folk Club
The Cross Keys Inn, Queen Street, Stonehouse
*Meets Every Second Friday*
**Contact** Billy Stewart
**Phone** 01698 359326

## Glasgow and Clyde Valley Other Events

### St Andrew's in the Square (Saints)
1 St Andrew's Square Glasgow
*Glasgow's newest venue for all music types. Regular sessions and ceilidhs, workshops and classes. Café bar open daily. Mon Fiddle class 7-9pm Bring a fiddle learn by ear Wed Traditional session 7.30pm*
**Phone** 0141 548 6020

## Glasgow and Clyde Valley Sessions

### Crown Hotel, Biggar
*Second and last Sunday of the month at 3pm*

### Scotia Bar
Stockwell St, GLASGOW
*Mondays singaround*
*Tuesdays Instrumental session*
**Phone** 0141 552 8681

### Clutha Vaults, GLASGOW
*Wednesdays first and third Wed in the month 9pm, Singaround.*
**Phone** 0141 569 7287

### Babbity Bowsters
Blackfriars St, GLASGOW
*Saturdays*
**Phone** 0141 552 5055

### Lanarkshire Songwriters Association
Wallace Cave, Lanark
*2nd and 4th Monday of each month*
**Contact** Billy Stewart
**Phone** 01698 359326

### Wiston Lodge, Lanark
*Second Thursday in the month from November onwards*
**Contact** Meg Beresford
**Phone** 01899 850228

## Highlands of Scotland Other Concerts

### Aros Centre
Portree, Isle of Skye
*Regular concerts throughout the year featuring local and visiting performers.*
**Phone** 01478 613649 Box Office
01478 613750
**Fax** 01478 613775
**Web** www.aros.co.uk

### Ceilidh Place
West Argyle Street, Ullapool
**Phone** 01854 612103

### Ben Nevis Inn
Achitee, Glen Nevis, Fort William
**Phone** 01397701227
**Web** www.ben-nevis-inn.co.uk

## Highlands of Scotland Sessions

### Clachnaharry Inn,
Clachnaharry, Ross-shire
*Thursdays Singers session 8pm - 9.30pm followed by mixed session 9.30 till late. Check with Fèis Rois*
**Phone** 01349 862600

### Edinbane Hotel
Edinbane near Dunvegan, Skye
*Traditional music most weekends, sessions visiting artists. Call Bill*
**Phone** 01470 582263

## Kingdom of Fife Folk Clubs

### Crail Folk Club
Upstairs in the Golf Hotel, Crail
*Meets 8pm Thursdays guests most weeks all welcome*
**Contact** Jill Saunderson
**Phone** 01333 450909
**Email** gks@st-andrews.ac.uk

### Dalgety Bay Folk Club
Dalgety Bay Sailing Club
*Meets 8pm Tickets purchased in advance £5*
**Contact** Marcus Stout
**Phone** 01383 822143
**Alt contact** Colin Hay
**Phone** 01383 822732
**Email** DBFolkClub@aol.com

### Dunfermline Folk Club
Thistle Tavern, Baldridge Burn, Dunfermline
*Wednesdays 8.30pm.*
*Tickets free unless stated.*
**Contact** Gifford Lind
**Phone** 01383 729673
**Alt contact** Jeanie Gardiner
**Phone** 01383 725872

### Kirkcaldy Folk Club
Path Tavern, Mid Street, Kirkcaldy
*Saturdays 8pm*
**Contact** Sandy Forbes
**Phone** 01592 200282

## Kingdom of Fife Other Music Events

### The No' Bad Crack Club
Cupar Arms Hotel, Cupar
*Last Tuesday in the month 7.30pm. Guests are well-known storytellers from various traditions. Entry £2.*
**Contact** Wendy Welch
**Phone** 01334 840234
**Email** jbeck69087@aol.com
**Alt contact** Margaret Tollick
**Phone** 01383 860559

### Scotland's Larder
Upper Largo
*Features traditional music evenings each Wednesday. Enjoy the best of Scottish food and listen to great music.*
**Contact** Christopher Trotter
**Phone** 01333 360414

## Kingdom of Fife Sessions

### Jinty's, Nethertown Road, Dunfermline
*Every 2nd Monday*

### Auchtermuchty
The Cycle Tavern, Burnside
*Wednesdays 9pm - midnight*
**Phone** 01337 828326

## Orkney Sessions

**Contact** the Tourist Information Centres below

### Kirkwall 6 Broad Street, Orkney KW15 1DH
**Phone** 01856 872856

### Stromness, Ferry Terminal Building, The Pier Head, Orkney, KW16 3AA
**Phone** 01856 850716

## Perthshire Folk Clubs

### The Taybank Folk Club
Taybank Hotel, Dunkeld
*Fridays 8pm Guests every second week £4 on guest nights Singers and musicians welcome every week.*
**Phone** 01350 727340

### Glenfarg Village Folk Club
Glenfarg Hotel
*Mondays 8.30pm No smoking. Ticket prices vary.*
**Contact** Graham Brotherstone
**Phone** 01383 738922

## Perthshire Sessions

### Maclean's Music Bar
Taybank Hotel, Tay Terrace, Dunkeld
**Phone** 01350 727686

### The Coach House, Killin
*Sunday*

### The Silver Broom
Canal St, Perth
*Wednesday, 9pm - midnight*

### Moulin Inn, Moulin, Pitlochry
*Friday*

## Scottish Borders Folk Clubs

### Denholm Folk Club
The Cross Keys, Hawick
*Meets Thursdays 8pm. Entry is free except on guest nights when tickets are £5/£2.50 conc.*
**Contact** Malcolm McEwan
**Phone** 01450 377165
01450 870305 (venue)

### Folk club at the Heriot Watt University
Scottish Borders Campus, Galashiels
*Meets every Tuesday evening 6.30 - 8.30 during term time in the new Students Union, and is open to anybody.*

## Scottish Borders Sessions

### Salmon Inn, Galashiels
*Last Saturday in the month open mic night*

### String Jam Club, Innerleithen,
*Thursdays 8pm*

### Neidpath Inn
St Ronan's Hotel, Peebles
*Alternate Thursdays 8pm*

### Crook Inn, Tweedsmuir
*1st Friday of the month, 8pm*

## Scottish Borders Accordion and Fiddle Club

### Kelso Accordion and Fiddle Club
Ednam House Hotel, Kelso
**Phone** 01573 224041

## Shetland Islands Sessions

### Shetland Fiddlers Society
Islesburgh Community Centre, Lerwick
*Wed May to September, Tuesdays*

### The Lounge
Douglas Arms, Fri Da Noost
*Wednesdays*
**Contact** Davy Gardener (info on other sessions)
**Phone** 01595 697550

### Barclay Arms Hotel
Sandwick by Scalloway
*May to July: Saturdays:*

### Asta Golf Club
*Every second Thursday Session hosted by the Portacabiners*
**Contact** James T Leask
**Phone** 01595 880231

## Western Isles Folk Clubs

### Stornoway Folk Club
*Meets occasionally check local press for information*

### Accordion and Fiddle Club
Lewis and Harris, The Sea Angling Club, Stornoway
**Phone** 01851 820295

### Borrodale Hotel
Daliburgh
*Every Saturday Accordion and pipes*
**Phone** 01878 700444

### Dark Island Hotel, Liniclate
*Every Saturday Accordion music*
**Phone** 01870 602414

## Western Isles Other Events

### An Lanntair, Stornoway,
*Occasional Concerts*
**Contact** Alex MacDonald
**Phone** 01851 703307

*See pages 366-370 for TMSA club listings.*

### An Lanntair, Lewis
**Mail address** An Lanntair, Town Hall, STORNOWAY, Isle of Lewis, HS1 2BX
**Contact** Alex MacDonald
**Fax** 01851 703307
**Email** lanntair@sol.co.uk
**Web** www.lanntair.com
*Promotes a year round programme with particular emphasis on traditional/ Gaelic arts.*
**AC** Scotland

### Ceilidh Dance - Scottish Bands, Stonehaven
Stonehaven Town Hall, STONEHAVEN, Kincardineshire, Scotland
**Contact** Robert Kerr
**Mail address** Invercowie House, Barclay Street, STONEHAVEN, AB39 2BH, Scotland
**Phone** 01569 762130
**Email** robert@invercowie.freeserve.co.uk
**Alt contact** Scott Begbie
**Alt address** 5 Amy Row, Cowie, STONEHAVEN, AB39 2RG, Scotland
**Phone** 01569 763488
*Regular ceilidhs with top Scottish bands. Tickets limited, advance booking advised.*
**AC** Scotland

### The Ceilidh Place
West Argyle Street, ULLAPOOL, Wester Ross, IV26 2XE, Scotland
**Contact** Robert Hicks
**Phone** 01854 612103
**Fax** 01854 612886
**Email** robert@ceilidh.demon.co.uk
*Major Scottish folk centre. Hotel, bookshop, café, bunkhouse, restaurant, gallery, venue for sessions, concerts, ceilidhs.*
**AC** Scotland

### Clydesdale Folk Club
Elphinstone Hotel, BIGGAR, Clydesdale, ML12, Scotland
**Fax** 01899 221192
**Contact** Chris McCosh
**Email** crisscross@zetnet.co.uk
*Last Thursday, 8pm.*
*Capacity 35-40.*
**AC** Scotland

### Crail Folk Club
Golf Hotel, CRAIL, Fife, Scotland
**Contact** Jill Saunderson
**Mail address** 36 Main Street, Colinsburgh, LEVEN, Fife, KY9 1LS, Scotland
**Phone** 01333 340494
**Email** gks@st-andrews.ac.uk
*Thursday fornightly. 8pm. Mostly guests.*
**AC** Scotland

### Dalgety Bay Folk Club
Dalgety Bay Sailing Club, Dalgety Bay, DUNFERMLINE, Fife, KY11, Scotland
**Contact** Colin Hay
**Mail address** 8 Doune Park, Dalgety Bay, DUNFERMLINE, Fife, KY11 9LX, Scotland
**Phone** 01383 822732
**Email** DBFolkClub@aol.com
*Friday evenings, monthly, 8pm. Traditional Irish and Scottish folk music.*
**AC** Scotland

### Edinburgh Folk Club
The Pleasance Caberat Bar, 60 The Pleasance, EDINBURGH, Scotland
**Contact** Frank Bechofer
**Mail address** 51 Barnton Park View, EDINBURGH, EH4 6HH, Scotland
**Phone** 0131 3394083
**Fax** 0131 3399261
**Email** efc@bechhofer.demon.co.uk
*Wednesday, 8pm. Diverse programme with the best of Scottish & other folk music. Tickets on the door.*
**AC** Scotland

### Edinburgh Shetland Fiddlers
Royal Scots Club, 29/31 Abercromby Place, EDINBURGH, Scotland
**Contact** Peter Brown
**Mail address** 20 Claremont Park, EDINBURGH, EH6 7PJ
**Phone** 0131 5541097
**Email** pjdbrown@hotmail.com
*1st & 3rd Sunday, 7.30-9.30pm. Session of mostly Shetland traditional music. For all ages & instruments (but mostly fiddle!)*
**AC** Scotland

### Glasgow Fiddle Workshop
Kinning Park Complex, Cornwall Street, GLASGOW, G41
**Contact** Sara Melville
**Mail address** 12 Whitehill Avenue, Stepps, GLASGOW, G33 6BL, Scotland
**Fax** 0141 779 9047
**Email** administrator@glasgowfiddle.f9.co.uk
**Web** www.glasgowfiddle.f9.co.uk
*Weekly classes in Scottish fiddle for all ages & abilities. Weekend events, ceilidhs, sessions, practice CDs, membership, etc.*
**AC** Scotland

### Haddington Folk Club
The Victoria Inn, 9 Court Street, HADDINGTON, East Lothian, Scotland
**Contact** Gordon Pearson
**Mail address** 53 Seggarsdean Court, HADDINGTON, East Lothian, Scotland
**Phone** 01620 822925
**Email** pearsong@btinternet.com
**Alt contact** Peter Brown
**Alt address** 20 Claremount Road, Leith, EDINBURGH, EH6 7PJ, Scotland
**Phone** 0131 554 1097
**Email** pjdbrown@hotmail.com
*Wednesday 8.30pm. Mainly traditional, singaround formatt.*
**AC** Scotland

### The Lemon Tree
The Lemon Tree, 5 West North Street, ABERDEEN, AB24 5AT, Scotland
**Phone** 01224 642230 - box
**Contact** Shona Powell
**Phone** 01224 647999 - admin
**Web** www.lemontree.org
*Major venue presenting a year round programme with awide range of music genres - folk, roots, blues, jazz, rock. See also Rootin Aboot Festival.*
**AC** Scotland

### Montrose Folk Club
Corner House Hotel, 131 High Street, MONTROSE, Scotland
**Contact** Ken Bruce
**Mail address** Five Furlongs, Main Road, Hillside, MONTROSE, DD10 9HH, Scotland
**Phone** 01674 830658
**Fax** 01674 673812
*Fornightly, Tuesdays, 8.30pm. All styles. Regular guests.Everyone, especially musicians, welcome.*
**AC** Scotland

### Music at The Manor Folk Club
The Manor Park Hotel, Monkton, BY PRESTWICK, Ayrshire, KA9 2RJ, Scotland
**Contact** Dave Dewar
**Mail address** 15 Portland Terrace, TROON, Ayrshire, KA10 6AJ
**Fax** 01292 313205
**Email** connectionscultural@hotmail.com
*1st Friday, 8pm. Scottish traditional music concerts(notJan, July, Aug).*
**AC** Scotland

### The Queen's Hall
Clerk Street, EDINBURGH, EH8 9JG
**Contact** Iain McQueen - Hall Manager
**Phone** 0131 668 3456
**Fax** 0131 668 2656
*Email queenshall@cableinet.co.uk*
*Alt contact Beth Caranagh - General Manager*
*Hall for hire. Capacity 8+ seated, 9+ standing. Open all year, would suit most touring artists.*
**AC** Scotland

### Sabhal Mor Ostaig
SLEAT, Isle of Skye, IV44 8RQ, Scotland
**Contact** Gavin Parsons
**Phone** 01471 888240
01471 888000
**Fax** 01471 888001
**Email** cg@smo.uhi.ac.uk
**Web** www.smo.uhi.ac.uk
*Gaelic college. Week-long courses in traditional, mainly West Highland, music, song and dance plus language courses during the summer.*
**AC** Scotland

### Sharkey's Session
Sharkey's Bar, 51 Old Rutherglen Road, GLASGOW, G5 9DT
**Contact** Benny McHugh
**Mail address** 89 Croptend Avenue, GLASGOW, G44 5PE, Scotland
**Phone** 0141 569 3557
0141 4180585
**Alt address** c/o 36 Kerrylemont Avenue, Toryglen, GLASGOW, G42, Scotland
*Mondays, 9pm. Music session run by Benny McHugh.*
**AC** Scotland

# Focus on Ireland

**The Arts Council/**
**An Chomhairle Ealaíon**
**Mail address** 70 Merrion Square, Dublin 2
**Phone** +353 1 618 0200
**Fax** + 353 1 676 1302
**Email** info@artscouncil.ie
**Web** www.artscouncil.ie

**The Arts Council of Northern Ireland**
**Mail address** MacNeice House, 77 Malone Road, Belfast BT9 6AQ
**Phone** 028 90 385200
**Fax** 028 90 661715
**Email** publicaffairs@artscouncil-ni.org
**Web** www.artscouncil-ni.org

Irish music is everywhere. There is a considerable presence throughout the British Isles and beyond with a vast array of artists working across Britain and Europe. There are "Irish scenes" in many English cities and numerous Irish artists tour the UK regularly.

The emphasis in this section is to provide routes to more information and to give an overview of the huge amount of traditional music throughout Ireland.

Together with a listing of the major information sources both in Ireland and across the British Isles, London based **Alan O'Leary** gives an overview of Irish music today, whilst **Becky Morris** in Belfast offers recommendations of venues and services. Thanks also to **Victor Ryan** of **AOIFE (Association of Irish Festival Events)** who has provided much of the information on Irish media and resources.

**Irish Music Magazine** is Ireland's leading independent folk and traditional magazine, with gig listings, reviews and interviews from around the world. Monthly sections on Irish and Celtic music in Ireland, UK, Europe and North America. It averages 80 pages a month, 11 issues a year, A4 full colour glossy.
**Contact** Sean Laffey (Editor)
**Mail address** 11 Clare Street, Dublin 2, Ireland
**Phone** +353 1 6624887
**Fax** +353 1 6624886
**Email** mrs@iol.ie
**Web** mag.irish-music.net
The Magazine's website has a links section covering sites on various instruments, set dancing, festivals, magazines and general Irish music sites.

**The Nenagh Singers Circle** provides a website list of Singing Clubs in Ireland. It doesn't claim to be comprehensive but is a way into such delights as **The Goilin Singers Club** in Dublin, **Inishowen Traditional Singers Circle**, **Wexford Traditional Singers Club**.
**Web** www.geocities.com/Broadway/Alley/4749/clubslist.html

**The ceili.ie website** offers Irish Music, Song and Dance- direct from Ireland. It has its roots in Set Dancing and provides a list of dance weekends, festivals and workshops.
**Web** www.ceili.ie/index.htm

**Ulstersongs** aims to promote the social singing tradition of (mainly) the North of Ireland.
**Web** http://members.aol.com/jmoul81075/ulstsong.htm

**Irish Traditional music in NW England:**
**Web** www.talented.fsnet.co.uk/links.htm links to artists, organisations, media, retail outlets, and Manchester and Liverpool music sites.

**The Irish Music Handbook** is available online at **www.musicnetwork.ie**

**Contemporary Music Centre** has a useful links page at **www.cmc.ie/links/links.html**

**Irish Traditional Music Archive** at **www.itma.ie**

**The Music In Northern Ireland** site is **www.nimusic.com**

## Comhaltas Ceolori Eireann (Irish Music Association)

***Headquarters:***
**Phone** +353 1 280 0295
**Email** enquiries@comhaltas.com
**Web** www.comhaltas.com

***London Regional Office:***
**Mail address** 50-52 Camden Square, London NW1 9XB
**Phone/Fax** 020 7916 8727
**Contact** Michael Nevin
**Phone** 020 8 360 3011
**Email** pnevin@goodplan.freeserve.co.uk

***Northern Regional Officer:***
**Contact** Joe Mullarkey
**Mail address** 9 Cross street, Farnworth, Bolton, Lancs.
**Phone** 01204 794036
**Email** joe@mullarky3.freesrve.co.uk
For a comprehensive guide to 'what's on' in the region send SAE to above address. Joe Mullarky edits the Comhaltas column in the **Irish Post**.

***Midlands Regional Officer:***
**Contact** Sean McDonagh
**Phone** 01582 597204
**Email** (Carmel Burke) carmel@burkecc.freeserve.co.uk

***Scottish Regional Officer:***
**Contact** Martin O'Neill
**Fax** 0709 21140703
**Email** martin.oneill@blueyonder.co.uk
**Web** www.johnnydohertycce.co.uk

***Provincial Secretary:***
**Contact** Ann Kelly
**Phone** 0115 9420337

## *Irish Music on the Radio*

### BBC Radio Ulster
FM92.4-95.4 MW 873/1341
*Friday 7.00-7.30pm. Traditional Music.*
Presented by Karen Na Haoine
**Email** karen.nahaoine@bbc.co.uk

*Saturday 10.05pm-12.00*
Mainly Music. Presented by Tony Mcauley and Colum Sands
**Email** tony.mcauley@bbc.co.uk
colum.sands@bbc.co.uk

*Sunday 6.05-7.00*
An Dlai Mhullaigh. Presented by Colm Macaindreasa
**Email** colm.macaindreasa@bbc.co.uk

### Radio Telefis Eireann
RTP Radio 1 MW567 and via Astra Satellite

*Saturday 9.30-10.15pm*
Ceilidh House. Presented by Kieran Hanrahan

*Saturday 10.15-11.00pm*
Failte Isteach. Presented by Donncha O'dulaing

*Sunday 8.10-8.55pm*
Mo Cheol Thu. Presented by Ciaran Mac Mathuna

### Downtown Radio
MW 1026
*Sunday 10.00-11.00pm*
Folkalpoint. Presented by Maurice Leyden

### Radio Na Gaeltachta
FM 93.5/94
*Range of Gaelic Music/Language programmes including Mora Dibh, broadcasts on ASTRA Satelite Channel 22*
*10.00am-12.00 Saturday and Sunday mornings.*
Details from **www.rnag.ie**



**NB** All telephone codes in Northern Ireland have changed recently
Country Code 028
Belfast Code 90
International dialling
+44 28 90 Belfast

***See Alan O'Leary's article on pages 137-138. Also see his Resource list on pages 138-140.***

***See Festival and Event information and Festival Listings on pages 254-257.***

**NB** All telephone codes in Northern Ireland have changed recently

| | |
|---|---|
| Country Code | 028 |
| Belfast Code | 90 |
| International dialling | +44 28 90 Belfast |

***See Alan O'Leary's article on pages 137-138. Also see his Resource list on pages 138-140.***

***See Festival and Event information and Festival Listings on pages 254-257.***

## *Media contacts in Ireland*

### BBC Northern Ireland
Ormeau Avenue, Belfast BT2 8HQ
**Phone** 028-903 3800
**Fax** 028-903 38806 (Newsdesk)
**Phone** 01-662 5500
**Fax** 01-662 5712 (Newsdesk)

### Radio na Gaeltachta
Casla, Co. na Gaillimhe
**Phone** 091-50 66 77
**Fax** 091-50 66 88 (News Desk)
**Email** rnag@rte.ie

### RTE
Donnybrook, Dublin 4
**Phone** 01-208 3111
**Fax** 01-208 3086 (News Desk)

### TG4
Baile na hAbann, Co. na Gaillimhe
**Phone** 091-50 50 50
**Fax** 091-50 50 05 (News Desk)
**Email** eolas@tnag.ie

### Today FM
124 Upper Abbey Street, Dublin 1
**Phone** 01-804 9000
**Fax** 01-804 9069 (News Desk)

### TV3
Westgate Business Park, Ballymount, Dublin 24
**Phone** 01-419 3333
**Fax** 01-419 3344 (News Desk)
**Email** kevin.macdermott@tv3.ie

### UTV Ulster Television
Havelock House, Ormeau Road
Belfast BT7 1EB
**Phone** 028-903 28122
**Fax** 028-902 38381 (News Desk)
**Email** newsroom@utv.com

### Community Arts Forum (CAN)
**Contact** Damian Mills (Editor)
81-87 Academy Street, Belfast BT1 2JS
**Phone** 028 902 429 10
**Fax** 028-903 122 64

### The Examiner
Academy Street, Cork City
**Phone** 021-27 27 22
**Fax** 021-27 54 77 (News Room)
**Email** ex_ed@examiner.ie

### Independent Newspapers
90 Middle Abbey Street, Dublin 1
**Phone** 01-705 5333
**Fax** 01-872 0304 (News Room)
**Email** newsroom@independent.ie

### Ireland on Sunday
50 City Quay, Dublin 2
**Phone** 01-671 8255
**Fax** 01-671 8882
**Email** info@irelandonsunday.iol.ie

### The Irish News
113-117 Donegal Street, Belfast BT1 2GE
**Phone** 028-903 22226
**Fax** 028-903 37505

### The Belfast Telegraph
124/144 Royal Avenue, Belfast BT1 1EB
**Phone** 028-902 64000
**Fax** 028-905 54506 (News Room)
**Email** editor@belfasttelegraph.co.uk

### The Evening Herald
90 Middle Abbey Street, Dublin 1
**Phone** 01-705 5333
**Fax** 01-872 0304 (News Room)
**Email** newsroom@independent.ie

### The Irish Sun
35/38 St. Stephen's Green, Dublin 2
**Phone** 01-602 8866
**Fax** 01-602 8869 (News Room)
**Email** news@the-sun.co.uk

### The Irish Times
10/16 D'Olier Street, Dublin 2
**Phone** 01-679 2022
**Fax** 01-677 2130 (News Room)
**Email** newsdesk@irish-times.ie

### The Mirror
46/56 Boucher Crescent
Belfast BT12 6QY
**Phone** 028-906 80000
**Phone** 028-906 80096 (News Room)

### The Newsletter
46/56 Boucher Crescent
Belfast BT12 6QY
**Phone** 028-906 80000

### The Sunday Tribune
15 Lower Baggot Street, Dublin 2
**Phone** 01-661 5555
**Fax** 01-661 5302 (News Room)
**Email** editorial@tribune.ie

### The Sunday World
18 Rathfarnham Road, Dublin 6
**Phone** 01-602 8800
**Phone** 01-490 1980
**Fax** 01-490 1838 (News Room)
**Email** sunworld@iol.ie
**Phone** 028-902 38118
**Fax** 028-902 38120 (News Room)

### The Star
62A Terenure Road North, Dublin 6W
**Phone** 01-490 1228
**Fax** 01-490 2193 (News Room)
**Email** news@the-star.ie

### The Sunday Business Post
Merchant's Quay, Dublin 8
**Phone** 01-679 9777
**Fax** 01-679 6496
**Email** sbpost@iol

*See Becky Morris' article below for more direct contacts.*

## A View From Belfast
By **Becky Morris**

### *Venues*
There isn't a folk club infrastructure as such in Northern (or Southern Ireland too for that matter) but (almost ) anything that would fit into a folk club in England would be welcomed as part of the general music policy for most music bars here. The plus side is that there can be plenty of work, the down side that they're not necessarily a listening audience, they'll enjoy the music (provided it's good ) but music is so commonplace here that they won't listen quietly and offer polite applause at the end of a number, they'll either go totally mental or not even bother to clap! There's a couple of exceptions.

**Downpatrick Folk Club**, currently run by Ian Clarke - is probably the closest you'll get to a British folk club in format, however it's only a capacity of 100 people with a maximum door entrance of a £5 so the acts they can put on are somewhat limited.
**Phone** 02844 811554

Another example would by **Culturlann McAdaim O Fiaich** on the Falls Road (no. 216), Belfast. You'll find obscure traditional Irish artistes here; a real treasure trove of stuff, you can guarantee the audience won't be the quietest in the world - but they do know their stuff.

If you're just after the craic, the following venues have a very varied bookings policy and don't usually advertise who's on - it's worth just dropping in if you're in town.

**The Menagerie**
130 University St, Belfast
**Phone** 028 90 235768
A typical week might include; Sun - String Quartet, Mon - Trad. session, Thursday - Drum and Bass, Fri - Dutch Blues Band, Sat - Paddy Keenan!

**Pat's Bar**, Clarendon Dock, Belfast - trad bias, regular sessions
The John Hewitt - home to 'The Liverpool Sessions', transferred after the demolishing of the Liverpool Bar. Live sessions 4/5 nights a week - lovely atmosphere and home to major concerts during the Open House Festival.

**The Hatfield**, Ormeau Road, Belfast - another session favourite.

**The Kitchen Bar** - Sessions on a Friday and Sunday - great food!
**Phone** 028 90 324901

**Maddens** - home to the serious traditional fans in town - sessions on a Friday and Saturday

**The Botanic** - lively covers stuff most weekends.

**Madison's Hotel** - Botanic Ave - Sunday lunchtime jazz

**The Rotterdam Bar**, Clarendon Dock, Belfast - once the home of traditional music in Belfast, a recent change in ownership means you're now more likely to get loud rocky blues stuff on a weekend and not much else.
**Phone** 028 90 746021

**Magennis's Bar**, next to St George's Market, music each weekend.
**Phone** 028 90 330295

**Irish Music magazine** provides an extensive sessions list covering the whole of Ireland.

Outside of Belfast, the following venues have a varied music policy and are more likely to have listening audiences than most.

### *In the north*

**Town and Country Inn**, Magherafelt

**Dufferin Arms**, Killyleagh

**The Ceili House**, 38 Church Place, Lurgan, Co Armagh
**Phone** 028 38 327624

**The Foyle Arts Centre**, Derry

### *In the south*

**Matt Molloy's**, Westport, Co Mayo
**Contact** Peter Molloy
**Phone** +353 98 26655

**Roisin Dubh**, Dominick Street, Galway
**Contact** John Mannion
**Phone** +353 91 586540

**McGrory's**, Culdaff, Co Donegal
**Contact** Neil McGrory
**Phone** +353 77 79104

**The Lobby**, Cork
**Contact** Pat Conway

**The Spirit Store**, George's Quay, Dundalk, Co Louth
**Contact** Mark Deary
**Phone** +353 42 9352697

**McCarthy's**, Baltimore, West Cork
**Contact** Declan McCarthy
**Phone** +353 282 0159

**The Glens Centre**, Manorhamilton, Co Leitrim
**Phone** +353 725 5833

**The Cobblestone**, Dublin

**Pepper's Bar**, Feakle, Co Clare

**The Cornerhouse**, Cork

**Dolan's** Limerick
**Phone** +353 61 314483

**HQ**, Hot Press Hall of Fame, Dublin

**Whelan's**, Vicar's Street, Dublin
**Phone** +353 1 478 0766
(and the craic for post event Dublin gigs - is usually to be found at The Harcourt Hotel, Harcourt St, Dublin
**Phone** +353 1 478 3677 )

**Limerick & Cork Universities** quite often have lunchtime concert series well worth checking out

### *Festivals*

### BEO 2001

at the National Concert Hall, Earlsfort Terrace, Dublin 2
**Phone** +353 1 475 1572 - August

### Celtic Flame

HQ, 57 Middle Abbey Street, Dublin 2
**Phone** +353 1 88 99 499 - February

*Irish Music Magazine provides a comprehensive list*

### *Belfast*

Most of the major folk, jazz, blues, and country names that will perform over here are brought over or presented by individual promoters who take all the risk themselves, hire the venues, PA etc. The sorts of venues that you're likely to find these gigs include:

**The Empire,** Botanic, Belfast (a 500-600 cap.) e.g. Sharon Shannon

**The Crescent Arts Centre**, University Road, Belfast (200ish cap.) e.g. Jazz nights

**The Limelight**, Ormeau Ave, Belfast (400ish cap.) - for the more indie end of the market.
**The Waterfront Hall** and **NTL Studio**, Lanyon Place, Belfast (2000 / 300 cap ) - e.g. Emmylou Harris / Luka Bloom

**The Whitla Hall**, University Road, Belfast (500ish) - mostly orchestral but used quite regularly during the Queens Festival.

**The Elmwood Hall**, University Road (1,000 ish) - again mostly used during Queens Festival

**The Errigle**, Ormeau Road, Belfast - upstairs room used by a variety of promoters for acoustic/folk/blues based bands.

### *Media - Northern Ireland*

One of the best points about listening to the radio here is that you don't have to remember a fixed time slot once a week for a 'specialist' music programme to cover folk stuff. It's not classed as something different, you're as likely to find a Dolores Keane track played next to a Madonna epic - makes for great listening. The BBC is as good a place to start as any;
**BBC Radio Ulster**, Ormeau Ave, Belfast

If you're promoting a gig, you could do worse that send half a dozen CDs/Press Releases to a variety of different presenters, they don't tend to work on a library system so it's worth sending individual CDs;
**John Bennett** - morning breakfast show - keen to include live sessions of people touring the province
**Liz Kennedy** - folk friendly producer for a variety of shows
**Joanne Murphy** - producer for 'folk show'
**Colum Sands** - presenter of 'folk show'
**Gerry Anderson** - mid-morning show, knows his music
**Sherrie McIlwaine** - late night show, anything slow/late-nighty!
**Across the Line** - for anything a bit out of the ordinary

The other two Belfast based radio stations are
**Downtown Radio**, Kiltonga Ind Est, Newtownards
**City Beat Radio**, Lamont Building, Stranmillis Embankment, Belfast
**Phone** 028 90 205967

Both will include listings if pushed and you might just get a bit of airplay but they're predominantly commercial stations. Saying that, though, Marc Mallett at City Beat is always open to new stuff and will slot in interviews where he can.
**Television** Again - it's not as hard to get TV coverage of an event as it would be in England, it'd be worth contacting producers at;
**UTV Life**, UTV
**The John Daly Show**, BBC
**The Kelly Show**, UTV (live on Friday



**NB** All telephone codes in Northern Ireland have changed recently
Country Code 028
Belfast Code 90
International dialling
+44 28 90 Belfast

*See Alan O'Leary's article on pages 137-138. Also see his Resource list on pages 138-140.*

*See Festival and Event information and Festival Listings on pages 254-257.*

**NB** All telephone codes in Northern Ireland have changed recently
Country Code 028
Belfast Code 90
International dialling
+44 28 90 Belfast

***See Alan O'Leary's article on pages 137-138. Also see his Resource list on pages 138-140.***

***See Festival and Event information and Festival Listings on pages 254-257.***

nights) alongside the various news programmes on both channels for the '...and finally' type slot.

## *Print*

There's a couple of glossy magazines that change editorship every couple of months and include listings but they tend to be read by club-goers and not necessarily the sort of people who'd attend a 'non-mainstream' gig. The best press angle here is to hit the key journalists at each of the three main papers:
**The Belfast Telegraph** - Neil Johnston
**The Irish News** - Tim Brannigan
**The Newsletter** - Geoff Harden for most folky stuff or James Elliott for anything a bit more off the wall.

Though based in the South - **Irish Music Magazine** contains a fairly comprehensive guide to what's on.
**Contact** 11 Clare Street, Dublin 2
**Phone** +353 1 662 4887

## *Production Companies*

90% of venues have an in-house PA, 90% of these leave a lot to be desired!
It's common practise if you're touring to bring in a rig specially, you need to remember though that hiring a rig over here does not necessarily include hiring an engineer - if you need someone to operate the desk then specify this at the time of hiring and be prepared to pay extra.

## *Useful PA Contacts*

Small pub gigs -
**Dougie Smith**
**Phone** 028 90 874607
07798 827484
Great especially for last minute stuff, probably the hardest working engineer in Belfast!

Small to medium gigs –
**Billy McGarritty**, a whole variety of stuff available including limited supply of lights
**Contact** Unit 3, Breezemount Storage, 78 Sainfield Road, Carryduff BT8 8EP
**Phone** 028 90 815122
07721 746801

Small to mega-big gigs
**Production House**
**Contact** John Willis or Neil Lewis
**Phone** 028 9077 4449
**Fax** 028 9077 1707
PA/Backline
**Ampec**
**Contact** John McDowell
**Phone** 028 9127 0221

## *Production/Tour Managers*

**Russell Allardice**, 31 Orpins Mill Road, Ballyclare BT39 0SX
**Phone** 0771 2579701

**Becky Morris**, Smallworld Music, PO Box 747, Belfast BT9 5ES
**Phone** 028 9038 2384

## *Stage Crew*

c/o **Smallworld Music**, PO Box 747, Belfast BT9 5ES
**Phone** 028 9038 2384
**Fax** 028 9029 5173

## *Event Security*

**Eventsec**, 138 University Street, Belfast BT7 1HH
**Phone** 028 9029 4981

## *Lights*

**Powerlight**
**Contact** Keith Shanks
10 Fernlea Park, Bangor, Co Down BT19 6XP
**Phone** 028 91 270113

**APT Lights**
**Contact** Andy Thompson (also suppliers of the biggest most easily and safely constructed stage in the country )
49 Ballymena Road, Cullybackey BT42 1DT

**Stage Services** (for anything extra like smoke machines etc.)
**Phone** 028 9077 7668
**Fax** 028 9077 1707

## *Festivals*

**Open House Festival**
**Contact** Kieran Gilmore, 31 Sheridan Drive, Bangor BT20 5NQ

**Global Notes** - series of "World Music" concerts promoted by Smallworld Music primarily within St George's Market, Belfast. Mailing List maintained for folk/roots world music concerts in the Belfast area.

**Ulster American Folk Park** hosts a couple of different events throughout the year, probably best known for its American/Bluegrass Weekend in the Autumn.
Cultra, Hollywood, Co Down
**Phone** 028 9042 8428

**Frankie Kennedy Winter School** - over the New Year week in Donegal!
**Feil en Phobail** (aka West Belfast Fleadh)
**Contact** Catriona Ruane, Ashton Centre, 5 Churchill Street, Belfast BT15 2BP
**Phone** 028 9074 3331

## *Travel*

Music friendly travel agents for internal/external travel arrangements;
**Grange Travel**, 134 Gt Victoria Street, Belfast
**Phone** 028 9032 1051
**Fax** 028 9024 6269

## *Specialist Music Photography*

**Contact** Rosie Mac
**Phone** 028 90 80 8112 (mobile)
0797 474 0304

**Becky Morris**
*Smallworld Music*

## Mc Grory's of Culdaff
INISHOWEN, Co Donegal, Ireland
Dunmore Productions
**Mail address** Glebe, Culdaff, INISHOWEN, Co Donegal, Ireland
**Phone** +353 77 79358
**Fax** + 353 77 79235
**Email** mrsmac@eircom.net
*Monthly folk club.*
**AC** Northern Ireland

## Black Nun Folk Club
The Edgewater Hotel, PORTSTEWART, Co Derry, Northern Ireland
**Contact** Dick Glasgow
**Mail address** 18 Main Street, BALLINTOY, Co Antrim, BT54 6LX, Northern Ireland
**Fax** 028 2076 3116
**Email** afm06@dial.pipex.com
**Web** www.causewaymusic.co.uk
*Usually 1st Monday. Traditional, folk & blues music.*
**AC** Northern Ireland

## Global Notes
**Contact** Smallworld Music
**Mail address** PO Box 747, BELFAST, BT9 5ES, N Ireland
**Phone** 028 9038 2384
**Fax** 028 9029 5173
**Email** Becksworld@btinternet.com
*Annual folk & world music events at various venues in Belfast.*
**AC** Northern Ireland

## The Jim McGill School of Traditional Music
18 Main Street, BALLINTOY, Co Antrim, BT54 6LX, Northern Ireland
**Contact** Dick Glasgow
**Fax** 028 2076 3116
**Email** afm06@dial.pipex.com
**Web** www.causewaymusic.co.uk
*Traditional music school. Tution in a variety of instruments in most primary schools on the Causeway Coast and the Glens of Antrim. Evening classes at various venues. Concerts, ceilidhs, pub sessions, folk club.*
**AC** Northern Ireland

## The Menagerie
130 Univeristy Street, BELFAST, BT7 8HH, Northern Ireland
**Phone** 028 9023 5678
**Contact** Smallworld Music
**Mail address** PO Box 747, BELFAST, BT9 5ES, N Ireland
**Phone** 028 9038 2384
**Fax** 028 9029 5173
**Email** Becksworld@btinternet.com
*Belfast's premiere licensed music venue. Live music Thursday - Monday.*
**AC** Northern Ireland

**NB** All telephone codes in Northern Ire and have changed recently
Country Code 028
Belfast Code 90
International dialling
+44 28 90 Belfast

***See Becky Morris's article on pages 374-375.***

Listed ceilidh and social dance bands in Wales include **Juice**, **Dragons Breath**, **This Way Up**, **Dawnswyr Pen Y Bont** and **Our Lady and The Apostles**.

# Focus on Wales

**The Arts Council of Wales** is based in three places; Colwyn Bay, Carmarthen and Cardiff. The staff there work in the five divisions of the Arts Council of Wales. These are Access Development, Artform Development, Finance and Resources, Lottery and Planning.
**Web** www.ccc-acw.org.uk

**Mail address** 9 Museum Place,
Cardiff CF10 3NX
**Phone** 02920 376500
**Fax** 02920 221447
**Minicom** 02920 390027
**Email** information@ccc-acw.org.uk

**Mail address** 6 Gardd Llydaw,
Jackson Lane, Carmarthen SA31 1QD
**Phone** 01267 234248
**Fax** 01267 233084

**Mail address** 36 Prince's Drive,
Colwyn Bay LL29 8LA
**Phone** 01492 533440
**Fax** 01492 533677
**Minicom** 01492 532288

**Taplas** magazine is a bi-monthly magazine principally for Wales and the Borders. News, interviews, articles and Checklist including gig guide and listings of regular clubs and workshops.
**Contact** Keith Hudson
**Mail address** 182 Broadway, Roath,
Cardiff CF24 1QJ
**Phone** 029 2049 9759
**Fax** 029 2048 4882

**Celfyddydau Mari Arts** hosts the **Taplas What's On guide** as well as providing lots of links to other Welsh music and dance sites.
**Web** www.folkwales.org.uk

**Celfyddydau Mari Arts** is an organisation providing a research, archiving, education & promotion service for all the traditional arts in Wales.
**Contact** Mick Tems
**Mail address** 1 Ty Clwyta Cottages,
Cross Inn, Llantrisant,
Rhondda Cynon Taf CF72 8AZ
**Phone/Fax** 01443 226892
**Email** mariarts@folkwales.org.uk

**trac** is the folk development organisation for Wales. It was set up in 1997 and began by commissioning a study on the state of folk music in Wales. This study showed that though a lot of activity exists, it is often fragmented and in ignorance of what is happening elsewhere. This situation is made more difficult by the geography of the country.

As a result, one of the main aims of **trac** is to provide a link between activities, encouraging the co-operation and cross fertilisation that the study recommends.

During 2001 **trac** will open an information line that will put people in touch with an ever expanding store of information on artists, venues, events and projects, drawing on the support of other organisations and their members.

Like other development agencies trac also aims to expose children to the best traditional skills at as early an age as possible, and is planning a Training the Trainers programme which will get under way later this year. Other pilot projects will aim to set new benchmarks for traditional music activity in Wales.

**trac** also feels it is necessary to raise the profile of artists from Wales, and has worked with the British Council and the Arts Council of Wales in providing material for a newsletter, tracks which has been distributed throughout the world. Two issues have been produced so far.
**Contact** Philip Freeman
**Mail address** Swn-y-Coed,
Llandinam, Powys, SY17 5DJ
**Phone/Fax** 01686 688102
**Email** freeman@mid-wales.com

## Venues and clubs

**Norwegian Church Arts Centre**, Cardiff Bay brings a range of top folk acts to the city. Further along the coast, **St Donats Arts Centre**, St Donats, Vale of Glamorgan hosts a programme of established folk & world music events from September to May. **Valley Roots** brings many established UK and Welsh acts to theatres in the South Wales valleys. Venues involved in the series include are the **Blackwood Miners Institute**, **Beaufort Theatre & Ballroom**, Ebbw Vale, **Borough Theatre**, Abergavenny and **Theatr Brycheiniog**, Brecon. Cardiff's major concert hall, **St David's Hall** (029 2087 8444) includes folk, roots & world music in its programme. **Pontardawe Arts Centre** programmes quarterly gigs in association with **Pontardawe Folk Festival**. On the club scene, **Clwb Gwerin Llantrisant Folk Club** has a mix of guest and open house nights. **Halfpenny Folk Club**, Gower has monthly guests and workshops in addition to club nights. **Newport Folk Club** is mainly English music and has bi-monthly national/international guests. Also see **Aberdare Acoustic Club**. Public dances are run by the **RUFF Ceilidh Club**, Cardiff.

**Theatr Hafren** is the principle North Powys theatre and presents a range of performances including a significant folk & roots programme. **Theatr Mwldan** presents touring folk acts. **gwerinABERfolk**, Aberystwyth runs bimonthly guest concerts at the **Coopers Arms** plus a weekly session. There is an open house session at **Fishguard Folk Club** on the Pembrokeshire Coast with emphasis on Welsh, Irish and maritime music.

In the North, **Llanelian Folk Club**, Colwyn Bay has international guests, mainly old timey, bluegrass, blues & related acoustic music. **The Folk Music Workshop**, Bangor runs Celtic traditional music workshops plus monthly Celtic folk evenings. Other clubs include **Denbigh Folk Club**, **Ruthin Acoustic Music**, **Conwy Folk Club** and monthly guests at **Jonkers**, Llangollen (01978 861158).

## Festivals

The major festivals in Wales include **Pontadawe Festival** (August) a world music & dance festival (including Welsh acts) and **Sesiwyn Faur Dolgellau** a free music festival which attracts 25,000 to Gwynedd and won of the Welsh Tourist Boards' Event Of The Year Award 2000. **Caerphilly International Festival** is in mid July and **The Big Cheese**, also at Caerphilly Castle, happens a few weeks later. **Gwyl Ifan** (June), Wales' largest folk dance festival, takes place in Cardiff. **Gower Folk Festival** (June) has a diverse range of popular folk & celtic acts and **Beyond The Border Storytelling Festival** (July), with a strong world music programme, happens at **St Donats Arts Centre**, Vale of Glamorgan. FMD casualties include **Miskin** at Easter which has moved to November for 2001and **Tredegar House Dance Festival** was cancelled in 2001. There are also some specialist festivals, such as **Gwyl Bibau Pencader Pipes Festival** (September) and smaller events such as **Rhuddlan Folk Day**.

• ***Thanks to Mick Tems, Philip Freeman, Danny KilBride, Gerard KilBride, Fflach Tradd and Sain for assustance with the above informations***

## Folk clubs, concert venues, sessions and dance in Wales

• ***Thanks to Celfyddydau Mari Arts for the following information.***

**Celfyddydau Mari Arts** operates a complete listing service for Wales and the Borders, in conjunction with **Taplas** magazine, at www.folkwales.org.uk

### *Folk Clubs*

**Whitchurch Folk Club**
Whitchurch Rugby Club, Cardiff
*Second Monday, 8.30pm*
**Contact** Fred McCormack
**Phone** 029 2061 1314.

**Conwy Folk Club** The Malt Loaf, Conwy. *Every Monday.*
**Contact** Denis Bennett
**Phone** 01492 877324

**The Goat Hotel**
Maerdy, near Betws-y-Coed.
*Every Monday.*

**Gilwern Folk Club**
Beaufort Arms, Gilwern
*Second and last Tuesdays.*
**Contact** Kevin Scourfield
**Phone** 01873 832074.

**BBC Folk Club (members only)**
BBC Club, Llandaff, Cardiff
*Second Tuesday, 9pm.*
**Contact** Dave Burns
**Phone** 029 2023 3509.

**gwerinABERfolk**
Coopers' Arms, Aberystwyth
*Every Tuesday.*
**Contact** Ian Gulley
Phone 01970 890321.

**Fishguard Folk Club**
Royal Oak, Fishguard
*Every Tuesday.*
**Contact** Gary Jones
**Phone** 01348 840181.

**Paxton Inn**
Llanarthne, near Carmarthen
*Every Tuesday.*

**Half Moon** Llanelli
*Every Tuesday.*
**Contact** Stan
**Phone** 01554 772626

**Llantrisant Folk Club**
The Windsor Hotel, Pontyclun
*Every Wednesday, 8.30pm.*
**Contact** Pat Smith
**Phone** 01443 226892.
**Email** folkclub@folkwales.org.uk

**Roath Folk Club**
St Peter's Hall, Roath, Cardiff
*Every Wednesday.*
**Contact** Bob Partridge
**Phone** 029 2062 7867.

**Aberdare Acoustic Music Club**
Full Moon, Aberdare
*Every Wednesday.*
**Contact** Steve Chandler
**Phone** 01685 877322

**Folk At The Twyn y Ffrwd**
The Twyn y Ffrwd, Abersychan
*Alternate Wednesdays.*
**Contact** Bob and Julie
**Phone** 01495 759652.

**Denbigh Folk Club**
Bull Hotel, Denbigh
*First and third Wednesdays.*
**Contact** Geoff Durno
**Phone** 01745 582265.

**Newport Folk Club**
Red Lion, Stow Hill, Newport, Gwent
*Every Thursday, 8.30pm.*
**Contact** Ken Potter
**Phone** 01633 680051.

**Abergavenny Folk Club**
Hen and Chickens, Abergavenny
*Alternate Thursdays.*
**Contact** Phil Dew
**Phone** 01873 855331.

**The Celtic Music and Dance Group**
Catholic Hall, Longcroft Road, Caldicot.
*Tuition in fiddle, whistle, guitar, bodhran, flute. Every Thursday, 8.30pm.*
**Contact** Donald
**Phone** 01291 423674
**Email** Suzanne.Moore@wales.gsi.gov.uk

**Cylch Canu**
Fforest Arms, Brechfa, nr Carmarthen
*Every Thursday.*
**Contact** Lyn Denman
**Phone** 01267 202474.

**Ruthin Acoustic Music**
Castle Hotel, Ruthin
*Every Thursday.*
**Contact** Campbell Finney
**Phone** 01824 750730.

**Wrexham Folk and Acoustic Music Club**
Nag's Head, Wrexham
*First and third Thursdays.*
**Contact** Goff Jones
**Phone** 01978 755478.

**Forest of Dean Folk Club**
The Gatehouse, Monmouth
*First and third Fridays, 8.30pm.*
**Contact** Sally Saysell
**Phone** 01291 641369.

**Valley Folk Club** Ivy Bush, Pontardawe. *Third Friday of month.*
**Contact** Martin Ellis
**Phone** 01792 865171.

**Red Lion** Llangynidr
*Last Friday in month.*
**Contact** Pippa Stayoung
**Phone** 01874 730135

**Folk and Country**
St Peter's Rugby Club, Newport Road, Cardiff
*Every Friday, 8.30pm.*
**Contact** Tony Brean
**Phone** 029 2049 9658

**Machynlleth Leisure Centre**
*First and third Fridays.*
**Contact** Tony Pearson
**Phone** 01654 703860

**Rhyl Folk Club** Costigans, Rhyl
*Every Friday.*
**Contact** Jeff Blythin
**Phone** 01745 588815

**Folk Music Workshop** St John's Methodist Church Hall, Bangor
*Every Friday.*
**Contact** Ramsay Isak
**Phone** 01248 421071

**Dyffryn Aman Folk Club**
Colliers Arms, Saron, nr Ammanford.
*Every Saturday.*
**Contact** 01269 592419

**The Discovery Session**
Windsor Arms, Pontyclun
*First Sunday, 1pm.*
**Contact** Celfyddydau Mari Arts
**Phone** 01443 226892.
**Email** mariarts@folkwales.org.uk

**The Platform Folk Club**
Ynysddu Hotel, Ynysddu, Gwent
*First Sunday.*
**Contact** Wynford Jones
**Phone** 01495 222935.
**Email** platform.folkclub@ukgateway.net

**Red Lion** St Asaph
*First Sunday in month.*

## Other venues with folk programme content

**Arts Centre** Aberystwyth
**Phone** 01970 623232

**Blackwood Miners' Institute**
**Phone** 01495 227206

**Beaufort Theatre** Ebbw Vale
**Phone** 01495 302112

**Borough Theatre** Abergavenny
**Phone** 01873 850805

**Cardiff International Arena**
**Phone** 02920 224488

**ECTARC** Llangollen
**Contact** Sharon Thomas
**Phone** 01978 861514

**Norwegian Church Arts Centre Cardiff**
**Phone** 029 2045 4899

**Pavilion Theatre** Rhyl
**Phone** 01745 330000

**Penyrheol Theatre** Gorseinon
**Phone** 01792 897030

**Pontardawe Arts Centre**
**Phone** 01792 863722

**Rhyn Park Arts Centre**
St Martins, near Oswestry
**Phone** 01691 791403

**Queen's Hall** Narberth
**Phone** 01834 861212.

**St David's Hall** Cardiff
**Phone** 029 2087 8444

**St Donats Arts Centre**
near Llantwit Major
**Phone** 01446 799100

**Theatr Brycheiniog** Brecon
**Phone** 01874 611622

**Theatr Clwyd** Mold
**Phone** 01352 755114

**Theatr Hafren** Newtown
**Phone** 01686 625447

**Theatr Llwyn** Llanfyllin
**Phone** 01938 810626

**Theatr Mwldan** Cardigan
**Phone** 01239 612687

**Wyeside Arts Centre**
Builth Wells
**Phone** 01982 552555

## Sessions in Wales

**Rising Sun Inn**
Coleford Road, Woodcroft, near Chepstow
*Irish session, First Monday 8.30pm.*
**Contact** Donald
**Phone** 01291 423674
**Email** suzanne.moore@wales.gsi.gov.uk

**New Inn** Rosebush, Pembrokeshire
*Every Monday.*

**The Nelson** Bangor, Gwynedd
*Every Monday.*

**Queen's Head** Monmouth
*Session (alternate Tuesdays).*
**Contact** 01600 712767

**The Pavilion** Pencader, Ceredigion
*Pibau Pencader (bagpipes) Every Tuesday, 7.30pm.*
**Contact** 01559 384962

**The Sportsman** Newtown, Powys
*Every Tuesday.*

**New Inn** Pontblyddyn, Flintshire
*Every Tuesday.*

**The Golden Fleece** Tremadog, Gwynedd
*Every Tuesday.*

**The Wildflower** Tre'r Ddol, Gwynedd
*Every Tuesday.*

**The Goldcroft** Caerleon, Gwent
*Session with Doed a Ddêl. Every Wednesday, 8.30pm.*
**Contact** 01633 815612.

**P.S. (formerly The Angel)**
Bridgend
*Session with Mabon and friends. Every Wednesday.*
**Contact** 01656 766667.

**Elan Valley Hotel** Rhayader
*First Wednesday in month.*

**Ship and Castle** Aberystwyth
*Every Wednesday.*

**Weston Vaults** Aberystwyth
*Every Wednesday.*

**White Lion**
Llanelian-yn-Rhos, Conwy
*Every Wednesday.*

**Sun Inn** Llangollen
*Every Wednesday.*

**The Conway**
Conway Road, Pontcanna, Cardiff
*Every Thursday, 8.30pm.*

**Mile End Inn**
Port Tennant, Swansea
*Every Thursday.*
**Contact** 01792 830246.

**The Hooker** Swansea
*Every Thursday.*

**New Ship Inn**
Drefach Felindre, near Cardigan
*Every Thursday.*

**Friendship Inn** Borth, Aberystwyth
*First Thursday of month.*

**Rhoslan** Llandudno
*Every Thursday.*

**The Mount** Llanwnda, nr Caernarfon
*Every Thursday.*

**Hollybrook Inn** Bronwydd, near Carmarthen
*Every Friday.*

**Powis Arms** Welshpool
*Every Friday.*

**The Nelson** Bangor, Gwynedd
*Every Friday.*

**Dolgellau** Gwynedd.
*Every Friday.*
**Contact** 01341 422063.

**Glan yr Afon** Milwr, Clwyd
*Every Friday.*

**New Inn** Llanbadarn Fynydd, Powys
*Every Saturday.*

**Red Lion** Tyn-y-Groes, near Conwy
*Irregular Saturdays.*
**Contact** Paul Hockaday
**Phone** 01492 876649.

**Windsor Arms** Pontyclun
*Discovery session for learners. First Sunday, 1pm.*
**Contact** Celfyddydau Mari Arts
**Phone** 01443 226892.
**Email** mariarts@folkwales.org.uk.

**Liverpool Arms** Conwy
*Every Sunday*

**Cross Keys** Selattyn, near Oswestry
*Every Thursday.*

**Red Lion** Rhosesmor, Flintshire
*Last Thursday in month.*
**Contact** Norman Dixon
**Phone** 01352 710864

## Dance in Wales

All of these are display teams, except the **Ruff Ceilidh Club** which organises public dances (Saturdays, Cardiff). However, most Welsh dance teams organise *twmpath* nights during the year. A *twmpath* is a social dance night, equivalent to a ceilidh/ barn dance in England. The word literally means 'hump' and comes from the days of open air dancing on the village green with the harper and fiddler sitting on a raised mound.

### Workmen's Hall
Pontymister, Gwent
*Ogam Igam. Welsh clog. Every Sunday afternoon.*
**Phone** 029 2075 0334.

### Alltwen Community Centre
Cam Carlam.
*International. Every Sunday.*
**Contact** Tony Craven
**Phone** 01792 862617.

### Cefnfaes Centre
Bethesda, Gwynedd
*Eryri Morris. Mixed Cotswold and Border. Every Monday.*
**Phone** 01248 681860.

### St Andrews Church Hall
off Caerphilly Rd, Birchgrove, Cardiff
*Ruff Country Dance Club. Every Monday, 8pm. British/US social.*
**Contact** Dave Parsons
**Phone** 01222 513440

### Christchurch Scout Hall
Roath, Cardiff
*English social. Every Monday.*
**Phone** 01446 735098.

### Capel Pendref Mold, Flintshire
*Dawnswyr Delyn. Welsh social. Every Monday.*
**Phone** 01352 752080.

### St Catherine's Scout Hall
Pontcanna, Cardiff
*Cobblers Awl. English/Welsh clog. Every Monday.*
**Phone** 029 2070 0170.

### Scout Hall Maitland Road, Cardiff
*Cardiff Morris Men. English/Welsh Morris. Every Tuesday.*
**Phone** 029 2071 1878.

### Rookwood Hospital
Llandaff, Cardiff
*Cardiff Ladies Morris. Every Tuesday, 7.30pm.*
**Phone** 029 2083 4337.

### New Inn Rugby Club
near Cwmbran
*Cwmni Gwerin Pontypwl. Welsh social. Every Tuesday.*
**Phone** 01633 761755.

### Hen Ysgol Arian Glas
Benllech
*Ffidl Ffadl. Welsh. Every Wednesday.*
**Phone** 01248 750561

### Clwb Ifor Bach Cardiff
*Twrch Trwyth. Welsh social. Every Wednesday.*

### Llantarnam Church Hall
Cwmbran
*Brandywine Cloggers. Appalachian. Every Wednesday.*
**Phone** 01633 856967.

### Presbyterian Church Hall
Victoria Drive, Llandudno Junction
*Conwy Morris. Mixed. Every Wednesday.*
**Phone** 01492 583834.

### Llanellen Village Hall
near Abergavenny
*Llanellen FDG. English/US social. Every Thursday.*
**Phone** 01873 854271.

### Garth Community Hall
Bassaleg
*Gwerinwyr Gwent. Welsh social. Every Thursday.*
**Phone** 01633 881461.

### Scout Hall Bryntirion, Bridgend
*Dawnswyr Gwerin Pen-y-Fai. Welsh social. Every Thursday*
**Contact** Mel Evans
**Phone** 01656 646276.

### Aelwyd Stryd yr Eglwys, Caernarfon
*Dawnswyr Aelwyd Caernarfon. Welsh social. Every Thursday.*
**Phone** 01286 673485.

### Catholic Hall Longcroft Road, Caldicot
*The Celtic Music and Dance Group. Every Thursday, 8.30pm. Irish and Scottish ceili and set dances.*
**Contact** Liz
**Phone** 01291 425880. **Email** Suzanne.Moore@wales.gsi. gov.uk

### Memorial Hall Coychurch
*Dawnswyr Penybont. Welsh social. Every Thursday.*
**Phone** 01656 660193.

### Ysceifiog Village Hall Holywell
*Clerical Error. Mixed border morris. Every Thursday.*

### Porth Rugby Club
*Dawnswyr Cwm Rhondda. Welsh social. Every Thursday.*
**Phone** 01443 433020.

### Derwenlas Powys
*Circle dance. Every Friday.*
**Phone** 01654 702655.

### RUFF Ceilidh Club
University of Wales Hospital Social Club Heath, Cardiff
*Saturdays, monthly.*
**Contact** Dave Parsons
**Phone** 029 2051 3440

**Fflach Tradd** and **Sain** are two Welsh record labels responsible for many notable albums by Welsh artists.

**Fflach Tradd**'s recent releases include those by renowned harpist **Llio Rhydderch**, **Ceri Rhys Matthews** and **Jonathan Shorland**, **KilBride Brothers**, **Sian Phillips** and **Rag Foundation**.
**Contact** Fflach, Llys-y-Coed, Heol Dinbych-y-Pysgod, Aberteifi, SA43 3AH
**Phone** 01239 614691
**Email** info@fflach.co.uk
**Web** www.fflach.co.uk

Welsh artists recorded on **Sain** include triple harpist **Robin Huw Bowen**, **Calennig**, **Crasdant**, **Cusan Tan**, **Gwerinos** and **Sian James**.
**Contact** Canolfan Sain, Llandrog, Caernarvon, Gwynedd, LL54 5TG.
**Phone** 01286 831 111
**Fax** 01286 831497
**Email** fideo@sain.wales.com

## Young Welsh Traditional Musician Awards

The first Young Welsh Traditional Musician Awards, created by **Gerard KilBride** (of the KilBride Brothers) and in partnership with **Teledu Elidir** will be held in Mid Wales, in the spring of 2002.

Young Musicians from Wales will be encouraged to take part in this timely and exciting project. It provides a showcase and a spring board for the best of Welsh Musical Youth and aims to strengthen and develope the vibrant living musical traditions of Wales.

Running along side the awards will be a new and dynamic educational support package, created under the framework of National Curriculum for Wales, with special emphasis on traditional music interlinked with Curriculum Cymreag.

The event will be broadcast bilingually on television and radio, both regionally and nationally, and can be followed via the Internet.

Further details will be announced in July 2001.

wales
venues

*See Celfyddydau Mari Arts' listings on pages 379-381.*

## Rooting around in Wales

**www.folkwales.org.uk**
*Celfyddydau Mari Arts*

**www.welshfolkdance.org.uk**
*Cymdeithas Ddawns Werin Cymru - Welsh Folk Dance Society*

**www.angelfire.com/music/pembs folk**
*Pembrokeshire Folk Index*

### Aberdare Acoustic Club
Black Lion Hotel, ABERDARE, Mid Glamorgan, Wales
**Contact** Steve Chandler
**Phone** 01685 877322
*Folk and acoustic music club.*
**AC** Wales

### The Beaufort Theatre
Beaufort Hill, Beaufort, EBBW VALE, Blaenau Gwent, NP23 5QQ, Wales
**Contact** Richard Hughes
**Phone** 01495 307354
01495 302112
**Fax** 01495 308966
**Email** beaufort.theatre@virgin.net
**Web** www.beauforttheatre.com
*Venue regularly programming top folk, roots, world & blues acts. 3360 capacity theatre plus 150 capacity ballroom. See also Valley Roots.*
**AC** Wales

### Blackwood Miners Institute
High Street, BLACKWOOD, NP2 1BB, Wales
**Phone** 01495 230075 - minicom booking
**Phone** 01495 227206
**Fax** 01495 226457
*Valley Roots venue. Wide range of folk concerts approx. monthly. Plus guitar workshops. 395 capacity, bar & disabled access.*
**AC** Wales

### Clwb Gwerin Llantrisant Folk Club
The Windsor Hotel, Pontyclun, LLANTRISANT, CF72 8DQ, Wales
**Contact** Mick Tems & Pat Smith
**Mail address** 1 Ty Clwyta Cottages, Cross Inn, LLANTRISANT, CF72 8AZ, Wales
**Fax** 01443 226892
**Mobile** 07773 075962
**Email** folkclub@folkwales.org.uk
**Web** www.folkwales.org.uk
*Wednesday. Guest & open house nights. Traditional & contemporary music from Wales & beyond.*
**AC** Wales

### Conwy Folk Club
The Malt Loaf, Rose Hill Street, CONWY, Wales
**Contact** Dennis Bennett
**Fax** 01492 877324
*Monday, 8.30pm. All types of singers & musicians welcome. Free admission & raffle.*
**AC** Wales

### Denbigh Folk Club
Bull Hotel, Hall Square, DENBIGH, Denbighshire, Wales
**Contact** Geoff Durno
**Mail address** Lothlorien, Upper Denbigh Road, ST ASAPH, Denbighshire, LL17 0BH
**Phone** 01745 582265
07974 665219
**Email** info@brynpolyw.co.uk
**AC** Wales

### Fishguard Folk Club
The Royal Oak, FISHGUARD, Pembrokeshire, Wales
**Contact** Gary Jones
**Phone** 01348 840181
**Web** www.pembrokeshire-folk-music.co.uk
*Tuesday, 8pm. Open house session; emphasis on Welsh & Irish music plus music associated with the sea.*
**AC** Wales

### Folk Music Workshop
Y Ffnnon, The Anglican Chapelaincy, Princes Road, BANGOR, Wales
**Contact** Ramsey Isak
**Phone** 01248 421071
07879 681292
**Email** ffynnon-gwerin@lineone.net
**Web** www.bangorweb.co.uk/ffynnogwerin
*Friday, 7.30pm. Celtic traditional music workshops, all instruments and levels. Monthly Celtic folk evenings.*
**AC** Wales

### gwerinABERfolk
The Coopers Arms, Northgate Street, ABERYSWYTH, Ceredigion, Wales
**Contact** Ian Gulley
*Phone 01970 890321*
*Tuesday, 8.30pm. Open session. Guest concert bi-monthly.*
**AC** Wales

### Halfpenny Folk Club
Greyhound Inn, Llanrhidian, GOWER, South Wales
**Contact** Joy Toole
**Phone** 01792 850803
*Sunday, 8.30pm. Traditional song & folk music club, guests monthly. Dance & instrumental workshops.*
**AC** Wales

### Llanelian Folk Club
The White Lion, Llanelian, Old Colwyn, COLWYN BAY, Wales
**Contact** Gill Williams
**Phone** 01492 515921
*Wednesday, 8pm. International guests; old timey, bluegrass, blues & related acoustic music.*
**AC** Wales

### Newport Folk Club
The Red Lion, Stow Hill, NEWPORT, Gwent, Wales
**Contact** Ken Potter
**Phone** 01633 680051
**Email** kenpotter@talk21.com
*Thursday, 8.30pm. Mainly English music. Bi-monthly national/ international guests.*
**AC** Wales

### Norwegian Church Arts Centre
Harbour Drive, CARDIFF, CF10 4PA, Wales
**Contact** Keith Hudson
**Mail address** 182 Broadway, Roath, CARDIFF, CF24 1QJ, Wales
**Phone** 029 2049 9759
07974 093541
**Fax** 029 2048 4882
**Alt contact** Karen Allen
**Phone** 029 2045 4899 - venue
**Fax** 029 2049 5122 - venue
*Monthly folk concerts, in association with Taplas. Contact Keith Hudson in first instance.*
**AC** Wales

### Pontardawe Arts Centre
Herbert Street, PONTADAWE, Nr Swansea, SA8 4ED, Wales
**Contact** Cathi Marcus - Arts & Ents
**Mail address** Neath Port Talbot County Borough Council, Afan Arts Centre, PORT TALBOT, SA12 1SW, Wales
**Phone** 07866 700709
01639 763149
**Fax** 01639 899914
**Email** c.marcus@neathporttalbot.gov.uk
**Alt contact** Angie Dickinson (Assistant Manager)
**Phone** 01792 863722
**Fax** 01792 864137
*Presenting venue for mixed arts programme including quarterly folk/ roots events. Programming in assocaition with Pontardawe Folk Festival. Neath Port Talbot County Borough Council*
**AC** Wales

### Ruthin Acoustic Music
The Castle Hotel, St Peters Square, RUTHIN, Denbighshire, Wales
Campbell Finney
**Phone** 01824 750730
**Email** campbellfinney@breathemail.net
**Web** www.ruthinmusic.co.uk
*Thursday, 8.30pm. Acoustic blues, rock, jazz, contemporary, folk rock. Contact re special guests.*
**AC** Wales

### St Donats Arts Centre
**Mail address** St Donats Castle, Vale of Glamorgan, CF61 1WF, Wales
**Contact** David Pepworth
**Phone** 01446 7991 (box office)
01446 799099 (admin)
**Email** marketing@stdonats.com
*14th century barn hosting folk & world music events, mainly established acts. Events programme runs September to May.*
**AC** Wales

### Theatr Brycheiniog
Brycheiniog, BRECON, Wales
**Phone** 01874 611622 - box office
01874 622838 - admin
*Theatre with studio space, gallery, bistro plus disabled access. 477 capacity. Varied programme including world, roots & folk events with top acts.*
**AC** Wales

### Theatr Hafren
Llanidloes Road, NEWTOWN, Powys, SY16 4HU, Wales
**Phone** 01686 625447
**Contact** Iain Kempton
**Web** www.theatrhafren.co.uk
*Principle North Powys theatre, presenting range of performances including significant folk & roots programme. Capcaity 556 seated/ 3+ cabaret style.*
**AC** Wales

### Theatr Mwldan
Bath House Road, CARDIGAN, SA43 1JY
**Phone** 01239 612687
**Contact** Dilwyn Davies
**Email** dilwyn@mwldan.co.uk
**Web** www.mwldan.co.uk
*Year round presenting venue.*
**AC** Wales



*See Celfyddydau Mari Arts' listings on pages 379-381.*

# organisations and resources

**Focus on:**

# Folk Arts Network (FAN)

**Folk Arts Network (FAN) is the national umbrella organisation supporting regional Folk Development Agencies in the UK.**

Since 1992 FAN has been assisting people working in the folk arts to:

- share information
- support and develop relationships
- collaborate with other related areas of the arts
- undertake specific projects
- act as an advisory body for the arts funding system

FAN runs an annual conference, Training in Traditions and initiates meetings between Regional Arts Boards and local folk practitioners. If you'd like more information about:

- becoming an assaociate of FAN
- receiving our newsletter
- meetings in your area
- previous meetings
- Arts Council of England's Folk Music Strategic Overview
- Training in Traditions

please email us at **fan@dmac.co.uk**

**Contact** The Administrator
**Mail address** Folk Arts Network Windsor Arts Centre, St. Leonards Road, Windsor, Berkshire, SL4 3BL
**Phone** 01753 858 577
**Email** fan@dmac.co.uk

# The English Folk Dance and Song Society (EFDSS)

**" ... putting English tradition into the hearts and minds of the people of England."**

**The English Folk Dance and Song Society (EFDSS),** a national membership-based educational charity, which for over 100 year has worked to promote, encourage, document and develop the folk music, dance, song and calendar traditions within England, which are some of the richest in the world.

The EFDSS is a forward thinking organisation that recognises and encourages the diversity of interest, influence and interpretation within the folk arts in England today.

The headquarters of the EFDSS are at Cecil Sharp House in Camden Town in London – a listed building that houses the Vaughan Williams Memorial Library.

The EFDSS promotes a diverse programme nationally aimed at stimulating the practice and enjoyment of folk music, dance, song and customs. It also acts as a national focal point for folk music activity, assisting with a wide range of enquiries, and co-operating with similar organisations within Britain and around the World.

The EFDSS is the trustee of the Vaughan Williams Memorial Library, the country's national archive and resource centre for folk music, dance and song.

This unique multi-media collection includes over 11,000 books and 6,000 recordings, as well as films, videos, photographs and manuscripts.

The EFDSS supports an ongoing programme of research, the results of which are constantly being added to the collections. The library provides help and advice to all levels of interest; including professional researchers, enthusiasts, educational establishments, performers, the media and the general public.

The EFDSS offers a national Education and Training Programme providing support and materials to teachers delivering the traditional dance element of the National Curriculum, plus a variety of accredited courses in music, dance and performance.

The EFDSS produces recordings, books, study guides and training materials, as well as two periodicals; English Dance and Song (a quarterly magazine) and the annual Folk Music Journal, and a web-based directory (Root Source - see www.rootsource.co.uk) – formerly the Folk Directory.

For details, advice or membership enquiries please check our website *www.efdss.org* or contact us at:

**Mail address** EFDSS,
Cecil Sharp House, 2 Regent's Park Road, London, NW1 7AY
**Phone** 020 7485 2206
**Main Fax** 020 7284 0534
**Library Fax** 020 7284 0523
**Email** efdss@efdss.org
**Web** www.efdss.org

# MODAL

Modal supports, develops awareness and aims to increase the profile for all musics in the UK that are regarded as 'outside the mainstream', in essence those musics that fall between rock/pop and classical.

Modal's primary activity is the production of an annual convention for this sector of the industry. The convention, held in Sheffield, consists of panel discussions, workshops, seminars, receptions, showcase performances, trade fair, film programme, radio broadcasts, exhibitions and a public access music event series - Modallive - featuring new and established acts. It acts as a forum for creative debate and the dissemination of good practice to the sector and also seeks to develop the creation of networks and to identify the major challenges and impediments to growth faced by the sector.

Attendance has quadrupled over the past four years with more than 500 delegates, artists and guests registering for this year's convention held in February 2001. Delegates are drawn from all areas of the music industry and wider arts world including promoters, record labels, venue and festival programmers, agents, managers, artists, printed and broadcast media, p.r., funding bodies, and government departments and organisations.

Modal also represents the non-mainstream music sector on a number of national advisory committees, acts as an information exchange for those working in the sector and advocates on a broad range of issues of relevance, in partnership where possible. This year, Modal is developing a major research project, *One Step Beyond*, which will seek to map the size, reach and economic value of the sector in the UK.

# The British Council

The British Council music team in the UK act as consultants to our 110 offices around the world to identify outstanding events and projects in the British music scene for international promotion.

We work with partners in all areas of music, including world, folk, jazz, club, electronic, early and contemporary classical. Our aim is to create cultural understanding and exchange between the UK and other countries, promote new images of Britain, establish long-term partnerships abroad and raise awareness of UK creativity amongst younger audiences.

Our music projects operate in varied and challenging contexts - from collaborations in Vietnam to workshops with schoolchildren in Southern Africa. Around 95% of the events we support are organised by the artists or their agents. We are not a funding body and when assessing which projects to support, the key relationship is always between the overseas partner and their local British Council office. On occasion, we take the lead to design events ourselves that complement our work in education and development and we identify UK artists who best meet the objectives of the project and complement the local context.

As well as supporting performance and outreach initiatives, we are also involved in developing the trade impact and potential of the UK's folk and roots music. The British Council has had a stand at WOMEX for the last three years that we invite all UK delegates to use as an informal meeting place and information point.

Roots music speaks volumes about a culture, and we find ourselves working more and more in this genre. There has never been a better time to celebrate the roots and folk music of the UK.

The defining lines between Britain's multicultural traditions are gently shifting, as different communities grow up side by side in changing political and cultural environments.

Devolution within the UK has also provided the exciting opportunity to reflect on the musical identities of four very different nations that combine to create the rich diversity of music in Britain today.

For more details on recent and upcoming projects and how we decide which projects to support, please visit our website at **http://music.britishcouncil.org**

# Visiting Arts

11 Portland Place, London, W1B 1EJ
**Phone** +44 (0) 20 7389 3019
**Fax** +44 (0) 20 7389 3016
**Email** office@visitingarts.demon.co.uk
**web** www.britishcouncil.org/visitingarts

**Purpose**
Visiting Arts is the national agency for promoting the flow of international arts into the UK and developing related cultural links abroad to help build cultural awareness and positive cultural relations. Activities include advice, information, training, consultancy, publications, special projects and project development. We cover the performing arts, visual, applied and media arts, crafts, design, literature, film, architecture and some museum activity.

**Geographical Interests**
Our interests span all regions of the world but we are particularly specialised and active in relation to East and Central Europe and the former Soviet Union, East and South East Asia, South Asia, Africa and Islamic countries. We have a special working relationship with the British Council which has offices in 110 countries, and links with complementary organisations across Europe. Our training and development focuses in particular on countries whose arts infrastructures are in transition. Current initiatives include China, Central Asia (the former Soviet Republics and Mongolia), the Caucasus (Armenia, Azerbaijan and Georgia), the Russian Federation, East and Central Europe, South East Europe, India, Vietnam and Southern Africa.

**Clients and Partners**
Visiting Arts works for and with a wide variety of organisations. We have completed major projects commissioned by the Hungarian, Israeli and Norwegian governments to produce definitive country arts and cultural directories, and have led reviews of cultural policy in the Russian Federation and Romania for the Council of Europe at the request of the respective governments. Study tours have been organised recently for Romanian and Vietnamese specialists for the European Union Phare programme and the Ford Foundation. Our overseas non-governmental clients and partners include the Soros Foundation network and the Ford Foundation. Other projects have included working with and co-ordinating programmes for the UK Foreign and Commonwealth Office and the British Council both in the UK and overseas.

**Other Activities**
Visiting Arts provides specialist information and training on the practical development and presentation of international arts and provides direct financial support to over 150 arts and cultural projects, tours or exhibitions coming to the UK and Europe each year. We produce a wide range of publications including a regular magazine and a series of comprehensive arts directories covering 38 countries. Our special projects have included the co-ordination of over 100 arts and cultural events to celebrate the 1998 ASEM2 Summit, the organisation of a major international conference, touring the Arts of East and South East Asia in Europe, and a cultural programme to celebrate the 50th anniversary of the independence of India and Pakistan in 1997. Recent programmes include Mutualities: Britain and Islam Cultural and Arts Programme, a promotion of Muslim arts, and an Asian visual artists-in-residence programme in the UK and Europe.

**The Organisation**
Visiting Arts is a company limited by guarantee (Registered in England and Wales number 4162404) with charitable status. The Board is chaired by Richard Lambert, Editor of the Financial Times. Visiting Arts is core-funded by the Arts Council of England, the Scottish Arts Council, the Arts Council of Wales, the Arts Council of Northern Ireland, the Foreign and Commonwealth Office and the British Council. The Department for Culture, Media and Sport also provides support. The Director of Visiting Arts is Terry Sandell who heads a team of specialists in cultural relations and wide-ranging areas of the arts and regions of the world.

***Editor's note*** *I have found Visiting Arts booklet* Cutting through the Red Tape *to be invaluable in recent years in dealing with the intricacies of bringing overseas artists into the country. Visiting Arts consider that this is in need of updating now and refer the reader to their website for the latest information on such matters.*

## Voluntary Arts Network (VAN)

VAN is the UK development agency for the voluntary arts. Around 56% of the population of the UK participates in the arts and crafts. The range of art forms is wide and varied and includes folk, roots and related music, other music, dance, drama, literature, media, visual arts, crafts and applied arts, and festivals.

We recognise that the arts are a key part of our culture and that they are vital to our health, social and economic development. They deserve support and encouragement to flourish.

To this end VAN works with policy makers, funders and politicians to improve the policy environment for everyone participating in the arts, from the smallest local groups to large national bodies. This includes around 300 national and regional umbrella bodies, and through them, their member groups of local voluntary arts practitioners.

VAN's services include:

- a quarterly newsletter providing information on opportunities, seminars
- funding and news about those in the voluntary arts
- briefing sheets that offer advice on issues relevant to the sector. These are aimed at demystifying arts, funding and management jargon handbooks - including information on funding, planning, legal issues, polices, publicity and contacts. Our publications provide invaluable help to both those organisations just setting out and those already well established. A list and the content of briefings and other publications is available on the website or direct from VAN.
- A directory listing all the national and regional organisations concerned with, or working for the voluntary arts in the UK is available on the website
- specialised arts management training (distance learning modules are also currently being created)
- www.voluntaryarts.org - our website is updated weekly and includes recent news, funding ideas, booklists, VAN publications, contacts, directory

**How to get in touch**

Our central office covers England, Scotland, Wales, Republic of Ireland and Northern Ireland. We currently have offices in Wales and Scotland and are setting up offices in Northern Ireland and England in 2001. These offices have close contact with voluntary arts organisations in those countries.
Contact **www.voluntaryarts.org**

**Voluntary Arts Network (UK Office)**
PO Box 200, Cardiff, CF1 9NU
**Phone** 01222 395 395
**Fax** 01222 397 397
**Email** info@voluntaryarts.org

**Voluntary Arts Wales (for projects in Wales)**
PO Box 200, Welshpool, Powys, SY21 7WN
**Phone** 01938 556 455
**Fax** 01938 556 451
**Email** lydia@vaw.org.uk

**Voluntary Arts Scotland**
PO Box 200, Edinburgh, H2 4WN
**Phone** 0131 220 4466
**Fax** 0131 220 4477
**Email** volartsscotland@charity.vfree.com

**Ginny Brink**
Information Officer
**Voluntary Arts Network (UK Office)**
PO Box 200, Cardiff, CF5 1YH
**Phone** 029 2039 5395
**Fax** 029 2039 7397
**Web** www.voluntaryarts.org

*The Voluntary Arts Network (VAN) is registered in Scotland as Company No.139147 and Charity No. SC 020345. VAN acknowledges funding from the Arts Councils of England, Northern Ireland, Scotland and Wales, the Carnegie UK Trust, the Esmee Fairbairn Charitable Trust and the Baring Foundation.*

## WOMEX 25th -28th October 2001, Rotterdam, The Netherlands

The Worldwide Music Expo WOMEX is the biggest professional conference, tradefair and showcase event exclusively dedicated to world, roots, folk, ethnic, traditional and local music of all kinds. After stopovers in Berlin, Brussels, Marseilles and Stockholm, WOMEX will now travel to Rotterdam in the Netherlands, the world's biggest harbour city and Europe's Cultural Capital of 2001. WOMEX 2001 host will be the Dunya Foundation, the venue will be De Doelen, Rotterdam's premier concert and congress-centre which can combine the WOMEX Conference, Showcases and Trade Fair together under one roof.

The first six WOMEX editions have affirmed the value and potential of networking across borders, whether these borders be musical, political, cultural or commercial.

WOMEX 2000 featured

- more than 1200 delegates from more than 70 countries, including more than 200 journalists
- more than 240 artists in 34 showcases on 3 stages
- more than 150 exhibitors in 99 trade fair stands the launch of the virtual WOMEX, the first internet fair for world music, co-financed by the European Community and the City Council of Berlin

For all deadlines, additional information and forms concerning registration, showcase, conference, trade fair and award proposals check the web site at **www.womex.com**
or contact WOMEX
c/o Piranha: womex@womex.com
**Phone** +49 30 318 6140
**Fax** +49 30 318 614 10

## International/ national organisations and institutions

### Anglo-American Dance Service (AADS)
**Mail address** Resedastraat 8, B-9920 LOVENDEGEM, Belgium
**Phone** +32 9 3729635
**Fax** +32 9 37229635
**Email** aads@village.uunet.be
**Web** http://gallery.uunet.be
*Promotors of Anglo-American dance in Western Europe. Dance courses and weekends, publishers and retailers of dance material and folk dance music.*

### Asian Music Circuit
**Mail address** Ground Floor Unit E, West Point, 33/34 Warple Way, LONDON, W3 0RG
**Phone** 020 8742 9911
**Fax** 020 8749 3948
**Email** info@amc.org.uk
**Web** www.amc.org.uk
*National organisation for the promotion of Asian music. Touring, concerts, workshops and education programme.*
**RAB** London Arts
***See feature in spotlight section.***

### Association of Festival Organisers
**Contact** Steve Heap
**Mail address** PO Box 296, AYLESBURY, Bucks, HP19 9TL
**Phone** 01296 394411
**Fax** 01296 392300
**Email** afo@mrscasey.co.uk
**Web** www.mrscasey.co.uk/afo
*National body recognised by the events industry and the arts. Association of community arts festival organisers. Conference last weekend in January.*
**RAB** Southern Arts Board
***See feature in festival section.***

### British Council - Performing Arts Department
**Mail address** 11 Portland Place, LONDON, W1B 4EJ
**Phone** 020 7389 3083
020 7389 3005
**Fax** 020 7389 3057
**Email** music@britishcouncil.org
**Web** http://music.britishcouncil.org
*The British Council is the UK's principal agency for international cultural relations, working with prtners in all forms of music including folk, world, jazz, club, electronic, early and contemporary classical.*
**RAB** Arts Council of England
***See feature in this section.***

### British Country Music Association
**Mail address** PO Box 240, HARROW, Middx, HA3 7PH
**Phone** 01273 559750
**Email** theBCMA@yahoo.com
*Information service on Country music.*

### British Library National Sound Archive - International Music Collection
**Contact** Janet Topp Fargion
**Phone** 020 7412 7427
**Fax** 020 7412 7441
**Email** janet.topp-fargion@bl.uk
**Web** www.bl.uk/collections/sound-archive
**Alt contact** Marie-Laure Manigand
**Email** marie-laure.manigand@bl.uk
*Collection of sound recording of traditional/ traditional-based music from the British Isles and the rest of the world. Accessible to the public through listening service by appointment. Catalogue available on website.*
**AC** Arts Council of England

### Celfyddydau Mari Arts
**Contact** Mick Tems
**Mail address** 1 Ty Clwyta Cottages, Cross Inn, LLANTRISANT, Rhondda Cynon Taf, CF72 8AZ, Wales
**Phone** 01443 226892
**Phone/Fax** 07773 075962
**Email** mariarts@folkwales.org.uk
**Web** www.folkwales.org.uk
*Research, archiving, education & promotion service for all the traditional arts in Wales. Also creation & performance of new work based on traditional themes.*
**AC** Wales
***See Focus on Wales.***

### Concertina Research and Resources
**Contact** Neil Wayne
**Mail address** The Cedars, BELPER, Derbys, DE56 1DP
**Phone** 01773 824157
**Email** concertinas@free-reed.co.uk
**Web** www.come.to/concertinas
*Research, advice and publications on all aspects of the concertina and other free reed instruments.*
**RAB** East Midlands Arts

### Consorcio Salamanca Javier Hernandez
**Mail address** C/ Pea Primera 18-24, 37002 SALAMANCA, Spain
**Phone** +923 281 601
**Fax** +923 281 603
**Email** conciertos@salamanca2002.org
**Web** www.salamanca2002.net / .org / .com
*Spanish company promoting folk/ roots events year round, including a festival.*

### Cymdeithas Offerynnau Traddodiadol Cymru - The Society for the Traditional Instruments of Wales
**Contact** Dewi Roberts
**Mail address** Cwrtiau, ABERGWYNGREGYN, Gwynedd, LL33 0LB, Wales
**Phone** 01248 681008
**Email** cotc@btinternet.com
*Membership based organisation promoting the instruments, instrumental traditions & related music of Wales. Primarily deals with triple harp, fiddle, flutes, whistles, pibgyrn, bagpipes through weekend workshops.*
***Musicians' Union member***
**AC** Wales

### ECTARC
**Contact** Sharon Thomas
**Mail address** LLANGOLLEN, Wales
**Phone** 01978 861514
**AB** Wales
*European Centre for Traditional and Regional Cultures*

### The Elphinstone Institute
**Contact**Dr Ian Russell - Director
**Mail address** University of Aberdeen, 24 High Street, ABERDEEN, AB24 3EB
**Phone** 01224 272996
**Fax** 01224 272728
**Email** elphinstone@abdn.ac.uk
**Web** www.abdn.ac.uk/elphinstone
*Institute exisiting to study, record and promote the cutural traditions and language of communities in the North of Scotland.*
**AC** Scotland
***See Traditional Music and Song in Spotlight section.***

### Folk Arts Network (FAN)
**Contact** Roger Watson - Chair
**Mail address** Windsor Arts Centre, St Leonards Road, WINDSOR, Berks, SL4 3BL
**Phone** 01753 858577
*National information network of 'folk development agencies'.*
***See feature in this section.***

## Folk For Multiple Sclerosis
**Contact** R S Hambleton
**Mail address** 17 Juniper Avenue, BRICKET WOOD, Herts, AL2 3LR
**Phone** 01923 672590
**Fax** 01923 404310 (phone first)
**Email** ffms@kestrel-folk.demon.co.uk
*Registered charity (1080774) raising money through folk activities to help sufferers of Multiple Sclerosis.*
**RAB** East England Arts

## Hirio Events
**Contact** Arianna Fioretti
**Mail address** Via Don Caustico 123, 10095 Grugliasco (TO), ITALY
**Phone** +39 11 415 9524
+39 335 591 5186
**Fax** +39 11 405 9700
**Email** hirio@hirio.com
**Web** www.hirio.com
*Italian company organisers and promoting all traditional music, mainly from Celtic areas, working all over Italy.*

## International Concertina Assocation
**Contact** Gill Noppen-Spacie
**Mail address** Dalecombe Cottage, 4 School Lane, Denby Dale, HUDDERSFIELD, HD8 8RX
**Phone** 01484 860877
**Fax** 01484 860852
**Web** www.harbour.demon.co.uk/ica
*Organisation seeking to promote the interests and development of music on all concertina systems. All ages, levels and abilities of players. Newsletter and extensive library/ archive. Help & support to individuals and groups.*

## Music for Change
**Contact** Tom Andrews
**Mail address** 27 Watling Street, CANTEBURY, Kent, CT1 2UD
**Phone** 01227 459243
**Email** music.forchange@virgin.net
**Web** www.musicforchange.org
*Music charity working with roots music in education and community projects.*
**RAB** South East Arts

## Musicians Union
**Contact** Ian Smith
**Mail address** 11 Sandyford Place, GLASGOW, G3 7NB, Scotland
**Phone** 0141 248 3723
0141 943 0767
**Fax** 0141 204 3510
**Email** is1@musiciansunion.org.uk
**RAB** Arts Council of England
***See Introduction section.***

## The Puppet Centre Trust
**Mail address** The Administration Battersea Arts Centre, Lavender Hill, LONDON, SW11 5TN
**Phone** 020 7228 5335
**Fax** 020 7228 8863
**Email** pct@puppetcentre.demon.co.uk
**Web** www.puppetcentre.com
*Registered charity, resource for anything to do with puppetry in all its forms. Enquiries, personnel, makers, performers, educational and other workshops referring to puppetry.*
**RAB** London Arts

## Scottish Culture and Traditions Assocation (SCaT)
**Contact** Malcolm Reavell - Secretary
**Mail address** Orphir, Swailend Bridge, Newmachar, ABERDEEN, AB21 7UU, Scotland
**Phone** 01651 862975
**Email** malcolm@appleonline.net
**Web** www.scat2000.co.uk
**Alt contact** Susan Kirkwood - President 78 Cairnfield Place, ABERDEEN, AB15 5NA, Scotland
**Phone** 01224 630979
**Email** skirkwooda@cix.co.uk
*SCaT is a voluntary organisation working in and around Aberdeen in traditional arts and language, and other related cultural activity. Activities include adult education,workshops, ceilidhs, concerts and performance groups.*
**AC** Scotland

## Scottish Folk Arts Group
**Contact** Willie Haines
**Mail address** c/o Blackfriars Music, 49 Blackfriars St, Off The Royal Mile, EDINBURGH, EH1 1NB
**Phone** 0131 557 3090
**Email** scotfolk@compuserve.com
**Web** www.scottishfolkdirectory.com
*Dedicated to the collection and presentation of contact and activity information in Scottish Folk Music and Folk Arts.*
**AC** Scotland
***See Focus on Scotland.***

## Scottish Music Information Centre
**Contact** Caitie Faulds
**Mail address** 1 Bowmont Gardens, GLASGOW, G12 9LR
**Phone** 0141 334 6393
**Fax** 0141 337 1161
**Email** info@smic.org.uk
**Web** www.smic.org.uk
*SMIC exists to document and promote Scottish music. Large library, some available for sale and hire. Extensive database of musicians, festivals, promoters, agents, services etc., covering all genres.*
**AC** Scotland

## Surdhwani National Arts Organisation
**Contact** Mrs Maitreyee Sarcar - Secretary
**Mail address** 3 Sherington Drive, Goldthorn Park, WOLVERHAMPTON, WV4 5DX
**Phone** 01902 658793
**Fax** 01902 830278
**Email** maitreyee@surdhwani.org.uk
**Web** www.surdhwani.org.uk
*National arts organisation dedicated to promoting Asian arts and culture in the UK.*
**RAB** West Midlands Arts

## trac
**Contact** Philip Freeman
**Mail address** Swn-y-Coed, LLANDINAM, Powys, SY17 5DJ
**Phone/Fax** 01686 688102
**Email** freeman@mid-wales.com
**Email** trac@btinternet.com
*Welsh traditional music & dance development agency.*
**AC** Wales
***See Focus on Wales.***

## Traditional Music and Song Association of Scotland (TMSA)
**Contact** Elspeth Cowie
**Mail address** 95-97 St. Leonard's Street, EDINBURGH, EH8 9QY
**Phone** 0131 667 5587
**Fax** 0131 662 9153
**Email** info@tmsa.demon.co.uk
**Web** www.tmsa.demon.co.uk/tmsa/
*Scottish traditional music and song development agency.*
**AC** Scotland
***See Focus on Scotland.***

## Vaughan Williams Memorial Library
**Mail address** Cecil Sharp House, 2 Regent's Park Road, LONDON NW1 7AY
**Phone** 020 7485 2206
**Fax** 020 7284 0523
**Email** library@efdss.org
**Web** www.efdss.org
***See Spotlight section; Traditional Music and Song and Calendar Customs. Also see London region for further details.***



***See Derek Schofield's Spotlight section on Traditional Music and Song on pages 144-149 for details of Organisations and Resources.***

***See Derek Schofield's Customs section on pages 220-221 for details of Vaughan Williams Memorial Library, The Folklore Society, School of Scottish Studies and the Museum of Welsh Life.***

## West Gallery Music Association
**Contact** Jacqueline Patten
**Mail address** Kerlistz, The Green, Morchard Bishop, CREDITON, Devon, EX17 6PD
**Phone** 01363 877503
**Email** patten@kerlistz.freeserve.co.uk
*Promotes village band & quire music of the 18th & 19th centuries via a newsletter, workshops, research, concerts, resources, etc.*
**RAB** South West Arts

## YaD Arts
**Contact** Josephine Burton
**Mail address** 49 Basildon Court, 28 Devonshire Street, LONDON, W1G 6PR
**Phone** 020 7486 5627
07775 656775
**Fax** 020 8944 6143
**Email** josephine@yadarts.com
**Web** www.yadarts.com
**Alt contact** Johnathan Walton
**Email** johnathan@yadarts.com
*Promotion of contemporary Jewish arts in Britain. Encouagement of dialogue between ethnic communities through live collaborative projects and multi-media events.*

# Regional and locally based organisations including education projects

## Acoustic Youth 2000
**Contact** Kerensa Newman
**Mail address** 7 St. Aubyn's Vean, TRURO, Cornwall TR1 2DX
**Phone** 01872 240475
07833 393928
**Email** kerensaay2k@supanet.com
**Web** www.acousticyouth.org
*Folk arts organisation run by and for young people. Workshops, concerts, etc at festival & venues across the country.*
**RAB** South West Arts

## Arts Alive
**Mail address** Further Up, Long Row, Lower Down, LYBURY NORTH, Shrops, SY7 8BB
**Phone** 01588 680388
**Fax** 01588 680398
**Email** info@artsalive.co.uk
**Web** www.artsalive.co.uk
*Rural touring scheme promoting live events in Shropshire and Herefordshire.*
**RAB** West Midlands Arts

## Awaken Village Interest in Dance (AVID)
**Contact** Peter Barnard
**Mail address** 1 Battle Green, Epworth, NR DONCASTER, DN9 1JT
**Phone** 01427 873937
**Email** peter_barnard.squeeze@virgin.net
*Informal session ceilidhs in village halls in North Lincs and North Notts every 2nd Tuesday or Wednesday of the month.*
**RAB** Yorkshire Arts

## Be@tts Inc
**Contact** Phil Plunkett
**Mail address** Loch Lomond Studio, Unt 20 Griffon Cn., Vale of Leven Ind E, DUMBARTON, G82 3PD, Scotland
**Phone** 01389 750555
**Email** phil@beattsinc.co.uk
**Web** www.beattsinc.co.uk
**Alt contact** Stuart Beattie/ Richy Plunkett
**Email** info@beattsinc.co.uk
*Custom built centre. Local talent promotion, community learning, education service & tuition. MU discounts.*
***Musicians' Union member***
**AC** Scotland

## Clocksback
**Contact** Ben Farmer
**Mail address** 27 Regent Street, LANCASTER, LA1 1SQ
**Phone** 01524 847135
**Email** ben@farmerboymusic.fsnet.co.uk
**Web** www.beulah.demon.co.uk/clocksback.html
*Organisation running workshops for adults and children in the Lancaster/ Morecambe area, a folk club and other community folk projects. See also Lancaster Clocksback/forward festivals. Bi-monthly newsletter. Please address emails to "Clocksback".*
**RAB** North West Arts

## Comhaltas Ceoltoiri Eireann (Jackfield Branch)
**Contact** David Harris - Chairman
**Mail address** 35 St Michaels Close, TELFORD, Shrops, TF7 5SD
**Phone** 01952 680249
**Email** david@g8ina.enta.net
**Web** www.g8ina.enta.net
*Traditional Irish music sessions every Thursday. Lessons for adults and children on Sundays and Tuesdays in Irish dance, language and music (most instruments).*
***Musicians' Union member***
**RAB** West Midlands Arts

## Cornish Music Project
**Contact** Hilary Coleman
**Mail address** 24 Valley Close, Newbridge, TRURO, Cornwall, TR1 3UN
**Phone** 01842 275058
**Web** www.cmp.kernow.eu.org
**Alt contact** Frances Bennett
**Email** sfbennett@aol.com
*Cornish music organisation aiming to nurture a sense of pride of place through a variety of music projects covering 4 areas - education, networking, celebration and research. Workshops, concerts and publications.*
***Musicians' Union member***
**RAB** South West Arts

## East Anglian Traditional Music Trust
**Contact** Katie Howson
**Mail address** 44 Old Street, Haughley, STOWMARKET, Suffolk, IP14 3NX
**Phone** 01449 673695
**Email** eamt@veteran.co.uk
*Projects, workshops and other events based on the traditional music and song of the East Anglian region.*
***Musicians' Union member***
**RAB** East England Arts
***See East England region.***

## The English Acoustic Collective
**Contact** Chris Wood
**Mail address** 40 Whitstable Road, FAVERSHAM, Kent, ME13 8DL
**Phone** 01795 537906
**Email** cw@rurecords.com
**Web** www.rufrecords.com
*Teaching organisation directed by Chris Wood, with a focus on individual development based on the best of our tradition. Annual summer school, last week of July plus other events during the year.*

## Essex Folk Association
**Contact** John New
**Mail address** 37 Sidwell Avenue, BENFLEET, Essex, SS7 1LF
**Phone** 01268 793905
**Email** john@essexfolknews.co.uk
**Web** www.essexfolknews.co.uk
*Aims to preserve, practise and promote traditional folk customs, music, dance & song in Essex and East London. Quarterly magazine.*
**RAB** East England Arts

### Folk South West
**Contact** Eddie Upton
**Mail address** The Stables, Montacute House, MONTACUTE, Somerset, TA15 6XP
**Phone** 01935 822911
**Fax** 01935 822024
**Email** folksw@folksw.org.uk
**Web** www.folksw.org.uk
*Folk development agency for SW England. Projects include education, events & publications.*
**RAB** South West Arts
***See South West region***

### Folk South-East
**Contact** John Smedley
**Mail address** 8 Bayham Road, SEVENOAKS, Kent, TN13 3XA
**Phone/Fax** 01732 460171
**Email** info@folksoutheast.org.uk
**Web** www.folksoutheast.org.uk
*The South-East's all-year-round folk festival. More than 30 concerts per year with a broad range of leading folk artists at various venues in Kent and Sussex.*
***Musicians' Union member***
**RAB** South East Arts
***See South East region***

### Folk Spots
**Contact** Alan Castle
**Mail address** 15 Repton Manor Road, ASHFORD, Kent, TN23 3HA
**Phone** 01233 626805
**Email** folkspots@btinternet.com
**Web** www.folkspots.btinternet.com
*Promotion & organisation of folk events.*
**RAB** South East Arts

### Folkus
**Contact** Alan Bell
**Mail address** 55 The Strand, FLEETWOOD, Lancs, FY7 8NP
**Phone** 01253 872317
**Fax** 01253 878382
**Email** alanbell@fylde-folk-fest.demon.co.uk
**Web** www.fylde-folk-festival.com
**Alt contact** Dave Jones
**Alt address** 4 Kingfisher Close, Swallowfields, Pleckgate, BLACKBURN, Lancs, BB1 8NP
**Phone** 01254 54877
*North West folk arts network. Presents and supportsfolk workshops, concerts, etc. in Lancashire.*
**RAB** North West Arts
***See North West region***

### Folkworks
**Mail address** 69 Westgate Road, NEWCASTLE-UPON-TYNE, NE1 1SG
**Phone** 0191 222 1717
**Fax** 0191 230 2484
**Email** folkworks@folkworks.co.uk
**Web** www.folkworks.co.uk
*Traditional music developemnt agency, organising tours and festivals, workshops, courses and summer schools plus extensive work in education.*
**RAB** Northern Arts
***See Northern region***

### Furness Tradition
**Contact** Gordon Jones
**Mail address** 60 Soutergate, ULVERSTON, Cumbria, LA12 7ES
**Phone** 01229 582704
**Fax** 01229 588290
**Email** kmode@onetel.net.uk
**Web** www.rootsworld.com/harbourtown
*Year round events focusing on Furness & South Lakeland traditions. Schools & educational workshops. Festival weekend in Ulverston.*
**RAB** Northern Arts

### Glasgow Fiddle Workshop
**Contact** Sara Melville
**Mail address** 12 Whitehill Avenue, Stepps, GLASGOW, G33 6BL, Scotland
**Phone** 0141 779 9047
**Email** administrator@glasgowfiddle.f9.co.uk
**Web** www.glasgowfiddle.f9.co.uk
*Weekly classes in Scottish fiddle for all ages & abilities. Weekend events, ceilidhs, sessions, practice CDs, membership, etc.*
**AC** Scotland

### Hands on Music Weekends
**Contact** Dave Townsend
**Mail address** PO Box 1162, EAST OXFORD DO, OX4 4WS
**Phone** 01865 714778, 07798 520552
**Fax** 01865 749428
**Email** homweekend@aol.com
*Regular weekend workshops on developing skills and exploring traditional music. See individual entries for details.*
***Musicians' Union member***
**RAB** Southern Arts

### Heart of England Music
**Contact** Stevie Horton
**Mail address** PO Box 1957, EATHORPE, Warks, CV33 9YG
**Phone/Fax** 01926 632946
**Phone** 07989 373698
**Email** mayhem.design@cwcom.net
**Web** www.heartofenglandmusic.co.uk
*Independent Midlands based non-profit initiative, supporting charities by publishing compilation albums and staging benefit concerts. Works mainly with folk and folk-rock artists.*
**RAB** West Midlands Arts

### Hertfordshire Folk Association
**Contact** Roger Barnes
**Mail address** 40 Battlefield Road, ST ALBANS, AL1 4DD
**Phone** 01727 851987
**Fax** 01727 853581
**Alt contact** Roger Swaine
**Alt address** 29 Turmore Dale, WELWYN GARDEN CITY, AL8 6HT
**Phone** 01707 324413
*Organisation promoting all forms of folk activity within Hertfordshire. Workshops, events plus Hatfield House summer dance festival.*
**RAB** East England Arts

### The Jim McGill School of Traditional Music
**Contact** Dick Glasgow
**Mail address** 18 Main Street, BALLINTOY, Co. Antrim, BT54 6LX, Northern Ireland
**Phone/Fax** 028 2076 3116
**Email** afmo6@dial.pipex.com
*Music tuition in most primary schools plus nightclasses and concerts, ceilis the Scottish way, sessions. See Black Nun Folk Club.*
**AC** Northern Ireland

### Kagemusha Taiko
**Contact** Jonathan Kirby
**Mail address** PO Box 128, EXETER, Devon, EX4 6YT
**Phone** 01392 494486
**Email** info@kagemusha.com
**Web** www.kagemusha.com
*Devon based organisation, dedicated to development/ nurture of an English style of Taiko drumming plus international artistic collaboration. 2 performing groups plus outreach work and short courses.*
**RAB** South West Arts

## Lancashire Voices
**Contact** Derek Gifford
**Mail address** 22 Stoney Brow, Roby Mill, UP HOLLAND, Lancs, WN8 0PE
**Phone** 01695 625097
**Email** derek.gifford@talk21.com
**Alt contact** Christopher Harvey
**Alt address** Cock Robin Music, 8/9 Cock Robin Cottages, High Field Road, CROSTON, Lancs, PR5 7HG
**Phone** 01772 601060
**Email** c.h.poll@btinternet.com

*Recording, archiving and promotion of contemporary Lancashire singers & poets.*

***Musicians' Union member***
**RAB** North West Arts

## Mythstories, Museum of Myth and Fable
**Contact** Dez Quarrell
**Phone** 01743 357140
**Email** dez@mythstories.com
**Web** www.mythstories.com
**Alt contact** Ali Quarrell
**Alt address** Rose Cottage, Church Road, WELSHPOOL, Powys, SY21 7LN
**Phone** 01938 554428
**Email** ali@mythstories.com

*Educational charity promoting literacy & literature through storytelling and related artforms. Cross media arts projects. See West End Words Festival and Storytelling Café. Venue due to move Sept 2001.*

**RAB** West Midlands Arts

## New Roots Competition
**Contact** Alison Macfarlane
**Mail address** 40 Warwick Road, ST ALBANS, Herts, AL1 4DL
**Phone** 01727 852111
**Email** alison.macfarlane@lineone.net

*Annual competition for young folk & roots music performers in the Eastern region.*

**RAB** East England Arts

## Nightjar Music/ The Music Pool
**Contact** Rob Strawson
**Mail address** The Courtyard, Edgar Street, HEREFORD, HR4 9JR
**Phone** 01432 278118
**Fax** 01432 356238
**Email** muspool@globalnet.co.uk
**Web** www.musicpool.org.uk

*Comprehensive community music provision.*

**RAB** West Midlands Arts

## Ryburn 3 Step
**Mail address** 103 Oldham Road, Ripponden, SOWERBY BRIDGE, W Yorks, HX6 4EB
**Phone** 01422 822569
**Email** ryburn3step@backshift.demon.co.uk
**Web** www.ryburn3step.org.uk

*Group of singers, dancers & musicians performing at & organising wide variety of folk events in W Yorks. Presentations, workshops and consultancy for schools and community organisiations.*

**RAB** Yorkshire Arts
***See Yorkshire region.***

## Sabhal Mor Ostaig
**Contact** Gavin Parsons
**Phone** 01471 888240, 01471 888000
**Fax** 01471 888001
**Email** cg@smo.uhi.ac.uk
**Web** www.smo.uhi.ac.uk

*Gaelic college. Week-long courses in traditional, mainly West Highland, music, song and dance plus language courses during the summer.*

**AC** Scotland

## South East Music Schemes and Spotlight South East
**Contact** Alison Maconochie
**Mail address** PO Box 2790, EASTBOURNE, BN20 7WF
**Phone** 01323 431283
**Email** sems@ukgateway.net
**Web** www.semusic.org

*Promotion of groups and individuals working in non-classical forms of music through an annual award scheme. Support includes subsized concerts/ bookings and administrative and marketing assistance.*

**RAB** South East Arts

## South Riding Folk Network
**Contact** May Cheadle
**Phone** 01433 631352
**Email** chair@folk-network.com
**Web** www.folk-network.com
**Alt contact** Cath James
**Phone** 0114 2680880
**Email** secretary@folk-network.com

*Regional voluntary group to support, promote and raise the profile of folk arts.*

**RAB** Yorkshire Arts

## Step In Time
**Contact** Kathryn Aldis
**Mail address** 88 Lowestoft Road, Worlingham, BECCLES, Suffolk, NR34 7RD
**Phone** 01502 712160
01502 518637
**Email** katealdis@netscape.net

*Community based musicians promoting traditional English music & dance to pre-school - 10 year olds through music, dance & craft workshops in schools, festivals, etc.*

***Musicians' Union member***
**RAB** East England Arts

## Stepback Project
**Contact** Anthony Allen
**Mail address** 89 Hollingbury Park Avenue, BRIGHTON, BN1 7JQ
**Phone** 01273 541453
07951 663570
**Fax** 01273 554189
**Email** brokenankles@btinternet.com
**Web** www.brokenankles.btinternet.co.uk

*Project teaching dance students through workshops, etc. Stage performances of traditional English based dance.*

**RAB** South East Arts

## TAPS
**Contact** Keith Holloway - Administrator
**Mail address** The Heritage Site, The Fairground, Weyhill, ANDOVER, Hants, SP10 0QN
**Phone** 01264 773317 - admin
01264 772570 - projects
**Fax** 0870 734 6005
**Email** taps@dmac.co.uk
**Web** www.tradarts.co.uk
**Alt contact** Roger Watson - Artistic Director
**Alt address** Windsor Arts Centre, St Leonards Road, WINDSOR, Berks, SL4 3BL
**Phone** 01753 858577
**Fax** 0870 7346005
**Email** roger.taps@dmac.co.uk

*Southern area folk development agency running community events. Education work at all levels; skills training for individuals & groups.Professional development and touring.*

***Musicians' Union member***
**RAB** Southern Arts
***See Southern region.***

## Tenterden Folk Day Trust

**Contact** Alan Castle
**Mail address** 15 Repton Manor Road, ASHFORD, Kent, TN23 3HA
**Phone** 01233 626805
**Email** tff@folkspots.btinternet.co.uk
**Web** www.folkspots/festival

*Educational projects, occasional events and festival. TFDT aims to preserve and advance the public education and appreciation of traditional and contemporary folk music, song, dance and other related traditions, crafts and folk arts as part of the living heritage.*

**RAB** South East Arts

## Trads (Traditional Arts Development South East)

**Contact** Gail Duff
**Mail address** Wynlic, Bull Lane, Lenham Heath, MAIDSTONE, Kent, ME17 2JA
**Phone** 01622 858460
0772 0592126
**Email** greenwillow@folkarts.fsnet.co.uk
**Alt contact** Bing Lyle
**Alt address** 45 Roundhill Crescent, BRIGHTON, East Sussex, BN2 3FQ
**Phone** 01273 689777

*Workshops, educational projects & community events in the South East using traditional performing arts as a base.*

**RAB** South East Arts
***See South East region.***

## Village Carols

**Contact** Ian Russell
**Mail address** PO Box 2099, SHEFFIELD, S35 0XU
**Phone** 01224 645486
**Fax** 01224 272728
**Email** ian.russell@abdn.ac.uk
**Web** www.sgpublishing.co.uk/gm/vc/vcabout.html

*Non-profit making organisation recording and promoting local carol singing traditions. Fieldwork & research, collection of source material and promotion of local carol singing. Publisher and retailer of CDs, books and tapes.*

**RAB** Yorkshire Arts

## Warwickshire Traditional Arts

**Contact** Graham Bradshaw
**Mail address** 250 Earlsdon Avenue North, COVENTRY, CV5 6GX
**Phone** 024 7671 1935
**Fax** 024 7671 1191
**Email** rootsrecs@btclick.com
**Alt contact** Dick Dixon
**Phone** 07831 890905
**Email** dick.dixon@warfolk.demon.co.uk

*Organisation and co-ordination of folk and traditional arts activities in Warwickshire, including Coventry.*

**RAB** West Midlands Arts

## Yorkshire Dales Workshops

**Mail address** 14 Oakburn Road, ILKLEY, Yorks, LS29 9NN
**Phone/Fax** 01943 609421
**Phone** 07760 287384
**Email** ydw@ydw.btinternet.co.uk
**Web** www.ydw.btinternet.co.uk

*Promotes participation in folk arts through practical workshops, courses & performances. Publisher of books, CDs and videos. Events throughout the year.*

**RAB** Yorkshire Arts
***See Yorkshire region.***

media

media
section

# media

# Rooting around the net By Kevin Sheils

rooting
on the net

As more and more of us have regular contact with the Internet, at home or in the workplace, its importance as a source of information regarding folk, roots and acoustic music and arts grows. Whether simply requiring information regarding who's on when and where, or needing to gather knowledge of, for example, the collections of ballads in various libraries for serious academic research, many now turn to the 'Web' for the answers.

This is not the place for a discussion of how to access the Internet or the merits of various Internet Service Providers, as many of you will already have access or friends who can help. There are also many specialist publications to advise on this.

**The Web**

When the Internet is referred to what is frequently meant is the World Wide Web, although there are other aspects to the Internet such as Newsgroups (Usenet) and Mailing Lists. I'll return to those other aspects later but will start with the Web itself and a simple description.

The Web is like a vast library with the attendant problems of finding the location of the "book" you want or even which "books" contain information pertinent to your interests. These "books", or to be precise web sites, are contained on many different computers around the world all linked by a vast network. Every web site is identified by a specific "address", known as a URL (Universal Resource Indicator) which needs to be entered into your web browser in order to access the site. These URLs are often in a form which makes sense to the user, for example the URL for this publication is www.direct-roots.com, the Internet itself converts this to a form that identifies the actual physical location of the computer where it is stored, and links your computer to the other. Once a site of interest is found the URL can be stored as a bookmark in your browser for quick access later.

Just as a physical book on a subject will often contain a bibliography listing related books, web sites frequently provide links to other related sites so that, once a site of interest is found, it's relatively easy to find more. This mutual linking of sites is one of the strengths of the web for speedy information retrieval but also one of its weaknesses. It's easy for anyone to set up a web site on almost any subject, keeping a site up to date is another matter. Links can easily become outdated unless they are regularly checked and maintained which can be an overhead for the person providing the links from the referring web site. Equally the owner of the target web site may not be aware of all other sites linking to it and therefore may not be in a position to ensure that changes are reflected throughout the Web. Bear this in mind when following links that don't work. Most web sites will provide an email address where you can advise them of broken links and will be happy to receive such notification.

**Where to start**

If you already have a good idea of what you want to find you will probably go to the relevant section of this publication and get a URL from the listings there. If however you aren't sure then you probably need to start at a site that will have plenty of links to take you further into the Web. Here are a few from my bookmarks to get you started. Remember these are just those I know of and find useful, there are many more and I am sure you will find, or already have, your own favourites.

**http://web.ukonline.co.uk/martin.nail/Folkmus.htm** A good start up place for English Folk and Traditional Music. Lots of links to artists, resources, regional listings etc as well as general help with search engines and the like.

**www.froots.demon.co.uk** Although mainly a commercial site for fRoots magazine its "Netrooting" section contains plenty of useful links with new ones added monthly.

**www.dirtylinen.com** Similar to the fRoots site but for the American Dirty Linen magazine so the links are mostly American angled. Good for Record Company contacts.

**http://www.ftech.co.uk/~webfeet**
The Web Feet English Folk Dance site.

As previously mentioned, you can look up URLs in the listings of the various Sections of this publication but below are listed some start up places for each Section taken from my own collection of bookmarks.

## *Regions*

There are many regional sites. These are included in the Regional Sections.

**General (English) sites**

These are a few sites that are not specific to a region but are national organisations or listings.

**www.efdss.org** *The English Folk Dance and Song Society*

**www.folklore-society.com**
*The Folklore Society*

**www.mrscasey.co.uk/afo**
*Association of Festival Organisers*

**www.bl.uk/collections/sound-archive** *The National Sound Archive at the British Library*

**www.entsweb.co.uk**
*EntsWeb, listing a variety of Entertainment Events*

A few sites are listed below. More are to be found in the Spotlight sections on each country.

## *Ireland*

**www.comhaltas.com**
*Comhaltas Ceoltóirí Éireann*

**www.itma.ie**
*The Irish Traditional Music Archive*

**mag.irish-music.net**
*Irish Music Magazine*

**www.iol.ie/~didly-didly**
*That magazine's editor's own web site*

**www.ceili.ie**
*Listings etc*

## *Scotland*

**www.tmsa.demon.co.uk**
*The Traditional Music and Song Association of Scotland*

**www.scottishfolkdirectory.com**
*Scottish Folk Directory*

**www.btinternet.com/~John.Slaven/folkmusicpage.htm**
*Folk Music In N.E. Scotland*

## *Wales*

**www.folkwales.org.uk**
*Celfyddydau Mari Arts*

**www.welshfolkdance.org.uk**
*Cymdeithas Ddawns Werin Cymru - Welsh Folk Dance Society*

**www.angelfire.com/music/pembsfolk** *Pembrokeshire Folk Index*

**Artistic Areas**

Here are some web sites that I have found useful in starting to search for information on the different artistic areas covered by Direct Roots. It is not intended to be exhaustive, or even the best sites, but simply what I found by easy searching and following links. Remember to check any of the classified listings also. Many more web sites can be found in the various articles in the Spotlight section.

**www.ftech.co.uk/~webfeet**
*Webfeet, English Ceilidh, Folk, Morris, Cajun, French Trad dance information*

**www.mustrad.org.uk**
*Musical Traditions on-line magazine*

**www.btinternet.com/~greenjack**
*Sabine Baring-Gould - Songs of the West, site dedicated to the famous collector*

**www.performance.salford.ac.uk/research/vmp/Index.htm**
*The Village Music Project*

**www.tradsong.freeserve.co.uk**
*Traditional Song Forum*

**www.folkworld.de**
*FolkWorld - Home of European Music, German based web magazine*

**www.folkworld.de/frog/index.html**
*FROG - the Folk & Roots Online Guide*

**www.users.zetnet.co.uk/mally/samba**
*Samba in Britain & Ireland*

**www.rootsworld.com/rw**
*RootsWorld, on line magazine. Some info accessible by subscribers only*

**www.globalvillageidiot.net**
*Global Village Idiot*

**africanmusic.org**
*African Music Encyclopedia*

**www.bbma.freeserve.co.uk**
*The British Bluegrass Music Association*

**folkmusic.about.com/musicperform/folkmusic**
*Site with info and links for bluegrass, old-timey, blues, cajun and more*

**www.blueflamecafe.com**
*Blue Flame Café, Encyclopædia of the Blues*

**www.pillard.demon.co.uk/foaotmad**
*The Friends Of American Old-Time Music and Dance*

**www.argonet.co.uk/users/johnmaher/Ring**
*The Morris Ring*

**www.langcen.cam.ac.uk/OMorris/OMhome.htm**
*Open Morris*

**home.clara.net/krt/homepage.htm**
*The Morris Federation*

**www.rapper.org.uk**
*Rapper Online*

Hopefully this publication will have sufficient web sites listed to satisfy your requirements but if your specific interest (artist, style etc) does not seem to be covered by a web site this may not mean that one doesn't exist, simply that we haven't been advised.

**What now?**
Well there are a number of search engines available on the Web. Simply input some keywords from your interest (e.g. "Melodeon Suppliers Northampton") press search and hopefully some web site addresses will be returned. There are two basic types of search engine, those that look up a database of registered sites and those that search the whole web looking for keywords anywhere.

**What else apart from web sites?**
Access to the Internet will generally also give you access to email and the various discussion groups available. If your Internet Service Provider doesn't provide these there are ways of handling them outside the limitations of your ISP.

**Email** should be self-explanatory and most will find it easy to use. Discussion Groups may require a bit of explanation. There are, in simple terms, three main types of discussion groups:

## *Newsgroups (Usenet), Mailing Lists and Web Based Discussions*

**Usenet**
Newsgroups are generally open to anyone to pop in and out, read and/or contribute, covering thousands of different interests and subjects. It is possible that the full range of newsgroups may not be available to you depending on your ISP. Some newsgroups may be of local interest only and may not be available from an ISP who does not normally serve that area. Others may be specific to the ISP's customers only.

Some newsgroups of interest to readers of this publication are
**uk.music.folk**
**rec.music.folk**
**rec.music.celtic**
**rec.folk-dancing**
**alt.music.world**

Many newsgroups have a charter outlining what is considered to be acceptable posting practice and a FAQ (Frequently Asked Questions) file somewhere on the Internet, but these can be difficult to find. A sensible approach when accessing Usenet, or a specific newsgroup, for the first time is to spend some time reading the messages ('lurking') to get a feel of the style of the contributors before leaping in. The Usenet community can be very quick at letting you know if your posting behaviour is unacceptable, but remember that not everyone has the same tolerance level.

If your ISP does not carry newsgroups, or the specific one you require, you can usually gain access through a web site. One place that carries an archive of postings is deja.com and this also allows reading and posting via the web page.

**Mailing Lists**
These are similar to Usenet newsgroups but are not openly accessible. You generally need to register as a subscriber via a web site and messages are then sent to and posted from your email account, either message by message or as a daily/weekly digest in one message. This tends to reduce the amount of "off-topic" material being posted.

Some mailing lists of interest to readers of this publication are
**folkbiz-uk** accessible at **www.yahoogroups.com**

**e-ceilidh** The English Ceilidh list accessible at **www.cix.co.uk/~net-services/ec**

There are also mailing lists and newsgroups discussing the work of various performers. If you need to know whether there is a mailing list or newsgroup on a specific subject or an artist, not listed above or elsewhere in this publication, then the easiest thing to do is ask on an appropriate newsgroup!

**Web based discussions**
Again these are similar to newsgroups but are accessed from a web site. Generally no registration is required and you will contribute via a posting form on the web site. There is an active discussion group at The Mudcat Café www.mudcat.org; again ask on a newsgroup if you want to find more.

The above should give you a good start in finding your way around the Internet. Check any URLs in the listing parts of **Direct Roots** but remember the Internet changes rapidly and information given here may become outdated.

**Kevin Sheils**
*Retired Telecom Manager, Folk concert MC and amateur web enthusiast.*

# Roots and the Media By Colin Irwin

Don't expect too many favours from the media.

Once away from the mainstream, music in its many peculiar shapes and forms is a total mystery to 99% of the media that shapes and dictates our daily attitudes, however hard we may think we fight to resist it. There is an argument that says we are better off without the media, that operating in specialist areas of the industry we should cherish our alternative status and celebrate the fact that most of the time they totally ignore us. Ignorance is bliss and all that.

All well and good except that if we do pretend it doesn't exist we are effectively inviting the media to keep recycling their worn out old clichés and stereotypes. We may groan when they trot out the hoary old jokes about specialist music fans, whether they be folkies, jazzers, dancers or whatever, but to the great big daft populous out there the more they repeat it the truer it becomes. And for anybody trying to attract new audiences that has a catastrophic effect. Sad but true, image is important and whole generations can be lost by a running joke on a comedy show on the telly, an ignorant send-up in a magazine and some absurd generic put-down on the radio.

It's time to fight back. The media can be manipulated, too, and things can be changed. Apart from anything else, papers and magazines desperately want to reflect public opinion and think they're on top of new developments. In the last couple of years **Eliza Carthy** has enjoyed acres of largely positive press, not necessarily because all the media thinks she's wonderful but because they have a good story to tell. Namely a) a young artist performing a style of music most of them fondly imagined had been ceremonially buried in 1969, b) she's willing to talk the hind legs off a donkey to promote it and c) she has blue hair.

You don't all have to dye your hair blue but aggressive tactics work. If you want to get people to a gig, festival or the opening of a teashop, then you have to tell them about it. Loud and clear. Some magazines and newspapers have specialist writers sympathetic to the cause but even they have to fight for space and whether fans or complete numbskulls who need force-feeding basic information, they need angles and stories to justify the story to their editors.

If you want coverage in a paper, imagine yourself as a punter, think of a fresh storyline to make the event different and newsworthy. Don't just send the press release and hope for the best, shape it into something urgent and exciting, whether one of the artists is making a comeback after being kidnapped by aliens or some selfish nasty residents association are trying to get the event cancelled.

Don't take no for an answer. Find out the right person to deal with the event - not some cub reporter, but a features/news editor or radio station manager - and pursue them to the ends of the earth until you convince them your event is a matter of crucial importance.

Offer them enticements. Free tickets or similar as a running prize will keep you in the news and the forefront of the minds of your potential audience.

Liaise with the artists or their representatives and persuade them to co-operate with interviews and promotional material in the press and radio in advance of their appearance. News and feature material doesn't grow on trees and if it's dressed up enticingly enough and comes knocking on their door it will be seen fit enough to fill a hole. Ideally, you will appoint a press officer to furnish them with all the material they need, invite them to the event itself, make them feel important and you never know, next year they may be calling you.

It may hurt, but it will pay to get the media on your side...

**Colin Irwin**
*Specialist Folk Music writer for MOJO and fRoots.*

# Press Release or Junk Mail? By Paul Saunders

At a guess, around 95% of press releases go into the waste bin within twenty seconds of being received. That is not a good result. Hours of hard work dismissed like piece of junk mail. It's made all the more surprising when you consider the media's voracious appetite for news. Anxious reporters working to daily, even hourly, deadlines. 'On air' lights about to be switched on and column inches to fill. For the media, no news really is bad news. What's more, creating stories is hard work - so if they can tell someone else's story they will. Provide them with the right story and they will probably use it in its entirety. So how do you get them to tell your story? Think of it this way - what you consider to be junk mail is a 'must have' offer to someone else out there. There are many ways of improving your chances of grabbing the media's' attention. However, before you plan an outrageous ascent of Nelson's Column in flippers and string vest, consider some basic principles that should be integral to all your press activities.

At the top of the list comes content. There is no such thing as pure news. A news story is only news if it is given an angle that is appropriate to the consumer and packaged accordingly. The commercial media are in the business of presenting relevant information to a clearly identified and targeted audience. Your feature, whether printed or broadcast, must appeal to their readers or listeners. If it doesn't, they won't use it. So if you want to publicise your festival in Back Street Heroes make sure the one who climbs Nelson's Column rides a Harley – ideally across Trafalgar Square. You stand a better chance of beating the bin if you can write a good headline to grabs your target's attention. Don't expect them to use it. You are not writing it for publication. That is their job - your job is to overcome the 'So what?' response.

Right up there alongside content is targeting. A good press release has to arrive with the right person at the right time in the manner that they would like to receive it. That last point is important - perhaps you can beat a deadline with email or fax but I know of a surprising number of journalists who do not have immediate access to either. So check out how they like to get their information. For your media strategy to work you will need to take account of the lead times and deadlines of the organisation. Colour

media
introduction

magazines can work four or more months ahead whereas the newsroom could be hourly and they will not appreciate you cluttering up their desk with something that is still three weeks away. Some like visuals with the release, others will ask if they want them.

You may also need to send press releases to more than one person e.g. the arts correspondent, the features editor and the news editor. On the other hand, some organisations are happy to receive just one release and circulate it, an approach that has good and bad things going for it. In larger establishments there may be several music and arts correspondents so writing the job title on the envelope is not enough. If you know the name, use it. If you don't, find out who it is. Keep a database with all this information and update it regularly – journalists do not like getting releases addressed to their predecessor or with their name spelt incorrectly.

Your media contact card should include:

- name, job title, organisation and contact details;
- timescales and advance notice requirements;
- deadlines;
- special interests;
- a note of articles and dates of covered stories.

Keeping track of who is doing what out there is a difficult job. It helps if you are an avid consumer of the media – newspapers, magazines, television, radio, the Internet. Staying up to date is probably the most difficult part of the job and requires varying amounts of time/money/motivation/stamina depending on what you want to achieve. Fortunately, you do not have to start from scratch. Whether you have a computerised system or still rely on pen and paper you can still build up a large address book from one of the many media contact databases on the market.

The list below gives an idea of what is available. The range, depth, completeness and accuracy of these publications vary considerably. Some are available on-line, others only as hard copy. Some are annuals, others offer monthly, half-yearly and even daily updates. Prices vary from under £20 to over £2500. You probably do get what you pay for but in truth I have never found one that is wholly accurate, up to date, classifies the information in the way that I need it or has a half-decent roots music section. Their strength is in listing mainstream media, including national and regional radio and television as well as newspapers and periodicals. I have found them useful for giving guidelines and essential background information as well as sparking some fruitful new directions. Whichever road you take, expect to have to do quite a lot of legwork yourself. Time spent picking up the telephone and checking out the details will pay dividends and save you wasted postage and effort.

**The Writers' & Artists' Yearbook**. Best-selling media guide includes national and regional newspapers, magazines UK & Ireland, plus magazines by category, separate sections for television and radio (national & regional). Plus syndicate, news and press agencies. Publishers: Black

**The Writer's Handbook.** For career writers with the emphasis on publication. Lists national and regional newspapers, magazines, news agencies, television and radio, production companies, US media contacts in the UK, Arts Councils and Regional Arts Boards and press cuttings agencies. Publishers: Macmillan

**Willings Press Guide.** Newspapers, magazines, journals and periodicals with contact details. Updated annually and published in March. Over 50,000 entries. Available in two separate volumes: UK and International. Book, CD and on-line. Published by Media Information and available from them.

**Phone** 01494 797300

**Benn's Media Directory.** Updated each year and published in February. Three volumes available separately: UK, Europe and worldwide. Current UK edition contains over 43,000 entries. Published by and available from United Business Media International
**Phone** 01732 362666

**Pims UK Media Directory.** Annual. Lists newspapers and magazines.
**Phone** 020 7226 1000

**The Media Guide 2001.** 10,000 contacts under five broad headings - The Internet, Press, Broadcasting, Cross Media and Outside Contacts. A big address book. Often only the telephone number is given – still the fastest point of contact in many situations. As one reviewer wrote, "Who knows when you will need the Association of Radical Midwives". Publisher: Fourth Estate. Available from retailers

**The Arts Council Press Contacts.** Exactly what the title suggests. Annual. Hard copy and CD. Available from The Arts Council of Great Britain.
**Phone** 020 7333 010

**Media Information.** Service providers with a wide range of information available to suit different needs and budgets from paper-based to on-line services.
**Phone** 01494 797260.

**BRAD.** Published monthly. Lists regional and local newspapers and magazines as well as national and overseas. Includes copy dates and deadlines, circulation and advertising specifications and rates. Available from Brad. **Phone** 0207 505 8273

**Media Contacts.** As the name suggests, a contact database. Mainstream arts emphasis. Contact details and background information. Hard copy and CD.
Telephone: 020 7379 9220

**PR Newswire Europe.** In-house maintained media contacts and postal/on-line press distribution services.
**Phone** 020 7490 8111

**M2 Presswire.** On-line press release distribution service.
**Phone** 01203 634700
**Email** info@presswire.net
**Web** www.presswire.net

Success in the press game can be partly attributed to luck but as golfer Jack Nicklaus famously said "The more I practise, the luckier I get." Experience and timing will always play a large part along with an instinct for a good story. Developing a good database won't make you a good writer of press releases but at least it could help to ensure that your story is released properly rather than simply escaping into the wild. Of course, you may not have time to practise, in which case you could always "get a man who does."

**Paul Saunders**
*runs a press and PR consultancy promoting roots music.*
**Phone** *01952 728283*
**Email** *info@heypressco.com*
**Web** *www.heypressco.com*

## National magazines – print and online

### Accordion World
**Contact** David Keen
**Mail address** 86 Brookdene Avenue, WATFORD, Herts, WD19 4LF
**Phone** 01923 236880
01895 859145
**Email** accordionworld@hotmail.com
*Bi-monthly accordion magazine, listings, profiles, ads, news, youth page.*
**RAB** South East Arts

### Blueprint - Magazine of the British Blues Connection
**Contact** Fran Leslie - Editor
**Mail address** 10 Messaline Avenue, LONDON, W3 6JX
**Phone** 020 8723 7376
**Fax** 020 8723 7380
**Email** info@blueprint-blues.co.uk
**Web** www.blueprint-blues.co.uk
**Alt contact** Jon Taylor - Reviews Editor
**Email** jon_blueprint@hotmail.com
*Monthly magazine with news, reviews and interviews, plus a national gig guide to UK blues events and an annual blues poll.*
**RAB** London Arts

### Blues & Rhythm - The Gospel Truth
**Contact** Tony Burke - Editor
**Mail address** 82 Quernby Way, BROMHAM, Beds, MK43 8QP
**Phone** 01234 826158
**Email** tonyburke@talk21.com
**Web** www.bluesworld.com
**Alt contact** Tony Watson
*Blues/ R&B fanzine. Published 10 times per year. Distribution covers UK, Europe and USA.*
**RAB** East England Arts

### British Bluegrass News
**Mail address** BBMA, 30 Six Acres Hemel Hempstead, Herts HP3 5HY
**Web** www.bbma.freeserve.co.uk
***See Bluegrass Section***

### Cajun Times
**Contact** Laraine Bridges
**Mail address** 20 Pensford Close, CROWTHORNE, Berks, RG45 6QR
**Phone** 01344 750069
**Fax** 01344 750208
**Email** ouisas@aol.com
*Quarterly Cajun & Zydedo music & dance magazine. Events & articles for the UK & Europe plus links to Louisiana.*
**RAB** Southern Arts

### Dance Expression
**Mail address** A E Morgan Publications, Stanley House, 9 West Street, EPSOM, Surrey, KT18 7RL
**Phone** 01372 741411
**Fax** 01372 744493
*General dance magazine with occasional coverage of folk dance.*

### English Dance & Song
**Contact** Dave Arthur
**Mail address** EFDSS, Cecil Sharp House, 2 Regent's Park Road, London NW1 7AY
**Phone** 020 7485 2206
**Fax** 020 7284 0534
**Email** info@efdss.org
*EFDSS Quarterly magazine*

### Facts & Fiction
**Contact** Pete Castle
**Mail address** 190 Burton Road, DERBY, DE1 1TQ
**Phone** 01332 346399
**Email** steelcarpet@lineone.net
*Quarterly storytelling magazine. £10 per year subscription, sample copy £2.50.*
***Musicians' Union member***
**RAB** East Midlands Arts

### Fiddle On Magazine
**Contact** Jed Mugford
**Mail address** 4 Lee Close, Kidlington, OXFORD, OX5 2XZ
**Phone** 01865 374624
**Email** jed@fiddleon.co.uk
**Web** www.fiddleon.co.uk
*Magazine for the fiddle player with articles, news, reviews, etc. 3 per year.*
**RAB** Southern Arts

### Folk Music Journal
**Contact** Mike Heaney
**Mail address** 5 Hanborough Close, Eynsham, WITNEY, Oxon, OX29 4NR
**Email** michael.heaney@ulib.ox.ac.uk
**Web** www.efdss.org
*Annual journal publishing scholarly articles and reviews. Contact for details on articles, reviews, ads.*
**RAB** Southern Arts

### fROOTS
**Mail address** PO Box 337, LONDON, N4 1TW
**Phone** 020 8340 9651
**Fax** 020 8348 5626
**Email** froots@froots.demon.co.uk
**Web** www.froots.demon.co.uk
*World's leading Folk, Roots and World Music monthly magazine.*
**AC** Arts Council of England
***See World Roots UK in Spotlight section.***

### Get Rhythm
**Contact** The Editor
**Mail address** PO Box 102, Forest Hall, Newcastle upon Tyne NE12 7WD
**Phone** 0191 245 3782
**Fax** 0191 245 3786
**Email** getrhythm@ukonline.co.uk
*Formerly NE based magazine, now gone national.*

### Irish Music Magazine
**Contact** Sean Laffey- Editor
**Mail address** 11 Clare Street, DUBLIN 2, Ireland
**Phone** +353 1 662 4887
**Fax** +353 1 662 4886
**Email** mrs@iol.ie
**Web** www.irish-music.net
**Alt address** Castlelake, CASHEL, Co Tipperary
**Phone** +353 6262685
+353 62 62967
*Ireland's leading independent folk & traditional music magazine. Irish & Celtic music in Ireland, UK, Europe and N America. Freelance copy always considered. Email or phone preferred contact. Please do not send pictures/ files on email. Send at least 2 copies of review CDs.*
**AC** Ireland

### The Living Tradition
**Contact** Pete Heywood
**Mail address** PO Box 1026, KILMARNOCK, Ayrshire, KA2 0LG, Scotland
**Phone** 01563 571220
**Fax** 01563 544855
**Email** living.tradition@almac.co.uk
**Web** www.folkmusic.net
**AC** Scotland

### MOJO
**Contact** The Editor
**Mail address** Mappin House, 4 Winsley Street, London W1W 8HF
**Phone** 020 7436 1515
**Fax** 020 7312 8296
**Email** mojo@ecm.emap.com
**Web** www.mojomagazine.co.uk
*National music magazine with some roots/world content.*

### Musical Traditions Internet Magazine
**Contact** Rod Stradling
**Mail address** 1 Castle Street, STROUD, Glos, GL5 2HP
**Phone** 01453 759475
**Email** rod@mustrad.org.uk
**Web** www.mustrad.org.uk
*Book & CD reviews, articles, news, comment, letters, links etc. CDs of traditional music published and sold. Review copies of CDs from traditional performers welcomed, not just 'trad' material by revivalists.*
**RAB** South West Arts

## Pukka Planet Productions
**Phone** 01206 751661
**Email** info@pukkaplanet.co.uk
**Web** www.pukkaplanet.co.uk
*Internet collective for free promotion of all things rootsy. Contact via website.*
**RAB** South East Arts

## Revolutions
**Contact** John Lonergan
**Mail address** 211 Western Road, LONDON, SW19 2QD
**Phone** 020 8646 7094
**Email** john@revolutionsuk.com
**Web** www.revolutionsuk.com
*Free weekly online roots music magazine. World, folk, blues, soul, reggae, latin, singer-songwriters & alternative country music.*
**RAB** London Arts

## Rock 'n' Reel
**Contact** Sean McGhee
**Mail address** PO Box 6, EGREMONT, CA25 5GA
**Phone** 01946 812496
**Fax** 01946 813415
**Email** rocknreel@zetnet.co.uk
**Web** www.rocknreel.co.uk
*Music magazine covering roots, rock, blues & beyond. Free CD with each issue.*
**RAB** North West Arts

## Roots & Branches
**Contact** Steve Morris
**Mail address** 54 Canterbury Road, WOLVERHAMPTON, WV4 4EN
**Phone/Fax** 01902 652759
**Email** brumbeat@waverider.co.uk
**Web** www.roots-and-branches.com
*Website for roots/ folk & related music. Radio show on WRC-AM and Midlands Digital Mulitplex.*
**RAB** West Midlands Arts

## RootsWorld Magazine
**Contact** Cliff Furnald
**Mail address** Box 1285, NEW HAVEN, CT 06505, USA
**Email** cliff@rootsworld.com
**Web** www.rootsworld.com
*US based online folk, world and roots magazine. Audio, reviews, interviews, articles. Published weekly.*

## Sambistas
**Web** www.sambistas.org.uk
*Website for Samba in Britain & Ireland. News & comprehensive band listings.*

## Songlines
**Contact** Simon Broughton - Editor
**Mail address** 38-42 Hampton Road, TEDDINGTON, Middx, TW11 0JE
**Phone** 020 8267 5124 - editorial
020 8367 5056 - advertising
**Fax** 020 8267 5844
**Email** songlines@haynet.com
**Alt contact** Galleon - subscriptions
**Alt address** PO Box 326, SITTINGBOURNE, Kent, ME9 8FA
**Phone** 01795 414827
**Fax** 01795 414555
**Email** songlines@galleon.co.uk
*Quarterly world music publication.*
***See World Roots UK***

## Taplas
**Contact** Keith Hudson
**Mail address** 182 Broadway, Roath, CARDIFF, CF24 1QJ
**Phone** 029 2049 9759
07974 093541
**Fax** 029 2048 4882
**Web** www.folkwales.org.uk/taplas.htm
*Bi-monthly folk music magazine, focusing principally on Wales and the Welsh Borders.*
**AC** Wales

## Traditional Music Maker
**Contact** Magnet Publishing Ltd
**Mail address** 28 Grafton Terrrace, LONDON, NW5 4JJ
*Monthly traditional music magazine, including folk, blues, country, etc.*
**RAB** London Arts

## UK Theatre Web
**Contact** Robert Iles
**Mail address** New House, High Street, FERNHAM, Oxon, SN7 7NY
**Phone** 01367 820828
**Fax** 01367 820827
**Email** info@uktw.co.uk
**Web** www.uktw.co.uk
*UK-wide on-line listings service.*
**RAB** Southern Arts

# Folk on Tap

023 8057 0082

*The Leading Quarterly Folk Music Magazine Of The South*

Folk on Tap was established in 1979 and is now in its 23rd year. It is a glossy 92-page A4 magazine, published four times a year on 1st January, 1st April, 1st July and 1st October.

**CONTENT**

» *features on international, national and local artistes*
» *news and articles on topical and other interesting issues*
» *regular columns written by national artistes*
» *articles on folk-related music genres such as blues and world music, and on folk-related musical instruments*
» *reviews and previews of festivals and live gigs*
» *national festival diary*
» *artistes' national tour guide*
» *diary listings of venues in the South*
» *comprehensive section of reviews of latest album releases*

**DISTRIBUTION**

The magazine is on sale in various venues in 14 counties in the south of England from Cornwall (West) to Kent (East) and from Buckinghamshire (North) to the Channel Isles (South), and by annual subscription both nationally and overseas.

**FREE INTRODUCTORY COPY**

Please send a C4 size s.a.e, stamped for 350gm, and we will send you a copy of the most recent back issue available (postage is currently 87p for second class or £1.09 for first class in the UK).

**COST**

Cover price for single issue: £2.40 (£3.00 by post)
Annual subscription: UK £9.50, Europe £11.50, USA £17.50

**ADVERTISING**

The rates are very competitive from £25 for a third-column to £90 for a full-page. Typesetting and design service available.

**CONTACT**

Editor: Sam Satyanadhan
Address: 3 Cranbury Road, Woolston, Southampton. Hampshire SO19 2HZ
Email: **editor@folkontap.co.uk**
Website: **http://www.folkontap.co.uk**
Telephone: **023 8057 0082**
Fax: **023 8043 7150**

www.folkontap.co.uk

## worldmusic.org.uk
**Contact** Barry Miller
**Mail address** 3 Hillside Drive, CHESTERFIELD, Derbys, S40 2DB
**Email** worldmusic@worldmusic.org.uk
**Web** www.worldmusic.org.uk
*Website for world music news, events, reviews and information.*
**RAB** East Midlands Arts

## www.freefolk.com
**Contact** Michael Raven
**Mail address** 126 Jug Bank, Ashley, MARKET DRAYTON, Shrops, TF9 4NJ
**Phone** 01630 672304
**Web** www.freefolk.com
*Bi-monthly online folk magazine with articles reviews, databases, etc.*
**RAB** West Midlands Arts

## Dirty Linen
**Mail address** PO Box 66600, Baltimore, Maryland, MD 21239-6600 USA
**Phone** +1 410 583 7973
**Fax** +1 410 337 6735
**Web** www.dirtylinen.com
*US magazine, bi-monthly. Extensive soverage of UK and Irish music.*

# Regional magazines – print and online

## AY2K
**Contact** Kerensa Newman
**Mail address** 7 St Aubyn's Vean, TRURO, Cornwall, TR1 2DX
**Phone** 01872 240475
07833 393928
**Email** kerensaay2k@supanet.com
*Quarterly folk magazine, written & produced by members of Acoustic Youth 2000.*
**RAB** South West Arts

## CONNECT (Somerset Dance Connections Magazine)
**Mail address** 11-13 Castle Street Bridgwater, Somerset TA6 3DD
**Phone** 01278 446409
**Fax** 01278 447402
**Email** somdanceco@aol.com
*Dance news and listings*
**RAB** South West Arts
***See South West region.***

## East Midlands Folk Pages
**Web** www.emfp.co.uk
*Website.*
**RAB** East Midlands Arts
***See East Midlands region.***

## EFN
**Contact** John New
**Mail address** 37 Sidwell Avenue South Benfleet, Essex SS7 1LF
**Phone** 01268 793905
**Email** john@essexfolknews.co.uk
*Folk / roots listings for Essex & East London. Available through clubs or by subscription - £2.60 for four issues.*
**Web** www.essexfolknews.co.uk
**RAB** East England Arts
***See East England Region***

## Fizgig
**Contact** Tom & Ali Beaumont
**Mail address** 11 Fortescue Close, Tattershall, LINCOLN, LN4 4LN
**Phone** 01526 343989
**Email** fizgigmusic@tinyonline.co.uk
**Web** users.tinyonline.co.uk/fizgig-tom/folk.htm
*On-line guide to folk music & gigs in Lincolnshire and the East Midlands. Artist profile, news & links. Listings.*
**RAB** East Midlands Arts

## Folk Buzz
**Email** folkbuzz@lineone.net
**Web** website.lineone.net/~folkbuzz
*Folk magazine & news from the North West and North Midlands. Folk song/ music, morris & social dance listings, CD/ book reviews.*
**RAB** North West Arts

## The Folk Diary
**Contact** Vic Smith
**Mail address** 26 Ferrers Road, LEWES, East Sussex, BN7 1PZ
**Phone/Fax** 01273 478124
**Email** tinvic@globanet.co.uk
**Web** www.users.globalnet.co.uk/~tinvic/pistols.htm
**Alt contact** Jim Marshall
**Alt address** 3 Chester Terrace, BRIGHTON
**Phone** 01273 559750
**Fax** 01273 559750
**Email** folk@brighton.co.uk
*Bi-monthly guide to the folk dance and song events in and around Sussex plus album reviews and services adverts. SAE to Jim or Vic for current issue.*
**RAB** South East Arts

## Folk in Kent
**Contact** Eddie Crook
**Mail address** 33 Chapel Street, EAST MALLING, Kent, ME19 6AP
**Phone** 01732 841178
**Email** folkinkent@cableinet.co.uk
*Quarterly magazine with information on folk song and dance activities in Kent.*
**RAB** South East Arts

## Folk London
**Contact** Sheila Finn - Editor
**Mail address** 4A Kenilworth Road, Petts Wood, ORPINGTON, Kent, BR5 1DY
**Phone/Fax** 01689 825263
**Phone** 07818 035658
**Email** sheila@folklon.fsnet.co.uk
**Web** www.grove-cottage.demon.co.uk/folklon/
**Alt contact** Gerry Milne - Distribution
**Alt address** Grove Cottage, Amyard Park Road, TWICKENHAM, Middx, TW1 3HG
**Phone** 020 8892 4621
**Email** gerry@grove-cottage.demon.co.uk
*Bi-monthly magazine, covering folk events, etc in London and the South East.*
**RAB** London Arts
***See London region***

## The Folk Mag
**Contact** Bob Taberner
**Mail address** 21 Oak Close, TIPTON, W Mids, DY4 0AY
**Phone** 0121 5566219
07714 980076
**Email** bob.taberner@btinternet.com
**Web** www.thefolkmag.co.uk
*Web-based folk magazine for Shrops, Staffs, West Mids, Warks, Worcs and Herefordshire.*
**RAB** West Midlands Arts

## Folk on Tap
**Contact** Sam Satyanadhan
**Mail address** 3 Cranbury Road, Woolston, SOUTHAMPTON, Hants, SO19 2HZ
**Phone** 023 8057 0082
**Email** editor@folk-on-tap.demon.co.uk
*Quarterly A4 64 page folk magazine. Listings mainly covering southern region.*
**RAB** Southern Arts
***See Southern region***

## Folk Roundabout
**Contact** Trevor Lister
**Mail address** 24 Ambleside Green, Acklam, MIDDLESBOROUGH, Cleveland, TS5 7DQ
**Phone** 01642 821776
**Email** trevor1@ntlworld.com
*North East England quarterly folk magazine, A5 format. Subscription £6 per year.*
**RAB** Yorkshire Arts
***See Northern region***

## folknet.co.uk
**Contact** Cliff Baylis
**Mail address** 77 Old Tovil Road, MAIDSTONE, Kent, ME15 6QE
**Phone/Fax** 01622 674725
**Phone** 07799 768797
**Email** cliff@folknet.co.uk
**Web** www.folknet.co.uk
*Website designers specialising in acoustic music. Supports artists, traders, instrument makers, clubs and venues.*
**RAB** South East Arts

## Folknews Kernow
**Contact** Christopher Ridley
**Mail address** Trenillocs, ST COLUMB, Cornwall, TR9 6JN
**Phone** 01637 880394
*Cornwall folk listings.*
**RAB** South West Arts
***See South West region***

## Folktalk
**Contact** Jim Hancock
**Mail address** 57 Lloyds Avenue, SCUNTHORPE, N Lincs, DN17 7BY
**Phone** 01724 844241
**Email** jim@folktalk.co.uk
**Web** www.folktalk.co.uk
*Folk magazine covering all aspects in Lincolnshire and Humberside. Distributed free at venues and events.*
**RAB** Yorkshire Arts

## Folkwords
**Contact** Folkworks
**Mail address** 69 Westgate Road Newcastle upon Tyne, NE1 1SG
**Phone** 0191 222 1717
**Fax** 0191 230 2484
**Email** folkworks@folkworks.co.uk
*The Folkworks Newsletter*
**RAB** Northern Arts
***See Northern Region***

## Folkwrite
**Contact** Flos Headford - Editor
**Mail address** 38 Upton Street, TREDWORTH, Glos, GL1 4LA
**Phone** 01592 240989
01452 310372
**Email** flos@madasafish.com
**Web** www.folkwrite.org.uk
**Alt contact** Clive Brooks - Subscriptions
**Alt address** 7 Pikes Pool Lane, Burcot, BROMSGROVE, B60 1LJ
*Quartley 52 booklet with articles, events, organisations & contacts in Glos & surrounding area.*
**RAB** South West Arts
***See South West region***

## Fyfe on Folk
**Contact** Pete Fyfe
**Mail address** 26 Cumberland Court, Cross Road, CROYDON, Surrey, CR0 6TE
**Phone** 020 8680 4302
**Email** petefyfe@aol.com
*Folk music magazine*
***Musicians' Union member***
**RAB** South East Arts

## Hot Tickets
**(London Evening Standard)**
**Contact** PA Newscentre
**Mail address** 292 Vauxhall Bridge Road, London SW1V 1AE
**Phone** 020 7963 7707
**Fax** 020 7963 7800
*Weekly Arts listings supplement to London evening paper.*
**RAB** London

## In Touch Magazine
**Contact** Dave Allton - Editor
**Mail address** 28 Columbia Gardens, BEDWORTH, Warks, CV12 9EF
**Phone** 024 7631 0877
0777 989 6291
**Email** in_touch34@hotmail.com
*Bi monthly magazine covering folk & acoustic music in Coventry/ Warks/ West Mids.*
**RAB** West Midlands Arts

## Lancashire Wakes
**Contact** Roy Smith
**Mail address** 7 Southgate, Fulwood, PRESTON, PR2 3HX
**Phone** 01772 716772
**Alt contact** Valerie Kite
**Alt address** 15 St Andrews Close, Leyland, PRESTON, PR5 2BJ
**Phone** 01772 422065
*Magazine covering the North-West area. Listings of callers, bands, morris teams and folk dance events.*
**RAB** North West Arts

## The Latest
**Mail address** Gloucester House 45 Gloucester Street, Brighton Sussex BN1 4EW
**Phone** 01273 818150
**Fax** 01273 818152
**Email** latest@thelatest.co.uk
*Brighton Listings magazine*
**RAB** South East Arts

## Leicester Folk Diary
**Contact** Peter Burnham
**Mail address** 77 Belvoir Drive, Aylestone, LEICESTER, LE2 8PB
**Phone** 0116 2915720
**Email** p.burnham@ntlworld.com
**Web** members.tripod.co.uk/ leicesterfolk
*Web-based diary of folk events in & around Leicestershire, links to other folk resources.*
**RAB** East Midlands Arts

## Magnet Publishing Ltd
**Contact** Brian Healey
**Mail address** 28 Grafton Terrrace, LONDON, NW5 4JJ
*Publishes 'Traditional Music Maker' magazine.*
**RAB** London Arts

## Mardles
**Contact** John Halliwell - general
**Mail address** 172 High Road, Trimley St Mary, FELIXSTOWE, Suffolk, IP11 0SS
**Phone** 01394 279753
**Email** halliwell@btinternet.com
**Alt contact** Gloria Helliwell - subsciptions
**Alt address** 320 Sidegate Lane, IPSWICH, Suffolk, IP4 3DW
**Phone** 01473 401439
*Magazine for folk dance, music & song in Suffolk & surrounding counties.*
**RAB** East England Arts
***See East England region***

## Puddingstone
**Contact** Mrs Libby Byne-Grey - editor
**Mail address** Musley House, 9 Holmfield Road, WARE, Herts, SG12 7NG
**Phone** 01920 460553
**Email** l.byne-grey@herts.ac.uk
**Alt contact** Roger Swaine
**Alt address** 29 Turmore Dale, WELWYN GARDEN CITY, Herts, AL8 6HT
**Phone** 01707 324413
*Hertfordshire folk association dance based magazine.*
**RAB** East England Arts

## rT-r2 Magazine
**Contact** Micheal Coughlan - Editor
**Mail address** Cambridge House, Cambridge Grove, Hammersmith, LONDON, W6 0LE
**Phone** 020 8741 0649
**Email** rt-r2@rt-r2.co.uk
**Web** www.rt-r2.co.uk
*Entertainment magazine (18-35) for Irish & second generation Irish in London.*
**RAB** London Arts

### Set and Turn Single

**Contact** Chris Turner
**Mail address** 9 Glendale Avenue, LONDON, N22 5HL
**Phone** 020 8889 0634
*Bi monthly folk dance magazine.*
**RAB** London Arts
***See Social Dance in Spotlight section.***

### Shire Folk

**Contact** Chris Mills
**Mail address** 5 Gladstone Road, HEADINGTON, Oxford, OX3 8LL
**Phone** 01865 769366
**Email** millses@btinternet.com
*Magazine covering all aspects of folk in Berks, Bucks, Herts & Oxon.*
**RAB** Southern Arts

### Shreds & Patches

**Contact** The Editor
**Mail address** 1 Herbert Avenue, Wellington, TELFORD, Shrops, TF1 2BT
**Phone** 01952 240989
**Email** mainwaring@enta.net
*Folk arts magazine for Shropshire & surrounding area. 3 times per year. Articles, reviews, listings & club details, adverts, etc.*
**RAB** West Midlands Arts

### Solent Waves

**Contact** David Roberts - editor
**Mail address** Symposia, Bishops Sutton, ALRESFORD, SO24 0AL
**Phone** 01962 735202
**Email** sw@symposia.freeserve.co.uk
**Alt contact** Joan Mash - distribution
**Alt address** 10 Marchwood Court, Broadsands Drive, GOSPORT, Hants, PO12 2UB
**Phone** 023 9250 3726
*Bi monthly small publication, listings, etc for folk music & dance.*
**RAB** Southern Arts

### Somers Publications

**Contact** Sam Simmons
**Mail address** 16 Barrett Rise, St James Park, MALVERN, Worcs, WR14 2UJ
**Phone** 01684 575704
*Folk publications including; What's On, Somers Directory, Somers Festivals, Somers Journal.*
**RAB** West Midlands Arts

### South Riding Folk Network News

**Contact** Paul Davenport
**Mail address** 6 Thompson Close, MATLBY, Yorks, S66 8QG
**Phone** 01709 813862
**Email** paul.davenport@virgin.net
*Quartley magazine of the SRFN.*
**RAB** Yorkshire Arts
***See Yorkshire region.***

### Spire Folk

**Contact** Barry Miller
**Mail address** 3 Hillside Drive, CHESTERFIELD, Derbys S40 2DB
**Email** spirefolk@spirefolk.org.uk
**Web** www.spirefolk.org.uk
*Folk, roots and world music website with local events, artist links, national & international news, etc.*
**RAB** East Midlands Arts

### The Stable Yard

**Contact** Sinclair Curdie
**Mail address** 1 The Stables Yard, 1103 Argyle Street, GLASGOW, G3 8ND, Scotland
**Phone** 0141 221 5522
**Fax** 0141 2215200
**Email** sinclair@thestableyard.net
**Web** www.thestableyard.net
**Alt contact** Graham Collins
**Email** graham@thestableyard.net
*Web services; site hostings, design, wap, etc.*
**AC** Scotland

### Stirrings

**Contact** Raymond Greenoaken
**Mail address** 11 Ratcliffe Road, SHEFFIELD, S11 8YA
**Phone** 0114 2661158
**Email** stirrings@taproot.demon.co.uk
**Web** www.stirrings.co.uk
*Quarterly magazine covering all aspects of folk in South Yorkshire and beyond.*
**RAB** Yorkshire Arts

### Tykes News

**Mail address** 408 Skipton Road, Uttley, KEIGHLEY, W Yorks, BD20 6HP
**Phone** 01535 606939
**Fax** 01535 211947
**Email** tykes@woodtyke.force9.co.uk
**Web** www.tabbytail.freeserve.co.uk/filofolk.htm
*Magazine of folk in and around Yorkshire.*
**RAB** Yorkshire Arts

### Unicorn Magazine

**Contact** Alan Creamer
**Mail address** 6 Dudley Street, LUTON, LU2 0NT
**Phone** 01582 733113
**Fax** 01582 404151
**Email** alan.creamer@virgin.net
**Alt contact** Theo Thomas
**Phone** 01582 882831
**Email** trpthomas@ao .com
*Quarterly folk magazine with listings, for Beds, Bucks, Cambs & Herts.*
**RAB** East Midlands Arts

### What's Afoot

**Contact** Colin Andrews
**Mail address** Bonny Green, Morchard Bishop, CREDITON, Devon, EX17 6PG
**Fax** 01363 877216
**Email** colin@bonnygreen.co.uk
**Web** www.bonnygreen.co.uk
**Alt contact** Dick Little - Advertising
**Alt address** Collaton Grange, Malborough, KINGSBRIDGE, Devon, TQ7 3DJ
*A5 magazine, 3 times per year. Articles, reviews, contacts, diary dates for Devon.*
**RAB** South West Arts

### What's On Folks

**Contact** Julia Winn
**Mail address** The Paw House, 30 Snoll Hatch Road, East Peckham, TONBRIDGE, Kent, TN12 5ED
**Phone** 01622 873142
*Bi-monthly folk music magazine covering Kent and bordering areas.*
**RAB** South East Arts

### What's On! Midland Folk Diary

**Contact** Joe Smith
**Mail address** 121 Morris Avenue, COVENTRY, CV2 5GS
**Phone** 024 7644 4405
*Monthly guide to folk events in the Midlands.*
**RAB** West Midlands Arts

## Additional Local Periodical Listings

*Thanks to Jacey Bedford's Folk Magazines in the UK Listings for the following additions.*
**Web** www.artifact.demon.co.uk/folkmags.htm

### Dorset Folk
**Contact** Steve Hunt
**Mail address** Meadow Cottage Chapel Lane, Woodlands, Dorset, BH21 8LU
**Phone** 01929 462405
*Quarterly folk magazine*
**RAB** South West

### East Surrey Newsletter
**Contact** Mike Rothon
**Mail address** 33 Glenthorne Avenue Croydon, Surrey CR0 7ET
**Phone** 020 8654 4430
*East Surrey Folk Association, two issues per year*
**RAB** South East

### Events South West
**Contact** Patrick Cunningham
**Mail address** 14 Gandy Street Exeter, Devon EX4 2LS
**Phone** 01392 258070
*What's On Folk Column*

### Folk in the South West
**Contact** Folk South West
**Mail address** The Stables, Montacute House, Montacute, Somerset TA15 6XP
**Phone** 01935 822911
**Fax** 01935 822024
**Email** folksw@folksw.org.uk

### Folknews
**Contact** Eric Storey
**Mail address** 133 Compass Road Hull, Yorks HU6 7AW
**Phone** 01482 804962
**Email** ericstorey@folknews.freeserve.co.uk
*North and East Yorkshire District EFDSS Quarterly*
**RAB** Yorkshire

### Folk North West
**Contact** Ken Bladon
**Mail address** 36 The Oaks, Eaves Green, Chorley, Lancashire PR7 3QU
**Phone** 01257 263678
**Email** four.fools@virgin.net
*North West Federation of Folk Clubs Quarterly*
***See North West Region***
**RAB** North West

### Leicester Mercury Folk Column
**Contact** Mike Polanth
**Mail address** Leicester Mercury St George Street, Leicester LE1 9FQ
**Phone** 0116 251 2512
**RAB** East Midlands

### Liverpool Daily Post Folk Column
**Contact** Jack Coutts
**Mail address** 7 Thomas Lane Liverpool L14 5NR
**Phone** 0151 220 0152
**RAB** North West

### Mersey and Deeside Folk
**Contact** Chris Warrington
**Mail address** 1 St Anne's Gardens Aigburth, Liverpool L17 6BP
**Phone** 0151 427 1907
*Two per year*
**RAB** North West

### Sussex Pie
**Contact** Kate & Doug Eaton
**Mail address** 2 Summerhill Hollington Park Road, St Leonards on Sea, E Sussex TN38 0GP
**Phone** 01424 714869
*Sussex Folk Association Events and News. Three per year*

### Venue Folk Column
**Contact** Tony Slinger
**Mail address** 64-65 North Road St Andrews, Bristol BS6 5AQ
**Phone** 0117 963 8280
**Fax** 0117 941 5884
**Email** editor@venue.co.uk
*Bristol Listings Magazine*
**RAB** South West

### West Surrey Newsletter
**Contact** David & Christine Sansom
**Mail address** 27 Crofton Close Ottershaw, Chertsey, Surrey KT16 0LR
**Phone** 01932 872617
*West Surrey Folk Association*
**RAB** South East

### What's On Supplement Folk Column
**(Kent Messenger Newspaper Group)**
**Contact** Doug Hudson
**Mail address** 182 Windmill Road Gillingham, Kent ME7 5PE
**Phone** 01634 574837
**Email** oneoffprod@aol.com
**RAB** South East

### Wiltshire Folk Association News
**Contact** Doug May
**Mail address** 8 Imber Avenue Amesbury, Salisbury, Wilts SP4 7JU
**Phone** 01980 625019
**RAB** Southern

## Directories and Yearbooks

### Root Source
**Web** www.rootsource.co.uk
*The English Folk Dance and Song Society's annual Folk Directory as been replaced by the Root Source database.*

### The White Book
**Contact** Sarah Hutchinson (Editor)
**Mail address** Inside Communications Ltd, 1st Floor, Bank House, 23 Warwick Road, Coventry CV1 2EW
**Phone** 024 7655 9590
**Fax** 024 7663 1185
**Email** Sarah_Hutchinson@mrn.co.uk
**Web** www.whitebook.co.uk
*Essential Events Industry handbook*

### AOIFE Yearbook
**Contact** Elizabeth McLoughlin (Administrator)
**Mail address** AOIFE Administration Office, 1 Upper Main Street, Arklow County Wicklow, Ireland
**Phone** 00 353 (0)402 32732
**Fax** 00 353 (0)402 91030
**Email** aoifeirl@iol.ie
*Yearbook of Irish festivals association*
***See Focus on Ireland***

### British Performing Arts Yearbook
**Mail address** Book Sales Dept. Rhinegold Publishing Ltd, Freepost London ,WC2H 8BR
**Phone** 020 7333 1721
**Fax** 020 7333 1769
**Email** sales@rhinegold.co.uk
**Web** www.rhinegold.co.uk
*Guide to venues, performers, festivals, services etc for the arts professional*

### The British Music Industry Directory
**Mail address** Harque Directories Ltd 433b Midsummer House, Midsummer Boulevard, Central Milton Keynes MK9 3BN
**Phone** 01908 662039
**Fax** 01908 660102
**Email** postmaster@harque.co.uk
**Web** www.music-directory.co.uk

### Music Week Directory
**Phone** 01858 438816
*Who's Who in the Music Industry*

### MBI World Directory
**Phone** 01858 438816
*Global Music Industry Directory*

### UK Choreographers Directory
**Mail address** Dance UK, Battersea Arts Centre, Lavender Hill, London SW11 TN
**Phone** 020 7228 4990
**Fax** 020 7223 0074

### The Directory of Folk and Related Arts in Yorkshire
**Contact** Liz Bowen
**Mail address** Yorkshire Dales Workshops, 14 Oakburn Road, ILKLEY, W Yorks, LS29 9NN
**Phone** 01943 609421
**Email** ydw@btinternet.com
**Web** www.ydw.btinternet.com
**RAB** Yorkshire Arts
***See Yorkshire region.***

### Scottish Folk Directory
**Mail address** The Scottish Folk Arts Group, 49 Blackfriars Street, Edinburgh, EH1 1NB, Scotland
**Phone/Fax** 0131 557 3090
**Email** sfag@scotfolk.org
**Web** www.scottishfolkdirectory.com
*Directory in its 32nd year. Now on line.*

### TMSA 2001 Scottish Traditional Music Festival Calendar
**Mail address** Traditional Music and Song Association of Scotland, 95-97 St.Leonard's Street, Edinburgh EH8 9QY
**Phone** 0131 667 5587
**Fax** 0131 662 9153
**Email** e.cowie@tmsa.demon.co.uk
**Web** www.tmsa.demon.co.uk/tmsa/home/tmsa.html
***See Focus on Scotland section for TMSA listings.***

### Artists and Agents
**Inc The Entertainment Event Organiser**
**Mail address** Richmond House Publishing Company Ltd, Douglas House, 3 Richmond Buildings London, W1V 5AE
**Phone** 020 7437 9556
**Fax** 020 7287 3463

### Guestlist Folk Performers Directory
**Contact** Jim Hancock
**Mail address** 57 Lloyd's Avenue, Scunthorpe, North Lincs. DN17 1BY
**Phone/Fax** 01724 844241
**Email** jim@guestlist.freeserve.co.uk
**Web** www.guestlist.freeserve.co.uk

### Directory of Storytellers
**Mail address** The Society for Storytelling, PO Box 2344, Reading, Berkshire, RG6 TFG
**Phone** 0118 935 1381
**Email** sfs@fairbruk.demon.co.uk
**Web** www.sfs.ork.uk

### Traditional Music Maker Yearbook and Festival Guide
**Mail address** Magnet Publishing Ltd. 28 Grafton Terrace, London, NW5 4JJ
**Phone** 020 7424 0027
**Fax** 020 7267 2457

### Small Scale Dance Companies Directory
**Mail address** The Place Dance Services, The Place, 17 Duke's Road London, WC1H 9AB
**Phone** 020 7383 3524
**Fax** 020 7388 5407
**Email** danceservices@the place. org.uk

### International Events Guide
**Mail address** Business Media Services, Centre Court, 1301 Stratford Road, Hall Green, Birmingham, B28 9HH
**Phone** 0212 6937000,
**Fax** 0121 6937100
**Web** www.eventsbook.co.uk

### The Showman's Directory
**Mail address** Lance Publications, Park House, Park Road, Petersfield, Hampshire, GU32 3DL
**Phone** 01730 266624,
**Fax** 01730 260117
**Web** www.showmans-directory.co.uk

### British Federation of Festivals Year Book
(ISBN 090153241X)
**Mail address** Festivals House, 198 Park Lane, Macclesfield, Cheshire, SK11 6UD
**Phone** 01625 428297,
**Fax** 01625 503229,
**Web** www.festivals.demon.co.uk

### Showcase International Music Book
**Mail address** Showcase Publications 38c The Broadway, Crouch End, London, N8 9SU
**Phone** 020 8348 2332,
**Fax** 020 8340 3750
**Web** www.showcase-music.com

### Marketing Yearbook
**Mail address** Hollis Directories, Harlequin House, 7 High Street, Teddington, Middlesex, TW11 8EL
**Email** gillie@hollis-pr.co.uk

### Hollis Sponsorship and Donation Yearbook
**Mail address** Hollis Directories, Harlequin House, 7 High Street, Teddington, Middlesex, TW11 8EL
**Email** spons@hollis-pr.co.uk

## Journalists and Radio/TV presenters

### Alan O'Leary
**Mail address** 68 Belleville Road, LONDON, SW11 6PP
**Phone/Fax** 020 7585 0357
**Email** alan.oleary@spydaradio.co.uk
**Web** www.virtuetv.com/radio/spydaradio/index.html
*Radio presenter of folk/ acoustic music and live sessions. 3 hour weekly show 'The Guest List'. Thursdays 7-10pm GMT. Please use home address for contact.*
**RAB** London Arts
***See Alan's article on Irish Music.***

### Andrew Cronshaw
**Mail address** Cloud Valley Music, 51 Hainault Court, Forest Rise, LONDON, E17 3NW
**Phone/Fax** 020 8521 4649
**Email** cloudval@aol.com
**Web** http://members.aol.com/cloudval
*Journalist.*
***Musicians' Union member***
**RAB** London Arts

### Andy Farquarson
**Mail address** The Green, BROADWELL, Warks, CV23 8HE
**Phone** 01926 814111
07949 231091
**Fax** 01926 811100
**Email** andyfarquarson@hotmail.com
*Freelance journalist. CD and gig reviews, articles on music/artists (folk, folkrock, world music).*
**RAB** West Midlands Arts

***Editor's note:*** *Just before going to press we were very sorry to hear that Mick Tems has been taken seriously ill. We wish him a speedy and full recovery.*

## Annie Windley
**Mail address** 3 Palace Road, Crouch End, LONDON, N8 8QH
**Phone** 020 8342 9360
07931 718876
**Email** annie.windley@virgin.net
*Freelance journalist.*
**RAB** London Arts

## B B Skone
**Contact** MJ Cawley
**Mail address** Ty Newydd, 1 Owen Street, PEMBROKE DOCK, Pembrokeshire, SA72 6SL, Wales
**Phone** 01646 682692
07773 994514
**Email** sd@mjcawley.freeuk.com
*News, reviews and previews service of live and recorded music, based in West Wales.*
**AC** Wales

## Bob Hall
**Mail address** Prospect Music, 5 Prospect Place, Totley Rise, SHEFFIELD, S17 4HZ
**Phone/Fax** 0114 2363309
**Email** prospect@boogie.demon.co.uk
**Web** www.boogie.demon.co.uk
**Alt contact** Lesley Carr
**Alt address** Able Records, Red House Cottage, Botley Road, SHEDFIELD, Hants, SO32 2HN
**Phone/Fax** 01329 833359
**Email** gone@globalnet.co.uk
*Radio and TV presenter.*
***Musicians' Union member***
**RAB** Yorkshire Arts

## Colin Irwin
**Mail address** 39 Fleece Road, LONG DITTON, Surrey, KT6 5JP
**Phone** 020 8398 8108
**Email** colinirwin@aol.com
*Freelance journalist specialising in folk & roots music; interviews, news, reviews, etc. Contributor to Mojo, Music Week, fROOTS, Teletext,*
**RAB** London Arts

## David Herron
**Mail address** 53 Wellington Road, TODMORDEN, W Yorks, OL14 5DY
**Phone** 01706 819697
**Email** davidherron98@yahoo.com
*Writer & journalist on folk music & activities. Articles/ interviews for regional/ national magazines incl. Living Tradition, Dance & Song.*
**RAB** North West Arts

## Fintan Vallely
**Mail address** 15 Castlewood Terrace, Rathmines, DUBLIN 6, Ireland
**Phone/Fax** +353 1 497 2979
**Fax** +353 86 603 9461
**Email** f@fidil.com
**Web** www.fidil.com
*Writer on Irish traditional music.*
**AC** Ireland

## Geoff Speed
**Mail address** 3 Monica Drive, WIDNES, Cheshire, WA8 8IP
**Phone** 0151 4246001
0151 4242471
**Fax** 0151 4242426
**Email** geoffspeed@compuserve.com
*BBC Local radio producer and presenter*
**RAB** North West Arts

## Jessica Taylor
**Mail address** Newsnight Review Room G680, Television Centre, Wood Lane, LONDON, W12 7RJ
**Phone** 020 8743 8000
**Fax** 020 8576 7164
**Email** jessica.taylor@bbc.co.uk
**RAB** London Arts

## John Crosby - Time Out (London)
**Mail address** Time Out, Universal House, 251 Tottenham Court Rd, LONDON, W1P 0AB
**Phone** 020 7813 3000
**Fax** 020 7813 6158
**Email** folklistings@timeout.com
**Web** www.timeout.com
*Folk critic and Roots (folk, blues, country & world) listings editor.*
**RAB** London Arts

## John O'Regan
**Mail address** 32 Singland Crescent, GARRYOWEN, Limerick, Ireland
**Phone** +353 61 417302
+353 61 318106
**Fax** +353 61 417398
**Email** jor32@hotmail.com
*Freelance writer comntributing to fRoots, MOJO, Irish Music. Presenter of "Regan's Rambles" folk/trad music show on Radio Galtee, Limerick*
**AC** Ireland

## Mick Tems
**Mail address** 1 Ty Clwyta Cottages, Cross Inn, LLANTRISANT, Rhondda Cynon Taf, CF72 8AZ, Wales
**Phone/Fax** 01443 226892
**Phone** 07773 075962
**Email** micktems@folkwales.org.uk
**Web** www.folkwales.org.uk
*Print & internet writer & designer specialising in the traditional arts in Wales & beyond.*
**AC** Wales

## Pete Fyfe
**Mail address** 26 Cumberland Court, Cross Road, CROYDON, Surrey, CR0 6TE
**Phone** 020 8680 4302
**Email** petefyfe@aol.com
*Freelance journalist.*
**RAB** South East Arts

## Pete Jennings
**Mail address** 12 Carleton Close, GT YELDHAM, Essex, CO9 4QJ
**Phone** 01787 238257
07778 366469
**Fax** 01787 238257
**Email** pete@gippeswic.demon.co.uk
**Web** www.gippeswic.demon.co.uk
**Alt address** BBC Radio Suffolk, St Matthews Street, IPSWICH, Suffolk, IP1 3EP
*Presents 'Suffolk Folk' for BBC Radio Suffolk.*
**RAB** East England Arts

## Rosie Upton
**Mail address** 24 Bearfield Buildings, BRADFORD ON AVON, Wilts, BA15 1RP
**Phone/Fax** 01225 865107
**Email** rosie@bearfld.demon.co.uk
*Freelance columist and journalist; folk, world music.*
**RAB** Southern Arts

## Roy Harris
**Mail address** 31 Carling Court, Haig Place, CARDIFF, CF5 4PH, Wales
**Phone** 029 2065 7311
**Fax** 029 2065 7312
**Email** reharris@ntlworld.com
*Freelance writer & reviewer.*
**AC** Wales

## Sean Laffey
**Contact** Castlelake Consultancy
**Mail address** Castlelake, CASHEL, Co Tipperary, Irish Republic
**Phone** +353 62 62685
+353 87982 1916
**Fax** +353 62 62967
**Email** slaffey@iol.ie
**Web** www.iol.ie/~didly-didly
*Editor of Irish Music Magazine and freelance writer for Irish American Post, plus contributor to other folk press.*

## REGIONAL TELEVISION STATIONS

### Newcastle
BBC North East & Cumbria Broadcasting Centre, Barrack Road, Newcastle upon Tyne, NE99 2NE
**Switchboard/reception** 0191 232 4141
0191 232 1313
**Opening Hours** 09.00-19.00 weekdays (manned 24hrs)
**Fax** 0191 232 5082 (radio)
0191 221 0112 (tv)
**Programmes** *Look North, Close Up North, North of Westminster, Out and About*

### Manchester
BBC North West, New Broadcasting House, Oxford Road, Manchester M60 1SJ
**Switchboard** 0161 200 2020
**Opening Hours** 09.00 - I8.30
**Fax** 0161 244 4388
**Programmes** *North West Tonight, Close Up North, Northwestminster, Out and About*

### Leeds
BBC North, Broadcasting Centre, Woodhouse Lane, LS2 9PX
**Switchboard/reception** 0113 244 1188
**Fax** 0113 243 9387 (Newsroom)
**Opening Hours** 8.30-18.30
**Programmes** *Look North, Close Up North, North of Westminster, Out and About*

### Birmingham
BBC West Midlands, Pebble Mill Road, Birmingham, B5 7QQ
**Switchboard external** 0121 432 8888
**Fax** 0121 432 8634
**Opening Hours** 06.00-24.00
**Programmes** *Midlands Today, Midlands Report, Midlands at Westminster, Out and About*

### Nottingham
BBC East Midlands, London Road , Nottingham, NG2 4UU
**Switchboard/reception** 0115 955 0500
**Fax** 0115 902 1984
**Newsline phone in** 0115 900 900
**Opening Hours** 09.00 - 18.00
**Programmes** *East Midlands Today, Midlands Report, Midlands at Westminster, Out and About*

### Norwich
BBC East, St Catherine's Close, All Saint's Green, Norwich, Norfolk, NR1 3ND
**Switchboard/reception** 01603 619 331
**Opening Hours** 09.00 - 18.00 (reception 09.00-19.00)
**Fax** 01603 667 865 (newsroom)
**Programmes** Look East Matter of Fact, East at Westminster, Out and About

### BBC London and South East
Clarendon Road, Borehamwood, Hertfordshire, WD6 1JF
**Switchboard/reception** 020 8953 6100
**Fax** 020 8228 8092
**Programmes** *Newsroom South East, First Sight, Around Westminster, Out and About*

### Southampton
BBC South, Broadcasting House, Havelock Road, Southampton SO14 7PU
**Switchboard/reception** 023 8022 6201
**Fax** 023 8033 9931 (newsroom)
**Opening hours** 09.00 - 19.00
**Programmes** *South Today, Southern Eye, South of Westminster, Out and About*

### Bristol
BBC West, Broadcasting House, Whiteladies Road , Bristol, BS8 2LR
**Switchboard/reception** 0117 973 2211
**Fax** 0117 974 1537 (newsroom)
**Opening Hours** 08.30-18.00 (manned 24hrs)
**Programmes** *News West, Close Up West, Out of Westminster, Out and About*

### Plymouth
BBC South West, Broadcasting House, Seymour Road, Mannamead, Plymouth PL3 5BD
**Switchboard/reception** 01752 229 201
**Fax** 01752 234 595
**Programmes** *News West, Close Up West, Out of Westminster, Out and About, Spotlight (nightly news programme), Close Up (Current Affairs), Spotlight on Westminster (Parliamentary prog), Out and About*

## REGIONAL RADIO STATIONS

### BBC Asian Network
Epic House, Charles Street, Leicester, LE1 3SH
**Frequencies** 1458AM, 828AM, 837AM
**Switchboard/reception** 0116 251 6688
**Fax** 0116 251 1463
**Opening Hours** 09.00 - 17.00 Mon - Thurs, 09.00 - 16.30 Fri, 09.00-12.30 Saturday

### BBC Radio Bristol & Somerset Sound,
PO Box 194, Bristol, BS99 7QT
**Frequencies** 95.5FM, 94.9FM, 104.6FM, 15.48AM
**Switchboard** 01179 741 111
**Fax (newsroom)** 01179 238 323
01179 732 549
01179 741 537
**Opening Hours** 08.30-18.30 (manned 24hrs)

### BBC Radio Cambridgeshire
PO Box 96, Hills Road, Cambridge, CB2 1LD
**Frequencies** 96FM, 95.7FM
**Switchboard** 01223 259 696
**Fax (news)** 01223 460 832
**Opening Hours** 09.00-17.00 Mon - Fri
***Peterborough Satellite Station***
**Phone** 01733 312 832

### BBC Radio Cleveland
PO Box 95FM, Newport Road, Middlesbrough, TS1 5DG
**Frequencies** 95FM 95.8FM
**Switchboard/reception** 01642 225 211
**Fax (News)** 01642 211 356
**Opening Hours** 09.00-I7.00 Mon to Fri

### BBC Radio Cornwall
Phoenix Wharf, Truro, Cornwall, TR1 1UA
**Frequencies** 103.9FM, 95.2FM, 96.0FM (Isles of Scilly)
**Switchboard/reception** 01872 275 421
**Fax (newsroom)** 01872 275 045
01872 240 679
**Opening Hours** 09.00 - 17.00 Mon-Fri

### BBC Coventry & Warwickshire
Holt Court, 1 Greyfriars Road, Coventry, CV1 2WR
**Frequencies** 94.8.FM, 104FM, 103.7FM
**Switchboard/reception** 024 7626 0086
**Fax** 024 7657 0100
**Phone in** 024 7623 1231
**Opening Hours** 09.00-17.00 Mon-Fri

## BBC Radio Cumbria
Annetwell Street, Carlisle, CA3 8BB
**Frequencies** 95.6FM, 96.1FM, 104.2FM
**Switchboard/reception** 01228 592 444
**Fax** 01228 511 195
**Opening Hours** 09.00 - 17.00 Mon-Fri

## BBC Radio Derby
PO Box 269, Derby, DE1 3HL
**Frequencies** 104.5FM, 95.3FM, 1116AM
**Switchboard/reception** 01332 375 000
**Fax** 01332 290 794
**Opening Hours** 09.00-17.00 Mon-Fri

## BBC Radio Devon
PO Box 5, Plymouth, PL1 1XT
**Frequencies** 103.4FM, 94.8FM, 95.8FM, 96.0FM
**Switchboard/reception** 01752 260 323
**Fax (newsroom)** 01752 234 5649
**Opening Hours** 08.45-19.00 Mon-Fri

## BBC Radio Essex
198 New London Road, Chelmsford, Essex, CM2 9XB
**Frequencies** 103.5FM, 95.3FM
**Switchboard/reception** 01245 616 000
**Fax (newsroom)** 01245 492 983
**Opening Hours** 09.30 - 17.00 Mon-Fri

## BBC Radio Gloucestershire
London Road, Gloucester, GL1 1SW
**Frequencies** 104.7FM, 1413AM
**Switchboard/reception** 01452 308 585
**Fax** 01452 309 491
**Phone in** 01452 307 575
**Opening Hours** 09.00 - 17.30 Mon-Fri

## BBC GMR
PO Box 951, Oxford Road, Manchester, M60 1SD
**Frequencies** 95.1FM, 104.6FM
**Switchboard** 0161 200 2000
**Opening Hours** 09.00-18.30 Mon-Fri
**Reception** 09.00 - 19.00 Mon-Fri
**Reception** 0161 244 4422

## BBC Radio Guernsey
Commerce House, Les Banques, St Peter Port, Guernsey, GY1 2HS
**Frequencies** 93.2FM, 1116AM
**Switchboard/reception** 01481 728 977
**Fax** 01481 713 557
**Opening Hours** 10.00 -13.00 Mon-Fri

## BBC Hereford & Worcester
Hylton Road, Worcester, WR2 5WW
**Frequencies** 104FM, 94.7FM, 104.6FM
**Switchboard/reception** 01905 748 485
**Opening Hours** 09.00-17.00 Mon-Fri (closed 13.00 - 14.00)

## BBC Radio Humberside
9 Chapel Street, Hull, HU1 3NU
**Frequencies** 95.9FM
**Switchboard/reception** 01482 323 232
**Fax** 01482 621 458
**Opening Hours** 09.00-17.00 Mon-Fri

## BBC Radio Jersey
18 Parade Road, St Helier, Jersey
**Frequencies** 88.8FM, 1026AM
**Switchboard** 01534 870 000
01534 870 111
**Fax** 01534 732 569
**Opening hours** 09.00-17.00 (Mon-Fri)
09.00 - 13.00 (Sat)
**Reception** 01534 870 000

## BBC Radio Kent
Sun Pier, Chatham, Kent, ME4 4EZ
**Frequencies** 96.7FM, 104.2FM, 97.6FM
**Switchboard/reception** 01634 830 505
**Fax** 01634 830 573
**Opening Hours** 09.00-17.00 Mon-Fri

## BBC Radio Lancashire
26 Darwen Street, Blackburn, Lancs, BB2 2EA
**Frequencies** 103.9FM, 95.5FM, 104.5FM
**Switchboard/reception** 01254 262 411
**Fax** 01254 680 821
**Opening Hours** 09.00-17.00 Mon-Fri

## BBC Radio Leeds
Broadcasting House, Woodhouse Lane, Leeds, LS2 9PN
**Frequencies** 92.4FM, 95.3FM, 774AM
**Switchboard/reception** 0113 244 2131
**Fax** 0113 242 0652
**Opening Hours** 08.30-19.00 Mon-Fri

## BBC Radio Leicester
Epic House, Charles Street, Leicester, LE1 3SH
**Frequencies** 104.9FM
**Switchboard/reception** 0116 251 6688
**Fax (newsroom)** 0116 251 1463
**Opening Hours** 09.00-17.00 Mon-Fri, 09.00-13.00 Saturday

## BBC Radio Lincolnshire
Radio Buildings, PO Box 219, Newport, Lincoln, LN1 3XY
**Frequencies** 94.9FM, 104.7FM, 1368AM
**Switchboard/reception** 01522 511 411
**Fax** 01522 511 058
**Opening Hours** 09.00-17.30 Mon-Fri, 09.00 - 13.00 Saturday

## BBC Radio Merseyside
55 Paradise Street, Liverpool, L1 3BP
**Frequencies** 95.8FM
**Switchboard** 0151 708 5500
**Fax** 0151 794 0988 (managers)
0151 794 0909 (newsroom)
**Phone in** 0151 709 9333
**Opening Hours** 09.00-17.30 Mon-Fri
**Reception** 0151 794 0975

## BBC Radio Newcastle
Broadcasting Centre, Barrack Rd, Newcastle upon Tyne, NE99 1RN
**Frequencies** 95.4FM, 96FM, 103.7FM, 104.4FM
**Switchboard** 0191 232 4141
**Fax** 0191 261 8907
**Opening Hours** 09.00-19.00 Mon-Fri (manned 24hrs)
**Reception** 0191 232 1313 (tv & radio)

## BBC Radio Norfolk
Norfolk Tower, Surrey Street, Norwich, NR1 3PA
**Frequencies** 95.1FM, 104.4FM
**Switchboard/reception** 01603 617 411
**Fax** 01603 633 692
**Opening Hours** 09.00 - 17.00 Mon-Fri

## BBC Radio Northampton
Broadcasting House, Abington Street, Northampton, NN1 2BH
**Frequencies** 104.2FM, 103.6FM
**Switchboard/reception** 01604 239 100
**Fax** 01604 230 709
**Opening Hours** 08.45-17.15 Mon-Fri

## BBC Radio Nottingham
London Road, Nottingham, NG2 4UU
**Frequencies** 95.5FM, 103.8FM
**Switchboard/reception** 0115 955 0500
**Fax** 0115 902 1983
**Opening Hours** 09.00 - 18.00 Mon - Fri

## BBC Southern Counties Radio
Broadcasting Centre, Guildford GU2 5AP
**Frequencies** 104 -104.8FM, 95 - 95.3FM
**Switchboard/reception** 01483 306 306
**Fax** (Newsroom) 01483 304 952
**Opening Hours** 09.00-17.30 Mon-Fri

### BBC Radio Sheffield
Ashdell Grove, 60 Westbourne Road, Sheffield, S10 2QU
**Frequencies** 104.1FM, 88.6FM, 94.7FM
**Switchboard/reception** 0114 268 6185
**Fax** 0114 266 4375
**Opening Hours** 09.00-17.30 Mon-Fri

### BBC Radio Shropshire
2-4 Boscobel Drive, Shrewsbury, SY1 3TT
**Frequencies** 96FM
**Switchboard/reception** 01743 248 484
**Fax** 01743 271 702
**Opening Hours** 09.00 - 17.00 Mon-Fri

### BBC Radio Solent
Broadcasting House, Havelock Road Southampton, SO14 7PW
**Frequencies** 96.1FM, 103.8FM
**Switchboard/reception** 023 8063 1311
**Fax** 023 8033 9648
**Opening Hours** 09.00-19.00 Mon-Fri

### BBC Radio Stoke
Cheapside, Hanley, Stoke on Trent ST1 1JJ
**Frequencies** 94.6FM, 104.1FM
**Switchboard/reception** 01782 208 080
**Phone in** 01782 208 008
**Opening Hours** 09.00 - 17.00 Mon-Fri

### BBC Radio Suffolk
Broadcasting House, St Matthew's Street, Ipswich, Suffolk, IP1 3EP
**Frequencies** 103.9FM, 104.6FM, 95.5FM
**Switchboard/reception** 01473 250 000
**Fax** 01473 210 887
**Opening Hours** 09.00 - 17.00 Mon-Fri

### BBC Thames Valley
269 Banbury Road, Oxford, OX2 7DW
**Frequencies** 95.2FM, 95.4FM, 104.1FM
**Switchboard/reception** 0645 311 444
**Fax** 0645 311 555
**Opening Hours** 09.00 -17.00 Mon-Fri

### BBC Three Counties Radio
PO Box 3CR, Luton, Bedfordshire LU1 5XL
**Frequencies** 95.5FM, 103.8FM, 104.5FM, 630AM
**Switchboard/reception** 01582 637 400
**Fax** 01582 401 467
**Opening Hours** 09.00 - 17.00 Mon-Fri

### BBC Radio Wiltshire Sound
Broadcasting House, Prospect Place Swindon, SN1 3RW
**Frequencies** 103.6FM, 104.3FM, 103.5FM, 104.9FM
**Switchboard/reception** 01793 513 626
**Fax** 01793 513 650
**Opening Hours** 09.00 - 17.00 Mon-Fri

### BBC Radio WM
PO Box 206, Birmingham, B5 7SD
**Frequencies** 95.6FM
**Switchboard** 0121 432 8484
**Fax** 0121 472 3174
0121 432 9939
**Opening Hours** 06.00-01.00
**Reception** 0121 432 9141
0121 432 9142

### BBC Radio York
20 Bootham Row, York, YO30 7BR
**Frequencies** 103.7FM, 104.3FM, 95.5FM
**Switchboard/reception** 01904 641 351
**Fax** 01904 540 337/ 540 339
**Opening Hours** 09.00 - 17.00 Mon-Fri

### Folkwaves BBC in the Midlands
**Mail address** PO Box 104.5, DERBY
**Phone** 01773 853428

*2 Hour radio folk show, Mondays 7.05pm. BBC Radio Derby, Lincoln, Nottingham & Leicester. Presented by Lester Simpson and Mick Peat.*

### Genevieve Tudor's Sunday Folk
**Contact** Genevieve Tudor
**Mail address** BBC Radio Shropshire, PO Box 96, Shropshire, SY1 3WW
**Phone** 01743 248484
**Fax** 01743 271702
**Email** genevieve.tudor@bbc.co.uk
**Web** www.bbc.co.uk/england/radio shropshire/folk.shtml

*Sunday 8-10pm. Mostly British Isles music & interviews with local to international performers.*

**RAB** West Midlands Arts

## The Mike Harding Show
By **John Leonard**

When we were asked to produce a folk music programme for BBC Radio 2 both Mike Harding and I went back to first principles and asked ourselves what it was about the music that first inspired us to listen. There is so little time available on our programme, just one hour a week, that it is virtually impossible to do a full service and represent all facets of folk music each week. So we decided that the aim of the programme should be to encourage excellence, try to introduce new people to the music and inspire them to make the same journey that we made.

The first real folk singer I ever heard was **Bob Dylan** at around his *Tambourine Man* period. As I explored his music I found out about his Roots; **Woody Guthrie**, **Jimmie Rodgers** and **Ramblin' Jack Elliott**. I discovered that some of his tunes were English, I listened to **Martin Carthy** singing *Lord Franklin* and from there it was a short step to other traditional music from these islands.

When we pick music for Mike's show we try and make it accessible. It has to be of exceptional quality and we hope that it will inspire listeners to make their own journey. If by playing **Kate Rusby** we lead people to **Nic Jones**, **Harry Cox** and **Shirley Collins**, by playing **Nanci Griffith** we introduce people to **Woody Guthrie**, **Guy Clark** and **Tom Russell** or by playing **Ry Cooder** listeners discover Cuban music, **Ali Farka Toure** and Tex Mex then we feel we are playing a role in helping to popularise folk music.

Give the programme a listen, write to congratulate or criticise and check out our folk web site at:
**www.bbc.co.uk/radio2**

# Commercial Independent Radio

By **John Ward**

'Commercial independent radio' and 'folk music' are not words you often find together. Part of the reason is that 'independent local stations' are often not that at all but, are in fact owned by a few large companies whose decisions about content are made from a central office many miles away. As a result of this, not much that is 'local' actually gets broadcast. This is frustrating for musicians performing in a town who, at one time, were likely to get a spot on the local station, and for those communities who enjoy a healthy folk scene and wish to see it promoted.

Unusually, for a change, it is not just folk music that is marginalized in this way but many other music genres. Those who run commercial radio generally believe that the top 40 of the last 40 years is all the public want to hear and that local music is uninteresting. Even many of the so called community stations which serve one town claim the public don't want to hear even the most popular local artist or know about local music clubs.

Can much be done to change this? Each commercial station has to agree to a Promise of Performance which stipulates what is to be included in its programming provision. This document can be found in your local library and while it is often vague and does not always mention particular genres, sometimes something can be found to support a challenge to their programming. Another proven strategy is to complain to your local MP who is likely to be anxious that they too are not appearing on local radio as much as they used too!

There are exceptions of course. Tommy Sands has been running his show every Saturday night in Belfast on Downtown Radio since 1977.

Also, digital radio is offering some hope particularly in the shape of MCE who broadcast all over Europe. They currently programme some folk and are set to feature more as long as the folk world shouts loud enough about its excellent and diverse music scene.

## FOLK AND ROOTS ON INDEPENDENT RADIO STATIONS

### ENGLAND

#### From the Wood
**Contact** Dave Wills
**Mail address** Gemini AM, Hawthorne House, Exeter Business Park, Exeter, Devon EX1 3QS
**Phone** 01392 444444
**Fax** 01392 444433

#### The Midday Programme
**Contact** The Producer
**Mail address** Medway FM, Berkley House, 186 High Street Rochester ME1 1EY
**Email** studio@medwayfm.com
**Web** www.medwayfm.com

#### Yorkshire Dales Radio
**Contact** Andrew Ingle
**Mail address** 62 Leeds Road, Otley LS21 1BT

#### Folkus
**Contact** Richard Tree
**Mail address** Kings Lynn Radio Blackborough End, Kings Lynn PE32 1SS

#### Plymouth Sound
**Contact** Brian Measures
**Mail address** Earl's Acre Plymouth PL3 4HX
**Email** mail@plymouthsound.com

#### Folkus
**Contact** Dave Cartwright
**Mail address** Radio Wyvern 5-6 Barbourne Terrace, Worcester

#### Mike Ganley
**Mail address** FM 107 - The Falcon 5 Valleys' Radio (Stroud) Ltd 6 Lansdown, Stroud, Gloucestershire GL5 1BE
**Web** www.thefalcon.org/

#### Shep Woolley
**Mail address** Radio Victory, Tipner Wharf, Twyford Avenue, Portsmouth Hampshire PO2 8PE

#### Back of Beyond
**Contact** Jim Trott
**Mail address** Island FM, 12 Westerbrook Street, Sampsons Guernsey GY2 4QQ
**Email** vikki@islandfm.guernsey.net
**Web** www.islandfm.guernsey.net

#### Shanty Jo Radio
**Contact** Castlelake Consultancy
**Mail address** Castlelake, CASHEL, Co Tipperary, Irish Republic
**Phone** +353 62 62685
+353 87982 1916
**Fax** +353 62 62967
**Email** slaffey@iol.ie
**Web** www.iol.ie/~didly-didly

*Net radio of Castlelake Consultancy, joint venture with VSL, Florida. Acoustic folk music from the British Isles and beyond. Offers a site where acoustic folk artists can present tracks.*

### ISLE OF MAN

#### The Folk Show
**Contact** John Kaneen
**Mail address** Manx Radio, Broadcasting House, Douglas, Isle of Man

### IRELAND

#### Downtown Radio
**Mail address** Newtownards, near Belfast

*101.6 FM and 1026 MW. Tommy Sands between 6.00pm and 8.00pm every Saturday.*

#### Tim Dennehy
**Mail address** Clare FM, Francis Street, Ennis, Co. Clare, Eire
**Email** tdennehy@clarefm.ie
**Web** www.clarefm.ie/index.htm

#### Maire Begley
**Mail address** Ceol agus Cedraigh, Maine Street, Tralee, Kerry, Eire

#### Living Tradition
**Contact** Collette Grufferty
**Mail address** Tipp FM, Davis Road Clonmel, Tipperary, Eire

#### Marcus Connaughton
**Mail address** RTE (Cork), Father Matthew Street, Cork, Ireland

#### Focal Point
**Contact** Maurice Leyden
**Mail address** Downtown Radio Newtownards, Co. Down Northern Ireland BT23 4ES
**Email** programmes@downtown.co.uk
**Web** www.downtown.co.uk

#### The Session
**Contact** Peter M Cunningham
**Mail address** Heartbeat 1521 Carn Business Park, Craigavon Co Armagh, Northern Ireland BT63 5RH

## SCOTLAND

### Room to Roam
**Contact** Clive Price
**Mail address** Heartland FM
Lower Oakfield, Lower Oakfield,
Perthshire PH16 2DS. Scotland
**Web** www.heartlandfm.co.uk

### Celtic Celebration
**Mail address** Heartland FM
Lower Oakfield, Lower Oakfield,
Perthshire PH16 2DS, Scotland
**Web** www.heartlandfm.co.uk

### Scene Around
**Mail address** Heartland FM
Lower Oakfield, Lower Oakfield,
Perthshire PH16 2DS, Scotland
**Web** www.heartlandfm.co.uk

### Folkus
**Contact** Don Catterall
**Mail address** Isles FM, PO Box 333
Stornoway, Isle of Lewis HS1 2TP

### Celtic Music New and Old
**Contact** Elsie Ross
**Mail address** Lochbroom FM
Mill Street Industrial Estate, Ullapool
Wester Ross IV26 2UN, Scotland
**Email** Radio@lochbroomfm.co.uk

**Web** www.lochbroomfm.co.uk

### Celtic Café
**Contact** Miranda Thow
**Mail address** Moray Firth Radio
PO Box 271, Inverness IV3 6SF
Scotland

### No Frontiers
**Contact** Maisie Dennison
**Mail address** Nevis Radio, Inverlochy,
Fort William, Inverness PH33 6LU
**Email** nevisradio@lochaber.sol.co.uk
**Web** www.nevisradio.co.uk

### Moray Forth Radio Folk Review
**Contact** Doug Mackenzie
**Mail address** Moray Forth Radio,
PO Box 271, Inverness IV3 6SF,
Scotland
**Web** www.morayfirth.co.uk

### The Sunday Show
**Contact** Andy Ross
**Mail address** Moray Forth Radio,
PO Box 271, Inverness IV3 6SF,
Scotland
**Web** www.morayfirth.co.uk

## WALES

### Radio Ceredigion
**Contact** Yr Awr Werin
**Mail address** Yr Hen Ysgol Cymraeg
Ffordd Alexandra, Aberystwyth
Ceredigion SY23 1LF, Wales

### The Folk Show
**Contact** Yvonne & John Hart
**Mail address** Radio Maldwyn, The
Park
Newtown, Powys SY16 2NZ
**Email** radio.maldwyn@uk.online.co.uk
**Web** www.magic756.com

### Dig the Roots
**Contact** Dave Robinson
**Mail address** Swansea Sound,
Victoria Road, Gowerton, Swansea
SA4 3AB
**Web** www.swanseasound.co.uk
**Email** info@swanseasound.co.uk

# working with the authorities

# The Overseas Labour Service

The Overseas Labour Service (OLS) is responsible for administering the issue of work permits to overseas nationals who wish to enter Great Britain to work. Although OLS works closely with the Home Office, it is a division within the Department for Education and Employment.

In the case of performers the **work permit scheme** aims to ensure that people who have performed at the highest level overseas and have an established international reputation are able to enter the country. Usually, the people concerned are engaged to perform or do work which only they can do. People from within the European Economic Area (EEA) do not need to apply for a work permit to perform in the UK.

Applications for a work permit for entertainers need to be made on form WP3. This can be obtained either by calling 01937 840731 and requesting the form be posted (including the WP3 Guidance Notes), or by downloading the application from the OLS website at www.dfee.gov.uk/ols.

The guidance notes will explain what information is required when submitting the application for consideration but some of the key points are as follows:

- Applications must be made by employers who are based in Great Britain and established in the entertainments industry. Very often the venue where the artist is performing will act as the employer. Employers applying for the first time should also include information confirming their trading status, such as a recent set of accounts.
- Performers requiring a work permit for the first time will need to provide evidence confirming their status as an established entertainer. This will usually take the form of press reviews but information from the internet is also acceptable.
- The salary paid to performers should reflect their status as entertainers of the highest calibre, and work permits are issued for the period of confirmed work.

Completed applications should be forwarded to:
Overseas Labour Service
Department for Education & Employment, W5, Moorfoot, Sheffield S1 4PQ

Alternatively these can be faxed on 0114 259 4987. As yet we are unable to accept electronic applications but this is currently being piloted with the intention of setting up this facility later in the year 2001.

In some circumstances (such as recognised festivals) entertainers from outside the EEA may enter the country permit free. In these cases please contact the Home Office for further advice.

Should you wish to know more information about the Work Permit Scheme please access our website at www.dfee.gov.uk/ols, or Email us at ents.ols@dfee.gov.uk. We can also be contacted by phone on 0114 259 3710.

# Taxation of non-UK resident entertainers

## The role of the Inland Revenue's Foreign Entertainers Unit (FEU)

**What is the Foreign Entertainers Unit (FEU)?**
FEU is the Inland Revenue's specialist unit which deals with the following;

- Managing the UK withholding tax system which applies to anyone who makes payments to/for non-UK resident entertainers (and sporting personalities)
- Agreeing the UK tax liabilities of individual non-UK resident entertainers (and sporting personalities) who perform in the UK

**To whom does the UK withholding tax apply?**

- Any individual or organisation which makes payments to/for an entertainer who performs in the UK (but is not resident here) must deduct withholding tax (currently at 22%) from all payments and pay that tax over to the Collector of Taxes(unless total payments made by any one payer to that entertainer are less than £1,000 - in which case payment may be made gross)
- Any non-UK resident entertainer who performs in this country should have withholding tax deducted from fees etc paid to them as a payment on account of their final UK tax liability

**Is withholding tax always the fixed rate (currently 22%)?**
Not necessarily. An entertainer (or anyone authorised on their behalf) may apply to FEU before the UK performance takes place to take into account any allowable expenses - e.g. agent commission, travel expenses etc - in arriving at the UK profit. That profit should then be taxed at the normal UK tax rates (including lower and higher rates if appropriate). Once agreed, that tax becomes the amount to be withheld by the payer.

**Can entertainers claim back the withholding tax deducted?**
If an application has been agreed as outlined above, the UK tax cannot be claimed back since the right amount should have been paid. If no application has been made and the entertainer feels that too much UK tax has been withheld, he or she can claim repayment of any overdeduction by completing a UK tax return (obtainable from FEU) after the end of the tax year.

**Does that mean that tax is paid twice on the same income i.e. in the UK and in an entertainer's home country?**
No. Tax should not be paid twice. What should happen is that the certificate of UK tax deducted (form FEU2), which the payer should give to the entertainer, should be sent by the entertainer to the Revenue authorities in the entertainer's home country. That country should give credit for the UK tax deducted so that tax is only paid once on the income connected with the UK activity.

**How can I get more information?**
This is available either from FEU, whose contact details are:

**Inland Revenue Foreign Entertainers Unit**
**Mail address** 2nd Floor, Royal House, Prince's Gate, 2 - 6 Homer Road, Solihull, West Midlands B91 3WG
**Phone** 0121 712 8601/2/3
**Fax** 0121 712 8662
**Email** sco.ir.birm@gtnet.gov.uk

or from the Inland Revenue's main website at **inrev.gov.uk/inland revenue/feu/index**

# What is MCPS?

Acting on behalf of its composer and publisher members, Mechanical Copyright Protection Society (MCPS) negotiates agreements with those who wish to copy music, ensuring where possible that the copyright owners - MCPS members - are rewarded through those agreements for the use of their music.

These agreements can take the form of blanket licences or licensing schemes (covering the use of all members' repertoire) or individually negotiated 'one-off' licences. MCPS collects and then distributes "mechanical" royalties generated from the copying of music onto many different formats.

**The Mechanical Right?**
For MCPS members it means that every time their musical work is copied, or that copy of the work is issued to the public, any mechanical royalties generated from its licensing will be collected by MCPS and paid on to the member.

This includes not only the recording of a song for sale on a record, tape, CD or any other sound carrier, but also where music is copied into TV and radio programmes, feature films, TV and radio commercials, videos (retail, corporate and educational), retail multi-media (e.g. computer games) and premium products (e.g. a free CD with a packet of cereal).

**The Copyright Designs & Patents Act, 1988**
The Copyright Designs and Patents Act 1988 gives a copyright owner five restricted acts in relation to his/her copyright musical work:-

- To copy the work.
- To issue copies of the work in public.
- To perform, show or play the work in public.
- To broadcast the work or include it in a cable programme service.
- To make an adaptation of the work or do any of the above in relation to an adaptation.

MCPS represents its composer and publisher members in relation to two of these restricted acts - to copy the work and to issue a copy of the work (distribution). In addition, copyright owners sometimes have the right to control the importation of copies of their musical works.

**Requirements for Membership of MCPS**
You are eligible for membership of MCPS if your musical works have been copied recently, or they are due to be copied imminently onto the following formats: CDs, records, tapes, videos (retail, corporate and educational), retail multi-media (e.g. computer games) TV and radio programmes, feature films, TV and radio commercials, and premium products (e.g. a free CD with a packet of cereal).

**Are you writing and producing music on your own label?**
If it's the case that you are the only person making copies, for example onto your own label, then it would not be practical for you to become a member of MCPS. This is because you would be both musical copyright owner and record company owner and so any mechanical royalties generated would be paid by yourself (as the record company owner) to yourself (as the musical copyright owner).

**Composers and MCPS**
As a composer you do not need to become a member of MCPS if you have already assigned your musical works to a music publisher. This is because when you assign your works, the publisher will collect any mechanical royalties generated and then pay any agreed share to you.

If you have assigned your musical works to a music publisher who is a member of MCPS then MCPS will pay the mechanical royalties to the publisher, who will pass on your share.

**If your music is being performed**, but not copied, then membership of MCPS is not relevant. In this case you should still consider membership of the **Performing Right Society (PRS)** (see page 421).

The Performing Right Society is a non-profit making membership organisation that collects licence fees from music users and distributes the money to its members - the writers and publishers of music.

## If you are a composer of music or a lyricist -

Music copyright owners have the right to control the use of their music and to earn from it, which is where PRS comes in. Membership of PRS is a practical way that composers, songwriters and music publishers can receive what is due to them for the public performance, broadcast and cable transmission of their music.

If you would like further information on becoming a member please contact PRS on **020 7306 4805** or, alternatively, check out the website: **www.prs.co.uk**

## If you run a music venue -

If you run a music venue or festival - or any public place where music is used - you need the PRS Music Licence. The PRS Music Licence entitles the owner to play or have performed just about any music on their premises, and our charges are based on the amount of music used, so you only pay for what you play

If you need a PRS Music Licence please call us free on **08000 68 48 28** or e-mail: **musiclicence@prs.co.uk.**

# The Performing Right Society

Established in 1914, the Performing Right Society (PRS) is a non-profit making membership organisation, which collects license fees from music users and distributes the money to its members - the writers and publishers of music.

Regardless of whether the music is performed live or by recorded means. Be it from a television, a juke box or through the internet a PRS licence is a legal requirement if that use is for a pubic performance i.e. outside a private home.

There are similar Performing Right Societies throughout the world. By agreement with them PRS represents their members in the UK and in turn the foreign societies collect the royalties PRS members earn in their territories. Because of these receptacle agreements, a PRS licence holder is entitled to play any of over 15 million musical works. Everything from advertising jingles to an entire symphony.

A Board of Directors who control its policy and administration runs the PRS. The elected board members nine writers and nine publishers and non-executive. There are also two executive board members one of who is the Societies Chief Executive. In addition, the Board appoints two external Directors from the world of commerce and industry.

In recent years, the folk, roots and acoustic music world has engaged with PRS and discussed the licensing, collecting of data and the distribution of funds to this genre of music. Much work has been done by individuals as well as the Musicians' Union and the AFO. The work is on-going and done in co-operation with the professional staff at PRS who offer the following bullet points as a basic guideline for the workings of the Performing Right Society.

1. If you write a piece of music you automatically have a copyright in it which lasts for your lifetime, and 70 years afterwards.
2. If anyone wants to make use of your music – perform, broadcast, record or arrange it – they must first have your permission, and you can charge a royalty in return.
3. In the UK, most composers, writers and music publishers assign the performing and broadcasting rights in their music to the Performing Right Society (PRS) to look after on their behalf.
4. PRS collects royalties for its members by charging fees to promoters, venue owners and broadcasters in return for issuing licences that cover the use of music.
   - Venues that use music regularly are licensed on a year-to-year basis. The fee payable depends on the type of venue and extent of music use. Club promoters should enquire with owners or managers whether there is a current PRS licence.
   - Festivals and other one-off events are licensed separately. Venues with a PRS music licence are not charged for PRS licensed festival events and need not declare them.
5. As far as possible, PRS gathers information about what music is played how and where so that the licence money can be paid to the members whose music is being used.
6. PRS staff regularly attend festivals and a sample of clubs to get returns from performers for this purpose.
7. PRS income also supports the Performing Right Society Foundation, which was launched in March 2000. The Foundation's aim is to encourage, promote and sustain music creation and its performance, of all genres, at all levels of activity. Support is focussed on organisations or groups (but not individuals) who are promoting music creators who live and work in the UK. There are a range of funding schemes available including Awards to Festivals, and Not-for-profit Promoters.
8. For further information please visit the PRS website at www.prs.co.uk, or The Foundation's website at **www.prsf.co.uk**, or call one of the phone numbers below

- To become a PRS member 020 7306 4805
- To get a PRS music licence (venues) 0800 684828
- To get a PRS music licence (festivals) 0845 3008060
- To find out more about the PRS Foundation 020 7306 4044

# Members of the Folk, Roots and Traditional Music Section of The Musicians' Union

**This list contains the known members of the Musicians' Union Folk Roots and Traditional Music Section at the time of going to press. If you are a member and are not on the list, please contact Ian Smith directly on 0141 248 3723 or at *folk@musiciansunion.org.uk* and we will ensure your listing in the next edition of** Direct Roots.

Adrian Jones
Adrian Y-Gof
Aidan O'Rourke
Aileen Hindley
Aimee Leonard
Al Summers
Alan Burke
Alan Burton
Alan Pyke
Alan Train
Alastair Mcdougald
Alex Debnam
Alicia Davies
Alison Finlay
Alison Heywood
Alison Macfarlane
Alistair Anderson
Alistair Hulett
Alistair Kildare
Alistair McCulloch
Alistair Russell
Allan Dunsmore
Allan Johnston
Aly Bain
Alyth McCormack
Amanda Hall
The Amazing Mr Smith
Amy Geddes
Andrea Preston
Andrew Hiles
Andrew Lambert
Andrew Mckay
Andrew Perkins
Andrew Webster
Andy Baines
Andy Cutting
Andy Knight
Andy May
Angelo Palladino
Anna-Wendy Stevenson
Anne Lister
Anne Martin
Anne Peck
Anne Summers
Annie Grace
Annie Mawson
Anthony Binns
Anthony Penneck
Ayo Ola Bamidele
Barbara Brown
Barry Coope
Barry Laing
Beard
Bernard Kearns
Bill Jones
Bill Nicoll
Bill Taylor
Billy Anderson
Bob Hall
Bram Taylor
Branco Stoysin
Brian Heywood
Brian Mcilvaney
Brian Miller
Brian O'Headhra
Brian Peters
Brian Rose
Brian Stafford
Brian Willoughby
Bruce Davies
Bruce Graham
Buz Collins
Cal Callaghan
Caleb Jarvis
Cara Dillon
Carlene Anglim
Carolyn Francis
Casey James
Caspar Cronk
Cath James
Catherine Mcgrother
Charles Spicer
Charlie MacKerron
Chris Bartram
Chris Girling
Chris Halliday
Chris Leslie
Chris Lowe
Chris Newman
Chris Parkinson
Chris Sherburn
Chris Turner
Christine Kydd
Christopher Dyson
Christopher Rogers
Christopher Stout
Christopher Taylor
Cliff Stapleton
Colin Harris
Colin Tommis
Colin Train
Colin Wilson
Collen Gregory
Cy Jack
Dai Thomas
Damian Woodings
Dan Evans
Dan Plews
Dan Quinn
Danny KilBride
Darren Tansley
Dave Bradbury
Dave Hunt
Dave Mallinson
Dave Mann
Dave Pegg
Dave Richardson
Dave Townsend
Dave Whetstone
David Benjafield
David Boag
David Brooks
David Camlin
David Chatterley
David Cripps
David Danford
David Fletcher
David Francis
David Gibb
David Grabham
David Grundy
David Harris
David Johnson
David Lim
David Oliver
David Cruickshank
David Sole
David Steele
David Sturt
David Thomas
David Toussaint
Davy Spillane
Deborah Scott
Den Couch
Derek Gifford
Derek Jones
Dewi Owen Jones
Diana Sanders
Diane Vickers
Dick Gaughan
Dirk Campbell
Donald Shaw
Dorothy Dearnley
Douglas Eunson
Douglas Keir
Duncan Mccrone
Ed Boyd
Eddie Upton
Eddy Sayer
Edward Mcguire
Eddie Walker
Edward Wolstenholme
Eileen Monger
Elaine Samuels
Eliza Carthy
Elspeth Cowie
Emily Slade
Emma Bell
Emyr Rhys
Eric Roche
Ewen Vernal
Fi Fraser

Finbar Furey
Fiona Branson
Francis Vickers
Frank Bogie
Frank McCracken
Fraser Fifield
Fraser Speirs
Freddy Macha
Gareth Banks
Gareth Turner
Gareth Warren
Gary Miller
Gavin Marwick
Gaye Anthony
Gaynor Butler
Geoffrey Tindall
Geoffrey Wright
George Futter
George Jukes
George Reid
Gerard Kearns
Gerard KilBride
Gerry Conway
Gerry Diver
Gerry Milne
Gina Mackey
Ginette Davis
Ginny Dowden
Gino Lupari
Glenn Miller
Graham Corbould
Graham Stacey
Guto Dafis
Guy Fletcher
Guy Hindley
Harry Macfadyen
Hazel Fairburn
Heather Hawthorn
Heather Innes
Heather Wells
Helen Holt
Helen Moody
Helen Thomson
Helene Hambrook
Holly Karlsen
Horse Mcdonald
Howard Evans
Hugh Bradley
Iain Fraser
Iain Maclachlan
Ian Dobson
Ian Hardie
Ian Smith
Ian Stephenson
Igor Outkine
Imogen Fernando
Ivitsky Molleson
Jacqueline Grant
Jacquellyn Nash
Jake Walton
James Armstrong
James Berriman
James Morrison
James O'Grady
Jane Clark
Jane Lawrence
Janet Woods
Jason Hill
Jeffery Davis
Jeffery Dennison
Jeffrey Dent
Jennifer Port
Jennifer Shotliff
Jennifer Wrigley
Jenny Crook
Jez Lowe
Jim Boyes
Jim Couza
Jim Darby
Jo Freya
Jo Hill
Joe Broughton
John Adams
John Addison
John Campbell
John Eaglesham
John Forrester
John Garner
John Howarth
John Kelly
John Kirkpatrick
John Malcolm
John Martin
John McCusker
John McNulty
John Pearson
John Peel
John Perkins
John Ramirez
John Smedley
John Ward
Johnny Collins
Johnny Handle
Jon Bamforth
Jonathan Brenner
Jonathan Isaacs
Jonathan Loomes
Jonathan Quick
Joseph Porter
Joseph Scurfield
Judith Brierley
Judith Linton
Jules Levy
Julian Burton
Julian Sutton
June Tabor
Karen Cormican
Karen Marshalsay
Karen Matheson
Karen Tweed
Karine Polwart
Kate Barfield
Kate Howden
Kate Rounding
Kate Rusby
Kathryn Aldis
Kathryn Tickell
Katie Howson
Keith Davis
Keith Gregson
Keith Holloway
Keith Jackman
Keith Osborne
Keith Smith
Kenneth Wheeler
Keri Simpson
Kevan Roberts
Kevin Conneff
Kevin Gladwell
Kevin Mackie
Kim Bretton
Laura Cunnell
Lawrence Evans
Leighton Jones
Lemon Otter
Len Dee
Leonard Scolley
Lester Simpson
Liam Hackett
Linda Long
Lizzie Segal
Luke Samuels
Lynda Swindlehurst
Lynne Percival
Maggie Holland
Mahrey Berthoud
Mairi Campbell
Malachy Duffin
Mandy Lilley
Margaret Callan
Marie Rogers
Marilyn Tucker
Mario Price
Mark Stevens
Mark Woolley
Martin Carthy
Martin Dale
Martin Fay
Martin Graebe
Martin Henning
Martin O'Neill
Martin Robertson
Martin Stoker
Mary English
Mary Humphreys
Mary MacMaster
Mary-Rose Merritt
Mathew Walklate
Matt Seattle
Matthew Swindlehurst
Mauricio Enrique Venegas
Max Rankin
Max Rankin
Michael Bailey
Michael Lempelius
Michael McGoldrick
Michael Muskett
Michael Roberts
Michael Ruff
Michael Sargeant
Michelle Short
Mike Bettison
Mike Chant
Mike Cosgrave
Mike Harding
Mike Parsons
Mike Smith
Modeste Hugues
Nancy Kerr
Neil Rogers
Neti Vaandrager
Nick Carpenter
Nick Chowlia
Nigel Eaton
Norma Waterson
Norrie Burnett
Oliver Blanchflower

Paddy Maloney
Pamela Bishop
Patrick Dunbar
Patrick Knock
Patsy Seddon
Paul Burgess
Paul Dengate
Paul Higgs
Paul Hoad
Paul Hurst
Paul Jones
Paul Sartin
Paul Saunders
Paul Stevens
Paul Wilson
Paula Smith
Pauline Cato
Penni Gillis
Pete Castle
Pete Coe
Pete Cooper
Pete Fyfe
Pete Morton
Peter Aston
Peter Glyde
Peter Jack
Peter Quinn
Phil Armitage
Phil Benson
Phil Cunningham
Phil Heaton
Phil Keys
Phil Wright
Philip Berthoud
Philip Cavanagh
Philip Martin
Philip Wright
Philippe Barnes
Pomegranate
Mackenney
Rab Noakes
Rachel Heffer
Rachel Pantin
Ravi Freeman
Ray Laidlaw
Rees Thomas
Rees Wesson
Ric Sanders
Richard Barton
Richard Beard
Richard Spong
Richard Stapleton
Richard Wilde
Rick Christian
Rob Gibson
Robb Johnson
Robert Harbron
Robert Mulford
Robert Wilson
Robin Willow
Rod Clements
Rod Meredith
Roger Digby
Roger Holt
Roger Nicholls
Roger Paton
Roger Smith
Ron Singh
Ronald Jamieson
Ronnie Hunter
Roy Bailey
Saffron Summerfield
Sally French
Sally Gladwell
Sally Horner
Sandra Kerr
Sandy Brechin
Sarah Allen
Sarah Crofts
Sarah Deere Jones
Sarah Matthews
Saskia Tomkins
Saul Rose
Seamus Curley
Seamus Heffernan
Sean Barry
Sean Keane
Shannon Smy
Shanty Jack
Shaun Black
Sheena Wellington
Sian Phillips
Sid Kipper
Simon Care
Simon Nelson
Simon Nicholls
Simon Nicol
Simon Rayner
Simon Thoumire
Sonia Oakes-Stuart
Steafan Hannigan
Stephen Campbell
Stephen Jones
Stephen Morris
Stephen Tyler
Steve Heap
Steve Hill
Steve Hunt
Steve Knightley
Steve Rusby
Steve Turner
Susan Shortland-Webb
Talitha Mackenzie
Terry Mann
Thomas Dolan
Thornton Holmes
Tim Dalling
Timothy Chipping
Timothy Laycock
Timothy Walker
Timothy Willets
Tom Brown
Tom McConville
Tom Napper
Toni Wood
Tony Backhouse
Tony Corcoran
Tony Kendall
Tony Molyneux
Tony Winn
Tracey Middleton
Travelling Charles Fyson
Trevor Carter
Trevor James
Trevor Lines
Troy Donockley
Ty Garner
Veronica Lowe
Vic Gammon
Vicki Swan
Vicky Brown
Vikki Clayton
Vincent Carr
Walid Rouissi
Wally Davies
Wendy Weatherby
William Nelis
William Whaley
Xenia Horne
Yves Langlois

notes

notes

notes

notes

notes

# PLEASE READ THE NOTES OVERLEAF BEFORE COMPLETING THIS FORM

**Please photocopy this if you need more forms, or download from www.direct-roots.com**

# FREE ENTRY in Direct Roots

The guide to folk, roots and related music and arts in the British Isles

**1 Name of artist (stage name), event, festival, club, venue, company etc.** (BLOCK CAPITALS)

______________________________

**2 Entry type** (PLEASE TICK APPROPRIATE SECTIONS)

☐ Artist ☐ Agent/Manager ☐ Promoter ☐ Festival
☐ Venue/Club ☐ Organisation ☐ Services ☐ Media
☐ Other (PLEASE GIVE DETAILS) ______________________________

**3 Venue address/Festival location** (e.g. The Red Lion, Gantry Road, Devon, E26 4RF or Beverley, East Yorkshire)

______________________________

**4 Contact details** (BLOCK CAPITALS)

Name ______________________________
Address ______________________________
______________________________
______________________________
______________________________
Postcode ______________________________
Tel 1 ______________________________
Tel 2 ______________________________
Fax ______________________________
Email ______________________________
______________________________

**5 Alternative contact details** (BLOCK CAPITALS)

Name ______________________________
Address ______________________________
______________________________
______________________________
______________________________
Postcode ______________________________
Tel 1 ______________________________
Tel 2 ______________________________
Fax ______________________________
Email ______________________________
______________________________

Website ______________________________

**6 Notes for contact details** ______________________________

______________________________

**7 Description of services and/or activities** (SEE NOTES) ______________________________

______________________________
______________________________

Date of event/festival 2002 ______________________________
Date of event/festival 2003 ______________________________

**8 Arts Boards and Arts Councils** (PLEASE TICK THE **REGION** or **COUNTRY** YOU ARE BASED IN)

☐ Eastern ☐ East Midlands ☐ London ☐ Northern
☐ North West ☐ Southern ☐ South East ☐ South West
☐ West Midlands ☐ Yorkshire
☐ **Northern Ireland** ☐ **Republic of Ireland** ☐ **Scotland** ☐ **Wales**

**9 Musicians' Union** (PLEASE TICK AS APPROPRIATE)

Are you currently a member? ☐ Yes ☐ No — Would you like details? ☐ Yes ☐ No
Are you a member of the MU Folk, Roots and Traditional Music section? ☐ Yes ☐ No — Would you like details? ☐ Yes ☐ No

**10 Signature and Date**

Please sign and date here if you agree to this information being included on the **Direct Roots** database and/or used in the **Direct Roots** directory.

Signature ______________________________ Date ____________
Print name ______________________________

Please send your completed form and any additional information (see notes overleaf) to:

**Direct Roots**
**22 Mattison Road**
**London N4 1BD**
**Fax 020 8292 1131**
**admin@direct-roots.com**

Please put any Email applications in same order as this form, or attach as a MSWord file. NO photo files or other attachments accepted.

# PLEASE READ THESE NOTES BEFORE COMPLETING THE FORM OVERLEAF

**Please photocopy this if you need more forms, or download from www.direct-roots.com**

Please send your completed form and any additional information (see notes overleaf) to:

**Direct Roots**
**22 Mattison Road**
**London N4 1BD**
**Fax 020 8292 1131**
**admin@direct-roots.com**

Please put any Email applications in same order as this form, or attach as a MSWord file. NO photo files or other attachments accepted.

## PLEASE READ THESE NOTES BEFORE COMPLETING THE FORM OVERLEAF

**1 Name of artist, event, festival, club, venue, company, etc.**
Please give artist (stage name), event, festival, club, venue, company, etc. as you wish to be listed.

**2 Entry type**
Tick the relevant box or boxes or suggest other description. See No. 7.

**3 Venue address/Festival location**
This is to identify the location of the venue, event or festival. Please use No. 4 for contact details.

**4 Contact details**
Please give details of artist, festival, venue etc. as you wish them to be listed.

**5 Alternative contact details**
Use this section if you want to name an alternative contact such as an agent.

**6 Notes for contact details**
Use this section for any notes you want to make on contact details (withholding personal numbers etc.).

**7 Description of services and/or activities**
Please give brief relevant description of your services (up to 30 words). For example:

**Artists**

- *Solo singer of mostly traditional songs accompanied by guitar and Anglo Concertina.*
- *Six piece global dance band drawing on mainly Latin influences.*
- *Caller for ceilidhs and barn dances.*
- *Street theatre duo mixing juggling, escapology and comedy.*
- *Appalachian dance team with Old Time band.*
- *Teacher of Flamenco dance.*

Brief additional notes on instrumentation, cultural origins of music, available workshops/classes, associations with other performers would be useful. You are welcome to attach a brief biography. Websites will be listed where given but will not be used for reference.

**Agents/Managers**
Please give brief description of your work (booking agent, personal management etc.) and any performance genre in which you specialise. List the artists that you represent with brief description as above. An attached roster is fine.

**Promoters**
Please give brief description of your work and any particular artistic policy.

**Festivals**
Please give dates for 2002 and 2003 if known with any formula for selecting dates (e.g. first Sunday in July).

Give a brief description of your event (World Music, Day of Dance, Cajun Dance Weekend) with details of type of venues used, style of music/dance and artistic policy if appropriate.

Include membership of any associations (AFO, CIOFF, TMSA etc.).

Enclose any available leaflet/programmes etc.

**Venues, clubs and regular events**
This covers regular events such as folk clubs, sessions, singarounds, concerts, dances, ceilidhs and any venue that has a programme of relevant music including arts centres, theatres, pubs, Local Authority premises etc. Please use section 3 to give details of the venue. Please use section 4 to give details of the organiser if different from the venue details.

Describe the nature of the event (folk club, ceilidh series etc.). Give time, day and frequency of regular meetings. Also please give details of artistic policy, facilities and capacity etc.

**Organisations** Give a brief description of your work including artistic and regional areas covered, policy, objectives etc.

**Services** This section covers those working as event suppliers, instrument makers and repairers, PA and lighting hire, record companies, distributors and retailers, professional services, marketing and all businesses offering services relevant to folk and roots music and arts. Please give a brief description of your services.

**Media** This section is for periodicals, directories, publications, publishers, radio programmes, journalists, publicists and all those specialising in promoting folk and roots music through the media. Please give a brief descrption of your work. Where relevant give publication dates, programme day and times etc.

**8 Arts Boards and Arts Councils**
Please tick the region or country in which you are based.

**9 Musicians' Union**
The Musicians' Union is delighted to support **Direct Roots** as a reference guide for musicians and others. Europe's largest representative organisation for musicians will work (in partnership) with **Direct Roots** to ensure that this is the most informed and widely used directory for this expanding genre. Ian Smith, Organiser of the MU Folk, Roots and Traditional Music Section will be sharing data with **Direct Roots** and completing the form overleaf is essential to your inclusion in this, the most comprehensive guide ever to be produced for folk, roots and related music. Further information about the Musicians' Union from **folk@musiciansunion.org.uk**

**10 Signature and date**
***Please ensure that you sign all forms and return.***
Return of details by Email will be taken as confirmation that you agree to inclusion in **Direct Roots**.